FIFTH EDITION

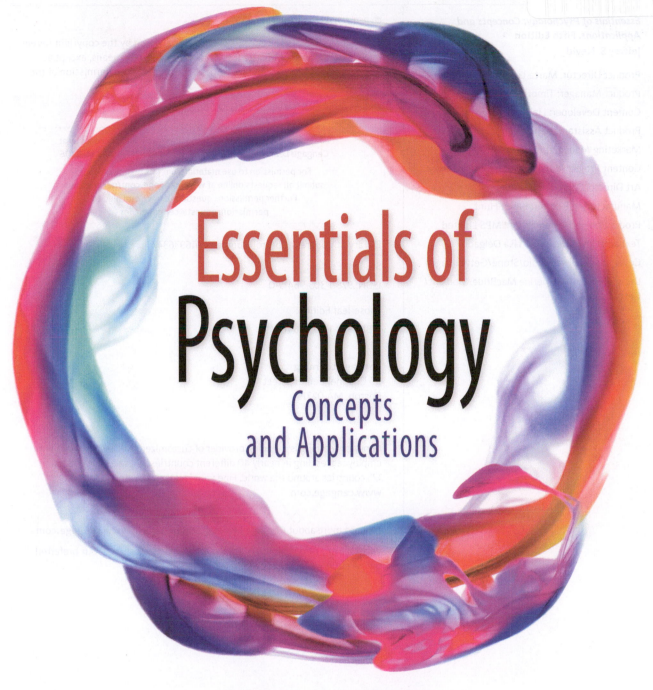

Essentials of
Psychology
Concepts
and Applications

Jeffrey S. Nevid

St. John's University

CENGAGE
Learning·

Australia • Brazil • Canada • Mexico • Singapore • United Kingdom • United States

Essentials of Psychology: Concepts and Applications, **Fifth Edition**

Jeffrey S. Nevid

Product Director: Marta Lee-Perriard

Product Manager: Timothy Matray

Content Developer: Liz Fraser

Product Assistant: Katie Chen

Marketing Manager: Andrew Ginsberg

Content Project Manager: Ruth Sakata Corley

Art Director: Vernon Boes

Manufacturing Planner: Karen Hunt

Production and Composition: MPS Limited

Text and Cover Designer: Lisa Delgado

Cover Image: Biwa Studio/Stone/Getty Images

Design Element: Catherine MacBride/Moment/Getty Images

For product information and technology assistance, contact us at **Cengage Learning Customer & Sales Support, 1-800-354-9706**

For permission to use material from this text or product, submit all requests online at **www.cengage.com/permissions**
Further permissions questions can be e-mailed to **permissionrequest@cengage.com**

Library of Congress Control Number: 2016936347

Student Edition:

ISBN: 978-1-305-96415-0

Loose-leaf Edition:

ISBN: 978-1-305-96417-4

Cengage Learning
20 Channel Center Street
Boston, MA 02210
USA

Cengage Learning is a leading provider of customized learning solutions with employees residing in nearly 40 different countries and sales in more than 125 countries around the world. Find your local representative at **www.cengage.com**

To learn more about Cengage Learning Solutions, visit **www.cengage.com**

Purchase any of our products at your local college store or at our preferred online store **www.cengage.com**

Printed at CLDPC, USA, 04-21

This text is dedicated to the thousands of psychology instructors who share their excitement and enthusiasm for the field of psychology with their students and seek to help them better understand the many contributions of psychology to our daily lives and to our understanding of ourselves and others. I consider myself fortunate to have the opportunity to be one of them.

About the Author

Dr. Jeffrey Nevid is professor of psychology at St. John's University in New York, where he teaches introductory psychology and other undergraduate and graduate courses. He received his doctorate from the State University of New York at Albany and completed a postdoctoral fellowship in evaluation research at Northwestern University. Dr. Nevid has accrued more than 200 research publications and presentations at professional conferences and has authored or coauthored more than a dozen textbooks in psychology and related fields. In addition to this text in introductory psychology, his other texts include *Abnormal Psychology in a Changing World*, published by Pearson Education; *Human Sexuality in a World of Diversity*, also published by Pearson Education; *Psychology and the Challenges of Life: Adjustment and Growth*, published by John Wiley & Sons; and *HLTH*, published by Wadsworth/Cengage Learning.

Dr. Nevid's research encompasses many areas of psychology, including health psychology, clinical and community psychology, social psychology, gender and human sexuality, adolescent development, and teaching of psychology. His publications have appeared in such journals as *Health Psychology, Journal of Consulting and Clinical Psychology, Journal of Community Psychology, Journal of Youth and Adolescence, Clinical Psychology and Psychotherapy, Journal of Nervous and Mental Disease, Behavior Therapy, Psychology & Marketing, Professional Psychology, Teaching of Psychology, International Journal for the Scholarship of Teaching and Learning, Sex Roles*, and *Journal of Social Psychology*, among others.

Dr. Nevid also served as an editorial consultant for the journals *Health Psychology* and *Psychology & Marketing* and as an associate editor of the *Journal of Consulting and Clinical Psychology*. He is actively involved in conducting research on pedagogical advances to help students succeed in their courses. His most recent research on effective learning and instruction has focused on journaling as a writing-to-learn assignment, the IDEA model of course assessment, accuracy of student confidence judgments on exams, and retrieval practice as a study tool.

Brief Contents

Contents

CHAPTER 1
The Science of Psychology   3

CHAPTER 2
Biological Foundations of Behavior   41

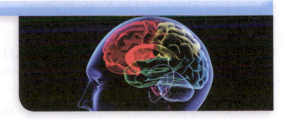

CHAPTER 3
Sensation and Perception 87

CHAPTER 4
Consciousness 133

CHAPTER 5
Learning   175

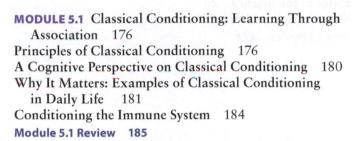

CHAPTER 6
Memory   211

CHAPTER 9
Human Development 323

CHAPTER 10
Psychology and Health 377

CHAPTER 11
Personality 411

CHAPTER 12
Social Psychology 449

CHAPTER 13
Psychological Disorders 487

CHAPTER 14
Methods of Therapy 527

Features

APPLYING PSYCHOLOGY IN DAILY LIFE

Preface

Welcome to the Fifth Edition of *Essentials of Psychology: Concepts and Applications*. I set out to accomplish three major purposes in writing this text:

1. To make the study of psychology accessible and engaging to beginning students in psychology
2. To provide students with a solid grounding in the knowledge base in psychology
3. To help students succeed in the course

The IDEA Model of Course Assessment: Mapping Acquired Skills to APA Learning Goals

This text offers a unique pedagogical framework, called the IDEA model of course assessment, which is grounded in the widely used taxonomy of educational objectives developed by renowned educational researcher Benjamin Bloom. Each chapter begins with a listing of learning objectives expressed in the form of action verbs tied to measurable learning outcomes. The action verbs represent four key acquired skills paralleling those in Bloom's taxonomy. The action verbs *identify, define,* and *describe* represent basic cognitive skills in Bloom's taxonomy (knowledge and comprehension, or remembering and understanding in the revised taxonomy). The action verb *apply* represents an intermediate level of skills development needed to apply knowledge to real-life situations and examples, and the action verbs *explain* and *evaluate* represent the highest or most complex level of skills acquisition in Bloom's taxonomy—skills needed to analyze, synthesize, and evaluate information (or analyzing, evaluating, and creating in the revised taxonomy).

These action verbs conveniently spell out the simple acronym IDEA:

Identify … key figures in the history of psychology, parts of nervous system, and so on.

Define or Describe … key concepts and features of major psychological theories.

Evaluate or Explain … underlying processes and mechanisms of behavior and mental processes.

Apply … psychological concepts to real-world examples.

The IDEA model is integrated with the *APA Guidelines for the Undergraduate Psychology Major, Version 2.0,* which identifies five major learning goals and corresponding student learning outcomes for undergraduate majors in psychology. Learning objectives in this text are mapped onto APA learning goals (see table later in the Preface) to ensure that beginning students in psychology are exposed to core concepts in the field and foundational areas of competence in the psychology major.

The IDEA model is also integrated with the test-item file so that instructors can select items measuring these particular outcomes—to *identify, define* or *describe, evaluate* or *explain,* and *apply* knowledge of psychology.

To help students accomplish these objectives, the text adopts a learning-centric approach to help students encode and retain key concepts in psychology. The keystones of this approach include the following concept-based pedagogical tools:

- **Concept Signaling** Key concepts, not just key terms, are identified and highlighted in the margins to help students encode and retain core concepts.

- **Concept Charts** These built-in study charts are "see-at-a-glance" capsulized summaries of key concepts to help reinforce new knowledge.

- **Concept Links** This feature highlights connections between key concepts across chapters. Concept links are integrated with the key concepts in the margins, so that students can see how core concepts are applied across different areas of psychology.

- **Concept Maps for Psychology** This online visual learning tool helps students visualize connections between key concepts in the text. Concept maps are available through Cengage Learning's *MindTap*. Concept maps are schematic diagrams comprising key concepts that are represented in boxed shapes called *nodes*, which are connected by links that typically take the form of verbs or conjunctions. Unlike other study charts, concept maps can be read either across or down the page to express a coherent knowledge structure. To encourage active learning, concept maps are presented in an incomplete (fill-in-the-blanks) form to engage students in the process of completing these knowledge structures. The answers are also available online.

What's New?

The Fifth Edition of *Essentials of Psychology* includes many new features and updates, including the following:

***New!* Psychology in our Digital World.** Students today are digital natives who have never known a time without cell phones or the Internet. When many of us started teaching, a *tablet* was something you took when you had a headache, a *cell phone* resembled a brick that only top corporate executives or military personnel carried, a *text* was something that instructors assigned in class, and a *web* was something that only spiders spun.

My how the world has changed in just the past generation! When I was writing the first edition of this text, "the facebook" was a social experiment in a Harvard dorm. Now, Facebook has more than 1.5 billion users worldwide. Psychologists today are actively exploring how personal technology is transforming our lives. This text brings this research to the attention of students who are experiencing these changes first-hand. In this text, students will learn what psychologists are discovering about the psychological impact of cell phones, the Internet, and social media. Previous editions of the text included early research in this area, but this new edition greatly expands the focus. Here is a sampling of psychological research on the effects of personal technology discussed in this edition:

- Laboratory evidence of effects that occur when students are physically separated from their cell phones (Chapter 1)

- Semantic analysis of the tone of Facebook postings as clues to how rainy days affect moods (Chapter 1)

- Data collection in the smartphone era—yes, there's an app for that (Chapter 1)

- How the brain responds to viewing Facebook pages (Chapter 4)

- Evidence from the Harvard iPhone app study showing that people tend to report unhappier moods when their minds are wandering than when they were focused on activities (Chapter 4)

- Risks posed by cell phone use during driving and the problem of inattention blindness (Chapter 4)

- Effects of Facebook use on student grades (Chapter 6)

- Evidence linking greater social media use to higher risk of eating disorders in young women (Chapter 8)

- Evidence linking greater social media use to more negative moods after signing off and to lower levels of happiness and life satisfaction overall (Chapter 8)

- Investigation of whether online connections strengthen or weaken real-life relationships (Chapter 9)

- Evidence of how Big Five traits relate to use of social networking sites (Chapter 11)

- Analysis of digital footprints ("likes" on Facebook) as a clue to an individual's personality traits (Chapter 11)

- Relationships between trait neuroticism and tendencies to present a fake or idealized image of oneself on Facebook profiles (Chapter 11)

- Displaying photographs and personal interests on social networking sites as a form of signaling racial identity among African American students (Chapter 11)

- Analysis of self-disclosure by adolescents and adults on social media pages (Chapter 12)

- How the reciprocity principle comes into play in rating desirability of people based on Facebook profiles (Chapter 12)

- Smartphone apps and Internet-based therapy modules as aids in helping people with psychological problems, such as the PTSD Coach (Chapter 14)

***New!* Integrated TED Talks.** I'm very appreciative of Cengage Learning's efforts to incorporate other learning resources within the *MindTap* platform and especially pleased that this edition features a number of TED talks on psychological content. Each talk is directly accessible from *MindTap*.

***New!* Thorough Updating.** Each edition of this text is thoroughly updated from start to finish. The field of psychology stands still for no author! New research developments are reported daily in professional journals and circulated widely in the popular media. As you thumb through the pages of this edition, you will find many hundreds of new findings from research appearing in the scientific literature in the past three years. Here is a sampling of new findings in the field from each chapter:

- 2015 APA report on ethnic minority percentages among working psychologists today (Chapter 1)

- New evidence of neurogenesis in the adult brain (Chapter 2)

- New research evidence that people can actually sniff happiness in others (Chapter 3)

- New recommended sleep guidelines from National Sleep Foundation (Chapter 4)

- 2015 UCLA study showing that only one of 85 undergraduates was able to correctly draw a logo they had seen countless times before—the Apple logo

- New evidence supporting the Flynn effect on IQ scores (Chapter 6)

- 2015 update on prevalence of obesity and being overweight in the United States (Chapter 8)

- 2015 recommendations from American Academy of Pediatrics about use of alcohol during pregnancy (Chapter 9)

- New research showing that socially isolated people and those living alone stand a higher risk of early death than more socially engaged people (Chapter 10)

- New evidence on changes in conscientiousness occurring in young adulthood (Chapter 11)

- New evidence that impression formation begins in a fraction of a second when someone catches a glimpse of someone, literally in the blink of an eye (Chapter 12)

- New evidence that the amygdala may be overreactive in people with anxiety-related disorders (Chapter 13)

■ Recent developments on the use of software programs, Internet-based resources, and smartphone apps in treating psychological problems (Chapter 14)

Targeting Effective Learning (EL): The Four E's of Effective Learning

The learning system adopted in this text is based on the *Four E's of Effective Learning:* (1) engaging interest; (2) encoding important information; (3) elaborating meaning; and (4) evaluating progress. This pedagogical framework is grounded in basic research on learning and memory and is supplemented by pedagogical research, including research I have conducted with my students.[1] The pedagogical framework was then tested in classrooms throughout the country.

The four key elements of effective learning, the "Four E's," are as follows:

■ Engaging Interest
■ Encoding Important Information
■ Elaborating Meaning
■ Evaluating Progress

Engaging Interest

Learning begins with focused attention. A textbook can be an effective learning tool only if it engages and retains student interest. Students are not likely to encode or retain information without focused attention.

Essentials of Psychology: Concepts and Applications is designed to generate interest as well as involve students directly in the material they read. Personal vignettes are used to draw readers into the material and to illustrate how concepts discussed in the chapter relate to their personal experiences. In addition, *"Did You Know That…"* chapter-opening features are designed to grab student attention and encourage further

reading. These chapter-opening questions whet the student's appetite for material presented in the chapter. Some questions debunk common myths and misconceptions, whereas others highlight interesting historical features or bring recent research developments into sharper focus. Accompanying page numbers are provided for easy cross-referencing to the chapter sections in which the information is discussed. A small sample follows:

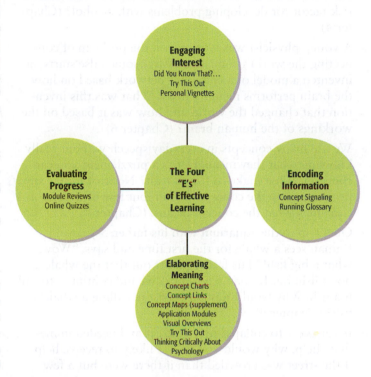

Did You Know That . . .

■ A major school of psychology was inspired by the view from a train? (Chapter 1)

■ It is impossible to tickle yourself? (Chapter 2)

■ You may be hooked on a drug you have with breakfast every morning? (Chapter 4)

■ If you want to remember something you observed, first close your eyes? (Chapter 6)

■ Albert Einstein used mental imagery in developing his theory of relativity? (Chapter 7)

■ People in different cultures smile differently? (Chapter 8)

■ Your personality traits help predict how well you are likely to do in college? (Chapter 11)

■ We literally begin forming an impression of other people in a fraction of a second of catching a glimpse of them? (Chapter 12)

■ People labeled as psychopaths are not psychotic? (Chapter 13)

■ Antidepressant drugs are used to treat many types of psychological disorders, not just depression? (Chapter 14)

---

[1]Nevid, J. S., & Carmony, T. M. (2002). Traditional versus modular format in presenting textual material in introductory psychology. *Teaching of Psychology, 29,* 237–238.

Nevid, J. S., & Lampmann, J. L. (2003). Effects on content acquisition of signaling key concepts in text material. *Teaching of Psychology, 30,* 227–229.

Nevid, J. S., & Forlenza, N. (2005). Graphing psychology: An analysis of the most commonly used graphs in introductory psychology textbooks. *Teaching of Psychology, 32,* 253–256.

Nevid, J. S. (2006, February). In pursuit of the "perfect lecture." *American Psychological Society Observer, 19*(2), 35–36, 42.

Nevid, J. S., & Mahon, K. (2009). Mastery quizzing as a signaling device to cue attention to lecture material. *Teaching of Psychology, 36,* 1–4.

Nevid, J. S., Pastva, A., & McClelland, N. (2012). Writing-to-learn assignments in introductory psychology: Is there a learning benefit? *Teaching of Psychology, 39,* 272–275.

Nevid, J. S., & McClelland, N. (2013). Using action verbs as learning outcomes: Applying Bloom's taxonomy in measuring instructional objectives in introductory psychology. *Journal of Education and Training Studies,* 1(2), 19–24.

Nevid, J. S., Cheney, B., & Thompson, C. (2015). "But I thought I knew that!" Student confidence judgments on course examinations in introductory psychology. *Teaching of Psychology, 42,* 330–334.

The Brain Loves a Puzzle. The use of thought-provoking puzzles in the text stimulates student interest and encourages them to read further. Each chapter poses a puzzle relating to the content of the chapter and provides clues students can use to find the solution. Here are some examples from the text:

- How could something so unpleasant as pain be a good thing? (Chapter 3)

- How might being "able to hold your liquor" be a genetic risk factor for developing problems with alcohol? (Chapter 4)

- A young physicist was working on the problem of connecting the world's computers. After some false starts, he invented a model of a computer network based on how the brain performs memory tasks. What was this invention that changed the world and how was it based on the workings of the human brain? (Chapter 6)

- We use many concepts in everyday speech without really knowing what they mean. Here's a puzzlement you can chew on: What makes a fruit a fruit? None of us has any problem using the concept of fruit, but few of us have a clear idea what the concept means. (Chapter 7)

- On a trip to the aquarium with his father, 5-year-old Kamau sees a whale for the first time and says, "Wow, what a big fish!" His father points out that the whale is not a fish, but Kamau seems puzzled and continues to call it a fish. Why would Kamau persist in calling a whale a fish? (Chapter 9)

- If you were to collapse on the street and needed immediate help, why would you be less likely to receive help if the street was crowded than if there were but a few people nearby? (Chapter 12)

- Genetics plays an important role in schizophrenia, but why is it the case that scientists have been unable to find the gene that causes schizophrenia and probably never will? (Chapter 13)

Try This Out Hands-On Exercises. These active learning exercises encourage students to apply psychological concepts to their own experiences. Whether the topic involves trying to read a magazine sideways, breaking through the "Magic 7" barrier, reading emotions in facial expressions or putting multitasking to the test, students work through problems, generate solutions, and test out beliefs. Some Try This Out activities offer suggestions for *service learning* through participation in research and volunteer experiences, whereas others involve self-scoring questionnaires that allow students to evaluate their own behavior and attitudes about specific issues (for example, "Are You an Optimist or a Pessimist?").

Encoding Important Information

Learning and retaining key concepts in text material requires that information first be encoded in memory. The pedagogical technique of signaling or cueing can help people encode important information. Textbook authors have long used certain forms of signaling, such as headings and highlighted key terms. This text also includes two other types of signaling devices, the *running glossary* and *concept signaling*.

Running Glossary. Key terms are highlighted in the text and defined in the margins. Students do not need to interrupt their reading to thumb through a glossary at the end of the text whenever they encounter an unfamiliar term. (A full glossary is presented at the end of the text as well.)

Concept Signaling. Concept signaling is a unique pedagogical feature designed to help students encode and retain key concepts by extracting and highlighting them in the margins of the text. Cued concepts are signposts to help students gauge that they are getting the key points as they make their way through the chapter. Although some students can easily extract key concepts from text material, others struggle with the process of encoding key points. They may come away knowing a few isolated facts, but may miss many of the major concepts that form the basic building blocks of knowledge in the field. Or they may feel "lost" in the middle of a chapter and become frustrated.

To evaluate the learning benefits of concept signaling, we conducted a controlled study in which students read two different text passages—one with key concepts highlighted in the margins and one without cued concepts. Our results showed that signaling key concepts by extracting them and highlighting them in the margins significantly improved quiz performance overall as well as on a subset of items that directly measured knowledge of key concepts (Nevid & Lampmann, 2003).

Not surprisingly, we found that signaling key concepts had no effects on learning surrounding material that was not signaled. This finding only reinforces what instructors have known for years—that students should not use pedagogical aids (whether they be summaries, interim quizzes, or cued concepts) as substitutes for reading the text in its entirety. Importantly, though, our results suggest that students may be better able to learn key concepts when they are signaled or highlighted in the text.

We also polled students in our study on which format they preferred—the one with signaled concepts or the one without. More than three of five students preferred concept signaling and found it easier to understand and more clearly presented than the standard (nonsignaled) format. (This was interesting in light of the fact that the content in the text passages was exactly the same in both formats.)

Elaborating Meaning

Though information must first be encoded to be learned, new learning needs to be strengthened to ensure long-term retention. Retention of newly acquired information can be strengthened through rote memorization, such as by rehearsal of particular words or phrases. But the types of deeper processing needed to build more enduring memories generally require *elaborative rehearsal* in which the person reflects on the meaning of the material and relates it to real-life applications and life experiences. This text provides several pedagogical features designed to facilitate elaborative rehearsal:

Learning Objectives. These important study aids are listed both at the beginning of the chapter and within the modules themselves. Sample answers to learning objectives are presented in the Recite It sections of Module Reviews using a fill-in-the-blanks format to foster active learning that encourages retrieval of key concepts. Research evidence consistently demonstrates the learning benefits of practicing retrieval skills. As noted earlier, learning objectives incorporate active learning verbs that follow the author's IDEA model of course assessment.

Concept Charts. These study charts summarize key concepts in tabular form. Concept Charts reinforce knowledge of major concepts and help students make relational connections between concepts.

Concepts are repeated in several forms to reinforce new learning—in the narrative itself, in Concept Charts, in marginal inserts of cued concepts, and in schematic diagrams. The use of different contexts for presenting information strengthens new learning.

Try This Out. These exercises not only engage student interest, but also encourage students to apply concepts they learn in the text to their own experiences.

Applying Psychology in Daily Life. Applications of psychological knowledge in daily life are integrated directly in the modules themselves in the Applying Psychology in Daily Life features. Examples include the following: "Psychology and Pain Management" (Chapter 3), "Putting Reinforcement into Practice" (Chapter 5), "Becoming a Creative Problem Solver" (Chapter 7), and "Taking the Distress Out of Stress" (Chapter 10).

Evaluating Progress

The text contains a number of study aids to help students evaluate their progress:

Module Review Sections. At the end of each module is a Module Review consisting of three sections, a Recite It section, a Recall It section, and a Think About It section.

Reciting new knowledge is a key feature of the SQ3R study method and an important, perhaps the most important, study tool. Recite It sections provide an opportunity for students to recite their knowledge of the learning objectives and then to compare their responses to sample answers given in the text.

The Recall It sections allow students to test their knowledge by taking a short quiz on several key concepts. The answers are given in Appendix B at the end of the text.

The Think About It features encourage critical thinking by posing thought-provoking questions to stimulate students to think more deeply about concepts presented in the text.

Visual Overviews. In addition, Visual Overview sections offer students a visual learning tool to help them review and strengthen their knowledge of new concepts and see relationships among concepts in summary form.

The Modular Approach

The text is organized in a modular format that breaks down each chapter into smaller instructional units called modules. Each module is a cohesive study unit organized around a set of key concepts in a particular area of study. The modular approach helps busy students better organize their study efforts by allowing them to focus on one module at a time rather than trying to tackle a whole chapter at once.

In our research, we found the majority of students preferred the modular format over the traditional format (57.3 percent versus 38.5 percent, with 4.2 percent expressing no preference) (Nevid & Carmony, 2002). In addition, students who preferred the modular format performed significantly better when material was presented in this format than in the traditional format. It stands to reason that when students prefer a particular format, they will become more engaged in reading texts based on that format—an outcome that may translate into improved performance in classroom situations.

Targeting Critical Thinking Skills

The text encourages students to challenge their preconceived assumptions about human behavior and to think critically about information they hear or read about in the media in the light of scientific evidence. The Thinking Critically About Psychology sections at the end of each chapter provide students with opportunities to sharpen their critical thinking skills. Students can practice these skills by answering questions that require them to analyze problems and evaluate claims in relation to information presented in the chapters. Students may then compare their answers to sample responses presented in Appendix A of the text. The Think About It sections in each Module Review pose thought-provoking questions that further reinforce critical thinking skills.

Built-In Study Method: SQ3R+

The SQ3R (Survey, Question, Read, Recite, Review) study method is a widely used technique for enhancing learning and encouraging students to adopt a more active role in the learning process. The SQ3R method is directly built into the text. The text not only incorporates the traditional elements of SQ3R but also adds another element, the Think About It feature, which fosters critical thinking skills.

■ **Survey and Question** Students can survey each chapter by reviewing the numbered listing of modules at the start of the chapter and by reading the introductory section in which material to be covered in the chapter is described. In addition, they can use the learning objectives as advance organizers to guide their reading and question themselves to ensure they have achieved these objectives.

- **Read** The writing style has been carefully developed for reading level, content, and style. Students are often addressed directly to engage them in the material and encourage them to examine how the information relates to their life experiences.

- **Recite and Review** Each module ends with a Module Review section that helps students review their knowledge of key concepts. Students should be encouraged to recite their knowledge of the learning objectives in the Recite It section of the Module Review before turning to the sample answers in the text for feedback. Students can then test their knowledge by completing a short quiz presented in the Recall It sections. These quizzes consist of fill-in, multiple-choice, matching, and short-answer questions. Concept Charts provide further opportunities for students to review the knowledge they have acquired.

- **Think About It** The text goes beyond review and recitation by posing thought-provoking questions in the Module Reviews that encourage reflection, critical thought, and self-exploration. These questions foster critical thinking (for example, "Do you believe that conventional intelligence tests are culturally biased? Why or why not?"), and encourage students to reflect on how the text material relates to their personal experiences (for example, "Are you a self-actualizer? Upon what evidence do you base your judgment? What steps could you take to become a self-actualizer?"). Instructors may wish to assign these questions as writing assignments.

Integrating Coverage of Diversity in Psychology

One primary objective of this text is to raise students' awareness of the importance of issues relating to diversity. Discussion of cultural and gender issues is therefore integrated within the main body of the text rather than relegated to boxed features. A proliferation of boxes tends to break the flow of the text and to introduce unnecessary clutter that many students find distracting; it might even inadvertently convey the impression that material relating to diversity is less important than other material because it is boxed off. For a reference guide to the integrated coverage of gender and sociocultural issues in the text, see the complete listings available in the Instructor's Manual that accompanies *Essentials of Psychology: Concepts and Applications.*

Ancillaries

Even the most comprehensive text is incomplete without ancillaries. The ones accompanying *Essentials of Psychology: Concepts and Applications* help make it a complete teaching package.

Teacher Ancillaries

Instructor's Resource Manual. The Instructor's Resource Manual (IRM) contains a variety of resources to aid instructors in preparing and presenting text material in a manner that meets their personal preferences and course needs. The IRM begins with a comprehensive preface, which covers preparation, pitfalls, planning, execution, resources, and best practices for both new and seasoned instructors. Each chapter provides a preview and a goals and activity planner to help organize classes. In addition, each chapter of the IRM contains a detailed outline, lecture suggestions, topics for discussion, classroom and individual activities with handouts, and ideas for writing assignments.

Test Bank. The test bank contains more than 2,400 items specifically developed for *Essentials of Psychology: Concepts and Applications.* Multiple-choice questions as well as essay questions with answers are written at both the chapter and the module level to provide flexibility for instructors. These questions are labeled by type (factual, conceptual, applied), learning objective, module reference number, and page reference for easier use in creating exams.

Acknowledgments

First, I am indebted to the thousands of psychologists and other scientists whose work has informed the writing of this text. Thanks to their efforts, the field of psychology has had an enormous impact in broadening our understanding of ourselves and enhancing the quality of our lives. On a more personal level, I owe a debt of gratitude to the many colleagues and publishing professionals who helped shape this manuscript into its present form. Let me begin by thanking the professional colleagues who reviewed the manuscript and helped me refine it through several stages of development:

Fred Nesbit, Sauk Valley Community College

Anne Duran, California State University, Bakersfield

Fred Leavitt, California State University, East Bay

Chitra Ranganathan, Framingham State College

Robert Stennett, Gainesville State College

John Lovell, California State University, East Bay

Shane Gomes, California State University, Los Angeles

Chrisanne Christensen, Southern Arkansas University

Second, I would like to thank the countless instructors and students who participated in our extensive market research conducted in the early stages of the text's development—including the instructors and students at Valencia Community College and the University of Central Florida, who provided us with great insight into their introductory psychology courses; the instructors who participated in the teleconference sessions and raised many important issues that impacted the day-to-day challenges of this course; and the 700-plus respondents who participated in our national survey on introductory psychology and this text. The overwhelming response we received from these professionals proved to be a rich resource throughout the development of the text.

The people at Cengage are consummate publishing professionals and I am very thankful for the supportive way in which they have welcomed me and worked so closely with me to update and strengthen the text to make it an ever more effective learning platform designed to engage students in the study of psychology and help them succeed in the course. In particular I would like to thank my editor, Timothy Matray, for his continuing guidance and support and developmental editor Tom Finn who helped strengthen and guide this text to make it an even more effective teaching and learning platform.

Jeff Nevid
New York, NY
jeffnevid@gmail.com

The Idea Model of Course Assessment: Mapping Acquired Skills to *APA Learning Goals for the Undergraduate Psychology Major, Version 2.0*

GOAL 1 Knowledge Base in Psychology

APA Learning Goals	Related Content in Text and Ancillaries	IDEA Model of Course Assessment: *Skills Acquired— to Identify . . . Define or Describe . . . Evaluate or Explain . . . and Apply*
1.1 Describe key concepts, principles, and overarching themes in psychology	Module 1.1	**Define** psychology and **explain** why psychology is a science. **Identify** the major contemporary perspectives in psychology, and **describe** each perspective.
	The interaction of heredity and environment: Module 2.7	**Evaluate** the role of genetics in behavior. **Describe** methods psychologists use to study the roles of genes and environment in behavior
	Free will versus determinism: Modules 11.3 and 11.4	**Describe** the social-cognitive theories of Rotter, Bandura, and Mischel. **Describe** the humanistic theories of Carl Rogers and Abraham Maslow.
	Interaction of mind and body: Modules 10.1 and 10.2	**Define** stress in psychological terms. **Identify** and **describe** the major sources of stress. **Define** the general adaptation syndrome, and **identify** its three stages. **Evaluate** the effects of stress on the body's immune system. **Identify** and **describe** psychological factors that buffer the effects of stress. **Apply** stress management techniques to daily life. **Identify** psychological factors linked to coronary heart disease. **Identify** psychological factors linked to cancer. **Apply** knowledge of the transmission of sexually transmitted disease to steps we can take to protect ourselves from these diseases.
1.2 Develop a working knowledge of psychology's content domains **Learning, Memory, and Cognition**	Module 5.1	**Define** learning in psychological terms. **Define** classical conditioning and describe the contributions of Ivan Pavlov. **Explain** the process by which conditioned responses become weaker or disappear. **Explain** how conditioned responses can be strengthened. **Define** stimulus generalization and discrimination, and describe their roles in classical conditioning. **Explain** classical conditioning from a cognitive perspective. **Apply** classical conditioning to examples discussed in the text.
	Module 5.2	**Define** operant conditioning, **identify** the major figures in its development, and **describe** their contributions. **Describe** different types of reinforcement and schedules of reinforcement. **Explain** the effects of different types of reinforcement on response rates. **Define** punishment, and **identify** the concerns that psychologists raise about the use of punishment in disciplining children. **Explain** the difference between escape learning and avoidance learning. **Apply** operant conditioning to examples discussed in the text.
	Module 5.3	**Define** cognitive learning, and describe several types of cognitive learning.
	Module 6.1	**Identify** and **describe** the basic processes and stages of memory. **Identify** and **describe** the different types of long-term memory. **Explain** the roles of the semantic network model and levels-of-processing theory in memory. **Apply** constructionist theory to **explain** memory distortions. **Identify** and discuss factors influencing the reliability of eyewitness testimony. **Explain** why the concept of recovered memory is controversial.
	Module 6.2	**Describe** the major theories and factors in forgetting. **Explain** why recognition tests of memory generally produce better results than recall tests. **Describe** the causes of amnesia and the two major types of amnesia.
	Module 7.1	**Define** thinking. **Identify** several ways in which we represent information in our minds. **Explain** the difference between logical and natural concepts. **Identify** and **describe** mental strategies we can use to solve problems more effectively. **Identify** and **describe** mental roadblocks that impede problem solving and decision making. **Describe** the basic processes of creative thought and **explain** the difference between divergent and convergent thinking. **Apply** skills of problem solving to become a creative problem solver.

Continued on following page

APA Learning Goals	Related Content in Text and Ancillaries	IDEA Model of Course Assessment: Skills Acquired— to Identify . . . Define or Describe . . . Evaluate or Explain . . . and Apply
	Module 7.2	**Identify** the basic components of language and the milestones in language development and **describe** the roles of nature and nurture in language development. **Evaluate** whether language is unique to humans and **evaluate** the linguistic relativity hypothesis in light of evidence.
	Module 7.3	**Define** intelligence, **identify** different tests of intelligence, and **evaluate** the characteristics of a good test of intelligence. **Evaluate** gender differences in cognitive abilities. **Describe** the characteristics of the two extremes of intelligence and the misuses of intelligence tests. **Describe** the major theories of intelligence and **evaluate** the roles of heredity and environment in intelligence.
Individual Differences	Module 11.1	**Define** the concept of personality. **Identify** and describe the three levels of consciousness and three structures of personality in Freud's psychoanalytic theory. **Identify** and **describe** the stages in Freud's theory of psychosexual development. **Describe** the personality theories of Jung, Adler, and Horney.
	Module 11.2	**Describe** the trait theories of Allport, Cattell, Eysenck, and the Big Five model. **Evaluate** the genetic basis of personality traits.
	Module 11.3	**Describe** the social-cognitive theories of Rotter, Bandura, and Mischel.
	Module 11.4	**Describe** the self-theory of humanistic theorist Carl Rogers. **Explain** the difference between the concepts of self in collectivistic and individualistic cultures. **Apply** suggestions for enhancing self-esteem.
	Module 11.5	**Identify** the two major types of personality tests, and **evaluate** self-report and projective personality tests.
Social bases of behavior	Module 12.1	**Identify** the major influences on first impressions, and **explain** why first impressions often become lasting impressions. **Identify** and **describe** cognitive biases that influence causal attributions. **Identify** three components of attitudes, and **describe** the sources of attitudes and the pathways involved in changing attitudes through persuasive appeals. **Describe** cognitive dissonance theory, and **explain** how cognitive dissonance can be reduced.
	Module 12.2	**Identify** factors that influence attraction. **Identify** the components of love identified in the triangular model of love. **Describe** the decision-making model of helping, and **identify** factors that influence helping behavior. **Define** prejudice, **explain** how it develops, and **apply** your knowledge to ways of reducing it. **Identify** factors that contribute to human aggression.
	Module 12.3	**Define** social identity and **evaluate** cultural factors involved in social identity. **Describe** the basic finding of Asch's classic study on conformity, and **identify** factors that influence conformity. **Explain** the psychological bases of manipulative sales tactics. **Describe** the findings of Milgram's classic study, and **evaluate** why his methods were controversial. **Evaluate** the effects of the presence of others on performance. **Define** groupthink, and **explain** how it can lead to wrong decisions.
Biological bases of behavior	Module 2.1	**Define** what a neuron is, **identify** the parts of the neuron, and **explain** how neurons communicate with each other. **Explain** how an action potential is generated. **Identify** key neurotransmitters and **describe** their functions. **Explain** the difference between agonists and antagonists.
	Module 2.2	**Describe** how the nervous system is organized. **Describe** the functions of the central nervous system and the divisions of the peripheral nervous system. **Explain** the differences in the functions of the sympathetic and parasympathetic divisions of the autonomic nervous system.

Continued on following page

APA Learning Goals	Related Content in Text and Ancillaries	IDEA Model of Course Assessment: *Skills Acquired— to Identify . . . Define or Describe . . . Evaluate or Explain . . . and Apply*
	Module 2.3	**Describe** how the brain is organized and the roles that particular brain structures play in behavior.
	Module 2.4	**Describe** methods scientists use to study the workings of the brain.
	Module 2.5	**Explain** how the two halves of the brain differ in their functions.
	Module 2.6	**Describe** how the endocrine system is organized and the roles that hormones play in behavior.
	Module 2.7	**Evaluate** the role of genetics in behavior. **Describe** methods psychologists use to study the roles of genes and environment in behavior.
	Module 6.3	**Identify** the key brain structures involved in memory and **explain** the roles of neuronal networks and long-term potentiation. **Explain** the role that genetics plays in memory.
Developmental processes	Module 9.1	**Identify** and **describe** the stages of prenatal development and major threats to prenatal development.
	Module 9.2	**Identify** reflexes present at birth. **Describe** the infant's sensory, perceptual, and learning abilities. **Describe** the development of the infant's motor skills in the first year of life.
	Module 9.3	**Identify** and **describe** three major types of temperament and three types of infant attachment styles. **Identify** and **describe** the major parenting styles. **Identify** and describe Erikson's stages of psychosocial development in childhood. **Describe** Piaget's stages of cognitive development . **Describe** Vygotsky's psychosocial theory of cognitive development.
	Module 9.4	**Describe** the physiological, cognitive, and psychosocial changes that occur during adolescence, and Erikson's beliefs about psychosocial development in adolescence. **Describe** Kohlberg's stages of moral reasoning, and **evaluate** his theory in light of Gilligan's criticism.
	Module 9.5	**Describe** the physical and cognitive changes that occur during adulthood and Erikson's stages of psychosocial development in early and middle adulthood.
	Module 9.6	**Describe** the physical and cognitive changes we can expect later in life and Erikson's views on psychosocial development in late adulthood. **Evaluate** the qualities associated with successful aging. **Identify** the stages of dying proposed by Kübler-Ross. **Apply** suggestions for living a longer and healthier life.
Historical and contemporary perspectives	Module 1.1	**Define** psychology and **explain** why psychology is a science. **Identify** early schools of psychology and the important contributors to these schools, and **describe** the major concepts associated with each school. **Identify** the major contemporary perspectives in psychology, and **describe** each perspective.
Sociocultural bases of behavior	Module 11.4	**Explain** the difference between the concepts of self in collectivistic and individualistic cultures.
	Module 12.2	**Define** prejudice, **explain** how it develops, and **apply** your knowledge to ways of reducing it. **Identify** factors that contribute to human aggression.
	Module 12.3	**Define** social identity and **evaluate** cultural factors involved in social identity.
		Sociocultural factors are integrated throughout the text, including research on ethnic differences in alcohol and drug use (Ch. 4), cultural display rules for emotional expression and cultural differences in smiling (Ch. 8); sociocultural differences in parenting styles (Ch. 9); Vygotsky's sociocultural theory (Ch. 9); acculturative stress of immigrant groups (Ch. 10), ethnic differences in cardiovascular disease (Ch. 10), ethnic identity and self-esteem (Ch. 11), cultural factors and self-identity in collectivistic versus individualistic cultures (Chs. 11 and 12); ethnic factors in self-disclosure (Ch. 12); sociocultural factors in conformity and aggressive behavior (Ch. 12); effects of stereotyping on stereotyped groups (Ch. 12); ethnic factors in access to mental health services (Ch. 13) and suicidal behaviors (Ch. 13); and multicultural factors in psychotherapy (Ch. 14), among others.

Continued on following page

APA Learning Goals	Related Content in Text and Ancillaries	IDEA Model of Course Assessment: *Skills Acquired—— to Identify . . . Define or Describe . . . Evaluate or Explain . . . and Apply*
1.3 Describe applications of psychology	**Applying Psychology in Daily Life features**	Becoming a Critical Thinker (Ch. 1) Looking Under the Hood: Scanning the Human Brain (Ch. 2) Psychology and Pain Management (Ch. 3) Getting Your Z's (Ch. 4) Putting Reinforcement into Practice (Ch. 5) Powering Up Your Memory (Ch. 6) Becoming a Creative Problem Solver (Ch. 7) Managing Anger (Ch. 8) Living Longer, Healthier Lives (Ch. 9) Taking the Distress Out of Stress (Ch. 10) Building Self-Esteem (Ch. 11) Compliance: Doing What Others Want You to Do (Ch. 12) Suicide Prevention (Ch. 13) Getting Help (Ch. 14)

GOAL 2   Scientific Thinking and Critical Thinking

2.1 Use scientific reasoning to interpret psychological phenomena	Module 1.3:	**Identify** the steps in the scientific method.
2.2 Demonstrate psychology information literacy	**The anatomy of a research study:** Breaks down the parts of a research study paper in psychology using an example of a contemporary research publication from a primary source	**Identify** and **describe** research methods that psychologists use and **evaluate** their strengths and weaknesses. **Describe** the ethical standards that govern research in psychology.
2.3 Engage in innovative and integrative thinking and problem solving		**Apply** critical thinking skills to **evaluate** claims made by others as well as online information.
2.4 Interpret, design, and conduct basic psychological research	Citing references in APA style Becoming A Critical Thinker	**Identify** and **describe** mental strategies we can use to solve problems more effectively.
	Modules 7.1 and 7.3	**Identify** and **describe** mental roadblocks that impede problem solving and decision making.
	The Brain Loves a Puzzle features throughout the text (one per chapter) encourage students to use critical thinking	**Describe** the basic processes of creative thought and **explain** the difference between divergent and convergent thinking. **Apply** skills of problem solving to become a creative problem solver.
	Thinking Critically about Psychology features in each chapter challenge students to apply critical thinking skills to evaluate claims	
	Think About It features in each Module Review further reinforce critical thinking skills	
	Statistics Appendix applies methods of scientific inquiry to test hypotheses based on theory	
2.5 Incorporate sociocultural factors in scientific inquiry	See examples of research on sociocultural factors listed above under APA Learning Goal 1.2	

Continued on following page

GOAL 3 Ethical and Social Responsiblity in a Diverse World

3.1 Apply ethical standards to evaluate psychological science and practice	Module 1.3	**Describe** the ethical standards that govern research in psychology.
3.2 Build and enhance interpersonal relationships	Module 8.4	**Define** emotional intelligence, and **evaluate** its importance.
3.3 Adopt values that build community at local, national, and global levels	Module 2.5: Learning Through Volunteering	**Explain** the difference between the concepts of self in collectivistic and individualistic cultures.
	Module 11.3	**Describe** the decision-making model of helping, and **identify** factors that influence helping behavior.
	Module 12.2	**Define** prejudice, **explain** how it develops, and **apply** your knowledge to ways of reducing it.
	Module 12.3: Our Social Selves: Who are We?	
	See examples of research on sociocultural factors listed above under APA Learning Goal 1.2	
4.1 Demonstrate effective writing for different purposes	**The anatomy of a research study (Module 1.3):** Breaks down the parts of a research article in psychology using an example of a contemporary research publication from a primary source	

GOAL 4 Communication

APA Learning Goal	Related Content in Text and Ancillaries
	Think About It: This Module Review feature provides critical thinking questions that can be assigned as writing assignments **Individualized feedback** from automatic scoring software for submitted student writing assignments helps students build more effective writing skills (Cengage *Write Experience*, optional)
4.2 Exhibit effective presentation skills for different purposes	**Statistics Appendix** provides examples of tables and graphs used for presenting data **Interactive Concept Maps** (online, one per chapter): An active learning exercise that provides examples of relational connections between concepts presented in a visual format **Use of various types of diagrams as learning tools throughout the text**—matrices (tabular presentation of concepts), network diagrams (flow charts and schematic diagrams), and hierarchical diagrams (ordered relationships among concepts)
4.3 Interact effectively with others	Module 5.2: Putting Reinforcement into Practice Module 8.4: Managing Anger Module 8.4: Factors Involved in Emotional Intelligence Module 8.4: Cultural Display Rules for Expressing Emotions Module 12.2: Cultural Differences in Self-Disclosure Module 12.3: The Nature of Prejudice and Ways of Reducing It Module 12.3: Resisting Persuasive Sales Pitches Instructor's Manual: Suggestions for group discussion

Continued on following page

5.1 **Apply** psychological content and skills to career goals	Module 1.1: Subfields in Psychology Module 8.1: Achievement Motivation vs. Avoidance motivation Module 11.2: Sizing Up Your Personality (relationship to occupational choice)
5.2 Exhibit self-efficacy and self-regulation	Module 7.1: Becoming a Creative Problem Solver Module 8.4: Emotional Intelligence Module 8.4: Managing Anger Module 11.4: Building Self-Esteem
5.3 Refine project-management skills	Statistics Appendix for building computational literacy
5.4 Enhance teamwork capacity	Module 12.3: Psychological Impediments to Group Task Performance (social loafing and groupthink) Module 12.3: Building Intergroup Cooperation in Social Groups
5.5 Develop meaningful professional direction for life after graduation	Weblinks to APA websites provide resources for pursuing career interests in psychology and related fields (Instructor's Resource Manual). **Building Effective Study Skills:** Study Tips for Getting the Most from This Course (and Your Other Courses) (Message to Students, in Preface) **Psychological perspectives on development of role identity:** See Module 9.4 for discussion of Erikson's concept of the identify crisis, and Marcia's taxonomy of identity statuses in the accompanying Thinking Critically About Psychology feature Module 11.5: What Should I Become? (Try This Out)

A Message to Students

Study Tips for Getting the Most from This Course (and Your Other Courses)

I often hear students say that they spend many hours reading their textbooks and attending classes, but their grades don't reflect the work that they do. I agree. Success is not a function of the time you put into your courses, but how well you use that time. Developing more effective study skills can help you become a more effective learner and get the most from this course as well as your other courses. Let's begin by discussing four key steps toward becoming an effective learner, which I call the four E's: (1) engaging interest; (2) encoding information; (3) elaborating meaning; and (4) evaluating progress.

The Four E's of Effective Learning

1. **Engaging Interest** Paying close attention is the first step toward becoming an effective learner. The brain does not passively soak up information like a sponge. When your attention is divided, it is difficult to process new information at a level needed to understand the complex material required in college-level courses and to retain this newly acquired knowledge. If you find your mind wandering during class or while studying, bring your attention back to the lecture or study material. Becoming an active note taker during class and when reading your text can help you remain alert and focused and avoid spacing out. Keep a notepad handy while reading the text and jot down key points as you read through the material.

2. **Encoding Information** Encoding is the process of bringing information into memory. To encode important information from your classes or assigned readings, make it a practice to stop and ask yourself, "What's the main point or idea? What am I hearing or reading? What am I expected to know?" Jot down the major concepts or ideas and review them later. Use the built-in study tools in your textbook, such as highlighted key terms or concepts, along with the Module Review sections, to identify main points and themes you need to learn.

3. **Elaborating Meaning** New learning is a fragile thing. Rehearsing or repeating the information to yourself in the form of rote memorization may help reinforce newly acquired knowledge, but a more effective way of reinforcing new learning and building more enduring memories is to work with these new concepts and ideas by elaborating their meaning, such as by linking them to real-life examples and using them to solve problems. Your teachers and parents may have encouraged you to demonstrate your understanding of new vocabulary words by using them in a sentence. When you learned formulas and other math skills in class, your teachers may have asked you to demonstrate this knowledge by using it to solve math problems in your textbooks or workbooks. Apply this principle to learning psychology. For every concept you read about in this text or learn in class, connect it to a real-life example or life experience. Your textbook authors and instructors provide many examples of concepts they use, but you can take this a step further by connecting these concepts to your own life experiences.

4. **Evaluating Progress** Keep track of your progress in the course. Most texts, including this one, have quizzes you can use to test yourself on the material you have just read. This text also offers online quizzes. Taking quizzes helps you gauge how you are doing and which areas you need to review further to improve your performance. Other built-in study tools that help you evaluate your progress include review sections and summaries. In this text, you'll find the Recite It section in the Module Review at the end of each module that provides brief answers to the learning objectives for the module. Recite your knowledge of the learning objectives before glancing at the sample answers in the text. Recitation is an important study skill that demonstrates you have acquired new knowledge. Recite your answers in your own words by jotting them down in a notebook or computer file as you read through the module or when you come to the Module Review. Use the answers provided in the text as feedback to determine if you have achieved the learning objectives or need further review of the related material in the text. Then test your knowledge by taking the brief quiz in the Recall It section of the Module Review.

Tips for Succeeding in Class

Read the Syllabus. Think of the syllabus as a road map or a pathway you need to follow to succeed in the course. Take note of the course assignments, grading system, and other course requirements or expectations. Use your course syllabus as a guide to planning your semester, making entries in your calendar for examination dates and required papers and other course assignments.

Prepare for Class by Completing the Assigned Reading. Instructors have good reasons for wanting you to read the assigned chapter or readings before coming to class. They know that students are better prepared for lectures when they have some familiarity with the topics discussed in class. When students have a working knowledge of the material before they come to class, instructors have more freedom to use class time to explore topics in greater depth and breadth, rather than simply to review basic concepts. However, lectures may not make much sense to students who lack basic knowledge about the material because they haven't kept up with their readings.

Attend Class. One of the most important steps to succeeding in college is attending classes regularly. Missing classes can quickly lead to falling behind. If you need to miss a class, notify your instructor beforehand and ask for any assignments you may miss. Then ask a classmate for the notes for the missed class, but only approach someone you believe is a good note taker.

Be Punctual. There may be nothing more distracting to your instructor and classmates than students who come late to class. Though your instructor may not say anything directly, coming late to class conveys a poor impression of yourself. It also makes it difficult to keep up with lecture material because it puts you in the position of playing catch-up. You wouldn't think of arriving at a movie theater in the middle of a movie, so why should you expect to be able to follow the lecture when you arrive after it starts? If you occasionally arrive late due to traffic or an unexpected demand, drop your instructor a note of apology explaining the circumstances. All of us, including your instructors, occasionally face similar situations. However, if you have trouble regularly arriving on time, talk to your instructor or adviser about arranging a schedule that works better for you, or consider taking online courses that don't require regular class attendance.

Ask Questions. Don't hesitate to ask questions in class. Failing to ask your instructor to clarify a particular point you don't understand can lead you to feel lost or confused during class. Also, make sure to ask your instructor about the material that will be covered on an exam, as well as the format used for the exam, such as essay, short-answer, or multiple-choice questions.

Become an Active Note Taker. Don't try to write down everything the instructor says or every word that pops up on a PowerPoint slide or an overhead. Very few people can write that fast. Besides, trying to copy everything verbatim can quickly lead you to fall behind. Focusing your attention on writing down everything also distracts you from thinking more deeply about material discussed in class. A better idea is to listen attentively and write down key points as clearly and concisely as you can, as well as the examples the instructor uses to illustrate these points. No one has perfect recall, so don't expect to remember every important point or concept discussed during a lecture. Write concepts down to review later. Some instructors use PowerPoint slides as a guide to or-

ganizing the content of the lecture. Think of PowerPoint slides as a table of contents for the lecture. The bullet points in the slides are merely starting points for the lecture. Your instructor will likely expound upon each point. If you spend class time just copying bullet points, you may miss important information about each point that is discussed in class. Become an active note taker, not a copy machine. Listen attentively and write down the main concepts and ideas and any examples the instructor may give.

Rephrase and Review Your Notes. An effective way of reinforcing new learning is typing your class notes into a computer file. But rather than typing them word for word, try rephrasing them in your own words. Reworking your notes in this way encourages deeper processing of the material, which is a key factor in strengthening memory of newly learned information. The more you think about the material, the more likely you'll be to remember it when exam time comes around.

Building Effective Study Skills

Where to Study. Select a quiet study space that is as neat, clean, and free of distractions as possible.

When to Study

- *Prevent procrastination.* Schedule regular study times and keep to your schedule.

- *Plan to study at times of the day you are most likely to be alert and best able to concentrate.* Don't leave it until the very end of the day when you are feeling tired or sleepy. Avoid studying directly after a big meal. Give your body time to digest your food. Likewise, avoid studying at a time of day when you're likely to be distracted by hunger pangs.

- *Avoid cramming for exams.* Cramming causes mental fatigue that can interfere with learning and retention. Establish a weekly study schedule to ensure you are well prepared for exams. Plan to review or brush up on the required material the day or two before the exam.

How to Study

- *Plan study periods of about 45 or 50 minutes.* Very few people can maintain concentration for longer than 45 minutes or so. Take a 5- or 10-minute break between study periods. Give your mind and body a break by getting up, stretching your legs, and moving around.

- *Establish clear study goals for each study period.* Goals can include topics you want to cover, pages in the textbook you want to read or review, questions you need to answer, problems you need to solve, and so on.

- *Sit properly to maintain concentration.* Sit upright and avoid reclining or lying down to prevent nodding off or losing focus. If your mind begins to wander, bring your thoughts back to your work. Or break the tendency to daydream by getting yourself out of your chair, gently stretch your muscles, take a quick walk around the room, and then return to studying.

How Much to Study. A convenient rule of thumb to use is to study two hours a week for each hour of class time. Like most rules of thumb, you may need to adjust it according to the amount of work you need to complete.

Read for Understanding. Slow down the pace of your reading so that you can pay close attention to the material you are trying to learn.

- Stop for a moment after every paragraph and pose questions to yourself about what you have just read. Jot down your answers to the questions you pose to yourself to reinforce this new learning.

- After reading a section of text, take a brief break and then review any concepts you don't fully understand to make sure you get the main points before moving to the next section or chapter. Yes, active reading takes more time and effort than just skimming, but it will make the time you spend reading more productive and meaningful.

Reach Out for Help. When you struggle to understand something, don't give up out of frustration. Ask your instructor for help.

Form Study Groups. Reach out to other students to form study groups. Studying as part of a group may induce you to hit the books more seriously.

Using This Textbook as a Study Tool

You are about to embark on a journey through the field of psychology. As with any journey, it is helpful to have markers or road signs to navigate your course. This text provides a number of convenient markers to help you know where you've been and where you're headed. Take a moment to familiarize yourself with the terrain you'll encounter in your journey. It centers on the unique organizational framework of the text—the *concept-based modular format*.

Use Modules to Organize Your Study Time. This text is organized in instructional units called modules to help you structure your study time more efficiently. The *modules* in each chapter break down the chapter into these smaller instructional units. Rather than try to digest an entire chapter at once, you can chew on one module at a time. Each module is organized around a set of key concepts. As you make your way through a module, you will be learning a set of basic concepts and how they relate to the theoretical and research foundations of the field of psychology.

Use Concept Signaling as at Tool to Learning Key Concepts. Key concepts in each module are highlighted or signaled in

the margins of the text to help ensure you learn the main points and ideas as you make your way through the text. Importantly, make sure to read all the surrounding material in the text, not just the material highlighted in the concept boxes in the margins. Your exams will likely test your knowledge of all the assigned material in the text.

Keep Notes as You Read. Taking notes in your own words strengthens deeper, more durable learning. Avoid underlining or highlighting whole sections of text. Let your brain—not your fingers—do the work. Highlight only the important sections of text you want to review further.

Use the Running Glossary to Learn Key Terms. Key terms are highlighted (boldfaced) in the text and defined in the margins for easy reference. To ensure you understand the meaning of these terms in context, see how they are used in the adjacent paragraphs of the text.

Review Your Progress. Each module begins with a set of learning objectives. Jot down these objectives in a notebook or computer file and try to answer them as you read along or when you come to the end of module. As noted earlier, you can check your answers against the sample answers in the *Recite It* sections of the Module Review. Then test yourself by taking the brief quizzes you'll find in the *Recall It* sections of the Module Reviews. If you find you are struggling with the quiz questions, review the corresponding sections of the text to strengthen your knowledge and then test yourself again.

Get the Study Edge with the SQ3R+ Study Method

This text includes a built-in study system called the SQ3R+ study method, a system designed to help students develop more effective study habits that expands upon the SQ3R method developed by psychologist Francis P. Robinson. SQ3R is an acronym that stands for five key study features: *survey, question, read, recite,* and *review*. This text adds an additional feature, the Think About It sections of the Module Reviews, which are the "+" in the SQ3R+ study method. Here's how the SQ3R+ study method works:

1. **Survey** Preview each chapter before reading it.

2. **Question** Pose questions to yourself as you read the text to ensure you are mastering the learning objectives. The learning objectives for each module test your ability to identify, define or describe, apply, and evaluate or explain your knowledge of psychology. To become a more active learner, use the learning objectives as a set of learning goals you want to achieve as you make your way through the chapter. Generate additional questions about the material you can pose to yourself to further assess your knowledge of the material.

3. **Read**   Read the module to master the learning objectives as well as to grasp key concepts and related information. To strengthen your understanding of text material, you may find it helpful to read each module a second or third time before an exam.

4. **Recite**   When you reach the end of the module, gauge how well you understand the material by using the Module Review section to evaluate your progress. Remember to recite your knowledge of the learning objectives before looking at the sample answers in the text. Hearing yourself speak the answers enhances retention of newly learned information.

5. **Review**   Establish a study schedule for reviewing text material on a regular basis. Test yourself each time you review or reread the material to boost long-term retention. Use the brief quiz in the *Recall It* section of the Module Review to test your knowledge.

6. **Think About It**   The Think About It feature in the Module Review poses thought-provoking questions that encourage you to apply critical thinking skills and to reflect on how the material relates to your own experiences. Thinking more deeply about these concepts and relating them to your life experiences helps strengthen new learning.

I hope this guide to college success will help you succeed not only in this course but in your other courses as well. I also hope you enjoy your journey through psychology. I began my own journey through psychology in my freshman year in college and have continued along this path with a sense of wonder and joy ever since.

Please email your comments, questions, or suggestions to me at jeffnevid@gmail.com.

Jeff Nevid
New York, NY

LEARNING OBJECTIVES

After studying this chapter, you will be able to...

1 **Define** psychology and **explain** why psychology is a science.

2 **Identify** early schools of psychology and the important contributors to these schools, and **describe** the major concepts associated with each school.

3 **Identify** the major contemporary perspectives in psychology and **describe** each perspective.

4 **Identify** specialty areas or subfields of psychology and emerging specialty areas.

5 **Describe** ethnic and gender characteristics of psychologists today and the changes that have occurred over time.

6 **Identify** the steps in the scientific method.

7 **Identify** research methods that psychologists use.

8 **Describe** the ethical standards that govern research in psychology.

9 **Apply** critical thinking skills to **evaluate** claims made by others as well as online sources.

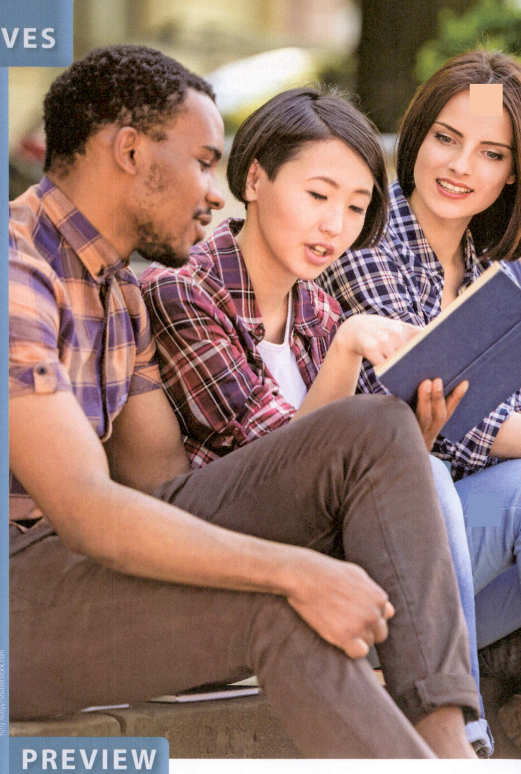

Yuriy Rudyy/Shutterstock.com

PREVIEW

The Science of Psychology

1

You. Me. Us.

This may be your first course in psychology, but it is probably not your first encounter with many of the topics psychologists study. Your earliest exposure to the subject matter of psychology probably began many years ago. Perhaps your first encounter with psychology came as you first wondered about why people do what they do or how their personalities differ. Perhaps you wondered why your third-grade classmate just couldn't seem to sit still and often disrupted the class. Or perhaps you were curious about how people relate to each other and how they influence each other's behavior. Or maybe you wondered mostly about yourself, about who you are and why you do the things you do. Perhaps one of the reasons you are taking this course is to learn more about yourself.

Psychologists study behavior in all its forms. One way of thinking about psychology is to understand that it involves the study of *you* (the behavior of other people), *me* (one's own behavior), and *us* (how our behavior is affected by groups and social influences). Psychologists are interested in studying behavior in nonhuman species as well. Studies of behavior of other animals can shed light on basic principles of behavior and may help inform our understanding of our own behavior as well.

You may find answers to many of the questions you have about yourself and others in this introductory course in psychology. But you will probably not find all the answers you are seeking. There is still so much we do not understand, so much that remains to be explored. This text, like the field of psychology itself, is really about the process of exploration—the quest for knowledge about behavior and mental processes.

As with any scientific discipline, psychology requires that opinions, assumptions, beliefs, and theories about the subject matter it studies be tested and scrutinized in the light of the available evidence. Psychologists seek answers to the questions they and others pose about human nature by using scientific methods of inquiry. Like other scientists, psychologists are professional skeptics. They have confidence only in theories that can be tied to observable evidence. As in all branches of science, investigators in the field of psychology gather evidence to test their theories, beliefs, and assumptions.

Before we go further with our exploration of psychology, let us define what we mean by the term *psychology*. Though many definitions of psychology have been proposed, the one most widely used today defines psychology as the science of behavior and mental processes. But what do these terms mean—*behavior* and *mental processes*?

Broadly speaking, anything an organism does is a form of behavior. Sitting in a chair is a form of behavior. Reading, studying, and watching TV are forms of behavior. Making yourself a sandwich and talking on the phone are forms of behavior. Smiling, dancing, and raising your arm are

Did you know that...

- One of the founders of modern psychology was such a poor student he was actually left back a grade in school? (p. 5)
- A movement that once dominated psychology believed that psychologists should turn away from the study of the mind? (p. 6)
- A major school of psychology was inspired by the view from a train? (p. 7)
- The school of psychology originated by Sigmund Freud holds that we are generally unaware of our true motives? (p. 8)
- People tend to post gloomier Facebook postings when it's raining outside than on sunny days? (p. 17)
- The popularity of women's names influences how other people judge their physical attractiveness? (p. 27)
- Pain patients reported a reduction in pain after they received a placebo ("sugar pill"), even though they were told it was a placebo? (p. 28)

also behaviors. Even thinking and dreaming are forms of behavior. Increasingly, people are interacting online, especially on social networking sites like Facebook. Online interactions are a form of social behavior and an area of increasing interest among psychologists and other social scientists.

Young people today are "digital natives" who have never known a time before the personal computer, the Web, or cell phones. They are an Internet surfing, iPoding, texting, Googling, Facebooking, and IMing generation (Nevid, 2011). Psychological attachment to cell phones is so strong that students in a recent laboratory study reported higher levels of anxiety and performed more poorly on a puzzle-solving task when they were physically separated from their cell phones than when their phones were in their possession (Clayton, Leshner, & Almond, 2015). Through the course of our study of psychology, we will examine what psychologists have learned about the psychological effects of electronic technology and social networking.

Mental processes are private experiences that constitute our inner lives. These private experiences include thoughts, feelings, dreams and daydreams, sensations, perceptions, and beliefs that others cannot directly observe or experience. Among the challenges psychologists face is finding ways of making such inner experiences available to scientific study.

Before we begin exploring how psychologists study behavior and mental processes, let us take the story of psychology back to its origins to see how it developed as a scientific discipline and where it stands today.

MODULE

1.1 Foundations of Modern Psychology

1 **Define** psychology and **explain** why psychology is a science.

2 **Identify** early schools of psychology and the important contributors to these schools, and **describe** the major concepts associated with each school.

3 **Identify** the major contemporary perspectives in psychology and **describe** each perspective.

CONCEPT 1.1
Psychology is the scientific discipline that studies behavior and mental processes.

CONCEPT 1.2
Although psychology is a relatively young science, interest in understanding the nature of mind and behavior can be traced back to ancient times.

This first module in the text sets the stage for our study of psychology. It describes the development of psychology as a scientific discipline. How did psychology develop? What were the important influences that shaped its development as a scientific discipline? Here we address those questions by recounting a brief history of psychology. Let us begin by noting that although psychology is still a young science, its origins can be traced back to ancient times.

Origins of Psychology

The story of psychology has no clear beginning. We cannot mark its birth on any calendar. We can speculate that the story very likely began when early humans developed the capacity to reflect on human nature. Perhaps they were curious, as many of us are today, about what makes people tick. But what they may have thought or said about the nature of human beings remains unknown, as no record exists of their musings.

The word **psychology** is derived from two Greek roots: *psyche*, meaning "mind," and *logos*, meaning "study" or "knowledge." So it is not surprising that serious inquiries into psychology can be traced back to ancient Greece, when philosophers began to record their thoughts about the nature of mind and behavior. Psychology remained largely an interest of philosophers, theologians, and writers for several thousand years. It did not begin to emerge as a scientific discipline until the late nineteenth century.

The founding of psychology as an experimental science is generally credited to a German scientist, Wilhelm Wundt (1832–1920) (Lamiell, 2013). Wundt (pronounced *Voont*) is deserving of the credit because in 1879 in the city of Leipzig, Germany, he established the world's first scientific laboratory dedicated to the study of psychology. With the founding of Wundt's laboratory, psychology made the transition from philosophy to science (Benjamin, 2000).

Wundt was in some respects an unlikely candidate to found a new science. As a boy, he was a poor student and was even required to repeat a grade. The problem for young Wundt was that he tended to daydream in class. He would often be found sitting with an open book in his hand, staring off into space rather than reading his assigned text (a practice this author hopes you don't emulate too closely when you open your psychology text). But he persevered, eventually graduating from medical school and, from there, launched a successful research career as a physiologist. Later, he would apply his scientific training to his true passion, the understanding of conscious experience. In establishing the first psychology laboratory, the man who had once been left back in school because he was so absorbed in his own thoughts became the first scientist of the mind.

Like any scientific discipline, the field of psychology is an unfolding story of exploration and discovery. In this text, you will encounter many of the explorers and discoverers who have shaped the continuing story of psychology. The bridge from ancient thought to the present starts with Wundt; there, we encounter his disciple Edward Titchener and structuralism, the school of thought with which both men were associated. (See ■ Figure 1.1 for a timeline of the early days of psychology.)

Wilhelm Wundt, Edward Titchener, and Structuralism

Wilhelm Wundt was interested in studying mental experiences. He used a method called **introspection**, which is an attempt to directly study consciousness by having people report on what they are consciously experiencing (Leahey, 2014). For example, he would present subjects with an object, such as a piece of fruit, and ask them to describe their impressions or perceptions of the object in terms of its shape, color, or texture and how the object felt when touched. Or subjects might be asked to sniff a scent and describe the sensations or feelings the scent evoked in them. In this way, Wundt and his students sought to break down mental experiences into their component parts, including sensations, perceptions, and feelings, and then discover the rules that determine how these elements come together to produce the full range of conscious experiences.

Edward Titchener (1867–1927), an Englishman who was a disciple of Wundt, brought Wundt's teachings and methods of introspection to the United States and other English-speaking countries. The school of psychology identified with Wundt and Titchener became known as **structuralism**, an approach that attempted to define the structure of the mind by breaking down mental experiences into their component parts.

The first American to work in Wundt's experimental laboratory was the psychologist G. Stanley Hall (1844–1924) (Johnson, 2000). In 1892, Hall founded the American Psychological Association (APA), now the largest organization of psychologists in the United States, and he served as its first president. Nine years earlier, in 1883, he had established the first psychology laboratory in the United States, which

Psychologists study what we do and what we think, feel, dream, sense, and perceive. They use scientific methods to guide their investigations of behavior and mental processes.

David Young-Wolff/PhotoEdit

Wilhelm Wundt.

Nicku/Shutterstock.com

CONCEPT 1.3
Structuralism, the early school of psychology associated with Wundt and Titchener, used introspection as a method of revealing the fundamental structures of mental experience in the form of sensations, perceptions, and feelings.

psychology The science of behavior and mental processes.

introspection Inward focusing on mental experiences, such as sensations or feelings.

structuralism The school of psychology that attempts to understand the structure of the mind by breaking it down into its component parts.

1860	• Gustav Fechner publishes *Elements of Psychophysics*
1875	• William James gives first psychology lecture at Harvard
1878	• G. Stanley Hall receives first Ph.D. in psychology in the U.S.
1879	• Wilhelm Wundt establishes first psychology laboratory
1883	• First American psychology laboratory established at Johns Hopkins University by G. Stanley Hall
1887	• G. Stanley Hall initiates the *American JOURNAL of Psychology*
1889	• James Mark Baldwin establishes first Canadian psychology laboratory at University of Toronto
1890	• James writes first psychology text, *Principles of Psychology*
1892	• American Psychological Association (APA) formed; G. Stanley Hall first president
1894	• Margaret Floy Washburn is first woman to receive a Ph.D. in psychology
1895	• Sigmund Freud publishes first work on psychology
1896	• Lightner Witmer establishes the first psychology clinic in the U.S.
1900	• Freud publishes *The Interpretation of Dreams*
1905	• Two Frenchmen, Alfred Binet and Théodore Simon, announce development of the first intelligence test, which they describe as "a measuring scale of intelligence" • Mary Whiton Calkins becomes first woman president of APA
1908	• Ivan Pavlov's work on conditioning first appears in an American scientific journal
1910	• Max Wertheimer and colleagues begin research on Gestalt psychology
1913	• Watson publishes the behaviorist manifesto, *Psychology as the Behaviorist Views It*
1920	• Francis Sumner is first African American to receive a Ph.D. in psychology in the U.S. • Henry Alston is first African American to publish his research findings in a major psychology journal in the U.S.

FIGURE 1.1 Timeline of the Early Days of Psychology

CONCEPT 1.4

William James, the founder of functionalism, believed that psychology should focus on how our behavior and mental processes help us adapt to the demands we face in the world.

CONCEPT 1.5

Behaviorism was based on the belief that psychology would advance as a science only if it turned away from the study of mental processes and limited itself to the study of observable behaviors that could be recorded and measured.

was housed at Johns Hopkins University (Benjamin, 2000). Although Hall played a pivotal role in the early days of psychology in the United States, Harvard psychologist William James is generally recognized as the father of American psychology.

William James and Functionalism

William James (1842–1910) was trained as a medical doctor but made important contributions to both psychology and philosophy. Although he too used introspection, he shifted the focus to the *functions* of behavior.

James founded **functionalism**, the school of psychology that focused on how behavior helps individuals adapt to demands placed upon them in the environment. Whereas structuralists were concerned with understanding the structure of the human mind, functionalists were concerned with the functions of mental processes (Willingham, 2007). Unlike the structuralists, James did not believe that conscious experience can be parceled into discrete elements. To James, consciousness is not like a jigsaw puzzle that can be pieced together from its component parts.

Functionalists examined the roles or functions of mental processes—*why* we do *what* we do. For example, James believed we develop habits, such as the characteristic ways in which we use a fork or a spoon, because they enable us to perform more effectively in meeting the many demands we face in daily life.

John Watson and Behaviorism

In the early 1900s, a new force in psychology gathered momentum called **behaviorism.** Its credo was that psychology should limit itself to the study of overt behavior that observers could record and measure. The founder of behaviorism was the American psychologist John Broadus Watson (1878–1958). Watson reasoned that because you can never observe another person's mental processes, psychology would never advance as a science unless it eliminated mentalistic concepts like mind, consciousness, thinking, and feeling. He rejected introspection as a method of scientific inquiry and proposed that psychology should become a science of behavior, not of mental processes (Tweney & Budzynski, 2000). In this respect, he shared with the ancient Greek philosopher Aristotle the belief that science should rely on observable events. The problem with introspectionism is that there is no way to directly observe a person's mental experiences or know how one person's feelings or sensations compare to another's.

Watson believed that the environment molds the behavior of humans and other animals. He even boasted that if he were given control over the lives of infants, he could determine the kinds of adults they would become:

> Give me a dozen healthy infants, well-formed, and my own specified world to bring them up in and I'll guarantee to take any one at random and train him to become any type of specialist I might suggest—doctor, lawyer, merchant-chief and, yes, even beggar-man and thief, regardless of his talents, penchants, tendencies, abilities, vocations, and the race of his ancestors. (Watson, 1924, p. 82)

No one, of course, took up Watson's challenge, so we never will know how "a dozen healthy infants" would have fared under his direction. Psychologists today, however, believe that human development is much more complex than Watson thought. Few would believe that Watson could have succeeded in meeting the challenge he posed.

Nonetheless, by the 1920s, behaviorism had become the main school of psychology in the United States, and it remained the dominant force in American psychology for several generations. Its popularity owed a great deal to the work of the Harvard University

 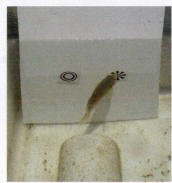

By reinforcing specific responses, we can teach a raccoon to shoot a basketball and a fish to peck at a particular shape. Still, the three-point shot might be beyond the raccoon's range.

Source: Courtesy of Ulrike Siebeck, reproduced with permission of the *Journal of Experimental Biology.* U. E. Siebeck, L. Litherland and G. M. Wallis, JEB 212, 2113–2119 (2009). http://jeb.biologists.org/cgi/content/full/212/13/2113

psychologist B. F. Skinner (1904–1990). Skinner studied how behavior is shaped by rewards and punishments, the environmental consequences that follow specific responses. Skinner showed he could train animals to perform simple behaviors by rewarding particular responses. A rat could learn to press a bar and a pigeon to peck a button if they were rewarded for these responses by receiving pellets of food. Skinner also showed how more complex behaviors could be learned and maintained by manipulation of rewards, which he called *reinforcers.* In some of his more colorful demonstrations of the use of reinforcement, he trained a pigeon to play a tune on a toy piano, and a pair of pigeons to play a type of ping-pong in which the birds rolled a ball back and forth between them. These methods can even be used to teach a raccoon to shoot a basketball and to train fish to tap a particular target shape (Carroll, 2009).

Although Skinner studied mainly pigeons and rats, he believed that the same principles of learning he observed in laboratory animals could be applied to humans as well. He argued that human behavior is as much a product of environmental consequences as the behavior of other animals. Everything we do, from saying "excuse me" when we sneeze, to attending class, to reading a book, represents responses learned through reinforcement, even though we cannot expect to recall the many reinforcement occasions involved in acquiring and maintaining these behaviors.

Max Wertheimer and Gestalt Psychology

In 1910, at about the time John Watson was appealing to psychologists to abandon the study of the mind, a young German psychologist, Max Wertheimer (1880–1943), was traveling by train through central Germany on vacation (Hunt, 1993). What he saw looking through the window of the train would lead him to found a new movement in psychology, which he called **Gestalt psychology**, the school of psychology that studies ways in which the brain organizes and structures our perceptions of the world.

What had captured Wertheimer's attention was the illusion that objects in the distance—telegraph poles, houses, and hilltops—appeared to be moving along with the train, even though they were obviously standing still. Wertheimer was intrigued to find out why the phenomenon occurred. He believed the illusion was not a trick of the eye but reflected higher-level processes in the brain that created a false perception of movement. He promptly canceled his vacation and headed back to his laboratory to begin studying this phenomenon. The experiments he conducted with two assistants, Wolfgang Köhler (1887–1967) and Kurt Koffka (1886–1941), led to major discoveries about the nature of perception—the processes by which we organize sense impressions and form meaningful representations of the world around us.

functionalism The school of psychology that focuses on the adaptive functions of behavior.

behaviorism The school of psychology that holds that psychology should limit itself to the study of overt, observable behavior.

Gestalt psychology The school of psychology that holds that the brain structures our perceptions of the world in terms of meaningful patterns or wholes.

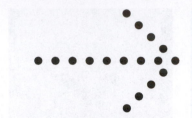

FIGURE 1.2 **What Is This?**

CONCEPT 1.6

Gestalt psychology was based on the principle that the human brain organizes our perceptions of the world, so that we perceive organized patterns or wholes, not individual bits and pieces of sense experiences added together.

CONCEPT LINK

Although the influences of Gestalt psychology extend to many areas of psychology, it is best known for its contributions to the study of perception. See Module 3.5.

CONCEPT 1.7

According to Freud, much of our behavior is determined by unconscious forces and motives that lie beyond the reach of ordinary awareness.

CONCEPT LINK

Freud's model of therapy, called psychoanalysis, is based on the belief that therapeutic change comes from uncovering and working through unconscious conflicts within the personality. See Module 14.1.

CONCEPT 1.8

Although some early schools of psychology have essentially disappeared, contemporary perspectives in the field, including the behavioral, psychodynamic, humanistic, physiological, cognitive, and sociocultural perspectives, continue to evolve and to shape our understandings of behavior.

gestalt A German word meaning "unitary form" or "pattern."

unconscious In Freudian theory, the part of the mind that lies outside the range of ordinary awareness and that contains primitive drives and instincts.

The Gestalt psychologists rejected the structuralist belief that mental experience could be understood by breaking it down into its component parts. The German word **gestalt** can be roughly translated as "unitary form" or "pattern." Gestalt psychologists believe the brain organizes our perceptions of the world by grouping elements together into unified or organized wholes, rather than as individual bits and pieces of sense experience (Sayim, Westheimer, & Herzog, 2010). The well-known Gestalt maxim that the "whole is greater than the sum of the parts" expresses this core belief. You perceive the dots in ■ Figure 1.2 not as a formless array of individual dots but as a representation of an arrow. When you see a large number of black objects flying overhead, you instantly recognize them as a flock of birds flying in formation. In other words, your brain interprets what your eyes see as organized patterns or wholes.

Sigmund Freud and Psychoanalysis

Around the time that behaviorism and Gestalt psychology were establishing a foothold in organized psychology, a very different model of psychology was emerging. It was based on the writings of an Austrian physician named Sigmund Freud (1856–1939). Freud's psychology focused not only on the mind, but also on a region of the mind that lay beyond the reach of ordinary consciousness—a region he called the **unconscious**. Freud conceived of the unconscious as the repository of primitive sexual and aggressive drives or instincts and of the wishes, impulses, and urges that arise from those drives or instincts (Kihlstrom, 2015). He believed that the motives underlying our behavior involve sexual and aggressive impulses that lie in the murky depths of the unconscious, hidden away from our ordinary awareness of ourselves. In other words, we may do or say things without understanding the true motives that prompted these behaviors.

Freud also believed that early childhood experiences play a determining role in shaping our personalities and behavior, including abnormal behaviors like excessive fears or phobias. He held that abnormal behavior patterns are rooted in unconscious conflicts originating in childhood. These conflicts involve a dynamic struggle within the unconscious mind between unacceptable sexual or aggressive impulses striving for expression and opposing mental forces seeking to keep this threatening material out of conscious awareness. Thus, Freud's view of psychology, and that of his followers, is often called the **psychodynamic perspective**.

Unlike Wundt, James, and Watson, Freud was a therapist, and his main aim was to help people overcome psychological problems. He developed a form of psychotherapy or "talk therapy" that he called **psychoanalysis** (discussed in Chapter 14). Psychoanalysis is a type of mental detective work. It incorporates methods, such as analysis of dreams and of "slips of the tongue," that Freud believed could be used to gain insight into the nature of the underlying motives and conflicts of which his patients were unaware. Freud maintained that once these unconscious conflicts were brought into the light of conscious awareness, they could be successfully resolved, or "worked through," during the course of therapy.

Contemporary Perspectives in Psychology

What do we find when we look over the landscape of psychology today? For one thing, we find a discipline that owes a great debt to its founders but is constantly reinventing itself to meet new challenges. Not all schools of thought have survived the test of time. Structuralism, for one, has essentially disappeared from the landscape; others maintain small groups of devoted followers who remain true to the original precepts. But by and large, the early schools of psychology—functionalism, behaviorism, Gestalt psychology, and psychoanalysis—have continued to evolve or have been consolidated within broader perspectives. Today, the landscape of psychology can be divided into six major perspectives: the behavioral, psychodynamic, humanistic, physiological, cognitive, and sociocultural.

The Behavioral Perspective

The linchpin of the **behavioral perspective** is behaviorism, the belief that environmental influences determine behavior and that psychology should restrict itself to the study of observable behavior. However, many psychologists believe that traditional behaviorism is too simplistic or limited to explain complex human behavior. Though traditional behaviorism continues to influence modern psychology, it is no longer the dominant force it was during its heyday in the early to mid-1900s.

Many psychologists today adopt a broader, learning-based perspective called **social-cognitive theory** (formerly called *social-learning theory*). This perspective originated in the 1960s with a group of learning theorists who broke away from traditional behaviorism (see Chapter 11). They believed that behavior is shaped not only by environmental factors, such as rewards and punishments, but also by *cognitive* factors, such as the value placed on different objects or goals (for example, getting good grades) and expectancies about the outcomes of behavior ("If I do X, then Y will follow."). Social-cognitive theorists challenged their fellow psychologists to find ways to study these mental processes rather than casting them aside as unscientific, as traditional behaviorists would. Traditional behaviorists may not deny that thinking occurs, but they do believe that mental processes lie outside the range of scientific study.

The behavioral perspective led to the development of a major school of therapy, **behavior therapy**. Behavior therapy involves the systematic application of learning principles that are grounded in the behaviorist tradition of Watson and Skinner. Whereas psychoanalysts are concerned with the workings of the unconscious mind, behavior therapists help people acquire more adaptive behaviors to overcome psychological problems such as fears and social inhibitions. Today, many behavior therapists subscribe to a broader therapeutic approach, called *cognitive-behavioral therapy*, which incorporates techniques for changing maladaptive thoughts as well as overt behaviors (see Chapter 14).

The Psychodynamic Perspective

The psychodynamic perspective remains a vibrant force in psychology. Like other contemporary perspectives in psychology, it continues to evolve. As we'll see in Chapter 11, "neo-Freudians" (psychodynamic theorists who have followed in the Freudian tradition) tend to place less emphasis on basic drives like sex and aggression than Freud did and more emphasis on processes of self-awareness, self-direction, and conscious choice.

The influence of psychodynamic theory extends well beyond the field of psychology. Its focus on our inner lives—our fantasies, wishes, dreams, and hidden motives—has had a profound impact on popular literature, art, and culture. Beliefs that psychological problems may be rooted in childhood and that people may not be consciously aware of their deeper motives and wishes continue to be widely endorsed, even by people not formally schooled in Freudian psychology.

The Humanistic Perspective: A "Third Force" in Psychology

In the 1950s, another force began to achieve prominence in psychology. Known as **humanistic psychology**, it was a response to the two dominant perspectives at the time, behaviorism and Freudian psychology. For that reason, humanistic psychology was called the "third force" in psychology. Humanistic psychologists, including the Americans Abraham Maslow (1908–1970) and Carl Rogers (1902–1987), rejected the deterministic views of behaviorism and psychodynamic psychology—beliefs that

psychodynamic perspective The view that behavior is influenced by the struggle between unconscious sexual or aggressive impulses and opposing forces that try to keep this threatening material out of consciousness.

psychoanalysis Freud's method of psychotherapy; it focuses on uncovering and working through unconscious conflicts he believed were at the root of psychological problems.

behavioral perspective An approach to the study of psychology that focuses on the role of learning and importance of environmental influences in explaining behavior.

social-cognitive theory A contemporary learning-based model that emphasizes the roles of cognitive and environmental factors in determining behavior.

behavior therapy A form of therapy that involves the systematic application of the principles of learning.

humanistic psychology The school of psychology that believes that free will and conscious choice are essential aspects of the human experience.

CONCEPT 1.11
Humanistic psychology emphasizes personal freedom and responsibility for our actions and the value of self-awareness and acceptance of our true selves.

CONCEPT 1.12
The physiological perspective examines relationships between biological processes and behavior.

CONCEPT 1.13
Evolutionary psychology subscribes to the view that our behavior reflects inherited predispositions or tendencies that increased the likelihood of survival of our early ancestors.

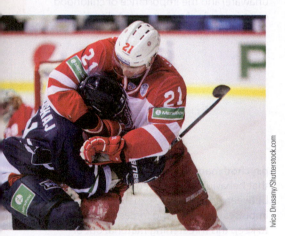
Ivica Drusany/Shutterstock.com

Evolutionary psychologists believe that behavioral tendencies that had survival value to ancestral humans, such as aggressiveness, may have been passed down the genetic highway to modern humans. Even our penchant for aggressive sports might reflect these genetic underpinnings.

humanistic perspective An approach to the study of psychology that applies the principles of humanistic psychology.

physiological perspective An approach to the study of psychology that focuses on the relationships between biological processes and behavior.

evolutionary psychology A branch of psychology that focuses on the role of evolutionary processes in shaping behavior.

cognitive perspective An approach to the study of psychology that focuses on the processes by which we acquire knowledge.

human behavior is determined by the environment (in the case of behaviorism) or by the interplay of unconscious forces and motives lying outside the person's awareness (in the case of Freudian psychology). Humanistic psychologists believe that free will and conscious choice are essential aspects of the human experience.

Psychologists who adopt a **humanistic perspective** believe that psychology should focus on conscious experiences, even if those experiences are subjective and cannot be directly observed and scientifically measured. Humanistic psychologists view each of us as individuals who possess distinctive clusters of traits and abilities and unique frames of reference or perspectives on life. They emphasize the value of self-awareness and of becoming an authentic person by being true to oneself (Grogan, 2013). They also stress the creative potentials of individuals and their ability to make choices that imbue their lives with meaning and purpose.

The Physiological Perspective

The **physiological perspective** examines relationships between biological processes and behavior. It is identified not with any one contributor but, rather, with many psychologists and neuroscientists who focus on the biological bases of behavior and mental processes.

Sitting atop your shoulders is a wondrous mass of tissue—your brain—that governs virtually everything you do. The brain is the center of the nervous system, an incredibly complex living computer that allows you to sense the world around you, to think and feel, to move through space, to regulate heartbeat and other bodily functions, and to coordinate what you see and hear with what you do. Your nervous system also allows you to visualize the world and imagine worlds that never were. As we'll find throughout this text, physiological psychology has illuminated our understanding of the biological bases of behavior and mental processes, including the roles of heredity, hormones, and the nervous system.

Evolutionary psychology is a movement within modern psychology that applies principles derived from Charles Darwin's theory of evolution to a wide range of behavior (Bolhuis & Wynne, 2009; Buss, 2008; Confer et al., 2010; Gallup & Frederick, 2010). Darwin (1809–1882) believed that all life forms, including humans, evolved from earlier life forms by adapting over time to the demands of their natural environments.

Evolutionary psychologists believe that behavioral *tendencies* or *predispositions*, such as aggressive tendencies, might be rooted in our genes, having been passed along from generation to generation from ancestral times all the way down the genetic highway to us. Aggressive traits may have helped early humans survive as hunters of wild game, even if they are no longer adaptive in modern society. Evolutionary psychologists examine behaviors in different species that may have been influenced by evolutionary processes, including aggression, mating practices, and even altruism (that is, self-sacrifice of the individual for the group). But they also recognize that environmental factors, especially cultural learning and family influences, play important roles in determining whether behavioral tendencies or predispositions lead to actual behavior (for example, whether or not a person acts aggressively).

The Cognitive Perspective

Psychologists working from a **cognitive perspective** study mental processes, including thinking, learning, memory, use of language, and problem solving. These processes enable people to gain knowledge about themselves and the world around them. The word *cognitive* comes from the Latin word *cognitio*, meaning "knowledge."

Cognitive psychologists make no apology for studying mental experience; they believe the methods they use to study thinking or cognition are well grounded in the scientific tradition. After all, no one has ever observed subatomic particles such as protons and neutrons, but that hasn't prevented physicists from conducting scientific studies that attempt to investigate their properties. Chapter 7 examines the intriguing research findings reported by cognitive psychologists.

The Sociocultural Perspective

Psychologists who adopt a **sociocultural perspective** examine how behavior and attitudes are shaped by social and cultural influences to which people are exposed. They focus on the influence of such factors as age, ethnicity, gender, sexual orientation, lifestyle, income level, disability status, and exposure to discrimination and prejudice.

The study of sociocultural factors in shaping behavior is especially relevant today because of the increasing diversity of American society. Ethnic minority groups now represent about one-third of the U.S. population, but are expected to grow to nearly half the population by the year 2050. The two fastest growing population groups in the United States are Hispanics (Latinos) and people with a multiracial identity, which include such high-profile individuals as President Barack Obama, singer Nicki Minaj, and baseball great Derek Jeter ("Hispanics to Total," 2014; Saulny, 2011).

The sociocultural perspective poses a number of questions to which we shall return later in the text: Does susceptibility to visual illusions vary across cultures? Are there gender differences in basic abilities in math or verbal skills? How does culture influence concepts of the self? Are there ethnic differences in drug use patterns, and if so, how might we account for them? Are there racial differences in intelligence, and if so, what do we make of them? What role does acculturation play in the psychological adjustment of immigrant groups?

Psychologists recognize that research samples need to be broadly representative of the populations to which they wish to generalize their findings. Much of the early research in psychology focused on White, middle-class samples, composed largely of male college students. We should not assume that findings based on narrowly defined groups of individuals necessarily generalize to other groups who have different life experiences.

Summary of Contemporary Perspectives

It's important to realize that no one perspective is necessarily right and the others wrong. Each major perspective in contemporary psychology focuses on different aspects of behavior or psychological functioning. Each has something unique to offer to our understanding of human behavior, and none offers a complete view. Given the complexity of human behavior and experience, it is not surprising that psychology has spawned multiple pathways for approaching its subject matter. It is also not surprising that many psychologists today identify with an *eclectic* approach to understanding human behavior—one that draws on theories and principles representing different perspectives. We should recognize, too, that contemporary psychology is not divided as neatly into different schools of thought as it seemed to be in its early days. There is considerable room for overlap among the different perspectives.

In addition to the six major perspectives that dot the landscape of contemporary psychology, a growing movement within psychology, called **positive psychology**, is directed toward the study of positive aspects of human experience, such as love, happiness, altruism, and hope (Donaldson, Csikszentmihalyi, & Nakamura, 2011; Hojjat & Cramer, 2013; McNulty & Fincham, 2012). Psychologists have devoted a great deal of attention to understanding human weaknesses and deficits, including emotional problems, effects of traumatic stress, and problem behaviors such as violence and drug addiction. Founded by psychologist Martin Seligman, positive psychology balances the scale by focusing on our virtues and strengths, not our flaws (Seligman et al., 2005). Throughout the text, we discuss aspects of positive psychology, including love, helping behavior, optimism, successful aging, happiness, self-esteem, self-actualization, and creativity.

In Concept Chart 1.1, the first of many such charts in the text, you'll find examples of the kinds of general questions that psychologists from each of the major contemporary perspectives might ask, as well as the kinds of questions they might

DNA ANALYSIS

CSL, CartoonStock ltd

CONCEPT 1.14
The cognitive perspective focuses on understanding the mental processes by which people gain knowledge about themselves and the world around them.

CONCEPT 1.15
The sociocultural perspective places behavior within a broad social context by examining the influences of ethnicity, gender, lifestyle, socioeconomic status, and culture.

© vadim kozlovsky/Shutterstock.com

sociocultural perspective An approach to the study of psychology that emphasizes the role of social and cultural influences on behavior.

positive psychology A contemporary movement within psychology that emphasizes the study of human virtues and assets, rather than weaknesses and deficits.

pose to learn more about specific topics. These topics are introduced here to help you distinguish among the various perspectives in contemporary psychology. They will be discussed further in later chapters.

Concept Chart 1.1 Contemporary Perspectives in Psychology: How They Differ

Perspective	General Questions	Questions About Specific Topics		
		Aggression	**Depression**	**Obesity**
Behavioral	How do early learning experiences shape our behavior as adults?	How is aggressive behavior learned? How is it rewarded or reinforced? Does exposure to violence in the media or among one's peers play a role?	How is depression related to changes in reinforcement patterns? What social skills are needed to establish and maintain social relationships that could serve as sources of reinforcement?	How might unhealthy eating habits lead to obesity? How might we change those habits?
Psychodynamic	How do unresolved conflicts from childhood affect adult behavior? How can people be helped to cope with these conflicts?	How is aggression related to unconscious impulses? Against whom are these impulses really directed?	How might depression be related to unresolved loss? Might it represent anger turned inward?	Might obesity relate to childhood conflicts revolving around unresolved needs for love and support? Might food have become a substitute for love?
Humanistic	How do people pursue goals that give their lives a sense of meaning and purpose?	Might violence be related to frustration arising when people are blocked from pursuing their goals? How might we turn this around to prevent violence?	Might depression be related to a lack of self-esteem or a threat to one's self-image? Might it stem from a sense of purposelessness or lack of meaning in life?	What sets the stage for obesity? Does food have a special meaning for obese people? How can we help them find other sources of satisfaction?
Physiological	How do biological structures and processes make behavior possible? What roles do nature (heredity) and nurture (environment) play in such areas as intelligence, language development, and aggression?	What brain mechanisms control aggressive behavior? Might brain abnormalities explain violent behavior in some people?	How are changes in brain chemistry related to depression? What genetic links might there be?	Is obesity inherited? What genes may be involved? How would knowledge of a genetic basis lead to new approaches to treatment or prevention?
Cognitive	How do people solve problems, make decisions, and develop language?	What thoughts trigger aggressive responses? What beliefs do aggressive people hold that might increase their potential for violence?	What types of thinking patterns are related to depression? How might they be changed to help people overcome depression or prevent it from occurring?	How does obesity affect a person's self-concept? What thoughts lead to eating binges? How might they be changed?
Sociocultural	How do concepts of self differ across cultures? How do social and cultural influences shape behavior?	What social conditions give rise to drug use and aggressive behavior? Does our society condone or even reward certain forms of violence, such as sexual aggression against women or spousal abuse?	Is depression linked to social stresses, such as poverty or unemployment? Why is depression more common among certain groups of people, especially women? Does it have to do with their expected social roles?	Are some groups at greater risk of obesity than others? Do cultural differences in dietary patterns and customs play a role?

MODULE REVIEW   1.1 Foundations of Modern Psychology

Recite It

1. **Define** psychology and **explain** why psychology is a science.

   Psychology is the science of (a) _____ and mental processes. Psychology is a science because it applies the scientific model in testing claims and beliefs in the light of (b) _____.

2. **Identify** early schools of psychology and the important contributors to these schools, and **describe** the major concepts associated with each school.

   (c) _____ is the earliest school of psychology. It was identified with Wilhelm (d) _____ and Edward Titchener, and it attempted to break down mental experiences into their component parts—sensations, perceptions, and feelings. Functionalism is the school of psychology founded by William (e) _____. It attempts to explain our behavior in terms of the (f) _____ it serves in helping us adapt to the environment.
   Behaviorism is the school of psychology begun by John (g) _____. It holds that psychology should limit itself to observable phenomena—namely, (h) _____.
   (i) _____ psychology is the school of psychology founded by Max (j) _____. It is grounded in the belief that the brain structures our perceptions of the world in terms of organized patterns or (k) _____.
   Psychoanalysis, the school of thought originated by Sigmund (l) _____, emphasizes the role of (m) _____ motives and conflicts in determining human behavior.

3. **Identify** the major contemporary perspectives in psychology and **describe** each perspective.

   The (n) _____ perspective focuses on observable behavior, the role of learning, and the importance of environmental influences on behavior.
   The (o) _____ perspective represents the model of psychology developed by Freud and his followers. It holds that our behavior and personalities are shaped by unconscious motives and conflicts that lie outside the range of ordinary awareness.
   The (p) _____ perspective reflects the views of humanistic psychologists such as Carl (q) _____ and Abraham (r) _____, who emphasized the importance of subjective conscious experience and personal freedom and responsibility.
   The (s) _____ perspective examines the ways in which behavior and mental experience are influenced by biological processes such as heredity, hormones, and the workings of the brain and other parts of the nervous system.
   The (t) _____ perspective focuses on mental processes that allow us to gain knowledge about ourselves and the world.
   The (u) _____ perspective examines how our behavior and attitudes are shaped by social and cultural influences.

Recall It

1. William James is to functionalism as _____ _____ is to structuralism.

2. The early school of psychology called structuralism
   a. rejected the use of introspection as a research method.
   b. focused on overt behavior.
   c. investigated the structure of the mind.
   d. was concerned with the functions of behavior.

3. Which of the early schools of psychology believed that psychology should be limited to the study of observable behavior?

4. Gestalt psychology focuses on
   a. the organization of the mind.
   b. the ways in which the brain organizes and structures our perceptions of the world.
   c. the functions of behavior.
   d. the role of self-actualization in motivating behavior.

5. Humanistic psychologists rejected the notion that unconscious processes and environmental influences determine our behavior. Rather, they emphasized the importance of _____ in understanding behavior.
   a. conscious choice
   b. heredity and physiological processes
   c. classical and operant conditioning
   d. the underlying structures of the mind

6. Which psychological perspective originated with Sigmund Freud?

Think About It

- Suppose you wanted to explain behavior in terms of how people's habits help them adapt to the environmental demands they face. What early school of psychology would you be adopting in your approach?

- Suppose you wanted to understand behavior in terms of underlying forces within the personality that influence behavior

even though the person may not be aware of them. What early school of psychology would this approach represent?

- Humanistic psychologists emphasize the importance of finding a purpose or meaning in life. What are your purposes in life? How can you make your own life more meaningful?

Recite It *answers placed at the end of chapter.*

MODULE

1.2 Psychologists: Who They Are and What They Do

4 Identify specialty areas or subfields of psychology and emerging specialty areas.

5 Describe ethnic and gender characteristics of psychologists today and the changes that have occurred over time.

When you think of a psychologist, do you form a mental image of someone working in a hospital or clinic who treats people with psychological problems? This image describes one particular type of psychologist—a clinical psychologist. But there are many types. Psychology is a diverse profession because of the large number of areas in the field and because of the many different roles psychologists perform. Some psychologists teach and conduct research. Others provide psychological services to individuals or to organizations, such as schools or businesses. Psychologists are usually identified with one particular specialty or subfield within psychology—for example, experimental, clinical, developmental, educational, or social psychology.

Some psychologists conduct **basic research**—research that seeks to expand our understanding of psychological phenomena even if such knowledge does not lead directly to any practical benefits. These psychologists typically work for universities or government agencies. Some psychologists conduct **applied research**—research intended to find solutions to specific problems. For example, a psychologist might apply research on learning and memory to studying methods of enhancing the educational experiences of children with intellectual disability. Still other psychologists work in applied areas of psychology in which they provide services to people or organizations. These include clinical, counseling, school, and industrial/organizational psychologists. Many of these applied psychologists also conduct research in the areas in which they practice. In this module, we take a closer look at the various types of psychologists.

CONCEPT 1.16
The field of psychology consists of an ever-growing number of specialty areas.

basic research Research focused on acquiring knowledge even if such knowledge has no direct practical application.

applied research Research that attempts to find solutions to specific problems.

Specialty Areas of Psychology

All psychologists study behavior and mental processes, but they pursue this knowledge in different ways, in different settings, and from different perspectives. The following sections provide a rundown of some of the major specialty areas within the field of psychology and some emerging ones.

Most psychologists earn doctoral degrees in their area of specialization, such as experimental psychology, clinical psychology, or social psychology. The PhD (doctor of philosophy) is the most common doctoral degree and is awarded after completion of required graduate coursework and a dissertation, which involves an original research project. Some psychologists seeking practice careers may earn a doctor of psychology degree (PsyD), a doctoral degree that is focused more on practitioner skills than on research skills. Others may pursue graduate programs in schools of education and be awarded a doctorate in education (EdD). In some specialty areas, such as school psychology and industrial/organizational (I/O) psychology, the master's degree is recognized as the entry-level degree for professional work in the field.

Major Specialty Areas

Concept Chart 1.2 provides an overview of the major specialties in psychology discussed in this section. ■ Figure 1.3 shows the percentages of psychologists working in major specialty areas, and ■ Figure 1.4 summarizes where psychologists work.

Experimental psychologists apply experimental methods to the study of behavior and mental processes. They study such processes as learning, sensation and perception, and cognition. Some experimental psychologists, called **comparative psychologists**, seek to understand animal behavior for its own sake and possibly for what it might teach us about human behavior (Dewsbury, 2000). Others, called **physiological psychologists** (also known as *biological psychologists*), study the biological bases of behavior.

Clinical psychologists evaluate and treat people with psychological disorders, such as depression and anxiety disorders. They may use psychotherapy to help people overcome psychological problems or cope better with the stresses they face in their lives. They may administer psychological tests to better understand people's problems or to evaluate their intellectual abilities or personalities.

Many conduct research in the field or train future psychologists. Others work in hospitals or clinics, while still others work in private practice or university settings. As Figure 1.3 shows, clinical psychologists represent the largest group of psychologists.

The professional roles of clinical psychologists in evaluating and treating psychological disorders often overlap with those of **psychiatrists**, medical doctors who complete residency training in the medical specialty of psychiatry. Unlike psychiatrists, however, psychologists cannot prescribe drugs. But even these lines may be blurring now that a small number of psychologists have been trained in a specialized program to prescribe drugs to treat psychological disorders (Bradshaw, 2008; Meyers, 2005).

Counseling psychologists help people who have adjustment problems that are usually not as severe as the kinds of problems that clinical psychologists treat. If you did not know what course of study to follow in college, or if you were having a difficult time adjusting to college, you might talk to a counseling psychologist about it. Counseling psychologists also help people make vocational decisions or resolve marital problems. Many work in college counseling centers or community-based counseling or mental health centers.

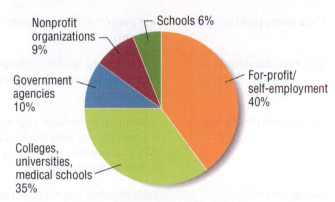

FIGURE 1.3 **Psychologists' Areas of Specialization**
Clinical psychologists make up the largest group of psychologists, followed by counseling psychologists and industrial/organizational psychologists.

Source: American Psychological Association, 2004.

Other 17.9%
Cognitive 1.1%
Experimental 1.5%
Health 1.6%
Educational 2.2%
Developmental 3.1%
School 4.0%
Industrial/Organizational 4.6%
Counseling 11.3%
Clinical 52.7%

Nonprofit organizations 9%
Schools 6%
Government agencies 10%
For-profit/self-employment 40%
Colleges, universities, medical schools 35%

FIGURE 1.4 **Where Psychologists Work**
The largest group of psychologists works in settings that provide psychological services. Many work at colleges and universities as teachers, researchers, administrators, or supervisors of psychologists in training. Some also work in schools or government agencies.

Source: American Psychological Association, 2003.

experimental psychologists Psychologists who apply experimental methods to the study of behavior and mental processes.

comparative psychologists Psychologists who study behavioral similarities and differences among animal species.

physiological psychologists Psychologists who focus on the biological underpinnings of behavior.

clinical psychologists Psychologists who use psychological techniques to evaluate and treat individuals with mental or psychological disorders.

psychiatrists Medical doctors who specialize in the diagnosis and treatment of mental or psychological disorders.

counseling psychologists Psychologists who help people clarify their goals and make life decisions or find ways of overcoming problems in various areas of their lives.

Concept Chart 1.2 Specialty Areas of Psychology

Types of Psychologists	Nature of Specialty	Typical Questions Studied
Experimental psychologists	Conduct research on learning, cognition, sensation and perception, biological bases of behavior, and animal behavior	How do various states of arousal affect learning? What brain centers are responsible for memory?
Clinical psychologists	Evaluate and treat people with psychological problems and disorders, such as depression and schizophrenia	How can we diagnose anxiety? Is depression treated more effectively with psychotherapy or drug therapy?
Counseling psychologists	Help people with adjustment problems	What kind of occupation would this student find fulfilling? Why does this person find it difficult to make friends?
School psychologists	Work in school systems to help children with academic problems or special needs	Would this child profit from special education, or would he or she be better off in a regular classroom?
Educational psychologists	Construct standardized psychological and educational tests (such as the SAT); improve course planning and instructional methods	Is this test a valid predictor of success in college? How can we teach algebra more efficiently?
Developmental psychologists	Study physical, cognitive, social, and personality development across the life span	At what age do children begin to walk or speak? What types of crises do people face in middle or later adulthood?
Personality psychologists	Study the psychological characteristics that make each of us unique	What is the structure of personality? How do we measure personality?
Social psychologists	Study the nature and causes of people's thoughts, feelings, and behavior in social situations	What are the origins of prejudice? Why do people do things as members of groups that they would not do as individuals?
Environmental psychologists	Study the ways in which people's behavior and mental processes influence, and are influenced by, their physical environments	What are the effects of city life on people? How does overcrowding affect people's health and behavior?
Industrial/organizational psychologists	Study the relationships between people and their work environments	How can we find out who would perform well in this position? How can we make hiring and promotion fairer? How can we enhance employees' motivation?
Health psychologists	Study the relationships between psychological factors and the prevention and treatment of physical illness	How can we help people avoid risky sexual behaviors? How can we help people quit smoking and start to exercise?
Consumer psychologists	Study relationships between psychological factors and consumers' preferences and purchasing behavior	Why do people select particular brands? What types of people prefer a particular type of product?

What are the different specialty areas in psychology? What types of questions do the different types of psychologists study?

Environmental psychologists suggest that by dimming the lights you may avoid turning a disagreement with someone into a heated argument.

Do you feel cheerier on pleasant spring days than in the "dog days" of summer? Environmental psychologists find a link between moods and outdoor temperature.

School psychologists work in school systems, where they help children with academic, emotional, and behavioral problems and evaluate students for placement in special education programs. They are also team players who work collaboratively with teachers and other professionals in providing a broad range of services for children.

Educational psychologists develop tests that measure intellectual ability or academic potential, help gear training approaches to students' learning styles, and create ways of helping students reach their maximum academic potential. Many also conduct research; among the issues they study are the nature of intelligence, how teachers can enhance the learning process, and why some children are more highly motivated than others to do well in school.

Developmental psychologists study people's physical, cognitive, social, and personality development throughout the life span. *Child psychologists* are developmental psychologists who limit their focus to child development.

Personality psychologists seek to understand the nature of personality—the cluster of psychological characteristics and behaviors that distinguishes us as unique individuals and leads us to act consistently over time. In particular, they study how personality is structured and how it develops and changes.

Social psychologists study how group or social influences affect behavior and attitudes. Whereas personality psychologists look within an individual's psychological makeup to explain behavior, social psychologists focus on how groups affect individuals and, in some cases, how individuals affect groups.

Environmental psychologists study relationships between the physical environment and behavior (Gifford, 2014). They study how weather affects people's moods and whether higher outdoor temperature spurs aggressive behaviors, as well as examine psychological effects of environmental factors such as air pollution, overcrowding, and noise (for example, Klimstra et al., 2011; Weir, 2012b).

Are your moods affected by the weather? Evidence from studies in environmental psychology shows that people tend to report more positive moods during pleasant spring weather and more negative moods during hotter summer months (Keller et al., 2005). People also tend to post gloomier comments on Facebook postings on rainy days than on days when the sun is shining (Coviello et al., 2014). Another recent study with more direct pocketbook implications showed that institutional investors who were charged with investing funds of large banks and financial firms were more likely to buy stocks on sunny days and sell them on cloudy ones, perhaps because sunnier days put them in a more cheerful, optimistic mood (Goetzmann et al., 2014).

Even indoor lighting can affect our behavior, as shown in a recent Canadian study in which college students showed stronger emotional responses in a laboratory

school psychologists Psychologists who evaluate and assist children with learning problems or other special needs.

educational psychologists Psychologists who study issues relating to the measurement of intelligence and the processes involved in educational or academic achievement.

developmental psychologists Psychologists who focus on processes involving physical, cognitive, social, and personality development.

personality psychologists Psychologists who study the psychological characteristics and behaviors that distinguish us as individuals and lead us to act consistently over time.

social psychologists Psychologists who study group or social influences on behavior and attitudes.

environmental psychologists Psychologists who study relationships between the physical environment and behavior.

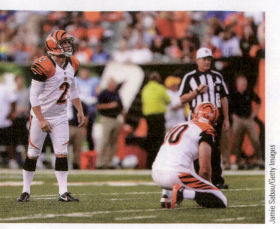

Jamie Sabau/Getty Images

The opposing team is about to call a time-out to "ice" the field goal kicker with the game on the line, giving him more time to think about the kick. Sport psychologists confirm a long-standing belief that athletes tend to choke in critical situations when they pay too much attention to their performance.

The Brain Loves a Puzzle

As you read ahead in the next few pages, use the information in the text to solve the following puzzle:

A student successfully completed all doctoral (PhD) requirements at Johns Hopkins University but was refused a doctorate. Undeterred, the student went on to a distinguished research career in psychology, even formulating a new theory of color vision. Why did the university refuse to grant her the doctoral degree?

industrial/organizational (I/O) psychologists Psychologists who study people's behavior at work.

health psychologists Psychologists who focus on the relationship between psychological factors and physical health.

study when they were tested under brighter lighting (Xu & Labroo, 2013). The lead investigator, Alison Jing Xu, believes these results have implications for how products are sold: "If you are selling emotional expressive products such as flowers or engagement rings it would make sense to make the store as bright as possible" (quoted in "The Way a Room Is Lit," 2014). On the other hand, if you want to avoid getting into a heated argument with someone, it may be best to first turn down the lights.

Industrial/organizational (I/O) psychologists study people at work. They are concerned with such issues as job satisfaction, personnel selection and training, leadership qualities, effects of organizational structure on productivity and work performance, and challenges posed by changes in the workplace. They may use psychological tests to determine the fit between applicants' abilities and interests and the jobs available within an organization or corporation. Some I/O psychologists perform human factors research in which they examine ways of making equipment (for example, airplane gauges and computer systems) more efficient and easier to use.

Health psychologists study how such psychological factors as stress, lifestyle, and attitude affect physical health. They apply this knowledge in developing disease prevention programs and interventions to improve the quality of life of patients with chronic diseases, such as heart disease, cancer, and HIV/AIDS.

Consumer psychologists are interested in understanding consumer behavior—why people purchase particular products and particular brands. They examine consumers' attitudes toward different products, ways of advertising or packaging products, even the choice of music stores play to put customers in a buying mood.

Emerging Specialty Areas

When G. Stanley Hall founded the American Psychological Association (APA) in 1892, it had 31 charter members (Benjamin, 1997); today, the membership exceeds 150,000. It's no wonder that psychology's interests and specialties cover so wide a range, including such emerging specialty areas as neuropsychology, geropsychology, forensic psychology, and sport psychology.

Neuropsychologists study relationships between the brain and behavior. Although some neuropsychologists limit their activities to research, *clinical neuropsychologists* use specialized tests to evaluate the cognitive effects of brain injuries and strokes. These tests can help them pinpoint the particular areas of the brain affected by injury or disease. Clinical neuropsychologists may also work with rehabilitation specialists in designing programs to help people who have suffered various forms of brain damage regain as much of their functioning as possible.

Geropsychologists focus on psychological processes associated with aging. They may work with geriatric patients to help them cope with the stresses of later life, including retirement, loss of loved ones, and declining physical health.

Forensic psychologists work within the legal system. They may perform psychological evaluations in child custody cases, testify about the competence of defendants to stand trial, develop psychological profiles of criminal types, give expert testimony in court on psychological issues, or assist attorneys in selecting potential jury members.

Sport psychologists apply psychological principles and techniques to sports and athletic competition (Aoyagi et al., 2012). They help athletes develop relaxation skills, and use positive self-talk and mental-focusing skills to overcome performance anxiety and enhance athletic performance (for example, Hatzigeorgiadis et al., 2011). They also study why athletes sometimes "choke" in critical game situations (focusing too much attention on what they are doing can ruin their performance) (Gray, 2011).

Some sport psychologists help athletes handle competitive pressures and balance travel, family, and life demands as well as team dynamics. Sport psychologists also counsel players who experience psychological difficulties adjusting to the rigors of competition.

Professional Psychology: Becoming More Diverse

The early psychologists shared more than just a yearning to understand behavior: Almost all of them were White males of European background. The ranks of women in the early days of psychology were slim, and the ranks of racial and ethnic minorities even slimmer. Back then, women and minority members faced many barriers in pursuing careers in psychology, as they did in numerous other professions.

Consider the puzzle posed about the woman who completed all doctoral degree requirements at Johns Hopkins University but was not awarded the doctoral degree. She was Christine Ladd-Franklin (1847–1930), the earliest woman pioneer in psychology. Christine completed all the requirements for a PhD at Johns Hopkins University in 1882, but the university refused to award her the degree because it did not issue doctoral degrees to women at that time. Nonetheless, she went on to pursue a distinguished research career in psychology, during which she developed a new theory of color vision. She finally received her PhD in 1926.

Another woman pioneer was Mary Whiton Calkins (1863–1930). A brilliant student of William James, Calkins completed all her PhD requirements at Harvard, but Harvard denied her a doctorate; like Johns Hopkins, it did not grant doctoral degrees to women. She was offered the doctorate through Radcliffe College, a women's academy affiliated with Harvard, but she refused it. Not easily deterred, she went on to a distinguished career in psychology—teaching and conducting important research on learning and short-term memory. In 1905, she became the first female president of the APA.

Margaret Floy Washburn (1871–1939) encountered similar discrimination when she pursued studies in psychology at Columbia University. In 1894, having found a more receptive environment at Cornell University, she became the first woman in the United States to earn a PhD in psychology. She wrote an influential book, *The Animal Mind*, and in 1921, became the second female president of the APA.

In 1909, Gilbert Haven Jones (1883–1966), an African American, received a doctorate in psychology from a university in Germany. It wasn't until 1920, however, at Clark University in Worcester, Massachusetts, that Francis Sumner (1895–1954) became the first African American to receive a doctorate in psychology in the United States. Sumner went on to a distinguished career in teaching and research. He helped

CONCEPT 1.17
Women and minority members faced difficult obstacles in pursuing careers in psychology in the early days of the profession.

consumer psychologists Psychologists who study why people purchase particular products and brands.

neuropsychologists Psychologists who study relationships between the brain and behavior.

geropsychologists Psychologists who focus on psychological processes involved in aging.

forensic psychologists Psychologists involved in the application of psychology to the legal system.

sport psychologists Psychologists who apply psychology to understanding and improving athletic performance.

Mary Whiton Calkins

Margaret Floy Washburn

Kenneth Clark

CONCEPT 1.18
Though the field of psychology has become more diverse, people of color are still underrepresented in professional psychology.

CONCEPT 1.19
The profession of psychology has undergone a major gender shift in recent years.

establish the psychology department at Howard University and served as its chairperson until his death in 1954.

In 1920, the same year Sumner earned his doctorate, J. Henry Alston became the first African American to publish his research findings (on the perception of warmth and cold) in a major U.S. psychology journal. It took another 50 years (until 1971) before the first—and, to this date, the only—African American psychologist, Kenneth Clark (1914–2005), was elected president of the APA. In 1999, Richard Suinn became the first Asian American psychologist to be elected president of the APA.

The professional ranks of psychology have become more diverse, but people of color still remain underrepresented in the profession. Minority representation constitutes only about 15 percent of the doctoral psychology workforce, which is less than half the percentage of minorities in the general population (APA, 2015; Lin, Stamm, & Christidis, 2015). We can expect minority representation to continue to tick upwards, as about 25 percent of new doctoral recipients now coming into the field are minority graduates (APA, 2010). ■ Figure 1.5 shows the racial and ethnic makeup of working psychologists today for the largest U.S. minority groups. Other minority groups are even less well represented in professional psychology. For example, there is only one Native American psychologist for every 30,000 Native Americans (Rabasca, 2000).

A different picture emerges when we examine gender shifts in professional psychology. Women comprise about two-thirds of active psychologists today. Women today account for more than two-thirds of doctorate recipients in psychology, as compared to about one in five in 1970 (see ■ Figure 1.6). This gender shift mirrors the increased representation of women in occupations traditionally dominated by men, including medicine and law. However, the gender shift is occurring at a faster rate in psychology than in other professions.

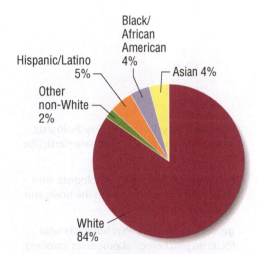

Note: Numbers do not sum to 100% because of rounding.

FIGURE 1.5 **Ethnicities of Doctorate Recipients in Psychology**
Although the psychology workforce is becoming more diverse, racial and ethnic minorities constitute only about 15 percent of working psychologists today.

Source: Lin, Stamm, & Christidis, 2015.

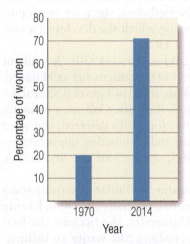

FIGURE 1.6 **Women PhD Recipients in Psychology**
Women represent more than three-quarters of new PhDs in psychology, as compared to about one-fifth in 1970.

Source: Christidis, P., Samm, K., & Lin, L. (2016 May). Latest class of psychologists is more diverse. *Monitor on Psychology, 47*(5), p. 24.

MODULE REVIEW   **1.2**   Psychologists: Who They Are and What They Do

Recite It

4. **Identify** specialty areas or subfields of psychology and emerging specialty areas.

   Subfields in psychology include clinical and counseling psychology, school psychology, industrial-organizational psychology, and experimental psychology, as well as emerging specialty areas such as geropsychology, (a) _____ psychology, and sport psychology.

5. **Describe** ethnic and gender characteristics of psychologists today and the changes that have occurred over time.

   Though psychology is now a more diverse discipline, African Americans and other minority groups remain (b) _____ in the professional ranks of psychologists. Unlike the early days of the profession, when (c) _____ were actively excluded from pursuing professional careers, they now constitute more than two-thirds of new PhDs in psychology.

Recall It

1. _____ research focuses on expanding our understanding and knowledge, whereas _____ research focuses on finding answers or solutions to particular problems.

2. Match the following types of psychologists with the type of work they do: (a) counseling psychologists; (b) developmental psychologists; (c) environmental psychologists; (d) consumer psychologists.

   i. study changes in behaviors and attitudes throughout the life cycle

   ii. study effects of outdoor temperature on aggression

   iii. study psychological characteristics of people who buy particular products

   iv. help students adjust to college life

3. A psychologist who works within the legal system is most likely to be a

   a. social psychologist.   c. forensic psychologist.

   b. neuropsychologist.   d. counseling psychologist.

4. The first African American to receive a doctorate in psychology in the United States was

   a. Mary Whiton Calkins.   c. Gilbert Haven Jones.

   b. Francis Sumner.   d. Kenneth Clark.

Think About It

▪ If you were uncertain about what career to pursue and wanted help sorting through the vocational choices best suited to you, what type of psychologist would you consult? Why?

▪ Suppose you read in a newspaper about a psychologist who was studying how people's behavior changes when they become part of an unorganized mob. What type of psychologist would this person likely be?

Recite It *answers placed at the end of chapter.*

MODULE

1.3 Research Methods in Psychology

6 **Identify** the steps in the scientific method.

7 **Identify** research methods psychologists use.

8 **Describe** the ethical standards that govern research in psychology.

9 **Apply** critical thinking skills to **evaluate** claims made by others as well as online sources.

Psychologists are trained to be skeptical of claims and arguments that are not grounded in evidence. They are especially skeptical of public opinion, common beliefs, and folklore, such as the widely held misconceptions listed in Table 1.1. What distinguishes psychology from other inquiries into human nature, including philosophy, theology, and poetry, is the use of scientific methods to gain knowledge. Psychologists adopt an **empirical approach**; that is, they base their beliefs on evidence gathered from experiments and careful observation.

The Scientific Method: How We Know What We Know

Like other scientific disciplines, psychology uses the scientific method in its pursuit of knowledge. The **scientific method** is a framework for acquiring knowledge based on careful observation and the use of experimental methods. It can be conceptualized in terms of four general steps that scientists use to test their ideas and to expand and

empirical approach A method of developing knowledge based on evaluating evidence gathered from experiments and careful observation.

scientific method A method of inquiry involving careful observation and use of experimental methods.

Table 1.1 Common Misconceptions About Psychology

Myth	Fact
Psychologists can read people's minds.	No, psychologists cannot read people's minds. As one prominent psychologist put it, "If you want to know what people are thinking, ask them. They just might tell you."
Psychology is not a true science.	Psychology is indeed a true science because it is grounded in the scientific method.
There can be only one true psychological theory; all the others must be false.	No one theory accounts for all forms of behavior. Theories are more or less useful to the degree they account for the available evidence and lead to accurate predictions of future behavior. Some theories account for some types of behavior better than others, but many have value in accounting for some forms of behavior.
The full moon drives people to lunacy.	Although the word *lunacy* derives from the Latin word for moon, *luna*, evidence fails to back up the widely held belief that the full moon is associated with bizarre behaviors, suicides, crimes, or increased hospital admissions (Belleville et al., 2012; Lilienfeld & Arkowitz, 2009).

CONCEPT 1.20

The scientific method is a framework for acquiring knowledge through careful observation and experimentation.

CONCEPT 1.21

Scientists use the scientific method to test out predictions derived from theory, observation, experience, and commonly held beliefs.

CONCEPT 1.22

Psychologists frame their research questions in the form of hypotheses, or specific predictions about the outcomes they expect to find.

CONCEPT 1.23

Psychologists gather evidence to test out their hypotheses.

CONCEPT 1.24

Psychologists evaluate the results of scientific studies by using statistical tests to determine whether relationships between variables or differences between groups are unlikely to be due to chance.

hypothesis A precise prediction about the outcomes of an experiment.

theory A formulation that accounts for relationships among observed events or experimental findings in ways that make them more understandable and predictable.

refine their knowledge: (1) developing a research question, (2) framing the research question in the form of a hypothesis, (3) gathering evidence to test the hypothesis, and (4) drawing conclusions about the hypothesis. ■ Figure 1.7 summarizes these steps.

1. *Developing a research question.* Psychologists generate research questions from many sources, including theory, careful observation, previous experience, and commonly held beliefs. For example, a researcher might be interested in the question "Does exposure to stress increase risk of the common cold?"

2. *Framing the research question in the form of a hypothesis.* An investigator reframes the research question in the form of a **hypothesis**—a precise prediction that can be tested through research. Hypotheses are often drawn from **theory.** For example, a researcher might theorize that stress weakens the immune system, the body's defense system against disease, leaving us more vulnerable to various kinds of illness, including the common cold. Based on this theoretical model, the investigator might frame the research question in the form of a testable hypothesis: "People who encounter high levels of stress in their lives will be more likely to develop a common cold after exposure to cold viruses than are people with lower levels of stress."

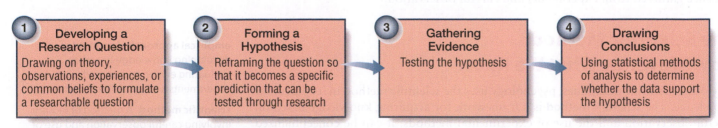

FIGURE 1.7 General Steps in the Scientific Method

Investigators may also develop hypotheses based on common beliefs or assumptions about behavior. Consider the commonly held belief that "opposites attract." An opposing belief is that people are attracted to those similar to themselves—that "birds of a feather flock together." A specific hypothesis drawn from the latter belief might be phrased as follows: "Most people choose romantic partners who are similar in educational level."

3. *Gathering evidence to test the hypothesis.* The investigator develops a research design or strategy for gathering evidence to provide a scientific test of the hypothesis. The type of research method used depends on the nature of the problem. In the stress and common cold example, the investigator might classify people into high-stress and low-stress groups and then expose them (with their permission, of course) to cold viruses to see if the high-stress group is more likely to develop a common cold. Using this methodology, researchers found that people under high levels of chronic stress were more likely to develop a cold after exposure to a cold virus than were people in a low-stress comparison group (Cohen et al., 1998).

4. *Drawing conclusions about the hypothesis.* Investigators draw conclusions about their hypotheses based on the evidence their research has produced. To test their hypotheses, they turn to **statistics**, the branch of mathematics involving methods of tabulating and analyzing numerical data. Investigators use statistical methods to determine whether relationships between variables (for example, stress and vulnerability to the common cold) or differences between groups (for example, an experimental group that receives a treatment versus a control group that does not) are *statistically significant* (relatively unlikely to have been due to chance). A **variable** is a factor that varies in an experiment, such as the dosage level of an experimental drug or the scores that participants receive on a measure of interest.

When research findings do not support the study's hypotheses, scientists may adjust the theories from which the hypotheses were derived. Research findings may suggest new avenues of research or revision of the psychological theories themselves.

Another important factor in drawing conclusions is **replication**, the attempt to duplicate findings reported by others to determine whether they will occur again under the same experimental conditions (Brandt et al., 2013; Stanley & Spence, 2014). Scientists have more confidence in findings that others can reliably replicate (Cesario, 2014; Simons, 2014).

Research Methods: How We Learn What We Know

The scientific method is a framework psychologists use to take their ideas for a test ride. Now let's consider the particular methods they employ to acquire knowledge about behavior and mental processes: the case study, survey, naturalistic observation, correlational, and experimental methods.

The Case Study Method

The **case study method** is an in-depth study of one or more individuals. The psychologist draws information from interviews, observation, or written records. Sigmund Freud, for example, based much of his theory of personality and abnormal behavior on data from intensive observation and study of the patients he treated in his clinical practice. The famed Swiss developmentalist Jean Piaget (1896–1980) developed a theory of cognitive development by closely observing and interviewing a small number of children. Many of the early findings on brain function came from studies of brain-injured patients that matched the types of injuries they sustained with particular deficits in memory functioning and motor skills.

Psychologists propose testable hypotheses that guide their research. For example, a psychologist might hypothesize that romantic partners with similar interests and attitudes are more likely to remain together than are couples with dissimilar interests and attitudes. Preferences for matching sweaters may have no bearing on the longevity of the relationship, however.

CONCEPT 1.25

Psychologists use a variety of research methods to learn about behavior and mental processes, including case study, survey, naturalistic observation, correlational, and experimental methods.

CONCEPT 1.26

Case studies can provide a wealth of information and suggest testable hypotheses, but they lack the controls found in scientific experiments.

statistics The branch of mathematics involving the tabulation, analysis, and interpretation of numerical data.

variable A factor or measure that varies within an experiment or among individuals.

replication The attempt to duplicate findings.

case study method An in-depth study of one or more individuals.

Problems with case studies can arise when investigators rely on people's memories of their past experiences, because memories can become distorted or filled with gaps. People may also withhold important information out of embarrassment or shame. To present a more favorable impression, some may even purposefully deceive a researcher. Interviewers themselves may hear only what they expect or want to hear, and observers may see only what they want or expect to see. In sum, though case studies can provide a treasure trove of information and lead to testable hypotheses, they lack the rigorous controls of scientific experiments.

The Survey Method

The **survey method** gathers information from target groups of people through the use of structured interviews or questionnaires. A **structured interview** is a questioning technique that follows a preset series of questions in a particular order. A **questionnaire** is a written set of questions or statements to which people can reply by marking responses on an answer form.

Psychologists and other researchers conduct survey research to learn about the characteristics, beliefs, attitudes, and behaviors of certain populations. In survey research, a **population** represents the total group of people who are the subjects of interest. For example, a population might consist of all people 18 years of age or older in the United States, or perhaps all high school seniors. Generally speaking, it is impractical to study an entire population; an exception would be a very small population that could be studied in its entirety, such as the population of students living in a particular dormitory. In virtually all cases, however, surveys are conducted on **samples**, or segments, of populations.

To draw conclusions about a population based on the results of a sample, the sample must be representative of the target population. Representative samples allow researchers to *generalize*, or transfer, their results from a sample to the population it represents. To create representative samples, researchers use **random sampling**, a technique whereby individuals are selected at random from a given population for participation in a sample. This often entails the use of a computer program that randomly selects names of individuals or households within a given population. Political polls reported in the media typically use random samples of voters to predict outcomes of elections.

Like case studies, surveys may be limited by gaps in people's memories. Participants may also give answers that they believe are socially desirable rather than reflective of what they truly feel or believe. This response style results from what is called **social desirability bias**. For example, many people exaggerate how frequently they attend church (Groves et al., 2009). Social desirability may be especially strong in situations where people have a considerable stake in what others think of them, such as on job interviews. Another form of bias in survey research is **volunteer bias**. This arises when people who volunteer to participate in surveys or other research studies are not representative of the population from which they are drawn.

The Naturalistic Observation Method

The **naturalistic observation method** takes the laboratory "into the field" to directly observe the behavior of humans or other animal species in their natural habitats or environments. The people or animal subjects serving as research participants may behave more "naturally" in their natural environments than they would in the artificial confines of the experimental laboratory. Psychologists have observed children at home with their parents to learn more about parent–child interactions and in school yards and classrooms to see how children relate to one another. Because people may act differently when they know they are being observed, the observers try to avoid interfering with the behaviors they are observing. To further minimize this potential bias, the observers may spend time allowing the subjects to get accustomed to

---

CONCEPT 1.27

Through survey research, psychologists can gather information about attitudes and behaviors of large numbers of people, but the information they obtain may be subject to memory gaps and biases.

survey method A research method in which structured interviews or questionnaires are used to gather information about groups of people.

structured interview An interview in which a set of specific questions is asked in a particular order.

questionnaire A written set of questions or statements to which people reply by marking their responses on an answer form.

population All the individuals or organisms that constitute particular groups.

samples Subsets of a population.

random sampling A method of sampling in which each individual in the population has an equal chance of being selected.

social desirability bias The tendency to respond to questions in a socially desirable manner.

volunteer bias The type of bias that arises when people who volunteer to participate in a survey or research study have characteristics that make them unrepresentative of the population from which they were drawn.

naturalistic observation method A method of research based on careful observation of behavior in natural settings.

them so that they begin acting more naturally before any actual measurement takes place. Observers may also position themselves so that the subjects cannot see them. Though the method of naturalistic observation may lack the controls available in controlled experiments, it can provide important insights into behavior as it occurs under natural conditions.

Problems with this method may arise if observers introduce their own biases. For example, if observers have a preconceived idea about how a parent's interaction with a child affects the child's behavior, they may tend to see what they expect to see. To guard against this, pairs of observers may be used to check for consistency between observers. Experimenters may also make random spot checks to see that observers are recording their measurements accurately.

Animals in laboratory or zoo-like environments may act differently than they do in their natural habitats. To learn more about chimp behavior, naturalist Jane Goodall lived for many years among chimpanzees in their natural environment. Gradually, she came to be accepted by the chimps. Her observations disputed the long-held belief that only humans use tools. For example, she watched as chimps used a stick as a tool, inserting it into a termite mound to remove termites, which they then ate. Not only did chimpanzees use tools, but they also showed other humanlike behavior, such as kissing when greeting one another.

Famed naturalist Jane Goodall spent many years carefully observing the behavior of chimpanzees in their natural environment.

The Correlational Method

Psychologists use the **correlational method** to examine relationships between variables. In Chapter 10, you will read about findings that show a *correlation*, or link, between optimism and better psychological adjustment among cancer patients. In Chapter 9, you will see that maternal smoking during pregnancy is correlated, unfortunately, with increased risk of sudden infant death syndrome (SIDS) in babies.

A **correlation coefficient** is a statistical measure of association between two variables. Correlation coefficients can vary from $+1.00$ to -1.00. Coefficients with a positive sign represent a positive correlation in which higher values on one variable are associated with higher values on the other variable (for example, people with higher levels of education tend to earn higher incomes; see ■ Figure 1.8).

CONCEPT 1.28
With the naturalistic observation method, researchers in the field can examine behavior as it unfolds, but they run the risk of influencing the behavior they are observing.

CONCEPT 1.29
With the correlational method, we can examine how variables are related to each other but cannot determine cause-and-effect relationships.

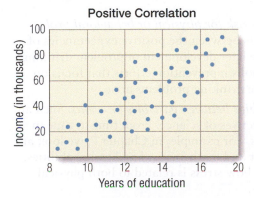

Generally speaking, people with higher levels of education tend to earn higher incomes.

Generally speaking, the longer a person is deprived of sleep, the less alert the person is likely to be.

FIGURE 1.8 Correlational Relationships
These graphs display positive and negative correlations. For a positive correlation, increases in one variable (educational level) are associated with increases in another (income level). For a negative correlation, increases in one variable (sleep deprivation) are associated with decreases in another (alertness). Each dot in these graphs represents the point of intersection of an individual's scores on the two plotted variables.

correlational method A research method used to examine relationships between variables, which are expressed in the form of a statistical measure called a correlation coefficient.

correlation coefficient A statistical measure of association between variables that can vary from -1.00 to $+1.00$.

A negative correlation, which is denoted by a negative sign, means the reverse: Higher values on one variable are associated with lower values on the other. For example, the longer people are deprived of sleep, the less alert they are likely to be. The size of the correlation expresses the strength or magnitude of the relationship between the variables. The stronger the relationship, the closer the correlation coefficient will be to either +1.00 (for a positive correlation) or −1.00 (for a negative correlation).

Correlations are useful because they allow us to predict one variable on the basis of the other. A perfect correlation of either +1.00 or −1.00 allows us to predict with certainty. Let's say we discovered a perfect correlation between certain genetic characteristics and the likelihood of developing a particular disease. If we knew you possessed these genetic characteristics, we would be able to predict with certainty whether you would develop the disease. However, virtually all of the relationships of interest to psychologists are less than perfect (that is, they vary in strength between 0.00 and either −1.00 or +1.00). For example, although intelligence is correlated with academic achievement, not everyone with a high score on intelligence tests succeeds in school. A zero correlation means that there is no relationship between the two variables; thus, one variable is of no value in predicting the other.

You may have heard the expression "correlation is not causation." The fact that two variables are correlated, even highly correlated, doesn't mean that one causes the other. For example, shoe size in children correlates strongly with vocabulary. While you may argue that some people seem to have more smarts in their little toes than others have in their whole brain, I don't think you'd argue that a growing foot causes vocabulary to expand. Rather, shoe size and vocabulary are correlated because older children tend to have larger feet and a larger vocabulary than younger children. Though the correlational method is limited in terms of specifying underlying causes, it has several benefits:

- *It offers clues to underlying causes.* Though correlational relationships cannot determine cause-and-effect relationships, they may point to possible causal factors that can be followed up in experimental research. For example, evidence of a correlation between smoking and lung cancer led to experimental studies with animals that showed that exposure to cigarette smoke induced the formation of cancerous lesions in the lungs.

- *It can identify groups of people at high risk for physical or behavioral problems.* Knowing that a relationship exists between the positive expectancies of adolescents toward alcohol use and the later development of problem drinking may direct us toward developing alcoholism prevention efforts that focus on changing attitudes of youngsters before drinking problems arise.

- *It increases understanding of relationships between variables or events.* Such an understanding is one of the major objectives of science. From time to time in this text, we explore such relationships. For example, in Chapter 7, we look at statistical relationships between gender and mathematical and verbal abilities, and in Chapters 10 and 12 we explore how stress is related to both physical and psychological health.

Data collection has entered the smartphone era, as investigators are now using smartphone apps to electronically prompt research participants to report on their thoughts, behaviors, moods, and activities as they go about their daily lives. These electronic reports are transmitted to researchers who use correlational methods of analysis to find patterns and relationships in the stream of data. Investigators are also mining social media sites (Gosling & Mason, 2015; Kosinski et al., 2016). For example, Cornell University researchers analyzed more than a half billion Twitter messages, looking to see if the use of happier words was linked to the time of day

(Weaver, 2012). The analysis showed that happy words indicative of a more positive mood were Tweeted most often during the early morning hours. But as the day dragged on, Twitter messages tended to become gloomier in tone. As researcher Michael Macy pointed out, "We found people are happiest around breakfast time in the morning and then it's all downhill from there." Do you also feel chipper in the morning when you awaken from a good night's sleep, but become grumpier as the daily grind wears you down mentally and physically?

The Experimental Method

In the **experimental method**, investigators directly explore cause-and-effect relationships by manipulating certain variables, called **independent variables**, and observing their effects on certain outcomes called **dependent variables**. Independent variables are manipulated, and their effects on the dependent variable or variables are measured. Dependent variables are so called because measures of these variables depend on the independent, or manipulated, variable. Experimenters attempt to hold constant all other factors or conditions to ensure that the independent variable alone is the cause of the observed effects on the dependent variable.

Consider an early experiment that examined whether the popularity of women's names affects judgments of their physical attractiveness. The experimenter paired women's photographs with either a currently popular name, such as Jessica, Jennifer, or Christine, or a traditional name that had fallen out of favor, such as Harriet, Gertrude, or Ethel (Garwood et al., 1980). The investigators found that college student participants rated the women depicted in the photographs who were assigned popular names as more attractive than those given out-of-fashion names. The experimenter controlled the *independent variable* (popularity of female names) by assigning women's photographs randomly to either currently popular or old-fashioned names. They measured the effects of the independent variable on the *dependent variable* (ratings of attractiveness).

Psychologists use **operational definitions** to define variables on the basis of the operations or procedures they use to measure those variables. Operational definitions establish an objective basis for determining what the variables of interest mean. In the study of female names, investigators operationalized the independent variable of name popularity by classifying names on the basis of whether they were currently popular or out-of-date. They operationalized physical attractiveness on the basis of scores on an attractiveness rating scale.

Experimenters typically use **control groups** to ensure that the effects of an independent variable are not due to other factors, such as the passage of time. For example, in a study examining the effects of alcohol intake on aggressive behavior, the experimental group would receive a dose of alcohol but the control group would not. The investigator would then observe whether the group given alcohol showed more aggressive behavior in a laboratory task than the control group.

In well-designed studies, experimenters use **random assignment** to place participants randomly in experimental groups or control groups. Random assignment balances experimental and control groups in terms of the background and personality characteristics of the people who constitute the groups. Random assignment gives us confidence that differences between groups in how they perform on dependent measures are due to the independent variable or variables and not to the characteristics of the people making up the groups. However, random assignment is not always feasible or ethically responsible. For example, ethical experimenters would never randomly assign children to be exposed to abuse or neglect to see what effects these experiences might have on their development. They may rely on correlational methods to examine these relationships even though such methods do not necessarily determine cause and effect.

CONCEPT 1.30

With the experimental method, researchers can explore cause-and-effect relationships by directly manipulating some variables and observing their effects on other variables under controlled conditions.

experimental method A method of scientific investigation involving the manipulation of independent variables and observation or measurement of their effects on dependent variables under controlled conditions.

independent variables Factors that are manipulated in an experiment.

dependent variables The effects or outcomes of an experiment that are believed to be dependent on the values of the independent variables.

operational definition A definition of a variable based on the procedures or operations used to measure it.

control groups Groups of participants in a research experiment who do not receive the experimental treatment or intervention.

random assignment A method of randomly assigning subjects to experimental or control groups.

placebo An inert substance or experimental condition that resembles the active treatment.

placebo effects Positive outcomes of an experiment resulting from a participant's positive expectations about the treatment rather than from the treatment itself.

single-blind studies In drug research, studies in which subjects are kept uninformed about whether they are receiving the experimental drug or a placebo.

double-blind studies In drug research, studies in which both participants and experimenters are kept uninformed about which participants are receiving the active drug and which are receiving the placebo.

prime A stimulus or cue that affects a person's subsequent behavior without the person being aware of its impact.

Experimenters may wish to keep research participants and themselves in the dark concerning which groups receive which treatments. In drug studies, subjects are typically assigned to receive either an active drug or a **placebo**—an inert pill, or "sugar pill," made to resemble the active drug. The purpose is to control for **placebo effects**—positive outcomes that reflect a person's hopeful expectancies about a drug rather than the chemical properties of the drug itself (Espay et al., 2015; Rutherford et al., 2014). Say you have a throat infection and are prescribed an antibiotic that you mistakenly believe produces an immediate effect. You might start feeling better within a few minutes or an hour or so because of the placebo effect, even though the drug itself wouldn't start to work medically for another 12 to 24 hours.

The placebo effect is an example of the power of suggestion. We see this power at work in research evidence that pain patients who are given mere placebos show actual biological changes in parts of the brain involved in processing pain (Atlas & Wager, 2014; Lu, 2015). Taking a placebo may block pain signals to the brain or lead to the release of *endorphins*, which are the brain's own pain-killing chemicals (Fox, 2014; Merchant, 2016).

Depressed patients in another study who responded positively to a placebo showed telltale changes in the brain associated with emotion regulation (Peciña et al., 2015). An even more compelling example of the power of suggestion comes from studies in which pain patients experienced a reduction of pain even though—now get this—they *knew* they were receiving a placebo (Schafer, Colloca, & Wager, 2015; Kam-Hansen et al., 2014). We should note that placebos typically have stronger effects on subjective states, such as pain and negative emotions, than they do on objectively measured medical conditions, such as high blood pressure (Meyer et al., 2015).

In drug studies, experimenters attempt to control for expectancy effects by preventing research participants from knowing whether they are receiving the active drug or a placebo. In **single-blind studies**, only the participants are kept in the dark. In **double-blind studies**, both the participants and the experimenters (prescribing physicians and other researchers) are "blinded" (kept uninformed) with respect to which participants are receiving the active drug. Keeping the experimenters "blind" helps prevent their own expectancies from affecting the results.

Unfortunately, the "blinds" in many double-blind studies are more like venetian blinds with the slats slightly open; that is, participants and experimenters are often able to tell whether a participant received a placebo or an active drug. Active drugs often have telltale side effects that give them away. Still, when conducted properly, the double-blind, randomized study is among the strongest research methods and is widely considered the "gold standard" when evaluating new medications (Perlis et al., 2010). To learn more about research methods, see Try This Out.

Anatomy of a Research Study: Clean Smell, Clean Hands?

We've all learned that regular hand washing is an important step in preventing the spread of infectious disease. But even in hospitals, where staff members are trained to wash their hands thoroughly and often, they don't always comply with hand hygiene procedures. Unfortunately, researchers find, the rate of compliance with health hygiene standards among health care workers is less than 50 percent (Erasmus et al., 2010). Staff training and peer pressure in hospital settings is often insufficient to ensure that health care workers follow established hand hygiene rules.

Short of having other staff members monitoring their colleagues by looking over their shoulders to make sure they follow the hand hygiene rules, would exposure to a subtle cue, called a **prime**, increase hand hygiene compliance? That was the question that guided research at a teaching hospital in Miami, Florida. There, as reported in 2016 in the scientific publication *Health Psychology*, investigators examined whether introducing a clean citric smell in an intensive care unit (ICU) on a surgical ward would increase HHC (hand hygiene compliance), as measured by the use of a hand-gel dispenser. Here we thoroughly examine the workings of their experiment.

Hypotheses (Predicted Outcomes)

A scientific hypothesis is a predicted outcome, but it is far from a wild guess. Hypotheses are informed by a careful review of theory and prior research. As we'll see in Chapter 3, psychological research demonstrates that behavior is influenced in subtle ways by odors, including bodily odors in human sweat. In some ways, we may be led around by our noses. For the Miami hospital study, we can frame testable hypotheses that exposure to primes associated with either the concept of cleanliness (a clean smell) or of obedience (a pair of observing human eyes) would increase the rate of compliance with hand hygiene in a hospital setting, in this case, a surgical intensive care unit (ICU).

Procedure (What They Did and How They Did It)

The participants in the study were 404 people entering the ICU. Participants included health care providers, including physicians and nurses, and hospital visitors. Anyone entering the ICU was expected to use a hand-gel dispenser before entering a patient room. Hand-gel dispensers were located directly in front of the entrance door, and several more were placed inside the ICU but before any of the patient rooms. Observers were discretely positioned both outside and inside the ICU in such a way that they could clearly see people entering the unit without being obvious themselves.

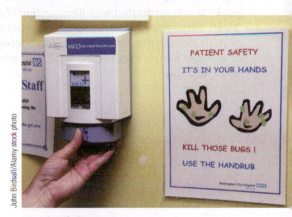

The observers checked off whether participants "washed hands" using a hand-gel dispenser or "didn't wash hands" before entering a patient room. A control group comprised 120 individuals entering the unit without any olfactory or visual prime. This control simulated the ordinary conditions in the hospital. Only 15 percent of controls were observed washing their hands using the hand-gel dispenser, representing a rather low rate of compliance with hygienic standards.

Hand-gel dispenser

The intervention phase consisted of exposure to either an olfactory prime ("clean" citrus smell) or to one of two visual primes, either a photograph of male or female eyes placed directly above the hand-gel dispenser. An aroma dispenser was used to disperse the olfactory prime. The particular aroma had earlier been tested with volunteers who selected it as the "cleanest and freshest" smell among ten different fragrances. The olfactory intervention was conducted on separate days. On some days, as determined by random assignment, the olfactory prime was present, but on other days it was not. For the second intervention phase, and again using random assignment, a picture of either a set of stern-looking, middle-age male eyes or a set of younger female eyes was placed above the dispenser. The experimenters decided to use stern, middle-age male eyes because of past research experience in which such harsher eyes had stronger effects on behavior than did either female eyes or younger male eyes.

Now that we've set the stage, what are your predictions of the results? Would a clean-smelling citrus scent in the air produce a significant uptick in the use of the hand-gel dispenser? Would people comply with hand hygiene expectations passing by a picture of stern male eyes or gentler female eyes? Let's have a look at what the experimenters found.

Results and Discussion (What They Found and What It Means)

The investigators used correlational analyses to examine relationships between hand washing (yes/no) and the experimental variables of the olfactory prime (citrus smell) and two visual primes, either stern-looking male eyes or younger female eyes. They also used a statistical means of controlling for the gender of participants, so as to ensure that the influence of the experimental variables was not dependent on the participant's gender.

Observing female and male eyes

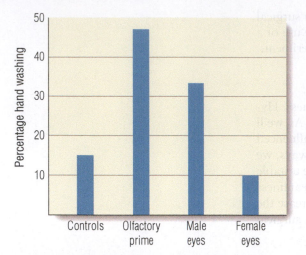

FIGURE 1.9 Percentage of Hand Washing Across Conditions
Significant improvements in the rate of hand washing was associated with introduction of a "clean" citrus smell and the posting of a photograph of stern-looking male eyes. However, a photograph of younger female eyes had no significant effect on hand washing.

The results—drum roll, please—showed a statistically significant increase in hand washing for participants in the citrus scent condition—47 percent versus 15 percent among controls (see ■ Figure 1.9). In the male eyes condition, one-third of participants (33 percent) washed their hands, a statistically significant difference as compared to controls. However, participants in the female eyes condition failed to show improvement in hand washing. Only 10 percent of these participants washed their hands, a result which was not significantly different from the control condition.

The results of this study suggest that subtle cues in the environment may have meaningful effects on behavior. Exposure to clean smells may bring into awareness the concept of cleanliness, inducing people to be more conscientious about their personal hygiene. Strategic placement of observing male eyes, especially stern-looking eyes, may have similar effects on compliance with hygienic standards. The study also has potentially important real-world implications. If the results stand up to future replications, it may encourage public institutions such as hospitals and schools to deploy olfactory or visual primes to increase compliance with expected hygienic behaviors.

As in all studies, this one leaves some unanswered questions that might be addressed in future research. For example, we don't know whether the participants were consciously aware of the primes and whether those who were aware of them were more likely to wash their hands. Nor did the investigators identify whether participants were visitors or hospital workers. It's conceivable that primes had stronger influences on hospital workers, who are trained to follow hygiene protocols, than on visitors. We also wonder whether stern-looking female eyes would produce similar effects as the stern-looking male eyes in this study or whether other images or smells might produce even stronger effects. Can you think of other primes that might exert an influence on cleanliness behaviors? All in all, the study raised our awareness about the role of subtle cues and suggested other directions that future researchers might pursue.

Citing References

Psychologists use a particular style for citing references that was developed by the American Psychological Association (see ■ Figure 1.10). Figure 1.10 shows the reference style for journal articles, using the hand-washing study as an example.

Before you move on, review Concept Chart 1.3, which summarizes the research methods we have discussed.

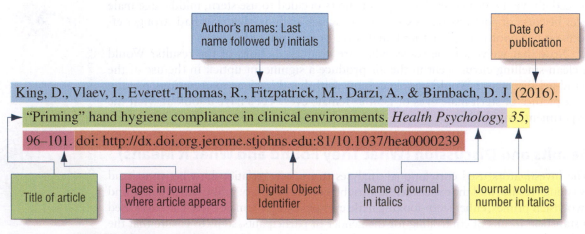

FIGURE 1.10 APA Reference Style

Concept Chart 1.3   How Psychologists Do Research

What Researchers Do	Comments	Approaches to Research Questions on Love
In the case study method, researchers interview or observe an individual (or small group of individuals) or examine historical records of the lives of particular individuals.	The accuracy of case studies may be jeopardized by gaps or errors in people's memories or by their efforts to make a favorable impression on a researcher.	A psychologist interested in the reasons people choose their mates might conduct in-depth interviews with several married people. 
In the survey method, researchers use questionnaires or interviews to obtain information about a particular group of people.	Psychologists may use surveys to explore the attitudes of thousands of people about such topics as abortion, premarital sex, or leisure pursuits. Results of surveys may be compromised by volunteer bias and other problems.	Psychologists might survey thousands of individuals about the characteristics of the people they have chosen as mates.
In the naturalistic observation method, researchers observe behavior in the field—that is, where it occurs naturally.	Psychologists attempt not to interfere with behaviors they are observing. They may spend considerable time allowing their research participants to become accustomed to them before they begin their observations.	Psychologists might observe from a distance how lovers walk together and how they look at each other. How do psychologists study love? Let us count the ways.
In the correlational method, researchers use statistical methods to reveal and describe positive and negative relationships (correlations) between variables.	This method may suggest the presence of cause and effect, but it does not demonstrate it. The degree to which variables are statistically associated is expressed as a correlation coefficient, which varies from −1.00 to +1.00.	Psychologists might study relationships between feelings of love, self-esteem, and sexual satisfaction.
In the experimental method, psychologists manipulate one or more independent variables (make changes in the participants' environments) and observe their effects on one or more dependent (measured) variables. Experiments are conducted to establish cause-and-effect relationships between independent and dependent variables.	Participants in experimental groups receive an experimental treatment; those in control groups do not. All other conditions are held constant to ensure that the independent variable alone is the cause of the observed effects. Random assignment to groups helps ensure that groups do not differ in characteristics that might affect the outcome.	Psychologists might expose dating partners to an experimental treatment in which they share an arousing experience, such as watching an emotionally powerful movie, and then measure the treatment's effects on the partners' feelings toward each other. (The control group would be exposed to a neutral movie.)

© AISPIX /Shutterstock.com

Ethical Principles in Psychological Research

Psychologists subscribe to a code of ethics that respects the dignity and welfare of their clients and those who participate in their research studies. This code recognizes that people have a basic right to make their own decisions and to exercise choices, including the choice of whether to participate in psychological research. Ethical guidelines also prohibit psychologists from using methods that would harm research participants or clients (American Psychological Association, 2002).

People who participate in experiments may be harmed not only by physical interventions, such as experimental drugs that have adverse effects, but also by

CONCEPT 1.31
Psychologists engaged in research must follow ethical guidelines that are designed to protect the welfare of research participants.

psychological interventions, such as being goaded into aggressive behavior that leads to feelings of guilt or shame. Invasions of privacy are another concern.

Today, nearly all institutions in which biomedical and behavioral research is conducted, such as hospitals, colleges, and research foundations, have **ethics review committees**. These committees, which are generally called institutional review boards (IRBs), are usually composed of professionals and laypeople. They must put their stamp of approval on all research proposals before the research can be carried out at their institutions. The committees review proposals to see that they comply with ethical guidelines and advise researchers concerning the potential harm of their proposed methods. In cases in which research participants may experience harm or discomfort, the IRB must weigh the potential benefits of the research against the potential harm. If the IRB believes that the proposed research might be unacceptably harmful, it will withhold approval.

One of the foremost ethical requirements is that investigators obtain **informed consent** from research participants before they begin participating in the study. This means that participants must be given enough information about the study's methods and purposes to make an "informed" decision about whether they wish to participate. Participants must also be free to withdraw from the study at any time.

Some research studies, including the famous Milgram studies on obedience to authority (see Chapter 12), deceived research participants as to the true purposes of the study. The APA's *Ethical Principles of Psychologists and Code of Conduct* (American Psychological Association, 2002) specifies the conditions that psychologists must meet to use deceptive practices in research. These conditions include a determination that the research is justified by its scientific, educational, or practical value; that no nondeceptive alternative research strategy is possible; that research participants are not misled about any research that can reasonably be expected to result in physical harm or severe emotional distress; and that participants receive an explanation of the deception at the earliest time that it is feasible to do so.

Psychologists must also protect the *confidentiality* of the records of research participants and of the clients they treat. That is, they must respect people's right to privacy. There are situations, however, when laws require psychologists to disclose confidential information acquired in research or clinical practice, as when a participant or a therapy client threatens to do physical harm to someone else.

Ethical guidelines also extend to the use of animals in psychological research. The design of research projects often precludes the use of human participants, and in such cases, the researchers use animals as subjects. For example, to determine which behaviors are instinctive and which are not, scientists have reared birds and fish in isolation from other members of their species; such research could not be conducted with humans because of the harmful effects of separating infants from their families. Scientists routinely test experimental drugs on animals to determine harmful effects before human trials are begun. And those who study the brain may destroy parts of the brains of laboratory animals, such as rats and monkeys, to learn how these parts of the brain are connected with behavior. (In Chapter 8, you will see how the surgical destruction of particular parts of the brain causes laboratory animals to either overeat or stop eating completely.)

Issues concerning the ethical treatment of animals in research studies have risen to the fore in recent years (Banyard & Flanagan, 2006; Kantowitz, Roediger, & Elmes, 2009). On one side of the debate are those who argue that significant advances in medicine and psychology could not have occurred without such research. Yet many psychologists believe it is unethical to kill animals or expose them to pain, regardless of the potential benefits of the research to humans. According to APA ethical guidelines, animals may not be harmed or subjected to stress unless there is no alternative way

© cubephoto/Shutterstock.com

ethics review committees Committees that evaluate whether proposed studies meet ethical guidelines.

informed consent Agreement to participate in a study following disclosure of information about the purposes and nature of the study and its potential risks and benefits.

to conduct the research and the goals of the research are justified by their intended scientific, educational, or practical value (American Psychological Association, 2002). Researchers must also obtain approval from their institutional review boards to ensure that ethical practices are followed.

MODULE REVIEW **1.3** Research Methods in Psychology

Recite It

6. Identify the steps in the scientific method.

The scientific method comprises four general steps that guide scientific research: (1) developing a research (a) _____, (2) formulating a (b) _____, (3) gathering (c) _____, and (4) drawing (d) _____.

7. Identify research methods psychologists use.

Research methods include the (e) _____ study method, the survey method, the (f) _____ observation method, the correlational method, and the experimental method.

8. Describe the ethical standards that govern research in psychology.

Psychologists are committed to protecting the welfare of research participants by following ethical guidelines that require (g) _____ consent, protect the (h) _____ of research records, and ensure that approval of research protocols from (i) _____ review committees is first obtained before undertaking research with humans or animals.

9. Apply critical thinking skills to evaluate claims made by others as well as online sources.

We can apply critical thinking skills when evaluating claims made by others by (j) _____ everything we hear or read, clarifying meaning of terms, avoiding oversimplifying, avoiding overgeneralizing, distinguishing between correlation and (k) _____, examining assumptions on which claims are based, examining sources of claims, questioning the evidence on which claims are based, and evaluating (l) _____ ways of explaining claims.

Recall It

1. Which of the following is *not* one of the four general steps in the scientific method?

a. developing a research question
b. testing the hypothesis
c. using the case study method as a starting point of investigation
d. drawing conclusions

2. A distinct advantage of the naturalistic observation method, when used correctly, is that it

a. allows us to establish cause-and-effect relationships.
b. does not require experimenters to follow ethical guidelines governing other forms of research.
c. allows us to generate hypotheses on the basis of intensive study of a person's life experiences.
d. provides a view of behavior that occurs in natural settings.

3. Which research method is best suited to providing evidence of cause-and-effect relationships?

4. Ethical guidelines in psychological research

a. provide a set of rules that govern research when obtaining approval from ethics review committees would cause critical delays in a project.
b. are designed to protect research participants from physical or psychological harm.
c. permit researchers to violate the principle of informed consent when experiments cannot be performed in accordance with that principle.
d. are a set of standards that apply to human research but not animal research.

Think About It

■ Perhaps you won't be surprised by research findings that adolescents with tattoos are more likely to engage in riskier behavior than their nontattooed peers (Roberts & Ryan, 2002). Tattooed youth are more likely to smoke cigarettes, engage in binge drinking, use marijuana, and join gangs. But does tattooing cause these risky behaviors? Can you think of other possible explanations for links between tattooing and high-risk behavior?

■ Can you think of another example in which two variables are correlated but not causally related?

■ Suppose you were interested in studying the relationship between alcohol use and grades among college students, but you couldn't experimentally control whether students used alcohol or how much they used. How might you use correlational methods to study this relationship? What might be the value of this type of research? Would you be able to conclude that alcohol use affects grades? Why or why not?

Recite It *answers placed at the end of chapter.*

APPLYING PSYCHOLOGY in Daily Life

Becoming a Critical Thinker

CONCEPT 1.32
Critical thinking involves adopting a skeptical, questioning attitude toward commonly held beliefs and assumptions and weighing arguments in terms of the available evidence.

Critical thinking involves adopting a questioning attitude in which you weigh evidence carefully and apply thoughtful analysis in probing the claims and arguments of others. It is a way of evaluating information by maintaining a skeptical attitude toward what you hear and read, even what you read in the pages of this text.

Critical thinking requires a willingness to challenge conventional wisdom and common knowledge that many of us take for granted. When you think critically, you maintain an open mind and suspend belief until you can obtain and evaluate evidence that either supports or refutes a particular claim or statement. You find *reasons* to support your beliefs, rather than relying on impressions or "gut feelings." In this text, you'll be able to hone your critical thinking skills by answering the questions posed in the Thinking Critically About Psychology sections, which appear at the end of every chapter.

Features of Critical Thinking

Critical thinkers maintain a healthy skepticism. They question assumptions and claims others make and demand to see the evidence upon which conclusions are based. Here are some suggestions for thinking critically about psychology:

1. *Question everything.* Critical thinkers do not blindly accept the validity of claims others make, even claims of authority figures such as political or religious leaders, scientists, or even textbook authors. They keep an open mind and weigh the evidence on which claims are made.

2. *Clarify meaning.* Whether a claim is true or false may depend on how we define the terms we use. Consider the claim "Stress is bad for you." If we define stress only in terms of the pressures and hassles of daily life, then perhaps there is some truth to that claim. But if we define stress more broadly to include any events that impose a pressure on us to adjust—even positive events such as the birth of a child or a promotion at work—then certain kinds of stress may actually be desirable (see Chapter 10). Perhaps we even need a certain amount of stress to be active and alert.

3. *Avoid oversimplifying.* Consider the claim "Alcoholism is inherited." In Chapter 4, we review evidence indicating that genetic factors may contribute to alcoholism. But the origins of alcoholism, as well as the origins of many other psychological and physical disorders, are more complex. Genetics alone does not tell the whole story. Many disorders involve the interplay of biological, psychological, and environmental factors, the nature of which we are only beginning to unravel.

© vector illustration/Shutterstock.com

critical thinking The adoption of a skeptical, questioning attitude and careful scrutiny of claims or arguments.

4. *Avoid overgeneralizing.* People from China and Japan and other East Asian cultures tend to be more reserved about disclosing information about themselves to strangers than are Americans or Europeans (see Chapter 12). Yet this doesn't mean that every person from these East Asian cultures is more withholding or that every American or European is more disclosing.

5. *Don't confuse correlation with causation.* As you'll see in Chapter 9, girls who show earlier signs of puberty than their peers (for example, early breast development) tend to have lower self-esteem, a more negative body image, and more emotional problems. But do physical changes associated with early puberty cause these negative psychological consequences, or might other factors be involved in explaining these links, such as how people react to these changes?

6. *Examine the assumptions on which claims are based.* Consider the claim that homosexuality is a psychological disorder. The claim rests in part on underlying assumptions about the nature of psychological disorders. What is a psychological disorder? What criteria are used to determine whether someone has a psychological disorder? Do gays, lesbians, or people with a bisexual orientation meet these criteria? Is there evidence to support these assertions? In Chapter 13, you will see that mental health professionals no longer classify homosexuality as a psychological disorder.

7. *Examine sources of claims.* In their publications, scientists cite the sources on which they base their claims. (See this book's reference list, which cites the sources used in its preparation.) When examining source citations, note such features as publication dates (to determine whether the sources are outdated or current) and the journals or other periodicals in which the sources may have appeared (to see whether they are well-respected scientific journals or questionable sources). Source citations allow readers to check the original sources for themselves to see if the information provided is accurate.

8. *Question the evidence on which claims are based.* Are claims based on sound scientific evidence or on anecdotes and personal testimonials that cannot be independently verified? In Chapter 6, we consider the controversy over so-called recovered memories—memories of childhood sexual abuse that suddenly reappear during adulthood, usually during the course of psychotherapy or hypnosis. Are such memories accurate? Or might they be tales spun of imaginary thread?

9. *Examine alternative ways of explaining claims.* Do you believe in the existence of extrasensory perception (ESP)? Some people claim to have extrasensory skills that enable them, simply by using their minds, to read other people's minds, to transmit their thoughts to others, or to move objects or change their shapes. Are such claims believable? Or might more mundane explanations account for these strange phenomena, such as coincidence, deliberate fabrication, or sleight of hand? In Chapter 3, we consider the case of a psychic who claims to have relied on her extrasensory ability in finding a missing person. Was it ESP? Or might there be other explanations?

Thinking Critically About Online Information

One of the features of the Internet is that any user can post information that others can access. Yet this freedom carries with it the risk that the information posted may be inaccurate or incomplete. The Internet may be an effective vehicle for

Think critically about online information. Check out the credibility of the source of the material and be wary of information provided by companies or marketers seeking to promote or sell particular products or services.

sandy young / Alamy stock photo

disseminating information that may not be accessible through other sources, such as information young people can use to arm themselves with skills to prevent sexually transmitted diseases (Keller & Brown, 2002).

Critical thinkers don't suspend their skeptical attitude when they go online. They check out the credentials of the source by asking questions such as these: Who is posting the material? Is the source a well-respected institution? Or is it an individual or group of individuals with no apparent credentials who may have a hidden agenda?

The most trustworthy online information comes from well-known scientific sources, such as leading scientific journals, government agencies like the National Institutes of Health, and major professional organizations like the American Psychological Association and the Association for Psychological Science. One reason articles in scientific journals are so trustworthy is that they undergo a process of peer review in which independent scientists carefully scrutinize them before they are accepted for publication. Many leading scientific organizations provide links to abstracts (brief descriptions) of recent works. Much of this information is available without charge.

Sad to say, many people never question the information that comes to them on the printed page or on their computer screens. But as critical thinkers, you *can* evaluate assertions and claims for yourself. The critical thinking sections found at the end of each chapter will give you an opportunity to sharpen your critical thinking skills.

THINKING CRITICALLY ABOUT PSYCHOLOGY

Here is the first critical thinking exercise you will encounter in this text. Based on your reading of the chapter, answer the following questions. Then, to evaluate your progress in developing critical thinking skills, compare your answers with the sample answers in Appendix A.

An experimenter claims that listening to a professor's lectures while you sleep can help improve your grades. The experimenter based this conclusion on the following data.

The experimenter invited students in a large introductory psychology class to participate in a study in which they would be given audiotapes of the professor's lectures and asked to play them back while they slept. Each of the 36 students who agreed to participate received a specially equipped audiotape player. Secured in the machine with tamper-proof sealing tape were recordings of each lecture given in the two weeks before the

final examination. The tape player automatically played the tape two hours after the students went to bed. At other times, the play button was deactivated so that the students could not play the tape.

After the final examination, the experimenter compared the grades of the participating students with those of a group of students selected from the same class who had not participated in the study. The results showed that participating students achieved higher test grades.

1. Do you believe the experimenter's claims are justified? Why or why not?

2. What other factors might account for the observed differences in test scores between the two groups?

3. How might you design the study differently to strengthen the experimenter's conclusion?

Recite It Answers for Chapter 1

Module 1.1   1. (a) behavior; (b) evidence; 2. (c) Structuralism; (d) Wundt; (e) James; (f) functions; (g) Watson; (h) behavior; (i) Gestalt; (j) Wertheimer; (k) wholes; (l) Freud; (m) unconscious; 3. (n) behavioral; (o) psychodynamic; (p) humanistic; (q) Rogers; (r) Maslow; (s) physiological; (t) cognitive; (u) sociocultural   **Module 1.2** 4. (a) forensic; 5. (b) underrepresented; (c) women   **Module 1.3** 6. (a) question; (b) hypothesis; (c) evidence; (d) conclusions; 7. (e) case; (f) naturalistic; 8. (g) informed; (h) confidentiality; (i) institutional; 9. (j) questioning; (k) causation; (l) alternative

VISUAL OVERVIEW
The Science of Psychology

MODULE 1.1

Foundations of Modern Psychology

Origins of Psychology

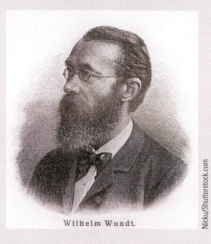

Wilhelm Wundt.

- **Wilhelm Wundt and Structuralism:** Breaking down mental experience into its components parts
- **William James and Functionalism:** Behavior tied to function
- **John Watson and Behaviorism:** Psychology as the science of observable behavior
- **Max Wertheimer and Gestalt Psychology:** "The whole is greater than the sum of the parts"
- **Sigmund Freud and Psychoanalysis:** Exploring the unconscious

Contemporary Perspectives in Psychology

- **Behavioral:** Focus on role of learning in explaining observable behavior
- **Psychodynamic:** Explores unconscious influences of unconscious conflicts on behavior
- **Humanistic:** Focuses on conscious experience and self-awareness
- **Physiological:** Focuses on the biological underpinnings of behavior
- **Cognitive:** Explores the mental processes by which we acquire knowledge of the world
- **Sociocultural:** Explores how behavior is influenced by social and cultural factors

Nicku/Shutterstock.com

MODULE 1.2

Psychologists: Who They Are and What They Do

Specialty Areas of Psychology

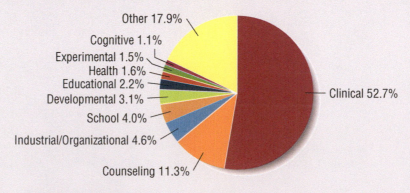

Other 17.9%
Cognitive 1.1%
Experimental 1.5%
Health 1.6%
Educational 2.2%
Developmental 3.1%
School 4.0%
Industrial/Organizational 4.6%
Counseling 11.3%
Clinical 52.7%

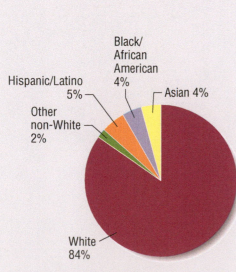

Black/African American 4%
Hispanic/Latino 5%
Asian 4%
Other non-White 2%
White 84%

Note: Numbers do not sum to 100% because of rounding.

- **Emerging Specialty Areas**

  Neuropsychology
  Geropsychology
  Forensic psychology
  Sport psychology
- **Ethnicities of Doctorate Recipients in Psychology:** Field becoming more diverse, but still comprising predominantly White, European Americans

Research Methods in Psychology

The Scientific Method

A framework for acquiring knowledge through careful observation and experimentation, comprising four general steps:

1 Developing a Research Question	**2** Forming a Hypothesis	**3** Gathering Evidence	**4** Drawing Conclusions
Drawing on theory, observations, experiences, or common beliefs to formulate a researchable question	Reframing the question so that it becomes a specific prediction that can be tested through research	Testing the hypothesis	Using statistical methods of analysis to determine whether the data support the hypothesis

Gathering Evidence: Types of Research Methods

- **Case Study Method:** Intensive study of individuals
- **Survey Method:** Measuring opinions and attitudes
- **Naturalistic Observation Method:** Taking research into the field
- **Correlational Method:** Examining relationships between variables
- **Experimental Method:** Exploring cause-and-effect relationships by manipulating independent variables and measuring their effects on dependent variables

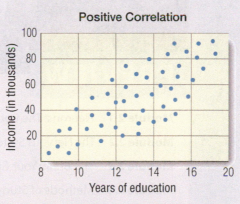

Generally speaking, people with higher levels of education tend to earn higher incomes.

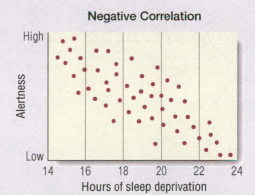

Generally speaking, the longer a person is deprived of sleep, the less alert the person is likely to be.

LEARNING OBJECTIVES

After studying this chapter, you will be able to . . .

1 **Define** what a neuron is, **identify** the parts of the neuron, and **explain** how neurons communicate with each other.

2 **Explain** how an action potential is generated.

3 **Identify** key neurotransmitters and **describe** their functions.

4 **Explain** the difference between antagonists and agonists.

5 **Describe** how the nervous system is organized.

6 **Describe** the functions of the central nervous system and the divisions of the peripheral nervous system.

7 **Explain** the differences in the functions of the sympathetic and parasympathetic divisions of the autonomic nervous system.

8 **Describe** how the brain is organized and the roles that particular brain structures play in behavior.

9 **Describe** methods scientists use to study the workings of the brain.

10 **Explain** how the two halves of the brain differ in their functions.

11 **Describe** how the endocrine system is organized and the roles that hormones play in behavior.

12 **Evaluate** the role of genetics in behavior.

13 **Describe** methods psychologists use to study the roles of genes and environment in behavior.

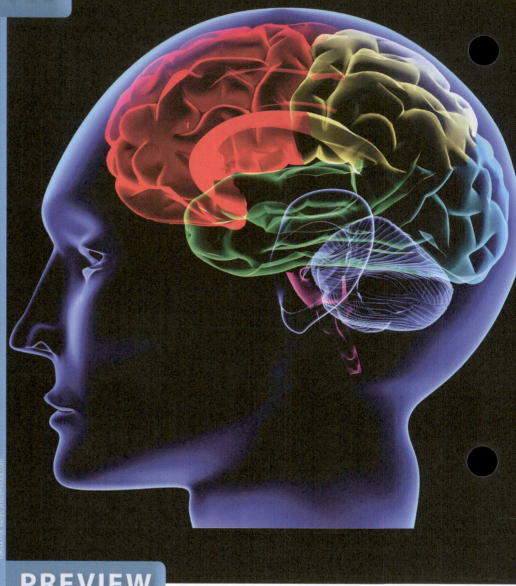

Yakobchuk Vasyl/Shutterstock.com

PREVIEW

Biological Foundations of Behavior

2

Do You Have Shopping on the Brain?

An MRI scanner may be about as far removed from a shopping mall as you can imagine, but it was used by consumer psychologists in a mock shopping mall study (Knutson et al., 2007). While participants were having their brains scanned, they were shown pictures of consumer products along with the prices of the items, which were pegged at about 75 percent below the retail value—a real bargain. The participants were then asked to think about whether they would like a chance to buy some of these products, using a $40 stash provided by the experimenters.

The investigators wanted to see what happens in the brain at the moment someone decides, "Yes, I want to buy that." They discovered that a particular cluster of nerve cells in the brain became active a moment before people make a conscious decision to buy a particular item. The nerve cells that were activated form part of the reward circuitry in the brain, a network of interconnected nerve cells that produce feelings of pleasure associated with consuming a good meal, experiencing satisfying sexual relations, or engaging in other enjoyable activities. In effect, deciding to buy a desired product activates the same brain pathways as those involved in producing other states of pleasure. This may be why people often experience pleasurable excitement when they shop.

Brain scans have long been used to evaluate pathological conditions affecting the brain, as we'll see later in this chapter. But researchers are now beginning to use advanced scanning methods to peer into the working brain to better understand the biological bases of ordinary behaviors such as shopping. They are probing the brain to find particular structures that may explain why some people become impulsive ("must have it now") shoppers whereas others are able to delay gratification. We can even imagine the possibility in the not-too-distant future of impulse shoppers deciding to have mild electrical currents applied to parts of their brains to tamp down unrestrained buying tendencies (Begley, 2011).

In this chapter, we take an inward journey of discovery to explore the biological bases of behavior. We study the organization and workings of the human brain, the most remarkable feat of engineering ever achieved. Weighing a mere three pounds on the average, it is a living supercomputer, far more elegant than any machine Silicon Valley wizards could hope to create. Even the most advanced computers lack the capacity for basic insights and creativity performed by the human brain. What computer has written noteworthy music or a decent poem? What computer is aware of itself or aware that it even exists? Such wonders remain the stuff of science fiction. We begin this inward journey by first studying the structure and workings of the basic unit of the nervous system—the nerve cell, or *neuron*.

Did you know that...

- The brain (and the rest of the nervous system) runs on electricity? (p. 44)
- Nerve impulses don't actually jump from one nerve to another, but are ferried by chemical messengers? (p. 45)
- Our bodies produce natural painkillers that are chemically similar to morphine and other narcotic drugs? (p. 48)
- Sometimes it's better not to use your brain before you respond? (p. 51)
- It is impossible to tickle yourself? (p. 62)
- Marketing researchers are looking for "whispers in the brain" to learn which ads on TV get people to pay attention and respond emotionally? (p. 65)
- Testosterone is produced in the bodies of both men and women? (p. 76)

2.1 Neurons: The Body's Wiring

1 **Define** what a neuron is, **identify** the parts of the neuron, and **explain** how neurons communicate with each other.

2 **Explain** how an action potential is generated.

3 **Identify** key neurotransmitters and **describe** their functions.

4 **Explain** the difference between antagonists and agonists.

CONCEPT 2.1

Neurons are the basic building blocks of the nervous system—the body's wiring through which messages are transmitted within the nervous system.

neurons Nerve cells.

brain The mass of nerve tissue encased in the skull that controls virtually everything we are and everything we do.

soma The cell body of a neuron that contains the nucleus of the cell and carries out the cell's metabolic functions.

Neurons do wondrous things, such as informing your **brain** when light strikes your eye and carrying messages from the brain that command your muscles to raise your arms and your heart to pump blood. They also enable you to think, plan, even to dream. They enable you to read this page and to wonder what will turn up in the next paragraph.

In this module, we first look at the structure of an individual neuron and then observe how neurons communicate with one another to transmit information within the nervous system.

The Structure of the Neuron

Neurons, the basic building blocks of the nervous system, are cells in the body that are specialized for transmitting information or messages in the form of electrical impulses. Each neuron is a single cell, consisting of a cell body (or *soma*), an axon, and dendrites. ■ Figure 2.1 illustrates these structures; Concept Chart 2.1 summarizes their functions. The **soma** is the main body of the cell. It

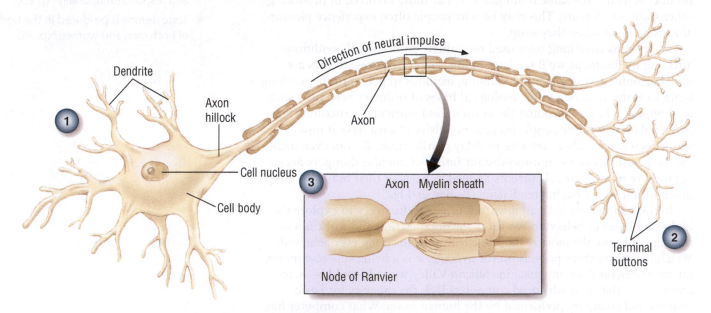

FIGURE 2.1 The Neuron

① A neuron or nerve cell consists of a cell body, or soma, which houses the cell nucleus; an axon, which carries the neural message; and dendrites, which receive messages from adjacent neurons. ② Terminal buttons are swellings at the end of the axon from which neurotransmitter molecules are released to ferry the message to other neurons. ③ Axons of many neurons are covered with a myelin sheath, which is a type of insulating layer that helps speed transmission of neural impulses.

Concept Chart 2.1   Parts of the Neuron

© sgame/Shutterstock.com

Part	Description	Function
Soma	Cell body containing the nucleus	Performs metabolic, or life-sustaining, functions of the cell
Axon	Long cable projecting from the soma	Carries neural impulses to the terminal buttons
Terminal buttons	Swellings at ends of axons	Release chemicals, called neurotransmitters, that carry neural messages to adjacent neurons
Dendrites	Fibers that project from the soma	Receive messages from neighboring neurons

CONCEPT 2.2
The nervous system has three types of neurons: sensory neurons, motor neurons, and interneurons.

CONCEPT 2.3
The nervous system has two types of cells, neurons and glial cells.

CONCEPT 2.4
Many axons are covered with a protective coating, called a myelin sheath, that speeds the transmission of neural impulses.

CONCEPT 2.5
The nervous system is a massive communication network that connects billions of neurons throughout your body.

houses the cell nucleus, which contains the cell's genetic material and carries out the *metabolic*, or life-sustaining, functions of the cell. Each neuron also has an **axon**, a long cable that projects trunklike from the soma and conducts outgoing messages to other neurons.

The axons of the neurons in your brain may be only a few thousandths of an inch long. Other axons, such as those that run from your spinal cord to your toes, are several feet long. Axons may branch off like the stems of plants, fanning out in different directions. At the ends of these branches are knoblike swellings called **terminal buttons**. It is here that chemicals called **neurotransmitters** are stored and released. These chemicals are synthesized in the soma and ferry outgoing messages to neighboring neurons at the **synapse**, the tiny gap that separates one neuron from another and serves as a connection point between neurons (the word *synapse* comes from a Greek word meaning "joining together").

Dendrites are treelike structures that project from the soma. Dendrites have receptor sites, or docking stations, that enable them to receive neurotransmitters released by neighboring neurons. Each neuron may receive messages from thousands of other neurons through its dendrites (Priebe & Ferster, 2010).

The nervous system has three types of neurons: sensory neurons, motor neurons, and interneurons. These different types play specialized roles in the nervous system.

Sensory neurons (also called *afferent neurons*) transmit information about the outside world to the spinal cord and brain. This information first registers on your sensory organs. So when someone touches your hand, sensory receptors within the skin transmit the message through sensory neurons to the spinal cord and brain, where the information is processed, resulting in the feeling of touch. Sensory neurons also carry information from your muscles and inner organs to your spinal cord and brain.

Motor neurons (also called *efferent neurons*) convey messages from the brain and spinal cord to the muscles that control the movements of your body. They also convey messages to your **glands**, causing them to release **hormones**—chemical substances that help regulate bodily processes.

Interneurons (also called *associative neurons*) are the most common type of neuron in the nervous system. They connect neurons to neurons. In the spinal cord, they connect sensory neurons to motor neurons. In the brain, they form complex assemblages of interconnected nerve cells that process information from sensory organs and control higher mental functions, such as planning and thinking.

A neuron is not the same thing as a nerve. A **nerve** is a bundle of axons from different neurons. An individual nerve—for example, the optic nerve, which transmits messages from the eyes to the brain—contains more than a million axons. Although individual axons are microscopic, a nerve may be visible to the naked eye. The cell bodies of the neurons that contain the axons are not part of the nerve itself.

axon The tubelike part of a neuron that carries messages away from the cell body toward other neurons.

terminal buttons Swellings at the tips of axons from which neurotransmitters are dispatched into the synapse.

neurotransmitters Chemical messengers that transport nerve impulses from one nerve cell to another.

synapse The small fluid-filled gap between neurons through which neurotransmitters carry neural impulses.

dendrites Rootlike structures at the end of axons that receive neural impulses from neighboring neurons.

sensory neurons Neurons that transmit information from sensory organs, muscles, and inner organs to the spinal cord and brain.

motor neurons Neurons that convey nerve impulses from the central nervous system to muscles and glands.

glands Body organs or structures that produce secretions called hormones.

hormones Secretions from endocrine glands that help regulate bodily processes.

interneurons Nerve cells within the central nervous system that process information.

nerve A bundle of axons from different neurons that transmit nerve impulses.

Neurons are not the only cells in the nervous system. Far more numerous are small cells called **glial cells** that act as a kind of glue to hold neurons together. The word *glial* is derived from the Greek word for "glue." Glial cells also support and nourish neurons in a number of ways, such as by removing their waste products, and may even assist them in communicating with one another (Fields, 2013; Smith, 2010; Unhavaithaya & Orr-Weaver, 2012).

Glial cells serve yet another important function: They form the **myelin sheath**, a fatty layer of cells that—like the insulation that wraps around electrical wires—acts as a protective shield on many axons. The insulation provided by the myelin sheath helps speed transmission of neural impulses, which allows muscles to move more efficiently and smoothly.

As shown in Figure 2.1, myelinated axons resemble a string of sausages that are pinched in at "the waist" at various points, creating gaps called **nodes of Ranvier**. The neural impulse appears to jump from node to node as it speeds down the axon. Because myelin sheaths are white, parts of the nervous system that contain myelinated axons are referred to as "white matter."

Multiple sclerosis (MS) is a chronic and often crippling disease of the central nervous system, affecting about one in one thousand adults, in which the body's own immune system attacks and eventually destroys the myelin sheath (Kwon, 2016). MS generally affects young adults between 20 and 40 years of age and is believed to be genetically influenced (Baranzini et al., 2010). The loss of myelin slows the transmission of nerve impulses, leading to a range of symptoms; in the most severe cases, the person loses the ability to speak, walk, write, or even breathe.

How Neurons Communicate

The human brain is densely packed with about one hundred billion neurons, which form trillions of connections among them. From the time we are born, as we begin learning about the world around us, our brains become an increasingly complex network of billions upon billions of interlaced neurons. These complex assemblages of brain cells are intricately weaved circuits that allow us to interpret the world around us, to respond to external stimuli, to organize our behavior, and to think, feel, and use language (Turk-Browne, 2013). Neurons perform all of these tasks by sending messages to one another. Let us break down the process into smaller steps to see how it works.

Let's take a close look at the workings of the neuron. Both inside and outside the neuron are electrically charged atoms and molecules called **ions**. Like the poles of a battery, ions have either a positive (+) or negative (−) charge. The movements of ions across the cell wall, or *cell membrane,* cause electrochemical changes in the cell that generate an electrical signal to travel down the cell's axon in the form of a neural impulse. The most important ions in this process are two types of positively charged ions, *sodium* ions and *potassium* ions. The movement of ions through the cell membrane is controlled by a series of gates, or tiny doors, that open to allow ions to enter the cell and close to shut them out.

When a neuron is at rest (not being stimulated), the gates that control the passage of sodium ions are closed. A greater concentration of positively charged sodium ions remains outside the cell, causing the cell to have a slightly negative charge, called a **resting potential**, relative to the surrounding fluid. The resting potential of a neuron is about −70 millivolts (mV) (a millivolt is one thousandth of a volt). Like a charged battery sitting on a shelf, a neuron in the resting state holds a store of potential energy that can be used to generate, or "fire," a neural impulse in response to stimulation. It awaits a source of stimulation that will temporarily reverse the electrical charges within the cell, causing it to fire.

When the cell is stimulated, usually by neurotransmitters released from adjoining neurons, sodium gates at the base of the axon open. Positively charged sodium ions from the surrounding fluid then rush in, which causes the area inside the cell membrane at the point of excitation to become less negatively charged. This process is called **depolarization**.

CONCEPT 2.6

A neuron fires when a stimulus triggers electrochemical changes along its cell membrane that lead to a chain reaction within the cell.

---

glial cells Small but numerous cells in the nervous system that support neurons and that form the myelin sheath found on many axons.

myelin sheath A layer of protective insulation that covers the axons of certain neurons and helps speed transmission of nerve impulses.

nodes of Ranvier Gaps in the myelin sheath that create noninsulated areas along the axon.

multiple sclerosis (MS) A disease of the central nervous system in which the myelin sheath that insulates axons is damaged or destroyed.

ions Electrically charged chemical particles.

resting potential The electrical potential across the cell membrane of a neuron in its resting state.

depolarization A positive shift in the electrical charge in the neuron's resting potential, making it less negatively charged.

When stimulation is sufficiently strong, as when enough of a neurotransmitter is present, depolarization quickly spreads along the cell membrane (Calderon de Anda et al., 2005). As this wave of depolarization reaches a critical threshold, the neuron abruptly shifts from a negative charge to a positive charge of about 140 mV. The sudden reversal of electrical charge is called an **action potential**, or *neural impulse*. The action potential typically begins at the juncture between the soma and the axon, which is called the *axon hillock*. It then shoots down the entire length of the axon as a wave of changing electrical charges. We refer to this action as a "firing" of the neuron, or as a *spike* (see ■ Figure 2.2).

Once an action potential reaches the end of an axon, it causes the release of neurotransmitters from the terminal buttons that carry the neural message to the next neuron. Action potentials are generated according to the **all-or-none principle**. A neuron will fire completely (generate an action potential) if sufficient stimulation is available, or it will not fire; there is no halfway point. Different axons generate action potentials of different speeds depending on such characteristics as their thickness (generally the thicker the axon, the faster the speed), and whether or not they are covered with a myelin sheath (which speeds transmission). Speeds of action potentials range from between two miles an hour to a few hundred miles an hour. Even the most rapid neural impulses are much slower than a speeding bullet, which travels at the rate of several hundred miles a minute. Even so, neural impulses race to their destinations at several hundred feet per second—fast enough to pull your hand in an instant from a burning surface, but perhaps not fast enough to avoid a burn (Aamodt & Wang, 2008).

For about one thousandth of a second (one millisecond) after firing, a neuron busies itself preparing to fire again. Sodium gates along the cell membrane close, preventing further inflows of positively charged sodium ions into the cell. The cell pumps out positively charged ions, mostly potassium ions, and as it rids itself of these positive ions, the neuron's negatively charged resting potential is restored. Then, in a slower process, the cell restores the electrochemical balance by pumping out sodium ions and drawing in some potassium ions, making it possible for another action potential to occur. During the time these changes are occurring, called a **refractory period**, the neuron, like a gun being reloaded, is temporarily incapable of firing. But *temporarily* truly means *temporarily*, for a neuron can "reload" hundreds of times per second.

Neurotransmitters: The Nervous System's Chemical Messengers

Neurons don't actually touch. Recall that neurons are separated by the tiny fluid-filled gap called a synapse, which measures less than a millionth of an inch across. Neural impulses or messages cannot jump even this tiniest of gaps. They must be transferred by neurotransmitters, the chemical agents or messengers that carry the message across the synapse. When a neuron fires, tiny vesicles (or sacs) in the axon's terminal buttons release molecules of neurotransmitters into the synaptic gap (also called the *synaptic cleft*) like a flotilla of ships casting off into the sea (see ■ Figure 2.3). Neurotransmitters carry messages that control activities ranging from contraction of muscles that move our bodies, to stimulation of glands to release hormones, to the psychological states of thinking and emotion.

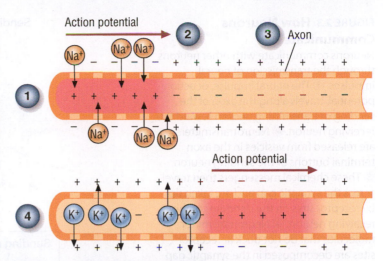

FIGURE 2.2 An Action Potential
Here we see how a neural impulse or action potential is generated. ① When a neuron in a resting state is stimulated, sodium gates in the cell membrane open, allowing positively charged sodium ions (Na⁺) to rush into the cell. ② With sufficient stimulation, the cell suddenly shifts from a negative to a positive charge. ③ The sudden reversal of charge is called an action potential or neural impulse that shoots down the axon, momentarily reversing charges all along the cell membrane. Once the action potential passes, sodium gates close, preventing further inflows of sodium ions. ④ The cell then pumps out positively charged ions, mostly potassium ions (K⁺). This restores the cells' negatively charged resting state, allowing it to fire again in response to stimulation.

CONCEPT 2.7
An action potential is generated according to the all-or-none principle—it is produced only if the level of excitation is sufficient.

CONCEPT 2.8
When the neural impulse reaches the axon's terminal buttons, it triggers the release of chemicals that either increase or decrease the likelihood that neighboring cells will fire.

action potential An abrupt change from a negative to a positive charge of a nerve cell, also called a *neural impulse*.

all-or-none principle The principle by which neurons will fire only when a change in the level of excitation occurs that is sufficient to produce an action potential.

refractory period A temporary state in which a neuron is unable to fire in response to continued stimulation.

FIGURE 2.3 How Neurons Communicate

Neurons communicate with other neurons through the transmission of neural impulses. ① The neural impulse, or action potential, travels along the axon of the sending or transmitting neuron toward the receiving neuron. ② Neurotransmitters are released from vesicles in the axon terminal buttons of the sending neuron. ③ These chemical messengers then travel across the synaptic gap and are taken up by receptor sites on the dendrites of the receiving neuron. ④ Neurotransmitter molecules that do not dock at receptor sites are decomposed in the synaptic gap or are reabsorbed by the transmitting neuron in a process called reuptake.

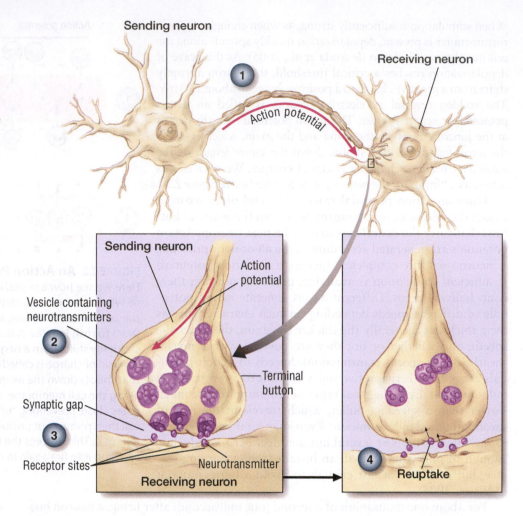

CONCEPT 2.9

Normal psychological functioning depends on the delicate balance of neurotransmitter activity in the brain.

CONCEPT LINK

Irregularities in neurotransmitter functioning are implicated in many psychological disorders, including eating disorders, depression, and schizophrenia. Eating disorders are discussed in Module 8.2, depression in Module 13.4, and schizophrenia in Module 13.5.

receptor site A site on the receiving neuron in which neurotransmitters dock.

reuptake The process by which neurotransmitters are reabsorbed by the transmitting neuron.

enzymes Organic substances that produce certain chemical changes in other organic substances through a catalytic action.

neuromodulators Chemicals released in the nervous system that influence the sensitivity of the receiving neuron to neurotransmitters.

antagonists Drugs that block the actions of neurotransmitters by occupying the receptor sites in which the neurotransmitters dock.

schizophrenia A severe and chronic psychological disorder characterized by disturbances in thinking, perception, emotions, and behavior.

hallucinations Perceptions experienced in the absence of corresponding external stimuli.

Each specific type of neurotransmitter has a particular chemical structure, or three-dimensional shape. It fits into only one kind of **receptor site**, like a key fitting into a lock. When neurotransmitters dock at receptor sites, they lock into place, causing chemical changes in the receiving (or *postsynaptic*) neuron. These changes have either an *excitatory effect* or an *inhibitory effect*. Excitatory effects make an action potential more likely to occur. Inhibitory effects put the brakes on an action potential, making it less likely to occur. Some neurotransmitters have excitatory effects; others, inhibitory effects; and still others, both excitatory and inhibitory effects. To function smoothly and efficiently, the nervous system depends on a balance between excitation and inhibition, or the turning on and off, of neurons (Chih, Engelman, & Scheiffele, 2005; Haider et al., 2006).

Several processes normally prevent excitatory neurotransmitters from continuing to stimulate a receiving cell. One process, called **reuptake**, is nature's own version of recycling. Through reuptake, neurotransmitters not taken up by the receiving cell are reabsorbed by their vesicles to be used again. In another process, **enzymes** in the synapse break down neurotransmitters, which are then eliminated from the body in the urine. In yet another process, terminal buttons release **neuromodulators**, chemicals that either increase or decrease the sensitivity of the receiving neuron to neurotransmitters.

Normal psychological functioning depends on the smooth transmission of messages among neurons in the brain. Your ability to think clearly, move your arms and legs at will, feel pain or emotions such as joy, fear, or anger—everything you do, feel, or think—depends on neurotransmitters. When the body produces too little or too much of a neurotransmitter, problems may occur. Sometimes receptor sites allow too many neurotransmitter molecules to dock, or they do not accept neurotransmitters properly. Excesses or deficits of particular neurotransmitters in the brain, or irregularities in how they function, are associated with many disorders. For example, irregularities in neurotransmitter functioning are linked to eating disorders (see Chapter 8) and to depression and schizophrenia (see Chapter 13).

Drugs or chemicals that block the actions of neurotransmitters by occupying their receptor sites are called **antagonists**. By locking into these receptor sites, antagonists prevent transmission of the messages the neurotransmitter carries. Consider *dopamine,* a neurotransmitter involved in controlling muscle contractions and in psychological processes involving learning, memory, and emotions (Berry et al., 2012; Flagel et al., 2011). It is of special interest to psychologists because irregularities in how the brain uses dopamine may help explain the development of **schizophrenia**, a severe mental disorder involving a break with reality (discussed in Chapter 13). People with schizophrenia may experience **hallucinations** ("hearing voices" or seeing things that are not there) and **delusions** (fixed, false ideas, such as believing that aliens have taken over their bodies). *Antipsychotic drugs*, which are antagonists that block receptor sites for dopamine, help control hallucinations and delusional thinking (see Chapter 13).

Parkinson's disease is a degenerative brain disease that leads to a progressive loss of motor functioning or physical movements. Parkinson's patients experience tremors (shakiness), muscle rigidity and stiffness, and difficulty walking and controlling the movements of their fingers and hands. These symptoms result from the death, for unknown reasons, of dopamine-producing cells in an area of the brain involved in regulating body movement (Laguna et al., 2015). Parkinson's typically strikes people later in life and affects an estimated 1 to 2 percent of people over the age of 60 (Okun, 2014). According to one expert, "Dopamine is like the oil in the engine of a car. . . . If the oil is there, the car runs smoothly. If not, it seizes up" (cited in Carroll, 2004, p. F5).

Parkinson's affects an estimated 1.5 million Americans, including former heavyweight boxing champion Muhammad Ali and actor Michael J. Fox. We don't yet know what causes dopamine-producing cells to die off, but scientists believe that mutations of particular genes are involved (Kazlauskaite et al., 2014; "New Parkinson's," 2014).

In contrast to antagonists that compete with neurotransmitters at the same receptor sites, other drugs, called **agonists**, enhance the activity of neurotransmitters. Agonists work by increasing either the availability or effectiveness of neurotransmitters or by binding to their receptor sites and mimicking their actions. As an example, the mild **stimulant** caffeine increases the availability of a neurotransmitter called *glutamate*. Glutamate is an excitatory neurotransmitter that keeps the central nervous system aroused (Weisz, Glowatzki, & Fuchs, 2009).

Stronger stimulants, such as **amphetamines** and cocaine, are agonists that increase the availability of the neurotransmitter dopamine in the brain by blocking its reuptake by the transmitting neuron. Dopamine plays many roles, including carrying messages in neural pathways in the brain that produce pleasurable feelings. Scientists believe that many drugs, including amphetamines and cocaine, as well as alcohol and opiates, produce pleasurable "highs" by increasing the availability of dopamine in the brain (Flagel et al., 2011). (We'll return to this topic in Chapter 4.) Investigators also believe the pleasurable excitement associated with falling in love involves release of dopamine (and other chemicals) in the brain (Ortigue et al., 2010).

Alcohol and antianxiety drugs like Valium act as agonists by increasing the sensitivity of receptor sites to the neurotransmitter *gamma-aminobutyric acid (GABA)*. GABA is the major *inhibitory* neurotransmitter in the adult brain; it helps regulate nervous system activity by preventing neurons from overly exciting their neighbors

Boxing legend Muhammad Ali developed Parkinson's disease, a degenerative brain disease that causes rigidity and tremors and affects the ability to control body movements.

Falling in love may inspire poetry, but feelings of pleasurable excitement new lovers experience may be better explained by chemical changes in the brain involving the neurotransmitter dopamine.

delusions Fixed but patently false beliefs, such as believing that one is being hounded by demons.

Parkinson's disease A progressive brain disease involving destruction of dopamine-producing brain cells and characterized by muscle tremors, shakiness, rigidity, and difficulty in walking and controlling fine body movements.

agonists Drugs that either increase the availability or effectiveness of neurotransmitters or mimic their actions.

stimulant A drug that activates the central nervous system, such as amphetamines and cocaine.

amphetamines A class of synthetically derived stimulant drugs, such as methamphetamine or "speed."

"I'll have a tall iced agonist to go." The caffeine in coffee is an agonist that enhances the actions of the excitatory neurotransmitter glutamate. What is the difference between drugs that work as agonists and those that work as antagonists?

antidepressants Drugs that combat depression by affecting the levels or activity of neurotransmitters.

endorphins Natural chemicals released in the brain that have pain-killing and pleasure-inducing effects.

(Gel et al., 2006). Thus, drugs that boost GABA's activity have calming or relaxing effects on the nervous system. Reduced levels of GABA in the brain may play a role in emotional disorders in which anxiety is a core feature, such as panic disorder (Kalueff & Nutt, 2006).

Neurotransmitters are also implicated in depression (Carver, Johnson, & Joormann, 2009; Sibille & Lewis, 2006). Drugs that help relieve depression, called **antidepressants**, serve as agonists that increase the availability of the neurotransmitters norepinephrine and serotonin in the brain. Norepinephrine (also called *noradrenaline*) is a chemical cousin of the hormone *epinephrine* (also called *adrenaline*). Norepinephrine does double duty as a neurotransmitter and a hormone (see Module 2.6). Serotonin, which works largely as an inhibitory neurotransmitter in the brain, serves to regulate mood states, feeling full after meals, and sleep. Serotonin also works as a kind of behavioral seat belt to curb impulsive behaviors, including impulsive acts of aggression (Crockett, 2009; Seo, Patrick, & Kennealy, 2008).

Did you know that the brain naturally produces neurotransmitters that are chemical cousins to narcotic drugs like morphine and heroin? These chemicals, called **endorphins** (short for *endogenous morphine*—morphine that "develops from within"), are inhibitory neurotransmitters. They lock into the same receptors in the brain as the drug morphine. (Narcotics and other psychoactive drugs are discussed further in Chapter 4.)

Endorphins are the body's natural painkillers. They are similar in chemical structure to narcotic drugs. Like morphine, heroin, and other narcotics, they deaden pain by fitting into receptor sites for chemicals that carry pain messages to the brain, thereby locking out pain messages. They also produce feelings of well-being and pleasure and may contribute to the "runner's high" experienced by many long-distance runners. Morphine and heroin are agonists, because they mimic the effects of naturally occurring endorphins on the body (Vetter et al., 2006).

MODULE REVIEW   2.1   Neurons: The Body's Wiring

Recite It

1. **Define** what a neuron is, **identify** the parts of the neuron, and **explain** how neurons communicate with each other.

   A (a) _____ is a nerve cell, the basic building block of the nervous system through which information in the form of neural impulses is transmitted. The parts of the neuron include the following: the cell body, or (b) _____, that houses the cell nucleus and carries out the metabolic work of the cell; the (c) _____, a long cable that conducts outgoing messages (neural impulses) to other neurons; (d) _____, which are the fibers that receive neural messages from other neurons; and terminal (e) _____ or swellings at the ends of the axon that release neurotransmitters in the synapse. When a neural impulse reaches the terminal buttons, it triggers the release of (f) _____, the chemical messengers that carry the message across the synapse (tiny gap between neurons) to neighboring neurons. Neurotransmitters have either excitatory or (g) _____ effects on neurons at which they dock.

2. **Explain** how an action potential is generated.

   Neural impulses are electrochemical events. When a neuron is stimulated beyond a threshold level, there is a rapid shift in its polarity from a negative to a (h) _____ charge. This reversal of charge, called an (i) _____ potential or neural impulse, is generated along the length of the axon to the terminal buttons.

3. **Describe** the functions of neurotransmitters in behavior and mental processes, and **identify** key neurotransmitters and their functions.

   Neurotransmitters are involved in psychological processes such as memory, learning, and regulation of emotions. Irregularities in the functioning of particular neurotransmitters are implicated in various disorders, including schizophrenia and depression. Key neurotransmitters include (j) _____, which is involved in controlling muscle contractions and in learning, memory, emotional processing, and regulating pleasurable sensations; _____, an excitatory neurotransmitter that maintains states of arousal in the central nervous system and is also involved in hearing; (k) _____, that tones down central nervous system activity; (l) _____, that plays key roles in regulation of mood states, feelings of satiety or fullness after a meal, sleep, and processes that curb impulsive behaviors;

and (m) _____, which help deaden pain and produce feelings of pleasure or well-being.

4. **Explain** the difference between antagonists and agonists.

Antagonists and agonists have opposite effects on neurotransmitters. (n) _____ block activity of certain neurotransmitters, whereas (o) _____ increase activity or availability of certain neurotransmitters.

Recall It

1. The function of a dendrite is to
    a. transmit signals to other neurons.
    b. receive signals from other neurons.
    c. conduct neural impulses along the length of the cell body.
    d. release neurotransmitters into the synapse.

2. What is the part of the neuron that performs the metabolic functions of the cell?

3. What are the three types of neurons in the human body?

4. When a neuron is at rest,
    a. greater concentration of sodium ions remains outside the nerve cell.

    b. the cell has a slightly positive charge (relative to surrounding fluid).
    c. the state is known as an action potential.
    d. it is in a state of depolarization.

5. Although nerve cells don't actually touch each other, they communicate by means of
    a. electrical impulses that travel from dendrites to receptor sites on adjacent neurons.
    b. neurotransmitters that carry the neural impulse across the synapse.
    c. interneurons that serve as relay stations between neurons.
    d. nerve cells that function independently and have no need to communicate with each other.

Think About It

■ How is a neuron in a resting state like a battery sitting on a shelf?

■ What is an action potential? How is it generated? What happens when it reaches the end of an axon?

■ A scientist develops a drug that blocks the actions of cocaine by locking into the same receptor sites as cocaine. So long as a person is taking the drug, cocaine will no longer produce a high. Would this drug be an antagonist or an agonist to cocaine? *Why?*

Recite It *answers placed at the end of chapter.*

To perform its many functions, the brain needs to communicate with the senses and muscles and other parts of our body. It does so through a complex network of neurons, of which the brain is a part, called the nervous system. The **nervous system** is an intricate network of neurons that functions as a communication network

nervous system The network of nerve cells and support cells for communicating and processing information from within and outside the body.

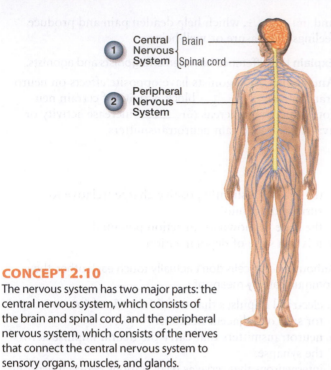

1. Central Nervous System — Brain, Spinal cord

2. Peripheral Nervous System

FIGURE 2.4 Parts of the Nervous System
The nervous system has two major divisions, the central nervous system and the peripheral nervous system. **1** The central nervous system, which consists of the brain and spinal cord, processes information it receives from the peripheral nervous system and issues commands carried through the peripheral nervous system to muscles and other organs in the body. **2** The peripheral system is a network of nerves connecting the central system to sensory organs, muscles, and glands throughout the body.

CONCEPT 2.10
The nervous system has two major parts: the central nervous system, which consists of the brain and spinal cord, and the peripheral nervous system, which consists of the nerves that connect the central nervous system to sensory organs, muscles, and glands.

for conducting information in the form of neural impulses. The nervous system is divided into two major parts: the *central nervous system*, consisting of the brain and spinal cord, and the *peripheral nervous system*, which connects the central nervous system to other parts of the body (see ■ Figure 2.4). Like a football team with every player having a specialized role to play, the different parts of the nervous system each have a role to perform and together, they work seamlessly to regulate vital bodily processes like respiration and heart rate, controlling bodily movements, sensing the world around us, and performing higher mental functions such as thinking, problem solving, and use of language. Concept Chart 2.2 shows the organization of the nervous system.

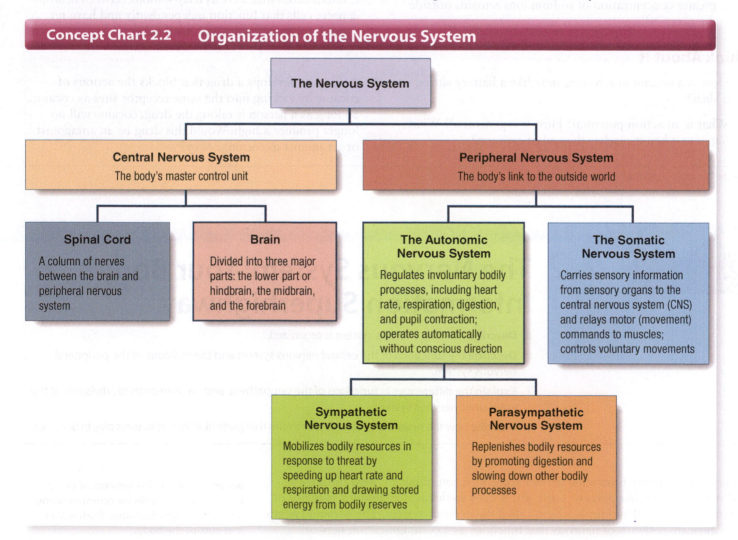

Concept Chart 2.2   Organization of the Nervous System

The Nervous System

Central Nervous System
The body's master control unit

Peripheral Nervous System
The body's link to the outside world

Spinal Cord
A column of nerves between the brain and peripheral nervous system

Brain
Divided into three major parts: the lower part or hindbrain, the midbrain, and the forebrain

The Autonomic Nervous System
Regulates involuntary bodily processes, including heart rate, respiration, digestion, and pupil contraction; operates automatically without conscious direction

The Somatic Nervous System
Carries sensory information from sensory organs to the central nervous system (CNS) and relays motor (movement) commands to muscles; controls voluntary movements

Sympathetic Nervous System
Mobilizes bodily resources in response to threat by speeding up heart rate and respiration and drawing stored energy from bodily reserves

Parasympathetic Nervous System
Replenishes bodily resources by promoting digestion and slowing down other bodily processes

The Central Nervous System: Your Body's Master Control Unit

You can compare the **central nervous system** to the central processing unit of a computer—the "brains" of the computer etched into a chip that controls the computer's central processing functions. The central nervous system is a master control system that regulates everything in your body, from the rate at which your heart beats, to the movements of your eyes as you scan these words, to your higher mental processes, such as thinking and reasoning. The central nervous system also enables you to sense the world around you and make sense of the sensations you experience (see Chapter 3).

The crowning glory of your central nervous system is your brain, that wondrous organ that regulates life processes and enables you to think, plan, and create. Fortunately, this tender mass of tissue is cushioned in a hard, bony shell called the skull.

As you'll see in Module 2.3, one way of studying the brain is by exploring its three major parts: the hindbrain, or lower brain—the brain's "basement"; the midbrain; and the forebrain, the highest region where thoughts and your sense of self "live." Here, let us consider the other major part of the central nervous system, the spinal cord—the brain's link to the peripheral nervous system.

The Spinal Cord

The **spinal cord**—a column of nerves nearly as thick as your thumb—is literally an extension of the brain. The spinal cord begins at the base of your brain and runs down the center of your back, ending just below the waist. It is a neural pathway that transmits information between the brain and the peripheral nervous system. It receives incoming information from your sense organs and other peripheral body parts and carries outgoing commands from your brain to muscles, glands, and organs throughout your body.

The spinal cord is encased in a protective bony column called the **spine**. Despite this protection, the spinal cord can suffer serious injury. In severe spinal cord injuries, signals cannot be transmitted between the brain and the peripheral organs, which may result in paralysis of the limbs and an inability to breathe on one's own. The person may become quadriplegic, losing control of his or her arms and legs. The spinal cord is not simply a conduit for neural transmission of signals between the brain and the peripheral nervous system. It also controls some *spinal reflexes* that let you respond as quickly as possible to particular types of stimuli. A **reflex** is an automatic, unlearned reaction to a stimulus; a **spinal reflex** is a reflex controlled at the level of the spinal cord—one that bypasses the brain. An example of a spinal reflex is the jerk your knee gives when a doctor who's examining you taps it lightly with a hammer. Some spinal reflexes, including the knee-jerk response, involve just two neurons—one sensory neuron and one motor neuron (see ■ Figure 2.5). In other cases, such as the reflexive withdrawal of the hand upon touching a hot object, a third neuron in the spinal cord, an interneuron, transmits information from the incoming sensory neuron to the outgoing motor neuron.

Spinal reflexes allow us to respond almost instantly and with great efficiency to particular stimuli. The knee-jerk reflex takes a mere 50 milliseconds from the time the knee is tapped until the time the leg jerks forward (as compared with the hundreds of milliseconds it takes to voluntarily flex your leg). To appreciate the value of spinal reflexes, recall the times you've pulled your hand away from a hot stove or blinked when a gust of wind sent particles of debris hurtling toward your eyeballs. By saving the many milliseconds it would take to send a message to your brain, have it interpreted, and have a command sent back along the spinal highway to motor neurons, spinal reflexes can spell the difference between a minor injury and a serious one.

CONCEPT 2.11
The spinal cord is an information highway that conducts information between the brain and the peripheral nervous system.

CONCEPT 2.12
Spinal reflexes are innate, automatic responses controlled at the level of the spinal cord that allow you to respond quickly to particular stimuli.

central nervous system (CNS) The part of the nervous system that consists of the brain and spinal cord.

spinal cord The column of nerves that transmits information between the brain and the peripheral nervous system.

spine The protective bony column that houses the spinal cord.

reflex An automatic, unlearned response to particular stimuli.

spinal reflex A reflex controlled at the level of the spinal cord that may involve as few as two neurons.

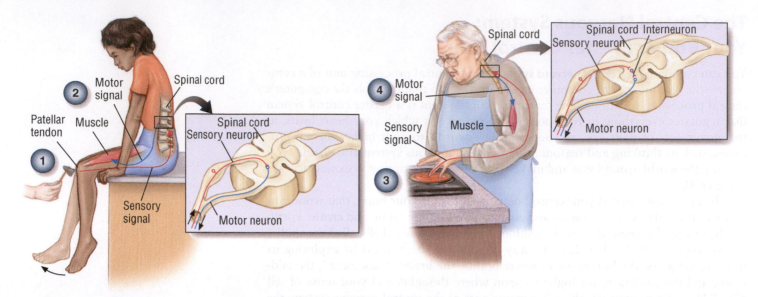

FIGURE 2.5 Anatomy of a Spinal Reflex

The Knee-Jerk Reflex

① Tapping the knee sends a signal through a sensory neuron to the spinal cord, where the information is transmitted to a motor neuron. ② The motor neuron carries signals to muscles in the thigh to contract, causing the leg to kick forward.

The Withdrawal Reflex

③ Touching a hot stove sends a signal through a sensory neuron to the spinal cord. ④ The information is relayed through an interneuron to a motor neuron, which signals muscles in the hand to contract, causing the hand to withdraw from a hot object.

CONCEPT 2.13

The somatic nervous system is the part of the peripheral nervous system that controls voluntary movements of muscles and relays information between the central nervous system and sensory organs.

CONCEPT 2.14

Like an automatic pilot, the autonomic nervous system, a division of the peripheral nervous system, automatically controls such involuntary bodily processes as heartbeat, respiration, and digestion.

peripheral nervous system (PNS) The part of the nervous system that connects the spinal cord and brain with the sensory organs, muscles, and glands.

somatic nervous system The part of the peripheral nervous system that transmits information between the central nervous system and the sensory organs and muscles; also controls voluntary movements.

autonomic nervous system (ANS) The part of the peripheral nervous system that automatically regulates involuntary bodily processes, such as breathing, heart rate, and digestion.

The Peripheral Nervous System: Your Body's Link to the Outside World

The central nervous system depends on the constant flow of information that it receives from your internal organs and sensory receptors, as well as on its ability to convey information to the muscles and glands that it regulates. These functions are performed by the **peripheral nervous system (PNS),** the part of the nervous system that connects your central nervous system with other parts of your body.

Without the peripheral nervous system, your brain would be like a computer chip disconnected from the computer hardware—a marvelous feat of engineering but unable to function. Without information transmitted from your sensory organs—your eyes, ears, tongue, nose, and skin—you would be unable to perceive the world. Without commands sent to your muscles, you would be unable to act upon the world. The PNS is divided into two parts, the **somatic nervous system** and the **autonomic nervous system (ANS).**

The Somatic Nervous System

The somatic nervous system transmits messages between your central nervous system and your sensory organs and muscles. It not only enables you to perceive the world, but it also ensures that your muscles will contract in response to an intentional command or a stimulus that triggers a reflex action. And, finally, it regulates subtle movements that maintain posture and balance.

The somatic nervous system is composed of sensory and motor neurons. As noted in Module 2.1, sensory neurons send messages from the sensory organs to the spinal cord and brain. In this way, information about stimuli that impinge upon our senses (light, sounds, odors, taste, pressure on our skin, and so on) is transmitted to the central nervous system. The brain then interprets these messages, allowing you to perceive a beautiful sunset or a threatening animal, distinguish a whisper from the rustling of the wind, determine whether you are sitting in a reclining or upright position, and experience sensations of warmth, cold, and pain.

The central nervous system processes the information it receives and sends messages back through motor neurons that control movements—such as walking and running, pulling your arm back reflexively upon touching a hot object, raising and lowering your arms at will—and the tiny, almost imperceptible, movements that regulate your balance and posture.

The Autonomic Nervous System

The autonomic nervous system (ANS) is the part of the peripheral nervous system that controls such internal bodily processes as heartbeat, respiration, digestion, and dilation of the pupils. The ANS does these tasks automatically, regulating these vital bodily processes without your having to think about them. (*Autonomic* means "automatic.") You can, however, exercise some voluntary control over some of these functions, as by intentionally breathing more rapidly or slowly.

The ANS is itself composed of two divisions, or branches, that have largely opposite effects, the *sympathetic nervous system* and the *parasympathetic nervous system*. The **sympathetic nervous system** speeds up bodily processes and draws energy from stored reserves. It serves as an alarm system that heightens arousal and mobilizes bodily resources in times of stress or physical exertion, or when defensive action might be needed to fend off a threat. It accelerates your heart rate and breathing rate and provides more fuel or energy for the body to use by releasing sugar (glucose) from the liver. Activation of the sympathetic nervous system is often accompanied by strong emotions, such as anxiety, fear, or anger. That is why we sense our hearts beating faster when we are anxious or angered.

The **parasympathetic nervous system** fosters bodily processes, such as digestion, that replenish stores of energy. Digestion provides the body with fuel by converting food into glucose (blood sugar), which cells use as a source of energy. The parasympathetic nervous system also helps conserve energy by slowing down other bodily processes. The sympathetic nervous system speeds up your heart; the parasympathetic slows it down. The sympathetic nervous system turns off (inhibits) digestive activity; the parasympathetic turns it on. The parasympathetic system is in command whenever you are relaxing or digesting a meal.

Your ability to appreciate a beautiful sunset is a function of your somatic nervous system transmitting visual information from the environment to the spinal cord and from there to the brain for processing.

CONCEPT 2.15
The autonomic nervous system is divided into two branches that have largely opposite effects: the sympathetic nervous system and the parasympathetic nervous system.

sympathetic nervous system The branch of the autonomic nervous system that accelerates bodily processes and releases stores of energy needed to meet increased physical demands.

parasympathetic nervous system The branch of the autonomic nervous system that regulates bodily processes, such as digestion, that replenish stores of energy.

| MODULE REVIEW | **2.2** | **The Nervous System: Your Body's Information Superhighway** |

Recite It

5. **Describe** how the nervous system is organized.

   The major divisions of the nervous system are the central nervous system, which consists of the brain and spinal cord, and the (a) _____ nervous system, which connects the central nervous system to the rest of the body. The peripheral nervous system is divided into the (b) _____ nervous system and (c) _____ nervous system.

6. **Describe** the functions of the central nervous system and the divisions of the peripheral nervous system.

   The (d) _____ nervous system is the master control unit that controls bodily processes and enables higher mental

functions, such as thinking, problem solving, and reasoning. The two divisions or branches of the (e) _____ nervous system are the somatic nervous system and autonomic nervous system. The (f) _____ nervous system relays messages between your central nervous system and your sensory organs and muscles. The (g) _____ nervous system (ANS) automatically controls vital bodily processes such as heartbeat, respiration, digestion, and dilation.

7. **Explain** the differences in functions of the sympathetic and parasympathetic divisions of the autonomic nervous system.

These two divisions have largely opposite effects. The **(h)** _____ nervous system speeds up bodily processes that expend energy, whereas the **(i)** _____ system slows down some bodily processes and fosters others, such as digestion, that replenish stores of energy.

Recall It

1. Name the two major divisions in the human nervous system.

2. The brain and spinal cord constitute the _____ nervous system.

3. Which part of the nervous system triggers changes that prepare the body to cope with stress?

4. The parasympathetic nervous system

   a. slows some bodily activity and allows for the replenishment of energy.
   b. is part of the central nervous system.
   c. is also known as the "fight-or-flight" mechanism.
   d. draws energy from bodily reserves to meet stressful demands on the body.

Think About It

■ As you're running to catch a bus, your breathing quickens and your heart starts pounding. Which part of your peripheral nervous system kicks into gear at such a time?

■ Were there any times in your life when a spinal reflex prevented serious injury?

Recite It _answers placed at the end of chapter._

MODULE

2.3 The Brain: Your Crowning Glory

8 **Describe** how the brain is organized and the roles that particular brain structures play in behavior.

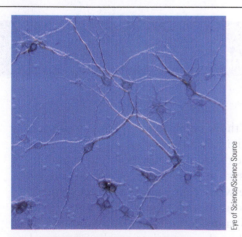

The adult brain continues to form thousands of new neurons each day. Scientists believe these new neurons are quickly put to use performing learning and memory functions.

Eye of Science/Science Source

A common misconception (myth really) is that we only use about 10 percent of our brain. The fact is that while we may not use all of the brain's resources at any given moment, we use the entirety of the brain to execute the many complex functions we perform during the course of a day (Chein & Schneider, 2012).

Another misconception is that the adult brain no longer forms new neurons. It was once thought that **neurogenesis** occurs only in the developing brain early in childhood. But recent evidence shows that the adult brain manufactures thousands, perhaps tens of thousands, of new neurons daily (Shors, 2014). We're not sure what functions these newborn neurons perform, but evidence suggests they play important roles in learning and memory (Bergmann & Frisén, 2013; Opendak & Gould, 2015).

Let us take a closer look at the various parts of the brain, beginning with our tour with the lowest level, the _hindbrain_—the part of the brain where the spinal cord enters the skull and widens. We then work our way upward, first to the _midbrain_, which lies above the hindbrain, and then to the _forebrain_, which lies in the highest part of the brain. Concept Chart 2.3 shows these major brain structures.

The Hindbrain

The lowest part of the brain, the **hindbrain**, is also the oldest part in evolutionary terms. The hindbrain includes the *medulla*, *pons*, and *cerebellum*. These structures control such basic life-support functions as breathing and heart rate.

The **medulla** and **pons** contain sensory neurons that transmit information from the spinal cord to the forebrain. The medulla is the section of the hindbrain that lies closest to the spinal cord. It forms the marrow, or core, of the **brainstem**, the "stem" or "stalk" that connects the spinal cord to the higher regions of the brain (see ■ Figure 2.6 on p. 56). (*Medulla* is a Latin word meaning "marrow.") The medulla controls such vital bodily processes as heart rate and breathing, and such reflexes as swallowing, coughing, and sneezing. The pons lies directly above the medulla. It contains nerve fibers that conduct information from the spinal cord and lower parts of the brain through the midbrain to the forebrain. It also helps regulate states of wakefulness and sleep.

Located behind the pons and resembling a sliced-open cauliflower, the **cerebellum** is involved in controlling balance and coordination. It enables a gymnast to do a back flip on the balance beam and a tennis player to land a serve (Brooks, Carriot, & Cullen, 2015). Injury to the cerebellum can lead to problems with balance and coordination as well as to difficulty initiating voluntary movements, such as being unable to lift an arm or a leg at will.

As we continue our brief tour of the brain, we come to the midbrain, the part of the brain that serves as a major relay station for information passing between the lower brain and the forebrain.

The Midbrain

The **midbrain**, which lies above the hindbrain, contains nerve pathways that connect the hindbrain with the forebrain. Structures in the midbrain perform important roles, including control of automatic movements of the eye muscles, which allows you to keep your eyes focused on an object as your head changes position in relation to the object. Parts of the midbrain make up the brainstem.

The **reticular formation** (also called the *reticular activating system*, or *RAS*) is a weblike network of neurons that rises from the hindbrain and passes through the midbrain to the thalamus in the forebrain. The reticular formation plays a key role in regulating states of attention, alertness, and arousal. It screens visual and auditory information, filtering out irrelevant information while allowing important information to reach the higher processing centers of the brain, even when we are asleep.

The Forebrain

The **forebrain**, located toward the top and front of the brain, is the largest part of the brain. The major structures in the forebrain are the *thalamus*, the *hypothalamus*, the *limbic system*, and the *cerebral cortex*.

The **thalamus** is a relay station near the middle of the brain. It consists of a pair of egg-shaped structures that route information from sense receptors for touch, vision, hearing, and taste (but not smell) to the processing centers of the brain located in the cerebral cortex. The thalamus first sorts through sensory information, sending information about vision to one area, information about hearing to another, and so on. From these relay stations in the thalamus, the information is then transmitted to the appropriate parts of the cerebral cortex for processing. The thalamus also plays an important role in regulating states of sleep and wakefulness (Jan et al., 2009) and receives input from the **basal ganglia**, a cluster of nerve cells that plays a key role in

CONCEPT 2.16
The brain is divided into three major parts: the hindbrain, the midbrain, and the forebrain.

CONCEPT 2.17
The hindbrain, the lowest part of the brain, contains structures that control basic bodily functions, such as breathing and heart rate.

CONCEPT 2.18
The midbrain contains nerve pathways for relaying messages between the hindbrain and the forebrain, as well as structures that control some automatic movements.

neurogenesis The process by which new neurons are formed.

hindbrain The lowest and, in evolutionary terms, oldest part of the brain; includes the medulla, pons, and cerebellum.

medulla A structure in the hindbrain involved in regulating basic life functions, such as heartbeat and respiration.

pons A structure in the hindbrain involved in regulating states of wakefulness and sleep.

brainstem The "stalk" in the lower part of the brain that connects the spinal cord to higher regions of the brain.

cerebellum A structure in the hindbrain involved in controlling coordination and balance.

midbrain The part of the brain that lies on top of the hindbrain and below the forebrain.

reticular formation A weblike formation of neurons involved in regulating states of attention, alertness, and arousal.

forebrain The largest and uppermost part of the brain; contains the thalamus, hypothalamus, limbic system, basal ganglia, and cerebral cortex.

thalamus A structure in the forebrain that serves as a relay station for sensory information and that plays a key role in regulating states of wakefulness and sleep.

basal ganglia An assemblage of neurons lying in the forebrain that is important in controlling movement and coordination.

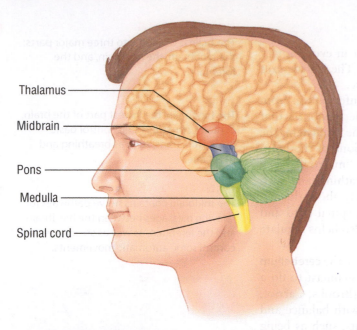

Thalamus

Midbrain

Pons

Medulla

Spinal cord

FIGURE 2.6 The Brainstem

The brainstem reaches from the top of the spinal cord up through the midbrain. It connects the spinal cord to the higher regions of the brain.

CONCEPT 2.19

The largest part of the brain, the forebrain, controls higher mental functions, such as thinking, problem solving, use of language, planning, and memory.

CONCEPT 2.20

The limbic system plays an important role in the regulation of memory and emotions.

CONCEPT 2.21

The cerebrum is divided into two hemispheres and is covered by a thin, outer layer, the cerebral cortex, which is responsible for higher mental functions.

hypothalamus A small, pea-sized structure in the forebrain that helps regulate many vital bodily functions, including body temperature and reproduction, as well as emotional states, aggression, and responses to stress.

limbic system A formation of structures in the forebrain that includes the hippocampus, amygdala, and parts of the thalamus and hypothalamus.

amygdala A set of almond-shaped structures in the limbic system believed to play an important role in aggression, rage, and fear.

regulating voluntary movement, such as walking and use of our hands (Chetrit et al., 2009).

Just beneath the thalamus is the **hypothalamus** (*hypo* meaning "under"), a pea-sized structure weighing a mere 4 grams. Despite its small size, the hypothalamus helps regulate many vital bodily functions, including hunger, thirst, daily sleep cycles, body temperature, bodily response to stress, reproductive processes, as well as emotional states and aggressive behavior. As we'll see in Module 2.6, the hypothalamus is part of the endocrine system, and it triggers release of hormones throughout the body. Electrical stimulation of particular parts of the hypothalamus in other mammals, such as rats, can generate, or "switch on," stereotypical behavior patterns that range from eating to attacking rivals, courting, mounting attempts, and caring for the young (Bandler, 2006; Falkner et al., 2016).

The **limbic system** is a group of interconnected structures that includes the *amygdala, hippocampus*, parts of the *thalamus* and *hypothalamus*, and other nearby interconnected structures (see Concept Chart 2.3). The limbic system is much more evolved in mammals than in lower animals. It plays important roles in both memory and emotional processing.

Referring again to Concept Chart 2.3, we find within the limbic system the **amygdala**, a set of two almond-shaped structures (*amygdala* is derived from the Greek root for "almond"). Among its functions, the amygdala triggers the emotional response of fear when we encounter a threatening stimulus or situation (see Chapter 8) (Agren et al., 2012; Wood, Ver Hoef, & Knight, 2014).

The **hippocampus** resembles a sea horse, from which it derives its name (the genus of sea horse is "hippocampus"). Located just behind the amygdala, the hippocampus plays an important role in the formation of new memories (Leutgeb, 2008; Reitz et al., 2009; Shors, 2014) (see Chapter 6).

Our journey through the brain now brings us to the uppermost part of the forebrain, the cerebral cortex. Because it is responsible for our ability to think, use language, calculate, organize, and create, we devote the entire next section to it.

The Cerebral Cortex: The Brain's Thinking, Calculating, Organizing, and Creative Center

The **cerebral cortex** forms the thin, outer layer of the largest part of the forebrain, which is called the **cerebrum**. The cerebrum consists of two large masses, the right and left **cerebral hemispheres**. The cerebral cortex covers the cerebrum like a cap and derives its name from the Latin words for brain ("cerebrum") and bark ("cortex"). A thick bundle of nerve fibers, called the **corpus callosum** (Latin for "thick body" or "hard body") connects the cerebral hemispheres and forms a pathway by which the hemispheres share information and communicate with each other. Structures in the brain that lie beneath the cerebral cortex are called *subcortical* structures (*sub* meaning "below" the cortex).

Though a mere one-eighth of an inch thick, no thicker than a napkin, the cerebral cortex accounts for more than 80 percent of the brain's total mass. The cortex owes its wrinkled or convoluted appearance to contours created by ridges and valleys. These contours enable its large surface area to be packed tightly within the confines of the skull (see Concept Chart 2.3). Its massive size in relation to the other parts of

Concept Chart 2.3   Major Structures of the Human Brain

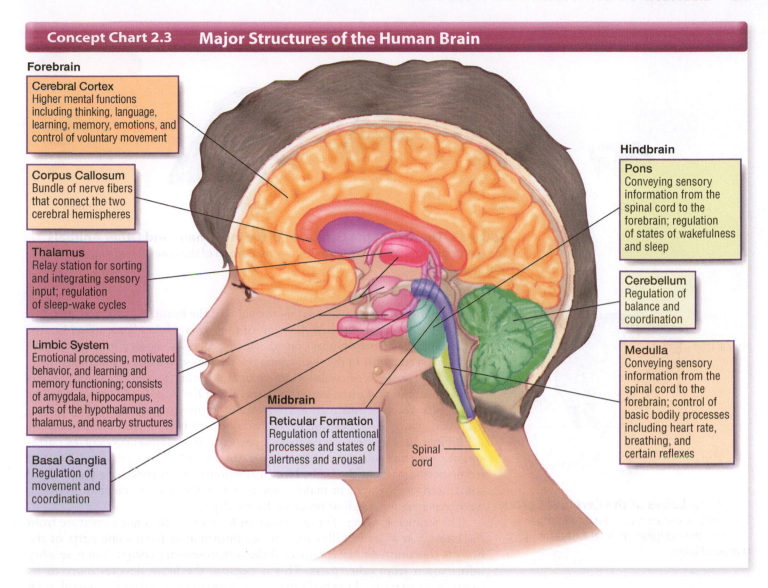

Forebrain

Cerebral Cortex
Higher mental functions including thinking, language, learning, memory, emotions, and control of voluntary movement

Corpus Callosum
Bundle of nerve fibers that connect the two cerebral hemispheres

Thalamus
Relay station for sorting and integrating sensory input; regulation of sleep-wake cycles

Limbic System
Emotional processing, motivated behavior, and learning and memory functioning; consists of amygdala, hippocampus, parts of the hypothalamus and thalamus, and nearby structures

Basal Ganglia
Regulation of movement and coordination

Midbrain

Reticular Formation
Regulation of attentional processes and states of alertness and arousal

Spinal cord

Hindbrain

Pons
Conveying sensory information from the spinal cord to the forebrain; regulation of states of wakefulness and sleep

Cerebellum
Regulation of balance and coordination

Medulla
Conveying sensory information from the spinal cord to the forebrain; control of basic bodily processes including heart rate, breathing, and certain reflexes

---

the brain reflects the amount of the brain devoted to higher mental functions, such as thinking, language use, and problem solving. Only in humans does the cortex account for so great a portion of the brain (see ■ Figure 2.7). The cortex also controls voluntary movement, states of motivation and emotional arousal, and processing of sensory information.

Each hemisphere of the cerebral cortex is divided into four parts, or *lobes,* as shown in ■ Figure 2.8. Thus, each lobe is represented in each hemisphere. The functions of the lobes are summarized in Table 2.1. Generally speaking, each of the cerebral hemispheres controls feeling and movement on the opposite side of the body.

The **occipital lobes,** located in the back of the head, process visual information, including visual cues that enable us to recognize objects and faces (Connor, 2010). We experience vision when a source of light stimulates receptors in the eyes and causes neurons in the occipital lobes to fire (discussed further in Chapter 3). Even a blow to the back of the head can produce visual experiences. Perhaps you have had the experience of "seeing stars" after being struck on this region of the head.

hippocampus A structure in the limbic system involved in memory formation.

cerebral cortex The wrinkled, outer layer of gray matter that covers the cerebral hemispheres; controls higher mental functions, such as thought and language.

cerebrum The largest mass of the forebrain, consisting of two cerebral hemispheres.

cerebral hemispheres The right and left masses of the cerebrum, which are joined by the corpus callosum.

corpus callosum The thick bundle of nerve fibers that connects the two cerebral hemispheres.

occipital lobes The parts of the cerebral cortex, located at the back of both cerebral hemispheres, that process visual stimuli.

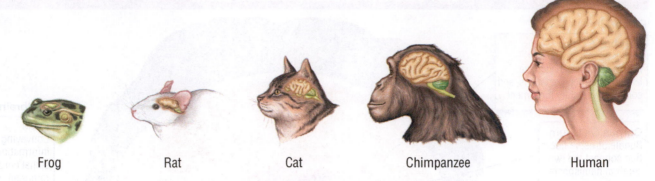

Frog   Rat   Cat   Chimpanzee   Human

FIGURE 2.7 **The Size of the Cerebral Cortex in Humans and Other Animals**
The cerebral cortex accounts for a much greater portion of the brain in humans than in other animals.

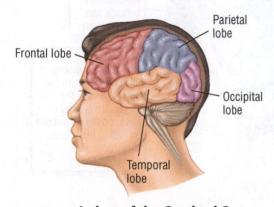

Frontal lobe

Parietal lobe

Occipital lobe

Temporal lobe

FIGURE 2.8 **Lobes of the Cerebral Cortex**
The cerebral cortex is divided into four parts, or lobes: the occipital, parietal, frontal, and temporal lobes.

CONCEPT 2.22
The corpus callosum is a bundle of nerve fibers connecting the two hemispheres of the brain, allowing them to share information.

CONCEPT 2.23
Each cerebral hemisphere has four main parts, or lobes: the occipital, parietal, frontal, and temporal lobes.

CONCEPT 2.24
Most of the cerebral cortex consists of association areas that are responsible for higher mental functions.

parietal lobes The parts of the cerebral cortex, located on the side of each cerebral hemisphere, that process bodily sensations.

The **parietal lobes** are located on the sides of the brain, directly above and in front of the occipital lobes. At the front of the parietal lobes lies a strip of nerve cells called the **somatosensory cortex,** which processes sensory information received from receptors in the skin, giving rise to our experience of touch, pressure, temperature (hotness or coldness), and pain. Like your eyes and ears, your skin is a sensory organ that provides information about the world. The somatosensory cortex also receives information from receptors in your muscles and joints to keep you aware of the position of the parts of your body as you move about.

■ Figure 2.9 illustrates how specific parts of the somatosensory cortex correspond to sensory information (touch, pressure, pain, and temperature) received from specific parts of the body. Electrical stimulation of particular parts of the somatosensory cortex can make it seem as though your shoulder or your leg were experiencing touch or pressure, for example.

The strange-looking "figure" shown in ■ Figure 2.10 is not a creature from the latest *Star Wars* installment. Sensory information from some parts of the body is transmitted to larger areas of the somatosensory cortex than is sensory information from other parts. This is because the brain devotes more of its capabilities to parts of the body that require greater sensitivity or control, such as the hands. Nor are the parts of the body represented in the somatosensory

Table 2.1	**The Lobes of the Cerebral Cortex**
Structure	**Functions**
Occipital lobes	Process visual information, giving rise to sensations of vision
Parietal lobes	Process information relating to sensations of touch, pressure, temperature (hot and cold), pain, and body movement
Frontal lobes	Control motor responses and higher mental functions, such as thinking, planning, problem solving, decision making, and accessing and acting on stored memories
Temporal lobes	Process auditory information, giving rise to sensations of sound

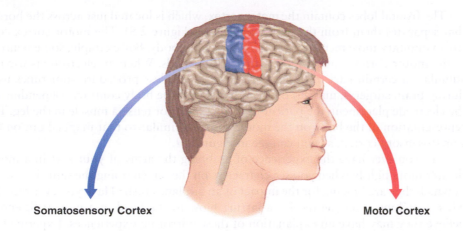

FIGURE 2.9 **Somatosensory Cortex and Motor Cortex**
Here we see how various parts of the body are mapped in the somatosensory cortex and the motor cortex. The mapping structure of the two cortexes is nearly a mirror image. But notice how body parts are not mapped onto these cortexes in relation to where they actually lie in the body. The size of the projections of the parts of the body in each cortex corresponds to the degree of sensitivity or need for control of these parts.

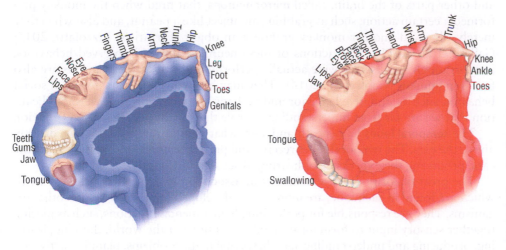

FIGURE 2.10 **A Creature from Star Wars?**
Actually, this is an artist's rendering of how we would appear if the size of our body parts were in proportion to the areas of the somatosensory cortex that process sensory information from these parts. Because much more cortex is devoted to the fingers and hands than to elbows or thighs, we can discern much finer differences in sensations of touch with our fingertips.

cortex in a way that directly corresponds to where they lie in the body. For example, sensory input from the genitals projects to an area that lies beneath the part receiving input from the toes, and the area that responds to stimulation of the tongue does not lie within the area that responds to stimulation of the lips. Why is this so? No one can say. But each of us knows the precise areas of our body that are touched. We know, for instance, when our lips are touched and not our tongues, and vice versa.

The **frontal lobes** are located in the front part of the brain, just behind the forehead. Scientists call the frontal lobes the "executive center" of the brain, because they believe they contain your "you"—the part that accesses your memories, mulls things over, has self-awareness, and decides that the red plaid shirt is just "too retro." Like the central processing unit of a computer, parts of the frontal lobes retrieve memories from storage, place them in active memory, manipulate them, and make decisions based on them. For example, your frontal lobes pull sensory memories about visual cues, sounds, odors, and even tastes from storage, so that the second time you see that oblong-shaped red pepper sitting innocently in your bowl of kung pao chicken, you remember not to bite into it. Your frontal lobes also allow you to solve problems, make decisions, plan actions, weigh evidence, and carry out coordinated actions.

Research evidence further indicates that the frontal lobes are involved in processing emotional states, such as happiness and sadness (Davidson et al., 2002). In addition, they enable you to suppress tendencies to act on impulse, such as when you restrain yourself from telling your boss or professor what you really think of him or her.

somatosensory cortex The part of the parietal lobe that processes information about touch and pressure on the skin, as well as the position of the parts of our bodies as we move about.

frontal lobes The parts of the cerebral cortex, located at the front of the cerebral hemispheres, that are considered the "executive center" of the brain because of their role in higher mental functions.

The frontal lobes contain the **motor cortex**, which is located just across the border that separates them from the parietal lobes (see Figure 2.9). The motor cortex controls voluntary movements of specific parts of the body. For example, some neurons in the motor cortex control movements of the hands. When an electrode is used to stimulate a certain part of the motor cortex (a painless procedure sometimes used during brain surgery), muscles on the other side of the body contract. Depending on the electrode placement, the patient may lift a finger or tense a muscle in the leg. The representation of the body on the motor cortex is similar to that mapped out on the somatosensory cortex, as you can see in Figure 2.9.

Did you ever have the experience of grabbing the arms of your seat in a movie theater more tightly when you see characters on the screen doing the same in a scene in which they are bracing for the impact of an airplane crash? Have you ever recoiled when watching someone receive a jarring blow to the head in a movie? Scientists believe they may have an explanation of these mirroring experiences. Experimental work with monkeys led to the discovery of specialized neurons in the motor cortex and other parts of the brain, called **mirror neurons**, that fired when the monkey performed a certain action, such as grabbing an object like a peanut, and also when they merely observed another monkey grabbing an object (Ferrari & Rizzolatti, 2015; Gallese et al., 2011). The actions of these neurons "mirror" observed behaviors, just as though an observer were actually performing them. Mirror neurons are also found in humans (Cook et al., 2014). They may be involved in some forms of social behavior, such as imitative behavior and perhaps even empathy, but we should caution that we are far from understanding the role they might play in human behavior.

The **temporal lobes** lie beneath and somewhat behind the frontal lobes, directly above the ears. The temporal lobes receive and process sensory information from the ears, producing the experience of hearing (discussed in Chapter 3).

The great majority of cortex consists of **association areas**. The association areas, which are found in each lobe, are more highly developed in humans than in other organisms. They are responsible for performing higher mental functions, such as piecing together sensory input to form meaningful perceptions of the world, thinking, learning, producing and understanding speech, solving math problems, planning activities, creating masterworks of architecture, and perhaps even composing the next hit song.

We cannot identify the precise locations where higher mental functions occur. Association areas are linked within intricate networks of neurons connecting many parts of the brain, the architecture of which we are only beginning to decipher (Stern, 2013).

motor cortex A region of the frontal lobes involved in regulating body movement.

mirror neurons Neurons that fire both when an action is performed and when the same action is merely observed.

temporal lobes The parts of the cerebral cortex lying beneath and somewhat behind the frontal lobes that are involved in processing auditory stimuli.

association areas Areas of the cerebral cortex that piece together sensory information to form meaningful perceptions of the world and perform higher mental functions.

MODULE REVIEW **2.3** **The Brain: Your Crowning Glory**

Recite It

8. **Describe** how the brain is organized and the roles that particular brain structures play in behavior.

We can divide the organization of the brain into three major sections. The (a) _____, which houses the medulla, pons, and cerebellum, is involved in controlling basic bodily functions. The (b) _____ houses nerve bundles that relay messages between the hindbrain and the forebrain; it also houses structures that help regulate automatic movement. The (c) _____ is the largest part of the brain; its major structures are the thalamus, the hypothalamus, the limbic system, and the cerebral cortex.

The (d) _____ relays sensory information to the cerebral cortex and helps regulate states of sleep and wakefulness.
The (e) _____ plays a key role in controlling many vital bodily processes.
The (f) _____ system, which includes the amygdala, hippocampus, and parts of the thalamus and hypothalamus, is involved in memory and emotional processing.
The (g) _____ cortex is responsible for processing sensory information, for higher mental functions such as thought, problem solving, and language, and for controlling voluntary movement, among other functions.

Each hemisphere of the cerebral cortex has four lobes: the frontal, parietal, temporal, and (h) _____ lobes. Each of the lobes is contained in each cerebral hemisphere. The (i) _____ _____ is a nerve bundle that connects the two hemispheres.

The occipital lobes are primarily involved with (j) _____; the parietal lobes, with sensations of (k) _____; the temporal lobes, with (l) _____; and the frontal lobes, with motor control and higher (m) _____ functions, including retrieving and acting on stored memories, solving problems, making decisions, and carrying out coordinated actions.

Recall It

1. The limbic system structure that resembles a sea horse and that plays an important role in memory functioning is
   a. the frontal cortex.
   b. the thalamus.
   c. the amygdala.
   d. the hippocampus.

2. Match the following parts of the brain with the functions they control: (a) medulla; (b) cerebellum; (c) thalamus; (d) cerebral cortex.
   i. balance and coordination
   ii. thinking and organizing
   iii. relay of sensory information to the cerebral cortex
   iv. heart rate and breathing

3. Which of the following is *not* correct? The cerebral cortex
   a. is the part of the brain most directly responsible for reasoning, language, and problem solving.
   b. is divided into four lobes.
   c. forms the outer layer of the cerebral hemispheres.
   d. accounts for a much smaller percentage of brain mass in humans than in other animals.

4. Which part of the cerebral cortex processes auditory information?

Think About It

■ Why does the text refer to your brain as your "crowning glory"?

■ A person suffers a serious fall and sustains severe damage to the back of the head. What sensory processes are most likely to be affected by the injury?

Recite It *answers placed at the end of chapter.*

2.4 Methods of Studying the Brain

9 **Describe** methods scientists use to study the workings of the brain.

Scientists use various methods of studying brain structures and their functioning. One method is to observe the effects of diseases or injuries on the brain. As a result of this type of observation, scientists have known for nearly two centuries that damage to the left side of the brain is connected with loss of sensation or movement on the right side of the body, and vice versa.

Over the years, scientists have also used invasive experimental methods to study the brain at work, including surgical procedures. Today, thanks to advanced technology, they have other, less invasive recording and imaging methods at their disposal. Concept Chart 2.4 summarizes these types of methods.

Recording and Imaging Techniques

Today, we have available a range of techniques that allow us to peer into the working brain and other parts of the body without invasive surgery. These techniques are used to diagnose brain diseases and examine brain damage, as well as to expand

CONCEPT 2.25
Modern technology provides ways of studying the structure and function of the brain without the need for invasive techniques.

CONCEPT LINK
Brain scans are used to help us better understand the biological bases of schizophrenia and other psychological disorders. See Module 12.5.

Concept Chart 2.4   Methods of Studying the Brain

Recording and Imaging Techniques	Description
EEG (electroencephalograph)	A device that uses electrodes attached to the skull to record brain wave activity
CT (computed tomography) scan	A computer-enhanced X-ray technique that can provide images of the internal structures of the brain
PET (positron emission tomography) scan	A method that can provide a computer-generated image of the brain, formed by tracing the amounts of glucose used in different parts of the brain during different types of activity
MRI (magnetic resonance imaging)	A method of producing computerized images of the brain and other body parts by measuring the signals they emit when placed in a strong magnetic field
Experimental Techniques	**Description**
Lesioning	Destruction of brain tissue in order to observe the effects on behavior
Electrical recording	Placement of electrodes in brain tissue to record changes in electrical activity in response to particular stimuli
Electrical stimulation	The use of a mild electric current to observe the effects of stimulating various parts of the brain

The Brain Loves a Puzzle

As you read ahead, use the information in the text to solve the following puzzle:

Why is it impossible to tickle yourself? Try it out for yourself. Why does tickling yourself fail to elicit the same tickling response that occurs when someone else tickles you?

Here's a ticklish question for you: Why is it that you can't tickle yourself? Researchers using a brain-imaging technique believe they have the answer.

EEG (electroencephalograph) A device that records electrical activity in the brain.

our understanding of brain functioning. Using these techniques, neuroscientists can examine the working brain while the subject is awake and alert.

The **EEG (electroencephalograph)** is an instrument that records electrical activity in the brain (see ■ Figure 2.11). Electrodes are attached to the scalp to measure the electrical currents, or *brain waves*, that are conducted between them. The EEG is used to study electrical activity in the brains of people with physical or psychological disorders and to explore brain wave patterns during stages of sleep.

The **CT (computed tomography) scan** (also called a *CAT* scan, for "**computed axial tomography**") is an imaging technique in which a computer measures the reflection of a narrow X-ray beam from various angles as it passes through the brain or other bodily structures; it thus produces a three-dimensional image of the inside of the body (see ■ Figure 2.12). The CT scan reveals brain abnormalities associated with structural problems such as blood clots, tumors, and brain injuries. We can also use it to explore structural abnormalities in the brains of people with schizophrenia or other severe psychological disorders.

Whereas the CT scan reveals information about the shape and size of structures in the brain, the **PET (positron emission tomography) scan** provides a computerized image of the brain and other organs at work. The subject receives an injection of a radioactive isotope that acts as a tracer in the bloodstream. How the tracer is metabolized (converted by cells into energy) in the brain reveals the parts of the brain that are more active than others. More active areas metabolize more of the tracer than less active ones (see ■ Figure 2.13). The PET scan can reveal which parts of the brain are most active when we are reading and writing, daydreaming, listening to music, or experiencing emotions. From these patterns, we can determine which parts of the brain are involved in particular functions.

MRI (magnetic resonance imaging) provides a detailed image of the brain or other body parts. To produce a brain image, a technician places the person's head within a doughnut-shaped device that emits a strong magnetic field, aligning the atoms that spin in the brain. A burst of radio waves directed at the person disrupts the atoms, which release signals as they become realigned. A computer then integrates the signals into an image of the brain.

A new form of MRI, called *functional MRI (fMRI)*, takes snapshots of the brain in action (see ■ Figure 2.14). Whereas traditional MRI is limited to mapping brain structures, functional MRI is used to study both the functions and the structures of the human brain. PET scans also map functions of brain structures, but fMRI is less invasive in that it does not require injections of radioactive isotopes.

In Figure 2.14, we see fMRI images of the working brain in response to different types of visual stimuli. Investigators use fMRI to identify specific parts of the brain that are activated when we perform particular tasks, such as seeing, hearing, thinking, remembering, using language, cooperating with others, and experiencing emotional states, even feelings of romantic love. That said, a full account of complex psychological processes like memory, thinking, and perception requires a better understanding of complex brain networks, not just individual brain structures (Gonsalves & Cohen, 2010; Poldrack, 2010). We may someday be able to tell what a person is thinking based on analyzing the person's brain activity (Naci, 2013).

Functional MRI may well have helped clear up a long-standing scientific mystery—why it is impossible to tickle yourself (Aamodt & Wang, 2008; Provine, 2004). Using this method, British researchers peered into the brains of people as they tickled themselves and as they were being tickled by a mechanical device. The part of the brain that processes sensations of touch, the somatosensory cortex, showed more activity when people were being tickled than when they tickled themselves. When we move our fingers to tickle ourselves, the brain center that coordinates these types of complex movements, the cerebellum, sends a signal that blocks some of the activity of the somatosensory cortex, which processes touch. But being tickled by an outside source comes as a surprise, so the cerebellum does not send a blocking signal to the cortex. Scientists believe this brain mechanism allows us to distinguish between stimuli we produce ourselves and unexpected outside stimuli that require closer attention by the cerebral cortex because they may pose a threat (Aamodt & Wang, 2008).

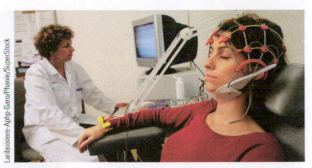

FIGURE 2.11 The Electroencephalograph (EEG)
The EEG is a device that records electrical activity in the brain in the form of brain wave patterns. It is used to study the brains of people with physical or psychological disorders and to explore brain wave patterns during stages of sleep.

CT (computed tomography) scan A computer-enhanced imaging technique in which an X-ray beam is passed through the body at different angles to generate a three-dimensional image of bodily structures (also called a CAT scan, short for computed axial tomography).

PET (positron emission tomography) scan An imaging technique in which a radioactive sugar tracer is injected into the bloodstream and used to measure levels of activity of various parts of the brain.

MRI (magnetic resonance imaging) A technique that uses a magnetic field to create a computerized image of internal bodily structures.

FIGURE 2.12 CT Scan
The CT scan provides a three-dimensional X-ray image of bodily structures. It can reveal structural abnormalities in the brain that may be associated with blood clots, tumors, brain injuries, or psychological disorders, such as schizophrenia.

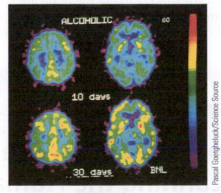

FIGURE 2.13 PET Scan
The PET scan measures the metabolic activity of the brain. More active regions are highlighted in yellow and red, whereas less active regions are shown in blues and greens. Here we see PET scan images of the brain of an alcoholic patient during withdrawal. By comparing relative levels of brain activity following 10 days (top row) and 30 days (bottom row) of withdrawal, we can observe that the brain becomes more active with greater length of time without alcohol.

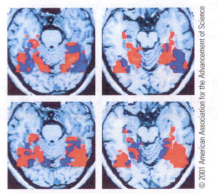

FIGURE 2.14
Using fMRI responses, investigators can detect distinct brain signals occurring when individuals look at different stimuli. The red areas indicate parts of the brain in which signals are elevated when people are shown images of faces. The blue areas denote brain regions in which signals are elevated when people are shown pictures of buildings. Eventually, perhaps, we may be able to tell what a person is thinking by decoding their brain images.

Human "Cyborgs"

Epilepsy patients fitted with electrodes implanted in their brains to record seizures used the implants to send signals to a computer, which allowed them to use their thoughts to issue commands to a computer. In one example, a patient moved a virtual spaceship back and forth on a computer screen simply by imagining that he was moving his tongue.

CONCEPT 2.26

Experimental methods used to study brain functioning include lesioning, electrical recording, and electrical stimulation.

lesioning In studies of brain functioning, the intentional destruction of brain tissue in order to observe the effects on behavior.

electrical recording As a method of investigating brain functioning, a process of recording the electrical changes that occur in a specific neuron or groups of neurons in the brain in relation to particular activities or behaviors.

electrical stimulation As a method of investigating brain functioning, a process of electrically stimulating particular parts of the brain to observe the effects on behavior.

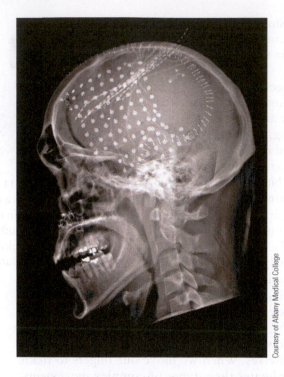

Courtesy of Albany Medical College

Experimental Methods

Scientists sometimes use invasive methods to investigate brain functioning. In one such method, called **lesioning**, the investigator destroys parts of the brain in experimental animals and then observes the effects. For example, destroying one part of a rhesus monkey's limbic system causes the animal to fly into a rage at the slightest provocation. But destroy another part of this system, and the monkey shows a placid response to all manner of provocation. Destroy one part of a rat's hypothalamus, and it gorges itself on food until it becomes extremely obese; destroy another part, and it stops eating. These experiments point to the parts of the brain engaged in these and other forms of behavior.

Other experimental techniques for studying brain function include *electrical recording* and *electrical stimulation*. In **electrical recording**, electrodes are implanted into particular neurons, groups of neurons, or nerves in specific parts of the brain. They provide a record of electrical changes in response to particular stimuli. Some experimental techniques are so refined that investigators can record electrical activity from a single brain cell. Using these methods, scientists discovered how individual neurons in the visual cortex respond to particular types of visual stimuli (see Chapter 3).

With the technique of **electrical stimulation**, investigators pass a mild electric current through particular parts of the brain and observe the effects. In this way, they can learn which parts of the brain are involved in controlling which behaviors. For example, we mentioned earlier how stimulation of parts of the hypothalamus in rats and other animals switches on stereotypical behavior patterns.

APPLYING PSYCHOLOGY

Looking Under the Hood: Scanning the Human Brain

Advances in cognitive neuroscience made possible by sophisticated brain-imaging techniques are broadening our understanding of how the brain works. Here we examine cutting-edge applications of brain-scanning technology that allow us to better understand how the brain works in different facets of our lives.

What's on Your Mind?

Using advanced scanning techniques, investigators are able to identify brain circuits in laboratory animals that correspond to the animals' past experiences (Bartho et al., 2004; Csicsvari et al., 2003). Research along these lines is still in its infancy, but

The Test
Research participants are shown mixed "positive" and "negative" images, like the images shown at right. Meanwhile, brain scans track differences in the patterns of activity among neurons in different parts of the brain.

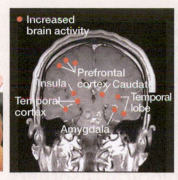

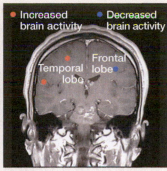

1. The Extrovert
"Positive" images stimulate these areas in people who are more social and show positive emotions.

2. The Neurotic
"Negative" images provoke these responses among people prone to anxiety and negative emotions.

FIGURE 2.15 **Scanning Your Personality**
The brains of people with different personality traits (extroversion versus neuroticism) show different patterns of activity in response to positive and negative images. Research along these lines may help us learn more about relationships between brain functioning and personality types.

Source: Adapted from Pepper, T. (2005, February 21). Inside the head of an applicant. *Newsweek*, pp. E24–E26. Photo Credits: Jeanne White/Science Source, Rubberball Productions/Getty Images, Medical Body Scans/Science Source, Medical Body Scans/Science Source

raises the possibility of identifying memory circuits in the human brain that hold particular memories that comprise a repository of our life experiences. (Chapter 6 discusses further the biological bases of memory.) We may one day be able to decode brain activity not only to locate particular memories but also to know what a person is thinking, just as though we were watching the person's thoughts float by on a computer screen (Haynes & Rees, 2006) (see Figure 2.14).

Reading Personality Traits on a Brain Scan

Brain scans may also reveal underlying personality traits. Recently, test subjects were shown a mix of positive and negative images, such as those in ■ Figure 2.15, while researchers tracked the neural activity in their brains using a high-tech imaging technique. The results showed differences in brain activity between people with different personality features or traits. In response to these positive and negative images, the brains of people who had personality traits of extraversion (were sociable, outgoing, and people-oriented) showed different patterns of activity than those who had traits of neuroticism (were anxious and worrisome). As the lead investigator, psychologist Turhan Canli said, "If I know what the conditions are under which I see [a certain] activation pattern, I can make a good prediction as to what this person's personality traits are" (quoted in Pepper, 2005).

How the Brain Responds to Advertisements

Not only might brain scans reveal what happens in the brain when people see something they want to buy, but they might also predict how people respond to advertisements, as well as their likelihood of buying or using particular products. In the emerging field of **neuromarketing**, researchers probe brain wave patterns to measure the brain's response to advertisements and other brand-related stimuli (Craig et al., 2011; Nevid, 2010). Marketers hope to find "whispers in the brain" detected by the EEG and other biometric tracking equipment to learn which particular ads evoke the strongest attentional and emotional responses (Singer, 2010) (see ■ Figure 2.16).

Advertisers take note. As scientists learn more about how neural markers relate to consumer behavior, marketers may begin applying this knowledge to develop more effective advertisements—even more popular TV shows—by tapping directly into brain responses. A recent study showed that particular brain wave patterns of viewers who were watching TV linked up with popularity ratings of particular programs (Dmochowski et al., 2014). Using brain scans, marketers may also be able to determine whether TV commercials produce the desired emotional responses in viewers that advertisers are seeking to elicit. Researchers say they can now tell

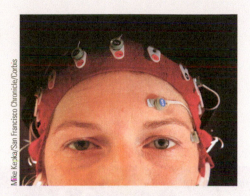

FIGURE 2.16 **How Your Brain Responds to TV Commercials**
Marketing researchers are now using biometric measures to probe consumer responses to advertisements. Here, a volunteer wearing a fabric cap containing EEG sensors and an eye-tracking device is exposed to marketing images on a TV monitor.

neuromarketing An emerging field of marketing that examines brain responses to advertisements and brand-related messages.

whether a person is feeling angry, sad, or disgusted just by looking at their brain scans (Fox, 2013; Kassam et al., 2013).

Neuromarketing techniques are also being used in political campaigns. For example, consultants today are measuring brain waves and coding facial expressions of people as they watch campaign commercials or speeches by political candidates, all in the interest of determining how well candidates connect to voters on a deeper emotional level (Randall, 2015). In the not-too-distant future, political candidates may come to rely on brain reading technology to fine-tune their public speaking or debating skills.

Diagnosing Psychological Disorders

Brain scans may also come into general use in diagnosing psychological or psychiatric disorders. Teams of experimenters are actively engaged in research exploring the use of brain scans in detecting signs of abnormal behavior patterns such as bipolar disorder, schizophrenia, and attention deficit/hyperactivity disorder (ADHD). Investigators hope to uncover signs of psychological disorders through scanning techniques, in much the same ways that scanning techniques are now used to reveal tumors and other physical disorders (Cyranoski, 2011). These techniques are presently limited to experimental use, but one day—perhaps one day soon—they may become as common as chest X-rays or even dental X-rays.

MODULE REVIEW **2.4** **Methods of Studying the Brain**

Recite It

9. Describe methods scientists use to study the workings of the brain.

(a) _____ is a method that involves destroying certain parts of the brains of laboratory animals in order to observe the effects. Electrical (b) _____ involves implanting electrodes in the brain to record changes in brain activity associated with certain activities or behaviors. Electrical (c) _____ entails passing a mild electric current through the brain so that the effects on specific parts of the brain can be observed. Less invasive methods include brain-imaging techniques such as the EEG, CT scan, PET scan, and (d) _____.

Recall It

1. Which of the following is a computer-enhanced imaging technique that uses X-ray beams to study structural abnormalities of the brain?

   a. fMRI
   b. PET scan
   c. CT scan
   d. MRI

2. Scientists who use the experimental technique of electrical recording to study brain functioning

   a. also make use of a radioactive isotope that can be detected in the bloodstream.
   b. implant electrodes in particular neurons, groups of neurons, or nerves in particular parts of the brain.
   c. send a narrow X-ray beam through the head.
   d. are unable to get precise measurements from a single brain cell.

3. Functional MRI (fMRI)

   a. is used to study both brain structure and brain functioning.
   b. involves an invasive technique known as lesioning.
   c. is a controversial procedure with ethical implications.
   d. is based on a sophisticated type of X-ray technique.

4. In the experimental technique for brain study called lesioning,

    a. parts of the brain of living organisms are destroyed.
    b. electrodes are surgically implanted in the brain.

    c. parts of the brain are electrically stimulated to observe the effects on behavior.
    d. connections between the brain and spinal cord are severed.

Think About It

■ What brain-imaging techniques do scientists use to study the functioning of the brain? To study the structures of the brain?

■ What is your opinion about using animals in experimental brain research? What safeguards do you think should be observed in this kind of research?

Recite It answers placed at the end of chapter.

MODULE

2.5 The Divided Brain: Specialization of Function

10 **Explain** how the two halves of the brain differ in their functions.

If you stub a toe on your left foot, cells in your right parietal lobe will "light up," producing sensations of pain. Conversely, a blow to your right foot will register in your left parietal lobe. This is because the sensory cortex in each hemisphere is connected to sensory receptors on the opposite sides of the body. Likewise, the motor cortex in your right frontal lobe controls the movements of the left side of your body, and vice versa. Thus, if we were to stimulate your left motor cortex in a certain spot, the fingers on your right hand would involuntarily contract. As we see next, evidence indicates that the right and left hemispheres are also specialized for certain types of functions.

The Brain at Work: Lateralization and Integration

The term **lateralization** refers to the division of functions between the right and left hemispheres (see Concept Chart 2.5). Generally speaking, the left hemisphere in most people appears to be dominant for language abilities—speaking, reading, and writing (Nielsen et al., 2013). The left hemisphere also appears to be dominant for tasks requiring logical analysis, problem solving, and mathematical computations. The right hemisphere in most people appears to be dominant for nonverbal processing, such as understanding spatial relationships (for example, piecing together puzzles, arranging blocks to match designs, reading maps), recognizing faces, interpreting people's gestures and facial expressions, perceiving and expressing emotion, and appreciating music and art.

Despite these differences, we shouldn't think people are either "left-brained" or "right-brained." The brain operates as a whole system and people don't typically have a stronger left brain or right brain (Novotney, 2013). We should also note that

CONCEPT 2.27

In most people, the left hemisphere is specialized for use of language and logical analysis, whereas the right hemisphere is specialized for spatial processing and other nonverbal tasks.

lateralization The specialization of the right and left cerebral hemispheres for particular functions.

Concept Chart 2.5   Lateralization of Brain Functions

Areas of Left-Hemisphere Dominance

Verbal functions (for right-handers and most left-handers), including spoken and written use of language, as well as logical analysis, problem solving, and mathematical computation

Areas of Right-Hemisphere Dominance

Nonverbal functions, including understanding spatial relationships (as presented, for example, in jigsaw puzzles or maps), recognizing faces and interpreting gestures, perceiving and expressing emotion, and appreciating music and art

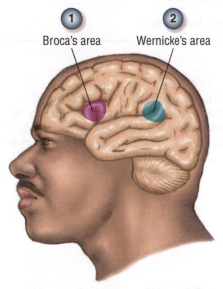

① Broca's area   ② Wernicke's area

FIGURE 2.17 Broca's and Wernicke's Areas

① Broca's area is an egg-shaped part of the frontal lobe that plays a key role in the production of speech. ② Wernicke's area, which is located in the temporal lobe, enables us to understand written or spoken language.

Broca's area An area of the left frontal lobe involved in speech.

functions of the left and right hemispheres largely overlap, and messages quickly zap back and forth between them across the corpus callosum.

Although one hemisphere may be dominant for a particular task, both hemispheres share the work in performing most tasks. Language dominance is associated with handedness (Hopkins & Cantalupo, 2008). The left hemisphere is dominant for language functions in about 95 percent of right-handed people and about 70 percent of left-handed people (Pinker, 1994; Springer & Deutsch, 1993; Tzourio-Mazoyer et al., 2010). For about 15 percent of left-handed people, the right hemisphere is dominant for language functions. The other 15 percent of left-handers show patterns of mixed dominance.

The French surgeon Paul Broca (1824–1880) was one of the pioneers in the discovery of the language areas of the brain. His most important discovery involved a male patient, 51 years old, who was admitted to the ward suffering from gangrene in his leg. The patient was also nearly unable to speak. He understood clearly what he heard, but his verbal utterances were limited primarily to one meaningless sound (*tan*).

The patient died a few days after being admitted. While conducting an autopsy, Broca found that an egg-shaped part of the left frontal lobe of the patient's brain had degenerated. The surgeon concluded that this area of the brain, now known as **Broca's area** in his honor, is essential to the production of speech (see ■ Figure 2.17) (Sahin et al., 2009; Wilson et al., 2011).

Broca's area is one of the brain's two vital language areas. The other, which is in the left temporal lobe, is **Wernicke's area** (see Figure 2.17). It is named after the German researcher Karl Wernicke (1848–1905). Wernicke's area is responsible for our ability to comprehend language in written or spoken form (Plaza et al., 2009). Wernicke's and Broca's areas are connected by nerve fibers, so that there is an ongoing interaction between understanding language and being able to produce it or express it (Wilson et al., 2011). Significant damage to Broca's area or

Wernicke's area, or to the nerve connections between them, can lead to different forms of **aphasia**—the loss or impairment of the ability to understand or express language.

Handedness: Why Are People Not More Even-Handed?

Though we may not be "right-brained" or "left-brained," most of us are primarily either right-handed or left-handed. About 90 percent of people are right-handed, with the remainder either left-handed or ambidextrous to some degree ("Genes Linked," 2013). We don't yet know what causes handedness, but evidence points to genetics playing an important role (Brandler et al., 2013; Klass, 2011). Not surprisingly given the likely role of genetics, handedness tends to run in families (see Table 2.2). However, handedness differs in about one in five sets of identical twins (one twin may be right-handed, the other left-handed). Identical twins have identical genes, so if handedness were purely genetic in origin, we would not observe this difference. Thus, other factors must also contribute to handedness. For example, social factors, such as family pressures on children to use their right hands for writing, may play a part in determining handedness.

Men are more likely to be left-handed than women (Papadatou-Pastou et al., 2008). The explanation of this gender difference remains unclear, although scientists suspect that sex-linked genetic factors and perhaps prenatal exposure to the male sex hormone testosterone are possible causal factors (Price, 2009b). We do know that handedness preferences begin to develop before birth. In an ultrasound-based study of more than 200 fetuses, researchers found that more than 95 percent of them sucked their right thumbs, whereas fewer than 5 percent sucked their left thumbs (Hepper, Shahidullah, & White, 1990). These percentages correspond closely to the distribution of right-handers and left-handers in the population.

Split-Brain Research: Can the Hemispheres Go It Alone?

Epilepsy is a neurological disorder in which sudden, violent neural discharges of electrical activity in the brain cause seizures. In many cases, these discharges resemble a neural ping-pong match—the electrical discharges begin in one cerebral hemisphere and thunder into the other. As they bounce back and forth, they create a kind of wild electrical storm in the brain. Fortunately, most people with epilepsy are able to avoid or control seizures with medication.

When the disorder fails to respond to conventional forms of treatment, surgery may become an option. In the 1960s, neurosurgeons treated some severe cases of epilepsy by severing the corpus callosum. The purpose was to stop the neural storm in the brain by preventing the electrical activity in one hemisphere from crossing into the other. The surgery prevents communication between the cerebral hemispheres.

Remarkably, patients who undergo the cutting of the corpus callosum, whom we call **split-brain patients,** retain their intellectual competence and distinctive personalities following surgery. Yet the two hemispheres appear to be of two minds about some things (Gazzaniga, 1999). We might sometimes joke that it seems as if our left hand doesn't know what our right hand is doing. For split-brain patients, this strikes

David Young-Wolff/PhotoEdit

The right hemisphere is dominant for spatial tasks, such as solving jigsaw puzzles, whereas the left hemisphere is dominant for verbal tasks, such as speaking, reading, and writing.

Table 2.2 Parents' Handedness and Child's Odds of Being Left-Handed

Parents Who Are Left-Handed	Child's Odds
Neither parent	1 in 50
One parent	1 in 6
Both parents	1 in 2

Source: Springer and Deutsch, 1993.

CONCEPT 2.28
Scientists suspect that handedness is strongly influenced by genetics.

Wernicke's area An area of the left temporal lobe involved in processing written and spoken language.

aphasia Loss or impairment of the ability to understand or express language.

epilepsy A neurological disorder characterized by seizures that involve sudden, violent discharges of electrical activity in the brain.

split-brain patients People with a corpus callosum that has been surgically severed.

Do you see Jacob or Edward? If you were a split-brain patient and focused on a point in the middle of the forehead of this composite face of two well-known characters, the image on the left (Edward) would project to the right hemisphere and the image on the right (Jacob) would project to the left hemisphere. If you were then asked whom you just saw, you would likely answer Jacob (since the left hemisphere is dominant for language). But if you were asked to point with your left hand to a picture of the person you just saw, you would be likely to point to Edward, because the right hemisphere is dominant for facial recognition, and controls movements on the left side of the body.

Source: Concept suggested by University of Oklahoma Elements of Psychology program.

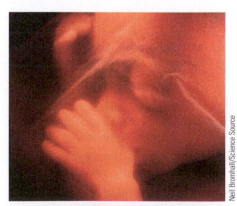

The proportions of fetuses sucking their right or left thumb parallel those of right-handed people in the population, suggesting that handedness preferences may begin to develop before birth.

close to home, as illustrated in landmark research conducted by Nobel Prize winner Roger Sperry and his colleague Michael Gazzaniga.

In one of these experiments, researchers placed a familiar object, such as a key, in the left hands of split-brain patients (Gazzaniga, 1992). When blindfolded, the patients could not name the object they were holding, although they were able to use the key to open a lock. The question is, *why*?

Recall that the somatosensory cortex in the right hemisphere processes sensory information from the left side of the body (the touch of a key placed in the left hand, for instance). Because the right hemisphere shares this information with the left hemisphere, speech centers in the left hemisphere can respond by naming the object that was felt. Thus, people whose brain functions normally have no trouble naming a familiar object placed in their left hand even if they cannot see it.

But in split-brain patients, the right hemisphere cannot transmit information to the speech centers in the left hemisphere, making it impossible to name the object being held in the left hand. The right hemisphere literally cannot "say" what the left hand is holding (Gazzaniga, 1995). But despite this lack of ability to name the object, the right hemisphere recognizes the object by touch and can demonstrate through hand movements how it is used.

In perception studies with split-brain patients, researchers briefly flash pictures of objects on a screen and then ask the patients to identify them by naming them or by selecting them from among a group of objects hidden behind the screen (see ■ Figure 2.18). The experimenters vary whether the stimuli are projected to the left or right visual cortex, which is located in the occipital lobes. If you look straight ahead and project a vertical line dividing your field of view into a right and a left half, the area to the left of the line represents your left visual field. Information presented to the left visual field crosses over and is processed by the right visual cortex. Conversely, information presented to the right of your field of view (to the right visual field) is projected to the left visual cortex. In people whose corpus callosum is intact, information is quickly exchanged between the hemispheres, but in split-brain patients, one hemisphere does not communicate with the other.

When an image is flashed to the right visual field of a split-brain patient, the left hemisphere processes the information, and the patient is able to name the object ("I saw a pencil"). This is not surprising when you consider that the left hemisphere in most people controls speech. But what happens when the picture of the object is flashed on the left side of the screen, which projects information to the right hemisphere, the one without language function? In this case, the patient cannot say what, if anything, is seen. The patient is likely to report, "I saw nothing." However, because the right hemisphere can recognize objects by touch, the patient is able to use the left hand to select the correct object from among those hidden behind the screen.

Findings from classic studies of split-brain patients provide additional evidence of the importance of the left hemisphere in speech and language production. Perhaps more revealing is the observation that split-brain patients appear to be quite normal in their outward behavior (Sperry, 1982). It seems as if their brains are able to adapt new strategies for processing information and solving problems that do not rely on communication between the hemispheres. As we will now see, this speaks to the remarkable ability of the human brain to adapt to new demands.

Brain Damage and Psychological Functioning

Many people have made remarkable recoveries from brain damage resulting from stroke or head trauma. Perhaps none is more remarkable than that of

FIGURE 2.18 **Split-Brain Study**

The right part of this figure shows that information from the right half of the visual field is transmitted to the occipital cortex in the left hemisphere; conversely, information from the left half of the visual field goes to the right occipital cortex for processing. In split-brain patients, information received by one hemisphere cannot be transferred to the other.

In a typical study with split-brain patients, investigators present a visual stimulus to each hemisphere individually.

❶ When an object, such as a pencil, is flashed in the right visual field, the visual information is transmitted to the patient's left hemisphere. Because the left hemisphere controls language, the patient can correctly name the object.

❷ When visual information is presented to the nonverbal right hemisphere, the patient is unable to name it.

❸ The patient is able to pick out the object by touch from a group of hidden objects when using the left hand, because the tactile information from the left hand projects to the right hemisphere, which has already "seen" the object.

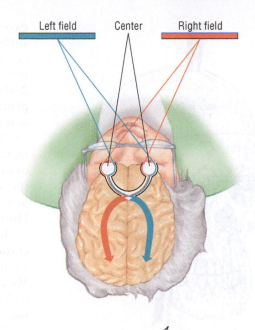

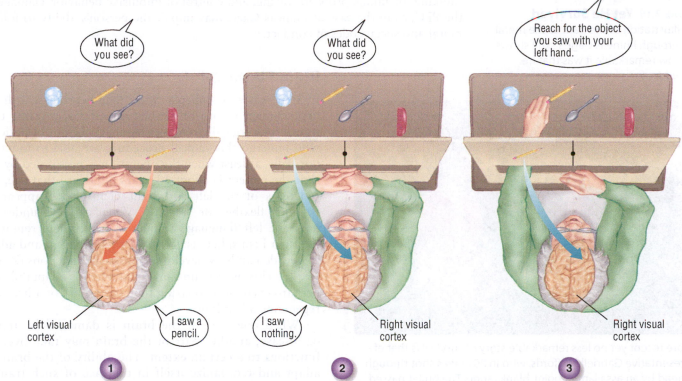

Phineas Gage, a nineteenth-century railroad worker whose case astounded the medical practitioners of his time (Kean, 2014). One day in 1848, Gage was packing blasting powder for a dynamite charge and accidentally set it off. The blast shot an inch-thick metal rod through his cheek and brain and out through the top of his head. Gage fell to the ground, but to the astonishment of his coworkers, he soon stood up, dusted himself off, and spoke to them. He was helped home, where his wounds were bandaged. Gage's wounds healed within

CONCEPT 2.29

The results of split-brain operations show that, under some conditions, the right hand literally doesn't know what the left hand is doing.

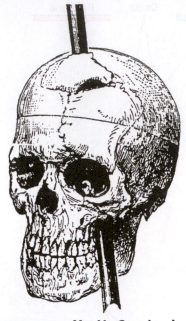

FIGURE 2.19 **Yet He Survived**
This illustration of the path of the metal rod through Phineas Gage's skull shows just how remarkable it was that he survived.

two months, and he was able to function despite the massive head injury he had suffered. Then, however, changes in his personality began to appear, which suggests to us that he suffered from subtle forms of brain damage. The formerly polite and conscientious worker became irritable, rude, and irresponsible (Holden, 2009). He started brawling and drinking heavily and "indulging in the grossest profanity" (Kean, 2014). Those who knew him before the accident said, "Gage is no longer Gage."

Gage's skull is now on display at Harvard University. The trajectory of the metal rod is obvious (see ■ Figure 2.19). With near-surgical precision, parts of the brain controlling vital bodily processes were spared, but the **prefrontal cortex (PFC)**, the area of the frontal lobes in front of the motor cortex, was damaged as were neural connections between the frontal lobes and other parts of the brain (Van Horn et al., 2012).

In the human brain, the PFC comprises about one-third of the entire cerebral cortex, which shouldn't surprise us given the central role it plays in many of the behaviors that make up what it is to be "human" (Huey, Krueger, & Grafman, 2006). We can think of the PFC as the "seat of intelligence" or the "executive control center" of the brain because it is involved in so many higher mental functions, including reasoning, decision making, weighing the consequences of our actions, creative thinking, planning, problem solving, and control of impulsive behavior. Damage to the PFC, as in the case of Phineas Gage, may impair the person's ability to follow moral and social codes of conduct.

Brain Plasticity

In some cases of epilepsy and other neurological disorders, damage to one of the hemispheres is so severe that it must be surgically removed. Remarkably, most patients who undergo this radical procedure are able to function normally, at least when the operation is performed by the time the patient is about 13 years old. Until that age, the functions of the left and right hemispheres appear to be quite flexible, or "plastic." When children under 13 have the left (language-dominant) hemisphere removed, the right hemisphere is able to reorganize itself and adapt to new demands by developing language functions (Zuger, 1997). This is an amazing example of adaptability—perhaps even more amazing than the ability of a lizard to regenerate a lost limb.

When one part of the brain is damaged by injury or disease, another part of the brain may take over its functions to a certain extent. The ability of the brain to adapt and reorganize itself in the face of such trauma is called **plasticity**. Seeking to capitalize on the brain's ability to heal itself, physicians are now stimulating healthy neurons in the brains of stroke victims, hoping that these neurons will take over the functions that stroke-damaged neurons are no longer able to serve (Nowak et al., 2010).

Saul Loeb-Pool/Getty Images

A more recent yet no less remarkable story of survival is that of Representative Gabrielle Giffords, who in 2011 was shot through the head by an assailant at point-blank range. The bullet passed through the left side of her brain, sparing critical brain structures needed for survival, but affecting areas involved in speech and movement. Here she is shown appearing before Congress two years after the shooting.

CONCEPT 2.30
Brain damage can result in subtle or profound consequences in physical and psychological functioning.

As with patients who undergo surgical removal of one of their cerebral hemispheres, plasticity is greatest among young children whose brains are not fully lateralized. How the brain accomplishes these feats of reorganization—whether in building new circuitry or altering existing circuitry—remains uncertain. Yet, as in the case of many brain injuries, there are limits to how well the brain can compensate for damage to brain tissue (see Try This Out).

Try This Out   Learning Through Volunteering

To learn firsthand about the effects of stroke and brain injuries, consider spending a few hours a week volunteering at a local rehabilitation center or clinic. Volunteers may assist occupational therapists, physical therapists, rehabilitation counselors, and other professionals. Or they may be asked to spend time with patients in the role of a companion or attentive listener. The work can be personally rewarding and give you the opportunity to see whether you might be well suited for a career in rehabilitation.

CONCEPT 2.31

The brain is capable of reorganizing itself to a certain extent to adapt to new functions, even in some cases in which half of it is surgically removed.

prefrontal cortex (PFC) The area of the frontal lobe that lies in front of the motor cortex and that is involved in higher mental functions, including thinking, planning, impulse control, and weighing the consequences of behavior.

plasticity The ability of the brain to adapt itself after trauma or surgical alteration.

MODULE REVIEW   2.5   The Divided Brain: Specialization of Function

Recite It

10. **Explain** how the two halves of the brain differ in their functions.

In most people, the left hemisphere appears to play a larger role in (a) _____ tasks, including the use of language and logic, whereas the right hemisphere is specialized for tasks involving (b) _____ processing, such as understanding spatial relationships, recognizing faces, and appreciating music and art.

Recall It

1. One long-established fact about the brain is that
   a. it is completely lateralized with respect to functions.
   b. the left part of the brain controls language, but only in right-handed people.
   c. the right side of the brain controls functioning in the left part of the human body, and vice versa.
   d. the functions of the left and right cerebral hemispheres do not overlap.

2. Whereas the _____ hemisphere appears to be dominant for language functions for most people, the _____ hemisphere appears to be dominant for nonverbal functions.

3. The part of the brain directly involved in speech production is
   a. the corpus callosum.   c. Broca's area.
   b. Wernicke's area.   d. the anterior fissure.

4. The part of the brain directly involved in comprehending written or spoken language is
   a. the prefrontal cortex.   c. the corpus callosum.
   b. Broca's area.   d. Wernicke's area.

5. Which of the following is *not* true?
   a. Handedness runs in families.
   b. Handedness is determined entirely by genetic factors.
   c. Researchers have found that the great majority of fetuses suck their right thumbs.
   d. Imposing right-handedness on left-handed children can lead to emotional problems.

Think About It

■ Why is it incorrect to say that someone is either right-brained or left-brained?

■ What are the risks of trying to impose right-handedness on left-handed children?

Recite It *answers placed at the end of chapter.*

2.6 The Endocrine System: The Body's Other Communication System

11 **Describe** how the endocrine system is organized and the roles that hormones play in behavior.

The nervous system is not the only means by which parts of the body communicate with each other. The *endocrine system* is also a communication system, although it is vastly slower than the nervous system. The messages it sends are conveyed through blood vessels rather than a network of nerves. The messengers it uses are hormones, which, as you may recall from Module 2.1, are chemical substances that help regulate bodily processes. Here we explore the endocrine system and the role that it plays in behavior.

Endocrine Glands: The Body's Pumping Stations

The **endocrine system** is a grouping of glands located in various parts of the body that release secretions, called hormones, directly into the bloodstream. ■ Figure 2.20 shows the location of many of the major endocrine glands in the body. Concept Chart 2.6 summarizes the functions of the hormones they release.

The endocrine system regulates important bodily processes, such as growth, reproduction, and metabolism. To do so, it relies on hormones to communicate its messages to organs and other bodily tissues. (The word *hormone* is derived from Greek roots that mean "to stimulate" or "to excite.")

Like neurotransmitters, hormones lock into receptor sites on target cells to trigger changes in these cells. For example, *insulin,* a hormone produced by the **pancreas**, regulates the concentration of glucose (sugar) in the blood. Like a key fitting into a lock, insulin opens glucose receptors on cells, allowing sugar to pass from the bloodstream into the cells where it is used as fuel. Unlike neurotransmitters, which are found only in the nervous system, hormones travel through the bloodstream system to their destinations.

One of the important functions of the endocrine system is helping to maintain an internally balanced state, or **homeostasis**, in the body. When the level of sugar in the blood exceeds a certain threshold, or set point—as may happen when you eat a meal rich in carbohydrates (sugars and starches)—the pancreas releases more insulin into the bloodstream. Insulin stimulates cells throughout the body to draw more glucose from the blood, which decreases the level of glucose in the body. As this level declines to its set point, the pancreas reduces the amount of insulin it secretes.

The two most important endocrine glands in the body, the hypothalamus and the **pituitary gland**, are located in the brain. The pituitary is often referred to as the "master gland" because it affects so many bodily processes. But even the so-called master gland operates under the control of another "master"—the hypothalamus.

The hypothalamus secretes hormones known as *releasing factors* that cause the nearby pituitary gland to release other hormones. For example, the hypothalamus releases *human growth hormone-releasing factor (hGRF)*, which stimulates the pituitary to release *growth hormone (GH)*, which in turn promotes physical growth. Other pituitary hormones cause other glands, such as the testes in men and ovaries

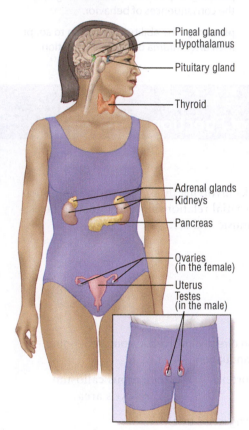

FIGURE 2.20 **Major Glands of the Endocrine System**
The endocrine system consists of glands that release secretions, called hormones, directly into the bloodstream.

endocrine system The body's system of glands that release their secretions, called hormones, directly into the bloodstream.

pancreas An endocrine gland located near the stomach that produces the hormone insulin.

homeostasis The tendency of systems to maintain a steady, internally balanced state.

pituitary gland An endocrine gland in the brain that produces various hormones involved in growth, regulation of the menstrual cycle, and childbirth.

in women, to release their own hormones. The process is akin to a series of falling dominoes.

In addition to the hypothalamus and pituitary, the brain houses another endocrine gland, the **pineal gland**, which releases *melatonin*, a hormone that helps regulate sleep–wake cycles (see Chapter 4). The **adrenal glands** are a pair of glands that lie above the kidneys. They have an outer layer, called the *adrenal cortex*, and a core, called the *adrenal medulla*. The pituitary hormone *ACTH* stimulates the adrenal cortex to secrete hormones called *cortical steroids*, which promote muscle development and stimulate the liver to release stores of sugar in times of stress. More energy thus becomes available in response to stressful situations, such as emergencies in

CONCEPT 2.32
Endocrine glands distributed throughout the body help coordinate many bodily functions.

CONCEPT 2.33
Hormones are released by endocrine glands directly into the bloodstream, and from there they travel to specific receptor sites on target organs and tissues.

Concept Chart 2.6	The Endocrine System
Gland/Hormone	**Function**
Pituitary gland	
Growth hormone	Stimulates growth, especially of bones
ACTH	Stimulates adrenal cortex to secrete cortical steroids
Oxytocin	Stimulates uterine contractions during childbirth and release of milk following childbirth
Hypothalamus	
Releasing factors	Stimulate the pituitary gland to release other hormones, including growth hormone
Pineal gland	
Melatonin	Helps regulate sleep–wake cycles
Pancreas	
Insulin	Facilitates entry of blood glucose (sugar) into cells; involved in regulation of blood sugar levels
Thyroid gland	
Thyroid hormones	Involved in regulating metabolic rate, growth, and maturation
Adrenal glands	
Cortical steroids	Help body cope with stress; promote muscle development; stimulate the liver to release stores of sugar
Epinephrine (adrenaline) and norepinephrine (noradrenaline)	Speeds up bodily processes, such as heart rate and breathing rate
Ovaries	
Estrogen	Fosters female sexual maturation; helps regulate menstrual cycle
Progesterone	Helps maintain pregnancy; helps regulate menstrual cycle
Testes	
Testosterone	Promotes sperm production; fosters male sexual differentiation during prenatal development; stokes sexual maturation in pubertal males

pineal gland A small endocrine gland in the brain that produces the hormone melatonin, which is involved in regulating sleep–wake cycles.

adrenal glands A pair of endocrine glands located just above the kidneys that produce various stress-related hormones.

CONCEPT 2.34
In concert with the nervous system, the endocrine system helps the body maintain a state of equilibrium, or homeostasis.

CONCEPT 2.35
The pituitary gland is often called the "master gland" because it helps regulate so many other endocrine glands.

CONCEPT 2.36
Hormones are linked to a wide range of behaviors and mood states.

gonads Sex glands (testes in men and ovaries in women) that produce sex hormones and germ cells (sperm in the male and egg cells in the female).

ovaries The female gonads, which secrete the female sex hormones estrogen and progesterone and produce mature egg cells.

testes The male gonads, which produce sperm and secrete the male sex hormone testosterone.

germ cells Sperm and egg cells from which new life develops.

thyroid gland An endocrine gland in the neck that secretes the hormone thyroxin, which is involved in regulating metabolic functions and physical growth.

which the organism faces the imminent threat of a predator attack. Other stress hormones, *epinephrine* and *norepinephrine,* are released by the adrenal medulla. They help prepare the body to deal with stress by speeding up bodily processes, such as heart rate and respiration rate.

As noted earlier in the chapter, some chemicals, like norepinephrine, do double duty: They function both as neurotransmitters in the nervous system and as hormones in the bloodstream. In the brain, norepinephrine—and to a lesser degree, epinephrine—function as neurotransmitters. Norepinephrine plays an important role in the nervous system in regulating mood, alertness, and appetite.

The **gonads** are the sex glands—**ovaries** in women and **testes** in men. The gonads produce the **germ cells**—egg cells in women and sperm in men. The ovaries also produce the female sex hormones *estrogen* and *progesterone,* which help regulate the menstrual cycle. Progesterone also stimulates growth of the female reproductive organs and helps the uterus maintain pregnancy.

The testes produce the male sex hormone, *testosterone,* which leads to the development of male sex organs in male fetuses. Following puberty in males, release of testosterone by the testes fosters growth of the male genitals, development of a beard, and deepening of the voice.

Though the nervous system and endocrine system are separate systems, they are closely intertwined. The brain regulates the activity of the endocrine system so that the body responds not as separate systems but as an integrated whole. The brain controls endocrine functions through the autonomic nervous system. In times of stress, for example, the sympathetic nervous system transmits commands from the brain to the adrenal medulla, leading to the release of the stress hormones epinephrine and norepinephrine that help prepare the body to deal with stress (discussed further in Chapter 10).

Hormones and Behavior

Though human behavior is more strongly influenced by learning and experience than by hormones, hormones do play a role. For example, the male sex hormone testosterone is linked to higher levels of dominance, competitiveness, and risk taking (Miller & Maner, 2010). Testosterone is also linked to greater physical aggressiveness in both men and women (Archer, 2006). Testosterone is produced in both men's and women's bodies, but in lesser amounts in women.

Ingestion of anabolic steroids (synthetic testosterone), which some people use to build up muscle mass, is also linked to increased aggressive and belligerent behavior. We should recognize, however, that testosterone is perhaps one of many factors interacting in complex ways that lead to aggressive behavior in humans. Deficiencies of testosterone can also lead to loss of sexual desire in both men and women.

Oxytocin, a hormone released by the pituitary gland, is involved in regulating uterine contractions during childbirth and release of mother's milk during nursing. But the hormone—dubbed the "trust molecule"—also affects the brain and appears to have psychological effects on a range of social behaviors such as trust, empathy, conformity, and generosity, as well as caregiving of mothers toward their infant children (for example, Chang et al., 2012; Lane et al., 2012; Zak, 2012). It may underlie feelings of safety and trust that help foster close social connections (Bartz, 2016; Carter, 2014). Oxytocin may also work to influence charitable giving by making strangers seem more like kin (Poulin, 2012).

Excesses and deficiencies in hormone levels are associated with many physical and psychological disorders. Thyroid hormones, produced by the **thyroid gland**, help regulate body metabolism, the rate at which the body turns food into energy. Excess thyroid hormones are associated with states of anxiety and irritability. Deficiencies of thyroid hormones can lead to sluggishness and weight gain and can retard intellectual development in children.

During the menstrual cycle, testosterone levels in women remain fairly stable, but levels of estrogen and progesterone shift dramatically. Most women, about three out of four, experience some form of **premenstrual syndrome (PMS)**—a constellation of physical and psychological symptoms in the days leading up to menstruation each month. These symptoms may include anxiety, depression, irritability, weight gain from fluid retention, and abdominal discomfort (Yonkers, O'Brien, & Eriksson, 2008). Nearly one in five women have PMS symptoms significant enough to affect daily functioning or cause significant emotional distress (Halbreich et al., 2006; Heinemann et al., 2010).

The causes of PMS remain unclear. We lack solid evidence that hormonal imbalances—too much or too little circulating estrogen or progesterone—are responsible for PMS. Scientists suspect that differences in sensitivity to these hormones, not their levels per se, may predispose some women to develop symptoms of PMS (Kiesner, 2009). PMS may also involve irregularities in the functioning of the neurotransmitter serotonin in the brain (Bäckström et al., 2003).

CONCEPT 2.37
Hormonal factors may be involved in explaining PMS, a syndrome affecting about three out of four women.

premenstrual syndrome (PMS) A cluster of physical and psychological symptoms occurring in the few days preceding the menstrual flow.

MODULE REVIEW | **2.6** The Endocrine System: The Body's Other Communication System

Recite It

11. Describe how the endocrine system is organized and the roles that hormones play in behavior.

The major (a) _____ glands are the pituitary gland, hypothalamus, pineal gland, thyroid, adrenal glands, pancreas, and (b) _____ (testes in males and ovaries in females).

Excesses of (c) _____ hormones can cause anxiety and irritability, whereas too little can lead to sluggishness and weight gain and can retard intellectual development in children. (d) _____ has been linked to aggressiveness. Female sex hormones appear to play a role in (e) _____.

Recall It

1. Name the body system that functions as a communication system by releasing chemical messengers directly into the bloodstream.

2. Which of the following do glands secrete directly into the body's bloodstream?

   a. neurotransmitters
   b. hormones
   c. neuromodulators
   d. glial cells

3. What term is used to describe an internally balanced state in the body?

4. Name the gland known as the "master gland" because of its role in regulating the activity of many other glands.

Think About It

■ Do you believe your behavior is influenced by your hormones? Why or why not?

■ Why does the text refer to the endocrine system as the body's other communication system?

Recite It *answers placed at the end of chapter.*

2.7 Genes and Behavior: A Case of Nature and Nurture

12 **Evaluate** the role of genetics in behavior.

13 **Describe** methods psychologists use to study the roles of genes and environment in behavior.

© Jip Fen/Shutterstock.com

Within every living organism is a set of inherited instructions that determines whether it will have lungs or gills, a penis or a vagina, blue or green eyes. This set of instructions, called a **genotype**, constitutes a master plan for building and maintaining a living organism. The genetic instructions are encoded in the organism's **genes**, the basic units of heredity that are passed along from parent to offspring.

Genes are composed of a complex, double-stranded, spiraling molecule called **deoxyribonucleic acid (DNA)**. They are linked together on long strands called **chromosomes** that reside in the cell nucleus. Scientists believe about 20,000 to 25,000 genes compose the entire *human genome,* or human genetic code (Lupski, 2007; Volkow, 2006). This full complement of genes is found in each body cell except for the germ cells (egg cells and sperm), which carry half of the person's genes. Children inherit half of their chromosomes and the genes they carry from their mothers and half from their fathers. During conception, the 23 chromosomes in the mother's egg cell unite with the 23 chromosomes in the father's sperm cell, forming the normal arrangement of 23 pairs of chromosomes in the cell nucleus. With the exception of identical twins, no two people share the same genetic code.

Having completed work on deciphering the human genome, scientists can now read the entire genetic script of a human being. Buried within the code are DNA sequences that may play important roles in determining a person's risk of developing many physical and mental disorders (Kendler, 2005a, 2005b). Scientists are focusing on understanding how genes work and tracking down the specific genes involved in particular physical and mental disorders. By further studying the human genome, they hope to gain insights into the genetic origins of disease and develop ways of blocking the actions of harmful genes and harnessing the actions of useful ones.

Genetic factors clearly determine physical characteristics such as eye and hair color, but what about their role in behavior? Is our behavior a product of our genes, our environment, or both?

genotype An organism's genetic code.

genes Basic units of heredity that contain an individual's genetic code.

deoxyribonucleic acid (DNA) The basic chemical material in chromosomes that carries an individual's genetic code.

chromosomes Rodlike structures in the cell nucleus that house an individual's genes.

nature–nurture debate The debate in psychology about the relative influences of genetics (nature) and environment (nurture) in determining behavior.

Genetic Influences on Behavior

Genes influence many patterns of behavior. Some dogs are bold or placid in temperament; others are yappy. They all share enough genes to make them dogs and not cats, but they may differ greatly from one another in their behavior and physical traits. People have selectively bred animals to enhance specific behavior patterns as well as physical traits. But what about human behavior?

One of the oldest discussions in psychology is the **nature–nurture debate.** Is our behavior governed by nature (genetics) or nurture (environment and culture)? Though the debate continues, most psychologists today believe that human behavior is influenced by a combination of genes and the environment. The contemporary version of the nature–nurture debate is framed in terms of the relative contributions of nature *and* nurture to particular behaviors than it is about nature *or* nurture.

Virtually all of our psychological traits are influenced to one degree or another by genetic factors (Johnson et al., 2009). Heredity influences many psychological traits, including intelligence, shyness, impulsivity, aggressiveness, sociability, and optimism, as well as aptitudes in music and art, whether we have a happy or sad disposition, the occupation we choose, and our tendency to be altruistic or helpful to others (for example, Bezdjian, Baker, & Tuvblad, 2011; Kelsoe, 2010; Reuter et al., 2010; Saphire-Bernstein et al., 2011).

Genetic factors are implicated in many psychological disorders, including anxiety disorders, mood disorders, alcohol and drug use disorders, and schizophrenia (for example, Duffy et al., 2014; Kendler et al., 2012; Mattheisen et al., 2014; Schizophrenia Working Group, 2014). However, our genes do not dictate what our lives or personalities become. Many factors determine who we are, how we act, and how we interact with others, including environmental as well as genetic influences and the interactions among these factors. A recent large-scale analysis of twin studies showed that about half of the variation in human traits could be explained by genetic factors and about half by environmental factors (Polderman et al., 2015).

The genotype, or genetic code, is a kind of recipe or set of instructions, not unlike a computer program, for creating a living being having particular features or traits. But the extent to which the genotype becomes expressed in the organism's observable traits, or **phenotype**, depends on a complex interaction of genes and the environment (Manuck & McCaffery, 2014). We can think of the role of genetics in terms of creating a *predisposition* or *likelihood*—not a certainty—that particular behaviors, abilities, personality traits, or psychological disorders will develop. Psychological traits, such as shyness, intelligence, or a predisposition to schizophrenia or alcoholism, appear to be **polygenic traits**. These traits are influenced by multiple genes interacting with the environment in complex ways.

Our genetic code remains the same throughout life, unchanged from the moment of fertilization, but environmental influences during our lifetime can lead to the release of chemicals in the body that determine which genes become active and which remain dormant (Franklin et al., 2011). Environmental factors such as family environments, life stress, and learning experiences can determine whether or not particular genetic factors become expressed in observable behaviors or psychological traits (Manuck & McCaffery, 2014; Mischel & Brooks, 2011). Recently, investigators reported that severe abuse in early childhood affects the expression of particular genes linked to emotional disorders, possibly setting the stage for the development of depression or other emotional problems later in life (Labonté et al., 2012).

Good parenting may have beneficial effects on genetic expression. Consider landmark research by psychologist David Reiss and his colleagues (Reiss et al., 2000). They showed that the degree to which genetic influences on the personality trait of shyness become expressed in the observed behavior of children depends on the interactions they have with their parents and other important people in their lives. Parents who are overprotective of a shy child may accentuate an underlying genetic tendency toward shyness, whereas those who encourage more outgoing behavior may help the child overcome it. One lesson we can draw from the gene–environment interaction is that good parenting may reduce or even negate the influence of bad genes, including genetic variations that put adolescents at higher risk of developing problems with substance abuse (Brody et al., 2009).

But how can we separate the effects of environment from those of genetics? Let us consider several methods scientists use to untangle these effects.

Kinship Studies: Untangling the Roles of Heredity and Environment

Scientists rely on several methods to examine genetic contributions to behavior, including familial association studies, twin studies, and adoptee studies. Concept Chart 2.7 provides a summary of these three basic types of kinship studies.

CONCEPT 2.38
The view most scientists today hold is that both heredity and environment interact in complex ways toward shaping our personalities and intellectual abilities.

CONCEPT 2.39
Genetic factors create predispositions that increase the likelihood that certain behaviors, abilities, or personality traits will emerge, but whether they do emerge depends largely on environmental influences and individual experiences.

CONCEPT LINK
Investigators believe that genetics influences many personality traits, from shyness to novelty seeking. See Module 11.2.

phenotype The observable physical and behavioral characteristics of an organism, representing the influences of the genotype and environment.

polygenic traits Traits that are influenced by multiple genes interacting in complex ways.

Concept Chart 2.7 Types of Kinship Studies

Type of Study	Method of Analysis	Evaluation
Familial association study 	Analysis of shared traits or disorders among family members in relation to their degree of kinship	Provides supportive evidence of genetic contribution to behavior when concordance is greater among more closely related family members than among more distantly related ones; limited because the closer their blood relationship, the more likely people are to share similar environments
Twin study 	Analysis of differences in the rates of overlap (concordance) for a given trait or disorder between identical and fraternal twins	Provides strong evidence of the role of genetic factors in behavior when concordance rates are greater among identical twins than among fraternal twins; may be biased by greater environmental similarity between identical twins than fraternal twins
Adoptee study 	Analysis of similarity in traits or psychological or physical disorders between adoptees and their biological and adoptive parents, or between identical twins reared apart and those reared together	The clearest way of separating the roles of heredity and environment, but may overlook common environmental factors for twins reared apart early in life

© Andresr/Shutterstock.com

© Kenneth Sponsler/Shutterstock.com

© Yurchyks/Shutterstock.com

CONCEPT 2.40

Scientists use three basic types of kinship studies to examine genetic influences on behavior: familial association studies, twin studies, and adoptee studies.

CONCEPT LINK

Similarities between identical twins as compared with fraternal twins provide evidence that genes contribute to intelligence. See Module 7.3.

familial association studies Studies that examine the degree to which disorders or characteristics are shared among family members.

Familial Association Studies

The more closely related people are, the more genes they have in common. Each parent shares 50 percent of his or her genes with his or her children, as do siblings with each other. More distant relatives, such as uncles, aunts, and cousins, have fewer genes in common. Therefore, if genes contribute to a given trait or disorder, we would expect to find more closely related people to be more likely to share the trait or disorder in question.

Familial association studies have been used to study family linkages in psychological disorders, such as schizophrenia. Consistent with a role for genetics in the development of this disorder, we find a greater risk of the disorder among closer blood relatives of schizophrenia patients than among more distant relatives. The risk among blood relatives rises from 2 percent among first cousins and uncles and aunts to 48 percent among identical twins. However, we should note a major limitation of this kind of study. The closer their blood relationship, the more likely people are to share common environments. Thus, researchers look to other types of studies, such as twin studies and adoptee studies, to help disentangle the relative contributions of heredity and environment.

© Andi Berger/Shutterstock.com

Twin Studies

In the case of **identical twins** (also called *monozygotic,* or *MZ,* twins), a fertilized egg cell, or **zygote**, splits into two cells, and each one develops into a separate person. Because their genetic code had been carried in the single cell before it split in two, identical twins have the same genetic makeup. In the case of **fraternal twins** (also called *dizygotic,* or *DZ,* twins), the mother releases two egg cells in the same month. They are fertilized by different sperm cells, and each fertilized egg cell then develops into a separate person. Fraternal twins thus share only 50 percent of their genetic makeup, as do other brothers and sisters.

In **twin studies**, researchers compare **concordance rates**, or percentages of shared traits or disorders. A higher rate of concordance (percentage of times both twins have the same disorder or trait) among MZ twins than among DZ twins strongly suggests a genetic contribution to the disorder or trait (Price & Jaffee, 2008). Identical twins are more likely than fraternal twins to share many psychological traits and even such disorders as schizophrenia (Hamilton, 2008; Kendler, 2005a).

Twin studies have a major limitation, however. The problem is that identical twins may be treated more alike than fraternal twins. Thus, environmental factors, not genes, may account for their higher rates of concordance. For example, identical twins may be encouraged to dress alike, take the same courses, and even play the same musical instrument. Despite this limitation, twin studies provide useful information on genetic contributions to personality and intellectual development.

Adoptee Studies

The clearest way to separate the roles of environment and heredity is to conduct **adoptee studies**. These studies (also called *adoption studies*) compare adopted children with both their adoptive parents and their biological parents. If they tend to be more like their adoptive parents in their psychological traits or the disorders they develop, we can argue that environment plays the more dominant role. If they tend to be more like their biological parents, we may assume that heredity has a greater influence.

When identical twins are separated at an early age and reared apart in separate adoptive families, we can attribute any differences between them to environmental factors since their genetic makeup is the same. This natural experiment—separating

identical twins Twins who developed from the same zygote and so have identical genes (also called monozygotic, or MZ, twins).

zygote A fertilized egg cell.

fraternal twins Twins who developed from separate zygotes and so have 50 percent of their genes in common (also called dizygotic, or DZ, twins).

twin studies Studies that examine the degree to which concordance rates between twin pairs for particular disorders or characteristics vary in relation to whether the twins are identical or fraternal.

concordance rates In twin studies, the percentages of cases in which both members of twin pairs share the same trait or disorder.

adoptee studies Studies that examine whether adoptees are more similar to their biological or adoptive parents with respect to their psychological traits or to the disorders they develop.

identical twins at an early age—does not happen often, but when it does, it provides a special opportunity to examine the role of nature and nurture. One landmark study showed a high level of similarity between identical twins reared apart and those reared together across a range of personality traits (Tellegen et al., 1988). These findings suggest that heredity plays an important role in personality development. Yet studies of twins reared apart may overlook common environmental factors. Because twins are rarely adopted at birth, they may have shared a common environment during infancy. Many continue to meet periodically throughout their lives. Thus, twins reared apart may have opportunities to be influenced by others in their shared environments or to influence each other, quite apart from their genetic overlap.

MODULE REVIEW **2.7** Genes and Behavior: A Case of Nature and Nurture

Recite It

12. **Evaluate** how genetics influences personality and behavior.

Genetic factors are major influences on animal behavior and temperament.

In humans, genetic factors (a) _____ in complex ways with environmental influences in determining personality and intellectual development.

13. **Describe** methods psychologists use to study the roles of genes and environment in behavior.

Three types of kinship studies are used to study the role of genetics in human behavior: (b) _____ association studies, which explore shared traits or disorders among family members; (c) _____ studies, which compare convergence rates for traits or disorders between monozygotic twins and dizygotic twins; and (d) _____ studies, which examine similarities between adopted children and their biological and adoptive parents.

Recall It

1. Scientists believe there are about _____ genes in the human genome.
   a. fewer than 5,000
   b. 10,000
   c. 20,000 to 25,000
   d. more than 100,000

2. In the long-standing debate in psychology over the nature–nurture issue, the central question is:
   a. How much of our genetic code do we have in common with others?
   b. Which is a more influential factor in human behavior—the genotype or the phenotype?
   c. Does heredity or environment govern human behavior?
   d. To what extent do rearing influences affect our genotype?

3. Polygenic traits are
   a. traits that are influenced by multiple genes.
   b. traits that are influenced by polygenic genes.

   c. traits that are determined by genetic defects.
   d. traits that are fully determined by combinations of genes.

4. What are the basic types of studies used to examine the influence of genetics on behavior?

5. Dizygotic (fraternal) twins result when
   a. a zygote is formed and then splits into two cells.
   b. two egg cells are fertilized by different sperm.
   c. two different sperm fertilize the same egg cell, which then divides in half.
   d. two zygotes are formed from the fertilization of the same egg cell.

Think About It

■ What aspects of your personality, if any, do you believe were influenced by your genetic inheritance?

■ What methods do researchers use to disentangle the influences of heredity and environment on behavior? What are the limitations of these methods?

Recite It *answers placed at the end of chapter.*

THINKING CRITICALLY ABOUT PSYCHOLOGY

Based on your reading of this chapter, answer the following questions. Then, to evaluate your progress in developing critical thinking skills, compare your answers to the sample answers found in Appendix A.

The case of Phineas Gage is one of the best-known case studies in the annals of psychology. In 1848, as you already know, Gage suffered an accident in which a metal rod pierced his cheek and brain and penetrated the top of his head. Yet not only did he survive this horrific accident, but he also managed to pick himself up and speak

to workers who came to his aid. Though he survived his injuries, his personality changed—so much so that people would remark, "Gage is no longer Gage."

1. Why do you think Gage's injury affected his personality but not the basic life functions that the brain controls, such as breathing and heart rate?

2. How might the nature of the injury that Gage sustained explain why this once polite and courteous man became aggressive and unruly?

Recite It Answers for Chapter 2

Module 2.1 1. (a) neuron; (b) soma; (c) axon; (d) dendrites; (e) buttons; (f) neurotransmitters; (g) inhibitory, 2. (h) positive; (i) action; 3. (j) dopamine, glutamate; (k) GABA; (l) seratonin; (m) endorphins, 4. (n) Antagonists; (o) agonists **Module 2.2** 5. (a) peripheral; (b) somatic; (c) autonomic, 6. (d) central; (e) peripheral; (f) somatic; (g) autonomic, 7. (h) sympathetic; (i) parasympathetic **Module 2.3** 8. (a) hindbrain; (b) midbrain; (c) forebrain; (d) thalamus; (e) hypothalamus; (f) limbic; (g) cerebral; (h) occipital; (i) corpus callosum; (j) vision; (k) touch; (l) hearing; (m) mental **Module 2.4** 9. (a) Lesioning; (b) recording; (c) stimulation, (d) MRI **Module 2.5** 10. (a) verbal; (b) nonverbal **Module 2.6** 11. (a) endocrine; (b) gonads; (c) thyroid; (d) Testosterone; (e) PMS **Module 2.7** 12. (a) interact; 13. (b) familial; (c) twin; (d) adoptee

Neurons

Parts of the Neuron

- **Soma:** Cell body
- **Axon:** "Cable" that conducts outgoing messages or action potentials
- **Dendrites:** Rootlike projections that receive messages from neighboring neurons
- **Terminal Buttons:** Knoblike structures at the end of axons that release neurotransmitters into the synapse
- **Myelin Sheath:** Protective coating of axons

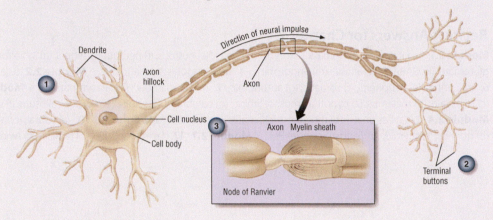

Dendrite

Axon hillock

Direction of neural impulse

Axon

Cell nucleus

Cell body

3

Axon Myelin sheath

Node of Ranvier

Terminal buttons

1

2

Transmission of Neural Impulses

- **Action Potentials:** Neural impulses or messages generated according to "all-or-none" principle
- **Neurotransmitters:** Chemical messengers that carry messages to neighboring neurons

The Nervous System

- **Central Nervous System (CNS):** The brain and spinal cord
- **Peripheral Nervous System (PNS):** The body's link to the outside world
- **Somatic Nervous System:** Part of PNS that relays sensory information from sensory organs to the CNS and motor (movement) commands from the CNS to muscles
- **Autonomic Nervous System (ANS):** Controls automatic bodily functions and processes
- **Sympathetic and Parasympathetic Divisions of ANS:** Have largely opposing effects on bodily processes

1 Central Nervous System {Brain Spinal cord}

2 Peripheral Nervous System

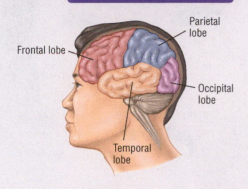

MODULES 2.3–2.5

The Brain

- **Hindbrain:** Consists of the medulla, pons, and cerebellum; involved in vital bodily functions
- **Midbrain:** Nerve pathways connecting hindbrain and forebrain; includes the reticular formation
- **Forebrain:** Includes the thalamus, the hypothalamus, other parts of the limbic system, and the cerebral cortex—the outer covering of the brain comprising four parts or lobes responsible for voluntary movement and higher mental functions
- **Methods of Studying the Brain:** Imaging techniques (EEG, CT scan, PET scan, MRI) and experimental techniques (lesioning, brain recording, electrical stimulation)
- **Brain Lateralization:** Specialization of function of the two cerebral hemispheres

MODULE 2.6

The Endocrine System

Major Endocrine Glands and Hormones

- **Pituitary:** Growth hormone, ACTH, oxytocin
- **Hypothalamus:** Releasing factors
- **Pineal Gland:** Melatonin
- **Pancreas:** Insulin
- **Thyroid:** Thyroid hormones
- **Adrenals:** Cortical steroids, epinephrine, norepinephrine
- **Ovaries in Women:** Estrogen, progesterone
- **Testes in Men:** Testosterone

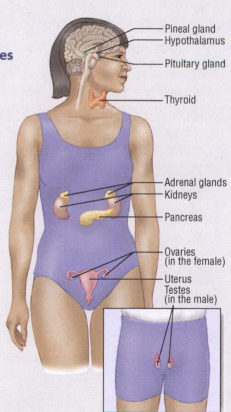

MODULE 2.7

Genes and Behavior

- **Genotype Versus Phenotype:** Genetic coding versus observable traits
- **Types of Kinship Studies:** Familial association study, twin studies, adoptee studies

LEARNING OBJECTIVES

After studying this chapter, you will be able to . . .

1 **Explain** the difference between sensation and perception.

2 **Define** the following basic terms in sensation: absolute and difference thresholds, signal detection theory, and stimulus adaptation.

3 **Identify** the parts of the eye, **describe** what happens when light enters the eye, and **explain** the roles of rods and cones.

4 **Describe** the two major theories of color vision.

5 **Explain** how the ear enables us to hear sounds.

6 **Explain** the perception of pitch and **identify** the main types and causes of deafness.

7 **Explain** how we sense odors and tastes.

8 **Identify** the various skin senses and **explain** the gate-control theory of pain.

9 **Describe** the functions of the kinesthetic and vestibular senses and **explain** how they work.

10 **Describe** the roles of attention, perceptual set, and modes of visual processing in perception.

11 **Identify** and **describe** the Gestalt principles of grouping objects into meaningful patterns or forms.

12 **Define** the concept of perceptual constancy and **apply** the concept to examples.

13 **Identify** and **describe** cues we use to judge distance and perceive movement, and **apply** these cues to examples.

14 **Identify** some common types of visual illusions and **explain** why it is the brain, not the eyes, that deceives us.

15 **Evaluate** evidence concerning the existence of subliminal perception and extrasensory perception.

tuipahn/Shutterstock.com

PREVIEW

Sensation and Perception

3

My Daughter, the Giant

One day, my infant daughter Daniella turned into a giant. Or so it seemed. I was making a video recording of her fledgling attempts to crawl. All was going well until she noticed the camera. She then started crawling toward this funny man holding the camera—me. As she approached, her image in the viewfinder grew larger and larger, eventually so large that she blotted out all other objects in my view. The image of my daughter that was cast upon my eyes was of a large and ever-growing giant! But I didn't panic. Despite the information my eyes were transmitting to my brain, I understood my daughter was not morphing into a giant. Fortunately, we tend to perceive objects to be of their actual size despite changes in the size of the image they project on our eyes as they grow nearer. Yet the sensation of seeing your infant grow to be a giant before your eyes can be an unsettling experience, especially when the "giant" then attempts to mouth the camera.

We are continually bombarded with stimuli from the outside world that impinge on our sensory organs. The world is a medley of lights and sounds that strike our eyes and ears, and of chemical substances that waft past our noses or land on our tongues as we consume food or drink liquids. In this chapter, you will see how your sense organs respond to external stimuli and transform these stimuli into sensory signals your brain uses to produce *sensations* of vision, hearing, touch, smell, and taste. You will learn how your brain assembles bits and pieces of sensory information into meaningful impressions of the world that are called *perceptions*. You will also learn how your brain senses changes in the position of your body, so you can move about without stumbling or losing your balance. Our sensory systems operate at blinding speeds, but the real marvel is how the brain processes all the information it receives from the body's sensory organs, making it possible for us not only to sense the world around us but also to make sense of it. As the example of my "giant" daughter demonstrates, sensation and perception are different processes. What we perceive may not correspond to what our eyes sense.

The study of sensation and perception is critical to psychology because our investigation of behavior and mental processes begins with input from the world around us and the way the senses and brain interpret that information. Let us proceed, first, to explore how our sensory systems operate. Then we will explore how the brain assembles the sensory information it receives to form perceptions that help us make sense of the sensations that fill our lives with the colors and sounds that form the rich tapestry of sensory experience.

Did you know that...

- Roy G. Biv is one of the most famous names psychology students learn, but he is not a real person? (p. 92)
- Wearing the color red makes you look sexier? (p. 97)
- Hearing may be our fastest sense? (p. 99)
- The bending of hair cells in the inner ear makes hearing possible, but these cells are not real hairs? (p. 100)
- Nearly one in five teens is already showing evidence of hearing loss due to years of living loudly? (p. 102)
- Exposure to bodily secretions of the opposite sex may have subtle effects on our behavior, even if we are not consciously aware of it? (p. 107)
- The mechanism that makes motion pictures possible lies in the viewer, not the projector? (p. 124)

3.1 Sensing Our World: Basic Concepts of Sensation

1 **Explain** the difference between sensation and perception.

2 **Define** the following basic terms in sensation: absolute and difference thresholds, signal detection theory, and stimulus adaptation.

CONCEPT 3.1

Sensation is the process by which physical stimuli that impinge on our sensory organs are converted into neural impulses the brain uses to create our experiences of vision, touch, hearing, taste, smell, and so on.

CONCEPT 3.2

Sensory receptors convert sources of sensory stimuli, such as light and sound, into neural impulses the brain can use to create sensations.

CONCEPT 3.3

Through the study of psychophysics, we learn how the properties of external stimuli relate to our sensations.

CONCEPT 3.4

Our sensory systems vary in the amounts of stimulation needed to detect the presence of a stimulus and the differences among stimuli.

sensation The process by which we receive, transform, and process stimuli from the outside world to create sensory experiences.

sensory receptors Specialized cells that detect sensory stimuli and convert them into neural impulses.

psychophysics The study of the relationship between features of physical stimuli, such as the intensity of light and sound, and the sensations we experience in response to these stimuli.

absolute threshold The smallest amount of a given stimulus a person can sense.

Sensation is the process by which we receive, transform, and process stimuli that impinge on our sensory organs into neural impulses, or signals, that the brain uses to create experiences of vision, hearing, taste, smell, touch, and so on.

Each of our sense organs contains specialized cells, called **sensory receptors**, that detect stimuli from the outside world, such as light, sound, and odors, and transform them into patterns of neural impulses the brain uses to create sensations of vision, hearing, and so on. We can think of the brain as a "coding machine" that processes these signals into the various sensations we experience (Max-Planck-Gesellschaft, 2011).

Sensory receptors are found throughout the body, in such organs as the eyes, ears, nose, and mouth, and in less obvious locations, such as the joints and muscles of the body and the entirety of the skin. In this module, we examine how sensory receptors respond to external stimuli and how they convert these stimuli into messages the brain uses to create the experience of sensation.

Our exploration of the process of sensation has its roots in **psychophysics**, the study of how physical sources of stimulation—light, sound, odors, and so on—relate to our experience of these stimuli in the form of sensations. Psychophysics began with the work of the nineteenth-century German scientist Gustav Theodor Fechner. Though Wilhelm Wundt is credited with establishing the first psychological laboratory in 1879, some historians believe that the publication of Fechner's *Elements of Psychophysics* in 1860 signaled the beginning of the scientific approach to psychology.

We begin our study of sensation by examining the common characteristics that relate to the functioning of our sensory systems: thresholds, signal detection, and sensory adaptation.

Absolute and Difference Thresholds: Is Something There? Is Something *Else* There?

Our sensory receptors are remarkably sensitive to certain types of stimuli. On a clear, dark night, we can detect a flickering candle 30 miles away. We can also detect about one drop of perfume spread through a small house. The **absolute threshold** is the smallest amount of a stimulus that a person can reliably detect. Table 3.1 lists absolute thresholds for the senses of vision, hearing, taste, smell, and touch.

People differ in their absolute thresholds. Some are more sensitive than others to certain kinds of sensory stimulation—for example, sounds or odors. Fechner sought to determine the absolute thresholds for various senses by presenting people with stimuli of different magnitudes, such as brighter and duller lights, and then asking them whether they could see them. According to this method, the absolute threshold is defined as the minimal level of stimulus energy that people can detect 50 percent of the time. Stimuli detected less than 50 percent of the time are

Table 3.1 Absolute Thresholds for Various Senses

Sense	Stimulus	Receptors	Threshold
Vision	Light energy	Rods and cones in the eyes	The flame from a single candle flickering about 30 miles away on a dark, clear night
Hearing	Sound waves	Hair cells in the inner ear	The ticking of a watch placed about 20 feet away from a listener in a quiet room
Taste	Chemical substances that contact the tongue	Taste buds on the tongue	About 1 teaspoon of sugar dissolved in 2 gallons of water
Smell	Chemical substances that enter the nose	Receptor cells in the upper nostrils	About one drop of perfume dispersed in a small house
Touch	Movement of, or pressure on, the skin	Nerve endings in the skin	The wing of a bee falling on the cheek from about 1 centimeter away

Source: Adapted from Galanter, 1962.

considered below the absolute threshold. Stimuli that can be detected more often are above the threshold.

The nineteenth-century German scientist Ernst Weber (1795–1878) (pronounced *Vayber*) studied the smallest differences between stimuli that people were able to perceive. The minimal difference between two stimuli that people can reliably detect is the **difference threshold,** or *just-noticeable difference (jnd)*. Just-noticeable differences apply to each of our senses.

How do difference thresholds apply to the range of stimuli we perceive with our senses? Weber summarized his findings in what is now known as **Weber's law.** According to this law, the amount you must change a stimulus to detect a difference is given by a constant fraction or proportion (called a *constant*) of the original stimulus. For example, Weber's constant for noticing a difference in weights is about 1/50 (or 2 percent). This means that if you were lifting a 50-pound weight, you would probably not notice a difference unless the weight were increased or reduced by about 2 percent (or 1 pound). But if you were lifting a 200-pound weight, the weight would have to be increased by about 4 pounds (2 percent) for you to notice the difference. Though the absolute weight needed to detect a difference is about quadruple as you increase the initial weight from 50 pounds to 200, the fraction remains the same (1/50).

Weber found that the difference threshold differed for each of the senses. People are noticeably more sensitive to changes in the pitch of a sound than to changes in volume. They will perceive the difference if you raise or lower the pitch of your voice by about one-third of 1 percent (1/333). Yet they will not perceive a difference in the loudness of a sound unless the sound is made louder or softer by about 10 percent. Table 3.2 lists Weber's constants for various senses.

Weber's constants have practical applications. If you're going to sing, you had better be right on pitch (hit the note precisely) or people are going to groan. However, if you raise the volume on your music system just a little, your next-door neighbor might not notice any difference. Then, too, if your neighbor is complaining about the loudness, lowering the volume of the music by a notch may not be noticeable.

CONCEPT 3.5
The ability to detect a stimulus depends not only on the stimulus itself, but also on the perceiver and the level of background stimulation.

© serhio/Shutterstock.com

difference threshold The minimal difference in the magnitude of energy needed for people to detect a difference between two stimuli.

Weber's law The principle that the amount of change in a stimulus needed to detect a difference is given by a constant ratio or fraction, called a constant, of the original stimulus.

Table 3.2 Examples of Weber's Constants

Sensation	Weber's Constant (Approximate)
Saltiness of food	1/5
Pressure on skin	1/7
Loudness of sounds	1/10
Odor	1/20
Heaviness of weights	1/50
Brightness of lights	1/60
Pitch of sounds	1/333

CONCEPT 3.6
Through the process of sensory adaptation, our sensory systems deal with repeated exposure to the same stimuli by becoming less sensitive to them.

signal-detection theory The belief that the detection of a stimulus depends on factors involving the intensity of the stimulus, the level of background stimulation, and the biological and psychological characteristics of the perceiver.

sensory adaptation The process by which sensory receptors adapt to constant stimuli by becoming less sensitive to them.

Signal Detection: More Than a Matter of Energy

Scientists who study psychophysics describe sounds, flashes of light, and other stimuli as *signals*. According to **signal-detection theory**, the threshold for detecting a signal depends not only on the properties of the stimulus itself, such as its intensity—the loudness of a sound, for example—but also on the level of background stimulation, or noise, and, importantly, on the biological and psychological characteristics of the perceiver. The sensitivity or degree of sharpness of an individual's sensory systems (for example, the acuity of your eyesight or hearing) partially determines whether a signal is detected. The organism's physical condition also plays a role. For instance, your sense of smell is duller when you have a cold and your nose is stuffed. Levels of fatigue or alertness also contribute to signal detection.

Psychological factors, including attention levels and states of motivation like hunger, also play important roles in signal detection. As you are walking down a darkened street by yourself late at night, you may be especially attentive to even the slightest sounds because they may signal danger. You may fail to notice the same sounds as you walk along the same street in broad daylight. If you haven't eaten for a while, you may be more likely to notice aromas of food wafting from a nearby kitchen than if you had just consumed a hearty meal.

Sensory Adaptation: Turning the Volume Down

Through the process of **sensory adaptation**, sensory systems become *less* sensitive to constant or unchanging stimuli. When you are wearing a new wristwatch or ring, you may at first be aware of the sensation of pressure your skin, but after a while you no longer notice it. We may be thankful for sensory adaptation when, after a few minutes of exposure, the water in a crisp mountain lake seems warmer or the odors in a locker room become less noticeable. However, sensory adaptation may not occur when we are repeatedly exposed to certain strong stimuli, such as the loud wail of a car alarm. In such cases, our sensory systems show no change in sensitivity to the stimulus. Concept Chart 3.1 reviews the basic concepts in sensation.

Concept Chart 3.1	Basic Concepts in Sensation
Sensation	The process of transforming stimuli that impinge on our sense organs into neural signals that the brain processes to create sensations of vision, touch, sound, taste, smell, and so on
Absolute threshold	The smallest amount of a stimulus that a person can reliably detect
Difference threshold	The minimal difference between two stimuli that people can reliably detect; also called *just-noticeable difference*
Weber's law	The amount of change in a stimulus needed to detect a difference, expressed as a constant ratio or fraction of the original stimulus
Signal-detection theory	The belief that the ability to detect a signal varies with the characteristics of the perceiver, the background, and the stimulus itself
Sensory adaptation	The process by which sensory systems adapt to constant stimuli by becoming less sensitive to them

MODULE REVIEW   **3.1** Sensing Our World: Basic Concepts of Sensation

Recite It

1. **Explain** the difference between sensation and perception.

   (a) _____ is the process of taking information from the world, transforming it into neural impulses, and transmitting these signals to the brain, where they are processed to produce experiences of vision, hearing, smell, taste, touch, and so on. (b) _____ is the process that makes sense of this sensory data, transforming sensory stimuli into (c) _____ impressions of the world.

2. **Define** the following basic terms in sensation: absolute and difference thresholds, signal detection theory, and stimulus adaptation.

An (d) _____ threshold is the smallest amount of a stimulus that a person can sense. A (e) _____ threshold, or just-noticeable difference (jnd), is the minimal difference in magnitude of energy needed for people to detect a difference between two stimuli. Signal (f) _____ accounts for factors that enable us to recognize that a signal is present. Stimulus (g) _____ is the process by which our sensory systems become less sensitive over time to constant or unchanging stimuli.

Recall It

1. Specialized cells in the sense organs, which are geared to detect stimuli in the external environment, are called

   a. feature detectors.   c. sensory receptors.
   b. threshold detectors.   d. signal detectors.

2. The smallest amount of stimulation that a person can reliably detect is called a(n)

   a. minimal sensory field   c. just-noticeable difference.
   b. absolute threshold.   d. vector of constants.

3. Jill notices a humming sound made by an air conditioner when she first enters a room, but within a few minutes she is no longer aware of the sound. What sensory process does this illustrate?

Think About It

■ You've probably noticed that when you draw a bath, it seems hotter at first than it does a minute or two later. Based on your reading of the text, explain this phenomenon.

■ Let's say you're using a recipe that calls for 15 grams of salt. According to Weber's constant for saltiness, which is 1/5, how much more salt must you add to make the recipe noticeably saltier?

Recite It answers placed at the end of chapter.

MODULE   **3.2** **Vision: Seeing the Light**

3 **Identify** the parts of the eye, **describe** what happens when light enters the eye, and **explain** the roles of rods and cones.

4 **Describe** the two major theories of color vision.

Vision is the process by which light energy is converted into signals (neural impulses) that the brain interprets to produce the experience of sight. Our sense of vision allows us to receive visual information from a mere few inches away, as when we read from a book held close to our eyes, to many billions of miles away, as when we observe twinkling stars on a clear night. To understand vision, we first need to consider the source of physical energy that gives rise to vision: light.

CONCEPT 3.7
Vision is the process by which light energy is converted into neural impulses that the brain interprets to produce the experience of sight.

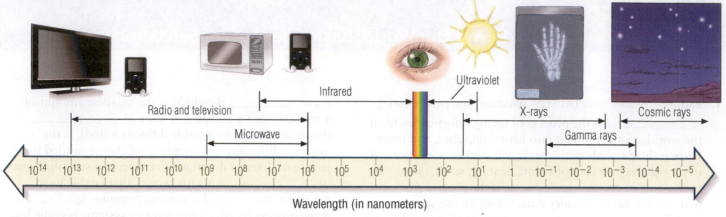

FIGURE 3.1 **The Electromagnetic Spectrum**
Visible light (represented by color bands) occupies only a small portion of the range of electromagnetic radiation that is called the electromagnetic spectrum.

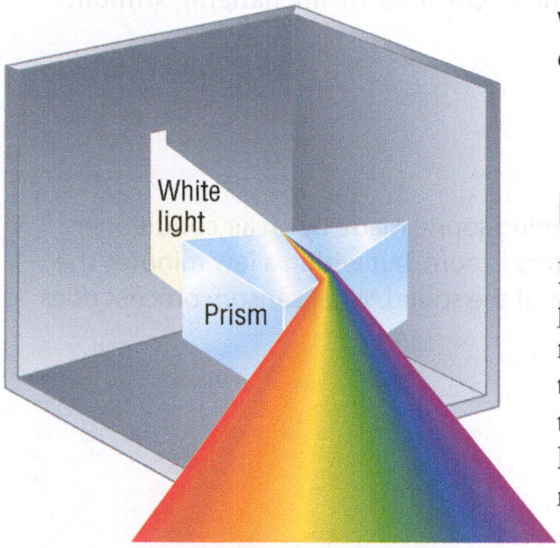

FIGURE 3.2 **The Color Spectrum**
A prism separates white light into the various hues that make up the part of the electromagnetic spectrum that is visible to humans.

Light: The Energy of Vision

Light is physical energy in the form of electromagnetic radiation (electrically charged particles). X-rays, ultraviolet waves, and radio waves are other forms of electromagnetic energy. Visible light is the portion of the spectrum of electromagnetic radiation that gives rise to our sense of vision. As you can see in ■ Figure 3.1, the visible spectrum occupies only a small portion of the full spectrum of electromagnetic radiation. It consists of the wavelengths from approximately 300 to 750 nanometers (a nanometer is one billionth of a meter).

Different wavelengths within the visible spectrum give rise to the experience of different colors (see ■ Figure 3.2). Violet has the shortest wavelength (about 400 billionths of a meter long), and red has the longest (about 700 billionths of a meter long). Psychology students are often told that they can remember the order of the colors of the spectrum by thinking of the name Roy G. Biv (standing for red, orange, yellow, green, blue, indigo, and violet).

The Eye: The Visionary Sensory Organ

The eye is the organ with receptor cells that respond to light. Light enters the eye through the **cornea**, a transparent covering on the eye's surface (see ■ Figure 3.3). A muscle called the **iris** contracts or expands to determine the amount of light that enters. The iris is colored, most often brown or blue, and gives the eye its color. The **pupil** of the eye is the black opening inside the iris. The iris increases or decreases the size of the pupil reflexively to adjust to the amount of light entering the eye. The brighter the light, the smaller the iris makes the pupil. Under darkened conditions, the iris opens to allow more light to enter the pupil so that we can see more clearly. Because these are reflex actions, they happen automatically (you don't have to think about them). The pupil is also tied into processes of attention. Your pupils expand when you focus attention on an object, which may help you to explore it more closely (Laeng, Sirois, & Gredeback, 2012).

The light enters the eye through the cornea and then passes through the pupil and **lens**. Through a process called **accommodation**, the lens changes its shape to adjust for the distance of the object, which helps focus the visual image on the inner surface of the eye called the **retina**. Like film in a camera, the retina receives the image as light strikes it. The retina contains light-sensitive receptor cells, called **photoreceptors**, that

CONCEPT 3.8
Light, a form of physical energy, is the stimulus to which receptors in the eyes respond, giving rise to our sense of vision.

CONCEPT 3.9
When energy in the form of light comes into contact with the photoreceptor cells in the retina, it is converted into neural signals that are transmitted to the brain.

CONCEPT 3.10
Rods, which are more sensitive to light than are cones, are responsible for peripheral vision and vision in dim light, whereas cones allow us to detect colors and to discern fine details of objects under bright illumination.

cornea A transparent covering on the eye's surface through which light enters.

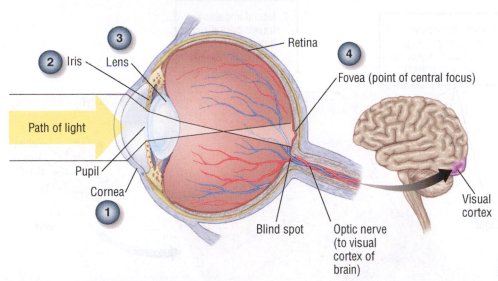

FIGURE 3.3 Parts of the Eye
① Light enters the eye through the cornea. ② The iris adjusts reflexively to control the size of the pupil. ③ The lens focuses the light on the retina, especially on the ④ fovea, the point of central focus that gives rise to clearest vision.

iris The pigmented, circular muscle in the eye that regulates the size of the pupil to adjust to changes in the level of illumination.

pupil The black opening inside the iris that allows light to enter the eye.

lens The structure in the eye that focuses light rays on the retina.

accommodation In perception, the process by which the lens changes its shape to focus images more clearly on the retina.

retina The light-sensitive layer of the inner surface of the eye that contains photoreceptor cells.

photoreceptors Light-sensitive cells (rods and cones) in the eye upon which light registers.

rods Photoreceptors that are sensitive only to the intensity of light (light and dark).

cones Photoreceptors that are sensitive to color.

bipolar cells A layer of interconnecting cells in the eye that connect photoreceptors to ganglion cells.

convert light energy into neural signals the brain uses to create visual sensations (Sejnowski & Delbruck, 2012).

When light hits the retina, it comes into contact with these photoreceptors that lie along the retina. There are two types of photoreceptors, called **rods** and **cones** because of their respective shapes (see ■ Figure 3.4). The eye has about 120 million rods and 6 million cones.

Have you ever noticed that when lighting is dim, you tend to make out the shapes of objects but not their colors? That's because cones are responsible for color vision but are less sensitive to light than rods are. Rods allow us to detect objects in low light. They are sensitive only to the intensity or brightness of light. They are also responsible for *peripheral vision*—the ability to detect objects, especially moving objects, at the edges (sides, as well as the top and bottom) of our visual field. Cones allow us to detect colors, as well as to discern fine details of objects in bright light. Some animals, including certain birds, have only cones in their eyes (Gaulin & McBurney, 2001). They can see only during daylight hours when the cones are activated. Because they become totally blind at night, they must return to their roosts as evening approaches.

The neural signals produced by the rods and cones pass back through a layer of interconnecting cells called **bipolar cells** and then through a layer of neurons called **ganglion cells** (see ■ Figure 3.5). The axon projecting from each ganglion cell makes up one nerve fiber in the **optic nerve**. The optic nerve, which consists of a million or so ganglion axons, transmits visual information to the brain. In the brain, this information is routed to the thalamus, a major relay station, and from there to the visual cortex. The visual cortex lies in the occipital lobes, the part of the cerebral cortex that processes visual information and produces the experience of vision.

The part of the retina where the optic nerve leaves the eye is the **blind spot,** a hole in the retina that contains no photoreceptors (rods or cones) (see ■ Figure 3.6). Thus, we cannot see images cast upon the blind spot (Miller et al., 2015).

Ralph C. Eagle Jr./Science Source

FIGURE 3.4 Rods and Cones
This close-up image of a portion of the retina shows cones (large reddish cone-like objects on the left side of the photograph) and rods (more numerous rod-like shaped objects).

ganglion cells Nerve cells in the back of the eye that transmit neural impulses in response to light stimulation, the axons of which make up the optic nerve.

optic nerve The nerve that carries neural impulses generated by light stimulation from the eye to the brain.

blind spot The area in the retina where the optic nerve leaves the eye and that contains no photoreceptor cells.

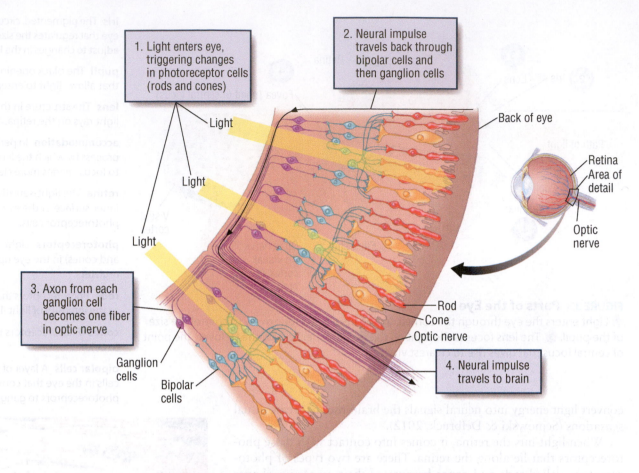

1. Light enters eye, triggering changes in photoreceptor cells (rods and cones)

2. Neural impulse travels back through bipolar cells and then ganglion cells

Light

Light

Light

3. Axon from each ganglion cell becomes one fiber in optic nerve

Ganglion cells

Bipolar cells

Back of eye

Retina

Area of detail

Optic nerve

Rod

Cone

Optic nerve

4. Neural impulse travels to brain

FIGURE 3.5 Conversion of Light into Neural Impulses
Light is converted into neural impulses that the brain uses to produce the sensation of vision.

By contrast, the **fovea** is the part of the retina that corresponds to the center of our gaze and that gives rise to our sharpest vision (see Figure 3.3). It contains only cones. Focusing our eyes on an object brings its image to bear directly on the fovea.

FIGURE 3.6 Blind Spot
Because there are no receptor cells in the blind spot—no rods or cones—images formed on the blind spot cannot be seen. You can demonstrate this for yourself by closing your left eye and, while focusing on the dot, slowly move the book farther away to about a distance of a foot. You'll notice there is a point at which the stack of money disappears. We are not typically aware of our blind spots because our eyes are constantly moving and because they work together to compensate for any loss of vision when an image falls on the blind spot.

fovea The area near the center of the retina that contains only cones and that is the center of focus for clearest vision.

Farther away from the fovea, the proportion of cones decreases while the proportion of rods increases. Rods show the opposite pattern. They are few and far between close to the fovea and more densely packed farther away from the fovea. The far ends of the retina contain only rods (see Try This Out).

Visual acuity, or sharpness of vision, is the ability to discern visual details. Many of us have impaired visual acuity. People who need to be unusually close to objects to discern their details are *nearsighted*. People who need to be unusually far away from objects to see them clearly are *farsighted*. Nearsightedness and farsightedness result from abnormalities in the shape of the eye. Nearsightedness can occur when the eyeball is too long or the cornea is too curved. In either case, distant objects are focused in front of the retina. Farsightedness can occur when the eyeball is too short so that light from nearby objects is focused behind the retina. People with nearsightedness or farsightedness can correct their vision by wearing eyeglasses or contact lenses.

Feature Detectors: Getting Down to Basics

In 1981, David Hubel and Torsten Wiesel received a Nobel Prize for unraveling a small piece of the puzzle of how we transform sensory information into rich visual experiences of the world around us. They discovered that the visual cortex contains nerve cells that respond only when an animal (in their studies, a cat) is shown a line with a particular orientation—horizontal, vertical, or diagonal (Hubel, 1988; Hubel & Wiesel, 1979). Some of these nerve cells respond only to lines that form right angles; others, to dots of light that move from right to left across the visual field; and yet others, to dots of light that move from left to right. Hubel and Wiesel made their discoveries by implanting a tiny electrode in individual cells in the cat's visual cortex. They then flashed different visual stimuli on a screen within the cat's field of vision and observed which cells fired in response to which types of stimuli. Neurons that respond to specific features of the visual stimulus are called **feature detectors**.

We do not see a world composed of scattered bits and pieces of sensory data, of lines, angles, and moving points of light. Somehow the visual cortex compiles information from various cells, combining them to form meaningful patterns. How do we go from recognizing specific features of a stimulus—its individual angles, lines, and edges—to discerning a meaningful pattern, such as letters, numbers, words, or the human face? Scientists believe that complex assemblages of neurons in the brain work together to analyze relationships among specific features of objects.

Hubel and Wiesel opened a door to understanding the beginning steps in this process at the level of the individual feature detector. Yet we are still a long way from understanding how the brain transforms sensory stimulation into the rich visual world we experience. We do know that the visual cortex is fast, very fast, in processing visual stimuli. It can recognize objects by sight, such as detecting that an object is an animal, in a mere 10th of a second, well before other parts of the brain figure out exactly what the object is (Perrinet & Bednar, 2015). This extraordinary speed of visual processing may have helped ancestral humans survive in a harsh environment by enabling them to nearly instantly detect the presence of an animal at a distance, an animal that might be a lurking predator.

Color Vision: Sensing a Colorful World

To be able to perceive different colors, color receptors in the retina of the eye must transmit different messages to the brain when visible lights having different wavelengths stimulate them. How are these messages transmitted? Two nineteenth-century

Try This Out
Reading Sideways

Hold a book or magazine to the side and try reading it. Did you notice that the words were blurry, if you could make them out at all? How does the distribution of rods and cones in the retina explain this phenomenon?

CONCEPT 3.11
Objects are seen most clearly when their images are focused on the fovea, a part of the retina that contains only cones.

CONCEPT 3.12
The brain's visual cortex contains cells so specialized that they fire only when they detect precise angles, lines, or points of light.

feature detectors Specialized neurons in the visual cortex that respond only to particular features of visual stimuli, such as horizontal or vertical lines.

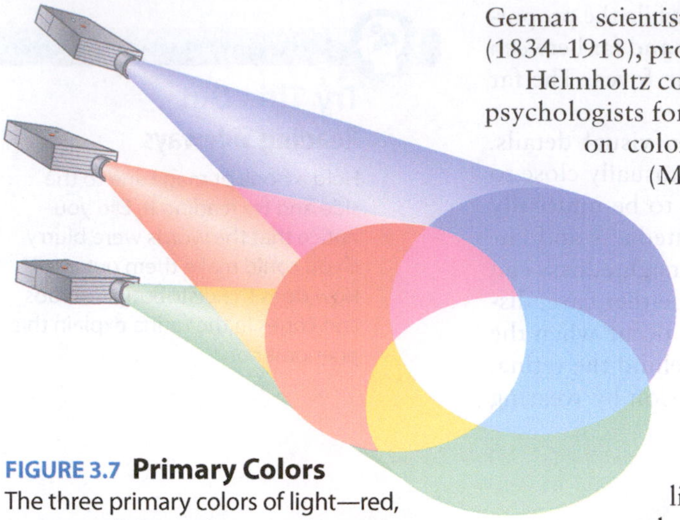

German scientists, Hermann von Helmholtz (1821–1894) and Ewald Hering (1834–1918), proposed different answers to this question.

Helmholtz contributed to many fields of science, but is perhaps best known to psychologists for his work on color vision. He was impressed by the earlier work on color vision by the English scientist Thomas Young (1773–1829) (Martindale, 2001). Young had reversed the process by which a prism breaks light down into component colors. He shone overlapping lights of red, green, and blue-violet onto a screen and found that he could create light of any color on the spectrum by varying the brightness of the lights (see ■ Figure 3.7). Where all three lights overlapped, there was white light—the color of sunlight.

Building on Young's work, Helmholtz proposed what is now known as the Young-Helmholtz theory, or **trichromatic theory** (from Greek roots meaning "three" and "color"). Helmholtz believed that Young's experimental results showed that the eyes have three types of color receptors—red, green, and blue-violet. We now call these color receptors *cones*. These three types of cones have differing sensitivities to different wavelengths of light. Blue-violet cones are most sensitive to short wavelengths; green cones, to middle wavelengths; and red cones, to long wavelengths. According to the trichromatic theory, the response pattern of these three types of cones allows us to see different colors. So when green cones are most strongly activated, we see green. But when a combination of different types of cones is activated, we see other colors, just as mixing paint of different colors produces yet other colors. For example, when red and green receptors are stimulated at the same time, we see yellow.

Hering developed a different theory of color vision based on his work with *afterimages*. An **afterimage** is what you see if you gaze at a visual stimulus for a while and then look at a neutral surface, such as a sheet of white paper.

Pause for a demonstration. The flag in ■ Figure 3.8 has all the shapes in the American flag, but the colors are off. Instead of being red, white, and blue, this flag is green, black, and yellow. Now, although you may not particularly wish to defend this oddly colored flag, gaze at it for a minute. (Time yourself; give yourself a full minute.) Then shift your gaze to a white sheet of paper. You are likely to see a more familiar flag; this is because red is the afterimage of green, white is the afterimage of black, and blue is the afterimage of yellow.

Hering's work with afterimages led him to develop the **opponent-process theory** of color vision. Opponent-process theory, like trichromatic theory, suggests that the eyes have three types of color receptors. According to this theory, however, each type of receptor consists of a pair of opposing receptors. Rather than there being separate receptors for red, green, and blue-violet, some receptors are sensitive to red or green; others, to blue or yellow; and others, to black or white. The black-white receptors detect brightness or shades of gray; the red-green and blue-yellow pairs detect differences in colors.

Hering believed that color vision arises from pairs of opposing processes. According to his theory, red-green receptors do not simultaneously transmit messages for red and green. Rather, they transmit messages for either one or the other. When the red cone is activated, the green one is blocked, or inhibited, and so we see red. Yet prolonged transmission of any one message, such as red or green, disturbs the balance of neural activity, making it more difficult to inhibit the opposing color receptor. Thus, according to Hering's theory, if you stare at the green, black, and yellow flag in Figure 3.8 for a minute or so, you will disturb the balance of neural activity, producing an *opponent process*. The afterimage of red, white, and blue you experience represents the eye's attempt to reestablish a balance between the two opposing receptors.

FIGURE 3.7 Primary Colors
The three primary colors of light—red, green, and blue-violet—combine to form white. Thomas Young showed that you could create any color of light by mixing these component colors and varying their brightnesses. For example, a combination of red and green light creates yellow.

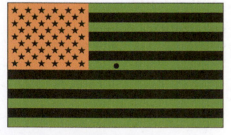

FIGURE 3.8 Afterimages
The colors in the American flag shown here can be set right by performing a simple experiment. Stare at the dot in the center of the flag for about 60 seconds. Then quickly shift your gaze to a white wall or white sheet of paper. You will then see the more familiar colors of the American flag as afterimages.

trichromatic theory A theory of color vision that posits that the ability to see different colors depends on the relative activity of three types of color receptors in the eye (red, green, and blue-violet).

afterimage The visual image of a stimulus that remains after the stimulus is removed.

opponent-process theory A theory of color vision that holds that the experience of color results from opposing processes involving two sets of color receptors, red-green receptors and blue-yellow receptors, and that another set of opposing receptors, black-white, is responsible for detecting differences in brightness.

Which model of color vision has it right—the trichromatic model or the opponent-process model? Contemporary research shows that both theories are right to a certain extent (Hergenhahn, 2009; Jacobs & Nathans, 2009). The trichromatic theory is correct at the receptor level, because the photochemistry of cones responds in the way described by trichromatic theory—some are sensitive to red light; others, to green light; and still others, to blue-violet light. But Hering's opponent-process theory is correct in terms of the behavior of cells that lie between the cones and the occipital lobe of the cerebral cortex—including bipolar and ganglion cells. These cells operate in an opponent-process fashion. Some are turned on by red light but are prevented (inhibited) from firing by green light. Others are turned on by green light but are inhibited by red light. Most authorities today believe that color vision includes elements of both trichromatic and opponent-process theories.

Trichromats are people with normal color vision who can discern all the colors of the visible spectrum—red, green, and blue-violet—as well as colors formed by various combinations of these hues.

Psychologists have begun to look at how colors affect judgments people make about us (Elliot & Maier, 2014). Investigators find that women tend to rate men as more attractive and sexually desirable when the men are shown wearing a red shirt than a shirt of a different color (Elliot et al., 2010). Women in red also tend to be judged by men as more sexually attractive and receptive (Pazda & Elliot, 2012; Pazda, Elliot, & Greitemeyer, 2012). There may be an evolutionary basis to this "look hot in red" effect. In nonhuman primates, displays of reddened genitalia serve as signals of sexual receptivity.

Related research shows that the color red may be used as a sexual signal. In a study in which women were led to expect they would be talking to an attractive man, they were more likely to choose to wear a red shirt for the occasion (Elliot, Greitemeyer, & Pazda, 2012).

Total color blindness is very rare, affecting about one out of every 40,000 people. These individuals are classified as **monochromats** because they see only in black and white, with the world appearing to them as though they were watching an old black-and-white movie or TV show. Because of a genetic defect, they have only one type of cone, so their brains cannot discern differences in wavelengths of light that give rise to perception of color. They detect only brightness, so objects appear in shades of gray. Much more common are **dichromats**—people who lack one of the three types of color receptors or cones, making it difficult for them to distinguish between certain colors. About 8 percent of men and about 1 percent of women have some form of color blindness (Bennett, 2009). The most common form is red-green color blindness, a genetic defect that makes it difficult to tell red from green (Martin, 2015). Much less common is blue-yellow color blindness, in which the person has difficulty distinguishing blues from yellows. ■ Figure 3.9 shows a plate from a test commonly used to assess color blindness.

People with red-green color blindness might put on one green sock and one red sock, as long as they were similar in brightness. But they would not confuse green with blue. Red-green color blindness appears to be a sex-linked genetic defect that is carried on the X sex chromosome. As noted, more males than females are affected by this condition. Because males have only one X chromosome whereas females have two, a defect on one X chromosome is more likely to be expressed in males than in females (Jacobs & Nathans, 2009). Concept Chart 3.2 provides an overview of vision.

Sexy? Or maybe it's just the shirt he's wearing.

CONCEPT 3.13

The major theories of color, trichromatic theory and opponent-process theory, may each partially account for color vision.

CONCEPT 3.14

The most common form of color blindness is red-green color blindness, in which people cannot tell reds from greens.

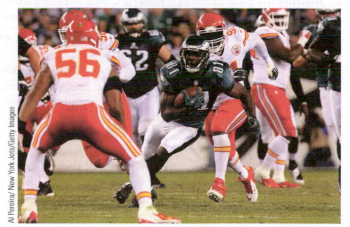

In a televised football game in which players on opposing teams wear red or green uniforms, color-blind viewers may not be able to tell which players are on which team as all the colors may appear the same.

trichromats People with normal color vision who can discern all the colors of the visual spectrum.

monochromats People who have no color vision and can see only in black and white.

dichromats People who can see some colors but not others.

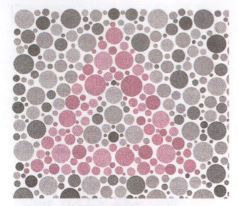

FIGURE 3.9 Color Blindness
What do you see? People with normal color vision will see the triangle in this array of dots. People with red-green color blindness will not perceive it.

Concept Chart 3.2	Vision
Source of Sensory Information	**Visible Light**
Receptor organs	The eyes. Light enters through the cornea and pupil and is focused on the retina.
Receptor cells	The retina has two kinds of photoreceptors. Rods are sensitive to the intensity of light, which is the basis of our sense of light and dark. Cones are sensitive to differences in the wavelengths of light, which is the basis of color vision. Visual information is transmitted to the brain by means of the optic nerve.
Color vision	Two major theories of color vision have been proposed, the trichromatic theory and the opponent-process theory. Each theory appears to account for some aspects of color vision.

MODULE REVIEW   3.2   Vision: Seeing the Light

Recite It

3. **Identify** the parts of the eye, **describe** what happens when light enters the eye, and **explain** the roles of rods and cones.

Light enters the eye through the (a) _____ and passes through the (b) _____ and then the (c) _____, which focuses the image on the retina. Light then stimulates photoreceptor cells, called (d) _____ and cones, which convert light energy into neural impulses carried first through (e) _____ cells and then ganglion cells that terminate in the (f) _____ nerve.
When we focus on an object, we bring its image to bear on the (g) _____, the cone-rich part of the retina in which we have our sharpest vision. (h) _____ allow us to see colors but are less sensitive to light than are rods.

Rods allow us to see objects in black and white in dim light; they are also responsible for (i) _____ vision.

4. **Describe** the two major theories of color vision.

The (j) _____ theory, or Young-Helmholtz theory, proposes that there are three kinds of color receptors (red, green, and blue-violet) and that all the colors in the spectrum can be generated by the simultaneous stimulation of a combination of these color receptors.
The (k) _____-_____ theory developed by Ewald Hering proposes that there are three pairs of receptors (red-green, blue-yellow, black-white) and that opposing processes within each pair determine our experience of color.

Recall It

1. Which of the following statements is true? Rods

   a. are most heavily concentrated around the fovea.
   b. are primarily responsible for color vision.
   c. allow us to discern fine details of objects under high illumination.
   d. are more sensitive to light than cones.

2. The photoreceptors in the retina that are responsible for peripheral vision and vision in dim light are called _____; those responsible for color vision and for discerning fine details in bright light are called _____.

3. In which lobe do we find the visual cortex?

4. Match the following parts of the eye with their respective functions: (a) iris; (b) pupil; (c) lens; (d) retina; (e) fovea; (f) blind spot.

   i. part of the eye that focuses the visual image on the retina
   ii. inner surface of the eye in which the photoreceptors are found
   iii. part of the retina from which the optic nerve leaves the eye
   iv. muscle controlling the size of the pupil
   v. area on the retina responsible for clearest vision
   vi. opening through which light enters the eye

Think About It

- Explain the phenomenon of afterimages by drawing upon Hering's opponent-process theory of color vision.

- Are you color blind? Do you know anyone who is? How has it affected your (his or her) life, if at all?

Recite It answers placed at the end of chapter.

3.3 Hearing: The Music of Sound

5 **Explain** how the ear enables us to hear sounds.

6 **Explain** the perception of pitch and **identify** the main types and causes of deafness.

The chattering of birds, the voices of children, the stirring melodies of Tchaikovsky—we sense all these sounds by means of hearing, or **audition**. We hear by sensing sound waves, which result from changes in the pressure of air or water. When sound waves impinge upon the ear, they cause parts of the ear to vibrate. These vibrations are then converted into electrical signals that are sent to the brain. We might think the human ear hears melodic tones or blaring car horns, but what it really senses are changes in pressure of molecules (Horowitz, 2012). It's the brain that converts these signals into recognizable sounds.

CONCEPT 3.15

Sound vibrations are the stimuli transformed by receptors in the ears into signals the brain uses to let you experience the sounds of the world around you.

Sound: Sensing Waves of Vibration

Like visible light, sound is a form of energy that travels in waves. Yet although light can travel through the empty reaches of outer space, sound exists only in a medium, such as air, liquids, gases, or even solids (which is why you may hear your neighbor's stereo through a solid wall). A vibrating object causes molecules of air (or other substances, such as water) to vibrate. For example, your voice is produced when your vocal cords vibrate. The resulting vibrations spread outward from the source in the form of sound waves that are characterized by such physical properties as *amplitude* (the height of the wave, which is a measure of the amount of energy in the sound wave) and *frequency* (the number of complete waves, or cycles, per second) (see ■ Figure 3.10).

The amplitude of sound waves determines their perceived loudness and is measured in *decibels* (dB). For each 10-decibel increase, loudness of sound increases tenfold. Thus, a sound of 20 decibels is actually 10 times louder than a sound of 10 decibels, not two times louder.

Light travels at 186,000 miles per second. Sound is a slowpoke by comparison. Sound travels through air at only about 1,130 feet per second (or 770 miles per *hour*). Therefore, it may take about 5 seconds for the thunder from lightning a mile away to reach your ears. But most of the sounds that matter to us—the voice of a teacher or a lover, the screeches and whines of cars and buses, and the sounds of music—are so close that they seem to reach us in no time at all. Within the human body, it is the sense of hearing that wins the race. Hearing appears to be our fastest sense, taking

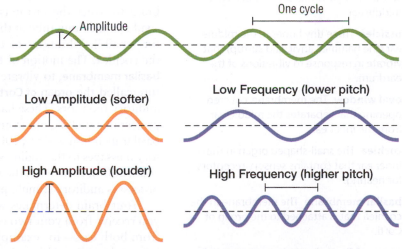

FIGURE 3.10 Sound Waves
Sound waves vary in such physical properties as amplitude, or height of the wave, and frequency, or number of complete cycles per second. Differences in amplitude give rise to perceptions of loudness, whereas differences in frequency lead to perceptions of pitch.

audition The sense of hearing.

only about 0.05 seconds for the brain to process an auditory signal, as compared to upwards of 0.25 seconds for processing visual images (Horowitz, 2012).

Why the need for speed? One explanation, based on evolutionary theory, posits that early humans were equipped to respond very quickly to certain sounds, such as the snapping of a twig at night, that might have signaled the stealthy approach of a lurking predator they couldn't see with their eyes (Horowitz, 2012).

Although sound travels more slowly than light, the vibrations that give rise to sound still occur many times a second. Deep within the cochlea of the inner ear, hair cells respond to sounds of different frequencies, providing signals the brain uses to produce the sensation of **pitch**, or how high or low a sound seems (Mann et al., 2014; Thiede et al., 2014).

The human ear senses sound waves that vary in frequency from about 20 to perhaps 20,000 cycles per second. Sound waves that are higher in frequency are perceived as being higher in pitch. Women's voices are usually higher than men's because their vocal cords tend to be shorter and thus vibrate more rapidly (at a greater frequency). The shorter strings on a harp (or in a piano) produce higher notes than the longer strings because they vibrate more rapidly.

The Ear: A Sound Machine

The ear is structured to capture sound waves, reverberate with them, and convert them into messages or electrical signals the brain can interpret (see ■ Figure 3.11) (Ashmore, 2004). Here's how it works: The outer ear funnels sound waves to the **eardrum**, a tight membrane that vibrates in response to them. The vibrations are then transmitted through three tiny bones in the middle ear called the **ossicles** (literally "little bones"). The first of these to vibrate, the "hammer" (*malleus*), is connected to the eardrum. It strikes the "anvil" (*incus*), which in turn strikes the "stirrup" (*stapes*), causing it to vibrate. The vibration is transmitted from the stirrup to the **oval window**, a membrane to which the stirrup is attached. The oval window connects the middle ear to a snail-shaped bony tube in the inner ear, called the **cochlea** (*cochlea* is the Greek word for "snail"). Vibrations of the oval window cause waves of motion in fluid within the cochlea. The motion of this fluid causes a structure within the cochlea, called the **basilar membrane**, to vibrate. The basilar membrane is attached to a gelatinous structure called the **organ of Corti**, which is lined with 15,000 or so **hair cells** that act as auditory receptors. These hair cells are not real hairs, but cells with 100 or so hairlike projections sticking out from their surfaces that bend in response to movements of the basilar membrane (Kros, 2005). These movements in turn trigger transmission of auditory messages to the auditory cortex in the brain by way of the **auditory nerve** (Gubbels et al., 2008). Located in the temporal lobes of the cerebral cortex, the auditory cortex processes auditory stimuli, producing the experience of sound (Voisin et al., 2006).

Your brain determines where a sound is coming from by comparing the sounds you receive from your two ears. Unless sounds originate from sources equally distant from both ears—for example, exactly in front of or above you—they reach one ear before the other. Although you might not be able to say exactly how much sooner you hear a sound in one ear than in the other, your brain can detect a difference as small as one ten-thousandth of a second. It uses such information to help locate the source of a sound. More distant sounds tend to be softer (just as more distant objects look smaller), which provides yet another cue for locating sounds.

Perception of Pitch: Perceiving the Highs and Lows

How do people distinguish whether one sound is higher or lower in pitch than another? As with perception of color, more than one theory is needed to help us understand how we perceive pitch. Two theories, *place theory* and *frequency theory,* help

---

CONCEPT 3.16

Sound waves cause parts of the ear to vibrate; this mechanical vibration in turn affects sensory receptors in the inner ear, called hair cells, triggering the transmission of auditory messages to the brain.

pitch The highness or lowness of a sound that corresponds to the frequency of the sound wave.

eardrum A sheet of connective tissue separating the outer ear from the middle ear that vibrates in response to auditory stimuli and transmits sound waves to the middle ear.

ossicles Three tiny bones in the middle ear (the hammer, anvil, and stirrup) that vibrate in response to vibrations of the eardrum.

oval window The membrane-covered opening that separates the middle ear from the inner ear.

cochlea The snail-shaped organ in the inner ear that contains sensory receptors for hearing.

basilar membrane The membrane in the cochlea that is attached to the organ of Corti.

organ of Corti A gelatinous structure in the cochlea containing the hair cells that serve as auditory receptors.

hair cells The auditory receptors that transform vibrations caused by sound waves into neural impulses that are then transmitted to the brain via the auditory nerve.

auditory nerve The nerve that carries neural impulses from the ear to the brain, which gives rise to the experience of hearing.

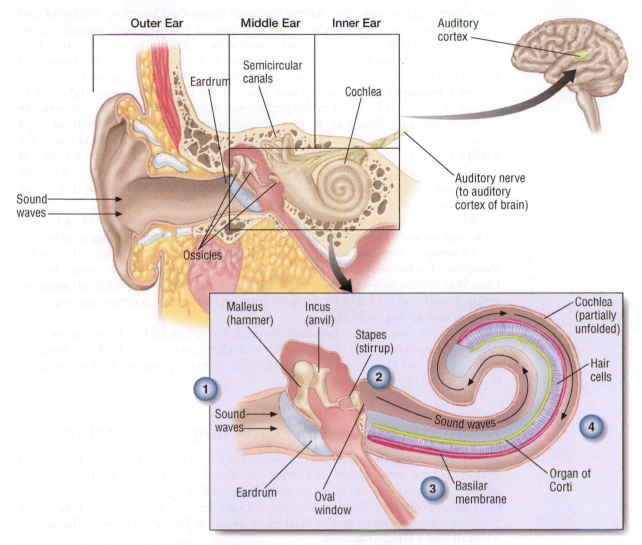

FIGURE 3.11 Conversion of Sound Waves into Neural Impulses
1 Sound waves are funneled by the outer ear to the eardrum, causing it to
vibrate. **2** These vibrations are transmitted through the ossicles, three tiny bones in
the middle ear, and then to the oval window, through which they are transmitted to the
cochlea within the inner ear. **3** Vibration of the oval window causes movement of fluid in
the cochlea, which in turn causes the basilar membrane to vibrate. **4** Hair-cell receptors
in the organ of Corti bend in response to these vibrations, triggering neural impulses that
travel through the auditory nerve to the brain.

explain how we detect high and low pitches, and a combination of the two, called
the *volley principle,* helps explain how we detect mid-range pitches.

Place theory, originally developed by Hermann von Helmholtz, suggests that people perceive a sound to have a certain pitch according to the place along the basilar
membrane that vibrates the most when sound waves of particular frequencies strike
the ear. It is as though neurons line up along the basilar membrane like so many keys
on a piano, standing ready to respond by producing sounds of different pitch when
they are "struck" (Azar, 1996).

Georg von Békésy (1957) won a Nobel Prize for showing that high-frequency
sounds cause the greatest vibration of hair cells close to the oval window, whereas
those with lower frequencies cause the greatest vibration farther down the basilar
membrane. Hair cells at the point of maximal vibration, like the crest of a wave,

CONCEPT 3.17
Perception of pitch may best be explained
by a combination of place theory, frequency theory, and the volley principle.

place theory The belief that pitch
depends on the place along the basilar
membrane that vibrates the most in
response to a particular auditory stimulus.

excite particular neurons that inform the brain about their location. The brain uses this information to code sounds for pitch. However, low-frequency sounds—those below about 4,000 cycles per second—cannot be coded for location because they do not cause the membrane to vibrate the most at any one spot. Yet we know that people can detect sounds with frequencies as low as 20 cycles per second.

Enter **frequency theory**, which may account for how we perceive the pitch of sounds of about 20 to 1,000 cycles per second. According to frequency theory, the basilar membrane vibrates at the same frequency as the sound wave itself. In other words, a sound wave with a frequency of 200 cycles per second would cause the basilar membrane to vibrate at that rate and generate a corresponding number of neural impulses to the brain. That is, there would be 200 neural impulses to the brain per second. But frequency theory also has its limitations. Most importantly, neurons cannot fire more frequently than about 1,000 times per second.

What, then, do we make of sounds with frequencies between 1,000 and 4,000 cycles per second? How do we bridge that gap? By means of the **volley principle**. In one of nature's many surprises, it seems that groups of neurons along the basilar membrane fire in volleys, or alternating succession. (Think of Revolutionary War or Civil War movies in which one group of soldiers stands and fires while an alternate group kneels and reloads.) By firing in rotation, groups of neurons combine their frequencies of firing to fill the gap.

In sum, frequency theory best explains pitch perception for low-frequency sounds, whereas place theory best explains pitch of high-frequency sounds. A combination of frequency and place theory, called the volley principle, suggests how we perceive the pitch of mid-range sounds.

Hearing Loss: Are You Protecting Your Hearing?

Nearly 30 million Americans suffer from hearing loss, and as many as 2 million are deaf. There are many causes of hearing loss and deafness, including birth defects, disease, advanced age, and injury, as well as the kind of injury caused by exposure to loud noise. Prolonged exposure to noise of 85 decibels can cause hearing loss, as can brief exposure to sounds of 120 decibels or louder. ■ Figure 3.12 shows the decibel levels of many familiar sounds.

The number of hearing-impaired individuals is expected to mushroom to an astounding 78 million by 2030, largely as the result of years of living loudly, a by-product of listening to earsplitting music piped through ear buds on personal music devices (Noonan, 2006). Excessive noise is also a source of stress that can lead to problems such as disturbed sleep, impaired work or academic performance, and even heart disease (Szalma & Hancock, 2011; University of Michigan, 2011).

The World Health Organization (WHO) reports that 1.1 billion young people worldwide—about 50 percent of young adults—are at risk of suffering serious hearing loss due to exposure to dangerously loud levels of sound from personal audio devices and concert venues (James, 2015; WHO, 2015). Unfortunately, many young people, as well as many of their parents, fail to heed warnings about the risks of hearing loss (see Table 3.3). A staggering proportion of teens—nearly one in five— are already showing signs of hearing loss, such as having difficulty discerning T's or K's (the word "talk" may sound like "aw") (Heffernan, 2011; Johnson, 2010). To protect the hearing of young ears, experts recommend turning down the volume to less than 60 percent of maximum and limiting use to an hour per day (James, 2015).

There are two main types of deafness: conduction deafness and nerve deafness. **Conduction deafness** is usually caused by damage to the middle ear. The eardrum may be punctured, or the three bones that amplify sound waves and conduct them to the inner ear may lose the ability to vibrate properly. People who experience conduction deafness may benefit from hearing aids that amplify sound waves.

CONCEPT 3.18
Loud noise can lead to hearing loss and impair learning ability.

frequency theory The belief that pitch depends on the frequency of vibration of the basilar membrane and the volley of neural impulses transmitted to the brain via the auditory nerve.

volley principle The principle that relates the experience of pitch to the alternating firing of groups of neurons along the basilar membrane.

conduction deafness A form of deafness, usually involving damage to the middle ear, in which there is a loss of conduction of sound vibrations through the ear.

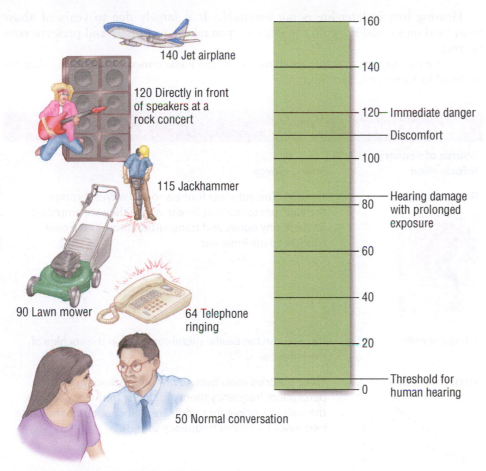

160
150
140 Jet airplane
140
120 Directly in front
of speakers at a
rock concert
120— Immediate danger
— Discomfort
100
115 Jackhammer
80 — Hearing damage
with prolonged
exposure
60
90 Lawn mower
64 Telephone
ringing
40
20
Threshold for
0 human hearing

50 Normal conversation

FIGURE 3.12 Sounds and Decibels
Permanent hearing loss may occur from prolonged exposure to sound over 85 decibels
(dB). Exposure to 120 dB or higher creates an immediate danger to hearing. Most people
can detect faint sounds at a decibel level just above 0 dB.

Nerve deafness is usually caused by damage to the hair cells of the inner ear or
to the auditory nerve. Exposure to loud sounds, disease, and aging can cause nerve
deafness. The ringing sensation that can follow exposure to loud noises may indicate
damage to hair cells. Cochlear implants, or "artificial ears," are sometimes successful
in transmitting sounds past damaged hair cells to the auditory nerve. They work
by converting sounds into electrical impulses. But these implants cannot correct for
damage to the auditory nerve itself. If the auditory nerve does not function, even
sounds that cause the hair cells on the basilar membrane to dance frantically will not
be sensed in the auditory cortex of the brain.

Chrisstockphoto/Alamy Stock Photo

Say what? A cause for concern is the
staggering proportion of teens, nearly
one in five, who are already showing
signs of hearing loss. What can you do to
protect your hearing?

Table 3.3 Now Hear This: Teens and Hearing Problems

Twenty-eight percent report having to turn up the volume on the television or radio to
hear well.

Twenty-nine percent report saying "what" or "huh" during normal conversations.

Seventeen percent report having had tinnitus, or ringing of the ears.

Source: CNN. (2006, March 14). "Poll: Teens Not Heeding Headphone Warning." Retrieved from www.cnn.com/2006/HEALTH
/conditions/03/14/ipod.hearingrisk/index.html

nerve deafness Deafness associated with
nerve damage, usually involving damage
to the hair cells or to the auditory nerve
itself.

Hearing loss in later life is not inevitable. It is largely due to years of abuse from loud music and noise. What steps are you taking to protect and preserve your hearing?

Before moving on, you may wish to review the basic concepts in hearing that are outlined in Concept Chart 3.3.

Concept Chart 3.3	Hearing
Source of Sensory Information	**Sound Waves**
Receptor organs	The ears. The outer ear funnels sound waves through the eardrum to the middle ear, where they are amplified by three tiny bones and transmitted through the oval window to the inner ear.
Receptor cells	Hair cells on the basilar membrane within the cochlea of the inner ear
Pitch perception	Three theories contribute to our understanding of pitch perception: frequency theory for lower frequency sounds, the volley principle for middle frequency sounds, and place frequency for higher frequency sounds.

© Wolfgang Amri/Shutterstock.com

© Jason Nemeth/Shutterstock.com

MODULE REVIEW **3.3** Hearing: The Music of Sound

Recite It

5. Explain how the ear enables us to hear sounds.

Sound waves enter the outer ear and are funneled to the **(a)** _____, causing it to vibrate. This mechanical energy is conveyed to tiny bones in the middle ear—the hammer, anvil, and stirrup—and then through the **(b)** _____ window to the **(c)** _____ in the inner ear. There, **(d)** _____ cells bend in response to the vibrations, triggering neural impulses that are transmitted to the brain.

6. Explain the perception of pitch and **identify** the main types and causes of deafness.

Perception of pitch is likely determined by a combination of the place on the **(e)** _____ membrane of greatest vibration (place theory), the **(f)** _____ of neural impulses (frequency theory), and the sequencing of firing of groups of neurons along the basilar membrane **(g)** (_____ principle).

The main types of deafness are **(h)** _____ deafness, usually caused by damage to the middle ear, and **(i)** _____ deafness, usually caused by damage to the hair cells of the inner ear or to the auditory nerve.

Recall It

1. Which characteristics of sound waves give rise to the perception of loudness and pitch?

2. Name the membrane in the inner ear that vibrates at different frequencies, giving rise to our perception of pitch.

3. Match these parts of the ear with the descriptions that follow:
   (a) eardrum; (b) ossicles; (c) cochlea; (d) basilar membrane;
   (e) organ of Corti; (f) hair cells.

   i. a membrane that separates the outer ear from the middle ear
   ii. sensory receptors for hearing
   iii. a gelatinous structure attached to the basilar membrane and lined with sensory receptors
   iv. the membrane in the cochlea that moves in response to sound vibration
   v. three small bones in the middle ear that conduct sound vibrations
   vi. a snail-shaped bony tube in the inner ear in which fluid moves in response to the vibrations of the oval window

Think About It

- What characteristics of sound waves give rise to the perception of loudness and pitch?

- What steps are you taking to protect your hearing from the damaging effects of noise? Are you doing enough?

Recite It *answers placed at the end of chapter.*

MODULE **3.4 Our Other Senses: Chemical, Skin, and Body Senses**

7 **Explain** how we sense odors and tastes.

8 **Identify** the various skin senses and **explain** the gate-control theory of pain.

9 **Describe** the functions of the kinesthetic and vestibular senses, and **explain** how they work.

We usually think of five senses—sight, hearing, smell, taste, and touch. Yet there are actually many more. Here we take a look at the chemical, skin, and body senses. These are the sensory systems that allow us to smell, taste, and touch and that keep us informed about the position and movement of our bodies.

The nose and tongue are like human chemistry laboratories. Smell and taste are chemical senses because they are based on the chemical analysis of molecules of substances that waft past the nose or that land on the tongue. The chemical senses allow us to perform chemistry on the fly.

Olfaction: What Your Nose Knows

Our sense of smell, or **olfaction**, depends on our ability to detect shapes of molecules of odorous chemical substances that waft into our nose. The work of detecting these chemical shapes is performed by millions of odor receptors that line our nasal passageways.

Like our other senses, olfaction is adaptive, allowing us to distinguish between the savory smells of a home-cooked meal and the rotten smells of spoiled food. The human olfactory system may not be as sensitive as that of dogs or cats, but it is nonetheless exquisitely sensitive. There are some 5 million odor receptors in the human nose, representing more than 1,000 distinct types. Just how many different odors the human nose can discern remains a point of controversy. Some scientists believe the nose can distinguish between a trillion or more distinct odors (Bushdid et al., 2014), but others maintain the number may be much, much lower, perhaps about 5,000 odors in total (Gerkin & Castro, 2015). But even accepting the lower estimate means we can distinguish among thousands of different substances based on odor.

Molecules of different chemical substances that waft into the nose fit into particular types of odor receptors as keys fit into locks, triggering olfactory messages that are carried to the brain by the **olfactory nerve**. This olfactory information is

CONCEPT 3.19
The sense of smell depends on receptors in the nose that detect thousands of chemical substances and transmit information about them to the brain.

olfaction The sense of smell.

olfactory nerve The nerve that carries impulses from olfactory receptors in the nose to the brain.

Try This Out
The Smell of Taste

Ever notice that food tastes bland when your nose is stuffed? To demonstrate how olfaction affects the sense of taste, try eating a meal while holding your nostrils closed. What effect does it have on your ability to taste your food? On your enjoyment of the meal?

Do certain odors make you feel happy? Investigators find that nearly everyone they studied could pick out a particular odor they associated with feeling happy or disgusted. Other investigators find that sniffing the odors of others can affect the receiver's emotional responses.

olfactory bulb The area in the front of the brain above the nostrils that receives sensory input from olfactory receptors in the nose.

processed by the brain, giving rise to sensations of odors corresponding to these particular chemical stimuli (Miyamichi et al., 2010) (see ■ Figure 3.13). The intensity of the odor appears to be a function of the number of olfactory receptors that are stimulated simultaneously.

Smell is the only sense in which sensory information does not go through the thalamus on its way to the cerebral cortex. Instead, olfactory information travels through the olfactory nerve directly to the **olfactory bulb**, a structure in the front of the brain above the nostrils. This information is then routed to the olfactory cortex in the temporal lobe and to several structures in the limbic system, which, as noted in Chapter 2, are a set of brain structures with important roles in emotion and memory. The connections between the olfactory system and the limbic system may account for the close relationship between odors and emotional memories. A whiff of chocolate pudding simmering on the stove or of someone's perfume may bring back strong feelings associated with childhood experiences or a particular person.

Olfaction is a key factor in the flavor of foods (see Try This Out) (Bakalar, 2012). Without the sense of smell, the flavor of a steak might not be all that different from that of cardboard. An apple might taste the same as a raw potato. A declining sense of smell in later life may be the major reason many older people complain that food doesn't taste as good as it once did.

Odors are also keyed into memory and emotions (Fields, 2012). A familiar scent can trigger recall of early memories and related emotions. A young woman reported that a mere sniff of a fragrance that her mother had favored would bring to mind loving memories of her mother. Investigators find that nearly every participant in their study could identify a particular odor they linked to feelings of happiness and disgust (Croy, Olgun, & Joraschky, 2011). What particular scents evoke emotional responses for you?

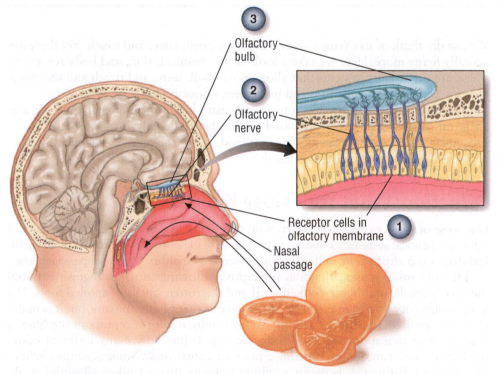

FIGURE 3.13 **Olfaction**
❶ Receptor cells (odor receptors) in the upper nose respond to the molecular shapes of particular chemical substances that enter the nose. ❷ Molecules fit particular odor receptors, triggering transmission of nerve impulses that travel through the olfactory nerve to the olfactory bulb in the brain. ❸ The olfactory bulb processes this information, giving rise to sensations of specific odors.

Can you sniff happiness in others? Perhaps so, based on results from a recent study showing that people who sniffed a vial of sweat taken from someone who was in a happy mood showed happier facial expressions themselves than they did when they sniffed sweat produced by a fearful person or one in an emotionally neutral state (de Groot et al., 2015). It seems that chemosignals in the natural secretions of others can rub off on our own emotional responses.

Our sensory organs were shaped over the course of millions of years of adaptation to the environment. Olfaction, among our other senses, is critical to our survival. It helps us avoid rotten and potentially harmful foods long before we put our tongue to them. In various animal species, olfaction serves other functions as well. Fur seals and many other animal species recognize their own young from the pack on the basis of smell. Salmon roam the seven seas but sniff out the streams of their birth at spawning time on the basis of a few molecules of water emitted by those streams.

Many animal and insect species emit chemical substances, called **pheromones**, that play important roles in regulating many behaviors, including attracting mates, marking territory, establishing dominance hierarchies, behaving aggressively, gathering food, and bonding with young (e.g., McCann et al., 2015; Shackelford & Goetz, 2012; Van Oystaeyen et al., 2014). Pheromones are found in bodily secretions, such as urine or vaginal secretions, and are detected by other members of the species through the sense of smell or taste.

Pheromones regulate sexual attraction and mating behaviors in many species of animals and insects (Mostafa, El Khouly, & Hassan, 2012). But do they serve similar purposes in humans? We know that humans are capable of detecting an invisible trail of body odors and that the brain uses that information to make judgments about the characteristics of people we encounter, including their gender, fertility, and age (Pazzaglia, 2015). We also know that the brain unconsciously processes these chemical signals even if we don't think we sensed an odor on a conscious level (Zhou et al., 2014). Yet we lack evidence needed to determine how, or indeed if, pheromones influence human sexual attraction or behavior. Suffice it to say that what the nose knows remains largely an open question. That said, an intriguing study suggests that, hormonally speaking, men may be led around by their noses when exposed to the scent of a woman.

Men in this study were asked to sniff a T-shirt previously worn by a woman (Miller & Maner, 2010). Some men smelled T-shirts that had been worn by women who were ovulating, which is the time of greatest female reproductive fertility. In many animal species, males show the greatest mating interest when females are at their peak fertility. Other men in the study sniffed T-shirts that had been worn by nonovulating women. The findings showed that men who had been exposed to scents of ovulating women had higher levels of testosterone than those who had sniffed scents of nonovulating women. This finding suggests that olfactory cues associated with female fertility are tied into male hormonal responses. Whether these influences actually affect men's sexual behavior or interest in women still remains to be determined.

Yet another intriguing study exposed men to chemical secretions in a woman's tears while they were making judgments of the sex appeal of images of women presented on a computer screen (Gelstein et al., 2011). Although tears are odorless, sniffing a woman's tears reduced the perceived sexiness that men attributed to the female images. Other men who sniffed women's tears while watching an emotional movie rated their level of sexual arousal lower, had lower physiological measures of sexual arousal, and even had lower testosterone levels—a hormone linked to sexual arousal—than did men exposed to control samples of saline. It appears that women's tears contain chemical signals that dampen men's sexual interest, even without conscious awareness or even without the physical presence of a crying woman.

Whatever role scents may play in sexual arousal in humans, we should recognize that we are primarily visual creatures when it comes to sexual arousal. As the prominent

CONCEPT 3.20
Pheromones are chemical secretions that play various roles in animal behavior, but their functions in human behavior remain unclear.

Adrian Samson/Stone/Getty Images

It turns out that chemical signals in women's tears dampen men's sexual interest. This effect holds even if men only sniff a woman's tears and do not actually see the woman.

pheromones Chemical substances that are emitted by many species and that have various functions, including sexual attraction.

biological anthropologist Helen Fisher put the issue, "For humans . . . it's usually love at first sight, not love at first smell. . . . There are many factors to sex appeal, and romance and scent is among them. But from studying the brain, I would argue that our brains are largely built for visual stimuli" (cited in Sweeney, 2009, p. E3).

Taste: The Flavorful Sense

Taste, like our other senses, plays an important role in adaptation and survival. We rely on both taste and smell to discriminate between healthy, nutritious food and spoiled or rotten food. (The sense organs are not perfect, however; some poisonous substances are undetectable by smell or taste.)

Though there are thousands of different flavors, there are but five primary tastes: sweet, sour, salty, bitter, and umami (the savory flavor associated with monosodium glutamate or MSG). The flavor of food results from a combination of these taste qualities, a food's aroma, and its texture and temperature.

Tastes are sensed by receptors called **taste cells**. These are nerve cells located within pores or openings on the tongue called **taste buds**. Most taste buds are found near the edges and back of the tongue. Yet people without tongues can also sense taste because additional taste receptors are located on the roof of the mouth, inside the cheeks, and in the throat. Some taste receptors are more sensitive to a specific taste quality; others respond to several tastes. Despite these sensitivities, the brain decodes stimulation arising from virtually any part of the tongue containing taste receptors to produce any of the primary tastes (Sugita & Shiba, 2005; Trivedi, 2012). Recent evidence indicates that particular clusters of neurons in the part of the cortex that processes taste stimuli respond specifically to particular taste qualities such as saltiness, sweetness, and bitterness (Miller, 2011).

Taste receptors differ from other neurons in that they regenerate very quickly—within a week to ten days. This is a good thing because people kill them off regularly by eating very hot food, such as pizza that is just out of the oven.

Why do some people like their food spicy, while others like it plain? Differences in cultural backgrounds play a part in taste preferences. For example, people from some cultures develop preferences for spicy foods. But why do people tend to sweat when they eat spicy foods? It turns out that the chemical that makes food spicy also activates receptors that detect warmth (Aamodt & Wang, 2008). These warmth receptors are found not only on the tongue but also throughout the body. So when you chew into a hot chili pepper, the brain senses warmth and produces a natural sweating response. No wonder we say spicy foods are hot.

Genetic factors influence taste sensitivities (Sandell & Breslin, 2006). Some people who douse their meat with salt may be nearly taste-blind to salt as the result of a genetic trait. Others are genetically predisposed to be extremely sensitive to salt, pepper, and other spices. Some inherit a sensitivity to bitter tastes that turns them off to sharp-tasting vegetables like Brussels sprouts (Pearson, 2006). Preference for sugary foods (a "sweet tooth") is also influenced by genetic factors (Eny et al., 2008).

Different species show differences in taste sensitivities. Cats appear to be taste-blind to sweetness, but pigs can sense sweetness. (It might be accurate to say that while humans may eat like pigs, pigs may eat like humans.) About one in four people (more women than men) are born with a very dense network of taste buds that makes them overly sensitive to certain tastes. These people, called "supertasters," have a greater than average number of taste buds and so experience tastes more intensely than do other people (Bartoshuk, 2007). They may recoil at the sharp or bitter tastes of many fruits and vegetables, such as broccoli, or may find sugary foods sickeningly sweet. Ethnic and gender differences come into play, as Asian women are the most likely to be supertasters, whereas Caucasian men are much less likely to belong to this group (Carpenter, 2000).

CONCEPT 3.21

Like the sense of smell, the sense of taste depends on receptors that detect chemical substances and transmit information about them to the brain.

Maridav/Shutterstock.com

Whether there are naturally sexy scents that induce sexual attraction in people remains a question that scientists (as well as fragrance companies) continue to explore.

taste cells Nerve cells that are sensitive to tastes.

taste buds Pores or openings on the tongue containing taste cells.

The Skin Senses: Your Largest Sensory Organ

You may not think of your skin as a sensory organ. But it is actually the body's largest sensory organ. It contains receptors for the body's **skin senses** that code for sensations of touch, pressure, warmth, cold, and pain. Some skin receptors respond to just one type of stimulation, such as pressure or warmth. Others respond to more than one type of stimulation.

Nearly a half million receptors for touch and pressure are distributed throughout the body. They transmit sensory information to the spinal cord, which relays it to the *somatosensory cortex,* the part of the cerebral cortex that processes information from our skin receptors and makes us aware of how and where we have been touched. Many touch receptors are located near the surface of the skin (see ■ Figure 3.14). They fire when the skin is lightly touched—for example, caressed, stroked, or patted. Other receptors at deeper levels beneath the skin fire in response to pressure.

Receptors for temperature are also found just beneath the skin. Scientists generally agree that specific receptors exist for warmth and cold. In one of nature's more interesting surprises, sensations of hotness are produced by simultaneous stimulation of receptors for warmth and cold. If you were to clutch coiled pipes with warm and cold water circulating through them, you might feel as though your hand were being burned. Then, if the pipes were uncoiled, you would find that neither one by itself could give rise to sensations of hotness.

Reflect for a moment about what it might mean if you did not experience pain. At first thought, not sensing pain might seem to be a good thing. After all, why go through life with headaches, toothaches, and backaches if you do not have to do so? Yet a life without pain could be a short one.

Pain is a sign that something is wrong. Without the experience of pain, you might not notice splinters, paper cuts, burns, and the many sources of injury, irritation, and infection that can ultimately threaten life if not attended to promptly. Pain is adaptive—that is, we use it to search for and do something about the source of pain and learn to avoid those actions that cause pain.

Pain receptors are located not just in the skin but also in other parts of the body, including muscles, joints, ligaments, and the pulp of the teeth—the source of tooth pain. We can feel pain in most parts of the body. Pain can be particularly acute where nerve endings are densely packed, as in the fingers and face.

People often try to control pain by rubbing or scratching a painful area or applying an ice pack. An explanation of why these methods may help involves a theory developed by psychologist Ronald Melzack and biologist Patrick Wall (1965, 1983). According to their **gate-control theory of pain**, a gating mechanism in the spinal cord opens and closes to let pain messages through to the brain or to shut them out. The "gate" is not an actual physical structure in the spinal cord but, rather, a pattern of nervous system activity that results in either blocking pain signals or letting them through.

Creating a bottleneck at the "gate" may block out pain signals. Signals associated with dull or throbbing pain are conducted through the neural gate by nerve fibers that are thinner and slower than the nerve fibers that carry sensory signals for warmth, cold, and touch. The signals carried by the faster and thicker nerve fibers can cause a bottleneck at the neural gate, thus blocking the passage of other messages. Rubbing or scratching an area in pain sends signals to the spinal cord through fast nerve fibers. Those signals may successfully compete for space with pain messages carried by thin fibers, which close the gate and temporarily block signals for dull and throbbing pain from reaching the brain. However, the first sharp pangs of pain you experience when you stub your toe or cut your finger are carried by large nerve pathways and apparently cannot be blocked out. This is a good thing, as it ensures that pain messages register quickly in the brain, alerting you instantly to the part of your body that has been injured.

CONCEPT 3.22
Sensory receptors in the skin are sensitive to touch, pressure, temperature, and pain, and transmit information about these stimuli to your brain.

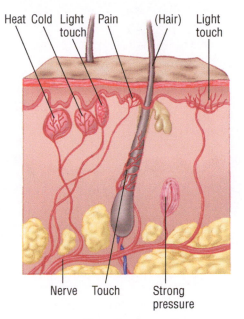

FIGURE 3.14 Your Largest Sensory Organ—Your Skin
The skin contains receptors that are sensitive to touch, pressure, warm and cold temperatures, and pain.

Used for centuries by Chinese physicians, the benefits of acupuncture are still being debated by Western scientists.

skin senses The senses of touch, pressure, warmth, cold, and pain that involve stimulation of sensory receptors in the skin.

gate-control theory of pain The belief that a neural gate in the spinal cord opens to allow pain messages to reach the brain and closes to shut them out.

CONCEPT 3.23
The gate-control theory of pain proposes that the spinal cord contains a gating mechanism that controls the transmission of pain messages to the brain.

Applying an ice pack to an injured area may help reduce pain. Based on your reading of the text, how would you explain this phenomenon?

acupuncture An ancient Chinese practice of inserting and rotating thin needles in various parts of the body in order to release natural healing energy.

An ice pack applied to the source of pain may help for several reasons. In addition to reducing inflammation and swelling—both of which contribute to the experience of pain—ice produces sensations of cold that help create a bottleneck at the gate in the spinal cord and thus, as in the earlier example, may temporarily block pain messages from reaching the brain.

The brain plays a critical role in controlling pain. In response to pain, the brain signals the release of *endorphins*. As you may recall from Chapter 2, endorphins are neurotransmitters that are similar in chemical composition to narcotic drugs, such as heroin. Like heroin, they have painkilling effects. They lock into receptor sites in the spinal cord that transmit pain messages, thereby closing the "pain gate" and preventing pain messages from reaching the brain.

The release of endorphins may explain the benefits of a traditional Chinese medical practice called **acupuncture**. The acupuncturist inserts thin needles at "acupuncture points" on the body and then rotates them. According to traditional Chinese beliefs, manipulation of the needles releases the body's natural healing energy. Although people with chronic pain who undergo acupuncture often report improvement, investigators question whether the benefits of acupuncture involve anything more than a strong placebo effect (Avins, 2012; Cloud, 2011a; Linde et al., 2009a; 2009b). Investigators doubt whether acupuncture provides any meaningful benefits over sham (fake) procedures in which needles are inserted in spots that are not acupuncture points in the body (Hinman et al., 2014; Schwenk, 2014; Vickers et al., 2012).

APPLYING PSYCHOLOGY

Psychology and Pain Management

CONCEPT 3.24
Psychological interventions may be helpful in managing pain.

CONCEPT LINK
Meditation is used to combat stress, relieve pain, and lower blood pressure. See Module 4.3.

The brain is a marvel of engineering. By allowing us to experience the first pangs of pain, it alerts us to danger. Without such a warning, we might not pull our hand away from a hot object in time to prevent burns. Then, by releasing endorphins, the brain gradually shuts the gate on pain.

Though we all experience pain in response to injury, more than 100 million Americans suffer from chronic pain, which includes back pain, headaches, and arthritis pain (Beck, 2011). Not surprisingly, the management of chronic pain is a rapidly growing field. New technologies and approaches to pain management are being introduced to clinical practice every year. Although pain has a biological basis, psychological methods can be used to reduce the suffering of pain patients and help them cope more effectively with chronic pain (for example, Burns et al., 2015; Connelly, 2013; Davis et al., 2015; Powers et al., 2013). In this module, we focus on psychological factors in pain management. However, before attempting to treat pain yourself, consult a health professional to determine the source of the pain and the appropriate course of treatment.

Distraction

Distraction not only helps direct attention away from pain, but it actually reduces pain signals traveling from the spinal cord to the brain (Sprenger et al., 2012). Fewer pain signals translate to lesser pain. So if you are faced with a painful medical or dental procedure, you might help keep your mind off your pain by focusing on a pleasing picture on the wall or some other stimulus or by letting your mind become absorbed in a pleasant fantasy. Chronic pain sufferers may find they are better able to cope with the pain if they distract themselves by exercising or perhaps by becoming immersed in a good book or video.

Creating a Bottleneck at the "Gate"

As noted earlier, the gate-control theory of pain holds that other sensory stimuli may temporarily block pain messages from passing through a neural gate in the spinal cord. You can attempt to create a traffic jam at the gate by lightly rubbing an irritated area. Interestingly, applying both heat and cold may help because each sends messages through the spinal cord that compete for attention. Cold packs have the additional advantage of reducing inflammation.

Changing Thoughts and Attitudes

What people say to themselves about their pain can affect how much pain they feel and how well they cope with it. Thinking pessimistic thoughts ("This will never get better") and catastrophic thoughts ("I can't take this anymore. I'm going to fall apart!") can worsen the feelings of pain (for example, Pinto et al., 2011). Findings from brain-scanning studies show higher levels of catastrophizing or thinking the worst are associated with greater levels of pain-related brain activity (Edwards et al., 2009).

Negative thinking can also lead to perceptions of lack of control, which in turn can produce feelings of helplessness and hopelessness. Psychologists help pain sufferers examine their thoughts and replace negative or pessimistic self-evaluations with rational alternatives—thoughts like "Don't give in to hopelessness. Focus on what you need to do to cope with this pain." Psychologists find that helping pain patients alter catastrophic thinking reduces the intensity of the pain they experience and improves their daily functioning (Turner, Mancl, & Aaron, 2006). Even if changing thoughts and attitudes does not eliminate pain, it can help people cope more effectively in managing their pain symptoms.

Obtaining Accurate Information

One of the most effective psychological methods for managing pain is obtaining factual and thorough information about the source of the pain and the available treatments. Many people try to avoid thinking about pain and its implications. Obtaining information helps people take an active role in controlling the challenges they face.

Meditation and Biofeedback

There are many forms of *meditation*, but most of them involve the narrowing of attention through repetition, such as repeating a particular word, thought, or phrase, or through maintaining a steady focus on one object, such as a burning candle or the design on a vase. Meditation can induce a relaxed, contemplative state. As discussed further in Chapter 4, meditation can be used to help relieve pain as well as the effects of stress on the body.

Psychologists find that providing people with feedback about their internal bodily functions ("biofeedback") helps them gain greater awareness and some degree of

CONCEPT 3.25
By providing information about changes in internal bodily processes, biofeedback training helps people gain some degree of conscious control over their physiological functioning.

Bonnie Kamin/PhotoEdit

biofeedback training (BFT) A method of learning to control certain bodily responses by using information from the body transmitted by physiological monitoring equipment.

electromyographic (EMG) biofeedback A form of BFT that involves feedback about changes in the level of muscle tension in the forehead or elsewhere in the body.

migraine headaches Prolonged, intense headaches brought on by changes in blood flow in blood vessels in the brain.

thermal biofeedback A form of BFT that involves feedback about changes in temperature and blood flow in selected parts of the body; used in the treatment of migraine headaches.

voluntary control over their internal bodily processes. In **biofeedback training (BFT)**, people are hooked up with physiological monitoring equipment that provides them with a continual stream of information about their internal bodily states. A rising tone may indicate increasing heart rate or muscle tension, while a lower tone indicates changes in the opposite direction. People use these biofeedback signals as cues to help them learn to modify their heart rates, blood pressure, muscle tension, body temperature, brain wave patterns, and other physiological processes (for example, Dalen et al., 2009; Nestoriuc & Martin, 2007; Weir, 2016).

One form of biofeedback training used to help relieve tension headache pain is **electromyographic (EMG) biofeedback**. In EMG, electrodes placed on the forehead or elsewhere on the body monitor muscle tension. A tone is used to indicate increases or decreases in muscle tension. By learning to lower the tone, people can relax their forehead muscles, which can help reduce pain associated with tension headaches.

People who suffer from **migraine headaches**, which affects an estimated 36 million Americans (Gelfand, 2014), may benefit from **thermal biofeedback**, a form of biofeedback training that teaches people to modulate the flow of blood to their extremities. Migraines involve intense, pulsating pain on one side of the head that is associated with changes in blood flow to the brain (Linde et al., 2005). In thermal biofeedback, a temperature-sensing device is attached to a finger. The device beeps more slowly (or more rapidly, depending on the settings) as the temperature in the finger rises. People learn to raise the temperature in their fingers, perhaps by imagining a finger growing warmer. The temperature rises as more blood flows to the limbs and away from the head. This change in blood flow may help relieve migraine pain.

Some of the benefits of BFT may be achieved through simpler forms of relaxation training that don't require expensive equipment, such as muscle relaxation techniques and deep breathing exercises. In Chapter 4, we discuss another psychological technique that can help control pain—hypnosis.

© Andersen Ross/Blend Images/Getty Images

Our kinesthetic sense allows us to fine-tune the movements of our body.

kinesthesia The sense that keeps us informed about movement of the parts of the body and their position in relation to each other.

vestibular sense The sense that keeps us informed about balance and the position of our body in space.

The Kinesthetic and Vestibular Senses: Of Grace and Balance

Kinesthesia is the body sense that allows you to ride a bicycle without watching the movements of your legs, type without looking at the keyboard, and wash the back of your neck without checking yourself in the mirror. It also makes it possible to touch your nose or your ears with your eyes closed or while blindfolded, or to swat away a mosquito that lands on your hand, even in darkness (University College London, 2010). Your kinesthetic sense keeps you continuously informed about the movements of the parts of your body and their positions in relation to one another. The sensory information that makes these tasks possible is processed by the brain based on information it receives from receptors in the joints, ligaments, tendons, skin, and muscles (Azañón et al., 2010).

You may occasionally watch what you are doing or think about what you are doing, but most of the time your movements are performed automatically based on this kinesthetic information.

Did you know there is a movement-sensing mechanism in your inner ear? The **vestibular sense** monitors the posture and movement of your body in space and enables you to maintain your balance (Ferrè, Lopez, & Haggard, 2014). It allows you to know whether you are moving faster or slower and to sense the position and rotation of your head, as when you are tilting your head or spinning around. You rely on your vestibular sense to know when the train or car in

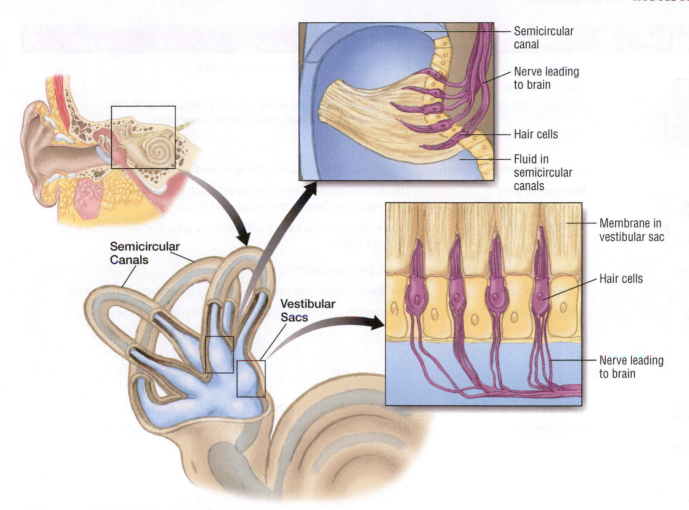

FIGURE 3.15 The Vestibular Sense
Hair-cell receptors in the inner ear bend in response to forces of gravity when we tilt our head and to movement of the head through space, triggering messages the brain uses to maintain our sense of balance and equilibrium and detect movement and orientation of our head in space.

which you are riding is speeding up, slowing down, coming to a stop, or reversing direction. Changes in the position of your head in space, such as when you rotate or tilt your head or move forward, backward, or sideways, cause movement of fluid within the **semicircular canals** in your inner ear, and shifts in the position of crystals in the **vestibular sacs** that connect the canals, which in turn stimulates tiny hair-cell receptors in your inner ear (see ■ Figure 3.15). These sensory receptors transmit messages to the brain that are decoded to allow you to sense the position and movement of your head in relation to the outside world (Day & Fitzpatrick, 2005).

If you spin around and around and come to an abrupt stop, you are likely to feel dizzy. The reason is that fluid in the semicircular canals in your inner ears keeps swirling about for a while after you stop, making it seem as if the world is still spinning. You may experience *motion sickness* when the vestibular and visual senses receive conflicting information about movement, as when you are riding in a car headed in one direction while observing a moving train headed in the other direction.

Concept Chart 3.4 reviews the chemical, skin, and bodily senses.

CONCEPT 3.26
Sensory receptors in your joints, ligaments, and muscles transmit information that the brain uses to keep you aware of the position and movement of parts of your body.

CONCEPT 3.27
Sensory organs within your inner ears respond to movements of your head, and provide the brain with sensory information it needs to help you maintain your balance and sense the position and movement of your body in space.

semicircular canals Three curved, tubelike canals in the inner ear that are involved in sensing changes in the direction and movement of the head.

vestibular sacs Organs in the inner ear that connect the semicircular canals.

Concept Chart 3.4 Chemical, Skin, and Body Senses

Olfaction

Ryan McVay/Lifesize/Getty Images

Source of sensory information	Molecules of the substance being sensed
Receptor organ	The nose
Receptor cells	Receptors in each nostril that can sense about 10,000 different substances on the basis of their molecular shapes

Taste

Christopher Robbins/ Rise/Getty Images

Source of sensory information	Molecules of the substance being sensed
Receptor organs	Mainly taste buds on the tongue, although there are additional receptors elsewhere in the mouth and throat
Receptor cells	Taste cells located in taste buds are nerve cells that are sensitive to different tastes.

Skin senses

Loop Delay/Getty Images

Source of sensory information	Touch, pressure, warmth, cold, and pain
Receptor organ	The skin (pain can also originate in many other parts of the body)
Receptor cells	Receptors that code for touch, pressure, warmth, cold, and pain

Kinesthesis

Thinkstock/Comstock Images/ Getty Images

Source of sensory information	Movement and relative position of body parts
Receptor cells	Receptors located mainly in joints, ligaments, and muscles

Vestibular sense

PCN Photography/Alamy Stock Photo

Source of sensory information	Motion of the body and orientation in space
Receptor organs	Semicircular canals and vestibular sacs in the inner ear
Receptor cells	Hair-cell receptors that respond to the movement of fluid in the semicircular canals and to shifts in position of crystals in vestibular sacs

MODULE REVIEW **3.4** Our Other Senses: Chemical, Skin, and Body Senses

Recite It

7. Explain how we sense odors and tastes.

Olfaction, or sense of smell, depends on receptors in the nostrils that are capable of sensing different (a) _____ substances on the basis of their (b) _____ shapes. This information is transmitted to the brain for processing, giving rise to the sensation of odor.

The sense of taste involves stimulation of (c) _____ receptors located in taste buds, mostly on the tongue. Some taste receptors are more sensitive to one basic type of taste (sweet, sour, salty, (d) _____, or umami) while others respond to several tastes. Stimulation of taste receptors is transmitted to the brain for processing these taste sensations.

8. Identify the various skin senses and **explain** the gate-control theory of pain.

The skin senses enable us to detect touch, (e) _____, temperature, and pain. Different receptors in the skin respond to these stimuli and transmit the information to the brain for processing. The **(f)** _____-_____ theory of pain holds that there is a gating mechanism in the spinal cord that opens to allow pain messages through to the brain to signal that something is wrong and closes to shut them off.

9. **Describe** the functions of the kinesthetic and vestibular senses, and **explain** how they work.

The **(g)** _____ sense enables you to sense the movement of various parts of your body and their positions in relation to one another. Receptors in the **(h)** _____, ligaments, and muscles transmit information about body movement and position to the brain for processing. The **(i)** _____ sense is the sensory system that enables you to detect your body's position and maintain your **(j)** _____. As the position of your head changes, messages are transmitted to the brain, which interprets them as information about the position of your body in space.

Recall It

1. Olfactory receptors in the nose recognize different chemical substances on the basis of their
   a. aromas.
   b. molecular shapes.
   c. density.
   d. vibrations.

2. Approximately how many different substances can our olfactory receptors sense?

3. What do we call chemicals that function as sexual attractants?

4. What kinds of sensory receptors are found in the skin?

5. The receptors that provide sensory information that helps us maintain our balance are located in
   a. joints and ligaments.
   b. the back of the eye.
   c. muscles.
   d. the inner ear.

6. John is learning to swing a golf club. He relies on his _____ sense to know how far back he is swinging the club.

Think About It

■ Selling cars is no longer simply a matter of performance, value, styling, and safety. Now aroma has entered the picture. General Motors, for example, has imbued some of its Cadillacs with a sweet scent they call "Nuance" (Hakim, 2003). Do you think people will be led by their noses when buying their next car?

■ Do you believe you are led around by your nose? How is your behavior affected by aromas?

Recite It answers placed at the end of chapter.

MODULE

3.5 Perceiving Our World: Principles of Perception

10 **Describe** the roles of attention, perceptual set, and modes of visual processing in perception.

11 **Identify** and **describe** the Gestalt principles of grouping objects into meaningful patterns or forms.

12 **Define** the concept of perceptual constancy and **apply** the concept to examples.

13 **Identify** and **describe** cues we use to judge distance and perceive movement and **apply** these cues to examples.

14 **Identify** some common types of visual illusions, and **explain** why it is the brain, not the eyes, that deceives us.

15 **Evaluate** evidence concerning the existence of subliminal perception and extrasensory perception.

Perception is the process by which the brain interprets sensory information, turning it into meaningful representations of the external world. Through perception, the brain attempts to make sense of the mass of sensory stimuli that impinge on our sensory organs. Were it not for perception, the world would seem like a continually changing hodgepodge of disconnected sensations—a buzzing confusion of lights, sounds, and other sensory impressions. The brain brings order to the mix

perception The process by which the brain integrates, organizes, and interprets sensory impressions to create representations of the world.

Is this the face of a man or a woman? Your answer may depend on the part of your visual field in which the image is projected.

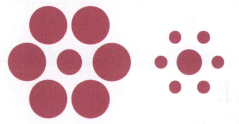

FIGURE 3.16 **Perception Versus Reality?**
Which of the circles in the middle of these two groupings is larger?

🔗 **CONCEPT LINK**
Our ability to divide our attention allows us to multitask, which can pose a risk when we combine driving with using a cell phone. See Module 4.1.

selective attention The process by which we attend to meaningful stimuli and filter out irrelevant or extraneous stimuli.

of sensations we experience, organizing them into coherent pictures of the world around us. To paraphrase Shakespeare, sensation without perception would be "full of sound and fury but signifying nothing."

Consider what you see on this page. When the dots of black ink register on your retina, your brain transforms these images into meaningful symbols that you perceive as letters. Perception is an active process in which the brain pieces together bits and pieces of sensory information to form orderly impressions or pictures of the world.

Though perceptions help us make sense of the world, they may not accurately reflect external reality. Look at the central circles in the left and right configurations in ■ Figure 3.16. Which of these two circles is larger? If you were to measure the diameter of each central circle with a ruler, you would find that they are exactly the same size. Yet you may perceive the central circle at the right to be larger than the one at the left. This is because the circle on the right is presented within an array of smaller circles, and your brain takes into account the context in which these shapes appear.

With perception, what you see is not necessarily what you get. Take a quick look at the gender-ambiguous facial image in the nearby photograph. Do you perceive it be a man's face, or a woman's? The answer may depend on which part of your visual field the image appears. Investigators recently discovered that if a series of gender-ambiguous images like this one are presented in a particular area of the visual field, say the upper right-hand corner, some people will perceive all the faces as male, whereas others will perceive the same faces as female (Afraz, Pashkam, & Cavanagh, 2010). We cannot yet explain why the visual processing centers in the brain of some people respond differently to ambiguous images than those in other people. But the lesson here is that perceptual experiences of the same stimuli do vary from person to person.

In this module, we explore basic concepts of perception, paying particular attention to visual perception—the area of perception that has captured the most research attention.

Attention: Did You Notice That?

Attention is the first step in perception. Through **selective attention**, you limit your attention to certain stimuli while filtering out other stimuli. When you focus attention on something, such as the sound of a person's voice, the brain filters out or ignores other stimuli (Sacchet et al., 2015). The process of selective attention prevents you from being flooded with extraneous information. It explains why you may perceive certain stimuli but not others. It allows you to focus on the words you are reading but not perceive the sounds of a car passing outside the window or the feeling of your toes touching the inside of your shoes. We also pay more attention to stimuli that are meaningful or emotionally significant. For example, a parent in a deep sleep may perceive the faint cry of an infant in the next room but be undisturbed by the wail of a siren from an ambulance passing just outside the house.

Our motivational states—whether we're hungry or thirsty, for example—play important roles in attention. When we are hungry, we are more likely than when we've just eaten to pay attention to odors wafting out of a restaurant. We also are more likely to notice billboards on the side of the road advertising nearby restaurants. I recall one professor who had the habit of dropping the words "midterm exam" into his lectures when he felt the class was nodding off. That seemed to motivate his students to pay closer attention.

Repeated exposure may increase attention to particular stimuli. Prenatal auditory exposure may explain why three-day-old infants prefer the sounds of their mother's voice—as measured by head turning—to the voices of other women (DeCasper & Fifer, 2008).

On the other hand, exposure to a constant stimulus can lead us to become *habituated,* or accustomed, to it. When you first turn on an air conditioner or fan, you may notice the constant humming sound it makes. But after a time, you no longer perceive it, even though the sound continues to impinge on the sensory receptors in your ears. Your brain has adapted to the constant stimulus by tuning it out. Habituation makes sense from an evolutionary perspective, because constant stimuli are less likely than changing stimuli to require an adaptive response.

Perceptual Set: Seeing What You Expect to See

Perceptual set is the tendency for perceptions to be influenced by expectations or preconceptions. Do you see the number 13 or the letter B in ■ Figure 3.17? In a classic study, Jerome Bruner and A. Leigh Minturn (1955) showed this figure to research participants after they had seen either a series of numbers or a series of letters. Among those who had viewed the number series, 83 percent said the stimulus was the number 13. Of those who had seen the letter series, 93 percent said the stimulus was a B. When faced with ambiguous stimuli, people often base their perceptions on their expectations and preconceptions. We might speculate that devoted fans of science fiction would be more likely than others to perceive flickering lights in the night sky as a UFO. ■ Figure 3.18 shows another example of a perceptual set.

FIGURE 3.17 What Do You See Here, the Letter B or the Number 13? Your answer may depend on your perceptual set.

CONCEPT 3.30

Our interpretations of stimuli depend in part on what we expect to happen in particular situations.

Modes of Visual Processing: Bottom-Up Versus Top-Down

As noted earlier, Hubel and Wiesel's (1979) work on feature detectors showed that specialized receptors in the visual cortex respond only to specific visual features, such as straight lines, angles, or moving points of light. Two general modes of visual processing, *bottom-up processing* and *top-down processing*, help account for how the brain transforms bits and pieces of visual stimuli into meaningful patterns.

In **bottom-up processing**, the brain assembles specific features of shapes, such as angles and lines, to form patterns that we can compare with stored images we have seen before. For example, the brain combines individual lines and angles to form a pattern we recognize as the number 4. Bottom-up processing may also be used to combine the individual elements of letters and words into recognizable patterns. But how is it that we can read handwriting in which the same letter is never formed twice in exactly the same way? This style of processing, called **top-down processing**, involves perceiving patterns as meaningful wholes—such as recognizing faces of people we know—without needing to piece together their component parts. We also use top-down and bottom-up types of processing for sounds or auditory stimulation (Tervaniemi et al., 2009). For example, we engage in bottom-up processing when trying to discriminate between different musical instruments in orchestral music or listening carefully for particular words in a song. We engage in top-down processing when we follow a melody in our head or hear the blending of instruments in a symphony or of words and lyrics in a song.

Top-down processing is based on acquired experience and knowledge with patterns, but it is not perfect. You may have had the experience of thinking you recognized someone approaching you from a distance, only to find you were mistaken as you got a closer look at the person. You made the mistake because of the tendency to perceive faces on the basis of their whole patterns rather than building them up feature by feature (see Figure 3.18). Despite the occasional miss, facial recognition is something the human brain does better than any computer system yet devised (Wagstaff, 2006). Can you think of other abilities the human brain does better than computers?

We now turn to the contributions of Gestalt psychologists to help us understand how the brain organizes our visual perceptions.

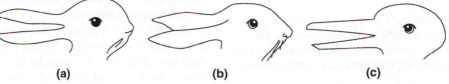

(a)   (b)   (c)

FIGURE 3.18 A Duck or a Rabbit? The figure in (a) appears to be a duck when you see it after viewing the figure in (c). But if you first observed the figure in (b), then the figure in (a) appears to be a rabbit.

Source: From H. R. Shiffman, *Sensation and Perception: An Integrated Approach,* Copyright © 2000 by John Wiley & Sons, Inc. Used by permission.

The Brain Loves a Puzzle

As you read ahead, use the information in the text to solve the following puzzle:

Frances Roberts/ Alamy stock photo

Did you ever notice the arrow in the FedEx logo? If not, why not?

perceptual set The tendency for perceptions to be influenced by one's expectations or preconceptions.

bottom-up processing A mode of perceptual processing by which the brain recognizes meaningful patterns by piecing together bits and pieces of sensory information.

top-down processing A mode of perceptual processing by which the brain identifies patterns as meaningful wholes rather than as piecemeal constructions.

Frances Roberts/ Alamy stock photo

Do you now see the arrow in the FedEx logo? We typically perceive letters as figures and white space as ground. If you are having trouble perceiving the arrow, try reversing the figure and ground. You should then perceive the arrow in the white space between the E and the X.

CONCEPT 3.31

The brain forms meaningful visual patterns using two different modes of processing visual stimuli: bottom-up processing and top-down processing.

CONCEPT 3.32

Gestalt psychologists described how the brain constructs meaning from sensations by organizing them into recognizable patterns.

 CONCEPT LINK

Gestalt therapy is a form of psychotherapy that helps individuals blend conflicting parts of the personality into an integrated whole or "Gestalt." See Module 14.1.

Try This Out
Your Neighborhood Gestalt

Take a walk through your neighborhood or local area. Look around you. How many examples of the Gestalt laws of perceptual organization can you identify?

laws of perceptual organization The principles identified by Gestalt psychologists that describe the ways in which the brain groups bits of sensory stimulation into meaningful wholes or patterns.

Gestalt Principles of Perceptual Organization

Max Wertheimer and the other early Gestalt psychologists conducted studies in which they observed the ways people assemble bits of sensory stimulation into meaningful wholes (Pomerantz & Portillo, 2011; Wagemans et al., 2012a, b). On this basis, they formulated **laws of perceptual organization**. Here we consider laws of figure–ground perception and laws of grouping.

Figure and Ground

Look around as you are walking down the street. What do you see? Are there people milling about? Are there clouds in the sky? Gestalt psychologists have shown that people, clouds, and other objects are perceived in terms of *figure,* and the background against which the figures are perceived (the street, for the people; the sky, for the clouds) serves as the *ground*. Figures have definite shapes, but ground is shapeless. We perceive objects as figures when they have shapes or other characteristics, such as distinctive coloring, which are set against a backdrop of the ground in which they appear (Peterson & Skow, 2008; Wagemans et al., 2012a, b).

Sometimes, however, when we perceive an outline, it may be unclear as to what constitutes the figure and what constitutes the ground. Does ■ Figure 3.19 show a vase, or does it show two profiles? Which is the figure, and which is the ground? Outline alone does not tell the tale, because the same outline describes a vase and human profiles. What other cues do you use to decide which is the figure and which is the ground?

Let's return to the puzzle we posed about the FedEx logo. Most of us have seen this logo countless times, but many people—you perhaps—have never noticed the arrow. (Hint: Focus on the Ex and perceive the arrow in white as a figure set against an orange background). Reversing figure and ground relationships leads us to perceive objects in different ways.

Now let's now consider ■ Figure 3.20, an ambiguous figure that can be perceived in different ways depending on how you organize your perceptions. What does the figure look like? Take a minute to focus on it before reading further.

FIGURE 3.19 Reversible Figure
Whether you see two profiles facing each other in this picture or a vase depends on your perception of figure and ground. See if you can shift back and forth between perceiving the profiles and the vase by switching the parts you take to be figure and those you take to be ground.

FIGURE 3.20 Ambiguous Figure
Do you see an old woman or a young one? If you have trouble switching between the two, look at Figure 3.22, in which figure and ground are less ambiguous.

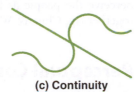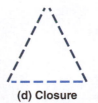

(a) Proximity   **(b) Similarity**   **(c) Continuity**   **(d) Closure**   **(e) Connectedness**

FIGURE 3.21 Gestalt Laws of Grouping
Gestalt psychologists recognized that people group objects according to certain organizational principles. Here we see examples of five such principles: proximity, similarity, continuity, closure, and connectedness.

Did you see an old woman or a young one? Are you able to switch back and forth? If you are struggling to switch between the two, here is a helpful hint: The old woman is facing forward and downward, while the young woman is facing diagonally away. Also, the old woman's nose is the young woman's chin, and her right eye is her counterpart's left ear. Whether you see an old woman or a young one depends on how you organize your perceptual experience—which parts you take to be the figure and which parts you take to be the ground. ■ Figure 3.22 provides an example in which figure and ground are less ambiguous.

Gestalt Laws of Grouping

People tend to group bits and pieces of sensory information into unitary forms or wholes (see Try This Out). Gestalt psychologists described several principles of grouping, including *proximity, similarity, continuity, closure,* and *connectedness.*

■ Figure 3.21(a) illustrates **proximity,** or nearness. Most observers would perceive the figure as consisting of three sets of parallel lines rather than six separate lines, although six lines are sensed. That is, we use the relative closeness of the lines as a perceptual cue for organizing them into a group.

How would you describe ■ Figure 3.21(b)? Do you perceive nine separate geometric shapes or two columns of X's and one column of ●'s? If you describe it in terms of X's and ●'s, you are using the principle of **similarity**—that is, grouping figures that are similar to one another (in this case, geometric figures that resemble each other). If you see four bare-chested young men at a football game who've painted their bodies in the colors of the home team, you are likely to perceive them as a group distinct from the other fans.

■ Figure 3.21(c) represents another way we group stimuli, **continuity,** which is the tendency to perceive a series of stimuli as a unified form when the stimuli appear to represent a continuous pattern. Here we perceive two intersecting continuous lines, one curved and one straight, rather than four separate lines.

Now, check ■ Figure 3.21(d). You sense a number of short lines, but do you perceive a meaningless array of lines or a broken triangle? If you perceive the triangle, your perception draws on the principle of **closure**—grouping disconnected pieces of information into a meaningful whole. You perceive a complete form even when there are gaps in the form. This illustrates the principle for which Gestalt psychologists are best known—that the whole is more than the sum of the parts.

■ Figure 3.21(e) gives an example of **connectedness**—the tendency to perceive objects as belonging together when they are positioned together or are moving together. Thus, you perceive three sets of connected triangles rather than six triangles with three interspersing lines. Perhaps you have noticed this tendency while watching two people walk down a street next to each other and being surprised when they suddenly walk off in different directions without saying goodbye. In such circumstances, we tend to

FIGURE 3.22 Old/Young Woman
The figure on the right shows the downward-looking "old woman" more clearly as figure than as ground, while the one on the left highlights the figural aspects of the "young woman" looking away from the perceiver. Now look back at Figure 3.20 and see if you can't switch back between the two impressions.

proximity The principle that objects that are near each other will be perceived as belonging to a common set.

similarity The principle that objects that are similar will be perceived as belonging to the same group.

continuity The principle that a series of stimuli will be perceived as representing a unified form.

closure The perceptual principle that people tend to piece together disconnected bits of information to perceive whole forms.

connectedness The principle that objects positioned together or moving together will be perceived as belonging to the same group.

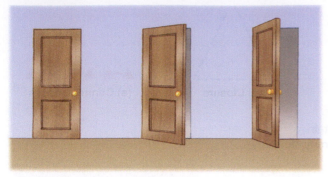

FIGURE 3.23 **Shape Constancy**
Perception of an object's shape remains the same even when the image it casts on the retina changes with the angle of view. You perceive three rectangular doors, despite the fact that the image each projects on the retina is different.

CONCEPT 3.33
We tend to perceive objects as having a constant size, shape, color, and brightness even when the image they cast on our retinas changes.

CONCEPT 3.34
Our perception of depth depends on both monocular and binocular cues for judging distance.

perceptual constancy The tendency to perceive the size, shape, color, and brightness of an object as remaining the same even when the image it casts on the retina changes.

shape constancy The tendency to perceive an object as having the same shape despite differences in the images it casts on the retina as the viewer's perspective changes.

size constancy The tendency to perceive an object as having the same size despite changes in the images it casts on the retina as the viewing distance changes.

color constancy The tendency to perceive an object as having the same color despite changes in lighting conditions.

brightness constancy The tendency to perceive objects as retaining their brightness even when they are viewed in dim light.

binocular cues Cues for depth that involve both eyes, such as retinal disparity and convergence.

retinal disparity A binocular cue for distance based on the slight differences in the visual impressions formed in both eyes.

perceive the people as belonging together because they are moving together (Ip, Chiu, & Wan, 2006; Sekuler & Bennett, 2001).

Perceptual Constancies

Here we focus on **perceptual constancy**—the tendency to perceive the size, shape, color, and brightness of an object as remaining the same even when the image it casts on the retina changes. We could not adjust to our world very well without perceptual constancy. The world is constantly shifting before our eyes as we look at objects from different distances and perspectives. Just turning our heads changes the geometry of an object projected on the retina. Yet we don't perceive objects as changing before our eyes. We perceive them as constant—a good thing, because, of course, they are constant. For example, the ability to perceive that a tiger is a tiger and not a housecat regardless of the distance from which the animal is viewed could be a lifesaving mechanism.

The tendency to perceive an object as being the same shape even when the object is viewed from different perspectives is **shape constancy**. If you observe a round bowl on a table from different angles, the image it casts on your retina changes shape. Nonetheless, you perceive the bowl as round. In other words, its shape remains constant despite the change in your angle of view. Similarly, you perceive a door as having an unchanging shape despite differences in the image it casts on your retina when it is open or closed (see ■ Figure 3.23).

Returning to the bowl, as you approach the bowl at eye level, its size—in terms of the size of the retinal image—grows. As you move farther away from it, the size of its retinal image decreases. Yet you continue to perceive the bowl as being the same size, just as I knew my daughter did not suddenly become a giant as she approached the camera. The tendency to perceive an object as being the same size despite changes in the size of the retinal image it casts is **size constancy** (Combe & Wexler, 2010).

Experience teaches people about distance and perspective. We learn that an object seen at a distance will look smaller than when it is close and that an object seen from different perspectives will appear to have different shapes. If we are wrong, please send out an all-points bulletin for a runaway giant infant.

People also perceive objects as retaining their color even when lighting conditions change. This tendency is called **color constancy**. For example, if your car is red, you perceive it to be red even though it may look grayish as evening falls. The tendency for perceived brightness or lightness of an object to remain relatively constant despite changes in illumination is called **brightness constancy** or *lightness constancy* (Wilcox & Duke, 2003). For example, a piece of white chalk placed in the shade on a sunny day reflects less light than does a black hockey puck placed directly in sunlight. Yet we perceive the chalk to be brighter than the hockey puck.

Cues to Depth Perception

How do we know that some objects are closer than others? The perception of distance, or depth perception, relies on cues involving both the individual eye (monocular cues) and both eyes working together (binocular cues) (Proffitt, 2006).

Binocular Cues for Depth

Having two eyes also comes in handy for judging distance. Some cues for depth, called **binocular cues**, depend on both eyes. Our eyes are a few inches apart, so each eye receives slightly different images of the world (Farell, 2006). The brain interprets differences in the two retinal images—the **retinal disparity** between them—as cues to the relative distances of objects. The closer an object, the greater the retinal disparity.

You can see for yourself how retinal disparity works by holding a finger an inch in front of your nose. First close your left eye and look at the finger only with your right eye. The finger looks as if it is off to the left. Then close your right eye and look at the finger with your left eye. The finger seems off to the right. The finger appears to move from side to side as you open and close each eye. The distance between the two apparent fingers corresponds to the retinal disparity between the two images that form on your retina. Now hold a finger straight ahead at arm's length away from your eyes. Again close one eye and focus on the finger. Then close that eye and open the other. The finger may still seem to "move," but there will be less distance between the two "fingers" because retinal disparity is smaller at greater distances.

Now let's try an experiment to illustrate the binocular cue of **convergence**, which depends on the muscular tension produced by turning both eyes inward to form a single image. Hold a finger once more at arm's length. Keeping both eyes open, concentrate on the finger so that you perceive only one finger. Now bring it slowly closer to your eyes, maintaining the single image. As you do, you will feel tension in your eye muscles. This is because your eyes are *converging,* or looking inward, to maintain the single image, as shown in ■ Figure 3.24. The closer the object—in this case, the finger—the greater the tension. Your brain uses the tension as a cue for depth perception.

Monocular Cues for Depth

Monocular cues depend on one eye only. When people drive, they use a combination of binocular and monocular cues to judge the distance of other cars and of the surrounding scenery. Although there are advantages to using binocular cues, most people can get by driving with monocular cues only, which include relative size, interposition, relative clarity, texture gradient, linear perspective, and shadowing:

- *Relative size.* When two objects are believed to be the same size, the one that appears larger is perceived to be closer, as in ■ Figure 3.25(a).
- *Interposition.* When objects block or otherwise obscure our view of other objects, we perceive the obscured object as farther away. Notice that in ■ Figure 3.25(b), we perceive the horses in front to be closer than the ones that are partially blocked.
- *Relative clarity.* Smog, dust, smoke, and water droplets in the atmosphere create a "haze" that makes distant objects appear blurrier than nearer objects, as in ■ Figure 3.25(c). You may have noticed how much closer faraway mountains appear on a really clear day.
- *Texture gradient.* The relative coarseness or smoothness of an object is used as a cue for distance. Closer objects appear to have a coarser or more detailed texture than more distant objects. Thus, the texture of flowers that are farther away is smoother than the texture of those that are closer, as in ■ Figure 3.25(d).

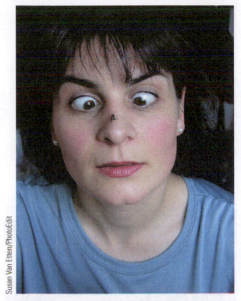

Susan Van Etten/PhotoEdit

FIGURE 3.24 Binocular Cues for Depth
When we rely on binocular cues for judging the depth of a nearby object, our eyes must converge on the object, which can give us that cross-eyed look.

convergence A binocular cue for distance based on the degree of tension required to focus two eyes on the same object.

monocular cues Cues for depth that can be perceived by each eye alone, such as relative size and interposition.

I have no depth perception. Is there a cop standing on the corner, or do you have a tiny person in your hair?

(a)

(b)

(c)

(d)

(e)

(f)

FIGURE 3.25 Monocular Cues for Depth
We use many different monocular cues to judge depth, including:

(a) Relative size

(b) Interposition

(c) Relative clarity

(d) Texture gradient

(e) Linear perspective

(f) Shadowing

- *Linear perspective.* Linear perspective is the perception of parallel lines converging as they recede into the distance. As we look straight ahead, objects and the distances between them appear smaller the farther away they are from us. Thus, the road ahead of the driver, which consists of parallel lines, appears to grow narrower as it recedes into the distance, as in ■ Figure 3.25(e). It may even seem to end in a point.

- *Shadowing.* Patterns of light and dark, or shadowing, create the appearance of three-dimensional objects or curving surfaces. Shadowing can make an object appear to be concave or convex. Notice how the dents that appear in ■ Figure 3.25(f) look like bumps when the image is turned upside down. We perceive objects that are lighter on top and darker on the bottom to be bumps, whereas the opposite is the case for dents (Gaulin & McBurney, 2001).

Motion Perception

CONCEPT 3.35
We use two basic cues in perceiving movement: the path of the image as it crosses the retina and the changing size of the object.

We use various cues to perceive motion. One is the actual movement of an object across our field of vision as the image it projects moves from point to point on the retina. The brain interprets the swath that the image paints across the retina as a sign of movement (Derrington, 2004). Another cue is the changing size of an object. Objects appear larger when they are closer. When you are driving and you see the cars ahead suddenly looming much larger, you perceive that you are moving faster than they are—so fast you may need to slam on the brakes to avoid a collision. When cars ahead grow smaller, they appear to be moving faster than you are.

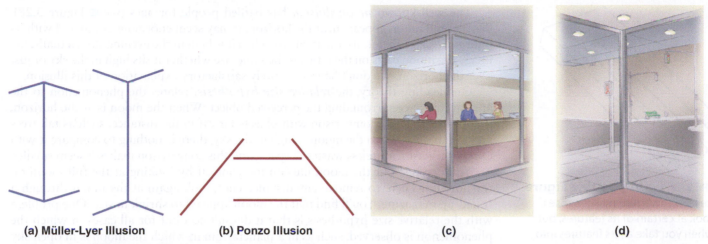

(a) Müller-Lyer Illusion   **(b) Ponzo Illusion**   **(c)**   **(d)**

FIGURE 3.26 Müller-Lyer Illusion and Ponzo Illusion
Visual illusions involve misperceptions in which our eyes seem to be playing tricks on us.

Visual Illusions: Do Your Eyes Deceive You?

Our eyes sometimes seem to play tricks on us in the form of **visual illusions**. ■ Figure 3.26 shows two well-known visual illusions: the *Müller-Lyer illusion* (a) and the *Ponzo illusion* (b). In both cases, what you think you see isn't exactly what you get when you pull out a ruler. Although the center lines in (a) are actually the same length, as are the center lines in (c) and (d), the line on the right in (a) seems longer, as does the center line in (d) as compared to the one in (c). The figure with the inward wings creates the impression of an outward corner of a room that appears to be closer (c). In the Müller-Lyer illusion, the figure with the outward wings suggests the inner corner of a room (d), which makes the center line seem farther away.

Although no one explanation may fully account for the Müller-Lyer illusion, a partial explanation may involve how the brain interprets size and distance cues.

As you'll recall from the discussion of size constancy, people tend to perceive an object as remaining the same size even as the image it projects on the retina changes in relation to distance from the observer. But when two objects of the same size appear to be at different distances from the observer, the one that is judged to be farther away is perceived to be larger. In the Müller-Lyer illusion, the figure with the outward wings suggests the inner corner of a room, which makes the center line seem farther away. The figure with the inward wings creates the impression of an outward corner of a room that appears to be closer to the observer. Because both center lines actually create the same size image on the retina, the brain interprets the one that appears to be farther away as being longer.

Now consider the Ponzo illusion (also called the railroad illusion). Which of the two horizontal lines in Figure 3.26(b) looks longer? Why do you think people generally perceive the line at the top to be longer? Converging lines may create an impression of linear perspective, leading us to perceive the upper line as farther away. As with the Müller-Lyer illusion, because lines of equal length cast the same size image on the retina, the one perceived as farther away is judged to be longer.

Another type of illusion involves *impossible figures*, such as the one in ■ Figure 3.27. Impossible figures fool the brain into creating the impression of a whole figure when the figure is viewed from certain perspectives. An impossible figure appears to make sense when you look at parts of it, but not when you try to take into account the characteristics of the whole figure.

Andia/Photoshot

To create the three-dimensional effect, as in the movie *Avatar*, slightly different images are projected to each eye. The brain pieces together the information to give the impression of depth.

CONCEPT 3.36
Visual illusions are misperceptions of visual stimuli in which it seems that our eyes are playing tricks on us.

visual illusions Misperceptions of visual stimuli.

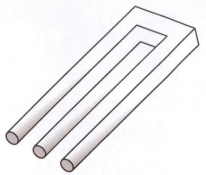

FIGURE 3.27 An Impossible Figure
Notice how the figure makes sense if you look at certain of its features, but not when you take all its features into account.

Russell Kord/Alamy stock photo

FIGURE 3.28 Moon Illusion
The moon illusion refers to the perception that the moon is larger when at the horizon than when it is high in the sky.

stroboscopic movement A type of apparent movement based on the rapid succession of still images, as in motion pictures.

The well-known *moon illusion* has baffled people for ages (see ■ Figure 3.28). When a full moon appears near the horizon, it may seem enormous compared with its "normal" size—that is, its apparent size when it is high in the evening sky. Actually, the image the moon casts on the retina is the same size whether it sits high in the sky or just over the horizon. We don't have an entirely satisfactory explanation of this illusion.

One leading theory, the *relative size hypothesis,* relates the phenomenon to the amount of space surrounding the perceived object. When the moon is at the horizon, it appears larger by comparison with objects far off in the distance, such as tall trees and mountains. When the moon is high in the sky, there is nothing to compare it with except the vast featureless wastes of space, and this comparison makes it seem smaller.

You can test out the moon illusion for yourself by looking at the full moon on the horizon. Then, to remove any distance cues, look again at the moon through a rolled-up magazine. You'll find that the moon appears to shrink in size. One problem with the relative size hypothesis is that it doesn't account for all cases in which the phenomenon is observed, such as in a planetarium in which the moon is in open sky without any intervening landscape cues.

We discussed how we perceive actual movement, but the illusion of **stroboscopic movement**, a form of apparent movement, puts the motion in motion pictures (see ■ Figure 3.29). We perceive the rapid progression of illuminated still images projected by a film projector to be a seamless "motion picture." The film itself contains a series of still images projected at more than 20 pictures, or "frames," per second. Each frame differs somewhat from the one shown before. This is nothing but a quick slide show; the "movie" mechanism lies within us—the viewers.

Visual illusions may also influence how much we eat (Wansink, 2013). In ■ Figure 3.30, the dark circle on the left appears larger than the one on the right, even though they are the same size (go ahead and measure them). Now imagine these are two plates and the circles represent portions of food placed on them. When portion sizes appear smaller, such as when food is placed on larger plates, people may have a tendency to eat more. Why not try out this principle at home by using luncheon plates rather than dinner plates when serving food?

Cultural Differences in Perceiving Visual Illusions

Suppose you lived in a culture in which structures with corners and angles were uncommon. Would you be as likely to experience the Müller-Lyer illusion as someone raised in, say, Cleveland or Dallas? To find out, Darhl Pedersen and John Wheeler (1983) tested two groups of Navajo Indians on the Müller-Lyer illusion. One group lived in rectangular houses that provided daily exposure to angles and corners. Another group lived in traditional rounded huts with fewer of these cues. Those living in the rounded huts were less likely to be deceived by the Müller-Lyer illusion, suggesting that prior experience plays a role in determining susceptibility to the illusion. Other studies have produced similar results. For example, the illusion was observed less frequently among the Zulu people of southern Africa, who also live in rounded structures (Segall, 1994).

© Andrew Davidhazy/Rochester Institute of Technology

FIGURE 3.29 Stroboscopic Movement
The perception of movement in "moving pictures" is a feature of the viewer, not the projector.

The **carpentered-world hypothesis** was put forth to account for cultural differences in susceptibility to the Müller-Lyer illusion (Segall, Campbell, & Herskovits, 1966). A carpentered world is one, like our own, that is dominated by structures (buildings, rooms, and furniture) in which straight lines meet at right angles. People living in noncarpentered worlds, which consist largely of rounded structures, are less prone to the illusion because of their limited experience with angular structures. Cultural experience, rather than race, seems the determinant. Zulus who move to cities where they become accustomed to seeing angular structures are more likely to be fooled by the illusion (Segall, Campbell, & Herskovits, 1963).

Studies with the Ponzo (railroad) illusion also show cultural differences. The illusion is less prominent among the people of Guam, an island with a hilly terrain and no long, uninterrupted highways or railroads (Leibowitz, 1971).

The lesson here goes beyond cultural differences in visual illusions. Perception is influenced not only by our sensory systems but also by our experience of living in a particular culture. People from different cultures may perceive the physical world differently. Consider a classic example offered by the anthropologist Colin Turnbull (1961). Turnbull took Kenge, an African pygmy guide, on his first trip outside the dense forest into the open plain. When Kenge saw buffalo several miles away on the plain, he took them to be insects. When he got closer to the animals and recognized them as buffalo, he was aghast at how the animals had been able to grow so quickly. Why would Kenge mistake a buffalo for an insect? In Kenge's culture, people lived in remote villages in a dense forest. He had never before had an unobstructed view of objects at a great distance. He lacked the experience needed to acquire size constancy for distant objects—to learn that objects retain their size even as the image they project on our eyes grows smaller.

Recent research shows that Westerners and East Asians tend to perceive the same visual scenes in different ways. Investigators found that Americans tend to focus more attention on objects in the foreground of visual scenes than do East Asians, whereas East Asians take in more of the background or contextual characteristics than do Americans (Chua, Boland, & Nisbett, 2005; Masuda & Nisbett, 2001). When it comes to West and East, Nisbett and his colleagues claim, we have two fundamentally different processing styles, a Western style of focusing on categorizing specific objects versus a more holistic Eastern style of attending to contextual information and making judgments about relationships among objects rather than simply classifying them (Chua, Boland, & Nisbett, 2005).

Next we focus on two controversies in perception that have sparked a continuing debate within both the scientific community and the society at large.

Controversies in Perception: Subliminal Perception and Extrasensory Perception

It created quite a stir during the 2000 U.S. presidential race when a campaign commercial for then candidate George W. Bush used what appeared to be a subliminal slur against his opponent, Vice President Al Gore (ABC News, 2000). The word *RATS* was flashed during an ad attacking Gore's health care plan. The producer of the ad claimed the message was not intended as a slur against Gore and simply represented a visual reminder of the word *bureaucrats* (*rats* being the last four letters of the word).

Whether or not it was intended as a slur, the commercial led people to wonder whether **subliminal perception** could affect people's attitudes and behaviors. In subsequent research, psychologists subliminally exposed research participants to four

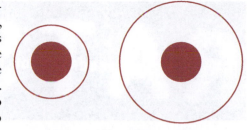

FIGURE 3.30 The Dinner Plate Illusion
Notice how the circle on the left appears larger, even though they are the same size. Now imagine the two circles are portions of food served on two plates of different sizes. If your eyes are fooled into thinking the portion of food looks larger, might you actually eat less?

CONCEPT 3.37

The susceptibility to visual illusions is influenced by cultural factors, such as the types of structures to which people in a particular culture are accustomed.

JJ pix/Alamy stock photo

According to the carpentered-world hypothesis, people living in cultures in which right-angled structures are rare are less prone to the Müller-Lyer illusion.

carpentered-world hypothesis An attempt to explain the Müller-Lyer illusion in terms of the cultural experience of living in a carpentered, right-angled world like our own.

subliminal perception Perception of stimuli that are presented below the threshold of conscious awareness.

CONCEPT 3.38

Though we sometimes perceive things we are not conscious of perceiving, there is no evidence that subliminal cues have significant effects on our daily lives.

extrasensory perception (ESP) Perception that occurs without benefit of the known senses.

parapsychology The study of paranormal phenomena.

telepathy Communication of thoughts from one mind to another that occurs without using the known senses.

clairvoyance The ability to perceive objects and events without using the known senses.

precognition The ability to foretell the future.

psychokinesis The ability to move objects by mental effort alone.

different stimuli: RATS, STAR, ARAB, or XXXX. They then showed them a picture of a fictional political candidate and asked them to rate the person's likeability and competence (Weinberger & Westen, 2008). Participants who were flashed the "RATS" stimulus rated the candidate more negatively than did participants in the other stimulus conditions.

An even more controversial topic is **extrasensory perception (ESP)** — perception that occurs without benefit of the known senses. Is it possible to read people's minds or to know the contents of a letter in a sealed envelope? Here we consider these long-standing controversies in light of the evidence that scientists have been able to gather.

Subliminal Perception: Did You See Something Flash By?

Does subliminal perception exist? Two-thirds of Americans think so (Onion, 2000). But does scientific evidence support this belief? The answer, researchers report, is yes, but it is a qualified yes.

Research evidence shows that people can detect a wide range of subliminal stimuli (visual images, sounds, and even some odors) without being consciously aware of them (Levy et al., 2014; Lin & Murray, 2014; Verwijmeren et al., 2011, 2013). Subliminal exposure to certain brand names may have subtle effects on our behavior, even making us think more creatively. Investigators flashed images of the logos of Apple and IBM at speeds too fast to be detected consciously. The investigators had earlier found the Apple brand to be more strongly associated with creativity. In their experiment, people who were flashed images of the Apple logo showed more creative responses in a follow-up task than those exposed to either an IBM logo or no logo at all (Fitzsimons, Chartrand, & Fitzsimons, 2008; Walker, 2008). In another research study, subliminal exposure to fast food images increased the participants' reading speed in a later reading task (Zhong, 2010). The upshot of this research is that we may be influenced by stimuli that whiz by us so quickly they don't register fully in consciousness.

How might we account for subliminal effects? One possibility is that people may be able to detect some features of a subliminally presented stimulus, even though they cannot report verbally what they have seen. Partial perception of a stimulus may help account for subliminal effects in laboratory studies, but we still lack any convincing evidence that subliminal messaging in advertising or motivational audiotapes actually influences purchase decisions or helps people become more successful in life, or has any meaningful impact on people's lives.

Extrasensory Perception: Is It for Real?

A man claims to be able to bend spoons with his mind. A woman claims to be able to find the bodies of crime victims aided by nothing more than a piece of clothing worn by the victim. Another woman claims to be able to foretell future events. The study of such *paranormal phenomena*—events that cannot be explained by known physical, psychological, or biological mechanisms—is called **parapsychology**. The major

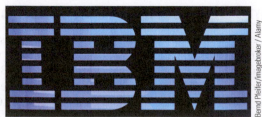

In a test of the effects of subliminal cues, research participants demonstrated more creative responses after they were flashed subliminal images of the Apple brand logo as compared with others who were exposed to either an IBM logo or no logo at all.

focus of paranormal psychology is *extrasensory perception*, the so-called "sixth sense" by which people claim they can perceive objects or events without using the known senses. The forms of paranormal phenomena most commonly identified with ESP are *telepathy, clairvoyance, precognition,* and *psychokinesis.*

Telepathy refers to the purported ability to project one's thoughts into other people's minds or to read what is in their minds—to perceive their thoughts or feelings without using the known senses. **Clairvoyance** is the perception of events that are not available to the senses. A clairvoyant may claim to know what someone across town is doing at that precise moment or to identify the contents of a sealed envelope. **Precognition** is the ability to foretell the future. **Psychokinesis** (formerly called *telekinesis*) is the ability to move objects without touching them. Strictly speaking, psychokinesis is not a form of ESP because it does not involve perception, but for the sake of convenience it is often classified as such.

Critical thinkers maintain an appropriate skepticism about claims of ESP or other paranormal phenomena that seem to defy the laws of nature. Many claims have proven to be hoaxes, whereas others may be explained as random or chance occurrences or mere statistical flukes, or based on findings that scientists cannot replicate (Galak et al., 2012; Hyman, 2010; LeBel & Peters, 2011; Ritchie, Wiseman, & French, 2012; Wagenmakers et al., 2011). Despite many decades of scientific study, we lack clear and convincing evidence supporting the existence of ESP that can withstand scientific scrutiny. As critical thinkers, we need to maintain a skeptical attitude and insist that claims of extrasensory abilities be reliably demonstrated under tightly controlled conditions before we are willing to accept them.

Concept Chart 3.5 provides an overview of many of the key concepts of perception discussed in this module.

Sean Pavone/Shutterstock.com

A recent study showed that people actually read more quickly after they were flashed images of a fast food restaurant. Stimuli in our environment that whiz by our eyes may have subtle effects on our behavior, even if they fail to fully register in consciousness.

CONCEPT 3.39

Claims of ESP remain just that—claims that have not met the rigorous tests of scientific inquiry.

Concept Chart 3.5	Overview of Perception	
Basic concepts in perception	Selective attention	The tendency to pay attention to types of sensory information that are important to us. Such factors as motivational states and repeated exposure influence whether we attend to particular stimuli.
	Perceptual set	The tendency for our expectations or preconceptions to influence our perceptions.
	Perceptual constancy	The tendency to perceive objects as unchanging in size, shape, color, and brightness despite changes in perspective, distance, or lighting conditions.
Modes of perceptual processing	Bottom-up	The process by which the brain forms perceptions by piecing together bits and pieces of sensory data to form meaningful patterns.
	Top-down	The process by which the brain forms perceptions by recognizing whole patterns without first piecing together their component parts.
Gestalt principles of perceptual organization	Figure–ground	The tendency to perceive the visual environment in terms of figures (objects) that stand out from the surrounding background, or ground.
	Proximity	The tendency to perceive objects as belonging together when they are close to one another.
	Similarity	The tendency to group objects that have similar characteristics.
	Continuity	The tendency to perceive a series of stimuli as a unified form when they appear to represent a continuous pattern.
	Closure	The tendency to group disconnected pieces of information into a meaningful whole.
	Connectedness	The tendency to perceive objects as belonging together when they are positioned together or are moving together.

(Continued)

Concept Chart 3.5   (Continued)

Cues for depth perception	Binocular cues	Retinal disparity	The disparity in the images of objects projected onto the retina, which the brain uses as a cue to the distance of the objects. Nearby objects produce greater retinal disparity.
		Convergence	Turning the eyes inward to focus on a nearby object, which creates muscular tension that the brain uses as a cue for depth perception. The closer the object, the more the eyes must converge to maintain the single image.
	Monocular cues	Relative size	An object that appears larger than another object believed to be of the same size is judged to be closer.
		Interposition	Objects that are obscured by other objects are perceived as being farther away.
		Relative clarity	Nearby objects are clearer than more distant objects.
		Texture gradient	The details of nearby objects appear to have a coarser texture than those of distant objects.
		Linear perspective	Objects and the spaces between them look smaller as they become more distant. Thus, parallel lines appear to converge as they recede into the distance.
		Shadowing	Shadows can create the appearance of curving surfaces or three dimensions, giving the impression of depth.
Controversies in perception		Subliminal perception	Perception of stimuli presented below the threshold of conscious awareness.
		Extrasensory perception (ESP)	Perception occurring without the benefit of the known senses.

MODULE REVIEW   3.5   Perceiving Our World: Principles of Perception

Recite It

10. Describe the roles of attention, perceptual set, and modes of visual processing in perception.

Through the process of (a) _____ attention, we tend to perceive the most meaningful stimuli impinging upon us at any one time. Attention is influenced by such factors as motivational states and repeated exposure.

The tendency for perceptions to be influenced by expectations and preconceptions is called perceptual (b) _____. The two general modes of visual processing are (c) _____-up processing, which involves piecing together specific features of visual stimuli to form meaningful patterns, and (d) _____-down processing, which involves recognizing patterns as meaningful wholes without first piecing together their component parts.

11. Identify and **describe** the Gestalt principles of grouping objects into meaningful patterns or forms.

The Gestalt principles of perceptual organization include laws of (e) _____–ground perception and laws of (f) _____ (proximity, similarity, continuity, closure, and connectedness). These principles allow us to perceive the world as comprised of (g) _____ or unified forms rather than isolated bits and pieces of sensory data.

12. Define the concept of perceptual constancy and **apply** the concept to examples.

Perceptual constancy is the tendency to perceive an object to be of the same shape, size, color, and (h) _____ even when the images it casts on the retina change in response to changes in viewing perspective, distance, and lighting.

13. Identify and **describe** cues we use to judge distance and perceive movement, and **apply** these cues to examples.

(i) _____ cues include retinal disparity and convergence. (j) _____ cues include relative size, interposition, relative clarity, texture gradient, linear perspective, and shadowing.

14. Identify some common types of visual illusions, and **explain** why it is the brain, not the eyes, that deceives us.

Examples of visual illusions include the Müller-Lyer illusion, the Ponzo illusion, and the (k) _____ illusion. The Müller-Lyer illusion and the Ponzo illusion appear to involve the brain's misperception of cues used in (l) _____ perception.

The brain may be fooled into perceiving apparent movement, as in the case of (m) _____ motion.

15. Evaluate evidence concerning the existence of subliminal perception and extrasensory perception.

Some limited forms of **(n)** _____ perception exist, but there is no evidence that exposure to subliminally presented messages in everyday life affects attitudes or behavior. There is no hard evidence acceptable to a majority of scientists that proves the existence of such forms of **(o)** _____ as telepathy, clairvoyance, precognition, and psychokinesis.

Recall It

1. The process by which the brain turns sensations into meaningful impressions of the external world is called ___.

2. The newborn infant's apparent preference for the sound of its mother's voice may be explained as a function of
    a. sensory facilitation.
    b. prenatal auditory exposure.
    c. inborn reflexes.
    d. the maximal adherence effect.

3. What is the term we use to describe the tendency for our expectations and preconceived notions to influence how we perceive events?

4. Name the Gestalt principle that describes the tendency to perceive objects as belonging together when they are positioned together or moving together.

5. Name the monocular cue by which we perceive objects to be closer to us when they obscure objects that are behind them.

6. Which of the following is *not* a monocular cue for depth?
    a. convergence   c. interposition
    b. relative clarity   d. shadowing

7. Subliminal perception involves
    a. acquiring knowledge or insight without using the known senses.
    b. perceiving information presented below the level of conscious awareness.
    c. perceiving stimuli in an underwater environment.
    d. sensory systems that can transmit all of a stimulus's features.

Think About It

- Drawing upon your understanding of Gestalt principles of perceptual organization, explain how perceptions differ from photographic images.

- Have you ever had any unusual experiences that you believe involved ESP? Think critically. What alternative explanations might account for these experiences?

Recite It *answers placed at the end of chapter.*

THINKING CRITICALLY ABOUT PSYCHOLOGY

Based on your reading of this chapter, answer the following questions. Then, to evaluate your progress in developing critical thinking skills, compare your answers to the sample answers found in Appendix A.

A few years ago, a police department asked a woman who claimed to have psychic abilities to help them locate an elderly man who had disappeared in a wooded area outside of town. Despite an extended search of the area, the police had been unable to locate the man. Working only from a photograph of the man and a map of the area, the woman circled an area of the map where she felt the man might be found. The police were amazed to discover the man's body in the area she had indicated. He had died of natural causes, and his body had been hidden by a dense thicket of bushes.

Critical thinkers adopt a skeptical attitude toward claims of ESP. They evaluate the evidence and consider more plausible alternative explanations. Consider these questions:

1. Do you believe this case demonstrates the existence of ESP? Why or why not?

2. What, if any, additional information would you need to help you evaluate the woman's claims or to generate alternative explanations?

Recite It Answers for Chapter 3

Module 3.1 1. (a) Sensation; (b) Perception; (c) meaningful, 3. (d) absolute, (e) difference; (f) signal detection; (g) adaptation **Module 3.2** 3. (a) cornea; (b) pupil; (c) lens; (d) rods ; (e) bipolar; (f) optic; (g) fovea; (h) Cones; (i) peripheral, 4. (j) trichromatic; (k) opponent-process **Module 3.3** 5. (a) eardrum; (b) oval; (c) cochlea; (d) hair, 6. (e) basilar; (f) frequency; (g) volley; (h) conduction, (i) nerve **Module 3.4** 7. (a) chemical; (b) molecular; (c) taste; (d) bitter, 8. (e) pressure (f) gate-control, 9. (g) kinesthetic; (h) joints; (i) vestibular; (j)balance **Module 3.5** 10. (a) selective; (b) set; (c) bottom; (d) top, 11. (e) figure; (f)grouping (g) whole, 12. (h) brightness 13. (i) Binocular; (j) Monocular, 14. (k) moon; (l) depth; (m) stroboscopic, 15. (n) subliminal; (o) ESP

Sensation and Perception

Basic Concepts of Sensation

- **Absolute Thresholds:** Is something there?
- **Difference Thresholds:** Is something different there?
- **Sensory Adaptation:** Getting duller with time
- **Signal Detection:** Picking up a signal

Sensory Receptors

- **Rods and cones for vision**
- **Hair cells for hearing**
- **Taste cells for taste**
- **Odor receptors for smell**
- **Skin receptors for skin senses**
- **Kinesthetic receptors in the joints, ligaments, and tendons**
- **Vestibular receptors in the inner ear**

Examples of Weber's Constants

Sensation	Weber's Constant (Approximate)
Saltiness of food	1/5
Pressure on skin	1/7
Loudness of sounds	1/10
Odor	1/20
Heaviness of weights	1/50
Brightness of lights	1/60
Pitch of sounds	1/333

Our Senses

The Senses

- **Vision:** Light energy → Receptor cells in retina → Neural impulses → Sight
- **Hearing:** Sound vibrations → Receptor cells in inner ear → Neural impulses along auditory nerve to auditory cortex → Sound
- **Chemical Senses:** Chemical substances → Transformed into neural impulses by receptors in nose and mouth → Smell and taste
- **Skin Senses:** Tactile stimuli → Receptors in skin → Neural impulses transmitted to somatosensory cortex → Touch, pressure, temperature, and pain
- **Kinesthesis:** Body receptors in joints, ligaments, and muscles → Neural signals to brain → Sense of position and movement of parts of the body
- **Vestibular Sense:** Gravitational forces → Stimulate receptors in the inner ear → Neural signals to brain → Sense of position of the body in space and maintenance of balance

Ralph C. Eagle Jr./Science Source

Perceiving Our World: Principles of Perception

Psychological Processes

- **Selective Attention:** Attending to important stimuli
- **Perceptual Set:** Expectations influence perceptions
- **Bottom-Up** and **Top-Down Processing:** Perceiving parts of patterns versus perceiving whole patterns
- **Gestalt Principles of Perceptual Organization:** Brain organizes sensations into recognizable wholes or patterns
- **Perceptual Constancy:** Objects retain their shapes and other properties even when the images they cast change with changing conditions

Perceptual Cues

- **Cues for Depth Perception:** *Monocular cues* depend on the individual eye (relative size, texture gradient, linear perspective, and so on). *Binocular cues* depend on both eyes working together (retinal disparity and convergence).
- **Cues for Motion Perception:** The two basic cues are the path of the image as it crosses the retina and changing size of the object.

Visual Illusions

- **When the Brain, Not the Eye, Plays Tricks on Us:** Examples include the Müller-Lyer illusion, the Ponzo illusion, the moon illusion, and apparent movement.

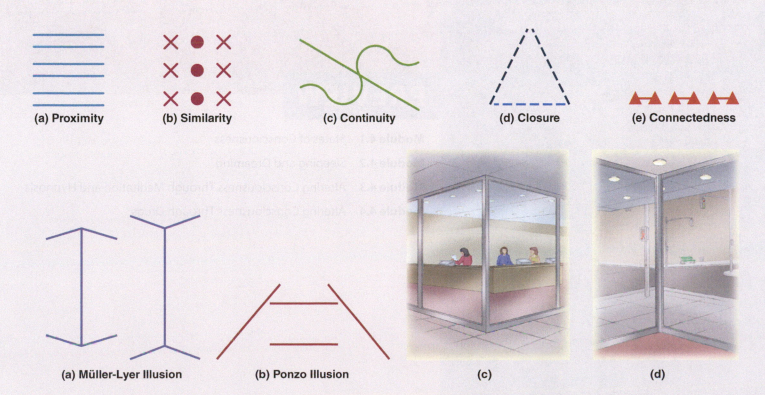

(a) Proximity   (b) Similarity   (c) Continuity   (d) Closure   (e) Connectedness

(a) Müller-Lyer Illusion   (b) Ponzo Illusion   (c)   (d)

LEARNING OBJECTIVES

After studying this chapter, you will be able to . . .

1 **Define** consciousness and **identify** and **describe** different states of consciousness.

2 **Explain** how the sleep–wake cycle is regulated.

3 **Describe** the characteristics of each stage of sleep and the brain wave patterns associated with each stage.

4 **Explain** why we sleep.

5 **Explain** why we dream.

6 **Evaluate** the effects of sleep deprivation.

7 **Identify** and **describe** different types of **sleep–wake** disorders.

8 **Define** and **describe** meditation and hypnosis.

9 **Identify** and **describe** the two major contemporary theories of hypnosis.

10 **Explain** the differences between physiological and psychological dependence, and between drug abuse and drug dependence.

11 **Identify** various types of drugs and **explain** how they affect us.

12 **Explain** the development of alcohol and drug abuse problems in terms of psychological, biological, and sociocultural factors.

13 **Describe** treatment programs to help people with drug problems.

Blend Images - Jose Luis Pelaez Inc/Getty Images

PREVIEW

Consciousness

Are You a Multitasker? Are You Good at It? (*Really?*)

Think about what you are doing right now. Is your attention fully absorbed in reading this page? Or is it divided between two or more tasks? While you are reading, are you also listening to music or musing about your plans for the weekend? We live in a multitasking world in which we keep one eye on one thing and another eye (or ear) on something else. The word *multitasking* entered the popular vocabulary with the introduction of computer systems that allowed users to perform two or more tasks at the same time, such as word processing and emailing. But with advances in technology, multitasking has spilled into our daily lives. We check text messages while watching TV, talk on cell phones while shopping, and send emails or IM our friends while listening to the latest hit song we just downloaded.

Computers are capable of handling multiple tasks without a hitch, but what about the human brain? How well equipped are we to divide our attention between two or more tasks at the same time? It turns out that while multitasking may be a time-saver, it comes at a significant cost in performance. Evidence from the research lab shows most people have difficulty multitasking effectively, especially when different tasks tap the same attentional resources (Lien, Ruthruff, & Johnston, 2006; Oberauer & Kliegl, 2004). Multitasking can also be dangerous in some situations, such as when talking on a cell phone while driving or texting while walking across the street.

Do you multitask while studying—dividing your attention between your textbook and the TV or smartphone? When it comes to mastering the challenging mental tasks needed to succeed in college, such as deciphering a lecture, studying for an exam, or decoding the basic principles of calculus or learning theory, multitasking can impair your performance and lead to poorer grades. When it comes to studying and multitasking, in a word, don't.

The very fact that we are capable of multitasking, whether or not we can do it well, means we can divide our consciousness, or state of mental awareness, between two or more activities at the same time. We can focus a part of our awareness on one task while directing another part to something else.

In this chapter, we set out on an inward exploration of human consciousness. We explore different states of consciousness and examine ways in which people seek to alter their ordinary waking states of consciousness, such as by practicing meditation, undergoing hypnosis, or using mind-altering drugs. We also consider the psychological and physiological effects of these drugs and the risks they pose.

Did you know that...

- Looking at Facebook creates a pattern of brain wave activity associated with states of pleasure? (p. 135)
- About one-third of adults fail to get the recommended 7 to 9 hours of sleep a night? (p. 145)
- Sleep deprivation can lead you to reach for a donut rather than a healthy snack? (p. 147)
- Training in mindfulness meditation helped build resilience in U.S. Marines preparing for deployment. (p. 152).
- It can be dangerous—indeed deadly—to let a person who blacks out from drinking too much "to just sleep it off"? (p. 160)
- Coca-Cola once contained cocaine? (p. 163)
- You may be hooked on a drug you have with breakfast every morning? (p. 165)
- More women die from lung cancer each year than from breast cancer? (p. 165)

4.1 States of Consciousness

1 **Define** consciousness and **identify** and **describe** different states of consciousness.

CONCEPT 4.1

Waking consciousness varies during the course of a day from focused awareness to divided consciousness to drifting consciousness.

CONCEPT 4.2

The selectivity of consciousness allows us to direct our attention to meaningful stimuli, events, or experiences while filtering out other stimuli.

CONCEPT LINK

Negative ways of thinking act like mental filters in our consciousness that put a slant on how we react to life events, which can set the stage for depression in the face of disappointing life experiences. See Module 13.4.

CONCEPT 4.3

States of drifting consciousness are associated with mental meanderings called daydreams.

CONCEPT 4.4

Our ability to divide consciousness allows us to perform more than one activity at a time.

CONCEPT 4.5

Altered states of consciousness may be induced in different ways, such as by practicing meditation or undergoing hypnosis, or by using mind-altering drugs.

consciousness A state of awareness of ourselves and of the world around us.

states of consciousness Levels of consciousness ranging from alert wakefulness to deep sleep.

focused awareness A state of heightened alertness in which one is fully absorbed in the task at hand.

William James is widely regarded as the father of American psychology. He was such an early figure in the field that the first psychology lecture he ever attended was the one he gave himself (Hothersall, 1995). At the time (1875), there were no psychology textbooks. It would be another 15 years, in fact, before the first textbook on psychology would be written, a book James himself would write, which he entitled *Principles of Psychology* (James, 1890/1970).

James was interested in the nature of **consciousness**, which he described as a stream of thoughts. To James, consciousness was not a fixed state or a collection of "chopped bits" of disconnected thoughts and experiences. Rather, it was a continuous process of thinking in which one thought flows into another, like water flowing continuously down a river (James, 1890/1970). Today, we view consciousness in much the same way James envisioned it, as a state of awareness of ourselves and of the world around us.

Your consciousness consists of whatever you happen to be aware of at any given moment in time—your thoughts, feelings, sensations, and perceptions of the outside world. Your awareness at this very moment is probably focused on reading these words. But your consciousness could quickly shift if, for example, you focused on the pressure of your backside against the chair in which you are sitting or listened carefully for a faint sound in the background.

During the course of a day, we experience different **states of consciousness**, or levels of awareness. At certain times of the day, we experience a state of focused awareness in which we are alert and absorbed in the task at hand. At other times, our consciousness follows a meandering or wandering course across a landscape of daydreams and fantasies. For perhaps a third of the day, we lapse into sleep, when our awareness of the external world is dimmed. In this module, we examine three states of consciousness you are likely to experience during the course of a day: focused awareness, drifting consciousness, and divided consciousness. In the next module, we enter the realm of sleep and dreams.

Focused Awareness

Consciousness is *selective*—we have the ability to direct our attention to certain objects, events, or experiences while filtering out extraneous stimuli. The selectivity of consciousness allows us to enter a state of heightened alertness called **focused awareness**, in which we are wide awake, fully alert, and completely engrossed in the task at hand. You may have experienced being so engrossed in watching a movie, or reading a book that's a real "page-turner," that you lost all awareness of time and any distracting external stimuli (traffic noises, rumbling air conditioners) and even disturbing internal stimuli (sensations of hunger or nagging aches and pains). Focused awareness allows us to perform at our best when completing tasks that require fixed attention, such as when you are learning a new skill or fully concentrating when studying for an exam (see Try This Out).

Scientists recently examined how the brain responds to using Facebook. It turns out that the brain responds differently when viewing Facebook pages than when watching beautiful nature scenes pass by or when performing stressful math problems (Mauri et al., 2011). Facebook use evokes a particular physiological response pattern called a "core flow state" that is characterized by a pleasurable arousal and focused awareness in which the person is completely absorbed in the activity at hand. This may help explain why Facebook keeps people mesmerized for hours.

Drifting Consciousness

It is difficult to maintain a state of focused awareness for an extended period of time. Before long, your mind may start drifting from thought to thought. This state of **drifting consciousness** may lead to **daydreaming**, a form of consciousness during a waking state in which your mind wanders off-task to a realm of dreamy thoughts, fantasies, or distracting stimuli (Forster & Lavie, 2014; Smallwood & Schooler, 2015). Generally, daydreams involve mundane facets of everyday life. Despite popular belief, relatively few involve sexual or romantic adventures.

Our minds tend to wander more when we are bored or performing unstructured activities, such as waiting for a bus. Daydreaming in class can disrupt recent memories, so it's best to maintain your focus if you want to remember the day's lecture (Delaney et al., 2010). We also tend to blink more when our mind wanders, which reduces the amount of information coming into the brain, making it more difficult for the brain to process information, including lecture material (Association for Psychological Science, 2010; Smilek, Carriere, & Cheyne, 2010).

But just how much time do we spend mind wandering or daydreaming? To find out, Harvard University researchers provided participants in a recent study with an iPhone app that texted them several times a day to report what they were doing, thinking, and feeling at the moment (Killingsworth & Gilbert, 2010). Data from more than 2,000 adults showed that, on average, people reported their minds wandering nearly half of the time (47 percent). The least frequent time spent mind wandering (no surprise!) was when participants were having sex.

These investigators also reported that a wandering mind is not a happy mind. People tended to report unhappier moods at times when their minds were wandering than when they were focused on activities (Schenkman, 2010). The results of the Harvard study suggests we may find greater happiness by focusing on what we're doing at the moment, rather than escaping into mental fantasies. Even people whose minds wandered to thinking about pleasant activities were not any happier than those who were thinking about their current activities.

Divided Consciousness

Learning a new skill typically requires focused awareness. When learning to drive, for example, you need to pay close attention to how far to turn the wheel when steering into a curve, how much pressure to apply to the brakes when stopping, and so on. But after a time, driving may become so routine that you experience a state of divided consciousness—dividing your attention between driving and other thoughts, such as trying to remember the words of a song or fantasizing about vacation.

Divided consciousness occurs when we simultaneously perform two different activities, each of which demands some level of attention. One of these activities is typically a mechanical task, such as driving or washing dishes. When we perform mechanical tasks, part of our mind seems to be on "automatic pilot" while the other part is free to think about other things.

A more complex but still automatic behavior is catching a fly ball, a skill requiring the brain to apply complicated geometric rules "on the fly" in order to determine the likely trajectory and landing point of a ball in midflight (Kistemaker, Faber, & Beek, 2009). The brain automatically performs the mental computations needed to determine the ball's trajectory, even if the player has no understanding of the underlying geometry.

What do you daydream about? Sexual adventures or wild flights of imagination? It turns out that most people daydream about the routine experiences of daily life.

Try This Out
Savoring Your Food

How does mental focusing affect your experience of eating a meal? Try this out: Focus your attention completely on your next meal. Avoid talking, watching TV, or reading while eating. Notice the shape, color, and texture of the food. Take a deep whiff of the aroma of the food before chewing. Then slowly chew each morsel, savoring the distinctive flavor of each bite. Mix different foods together in your mouth to appreciate their distinctive flavors and how they blend together in a mélange of taste. What differences do you notice between this experience and your usual dining experience?

drifting consciousness A state of awareness characterized by drifting thoughts or mental imagery.

daydreaming A form of consciousness during a waking state in which one's mind wanders to dreamy thoughts or fantasies.

divided consciousness A state of awareness characterized by divided attention to two or more tasks or activities performed at the same time.

The ability to divide consciousness allows us to perform two tasks at once. But the combination of driving and using a phone is associated with a threefold increase in the risk of motor vehicle accidents. Texting is especially dangerous while driving, so much so that reaction times of drivers when texting are reduced by an average of 30 percent.

inattentional blindness The failure to notice something right in front of your eyes because your attention is directed elsewhere.

altered states of consciousness States of awareness during wakefulness that are different than the person's usual waking state.

Divided attention also comes into play in the phenomenon of **inattentional blindness**, the failure to notice something right in front of your eyes because your attention is directed elsewhere. The most famous example is that of viewers failing to notice a dancing gorilla that appears in a video clip of basketball players passing a ball to each other when they are instructed to count the number of passes one of the teams makes. Even expert observers are vulnerable to inattentional blindness. Investigators had a group of radiologists perform a task that was very familiar to them—finding lung-nodules in a series of X-ray films (Drew, Võ, & Wolfe, 2013). Unbeknownst to the doctors, the experimenters slipped in an image of a gorilla in the last film. Most of these expert observers (83 percent) failed to notice the gorilla, even though the image was 48 times the size of the typical nodule and most of observers had looked directly at the image.

The brain can abruptly shift consciousness from a state of divided awareness to focused awareness when necessary. If you are driving while carrying on a conversation with a passenger and suddenly encounter a blinding rainstorm, you can quickly shift full attention to driving. However, divided attention on the road raises important safety concerns, even in the calmest weather. Drivers who use hand-held cell phones are three times more likely to have accidents than those who do not ("By the Numbers," 2014). The problem is not simply fiddling with the phone. Using a hands-free device doesn't eliminate the increased risk use of either a hands-free or handheld phone can be dangerously distracting, taking your attention off the road and leading to a serious loss of concentration called "inattention blindness" (Strayer & Drews, 2007). As psychologist David Strayer, a leading researcher in the field, says, "It's not that your hands aren't on the wheel. . . . It's that your mind is not on the road" (cited in Parker-Pope, 2009). However, ordinary conversations with passengers are not nearly as distracting as talking on a cell phone or texting while driving (Drews, Pasupathi, & Strayer, 2008; Strayer & Drews, 2007).

Why is cell phone use so dangerously distracting to drivers? One reason is that the brain lacks the attentional resources needed to perform two high-level tasks at the same time (Stothart, Mitchum, & Yehnert, 2015). We may be able to work out on the treadmill while watching TV, but performing higher-level or more complex tasks like driving requires attentional resources that cannot be split effectively with other high-level tasks, such as using a cell phone.

The hazards of divided driving involve more than cell phone use (Klauer et al., 2014). Fussing with a child in the backseat, putting on makeup, and eating or drinking can be dangerously distracting (see Table 4.1). Texting during driving is especially risky, as it delays reaction times of drivers by an average of 30 percent (Drews, Pasupathi, & Strayer, 2008). More than a third of drivers in a recent survey said they had read a text or email while driving during the previous 30 days (Richtel, 2015). It's not just drivers who are driven to distraction. Visits to the ER for injuries caused by cell phone-distracted walking have jumped by about eightfold during the past 15 years (Brody, 2015).

Keeping your eyes and mind on the road at all times can help save a life, quite possibly your own. Sadly, more than 3,000 people in the United States lose their lives annually, and about 400,000 are injured due to motor vehicle crashes involving a distracted driver ("Distracted Driving," 2013; NHSTA, 2013). One problem with factoring in these statistics is that while people are generally aware of risks posed by divided attention, they tend to underestimate how risky divided attention is for them relative to other people (Finley, Benjamin, & McCarley, 2014). Sadly, underestimating the risk of divided attention while driving can lead to deadly consequences.

Changes in the level of ordinary awareness in the waking state are called **altered states of consciousness**. Altered states of consciousness may occur when we daydream, meditate or undergo hypnosis, or use mind-altering drugs like alcohol and marijuana. Repetitive physical activity, such as long-distance running or lap swimming, also may induce an altered state of consciousness—one in which the outside

Table 4.1 Driving While Distracted

A Canadian survey asked drivers whether they had engaged in the following behaviors while driving, and whether they had observed other drivers engaging in the same behaviors.

Behaviors	Yourself (%)	Another Driver (%)
Drinking beverages (for example, coffee, soft drinks)	65	74
Eating	53	66
Using a cell phone	35	79
Arguing with passengers	27	41
Disciplining children	18	33
Reading	8	26
Putting on makeup, shaving, or combing hair	8	43
Using PDAs, laptops, or other high-tech devices	5	21

Source: Adapted from *2003 Nerves of Steel* survey, commissioned by the Steel Alliance and the Canada Safety Council, retrieved from www.safety-council.org/info/traffic/distract.html.

© Simon Marcus/Corbis

Multitasking may be an efficient use of attentional resources when performing routine or well-practiced tasks, such as washing the dishes or jogging along a familiar path. But when it comes to multitasking and studying, in a word, don't.

Try This Out
Putting Multitasking to the Test

How distracting is multitasking during studying? Let's put it to the test. Read a page in this text with full attention on your reading. Then jot down on a piece of paper or type into the computer everything you learned—concepts, definitions, key points, research findings—without looking back at the text. Then read the following page in the text while listening to one of your favorite musical groups while you are reading. After reading the page, jot down everything you learned. Then compare the two documents. Does the first provide a more complete and accurate account of the text material? To what extent did multitasking interfere with your ability to learn and remember what you were reading?

world seems to fade out of awareness. In some altered states, the person may experience changes in the sense of time (time may seem to stand still or speed up) and in sensory experiences (colors may seem more vibrant or, as in some drug-induced states, the person may hear voices or see visions). In Modules 4.2 to 4.4, we explore the range of human consciousness, from states of sleep and wakefulness to altered states of consciousness. Concept Chart 4.1 offers an overview of these different levels or states of consciousness.

Concept Chart 4.1 States of Consciousness

	States of Consciousness	Level of Alertness/Attention	Examples or Features
GILKIS - Damon Hyland/Gallo Images/Getty Images	Focused awareness	High; fully awake and alert	Learning a new skill; watching an engrossing movie
© Yuri Arcurs/Shutterstock.com	Drifting consciousness	Variable or shifting	Daydreaming, or letting one's thoughts wander

(Continued)

Concept Chart 4.1 (Continued)

	States of Consciousness	Level of Alertness/ Attention	Examples or Features
Caterina Bernardi/ Getty Images	Divided consciousness	Medium; attention split between two activities	Thinking of other things while exercising or driving a car
© Gravicapa/ Shutterstock.com	Sleeping and dreaming	Low	During sleep, the person is generally unaware of external surroundings but may respond to certain stimuli
© iStockphoto.com/ nicolas hansen	Waking states of altered consciousness	Variable	Changes in consciousness associated with hypnosis, meditation, and drug use

MODULE REVIEW 4.1 States of Consciousness

Recite It

1. **Define** consciousness and **identify** and **describe** different states of consciousness.

   Consciousness is our current (a) _____ of ourselves and of the world around us.
   States of consciousness include (b) _____ awareness (full mental absorption), (c) _____ consciousness (daydreaming), (d) _____ consciousness (splitting of consciousness between two or more tasks), sleep and dreaming (states of (e) _____), and (f) _____ states of consciousness (changes in typical level of awareness while awake).

Recall It

1. The nineteenth-century psychologist William James likened consciousness to

   a. water flowing continuously down a river.
   b. a drifting cloud.
   c. a swirling ocean.
   d. a state of tranquility.

2. The ___ of consciousness allows us to focus on meaningful stimuli, events, and experiences.

3. The state of awareness in which we are completely alert and engrossed in a task is known as

   a. daydreaming.
   b. divided consciousness.
   c. altered consciousness.
   d. focused awareness.

Think About It

- What steps can you take to reduce your risk of driving while distracted? Did the discussion in the module change your views on the issue? Why or why not?

Recite It answers placed at the end of chapter.

4.2 Sleeping and Dreaming

2 Explain how the sleep–wake cycle is regulated.

3 Describe the characteristics of each stage of sleep and the brain wave patterns associated with each stage.

4 Explain why we sleep.

5 Explain why we dream.

6 Evaluate the effects of sleep deprivation.

7 Identify and **describe** different types of sleep–wake disorders.

We spend about a third of our lives sleeping. During sleep, we enter our own private theater of the mind—a realm of dreams in which the mind weaves tales ranging from the mundane and ordinary to the fantastic and bizarre. The laws of the physical world don't apply when we dream. Objects change shape, one person may be transformed into another, and scenes move abruptly without regard to the physical limits of time and place. Though we've learned much about sleeping and dreaming, many mysteries remain. We lack a consensus about such basic questions as "Why do we sleep?" and "Why do we dream?" In this module, we venture into the mysterious domain of sleep and dreams. We begin by examining the bodily mechanisms responsible for our sleep–wake cycles.

During sleep, we are relatively unaware of our external surroundings. Passing sounds do not register in our awareness unless they are very loud or blaring and interrupt our sleep. Despite the fact that our awareness of the world is dimmed while we sleep, we may still be responsive to certain types of stimuli that are personally meaningful or relevant. As noted in Chapter 3, people may sleep soundly through the wail of a passing ambulance but be awakened instantly by their child's soft cry.

Sleep and Wakefulness: A Circadian Rhythm

Many bodily processes—sleep–wake cycles, as well as body temperature, hormonal secretions, blood pressure, and heart rate—fluctuate daily in a pattern called a **circadian rhythm**. The word *circadian* is derived from the Latin roots *circa* ("about") and *dies* ("day"). Circadian or daily rhythms are found in virtually all species, including organisms as varied as single-celled paramecia, fruit flies, humans and other mammals, and even trees. Circadian rhythms are synchronized with the 24-hour cycle of day and night (Sanchez-Romera et al., 2014). In humans, the sleep–wake cycle operates on a circadian rhythm that is about 24 hours in length.

Do you feel happier upon awakening than you do later in the day? Though late-day fatigue may play a role, there might also be a circadian basis to this mood effect. Based on coding the emotional content of words used in millions of public Twitter messages from around the world, investigators found that people tend to use happier words earlier in the day, which may reflect a change from positive moods upon awakening to more sour moods as the day drags on (Golder & Macy, 2011).

It may surprise you to learn that the human body does not maintain a steady 98.6 degree temperature. Body temperature follows a circadian rhythm, falling a few degrees during the middle of the night, then rising in the early morning hours and peaking at around midday.

CONCEPT 4.6

At the lower end of the continuum of awareness are states of sleeping and dreaming.

Ian Dagnall/Alamy Stock Photo

Circadian rhythms may explain why people tend use happier words in Twitter messages posted earlier in the day.

circadian rhythm The pattern of fluctuations in bodily processes that occur regularly each day.

A small area of the hypothalamus called the *suprachiasmatic nucleus (SCN)* is an internal body clock that regulates our sleep–wake cycles (Dubovsky, 2014; Jones, Tackenberg, & McMahon, 2015). The SCN syncs with the daily light/dark cycle and responds to light impinging on the retina (Azzi et al., 2014; Kramer, 2015). When light enters the eye, its energy is transformed into neural impulses that travel to the SCN. The SCN in turn regulates the pineal gland, which, as noted in Chapter 2, releases the hormone *melatonin*.

Melatonin helps synchronize the body's sleep–wake cycle by making us feel sleepy. Exposure to darkness during evening hours stimulates the brain's production of melatonin. During exposure to bright light, melatonin production falls off, which helps us stay awake and alert during daylight hours. (This might also explain why we often feel sleepy on cloudy days.)

Frequent time shifts can play havoc with the body's circadian rhythms. If you've ever traveled by plane across several time zones, you've probably experienced jet lag. **Jet lag** occurs when a change in local time conflicts with your internal body clock, making it difficult to fall asleep earlier than usual or to stay awake later than usual, depending whether you've lost time by traveling east or gained time by traveling west. Jet lag is associated not only with disruption of sleep–wake cycles but also with irritability, fatigue, and difficulty in concentrating.

The Stages of Sleep

The electroencephalograph (EEG) is one of several devices researchers use to determine how our bodies respond when we sleep. The EEG tracks brain waves, which vary in intensity or amplitude (height of the wave) and speed or frequency (wave cycles per second). When you are awake and alert, your brain wave pattern is dominated by fast, low-amplitude *beta waves*. As you close your eyes and relax in bed, you enter a state of relaxed wakefulness. In this state, your brain wave pattern is dominated by slower, rhythmic cycles called *alpha waves*. When people sleep, the EEG shows they progress through several distinct stages of sleep characterized by different brain wave patterns (see ■ Figure 4.1).

Stages 1 to 4: From Light to Deep Sleep

In Stage 1 sleep, brain waves become small and irregular with varying frequencies. The sleeper can be easily awakened during this stage and may not even realize she or he had been sleeping. Stage 2 sleep begins about 2 minutes after Stage 1 sleep and is characterized by bursts of brain wave activity represented by spindle-shaped waves called *sleep spindles*. People spend more than half of their sleep time in Stage 2 sleep. This is a deeper stage of sleep, but the person can still be readily awakened. Stages 3 and 4 of sleep, called *delta sleep* or *slow-wave sleep (SWS)*, are characterized by the appearance of large, slow brain waves called *delta waves*. This is the period of deep sleep in which it is difficult to awaken the person. The distinction between Stage 3 and Stage 4 is based on the proportion of delta waves. In Stage 3, delta waves constitute 50 percent or fewer of the brain wave patterns; in Stage 4, they constitute more than 50 percent.

REM Sleep: The Stuff of Which Dreams Are Made

Rapid eye movement (REM) sleep is the stage of sleep in which one's eyes dart about under closed eyelids. After Stage 4 sleep, the sleeper briefly recycles through Stages 3 and 2 and from there enters REM sleep. REM is the stage of sleep most closely associated with dreaming. Dreams also occur during Stages 1 to 4—which are collectively called non-REM (NREM) sleep—but they are generally briefer, less frequent, and more thought-like than those experienced during REM sleep.

jet lag A disruption of sleep–wake cycles caused by the shifts in time zones that accompany long-distance air travel.

rapid-eye-movement (REM) sleep The stage of sleep that involves rapid eye movements and that is most closely associated with periods of dreaming.

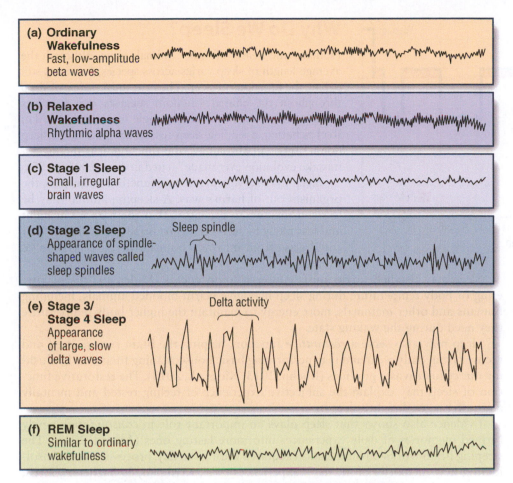

(a) Ordinary Wakefulness
Fast, low-amplitude beta waves

(b) Relaxed Wakefulness
Rhythmic alpha waves

(c) Stage 1 Sleep
Small, irregular brain waves

(d) Stage 2 Sleep
Appearance of spindle-shaped waves called sleep spindles

Sleep spindle

(e) Stage 3/ Stage 4 Sleep
Appearance of large, slow delta waves

Delta activity

(f) REM Sleep
Similar to ordinary wakefulness

FIGURE 4.1 **Brain Wave Patterns During Wakefulness and Sleep**
Here we see the characteristic brain wave patterns associated with each stage of sleep: (a) Ordinary wakefulness—fast, low-amplitude beta waves; (b) relaxed wakefulness—rhythmic alpha waves; (c) Stage 1 sleep—small, irregular brain waves with varying frequencies; (d) Stage 2 sleep—sleep spindles; (e) Stage 3 and Stage 4 sleep—large, slow, delta waves; and (f) REM sleep—rapid, active pattern similar to that in ordinary wakefulness.

The brain becomes more active during REM sleep, which is why it is sometimes called *active sleep*. As Robert Stickgold, a leading sleep researcher, explains, "During sleep, our brain is very active. Much of that activity helps the brain to learn, to remember, and to make connections" (cited in Stickgold & Wehrwein, 2009).

Brain wave patterns during REM sleep are similar to those during states of alert wakefulness. REM sleep is also called *paradoxical sleep*. What makes it paradoxical is that despite a high level of brain activity, muscle activity is blocked to the point that the person is practically paralyzed. This is indeed fortunate, as it prevents injuries that might occur if dreamers were to suddenly bolt out of bed and act out their dreams.

Sleep cycles generally repeat about every 90 minutes. The average person has about four or five sleep cycles during a night's sleep. It may take about an hour to reach Stage 4 sleep in the first cycle and then another 30 or 40 minutes to reach REM. As the night goes on, the amount of time spent in REM sleep increases (see ■ Figure 4.2). Moreover, Stage 4 sleep disappears during the course of the night, which means that we progress faster to REM sleep as the night wears on.

Concept Chart 4.2 summarizes the different states of wakefulness and stages of sleep.

The sleeping brain may not be awake, but it is actively working on consolidating new memories from information acquired during the day.

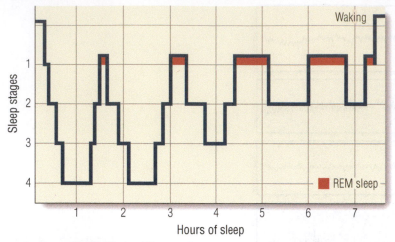

FIGURE 4.2 REM Sleep Through the Night
Notice how periods of REM sleep become longer as sleep progresses through the night.

Milton J. Micaller/Getty Images

CONCEPT 4.10
Sleep may serve many functions, including a protective function, an energy conservation function, a restorative function, and a memory consolidation function.

 **CONCEPT LINK**
Newly learned material may be better retained when you have the chance to sleep on it. See Module 6.2.

Why Do We Sleep?

Humans and nearly all other animals sleep, although the average length of sleep varies across species. Scientists still debate the functions of sleep. The near universality of sleep throughout the animal kingdom suggests that it serves an important function in the struggle to survive. As Alan Rechtschaffen, a leading sleep researcher, puts it, "If sleep doesn't serve an absolutely vital function, it is the biggest mistake evolution ever made" (cited in Azar, 2006, p. 55).

Sleep may serve a *protective* function in keeping the organism out of harm's way. A sleeping animal may be less conspicuous to predators that roam about at night and less likely to suffer dangerous falls or accidents that could arise from moving about in the dark (Gaulin & McBurney, 2001).

Sleep may also help an organism conserve bodily energy (Miller, 2009). The lowering of body temperature during sleep may give warm-blooded animals, including humans and other mammals, more energy to maintain the higher body temperature they need during the waking state.

Sleep may also serve a *restorative* function, helping the brain restore itself and recover from daily wear and tear, performing basic housecleaning functions by flushing out cellular waste products (Kuehn, 2013; Xie et al., 2013). The restorative function of sleep may explain the subjective experience of feeling rested and mentally alert after a good night's sleep.

Evidence also shows that sleep plays an important role in *consolidating* newly formed memories of daily experiences into more lasting ones (Arnold, 2011). The sleeping brain works on information acquired during the day, processing and consolidating new memories of the day's experiences (Wei, Krishnan, & Bazhenov, 2016;

Concept Chart 4.2	Wakefulness and Sleep	
State of Wakefulness/ Stage of Sleep	**Characteristic Brain Wave Pattern**	**Key Features**
Alert wakefulness	Fast, low-amplitude beta waves	State of focused attention or active thought
Relaxed wakefulness	Slower, rhythmic alpha waves	State of resting quietly with eyes closed
Stage 1 sleep	Small, irregular brain waves with varying frequencies	Light sleep from which the person can be easily awakened
Stage 2 sleep	Sleep spindles	Deeper sleep, but the sleeper is still readily awakened
Stage 3 sleep	Large, slow delta waves	Deep sleep (called delta sleep or slow-wave sleep) from which it is difficult to arouse a sleeper
Stage 4 sleep	Dominance of delta waves	Deepest level of sleep
REM sleep	Rapid, active pattern, similar to that in alert wakefulness	Sleep in which the brain becomes more active but muscle activity is blocked (also called active sleep or paradoxical sleep); stage associated with dreaming

Wilhelm et al., 2011). Even while infants sleep in their cribs, their brains are processing what they learned during the day (Friedrich et al., 2015).

Would you like to improve your ability to remember newly learned material? Here's a suggestion bolstered by research: Sleep on it. In a research study, participants who learned a word list in the evening and then went to sleep before being tested the following morning did better than others who learned the material in the morning but were tested later that evening before they had a chance to sleep (Ellenbogen et al., 2006).

Dreams and Dreaming

A dream is an imaginative creation of the brain during sleep, a kind of nightly excursion into a world of fantasy (Hartmann, 2012). The dreams that occur later in the night tend to be longer, more elaborate, and more emotionally impactful (Malinowski & Horton, 2014). But why do we dream? The short answer is that no one really knows. In all likelihood, dreaming has multiple functions, as sleep does.

Like REM sleep, deep sleep plays an important role in memory consolidation, the process by which freshly formed memories become lasting ones (Datta, 2011; Tononi & Cirelli, 2014). The brain may replay waking experiences during dreams in order to strengthen new memories (Ji & Wilson, 2007; Miller, 2007).

Dreams may have other functions as well. Ernest Hartmann, a leading dream investigator, believes that dreams help us sort through possible solutions to everyday problems and concerns and work through emotional crises or traumas (Hartmann, 2011). Consistent with this view, the content of many dreams involves difficulties encountered while trying to perform a task (Maggiolini et al., 2010).

Another prominent view of dreaming, called the **activation-synthesis hypothesis** (Hobson, 1999), holds that dreams represent an attempt by the cerebral cortex to make sense of random discharges of electrical activity in the brain during REM sleep. The electrical activity arises from the brain stem, the part of the brain responsible for such basic functions as breathing and heart rate (see ■ Figure 4.3). According to this hypothesis, the cerebral cortex creates a story line based on the individual's storehouse of knowledge and memories to explain these random signals emanating from lower brain structures and the emotions and sensory experiences they generate.

Interestingly, parts of the brain that show decreased activity during REM sleep include regions of the cerebral cortex involved in logical thought. This pattern of neural activity suggests why dreams may lack the logical ordering of events of ordinary conscious thought—why they may form from bits and pieces of emotionally charged memories and vivid imagery that unfold in a chaotic sequence of events.

Even if dreams emanate from a hodgepodge of electrical discharges from the deep recesses of the brain, they may be filled with personal meaning because they are based on individual memories and associations. But what, if anything, do they mean?

Sigmund Freud (1900) believed he had an answer to this question in arguing that dreams represent a form of *wish fulfillment*. Dreams are expressed in the form of symbols that represent a sleeper's deeper or underlying wishes, usually of a sexual or aggressive nature. He called dreams the "royal road" to the unconscious mind, but believed you need a kind of psychological road map to interpret them because dream symbols mask their true meanings. Freud distinguished between two types of dream content:

1. *Manifest content*. The manifest content refers to events that occur in a dream. You might dream, for example, of driving fast and getting a speeding ticket from a police officer.

2. *Latent content*. This is the true, underlying meaning of a dream, disguised in the form of dream symbols. The disguise conceals the dream's real meaning, thereby helping preserve sleep by preventing emotionally threatening material from waking you up. Driving fast might symbolize an unacceptable sexual wish. The police officer, a symbol of male authority, might represent your father punishing you for having the sexual wish.

CONCEPT 4.11
Though we all dream while asleep, the question of why we dream remains unanswered.

activation-synthesis hypothesis The proposition that dreams represent the brain's attempt to make sense of the random discharges of electrical activity that occur during REM sleep.

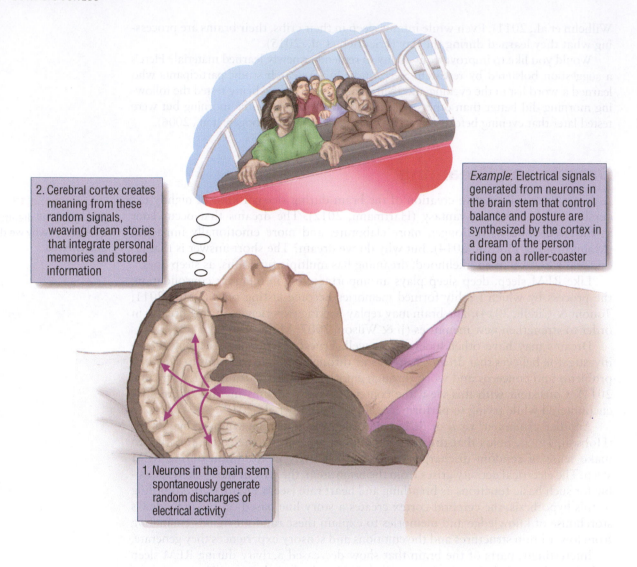

2. Cerebral cortex creates meaning from these random signals, weaving dream stories that integrate personal memories and stored information

Example: Electrical signals generated from neurons in the brain stem that control balance and posture are synthesized by the cortex in a dream of the person riding on a roller-coaster

1. Neurons in the brain stem spontaneously generate random discharges of electrical activity

FIGURE 4.3 **Activation-Synthesis Hypothesis**
According to the activation-synthesis hypothesis, dreams arise when the cerebral cortex attempts to make sense of random electrical discharges emanating from the brain stem during REM sleep.

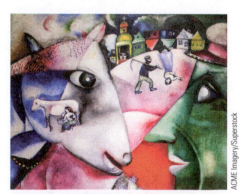

ACME Imagery/Superstock

Why do we dream? Although speculations about dreams abound, their meaning remains a mystery.

In Freud's view, phallic objects such as trees, skyscrapers, snakes, and guns are symbols of male genitalia, whereas enclosed objects such as boxes, closets, and ovens symbolize female genitalia. But Freud believed we shouldn't rush to judgment when interpreting dream symbols—that sometimes "a cigar is just a cigar." Freud also recognized that the same dream events might have different meanings for different people, so individual analysis is necessary to ferret out their meanings (Pesant & Zadra, 2004).

Dream interpretation makes for an interesting exercise, but how do we know that our interpretations are accurate? Unfortunately, although the meaning of dreams has been studied and debated for more than a century since Freud's initial work, we still lack any objective means of verifying the accuracy of dream interpretations. Nor do we have any evidence that dreams serve the function of preserving sleep, as Freud proposed. At the very least, we should credit Freud with raising our awareness that dreams may have a psychological meaning and may express emotional issues.

Try This Out   Dream a Little Dream for Me

Can you determine what you are going to dream about? To find out, try this experiment:

1. Before retiring for the night, select a topic to dream about—for example, meeting a famous person or playing your favorite sport—and put a pen and pad within handy reach of your bed.

2. For 10 or 15 minutes before retiring, mentally rehearse the dream by fantasizing about the topic.

3. Upon retiring, say to yourself, "I think I'll dream some more about this."

4. As you grow sleepier, return to the fantasy, but don't resist letting your mind wander off.

5. When you awake, whether in the middle of the night or the next morning, lie still while you recollect what you dreamed about, then immediately reach for your pen and pad and write down the dream content.

6. Evaluate your results. Were you able to program your dream in advance?

Whatever the underlying meaning of dreams may be, investigators find that some people report **lucid dreams**—dreams in which the person is aware that he or she is dreaming (Bourke & Shaw, 2014). Relatively few people report lucid dreams, but those who do may have a greater capacity for self-reflection than the rest of us—a skill that may carry into the sleeping state (Filevich et al., 2015). Some lucid dreamers report that they are able to direct the action of their dreams while they are dreaming (Yates, 2011). Here's one report from a lucid dreamer:

> "I moved my eyes, and I realized that I was asleep in bed. When I saw the beautiful landscape start to blur, I thought to myself, 'This is my dream; I want it to stay!' And the scene reappeared. Then I thought to myself how nice it would be to gallop through this landscape. I got myself a horse. . . . I could feel myself riding the horse and lying in bed at the same time." (cited in Voss, 2011)

Is it possible to determine what you dream about before you fall asleep? This remains an open question, but it is one you can test out for yourself by performing a mini-experiment (see Try This Out).

Sleep Deprivation: Getting By on Less

People vary in their need for sleep, but most adults require between 7 and 9 hours of sleep to feel fully refreshed and to function at their best (CDC, 2015; see Table 4.2). Most adults do sleep at least 7 hours a night, but many do not (O'Connor, 2015). About one in three adults report sleeping 6 hours or less a night (see ■ Figure 4.4). College students average only 6 to 6.9 hours of sleep a night (Markel, 2003). Among high school students, only about 30 percent get the minimum recommended level of 8 hours of sleep on an average school night, and among 15-year-olds, nearly 40 percent get fewer than 7 hours of sleep nightly (CDC, 2011a; Keyes et al., 2015).

Sleep patterns change during the life cycle. Newborn infants sleep for about two-thirds of the day. Infants spend about one-half of their sleep time in REM sleep, whereas adults spend about one-fifth. Infants and children spend more time in REM during sleep than adults (Scriba et al., 2013). As they mature, the proportion of REM sleep declines and periods of NREM sleep and wakefulness increase. The amounts of REM sleep, deep sleep, and total sleep decline over time during adulthood. By the time we reach our 60s or 70s, we may require only 6 hours of sleep per night.

© wizdata1/Shutterstock.com

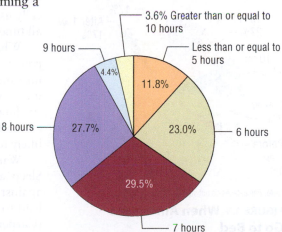

FIGURE 4.4 How Long We Sleep
About one in three adults fail to get the recommended 7 to 9 hours of sleep a night.

Source: Liu et al., 2016.

lucid dreams Dreams in which the dreamer is aware that he or she is dreaming.

Getting enough sleep? Compare your own sleep habits with the recommended duration of sleep in Table 4.2 for your age group.

Table 4.2 Are You Getting Enough Sleep?

Age Groups	Recommended Daily Duration of Sleep
Newborns	14–17 hours
Infants (4–11 months)	12–15 hours
Toddlers (1–2 years)	11–14 hours
Preschoolers (3–5 years)	10–13 hours
School-aged children (6–13 years)	9–11 hours
Teens (14–17 years)	8–10 hours
Adults (18–64 years)	7–9 hours
Older adults (65+ years)	7–8 hours

Source: Hirshkowitz et al., 2015.

CONCEPT 4.12
Though people vary in how much sleep they need, most adults require 7 to 9 hours of sleep to feel refreshed and to perform at their best.

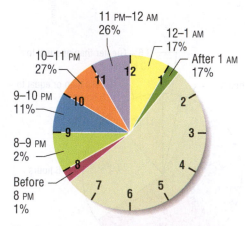

Note: Percentages do not sum to 100% due to rounding.

FIGURE 4.5 When Americans Go to Bed
Living in a 24/7 world in which we can watch movies and news all night long or even order a pizza at 2:00 A.M. has taken its toll on Americans' sleep habits. One reason that many Americans don't get enough sleep is that they are going to bed too late.

Source: Adapted from Sleepless in America, a survey conducted by the ACNielsen Company, April 2005.

In 2015, the National Sleep Foundation issued a new set of recommended guidelines for number of hours of sleep needed by most people to maintain health and well–being (Hirshkowitz et al., 2015). Are you meeting these guidelines on a regular basis? Do you feel rested and refreshed in the morning and able to function at your best? If not, how might sleep deprivation be affecting you? How can you change your sleep habits to ensure you are getting enough sleep?

It's no surprise that many Americans feel sleepy, especially because many of them don't get to bed until the wee hours of the morning (see ■ Figure 4.5). Lifestyle factors, such as demanding work schedules and caregiving responsibilities, also make it difficult for people to get the sleep they need.

Do smartphones contribute to sleep deprivation? Investigators suspect that the presence of always-on (and always nearby) smartphones may be disrupting normal sleep patterns ("The Psychological Toll," 2014). A recent study of employees who typically use their smartphones for business-related work and need to have them nearby at all times tend to sleep more poorly than do other workers (Lanaj et al., 2014).

Whatever the cause, sleep deprivation makes it more difficult to concentrate and pay attention, to respond quickly, to solve problems, and to remember newly learned information (Florian et al., 2011; Kuehn, 2013; Lim & Dinges, 2010). Driver drowsiness, which often occurs among sleep-deprived drivers, accounts for about one in six fatal car crashes, which translates to about 7,500 fatal motor vehicle crashes annually on the nation's roads ("Drowsy Driving," 2013). These accidents are most likely to occur in the early-morning hours when drivers are typically at their sleepiest.

Want to reduce your chances of catching the common cold? Get more sleep. Sleep appears to bolster the body's immune system, the body's defense system against disease-causing microbes. But getting too little sleep on a regular basis can lead to poorer immune system functioning and increased risk of infectious disease (Carpenter, 2013; Irwin, 2015). Investigators in a recent study found that research participants who slept fewer than 7 hours a night were nearly three times more likely to develop the common cold after exposure to a cold virus than those who slept 8 hours or more (Cohen et al., 2009). Not surprisingly, you may find yourself more susceptible to the common cold and other physical health problems when you've gone without your necessary quota of sleep.

Job performance may also suffer for sleep deprived workers, even if the workers themselves don't feel tired (Pomplun et al., 2012). Eliminating extended work shifts for sleep-deprived medical interns reduces potentially dangerous medical errors due to lack of attention (Lockley et al., 2004).

Sleep deprivation can also affect your waistline, leading you to reach for a donut rather than a healthy snack and to buy more high-calorie (comfort) foods (Chapman et al., 2013; Matthews, 2012). When people are sleep deprived, they show more interest in sweets than healthier food choices and also show less activity in the prefrontal cortex, the part of the brain that curbs impulsive behaviors, including impulsive eating.

It's not just the total amount of sleep that affects our daily functioning, but also the type of sleep. Missing out on REM sleep can impair learning ability and memory functioning (Greer, 2004). REM sleep also helps boost creative problem-solving ability, which is yet another reason not to skimp on getting a full night's sleep (Mednick et al., 2009).

Although temporary periods of sleep deprivation are not linked to lasting ill effects, burning the candle at both ends is potentially hazardous to your health. Prolonged periods of sleep deprivation increase the risk of hypertension (high blood pressure), a serious cardiovascular disorder and potential killer (Bakalar, 2006a; Motivala & Irwin, 2007). However, we shouldn't become alarmed if we miss a few hours of sleep; rather, we should restore our normal sleep pattern the following night.

Sleep–Wake Disorders: When Normal Sleep Eludes Us

Many of us are troubled by sleep problems that prevent us from getting a good night's sleep and remaining alert or maintaining wakefulness during the day. These problems are classified within a diagnostic category of psychological or mental disorders called **sleep–wake disorders** (Reynolds & O'Hara, 2013).

The most common sleep–wake disorder, called *insomnia disorder*, involves a pattern of chronic **insomnia** affecting an estimated 6 to 10 percent of American adults (Bootzin & Epstein, 2011; Smith & Perlis, 2006). People with insomnia disorder may have difficulty falling asleep, remaining asleep, or returning to sleep after nighttime awakenings. Insomnia prevents achieving restorative sleep, the type of sleep that leaves us feeling refreshed and alert in the morning (Harvey & Tang, 2012).

Insomnia may be caused by many factors, including substance abuse, physical illness, and psychological disorders like depression. If the underlying problem is resolved, chances are that sleep patterns will return to normal. Problem sleep habits, such as bringing worries and concerns to bed and playing havoc with the body's natural sleep–wake cycle by making frequent changes in sleep and waking times, are another major cause of insomnia.

Worrying is accompanied by increased bodily arousal, which can prevent normal sleep. The thoughts we have while tossing and turning, such as thinking that it is absolutely necessary to get a full night's sleep can also bump up the person's anxiety level to a level of interfering with sleep (Sánchez-Ortuño & Edinger, 2010). The harder the person tries to fall asleep, the more difficult it becomes. The lesson here is that sleep is a natural function that cannot be forced. Ruminating about your concerns while trying to fall asleep can also contribute to problems falling asleep.

Narcolepsy, a sleep–wake disorder affecting about one in 2,000 people, is characterized by sudden, unexplained "sleep attacks" during daytime hours (APA, 2013; Scammell, 2015). A person with narcolepsy may be fully awake and engaged in conversation one moment and then fall fast asleep and slump to the floor the next. In contrast to the normal sleep pattern in which REM sleep occurs after several stages of non-REM sleep, REM sleep usually begins almost immediately after the onset of a narcoleptic attack. The sleep episode usually lasts for about 15 minutes. In some cases, the sleep attack is preceded by frightening hallucinations that may involve several senses—visual, auditory, tactile, or kinesthetic (body movement).

CONCEPT 4.13
The amount of REM sleep you get affects your ability to function at your best.

CONCEPT 4.14
Sleep–wake disorders are a class of psychological or mental disorders involving patterns of disturbed sleep.

sleep–wake disorders A diagnostic category of psychological or mental disorders involving disturbed sleep patterns.

insomnia Difficulty falling asleep, remaining asleep, or returning to sleep after nighttime awakenings.

narcolepsy A sleep–wake disorder characterized by sudden unexplained "sleep attacks" during the day.

Sleep deprivation not only leaves you feeling groggy; it also slows your reaction times and impairs your concentration, memory, and problem-solving ability.

© iStockphoto.com/Pawel Gaul

Sleep attacks can be very dangerous. Household accidents due to falls are common. Even more disturbing, some patients report narcoleptic attacks while driving. Genetics plays a role in narcolepsy, which, scientists suspect, is caused in many cases by a loss of brain cells in an area of the hypothalamus that produces a chemical needed to maintain wakefulness (De la Herran-Arita et al., 2013; Hor et al., 2011). The available treatments include daytime naps and the use of drugs that help maintain wakefulness.

People with **sleep apnea** momentarily stop breathing many times during a night's sleep, even hundreds of times. (The word *apnea* means "without breath.") Sleep apnea, which affects an estimated 28 million Americans, mostly commonly occurs among middle age and older adults and obese people (Chen et al., 2015; O'Connor, 2012).

Sleep apnea is caused by a structural defect, such as an overly thick palate or enlarged tonsils, that partially or fully blocks the flow of air through the upper airways. With complete blockage, people may stop breathing for perhaps 15 seconds or as long as 90 seconds. They usually awaken the next morning with no memory of these breath stoppages. However, their fitful sleep patterns deprive them of solid sleep so that they are sleepy during the day and have difficulty functioning at their best. For reasons that remain unclear, people with sleep apnea are at greater risk of serious health problems, such as cardiovascular problems and diabetes (Kendzerska et al., 2014; Macey et al., 2013; Strollo et al., 2014). They also snore very loudly (described as "industrial-strength" snoring) because of narrowed airways. The disorder is often treated with a nose mask that exerts pressure to keep the upper airway passages open during sleep and sometimes with surgery to open narrowed airways (Raymond, 2013).

People with **nightmare disorder** have frequent, disturbing nightmares (APA, 2013). Children are especially prone to nightmare disorder. Nightmares are storylike dreams that contain threats to a dreamer's life or safety. The action of the nightmare may be vivid and intense—falling through space or fleeing from attackers or giant insects. Nightmares typically take place during REM sleep. People are usually more susceptible to nightmares when they are under emotional stress, have high fevers, or are suffering from sleep deprivation.

People with **sleep terror disorder** have frequent "night terrors," which are more intense episodes than ordinary nightmares (APA, 2013). Unlike nightmares, which occur mainly during REM sleep, night terrors occur during deep sleep. The disorder primarily affects children, and occurs more often in boys than girls. Night terrors begin with a loud panicky scream. The child may sit up in bed, appear dazed and frightened, and be able to remember only fragmentary dream images, rather than the detailed dream stories that are typically remembered after nightmares. Most young children with sleep terrors outgrow the problem by adolescence (Geller, 2015; Petit et al., 2015).

Children occasionally have **sleepwalking disorder** episodes, but persistent sleepwalking may be indicative of a sleep–wake disorder found more commonly in children than adults. Sleepwalking disorder is believed to affect between 1 and 5 percent of children (APA, 2013). Adults too may have occasional sleepwalking episodes, with about 4 percent of adults reporting at least one episode of sleepwalking during the preceding year (Ohayon et al., 2012).

Sleepwalkers remain asleep even though their eyes are open. They may appear to have an expressionless look on their face. Though sleepwalkers generally avoid knocking into things, accidents sometimes occur. The following morning, sleepwalkers usually remember nothing of their nighttime wanderings. Sleepwalking typically occurs during deep, dreamless sleep, so the sleepwalker does not appear to be enacting a dream. Despite a belief to the contrary, there is no harm in awakening a sleepwalker.

Sleep–wake disorders are often treated with sleep medications. However, drugs used to treat insomnia can lead to physiological dependence and should only be used

sleep apnea Temporary cessation of breathing during sleep.

nightmare disorder A type of sleep–wake disorder involving a pattern of frequent, disturbing nightmares.

sleep terror disorder A type of sleep–wake disorder involving repeated episodes of intense fear during sleep, causing the person to awake abruptly in a terrified state.

sleepwalking disorder A sleep–wake disorder characterized by repeated episodes of sleepwalking.

for a brief period of time, perhaps a few weeks at most. Alternatively, psychological techniques that focus on changing problem sleep habits (see Applying Psychology in Daily Life) are just as effective as sleep medications in treating insomnia in the short term and more effective over the long term (see Bootzin & Epstein, 2011; Harvey et al., 2014; Kaldo et al., 2015; McCrae et al., 2014). Stimulant drugs may be used to help maintain wakefulness in people with narcolepsy.

APPLYING PSYCHOLOGY *in Daily Life*

Getting Your Z's

Many people have difficulty falling asleep or getting enough sleep to feel refreshed upon awakening. Because insomnia may result from an underlying medical or psychological disorder, it is best to have the condition evaluated by a health professional. In many cases, however, insomnia reflects unhealthy sleep habits, which can be changed. Evidence shows that making healthy changes in sleep habits and thinking patterns helps people overcome insomnia (see, for example, Blom et al., 2015; Harvey et al., 2014; Järnefelt et al., 2014; Kaldo et al., 2015; Trauer et al., 2015; Wu et al., 2015).

Here are some suggestions for developing healthier sleep habits (adapted from Brody, 2006; Nevid & Rathus, 2013; Wollon, 2015):

- *Adopt a regular sleep schedule.* Help get your internal body clock in sync by going to bed and awakening as close as possible to the same times every day, including weekends and holidays.

- *Don't try to force sleep.* Sleep is a natural process that cannot be forced. If you are wide-eyed and full of energy, allow your body and mind to wind down before going to bed.

- *Establish a regular bedtime routine.* Adopt a regular routine before going to bed. You may find that reading, watching TV, or practicing a relaxation or meditation technique helps prepare you for sleep.

- *Establish proper cues for sleeping.* Make your bed a cue for sleeping by limiting other activities in bed, such as eating, reading, watching TV, or talking on the telephone as much as possible.

- *Avoid tossing and turning.* If you cannot fall asleep within 10 to 20 minutes, don't continue tossing and turning. Get out of bed, move to another room, and achieve a state of relaxation by reading, listening to calming music, or meditating. When you are feeling relaxed, return to bed. Repeat this process as necessary until you are able to fall asleep.

- *Avoid daytime naps if you miss sleep.* Many people try to make up for nighttime sleeplessness by napping during the day. Napping can throw off your natural body clock, making it more difficult to fall asleep the following night.

- *Don't take your problems to bed.* Retiring to bed should be conducive to sleeping, not to mulling over your problems or organizing your daily schedule. Tell yourself you'll think about tomorrow, tomorrow. Or, before you go to bed, write reminder notes to yourself about the things you need to do the following day.

- *Limit screen time, especially before bed.* Light from e-readers, tablets, smartphones, and TVs can disrupt sleep by interfering with the body's circadian clock (Chang et al., 2014). Basically, any source of light can disturb sleep, so

CONCEPT 4.15
Developing healthy sleep habits can help people overcome insomnia not caused by underlying physical or psychological problems.

Simon Potter/Polka Dot/Jupiter Images

What's wrong with this picture? If you have a problem with insomnia, you might find it helpful to make your bed a stronger cue for sleep by limiting other activities in bed, such as eating, reading, watching TV, or talking on the phone.

Consuming caffeine in the evening affects the timing of the body's circadian rhythm clock that regulates sleep–wake cycles, making it more difficult to fall asleep.

it makes sense to reduce exposure to bright light (including bright bathroom light) before going to bed (O'Connor, 2015).

- *Use mental imagery.* Picturing relaxing scenes in your mind—for example, imagining yourself basking in the sun on a tropical beach or walking through a pristine forest—can help you slip from ordinary consciousness into the realm of sleep.

- *Adopt a regular exercise program.* Vigorous exercise can help relieve the stresses of daily life and prepare the body for restful sleep. But avoid exercising for several hours before sleep, as exercise increases states of bodily arousal.

- *Limit your intake of caffeine, especially in the afternoon and evening.* The caffeine in coffee, tea, and other substances can increase states of bodily arousal for up to 10 hours. Laboratory evidence shows that consumption of caffeine in the evening affects the timing of the body's circadian rhythm clock that regulates our sleep–wake cycles (Burke et al., 2015). Also, you should avoid smoking, not only because of its harmful effects on your health but also because tobacco contains nicotine, a mild stimulant.

- *Practice rational "self-talk."* Disturbing thoughts you silently mumble to yourself under your breath can lead to anxiety and worry that may keep you up well into the night. Replace such anxious self-talk with coping thoughts. For example, instead of thinking "I must get to sleep or I'll be a wreck tomorrow," substitute a thought like "I might not feel as sharp as usual but I'm not going to fall apart. I've gotten by with little sleep before and can do so again." Don't fall into the trap of blowing things out of proportion.

MODULE REVIEW   4.2   Sleeping and Dreaming

Recite It

2. Explain how the sleep–wake cycle is regulated.

The suprachiasmatic nucleus (SCN), a clocklike mechanism in the (a) _____, regulates our sleep–wake cycles according to a circadian rhythm that approximates the 24-hour day.

3. Describe the characteristics of each stage of sleep and the brain wave patterns associated with each stage.

There are five stages of sleep: Stage 1 or light sleep, characterized by small, irregular brain waves of varying frequency; Stage 2, characterized by sleep (b) _____; Stages 3 and 4, or deep sleep, characterized by larger, slower (c) _____ waves; and (d) _____ sleep, during which the brain is relatively active and when most dreaming occurs.

4. Explain why we sleep.

Though no one knows for sure, sleep experts suspect that sleep serves several functions, including a protective function, an energy (e) _____ function, and a (f) _____ function.

5. Explain why we dream.

Again, no one can say for sure, but theories include the belief that dreams are needed to (g) _____ memories and experiences that occur during the day; Hartmann's view that dreams help people work out their everyday problems; the (h) _____-_____ hypothesis; and Freud's view that dreaming helps preserve sleep by disguising potentially threatening wishes or impulses in the form of dream (i) _____.

6. Evaluate the effects of sleep deprivation.

Sleep deprivation can result in slow (j) _____ times, impaired concentration, memory, and (k) _____-solving ability, and difficulty retaining newly learned information. Sleep deprivation can also lead to motor vehicle and other accidents and impair health.

7. Identify and **describe** different types of sleep–wake disorders.

Sleep–wake disorders involve patterns of disturbed sleep, including (l) _____ (difficulty falling asleep or resuming sleep), **(m)** _____ (sudden sleep attacks), sleep **(n)** _____ (momentary suspensions of breathing while asleep), **(o)** _____ disorder (frightening dreams), sleep **(p)** _____ disorder (terror attacks during sleep), and **(q)** _____ (walking around while asleep).

Recall It

1. The sleep–wake cycle operates according to a _____ cycle.

2. Deep sleep, which is characterized by delta brain wave patterns, occurs during

   a. Stages 1 and 2 of sleep.
   b. Stages 2 and 3 of sleep.
   c. Stages 3 and 4 of sleep.
   d. REM sleep.

3. Sleep may help the body replenish resources expended during wakefulness. What is this function of sleep called?

4. Match each of the sleep–wake disorders listed on the left with the appropriate description on the right:

   I. narcolepsy
   II. sleep terror disorder
   III. sleep apnea
   IV. nightmare disorder

   a. frequent, frightening dreams that usually occur during REM sleep
   b. intense nightmares that occur during deep sleep and primarily affect children
   c. sudden, unexplained "sleep attacks" during the day
   d. temporary cessation of breathing during sleep

Think About It

- Have you experienced jet lag? How did it affect you? What might you do differently in the future to cope with it? One suggestion is to gradually alter your body clock by adjusting the time you go to bed by an hour a day for several days before your trip. If you will be away for only a brief time, you might be better off to follow your body clock as much as possible during the trip.

- Many college students disrupt their normal sleep–wake cycles by staying up to all hours of the night and then napping during the day to catch up on missed sleep. They may feel as though they are continually suffering from jet lag. What would you suggest to help someone get his or her sleep cycle back on track?

- How would you rate your sleep habits? What specific changes can you make to improve them?

- Apply each of the major theories of dreaming—Hartmann's belief that dreams allow us to sort through potential solutions to everyday problems and concerns, Freud's wish-fulfillment theory, and the activation-synthesis hypothesis—to a particular dream or dreams you are able to recall. Which of these theories do you believe best accounts for your dream or dreams?

Recite It *answers placed at the end of chapter.*

MODULE **4.3** **Altering Consciousness Through Meditation and Hypnosis**

8 **Define** and **describe** meditation and hypnosis.

9 **Identify** and **describe** the two major contemporary theories of hypnosis.

We venture now from considering states of ordinary wakefulness and sleep to considering states of altered consciousness. Some people use psychoactive drugs to achieve altered states of consciousness, whereas others may practice meditation or undergo hypnosis. You might not think of meditation and hypnosis as having much in common, but both involve rituals that focus on the narrowing of attention or concentration to achieve an altered state of consciousness.

CONCEPT 4.16
Meditation involves practices that induce an altered state of consciousness through techniques of focused attention.

 **CONCEPT LINK**

As a form of relaxation, meditation can help tone down the body's response to stress. See Module 10.1

Meditation can induce a relaxed but alert state.

meditation A process of focused attention that induces a relaxed, contemplative state.

transcendental meditation (TM) A form of meditation in which practitioners focus their attention by repeating a particular mantra.

mantra A sound or phrase chanted repeatedly during transcendental meditation.

mindfulness meditation A form of meditation in which one adopts a state of nonjudgmental attention to the unfolding of experience on a moment-to-moment basis.

hypnosis An altered state of consciousness characterized by focused attention, deep relaxation, and heightened susceptibility to suggestion.

hypnotic age regression A hypnotically induced experience that involves reexperiencing past events in one's life.

hypnotic analgesia A loss of feeling or responsiveness to pain in certain parts of the body occurring during hypnosis.

Meditation: Achieving a Peaceful State by Focusing Your Attention

People from many different cultures practice **meditation**, which, as you may recall from Chapter 3, is a process of focused attention that induces a relaxed, contemplative state. To remove all other thoughts from consciousness, practitioners of meditation narrow their attention to a single object or thought. The particular meditative technique used varies among cultures. In ancient Egypt, practitioners stared at an oil-burning lamp, a custom that may have inspired the tale of Aladdin's lamp. Yogis focus on the design of a vase or other graphic symbols. Other practitioners focus on a burning candle.

In **transcendental meditation (TM)**, practitioners focus their attention by repeating a phrase or sound (such as *ommm*), which is known as a **mantra**. In **mindfulness meditation**, they learn to focus entirely on their unfolding experience on a moment-to-moment basis (Ameli, 2014; van der Velden et al., 2015). Mindfulness is about being present in the moment rather than standing back and evaluating your thoughts or experiences, such as by thinking, "Am I doing this right?" The Dalai Lama, the Buddhist spiritual leader, likens mindfulness to "watching a river flow by" (Gyatso, 2003, p. A29). Perhaps there is a meeting of the twain when it comes to East and West. Recall the Harvard iPhone app study discussed earlier in the chapter that connects focusing on the "here and now" to greater happiness (Killingsworth & Gilbert, 2010).

Many healthful benefits to mind and body are associated with meditation, including combating daily stress, lowering blood pressure, and relieving chronic pain, insomnia, and anxiety and depression (see, for example, Armstrong & Rimes, 2016; Cherkin et al., 2016; Davis et al., 2015; Dimidjian & Segal, 2015; Khoury et al., 2015; Meadows et al., 2014; Polusny et al., 2015; van der Velden et al., 2015). Meditation produces physical changes in the brain linked to improved memory and emotional processing, changes we can observe even when the person is not actively meditating (Creswell et al, 2016; Desbordes et al., 2012). A recent study using mindfulness training with U.S. Marines preparing for deployment showed improved physiological markers of resilience to stress (Johnson et al., 2014).

Some practitioners of meditation believe it does more than just relax the body and mind. They believe it expands their consciousness and allows them to experience a deeper state of awareness or a state of inner peace. Perhaps meditation achieves these effects by helping people tune out the outside world, thus allowing them more opportunity for inward focus. Yet many people practice meditation not to expand consciousness but to find relief from the stress of everyday life.

Hypnosis: "You Are Now Getting Sleepier"

Hypnosis is derived from the Greek word *hypnos,* meaning "sleep." Though definitions of **hypnosis** abound, it is most commonly defined as an altered state of consciousness characterized by focused attention, deep relaxation, and heightened susceptibility to suggestion. Techniques for inducing hypnosis vary, but they usually involve a narrowing of attention to the hypnotist's voice.

People who undergo hypnosis may feel sleepier, but they are not asleep. During a hypnotic induction, the hypnotist may ask a person to focus on an object, such as a swinging watch, and listen only to the sound of his or her voice. The hypnotist may also suggest that the person's eyelids are getting heavier and heavier and that the person is becoming sleepy.

Once the person becomes deeply relaxed, the hypnotist begins giving the person hypnotic suggestions that may lead to unusual experiences. These experiences include **hypnotic age regression** (reliving past events, usually from childhood) and **hypnotic analgesia** (loss of feeling or responsiveness to pain in certain parts of the body). Other hypnotic experiences include distortions of reality—seeing, hearing, or feeling something that is not present in reality (a *positive* hallucination), or not perceiving something, such as a pen or a chair, that truly does exist (a *negative* hallucination). Another kind of hypnotic experience in response to hypnotic suggestions is **posthypnotic amnesia**, an inability to recall what happened during hypnosis. Yet another type of hypnotic experience is **posthypnotic suggestion**, in which the hypnotist plants the idea that, after coming out of the hypnotic state, people will respond in particular ways (such as touching their ears or scratching their heads) when they hear a cue word—for example, *elephant*. A person may respond in the suggested way but deny any awareness of having performed the behavior.

Theories of Hypnosis

Despite more than 100 years of scientific study, there is still no consensus about what hypnosis is or even how it should be defined (Vaitl et al., 2005). There is still a debate about whether hypnosis involves anything more than a role a subject performs to please the hypnotist by following the hypnotist's every suggestion (Blakeslee, 2005). This point of view, generally called the *role-playing model,* proposes that hypnosis is a social interaction between a hypnotist and a willing person who assumes the role of a "good" hypnotic subject—one who faithfully follows the hypnotist's directions. This doesn't mean that hypnotic subjects are faking their responses, any more than you are faking by adopting the role of a good student, as when you raise your hand before speaking in class.

An alternative view of hypnosis is that it is a *trance state*—an altered state of awareness characterized by heightened *suggestibility*. Suggestibility is the readiness with which one complies with suggestions offered by others, including a hypnotist. Yet many psychologists reject the view that hypnosis is a trance state, or even that it constitutes an altered state of consciousness (Kihlstrom, 2005; Lynn et al., 2008).

Some research supports the role-playing model. For example, when subjects are given a role-playing explanation of hypnosis before a hypnotic induction takes place, their later responses to hypnotic suggestions are either reduced or eliminated (Wagstaff & Frost, 1996). On the other hand, patterns of brain activity in people who are hypnotized differ from those who are merely instructed to *act* as if they were hypnotized (Kosslyn et al., 2000). More research in this area is needed, but there appears to be something more to hypnosis than mere role-playing (Bryant & Mallard, 2002).

One leading theorist who believed that hypnosis is a special state of consciousness was the psychologist Ernest Hilgard (1977, 1994). His **neodissociation theory** rests on the belief that there are multiple levels of awareness that can become split off or dissociated from one another. Hypnosis induces a splitting of consciousness into two parts, a part that carries out the hypnotist's suggestions and another part, called the **hidden observer**, that stands apart, monitoring everything that happens. In hypnotic analgesia, for example, the person experiences a splitting off, or dissociation, of consciousness into one part that is aware of the pain (the hidden observer) and another part (the dissociated part) that is not.

The belief that hypnotists have special powers that give them control over a hypnotized subject may be part of the mystique of hypnosis, but it is not consistent with contemporary views. It is a widely held myth that hypnosis can cause people to commit murder or other immoral and illegal acts they wouldn't otherwise perform. On the contrary, hypnosis depends on the willingness of subjects to go along with imagining the alternate realities suggested by a hypnotist. In hypnotic age regression, for instance, people do not actually relive childhood incidents or experiences; they merely imagine that they are again children (Barber, 1999). The effects of hypnotic suggestions may have more to do with the efforts and skills of the people who are hypnotized than with those of the hypnotist (Kirsch & Lynn, 1995).

Though most people can be hypnotized to some extent, some are more hypnotizable, or susceptible to suggestions, than others. People who are highly hypnotizable

B. BOISSONNET/BSIP/Alamy stock photo

The clinical use of hypnosis ranges from treating those with chronic pain to helping people stop smoking.

CONCEPT 4.17
Hypnosis is not sleep but, rather, a relaxed state of focused attention in which a person may become more responsive to suggestions.

CONCEPT 4.18
Two theoretical models that have guided recent research on hypnosis are the role-playing model and neodissociation theory.

posthypnotic amnesia An inability to recall what happened during hypnosis.

posthypnotic suggestion A hypnotist's suggestion that the subject will respond in a particular way following hypnosis.

neodissociation theory A theory of hypnosis based on the belief that hypnosis represents a state of dissociated (divided) consciousness.

hidden observer Hilgard's term for a part of consciousness that remains detached from the hypnotic experience but aware of everything that happens during it.

Concept Chart 4.3 — Altering Consciousness Through Meditation and Hypnosis

	Technique	Method of Induction	Key Points
	Meditation	Narrowing attention to a single object, word, or thought, or performing a repetitive ritual	Meditation relaxes the body and mind, helps combat stress, and can help people cope with pain. Some people believe it leads to a state of inner peace or spiritual enlightenment, while others practice it for its stress- and pain-relieving effects.
	Hypnosis	Narrowing attention to the hypnotist's voice or repetitive stimulus	Debate about the nature of hypnosis continues. Role-playing theory and neodissociation theory have emerged as the major contemporary theories of hypnosis.

© Naffarts/Shutterstock.com

© Tatiana Popova/Shutterstock.com

CONCEPT 4.19
The effectiveness of hypnosis may have more to do with the psychological characteristics of a hypnotized subject than with the skills of the hypnotist.

tend to have a well-developed fantasy life, a vivid sense of imagination, a tendency to be forgetful, and a positive attitude toward hypnosis (Barber, 1999). These characteristics help them to think along with the hypnotist—to imagine whatever the hypnotist suggests, perhaps so vividly that it seems real to them.

Many helping professionals today use hypnosis in treating a wide range of problems, including pain and anxiety, weight management, and smoking cessation (see, for example, Carmody et al., 2008; Hammond, 2007; Jensen, 2008; Pittler & Ernst, 2005). Hypnosis may even boost the body's immune system to function better during times of stress (Kiecolt-Glaser et al., 2001; Patterson & Jensen, 2003). Although hypnosis may have therapeutic benefits, it should only be used as an adjunctive treatment, not as a substitute for conventional treatments.

For a summary of altering consciousness through meditation and hypnosis, see Concept Chart 4.3.

MODULE REVIEW   4.3   Altering Consciousness Through Meditation and Hypnosis

Recite It

8. Define and **describe** meditation and hypnosis.

Meditation is an altered state of (a) _____ induced by narrowing (b) _____ to a single object, word, or thought or performing a repetitive ritual. Meditation produces a relaxed state that may have therapeutic benefits in relieving stress and pain.

Although there is no consensus about the nature of hypnosis, it has traditionally been defined as an altered state of consciousness characterized by focused attention, deep relaxation, and heightened (c) _____ to suggestion.

Hypnosis is increasingly being used within mainstream psychology and medicine.

9. Identify and **describe** the two major contemporary theories of hypnosis.

The two major contemporary views of hypnosis are the (d) _____ model, which proposes that hypnosis is a form of social role-playing, and (e) _____ theory, which holds that hypnosis is a state of divided consciousness.

Recall It

1. Name the type of meditation in which practitioners focus their attention by repeating a mantra.

2. What is the term used to describe the loss of feeling or responsiveness to pain as a result of hypnotic suggestion?

3. The concept of a "hidden observer" is a central feature of which theory of hypnosis?

Think About It

■ Have you ever practiced meditation? How did it affect your state of consciousness?

■ Were you ever hypnotized? If so, what was the experience like? Whether or not you've experienced hypnosis, has

reading this module changed any of your views about hypnosis? If so, how?

■ Do you believe the concept of the "hidden observer" is an example of a special state of consciousness? Why or why not?

Recite It *answers placed at the end of chapter.*

MODULE 4.4 Altering Consciousness Through Drugs

10 **Explain** the differences between physiological and psychological dependence, and between drug abuse and drug dependence.

11 **Identify** various types of drugs and **explain** how they affect us.

12 **Explain** the development of alcohol and drug abuse problems in terms of psychological, biological, and sociocultural factors.

13 **Describe** treatment programs to help people with drug problems.

Most people who want to change their states of waking consciousness don't turn to meditation or hypnosis. They are more likely to pop a pill, drink an alcoholic beverage, or smoke a joint.

Psychoactive drugs are chemical substances that act on the brain to affect emotional or mental states. They affect mood, thought processes, perceptions, and behavior. People use psychoactive drugs for many reasons: to change their level of alertness (stimulants to perk them up; depressants to relax them and make them drowsy so they can fall asleep), to alter their mental states by getting "high" or induce feelings of intense pleasure (a euphoric "rush"), to blunt awareness of the stresses and strains of daily life, or to seek some type of inner truth. Some psychoactive drugs, including heroin, cocaine, and marijuana, are illegal or *illicit*. Others, such as alcohol and nicotine (found in tobacco), are legally available, but restrictions are placed on their use or sale. Another legal psychoactive drug, caffeine, is so widely used that many people don't realize they are ingesting a psychoactive drug when they drink a caffeinated beverage or eat a chocolate bar (yes, chocolate contains caffeine).

Nearly half of adult Americans admit to having used an illicit drug at some point in their lives, with marijuana topping the list of the most widely used illicit substances. Nearly one in ten Americans age 12 and older currently uses illicit drugs (SAMHSA, 2015). Marijuana use among the nation's youth is on the rise, with more high school seniors today reporting they are using marijuana than smoking cigarettes (Lanza, 2015; MMWR, 2015).

CONCEPT 4.20
Psychoactive substances—depressants, stimulants, and hallucinogens—are drugs that alter the user's mental state.

psychoactive drugs Chemical substances that affect a person's mental or emotional state.

The use of illicit (illegal) drugs pales in comparison to use of two psychoactive substances adults may use legally—alcohol and tobacco. Alcoholic beverages contain alcohol, which is classified as a depressant drug, and products containing tobacco, such as cigarettes and cigars, contain the stimulant drug nicotine. Despite the fact that all states prohibit drinking by people under the age of 21, nearly three in four high school seniors (70 percent) have tried alcohol, as have more than one in three (37 percent) eighth-graders (Johnston et al., 2010b). More than half of high school students report having been drunk at least once. One in five high school students smoke, and some 1,000 teenagers begin smoking on any given day, setting the stage for addiction, serious health consequences, and premature death (SAMHSA, 2010b).

Drug Abuse: When Drug Use Causes Harm

CONCEPT 4.21
Drug use becomes abuse when it becomes maladaptive and either causes or contributes to personal, occupational, or health-related problems.

Drug use becomes **drug abuse** when repeated use causes or aggravates personal, occupational, or health-related problems. Drug abuse involves the maladaptive or dangerous use of a chemical substance. If drug use impairs a person's health or ability to function at home, in school, or on the job, or if it becomes associated with dangerous behavior such as drinking and driving, the person has crossed the line from use to abuse. If you repeatedly miss school or work because you are drunk or "sleeping it off," you are abusing alcohol. You may not admit you have a drug problem, but you do. People who abuse more than one drug at a time are called **polyabusers**.

CONCEPT 4.22
People who are psychologically dependent on drugs use them habitually or compulsively to cope with stress or to relieve negative feelings.

Drug Dependence: When the Drug Takes Control

Drug abuse often leads to **drug dependence**, a more severe drug-related problem characterized by impaired control over the use of a drug. People who become dependent on a drug feel compelled to use the drug or powerless to stop using it, even when they know the drug use is ruining their lives. About one in ten adults in the United States will develop a drug abuse or dependence disorder at some point in their lives (Compton et al., 2005).

Drug dependence is usually, but not always, associated with *physiological dependence* (also called *chemical dependence*). In **physiological dependence**, a person's body chemistry changes as the result of repeated use of a drug so that the body comes to depend on having a steady supply of the drug. When physiologically dependent people abruptly stop their drug use, they may experience a cluster of unpleasant and sometimes dangerous symptoms called a **withdrawal syndrome** (also called an *abstinence syndrome*). Another frequent sign of physiological dependence is **tolerance**, the need to increase the amount of a drug so that it has the same effect.

Professionals use the terms *drug abuse* and *drug dependence* to describe the different types of substance-use disorders. Laypeople more often use the term *drug*

drug abuse Maladaptive or dangerous use of a chemical substance.

polyabusers People who abuse more than one drug at a time.

drug dependence A severe drug-related problem characterized by impaired control over the use of the drug.

physiological dependence A state of physical dependence on a drug caused by repeated usage that changes body chemistry.

withdrawal syndrome A cluster of symptoms associated with abrupt withdrawal from a drug.

tolerance A form of physical habituation to a drug in which increased amounts are needed to achieve the same effect.

When does use become abuse? Many people use alcohol socially, but when does use cross over into abuse? According to mental health professionals, drug use becomes drug abuse when it leads to damaging or dangerous consequences.

addiction, but it has different meanings to different people. Here, let us define **drug addiction** (also called *chemical addiction*) as a pattern of drug dependence accompanied by physiological dependence. By this definition, we consider people to be addicted when they feel powerless to control their use of the drug *and* have developed signs of physiological dependence—typically a withdrawal syndrome.

Let's also point out that people can become *psychologically* dependent on a drug without becoming physiologically dependent on it. **Psychological dependence** is a pattern of compulsive or habitual use of a drug that serves a psychological need, such as lessening anxiety or escaping from stress. People who are psychologically dependent on a drug come to rely on it to counter unpleasant feelings or to cope with personal problems or conflicts with others. Some drugs, such as nicotine, alcohol, and heroin, can lead to both psychological and physiological dependence. Some other drugs, including hallucinogens, can produce psychological dependence but are not known to produce physiological dependence.

Now let us turn to the major classes of psychoactive drugs: depressants, stimulants, and hallucinogens.

Depressants

Depressants are drugs that reduce central nervous system activity, which in turn depresses (slows down) such bodily processes as heart rate and respiration rate. The major types of depressants are alcohol, barbiturates and tranquilizers, and opioids. Psychologically, depressants induce feelings of relaxation and provide relief from states of anxiety and tension. Some depressants also produce a "rush" of pleasure. In high doses, depressants can kill by arresting vital bodily functions, such as breathing. Depressants are highly addictive and can be dangerous, even lethal, in overdose or when mixed with other drugs. The deaths of famed entertainers Marilyn Monroe and Judy Garland were blamed on the deadly mix of barbiturates and alcohol.

Alcohol: The Most Widely Used and Abused Depressant

Alcohol is an **intoxicant**—a chemical substance that produces a state of drunkenness. The more a person drinks, the stronger the intoxicating effects become. Table 4.3 summarizes how increasing blood alcohol levels affect behavior. Many people underestimate their blood alcohol concentration when they are drinking, especially when drinking heavily, believing they are not as intoxicated as they really are (Grant et al., 2012).

Consuming even one alcoholic drink impairs driving ability. With heavier doses, the depressant effects of the drug on the central nervous system can induce a state of stupor, unconsciousness, and even death.

Women typically become intoxicated at lower doses of alcohol than men do. One reason is that women usually weigh less than men, and the less people weigh, the less alcohol it usually takes to produce intoxication. The rule of thumb is that a single drink for a woman is equal in its effects to two drinks for a man (Springen & Kantrowitz, 2004). Another reason for this gender difference is that women have less of an enzyme that breaks down alcohol in the stomach than men do and thus more pure alcohol reaches the bloodstream. Yet women's greater sensitivity to alcohol can work in their favor in that it may serve as a biological constraint on excessive drinking.

Alcohol directly affects the brain, clouding judgment and impairing concentration and attention, as well as the ability to weigh the consequences of behavior. Thus, people may do or say things when they are drinking that they might not otherwise, including unsafe sexual behavior (Orchowski, Mastroleo, & Borsari, 2012; Purdie et al., 2011). The slogan from a public health campaign bears repeating: "First you get drunk. Then you get stupid. Then you get AIDS."

The Brain Loves a Puzzle

As you read ahead, use the information in the text to solve the following puzzle:

How might being "able to hold your liquor" be a genetic risk factor for developing problems with alcohol?

CONCEPT 4.23
Depressants are addictive drugs that can be deadly when used in high doses or when mixed with other drugs.

CONCEPT 4.24
Alcohol is a depressant drug that slows down central nervous system activity and affects higher cognitive functions, such as the ability to weigh the consequences of behavior.

CONCEPT LINK

Maternal use of alcohol during pregnancy can cause fetal alcohol syndrome, which is a leading cause of intellectual disability (formerly called mental retardation). See Module 9.1.

Consuming even one alcoholic drink impairs driving ability.

drug addiction Drug dependence accompanied by signs of physiological dependence, such as the development of a withdrawal syndrome.

psychological dependence A pattern of compulsive or habitual use of a drug to satisfy a psychological need.

depressants Drugs, such as alcohol and barbiturates, that dampen central nervous system activity.

intoxicant A chemical substance that induces a state of drunkenness.

Table 4.3 Progressive Effects of Blood Alcohol Levels

Blood Alcohol Concentration (%)	Effects/Risks
0.01–0.05	Relaxation, sense of well-being, loss of inhibition, impaired alertness and judgment
0.06–0.10	Pleasure, numbness of feelings, nausea, sleepiness, emotional arousal, and impaired coordination (especially for fine motor skills)
0.11–0.20	Mood swings, anger, sadness, mania, impaired reasoning and depth perception, and inappropriate social behavior (obnoxiousness)
0.21–0.30	Aggression, reduced sensations, depression, stupor, slurred speech, lack of balance, and loss of temperature regulation
0.31–0.40	Unconsciousness, coma, possible death, loss of bladder control, and difficulty breathing
0.41 and greater	Slowed heart rate, death

Source: Adapted from *Teacher's Guide: Information about Alcohol*, National Institutes of Health, National Institute on Alcohol Abuse and Alcoholism, 2003.

Alcohol can release inhibitions, leading to aggressive or impulsive behavior or sexually risky behaviors. Alcohol use is implicated in many forms of aggressive behavior, from rape and spousal abuse to robbery, assault, and even homicide (Bartholow & Heinz, 2006; Buddie & Testa, 2005). Yet not everyone who drinks becomes aggressive or acts foolishly or recklessly. Individual differences play a large role. We examine relationships between alcohol and violent behavior in Chapter 12.

Nearly 90,000 people in the United States die from alcohol-related causes each year, mostly from motor vehicle crashes and alcohol-related diseases such as liver disease and heart disease (Kleiman, Caulkins, & Hawken, 2012; Lerner, 2011). One reason drinking and driving is so dangerous is that alcohol impairs depth perception, making it more difficult to judge distances between cars (Nawrot, Nordenstrom, & Olson, 2004). Excessive use of alcohol accounts for about 1 in 10 deaths among adults age 20 to 64 (CDC, 2014; "Heavy Toll," 2014; Stahre et al., 2014).

Alcohol-related accidents are also the leading cause of death among young people in the 17- to 24-year-old age range (Ham & Hope, 2003). All in all, alcohol plays a role in about one in three suicides and accidental deaths in the United States (Dougherty et al., 2004; Sher, 2005; Shneidman, 2005).

Alcoholism. Most people who drink alcohol do so in moderation. However, statistics show that about 8 million Americans suffer from **alcoholism**, a form of chemical dependence in which the body becomes physically dependent on alcohol and the person becomes unable to control the use of the drug. Relatively few people with alcoholism, perhaps only 5 percent, fit the stereotype of the "skid-row bum." Most have families and work for a living. They are the kinds of people you're likely to meet in your daily life—neighbors, coworkers, friends, and even family members. Yet, alcoholism is an equal opportunity destroyer, leading to devastating health problems, motor vehicle accidents, and ruined careers and marriages. Alcoholism typically begins in early adulthood, usually between the ages of 20 and 40, although it may develop earlier in life, even during childhood in some cases.

CONCEPT 4.25
Alcohol can reduce inhibitions, which may lead to aggressive or impulsive behavior.

CONCEPT 4.26
Only a small percentage of people with alcoholism fit the stereotype of the "skid-row" bum.

alcoholism A chemical addiction characterized by impaired control over the use of alcohol and physiological dependence on it.

Alcohol abuse involving regular, heavy consumption of alcohol can damage nearly every major organ and body system. Heavy drinking often has its most damaging effects on the liver, the organ that primarily metabolizes (breaks down) alcohol. *Cirrhosis of the liver,* an irreversible scarring of liver tissue typically caused by alcohol abuse, accounts for about 30,000 deaths annually in the United States (Busuttil & Klintmalm, 2015).

Ironically, despite health risks associated with heavy drinking, moderate use of alcohol (one to two drinks a day for men, one drink for women) is associated with lower risk of heart disease and strokes and lower death rates overall (Bollmann et al., 2014; Gémes et al., 2015; Goncalves et al., 2015). However, most health officials draw the line at encouraging moderate drinking because of concerns it may lead to heavier drinking, which clearly has unhealthy effects.

College Drinking. Alcohol, not cocaine, heroin, or marijuana, is the BDOC—big drug on campus. About six in ten college students drink alcohol at least once monthly, even though most of them are under the legal drinking age (see Table 4.4). College students tend to drink more than their peers who do not attend college (Slutske, 2005). Factors associated with college life such as living away from home and being exposed to peers who drink contribute to increased drinking during the first year of college (White et al., 2008).

Sadly, alcohol use and abuse takes a significant toll on college campuses, claiming the lives of about 1,800 college students in the United States each year, with most deaths resulting from alcohol-related motor vehicle accidents and overdoses (NIH, 2015). Alcohol use in college students also accounts for nearly 700,000 physical assaults and nearly 100,000 reported sexual assaults annually in the United States (Hingson, Zha, & Weitzmanet, 2009). Drinking at college parties is also a major risk factor for engaging in unsafe sexual behaviors (Bersamin et al., 2012).

Binge Drinking: A Dangerous College Pastime. A major alcohol-related concern on college campuses is binge drinking. *Binge drinking* is usually defined as having five or more drinks (for men) or four or more drinks (for women) on one occasion. Binge drinking is on the rise among college students, with more than two out of five college students reporting binge-drinking episodes during the past month (Patrick & Schulenberg, 2011; Squeglia et al., 2012). Binge drinking is also up sharply among high school students, with one in four seniors (24 percent) reporting an episode of binge drinking during the preceding two-week period (Johnston et al., 2012a).

Excessive drinking on campus is also associated with the "Greek" culture of fraternities and sororities (Park et al., 2009). However, many "Greek" organizations today either ban alcoholic behaviors or encourage more responsible drinking by

Women absorb more pure alcohol into their bloodstreams than men do. They become about as intoxicated from one drink as men become from two.

Table 4.4	**Alcohol Use Among College Students (approx. percentages)**
60%	Percentage who have used alcohol within the past 30 days
66%	Percentage who drink alcohol who have engaged in binge drinking within the past 30 days
25%	Percentage who report academic problems linked to drinking
20%	Percentage who meet diagnostic criteria for alcohol use disorder

Source: National Institutes of Health, National Institute on Alcohol Abuse and Alcoholism, 2015.

Heavy drinking among college students is associated with poor grades, in part because students who drink heavily tend to get too little sleep.

CONCEPT 4.27

Binge drinking is linked to increased risks of alcohol dependence, alcohol overdoses, unsafe or unplanned sex, and driving while impaired, among other problems.

Samantha Spady, a 19-year-old Colorado State University sophomore, died from alcohol poisoning after an evening of heavy drinking with her friends. At the time of her death, she had a blood alcohol concentration over five times the legal limit for driving.

their members. Still, drinking has become so ingrained in Greek or non-Greek college life that it is virtually as much a part of the college experience as attending a dance or basketball game.

Binge drinking is not only damaging to health, but it is also associated with poorer academic performance in college, including missing class, falling behind in course work, receiving lower grades, and increasing the risk of developing alcohol and drug problems (CDC, 2012c; Friedmann, 2013).

For many college students, turning 21 (the legal drinking age) becomes an occasion for excessive and potentially dangerous drinking that can lead to blackouts and sexually risky behaviors (Neighbors et al., 2012). A recent survey of college students showed that people on their 21st birthdays consumed an average of about ten alcoholic drinks (Brister, Sher, & Fromme, 2011).

Heavy drinking in college students is associated with lower GPAs, in part because students who drink heavily tend to get too little sleep (Singleton & Wolfson, 2009). Binge drinkers create additional risks for themselves, such as by driving under the influence and engaging in unplanned sexual activities, which can result in unwanted pregnancies and sexually transmitted infections. Not surprisingly, evidence shows that students who are strongly committed to academic achievement are less likely to engage in binge drinking or other problem drinking behaviors than less committed students (Palfai & Weafer, 2006).

Binge drinking and related drinking games (for example, beer chugging) are a serious concern for many reasons, including placing drinkers at risk of coma and even death from alcohol overdose (Zamboanga et al., 2014). Blackouts and seizures may also occur with consumption of large amounts of alcohol. Choking on one's own vomit is a frequent cause of alcohol-induced deaths. Although heavy drinking can cause people to vomit reflexively, the drug's depressant effects on the central nervous system interfere with the normal vomiting response. As a result, vomit accumulates in the air passages, which can lead to asphyxiation and death.

Prompt medical attention is needed if a person overdoses on alcohol. But how can you tell if a person has drunk too much? Table 4.5 lists some signs of alcohol overdose. A person who is unresponsive or unconscious should not be left alone. Don't simply assume that he or she will "sleep it off." Stay with the person until you or someone else can obtain medical attention. Most important, call a physician or local emergency number immediately and ask for advice.

It may seem easier to walk away from the situation and let the person "sleep it off." You may think you have no right to interfere. You may have doubts about whether the person is truly in danger. But ask yourself, if you were in the place of a person who showed signs of overdosing on alcohol, wouldn't you want someone to intervene to save your life?

Table 4.5 **Signs of Alcohol Overdose**

Failure to respond when talked to or shouted at
Failure to respond to being pinched, shaken, or poked
Inability to stand unaided
Failure to wake up
Purplish or clammy skin
Rapid pulse rate, irregular heart rhythm, low blood pressure, or difficulty breathing

Barbiturates and Tranquilizers

Barbiturates are calming or sedating drugs that have several legitimate medical uses. They are used to regulate high blood pressure, to block pain during surgery, and to control epileptic seizures. Yet they are also highly addictive and used illicitly as street drugs to induce states of euphoria and relaxation. Among the more widely used barbiturates are amobarbital, pentobarbital, phenobarbital, and secobarbital. Methaqualone (street names, "ludes" and "sopors") is a sedating drug with effects similar to those of barbiturates, and with similar risks.

Barbiturates can induce drowsiness and slurred speech, and impair motor skills and judgment. Overdoses can lead to convulsions, coma, and death. The mixture of barbiturates or methaqualone with alcohol can be especially dangerous and potentially lethal. People who are physiologically dependent on barbiturates or methaqualone should withdraw under careful medical supervision, because abrupt withdrawal can cause convulsions and even death.

Tranquilizers are a class of depressants widely used to treat anxiety and insomnia. Though they are less toxic than barbiturates, they can be dangerous in high doses, especially if combined with alcohol or other drugs. They also carry a risk of addiction, so they should not be used for extended periods of time. The most widely used tranquilizers include Valium, Xanax, and Halcion, which are members of the *benzodiazepine* family of drugs. Benzodiazepines act by boosting the availability of the neurotransmitter GABA in the brain (see Chapter 2). GABA, an inhibitory neurotransmitter, reduces excess nervous system activity.

Opioids

Opioids (also called *opiates*) are **narcotics**—addictive drugs that have pain-relieving and sleep-inducing properties. They include morphine, heroin, and codeine, naturally occurring drugs derived from the poppy plant. Synthetic opioids, including Demerol, Percodan, and Darvon, are manufactured in a laboratory to have effects similar to those of natural opiates. Opiates produce a "rush" of pleasurable excitement and dampen awareness of personal problems, which are two main reasons for their popularity as illicit street drugs. They have legitimate medical uses as painkillers and are prescribed to deaden postsurgical pain and to manage other pain conditions. However, naturally occurring opiates like heroin and morphine and synthetic opiates like OxyContin and Vicodin are also abused as street drugs when they are obtained and used illegally.

Opiates are similar in chemical structure to endorphins and lock into the same receptor sites in the brain. You'll recall from Chapter 2 that endorphins are neurotransmitters that block pain and regulate states of pleasure. Opiates mimic the actions of endorphins by stimulating brain centers that produce feelings of pleasure.

About 1.6 percent of adults in the United States (aged 12 or older) report using heroin, the most widely used and abused opiate, at some point in their lives (SAMHSA, 2015). Nearly 1 million Americans are believed to be addicted to heroin (Krantz & Mehler, 2004). Today, the burden of heroin addiction is shifting from decaying inner-city communities to more rural areas and is primarily affecting Caucasian men and women in their late 20s (Cicero et al., 2014).

Heroin induces a euphoric rush that lasts perhaps 5 to 15 minutes. The rush is so intense and pleasurable that users liken it to the pleasure of orgasm. After the rush fades, a second phase sets in that is characterized by a relaxed, drowsy state. Worries and concerns seem to evaporate, which is why heroin often appeals to people seeking a psychological escape from their problems. This mellow state soon fades, too, leading habitual users to seek another "fix" to return to the drugged state. Tolerance develops, and users begin needing higher doses, which can lead to dangerous overdoses. Physical dependence often develops within only a few weeks of regular use (Brady, McCauley, & Back, 2016). The life of a heroin addict is usually organized

CONCEPT 4.28
Barbiturates and tranquilizers are depressants that help calm the nervous system, but they are addictive and potentially dangerous in high doses, especially when mixed with other drugs, such as alcohol.

CONCEPT 4.29
Opioids, such as morphine and heroin, are depressants that induce a euphoric high.

narcotics Addictive drugs that have pain-relieving and sleep-inducing properties.

CONCEPT 4.30

Stimulants increase activity in the central nervous system, heightening states of alertness and in some cases producing a pleasurable "high."

🔗 CONCEPT LINK

Although stimulant drugs can become drugs of abuse, they are also used therapeutically in the treatment of attention deficit/hyperactivity disorder (ADHD). See Module 14.2.

Adderall, a stimulant used to treat ADHD, has become widely abused among college students who use it as a "study drug." However, misuse of the drug can lead to addiction and adverse side effects.

stimulant A drug that activates the central nervous system, such as amphetamines and cocaine.

around efforts to obtain and use the drug. Many turn to crime or prostitution to support their habit.

Although alcohol abuse and binge drinking remain the most common drug-related problems on high school and college campuses, abuse of prescription drugs—obtained from physicians who overprescribe them or from illicit street dealers—has become a serious problem among the nation's youth (Bakes, 2013; NCPIE, 2013a). Among the most widely abused prescription drugs are synthetically derived opiates such as OxyContin, Hydrocodone, and Vicodin, depressants such as Valium and Xanax, and stimulants such as Adderall and Concerta. Not only is nonmedical use of these drugs illegal, but it can also lead to addiction, overdose, damage to internal organs, and even death (NCPIE, 2013b). Perhaps this message is getting across, as the percentage of 18- to 25-year-olds reporting nonmedical use of prescription pain relievers has begun to decline (SAMHSA, 2013).

Stimulants

Stimulants are drugs that heighten the activity of the central nervous system. They include amphetamines, cocaine, MDMA ("Ecstasy"), nicotine, and caffeine. They can lead to both physiological and psychological dependence. Drugs such as amphetamines and cocaine are used to produce a pleasurable "high."

Stimulants such as Adderall and Concerta have therapeutic uses in treating attention deficit/hyperactivity disorder (ADHD), but as noted previously, they too can become drugs of abuse when used for nonmedical purposes. Some college students misuse Adderall as a kind of "study drug" to boost their attention and alertness while studying (Keeler, 2012). Students who misuse the drug may not realize it has a strong addiction potential and can cause adverse side effects, such as loss of appetite, headaches, increased blood pressure, dry mouth, and difficulty falling asleep.

Amphetamines

Like the synthetic opioids, *amphetamines* are not found in nature; they are chemicals manufactured in a laboratory. They activate the sympathetic branch of the autonomic nervous system, causing heart rate, breathing rate, and blood pressure to rise. At low doses, they boost mental alertness and concentration, reduce fatigue, and lessen the need for sleep. At high doses, they can induce an intense, pleasurable rush.

Amphetamines act on the brain by boosting availability of the neurotransmitters norepinephrine and dopamine in the brain. Increased availability of these chemicals keeps neurons firing, which helps maintain high levels of arousal and alertness. Amphetamines also produce pleasurable feelings by directly stimulating the reward pathways in the brain, the brain circuitry responsible for feelings of pleasure.

The most widely used amphetamines are amphetamine sulfate (brand name, Benzedrine; street name, "bennies"), methamphetamine (Methedrine, or "speed"), and dextroamphetamine (Dexedrine, or "dexies"). They can be used in pill form, smoked in a relatively pure form of methamphetamine called "ice" or "crystal meth," or injected in the form of liquid methamphetamine.

About 5 percent of U.S. adults (aged 12 or older) have used "meth" at some point in their lives (SAMHSA, 2015). Some 1.5 million are regular users (Jefferson, 2005). Amphetamine overdoses, which often occur as users develop tolerance to the drug and keep increasing the amount they consume, can have dangerous, even fatal, consequences. In high doses, amphetamines can cause extreme restlessness, loss of appetite, tremors, and cardiovascular irregularities that may result in coma or death. High doses of amphetamines can also induce *amphetamine psychosis*, a psychotic reaction characterized by hallucinations and delusions that resembles acute episodes of schizophrenia. Brain-imaging studies show that "meth" can damage the brain, causing deficits in learning, memory, and other functions (Thompson et al., 2004; Toomey et al., 2003). Long-term use can also lead to stroke, liver damage, and other serious health problems.

Cocaine

Cocaine is a natural stimulant derived from the leaves of the coca plant. The drug can be administered in several ways. It can be sniffed in powder form, smoked in a hardened form called *crack,* injected in liquid form, or ingested as a tea brewed from coca leaves. You may be surprised to learn that when Coca-Cola was introduced in 1886, it contained cocaine and was soon being marketed as "the ideal brain tonic." (Cocaine was removed from Coca-Cola in the early twentieth century, but the beverage is still flavored with a nonpsychoactive extract from the coca plant.)

Cocaine produces states of pleasure primarily by working on the neurotransmitter dopamine, a brain chemical that directly stimulates reward or pleasure pathways in the brain (Flagel et al., 2011). These brain circuits provide reinforcement for behaviors essential to our survival. For example, when we are hungry and have something to eat, or thirsty and have something to drink, reward pathways in the brain become flooded with dopamine, leading to feelings of pleasure or satisfaction.

As we can see in ■ Figure 4.6, cocaine blocks the reuptake of dopamine in the synapse between neurons. As a result, more dopamine molecules remain active in the synapse for longer periods of time, overstimulating neurons that produce states of pleasure, which may result in a euphoric drug high. Dopamine helps alert us to the

CONCEPT 4.31
Cocaine is a highly addictive stimulant that induces a euphoric high by directly stimulating reward pathways in the brain.

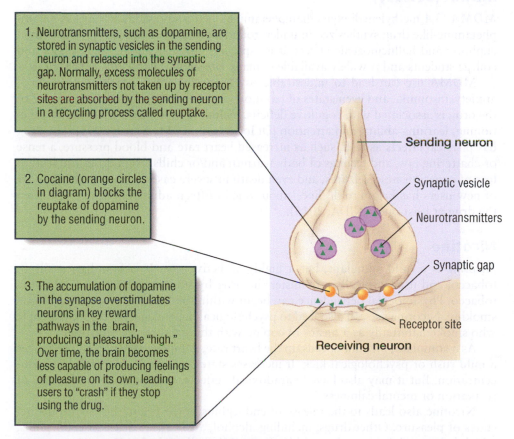

1. Neurotransmitters, such as dopamine, are stored in synaptic vesicles in the sending neuron and released into the synaptic gap. Normally, excess molecules of neurotransmitters not taken up by receptor sites are absorbed by the sending neuron in a recycling process called reuptake.

2. Cocaine (orange circles in diagram) blocks the reuptake of dopamine by the sending neuron.

3. The accumulation of dopamine in the synapse overstimulates neurons in key reward pathways in the brain, producing a pleasurable "high." Over time, the brain becomes less capable of producing feelings of pleasure on its own, leading users to "crash" if they stop using the drug.

Sending neuron
Synaptic vesicle
Neurotransmitters
Synaptic gap
Receptor site
Receiving neuron

FIGURE 4.6 How Cocaine Works in the Brain
Cocaine blocks the normal recycling process of dopamine (the circles in the diagram), resulting in a buildup of the neurotransmitter in the synapse.

Source: National Institute on Drug Abuse, U.S. Department of Health and Human Services, National Institutes of Health, 2004.

IT RELIEVES EXHAUSTION

Coca-Cola

Bettmann/Corbis

Coca-Cola originally contained an extract of cocaine and was promoted as a mental tonic to relieve exhaustion. Though cocaine was removed from the beverage more than 100 years ago, it now contains small amounts of the mild stimulant caffeine.

CONCEPT 4.32
Nicotine, a stimulant, is an addictive substance found in tobacco.

presence of objects we may want, such as chocolate if we are chocolate lovers, and to objects we may fear, such as creepy crawlers (Angier, 2009). A person with cocaine addiction may experience a rush of dopamine when a crack pipe is presented, making the drug and related paraphernalia more difficult to ignore.

Although amphetamines and cocaine have similar effects, the high induced by cocaine, especially in the form of crack, is typically shorter lived. Smoking crack delivers the drug almost instantaneously to the brain, producing an immediate, intense high. But the high fades within 5 or 10 minutes, leaving the user craving more.

Regular use of cocaine can have damaging effects on the heart and circulatory system and other body organs. High doses can result in life-threatening or fatal consequences. Prolonged use may also lead to psychological problems, such as anxiety, irritability, and depression. At high doses, cocaine can induce a type of psychosis, called *cocaine psychosis*, characterized by hallucinations and delusions of persecution (unfounded beliefs that one is being pursued by others or by mysterious forces).

Cocaine is highly addictive and can lead to a withdrawal syndrome involving intense cravings for the drug, feelings of depression, and an inability to experience pleasure in the activities of everyday life. People addicted to cocaine will often return to using the drug to gain relief from these unpleasant withdrawal symptoms. Tolerance also develops quickly, yet another sign of the physically addicting properties of cocaine. Users may also become psychologically dependent on the drug, using it compulsively to deal with life stress.

MDMA (Ecstasy)

MDMA (3,4-methylenedioxymethamphetamine), better known as *Ecstasy,* is an amphetamine-like drug synthesized in underground laboratories. MDMA produces mild euphoric and hallucinogenic effects. It is especially popular among high school and college students and is widely available in many late-night dance clubs in U.S. cities.

MDMA use can lead to undesirable psychological effects, such as depression, anxiety, insomnia, and even states of paranoia or psychotic symptoms. Heavy use of the drug is associated with cognitive deficits, including problems with memory functioning, learning ability, and attention (Di Iorio et al., 2011; Eisner, 2005). The drug has physical effects as well, such as increased heart rate and blood pressure, a tense or chattering jaw, and feelings of body warmth and/or chills. High doses can lead to loss of consciousness, seizures, and even death in severe cases. Although the number of new users has begun to decline, about one in fifteen adult Americans have tried the drug at least once (NIDA, 2013).

Nicotine

Nicotine is a mild stimulant, but a highly addictive one. It is found naturally in tobacco, and users typically administer the drug by smoking, snorting, or chewing tobacco. Physiological dependence can begin within the first few weeks of cigarette smoking. Nicotine use can also lead to psychological dependence, as we see in people who smoke habitually as a means of coping with the stress of everyday life.

As a stimulant, nicotine speeds up the heart rate, dampens appetite, and produces a mild rush or psychological kick. It increases states of arousal, alertness, and concentration. But it may also have "paradoxical" effects, such as inducing feelings of relaxation or mental calmness.

Nicotine also leads to the release of endorphins in the brain, thereby producing states of pleasure. Other drugs, including alcohol, also cause release of endorphins, which helps explain their pleasurable effects (Mitchell et al., 2012).

You certainly know that smoking is dangerous. But just how dangerous is it? So dangerous that it kills about 480,000 Americans each year, making it the leading preventable cause of death in the nation (CDC, 2015a). Overall, smoking accounts for about one in five deaths in the United States and cuts about ten years off the average smoker's lifespan (Benowitz, 2010; Jha et al., 2013). Smoking is responsible for nearly one in three cancer deaths in the United States, mostly due to lung cancer, the leading cancer killer of both men and women. It may surprise you to learn that more women die annually from lung cancer than from breast cancer. The toxic substances in cigarette smoke wend their way through the body, damaging virtually every organ in the body. The heartbreaking news about smoking is that it is also a major contributor to cardiovascular disease (heart and artery disease), the biggest killer of all. Smoking is also a causative factor in diabetes, colorectal cancer, ectopic pregnancy, erectile dysfunction, and even tooth loss (e.g., Dietrich et al., 2015; Tavernisejan, 2014). Overall, smoking triples the likelihood of dying between the ages of 25 and 79 (Jha et al., 2013).

If present trends in tobacco use continue, about 1 billion people worldwide, most from poor or middle-income countries, will die from tobacco use during the twenty-first century (Jha & Peto, 2014). That said, there is good news, very good news in fact, to report on the smoking front, as the smoking rate in the United States has been declining steadily for several decades and is now down to 16.8 percent among adults, which is the lowest recorded level in more than 50 years (CDC, 2015a; Fox, 2015). Smoking control efforts have reaped major health benefits, saving an estimated 8 million people from premature death and extending life spans on the average by 19 to 20 years (Holford et al., 2014). Tempering the good news, though, is that about one in six adult Americans still continue to smoke. Smoking is more prevalent among men than women, among younger adults, and among less-educated people.

Smoking among teens is also on the decline, but still remains much too high, as nearly one in five (18 percent) high school seniors report that they smoke (CDC, 2015b; Kuehn, 2013). Use of tobacco products often begins in adolescence and is difficult to stop once a pattern of regular use is established. Estimates are that about one in three young people who begin smoking will eventually die of smoking-related diseases. On the other hand, quitting smoking greatly reduces (but unfortunately, doesn't eliminate) the increased risk of death associated with tobacco use (Thun et al., 2013).

Caffeine

Caffeine, a mild stimulant found in coffee, tea, cola drinks, chocolate, and other substances, is our most widely used psychoactive drug. Regular use of caffeine leads to physiological dependence. If your daily routine includes one or more cups of coffee or caffeinated tea and you feel on edge or have headaches when you go without your daily supply of caffeine, chances are you're physiologically dependent, or "hooked," on caffeine. Drinking just a cup or two of coffee or tea or even a few cans of caffeinated soft drinks each day can lead to dependence. The good news is that most caffeine users are able to maintain control over their use of the drug despite being physiologically dependent on it. In other words, they can limit their coffee or tea intake and can use the drug in moderation without it significantly interfering with their daily lives.

Fortunately, too, caffeine is not known to be associated with health risks (other than during pregnancy) when used in moderation. However, we recently learned that coffee drinking, especially heavier drinking, is linked in some genetically predisposed individuals to an increased risk of heart attacks (Cornelis et al., 2006). Caffeine has some desirable effects, such as enhancing wakefulness and mental alertness, although negative effects, such as jitteriness or nervousness, can occur at higher dosages (from 200 to 600 milligrams).

Hallucinogens

Hallucinogens are drugs that alter sensory perceptions, producing distortions or hallucinations in visual, auditory, or other sensory forms. They are also called *psychedelics,* a word that literally means "mind revealing." Hallucinogens may induce feelings of relaxation and calmness in some users but cause feelings of paranoia or

Caffeine is the most widely used psychoactive drug. Most regular users can control their use of the drug despite being physiologically dependent on it.

CONCEPT 4.33
Caffeine, a mild stimulant found in coffee, tea, cola drinks, chocolate, and other substances, is the most widely used psychoactive drug.

CONCEPT 4.34
Hallucinogens alter or distort sensory perceptions and produce feelings of relaxation in some people but paranoid or panicky feelings in others.

hallucinogens Drugs that alter sensory experiences and produce hallucinations.

panic in others. Though they are not known to produce physiological dependence, they can lead to psychological dependence when users come to depend on them for help in coping with problems or stressful life experiences. Hallucinogens include LSD, mescaline, psilocybin, PCP, and marijuana. Of these, the two most widely used are LSD and marijuana. The percentage of current users of hallucinogens (excluding marijuana) is estimated to be about 0.5 percent (1 in 200 people) (SAMHSA, 2014).

LSD

LSD (lysergic acid diethylamide; street name, "acid") produces vivid hallucinations and other sensory distortions. The experience of using the drug is called a "trip," and it may last as long as 12 hours. More than a half million Americans report having used LSD (NIDA Notes, 2004).

LSD has various effects on the body, including pupil dilation and increases in heart rate, blood pressure, and body temperature. It may also produce sweating, tremors, loss of appetite, and sleeplessness. The psychological effects on the user are variable and unpredictable. Users often report distortions of time and space. Higher doses are likely to produce more vivid displays of colors and outright hallucinations. Brain scans of people under the influence of LSD suggest that visual hallucinations are a form of seeing things from one's imagination rather than the outside world (Carhart-Harris et al., 2016; Science News, 2016).

The psychological effects depend not only on the amount used but also on the user's personality, expectancies about the drug, and the context in which it is used. Some users experience "bad trips," in which they suffer intense anxiety or panic or have psychotic reactions, such as delusions of persecution. Others have flashbacks, which involve a sudden reexperiencing of some of the perceptual distortions of an LSD trip.

Mescaline, Psilocybin, and PCP

For centuries, Native Americans have used the hallucinogens *mescaline* (derived from the cactus plant) and *psilocybin* (derived from certain mushrooms) for religious purposes. *PCP* (phencyclidine), or "angel dust," is a synthetic drug that produces **delirium**, a state of mental confusion characterized by excitement, disorientation, and difficulty in focusing attention. PCP can produce distortions in the sense of time and space, feelings of unreality, and vivid, sometimes frightening, hallucinations. It may lead to feelings of paranoia and blind rage, and prompt bizarre or violent behavior. High doses can lead to coma and death.

Marijuana

Marijuana ("pot," "weed," "grass," "reefer," "dope") is derived from the cannabis plant. The psychoactive chemical in marijuana is THC (delta-9-tetrahydrocannabinol). The leaves of the plant are ground up and may be smoked in a pipe or rolled into "joints." The most potent form of the drug, called hashish ("hash"), is derived from the resin of the plant, which contains the highest concentration of THC. Though marijuana and hashish are usually smoked, some users ingest the drug by eating parts of the plant or foods into which the cannabis leaves have been baked.

Marijuana is generally classified as a hallucinogen because it alters perceptions and can produce hallucinations, especially in high doses or when used by susceptible individuals. At lower doses, users may feel relaxed and mildly euphoric. It may seem as if time is passing more slowly. Bodily sensations may seem more pronounced, which can create anxiety or even panicky feelings in some users (for example, a pronounced sense of the heartbeat may cause some users to fear they are having a heart attack). High doses can cause nausea and vomiting, feelings of disorientation, panic attacks, and paranoia.

Although legal in some states, marijuana remains illegal throughout much of the United States and is the nation's most widely used illicit drug. More than 40 percent of adult Americans report having used marijuana at some point in their lives, and about

delirium A mental state characterized by confusion, disorientation, difficulty in focusing attention, and excitable behavior.

7.5 percent are current (past-month) users (SAMHSA, 2010a, b; 2015). Marijuana use is also rising among teens, portending higher rates of use in future years (Lanza et al., 2015).

Whether marijuana leads to physiological dependence remains unclear. However, increasing evidence points to a definable withdrawal syndrome in long-term heavy users when they abruptly stop using the drug (Allsop et al., 2012; Mason et al., 2012). Marijuana can also lead to psychological dependence if people come to rely on it to deal with daily stress or personal problems. Whether marijuana use plays a causal role in leading to harder drug use also remains an open question.

Regardless of its legality, marijuana use carries certain risks. It increases heart rate and possibly blood pressure, which can be potentially dangerous for people with cardiovascular problems. It impairs motor performance and coordination and can cause perceptual distortions, making driving under the influence of marijuana especially dangerous, as well as illegal (Bergeron, Langlois, & Cheang, 2014). Regular use of marijuana can also impair cognitive functioning, including learning and memory, and regular, long-term use can lead to brain abnormalities (Batalla et al., 2013; Filbey et al., 2014; Moore, 2014). It remains unclear whether there is any safe level of marijuana use or whether brain changes associated with heavy, long-term use are permanent (Weir, 2015). Finally, it is important to note that smoking marijuana introduces cancer-causing agents into the body.

In Concept Chart 4.4, you'll find a listing of the major types of psychoactive drugs in terms of their potential for psychological and physiological dependence, major psychological effects, and major risks.

The hallucinogen LSD can produce vivid perceptual distortions and outright hallucinations. Some users experience "bad trips," which are characterized by panicky feelings and even psychotic states.

CONCEPT 4.35
Marijuana induces feelings of relaxation and mild euphoria at low doses, but it can produce hallucinations in high doses or when used by susceptible individuals.

Concept Chart 4.4   Major Types of Psychoactive Drugs

	Drug	Potential for Psychological/ Physiological Dependence	Major Psychological Effects	Major Risks
Depressants	Alcohol	Yes/Yes	Induces relaxation, mild euphoria, and intoxication; relieves anxiety; reduces mental alertness and inhibitions; impairs concentration, judgment, coordination, and balance	With heavy use, can cause liver disorders and other physical problems; in overdose, can cause coma or death
	Barbiturates and tranquilizers	Yes/Yes	Reduces mental alertness; induces relaxation and calm; may produce pleasurable rush (barbiturates)	High addictive potential; dangerous in overdose and when mixed with alcohol and other drugs
	Opioids	Yes/Yes	Induces relaxation and a euphoric rush; may temporarily blot out awareness of personal problems	High addictive potential; in overdose, may cause sudden death
Stimulants	Amphetamines	Yes/Yes	Boosts mental alertness; reduces need for sleep; induces pleasurable rush; causes loss of appetite	In high doses, can induce psychotic symptoms and cardiovascular irregularities that may lead to coma or death
	Cocaine	Yes/Yes	Effects similar to those of amphetamines but shorter lived	High addictive potential; risk of sudden death from overdose; in high doses, can have psychotic effects; risk of nasal defects from "snorting"
	MDMA ("Ecstasy")	Yes/Yes	Mild euphoria and hallucinogenic effects	High doses can be lethal; may lead to depression or other psychological effects; may impair learning, attention, and memory

(Continued)

Concept Chart 4.4 (Continued)

	Drug	Potential for Psychological/ Physiological Dependence	Major Psychological Effects	Major Risks
Stimulants	Nicotine	Yes/Yes	Increases mental alertness; produces mild rush but paradoxically may have relaxing and calming effects	Strong addictive potential; implicated in various cancers, cardiovascular disease, and other physical disorders
	Caffeine	Yes/Yes	Increases mental alertness and wakefulness	In high doses, can cause jitteriness and sleeplessness; may increase risk of miscarriage during pregnancy
Hallucinogens	LSD	Yes/No	Produces hallucinations and other sensory distortions	Intense anxiety, panic, or psychotic reactions associated with "bad trips"; flashbacks
	Marijuana	Yes/?	Induces relaxation and mild euphoria; can produce hallucinations	In high doses, can cause nausea, vomiting, disorientation, panic, and paranoia; possible health risks from regular use

CONCEPT 4.36

Drug abuse and dependence are complex problems arising from an interplay of social, biological, and psychological factors.

Understanding Drug Abuse

People use drugs for many reasons, not simply to change their states of consciousness. To better understand the problems of drug use and abuse, we need to consider social, biological, and psychological factors. Pleasurable effects of drugs, peer pressure, and exposure to family members who smoke or use alcohol or other drugs are all important influences in leading young people to begin experimenting with these substances (Hu, Davies, & Kandel, 2006; Read et al., 2003).

Sociocultural Factors

Young people who feel alienated from mainstream culture may identify with subcultures in which drug use is sanctioned or encouraged, such as the gang subculture. Though initiation into drug use may be motivated by the desire to "fit in" or appear "cool" in the eyes of peers, people generally continue using drugs because of the pleasurable or reinforcing effects of the drugs themselves. With prolonged use of a drug, the body comes to depend on a steady supply of it, leading to physiological dependence. As people become chemically dependent, they may continue using drugs primarily to avoid unpleasant withdrawal symptoms and cravings that occur when they stop using them.

Unemployment is another social factor linked to drug abuse. Yet this relationship may be two-sided: Drug abuse may increase the likelihood of unemployment, while unemployment may increase the likelihood of drug abuse.

Use of alcohol and other drugs is strongly affected by cultural norms. Cultural beliefs and customs may either encourage or discourage drinking. Some ethnic groups—Jews, Greeks, Italians, and Asians, for example—have low rates of alcoholism, largely because of tight social controls imposed on excessive and underage drinking. In traditional Islamic cultures, alcohol is prohibited altogether.

Ethnic and racial groups also differ in reported use of illicit drugs. ■ Figure 4.7 shows reported rates of cocaine and marijuana use by African Americans and (non-Hispanic) White Americans. The data are drawn from an ongoing survey of American households. Later in the chapter, we will ask you to think critically about these data. Do they in fact demonstrate that race or ethnicity is responsible for these differences?

Acculturation plays a part in explaining drug use and abuse (Pokhrel et al., 2013). For example, traditional Hispanic cultures place severe restrictions on women's use of alcohol, especially on heavy drinking. Not surprisingly, highly acculturated Hispanic

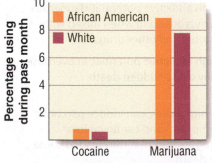

FIGURE 4.7 Ethnicity and Drug Use
This figure shows the percentages of people in two ethnic groups who reported using illicit drugs during the past month. The data are from an ongoing federally sponsored study of drug use patterns in the United States. But can we infer from these data that drug use—especially cocaine use—is a problem associated with minority group status?

Source: Based on 2013 data from National Survey on Drug Use and Health, SAMSHA

American women who have been exposed to the loose constraints on female drinking in mainstream U.S. society are much more likely to drink heavily than are relatively unacculturated Hispanic American women (Caetano, 1987).

Biological Factors

Genetic factors play an important role in many addictive disorders, including alcoholism, heroin dependence, cocaine dependence, and even nicotine (smoking) dependence (Anstee et al., 2013; "Gene Mutation," 2013; Kendler et al., 2012; Ray, 2012). Consistent with a genetic contribution, we have learned that identical twins are more likely to share alcoholism in common than are fraternal twins (MacKillop, McGeary, & Ray, 2010).

No single gene is responsible for alcoholism or other forms of substance abuse or dependence. Rather, scientists believe that multiple genes act together with environmental influences in leading to problems of alcohol and drug abuse and dependence (Kendler et al., 2008, 2012). Some people may be genetically predisposed to reap greater pleasure from alcohol or other drugs, which raises their risk potential. Others may inherit a greater tolerance for alcohol's negative effects (the nausea and so on), making it more difficult for them "to know when to say when" (Corbett et al., 2005; Radel et al., 2005). Ironically, having a greater ability to hold one's liquor appears to put one at greater risk of developing problems with alcohol (Edenberg et al., 2005).

People who inherit a greater sensitivity to the negative effects of alcohol—those whose bodies more readily "put the brakes" on excess drinking—may be less likely to develop problems with alcohol abuse or dependence. As noted, some people may also possess a genetically greater capacity for reaping pleasure from alcohol, thereby raising their risk of problem drinking.

We also need to consider the role of neurotransmitters. Many psychoactive drugs, including cocaine, amphetamines, alcohol, and opiates, produce pleasurable or euphoric effects by increasing the availability of the neurotransmitter dopamine in the brain—a neurotransmitter involved in activating the brain's reward or pleasure circuits (Connor, 2010; Gallistel, 2006). Even the mere mention of words associated with alcohol (such as "keg" or "binge") may activate brain circuits associated with pleasure or reward in people who suffer from alcohol dependence.

Regular use of these drugs can damage brain circuits that produce states of pleasure and may even impair the brain's ability to produce dopamine on its own. As a result, drug abusers may find it difficult to reap pleasure from ordinarily pleasurable activities, such as enjoying a good meal or socializing with others. The brain comes to depend on having these drugs available to produce feelings of pleasure or erase negative feelings, such as anxiety or depression. Without drugs, life may seem drab and unfulfilling, or even no longer worth living.

Drugs also have complex effects on other neurotransmitters, including endorphins. Opioids lock into the same receptor sites as endorphins. Over time, the brain becomes habituated to a supply of opiates and may suppress its natural production of endorphins. People who are dependent on these drugs come to rely on them to perform pain-relieving and pleasure-producing functions normally performed by endorphins. Habitual users who quit using the drugs may find that little aches and pains become magnified until the body resumes adequate production of endorphins.

Psychological Factors

Psychological factors, such as feelings of hopelessness, thrill seeking, and the desire to escape troubling emotions, are major contributors to the development of drug use and dependence. Young people from troubled backgrounds may turn to drugs out of a sense of futility and despair. People with a high need for thrills or sensations—those who become easily bored with the ordinary activities that fill most people's days—may come to rely on drugs to provide the stimulation they seek.

Some people use alcohol or other drugs as a form of self-medication to relieve anxiety, such as social anxiety, to dull emotional pain, to cope with negative experiences,

Many problem drinkers use alcohol as self-medication in the attempt to wash away their problems or troubling emotions.

or to temporarily escape from life's problems (Cludius et al., 2013; Tomlinson et al., 2006). Cognitive factors, such as holding positive attitudes toward drugs or positive expectancies about the effects they produce (for example, making one more outgoing or socially confident), also contribute to drug use and abuse, especially among young people (for example, Pabst et al., 2014).

Drug Treatment

CONCEPT 4.37
Effective drug treatment requires a multi-faceted approach to helping people free themselves of chemical dependence and develop more adaptive ways of coping with their problems.

The most effective drug treatment programs use a variety of approaches in dealing with the wide range of problems faced by people with drug abuse problems. People with chemical dependencies may first need to undergo **detoxification**, a process in which their bodies are cleared of addictive drugs. To ensure that medical monitoring is available, detoxification usually requires a hospital stay.

Follow-up services, including professional counseling, can assist people in remaining free of drugs by helping them confront the psychological problems that may underlie their drug abuse, such as depression and low self-esteem. Self-help programs such as Alcoholics Anonymous (AA) and Narcotics Anonymous (NA) may also help motivate individuals to maintain abstinence and rebuild their lives free of drugs, especially those who have committed themselves to the goal of abstinence (Ferri, Amato, & Davoli, 2006; Bergman et al., 2013).

Therapeutic drugs may be used in combination with psychological counseling to fight drug addiction (Müller et al., 2014). Nicotine replacement therapy —for example, the nicotine patch—is used to help quell withdrawal symptoms in smokers making the attempt to quit smoking (Koegelenberg et al., 2014). The synthetic opioid *methadone* does not produce the rush associated with heroin but can curb withdrawal symptoms when users stop taking heroin. Taken daily, methadone can help heroin abusers get their lives back on track (Veilleux et al., 2010). Some therapeutic drugs prevent opioids and alcohol from producing a high (Jonas et al., 2014; Mann et al., 2014).

detoxification A process of clearing drugs or toxins from the body.

MODULE REVIEW   **4.4**   **Altering Consciousness Through Drugs**

Recite It

10. **Explain** the differences between physiological and psychological dependence, and between drug abuse and drug dependence.

   Drug use becomes drug (a) _____ when it involves the maladaptive or dangerous use of a drug (use that causes or aggravates personal, occupational, or physical problems). Drug (b) _____ is a state of impaired control over the use of a drug. It is often accompanied by signs of physiological dependence. (c) _____ dependence means that the person's body has come to depend on having a steady supply of the drug. When (d) _____ _____ people rely on a drug as a way of coping with anxiety, stress, and other negative feelings.

11. **Identify** various types of drugs and **explain** how they affect us.

   (e) _____, such as alcohol, barbiturates, tranquilizers, and opioids, are addictive drugs that (f) _____ the activity of the central nervous system. They have a range of effects, including reducing states of bodily arousal, relieving anxiety and tension, and, in the case of barbiturates

and opioids, producing a pleasurable or euphoric rush. (g) _____, which include amphetamines, cocaine, MDMA ("Ecstasy"), nicotine, and caffeine, (h) _____ the activity of the nervous system. Stimulants may induce feelings of euphoria, but they also can lead to physiological dependence. Cocaine directly stimulates reward pathways in the brain, producing states of euphoria, but it is a highly addictive and dangerous drug. (i) _____ ("Ecstasy") is a chemical knockoff of amphetamines that can have serious psychological and physical consequences. (j) _____, a mild stimulant, is the addictive substance found in tobacco. Though regular use of caffeine may lead to psychological dependence, most users can maintain control over their consumption of it. (k) _____ are drugs that alter sensory perceptions and produce hallucinations. They include LSD, mescaline, psilocybin, PCP, and marijuana. PCP ("angel dust") is a synthetic drug that produces delirium—a state of confusion and disorientation that may be accompanied by hallucinations and violent behavior. (l) _____, the most widely used illicit drug, has a range of effects depending on dosage level.

12. **Explain** the development of alcohol and drug abuse problems in terms of psychological, biological, and sociocultural factors.

In addition to the reinforcing effects of the drugs themselves, social, biological, and psychological factors contribute to drug abuse. Among the contributing social factors are peer (m) _____ and exposure to family members and friends who use drugs. Biological factors

include high (n) _____ for negative drug effects. Psychological factors include feelings of (o) _____ and the desire to escape troubling emotions.

13. **Describe** treatment programs to help people with drug problems.

Approaches to treating people with drug problems include (p) _____ programs, professional counseling, use of therapeutic drugs, and self-help programs such as (q) _____ _____ and (r) _____ _____.

Recall It

1. Chemical substances that alter mental states are called _____ drugs.

2. When repeated use of a drug alters a person's body chemistry so that the body comes to rely on having a steady supply of the drug, the condition is called

   a. drug abuse.
   b. drug misuse.
   c. psychological dependence.
   d. physiological dependence.

3. Alcohol and heroin belong to which class of drugs?

4. The most widely used and abused type of depressant is

   a. nicotine.
   b. alcohol.
   c. heroin.
   d. caffeine.

5. What types of drugs are used to treat anxiety and insomnia but that can become addictive when used for extended periods of time.

6. Psychoactive drugs induce pleasurable effects by increasing brain concentrations of which neurotransmitter?

Think About It

■ What roles does reinforcement play in problems of drug abuse and dependence?

■ Should marijuana be legalized? Why or why not?

Recite It answers placed at the end of chapter.

THINKING CRITICALLY ABOUT PSYCHOLOGY

Based on your reading of this chapter, answer the following questions. Then, to evaluate your progress in developing critical thinking skills, compare your answers to the sample answers found in Appendix A.

Do statistics lie? Although statistics may not actually lie, they can certainly mislead if we don't apply critical thinking skills when interpreting them. Recall Figure 4.7 from p. 168, which showed racial/ethnic differences in reported use of cocaine and marijuana. These survey results showed that African Americans were more

likely to report using these drugs within the past month than were (non-Hispanic) White Americans. Now apply your critical thinking skills to answer the following questions:

1. Does this evidence demonstrate that ethnicity accounts for differences in rates of drug use? Why or why not?

2. What other explanations might account for these findings?

Recite It Answers for Chapter 4

Module 4.1 1. (a) awareness; (b) focused; (c) drifting; (d) divided; (e) unconsciousness; (f) altered **Module 4.2** 2. (a) hypothalamus, 3. (b) spindles; (c) delta; (d) REM., 4. (e) conservation; (f) restorative 5. (g) consolidate; (h) activation-synthesis; (i) symbols, 6. (j) reaction; (k) problem, 7. (l) insomnia; (m) narcolepsy; (n) apnea; (o) nightmare; (p) terror; (q) sleepwalking **Module 4.3** 8. (a) consciousness; (b) attention; (c) susceptibility, 9. (d) role-playing; (e) neodissociation **Module 4.4** 10. (a) abuse; (b) dependence; (c) Physiological; (d) psychologically dependent, 11. (e) Depressants; (f) reduce; (g) Stimulants; (h) heighten; (i) MDMA; (j) Nicotine; (k) Hallucinogens; (l) Marijuana 12. (m) pressure; (n) tolerance; (o) hopelessness, 13. (p) detoxification; (q) Alcoholics Anonymous; (r) Narcotics Anonymous

MODULE 4.1

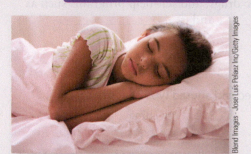

Blend Images – Jose Luis Pelaez Inc/Getty Images

States of Consciousness

- **Focused Awareness:** Fully alert and absorbed
- **Drifting Consciousness:** Meandering thoughts
- **Divided Consciousness:** Dividing consciousness between two or more tasks
- **Sleeping and Dreaming:** Dimmed consciousness during sleep
- **Waking States of Altered Consciousness:** Changes in usual states of awareness during wakefulness

MODULE 4.2

Sleeping and Dreaming

Stages of Sleep

- **Non-REM Sleep (Stages 1 to 4):** Changing brain wave patterns leading to slow wave sleep
- **REM Sleep:** Active brain wave patterns associated with dreaming

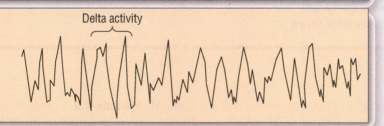

(a) Ordinary Wakefulness
Fast, low-amplitude beta waves

(b) Relaxed Wakefulness
Rhythmic alpha waves

(c) Stage 1 Sleep
Small, irregular brain waves

(d) Stage 2 Sleep
Appearance of spindle-shaped waves called sleep spindles

Sleep spindle

(e) Stage 3/ Stage 4 Sleep
Appearance of large, slow delta waves

Delta activity

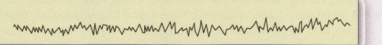

(f) REM Sleep
Similar to ordinary wakefulness

Functions of Sleep

- **Protective Function:** Keeping out of harm's way
- **Energy-Conservation Function:** Preserving energy needed to find food
- **Restorative Function:** Replenishing spent bodily resources
- **Memory Consolidation Function:** Converting fresh memories into more durable memories

Theories of Dreaming

- **Problem-Solving Hypothesis:** Dreams as attempts to solve problems of daily living
- **Activation-Synthesis Hypothesis:** The cortex trying to make sense of random electrical discharges from the brain stem
- **Wish-Fulfillment Hypothesis:** Freud's view of dreams as disguised sexual or aggressive wishes

Problems with Sleep

- **Sleep Deprivation:** Can cause significant problems if it becomes a pattern

- **Sleep–Wake Disorders:** Disturbances of normal sleep, including insomnia disorder, narcolepsy, sleep apnea, nightmare disorder, sleep terror disorder, and sleepwalking.

MODULE 4.3

Altering Consciousness Through Meditation and Hypnosis

Types of Meditation

- **Transcendental Meditation:** Repeating a mantra to induce a meditative state
- **Mindfulness Meditation:** Passively attending to the flow of thoughts

Theories of Hypnosis

- **Role-Playing Theory:** Hypnosis as a social interaction
- **Neodissociation Theory:** Hypnosis as splitting of consciousness

B. BOISSONNET/BSIP/Alamy stock photo

MODULE 4.4

Altering Consciousness Through Drugs

Types of Drugs

- **Depressants:** Alcohol, barbiturates, tranquilizers, opioids
- **Stimulants:** Amphetamine, cocaine, nicotine, caffeine
- **Hallucinogens:** LSD, mescaline, psilocybin, PCP, marijuana

Factors in Drug Use and Abuse
Multiple Factors Involved

- **Social Factors:** Alienation, unemployment, cultural norms, acculturation
- **Biological Factors:** Genetic influences, effects on neurotransmitters in the brain
- **Psychological Factors:** Feelings of hopelessness, sensation seeking, desire to escape troubling emotions

1. Neurotransmitters, such as dopamine, are stored in synaptic vesicles in the sending neuron and released into the synaptic gap. Normally, excess molecules of neurotransmitters not taken up by receptor sites are absorbed by the sending neuron in a recycling process called reuptake.

2. Cocaine (orange circles in diagram) blocks the reuptake of dopamine by the sending neuron.

3. The accumulation of dopamine in the synapse overstimulates neurons in key reward pathways in the brain, producing a pleasurable "high." Over time, the brain becomes less capable of producing feelings of pleasure on its own, leading users to "crash" if they stop using the drug.

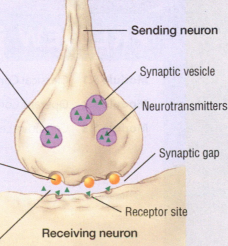

- Sending neuron
- Synaptic vesicle
- Neurotransmitters
- Synaptic gap
- Receptor site
- Receiving neuron

LEARNING OBJECTIVES

After studying this chapter, you will be able to . . .

1 **Define** learning in psychological terms.

2 **Explain** how conditioned responses are acquired and **describe** the contributions of Ivan Pavlov.

3 **Explain** the process by which conditioned responses become weaker or disappear.

4 **Explain** how conditioned responses can be strengthened.

5 **Define** stimulus generalization and discrimination and **describe** their roles in classical conditioning.

6 **Explain** classical conditioning from a cognitive perspective.

7 **Apply** classical conditioning to examples discussed in the text.

8 **Define** operant conditioning, **identify** the major figures in its development, and **describe** their contributions.

9 **Describe** different types of reinforcement and schedules of reinforcement.

10 **Explain** the effects of different types of reinforcement on response rates.

11 **Define** punishment and **explain** why psychologists raise concerns about the use of punishment in disciplining children.

12 **Explain** the difference between escape learning and avoidance learning.

13 **Apply** operant conditioning to examples discussed in the text.

14 **Define** cognitive learning and **describe** several types of cognitive learning.

JAKOBCHUK VIACHESLAV/Shutterstock.com

PREVIEW

Learning

Confessions of an Egg Hater

I hate eggs. It's not just the taste of eggs I can't stand. The smell, the feel, the very sight of eggs is enough to make me sick. Watching other people eat eggs can make me nauseous. It's not that I'm allergic to eggs. I like all kinds of baked goods that are made with eggs. I'm fine with eggs as long as they are cooked into other foods so they are no longer recognizable as, well, eggs. But eggs themselves, especially runny eggs, fill me with disgust.

I wasn't born with a disgust for eggs. Nor did I always dislike eggs. My parents tell me I was actually quite fond of eggs as a young child. But somewhere along the line, I acquired an aversion to eggs. Chances are I had an unpleasant experience with eggs. No, I don't think I was chased around a barn by a clutch of crazed chickens. Most likely, I had an experience in which eggs made me sick. Or perhaps I was forced to eat eggs when I wasn't feeling well. In any event, I have no memory of it. All I know is that I hate eggs and have hated them for as long as I can recall.

I have described my aversion to eggs to introduce you to the topic of learning. Some responses, such as pulling your hand away from a hot stove, are reflexive. We don't learn reflexes; we are biologically equipped to perform them automatically. Other behaviors develop naturally as the result of maturation. As a child's muscles mature, the child becomes capable of lifting heavier weights or throwing a ball a longer distance. But other responses, such as my aversion to eggs, are acquired through *experience*.

Psychologists generally define *learning* as a relatively permanent change in behavior that results from experience. Through experience, we learn about the world and develop new skills, such as riding a bicycle or cooking a soufflé. Acquired taste preferences or aversions, including my aversion to eggs, are also learned behaviors. Note the use of the term *relatively permanent* in the definition of learning. For learning to occur, changes in behavior must be enduring. But change need not be permanent. It is possible to unlearn behavior. For example, you would need to unlearn the behavior of driving on the right side of the road if you wanted to drive in a country where people drive on the left side of the road.

Learning is adaptive—it enables organisms to adapt their behavior to the demands they face in the environment. Through learning, organisms acquire behaviors that increase their chances of survival. Even taste aversions can be adaptive. They prevent animals, including humans, from eating foods that have sickened or poisoned them in the past. But not all learned responses are adaptive. My own aversion to eggs limits the range of foods I might enjoy. By and large, however, learning helps prepare organisms to meet the demands that their environments impose on them.

Psychologists study many forms of learning, including three major types that are the focus of this chapter: classical conditioning, operant conditioning, and cognitive learning.

Did you know that...

- Déjà vu may be a learned response? (p. 179)

- Principles of learning discovered by Ivan Pavlov based on his studies of digestion in dogs help explain the development of phobias in people? (p. 182)

- Salivating to the sound of a tone may not be harmful, but salivating at the sight of a Scotch bottle may well be dangerous to people battling alcoholism? (p. 183)

- Principles of classical conditioning were put into practice on a ranch to prevent coyotes from killing sheep? (p. 184)

- The concept of a discriminative stimulus is a useful thing to keep in mind when asking someone for money or a favor? (p. 190)

- Schedules of reinforcement explain why people continue to buy lottery tickets although they hardly, if ever, win anything? (p. 193)

- Use of even mild forms of punishment, including spanking, smacking, or pushing, increases the risk that children will go on to develop emotional problems in adulthood? (p. 196)

5.1 Classical Conditioning: Learning Through Association

1 **Define** learning in psychological terms.

2 **Explain** how conditioned responses are acquired and **describe** the contributions of Ivan Pavlov.

3 **Explain** the process by which conditioned responses become weaker or disappear.

4 **Explain** how conditioned responses can be strengthened.

5 **Define** stimulus generalization and discrimination and **describe** their roles in classical conditioning.

6 **Explain** classical conditioning from a cognitive perspective.

7 **Apply** classical conditioning to examples discussed in the text.

The Brain Loves a Puzzle

As you read ahead, use the information in the text to solve the following puzzle:

A recovering heroin addict in New York City was trying to get his life back on track. One day he took the subway to begin work at a new job site. Just as the subway doors opened at a particular station, he suddenly experienced intense cravings for heroin and shortly thereafter experienced a full-blown relapse. Why do you suppose he experienced these strong cravings at a particular subway stop? What principles of learning explain these cravings?

vdbvsl/Alamy stock photo

CONCEPT 5.1

Pavlov's discovery that dogs would salivate to particular sounds in his laboratory led him to identify a process of learning called classical conditioning.

Do your muscles tighten at the sound of a dentist's drill? Do you suddenly begin to salivate when passing by your favorite bakery? You weren't born with these responses—you learned them. But how does **learning** occur?

To understand how responses are learned, we need to consider the work of the Russian physiologist Ivan Pavlov (1849–1936). Pavlov discovered the form of learning we call **classical conditioning**. Pavlov, who at the time was studying digestive processes in dogs, made this discovery when he observed that dogs would salivate to sounds in his laboratory that had become associated with food, such as the sound of metal food carts being wheeled into his laboratory.

Milkovasa/Shutterstock.com

You can think of classical conditioning as *learning by association*. If you associate the sound of a dentist's drill with pain because of past dental treatment, the sound of the drill will probably cause you to respond with the muscle tension that is a natural reflex to pain. If you associate a certain bakery with a particularly tasty treat, you may find yourself salivating simply by driving by the bakery. In other words, you learn to connect or associate two stimuli—the sound of the dental drill and pain, for instance (Chance, 2009). Although classical conditioning is a relatively simple form of learning, it plays important roles in our lives—as you will see in this module.

Principles of Classical Conditioning

Pavlov performed many experiments in classical conditioning. In a typical experiment, he harnessed dogs in an apparatus similar to the one shown in ■ Figure 5.1. When food is placed on a dog's tongue, the dog naturally salivates. This reflexive behavior is called an **unconditioned response (UR or UCR)** (*unconditioned* means "unlearned"). A stimulus that elicits an unconditioned response—in this case, the dog's food—is called an **unconditioned stimulus (US or UCS)** .

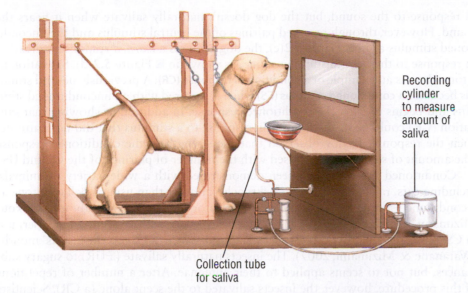

FIGURE 5.1 Apparatus Similar to One Used in Pavlov's Experiments on Conditioning
In Pavlov's studies, a research assistant positioned behind a mirror sounded a tone as food was placed on the dog's tongue. After several pairings of the tone and food, the dog acquired a conditioned response of salivation. The amount of saliva dripping through a tube to a collection vial was taken as the measure of the strength of the conditioned response.

■ Figure 5.2 outlines the steps involved in a Pavlovian experiment. As you can see in ■ Figure 5.2(b), the introduction of a **neutral stimulus (NS)**, such as the tone produced by striking a tuning fork or ringing a bell, does not initially elicit a response of salivation. It may produce other responses, however. A dog's ears may turn up

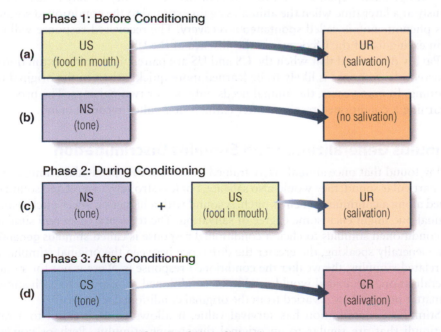

FIGURE 5.2 Diagramming Classical Conditioning
In classical conditioning, a neutral stimulus (the tone) is paired with an unconditioned stimulus (food) that normally elicits an unconditioned response (salivation). With repeated pairings, the neutral stimulus becomes a conditioned stimulus that elicits the conditioned response of salivation.

learning A relatively permanent change in behavior acquired through experience.

classical conditioning The process of learning by which a previously neutral stimulus comes to elicit a response identical or similar to one that was originally elicited by another stimulus as the result of the pairing or association of the two stimuli.

unconditioned response (UR) An unlearned response to a stimulus.

unconditioned stimulus (US) A stimulus that elicits an unlearned response.

neutral stimulus (NS) A stimulus that before conditioning does not produce a particular response.

Ivan Pavlov (right) in his laboratory

CONCEPT 5.2

Through a process of extinction, conditioned responses gradually weaken and eventually disappear as a result of the repeated presentation of the conditioned stimulus in the absence of the unconditioned stimulus.

CONCEPT LINK

A therapy technique called gradual exposure makes use of the principle of extinction to help people overcome phobias. See Module 14.1.

CONCEPT 5.3

Extinguished responses are not forgotten but may return spontaneously in the future if the conditioned stimulus is presented again.

CONCEPT 5.4

Stimulus generalization has survival value by enabling organisms to generalize their learned responses to new stimuli that are similar to an original threatening stimulus.

conditioned response (CR) An acquired or learned response to a conditioned stimulus.

conditioned stimulus (CS) A previously neutral stimulus that comes to elicit a conditioned response after it has been paired with an unconditioned stimulus.

extinction The gradual weakening and eventual disappearance of a conditioned response.

spontaneous recovery The spontaneous return of a conditioned response following extinction.

reconditioning The process of relearning a conditioned response following extinction.

in response to the sound, but the dog doesn't naturally salivate when it hears the sound. However, through repeated pairings of the neutral stimulus and the unconditioned stimulus as in ■ Figure 5.2(c), the dog acquires a *learned* response: salivation in response to the neutral stimulus alone, as shown in ■ Figure 5.2(d). Salivation to a tone alone is an example of a **conditioned response (CR)**. A previously neutral stimulus becomes a **conditioned stimulus (CS)** when it is paired with an unconditioned stimulus and begins to elicit the conditioned response. In addition to showing that salivation (CR) could be made to occur in response to a stimulus that did not naturally elicit the response, Pavlov observed that the strength of the conditioned response (the amount of salivation) increased with the number of pairings of the CS and US.

Conditioned salivation has been demonstrated with a wide variety of animals, including cats, rats, and yes, even cockroaches. Rather than using a bell or a tone as a conditioned stimulus (CS), Japanese investigators Hidehiro Watanabe and Makoto Mizunami stimulated the antennae of cockroaches with a scent of peppermint (a CS) while they placed droplets of a sugary substance (a US) on the insects' mouths (Watanabe & Mizunami, 2007). The insects naturally salivate (a UR) to sugary substances, but not to scents applied to their antennae. After a number of repetitions of this procedure, however, the insects salivated to the scent alone (a CR). Scientists hope that by studying simpler organisms like insects, they will learn more about the mechanisms of conditioning at the neuronal level (Fountain, 2007).

We next examine other characteristics of classical conditioning: extinction and spontaneous recovery, stimulus generalization and discrimination, and stimulus characteristics that strengthen conditioned responses.

Extinction and Spontaneous Recovery

Pavlov noticed that the conditioned response of salivation to the sound of a bell or a tuning fork would gradually weaken and eventually disappear when he repeatedly presented the sound in the absence of the US (food). This process is called **extinction**. The extinguished response is not forgotten or lost to memory. It may return spontaneously at a later time when the animal is again exposed to the conditioned stimulus. This phenomenon is called **spontaneous recovery**. The recovered response will once again extinguish if the CS occurs in the absence of the US.

Pavlov discovered that when the CS and US are paired again after extinction has occurred, the response is likely to be learned more quickly than in the original conditioning. In many cases, the animal needs only one or two pairings. The process of relearning a conditioned response after extinction is called **reconditioning**.

Stimulus Generalization and Stimulus Discrimination

Pavlov found that once animals were trained to salivate to a particular stimulus, such as a particular sound, they would also salivate, but less strongly, to a related sound that varied along a continuum, such as pitch. A sound with a higher or lower pitch than the original one might elicit some degree of salivation. The tendency of stimuli similar to the conditioned stimulus to elicit a conditioned response is called **stimulus generalization**. Generally speaking, the greater the difference between the original stimulus and the related stimulus, the weaker the conditioned response is. Were it not for stimulus generalization, the animal would need to be conditioned to respond to each stimulus no matter how slightly it varied from the original conditioned stimulus.

Stimulus generalization has survival value. It allows us to respond to a range of stimuli that are similar to an original threatening stimulus. Perhaps you were menaced or bitten by a large dog when you were young. Because of stimulus generalization, you may find yourself tensing up whenever you see a large dog approaching. Not all large dogs are dangerous, of course, but stimulus generalization helps prepare us just in case.

Have you ever walked into a room and suddenly felt uncomfortable or anxious for no apparent reason? Your emotional reaction may be a conditioned response to generalized stimuli in the environment that are similar to cues associated with unpleasant experiences in the past. Perhaps, too, you may have experienced déjà vu—a feeling of having been in a place before when you've never actually been there. Stimulus generalization provides an explanation of these experiences. The feeling of familiarity in novel situations may be a conditioned response evoked by cues or stimuli in these novel environments that resemble conditioned stimuli encountered in other situations. A fleeting odor, the way light bounces off a ceiling, even the color of walls—all may be cues that evoke conditioned responses acquired in other settings.

Stimulus discrimination, the ability to differentiate among related stimuli, represents the opposite side of the coin to stimulus generalization. This ability allows us to fine-tune our responses to the environment. Suppose, for example, an animal in a laboratory study receives a mild shock shortly after exposure to a CS (a tone) (Domjan, 2005). After a few pairings of the tone and shock, the animal shows signs of fear (for example, cowering, urinating) to the tone alone. The tone is the CS, the shock is the US, and the pairing of the two leads to the acquisition of the conditioned response (CR) of fear to the tone alone. Now, let's say the pairings of the tone and the shock continue but are interspersed with a tone of a higher pitch that is not accompanied by a shock. What happens next is that the animal learns to discriminate between the two stimuli, responding with fear to the original tone but remaining calm when the higher-pitched tone is sounded.

Stimulus discrimination in daily life allows us to differentiate between threatening and nonthreatening stimuli. For example, through repeated noneventful encounters with certain breeds of dogs, we may learn to respond with fear to a large dog of an unfamiliar breed but not to the friendly Labrador that lives next door.

■ Figure 5.3 illustrates the processes of stimulus generalization and stimulus discrimination.

Concept Chart 5.1 presents an overview of the major concepts in classical conditioning.

Stimulus Characteristics That Strengthen Conditioned Responses

Psychologists have identified several key factors relating to the timing and intensity of stimuli that serve to strengthen conditioned responses:

1. *Frequency of pairings.* Generally, the more often the CS is paired with the US, the stronger and more reliable the CR will be. In some cases, however, even a single pairing can produce a strong CR. An airline passenger who

Nico Kai/The Image Bank/Getty Images

In a case example, a man developed a conditioned fear of enclosed spaces (claustrophobia) after he became trapped behind a refrigerator and nearly suffocated while helping a friend move. Through stimulus generalization, the phobia generalized to related stimuli, including riding on small, crowded elevators. As the result of stimulus discrimination, however, he did not experience any fear of riding on larger, uncrowded elevators.

CONCEPT 5.5

By learning to differentiate among related stimuli, we are able to fine-tune our responses to the environment.

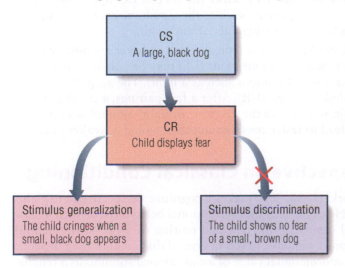

FIGURE 5.3 Stimulus Generalization and Discrimination

In stimulus generalization, a conditioned response generalizes to stimuli that are similar to the original conditioned stimulus. In stimulus discrimination, the organism differentiates between related stimuli.

stimulus generalization The tendency for stimuli that are similar to the conditioned stimulus to elicit a conditioned response.

stimulus discrimination The tendency to differentiate among stimuli so that stimuli that are related to the original conditioned stimulus, but not identical to it, fail to elicit a conditioned response.

Concept Chart 5.1 Key Concepts in Classical Conditioning

Concept	Description	Example: Fear of Dentistry
Classical conditioning	A form of learning in which a response identical or similar to one originally elicited by an unconditioned stimulus (US) is made in response to a conditioned stimulus (CS) based on the pairing of the two stimuli	The pairing of pain during dental procedures with environmental stimuli in the dentist's office leads to the development of a fear response to the environmental cues alone.
Extinction	Gradual weakening and eventual disappearance of the conditioned response (CR) when the CS is repeatedly presented without the US	The use of anesthetics and painless dental techniques leads to the gradual reduction and elimination of fear of dentistry.
Spontaneous recovery	Spontaneous return of the CR some time after extinction occurs	Fear of dentistry returns spontaneously a few months or a few years after extinction.
Stimulus generalization	CR evoked by stimuli that are similar to the original CS	A person shows a fear response when visiting the office of a new dentist.
Stimulus discrimination	CR not evoked by stimuli that are related but not identical to the CS	A person shows a fear response to the sight of a dentist's drill but not to equipment used for cleaning teeth.

CONCEPT 5.6
The strength of a classically conditioned response depends on the frequency of pairings and the timing of the stimuli, as well as the intensity of the US.

experiences a sudden free fall during a flight may develop an immediate and enduring fear of flying.

2. *Timing.* The strongest CRs occur when the CS is presented first and remains present throughout the administration of the US. Weaker CRs occur when the CS is presented first (for example, a tone, as in the case of fear conditioning described above) but is withdrawn before the US (for example, a shock) is introduced. Other timing sequences, such as the simultaneous presentation of the CS and US, produce even weaker CRs, if any at all.

3. *Intensity of the US.* A stronger US will typically lead to faster conditioning than a weaker one. For example, a puff of air (US) may be paired with a CS (for example, a tone or a visual stimulus such as a light). The air puff produces a reflexive eyeblink response (UR). After a few pairings, a conditioned eyeblink (CR) occurs in response to the CS (tone or light) alone. Use of a stronger air puff will lead to faster conditioning than would a weaker one.

A Cognitive Perspective on Classical Conditioning

Psychologist Robert Rescorla (1988, 2009) takes a cognitive perspective in explaining classical conditioning. He challenged the conventional behaviorist view that classical conditioning is based simply on the repeated pairing of a previously neutral stimulus and an unconditioned stimulus. Rescorla argued that conditioning depends on a cognitive factor—the informational value of a conditioned stimulus as a reliable

CONCEPT 5.7
In Rescorla's view, classical conditioning involves a cognitive process by which organisms learn to anticipate events based on cues, called conditioned stimuli, that come to reliably predict the occurrence of these events.

signal for *predicting* the occurrence of the unconditioned stimulus. Humans and other animals actively seek information that helps them make predictions about important events in their environments. Conditioned stimuli are signals or cues that organisms use to make these predictions. The more reliable the signal, the stronger the conditioned response.

Recent evidence suggests that in humans, conscious awareness of the link between the two stimuli, the CS and the US, may be critical in learning conditioned responses (Weidemann, Satkunarajah, & Lovibond, 2016). To acquire a conditioned response, we may first need to attend to the relationship between the two stimuli.

Rescorla's model has important survival implications. Dogs and other animals may be more likely to survive if they learn to respond with salivation to cues that food is present, because salivation prepares them to swallow food. Animals are also more likely to survive if they learn to respond with fear (heightened bodily arousal) to cues that reliably signal the presence of threatening stimuli. Consider an animal that hears a sound or gets a whiff of an odor (a CS) previously associated with the presence of a particular predator (a US). By responding quickly with heightened arousal to such a stimulus, the animal is better prepared to take defensive action if the predator appears. Thus, we can think of classical conditioning as a kind of built-in early warning system.

Rescorla's model also explains why you are likely to develop a fear of dentistry more quickly if you experience pain during each dental visit than if you have pain only every now and then. In other words, the more reliably the CS (a dental cue) signals the occurrence of the US (pain), the stronger the conditioned response is likely to be.

Why It Matters: Examples of Classical Conditioning in Daily Life

Pavlov's studies might merit only a footnote in the history of psychology if classical conditioning were limited to the salivary responses of dogs. However, classical conditioning helps us explain such diverse behaviors as phobias, drug cravings, and taste aversions. John B. Watson, the founder of behaviorism, believed that Pavlov's principles of conditioning could explain emotional responses in humans. In 1919, Watson set out with Rosalie Rayner, a student who was later to become his wife, to prove that a fear response could be acquired through classical conditioning. After taking a look at Watson and Rayner's experiment, we consider other examples of conditioning in humans.

Classical Conditioning of Fear Responses

As their subject, Watson and Rayner selected an 11-month-old boy whom they called Albert B., but who is better known in the annals of psychology as Little Albert (Watson & Rayner, 1920). Albert had previously shown no fear of a white rat that was placed near him and had even reached out to stroke the animal (see ■ Figure 5.4). In the experimental procedure, the rat was placed close to Albert, and as he reached for it, the experimenters banged a steel bar with a hammer just behind his head, creating a loud gong. Watson believed that loud sounds naturally make infants cringe and shudder with fear. Sure enough, Albert showed signs of fear when the bar was struck—crying and burying his face in the mattress. Watson and Rayner then repeatedly paired the rat and the loud sound, which resulted in Albert developing a fear response to the sight of the rat alone.

CONCEPT 5.8
Classical conditioning helps explain the development of conditioned emotional reactions, such as conditioned fear responses.

CONCEPT LINK
Clinicians apply principles of classical conditioning to explain the development of excessive fear reactions, or phobias. See Module 13.2.

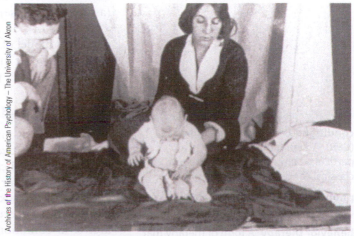

Archives of the History of American Psychology – The University of Akron

John Watson and Rosalie Rayner with Little Albert

Before Conditioning	During Conditioning	After Conditioning	Stimulus Generalization
Child shows no fear of white rat	White rat (CS) is paired with loud sound (US) that naturally evokes fear response	Child shows fear (CR) of white rat alone (CS)	Child shows fear reaction (CR) to related stimuli

FIGURE 5.4 The Conditioning of "Little Albert"

Advertising Archives

There's a common expression that "sex sells." How might you use the principles of classical conditioning to explain the role of sexual stimuli in advertising?

conditioned emotional reaction (CER) An emotional response to a particular stimulus acquired through classical conditioning.

phobias Excessive fears of particular objects or situations.

behavior therapy A form of therapy that involves the systematic application of the principles of learning.

Such an acquired fear response is called a **conditioned emotional reaction (CER)**. Later experiments showed that Albert's fear response had generalized to other furry stimuli, including a dog, a rabbit, and even a Santa Claus mask that Watson had worn.

Let us examine the Watson and Rayner study by applying what we know about classical conditioning. Before conditioning, Albert showed no fear of the white rat; it was a neutral stimulus. The unconditioned stimulus (US) was the loud banging sound, a stimulus that naturally elicits a fear response (UR) in young children. Through repeated pairings of the white rat and the banging sound (US), the white rat alone (CS) came to elicit a fear response (CR).

Though the Little Albert experiment is among the most famous studies in psychology, it would not pass muster with the stricter ethical standards in place today. Exposing a child to intense fear, even with the parents' permission, fails to adhere to the responsibility investigators have to safeguard the welfare of research participants. In addition, Watson and Rayner made no attempt to undo or extinguish Albert's fears, as ethical codes would now require, although they did discuss techniques they might use to do so. We cannot say for sure what became of Little Albert, but investigators report that, sadly, the child they believe may have been Albert succumbed to a childhood illness at the age of 6 (Beck, Levinson, & Irons, 2009).

Excessive fears, or **phobias**, such as Albert's fear of white rats or a person's fear of dentistry, can be acquired through classical conditioning. In one case example, a 34-year-old woman had been terrified of riding on elevators since a childhood incident occurred in which she and her grandmother were trapped on an elevator for hours. For her, the single pairing of previously neutral stimuli (cues associated with riding on elevators) and a traumatic experience was sufficient to produce an enduring phobia (fear of elevators). In some cases, the original conditioning experiences may be lost to memory, or they may have occurred even before language developed (as in Albert's case).

Early work on the conditioning of fear responses set the stage for the development of a model of therapy called **behavior therapy** (discussed in Chapter 14), which is the systematic application of the principles of learning to help people overcome phobias and other problem behaviors.

Classical Conditioning in Advertising

John Watson also made his mark in the world of advertising, working as an executive at a major advertising firm after leaving academia. Watson's success in this field rested on his application of the principles of classical conditioning. He suggested that manufacturers pair their products in print advertisements with emotionally arousing cues, especially sexual stimuli. His advertising campaign for a popular toothpaste of the time, Pebeco, featured a seductively dressed young woman smoking a cigarette. In conditioning terms, the toothpaste represents the CS and the attractive young woman, the US. Today, thanks in part to Mr. Watson, we are bombarded with advertisements and television commercials that pair products with sexual cues and other emotionally arousing stimuli. Advertisers hope their products will elicit sexual arousal and positive emotions that will in turn spur sales. Can you think of commercials on TV that pitch products with sexual cues?

Classical Conditioning of Positive Emotions

It's not just negative emotions like fear that can be classically conditioned. Perhaps you've had the experience of hearing a certain song on the radio and suddenly smiling or feeling cheerful, or even experiencing a tinge of sexual arousal. Chances are the song evoked past experiences associated with pleasant emotions or sexual arousal. Similarly, feelings of nostalgia may be conditioned responses elicited by subtle cues in the environment that had come to be associated with pleasant experiences in the past. These cues, perhaps just a whiff of perfume or the mist in the air on a spring day, may induce nostalgic feelings.

Classical Conditioning of Drug Cravings

People with chemical dependencies frequently encounter drug cravings, especially when they undergo drug withdrawal or go "cold turkey." Though cravings may have a physiological basis (they constitute part of the withdrawal syndrome for addictive drugs), classical conditioning can also contribute to these strong desires. Cravings may be elicited by cues (conditioned stimuli) in the environment associated with prior drug use. People battling alcoholism may experience strong cravings for the drug when they are exposed to drug-related conditioned stimuli, such as the sight of a bottle of alcohol. Cravings may be elicited by conditioned stimuli long after withdrawal symptoms have passed, such as cues associated with a subway station where a drug abuser formerly bought drugs (see earlier The Brain Loves a Puzzle).

Consider also the person suffering from alcoholism who salivates at the very sight of a liquor bottle. Salivating to the sound of a tone may be harmless enough, but salivating when looking at a picture of a Scotch bottle in a magazine can be dangerous to a person struggling with alcoholism. Not surprisingly, drug counselors encourage recovering drug and alcohol abusers to avoid cues associated with their former drug use patterns.

Classical Conditioning of Taste Aversions

The principles of classical conditioning can also be used to explain a **conditioned taste aversion**, including my disgust for eggs (Garcia & Koelling, 2009; Limebeer & Parker, 2006). Do you have an acquired taste aversion? Can you trace how it developed?

Psychologist John Garcia was the first to demonstrate experimentally the role of classical conditioning in the acquisition of taste aversions. Garcia and colleague Bob Koelling noticed something unusual in the behavior of rats that had been exposed to nausea-inducing radiation. The rats developed an aversion or "conditioned nausea" to flavored water sweetened with saccharine when the water was paired with the nausea-producing radiation (Garcia & Koelling, 1966). In classical conditioning terms, the radiation was the US; the nausea it produced was the UR; the flavored water was the CS; and the aversion (nausea) the CS elicited on its own was the CR.

In related work, Garcia demonstrated that aversion to particular foods could be classically conditioned by giving rats a nausea-inducing drug soon after they ate the foods (Garcia & Koelling, 1971). Moreover, taste aversions were acquired even when the CS (the taste of the food) was presented a few hours before the presentation of the US (the nausea-inducing stimulus) (Domjan, 2005). This discovery shocked Garcia's experimental colleagues, who believed that classical conditioning could occur only when the CS is followed almost immediately by the US. Moreover,

Mario Tama/Getty Images

Drug cravings may be conditioned responses elicited by exposure to cues (conditioned stimuli) associated with drug-using behavior.

conditioned taste aversion An aversion to a particular food or beverage acquired through classical conditioning.

In a field experiment by psychologist John Garcia (shown here), investigators left sheep carcasses on the range after injecting them with a nausea-producing chemical. After eating meat from these carcasses and becoming sickened, coyotes developed a conditioned taste aversion to sheep meat.

Thomas Kitchin

John Garcia

Garcia and his team were able to demonstrate that a conditioned taste aversion could be acquired on the basis of a single pairing of the flavor of a food or drink with a nausea-inducing stimulus.

Like other forms of classical conditioning, conditioned taste aversions have clear survival benefits. Our ancestors lived without benefit of refrigeration or preservatives. Acquiring an aversion to foods whose rancid smells and tastes sickened them would have helped them avoid such foods in the future. Similarly for us, learning to become averse to tastes and aromas of foods that sicken us prompts us to avoid such foods in the future.

In a classic study that literally applied principles of classical conditioning on the open range, John Garcia and his colleagues came up with an ingenious way to help sheep ranchers protect their sheep from coyotes (Gustavson & Garcia, 1974; Gustavson et al., 1974). At the time of the study, free-ranging coyotes were killing thousands of sheep, and ranchers seeking to protect their flocks were killing so many coyotes that their survival as a species was endangered. It was therefore important to find a way of stopping the coyotes' destructive behavior without killing them. As an experiment, the researchers injected sheep carcasses with a poison that would sicken but not kill the coyotes and scattered the carcasses over the range. Not only did sheep killings drop, but some coyotes also developed such an aversion to the taste of the sheep meat that they ran away just at the sight or smell of sheep.

Conditioning the Immune System

In a landmark study, Robert Ader and Nicholas Cohen (1982) showed that classical conditioning even extends to the workings of the **immune system**. The immune system protects the body from disease-causing organisms. The researchers had laboratory rats ingest saccharin-sweetened water (CS) while at the same time giving them a drug (US) that suppressed immune system responses (UR). After several pairings of the CS and US, immune suppression (CR) occurred when the rats drank the sweetened water alone (CS).

Conditioned immune suppression can be made to occur in response to other conditioned stimuli, such as odors and sounds, as well as in humans (Kusnecov, 2001; Pacheco-Lopez et al., 2005). For example, a group of healthy people was given an immune-suppressant drug as an unconditioned stimulus, which was paired with a distinctively flavored drink as a conditioned stimulus during four separate sessions

CONCEPT 5.11

Investigators have found that even immune system responses can be classically conditioned.

immune system The body's system of defense against disease.

spread over three days (Goebel et al., 2002). Afterward, presenting the drink without the active drug succeeded in suppressing immune system responses, thereby demonstrating the acquisition of a conditioned response.

The ability to acquire an immune-suppressant response through classical conditioning may have important health implications for humans. In people who receive organ transplants, the immune system attacks the transplanted organs as foreign objects. Perhaps classical conditioning can be used to suppress the tendency of the body to reject transplanted organs, lessening the need for immune-suppressant drugs. It is also conceivable that classical conditioning may be used to give the immune system a boost in its fight against disease, perhaps even to strengthen the body's ability to defend itself against cancer. However, we need further research to determine the value of classical conditioning in medical treatment.

MODULE REVIEW   5.1   Classical Conditioning: Learning Through Association

Recite It

1. **Define** learning in psychological terms.

   Psychologists generally define learning as a relatively (a) _____ change in behavior that results from (b) _____.

2. **Explain** how conditioned responses are acquired and **describe** the contributions of Ivan Pavlov.

   Conditioned responses are acquired on the basis of classical conditioning, a form of learning in which a response that is the same as or similar to one originally elicited by an (c) _____ stimulus (US) is made to occur to a (d) _____ stimulus (CS) on the basis of pairing the two stimuli. Pavlov discovered classical conditioning based on his experiments on the salivation reflex in dogs in which he demonstrated that dogs would salivate to a previously (e) _____ stimulus (a bell or tone) after it was repeatedly paired with an (f) _____ stimulus that naturally elicits salivation (food placed on the animal's tongue).

3. **Explain** the process by which conditioned responses become weaker or disappear.

   (g) _____ is the process by which learned responses gradually weaken and eventually disappear when the conditioned stimulus (CS) is presented repeatedly in the absence of the unconditioned stimulus (US). Spontaneous (h) _____ is the return of the conditioned response some time after extinction.

4. **Explain** how conditioned responses can be strengthened.

   Conditioned responses can be strengthened based on manipulation of the (i) _____ of pairings of the conditioned stimulus and unconditioned stimulus, the (j) _____ of the

presentation of the two stimuli, and the (k) _____ of the unconditioned stimulus.

5. **Define** stimulus generalization and discrimination and **describe** their roles in classical conditioning.

   Stimulus (l) _____ is the tendency of stimuli that are similar to the conditioned stimulus to elicit a conditioned response. Stimulus generalization enables us to respond in a like way to stimuli that resemble the original (m) _____ stimulus.

   Through stimulus (n) _____, organisms learn to differentiate stimuli such that those that are related to the conditioned stimulus, but not identical to it, fail to elicit a conditioned (o) _____.

6. **Explain** classical conditioning from a cognitive perspective.

   Developed by Robert Rescorla, the cognitive perspective on classical conditioning holds that conditioning depends on the (p) _____ value that the conditioned stimulus acquires in predicting the occurrence of the unconditioned stimulus. According to this model, humans and other animals actively seek information that helps them make (q) _____ about important events in their environment; conditioned stimuli are cues that they use to make these predictions.

7. **Apply** classical conditioning to examples discussed in the text.

   Examples include the acquisition of fear responses and taste (r) _____. Classical conditioning also plays a role in positive emotions, drug (s) _____, and immune system responses.

Recall It

1. What is the process called by which conditioned responses occur in response to stimuli that are similar to conditioned stimuli?

2. Which of the following does *not* affect the strength of conditioned responses?
   a. frequency of pairings of the CS with the US
   b. timing of the presentation of the CS and US
   c. intensity of the US
   d. alternation of a US–CS presentation with a CR–UR presentation

3. In John Garcia's study of conditioned taste aversion, rats refused to drink from the plastic water bottles in the chambers in which they were given radiation because they associated the plastic-tasting water with the nausea from the radiation. In classical conditioning terms, the radiation in Garcia's research on taste aversion is the _____.
   a. UR   c. US
   b. CS   d. CR

4. Rescorla's cognitive model of classical conditioning emphasizes the role of
   a. repeated pairings of the CS and US as the key factor in classical conditioning.
   b. the informational value of the CS as a signal or cue.
   c. the relationship between the strength of conditioning and the intensity of the US.
   d. the role of the US as a predictor of the CS.

5. In Watson and Rayner's study of "Little Albert," the child became frightened of a white rat and similar stimuli because
   a. children are naturally afraid of white rats.
   b. a loud noise occurred whenever the rat was in Albert's presence.
   c. the rat was repeatedly paired with a neutral stimulus.
   d. Albert had a traumatic experience with a rat.

Think About It

■ Can you think of any examples of classical conditioning in your daily life? For example, some people experience emotional reactions when they hear certain music or sounds or get a whiff of certain odors. How might you explain the origins of these responses in classical conditioning terms?

■ What do you fear? Do these fears interfere with your daily life? Based on your reading of the chapter, what do you think might be the origin of these fears? How are you coping with them? Have you talked to anyone about them? Is there anyone you might contact to help you overcome them, such as a college health official or a health care provider in your area?

Recite It answers placed at the end of chapter.

MODULE

5.2 Operant Conditioning: Learning Through Consequences

8 **Define** operant conditioning, **identify** the major figures in its development, and **describe** their contributions.

9 **Describe** different types of reinforcement and schedules of reinforcement.

10 **Explain** the effects of different types of reinforcement on response rates.

11 **Define** punishment, and **explain** why psychologists raise concerns about the use of punishment in disciplining children.

12 **Explain** the difference between escape learning and avoidance learning.

13 **Apply** operant conditioning to examples discussed in the text.

Classical conditioning can explain how we learn relatively simple, reflexive responses, such as salivation and eyeblinks, as well as emotional responses associated with fear and disgust. But classical conditioning cannot explain how we learn the more complex behaviors that are part and parcel of our daily experiences. You get up in the morning, dress, go to work or school, prepare meals, take care of household chores, run errands, socialize with friends, and perhaps have an hour or two to relax at the end of the day. To account for such behaviors, we need to consider a form of learning called *operant conditioning*. With classical conditioning, we examined learning that results from the association between stimuli before a response occurs. With operant conditioning, we explore learning that results from the association of a response with its consequences. As you will see with this form of learning, responses are acquired and strengthened by the effects they produce in the environment.

We focus on the contributions of two American psychologists: Edward Thorndike, whose law of effect was the first systematic attempt to describe how behavior is affected by its consequences, and B. F. Skinner, whose experimental work laid out many of the principles of operant conditioning.

Thorndike and the Law of Effect

Edward Thorndike (1874–1949) studied learning in animals because he found them easier to work with than people. He constructed a device called a "puzzle box"—a cage in which the animal (usually a cat) had to perform a simple act (such as pulling a looped string or pushing a pedal) to make its escape and reach a dish of food placed within its view just outside the cage (see ■ Figure 5.5). The animal would first engage in seemingly random behaviors until it accidentally performed the response that released the door. Thorndike argued that the animals did not employ reasoning, insight, or any other form of higher intelligence to find their way to the exit. Rather, it was through a random process of *trial and error* that they gradually eliminated useless responses and eventually chanced upon the successful behavior. Successful responses were then "stamped in" by the pleasure they produced and became more likely to be repeated in the future.

Based on his observations, Thorndike (1905) proposed a principle that he called the **law of effect**, which holds that the tendency for a response to occur depends on the effects it has on the environment (Brown & Jenkins, 2009). Specifically, Thorndike's law of effect states that responses that have satisfying effects are strengthened and become more likely to occur again in a given situation, whereas responses that lead to discomfort are weakened and become less likely to recur. Modern psychologists call the first part of the law of effect *reinforcement* and the second part *punishment* (Benjamin, 1988).

Thorndike went on to study how the principles of animal learning that he formulated could be applied to human behavior and especially to education. He believed that although human behavior is certainly more complex than animal behavior, it, too, can be explained on the basis of trial-and-error learning in which accidental successes become "stamped in" by positive consequences.

B. F. Skinner and Operant Conditioning

Thorndike laid the groundwork for an explanation of learning based on the association between responses and their consequences. It would fall to another American psychologist, B. F. Skinner (1904–1990), to develop a more formal model of this type of learning, which he called **operant conditioning**.

Skinner was arguably not only the most famous psychologist of his time but also the most controversial. What made him famous was his ability to bring behaviorist principles into the public eye through his books, articles in popular magazines, and public appearances. What made him controversial was his belief in **radical behaviorism**, which holds that behavior, whether animal or human, is completely determined by environmental and genetic influences. Free will, according to Skinner, is but an illusion

FIGURE 5.5 Thorndike's Puzzle Box
Cats placed in Thorndike's puzzle box learned to make their escape through a random process of trial and error.

CONCEPT 5.12
According to Thorndike's law of effect, we are more likely to repeat responses that have satisfying effects and are less likely to repeat those that lead to discomfort.

CONCEPT 5.13
B. F. Skinner believed that human behavior is completely determined by environmental and genetic influences and that the concept of free will is but an illusion or myth.

law of effect Thorndike's principle that responses that have satisfying effects are more likely to recur, whereas those that have unpleasant effects are less likely to recur.

operant conditioning The process of learning in which the consequences of a response determine the probability that the response will be repeated.

radical behaviorism The philosophical position that free will is an illusion or myth and that human and animal behavior is completely determined by environmental and genetic influences.

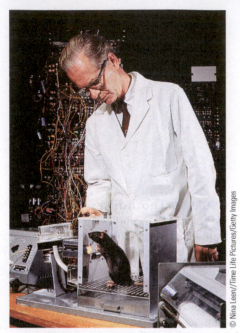

B. F. Skinner

CONCEPT 5.14

Skinner showed how superstitious behavior can be learned through the coincidental pairing of responses and reinforcement.

Skinner box An experimental apparatus developed by B. F. Skinner for studying relationships between reinforcement and behavior.

operant response A response that operates on the environment to produce certain consequences.

reinforcer A stimulus or event that increases the probability that the response it follows will be repeated.

superstitious behavior In Skinner's view, behavior acquired through coincidental association of a response and a reinforcement.

or a myth. Though the staunch behaviorism he espoused was controversial in his own time and remains so today, there is no doubt that his concept of operant conditioning alone merits him a place among the pioneers of modern psychology.

Like Watson, Skinner was a strict behaviorist who believed that psychologists should limit themselves to the study of observable behavior. Because "private events," such as thoughts and feelings, cannot be observed, he believed they have no place in a scientific account of behavior. For Skinner, the mind was a "black box" whose contents cannot be illuminated by science.

Skinner allowed that some responses occur reflexively, as Pavlov had demonstrated. But classical conditioning is limited to explaining how new stimuli can elicit existing behaviors, such as salivation. It cannot account for new behaviors, such as the behavior of the experimental animals in Thorndike's puzzle box. Skinner found in Thorndike's work a guiding principle that behavior is shaped by its consequences. However, he rejected Thorndike's mentalistic concept that consequences influence behavior because they produce "satisfying effects." Skinner proposed that organisms learn responses that *operate* on the environment to produce consequences; he therefore called this learning process *operant conditioning*.

Skinner studied animal learning using a device we now call a **Skinner box**. The Skinner box is a cage that contains a food-release mechanism the animal activates when it responds in a certain way—for example, by pressing a lever or pushing a button.

Through *operant conditioning*, organisms learn responses, such as pressing a bar, that produce changes in the environment (release of food). In this form of learning, the consequences of a response determine the likelihood that the response will occur again. The response itself is called an **operant response** or, more simply, an "operant." Behaviors that produce rewarding effects are strengthened—that is, they become more likely to occur again. In effect, a well-trained operant response becomes a habit (Staddon & Cerutti, 2003). For example, if your teacher responds to a question only if you first raise your hand, you will become more likely to develop the habit of raising your hand before asking a question.

Operant conditioning is also called *instrumental learning* because the behavior is instrumental in bringing about rewarding consequences. The term **reinforcer** refers to a stimulus or event that increases the likelihood that the behavior it follows will be repeated. For example, the act of answering questions when students raise their hands is a reinforcer.

Skinner observed that the longer reinforcement is delayed, the weaker its effects will be. A rat or a pigeon in the Skinner box or a child in the classroom will learn the correct responses faster when reinforcement follows the response as quickly as possible. In general, learning progresses more slowly as the delay between response and reinforcement increases.

Skinner also showed how operant conditioning could explain some forms of **superstitious behavior**. Consider a baseball player who hits a home run after a long slump and then wears the same pair of socks he had on at the time for good luck in every remaining game of the season. The superstitious behavior could be understood in terms of mistaking a mere coincidence between a response (wearing a particular pair of socks) and a reinforcement (home run) for a connection between the two.

Many commonly held superstitions, from not stepping on cracks in the sidewalk to throwing salt over one's shoulder for good luck, are part of our cultural heritage, handed down from generation to generation. Perhaps there was a time when these behaviors were accidentally reinforced, but they have become so much a part of our cultural tradition that people no longer recall their origins.

In the next sections, we review the basic principles of operant conditioning.

Principles of Operant Conditioning

Experimental work by Skinner and other psychologists established the basic principles of operant conditioning, including those we consider here: positive and negative reinforcement, primary and secondary reinforcers, discriminative stimuli, shaping, and extinction.

Positive and Negative Reinforcement

Skinner distinguished between two types of reinforcement, *positive reinforcement* and *negative reinforcement*. In **positive reinforcement**, a response is strengthened by the introduction of a stimulus after the response occurs. This type of stimulus is called a *positive reinforcer* or *reward*. Examples of positive reinforcers include food, money, and social approval. You are more likely to continue working at your job if you receive a steady paycheck (a positive reinforcer) than if the checks stop coming. You are more likely to study hard for exams if your efforts are rewarded with good grades (another positive reinforcer) than if you consistently fail (see ■Figure 5.6).

In **negative reinforcement**, a response is strengthened when it leads to the removal of an "aversive" (unpleasant or painful) stimulus. Negative reinforcers are aversive stimuli such as loud noise, cold, pain, nagging, or a child's crying. We are more likely to repeat behaviors that lead to their removal. A parent's behavior in picking up a crying baby to comfort it is negatively reinforced when the baby stops crying; in this case, the aversive stimulus of crying has been removed.

Many people are confused about the meaning of negative reinforcement because the term "negative" implies punishment. However, remember that any form of reinforcement, whether positive or negative, actually strengthens behavior. The difference is that with positive reinforcement, behaviors are strengthened when they are followed by the *introduction* or presentation of a stimulus, whereas with negative reinforcement, behaviors are strengthened when they lead to the *removal* of a stimulus. It may be helpful to think of it this way: A positive reinforcer is something added after a response occurs, whereas a negative reinforcer is something removed after a response occurs. A positive reinforcer is typically a rewarding stimulus (for example, food or praise), whereas a negative reinforcer is typically an unpleasant or aversive stimulus (for example, pain or crying).

Negative reinforcement can be a "two-way street." Crying is the only means infants have of letting us know when they are hungry or wet or have other needs. It is also an aversive stimulus to anyone within earshot. It is a negative reinforcer because parents will repeat behaviors that succeed in stopping the infant's crying. The baby's crying is positively reinforced by the parents' responses. (Like Skinner's pigeons, parents may need to do some "pecking around" to find out what Junior wants: "Let's see, he's not wet, so he must be hungry.")

CONCEPT 5.15

In positive reinforcement, the introduction of a reward (positive reinforcer) after a response occurs strengthens the response. In negative reinforcement, the removal of an aversive stimulus (negative reinforcer) after a response occurs strengthens the response.

CONCEPT LINK

Negative reinforcement helps account for the avoidance of fearful stimuli or situations in people with phobias and may contribute to the development of obsessive-compulsive disorder. See Module 13.2.

CONCEPT LINK

Behavior therapists use methods based on the principles of reinforcement to strengthen desirable behavior and weaken or eliminate undesirable behavior. See Module 14.1.

positive reinforcement The strengthening of a response through the introduction of a stimulus after the response occurs.

negative reinforcement The strengthening of a response through the removal of a stimulus after the response occurs.

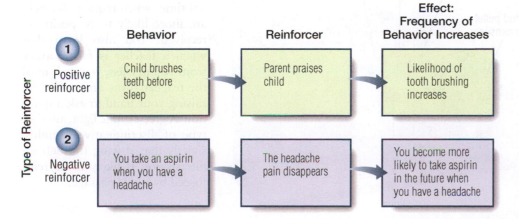

FIGURE 5.6 Types of Reinforcers Positive and negative reinforcers strengthen the behaviors they follow. Can you think of examples of how positive and negative reinforcers influence your behavior? Introducing a positive reinforcer strengthens the behavior it follows. The removal or elimination of a negative reinforcer also strengthens the preceding behavior.

Negative reinforcement may have undesirable effects in some situations. Consider a child who throws a tantrum in a toy store when the parent refuses the child's request for a particular toy. The child may have learned from past experience that tantrums get results. In operant learning terms, when a tantrum does get results, the child is positively reinforced for throwing the tantrum (because the parent "gives in"), while the parent is negatively reinforced for complying with the child's demands because the tantrum stops. Unfortunately, this pattern of reinforcement only makes the recurrence of tantrums more likely.

Primary and Secondary Reinforcers

At 16 months of age, my daughter Daniella became intrigued with the contents of my wallet. It wasn't those greenbacks with the pictures of Washington and Lincoln that caught her eye. No, she ignored the paper money but was fascinated with the holograms on the plastic credit cards. The point here is that some stimuli, called **primary reinforcers**, are intrinsically rewarding because they satisfy basic biological needs or drives. Their reward or reinforcement value does not depend on learning. Primary reinforcers include food, water, sleep, relief from pain or loud noise, oxygen, sexual stimulation, and novel visual stimuli, such as holograms.

Other reinforcers, called **secondary reinforcers**, acquire their reinforcement value through a learning process by which they become associated with primary reinforcers (Chance, 2009). Money is a secondary reinforcer (also called a *conditioned reinforcer*). It acquires reinforcement value because we learn it can be exchanged for more basic reinforcers, such as food or clothing. Other examples of secondary reinforcers include good grades, awards, recognition, smiles, and praise. Much of our daily behavior is influenced by secondary reinforcers in the form of expressions of approval from others.

Discriminative Stimuli

Put a rat in a Skinner box and reinforce it with food when it presses a bar, but only if it makes that response when a light is turned on (see ■ Figure 5.7). When the light is off, it receives no reinforcement no matter how many times it presses the bar. How do you think the rat will respond? Clearly, the rate of response will be much higher when the light is on than when it is off. The light is an example of a **discriminative stimulus**, a cue that signals that reinforcement is available if the subject makes a particular response.

Our physical and social environment is teeming with discriminative stimuli. When is the better time to ask someone for a favor: when the person appears to be down in the dumps or is smiling and appears cheerful? You know the answer. The reason you know is that you have learned that a person's facial cues serve as discriminative stimuli that signal times when requests for help are more likely to be positively received. You also learn that when a teacher is facing away from you in class, you wait until the teacher turns around before raising your hand to ask a question. A green traffic light, another type of discriminative stimulus, signals that driving through an intersection is likely to be reinforced by a safe passage.

Reinforcement is not a one-way street. Who is reinforcing whom? Children and parents continually reinforce each other. By stopping a tantrum when she gets her way, the child negatively reinforces the parent. Unwittingly, perhaps, the parent positively reinforces tantrum-throwing behavior by giving in. How would you suggest the parent change these reinforcement patterns?

CONCEPT 5.16
Some reinforcers are rewarding because they satisfy basic biological needs; other reinforcers acquire reward value as the result of experience.

FIGURE 5.7 Discriminative Stimulus in a Skinner Box
Here we see a rat in a Skinner box, an apparatus used to study operant conditioning. When the rat presses the bar, it receives a pellet of food or a drop of water as a reinforcer. The light is a discriminative stimulus, a cue that signals that the reinforcer is available. The rat learns to press the lever only when the light is on.

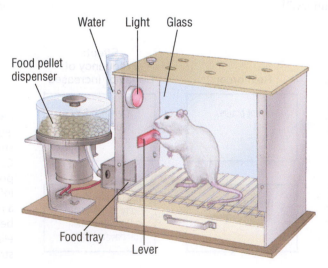

Water   Light   Glass
Food pellet dispenser
Food tray
Lever

Shaping

Rats don't naturally press levers or bars. If you place a rat in a Skinner box, it may eventually happen upon the correct response through trial and error. However, the experimenter can hasten the learning process by using the technique of **shaping**. Shaping involves learning in small steps through applying the *method of successive approximations* in which the  experimenter reinforces a series of ever-closer approximations of the target response (Kreuger & Dayan, 2009). The experimenter may at first reinforce the rat when it moves to the part of the cage that contains the bar. Once this behavior is established, reinforcement occurs only if the animal moves closer to the bar, then closer still, then touches the bar with its paw, and then actually presses the bar. If you have ever observed animal trainers at work, you will recognize how shaping is used to train animals to perform a complex sequence of behaviors.

We put the method of successive approximations into practice in our daily lives when we attempt to teach someone a new skill, especially one involving a complex set of behaviors. When teaching a child to swim, the instructor may deliver verbal reinforcement (telling the child he or she is doing "great") each time the child successfully performs a new step in the series of steps needed to develop proper form.

Extinction

You'll recall from Module 5.1 that extinction of classically conditioned responses occurs when the conditioned stimulus is repeatedly presented in the absence of the unconditioned stimulus. Similarly, in operant conditioning, extinction is the process by which responses are weakened and eventually eliminated when the response is repeatedly performed but is no longer reinforced. Thus, the bar-pressing response of a rat in the Skinner box will eventually be extinguished if reinforcement (food) is withheld. If you repeatedly raise your hand in class but aren't called upon, you will probably stop raising your hand in time.

Schedules of Reinforcement

In the Skinner box, an animal can be reinforced for each peck or bar press, or for some portion of pecks or bar presses. One of Skinner's major contributions was to show how these different **schedules of reinforcement**—predetermined plans for timing the delivery of reinforcement—influence learning.

In a **schedule of continuous reinforcement**, reinforcement follows each instance of the operant response. The rat in the Skinner box receives a food pellet every time it presses the lever. Similarly, if a light comes on every time you flick a light switch, you will quickly learn to flick the switch each time you enter a darkened room. Operant responses are learned most rapidly under a schedule of continuous reinforcement. However, continuous reinforcement also leads to rapid extinction when reinforcement is withheld. How long will it take before you stop flicking the light switch if the light fails to come on because the bulb needs replacing? Just one or two flicks of the switch without results may be sufficient to extinguish the response. But extinction does not mean the response is forgotten or lost to memory. It is likely to return quickly once reinforcement is reinstated—that is, once you install a new bulb.

Responses are more resistant to extinction under a **schedule of partial reinforcement** than under a schedule of continuous reinforcement. In a schedule of partial reinforcement, only a portion of responses is reinforced. Because this makes it more

---

A teacher facing the class is a discriminative stimulus for students raising their hands to ask a question. Students learn that teachers are more likely to reinforce hand raising when they looking directly at them than when they are looking at their notes.

CONCEPT 5.17

Discriminative stimuli set the stage for reinforcement, which is a useful thing to know if you want to ask someone for a favor.

CONCEPT 5.18

Organisms can learn complex behaviors through a process of shaping, or reinforcement of successive approximations to the desired behaviors.

CONCEPT 5.19

In operant conditioning, extinction is the weakening and eventual elimination of a response that occurs when the response is no longer reinforced.

CONCEPT 5.20

The schedule by which reinforcements are dispensed influences the rate of learning and resistance to extinction.

primary reinforcers Reinforcers, such as food or sexual stimulation, that are naturally rewarding because they satisfy basic biological needs or drives.

secondary reinforcers Learned reinforcers, such as money, that develop their reinforcing properties because of their association with primary reinforcers.

discriminative stimulus A cue that signals that reinforcement is available if the subject makes a particular response.

shaping A process of learning that involves the reinforcement of increasingly closer approximations of the desired response.

schedules of reinforcement Predetermined plans for timing the delivery of reinforcement.

schedule of continuous reinforcement A system of dispensing a reinforcement each time a response is produced.

schedule of partial reinforcement A system of reinforcement in which only a portion of responses is reinforced.

CONCEPT 5.21
There are four types of partial-reinforcement schedules: fixed-ratio, variable-ratio, fixed-interval, and variable-interval schedules.

unlikely that an absence of reinforcement will be noticed, it takes a longer time for the response to fade out.

Schedules of partial reinforcement are much more common than schedules of continuous reinforcement in daily life. Think what it would mean to be reinforced on a continuous basis. You would receive a reinforcer (reward) each time you came to class, cracked open a textbook, or arrived at work on time. However desirable this rate of reinforcement might seem, it is no doubt impossible to achieve in daily life. Fortunately, partial-reinforcement schedules produce overall high response rates and have the added advantage of greater resistance to extinction.

Partial reinforcement is administered under two general kinds of schedules: *ratio schedules* and *interval schedules*. In ratio schedules, reinforcement is based on the *number* of responses. In interval schedules, reinforcement is based on the *timing* of responses. For each type, reinforcement can be administered on either a *fixed* or *variable* basis.

■ Figure 5.8 shows typical rates of response under different schedules of partial reinforcement. Notice how much faster response rates are in ratio schedules than in interval schedules. To account for this difference, remember that in ratio schedules, reinforcement depends on the number of responses and not on the length of time elapsed since the last reinforcement, as is the case with interval schedules.

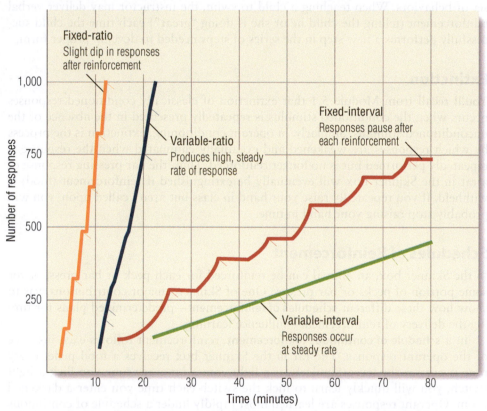

FIGURE 5.8 **Rates of Response Under Different Schedules of Partial Reinforcement**
Here we see rates of response we typically find under different schedules of partial reinforcement. The diagonal lines that intersect with these response curves show the times at which reinforcement is given. Notice how ratio schedules produce much faster response rates than interval schedules. However, there is usually a short pause following each reinforced set of responses under fixed-ratio schedules. Fixed-interval schedules produce a "scalloped" effect with long pauses following each reinforcement, whereas variable-interval schedules typically produce a slow but steady rate of response.

Source: Adapted from Skinner, 1961.

Fixed-Ratio Schedule

In a fixed-ratio (FR) schedule, reinforcement is given after a specified number of correct responses. For example, in an "FR-6" schedule, reinforcement is given after each sixth response. The classic example of fixed-ratio schedules is piecework, in which workers are paid according to the number of items they produce. Fixed-ratio schedules produce a constant, high level of response, with a slight dip in responses occurring after each reinforcement (see Figure 5.8). On fixed-ratio schedules, the faster people work, the more items they produce and the more money they earn. However, quality may suffer if quantity alone determines how reinforcements are dispensed.

Alex Hinds/Alamy Stock Photo

Many customer loyalty programs operate on a fixed-ratio schedule of reinforcement, offering rewards to customers who meet a reward criterion based on the number of purchases. A "buy 10 coffees, get one free" program represents an FR-10 schedule of reinforcement. What rate of responding do you expect from this type of reinforcement schedule?

Variable-Ratio Schedule

In a variable-ratio (VR) schedule, the number of correct responses needed before reinforcement is given varies around some average number. For example, a "VR-20" schedule means that reinforcement is administered after an average of every 20 responses. In some instances, reinforcement may be delivered after only 2, 5, or 10 responses; at other times, 30 or 40 responses may be required. Gambling is a form of behavior that is reinforced on a variable-ratio schedule. With a slot machine, for instance, a win (reinforcement) may occur after perhaps 1, 2, 10, or 50 or more tries.

Variable-ratio schedules typically produce high, steady rates of response (see Figure 5.8). They are also more resistant to extinction than fixed-ratio schedules because one cannot reliably predict whether a given number of responses will be rewarded. Perhaps this explains why many people routinely play slot machines or buy state lottery tickets even though they may win only piddling amounts every now and then. As an advertisement for one state lottery puts it, "Hey, you never know."

Fixed-Interval Schedule

In a fixed-interval (FI) schedule, reinforcement is given only for a correct response made after a fixed amount of time has elapsed since the last reinforcement. On an "FI-30" schedule, for example, an animal in a Skinner box receives a food pellet if it makes the required response after an interval of 30 seconds has elapsed since the last food pellet was delivered, regardless of the number of responses it made during the 30-second interval. Fixed-interval schedules tend to produce a "scalloped" response pattern in which the rate of response typically dips just after reinforcement and then increases as the end of the interval approaches (see Figure 5.8). An example of this effect with humans would be workers who receive monthly performance reviews and show more productive behaviors in the days leading up to their evaluations than immediately afterward.

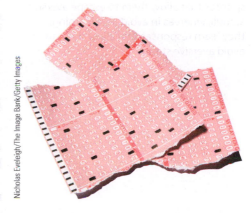

Nicholas Eveleigh/The Image Bank/Getty Images

Variable-Interval Schedule

In a variable-interval (VI) schedule, the amount of time that must elapse before reinforcement can be given for a correct response is variable rather than fixed. A "VI-60" schedule, for example, means that the period of time that elapses before reinforcement is given varies around an average of 60 seconds across occasions (trials). On any one occasion, the interval could be as short as 1 second or as long as 120 seconds, but the average across all occasions would be 60 seconds. Variable-interval schedules tend to produce a slow but steady rate of response. Because reinforcement doesn't occur after predictable intervals on this schedule, responses tend to be more resistant to extinction than they would be on a fixed-interval schedule.

Checking email is positively reinforced by receiving messages and is typically maintained on a VI schedule of reinforcement because messages tend to occur unpredictably over time. With VI schedules, we expect a slow, consistent pattern of responding, such as checking email every few hours, but for people with more frequently occurring messages, checking may occur every few minutes.

CONCEPT 5.22

In escape learning, organisms learn responses that allow them to escape aversive stimuli, whereas in avoidance learning, they learn responses that allow them to avoid aversive stimuli.

escape learning The learning of behaviors that allow an organism to escape from an aversive stimulus.

avoidance learning The learning of behaviors that allow an organism to avoid an aversive stimulus.

punishment The introduction of an aversive stimulus or the removal of a reinforcing stimulus after a response occurs, which leads to the weakening or suppression of the response.

Teachers who use surprise ("pop") quizzes to encourage regular studying behavior are applying variable-interval schedules of reinforcement. Because students never know the exact days on which quizzes are given, they are more likely to receive reinforcement (good grades) when they prepare for each class by studying regularly. With scheduled tests, reinforcement is based on a fixed-interval schedule; that is, rewards for studying become available only at the regular times the tests are given. In this case, we expect to find the scalloped rate of response that is typical of fixed-interval reinforcement—an increased rate of studying, or perhaps even cramming, just before the test and a decline afterward.

Escape Learning and Avoidance Learning

In **escape learning**, an organism learns to *escape* an aversive stimulus by performing an operant response. The escape behavior is negatively reinforced by the removal of the aversive stimulus. A rat may be taught to press a bar to turn off an electric shock. We may learn to escape from the heat of a summer day by turning on a fan or air conditioner.

In **avoidance learning**, the organism learns to perform a response that *avoids* an aversive stimulus. The rat in a Skinner box may receive a signal (for example, a tone) that a shock is about to be delivered. The animal learns to avoid the shock by performing the correct response, such as pressing a bar. You open an umbrella before stepping out in the rain to avoid the unpleasant experience of being drenched.

Like other forms of learning, escape learning and avoidance learning may be adaptive in some circumstances but not in others. We learn to apply sunscreen to avoid sunburn, which is adaptive. But skipping regular dental visits to avoid unpleasant or painful dental procedures is not adaptive, as it can lead to more serious dental problems or even to tooth loss. People may turn to alcohol or other drugs to escape from their problems or troubling emotions. But the escape is short lived, and problems resulting from drug or alcohol abuse can quickly compound the person's initial difficulties.

You may at this point wish to review the key concepts in operant conditioning outlined in Concept Chart 5.2.

Punishment

Skinner observed that behaviors that are not reinforced or that are punished are less likely to be repeated. **Punishment** is the flip side of reinforcement: It weakens the behavior it follows, whereas reinforcement strengthens the preceding behavior. Just as there are positive and negative forms of reinforcement, there are also positive and negative forms of punishment. In *positive punishment,* an aversive or unpleasant stimulus is imposed as a consequence of an undesirable behavior, which over time tends to reduce the frequency of the undesirable behavior. Examples include a parent who scolds or spanks a child who "talks back," or the imposition of penalties in the form of monetary fines for speeding or illegal parking.

In *negative punishment,* a reinforcing stimulus is removed as a consequence of an undesirable behavior, which over time tends to reduce the frequency of the undesirable behavior. Examples include turning off the TV when a child misbehaves, taking away privileges (for example, grounding teenagers), or removing the misbehaving child from a reinforcing environment ("a time-out"). The use of punishment, whether positive or negative, tends to reduce the frequency of the behavior it follows.

Punishment is often confused with negative reinforcement, because both rely on aversive stimuli. But here's the difference: With punishment, the *introduction* of an aversive stimulus or the *removal* of a pleasant stimulus (for example, a time-out) after a behavior

Concept Chart 5.2 — Key Concepts in Operant Conditioning

Concept	Description	Example
Nature of operant conditioning	A form of learning in which responses are strengthened by the effects they have in the environment	If students receive answers to their questions only when they raise their hands before asking them, hand-raising behavior is strengthened.
Discriminative stimulus	A stimulus that indicates that reinforcement will be available if the correct response is made	A child learns to answer the phone when it rings and to wait for a dial tone before dialing.
Positive reinforcer	A stimulus or event that makes the response it follows more likely to occur again	Praising children for picking up their clothes increases the likelihood that they will repeat the behavior.
Negative reinforcer	An aversive stimulus whose removal strengthens the preceding behavior and increases the probability that the behavior will be repeated	The annoying sound of a buzzer on an alarm clock increases the likelihood that we will get out of bed to turn it off.
Primary reinforcer	A stimulus that is innately reinforcing because it satisfies basic biological needs or drives	Food, water, and sexual stimulation are primary reinforcers.
Secondary reinforcer	A stimulus whose reinforcement value derives from its association with primary reinforcers	Money, which can be exchanged for food and clothing, is a secondary reinforcer.
Shaping	A process of learning that involves the reinforcement of increasingly closer approximations to the desired response	A boy learns to dress himself when the parent reinforces him for accomplishing each small step in the process.
Extinction	The gradual weakening and elimination of an operant response when it is not reinforced	A girl stops calling out in class without first raising her hand when the teacher fails to respond to her.
Schedule of continuous reinforcement	A schedule for delivering reinforcement every time a correct response is produced	A girl receives praise each time she puts her clothes away.
Schedule of partial reinforcement (fixed-ratio, variable-ratio, fixed-interval, or variable-interval schedule)	A schedule of delivering reinforcement in which only a portion of responses is reinforced	A boy receives praise for putting his clothes away every third time he does it (fixed-ratio schedule).
Escape learning	Learning responses that result in escape from an aversive stimulus	A motorist learns detours that provide an escape from congested traffic.
Avoidance learning	Learning responses that result in avoidance of an aversive stimulus	A person leaves for work an hour early to avoid heavy traffic.

occurs *weakens* or *suppresses* the behavior (for example, hitting other children in the playground). With negative reinforcement, the *removal* of an aversive stimulus (a baby's crying) after a behavior occurs *strengthens* the behavior (picking up the baby). See Figure 5.9.

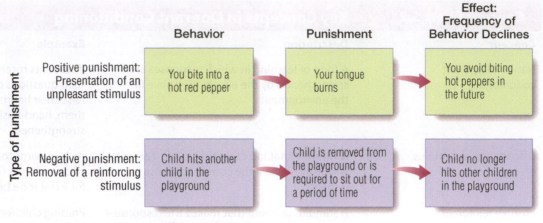

FIGURE 5.9 Types of Punishment
Punishment involves the introduction of an aversive stimulus or the removal of a reinforcing stimulus to weaken or suppress a behavior.

CONCEPT 5.23

Though punishment may suppress or weaken behavior, psychologists generally advise parents not to rely on punishment as a means of disciplining their children.

Psychologists and pediatricians encourage parents to reinforce their children for desirable behavior, rather than rely on punishment as a form of discipline. Punishment, especially physical punishment, has many drawbacks, including the following:

- *Punishment may suppress undesirable behavior, but it doesn't eliminate it.* The punished behavior often returns when the punishing stimulus is withdrawn. For example, the child who is punished for misbehavior may perform the undesirable behavior when the parents aren't looking.

- *Punishment does not teach new behaviors.* Punishment may suppress an undesirable behavior, but it does not help the child acquire a more appropriate behavior in its place.

- *Punishment can have undesirable consequences.* Punishment, especially physical punishment, can lead to strong negative emotions in children, such as anger, hostility, and fear directed toward the parent or other punishing agent. Fear may also generalize. Children repeatedly punished for poor performance in school may lose confidence in themselves or develop a fear of failure that handicaps their academic performance. They may cut classes, withdraw from challenging courses, or even drop out of school.

- *Punishment may become abusive.* Stopping a child's undesirable behavior, at least temporarily, may reinforce the parents for using spanking and other forms of physical punishment. Reinforcement may lead to using more frequent and harsh physical punishment that can cross the line between discipline and abuse. Parents may also employ ever-harsher forms of punishment when milder punishments fail. Although severe abuse generally results in more emotional and physical harm to children, even milder forms of punishment such as spanking, smacking, or pushing increases the risk that children will develop emotional problems in adulthood, including anxiety disorders and mood disorders (Afifi et al., 2012; Kish & Newcombe, 2015). Children who suffer abuse and physical punishment may harbor intense rage or resentment toward the punisher, which they may vent by responding aggressively against that person or other, less physically imposing targets, such as peers or siblings.

- *Punishment may represent a form of inappropriate modeling.* When children observe their parents resorting to physical punishment to enforce compliance with their demands, the lesson they learn is that using force is an acceptable way of resolving interpersonal problems.

Table 5.1 Comparing Reinforcement and Punishment

Technique	What Happens?	When Does This Occur?	Example	Consequence of Behavior
Positive reinforcement	A positive event or stimulus is added or introduced.	After a response	Your instructor smiles at you (a positive stimulus) when you answer a question correctly.	You become more likely to answer questions in class.
Negative reinforcement	An aversive stimulus is removed.	After a response	Buckling the seat belt turns off the annoying buzzer.	You become more likely to buckle your seat belt before starting the engine.
Punishment (application of aversive stimulus)	An aversive stimulus is applied.	After a response	A parent scolds a child for slamming a door.	The child becomes less likely to slam doors.
Punishment (removal of a reinforcing stimulus)	A reinforcing stimulus is removed.	After a response	A child loses TV privileges for hitting a sibling.	The child becomes less likely to engage in hitting.

Do the drawbacks of punishment mean that it should never be used? There may be some occasions when punishment is appropriate. Parents may need to use punishment to stop children from harming themselves or others (for example, by running into the street or hitting other children in the playground). But parents should avoid using harsh physical punishment. Examples of milder punishments include (1) *verbal reprimand* ("No, Johnny, don't do that. You can get hurt that way."); (2) *removal of a reinforcer,* such as grounding teenagers or taking away a certain number of points or tokens that children receive each week that are exchangeable for tangible reinforcers (for example, toys, special activities); and (3) *time-out,* or temporary removal of a child from a reinforcing environment following misbehavior.

Parents who use punishment should help the child understand why he or she is being punished. Children may think they are being punished because they are "bad." They may think negatively of themselves or fear that their mother and father no longer love them. Parents need to make clear exactly what behavior is being punished and what the child can do differently in the future. In this way, parents can help children learn more desirable behaviors. Punishment is also more effective when it is combined with positive reinforcement for alternative desirable behaviors. Before going further, you may wish to review Table 5.1, which compares reinforcement and punishment.

Psychologists advocate the use of positive reinforcement rather than punishment when disciplining children. Scolding, a form of punishment, may temporarily suppress an undesirable behavior, but it does not help the child acquire more adaptive behaviors in its place.

Why It Matters: Applications of Operant Conditioning

In many ways, the world is like a huge Skinner box. From the time we are small children, reinforcements and punishments mold our behavior. We quickly learn which behaviors earn approval and which incur disapproval. How many thousands upon thousands of reinforcements have shaped your behavior over the years? Would you be taking college courses today were it not for the positive reinforcement you received from an early age for paying attention in class, doing your homework, studying for exams, and getting good grades? Who were the major reinforcing agents

CONCEPT 5.24
Principles of operant conditioning are used in biofeedback training, behavior modification, and programmed instruction.

in your life? Your mother or father? A favorite uncle or aunt? Your teachers or coaches? Yourself?

Psychologists have developed a number of applications of operant conditioning, including biofeedback training, behavior modification, and programmed instruction.

Biofeedback Training: Using Your Body's Signals as Reinforcers

As discussed in Chapter 3, *biofeedback training* is a technique for teaching people to change certain bodily responses, including heart rate and types of brain waves. Biofeedback training relies on operant conditioning principles. Physiological monitoring devices record changes in bodily responses and transmit the information to the user, typically in the form of auditory signals that provide feedback regarding desirable changes in these responses. The feedback reinforces behaviors (for example, thinking calming thoughts) that bring about these desirable changes.

Behavior Modification: Putting Learning Principles into Practice

Behavior modification (B-mod) is the systematic application of learning principles to strengthen adaptive behavior and weaken maladaptive behavior. For example, Skinner and his colleagues applied operant conditioning principles in a real-world setting by establishing the first **token economy program** in a mental hospital. In a token economy program, patients receive tokens, such as plastic chips, for performing desired behaviors, such as dressing and grooming themselves, making their beds, or socializing with others. The tokens are exchangeable for positive reinforcers, such as extra privileges.

Behavior modification programs are also applied in the classroom, where they have produced measurable benefits in academic performance and social interactions, and in reductions in aggressive and disruptive behaviors and truancy. Teachers may use tokens or gold stars to reward students for appropriate classroom behavior and academic achievement. Children can use the tokens or gold stars at a later time to "purchase" small prizes or special privileges, such as more recess time.

Parent training programs bring behavior modification into the home. After training in using B-mod techniques, parents reward children's appropriate behaviors and punish noncompliant and aggressive behaviors with time-outs and suspension of privileges and rewards.

behavior modification (B-mod) The systematic application of learning principles to strengthen adaptive behavior and weaken maladaptive behavior.

token economy program A form of behavior modification in which tokens earned for performing desired behaviors can be exchanged for positive reinforcers.

programmed instruction A learning method in which complex material is broken down into a series of small steps that learners master at their own pace.

computer-assisted instruction A form of programmed instruction in which a computer is used to guide a student through a series of increasingly difficult questions.

Programmed Instruction

Skinner applied operant conditioning to education in the form of **programmed instruction**. In programmed instruction, the learning of complex material is broken down into a series of small steps. Learners proceed to master each step at their own pace. Skinner even designed a "teaching machine" that guided students through a series of questions of increasing difficulty. After students responded to each question, the correct response would immediately appear. This provided immediate reinforcement for correct responses and allowed students to correct any mistakes they had made. Because questions were designed to build upon each other in small steps, students would generally produce a high rate of correct responses and thus receive a steady stream of reinforcement. The types of teaching machines Skinner introduced paved the way toward development of **computer-assisted instruction**, a form of computer-based instruction in which the computer guides the student through an inventory of increasingly more challenging questions (Johnson & Rubin, 2011; Westera, 2012).

APPLYING PSYCHOLOGY *in Daily Life*

Putting Reinforcement into Practice

When you smile at someone who compliments you or thank someone for doing you a favor, you are applying positive reinforcement, one of the principles of operant conditioning. Showing appreciation for desired behavior increases the likelihood that the behavior will be repeated.

To modify behavior through reinforcement, it is important to establish a clear *contingency*, or connection, between the desired behavior and the reinforcement. For example, parents can use a desired activity as a reinforcer (for example, time playing video games) for completing daily homework assignments. *Contingency contracting*, which involves an exchange of desirable reinforcers, is a more formal way of establishing a contingency. In contingency contracting, two people in a relationship list the behaviors of the other that they would like changed. They then agree to reinforce each other for carrying out the desired behavioral changes by making a quid pro quo contract, as in this example between two college roommates:

> *Carmen:* I agree to keep the music off after 8:00 p.m. every weekday evening if you agree to forbid your friends to smoke in the apartment.
>
> *Lukisha:* I agree to replace the toilet paper when we run out if you, in return, clean your hair out of the bathroom sink.

CONCEPT 5.25
To modify behavior through reinforcement, it is important to establish a clear connection, or contingency, between the desired behavior and the reinforcement.

Applying Reinforcement

As noted in our earlier discussion of behavior modification programs, teachers and parents apply reinforcement to help children develop more appropriate behaviors. Here are some guidelines for enhancing the effectiveness of reinforcement (adapted from Eberlein, 1997, and Samalin & Whitney, 1997):

1. *Be specific.* Identify the specific behavior you want to increase, such as having 5-year-old Johnny put the blocks back on the shelf after playing with them.

2. *Use specific language.* Rather than saying "Johnny, I'd like you to clean your room when you finish playing," say "Johnny, when you finish with the blocks, you need to put them back on the shelf."

3. *Select a reinforcer.* Identify a reinforcer that the child values, such as access to TV or gold stars the child can accumulate and later redeem for small gifts. The reinforcer should be one that is readily available and that can be used repeatedly.

4. *Explain the contingency.* "Johnny, when you put back all of the blocks on the shelf, you'll get a gold star."

5. *Apply the reinforcer.* Reinforce the child immediately after each occurrence of the desired behavior. If the child cannot achieve the desired standard of behavior (for example, a few blocks are left on the floor), demonstrate how to do so and give the child the opportunity to perform the behavior satisfactorily. Pair the reinforcer with praise: "Johnny, you did a great job putting away those blocks."

6. *Track the frequency of the desired behavior.* Keep a running record of the behavior in terms of how often it occurs each day.

7. *Wean the child from the reinforcer.* After the desired response is well established, gradually eliminate the reinforcer but continue using social reinforcement (praise) to maintain the behavior: "Johnny, I think you did a good job in putting the blocks where they belong."

Skjold Photographs/PhotoEdit

Hugs are a form of positive reinforcement when they follow desirable behavior.

Giving Praise

Praise can be a highly effective reinforcer in its own right. Here are some guidelines for using praise to strengthen desirable behavior in children:

- *Connect.* Make eye contact with the child and smile when giving praise.
- *Use hugs.* Combine physical contact with verbal praise.
- *Be specific.* Connect praise with the desired behavior (Belluck, 2000). Rather than offering vague praise—"You're a great older brother"—connect it with the noteworthy effort or accomplishment. Say, for example, "Thanks for watching your little brother while I was on the phone. It was a big help."
- *Avoid empty flattery.* Children can see through empty flattery. Empty flattery may prompt them to think, why do people need to make up stuff about me? What is so wrong with me that people feel they need to cover up (Henderlong & Lepper, 2002)? Indiscriminant praise can also have the unfortunate effect of leading to an inflated sense of self-importance (Baumeister et al., 2003).
- *Reward the effort, not the outcome.* Instead of saying "I'm so proud of you for getting an A in class," say "I'm so proud of you for how well you prepared for the test." Praising the accomplishment, not the effort, may convey the message that the child will be prized only if he or she continues to get A's.
- *Avoid repeating yourself.* Avoid using the same words each time you praise the child. If you tell Timmy he's terrific each time you praise him, the praise will soon lose its appeal.
- *Don't end on a sour note.* Don't say "I'm proud of how you cleaned your room by yourself, but next time I think you can do it faster."

MODULE REVIEW **5.2** Operant Conditioning: Learning Through Consequences

Recite It

8. **Define** operant conditioning, **identify** the major figures in its development, and **describe** their contributions.

   Operant conditioning is a form of learning in which the (a) _____ of behavior influence the strength or likelihood that the behavior will occur.
   Edward Thorndike developed the law of (b) _____, which holds that responses that have satisfying effects will be strengthened whereas those that lead to discomfort will be weakened.
   B. F. Skinner developed the principles of (c) _____ conditioning, including the roles of positive and negative reinforcement and of schedules of reinforcement.

9. **Describe** different types of reinforcement and schedules of reinforcement.

   (d) _____ reinforcement strengthens behavior when reinforcement (for example, a reward) is presented after the response occurs, whereas (e) _____ reinforcement strengthens behavior when an unpleasant or painful stimulus is removed after the response occurs.
   (f) _____ of reinforcement are predetermined plans for timing the delivery of reinforcement. In (g) _____ reinforcement, reinforcement is given after every correct response. In a partial-reinforcement schedule, only a portion of correct responses is reinforced. In (h) _____ reinforcement, reinforcement is administered intermittently under either a (i) _____ or interval schedule.
   In a (j) _____-ratio schedule, reinforcement follows a specified number of correct responses. In a (k) _____-ratio schedule, the number of correct responses needed before reinforcement is given varies around some average number.
   In a fixed-(l) _____ schedule, a specified period of time must pass before a correct response can be reinforced. In a variable-(m) _____ schedule, the period of time that must elapse before a response can be reinforced varies around some average interval.

10. **Explain** the effects of different types of reinforcement on response rates.

A schedule of (n) _____ reinforcement produces the most rapid learning but also the most rapid extinction of a response when reinforcement is withheld.

(o) _____ is slower under a partial reinforcement schedule, but resistance to extinction varies with the particular type of schedule. Response rates also vary with the particular type of partial reinforcement schedule.

11. **Define** punishment, and **explain** why psychologists raise concerns about the use of punishment in disciplining children.

(p) _____ is the introduction of a painful or aversive stimulus (or (q) _____ of a rewarding stimulus) following a response, which weakens or suppresses the response. The reasons psychologists are concerned about using punishment to discipline children include the following: Punishment may only suppress behavior, not

(r) _____ it; it doesn't teach new and more appropriate behaviors; it can have undesirable emotional and behavioral consequences; it may cross the line into abuse; and it can model inappropriate ways of resolving conflicts.

12. **Explain** the difference between escape learning and avoidance learning.

Through (s) _____ learning, organisms learn responses that allow them to escape from aversive stimuli, such as pain, whereas through (t) _____ learning, organisms learn to avoid these types of stimuli. Escape learning and avoidance learning may be adaptive in some situations but not in others.

13. **Apply** operant conditioning to examples discussed in the text.

Principles of operant conditioning are used in (u) _____ training, behavior modification, and programmed instruction.

Recall It

1. In operant conditioning, learning results from the association of a behavior with

    a. its consequences.   c. cognitions.
    b. conditioned stimuli.   d. unconditioned stimuli.

2. B. F. Skinner's belief that all behavior is determined by environmental and genetic influences and that free will is an illusion or myth is called _____ _____.

3. Skinner demonstrated that superstitious behavior can be acquired through the coincidental pairing of a(n) _____ with a(n) _____.

4. In negative reinforcement, a behavior is strengthened by the

    a. introduction of a negative reinforcer.
    b. extinction of a positive stimulus.
    c. introduction of a positive reinforcer.
    d. removal of an aversive stimulus.

5. Operant responses are learned most rapidly under a schedule of _____ reinforcement; responses are most resistant to extinction under a schedule of _____ reinforcement.

    a. continuous; continuous
    b. partial; partial
    c. continuous; partial
    d. partial; continuous

Think About It

■ B. F. Skinner believed that free will is but an illusion. Do you agree? Explain.

■ The parents of a 13-year-old boy would like him to help out more around the house, including doing his share of the dishes. After a meal at which it is his turn to do the dishes, he first refuses, pleading that he has other things to do that are more important. Frustrated with his refusal, his parents start yelling at him and continue until he complies with their request. But as he washes the

dishes, his mother notices that he is doing a very poor job, so she relieves him of his duty and finishes the job herself. What type of reinforcement did the parents use to gain the boy's compliance? What behaviors of the parents did the boy reinforce by complying with their request? What behavior did the mother inadvertently strengthen by relieving the boy of his chores? Based on your reading of the text, how would you suggest this family change these reinforcement patterns?

Recite It answers placed at the end of chapter.

5.3 Cognitive Learning

14 **Define** cognitive learning and **describe** several types of cognitive learning.

Let's say you wanted to learn the way to drive to your friend's new house. You could stumble around like Thorndike's laboratory animals until you happened upon the correct route by chance. Then again, you could ask for directions and form a mental image of the route ("Let's see, you make a left at the blue house on the corner, then a right turn at the stop sign, and then . . ."). Forming a mental road map allows you to perform new behaviors (for example, driving to your friend's house) even before you have had the opportunity to be reinforced for it. Many psychologists believe that we need to go beyond classical and operant conditioning to explain this type of learning, which is called **cognitive learning**. Cognitive learning involves mental processes that cannot be directly observed—processes such as thinking, information processing, problem solving, and mental imaging. Psychologists who study cognitive learning maintain that humans and other animals are, at least to a certain extent, capable of new behaviors without actually having had the chance to perform them or being reinforced for them.

In Chapter 7, we elaborate on cognitive processes involved in information processing, problem solving, and creativity. Here we focus on three types of cognitive learning: insight learning, latent learning, and observational learning.

Insight Learning

CONCEPT 5.26
By reworking a problem in your mind, you may come to see how the various parts fit together to form a solution.

In an early experiment with a chimp named Sultan, German psychologist Wolfgang Köhler (1927) placed a bunch of bananas outside the animal's cage beyond its reach. Sultan, who was obviously hungry, needed to use a nearby object, a stick, as a tool to obtain the fruit. Before long, the chimp succeeded in using the stick to pull in the bananas. Köhler then moved the bananas farther away from Sultan, beyond the reach of the stick, but made a longer stick available to him. Sultan looked at the two sticks and held them in his hands. He tried reaching the bananas with one of the sticks and then the other, but to no avail. The bananas were too far away. He again held the two sticks, tinkered with them a bit, then attached one to the other to form a longer stick (the sticks were attachable), and *voilà*—the problem was solved. Sultan used the longer stick to pull the bananas into the cage. Unlike the animals in Thorndike's or Skinner's operant conditioning studies, Sultan did not gradually happen upon the reinforced response through an overt process of trial and error. Köhler believed Sultan had solved the problem on the basis of *insight,* the sudden flash of inspiration that reveals the solution to a problem.

cognitive learning Learning that occurs without the opportunity of first performing the learned response or being reinforced for it.

insight learning The process of mentally working through a problem until the sudden realization of a solution occurs.

Insight learning is the process of mentally working through a problem until the sudden realization of a solution occurs. We may call this moment of sudden insight the "Aha!" phenomenon (Topolinski & Reber, 2010). But insight learning may not depend on a flash of inspiration or arise "out of the blue." Insight may occur by restructuring or reorganizing a problem in your mind until you see how the various parts fit together to form a solution (Kounios & Beeman, 2009). As the nineteenth-century scientist Louis Pasteur famously said, "Chance favors only the prepared mind." When it comes to insight learning, the prepared mind—the one that mulls over the problem from different angles—may be better able to arrive at that Aha! moment of apparently sudden inspiration.

In the behaviorist view, "insight" is neither sudden nor free of prior reinforcement. What you don't see, behaviorists claim, is the history of reinforced behavior leading to an apparently sudden flash of "insight." In this view, insight learning is nothing more than the chaining of previously reinforced responses. Perhaps there is room for compromise between these positions. Insight learning may arise from a *mental* process of trial and error—the working out in your mind of possible solutions to a problem based on responses that succeeded (were reinforced) in the past.

Latent Learning

In an early study of the role of cognitive processes in learning, Edward Tolman and C. H. Honzik (1930) trained rats to run a maze. Some rats were rewarded with food placed in goal boxes at the end of the maze; others went unrewarded for their efforts. Each day for 10 days, the rats were put in the maze and the experimenters counted the number of wrong turns they made. The rewarded rats quickly learned the maze, but the unrewarded rats did not. They seemed to wander aimlessly through the maze, making many wrong turns. This evidence points to the importance of reinforcement in shaping learned behavior.

Yet the experimenters noticed something that didn't fit classical notions of conditioning. On the 11th day, food was placed in the goal boxes of some of the previously unrewarded rats. The very next day, these rats ran the maze with even fewer errors than the rats that had been rewarded during the previous 10 days (see ■ Figure 5.10). The investigators argued that a single reinforced trial could not account for this dramatic improvement in performance. These rats must have learned

CONCEPT 5.27
Latent learning occurs without apparent reinforcement and is not displayed until reinforcement is provided.

Ariel Skelley/Blend Images/Getty Images

Do you know the words of songs you have heard repeatedly, even if you never attempted to learn them or practice them? What form of learning does this represent?

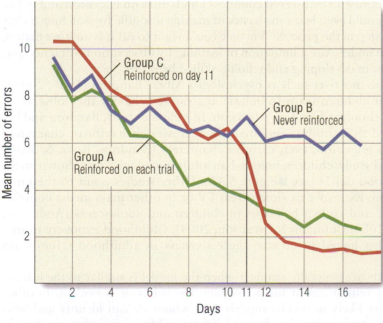

FIGURE 5.10 Tolman and Honzik's Study of Latent Learning
Notice the sharp reduction in errors that occurred among the rats that had not previously received reinforcement when on the 11th day they were reinforced for reaching the goal. Tolman argued that learning had occurred in these rats during the previous trials but that it had remained hidden until rewarded.

CONCEPT 5.28

In observational learning, behaviors are acquired by observing and imitating the behaviors of others.

A stroke of insight may appear to occur at random, but we should bear in mind what the nineteenth-century scientist Louis Pasteur famously said, "Chance favors only the prepared mind."

OMIKRON/Science Source

"Next time we'll do a soufflé." We learn a wide range of skills by carefully observing and imitating behavior of others. But practice and aptitude also count in developing skilled behaviors.

Peter Kramer/NBC/NBC NewsWire/Getty Images

latent learning Learning that occurs without apparent reinforcement and that is not displayed until reinforcement is provided.

cognitive map A mental representation of an area that helps an organism navigate its way from one point to another.

observational learning Learning by observing and imitating the behavior of others (also called *vicarious learning* or *modeling*).

the maze earlier, without any reinforcement, but only demonstrated what they had learned when they were later reinforced for doing so. This type of learning, **latent learning**, is a kind of "hidden" or implicit learning that occurs without apparent reinforcement and is not revealed at the time learning occurs. The learned behavior is displayed only at some later time when it is reinforced.

What had the rats learned during those unreinforced trials? The lead investigator, psychologist Edward Tolman (1886–1959), believed he had an answer. He argued that the rats had developed a **cognitive map**—a mental representation of the maze that allowed them to find their way to the goal box once a reward became available. Tolman's research laid a foundation for the view that humans and other animals create mental representations of the world around them, a theme we will pick up in Chapter 7, when we explore the field of cognitive psychology.

Early work on latent learning opened the door to more recent research showing that learning can occur without conscious awareness or reinforced practice (Goschke & Bolte, 2012). A common example is learning the lyrics to a song you may have heard repeatedly on the radio, even though you never made an effort to learn them or ever practiced them. Learning the lyrics may remain "latent" until someone prompts you to recite them at a party.

Observational Learning

In preschool, Jenny sees that the teacher praises Tina for picking up the blocks after playing with them. Tina's behavior provides Jenny with a cue that she can use to guide her own behavior. In **observational learning** (also called *vicarious learning* or *modeling*), we acquire new behaviors by imitating behaviors we observe in others. The person whose behavior is observed is called a *model*.

Through observational learning, we become capable of behaviors even before we have had the chance to perform them ourselves. I have never fired a gun, but I expect I can do so because I've observed countless gun battles on television and in the movies. I expect I could even learn the basics of making a soufflé by watching a chef demonstrate each step in the process. Whether you'd want to eat it is another matter, which only goes to underscore a limitation of learning by observation—practice and aptitude also count in developing and refining skilled behavior.

Social-cognitive theorists such as psychologist Albert Bandura (1986, 2008a, 2009) believe that children learn to imitate aggressive behavior they observe in the home, in the schoolyard, and on television. In a classic study, Bandura and his colleagues showed that children imitated the aggressive behavior of characters they observed on television, even cartoon characters (Bandura, Ross, & Ross, 1963). In a related study, children imitated an adult model who was shown striking a toy (the "Bobo doll") (see ■Figure 5.11). Other studies point to the same general conclusion: Exposure to violence on TV or in other mass media contributes to aggressive and violent behavior in children and adolescents (Anderson, Dallal, & Must, 2003; Uhlmann & Swanson, 2004). Childhood exposure to media violence is also linked to greater aggressiveness in adulthood (Huesmann et al., 2003).

Modeling effects are generally stronger when the model is similar to the learner and when positive reinforcement for performing the behavior is evident. In other words, we are more likely to imitate models with whom we can identify and who receive rewards for performing the observed behavior. Modeling influences a wide range of behavior, from learning what outfit to wear at a social occasion, to how to change a tire, to how to cook a soufflé (see Try This Out). People even express more positive opinions of a piece of music when they observe a model with whom they share other opinions expressing favorable opinions of the music (Hilmert, Kulik, & Christenfeld, 2006).

People also develop styles of dealing with conflicts in intimate relationships based on their observations during childhood of how their mothers and fathers dealt with marital disagreements (Reese-Weber & Marchand, 2002). For example, young people may learn to imitate an attack style for handling disputes that they had observed in the relationship between their parents or between their parents and themselves (Reese-Weber, 2000).

Does the idea of holding a rat make you squirm? Does the sight of a crab on the beach make you want to run in the other direction? How about touching an insect? Many of us have fears of various creatures even though we have never had any negative experience with them. These fears may be acquired by modeling—that is, by observing other people squirm or show fright when confronted with them.

Concept Chart 5.3 provides an overview of the three types of cognitive learning.

FIGURE 5.11 Imitation of Aggressive Models
Research by psychologist Albert Bandura and his colleagues shows that children will display aggressive behavior after exposure to aggressive models. Here we see a boy and girl striking a toy "Bobo doll" after observing an adult model strike the doll.

Concept Chart 5.3 Types of Cognitive Learning

Type of Learning		Description	Example
Insight learning		The process of mentally dissecting a problem until the pieces suddenly fit together to form a workable solution	A person arrives at a solution to a problem after thinking about it from a different angle.
Latent learning		Learning that occurs but remains "hidden" until there is a reward for performing the learned behavior	A person learns the words of a song playing on the radio but doesn't sing them until friends at a party begin singing.
Observational learning		Learning by observing and imitating the behavior of others	Through observation, a child learns to imitate the gestures and habits of older siblings.

© Michael D Brown/Shutterstock.com
Alex Dvihally/Shutterstock.com
© Monkey Business Images/Shutterstock.com

MODULE REVIEW **5.3** **Cognitive Learning**

Recite It

14. Define cognitive learning and **describe** several types of cognitive learning.

In cognitive learning, an organism learns a behavior before it can perform the behavior or be (a) _____ for it. Cognitive learning depends on (b) _____ processes such as thinking, problem solving, and mental imaging. (c) _____ learning is a mental process in which the restructuring of a problem into its component parts leads to the sudden realization of a solution to the problem. (d) _____ learning is a kind of "hidden" learning that occurs without apparent reinforcement and is not displayed until reinforcement is provided. In (e) _____ learning, behaviors are acquired by observing and imitating the behaviors of others.

Recall It

1. What type of learning involves thinking, information processing, mental imaging, and problem solving?

2. The chimp named Sultan learned to reach bananas by attaching two sticks together. This type of learning is called

   a. insight learning.
   b. latent learning.
   c. observational learning.
   d. classical conditioning.

3. What is the type of cognitive learning that occurs without any apparent reinforcement and that is not displayed at the time it is acquired?

4. Observational learning

   a. is also known as latent learning.
   b. involves imitating the behavior of others.
   c. may lead to the acquisition of useful new skills but not to fear responses.
   d. is based on the principles of operant conditioning.

Think About It

■ Do you believe that learning can occur by insight alone? Why or why not?

■ Who were the major modeling influences in your life? What behaviors, positive or negative, did you acquire by observing these models?

Recite It *answers placed at the end of chapter.*

THINKING CRITICALLY ABOUT PSYCHOLOGY

Based on your reading of this chapter, answer the following questions. Then, to evaluate your progress in developing critical thinking skills, compare your answers to the sample answers found in Appendix A.

Recall the experiment described on p. 184 in which psychologist John Garcia and his colleagues left sheep carcasses on the open range that were laced with a poison that sickened coyotes when they ate the tainted meat. Apply your critical thinking skills to break down this study in classical conditioning terms.

1. What was the unconditioned stimulus in this example?

2. What was the conditioned stimulus?

3. What was the unconditioned response?

4. What was the conditioned response?

Recite It Answers for Chapter 5

Module 5.1 1. (a) permanent; (b) experience, 2. (c) unconditioned; (d) conditioned; (e) neutral; (f) unconditioned, 3. (g) Extinction; (h) recovery, 4. (i) frequency; (j) timing; (k) intensity, 5. (l) generalization; (m) conditioned; (n) discrimination; (o) response, 6. (p) informational; (q) predictions, 7. (r) aversions; (s) cravings   **Module 5.2** 8. (a) consequences; (b) effect; (c) operant, 9. (d) Positive; (e) negative; (f) Schedules; (g) continuous; (h) partial; (i) ratio; (j) fixed; (k) variable; (l) interval; (m) interval, 10. (n) continuous; (o) Extinction, 11. (p) Punishment; (q) removal; (r) eliminate, 12. (s) escape; (t) avoidance, 13. (u) biofeedback   **Module 5.3** 14. (a) reinforced; (b) mental; (c) Insight; (d) Latent; (e) observational

Classical Conditioning: Learning Through Association

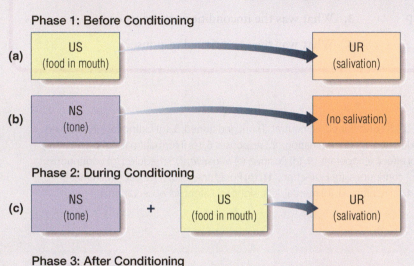

Phase 1: Before Conditioning

(a) US (food in mouth) → UR (salivation)

(b) NS (tone) → (no salivation)

Phase 2: During Conditioning

(c) NS (tone) + US (food in mouth) → UR (salivation)

Phase 3: After Conditioning

(d) CS (tone) → CR (salivation)

Key Concepts

- **How It Works:** Pairing an unconditioned stimulus (US) and a neutral stimulus (NS) results in acquisition of a conditioned response (CR) to the neutral stimulus, which is then called a conditioned stimulus (CS).
- **Extinction:** Weakening of a response following repeated exposure to the CS alone
- **Spontaneous Recovery:** The return of the CR after a lapse of time following extinction
- **Stimulus Generalization:** CR occurs in response to stimuli similar to the original CS
- **Stimulus Discrimination:** CR fails to occur to stimuli different from the original CS

Examples of Classical Conditioning

- **Conditioned Emotional Reaction:** Conditioned emotional response, such as fear, to a particular object
- **Drug Cravings:** Cravings elicited by conditioned stimuli in the environment
- **Taste Aversions:** Conditioned aversions to foods and beverages
- **Immune System Responses:** Immune system responses may be influenced by conditioning.

Operant Conditioning: Learning Through Consequences

Key Concepts

- **Positive Reinforcement:** The strengthening of a response by means of presenting a rewarding stimulus after the response occurs
- **Negative Reinforcement:** The strengthening of a response by means of removing an unpleasant stimulus after a response occurs
- **Primary Reinforcers:** Stimuli that are naturally reinforcing
- **Secondary Reinforcers:** Stimuli that acquire reinforcement value through experience
- **Discriminative Stimuli:** Stimuli that signal the occasion for reinforcement
- **Shaping:** Rewarding gradual approximations to the desired behavior
- **Extinction:** Weakening of a response through withdrawal of reinforcement
- **Schedules of Reinforcement:** Systems for dispensing reinforcements, such as fixed-ratio, variable-ratio, fixed-interval, and variable-interval schedules
- **Punishment:** Introduction of an unpleasant stimulus or removal of a reinforcing stimulus after a response occurs, resulting in the weakening or suppression of the response

Applications of Operant Conditioning

- Biofeedback Training
- Behavior Modification
- Programmed Instruction

Cognitive Learning

Types of Cognitive Learning

- **Insight Learning:** The "Aha!" phenomenon, or sudden realization of a solution to a problem
- **Latent Learning:** Learning not expressed outwardly in behavior until the response is reinforced
- **Observational Learning:** Learning by observing and imitating other people's behavior; also called vicarious learning or modeling

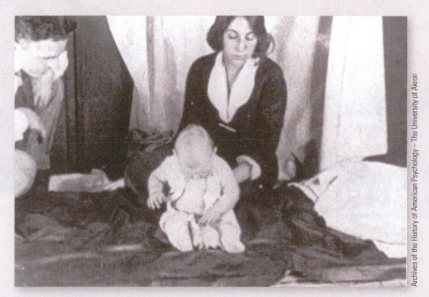

Archives of the History of American Psychology – The University of Akron

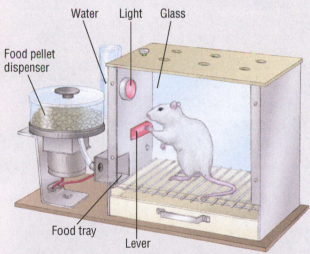

Water   Light   Glass

Food pellet dispenser

Food tray   Lever

© Albert Bandura/Stanford University

© Albert Bandura/Stanford University

© Albert Bandura/Stanford University

LEARNING OBJECTIVES

After studying this chapter, you will be able to . . .

1. **Identify** and **describe** the basic processes and stages of memory.

2. **Identify** and **describe** the different types of long-term memory.

3. **Explain** the roles of the semantic network model and levels-of-processing theory in memory.

4. **Apply** constructionist theory to **explain** memory distortions.

5. **Identify** factors influencing the reliability of eyewitness testimony.

6. **Explain** why the concept of recovered memory is controversial.

7. **Describe** the major theories and factors in forgetting.

8. **Explain** why recognition tests of memory generally produce better results than recall tests.

9. **Describe** the causes of amnesia and the two major types of amnesia.

10. **Identify** the key brain structures involved in memory and **explain** the roles of neuronal networks and long-term potentiation.

11. **Explain** the role that genetics plays in memory.

12. **Apply** knowledge of how memory works to power up your memory.

sl © Yi Lu/Viewstock/Corbis

PREVIEW

Memory

Now Try This . . .

Take a few minutes to see how many digits of *pi* you can recite from memory: 3.14159265358979323846264338327950 2 . . .

Where did you top off? Six digits? Ten? Twenty? Thirty? You probably fell well short of the world record set by a Japanese man, who was able to recite 40,000 digits of *pi* from memory (Takahashi et al., 2006). Like this man, we have other cases of memory competitors who could perform remarkable feats of memory. For example, a man in the United States was able to recite each card (suit and number) in the order in which it appeared in a shuffled deck of 52 cards ("Instant Recall," 2000). Another, a finalist in a memory competition, was able to memorize 501 digits in five minutes (Carey, 2014).

Perhaps the most prodigious memory ever studied was that of a Russian man known only by his first initial, S. He could repeat 70 randomly selected numbers in the precise order in which he had just heard them (Luria, 1968). He could memorize lists of hundreds of meaningless syllables and recite them not only immediately after studying them but also when tested again some 15 years later. He memorized long mathematical formulas that were utterly meaningless to him except as an enormously long string of numbers and symbols. After but a single reading, he could recite stanza after stanza of Dante's *Divine Comedy* in Italian, even though he could not speak the language (Rupp, 1998).

Imagine what it would be like to have such an extraordinary memory— to be able to remember everything you read word for word or to recall lists of facts you learned years ago. Yet if S.'s life story is any indication, it may be just as well you don't possess such a prodigious memory. S.'s mind was so crammed with meaningless details that he had difficulty distinguishing between the trivial and the significant (Turkington, 1996). He had trouble holding conversations because individual words opened a floodgate of associations that distracted him from what the other person was saying. He couldn't shift gears when new information conflicted with fixed images he held in memory. For example, he had difficulty recognizing people who had changed small details of their appearance, such as by getting a haircut or wearing a new suit. Unfortunately, S.'s life didn't end well. He spent the last years of his life confined to a mental hospital. Most of us will probably never possess the memory of someone like S., nor would we even want to. Yet learning how our memory works and what we can do to improve it can help us meet many of life's challenges, from performing better in school or on the job to remembering to water the plants before leaving the house.

Our study of memory begins with a discussion of the underlying processes that make memory possible. We then consider the loss of information that results from forgetting and discuss how the brain creates and stores memories. We end with some practical suggestions for improving your memory.

Did you know that...

- A man memorized lists of hundreds of meaningless syllables and was able to recite them again 15 years later? (p. 211)
- A good way to retain information you've just learned is to sleep on it? (p. 215)
- Fewer than half of the people tested in a research study could pick out the correct drawing of a penny? (p. 228)
- Only one of 85 college students tested in a recent study were able to correctly draw the Apple logo from memory? (p. 228)
- Scientists believe that when it comes to memory, cells that fire together, wire together? (p. 234)
- If you want to remember something you observed, first close your eyes? (p. 236)
- You are more likely to earn a good grade by spacing your study sessions than by cramming for a test? (p. 237)

6.1 Remembering

1 **Identify** and **describe** the basic processes and stages of memory.

2 **Identify** and **describe** the different types of long-term memory.

3 **Explain** the roles of the semantic network model and levels-of-processing theory in memory.

4 **Apply** constructionist theory to **explain** memory distortions.

5 **Identify** factors influencing the reliability of eyewitness testimony.

6 **Explain** why the concept of recovered memory is controversial.

In Chapter 5, we defined learning as a relatively permanent change in behavior that occurs as the result of experience. But learning could not occur without memory. **Memory** is the system by which we retain information and bring it to mind. Without memory, experience would leave no mark on our behavior; we would be unable to retain the information and skills we acquire through experience. In this module, we focus on the factors that make memory possible.

Human Memory as an Information Processing System

CONCEPT 6.1
The three basic processes that make memory possible are encoding, storage, and retrieval.

Many psychologists conceptualize human memory as a type of information processing system that has three basic processes: *encoding, storage,* and *retrieval.* These processes allow us to take information from the world, encode it in a form that can be stored in memory, and later retrieve it when it is needed (see ■ Figure 6.1). As we shall see, these underlying processes work through a sequence of stages leading to the formation of enduring memories.

Memory Encoding: Taking in Information

Information about the outside world comes to us through our senses. But for this information to enter memory, it must undergo a process of **memory encoding**, or conversion into a form we can store in memory. Encoding is akin to the process by which a computer converts keyed input into bits of information that can be stored in its memory (Payne & Kensinger, 2010).

memory The system that allows us to retain information and bring it to mind.

memory encoding The process of converting information into a form that can be stored in memory.

We encode information in different ways, including *acoustically* (coded by sound), *visually* (coded by forming a mental picture), and *semantically* (coded by meaning). We encode information acoustically by converting auditory signals into strings of recognizable sounds. For example, you use acoustic coding when trying

Information →	**1 Encoding** Converting information into a form usable in memory	→ **2 Storage** Retaining information in memory	→ **3 Retrieval** Bringing to mind information stored in memory

FIGURE 6.1 Three Basic Processes of Memory
Human memory can be represented as an information processing system consisting of three basic processes: encoding, storage, and retrieval of information.

to keep a phone number in mind by repeating it to yourself. Or you might encode this information visually by picturing a mental image of the digits of the telephone number. But visual coding tends to fade more quickly than auditory coding, so it is generally less efficient for remembering strings of numbers. We tend to use visual coding to form lasting memories of people's faces. We use acoustic codes to retain familiar melodies and rhymes.

Encoding information semantically—by meaning—involves transforming sounds and visual images into meaningful words. When you hold a conversation, you bring into memory the meaning of what the other person is saying, not the sounds the person makes while speaking. Semantic encoding helps preserve information in memory. You're more likely to remember information when you make a conscious effort to understand what it means than when you simply rely on rote memorization (just repeating the information verbatim).

Memory Storage: Retaining Information in Memory

Memory storage is the process of retaining information in memory. Some memories—your first kiss or your wedding, for example—may last a lifetime. But not all information becomes an enduring or long-term memory. As we shall see when we discuss the stages of memory, some information is retained for only a fraction of a second.

Memory Retrieval: Accessing Stored Information

Memory retrieval is the process of accessing stored information to make it available to consciousness. Retrieving long-held information is one of the marvels of the human brain. At one moment, we can summon to mind the names of the first three presidents of the United States and, at the next moment, recall our Uncle Roger's birthday. But memory retrieval is far from perfect ("Now, when is Uncle Roger's birthday anyway?"). Though some memories seem to be retrieved effortlessly, others depend on using certain clues, called **retrieval cues**, to jog them into awareness. Retrieval cues are associated with situations in which memories were originally formed. You may jog your memory of what you learned in class yesterday by bringing to mind where you sat, what you were wearing, and so on.

Memory Stages

Some memories last but a few seconds whereas others endure for a lifetime. The **three-stage model** of memory proposes three distinct stages that account for the length of time that information is held in memory: *sensory memory, short-term memory,* and *long-term memory* (Atkinson & Shiffrin, 1971).

Sensory Memory: Getting to Know What's Out There

Sensory memory is a memory system for storing sensory information for a very short period of time, ranging from a fraction of a second to as long as 3 or 4 seconds. Visual, auditory, and other sensory stimuli constantly strike your sensory receptors, forming impressions you briefly hold in sensory memory in a kind of temporary storage device called a **sensory register**. The sensory impression then disappears and is replaced by the next one. Visual stimuli encoded in the form of mental images enter a sensory register called **iconic memory**. Iconic memory is a type of photographic memory for holding a visual image of an object or a scene in mind for a mere fraction of a second. This visual image can be so clear that people may report exact details as though they were looking at a picture.

The three-stage model of memory proposes three stages of memory organized around the length of time that information is held in memory: sensory memory, short-term memory, and long-term memory.

© Timothy Boomer/Shutterstock.com

memory storage The process of retaining information in memory.

memory retrieval The process of accessing and bringing into consciousness information stored in memory.

retrieval cues Cues associated with the original learning that facilitate the retrieval of memories.

three-stage model A model of memory that posits three distinct stages of memory: sensory memory, short-term memory, and long-term memory.

sensory memory The storage system that holds memory of sensory impressions for a very short time.

sensory register A temporary storage device for holding sensory memories.

iconic memory A sensory store for holding a mental representation of a visual image for a fraction of a second.

Some people can recall a visual image they have previously seen as accurately as if they are still looking at it. This form of visual memory is called **eidetic imagery**, or *photographic memory*. (The term *eidetic* is derived from the Greek word *eidos*, meaning "image.") Eidetic imagery is rare and almost exclusively limited to children (Rothen, Meier, & Ward, 2012). Although eidetic images may be quite vivid, they are not perceived as clearly as actual photographs (Jahnke & Nowaczyk, 1998).

Auditory stimuli encoded as mental representations of sounds are held in a sensory register called **echoic memory**. An auditory stimulus, such as the sound of an ambulance siren, for example, creates an echo-like impression in your mind for a few seconds after you hear it. Sounds held in echoic memory tend to last about 2 or 3 seconds longer than visual images. Although most sensory impressions fade quickly, some enter a longer storage system, called short-term memory.

Short-Term, or Working, Memory: The Mind's Blackboard

Many sensory impressions don't just fade away into oblivion. They are transferred into **short-term memory (STM)** for further processing. Short-term memory is a storage system for retaining and processing information for a maximum of about 30 seconds. It relies on both visual and acoustic coding, but mostly on acoustic coding. For example, you may try to remember directions by repeating them to yourself (turn right, then left, then right, then left again) just long enough to write them down.

Many psychologists refer to short-term memory as working memory because it is the memory system we use to work on information held in mind for a brief period of time. Think of working memory as a kind of mental blackboard or scratch pad of the mind. We engage working memory whenever we form an image of a person's face and hold it in memory for the second or two it takes the brain to determine whether we know the person. We also use working memory to perform mental arithmetic (for example, adding or subtracting in our head) or holding a conversation. When we have a conversation with someone, we hold in mind the impressions of the sounds we hear the other person speaking just long enough to convert them into recognizable words. Humans are not the only species that have a working memory—even rats have them (Fassihi et al., 2014).

Just how much information can most people hold in short-term memory? Psychologist George Miller conducted landmark studies in the 1950s to determine the storage capacity of STM. He determined that people can retain about seven bits of information in short-term memory, plus or minus two. Miller referred to this limit as the "Magic 7." This means that most people can hold in mind five to nine bits or pieces of information at any one time.

The magic number seven appears in many forms in human experience, including the "seven ages of man" in Shakespeare's *As You Like It*, the Seven Wonders of the World, the Seven Deadly Sins, and even the seven dwarfs of Disney fame. People can normally repeat a maximum of six or seven single-syllable words they have just heard. Think about the "Magic 7" in the context of your daily experiences. Telephone numbers are seven-digit numbers, which means you can probably retain a telephone number in short-term memory just long enough to dial it. People vary in working memory capacity, with some people having somewhat greater capacity than others (Draheim, Hicks, & Engle, 2016; Richmond, Redick, & Braver, 2015; Unsworth et al., 2014). But we can all learn simple memory techniques to retain much longer sequences of letters or numbers. Take the challenge in the nearby Try This Out feature to learn about this memory tip before reading further.

Were you better able to remember the 24 digits in Row 7 than the 8 digits in Row 5 or the 10 in Row 6? If that was the case, you probably recognized that each

---

CONCEPT 6.3

People can normally retain a maximum of about seven items in short-term memory at any one time.

Most of us can retain about seven bits of information in short-term memory, plus or minus two. You probably are able to retain in memory a seven-digit telephone number, at least for the few seconds it takes to dial it.

eidetic imagery A lingering mental representation of a visual image (commonly called *photographic memory*).

echoic memory A sensory store for holding a mental representation of a sound for a few seconds after it registers in the ears.

short-term memory (STM) The memory subsystem that allows for retention and processing of newly acquired information for a maximum of about 30 seconds (also called *working memory*).

chunking The process of enhancing retention of a large amount of information by breaking it down into smaller, more easily recalled chunks.

Try This Out   Breaking Through the "Magic 7" Barrier

At right are seven rows containing series of numbers. Read aloud the series in the first row. Then look away and repeat the numbers out loud in the order in which they appeared. Check whether your answer was correct or incorrect, and record it in the appropriate "yes" or "no" column. Repeat this procedure for each of the remaining rows.

How well did you do? Chances are you had little trouble with the first four series consisting of four to seven numbers. But you probably stumbled as you bumped up against the "Magic 7" barrier in the next two series, which have 8 and 10 digits. You may have had even more success with the last series, consisting of 24 digits. Why might you perform better with 24 digits than with 8 or 10? An explanation is offered in the nearby section of the text.

Get It Right?

Row 1:	6293	___Yes ___No
Row 2:	73932	___Yes ___No
Row 3:	835405	___Yes ___No
Row 4:	3820961	___Yes ___No
Row 5:	18294624	___Yes ___No
Row 6:	9284619384	___Yes ___No
Row 7:	202020252030203520402045	___Yes ___No

set of 4 digits could be grouped together as individual years in a series of years that increased each time by five (2020, 2025, 2030 . . .). The grouping of a larger number of bits of information into a smaller number to aid recall is called **chunking** (Chen & Cowan, 2005). Children typically learn the alphabet by chunking series of letters. That's why they often say the letters *lmnop* as if they were one word (Rupp, 1998).

Most information that passes through short-term memory fades away after about 30 seconds or is transferred to long-term memory. But you can extend short-term memory beyond 30 seconds by engaging in **maintenance rehearsal**, as when you try to remember a person's name by rehearsing it again and again in your mind. But when your rehearsal is interrupted, even for a few seconds, the contents of short-term memory quickly fade away. This is why it is difficult to keep a particular thought in mind and follow what someone is saying in conversation at the same time.

Long-Term Memory: Preserving the Past

Long-term memory (LTM) is a storage system that allows you to retain information for periods of time beyond the capacity of short-term memory. Though some information may remain in long-term memory for only days or weeks, other information may remain for a lifetime. The storage capacity of short-term memory is limited, but long-term memory is virtually limitless in what it can hold. In all likelihood, we can always squeeze more facts and more experiences into long-term memory.

Consolidation is the process by which the brain converts unstable, fresh memories into stable, long-term memories. The first 24 hours after information is acquired are critical for consolidation to occur. We noted in Chapter 4 that sleep plays an important role in memory consolidation (Wei, Krishnan, & Bazhenov, 2016). So if you want to do well on your exams, make sure to get enough sleep so that your brain can consolidate new learning acquired during the day. Sleep even helps consolidate new memories in other animals, such as birds (Brawn, Nusbaum, & Margoliash, 2010). Sleep also helps you access information held in memory so that it becomes easier to recall the next day (Dumay, 2015).

Short-term memory relies largely on acoustic coding, but long-term memory depends more on semantic coding, or coding by meaning. One way of transferring information from short-term to long-term memory is through maintenance rehearsal, which, as we've noted, is the repeated rehearsal of words or sounds. But a better way is through **elaborative rehearsal**, a method of rehearsal in which you

The Brain Loves a Puzzle

As you read ahead, use the information in the text to solve the following puzzle:

A young physicist was working on the problem of connecting the world's computers. After some false starts, he invented a model of a computer network based on how the brain performs memory tasks. What was this invention that changed the world and how was it based on the workings of the human brain?

© iStockphoto.com/Alex Slobodkin

maintenance rehearsal The process of extending retention of information held in short-term memory by consciously repeating the information.

long-term memory (LTM) The memory subsystem responsible for long-term storage of information.

consolidation The process of converting short-term memories into long-term memories.

elaborative rehearsal The process of strengthening new memories by forming meaningful associations between the information and existing memories or knowledge.

Andrew Brusso/Corbis

Do you know this man? He's Tim Berners-Lee, who modeled his creation, the World Wide Web, on the workings of the human brain in linking related concepts to each other within semantic networks.

semantic network model A representation of the organizational structure of long-term memory in terms of a network of associated concepts.

levels-of-processing theory The belief that how well or how long information is remembered depends on the depth of encoding or processing.

focus on the *meaning* of the material. A friend of mine has a telephone number that ends with the digits 1991, a year I remember well because it was the year my son Michael was born. I have no trouble remembering my friend's number because I associate it with something meaningful (my son's birth year). But I need to look up other friends' numbers that end in digits that have no personal significance for me.

How do we manage to organize our long-term memory banks so we can retrieve what we want to know when we want to know it? Imagine being in a museum where bones, artifacts, and other holdings were strewn about without any organization. It would be difficult, perhaps impossible, to find the exhibit you were looking for. Now imagine how difficult it would be to retrieve specific memories if they were all scattered about in LTM without any rhyme or reason. Fortunately, LTM is organized in ways that provide relatively quick access to specific memories.

A leading conceptual model of how LTM is organized is the **semantic network model**, which holds that information is retained within networks of interlinking concepts (Collins & Loftus, 1975). We understand the meaning of something by linking it to related things. For example, the concept of "animal" might be linked to concepts of "fish" and "bird," which in turn might be linked to associated concepts such as "salmon" and "robin," respectively. The act of thinking of a particular concept causes a ripple effect throughout the semantic network. This rippling effect, called *spreading activation*, triggers recall of related concepts (Willingham, 2007). In other words, think "fish" and certain related concepts, such as "salmon" or "cod," suddenly begin springing to mind, which in turn triggers other associations such as "pink," "tastes fishy," and so on. These semantic networks may be held together by certain keywords, such as fish, that link to related concepts (Vitevitch & Goldstein, 2014).

Recall the puzzle about the invention that changed the world? The invention was the World Wide Web in the early 1990s, and the inventor was a young physicist named Tim Berners-Lee. He modeled his creation on the workings of the human brain. As Berners-Lee later wrote in his memoir, "Suppose all the information stored on computers everywhere were linked, I thought. Suppose I could program my computer to create a space in which anything could be linked to anything. All the bits of information in every computer . . . on the planet . . . would be available to me and to anyone else . . ." (Berners-Lee, 1999, p. 4). Today, whenever you go surfing on the Web by clicking on one hyperlink after another, you are modeling what your brain does naturally—linking information in networks of interlinking concepts called semantic networks.

Why should elaborative rehearsal (rehearsal by meaning) result in better transfer of information from short-term to long-term memory than maintenance rehearsal (rehearsal by repetition)? One explanation, called the **levels-of-processing theory**, holds that the level at which information is encoded or processed determines how well or how long information is stored in memory (Craik & Lockhart, 1972). In this view, information is better retained when it is processed more "deeply," or encoded on the basis of its meaning. By contrast, shallow processing is encoded by superficial characteristics, such as the rhyming of words (Willingham, 2007).

We began our discussion of how memory works by recognizing that memory depends on underlying processes (encoding, storage, retrieval) that proceed through a series of stages (sensory memory, short-term memory, long-term memory). Concept Chart 6.1 summarizes these processes and stages; ■ Figure 6.2 shows the three stages in schematic form. Through these processes, we form long-term memories that we can recall at will or with some help (retrieval cues). Next we focus on the contents of long-term memory—the kinds of memories that enrich our lives.

Concept Chart 6.1   Stages and Processes of Memory

Memory Stage	Memory Process		
	Encoding	Storage	Retrieval
Sensory memory	Iconic and echoic	Very brief, from a fraction of a second to 3 or 4 seconds	No retrieval; information is either lost or transferred to short-term memory.
Short-term memory	Acoustic and visual, but primarily acoustic	A maximum of about 30 seconds, but maintenance rehearsal or elaborative rehearsal can maintain the memory longer or convert it into long-term memory	No retrieval; information is either lost or transferred to long-term memory.
Long-term memory	Acoustic, visual, and semantic, but primarily semantic	Long-term, possibly lifelong	Retrieval is assisted by retrieval cues and activation of semantic networks.

Yakobchuk Vasyl/Shutterstock.com
© Alexander Kalina/Shutterstock.com
© Andreja Donko/Shutterstock.com

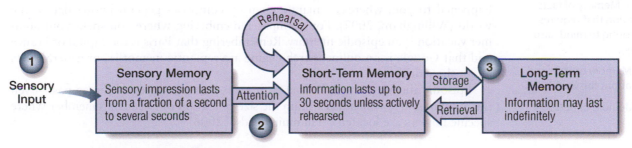

FIGURE 6.2 Three-Stage Model of Memory
The three-stage model of memory is a useful framework for understanding the relationships among the three memory systems. **1** Sensory input (visual images, sounds, and so on) creates impressions held briefly in sensory memory. **2** By directing attention to sensory information, we can bring this information into short-term memory, where we can keep it in mind for a brief period of time. We use two general types of rehearsal strategies (maintenance rehearsal and elaborative rehearsal) to transfer information held in short-term memory into long-term memory. **3** Once information is stored in long-term memory, it must be retrieved and brought back into short-term memory before it can be used.

What We Remember: The Contents of Long-Term Memory

What types of memories are stored in long-term memory? At the broadest level, we can distinguish between two types of long-term memory: *declarative memory*, or "knowing that," and *procedural memory*, or "knowing how" (see ■ Figure 6.3) (Cabeza & Moscovitch, 2013; Rupp, 1998).

CONCEPT 6.5
According to the levels-of-processing theory, information is better retained in memory when it is encoded or processed at a "deeper" level.

CONCEPT 6.6
The two major types of long-term memory are declarative memory ("knowing that") and procedural memory ("knowing how").

CONCEPT 6.7
Declarative memory consists of semantic memory (memory of facts) and episodic, or autobiographical, memory (memory of life events and experiences).

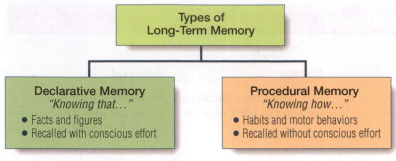

FIGURE 6.3 **Types of Long-Term Memory**

This organizational chart shows how long-term memory can be divided into two general types, declarative memory and procedural memory.

CONCEPT 6.8
Prospective memory, or remembering to remember, has important applications in daily life, involving everything from remembering appointments to remembering to call people on their birthdays.

declarative memory Memory of facts and personal information that requires a conscious effort to bring to mind (also called *explicit memory*).

semantic memory Memory of facts and general information about the world.

episodic memory Memory of personal experiences.

Declarative Memory: "Knowing That"

Declarative memory (also called *explicit memory*) is memory of facts and personal information that requires a conscious effort to bring to mind. Declarative memory allows us to know "what" and "that." We know that there are 50 states in the United States, that we live on such and such a street, and that water and oil don't mix. We know what elements are found in water and what colors are in the American and Canadian flags. We can group declarative memories into two general categories: (1) type of memory (*semantic* or *episodic memory*) and (2) time frame (*retrospective* or *prospective memory*) (see ■ Figure 6.4).

Semantic memory is memory of facts. We can liken semantic memory to a mental encyclopedia or storehouse of information we carry around in our heads. It allows us to remember who wrote *The Grapes of Wrath,* which film won the Academy Award for best picture last year, how to spell the word *encyclopedia,* and what day Japan attacked Pearl Harbor. Semantic memories are not indelibly imprinted in our brains, which is why you may no longer remember last year's Oscar winner or that John Steinbeck wrote *The Grapes of Wrath.* Semantic memories are better remembered when they are retrieved and rehearsed from time to time. So if you stumbled when it came to remembering the name of the author of *The Grapes of Wrath,* reminding you of it today will probably help you remember it tomorrow.

Episodic memory (also called *autobiographical memory*) is memory of personal experiences that constitute the story of your life—everything from memories of what you had for dinner last night to the time you fell from a tree when you were 10 years old and needed 15 stitches. Episodic memory is a personal diary of things that have happened to you, whereas semantic memory comprises general knowledge of the world (Willingham, 2007). For example, remembering where you spent your summer vacation is an episodic memory. Remembering that Paris is the capital of France and that Google is an online search engine are semantic memories, or general facts about the world.

Episodic memory is not limited to human remembrances of things past. Even the hummingbird, which has a brain the size of a grain of rice, can remember where specific flowers are located ("Hummingbirds," 2006).

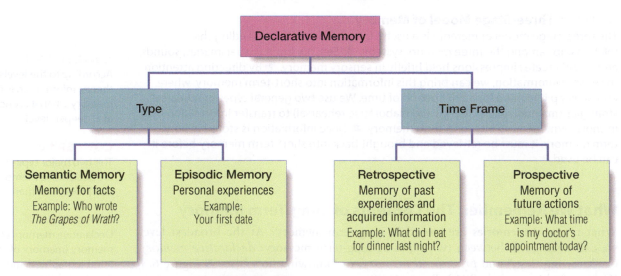

FIGURE 6.4 **Declarative Memory**
Here we see a diagram of the different types of declarative memory.

Retrospective memory is memory of your past experiences, such as where you went to school, as well as information you previously learned, including the knowledge you have acquired of the principles of psychology. **Prospective memory** is the process of remembering to remember (Dismukes, 2012; McDaniel et al,. 2013). You rely on prospective memory to remember things you need to do, or intend to do, in the future, such as remembering to take your medication, to pay your cell phone bill on time, or to call your Mom on her birthday. Some of our most embarrassing lapses of memory involve forgetting to do things. ("Sorry, I forgot to call the restaurant for reservations. It just slipped my mind.") Failures of prospective memory can also have dangerous consequences, as in the case of air traffic controllers who forget to instruct pilots to perform aircraft separation maneuvers (Loft, 2014).

Procedural Memory: "Knowing How"

Procedural memory is memory of how to do things, such as how to ride a bicycle, climb stairs, tie shoelaces, perform mathematical operations, or play a musical instrument. Whereas declarative memory is brought to mind by conscious effort, procedural memory is engaged without any conscious effort. Another difference between these two types of memory is that declarative memory involves information that can be verbalized, whereas procedural memory involves motor or performance skills that cannot be explained in words, at least not easily. Try, for example, to describe how you move your muscles when riding a bicycle. Touch-typing requires procedural memory of the positions of the keys on the keyboard. Even though you may not be able to name the keys in each row, you remember which fingers to move to strike the keys corresponding to each of the letters.

Implicit memory—memory evoked without any conscious effort to remember—is closely related to procedural memory and may even be a form of procedural memory. Hearing a familiar song on the radio may evoke pleasant feelings associated with past experiences even though you made no conscious attempt to recall these experiences. In contrast, **explicit memory** requires a conscious or *explicit* effort to bring it to mind ("Hmm, what is the capital of Finland?").

We rely on muscle memory, a form of procedural memory, whenever we perform complex motor skills such as riding a bike, dancing, typing, climbing stairs, hitting or throwing a baseball, or playing tennis.

The Reliability of Long-Term Memory: Can We Trust Our Memories?

We might think our memories accurately reflect events we've experienced. But memory may not be as reliable or accurate as we might think. Although about two-thirds of people reported in a recent survey that they believe that memory works like a video camera for recording and later playing back life experiences, memory scientists take a different view of how memory works (Aamodt & Wang, 2008; Simons & Chabris, 2011).

The leading view of memory today, called **constructionist theory**, holds that memory is a process by which the brain stitches together bits and pieces of stored information in reconstructing personal experiences. Reconstruction, however, can lead to memory distortions. You may feel that your life memories are accurate representations of events as they actually happened, but evidence shows that memories are often distorted. The brain may invent details to weave a more coherent story of past experiences. Or it may edit past experiences when retrieving them by inserting newer information (Bridge & Voss, 2014). Says memory researcher Donna Jo Bridge, "When you think back to when you met your current partner, you may recall this feeling of love and euphoria. . . . But you may be projecting your current feelings back to the original encounter with this person" (cited in "Your Memory," 2014).

Memory is something like the old game of telephone in which one person whispers something in the ear of the next person in line and by the time the message

retrospective memory Memory of past experiences or events and previously acquired information.

prospective memory Memory of things one plans to do in the future.

procedural memory Memory of how to do things that require motor or performance skills.

implicit memory Memory accessed without conscious effort.

explicit memory Memory accessed through conscious effort.

constructionist theory A theory that holds that memory is not a replica of the past but a representation, or *reconstruction*, of the past.

CONCEPT 6.9

We can distinguish between two types of memory, implicit and explicit memory, that differ in terms of whether we make a conscious effort to bring information to mind.

CONCEPT 6.10

The constructionist theory holds that memory is a process of reconstructing past events and experiences, not of replaying them exactly as they occurred.

Like impressionist paintings, our memories are impressions of our past experiences, not verbatim copies.

gets to the last person in line, it bears little resemblance to the original message. Research evidence shows that memories of past events change through the process of remembering them, and like the game of telephone, we may then only remember the preceding version (Bridge & Paller, 2012). Over time, the original memory may become so distorted that it basically becomes a false memory.

Constructionist theory holds that memories are not verbatim copies of reality, but are pieced together or reconstructed from bits and pieces of past events. Two people may witness the same event but have very different memories of the event based on how they pieced together their memories. From this perspective, it's not surprising that recollections of childhood experiences are not precise recordings of what actually happened, but rather reconstructions based on pieces of information from many sources—from old photographs, from what your mother told you about the time you fell from the tree when you were 10, and so on.

Constructionist theory leads us to expect that memories are more like impressionist paintings than mental snapshots of life experiences. Some memories may be flawed or distorted in various ways or completely false (Bernstein & Loftus, 2009). Even so, we shouldn't presume that all memories are distorted. Some may be more or less accurate reflections of events, but it's difficult to know what is true from what we merely believe is true. Believing that a memory is accurate doesn't make it so.

The constructionist account of memory provides an interesting perspective on how *negative stereotyping*—ascribing negative traits to people of certain groups—can influence perceptions and attitudes of people subjected to stereotyping. Investigators Cara Averhart and Rebecca Bigler (1997) examined the influence of racial stereotypes on memory in African American children of elementary school age. They used a memory test in which children recalled information embedded in stories in which light- and dark-complexioned African American characters were associated with either positive ("nice") or negative ("mean") attributes. The results showed that children had better memory for stories in which more favorable attributes were associated with light-complexioned characters and more negative characteristics were associated with dark-complexioned characters. The memory bias was even greater among children who rated themselves as having light skin tones. The results support a constructionist view that people are better able to recall information that is consistent with their existing concepts or *schemas*, even when these schemas are grounded in prejudice.

Try This Out What's in the Photograph?

Look briefly at the photograph of a professor's office that appears in ■ Figure 6.5. Then continue with your reading of the chapter. After a few minutes, return here, and without looking at the photo again, list all the objects you saw in the office.

_____

_____

_____

_____

_____

Now look again at the photo. Did you list any objects not actually present in the office but that may have fit your concept, or schema, of what a professor's office looks like, such as filing cabinets and bookshelves? Investigators who used this photograph in a similar experiment found that many subjects remembered seeing such objects, demonstrating that their memories were affected by their existing schemas (Brewer & Treyens, 1981).

FIGURE 6.5 Professor's Office

A schema is an organized knowledge structure or set of beliefs about the world, such as the concepts in the study cited previously that black/dark is associated with negative characteristics and white/light with positive characteristics. The schemas we develop reflect our experiences and expectancies. You can test for yourself whether your memory schemas lead to distorted memories by completing the exercise in the nearby Try This Out feature titled "What's in the Photograph?"

In the next sections, we take a look at two controversial issues that call into question the credibility of long-term memory: eyewitness testimony and recovery of repressed memories. These issues place memory research squarely in the public eye. First, however, we examine another type of long-term memory: flashbulb memories, which are emotionally charged memories that seem indelibly etched in the brain.

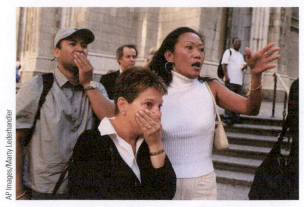

Emotionally charged experiences, such as the horrific attacks of September 11, 2001, can create "flashbulb memories" that seem permanently etched into our brains.

Flashbulb Memories: What Were You Doing When . . . ?

Extremely stressful or emotionally arousing personal or historical events may leave vivid, lasting, and highly detailed memories called **flashbulb memories**. We call them flashbulb memories because they seem to have been permanently seared into the brain by the pop of the flashbulb on an old-fashioned camera. Many of us share a flashbulb memory of the World Trade Center disaster. We remember where we were and what we were doing at the time we heard of the attack, just as though it had happened yesterday. Many baby boomers share the flashbulb memory of the assassination of President John F. Kennedy in 1963.

Flashbulb memories may seem like accurate representations of events as they unfolded, but evidence shows they are prone to the same kinds of distortions that affect other types of memory (Hirst et al., 2015). For example, a study of flashbulb memories of the terrorist attacks of September 11, 2001, showed they were not any more accurate than ordinary memories (Talarico & Rubin, 2003). Moreover, flashbulb memories may not be as fixed in the mind as people suspect, as evidence shows they may change over time (Hirst & Phelps, 2016).

CONCEPT 6.11
Emotionally arousing events may leave vivid, lasting impressions in memory, called flashbulb memories, that seem permanently etched into our brains.

CONCEPT LINK
People who develop post-traumatic stress disorder, or PTSD, following emotionally traumatic events may reexperience the traumatic event in the form of intrusive memories or images of the trauma. See Module 10.1.

CONCEPT 6.12
Memory reports of eyewitnesses may be flawed, even when eyewitnesses are convinced of the accuracy of their recollections.

Eyewitness Testimony: "What Did You See on the Day in Question?"

In reaching a verdict, juries give considerable weight to eyewitness testimony. Yet memory researchers find that eyewitness testimony can be as flawed and strewn with error as other forms of memory. Psychologist Elizabeth Loftus (2004), a leading expert on eyewitness testimony, points out that a shockingly high number of people are wrongly convicted of crimes each year because of faulty eyewitness testimony.

Imagine your brother or sister told you about an incident you had as a child in which you fell off a swing. If he or she insisted that it really did happen, you might start to believe it. Similarly, people can be led to believe events occurred in their past that never actually happened. Investigators find they can induce false memories in many people— memories of events that never actually occurred (Paz-Alonso, Gallego, & Ghetti, 2013; Ramirez et al., 2013).

Memories can be altered by later exposure to misleading information about these events (Chan, Thomas, & Bulevich, 2009; Frenda, Nichols, & Loftus, 2011). Loftus described this phenomenon as the **misinformation effect**. In a landmark study, she and her colleagues had subjects view a film of a car accident that occurred at an intersection with a stop sign (Loftus, Miller, & Burns, 1978). Some subjects were then given misleading information telling them that the traffic sign was a yield sign. When subjects were later asked what traffic sign they saw at the intersection, those given the false information tended to report seeing the yield sign (see ■ Figure 6.6). Subjects who were not given the false information were much more likely to recall

Memory researcher Elizabeth Loftus

flashbulb memories Enduring memories of emotionally charged events that seem permanently seared into the brain.

misinformation effect A form of memory distortion that affects eyewitness testimony and that is caused by misinformation provided during the retention interval.

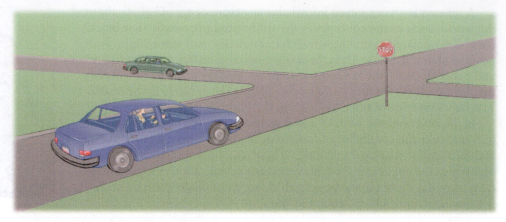

FIGURE 6.6 **Misinformation Effect**

If you were one of the subjects in this study, do you think your memory would be based on what you had actually seen (the stop sign) or on what you were later told you had seen (a yield sign)?

the correct traffic sign. This research calls into question the credibility of eyewitness testimony, especially when witnesses are subjected to leading or suggestive questioning that might "plant" ideas in their heads.

Because eyewitness testimony may often be flawed, should we eliminate it from court proceedings? Loftus (1993) argued that if we dispense with eyewitness testimony, many criminals would go free. As an alternative, we can attempt to increase the accuracy of eyewitness testimony. One way of boosting accuracy is to find corroborating evidence or independent witnesses who can back up each other's testimony. The accuracy of eyewitness testimony depends upon a number of factors, including the following:

1. *Ease of recall.* People who take longer to answer questions in giving testimony are less likely to be accurate in their recall than those who respond without hesitation (Sauerland & Sporer, 2009). Similarly, eyewitnesses who are quicker identifying a perpetrator from a lineup tend to be more accurate than those who take longer (Wells & Olson, 2003).

2. *Degree of confidence.* Highly confident witnesses ("Yes, that's the guy. Definitely.") are generally more accurate than less confident witnesses ("I think it's the guy, but I'm not really sure.") (Brewer & Wells, 2011). But confidence appears to be a better indicator of accuracy at the time when an initial identification is made, rather than during later court proceedings (Wixted et al., 2015). We also should note that even highly confident witnesses are sometimes wrong.

3. *General knowledge about a subject.* People who are knowledgeable about a subject are more likely than those who know less about the subject to be reliable witnesses. For example, when asked by a police officer to identify a motor vehicle involved in a crime, a person familiar with the various makes and models of automobiles may be better equipped to give a reliable answer than one who knows little or nothing of vehicles.

4. *Racial identification.* People are generally better able to recognize and remember faces of people of their own race than the faces of people of other races (Hehman, Mania, & Gaertner, 2010; Van Bavel & Cunningham, 2012). Consequently, eyewitnesses may be more prone to make mistakes when identifying members of other races.

5. *Types of questions.* Leading or suggestive questions by investigators can result in the misidentification of perpetrators, whereas open-ended questions—for

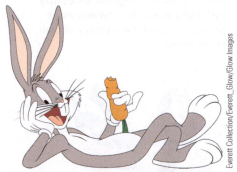

"Me at Disneyland? What's up with that, Doc?" About one in three people who were shown a phony ad featuring a picture of Bugs Bunny just outside the Magic Kingdom at Disneyland later said they believed or remembered that they had once met Bugs at Disneyland (Loftus, 2004). But such meetings could never have occurred because the character of Bugs is owned by the Disney rival Time Warner. These findings suggest how easy it can be to create false memories in the minds of some people.

Everett Collection/Everett_Glow/Glow Images

example, "What did you see?"—tend to increase the accuracy of eyewitness testimony (Fruzzetti et al., 1992; Loftus, 1997). On the other hand, open-ended questions tend to elicit fewer details from witnesses.

6. *Facial characteristics.* Faces with distinctive features are much more likely to be accurately recognized than nondistinctive faces (Wells & Olson, 2003). Also, highly attractive or highly unattractive faces are more likely to be accurately identified than are those of average attractiveness.

Recovery of Repressed Memories

Controversy has swirled around the credibility of memories that suddenly surface in adulthood. In most cases, such memories come to light during hypnosis or psychotherapy. On the basis of recovered memories of sexual trauma in childhood, authorities have brought charges of sexual abuse against hundreds of people. A number of these cases have resulted in convictions and long jail sentences, even in the absence of corroborating evidence. But should recovered memories be taken at face value?

Although it is possible that some people may forget traumatic events such as sexual assault (Brewin & Andrews, 2014), it is unusual, even rare, for someone to completely forget childhood traumas (McNally & Geraerts, 2009). Techniques used in therapy to recover memories of childhood sexual abuse, such as hypnosis and dream interpretation, may actually foster false memories of these events (Geraerts et al., 2009; Patihis et al., 2014). Events that never happened can enter a person's memory and seem just as real and accurate as memories of events that did occur (Leding, 2012). In all likelihood, some recovered memories are genuine, whereas others are undoubtedly false (Erdlyi, 2010). The problem is that we lack tools to reliably differentiate true memories from false ones (McNally & Geraerts, 2009). From a constructionist standpoint, we should not be surprised that memories may be distorted, even when the person believes them to be true.

CONCEPT 6.13

Research showing that false memories may seem as real as actual events calls into question the credibility of recovered memories of childhood abuse.

CONCEPT LINK

Though we may question the validity of recovered memories of childhood abuse, sexual or physical abuse in childhood does play an important role in many psychological disorders, such as dissociative identity disorder. See Module 13.3.

CONCEPT 6.14

Though some recovered memories of childhood abuse may be genuine, we lack the tools to determine which are true.

MODULE REVIEW   6.1   Remembering

Recite It

1. **Identify** and **describe** the basic processes and stages of memory.

   The three basic memory processes are (a) _____ (converting stimuli into a form that can be stored in memory), (b) _____ (retaining information in memory), and (c) _____ (accessing stored information). We encode information by means of (d) _____ codes (coding by sounds), (e) _____ codes (coding by mental imaging), and (f) _____ codes (coding by meaning). The three stages of memory are (g) _____ memory (momentary storage of sensory impressions), (h) _____-_____ memory (working memory of information held in awareness for up to about 30 seconds), and (i) _____-_____ memory (long-term or permanent storage of information).

2. **Identify** and **describe** the different types of long-term memory.

   The two major types of long-term memory are (j) _____ memory ("knowing what or that") and (k) _____ memory ("knowing how").

   Declarative memory is brought to mind by conscious effort, whereas (l) _____ memory is engaged without any conscious effort.

3. **Explain** the roles of the semantic network model and levels-of-processing theory in memory.

   The (m) _____ network model posits that information is held in long-term memory in networks of interlinking concepts. Through a process of (n) _____ activation, thinking of one concept brings related concepts within that semantic network to mind.
   Levels-of-processing theory proposes that deeper processing (o) (_____ rehearsal) leads to more enduring memory than superficial processing (p) (_____ memorization).

4. **Apply** constructionist theory to **explain** memory distortions.

   Constructionist theory holds that memory is a representation, or reconstruction, of past events or experiences, not a verbatim (q) _____ of past experiences. Reconstructing or piecing together memories of past experiences can lead to simplifications, omissions of (r) _____, or even outright fabrications.

knowledge about the subject, same-(t)_____ identification, and leading or suggestive questioning.

5. **Identify** factors influencing the reliability of eyewitness testimony.

Factors affecting the accuracy of eyewitness testimony include ease of (s) _____, confidence in memory, general

6. **Explain** why the concept of recovered memory is controversial. Some recovered memories may be credible, but others are not. We presently lack the tools to determine which are (u) _____ and which are not.

Recall It

1. What is the type of memory that corresponds to "knowing how"?

2. Which of the following is *not* correct?
   a. Constructionist theory suggests that memory recall may not be accurate.
   b. Information is best recalled when it is consistent with a person's memory schemas.
   c. Eyewitness testimony may be influenced by misinformation.
   d. Flashbulb memories are immune to distortion.

3. Match the concepts on the left with their descriptions on the right:

   I. sensory memory
   a. process by which short-term memory is converted to long-term memory

   II. short-term memory
   b. also known as "working" memory

   III. consolidation
   c. process that uses semantic coding to transfer short-term memory to long-term memory

   IV. elaborative rehearsal
   d. storage system for fleeting iconic and echoic memories

Think About It

■ Why is it incorrect to say that memory works like a mental camera?

■ What factors influence the accuracy of eyewitness testimony?

Recite It *answers placed at the end of chapter.*

MODULE

6.2 Forgetting

7 **Describe** the major theories and factors in forgetting.

8 **Explain** why recognition tests of memory generally produce better results than recall tests.

9 **Describe** the causes of amnesia and the two major types of amnesia.

CONCEPT 6.15
The oldest theory of forgetting, decay theory, may explain memory loss that occurs due to the passage of time, but it fails to account for why some memories are more enduring.

Everyone is forgetful. Some of us are more forgetful than others. But why do we forget? Is it simply a matter of memories fading over time? Or are there other factors that account for forgetfulness? Degenerative brain diseases, such as Alzheimer's disease, are one cause of forgetfulness; another is amnesia, a memory disorder we discuss at the end of this module. Our main focus here, however, is on normal processes of forgetting. We recount several leading theories of forgetting and highlight the factors that make it easier or harder to remember information. We begin with decay theory.

Decay Theory: Fading Impressions

The belief that memories consist of traces laid down in the brain that gradually deteriorate and fade away over time dates back to the writings of the Greek philosopher Plato some 2,500 years ago (Willingham, 2007). This theory of forgetting, now known as **decay theory** (also called *trace theory*), was bolstered by early experimental studies conducted by one of the founders of experimental psychology, Hermann Ebbinghaus (1850–1909).

An interesting aspect of Ebbinghaus's experimental work on forgetting is that the only subject in his early studies was himself. To study the processes of memory and forgetting, Ebbinghaus knew he had to eliminate any earlier associations to the material to be remembered. He devised a method for testing memory that used nonsense syllables (combinations of letters that don't spell out anything), such as *nuz* and *lef* (Ebbinghaus, 1885). He presented these lists of syllables to himself and determined the number of trials it took for him to recall them perfectly. He then tested himself again at different intervals to see how much he would forget over time. The results showed a decline in memory that has since become known as the *Ebbinghaus forgetting curve* (see ■ Figure 6.7). Forgetting occurred rapidly in the first few hours after learning and then declined more gradually. It seemed as though memories simply faded over time. By the end of the first day, 66 percent of the information had been lost, and after a month, nearly 80 percent was gone (Rupp, 1998).

Ebbinghaus also employed a **savings method** to test his memory retention. He first counted the number of times needed to rehearse a list of nonsense syllables in order to commit it to memory. Then he counted the number of times it took to relearn the list after a period of time had elapsed. If it took ten repetitions to learn the list the first time and five the second, the savings would be 50 percent.

Memory researchers recognize that when people attempt to memorize information, they generally retain more information when they space their study sessions than when they cram them together within a single day (Cepeda et al., 2006). One reason for this effect, called the **massed versus spaced practice effect**, is that massed, or crammed, practice causes mental fatigue that interferes with learning and retention. A practical implication of this effect should be obvious: When studying for exams, don't cram. Rather, space out your study sessions. You'll learn more and remember more of what you learn. Also, spaced practice produces the same learning benefits for other animals, which is useful to keep in mind when trying to train your dog (Aamodt & Wang, 2008).

Decay theory helps account for memory loss due to the passage of time. However, a major weakness of the theory is that it fails to account for the unevenness with which memory decays over time. Some memories remain well preserved over time, whereas others quickly fade. One reason for this unevenness is that more distinctive or unusual information tends to be remembered better over time (Hunt & Worthen, 2006; Unsworth, Heitz, & Parks, 2008). You're likely to remember your first date better than your 14th. You're also more likely to later recall the name of a man you were introduced to at a party if the man's name was Oscar than if it had been Michael or Chris.

Ebbinghaus studied retention of meaningless syllables. When we examine recall of more meaningful information, such as poetry or prose, we find a more gradual loss of memory over time. Then again, little if any forgetting may occur for important life events and knowledge we acquire about our work or career. Another factor that helps explain forgetting is interference (Wixted, 2005).

Interference Theory: When Learning More Leads to Remembering Less

Chances are you have forgotten what you ate for dinner a week ago Wednesday. The reason for your forgetfulness, according to **interference theory**, is interference from memories of dinners that preceded and followed that particular dinner. On the other hand, you are unlikely to forget your wedding day because it is so unlike

FIGURE 6.7 Ebbinghaus Forgetting Curve
Ebbinghaus showed that forgetting occurs most rapidly shortly after learning and then gradually declines over time.

decay theory A theory of forgetting that posits that memories consist of traces laid down in the brain that gradually deteriorate and fade away over time (also called *trace theory*).

savings method A method of testing memory retention by comparing the numbers of trials needed to learn material with the number of trials needed to relearn the material at a later time.

massed versus spaced practice effect The tendency for retention of learned material to be greater with spaced practice than with massed practice.

interference theory The belief that forgetting is the result of the interference of memories with each other.

any other day in your life (except for those, perhaps, who have taken many walks down the aisle). Interference theory helps explain why some events may be easily forgotten while others remain vivid for a lifetime. The greater the similarity between events, the greater the risk of interference. There are two general kinds of interference, *retroactive interference* and *proactive interference*.

Interference occurring after material is learned but before it is recalled is called **retroactive interference**. Perhaps you have found that material you learned in your 9:00 A.M. class, which seemed so clear when you left the classroom, quickly began to fade once you started soaking in information in the next class. In effect, new memories retroactively interfere with unstable earlier memories that are still undergoing the process of memory consolidation (Wixted, 2004).

Proactive interference is caused by the influence of previously learned material. Because of proactive interference, you may have difficulty remembering a new area code (you keep dialing the old one by mistake). Or you may forget to advance the year when writing checks early in a new year. ■ Figure 6.8 illustrates retroactive and proactive interference.

Though some interference is unavoidable, we can take steps to minimize its disruptive effects:

Want to do well on your exams? Study, yes, but don't skimp on sleep.

- *Sleep on it*. Want to improve your recall of newly learned material? Sleep on it. Sleep is believed to play an important role in converting fragile new memories into lasting ones (Cohen et al., 2012). By first learning course material and then sleeping on it, you may retain more of what you learn.

- *Rehearse fresh memories*. New long-term memories are fragile. Practicing or rehearsing fresh memories aloud or silently can strengthen them, making them more resistant to the effects of interference. Repeated practice beyond the point necessary to reproduce material without error is called **overlearning**. Apply the principle of overlearning to reviewing the material in this text, such as by rehearsing your knowledge of the key concepts in each chapter two or more times after you can demonstrate your knowledge without any errors.

retroactive interference A form of interference in which newly acquired information interferes with retention of material learned earlier.

proactive interference A form of interference in which material learned earlier interferes with retention of newly acquired information.

overlearning Practice repeated beyond the point necessary to reproduce material without error.

1 Retroactive Interference

| Study philosophy at 9 A.M. | Study psychology at 11 A.M. | Test in philosophy the next day |

2 Proactive Interference

| Study philosophy at 9 A.M. | Study psychology at 11 A.M. | Test in psychology the next day |

FIGURE 6.8 Retroactive and Proactive Interference
In 1 retroactive interference, new learning (psychology in the first example) interferes with recall of previously learned material (philosophy). In 2 proactive interference, previously learned material (philosophy in the second example) interferes with recall of new material (psychology).

- *Give yourself a break.* Try not to schedule one class directly after another. Give your recent memories time to consolidate in your brain.
- *Avoid sequential study of similar material.* Try not to study material that is similar in content in back-to-back fashion—for example, avoid scheduling a French class right after a Spanish one.

Interference may help explain the **serial position effect**, the tendency to recall the first and last items in a list, such as a shopping list, better than those in the middle of the list. The unfortunate items in the middle are often forgotten. Putting the serial position effect to the test, researchers asked college students to recall as many presidents as they were able to remember (Roediger & DeSoto, 2014). Students tended to recall the first few presidents and the last few, but not those in the middle. There were a few exceptions, however. Can you guess which "middle" presidents were more likely to be remembered? The answer, not surprisngly, was perhaps the most revered president, Abraham Lincoln (#16), and the two presidents who succeeded him, Andrew Johnson and Ulysses S. Grant.

Interference is the likely culprit in serial position effects. Items compete with one another in memory, and interference is greatest in the middle of a list than at either end of the list. For example, in a list of seven items, the fourth item may interfere with the item that it follows and the item that it precedes. But interference is least for the first and last items in the list—the first, because no other item precedes it; the last, because no other item follows it. The tendency to recall items better when they are learned first is called the **primacy effect** (Davelaar et al., 2005). The tendency to recall items better when they are learned last is called the **recency effect**. As the delay between a study period and a test period increases, primacy effects become stronger whereas recency effects become weaker (Knoedler, Hellwig, & Neath, 1999). This recency–primacy shift means that as time passes after you have committed a list to memory, it becomes easier to remember the early items but more difficult to remember the later-appearing items in the list.

In sum, evidence shows that both the passage of time and interference contribute to forgetting. But neither decay theory nor interference theory can determine whether forgotten material becomes lost to memory or just more difficult to retrieve. Some forgotten material can be recovered if subjects are given retrieval cues to jog their memories, such as exposure to stimuli associated with the original situations in which the memories were formed. This brings us to a third model of forgetting, retrieval theory.

Retrieval Theory: Forgetting as a Breakdown in Retrieval

Retrieval theory posits that forgetting is the result of failing to access stored memories. Let us consider two principal ways in which the retrieval process can break down, *encoding failure* and *lack of retrieval cues.*

Encoding Failure: What Image Is on the Back Side of a Nickel?

Memories cannot be retrieved if they were never encoded in the first place. The failure to encode information may explain why people often cannot recall details about common objects they use every day. For example, do you know what image appears on the back of a nickel? Before you rummage through your pockets, let me tell you it is an image of Monticello, the home of Thomas Jefferson, whose image is on the front of the coin. You may have glanced at this image of Monticello countless times but never brought it into memory because you failed to encode it. We tend to encode only as much information as we need to know (Rupp, 1998). Because we don't need

Hill Street Studios/Blend Images/Getty Images

This man remembered the broccoli his wife asked him to pick up at the store, but not the tuna. Based on your knowledge of the serial position effect, why do you suppose he remembered the broccoli and not the tuna?

© JohnKwan/Shutterstock.com

serial position effect The tendency to recall items at the start or end of a list better than items in the middle of a list.

primacy effect The tendency to recall items better when they are learned first.

recency effect The tendency to recall items better when they are learned last.

retrieval theory The belief that forgetting is the result of a failure to access stored memories.

CONCEPT 6.17
The serial position effect explains why we are more likely to forget the middle items in a list than those at the beginning or end.

CONCEPT 6.18
Memory retrieval may be impaired by a failure to encode information and by a lack of retrieval cues to access stored memories.

to encode more specific details of a coin to recognize one or use it correctly, such information may not be encoded and thus cannot be retrieved (see also the Try This Out titled "What Does a Dime Look Like"?).

Events that stand out tend to be better remembered. You are also more likely to remember events that occur irregularly (for example, visits to a doctor because of an injury) than regularly occurring events (for example, routine medical checkups). Events that are similar are generally encoded in terms of their common features rather than their distinctive characteristics. Because similar events tend to be encoded in similar ways, it becomes more difficult to retrieve memories of the specific events.

Try This Out **What Does a Dime Look Like?**

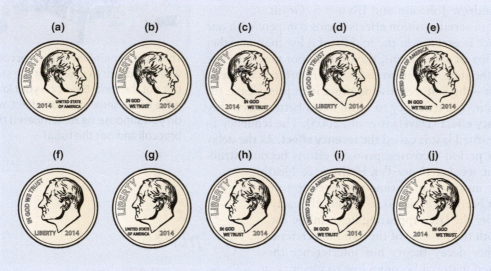

FIGURE 6.9 **What Image Appears on the Front of a Dime?**

How well do you remember the features of common coins you may have in your pocket at this very moment? In a classic study, researchers Raymond Nickerson and Marilyn Jager Adams (1979) decided to find out. They showed subjects an array of drawings of a penny, only one of which was correct. Fewer than half of their subjects were able to pick out the correct

one. Here's an opportunity to test your knowledge of the image on another coin you've handled countless times in your life. Without looking at the coins in your pocket, can you tell which drawing of a dime in ■ Figure 6.9 is the correct one? The answer appears on p. 239.

Don't be too hard on yourself if you failed to identify the correct image. In all likelihood, you never encoded the correct image in the first place. We tend to encode only as much detail as we need to identify common objects.

If you'd like another try, see if you can identify the correct image of the Apple logo from those images shown in ■ Figure. 6.10.

Investigators found that fewer than half of the UCLA students they tested picked the correct image when it was shown along with a set of similar logos (Blake, Nazarian, & Castel, 2015). Only one of the 85 students was able to draw the correct logo on a blank piece of paper. Go ahead and try it yourself. Take out a piece of paper and draw the Apple logo without looking at it.

Adam Blake, Meenely Nazarian, Alan Castel/UCLA Psychology

FIGURE 6.10 **Examples of Incorrect Logos Shown in Study**

Lack of Retrieval Cues: What's His Name?

Information may be encoded in memory but remain inaccessible because of a lack of appropriate retrieval cues. A common and often embarrassing difficulty with memory retrieval is recalling proper names. Proper names have no built-in associations, no convenient retrieval cues or "handles" that can be used to distinguish among the many Jennifers, Susans, Davids, and Petes of the world. A lack of retrieval cues may account for a common experience called the **tip-of-the-tongue (TOT) phenomenon**, in which the information seems to be at the tip of one's tongue but just outside one's reach. If you've ever felt frustrated trying to recall something you're certain you know but just cannot seem to bring to mind, you've experienced the TOT phenomenon. People who experience TOTs (and that includes most of us) may have partial recall of the information they are trying to retrieve, which is why they feel so sure the information is stored somewhere in their memory (Farrell & Abrams, 2011). They may recall the first few letters or sounds of the word or name ("I know it starts with a *B*"), or perhaps a similar-sounding word comes to mind. TOTs may result not only from a lack of available retrieval cues but also from more general difficulties with word retrieval. TOTs tend to increase later in life, when word retrieval typically becomes more difficult (Theocharopoulou et al., 2015).

william87/Getty Images

"What's his name? Wait, I've got it on the tip of my tongue."

Motivated Forgetting: Memories Hidden From Awareness

Sigmund Freud believed that certain memories are not forgotten but are kept hidden from awareness by **repression**, or motivated forgetting. In Freud's view, repression is a psychological defense mechanism that protects the self from awareness of threatening material, such as unacceptable sexual or aggressive wishes or impulses. Were it not for repression, Freud believed, we would be flooded with overwhelming anxiety whenever such threatening material entered consciousness. Repression, or motivated forgetting, is not simple forgetting; the repressed contents do not disappear but remain in the unconscious mind, hidden from awareness.

Freud's concept of repression does not account for ordinary forgetting—the kind that occurs when you try to retain information you read in your psychology textbook. Another problem with this concept is that people who are traumatized by rape, combat, or natural disasters, such as earthquakes or floods, tend to retain vivid if somewhat fragmented memories of these experiences. They often find it difficult to put such anxiety-evoking events out of their minds, which is the opposite of what we might expect from Freud's concept of repression. Moreover, because repression operates unconsciously, we may lack direct means of testing it scientifically. Nonetheless, many memory researchers believe that repression can occur under some conditions (Willingham, 2007).

Measuring Memory: How It Is Measured May Determine How Much Is Recalled

Students who are given the choice generally prefer multiple-choice questions to questions that require a written essay. Why? The answer has to do with the different ways in which memory is measured.

The methods used to measure memory can have an important bearing on how well you are able to retrieve information stored in memory. In a *recall task,* such as

tip-of-the-tongue (TOT) phenomenon
An experience in which people are sure they know something but cannot seem to bring it to mind.

repression In Freudian theory, a type of defense mechanism involving motivated forgetting of anxiety-evoking material.

CONCEPT 6.21
The methods used to measure memory, such as recall tasks and recognition tasks, affect how much we are able to recall.

CONCEPT 6.22
There are two general types of amnesia: retrograde amnesia (loss of memory of past events) and anterograde amnesia (loss or impairment of the ability to form or store new memories).

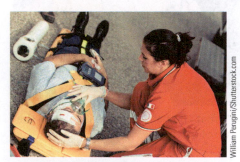

Amnesia is often caused by a traumatic injury to the brain. This man was involved in a motor vehicle crash in which he was knocked unconscious. He may remember nothing about the accident, or even about events leading up to the accident, when he regains consciousness.

free recall A type of recall task in which individuals are asked to recall as much information as they can about a particular topic in any order.

recognition task A method of measuring memory retention that assesses the ability to select the correct answer from among a range of alternative answers.

amnesia Loss of memory.

retrograde amnesia Loss of memory of past events.

anterograde amnesia Loss or impairment of the ability to form or store new memories.

an essay question, you are asked to reproduce information you have committed to memory. There are three basic types of recall task. In **free recall**, you are asked to recall as much information as you can in any order you wish (for example, randomly naming starting players on your college's basketball team). In a *serial recall* task, you are asked to recall a series of items or numbers in a particular order (for example, reciting a telephone number). In *paired-associates recall,* you are first asked to memorize pairs of items, such as pairs of unrelated words like *shoe–crayon* and *cat–phone*. You are then presented with one item in each pair, such as the word *shoe,* and asked to recall the item with which it was paired (*crayon*). If you've ever taken a foreign language exam in which you were presented with a word in English and asked to produce the foreign word for it, you know what a paired-associates recall task is.

In a **recognition task**, you are asked to pick out the correct answer from among a range of alternative answers. Tests of recognition memory, such as multiple-choice tests, generally produce much better retrieval than those of recall memory, largely because recognition tests provide retrieval cues. You're more likely to remember the name of the author of *Moby Dick* if you see the author's name among a group of multiple-choice responses than if you are asked to complete a recall task, such as a fill-in-the-blank item in which you are required to insert the author's name (Herman Melville).

Amnesia: Of Memories Lost or Never Gained

A medical student is brought by ambulance to the hospital after falling from his motorcycle and suffering a blow to his head. His parents rush to his side, keeping a vigil until he regains consciousness. Fortunately, he is not unconscious for long. As his parents are explaining what has happened to him, his wife suddenly bursts into the hospital room, throwing her arms around him and expressing her great relief that he wasn't seriously injured or killed. When his wife, whom he had married only a few weeks earlier, leaves the room, the medical student turns to his mother and asks, "Who is she?" (cited in Freemon, 1981, p. 96).

How can we explain this severe loss of memory? The medical student suffered from a type of **amnesia**, or memory loss. The term *amnesia* is derived from the Greek roots *a* ("not") and *mnasthai* ("to remember").

Types of Amnesia

The medical student suffered from **retrograde amnesia**, or loss of memory of past events. A football player knocked unconscious by a blow to the head during a game may remember nothing beyond suiting up in the locker room. A boxer knocked cold in the ring may not remember the fight. A blow to the head can interfere with *memory consolidation*—which, as we noted in Module 6.1, is the process of converting unstable, short-term memories into stable and enduring ones. When this process is disrupted, memories of events occurring around the time of the disruption may be lost permanently. Some cases go beyond problems with memory consolidation. The medical student's memory loss extended beyond the time of his head injury to before he had met his wife. In such cases, whole chunks of memory are lost. Nonetheless, recent memories are generally more susceptible to retrograde amnesia than remote events (James & MacKay, 2001). In another form of amnesia, **anterograde amnesia**, people cannot form or store new memories or have difficulty doing so.

Causes of Amnesia

Amnesia may be caused by physical or psychological factors. Physical causes include blows to the head, degenerative brain diseases (such as Alzheimer's disease; see Chapter 9), blockage of blood vessels to the brain, infectious diseases, and chronic alcoholism. Amnesias in some cases may be reversed if the underlying physical problem is successfully treated.

Concept Chart 6.2   Forgetting: Key Concepts

Image Source/Jupiter Images

	Concept	Description	Example
Theories of Forgetting	Decay theory	Gradual fading of memory traces as a function of time	Facts you learned in school gradually fade out of memory over time.
	Interference theory	Disruption of memory caused by interference of previously learned material or newly learned material	After sitting through your biology lecture, you forget what you learned in chemistry class the hour before.
	Retrieval theory	Failure to access material stored in memory because of encoding failure or lack of retrieval cues	You have difficulty remembering something you know is stored in memory.
	Motivated forgetting	Repression of anxiety-provoking material	You cannot remember a traumatic childhood experience.
Measuring Methods	Recall task	Test of the ability to reproduce information held in memory	You recite a phone number or the capitals of U.S. states or the provinces of Canada.
	Recognition task	Test of the ability to recognize material held in memory	You recognize the correct answer in a multiple-choice question.
Types of Amnesia	Retrograde amnesia	Loss of memory of past events	After suffering a blow to the head in a car accident, you are unable to remember details of the accident itself.
	Anterograde amnesia	Loss or impairment of the ability to form or store new memories	Because of a brain disorder, you find it difficult to retain new information.

Amnesia resulting from psychological causes is called **dissociative amnesia**. *Dissociation* means "splitting off." Memories of a traumatic experience may become "dissociated" (split off) from consciousness, producing a form of amnesia for events occurring during a specific time (see Chapter 13). These events may be too emotionally troubling—provoking too much anxiety or guilt—to be consciously experienced. A soldier may have at best a dim memory of the horror he experienced on the battlefield and remember nothing of his buddy being killed; yet his memory of other past events remains intact. Rarely is dissociative amnesia of the type that fuels many a daytime soap opera, the type in which people forget their entire lives—who they are, where they live, and so on.

Concept Chart 6.2 provides an overview of the key concepts of forgetting.

dissociative amnesia A psychologically based form of amnesia involving the "splitting off" from memory of traumatic or troubling experiences.

MODULE REVIEW   6.2   Forgetting

Recite It

7. Describe the major theories and factors in forgetting.

(a) _____ theory holds that forgetting results from the gradual deterioration of memory traces in the brain.

(b) _____ theory is the belief that forgetting results from the interference of memories with each other.

(c) _____ theory holds that forgetting is the result of a failure to access stored memories.

(d) _____ forgetting, or repression, is the Freudian belief that people banish anxiety-provoking material from conscious awareness.

8. **Explain** why recognition tests of memory generally produce better results than recall tests.

(e) _____ tasks (such as multiple-choice questions) generally produce better memory retrieval than (f) _____ tests (free recall, serial recall, or paired-associates recall) because they provide more retrieval cues that help jog memory.

9. **Describe** the causes of amnesia and the two major types of amnesia.

Amnesia, or memory loss, may be caused by psychological factors or by physical factors such as degenerative brain diseases and brain trauma. There are two general types of amnesia: (g) _____ amnesia (loss of memory for past events) and (h) _____ amnesia (inability to form new memories).

Recall It

1. What type of interference accounts for why you may forget to advance the year when writing checks early in a new year?

2. Which of the following is *not* a helpful way to reduce the effects of interference on memory?
   a. Avoid overlearning.
   b. Study material just before going to bed.
   c. Rehearse or practice material repeatedly.
   d. Avoid studying similar content simultaneously.

3. When it comes to remembering what you've learned, _____ practice is preferable to _____ practice.

4. Memory loss in which earlier life events are forgotten is known as
   a. dissociative amnesia.
   b. retrograde amnesia.
   c. retroactive amnesia.
   d. anterograde amnesia.

Think About It

■ Have you had any tip-of-the-tongue experiences? Were you eventually able to retrieve the memory you were searching for? If so, how were you able to retrieve it?

■ Why is it not a good idea to apply the principle of "massed practice" when preparing for exams? What study techniques are likely to be more effective?

Recite It answers placed at the end of chapter.

MODULE

6.3 The Biology of Memory

10 **Identify** the key brain structures involved in memory and **explain** the roles of neuronal networks and long-term potentiation.

11 **Explain** the role that genetics plays in memory.

12 **Apply** knowledge of how memory works to power up your memory.

How are memories formed in the brain? Where are they stored? Breakthrough research is beginning to answer these and other questions that probe the biological underpinnings of memory. In this module, we examine what is presently known about those underpinnings.

Brain Structures in Memory: Where Do Memories Reside?

Psychologist Karl Lashley (1890–1958) spent much of his career attempting to track down the elusive **engram**, the term he used to describe a physical trace or etching in the brain where he believed a memory is stored. A rat that learns to run a maze, for example, should have an engram somewhere in its brain containing a memory trace of the correct route leading to the exit or goal box.

Lashley spent years training rats to run mazes, then surgically removing parts of their cerebral cortexes, and testing them again to see if their memories for mazes

engram Lashley's term for the physical trace or etching of a memory in the brain.

remained intact. He reasoned that if removal of a part of the cortex wiped away a given memory, that part must be where the particular memory was stored. Despite years of painstaking research, he found that rats continued to run mazes they had learned previously regardless of the parts of the cortex he removed. The rats simply did not forget. He concluded that memories are not housed in any specific brain structure but must be scattered about the brain.

Neuronal Networks: The Circuitry of Memory

Memory scientists today believe that memories are not etched into particular neurons in the brain but rather are encoded and stored in memory circuits that are housed throughout the brain in complex networks of neurons called **neuronal networks** (also called *neural networks*) (Lu & Zuo, 2015; Miller, 2015). In simplest terms, think of these memory networks as intricate webs of connections among neurons in the brain. We just don't know how many neurons are involved in storing any individual memory—perhaps only few thousand or fewer, or perhaps even hundreds of millions of neurons dispersed in complex networks throughout the brain (Quiroga, Fried, & Koch, 2013).

The Hippocampus: A Storage Bin for Memory

The hippocampus, a seahorse-shaped structure in the forebrain, is essential to forming memories of facts and general information (semantic memory) and life experiences (episodic memory) (Buzsáki, 2013; Merkow, Burke, & Kahana, 2015).

The hippocampus doesn't seem to be involved in procedural memory, the kind of memory process we draw upon when riding a bicycle or using tools. Nor does the hippocampus appear to be the final destination for new memories. Rather, it appears to be a temporary storage bin for holding new memories, perhaps for a few weeks or months, before they are moved and filed away in the cerebral cortex and other parts of the brain for long-term storage (Aamodt & Wang, 2008; Stickgold & Wehrwein, 2009).

If you suffered extensive damage to your hippocampus, you might develop anterograde amnesia and be unable to form new memories. Depending on the extent of the damage, you might retain earlier memories but each new experience would fail to leave any mark in your memory (Thompson, 2005).

Memory also depends on other brain structures, including the thalamus and the amygdala. Damage to the thalamus can result in amnesia. The amygdala plays an important part in encoding emotional experiences, such as fear and anger. Scientists believe the amygdala and hippocampus are especially active during emotionally charged experiences, which serves to strengthen and preserve memories of such meaningful life events (Hassert, Miyashita, & Williams, 2004). All in all, there is no one memory center in the brain, no one part of the brain entirely responsible for memory formation.

Strengthening Connections Between Neurons: The Key to Forming Memories

Locating neuronal networks corresponding to particular memories makes finding the proverbial needle in the haystack seem like child's play. The human brain contains billions of neurons and trillions of synapses among them. Individual neurons in the brain can have thousands of synaptic connections with other neurons. In tracking down specific networks of cells where memories are formed, researchers turned to a relatively simple animal, a large sea snail (*Aplysia*) that possesses a mere 20,000 neurons.

The landmark research that Eric Kandel, a molecular biologist and Nobel Prize winner, performed on *Aplysia* represented a major step forward in unraveling the

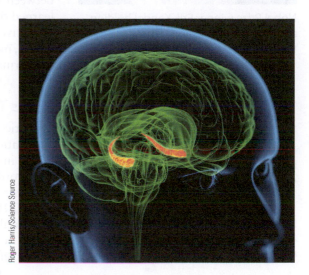

Roger Harris/Science Source

CONCEPT 6.23
Memories are stored in complex networks of interconnected brain cells called neuronal networks.

CONCEPT 6.24
Damage to the hippocampus could prevent you from forming new memories, so that you might be unable to remember someone you've just met.

CONCEPT LINK
The hippocampus plays a role in remembering the context in which fearful responses were experienced. See Module 8.4.

neuronal networks Memory circuits in the brain that consist of complicated networks of nerve cells.

Nobel Prize winner Erik Kandel holding an *Aplysia*, the sea snail he used to study the biological bases of memory.

Eric R. Kandel

biological bases of memory (Kandel, 1995; Kandel & Hawkins, 1993). Because learning results in the formation of new memories, Kandel needed to first demonstrate that these animals were capable of learning new responses. To accomplish this, he and his colleagues first desensitized the snails to receiving a mild squirt of water. After a number of trials, the animals became habituated to the water squirt so that it no longer caused them to budge. In the second phase of the experiment, the researchers paired the squirt with a mild electric shock. The animals showed they could learn a simple conditioned response—reflexively withdrawing their gills (their breathing apparatus) when squirted with water alone. This self-defensive maneuver is the equivalent of the snails' battening down the hatches in anticipation of impending shock (Rupp, 1998).

Kandel observed that the amount of neurotransmitters released into synapses between the nerve cells that control the withdrawal reflex increased as the animals learned the conditioned response. The added neurotransmitter kicked the reflex into overdrive, making it more likely to fire. In effect, these synapses became stronger—that is, more capable of transmitting neural messages. Kandel had shown that memory formation involves biochemical changes occurring at the synaptic level.

"Cells That Fire Together, Wire Together"

CONCEPT 6.25
The key to forming memories may lie in strengthening the interconnections between the neurons that form neuronal networks in the brain.

CONCEPT 6.26
Scientists suspect that long-term potentiation (LTP) may be needed for long-term memory to occur.

Synaptic connections between neurons can be strengthened by repeated electrical stimulation. In effect, neurons that "fire together, wire together." A long-lasting increase in the strength of synaptic connections is called **long-term potentiation (LTP)**. The word *potentiation* simply means strengthening. When synaptic connections become stronger, neurons are better able to communicate with each other (Monaco et al., 2014; Sejnowski & Delbruck, 2012).

The ability to form long-term memories appears to depend on strengthening synaptic connections between neurons within complex brain circuits (Craddock, Tuszynski, & Hameroff, 2012). In other words, we remember life experiences or newly learned information (such as the meaning of the word *potentiation*) when groups of neurons in the brain form connections in which the particular memory is embedded or encoded (Tayler et al., 2012). We can think of a memory as a pattern of neural activity within a particular brain circuit. Retrieving a particular memory from storage ("Let's see, what does potentiation mean?") brings the information to mind by reactivating the corresponding pattern of brain activity.

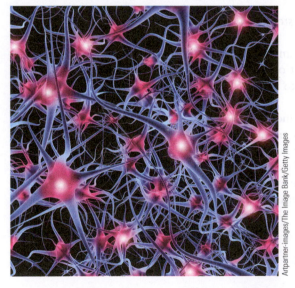

Artpartner-images/The Image Bank/Getty Images

Scientists believe the process of LTP plays a key role in converting short-term memory into long-term memory (Hutchison, Chidiac, & Leung, 2009). But just how are synaptic connections strengthened? One way is to repeatedly practice or rehearse information you want to remember (studying, anyone?). However, mere repeated practice or rote memorization may not be sufficient to remember complex material, such as the principles of memory discussed in this chapter. We may need to strengthen newly formed memories by elaborating on the meaning of the material—for example, by thinking of examples of the concepts discussed in this chapter or by relating them to your own personal experiences.

CONCEPT 6.27
Scientists have begun to unravel the genetic bases of memory, which may lead to the development of safe drugs that can help preserve or restore memory functioning.

long-term potentiation (LTP) The long-term strengthening of neural connections as the result of repeated stimulation.

Genetic Bases of Memory

Promising research with genetic engineering is offering new insights into how memory works. Transforming short-term memory into long-term memory depends on the production of certain proteins that are regulated by certain genes (Ramamoorthi et al., 2011). Learning more about how these genes functions will help unravel the molecular bases of memory, perhaps leading to a time when we will be able to directly manipulate "memory genes" to enhance learning and memory ability. Scientists have already been able to boost memory ability in mice by means of genetic

Concept Chart 6.3   Biology of Memory: Key Concepts

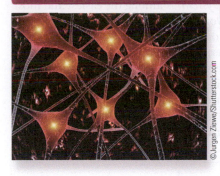

©Jurgen Ziewe/Shutterstock.com

Concept	Description
Lashley's engram	Despite years of research, Karl Lashley failed to find evidence of an *engram*, his term for a physical trace or etching in the brain where he believed a memory is stored.
Neuronal networks	Memory scientists believe that memories may "reside" in complex networks of neurons distributed across different parts of the brain.
Biological underpinnings of memory	The hippocampus is a key brain structure in converting short-term memory into long-term memory. The conversion of short-term to long-term memory appears to depend on long-term potentiation, the process of strengthening synaptic connections between neurons in which memories are embedded.
Genetic factors in memory	Conversion of short-term memory to long-term memory depends on brain proteins whose production is regulated by certain genes. Advances in genetic engineering show that it is possible to enhance learning and memory ability in nonhuman organisms by genetic manipulation.

engineering (tinkering with genes) (Zhu et al., 2011). Further advances in genetic engineering might also one day reap benefits in helping people suffering from memory loss, such as those with Alzheimer's disease.

Scientists hope that knowledge gained about the role of brain proteins in memory and the genes that help regulate their production may eventually lead to the development of drugs to treat or even cure Alzheimer's disease and other memory disorders. Perhaps we'll even have drugs that boost the memory functioning of normal individuals. In the meantime, think critically if you encounter claims about so-called memory-enhancing drugs. We have no compelling scientific evidence that any drug or supplement available today enhances memory in normal individuals (Begley, 2011a).

Concept Chart 6.3 summarizes some of the key concepts relating to the biology of memory.

APPLYING PSYCHOLOGY *in Daily Life*

Powering Up Your Memory

Even if you never compete in a memory championship, you can learn to boost your memory power. Techniques specifically aimed at enhancing memory are called *mnemonics*, some of which have been practiced since the time of the ancient Greeks. Yet perhaps the most important ways to power up your memory are to take care of your health and to adopt more effective methods of studying, such as the SQ3R+ system (see "A Message to Students" in the preface of the text).

Using Mnemonics to Improve Memory

A **mnemonic** is a device for improving memory. The word *mnemonic* is derived from the name of the Greek goddess of memory, Mnemosyne, and is pronounced neh-MAHN-ik (the first *m* is silent). Here are some of the most widely used mnemonic devices.

CONCEPT 6.28
You can boost your memory power in many ways, such as by using mnemonics, focusing your attention, practicing repeatedly, taking care of your health, and adopting effective study habits.

mnemonic A device for improving memory.

Acronyms and Acrostics

The method of acronyms (also called the *first-letter system*) is among the easiest and most widely used mnemonic devices. An **acronym** is a word composed of the first letters of a series of words. The acronym HOMES can help you remember the names of the Great Lakes (Huron, Ontario, Michigan, Erie, and Superior). In Chapter 3, you learned the acronym Roy G. Biv, which spells out the first letters of the colors of the spectrum. You might try devising some acronyms to help you retain information you learned in class.

An **acrostic** is a verse or saying in which a letter of each word, typically the first letter, stands for something else. Generations of musicians have learned the lines of the treble clef staff (E, G, B, D, and F) by committing to memory the acrostic "*Every Good Boy Does Fine.*"

Popular Sayings and Rhymes

Popular sayings and poems help us remember a variety of things, including when to turn the clock forward or back ("Fall back, spring forward"). Rhymes can be used as a mnemonic for remembering specific information. A common example is the rhyme for remembering the number of days in each month: "Thirty days hath September, April, June, and November . . . ."

Visual Cues and Visual Imagery

Visual cues can help us remember to remember. When you need to remember to do something, pin a reminder note where you will be most likely to notice it, such as on your shoes, the front door, or the steering wheel of your car.

Visual imagery can help us remember new words, names, and word combinations. For example, to remember the word *hippocampus,* think of an associated image, such as the image of a hippopotamus. To remember the name Bill Smith, picture a blacksmith who has a mouth shaped like a duck's bill (Turkington, 1996). The well-known memory expert Harry Lorayne (2002) recommended linking imagery to tasks that need to be remembered. For example, if you want to remember to mail a letter, picture the letter on the handle of the front door. Seeing the front door handle may cue you to take the letter to the mailbox.

Close Your Eyes to Boost Recall

British investigators reported that people recalled more details of a burglary they had earlier viewed on a video by closing their eyes when recalling the event (Nash et al., 2015). Closing your eyes may help boost memory recall of events you witness or in which you participate, perhaps because it helps you recall visual images associated with the event.

Chunking

Chunking, which we discussed in Module 6.1, is one of the easiest ways to remember a series of numbers. To use it, break down a number series into more easily remembered bits. For example, the number 7362928739 may be difficult to remember as one long series. The task becomes easier when the digits are chunked like a telephone number into three bits: 736-292-8739. Learning the zip code 10024 becomes easier when it is chunked into 100-24.

General Suggestions for Improving Memory

Though mnemonic devices can help you remember bits and pieces of information, they are of little use when it comes to remembering more complex material, such as the content of your college courses. But keeping to the following guidelines and adopting good study habits will help you keep your learning and memory processes as sharp as possible (Herrmann & Palmisano, 1992; Turkington, 1996).

acronym A word composed of the first letters of a series of words.

acrostic A verse or saying in which the first or last letter of each word stands for something else.

Pay Attention

One of the best ways to boost your learning or memory ability is to pay close attention. Paying attention not only means focusing more closely on the material at hand, but it also means placing yourself in a quiet area that is conducive to studying and free of distractions (no TV, radio, phone, Internet, and so on).

What about lightening up on time spent on Facebook or other social media sites? College freshmen in a recent study who reported greater Facebook use tended to have poorer grades than did less frequent users (Junco, 2015). Before jumping to conclusions that Facebook is to blame, we should recognize that this research is correlational (relating one variable, Facebook use, to another, grades), and so we can't prove a causal link. Can you think of a rival hypothesis to explain the Facebook/poor grades link? For example, might poorer students tend to spend more time on social media? Also, before singling out Facebook for blame, we should recognize that any significant distraction, whether it be watching TV or just hanging out, may detract from a student's grades if it drains time needed to meet academic responsibilities.

Practice, Practice, Practice

You may have heard the old saying that the way to get to Carnegie Hall is to practice. Well, a good way to retain information is to rehearse it, and then rehearse it some more. Repeating information out loud or silently can help convert it from a short-term memory into a more enduring long-term memory. Make it a practice to "overlearn" material by repeating it two or more times beyond the point necessary for minimal proficiency.

You can also use elaborative rehearsal to strengthen retention of material you want to remember. One way of doing this is to relate the material to your personal experiences. Find examples in your own life of the concepts discussed in this chapter, such as declarative memory, procedural memory, implicit memory, and the tip-of-the-tongue phenomenon.

Spaced practice is more effective than massed practice at boosting retention. Spacing study sessions throughout the semester is a better strategy for preparing for exams than cramming at the end. Moreover, don't try to retain all the material in a chapter at one time. Break it down by sections or parts and rehearse your knowledge of each part. Then rehearse how the parts relate to each other as a whole.

Use External Memory Aids

Our daily lives are so packed with bits and pieces of information to be remembered that it makes sense to use whatever resources we can. Yes, you could use a mnemonic device to remember to tell your roommate that her mother called. But writing a reminder note to yourself will allow you to expend your mental efforts more profitably on something else. Other types of notes, such as class notes and Post-it notes, are tools that you can use to retain more information. External memory aids, such as electronic organizers and computerized to-do lists, may also be helpful. You might even try putting objects, such as your key ring, in conspicuous places (thereby reducing occurrences of the common cry, "Now, where did I leave those keys?").

Link Time-Based Tasks to External Cues

Linking time-based tasks to external cues or activities can help boost prospective memory (Marsh, Hicks, & Cook, 2005). For example, if you need to take medication in the early evening, link it with having dinner. Even the time-honored tradition of tying a string around your finger may be helpful.

Mentally Rehearse What You Intend to Do

Picturing in your mind what you plan to do may increase the likelihood of performing the intended action (Dismukes, 2012). Before leaving the house in the morning, practice saying to yourself the intended action—for example, "I intend to pick up my clothes from the dry cleaners today." Then form a mental image of yourself performing the intended action.

Don't Memorize—Just Google It

Many people today are letting Google do the work for them when it comes to finding and accessing information they need. A few generations ago, schoolchildren learned largely through rote memorization, such as by committing to memory all the state capitals in the United States. Today, schoolchildren learn to use search engines to access information on the Internet, allowing them to focus more of their time and effort on organizing and integrating information in useful and potentially creative ways. We live in an information society in which it may be more important to know how to use technology that puts information at our fingertips than to put effort into memorization.

Control Stress

Though we may need some level of stress to remain active and alert, prolonged or intense stress can interfere with the transfer of new learning into long-term memory. The stress management techniques discussed in Chapter 10 can help you keep stress within manageable levels.

Adopt Healthy Habits

Adopting a healthier lifestyle, such as by following a healthy diet, maintaining a regular sleep schedule, and exercising regularly, may help enhance your memory. You should also avoid eating a large meal before cracking open your textbook, because consumption of large amounts of food puts your body in a restful mood that facilitates digestion, not mental alertness. On the other hand, avoid studying on an empty stomach, as hunger pangs make it more difficult to concentrate and retain new information. Remember, too, that using alcohol and other drugs does not mix with the mental alertness needed to learn and retain information. Finally, make sure to get enough sleep. Skipping sleep to cram for exams may make it more difficult to retain the information you've learned.

MODULE REVIEW   **6.3**   The Biology of Memory

Recite It

10. **Identify** the key brain structures involved in memory and **explain** the roles of neuronal networks and long-term potentiation.

    Memories are stored within complex circuits of nerve cells in the brain called **(a)** _____ networks.
    The **(b)** _____ appears to play a key role in the formation and temporary storage of declarative memories. Long-term memories are stored in other parts of the brain, especially in the **(c)** _____ _____.
    LTP (long-term **(d)** _____) is the biochemical process by which repeated stimulation strengthens synaptic connections between nerve cells. Forming long-term memories may depend on the process of potentiating or strengthening **(e)** _____ connections in brain circuits in which memories are encoded and stored.

11. **Explain** the role that genetics plays in memory.

    Genes regulate production of **(f)** _____ involved in transforming short-term memory into long-term memory.

12. **Apply** knowledge of how memory works to power up your memory.

    You can power up your memory by using memory strategies (for example, mnemonics, acronyms and **(g)** _____, popular sayings and rhymes, visual cues and visual memory, chunking) and by applying general suggestions (for example, paying attention, repeated practice, use of external memory aids, linking time-based tasks to external cues, mental rehearsal, use of online search engines, controlling stress, and adopting **(h)** _____ habits).

Recall It

1. Researchers today believe that memories are stored in constellations of brain cells known as _____.

2. Which of the following does *not* seem to be a function of the hippocampus?
   a. converting short-term memories into long-term declarative memories
   b. forming procedural memories
   c. creating long-term memories of facts (semantic memory) and life experiences (episodic memory)
   d. serving as a temporary storage area for new memories

3. The strengthening of synaptic connections that may underlie the conversion of short-term memory into long-term memory is called _____.

4. Researchers are finding genetic influences in memory. How do genes appear to influence memory functioning?
   a. Genes regulate the production of certain proteins that are critical to long-term memory.
   b. A memory gene leads to the production of specialized neurotransmitters involved in learning and memory.
   c. Genes regulate the production of a memory molecule that allows new memories to form.
   d. Memories are directly encoded in genes, which are then passed from one generation to the next.

Think About It

- Why did Lashley's search for engrams prove elusive?

- Suppose memory boosters are found that would allow you to preserve perfect memories of everything you read and experience. Though memory pills might help you around exam time, would you really want to retain crystal-clear memories of every personal experience, including disappointments, personal tragedies, and traumatic experiences? What do you think?

Recite It answers placed at the end of chapter.

THINKING CRITICALLY ABOUT PSYCHOLOGY

Based on your reading of this chapter, answer the following questions. Then, to evaluate your progress in developing critical thinking skills, compare your answers to the sample answers found in Appendix A.

1. Two men observe an accident in which a car hits a pedestrian and speeds away without stopping. They both are alert enough to glance at the car's license plate before it disappears around the corner. Later, when interviewed by the police, the first man says, "I only got a glimpse of it but tried to picture it in my mind. I think it began with the letters QW." The second man chimes in, "Yes, but the whole plate number was QW37XT." Why do you think the second man was able to remember more details of the license plate than the first man?

2. An English-speaking singer gives a concert in Italy and includes a popular Italian folk song in her repertoire. Her rendition is so moving that an Italian woman from the audience later comes backstage to congratulate the singer, telling her, "That song was one of my favorites as a little girl. I've never heard it sung so beautifully. But when did you learn to speak Italian so well?" The singer thanks her for the compliment but tells her she doesn't speak a word of Italian. Drawing on your knowledge of memory processes, explain how the woman was able to learn a song in a language she couldn't speak.

Answer to Try This Out (p. 228)
Drawing (h) shows the correct image of a dime in Figure 6.9.

Recite It Answers for Chapter 6
Module 6.1 1. (a) encoding; (b) storage; (c) retrieval; (d) acoustic; (e) visual; (f) semantic; (g) sensory; (h) short-term; (i) long-term, 2. (j) declarative; (k) procedural; (l) procedural, 3. (m) semantic; (n) spreading; (o) elaborative; (p) rote, 4. (q) copy; (r) details, 5. (s) recall; (t) race, 6. (u) accurate
Module 6.2 7. (a) Decay; (b) Interference ; (c) Retrieval; (d) Motivated, 8. (e) Recognition; (f) recall, 9. (g) retrograde; (h) anterograde
Module 6.3 10. (a) neuronal; (b) hippocampus; (c) cerebral cortex; (d) potentiation; (e) synaptic, 11. (f) proteins, 12. (g) acrostics; (h) healthy

Remembering

Memory Processes

- **Encoding:** Bringing information into memory
- **Storage:** Maintaining information in memory
- **Retrieval:** Accessing stored information

Information →

1 Encoding
Converting information into a form usable in memory

2 Storage
Retaining information in memory

3 Retrieval
Bringing to mind information stored in memory

Stages of Memory

- **Sensory Memory:** Storage bin for fleeting sensory impressions
- **Short-Term Memory:** Holding in mind and working on information for upward of 30 seconds
- **Long-Term Memory:** Consolidating fresh memories into lasting ones

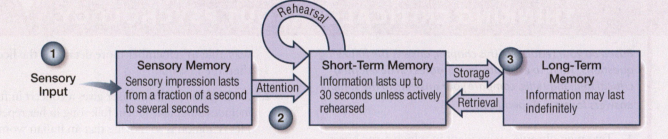

Rehearsal

1 Sensory Input →
Sensory Memory
Sensory impression lasts from a fraction of a second to several seconds

Attention →

2

Short-Term Memory
Information lasts up to 30 seconds unless actively rehearsed

Storage →
← Retrieval

3 **Long-Term Memory**
Information may last indefinitely

Types of Long-Term Memory

- **Declarative Memory:** "Knowing that"
- **Type:** Semantic memory versus episodic memory
- **Time Frame:** Retrospective versus prospective
- **Procedural memory:** "Knowing how"

Techniques for Strengthening New Memories

- **Maintenance Rehearsal:** Repeated rehearsal or rote memorization
- **Elaborative Rehearsal:** Elaborating meaningful connections

Issues in Memory Research

- **Reliability of Long-Term Memory:** Memory as a construction of experience, not a copy
- **Repressed Memory:** Suddenly recovered memories, but may not be accurate
- **Flashbulb Memory:** Events frozen in time, but still prone to biases
- **Eyewitness Testimony:** Many factors affect reliability
- **Misinformation Effect:** Creating false memories

Forgetting

Theories of Forgetting

- **Decay Theory:** Memories fading gradually over time
- **Interference Theory:** Two types, retroactive and proactive interference
- **Retrieval Theory:** Difficulty accessing stored memories; lack of retrieval cues
- **Motivated Forgetting:** Memories hidden from awareness

Measuring Memory

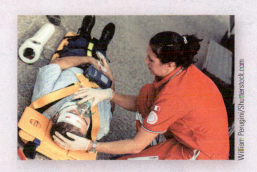

- **Recall Tasks:** Includes three types (free recall, serial recall, and paired-associates recall)
- **Recognition Tasks:** Recognizing correct answers, as in multiple-choice tests
- **Types of Amnesia**
  - **Retrograde Amnesia:** Gaps in memory for past events
  - **Anterograde Amnesia:** Difficulty forming new memories

William Perugini/Shutterstock.com

The Biology of Memory

Key Concepts

Lashley's Engram: Elusive search for memory traces in the brain

- **Neuronal Networks:** Complex assemblages of neurons in which memories are stored
- **Long-Term Potentiation (LTP):** Memories strengthened at the synaptic level through repeated stimulation
- **Brain Structures:** Many brain structures involved, including the hippocampus and the cerebral cortex
- **Genetic Factors:** Genes codes for particular proteins needed to convert short-term memory into long-term memory

Eric R. Kandel

LEARNING OBJECTIVES

After studying this chapter, you will be able to . . .

1 **Define** thinking.

2 **Describe** several ways in which we represent information in our minds.

3 **Explain** the difference between logical and natural concepts.

4 **Identify** and **describe** mental strategies we can use to solve problems more effectively.

5 **Identify** and **describe** mental roadblocks that impede problem solving and decision making.

6 **Describe** the basic processes of creative thought and **explain** the difference between divergent and convergent thinking.

7 **Apply** skills of problem solving to become a creative problem solver.

8 **Identify** and **describe** the basic components of language and the milestones in language development, and **describe** the roles of nature and nurture in language development.

9 **Evaluate** the linguistic relativity hypothesis and whether language is unique to humans.

10 **Define** intelligence, **identify** different tests of intelligence, and **evaluate** the characteristics of a good test of intelligence.

11 **Evaluate** gender differences in cognitive abilities.

12 **Describe** the characteristics of the two extremes of intelligence and the misuses of intelligence tests.

13 **Describe** the major theories of intelligence and **evaluate** the roles of heredity and environment in intelligence.

bikeriderlondon/Shutterstock.com

PREVIEW

Thinking, Language, and Intelligence

7

Two Sticky Inventions

While working on adhesives, Arthur Fry, a chemist for the company 3M, came upon an unusual compound: an adhesive that could be used to stick paper to other objects. It was not nearly as strong as other adhesives then available, such as the adhesive in Scotch tape (Bellis, 2001), and 3M did not at first see any commercial use for it. Nothing more might have been made of the new compound had Fry not had a continuing problem finding his place in his church hymnal. The slips of paper he used as bookmarks often fell to the floor, leaving him scrambling to find his place. Then it dawned on him that the unusual compound he had developed in the lab might be of help in keeping bookmarks in place. What product that many people now use in their daily lives is based on Fry's adhesive?

Here's another story about a sticky invention (Bellis, 2001). In 1948, a man in Switzerland took his dog out for a nature walk. Both returned covered with burrs, the plant seed sacs that stick to clothing and animal fur. The man decided to inspect the burrs under a microscope to determine what made them so sticky. It turned out that they contained tiny hooks that grabbed hold of small loops in the fabric of his clothing. The man, George de Mestral, looked up from the microscope and a smile crossed his face. He knew in a flash what he must do. What do you think de Mestral did with his discovery of how burrs stick to fabrics? What widely used product resulted from this discovery? You may never have heard of Arthur Fry or George de Mestral. But chances are you make use of their discoveries in your daily life. Arthur Fry's sticky compound is the adhesive in Post-it Notes. George de Mestral's discovery led him to develop the fastening fabric we now call Velcro.

The insights of Fry and de Mestral are examples of the creative mind at work. Creativity is a form of thinking in which we combine information in new ways that provide useful solutions to problems. Creative thought is not limited to a few creative geniuses. It is a basic mental capability available to nearly all of us. This chapter focuses on creativity and other aspects of thinking, including concept formation, problem solving, and decision making.

We start out by thinking about thinking, the process by which we represent and manipulate information in our minds. We then examine language development and how language affects our thinking. We also venture into the controversy about whether humans are the only species to use language. Next, we explore the nature and measurement of intelligence—the mental ability or abilities used to solve problems, learn from our experiences, and adapt to the demands of the environment. We end by focusing on skills you can use to become a more creative problem solver.

Did you know that...

- Despite the fact that we spend most of our time thinking, a recent study suggests that most people don't enjoy spending time alone with their thoughts? (p. 244)

- Albert Einstein used mental imagery when developing his theory of relativity? (p. 245)

- Alexander Graham Bell used an analogy based on the human ear to develop the design for the first telephone? (p. 251)

- Children learn to speak in grammatically correct sentences long before they learn the rules of grammar in school? (p. 257)

- Humans may have learned to talk with their hands before they learned to speak with their mouths? (p. 260)

- A worldwide study of math abilities showed girls and boys have about the same ability, but girls tend to have less confidence in their math skills? (p. 265)

- Men tend to have the upper hand in map reading, but women generally have an edge when it comes to finding lost keys? (p. 265)

- A leading psychological theory of intelligence proposes not one but many different intelligences? (p. 268)

- IQ scores worldwide have been rising steadily for more than a hundred years? (p. 272)

7.1 Thinking

1 **Define** thinking.

2 **Describe** several ways in which we represent information in our minds.

3 **Explain** the difference between logical and natural concepts.

4 **Identify** and **describe** mental strategies we can use to solve problems more effectively.

5 **Identify** and **describe** mental roadblocks that impede problem solving and decision making.

6 **Describe** the basic processes of creative thought and **explain** the difference between divergent and convergent thinking.

7 **Apply** skills of problem solving to become a creative problem solver.

Do you enjoy being alone with your thoughts? A recent study suggests that most people would rather do most anything else other than spending time just thinking.

CONCEPT 7.1

When we think, we represent information in our minds in the form of images, words, and concepts, and manipulate that information to solve problems, make decisions, and produce creative works.

CONCEPT 7.2

Mental images help us perform various cognitive functions, such as remembering directions and seeking creative solutions to problems.

CONCEPT LINK

Behavior therapists use mental imagery in treating phobic individuals by having them practice imaginal encounters with a series of increasing fearful stimuli. See Module 14.1.

cognitive psychology The branch of psychology that focuses on such mental processes as thinking, problem solving, decision making, and use of language.

thinking The process of mentally representing and manipulating information.

mental image A mental picture or representation of an object or event.

g-stockstudio/Shutterstock.com

Thinking, or *cognition,* is the major focus of study in **cognitive psychology,** the branch of psychology that explores how we acquire knowledge about the world. Cognitive psychologists investigate how we think, process information, use language, and solve problems.

The human mind is continually thinking, but what exactly is thinking? Psychologists generally define **thinking** as the process of representing and manipulating information in our mind. When we think, we represent information in our minds in the form of mental images, words, or concepts (such as abstract concepts like truth and beauty, or concrete objects like chairs and tables). We manipulate information we hold in mind when we solve problems, make decisions, and engage in creative activities.

We spend most of our waking hours thinking (try keeping your mind blank for any period of time). But researchers find that people generally don't enjoy spending time doing nothing else but thinking (Wilson et al., 2014). Participants in this study preferred performing routine tasks, and some even preferred administering mild electric shocks to themselves rather than spending time just thinking, even for brief periods of time ranging from 6 to 15 minutes. Perhaps the mind needs to be engaged in doing something rather than just thinking about something. Why not try a personal experiment to see whether you enjoy being alone with your thoughts for say 15 to 30 minutes?

Mental Images: In Your Mind's Eye

A **mental image** is a mental picture or representation of an object or event. We can form mental images of many different objects—faces of familiar people, the layout of the furniture in their homes, the letters of the alphabet, a graduation or religious ceremony. A mental image is not an actual or photographic representation. Rather, it is a reconstruction of the object or event from memory.

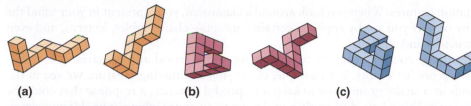

FIGURE 7.1 Mental Rotation

Are the objects in each pair the same or different? Answering this question depends on your ability to rotate objects in your mind's eye.*

*Answer: The objects in pairs (a) and (b) are the same; those in pair (c) are different.

Thanks to the creative insight of George de Mestral, an ordinary nature walk led to the development of a fastening device millions of people use today.

We also manipulate visual images in our minds in performing many cognitive tasks, such as recalling directions (Pearson, 2014). Yes, you could use verbal descriptions alone ("Let's see, that was two lefts and a right, right?"). But using a mental image—for example, picturing the church where you make a left turn and the gas station where you make a right—might work better.

Mental imaging can also lead to creative solutions to puzzling problems, as was the case with one of the greatest geniuses of the past 100 years, the scientist Albert Einstein (Isaacson, 2007). Many of his creative insights derived from the use of mental imaging in the form of thought experiments. The creative journey that led to his landmark theory of relativity began at age 16 when he pictured in his mind what it might be like to ride a light beam at the speed of light. He later was to say that words did not play any role in his creative thinking. Words, he said, only came into play after he was able to create mental images of new ideas he had formulated in thought experiments.

■ Figure 7.1 provides an opportunity to test your ability to manipulate mental images. Investigators find gender differences in mental imagery. In one early study, women reported more vivid images of past experiences and greater use of imagery to remember past experiences than men did, but men more often reported using imagery to solve problems (Harshman & Paivio, 1987). Women also tend to outperform men in remembering the spatial location of objects (Aamodt & Wang, 2008). Perhaps that's why husbands seem so often to ask their wives where they have put their keys or their glasses. Women may be better at recalling where things are placed because of their greater skill in visually scanning an image of a particular location in their minds.

Mental imagery is not limited to visual images. Most people can experience mental images of other sensory experiences, such as "hearing" in their minds the rousing first chords of Beethoven's Fifth Symphony or recalling the taste of a fresh strawberry or the feel of cotton brushing lightly against the cheek. Yet people generally have an easier time forming visual images than images of other sensory experiences.

Some information is better represented by words and concepts than by images. Abstractions like justice, honor, liberty, and respect fall into this category. After all, we may describe in words what we mean by the term *justice,* but what sort of mental image would represent what justice might look like?

Forming a mental map in your mind can help you follow some simple navigational directions. Of course, with more complex directions, GPS would help.

CONCEPT 7.3

Concepts are mental categories we use for grouping objects, events, and ideas.

concepts Mental categories for classifying events, objects, and ideas on the basis of their common features or properties.

Concepts: What Makes a Bird a Bird?

What makes a bird a bird? Or a fruit a "fruit? You see objects moving along a road and represent them in your mind by using **concepts** such as "trucks" and "cars." Concepts are mental categories we use to group objects, events, and ideas according to their

Is a penguin a bird? Although a penguin doesn't fly, it is classified as a bird, yet people may not recognize it as a bird if it does not closely resemble the model of a bird they have in mind, such as a robin.

CONCEPT 7.4
Cognitive psychologists classify concepts in two general categories, logical concepts and natural concepts.

CONCEPT 7.5
People determine whether objects belong to particular categories by comparing the object with models or examples of category members.

logical concepts Concepts with clearly defined rules for membership.

natural concepts Concepts with poorly defined or fuzzy rules for membership.

common features. When you look around a classroom, you represent in your mind the many objects you see by applying certain concepts—chairs, tables, lecterns, and even instructors and students.

Forming concepts helps us to make sense of the world and prepares us to anticipate or predict events. For example, classifying a slithering creature we see in the woods as a snake prompts us to keep a respectful distance, a response that could be a lifesaver. Think how differently you'd react to an approaching animal if you classified it as a skunk rather than a rabbit. Any species that failed to differentiate between something poisonous and something nutritious, or between a harmless creature or predator, would quickly become extinct (Ashby & Maddox, 2005).

Imagine, too, what it would be like if you were unable to form concepts. Each time you encountered a four-legged furry creature that went "woof," you wouldn't know whether to pet it or to run from it. Nor would you know whether a spherical object placed before you is one to be eaten (a meatball) or played with (a ball).

Concepts also help us respond more quickly to events by reducing the need for new learning each time we encounter a familiar object or event. Having acquired the concept *ambulance,* we immediately know how to respond when we see one pulling up behind us on the road.

We can classify concepts into two major types, *logical concepts* and *natural concepts.* **Logical concepts** have clearly defined rules for determining membership. Schoolchildren learn that the concept of a triangle applies to any three-sided form or figure. If a figure has three sides, it must be a triangle. However, most concepts we use in everyday life are **natural concepts,** in which the rules for determining how they are applied are poorly defined or fuzzy. Abstract concepts such as justice, honor, and freedom are classified as natural concepts because people typically use them without relying on a strict set of rules to determine how the concepts are applied.

We use many concepts in everyday speech without really knowing what they mean. Here's a puzzlement you can chew on: What makes a fruit a fruit? None of us has any problem using the concept of fruit, but few of us have a precise idea what the concept of "fruit" means. They might readily agree that an apple is a fruit, but be unsure whether a pumpkin, an avocado, or an olive is a fruit (they all are). Botanists, however, use the term *fruit* as a logical concept that they apply only to objects that meet the formal botanical definition (e.g., the ripened reproductive parts of seed plants). But what makes a fruit a fruit in the way most people use the concept? Typically, people base their judgment on taste (fruits are typically sweet, whereas vegetables are generally savory) rather than a botanical criterion.

How do people apply natural concepts? How do they determine that a particular animal—say, an ostrich or a penguin—is a bird? One commonly used basis for categorization involves judgments of probability—that is, judgment of the likelihood that a particular object belongs to a particular category (Willingham, 2007). In forming these judgments, we may compare an object's characteristics with those of a model or example of a category member to determine whether the object is a good fit to the category. For instance, we may think of a robin as a model or "best example" of a bird. We might then classify a sparrow as a bird more readily than we would an ostrich or a penguin because the sparrow has more robin-like features (sparrows fly; ostriches and penguins don't).

We now turn to consider how we act on information we represent in our minds, beginning with problem solving. Before we go any further, take a moment to answer a few brain teasers, which are intended to probe how you think through problems. The answers are provided at other points in the chapter.

1. Do you perceive two interlocking squares in ■ Figure 7.2? Or might this figure represent something else?
2. Emily and Sophia played six games of chess, and each of them won four. There were no ties. How is that possible? (adapted from Willingham, 2007)

3. An airliner from France crashes just off the coast of New Jersey within the territorial waters of the United States. Although all of the passengers and crew were French citizens, none of the survivors was returned to France for burial. Why not?

4. A man used a key that allowed him to enter but could not be used to open any locks. What kind of key was it?

5. ■ Figure 7.3 shows a classic problem called the nine-dot problem. Your task is to draw no more than four lines that connect all the dots without lifting your pen or pencil from the paper.

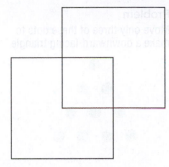

FIGURE 7.2 Two Interlocking Squares?

Source: Adapted from de Bono, 1970.

FIGURE 7.3 The Nine-Dot Problem

Problem Solving: Applying Mental Strategies to Solving Problems

Problem solving is a cognitive process in which we employ mental strategies to solve problems. As you may recall from Chapter 5, psychologist Edward Thorndike observed that animals placed in his puzzle box used trial and error to solve the problem of escaping from the enclosed compartment. The animals would try one response after another until they stumbled on the action that activated the escape mechanism. Solving a problem by trial and error is a "hit-or-miss" approach of trying one solution after another until finding the correct one.

Some people solve problems by trial and error, whereas others report "Eureka!"-type experiences in which solutions just seem to suddenly "pop" into their minds. You'll recall from Chapter 5 that the Gestalt psychologist Wolfgang Köhler referred to this sudden awareness of a solution to a problem as *insight*. Cognitive psychologists believe that insight results from restructuring a problem in our mind so that its elements fit together to render a solution. Restructuring may occur when the person sees the problem from a different perspective, takes new information into account, or recognizes connections between elements of the problem that were previously overlooked. Recall the question of how Emily and Sophia would each win four games of chess if they played six games and there were no ties. The answer is that Emily and Sophia did not play against each other. The solution comes from restructuring the problem so that it does not depend on their playing each other. ■ Figure 7.4 shows another type of insight problem.

Though we sometimes arrive at correct solutions through trial and error or insight, these approaches to problem solving have certain drawbacks. Trial and error is tedious. You must try one solution after another until you happen on the right one. And mulling over a problem while waiting for a sudden flash of insight to occur may require quite a long wait. How might we approach problem solving more efficiently? Here we consider two problem-solving strategies—*algorithms* and *heuristics*—that may prove helpful. We also explore common pitfalls that can impede our problem-solving efforts.

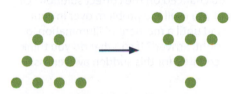

FIGURE 7.4 An Insight Problem
Your task here is to move only three of the dots to make a downward-facing triangle. You can try it using a stack of poker chips. If you get stuck, see ■ Figure 7.5 on p. 248 for the answer.

Source: Metcalfe, 1986.

Algorithms

An **algorithm** is a step-by-step set of rules for solving a problem. You probably first became acquainted with algorithms when you learned the basic rules (algorithms) of arithmetic, such as carrying the number to the next column when adding columns of numbers. So long as you applied the rules precisely to an arithmetic problem, you were guaranteed to get the right answer. But the major drawback to using algorithms in solving life problems is finding one that precisely fits the particular problem. Even if you lack a precise algorithm, you might still boost your chances of solving a problem by using an imprecise or working algorithm, which is a general set of guidelines for solving a particular problem. For example, a working algorithm for achieving a

CONCEPT 7.6
Algorithms and heuristics are problem-solving strategies that can help you solve problems more efficiently.

problem solving A form of thinking focused on finding a solution to a particular problem.

algorithm A step-by-step set of rules that will always lead to a correct solution to a problem.

Problem
Move only three of these dots to
make a downward-facing triangle

Solution

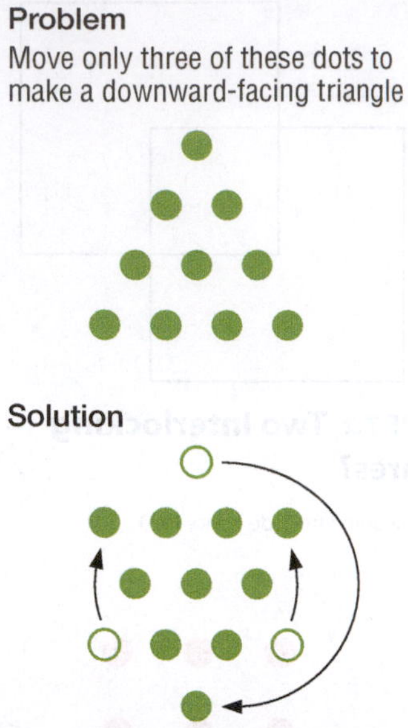

FIGURE 7.5 **Solution to the Insight Problem in Figure 7.4**
Assuming you solved the problem, did you rely on the trial-and-error method—moving the dots (or chips) around until you chanced on the correct solution? Or did you mull the problem over in your mind until a moment of illumination, or insight, arrived? If so, what do you think accounted for this sudden awareness?

heuristic A rule of thumb for solving problems or making judgments or decisions.

mental set The tendency to rely on strategies that worked in similar situations in the past but that may not be appropriate to the present situation.

functional fixedness The tendency to perceive objects as limited to the customary functions they serve.

good grade in introductory psychology would be to set aside a certain number of hours to study the text and other readings each week, attend class regularly, and participate in a study group. Will this guarantee success? Perhaps not. But the odds are in your favor.

Heuristics

A rule of thumb used to solve problems or make judgments or decisions is called a **heuristic**. Heuristics do not guarantee a solution, but they may help you arrive at one more quickly (Schwab, 2009). Using the *means–end heuristic,* we evaluate our current situation and compare it with the end result we want to achieve. We then develop a plan to reduce the distance between the two, step by step. In using a *backward-working heuristic,* for instance, we start with a possible solution and then work backward to see if the data support the solution. A psychologist seeking the causes of schizophrenia might approach the problem by proposing a model (schizophrenia as a genetic disease) and then determining whether the available data fit the model.

When using another heuristic, *creating subgoals,* we break a larger problem down into smaller, more manageable problems. Scientists use this strategy when they assign different teams to work on different parts of a problem. In AIDS research, for example, one team might work on how HIV penetrates the cell, another on how it reproduces, and so on. Solving the riddle of HIV may depend on knowledge gained from achieving each of the subgoals.

Mental Roadblocks to Problem Solving

Chris is sitting in the front passenger seat of a car waiting for the driver to return when the car suddenly begins to roll backward down a hill. In panic, he tries to climb over the gearshift lever, clumsily reaching with his foot for the brake pedal to stop the car. Unfortunately, he cannot reach the brake pedal in time to prevent the car from slamming into a pole. What could he have done differently in this situation? Why do you think he responded the way he did (adapted from Levine, 1994)?

Perhaps Chris should have realized that a much simpler solution was available: pulling the emergency brake. Yet Chris was locked into a preconceived way of solving the problem: depressing the brake pedal. This solution works well if you're sitting in the driver's seat but may not be effective if you need to climb over from the passenger side. The tendency to rely on strategies that worked well in similar situations in the past is called a **mental set**.

In some instances, as when a new problem is similar to an old one, a mental set may help you reach an appropriate solution more quickly. But a mental set can be an impediment to problem solving if a new problem requires a solution different from an old one, as the example of Chris illustrates.

Another impediment to problem solving is **functional fixedness**, the inability to see how familiar objects can be used in new ways (German & Barrett, 2005). Suppose you're working at your desk and a gust of wind blows in from an open window, scattering your papers about (Levine, 1994). Would functional fixedness prevent you from recognizing new uses for familiar objects? Or would you reach for objects that don't ordinarily serve as paperweights, such as your eyeglasses or wallet, and use them to hold down your papers long enough for you to get up and close the window? The box-candle problem and the two-string problem are classic examples of functional fixedness (see ■ Figures 7.6 and 7.7).

Yet another impediment to problem solving is the tendency to allow irrelevant information to distract one's attention from the relevant information needed to solve the problem. Recall the problem on p. 250, which stated that none of the survivors of the crash of the French airliner were buried in France. Did the geographical details

FIGURE 7.6 The Two-String Problem
Two strings hang from the ceiling but are too far apart to be touched at the same time. The task is to tie them together. Except for the string and the pliers on the table, the room is empty. How would you tie the strings together? The solution is shown in ■ Figure 7.8.

FIGURE 7.7 The Box-Candle Problem
Using only the material you see on the table, figure out a way to mount a candle on the wall so that it doesn't drip wax on the floor when it burns. The answer is shown in ■ Figure 7.9.

Source: Adapted from Duncker, 1945.

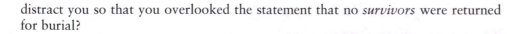

distract you so that you overlooked the statement that no *survivors* were returned for burial?

Why It Matters: Mental Roadblocks in Decision Making

We constantly need to make decisions, ranging from everyday ones—"What should I wear?" and "What should I have for dinner?"—to important life decisions—"What should I major in?" or "Should I get married?" and "Should I take this job or stay in college?" **Decision making** is a form of problem solving in which we must select a course of action from among the available alternatives.

We may think we always make logical, well-reasoned decisions, but researchers find that decision making is often influenced by underlying *cognitive biases* that hamper our ability to make rational or sound choices (Kahneman & Frederick, 2005). An example of a cognitive bias is the **confirmation bias**, which is the tendency to stick to an initial hypothesis even in the face of strong contrary evidence (Cook & Smallman, 2008). The confirmation bias leads us to place greater weight on information that confirms our prior beliefs and expectations than on information that disputes it (Hernandez & Preston, 2012). Consider a juror who decides whether a defendant is guilty based on the preliminary evidence and then fails to reconsider that decision even when strong contradictory evidence is presented at trial.

Though heuristics may help us solve problems, they can sometimes lead to bad decisions. One example is the **representativeness heuristic**, which can lead us to make more of something than we should (Kahneman & Frederick, 2005). We apply this heuristic whenever we assume that a given sample of behaviors is representative of a larger population. So we might base a decision about which movie to see on the opinion of someone we just happened to overhear talking about it. The result might be that we end up seeing a bad movie or passing up a good one, an unhappy consequence but a relatively benign one. But the representativeness heuristic can have more profound consequences. It can lead us to reject attending a particular college

CONCEPT 7.7
Mental set and functional fixedness are examples of cognitive tendencies that can impede problem solving.

CONCEPT 7.8
We may think we approach decision making in a logical way, but underlying biases in our thinking often hamper our ability to make rational decisions.

decision making A form of problem solving in which we must select a course of action from among the available alternatives.

confirmation bias The tendency to maintain allegiance to an initial hypothesis despite strong evidence to the contrary.

representativeness heuristic A rule of thumb for making a judgment that assumes a given sample is representative of the larger population from which it is drawn.

CONCEPT 7.9

The confirmation bias, the representativeness heuristic, and the availability heuristic are examples of biases in thinking that can lead us to make bad decisions.

Try This Out

The Coin Toss

A quarter is tossed six times. It lands heads up three times and tails up three times. Which of these sequences is most likely to have occurred?

1. HHHTTT
2. HTHTHT
3. TTTHHH
4. HTTHHT

Did you select the last sequence? Many people do. The representativeness heuristic leads people to judge the irregular sequence in the last item to be more representative of a random order than the others. Yet the laws of probability teach us that each of these sequences is equally likely to have occurred.

availability heuristic The tendency to judge events as more likely to occur when information pertaining to them comes readily to mind.

because we were unimpressed with the one or two students we happened to meet on a campus tour. In one example, a young woman was on her way to the admissions office for a college tour but turned around to head home after running into a student who happened to be wearing what she considered to be an unfashionable pair of shoes (Gardner, 2006).

The representativeness heuristic also underlies the tendency to judge people by first impressions. Consequently, we might decide not to pursue a relationship with someone based on a brief conversation or even on how the person dressed on a particular occasion. In this case, we are making an inference that the sample of behavior we observe is representative of the person's behavior in general, which may not be the case. The Try This Out feature offers an example of how the representativeness heuristic may bias your thinking.

The **availability heuristic** is the tendency to base decisions on examples we most easily recall or bring to mind. For example, we might buy a particular brand because we recall having seen it advertised on TV. The availability heuristic also comes into play in the judgments we make about risks we face in our daily lives (Paulos, 2009). Consider the many uncertainties we face in life. Driving to work, flying on an airplane, eating a fat-filled dessert—all entail some degree of risk. Even getting out of bed in the morning incurs some degree of risk (you could fall). The availability heuristic can lead to errors in judging relative risks. For example, the vivid images of a plane crash we see on a television news program may stick in our minds, leading us to overestimate the risk we face flying on a commercial airliner.

Creativity: Are You Tapping Your Creative Potential?

Creativity is a form of thinking that leads to original, practical, and meaningful solutions to problems or that generates new ideas or artistic expressions. Thinking of a new product or a clever way of doing something are examples of creative thought when they lead to practical applications.

FIGURE 7.8 Solution to the Two-String Problem
The solution? Think of an alternate use for the pliers. By attaching them as a weight to the end of one of the strings, you can swing the string as a pendulum. Then move to the other string and wait for the swinging string to come close enough to catch it so that you can tie the two strings together.

Source: Adapted from Maier, 1931.

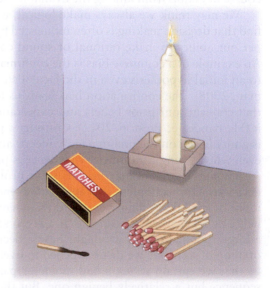

FIGURE 7.9 Solution to the Box-Candle Problem

Creativity is not limited to a few geniuses in the arts or sciences. We all have the potential to think in creative ways (Lehrer, 2012). A parent who invents a new playtime activity for a 4-year-old, a chef who combines ingredients in innovative ways, a worker who improves on a production method—all demonstrate creativity.

Creativity is distinct from general intelligence (Kim, 2005; Nettelbeck & Wilson, 2005). Although most creative people have at least average intelligence, people at the higher echelons of intelligence are not necessarily any more creative than those of average intelligence. As psychologist Robert Sternberg (2001b) notes, highly intelligent people may perform efficiently and productively, though not necessarily creatively.

Creativity is measured in different ways but most commonly through tests that tap *divergent thinking*. **Divergent thinking** is the wellspring of invention; it is the ability to conceive of new ways of viewing situations and new uses for familiar objects. By contrast, **convergent thinking** is the attempt to find the one correct answer to a problem. Refer back to Problem 1 on p. 246. The answer (two interlocking squares) seems so obvious we may not think of any alternatives. Yet by thinking divergently, we can find other answers: three squares (note the one in the area of intersection), two L-shaped pieces separated by a square (see ■ Figure 7.10), and a rectangle divided into two pieces that have been pushed askew.

Tests that tap divergent thinking were originated by psychologist J. P. Guilford and his colleagues. One widely used measure, the Alternate Uses Test, instructs subjects to list as many possible uses as they can for a common object, such as a shoe (Guilford et al., 1978). The person's score is based on the number of acceptable responses the person is able to generate.

When we think creatively, we use cognitive processes to manipulate or act on stored knowledge. Investigators identify a number of cognitive processes that underlie creative thinking, including the use of *analogy, conceptual combination,* and *conceptual expansion* (Costello & Keane, 2001; Mumford, Medeiros, & Partlow, 2012; Ward, 2004, 2007):

1. *Analogy.* An *analogy* is a comparison between two things based on their similar features or properties—for example, likening the actions of the heart to those of a pump. Alexander Graham Bell showed a creative use of analogy when he invented the telephone (Levine, 1994). In studying the human ear, Bell had noticed how sounds were transmitted when the membrane known as the eardrum vibrated. He applied this idea in his design of the telephone.

2. *Conceptual combination.* Combining two or more concepts into one can result in novel ideas or applications that reflect more than the sum of the parts. Examples of **conceptual combinations** include "cell phones," "veggie burgers," and "home page." Can you think of other ways in which concepts can be creatively combined?

3. *Conceptual expansion.* One way of developing novel ideas is to expand familiar concepts. Examples of **conceptual expansion** include an architect's adaptation of an existing building to

FIGURE 7.10 Divergent Thinking
Compare Figure 7.2 on p. 247 with the cutout shown here. Now imagine these two L-shaped figures pushed together so that they are separated by a square.

CONCEPT 7.10
Creativity is a cognitive ability found in varying degrees in most people.

CONCEPT 7.11
Creativity involves using cognitive processes to manipulate or act on stored knowledge.

CONCEPT 7.12
When people approach creative tasks, they tend to expand on what is familiar to them.

creativity Originality of thought associated with the development of new, workable products or solutions to problems.

divergent thinking The ability to conceive of new ways of viewing situations and new uses for familiar objects.

convergent thinking The attempt to narrow down a range of alternatives to converge on the one correct answer to a problem.

conceptual combinations Combinations of two or more concepts into one concept, resulting in the creation of a novel idea or application.

conceptual expansion Expanding familiar concepts by applying them to new uses.

"Never, ever, think outside the box."

Concept Chart 7.1	Cognitive Processes in Thinking	
Cognitive Process	**Definition**	**Description**
Mental imaging	Forming mental representations of objects or events	Images can be formed based on various sensory experiences, including vision, hearing, taste, and touch. Mental images can be manipulated to help us solve certain kinds of problems.
Concept formation	Grouping objects, events, and ideas on the basis of their common features	Most concepts are natural concepts, which have fuzzy or imprecise rules for membership. Logical concepts are those that have strict rules for membership.
Problem solving	The process of arriving at a solution to a given problem	Strategies include algorithms and heuristics. Pitfalls include mental set and functional fixedness.
Decision making	The process of deciding which of two or more courses of action to take	Decision making is often influenced by errors in thinking associated with the confirmation bias, the representativeness heuristic, and the availability heuristic.
Creativity	The generation of novel, workable products or ideas	Creativity applies cognitive processes that act on or manipulate stored knowledge. These processes include the use of analogy, conceptual combination, and conceptual expansion.

a new use, a writer's creation of new scenes using familiar characters, and a chef's variation on a traditional dish that results in a new culinary sensation.

Creativity typically springs from the expansion or modification of familiar categories or concepts. The ability to take what we know and to modify and expand on it is one of the basic processes of creative thinking.

Before going further, you may wish to review the cognitive processes involved in thinking, which are outlined in Concept Chart 7.1.

APPLYING PSYCHOLOGY in Daily Life

Becoming a Creative Problem Solver

The range of problems we face in our personal lives is virtually limitless. Consider some common examples: getting to school or work on time; helping a friend with a personal problem; resolving disputes; and juggling school, work, and family responsibilities. Creative problem solvers challenge preconceptions and consider as many alternative solutions to a problem as possible. Were you stumped by the problem on p. 247 about the key that opened no locks but allowed the man to enter? Perhaps it was because you approached the problem from only one vantage point—that the key was a door key. Solving the problem requires that you consider an alternative that may not have seemed obvious at first—that the key was an enter key on a keyboard. Speaking of keys, here are some key steps toward becoming a creative problem solver.

Adopt a Questioning Attitude

Finding creative solutions to problems begins with adopting a questioning attitude. The creative problem solver asks, "What alternatives are available? What has worked in the past? What hasn't worked? What can I do differently?"

Gather Information

Creative problem solvers acquire the information and resources they need to explore possible solutions. People today have access to a wider range of information resources than ever before, including newspapers and magazines, college courses, and, of course, the Internet. Want to know more about combating a common problem like insomnia? Why not search the Internet to see what information is available? However, think critically about the information you find.

Avoid Getting Stuck in Mental Sets

Here's a question for you: "If there were three apples and you took away two, how many would you have?" If you answered one, chances are you had a mental set to respond to this type of problem as a subtraction problem. But the question did not ask how many apples were left. The answer is that you would have two apples—the two you took away.

To avoid slipping into a mental set that impairs problem-solving efforts, think through each question carefully. Ask yourself: What am I required to do? What type of problem is this? What problem-solving strategy would work best for this type of problem?

Put these skills into practice by responding to a few brainteasers (the answers are given under the heading "Answers to Brainteasers" on p. 275) (National Institute of Environmental Health Sciences, 2001):

1. How many two-cent stamps are there in a dozen?
2. You are holding two U.S. coins that total 55 cents. One of the coins is not a nickel. What are the coins you are holding?
3. A farmer has 18 cows and all but 11 of them died. How many were left?

Generate Alternatives

Creative problem solvers generate as many alternative solutions to a problem as possible. They don't rely on their first gut reaction. Consider this puzzle: A bat and a ball cost $1.10 together, and the bat costs one dollar more than the ball. How much does the ball cost?

Most people immediately jump to the wrong answer based on the first thought that comes to mind: 10 cents. (The correct answer is 5 cents. Do the math.) If you got it wrong, don't feel badly. About half of the undergraduates in some of the nation's best colleges (for example, MIT, Princeton, Harvard) get it wrong (Kahneman & Klein, 2009). Solving a problem like this requires you avoid a knee-jerk response and carefully think through the problem (May 2016). It's a normal tendency to go with your gut feelings, not only with puzzles, but also with many decisions you face. However, creative problem solvers carefully think through problems and generate as many solutions as possible. They may decide upon their original solution, or they

CONCEPT 7.13
Creative problem solvers challenge preconceptions and consider as many alternative solutions to a problem as possible.

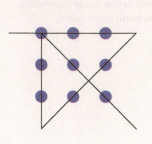

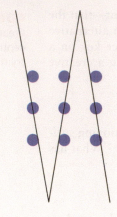

The nine-dot problem

may decide that one of the alternatives works best. Here are a few suggestions for generating alternatives:

1. *Personal brainstorming.* Alex Osborne (1963) introduced the concept of brainstorming to help business executives and engineers solve problems more creatively. The basic idea is to encourage divergent thinking. **Brainstorming** encourages people to propose as many solutions to a problem as possible without fear of being judged negatively by others, no matter how far-fetched their proposals may seem. There are three general rules for brainstorming:

   Rule 1: Write down as many solutions to the problem as you can think of. Quantity counts more than quality.

   Rule 2: Suspend judgment. Don't evaluate any of the possible solutions or strike them off your list.

   Rule 3: Seek unusual, remote, or even weird ideas. Today's strange or oddball idea may turn into tomorrow's brilliant solution.

2. *After generating your list, put it aside for a few days.* When you return to it, ask yourself which solutions are worth pursuing. Take into account the resources or additional information you will need to put these solutions into practice.

3. *Find analogies.* Finding a situation analogous to the present problem can lead to a creative solution. Ask yourself how the present problem is similar to problems you've encountered before. What strategies worked in the past? How can they be modified to fit the present problem? This is a constructive use of mental sets—using past solutions as a guide, not an impediment, to problem solving.

4. *Think outside the box.* Recall the nine-dot problem in Figure 7.3 (p. 247). People have difficulty with this problem because of a tendency to limit the ways they think about it. If you didn't solve the nine-dot problem, you're in good company. In a laboratory test, none of the research participants who were given several minutes to solve the problem were able to do so (MacGregor, Ormerod, & Chronicle, 2001). The problem is solvable only if you think "outside the box"—literally, as shown above. Creative problem solvers make an effort to conceptualize problems from different perspectives, steering problem-solving efforts toward finding new solutions (Ormerod, MacGregor, & Chronicle, 2002).

Sleep on It

People facing difficult problems may benefit from the age-old wisdom of "sleeping on it." Learning new information and then sleeping on it may help you retain more of what you learn. Investigators find that sleep enhances insight and creative thinking of research subjects challenged with solving difficult math problems (Wagner et al., 2004). Indeed, the cognitive benefits of getting a good night's sleep may account for the experiences of many famous scientists and artists whose inspired ideas occurred upon awakening from a deep sleep (Komaroff, 2004).

Test It Out

Try out possible solutions to see how they work. Gather information that will help you evaluate what you need to do differently to achieve a better solution. If you get stuck, take time away from the problem. Allow the problem to "incubate" in your mind. When you return to it, you may have a fresh perspective that will help you discover a workable solution.

brainstorming A method of promoting divergent thinking by encouraging people to propose as many solutions to a problem as possible without fear of being judged negatively by others, no matter how far-fetched their proposals may be.

MODULE REVIEW   7.1   Thinking

Recite It

1. **Define** thinking.

   Psychologists generally define thinking as the mental (a) _____ and (b) _____ of information.

2. **Describe** several ways in which we represent information in our minds.

   These include use of mental (c) _____ (picturing information in mind), (d) use of _____ (naming an object or a person), and (e) _____ _____ (classifying an object in a particular category).

3. **Explain** the difference between logical and natural concepts.

   (f) _____ concepts have clearly defined rules for membership, whereas (g) _____ concepts have poorly defined or fuzzy criteria for membership.

4. **Identify** and **describe** mental strategies we can use to solve problems more effectively.

   Problem-solving strategies involve use of (h) _____ (sudden realization of a solution), (i) _____ and (j) _____ (trying out one possible solution after another), (k) _____ (a step-by-step set of rules for solving a problem), and (l) _____ (rules of thumb used to solve problems).

5. **Identify** and **describe** mental roadblocks that impede problem solving and decision making.

   These roadblocks include mental (m) _____ (preset ways of solving problems that may apply to the present situation) and (n) _____ fixedness (failure to recognize alternate uses for objects).
   The (o) _____ bias leads people to discount evidence that contradicts their prior beliefs and expectations. The (p) _____ heuristic leads people to make more of a given sample than they should. The (q) _____ heuristic leads people to make snap decisions based on whatever information comes most readily to mind.

6. **Describe** the basic processes of creative thought and **explain** the difference between divergent and convergent thinking.

   (r) _____ thinking involves finding the one right answer or solution to a problem, whereas (s) _____ thinking taps into creative thinking involved in finding new ways of thinking about problems or using familiar objects.
   Cognitive processes in creative thinking include analogy, conceptual (t) _____, and conceptual (u) _____.

7. **Apply** skills of problem solving to become a creative problem solver.

   These skills include adopting a (v) _____ attitude, gathering information, avoiding getting stuck in mental sets, generating alternatives, sleeping on it, and (w) _____ out possible solutions.

Recall It

1. When we think, we form mental representations of information in the form of images, words, and _____.

2. A category with clearly defined rules for membership is called a _____ concept, whereas a category with poorly defined rules for membership is a _____ concept.

3. One mental roadblock to problem solving is the inability to see how a familiar object can be used in new ways. This impediment is known as

   a. a mental set.   c. an incubation period.
   b. functional fixedness. d. confirmation bias.

4. Merging two or more concepts to produce novel ideas or applications is called

   a. conceptual expansion.
   b. creative combination.
   c. divergent thinking.
   d. conceptual combination.

Think About It

■ Have you ever used mental imagery to find a creative solution to a problem? Might you use it in the future? Why or why not?

■ How might you apply the concepts of analogy, conceptual combination, and conceptual expansion to develop a novel idea, application, or service?

Recite It answers placed at the end of chapter.

7.2 Language

8 **Identify** and **describe** the basic components of language and the milestones in language development, and **describe** the roles of nature and nurture in language development.

9 **Evaluate** the linguistic relativity hypothesis and whether language is unique to humans.

The Brain Loves a Puzzle

As you read ahead, use the information in the text to solve the following puzzle:

Why do you suppose that traffic lights use colors rather than words like "stop" or "go"?

jeff gynane/Shutterstock.com

CONCEPT 7.14

Language consists of four basic components: phonemes, morphemes, syntax, and semantics.

language A system of communication composed of symbols (words, hand signs, and so on) that are arranged according to a set of rules (grammar) to form meaningful expressions.

grammar The set of rules governing how symbols in a given language are used to form meaningful expressions.

phonemes The basic units of sound in a language.

morphemes The smallest units of meaning in a language.

syntax The rules of grammar that determine how words are ordered within sentences or phrases to form meaningful expressions.

semantics The set of rules governing the meaning of words.

The term **language** refers to a system of communication consisting of symbols—words or hand signs (as in the case of American Sign Language)—arranged according to a set of rules, called a **grammar**, to express meaning (Gertner, Fisher, & Eisengart, 2006). The ability to use language is a remarkable cognitive ability so tightly woven into the human experience, says prominent linguist Steven Pinker (1994, p. 17), that "it is scarcely possible to imagine life without it. Chances are that if you find two or more people together anywhere on earth they will soon be exchanging words. When there is no one to talk with, people talk to themselves, to their dogs, even to their plants."

In this module, we examine the remarkable capacity of humans to communicate through language. We consider the basic components of language, developmental milestones in language acquisition, and leading theories of language acquisition. We also consider the question of whether language is a uniquely human characteristic.

Components of Language

The basic units of sound in a spoken language are called **phonemes**. English has about 40 phonemes to sound out the 500,000 or so words found in modern unabridged English dictionaries. The word *dog* consists of three phonemes: "d," "au," and "g." Phonemes in English correspond both to individual letters and to letter combinations, including the "au" in *dog* and the sounds "th" and "sh." The same letter can make different sounds in different words. The "o" in the word *two* is a different phoneme from the "o" in the word *one*. Changing one phoneme in a word can change the meaning of the word. Changing the "r" sound in *reach* to the "t" sound makes it *teach*. Different languages have different phonemes. In some African languages, various clicking sounds are phonemes. Hebrew has a guttural "chhh" phoneme, as in the expression *l'chaim* ("to life").

Phonemes are combined to form **morphemes**, the smallest units of meaning in a language. Simple words such as *car*, *ball*, and *time* are morphemes, but so are other linguistic units that convey meaning, such as prefixes and suffixes. The prefix "un," for example, means "not," and the suffix "ed" following a verb means that the action expressed by the verb occurred in the past. More complex words are composed of several morphemes. The word *pretested* consists of three morphemes: "pre," "test," and "ed."

Language requires more than phonemes and morphemes. It also requires **syntax**, the rules of grammar that determine how words are ordered within sentences and phrases to form meaningful expressions, and **semantics**, the set of rules governing the meaning of words. The sentence "buy milk I" sounds odd to us because it violates a basic rule of English syntax—that the subject ("I") must precede the verb ("buy"). We follow rules of syntax in everyday speech even if we are not aware of them or cannot verbalize them. But even when our speech follows proper syntax, it may still lack meaning. The famed linguist Noam Chomsky, to whose work we will return shortly, illustrated this point with the example "Colorless green ideas sleep furiously." The sentence may sound correct to our ears because it follows the rules of English syntax, but it doesn't convey any meaning. The same word may convey very different meanings depending on the context in which it is used. "Don't *trip* going down the stairs" means something very different from "Have a good *trip*."

Language Development

Children the world over develop language in basically the same stages, which unfold at basically the same ages. Until about 6 months of age, infants are limited to nonlinguistic forms of communication—crying and cooing. At around that time, the first sounds resembling human speech appear in the form of babbling. The child then progresses through stages of one- and two-word phrases, and between the ages of 2 and 3 begins developing more complex speech patterns (see Concept Chart 7.2). By around 30 months of age, children are speaking in full sentences and have a vocabulary of about 550 words (Golinkoff & Hirsh-Pasek, 2006).

The similar course of language development across cultures and the ease with which children naturally acquire language suggest that language depends on an innate mechanism that may be hardwired in the human brain. Noam Chomsky (1965) called this mechanism the **language acquisition device**. We acquire the ability to speak, much as we do the ability to walk and jump, because we have an inborn propensity to develop it. As psychologist Steven Pinker (1994) put it, "We don't teach our children to sit, stand, and walk, and they do it anyway." Children learn to use the rules of grammar without any formal instruction. In English-speaking cultures, they begin placing the subject before the verb long before they learn what the terms *subject* and *verb* mean. According to Chomsky and Pinker,

CONCEPT 7.15
Young children pass through a series of milestones of language acquisition, from crying and cooing to babbling, to one- and two-word phrases, and then to more complex speech.

Noam Chomsky

language acquisition device Chomsky's concept of an innate, prewired mechanism in the brain that allows children to acquire language naturally.

Concept Chart 7.2	Milestones in Language Acquisition	
Age (Approximate)	**Vocal Activity**	**Description**
Birth	Crying	Crying expresses distress.
2 months	Cooing	Infant begins making cooing sounds (e.g., "aah" and "oooh").
6 to 12 months	Babbling	Phonemes, the basic units of sound, appear.
12 months	One-word phrases	Babies imitate sounds and can understand some words; they begin to say single words.
18 to 24 months	Two-word phrases or sentences	Vocabulary grows to about 50 words, and babies emit two-word phrases or sentences.
24 to 36 months	Complex speech	Sentences become longer and more complex and include plurals and past tense; speech shows elements of proper syntax.

children are able to learn grammatical structures as rapidly and easily as they do because the human brain contains the basic blueprints or neural circuitry for using grammar.

Critics point out that Chomsky's language acquisition device is not an actual physical structure in the brain but a hypothesis—an abstract concept of how language centers in the brain work—and that it does not explain the mechanisms by which language is produced. In fairness to Chomsky, we should point out that brain mechanisms responsible for language are extremely complex, consisting of complicated circuits in many areas of the brain that link together to produce language in ways we don't yet understand. However, the pieces of the puzzle may be starting to fall into place. Scientists are beginning to chart specialized neural networks in the brain responsible for speech and language processing (Friederici & Singer, 2015).

Regardless of the brain mechanisms involved in language production, both nature and nurture are necessary for language to develop. Our ability to use language depends not only on having a biological capacity for language production but also on experience with the sounds, meanings, and structures of human speech (Berko Gleason & Ratner, 2009). Children naturally acquire language by listening to the speech of others, well before they learn rules of formal grammar in school (Pancsofar & Vernon-Feagans, 2006; Sakai, 2005). They also enlarge their vocabularies by imitating the words others use to refer to particular objects. Parents can help children develop language skills by talking and reading to them frequently. They can also use principles of operant conditioning and observational learning (discussed in Chapter 5) by modeling proper language use and rewarding children for imitating it.

However language develops, it is clear that language and thinking are closely intertwined. The brain has a remarkable capacity for processing words, but its ability to process colors is much faster (Rayner et al., 2016). This is the reason that traffic lights use colors rather than words. Speaking of color perception, we will see next that the ability to distinguish different colors has a bearing on the question of whether language determines how we think.

Culture and Language: Does the Language We Use Determine How We Think?

Does the language we speak affect how we think? Might French Canadians, Chinese, and Africans see the world differently because of the vocabulary and syntax of their native languages? According to the **linguistic relativity hypothesis**, the answer is yes. This hypothesis—also called the *Whorfian hypothesis* after Benjamin Whorf, the amateur linguist who developed it—holds that the language we use determines how we think and how we perceive reality. Whorf (1956) pointed out that some cultures have many different words for colors, whereas others have only a few. English has 11 words for basic colors: black, white, red, green, yellow, blue, brown, purple, pink, orange, and gray (Adelson, 2005). At the other end of the spectrum is the Navajo language, which has no separate words for blue and green.

If we had only a few words to describe colors, would we be able to identify the many different colors in the color spectrum? The answer is yes, based on landmark research conducted by Eleanor Rosch (Rosch, 1975; Rosch-Heider & Olivier, 1972). Rosch and her colleagues showed that members of a preliterate tribe in New Guinea, whose language contained but two color names, were just as capable of recognizing many different colors as English-speaking subjects. This finding suggests that people

---

CONCEPT 7.16
Language development depends on both a biological capacity for language production and experience with the sounds, meanings, and structures of human speech.

CONCEPT 7.17
The belief that the language we speak determines how we think and perceive the world is a controversial viewpoint that has not been supported by research evidence.

linguistic relativity hypothesis The proposition that the language we use determines how we think and how we perceive the world (also called the *Whorfian hypothesis*).

have the capacity to recognize colors regardless of differences in the words they use to describe them.

Overall, research evidence does not support the original version of the Whorfian hypothesis, which holds that language determines how we think and perceive the world (Pinker, 2003; Siegal, Varley, & Want, 2001). But a weaker version of the theory does have merit, a version that proposes that the culture in which we are raised and the language we use are important influences that shape how we think and how we perceive the world (Adelson, 2005; Fiedler, 2008). For example, English speakers tend to perceive blue- and green-colored shapes as different from each other, but speakers of African languages that use a single term to describe blue and green tend to perceive these shapes as belonging to the same category of shapes (Özgen, 2004).

Language can influence thinking in other ways. Consider this sentence: "A person should always be respectful of *his* parents." If the very concept of personhood embodies maleness, where does that leave females? As *nonpersons*? If Adriana sees that *he* is used when referring to professionals like doctors, engineers, or scientists, might she get the idea that such careers are not as available to her as they are to her brother?

Is Language Unique to Humans?

Do animals other than humans use language? Consider the case of Koko, a gorilla trained to use American Sign Language (ASL). Apes lack the vocal apparatus needed to form human sounds, so researchers have turned to nonverbal means of expression, such as sign language used by people with impaired hearing, to communicate with them. One day Koko flashed the ASL sign for pain and pointed to her mouth ("Koko the Gorilla," 2004). Dentists were summoned and soon discovered that Koko had a decayed tooth. They removed the tooth to relieve the pain.

Koko was able to communicate with humans, but was she using language? In the 1960s, investigators Beatrice and Allen Gardner trained a chimpanzee named Washoe to use about 160 signs, including signs for "apple," "tickle," "flower," and "more" (Gardner & Gardner, 1969, 1978). Washoe learned to combine signs into simple phrases, such as "more fruit" and "gimme flower." She even displayed a basic grammar by changing the position of the subject and object in her signing to reflect a change in meaning. For example, when she wanted her trainer to tickle her, she would sign, "You tickle Washoe." But when she wanted to do the tickling, she would sign, "Washoe tickle you" (Gardner & Gardner, 1978).

David Premack developed an artificial language in which plastic chips of different sizes, colors, and shapes symbolize different words (see ■ Figure 7.11). Using shaping and reinforcement techniques, he trained a chimp named Sarah to communicate by placing the chips on a magnetic board. Sarah learned to form simple sentences. For example, she would request food by putting together a sequence of chips that signaled "Mary give apple Sarah" (Premack, 1971).

Perhaps the most remarkable demonstration of simian communication involved Kanzi, a male pygmy chimpanzee (Savage-Rumbaugh, Shanker, & Taylor, 1998; Shanker & Savage-Rumbaugh, 1999). Kanzi's mother was trained to communicate by pushing geometric symbols into a keyboard, but Kanzi received no special training himself. He appeared to have learned the keyboard system simply by observing his mother's training sessions. At age 2, Kanzi stunned his trainers when he suddenly began manipulating symbols on the keyboard to ask for a specific fruit. By age 6, he was using some 200 symbols to communicate.

So, can apes acquire and use language? Critics claim that Washoe, Sarah, and others merely learned to imitate gestures and other responses for which they were

Eleanor Rosch's research findings ran contrary to the Whorfian hypothesis. Members of a New Guinea tribe, even though they used only two words to distinguish among different colors, were just as able as English-speaking subjects to identify different colors.

CONCEPT 7.18
Though research findings have not supported the original form of the linguistic relativity hypothesis, a weaker version which holds that culture and language influence thinking has merit.

CONCEPT LINK
People from Eastern and Western cultures tend to perceive the same visual scenes in different ways, as we examined in Chapter 3. See Module 3.5.

Mary · Sarah · Apple · Banana · Not · Give

FIGURE 7.11 Examples of Materials Used in Premack's Study

Questions remain about whether an ape's ability to manipulate symbols on a keyboard, as Panbanisha, a female bonobo, is demonstrating here, is tantamount to human language.

CONCEPT 7.19

Whether humans are unique in possessing the ability to communicate through language remains a controversial question.

reinforced, rather than learning the complex syntax and morphemes of a true human language like ASL (Pinker, 1994; Terrace, 2005). A chimp signing "me cookie" is no different, critics say, than a pigeon learning to perform a series of responses to obtain a food pellet. Perhaps the question of whether apes can use language depends on how broadly we define language. If our definition includes communicating through the use of symbols and gestures, then apes as well as other nonhuman species may indeed be able to use language. But if our definition hinges on the use of complex syntax and grammatical structures, then the ability to use language may be unique to humans. The language abilities of Kanzi and other chimps may involve a kind of primitive language similar to that used by human infants or toddlers, not the complex forms of language that children naturally acquire as they mature (Yule, 2014).

Even so, ape communication may hold clues to the origins of human language (Pollick & de Waal, 2007). Apes frequently gesture with their hands, which may represent a useful starting point to study the development of human language (Roberts et al., 2014; Tierney, 2007; Wade, 2007). Humans may have learned to talk with their hands before they learned to speak with their mouths (Wargo, 2008). People continue to use their hands for emphasis when they speak.

MODULE REVIEW 7.2 Language

Recite It

8. Identify and **describe** the basic components of language and the milestones in language development, and **describe** the roles of nature and nurture in language development.

The major components of language are (a) _____ (basic units of sounds), morphemes (basic units of meaning), (b) _____ (the rules of grammar that determine how words are ordered in sentences and phrases to express meaning), and (c) _____ (the set of rules governing the meaning of words).

The major milestones in language development include crying, cooing, babbling, use of (d) _____-_____ phrases, use of two-word phrases or sentences, and use of more complex sentences.

According to Noam (e) _____, language development depends on an innate mechanism that is "prewired" in the human brain. Language development also depends on

exposure to the speech of others. Thus, both nature and (f) _____ are necessary.

9. Evaluate the linguistic relativity hypothesis and whether language is unique to humans.

In its original form, this hypothesis (also called the Whorfian hypothesis) holds that language determines how we (g) _____ and how we (h) _____ the world. Research findings fail to support this version of the hypothesis, but a weaker version, which maintains that culture and language influence thinking, has some merit.

Research with chimps and gorillas has shown that these primates are capable of learning elementary forms of communication—for example, manipulating symbols to request food—but questions remain about whether these communication skills are equivalent to human (i) _____.

Recall It

1. The set of rules governing the proper use of words, phrases, and sentences is called
   a. language.
   b. grammar.
   c. cultural determinism.
   d. syntax.

2. The basic units of sounds in a language are called
   a. phonemes.
   b. morphemes.
   c. semantics.
   d. syntax.

3. The belief that language determines how we think and perceive reality is called the linguistic _____ hypothesis.

4. Apes have been taught American Sign Language (ASL) because

   a. researchers have agreed to use this universal language.
   b. sign language is easier to acquire than spoken language.

c. they lack the vocal apparatus needed to form human sounds.

d. sign language is more effective than spoken language in communicating basic needs.

Think About It

- In what ways are sexist biases reflected in the language we use in ordinary speech?

- Do you believe that chimps that learn to use signs are capable of communicating through language? Why or why not?

Recite It answers placed at the end of chapter.

MODULE

7.3 Intelligence

10 **Define** intelligence, **identify** different tests of intelligence, and **evaluate** the characteristics of a good test of intelligence.

11 **Evaluate** gender differences in cognitive abilities.

12 **Describe** the characteristics of the two extremes of intelligence and the misuses of intelligence tests.

13 **Describe** the major theories of intelligence and **evaluate** the roles of heredity and environment in intelligence.

Perhaps no subject in psychology has sparked as much controversy as intelligence. Psychologists have long argued about how to define it, how to measure it, what factors govern it, whether different racial and ethnic groups have more or less of it, and, if so, what accounts for these differences. These debates are still very much at the forefront of contemporary psychology.

What Is Intelligence?

Just what is **intelligence**? Is it the ability to acquire knowledge from books or formal schooling? Or might it be "street smarts"—practical intelligence of the kind we see in people who survive by their wits rather than by knowledge acquired in school? Is it the ability to solve problems? Or is it the ability to adapt to the demands of the environment? Psychologists believe intelligence may be all these things and more. Though definitions of intelligence vary, a central belief of each is that intelligence is the ability to adapt to the environment. Perhaps the most widely used definition of intelligence is the one offered by psychologist David Wechsler (1975): "Intelligence is the global capacity of the individual to act purposefully, to think rationally, and to deal effectively with the environment."

Some theorists believe there are many different forms of intelligence, perhaps even multiple intelligences. Before we explore theories of intelligence, let us consider the history and nature of intelligence testing in modern times as well as extremes of intelligence.

CONCEPT 7.20
Though theorists define intelligence in different ways, one widely used definition holds that intelligence is the capacity to act purposefully, think rationally, and deal effectively with the environment.

CONCEPT LINK
Some theorists believe that the ability to recognize and manage emotions is a form of intelligent behavior called emotional intelligence. See Module 8.4.

CONCEPT 7.21
Alfred Binet and Theodore Simon developed the type of intelligence test in use today. Their work led to the concept of an intelligence quotient.

intelligence The capacity to think and reason clearly and to act purposefully and effectively in adapting to the environment and pursuing one's goals.

wavebreakmedia/Shutterstock.com

© Archives of the History of American Psychology – The University of Akron

Henry Goddard, the early psychologist who brought the Binet-Simon intelligence test to the United States, also held another important distinction. He briefly served as coach of the USC football team. He remains to this day the only undefeated head coach in USC history.

CONCEPT 7.22

The Stanford-Binet Intelligence Scale and the Wechsler scales are the major tests of intelligence in use today.

mental age A representation of a person's intelligence based on the age of people who are capable of performing at the same level of ability.

intelligence quotient (IQ) A measure of intelligence based on performance on tests of mental abilities, expressed as a ratio between one's mental age and chronological age or derived from the deviation of one's scores from the norms for those of one's age group.

How Is Intelligence Measured?

The type of intelligence test used today originated with the work of a Frenchman, Alfred Binet (1857–1911). In 1904, school officials in Paris commissioned Binet to develop methods of identifying children who were unable to cope with the demands of regular classroom instruction and who required special classes to meet their needs. Today, we might describe such children as having learning disorders or mild intellectual disability.

To measure mental abilities, Binet and a colleague, Theodore Simon (1872–1961), developed an intelligence test consisting of memory tasks and other short tasks representing the kinds of everyday problems children might encounter, such as counting coins. By 1908, Binet and Simon had decided to scale the tasks according to the age at which a child should be able to perform them successfully. A child began the testing with tasks scaled at the lowest age and then progressed to more difficult tasks, stopping at the point at which he or she could no longer perform them. The age at which the child's performance topped off was considered the child's **mental age**.

Binet and Simon calculated intelligence by subtracting the child's mental age from his or her chronological (actual) age. Children whose mental ages sufficiently lagged behind their chronological ages were considered in need of special education. In 1912, a German psychologist, William Stern, suggested a different way of computing intelligence, which Binet and Simon adopted. Stern divided mental age by chronological age, yielding a "mental quotient." It soon was labeled the **intelligence quotient (IQ)**. IQ is given by the following formula, in which MA is mental age and CA is chronological age:

$$IQ = \frac{MA}{CA} \times 100$$

Thus, if a child has a mental age of 10 and a chronological age of 8, the child's IQ would be 125 (10/8 = 1.25 × 100 = 125). A child with a mental age of 10 who is 12 years of age would have an IQ of 83 (10/12 = .8333 × 100 = 83).

Researchers following in Binet's footsteps developed intelligence tests that could be used with groups other than French schoolchildren. Henry Goddard (1865–1957), a research director at a school for children with mental retardation (now labeled *intellectual disability*), brought the Binet-Simon test to the United States and translated it into English for use with American children. Early in his career, Goddard taught at the University of Southern California (USC), where he also briefly served as the school's first head football coach and remains to this day the only undefeated head coach in USC football history (Benjamin, 2009). (His 1888 team had a record of two wins and no losses against a local athletic club team.)

During World War I, the U.S. Army developed group-administered intelligence tests used to screen millions of recruits. At about the same time, Stanford University psychologist Lewis Terman (1877–1956) adapted the Binet-Simon test for American use, adding many items of his own and establishing criteria, or **norms**, for comparing an individual's scores with those of the general population. The revised test, known as the Stanford-Binet Intelligence Scale (SBIS), was first published in 1916.

The Stanford-Binet Intelligence Scale is still commonly used to measure intelligence in children and young adults. However, tests developed by David Wechsler (1896–1981) are today the most widely used intelligence tests in the United States and Canada. Wechsler, a psychologist at Bellevue Hospital in New York, developed tests of intelligence for preschool children, school-age children, and adults (Wechsler Adult Intelligence Scale, now in a fourth edition called the WAIS-IV; see ■ Figure 7.12). The Wechsler scales introduced the concept of the *deviation IQ*—an IQ score based on the deviation, or difference, of a person's test score from the norms for the person's age

Sample Subtests

Comprehension
Why do people need to obey traffic laws? What does the saying, "The early bird catches the worm," mean?

Vocabulary
What does *capricious* mean?

Arithmetic
John wanted to buy a shirt that cost $31.50, but only had 17 dollars. How much more money would he need to buy the shirt?

Similarities
How are a stapler and a paper clip alike?

Picture Completion
What's missing from this picture?

Digit Span
Listen to this series of numbers and repeat them back to me in the same order:
6 4 5 2 7 3

Listen to this series of numbers and then repeat them backward:
9 4 2 5 8 7

Letter-Number Sequencing
Listen to this series of numbers and letters and repeat them back, first saying the numbers from least to most, and then saying the letters in alphabetical order:
S-2-C-1

Block Design
Using these blocks, match the design shown.

FIGURE 7.12 Examples of Items Similar to Those on the Wechsler Adult Intelligence Scale

group, rather than on the ratio of mental age to chronological age. The Wechsler scales are standardized in such a way that an average score is set at 100. The contemporary version of the Stanford-Binet Intelligence Scale also uses the deviation method to compute IQ scores.

What Are the Characteristics of a Good Test of Intelligence?

Like all psychological tests, tests of intelligence must be standardized, reliable, and valid. If they do not meet these criteria, we cannot be confident of the results.

Standardization

Standardization is the process of establishing norms for a test by administering it to large numbers of people. These large numbers make up the *standardization sample*. The standardization sample must be representative of the population for whom the test is intended. As noted earlier, norms are the criteria, or standards, used to compare a person's performance with the performance of others. You can determine how well you do on an intelligence test by comparing your scores with the norms for people in your age group in the standardization sample.

As noted previously, IQ scores are based on the deviation of a person's score from norms for others of the same age, and the mean (average) score is set at 100. IQ scores are distributed around the mean in such a way that two-thirds of the scores in the general population fall within an "average" range of 85 to 115. In ■ Figure 7.13, we can see that distribution (spread) of IQ scores follows the form of a bell-shaped

CONCEPT 7.23
Like all psychological tests, intelligence tests must be standardized, reliable, and valid if we are to be confident of the results.

norms The standards used to compare an individual's performance on a test with the performance of others.

standardization The process of establishing norms for a test by administering the test to large numbers of people who constitute a standardization sample.

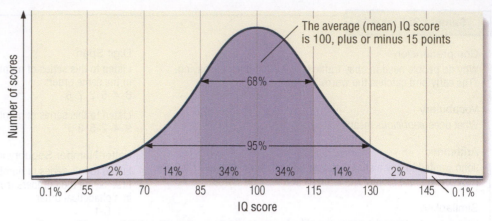

FIGURE 7.13 **Normal Distribution of IQ Scores**
The average (mean) IQ score is 100, plus or minus 15 points. The percentages shown are rounded off.

curve. Relatively few people score at either the very high or very low end of the curve, with most bunching up in the middle of the distribution.

Standardization has another meaning in test administration. It also refers to uniform procedures that must be followed to ensure that the test is used correctly.

Reliability

Reliability refers to the consistency of test scores over time. You wouldn't trust a bathroom scale that gave you different readings each time you used it. Nor would you trust an IQ test that gave you a score of 135 one day, 75 the next, and 105 the day after that. A reliable test is one that produces similar results over time. One way of assessing reliability is the *test–retest method*. With this method, the subject takes the same test again after a short interval. Because familiarity with the test questions can result in consistent performance, psychologists sometimes use the *alternate-forms method*. When this method is used, subjects are given a parallel form of the test.

Validity

Validity is the degree to which a test measures what it purports to measure. A test may be reliable—producing consistent scores over time—but not valid. For example, a test that measures head size may be reliable, yielding consistent results over time, but invalid as a measure of intelligence.

There are several types of validity. One type is *predictive validity,* the degree to which test scores accurately predict future behavior or performance. IQ tests are good predictors of academic achievement in school and performance on general aptitude tests, such as the Scholastic Aptitude Test (SAT) (Kaufman & Lichtenberger, 2006; Vock, Preckel, & Holling, 2011). But that's not all. It turns out that IQ also predicts long-term health and longevity, perhaps because people who tend to do well on IQ tests have the kinds of problem-solving and learning skills needed to acquire and practice healthier behaviors (Gottfredson & Deary, 2004). Measures of general intelligence, such as IQ tests, also predict job performance and other measures of success in adulthood (Brant et al., 2013; Greer, 2004; Kuncel, Hezlett, & Ones, 2004).

Misuses of Intelligence Tests

Even Binet, the father of the modern IQ test, was concerned that intelligence tests may be misused if teachers or parents lose interest or hope in children with low IQ scores and set low expectations for them. Low expectations can in turn become

CONCEPT 7.24
Intelligence tests are misused when children with low scores are labeled as innately incapable or inferior, when too much emphasis is placed on IQ scores, and when cultural biases in the tests put children at a disadvantage.

reliability The stability of test scores over time.

validity The degree to which a test measures what it purports to measure.

self-fulfilling prophecies, as children who are labeled as "dumb" may give up on themselves and become underachievers.

Misuse also occurs when too much emphasis is placed on IQ scores. Though intelligence tests do predict future academic performance, they are far from perfect predictors, and they should not be used as the only basis for placing children in special education programs. Some children who test poorly may be able to benefit from regular classroom instruction. Placement decisions should be based on a comprehensive assessment—one that takes into account not only the child's performance on intelligence tests but also the child's cultural and linguistic background and ability to adapt to the academic environment.

Intelligence tests may be biased against children who are not part of the White majority culture. Children from different cultural backgrounds may not have had any exposure to the types of information assessed by standard IQ tests, such as knowledge of famous individuals. Several **culture-fair tests**—tests designed to eliminate cultural biases—have been developed. They consist of nonverbal tasks that measure visual-spatial abilities and reasoning skills. However, these tests are not widely used, largely because they don't predict academic performance as well as standard IQ tests. This is not surprising, because academic success in the United States and other Western countries depends heavily on linguistic and knowledge-acquisition skills reflected in standard IQ tests. Moreover, it may be impossible to develop a purely culture-free IQ test because the skills that define intelligence depend on the values of the culture in which the test is developed (Benson, 2003). Nor should we assume that all people in the same culture have the same experience with test-taking skills or familiarity with the types of materials used on the tests. At best, we may only be able to develop *culture-reduced tests*, not entirely culture-fair or culture-free tests (Sternberg & Grigorenko, 2008).

Who's smarter—men or women? Let's call this age-old battle a draw, because evidence shows that men and women perform similarly on tests of general intelligence and problem-solving ability. However, gender differences do emerge on some specific cognitive abilities.

Gender Differences in Cognitive Abilities

Who's smarter—men or women? Before you jump to defend your gender, note that the evidence teaches us that men and women perform similarly on tests of both general intelligence (IQ) and problem-solving ability (Halpern, 2004; Saggino et al., 2014). As former American Psychological Association president Diane Halpern points out, "There is no evidence that one sex is smarter than the other" (Halpern, 2004, p. 139).

There are some gender differences in cognitive abilities and personality, but they tend to be rather small in magnitude (Zell, Krizan, & Teeter, 2015). That is, males and females tend to be much more alike in their psychological characteristics and abilities than they are different. Still, girls do hold an edge in verbal skills such as reading, writing, and spelling and they generally get higher grades in language classes (Voyer & Voyer, 2014). Boys are more likely to have problems in reading that range from reading below grade level to more severe disabilities such as **dyslexia** (American Psychiatric Association, 2013).

Boys have traditionally held an advantage in math skills, but this gender gap has narrowed so much in recent years that there is now essentially no difference in math performance between boys and girls on standardized tests and little difference in their math grades in school (Hyde, 2014; Voyer & Voyer, 2014). But an important gender difference exists in self-confidence. A worldwide study of math abilities of students in 69 countries showed that girls generally had less confidence in their math skills than boys, even though they had no less ability (Else-Quest, Hyde, & Linn, 2010; Szymenowicza & Furnham, 2011). The lead researcher, psychologist Nicole Else-Quest, commented that ". . . girls are likely to perform as well as boys when they are encouraged to succeed" (cited in American Psychological Association, 2010).

As for a male advantage, males typically outperform females in some visual-spatial skills, such as map reading and mental rotation of three-dimensional figures,

CONCEPT 7.25
Researchers find that, on average, girls outperform boys on some verbal skills, whereas boys typically do better on some visual-spatial tasks.

culture-fair tests Tests designed to eliminate cultural biases.

dyslexia A learning disorder characterized by impaired ability to read.

like the ones shown in Figure 7.1 (Campos, 2014; Sneider et al., 2015; Zell, Krizan, & Teeter, 2015). The male advantage in mental rotation is even observed in infants (Quinn & Liben, 2008). The ability to perceive relationships among three-dimensional objects may explain why both boys and men tend to excel in tasks requiring certain visual-spatial skills, such as playing chess, solving geometry problems, and finding embedded shapes within geometric figures. What might account for these gender differences? Although we cannot say with certainty, one possibility is that the male brain may be more highly specialized for certain kinds of visual-spatial skills. Male fetuses are exposed to higher levels of testosterone, which may spur development of neural connections in the brain involved in performing spatial tasks.

Women, again on average, are better skilled at remembering where objects are located, which may explain why women tend to be better at finding lost keys (Lovén, Herlitz, & Rehnman, 2011). But notice the qualifying phrase "on average." Many individuals exhibit abilities in which the opposite gender tends to excel: Many women excel in math and science, and many men shine in writing and verbal skills. In fact, greater variations in cognitive abilities exist within genders than between genders. Thus, it is important to avoid using traditional stereotypes to limit the interests and vocations that boys and girls may pursue.

We also need to take into account psychosocial factors to explain differences in cognitive skills. Parents who hold the stereotypical view that "girls are not good at math and science" may not encourage their daughters to develop math skills or take science courses. Negative expectancies may then become self-fulfilling prophecies, as they may lead girls to doubt their abilities in math or science and discourage them from developing interests in these areas. Our culture appears to train women to perform a simple deduction based on a faulty premise that math is "masculine" (Nosek, Banaji, & Greenwald, 2003):

Math = Male
Me = Female
Therefore Math ≠ Me

The narrowing of gender differences in math and science in recent years lends further credence to the influence of social or cultural factors. In all likelihood, both biological and psychosocial factors account for gender differences in cognitive abilities.

© Rhoda Sidney/The Image Works

Yes, math is me. What messages do we communicate to young women about their abilities in math and science? How might cultural expectations keep young women from developing interests in these areas?

Extremes of Intelligence: Intellectual Disability and Giftedness

Low IQ scores alone are not sufficient to determine **intellectual disability** (formerly called mental retardation), a psychological disorder in which there is a general delay in the development of intellectual and social skills. Generally speaking, a person with intellectual disability has an IQ score of approximately 70 or below and significant difficulty coping with tasks appropriate to his or her age and life situation (APA, 2013). The kinds of educational and support services needed by children with intellectual disability depend to a large extent on the severity of their intellectual deficits.

Table 7.1 shows the general capabilities of school-age children in relation to the level of intellectual disability. Most people with intellectual disability fall in a mild range of severity and are capable of meeting basic educational challenges, such as reading and solving arithmetic problems. Many children with intellectual disability are placed in regular classrooms, a practice called **mainstreaming**. Those with severe intellectual deficits require more supportive programs, which may include institutional placement, at least until the person can function in less restrictive settings in the community.

CONCEPT 7.26

Most people with intellectual disability (formerly called *mental retardation*) are able to acquire basic reading and arithmetic skills and can learn to function relatively independently and perform productive work.

intellectual disability A generalized deficit or impairment in intellectual and social skills.

mainstreaming The practice of placing children with special needs in a regular classroom environment.

Table 7.1 Levels of Intellectual Disability and Capabilities of School-Age Children

Level of Intellectual Disability (approx. IQ Range)	Approx. Percentage of Cases	Typical Capabilities of School-Age Children
Mild (50–69)	85%	Able to acquire reading and arithmetic skills to about a sixth-grade level and can later function relatively independently and engage in productive work
Moderate (35–49)	10%	Able to learn simple communication and manual skills, but have difficulty acquiring reading and arithmetic skills
Severe (20–34)	4%	Capable of basic speech and may be able to learn repetitive tasks in supervised settings
Profound (below 20)	2%	Severe delays in all areas of development, but some may learn simple tasks in supervised settings

Note: IQ ranges and prevalence data based on the following: *International Statistical Classification of Diseases and Related Health Problems, 10th Revision (ICD-10) Version for 2010.* Geneva, Switzerland: World Health Organization; King et al., 2009.

The causes of intellectual disability include both biological and environmental factors. Biological causes include genetic or chromosomal disorders, brain damage, and exposure to lead. The most common environmental cause is a deprived family environment, one lacking in verbal interactions between the child and the parents and lacking in intellectually stimulating play activities.

People at the upper end of the IQ spectrum (typically about 130 or higher) are generally classified as intellectually gifted. As children, they may benefit from enriched educational programs that allow them to progress at a faster pace than standard programs. Today, the concept of giftedness includes not only children with high IQ scores but also those with special talents, such as musical or artistic ability—skills not typically assessed by standard IQ tests. Gifted children may play musical instruments as well as highly trained adults, or solve algebra problems at an age when their peers have not yet learned to carry numbers in addition.

Theories of Intelligence

Does intelligence consist of one general ability or a cluster of different abilities? Might there be different forms of intelligence or even different intelligences? Throughout the history of modern psychology, theorists have attempted to explain intelligence. There are perhaps as many theories about it as there are theoreticians. Here we consider several major theories.

CONCEPT 7.27
Psychologists have been debating the nature of intelligence ever since intelligence tests were first introduced.

Spearman's "g": In Search of General Cognitive Ability

British psychologist Charles Spearman (1863–1945) observed that people who scored well on one test of mental ability tended to score well on other tests (Spearman, 1927). He reasoned that there must be an underlying general factor of intelligence that allows people to do well on mental tests, a factor he labeled "g" for general intelligence. However, he also believed that intelligence includes specific abilities that, along with "g," contribute to performance on individual tests. For example, a person's performance on an arithmetic test might be determined by both this general factor of intelligence and by specific mathematical abilities. Intelligence tests, such as the SBIS and the Wechsler scales, were developed to measure Spearman's concept of general intelligence, or "g," which is expressed as an IQ score.

Table 7.2 Gardner's Multiple Intelligences

Types of Intelligence	Description	Groups with High Levels of the Intelligence
Linguistic	Ability to understand and use words	Writers, poets, effective public speakers
Logical-mathematical	Ability to perform mathematical, computational, or logical operations	Scientists, engineers, computer programmers
Musical	Ability to analyze, compose, or perform music	Musicians, singers, composers
Spatial	Ability to perceive spatial relationships and arrange objects in space	Painters, architects, sculptors
Bodily-kinesthetic	Ability to control bodily movements and manipulate objects effectively	Dancers, athletes, race car drivers, mechanics
Interpersonal	Ability to relate effectively to others and to understand others' moods and motives	Industrial and political leaders, effective supervisors
Intrapersonal	Ability to understand one's own feelings and behavior (self-perception)	Psychologically well-adjusted people
Naturalist	Ability to recognize objects and patterns in nature, such as flora and fauna	Botanists, biologists, naturalists

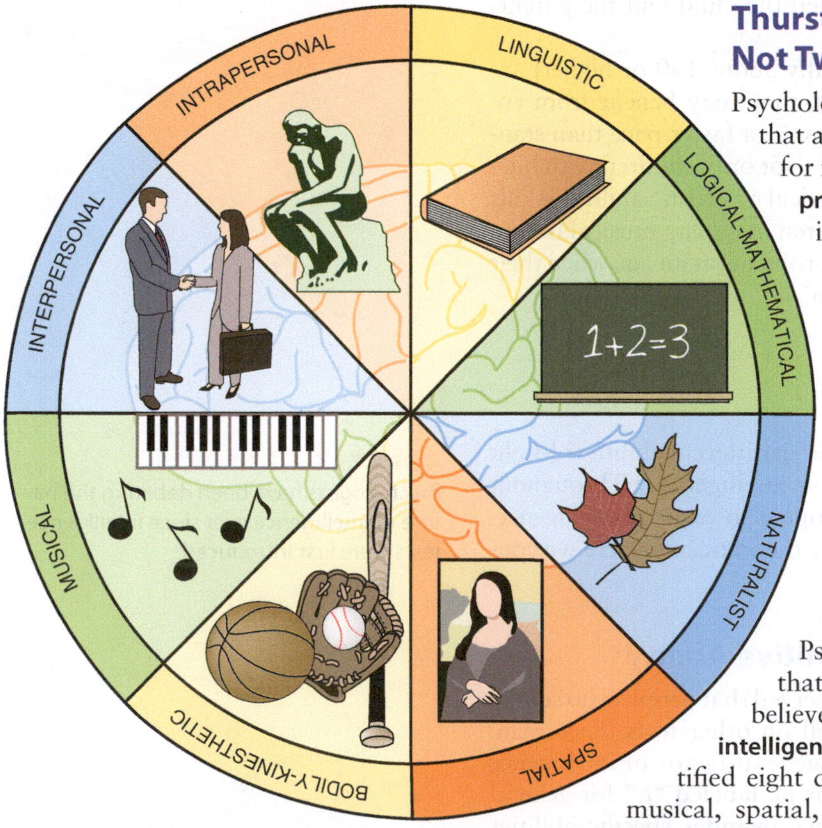

FIGURE 7.14 **Gardner's Model of Multiple Intelligences**

Source: From D. J. Martin and K. S. Loomis, *Building Teachers*, Figure 5.5, p. 136. Copyright © 2007 Wadsworth, a part of Cengage Learning. Reproduced by permission. www.academic.cengage.com.

Thurstone's Primary Mental Abilities: Not Two Factors, but Seven

Psychologist Louis L. Thurstone (1887–1955) did not believe that any one large, dominating factor like "g" could account for intelligence. Rather, his studies pointed to a set of seven **primary mental abilities**: verbal comprehension, numerical ability, memory, inductive reasoning, perceptual speed, verbal fluency, and spatial relations (Thurstone & Thurstone, 1941). Although Thurstone did not deny the existence of "g," he argued that a single IQ score does not hold much value in assessing intelligence. He and his wife, Thelma Thurstone, developed a test called the *Primary Mental Abilities Test* to measure the seven primary abilities they believed constitute intelligence.

Gardner's Model of Multiple Intelligences

Psychologist Howard Gardner (b. 1943) rejects the view that there is a single entity called "intelligence." Rather, he believes there exist different types of intelligence, **multiple intelligences**, that vary from person to person. Gardner identified eight different intelligences: linguistic, logical-mathematical, musical, spatial, bodily-kinesthetic, interpersonal, intrapersonal, and naturalist (Gardner, 1998, 2006, 2011) (see Table 7.2 and ■ Figure 7.14). These separate intelligences are believed to be independent of one another. Thus, a person could score high in some intelligences but low in others. For example, you might have a high level of linguistic, or verbal, intelligence but a lower level of intelligence in mathematics, music, or spatial relationships. Some people have good "people skills" (interpersonal intelligence) but may not be highly skilled at mathematical and logical tasks.

Gardner's model has had enormous influence, especially in educational settings (Davis et al., 2011). Many schools today seek to cultivate specific intelligences that go beyond verbal and mathematical abilities. However, a frequent criticism of the model is that it fails to account for how multiple intelligences interact with each other. Most cognitive activities involve the interaction of multiple abilities, not just one isolated type of intelligence. For example, the ability to relate effectively to others (interpersonal intelligence) depends in part on the linguistic skills needed to express oneself clearly (linguistic intelligence).

We also need to consider why we need to specify eight separate intelligences (Gardner now believes there may be nine). Might there be more or fewer? Why musical intelligence but not, say, culinary intelligence, sports intelligence, or simply practical intelligence (that is, common sense or "street smarts")? Evidence suggests that some forms of intelligence (for example, bodily-kinesthetic) stand on their own as distinctive abilities, but others show closer relationships (for example, linguistic and logical/mathematical) than Gardner's model of multiple intelligences might suggest (Visser, Ashton, & Vernon, 2006). We should also recognize that people who have a high level of intelligence in one area—verbal skills, for instance—may also excel at mathematical and logical skills.

CONCEPT 7.28
Though IQ tests were developed to measure Spearman's concepts of general intelligence, or "g," theorists like Thurstone believed that intelligence consists of a range of mental abilities that cannot be measured by one general IQ score.

CONCEPT 7.29
According to Gardner's model of multiple intelligences, we possess separate intelligences that we rely on to perform different types of tasks.

Sternberg's Triarchic Theory of Intelligence

Whereas Gardner focuses on different types of intelligence, psychologist Robert Sternberg (b. 1949) emphasizes how we bring together different aspects of our intelligence to meet the demands we face in our daily lives. Sternberg (2001a, 2003) proposes a **triarchic theory of intelligence**, which holds that intelligence has three aspects: analytic, creative, and practical (see ■ Figure 7.15).

CONCEPT 7.30
Sternberg's triarchic theory of intelligence focuses on how we bring together the analytic, creative, and practical aspects of our intelligence to solve the range of problems we face in everyday situations.

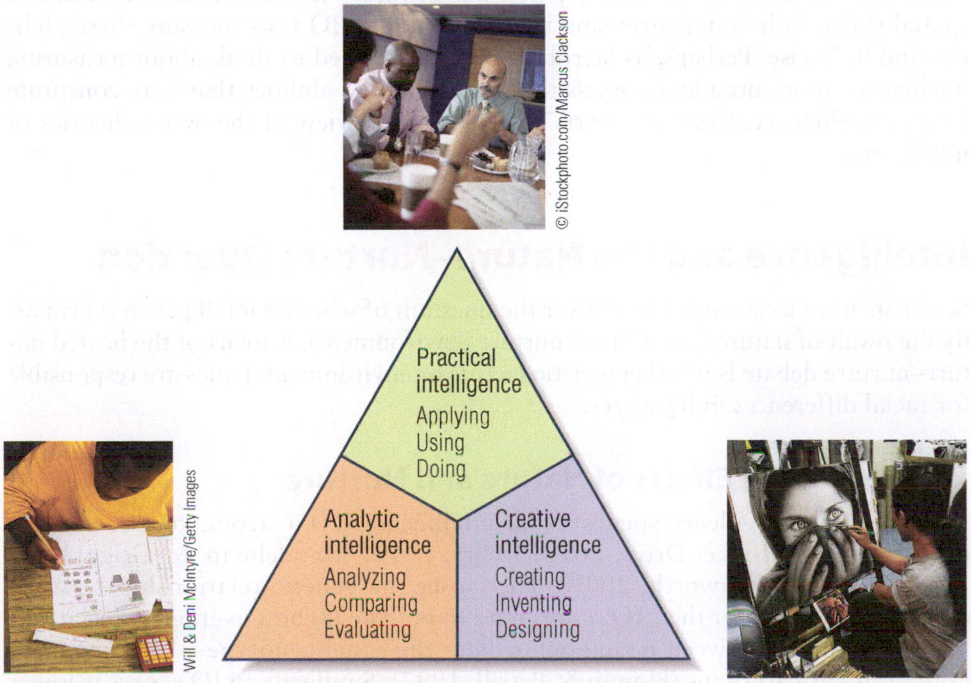

FIGURE 7.15 **Sternberg's Triarchic Model of Intelligence**

primary mental abilities Seven basic mental abilities that Thurstone believed constitute intelligence.

multiple intelligences Gardner's term for the distinct types of intelligence that characterize different forms of intelligent behavior.

triarchic theory of intelligence Sternberg's theory of intelligence that posits three aspects of intelligence: analytic, creative, and practical.

Sternberg believes that people with high levels of intelligence are better able to integrate or organize these three aspects of intelligence in their daily lives. *Analytic intelligence* is the kind of intelligence measured by traditional intelligence tests. It comes into play when you analyze and evaluate familiar problems, break them down into their component parts, and develop strategies to solve them. *Creative intelligence* allows us to invent new ways of solving unfamiliar problems. *Practical intelligence* is the ability to apply what we know to everyday life—the common sense, or "street smarts," that traditional intelligence tests fail to measure. Sternberg argues that we need all three types of intelligence to succeed in life. He also believes we need to supplement standard intelligence tests with measures of creative intelligence and practical intelligence.

Overview of Theories of Intelligence

Scientists continue to debate just how much importance to place on the general factor of intelligence, or "g," in explaining mental abilities (see Ashton & Leeb, 2014; Hampshire et al., 2012, 2014; Willis, Dumont, & Kaufman, 2011, among many others). Gardner's and Sternberg's models of intelligence take us in a different direction. They raise our awareness that traditional intelligence tests that seek to measure general intelligence fail to capture important dimensions of intelligence, such as how people use their intelligence to meet the challenges and demands they face in everyday life. Though Gardner's and Sternberg's theories prompted renewed interest in the nature of intelligence, they remain to be fully tested (Reeve & Bonaccio, 2011). In sum, we lack a consensus among psychologists about whether there exist separate types of intelligence, such as Gardner's multiple intelligences or Sternberg's practical intelligence, and just how many different types of "intelligences" there might be.

What can we conclude about these various theories of intelligence? First, it is clear that human intelligence consists of multiple abilities, perhaps even multiple intelligences. Second, we need to take into account cultural contexts in which intelligent behavior occurs. The abilities a society values determine how intelligence is defined and measured. Our society places a high value on verbal, mathematical, and spatial skills, so it is not surprising that conventional IQ tests measure these abilities and little else. Perhaps, as Sternberg argues, we need to think about measuring intelligence more broadly to assess the wider range of abilities that may constitute human intelligence. Concept Chart 7.3 offers an overview of the major theories of intelligence.

Intelligence and the Nature–Nurture Question

Scientists have long sought to answer the question of whether intelligence is primarily the result of nature (genetics) or nurture (environment). A focus of the heated nature–nurture debate is whether genetic factors or environmental ones are responsible for racial differences in IQ scores.

Separating the Effects of Nature and Nurture

A large body of evidence suggests that intelligence has a strong genetic component (Briley & Tucker-Drob, 2013; Deary, 2012; Mandelman & Grigorenko, 2011; Plomin & Haworth, 2009). The closer the genetic relationship between two people, the closer their IQ scores tend to be. The highest average correlations in IQ scores are between people who share the same genotype—MZ (monozygotic or identical) twins (Plomin & Petrill, 1997). Similarity in IQ scores is lower

Concept Chart 7.3 Theories of Intelligence

Theorist	Major Concepts	Comments
Spearman	Intelligence involves general cognitive ability, or "g."	Traditional intelligence tests are designed to measure "g" in the form of an IQ score.
Thurstone	Intelligence consists of seven primary mental abilities.	Thurstone argued that a single IQ score cannot capture the broad range of mental abilities that constitutes intelligence.
Gardner	Multiple intelligences are needed to account for the range of mental abilities.	Gardner's theory has popular appeal but does not account for the interrelationships among the different intelligences. It also does not draw the line in determining how many separate intelligences are needed to account for the full range of mental abilities.
Sternberg	Sternberg's triarchic theory proposes three aspects of intelligence: analytic, creative, and practical.	The triarchic theory is important because it provides a much-needed focus on how people use their intelligence in everyday life.

among biologically related siblings and DZ (dizygotic or fraternal) twins who share 50 percent of their genes in common, and is lower still among nonbiologically related pairs, such as adoptee siblings raised together. IQ scores of MZ twins who are raised in separate households are even more similar than those of DZ twins who are raised together.

Adoptee studies provide yet more evidence of the role of genetics in determining IQ. Studies have consistently shown that the IQ scores of adopted children are closer to those of their biological parents than to those of their adoptive parents (Bishop et al., 2003).

Heredity doesn't tell the whole story, however. Correlations in IQ scores between MZ twins are greater among those twin pairs raised together than those raised apart (Plomin & Petrill, 1997). Think about that for a moment. MZ twins share the same genes, so differences in correlations between MZ twins raised together and those raised apart points to environment factors playing a role in shaping IQ. Just what kinds of environmental influences have a bearing on a child's intellectual development? Recently, investigators pointed to such environmental influences as preschool programs, early educational interventions, and interactive reading with parents, all of which have been shown to raise intelligence levels of young children, in effect making them smarter (Protzko, Aronson, & Blair, 2013). All in all, genetic and environmental factors interact in complex ways in determining intelligence (Deary, 2012; Sternberg & Grigorenko, 2008). But just how much of intelligence is explained by genetics and how much by environment?

To break down the respective roles of heredity and environment, we first need to understand the concept of **heritability**. The heritability of a trait is the degree to which genetic factors explain the variability or differences of that trait among

© Andrey Arkusha/shutterstock.com

IQ scores of identical twins tend to be more similar than those between other siblings, but whether identical twins are raised together or apart also has a bearing on how similar their IQ scores are likely to be.

CONCEPT 7.31

Evidence indicates that genetic and environmental factors interact in complex ways in shaping intelligence.

heritability The degree to which heredity accounts for variations on a given trait within a population.

people. Intelligence (IQ) has a heritability of about 50 percent, which means that genetics explains about 50 percent of the differences (variability) among people in IQ scores (Mandelman & Grigorenko, 2011). The remaining 50 percent would be explained by nongenetic factors, such as environment influences. But let's be careful about how to interpret these findings. A heritability of 50 percent does not mean that 50 percent of any given person's IQ results from genetic factors and the rest from environmental or other influences. We need to bear in mind that heritability estimates apply only to the population on the whole, not to any given individual in the population.

Racial Differences in IQ

White Americans of European background typically score higher on IQ tests than African Americans—about 15 points higher, on the average (Fagan & Holland, 2002). This racial gap in IQ scores exists even when differences in income levels are taken into account. But are these racial differences in IQ genetic or environmental in origin?

Increasing evidence points to environmental, rather than genetic, factors in explaining racial or ethnic group differences in IQ (Cottrell, Newman, & Roisman, 2015; Nisbett et al., 2012b). For one thing, ethnic minority children from disadvantaged backgrounds may lack exposure to books and other educational materials to develop their intellectual potential. For another, they may lack the kinds of opportunities that more advantaged children have to develop the types of skills tested on traditional IQ tests, such as vocabulary skills and abstract reasoning skills.

The racial gap in IQ has also narrowed over the past few decades, a trend that cannot easily be explained by genetic factors (Nisbett et al., 2012b; te Nijenhuis, 2013). We need to look at environmental influences to explain the narrowing of the racial gap in IQ scores, such as increased accessibility to enriched educational programs for children from different backgrounds (Nisbett et al., 2012a, b). Consider too that average IQs of population groups change over time. IQ scores overall in the United States and worldwide have been rising steadily for more than a hundred years, about three IQ points per decade, most probably because of favorable environmental changes such as improved nutrition and expanded educational opportunities (Flynn, 2013; Pietschnig & Voracek, 2015; Trahan et al., 2014).

Perhaps the most telling evidence of environmental influences comes from a classic study of African American and interracial children who were adopted and raised by upper-middle-class White American families. The IQ scores of these adopted children were about 15 points higher on the average than would be expected of the average African American child from a socially disadvantaged background (Waldman, Weinberg, & Scarr, 1994). The investigators attributed the better performance of the African American adoptees to the social and cultural effects of being raised in an environment that places a strong value on educational achievement—effects that basically canceled out the oft-cited 15-point gap in IQ between these groups.

We still have much to learn about the role of genetics in intelligence. As psychologist Robert Sternberg and his colleagues argue, we cannot yet say how large a role genetic factors may play in determining racial or ethnic differences

CONCEPT 7.32

A gap between the IQ scores of African Americans and Euro-Americans has provoked a heated debate over the origins of these differences.

Parental emphasis on education can have an important bearing on a child's intellectual development.

Gallo Images - Anthony Strack/Getty Images

in intelligence (Sternberg, Grigorenko, & Kidd, 2005). Whatever the role of heredity might be, environmental factors make an important contribution to explaining ethnic/racial gaps in IQ. "Changing the environment," says Michael Rutter, a leading researcher in the field, "can make an enormous difference" in a child's intelligence (cited in Kirp, 2006, p. 15). Unfortunately, children living in deprived or chaotic family circumstances may fail to reach their genetic potentials.

Let us also note that group differences in IQ tell us nothing about individual potential. Any group, no matter what its average IQ scores may be, can produce its share of intellectually gifted people. We also need to recognize that children from groups such as African Americans that place a strong value on creative expression may not give the obvious answers to questions on IQ tests. Psychologist Janet Helms (1992) points out that the use of different reasoning or test-taking strategies is not evidence of lack of intelligence.

MODULE REVIEW 7.3 Intelligence

Recite It

10. Define intelligence, **identify** different tests of intelligence, and **evaluate** the characteristics of a good test of intelligence.

One widely used definition holds that intelligence is the capacity to act (a) _____, think rationally, and deal effectively with the environment.
Standardized intelligence tests, such as the (b) _____-Binet Intelligence Scale and the (c) _____ scales of intelligence, are generally used to measure intelligence.
The basic requirements of a good intelligence test are standardization (generation of (d) _____ based on samples representative of the population), (e) _____ (stability of test scores over time), and (f) _____ (the test's ability to measure what it purports to measure).

11. Evaluate gender differences in cognitive abilities.

Girls tend to outperform boys on some (g) _____ skills, such as reading, writing, and spelling. Boys hold an edge in some (h) _____-_____ tasks and math skills, though the gap in math abilities is narrowing. However, boys and girls perform similarly on tests of general (i) _____ and problem-solving skills.
Intelligence tests are (j) _____ when children with low scores are labeled as innately incapable or inferior, when too much emphasis is placed on

IQ scores, and when (k) _____ biases in tests put children from diverse cultural backgrounds at a disadvantage.

12. Describe the characteristics of the two extremes of intelligence and the misuses of intelligence tests.

Intellectual disability is generally identified on the basis of a low IQ score (typically (l) _____ or below) and delayed or impaired social skills. Giftedness is usually associated with IQ scores of about (m) _____ or above or with evidence of special talents.

13. Describe the major theories of intelligence and **evaluate** the roles of heredity and environment in intelligence.

Major theories of intelligence include Spearman's concept of general intelligence, or (n) _____ (o) _____ theory of primary mental abilities, Gardner's model of (p) _____ intelligences, and Sternberg's (q) _____ theory. Some theorists favor the view that intelligence consists of a general cognitive ability, whereas others favor a model based on multiple abilities or even multiple intelligences.
Most experts believe that intelligence is based on a complex interaction of (r) _____ (genetic influences) and (s) _____ (environmental influences).

Recall It

1. Match the terms on the top with the definitions below:

   I. standardization
   II. validity
   III. mainstreaming
   IV. Spearman's "g"
   a. a test's ability to measure what it is designed to measure
   b. the practice of placing children with mild levels of intellectual disability in regular classrooms
   c. an underlying general factor of intelligence
   d. the generation of test norms based on representative samples of the population

2. Problems with intelligence tests include potential ___ biases in test content.

3. What is the name of Sternberg's theory of intelligence?

4. In recent years, IQ scores have been

   a. falling in many countries, but rising in the United States.
   b. rising in many countries, but falling in the United States.
   c. falling in the United States and many other countries.
   d. rising in the United States and many other countries.

Think About It

■ Do you believe that conventional intelligence tests are culturally biased? Why or why not?

■ In what ways are intelligence tests useful? In what ways might they be misused?

Recite It answers placed at the end of chapter.

THINKING CRITICALLY ABOUT PSYCHOLOGY

Based on your reading of this chapter, answer the following questions. Then, to evaluate your progress in developing critical thinking skills, compare your answers to the sample answers found in Appendix A.

1. An ambulance is heading toward the hospital on a country road, carrying an injured man who needs emergency surgery. When the ambulance comes around a bend, the driver notices a large flock of sheep blocking the road. The driver starts pounding on the horn and sounding the siren to part the sheep, but to no effect. A medical technician jumps out of the ambulance and tries to shove the rearmost sheep out of the way, hoping the others will follow. The driver starts screaming at the shepherd, imploring him to clear the road. The shepherd also starts screaming, but the sheep just keep on bleating. Suddenly, the shepherd raises his hand to signal the ambulance to stop. He then succeeds in clearing a path for the ambulance, but not by parting the sheep or by guiding the ambulance past them (adapted from Levine, 1994):

   a. How did the shepherd clear the road for the ambulance?

   b. What impediment to problem solving does the behavior of the medical technician represent?

2. John receives an inheritance, which he decides to invest in the stock market. Like many other investors, he decides to open an online trading account. At first, he does well. Then he begins to trade more actively, buying and selling stocks almost daily. His losses soon begin to mount. Concerned, he consults a financial adviser, who asks him about his trading strategy. John recounts that he buys stocks in companies he hears positive things about and sells stocks in companies whenever he notices negative news items.

   a. What cognitive error(s) in decision making might explain John's losses in the stock market?

   b. How would you advise him to avoid such errors in the future?

Answers to Brainteasers (p. 253)

1. There are 12 two-cent stamps, because a dozen of anything is 12.
2. You are holding a 50-cent piece and a nickel. One of the two coins (the 50-cent piece) is not a nickel.
3. There are 11 cows left. All but 11 died.

Recite It Answers for Chapter 7

Module 7.1 **1.** (a) representation; (b) manipulation, **2.** (c) images; (d) words; (e) concept formation, **3.** (f) Logical; (g) natural, **4.** (h) insight; (i) trial; (j) error; (k) algorithms; (l) heuristics, **5.** (m) sets; (n) functional; (o) confirmation; (p) representativeness; (q) availability, **6.** (r) Convergent; (s) divergent; (t) combination; (u) expansion, **7.** (v) questioning; (w) testing   **Module 7.2** **8.** (a) phonemes; (b) syntax; (c) semantics; (d) one-word; (e) Chomsky; (f) nurture, **9.** (g) think; (h) perceive; (i) language   **Module 7.3** **10.** (a) purposefully; (b) Stanford; (c) Wechsler; (d) norms; (e) reliability; (f) validity, **11.** (g) verbal; (h) visual-spatial; (i) intelligence; (j) misused; (k) cultural, **12.** (l) 70; (m) 130, **13.** (n) "g"; (o) Thurstone's; (p) multiple; (q) triarchic; (r) nature; (s) nurture

"Never, ever, think outside the box."

Thinking

What Is Thinking?

- Thinking is the mental representation and manipulation of information.
- We can represent information in the form of images, words, and concepts used to categorize objects and events.
- Thinking takes many forms, including problem solving, decision making, and creativity.

Examples of Problem-Solving Strategies

- **Heuristics:** Rules of thumb for solving problems and making decisions
- **Algorithms:** Step-by-step recipes for solving problems

Mental Roadblocks to Problem Solving and Decision Making

- **Mental Sets:** Using what's worked before, but may not work now
- **Functional Fixedness:** Failing to see new uses for familiar objects
- **Confirmation Bias:** Filtering evidence to confirm prior beliefs
- **Representativeness Heuristic:** Basing decisions on a limited sample
- **Availability Heuristic:** Basing decisions on what most easily comes to mind

Processes in Creative Thought

- **Divergent Thinking:** Conceiving new ideas and uses for familiar objects
- **Analogy:** Using an analogy to draw upon knowledge of solutions to similar problems
- **Conceptual Combination:** Putting together two or more different concepts to form new ideas or applications
- **Conceptual Expansion:** Taking existing concepts and expanding them to new uses

Language

Parts of Language

- **Phonemes:** Basic units of sound in a language
- **Morphemes:** Basic units of meaning in a language
- **Semantics:** Rules governing meaning of words
- **Syntax:** Rules of grammar for ordering words

Factors in Language Development

- **Biological Capacity for Speech:** The brain is prewired for speech
- **Experience with Human Speech:** Development of language depends on hearing human speech

Intelligence

Defining Intelligence

- Thinking Rationally
- Acting Purposefully
- Dealing Effectively with Environmental Demands

Standardized Tests of Intelligence

- **Widely Used Tests:** Stanford-Binet Intelligence Scale, Wechsler scales of intelligence
- **Standards of Good Intelligence Tests:** Reliability, validity, and norming (standardization)

Theories of Intelligence

- **Spearman's "g:"** General ability
- **Thurstone's Primary Mental Abilities:** Seven primary abilities
- **Gardner's Multiple Intelligences:** Multiple forms of intelligence, not just one
- **Sternberg's Triarchic Theory:** Analytic intelligence, creative intelligence, practical intelligence

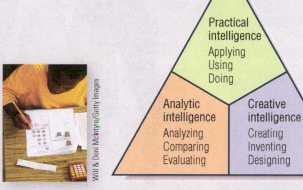

Practical intelligence
Applying
Using
Doing

Analytic intelligence
Analyzing
Comparing
Evaluating

Creative intelligence
Creating
Inventing
Designing

Extremes of Intelligence

- **Intellectual Disability:** Low IQ and general delay in development of intellectual and social skills
- **Giftedness:** High IQ or special talents not measured by IQ tests

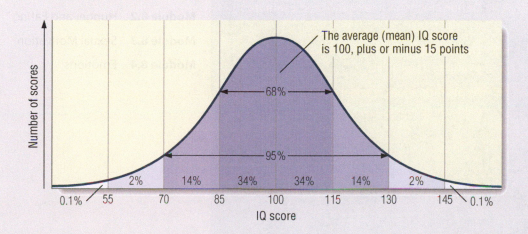

The average (mean) IQ score is 100, plus or minus 15 points

Number of scores

68%

95%

0.1%   2%   14%   34%   34%   14%   2%   0.1%

55   70   85   100   115   130   145

IQ score

LEARNING OBJECTIVES

After studying this chapter, you will be able to . . .

1 **Define** the concept of motivation and **describe** several major theories of motivation.

2 **Identify** different types of psychosocial needs.

3 **Describe** Maslow's hierarchy of needs and **identify** the needs at each level in the hierarchy.

4 **Explain** how hunger and appetite are regulated.

5 **Identify** causal factors in obesity.

6 **Identify** and **describe** the types and causes of eating disorders.

7 **Identify** and **describe** the four phases of the sexual response cycle.

8 **Describe** how researchers characterize the continuum of sexual orientation.

9 **Describe** the causes of sexual dysfunctions.

10 **Identify** the basic components of emotions and the six basic emotional expressions.

11 **Describe** the roles of gender and cultural factors in emotions.

12 **Identify** factors involved in human happiness.

13 **Explain** how the brain processes emotions.

14 **Describe** the major theories of emotion and **identify** the major theorists.

15 **Define** emotional intelligence and **evaluate** its importance.

16 **Describe** the polygraph technique and **evaluate** its reliability.

17 **Apply** techniques of anger management for controlling anger.

Michael Steele/Getty Images

PREVIEW

Motivation and Emotion

8

The Woman who Showed No Fear

Imagine what it would be like to be unable to experience fear—to be mildly amused when others at a 3D horror movie are jumping out of their seats or to remain calm even in the face of an immediate threat to your life. Let me introduce you to a person without any fear, a 44-year-old woman referred to in a medical journal as S.M. (Feinstein et al., 2010; Neuroscience News, 2010).

A team of researchers tried as they might to shake her up, exposing her to situations that would frighten most people. They exposed her to snakes and spiders and even took her to one of the world's scariest haunted houses. They had her watch a series of horror movies. But for all these tests and measures, one thing remained constant: She showed no fear. She also recounted an experience in which she had been held up at knifepoint in a darkened park, but didn't feel any fear. She was able, however, to experience a range of other emotions, including happiness and sadness.

The case study of S.M. illustrates the close connections between brain and behavior. The researchers who studied S.M. believe her fearlessness was due to the lack of an amygdala, small structure in the brain's limbic system that plays a pivotal role in triggering fear. In S.M.'s case, the amygdala had failed to develop because of a rare genetic condition.

In this chapter, we study fear and other emotions. The concepts of emotion and motivation are closely connected and actually share a common Latin root, *movere,* meaning "to move." Both motives and emotions move us to act or to prepare for action. The hunger motive, for example, moves us toward finding and consuming food. The emotion of fear, perhaps our most basic emotion, motivates us to avoid threatening objects or situations, whereas love, the emotion that "makes the world go round," moves us toward approaching objects of our desire. Anger prompts us to respond aggressively to provocation. In this chapter, we explore these motivating factors in our lives—our motives and our emotions.

Did you know that...

- People tend to eat more food when it is served in larger portion sizes or on larger plates? (p. 289)
- Among children, Ronald McDonald is the second most recognized personality figure, after Santa Claus? (p. 290)
- Obesity shaves off as many as eight years from the average person's lifespan? (p. 289)
- In a recent study, people who counted their bites lost weight? (p. 292)
- In a recent study, a group of college women who spent more time on Facebook showed higher levels of problem eating behaviors? (p. 294)
- The male sex hormone testosterone energizes sexual drives in both men and women? (p. 300)
- People in different cultures smile differently? (p. 306)
- Money does not breed happiness? (p. 307)
- Practicing smiling can lift your mood? (p. 309)
- Responding without thinking can be a lifesaver in some situations? (p. 312)

8.1 Motivation: The "Whys" of Behavior

1 **Define** the concept of motivation and **describe** several major theories of motivation.

2 **Identify** different types of psychosocial needs.

3 **Describe** Maslow's hierarchy of needs and **identify** the needs at each level in the hierarchy.

CONCEPT 8.1

Motivation refers to the "whys" of behavior—factors that activate, direct, and sustain goal-directed behavior.

The term **motivation** refers to factors that *activate*, *direct*, and *sustain* goal-directed behavior. If, after a few hours of not eating, you get up from your chair and go to the kitchen to fix yourself a snack, we might infer that the *motive* for your behavior is hunger. The hunger motive activates your behavior (causing you to stand), directs it (moving you toward the kitchen), and sustains it (as you make yourself a snack and consume it) until you've achieved your goal (satisfying your hunger).

Motives are the "whys" of behavior—the needs or wants that drive behavior and explain why we do what we do. We don't actually observe a motive; rather, we infer that one exists based on the behavior we observe.

In this module, we focus on the biological and psychological sources of motivation and the various theories psychologists have constructed to explain motivated behavior. None of these theories offers a complete explanation of motivated behavior, but each contributes something to our understanding of the "whys" of behavior.

Biological Sources of Motivation

We need oxygen to breathe, food for energy, water to remain hydrated, and protection from the elements. These basic biological needs motivate much of our behavior. Biological needs are inborn. We don't learn to breathe or to become hungry or thirsty. Nonetheless, learning and experience influence how we satisfy our biological needs, especially our need for food. Eating tamales or mutton stew might satisfy our hunger, but our cultural background and learning experiences influence our food choices and the ways in which we prepare and consume it.

CONCEPT 8.2

Instinct theorists believe that humans and other animals are motivated by instincts—fixed, inborn patterns of response that are specific to members of a particular species. However, most psychologists reject instincts as a motivator of complex human behavior.

Instincts: Behavior Programmed by Nature

Birds build nests, and salmon return upstream to their birthplaces to spawn. They do not acquire these behaviors through experience or by attending nest-building or spawning schools. These are **instinctive behaviors**—fixed, inborn patterns of response that are specific to members of a particular species. **Instinct theory** holds that behavior is motivated by instincts.

Though we can find many examples of instinctive behaviors in other species, do instincts motivate human behavior? One theorist who thought so was Sigmund Freud, who believed that human behavior is motivated primarily by sexual and aggressive instincts (see Chapters 1 and 11). Another was William James (1890), the father of American psychology, who compiled a list of 37 instincts that he believed could explain much of human behavior. His list included physical instincts, such as sucking, and mental instincts, such as curiosity, jealousy, and even cleanliness. Other early psychologists, notably William McDougall (1908), expanded on James's list. The list kept growing and growing, so much so that by the 1920s, it had ballooned to some 10,000 instincts covering a wide range of human behavior (Bernard, 1924).

motivation Factors that activate, direct, and sustain goal-directed behavior.

motives Needs or wants that drive goal-directed behavior.

instinctive behaviors Genetically programmed, innate patterns of response that are specific to members of a particular species.

instinct theory The belief that behavior is motivated by instinct.

The instinct theory of human motivation has long been out of favor. One reason for its decline is that the list of instincts simply grew too large to be useful. Another is that explaining behavior on the basis of instincts is merely a way of describing it, not explaining it. For example, saying a person is lazy because of a laziness instinct or stingy because of a stinginess instinct doesn't really explain the person's behavior. It merely attaches a label to it. Perhaps most important, psychologists recognized that human behavior is much more variable and flexible than would be the case if it were determined by instinct. Moreover, instinct theory fails to account for the important roles of culture and learning in determining human behavior. Though instincts may account for some stereotypical behavior in other animals, most psychologists reject the view that instincts motivate complex human behavior.

Needs and Drives: Maintaining a Steady Internal State

By the early 1950s, **drive theory** had replaced instinct theory as the major model of human motivation. Its foremost proponent, psychologist Clark Hull (1943, 1952), believed we have biological needs that demand satisfaction, such as the needs for food, water, and sleep. A **need** is a state of deprivation or deficiency. A **drive** is a state of bodily tension, such as hunger or thirst, arising from an unmet need. The satisfaction of a drive is called **drive reduction**.

Drive theory is based on the principles of *homeostasis,* the tendency of the body to maintain a steady internal state (see Chapter 2). Homeostatic mechanisms in the body monitor temperature, oxygen, and blood sugar, and maintain them at steady levels. According to drive theory, whenever homeostasis is disturbed, drives activate the behavior needed to restore a steady balance. For example, when our blood sugar level drops because we haven't eaten in a while, we become hungry. Hunger is the drive that motivates us to seek nourishment, which restores homeostasis. Although drive theory focuses on biological needs, some needs, such as the needs for comfort and safety, have a psychological basis.

Though needs and drives are related, they are distinct from each other. We may have a bodily need for a certain vitamin but not become aware of it until we develop a vitamin deficiency disorder. In other words, the need may exist in the absence of a corresponding drive. Moreover, the strength of a need and the drive to satisfy it may differ. People who fast for religious or other reasons may find they are less hungry on the second or third day of a fast than on the first, even though their need for food is even greater.

Unlike instinct theory, drive theory posits an important role for learning, especially operant conditioning (discussed in Chapter 5). We learn responses (such as ordering a pizza when we're hungry) that are reinforced by drive reduction. A behavior that results in drive reduction is more likely to be repeated the next time the need arises. Drives may also be acquired through experience. Biological drives, such as hunger, thirst, and sexual desire, are called **primary drives** because they are considered inborn; drives that are the result of experience are called **secondary drives**. For example, a drive to achieve monetary wealth is not something we are born with; we acquire it as a secondary drive because we learn that money can be used to satisfy many primary and other secondary drives.

Optimal Level of Arousal: What's Optimal for You?

Drive theory focuses on drives that satisfy survival needs, such as needs for food and water. But classic experiments by psychologist Harry Harlow and his colleagues challenged the notion that all drives satisfy basic survival needs. When they placed a mechanical puzzle in a monkey's cage, they found that the monkey began manipulating it and taking it apart, even though the animal didn't receive any food or other obvious reinforcement for its efforts (Harlow, Harlow, & Meyer, 1950). Human babies, too,

CONCEPT 8.3
Drive theorists maintain that we are motivated by drives that arise from biological needs that demand satisfaction.

drive theory The belief that behavior is motivated by drives that arise from biological needs that demand satisfaction.

need A state of deprivation or deficiency.

drive A state of bodily tension, such as hunger or thirst, that arises from an unmet need.

drive reduction Satisfaction of a drive.

primary drives Innate drives, such as hunger, thirst, and sexual desire, that arise from basic biological needs.

secondary drives Drives that are learned or acquired through experience, such as the drive to achieve monetary wealth.

CONCEPT 8.4
Stimulus motives prod organisms to explore their environments and manipulate objects.

CONCEPT 8.5
Arousal theory postulates a biologically based need to maintain stimulation at an optimal level.

🔗 **CONCEPT LINK**

People with antisocial personalities may become quickly bored with routine activities because of a biological predisposition that leads them to crave higher levels of stimulation to maintain their optimum level of arousal. See Module 13.6.

manipulate objects placed before them. They shake rattles, turn knobs, push buttons on activity toys, and mouth new objects, even though none of these behaviors is connected with satisfaction of their basic survival needs.

The work of Harlow and others suggests that humans and many other animals may have innate, biologically based needs for exploration and activity. These needs, which prod organisms to explore their environments and manipulate objects—especially unusual or novel objects—are called **stimulus motives**. Stimulus motives don't disappear as we get older. Adults seek to touch and manipulate interesting objects, as attested to by the many grown-ups who try their hand at the latest gizmos displayed at stores like Brookstone.

Other basic drives like hunger motivate behaviors that lead to reduced states of bodily arousal. For example, when we are hungry, the brain creates a state of heightened arousal that lasts until we satisfy our hunger; after eating, we may feel tranquil or sleepy. However, stimulus motives instigate behaviors that lead to increased, not decreased, arousal. In other words, even when our basic needs for food and water are met, we are motivated to seek out stimulation that heightens our level of arousal.

According to some theorists, stimulus motives represent a biologically based need that serves to maintain the organism at an *optimal* level of arousal (Hebb, 1955; Zuckerman, 1980). This theory, called **arousal theory**, holds that whenever the level of stimulation dips below an organism's optimal level, the organism seeks ways of increasing it. When stimulation exceeds an optimal level, the organism seeks ways of toning it down.

The optimal level of arousal varies from person to person. Some people require a steady diet of highly stimulating activities, such as mountain climbing, snowboarding, bungee jumping, or parasailing. Others are satisfied to spend quiet evenings at home, curled up with a good book or relaxing by watching TV.

People with a high need for arousal see life as an adventure. To maintain their optimal level of stimulation, they seek exciting experiences and thrills. Psychologist Marvin Zuckerman (2004) calls such people *sensation seekers*. Sensation seekers tend to get bored easily and may have difficulty restraining their impulses. They may limit their sensation seeking to reasonably safe activities, but the desire for stimulation leads some to engage in risky behaviors, or develop problems with alcohol or drugs, or engage in illegal activities (see, for example, Cicognani & Zani, 2011; Weiland et al., 2012). It's no surprise that surfers tend to score higher than golfers on measures of sensation seeking (Diehm & Armatas, 2004). Sensation seeking appears to have a strong genetic component—the taste for thrills may be something we are born with (Derringer et al., 2010).

Psychological Sources of Motivation

If motivation were simply a matter of maintaining homeostasis in our bodies, we would rest quietly until prompted again by hunger, thirst, or some other biological drive. But we don't sit idly by when our bellies are full and our other biological needs are met. We are also motivated by psychological needs, such as the need for friendship or achievement. We perceive certain goals as desirable or rewarding even though attaining them will not satisfy any biological needs. Clearly, such motivated behaviors are best addressed by considering the role of psychological factors in motivation. These factors include incentives and psychosocial needs.

Incentives: The "Pull" Side of Motivation

According to **incentive theory**, our attraction to particular goals or objects motivates much of our behavior. **Incentives** are rewards or other stimuli that motivate us to act. The attraction, or "pull," exerted by an incentive stems from our perception that it can satisfy a need or is in itself desirable.

stimulus motives Internal states that prompt inquisitive, stimulation-seeking, and exploratory behavior.

arousal theory The belief that whenever the level of stimulation dips below an organism's optimal level, the organism seeks ways of increasing it.

incentive theory The belief that our attraction to particular goals or objects motivates much of our behavior.

incentives Rewards or other stimuli that motivate us to act.

In contrast to drive theory, which explains how unmet biological needs push us in the direction of satisfying them, incentive theory holds that incentives motivate us by pulling us toward them. Incentive theory thus focuses on the lure, or "pull," of incentives in motivating behavior, rather than the "push" of internal need states or drives. You may crave a scrumptious-looking dessert even though you've just eaten a full meal and no longer feel "pushed" by the drive of hunger. You may feel drawn to buy the latest fashions or technological gizmos even though obtaining these objects will not satisfy any biological need.

The strength of the "pull" that a goal or reward exerts on our behavior is its **incentive value**. Incentive values are influenced by many factors, including an individual's learning experiences and expectancies. We place more value on a goal if we have learned from past experience to associate it with pleasure and if we expect it will be rewarding when we obtain it. Many employers spur employee productivity by offering them such incentives as bonuses, merit pay increases, stock options, and awards. Marketers manipulate the incentive value of the products they want us to buy. They try to persuade us that to be cool, healthy, sexy, or successful, we need to use their products.

Cultural influences play a large part in determining incentive values. Some cultures place great value on individual achievement and accumulation of wealth. Others place a premium on meeting obligations to one's family, religious group, employer, or community.

What incentives motivate your behavior—a college diploma, wealth, the man or woman of your dreams, status, or respect of your family or community? Which incentives have the strongest "pull" on your behavior?

CONCEPT 8.6
Incentives motivate us by exerting a pull on our behavior; their strength varies in relation to the value we place on them.

incentive value The strength of the "pull" of a goal or reward.

Try This Out   Are You a Sensation Seeker?

Do you pursue thrills and adventure? Or do you prefer quiet evenings at home? To evaluate whether you fit the profile of a sensation seeker, circle the number on each line that best describes you.

Interpreting your responses. Responses above 5 indicate a high level of sensation seeking; those 5 or below indicate a low level. On which side of the continuum do your responses lie? Draw a line connecting your responses. The farther to the right the line falls, the stronger your personality fits the profile of a sensation seeker.

Prefer a job in one location	1 2 3 4 5 6 7 8 9 10	Prefer a job with lots of travel
Prefer staying out of the cold	1 2 3 4 5 6 7 8 9 10	Enjoy a brisk walk on a cold day
Prefer being with familiar people	1 2 3 4 5 6 7 8 9 10	Prefer meeting new people
Like to play it safe	1 2 3 4 5 6 7 8 9 10	Like living "on the edge"
Would prefer not to try hypnosis	1 2 3 4 5 6 7 8 9 10	Would like to try hypnosis
Would prefer not to try parachute jumping	1 2 3 4 5 6 7 8 9 10	Would like to try parachute jumping
Prefer quiet evenings at home	1 2 3 4 5 6 7 8 9 10	Prefer going out dancing at night
Prefer a safe and secure life	1 2 3 4 5 6 7 8 9 10	Prefer experiencing as much as possible
Prefer calm and controlled people	1 2 3 4 5 6 7 8 9 10	Prefer people who are a bit wild
Like to sleep in a comfortable room with a good bed	1 2 3 4 5 6 7 8 9 10	Enjoy camping out
Prefer avoiding risky activities	1 2 3 4 5 6 7 8 9 10	Like to do things that are a little dangerous

Source: Adapted from Zuckerman, 1980.

CONCEPT 8.7
Many psychologists believe we are motivated to satisfy not only biological needs, but also psychosocial needs, such as the need for achievement.

Jeff Greenberg/PhotoEdit

How strong is your need for achievement—your need not just to succeed, but to excel?

psychosocial needs Needs that reflect interpersonal aspects of motivation, such as the need for friendship or achievement.

need for achievement The need to excel in one's endeavors.

extrinsic motivation Motivation reflecting a desire for external rewards, such as wealth or the respect of others.

intrinsic motivation Motivation reflecting a desire for internal gratification, such as the self-satisfaction derived from accomplishing a particular goal.

achievement motivation The motive or desire to achieve success.

avoidance motivation The motive or desire to avoid failure.

hierarchy of needs Maslow's concept that there is an order to human needs, which starts with basic biological needs and progresses to self-actualization.

Psychosocial Needs

The fulfillment of basic biological needs is necessary for survival, but human beings seek more out of life than mere survival. We are social creatures who are motivated to satisfy **psychosocial needs** (also called *interpersonal needs*). One example is the need to be with other people (also called the *need for affiliation*). This need motivates us to seek out social contacts with others, form social relationships, and belong to groups. Here we focus on the most widely studied of the psychosocial needs—the need to excel at what we do, which is known as the **need for achievement**.

Some people strive relentlessly to get ahead, to earn vast sums of money, to invent, to create—in short, to achieve. People with a high need for achievement are found in many walks of life, from business and professional sports to academia and the arts. They have a strong desire to excel at what they do. They are driven and ambitious and take pride in accomplishing their goals.

People with a high need for achievement set challenging but realistic goals for themselves, according to Harvard psychologist David McClelland (1958, 1985). Goals that are too easily achieved are of no interest to them, nor are goals that are patently unobtainable. Such people may not always succeed, but they take failure in stride and keep pushing ahead. By contrast, people with a low need for achievement are motivated by a desire to avoid failure. They set goals either so low that anyone can achieve them or so unrealistically high that no one can achieve them. If the bar is set too high, who can blame them if they fail? When they meet with failure, they are more likely to quit than to persevere.

The need for achievement is driven by *extrinsic motivation, intrinsic motivation,* or both (Ryan & Deci, 2000; Story et al., 2009). **Extrinsic motivation** reflects a desire for external rewards, such as money or the respect of one's peers or family. **Intrinsic motivation** reflects a desire for internal gratification, such as the self-satisfaction or pleasure derived from accomplishing a particular goal or performing a certain task. In other words, extrinsic motivation is a "means to an end," whereas intrinsic motivation is an "end in itself" (Schunk, Pintrich, & Meece, 2008).

In achievement situations, we may be pulled in opposite directions by two kinds of motives: **achievement motivation** (the desire to achieve success) and **avoidance motivation** (the desire to avoid failure). Achievement motivation leads us to undertake challenges that run the risk of failure but that may also lead to success. People with a higher need for achievement tend to be more persistent in their efforts and work harder toward achieving their goals than those with lower achievement motivation. On the other hand, avoidance motivation may reduce the chance of failure, but at the cost of limiting the likelihood of success. People who are high in avoidance motivation tend to avoid taking chances that might result in failure. Avoidance motivation prompts them to stick with the sure and safe path. Not surprisingly, researchers link higher levels of avoidance motivation to more negative outcomes, including lower levels of emotional well-being (Roskes et al., 2014).

Achievement motivation develops early in life and is strongly influenced by parents. Children who develop a high need for achievement typically have parents who encourage them to become independent, to attempt difficult tasks, and to set high standards for performance. They reward their children by praising them or using other reinforcements for their persistence at achieving difficult tasks and encourage them to strive to achieve even more challenging tasks (Bempechat & Shernoff, 2012; Dweck, 1997).

The Hierarchy of Needs: Ordering Needs from the Lowest to the Highest Level of Human Experience

We have seen that both biological and psychological needs play important roles in human motivation. But how do these needs relate to each other? We now consider a model that bridges both sources of motivation—the **hierarchy of needs** developed by humanistic psychologist Abraham Maslow (1943, 1970) (see ■ Figure 8.1).

Maslow's hierarchy of basic needs consists of five levels: (1) *physiological needs,* such as hunger and thirst; (2) *safety needs,* such as the need for secure housing; (3) *love and belongingness needs,* such as the need for intimate relationships; (4) *esteem needs,* such as the need for the respect of one's peers; and (5) *the need for self-actualization,* which is a need that motivates people to fulfill their unique potentials and become all they are capable of being. In Maslow's view, our needs are ordered in such a way that we are motivated to meet basic needs before moving upward in the hierarchy. In other words, once we fill our bellies, we strive to meet higher-order needs, such as our needs for security, love, achievement, and **self-actualization**.

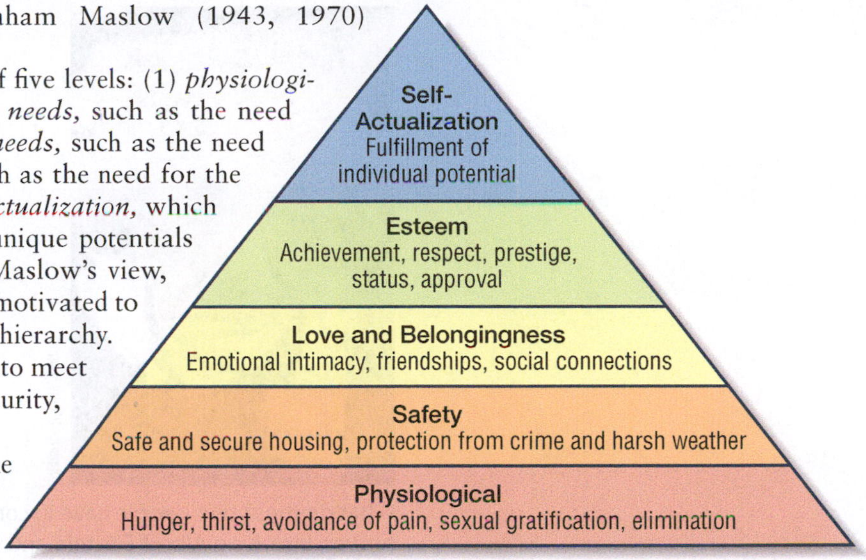

Because no two people are perfectly alike, the drive for self-actualization leads people in different directions (Kenrick et al., 2010). For some, self-actualization may mean creating works of art; for others, it means striving on the playing field, in the classroom, or in the corporate setting. Not all of us climb to the top of the hierarchy; we don't all seek self-actualization. We shouldn't think of self-actualization as an end state, but rather as a journey in pursuit of one's inner potential. What might your own inner potential be? Are you seeking to fulfill that need? *Why or why not?*

Maslow's hierarchical model of needs has intuitive appeal. We generally seek satisfaction of basic needs for food, drink, and shelter before concerning ourselves with psychologically based needs like belongingness. However, our needs may not be ordered in as fixed a manner as Maslow's hierarchy suggests. An artist might go for days with little if any nourishment in order to complete a new work. People may forgo seeking satisfaction of their need for intimate relationships to focus their energies on seeking status or prestige in their careers. Maslow might counter that the emptiness of their emotional lives would eventually motivate them to fill the gap.

Another problem with Maslow's model is that the same behavior may reflect multiple needs. Perhaps you are attending college to satisfy physiological and safety needs (to prepare for a career so that you can earn money to live comfortably and securely), love and belongingness needs (to form friendships and social ties), esteem needs (to achieve status or approval), and self-actualization needs (to fulfill your intellectual or creative potential). Despite its limitations, Maslow's model leads us to recognize that human behavior is motivated by higher pursuits as well as satisfaction of basic needs.

Maslow did not believe the hierarchy of needs captures all of human striving. Later in his career, he proposed other needs that motivate human behavior, including *cognitive needs* (needs to know, understand, and explore), *aesthetic needs* (needs for beauty, symmetry, and order), and *self-transcendence* (needs to connect to something beyond the self and help others realize their own potential) (Maslow, 1969, 1971, 1987). Whereas self-actualization is directed toward fulfilling one's own potential, self-transcendence represents a higher level need expressed through commitment to ideals, purposes, or causes that go beyond the self (Koltko-Rivera, 2006). Although Maslow believed there is an interrelationship between his original needs and these additional needs, he did not specify how both sets of needs should be combined (Maslow, 1969; Ward & Lasen, 2009).

Before going forward, you may wish to review the sources of motivation outlined in Concept Chart 8.1.

FIGURE 8.1 **Maslow's Hierarchy of Needs**

CONCEPT 8.8

Maslow conceptualized human needs in the form of a hierarchy that ranges from biological needs at the base to the need for self-actualization at the top.

CONCEPT LINK

Maslow was a humanistic theorist who believed that the distinctly human drive toward self-actualization shapes our personality as well as our behavior. See Module 11.4.

self-actualization The motive that drives individuals to express their unique capabilities and fulfill their potentials.

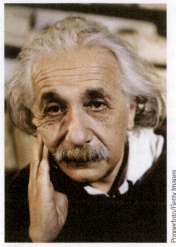

Popperfoto/Getty Images

Marvin Koner/Corbis

What do these two people have in common? Maslow identified a number of historical figures, including Albert Einstein and Eleanor Roosevelt, whom he believed showed qualities of self-actualization. However, you needn't be a notable historical figure to become a self-actualizer. Maslow believed we all have the ability to follow our unique paths toward achieving self-actualization.

Concept Chart 8.1	**Sources of Motivation**	
	Source	**Description**
Biological Sources	Instincts	Instincts are fixed, inborn response patterns that are specific to members of a particular species.
	Needs and drives	Unmet needs create internal drive states, which motivate behavior that leads to drive reduction.
	Stimulus motives and optimal level of arousal	Stimulus motives arise from biologically based needs to be curious and active and to explore the environment. Arousal theory holds that we are motivated to maintain a level of stimulation that is optimal for us.
Psychological Sources	Incentives	The value we place on goals or objects creates a lure, or "pull," to obtain them.
	Psychosocial needs	These psychologically based needs include needs for achievement and social relationships.

© Dainis/Shutterstock.com

© photogl/Shutterstock.com

Note: According to Maslow, human needs are organized within a hierarchy that ranges from basic biological needs at the base to the need for self-actualization at the pinnacle.

MODULE REVIEW   8.1   Motivation: The "Whys" of Behavior

Recite It

1. **Define** the concept of motivation and **describe** several major theories of motivation.

(a) _____ is the set of factors or internal processes that activate, direct, and sustain behavior toward the satisfaction of a need or the attainment of a goal.

Instinct theory proposes that behavior is motivated by (b) _____ programmed, species-specific, fixed patterns of responses called instincts. Though this model may have value in explaining some forms of animal behavior, human behavior is too (c) _____ to be explained by instincts.

(d) _____ theory asserts that animals are driven to satisfy unmet biological needs, such as hunger and thirst. The theory is limited, in part because it fails to account for motives involving the desire to (e) _____ states of arousal. According to (f) _____ theory, the optimal level of arousal varies from person to person. To maintain arousal at an (g) _____ level, some people seek exciting, even potentially dangerous, activities, while others seek more tranquil ones.

(h) _____ theory focuses on the "pull," or lure, of goals or objects that we perceive as attractive, whereas (i) _____ theory focuses on the "push" of unmet biological needs.

2. **Identify** different types of psychosocial needs.

(j) _____ needs are distinctly human needs that are based on psychological rather than biological factors.

They include the need for social relationships and the need for (k) _____

People with a high need for achievement are hard-driving and ambitious. They set challenging but (l) _____ goals for themselves. They accomplish more than people with similar abilities and opportunities but a lower need for achievement.

3. **Describe** Maslow's hierarchy of needs and **identify** the levels of needs at each level in the hierarchy.

Maslow believed we are motivated to meet more basic (m) _____ needs, such as hunger and thirst, before fulfilling higher psychological needs. His hierarchy comprises five levels of need organized from bottom to top: physiological needs, safety and security needs, love and belongingness needs, esteem needs, and (n) _____-needs.

Recall It

1. What is the term used to describe factors that activate, direct, and sustain goal-directed behavior?

2. Match the terms on the left with the definitions on the right:

   I. primary drive   a. a drive acquired through experience

   II. secondary drive   b. the tendency to maintain a steady internal state

   III. need   c. a state of deprivation or deficiency

   IV. homeostasis   d. an innate biological drive

3. What types of motives prompt exploration of the environment and manipulation of objects, especially novel or unusual objects?

4. The strength of the "pull" that a goal or reward exerts on our behavior is called its _____ _____.

5. At the top of Maslow's hierarchy of needs is the need that motivates people to fulfill their unique potentials and become all they are capable of being. This is known as the need for

   a. esteem.   c. love and belongingness.
   b. achievement.   d. self-actualization.

Think About It

■ Do you believe that human behavior is motivated by instinct? Why or why not?

■ Are you a self-actualizer? Upon what evidence do you base your judgment? What steps could you take to become a self-actualizer?

Recite It *answers placed at the end of chapter.*

MODULE 8.2 Hunger and Eating

4 **Explain** how hunger and appetite are regulated.

5 **Identify** causal factors in obesity.

6 **Identify** and **describe** the types and causes of eating disorders.

Hunger, one of the most basic drives and one of the most difficult to ignore, motivates us to eat. But what makes us hungry? If your stomach is growling at this moment, you are unlikely to pay close attention to what you are reading. But there's a lot more to hunger than a grumbling stomach.

What Makes Us Hungry?

CONCEPT 8.9
The hypothalamus detects decreases in blood sugar levels and depletion of fat from fat cells, which leads to the feelings of hunger that motivate eating.

CONCEPT 8.10
Neurotransmitters and hormones play important roles in regulating appetite.

The Brain Loves a Puzzle

As you read ahead, use the information in the text to solve the following puzzle:

Recent evidence suggests that obesity may be catching. How is that possible?

lateral hypothalamus A part of the hypothalamus involved in initiating, or "turning on," eating.

ventromedial hypothalamus A part of the hypothalamus involved in regulating feelings of satiety.

It may seem that pangs of hunger arise from the grumblings of an empty stomach, but it is the brain, not the stomach, that controls hunger. It works like this: When we haven't eaten for a while, our blood sugar levels drop. When this happens, fat is released from *fat cells*—body cells that store fat—to provide fuel that cells use until our next meal. The *hypothalamus*, a small structure in the forebrain that helps regulate hunger and many other bodily processes (discussed in Chapter 2), detects these changes and triggers a cascading series of events, leading to feelings of hunger that motivate eating behaviors. Eating restores an internally balanced state, or homeostasis, by bringing blood sugar levels back into balance and replenishing fat cells.

Different parts of the hypothalamus play different roles in regulating hunger and eating (see ■ Figure 8.2). Stimulating the **lateral hypothalamus** causes a laboratory animal to start eating even if it has just consumed a full meal. If the lateral hypothalamus is surgically destroyed, the animal will stop eating and eventually starve to death. Thus, we know that the lateral hypothalamus is involved in initiating, or "turning on," eating.

Another part of the hypothalamus, the **ventromedial hypothalamus**, acts as an off switch that signals when it is time to stop eating. When this area is destroyed, animals will overeat and eventually become severely obese.

A mixture of brain chemicals, including neurotransmitters and hormones, are involved in regulating hunger and appetite (Kern et al., 2012). One of these chemicals, the neurotransmitter *neuropeptide Y (NPY)*, works on the hypothalamus to stimulate appetite and eating. When we haven't eaten in a while, the brain releases more NPY. The hormone *leptin* (from the Greek word *leptos*, meaning "thin") is released by fat cells in the body and acts to curb hunger when we've had enough to eat. One way leptin works is by reducing the brain's production of NPY.

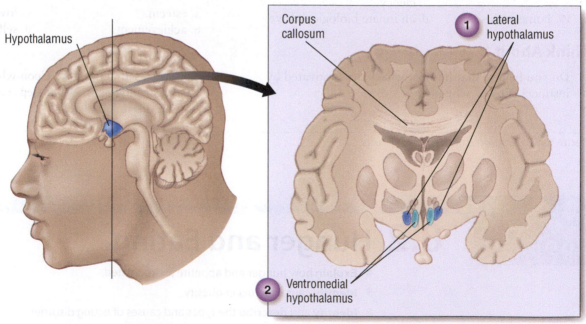

Location of the Hypothalamus

Cross-section Showing Parts of the Hypothalamus

FIGURE 8.2 Parts of the Hypothalamus Involved in Hunger and Eating
The hypothalamus plays a key role in regulating hunger and eating behavior. ❶ The lateral hypothalamus stimulates appetite and eating behavior. ❷ The ventromedial hypothalamus signals satiety and works like an off switch for eating.

Obesity: A National Epidemic

Many of us consume more calories in food than the body burns to maintain bodily processes and perform physical activity. An imbalance between calories consumed ("energy in") and calories burned ("energy out") leads to the accumulation of body weight, which over time can lead to obesity (Gordon-Larsen, 2008).

More Americans are either overweight or obese than ever before. More than two-thirds of U.S. adults (about 69 percent) are either overweight or obese, and more than one in three (about 35 percent) qualify as obese (CDC, 2015b; Yang & Colditz, 2015) (see ■ Figure 8.3). About one-third of children and teens in the United States are either overweight or obese (Tavernise, 2012; Weir, 2012a). Rates of obesity appear to have stabilized in recent years, but the prevalence of abdominal obesity (noted by expanding waistlines)—a type of obesity strongly linked to medical problems and early death—is still on the rise (Ford, Maynard, & Li, 2014; Ogden et al., 2014). The obesity epidemic is worldwide, with the numbers of overweight people throughout the world now estimated to top two billion (Ng et al., 2014).

Why should it matter if we weigh too much? It matters because obesity is a major health risk factor for many serious and life-threatening health problems, including cardiovascular disease (heart and artery disease), respiratory illnesses, diabetes, and some types of cancer (for example, Apovian, 2016; CDC, 2009c; Taubes, 2012). Not surprisingly, obesity is associated with a greater risk of premature death (Berrington de Gonzalez et al., 2010; Flegal et al., 2013). All told, obesity accounts for more than 100,000 excess deaths annually in the United States and shaves up to eight years off the average person's life expectancy (Flegal et al., 2005; Grover et al., 2015).

Why the uptrend in obesity? Research evidence points to too little exercise as the main culprit (Ladabaum et al., 2014). Many of us have become "couch potatoes" and "cyberslugs" who sit around too much and exercise too little. Eating too much high-fat, high-calorie food also plays a part, as does increased portion size.

Portion size, which is way up in many restaurants today, is a powerful food cue that can influence how much we eat. People tend to consume more food when it is offered in larger portion sizes or served on larger plates (Geier, Rozin, & Doros, 2006; Nassauer, 2013). A recent study found that diners at a Chinese buffet who were given larger plates served themselves about 50 percent more food than those given smaller plates (Wansink & van Ittersum, 2013). The researchers in this study believe there is a tendency people have to fill their plates to about the 70 percent full level. (Hint: If you want to monitor your own food consumption, use luncheon-size plates when serving yourself rather than dinner plates.)

In a recent research example, college students were given tubes of Lay's stackable potato chips to munch while watching TV (Geier, Wansink, & Rozin, 2012). Some of the students received tubes with reddish-colored potato chips interspersed among the other chips, whereas others were given regular tubes of potato chips without the reddish chips. It turned out that students who received the tubes with reddish chips ate fewer than half the number of potato chips as those given the regular tubes. These reddish chips may have interrupted automatic eating or helped students monitor how much they were eating.

Many causal factors contribute to obesity, including diet and exercise patterns, as well as genetics (Hamre, 2013). Genetic variations among people contribute to obesity and to how fat is distributed in the body (Locke et al., 2015; Shungin et al., 2015). Body weight is influenced by the person's *basal metabolic rate* (also called *basal metabolism*), the rate at which the body burns calories while at rest. The slower the body's metabolic rate, the more likely the person is to gain weight easily. Genetic variations also help explain why some people have slower metabolic rates than others, leading to the accumulation of more fat in their bodies (Vogel, 2015).

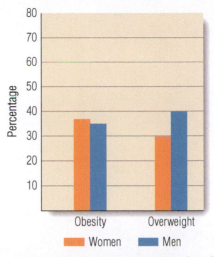

FIGURE 8.3 **America's Vast Waistland** More than two-thirds of American adults are either overweight or obese, and more than one in three qualifies as obese. What are the health risks associated with excess weight?

Source: Adapted from Yang & Colditz, 2015.

Get moving America! Lack of exercise is perhaps the major culprit accounting for America's expanding waistline.

Clynt Garnham Food & Drink/ Alamy Stock Photo

studiomode/Alamy Stock Photo

Are you likely to consume more cookies if they are packaged in larger size bags than smaller, single-serving size bags? How do subtle food cues influence how much you eat?

CONCEPT 8.11

Obesity is a complex health problem in which behavioral patterns, genetics, and environmental and emotional factors all play a role.

CONCEPT LINK

Obesity is a major risk factor in coronary heart disease, the leading killer of Americans. See Module 10.2.

© Steven Frame/Shutterstock.com

set point theory The belief that brain mechanisms regulate body weight around a genetically predetermined "set point."

According to **set point theory**, the brain regulates body weight around a genetically predetermined level or "set point." The theory proposes that when we gain or lose weight, the brain adjusts the basal metabolic rate to keep our weight around a set point (Major et al., 2007). If we lose weight, the brain slows the body's metabolic rate, and as this rate slows, the body conserves stores of fat. This may explain why dieters often find it hard to continue losing more weight or even maintain the weight they've lost. The body's ability to adjust its metabolic rate downward when caloric intake falls off may be a bane to many dieters today, but it may have helped ancestral humans survive times of famine.

The number of fat cells in one's body is another factor in obesity. Obese people typically have far more fat cells than do people of normal weight. Severely obese people may have 200 billion or more fat cells, as compared with the 25 billion or 30 billion fat cells in normal weight people. When we haven't eaten in a while, the body draws stored energy in the form of fat from its fat cells. The depletion of fat cells is an important trigger for hunger, which in turn motivates eating to restore the balance of stored fat. Because obese people typically have a great many more fat cells than normal weight individuals, they may feel hungry sooner after eating than normal weight people. Consequently, they may be more strongly motivated to consume excess quantities of food. Unfortunately, we don't shed fat cells even when we lose weight (Hopkin, 2008).

Eating habits, such as eating quickly, eating larger portions, and eating until feeling stuffed, represent behavioral factors that can lead to overweight and obesity (Maruyama et al., 2008). Environmental factors also contribute to the problem. We live in a food-absorbed environment in which we are constantly bombarded by food cues—TV commercials showing displays of tempting foods, aromas permeating the air as we walk by the bakery, and on and on. Consider that, among children, Ronald McDonald is the second most widely recognized figure, after Santa Claus (Parloff, 2003). Laboratory research shows that exposure to food advertisements increases food consumption in both children and adults (Harris, Bargh, & Brownell, 2009).

Emotional states, such as anger, fear, and depression, can also prompt excessive eating. Many of us overeat in anger, or when we're feeling lonely, bored, or depressed. Have you ever tried to quell anxiety over an upcoming examination by finishing off a carton of ice cream? We may find we can soothe our negative feelings, at least temporarily, by treating ourselves to food.

Might obesity be catching? Investigators find that obesity tends to be shared among people in social networks comprising friends, neighbors, spouses, and family members (Christakis & Fowler, 2007). And judging by the results of a recent study, when we dine with an overweight person, we're likely to order more fattening foods. Cornell undergrads who had lunch with a female experimenter who donned a fat suit ate more pasta than salad even when the experimenter herself ate more salad (Holohan, 2014). Findings like these suggest that the people we socialize with influence what we eat, how much we eat, and the judgments we make about the acceptability of obesity. Environmental factors such as the prevalence of obesity in our social networks and the communities in which we live may be an even stronger determinant of obesity than genetic factors (Barabási, 2007; Lazaros et al., 2012). But if social networks can encourage unhealthy eating, the opposite side is also true—friends who make healthy eating choices can serve as positive role models.

What's the bottom line (or curve) on the causes of obesity? Behavioral patterns, genetics, environmental factors, and emotional cues all play a role. Yet even people whose genes predispose them to weight problems can achieve and maintain a healthy body weight by eating sensibly and exercising regularly. Regular physical activity not only burns calories, but it also increases the metabolic rate because it builds muscles, and muscle tissue burns more calories than fatty tissue. Thus, regular exercise combined with gradual weight reduction can help offset the reduction in the body's metabolic rate that may occur when we begin losing weight. It seems more Americans are getting the message, as evidence shows reductions in caloric intake in recent years (Beck & Schatz, 2014).

Health experts recognize that "quickie" diets are not the answer to long-term weight management. The great majority of people eventually regain any weight they lose on a diet. Diet or weight-loss drugs offer at best only a temporary benefit and may carry a risk of serious side effects. Long-term success in losing excess weight and keeping it off requires a lifelong commitment to following a sensible, healthy diet combined with regular exercise (Lamberg, 2006; Van Horn, 2014; Wadden et al., 2014).

Modern technology may also be helpful. Duke University researchers found that texting helped people monitor their weight loss efforts (Steinberg et al., 2013). Participants in a weight-loss program received a daily text in the morning, prompting them to enter their total number of steps from the previous day (the target was 10,000 steps as measured by a pedometer), whether they had eaten at a fast restaurant, and how many sugary drinks they had consumed. They received a personalized reply along with a weight control tip for the day. Most participants found the daily texts helpful in meeting their program goals.

We also need to become calorie conscious. For example, we need to recognize that "low fat" does not necessarily mean "low calorie." (Check the nutritional labels.) Even if obesity is not a current concern in your life, adopting healthy eating and exercise habits can help you avoid weight problems in the future (see Table 8.1)

CONCEPT 8.12

Effective weight management requires a lifelong commitment to healthy eating and exercise habits that balance caloric intake with energy output.

Eating Disorders

Karen, the 22-year-old daughter of a famed English professor, felt her weight was "just about right" (Boskind-White & White, 1983). But at 78 pounds on a 5-foot frame, she looked more like a prepubescent 11-year-old than a young adult. Her parents tried to persuade her to seek help with her eating behavior, but she continually denied she had a problem. Ultimately, however, after she lost yet another pound, her parents convinced her to enter a residential treatment program where her eating could be closely monitored. Nicole, 19, wakes up each morning hoping this will be the day she begins living normally—that today she'll avoid gorging herself and inducing herself to vomit. But she doesn't feel confident that her eating behavior and purging are under her

Table 8.1 Suggestions for Maintaining a Healthy Weight

Watch your fat intake.	Limit your total daily fat intake to less than 30 percent of calories consumed, and keep your intake of saturated fat to less than 10 percent. This means that if you consume 2,000 calories a day on the average, limit your fat intake to 66 grams of fat and saturated fat to 22 grams. (Note that 1 gram of fat contains 9 calories.)
Control portion size.	To maintain a healthy weight, you need to strike a balance between calories consumed and calories expended. Controlling portion size will help you maintain this caloric balance.
Slow down your eating.	It takes about 15 minutes for your brain to register that your stomach feels full. Give it a chance to catch up to your stomach. Put the fork down between bites to slow the pace of your eating.
Count your bites.	Like counting steps to monitor your daily activity, counting bites can help you keep tabs on how much you eat. In a pilot test, Brigham Young University researchers found that people who counted bites and then set a lower daily target level of bites lost about 4 pounds in a month's time (Crookston et al., 2015).
Beware of hidden calories.	Check product labels for calories. Fruit drinks, for instance, are loaded with hidden calories. Try diluting fruit drinks with water, or substitute the actual fruit itself. Also, many processed foods, especially baked goods, are loaded with calories as the result of high sugar and fat content.
Make physical activity a part of your lifestyle.	Health experts recommend at least 30 minutes a day of moderate physical activity—activity equivalent in strenuousness to walking three to four miles per hour. This doesn't mean you need to work out in a gym or jog around a park every day. Taking a brisk walk from your car to your office or school, climbing stairs, or doing vigorous work around the house can help you meet your daily exercise needs. But additional aerobic exercise—like running, swimming, or using equipment specially designed for aerobic exercise—may help even more. Before starting any exercise program, discuss your health needs and concerns with a health care provider.

© Monkey Business Images/Shutterstock.com

CONCEPT 8.13

Eating disorders, such as anorexia nervosa and bulimia nervosa, disproportionately affect young women, in large part because of a cultural obsession to achieve unrealistic standards of thinness.

control. The disordered eating behavior of Karen and Nicole are characteristic of the two major types of eating disorders: *anorexia nervosa* and *bulimia nervosa*.

Anorexia nervosa affects about 0.9 percent of women in our society (about 9 in 1,000), according to the most recent population-based survey (Hudson et al., 2006). Estimates are that about 1 to 3 percent of women are affected by bulimia nervosa at some point in their lives (American Psychiatric Association, 2013). Prevalence rates among men are estimated at about 0.3 percent (3 in 1,000) for anorexia nervosa and 0.3 percent or less for bulimia nervosa (American Psychiatric Association, 2013; Hudson et al., 2006).

Anorexia Nervosa

Anorexia nervosa involves self-starvation resulting in an unhealthy and potentially dangerously low body weight. It is characterized by both an intense fear of becoming fat and a distorted body image. Anorexia is found predominantly in young women. The young woman may believe she is too fat, even though others may see her as little more than "skin and bones."

Anorexia nervosa is a dangerous medical condition and poses serious risks, including cardiovascular problems, such as irregular heartbeat and low blood pressure; gastrointestinal problems, such as chronic constipation and abdominal pain; loss of menstruation; and even deaths due to suicide or to medical complications associated with severe weight loss. Sadly, between 5 percent and 20 percent of cases of anorexia nervosa result in death, resulting from either suicide or malnutrition due to starvation (Arcelus et al., 2011; Franko et al., 2013; Haynos & Fruzzetti, 2011).

In a typical case, the young woman begins to notice some weight gain in adolescence. She becomes overly concerned about getting fat. She resorts to extreme dieting and perhaps excessive exercise to reduce her weight to a prepubescent level. She denies that she is too thin or losing too much weight, despite the concerns of others. In her mind's eye, she is heavier than she actually is.

Bulimia Nervosa

Bulimia nervosa is characterized by a repetitive pattern of binge eating followed by purging. Purging usually involves self-induced vomiting but may take other forms, such as excessive use of laxatives. Some individuals with bulimia purge regularly after meals, not just after binges. Some engage in excessive, even compulsive, exercise regimens to try to control their weight. Like those with anorexia, people with bulimia are obsessed with their weight and are unhappy with their bodies. But unlike those with anorexia, they typically maintain a relatively normal weight (Bulik et al., 2012).

Bulimia usually begins in late adolescence following a period of rigid dieting to lose weight. Bingeing may alternate with strict dieting. The binge itself usually occurs in secret. During the binge, the person consumes enormous amounts of foods that are sweet and high in fat. Repeated purging, especially self-induced vomiting, can cause serious medical complications, including potentially dangerous potassium deficiencies, esophageal damage, decay of tooth enamel, skin problems, and gastrointestinal and cardiovascular disorders (Forney et al., 2016).

Causal Factors in Eating Disorders. What underlies the development of anorexia nervosa and bulimia nervosa? One of the principal factors is social pressure on young women to achieve an unrealistic standard of thinness (Brannan & Petrie, 2011; Chernyak & Lowe, 2010). The constant barrage of media images of ultrathin models conveys powerful messages to girls and young women, affecting how they view their own bodies and leading to feelings of body dissatisfaction and disordered eating behaviors (Bell & Dittmar, 2011; Tiggemann & Miller, 2010). Even girls as young as 3 have begun to internalize a thinness ideal (Harriger et al., 2010). Whereas college women are more likely than college men to believe they are overweight, the reverse is true for self-perceptions of being underweight (see ■ Figure 8.4) (American College Health Association, 2011).

Social pressure to achieve and maintain a slender figure falls most heavily on women in our society, especially young women. Concerns about weight can be expressed in different ways, such as feelings of guilt or shame associated with eating treats or even purchasing them. About one in seven college women surveyed by a team of investigators said they

AP Images/Eugenio Savio

Brazilian fashion model Ana Carolina Reston was just 21 when she died in 2006 from medical complications due to anorexia. At the time of her death, the 5-foot, 7-inch young woman weighed only 88 pounds. Unfortunately, the problem of anorexia and other eating disorders among fashion models is widespread, as it is in other situations in which pressure is imposed to attain unrealistic standards of thinness.

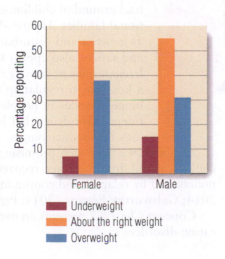

FIGURE 8.4 Student's Self-Description of Weight
College women more often think of themselves as overweight than do college men, but the reverse is the case when it comes to self-perceptions of being underweight.

Note: Refers to question, "How would you describe your weight." Because of missing or invalid data, the response categories by sex do not always equal the total.

Source: Data derived from American College Health Association National College Health Assessment—Reference Group Data Report, Fall 2011.

Christin Gilbert/age fotostock/superstock

Is Facebook a downer? Evidence links greater use of Facebook to more negative moods, to lower levels of happiness and life satisfaction and to more problem eating behaviors.

would be embarrassed to buy a chocolate bar in a store (Rozin, Bauer, & Catanese, 2003).

Social media use may also be a contributing factor to eating disorders. Investigators tracked Facebook use of a sample of college women (Smith, Hames, & Joiner, 2013). It turned out that college women who more often used Facebook to compare themselves with others showed greater body dissatisfaction, which in turn linked up with more frequent bulimic symptoms as well as overeating. Other investigators find that college women who spend more time on Facebook also tend to show higher levels of problem eating behaviors (Mabe, Forney, & Keel, 2014). Investigators also link greater use of social media sites like Facebook to more negative moods after logging off, to lower levels of general happiness and life satisfaction, and to increased risk of depression (Kross et al., 2013; Lin et al., 2016; Sagioglou & Greitemeyer, 2014). The take-away message is that regularly comparing yourself to others on social media sites may be damaging to managing your eating behavior as well as your emotional well-being.

Eating disorders are much less common in non-Western countries that lack our cultural emphasis on thinness. They also appear to be less common among women of color for whom body image is not as closely tied to a slender form as it is among Euro-American women (Overstreet, Quinn, & Agocha, 2010). Identification with African American culture may serve as kind of protective factor against disturbed eating behaviors (Henrickson, Crowther, & Harrington, 2010).

Many of the men affected by eating disorders participate in certain sports, such as competitive wrestling, in which they face pressures to maintain their weight within a narrow range. Body dissatisfaction also occurs in boys and men and is often linked to a desire to have a muscular build (Blashill & Wilhelm, 2013). Exposure to media images of heavily muscled men can damage the image that boys and men have of their own bodies (Hargreaves & Tiggemann, 2009; Hobza & Rochlen, 2009).

Jill Greenberg Studio, Inc

If a slender woman like the one on the left had the same proportions as the original Barbie doll, she would look like the woman on the right. To achieve this, she would need to grow nearly a foot in height, increase her bust size by 4 inches, and reduce her waist by 5 inches. What message do you think the classic Barbie doll sends to the average young woman?

Other factors also contribute to eating disorders. Negative emotions such as depression and anxiety can trigger binge-eating episodes (Merwin, 2011). Many young women with eating disorders have issues relating to perfectionism and control (Farstad, McGeown, & von Ranson, 2016; La Mela et al., 2015; Martinez & Craighead, 2015; Wade et al., 2015). They may place unreasonable pressures on themselves to achieve a "perfect body" or think that the only part of their lives they can control is their dieting. Eating disorders also frequently develop against a background of childhood sexual or physical abuse or living in dysfunctional families (Holtom-Viesel & Allan, 2014). Biological factors, such as genetics and disturbances in brain mechanisms that control hunger and satiety, also appear to contribute to eating disorders (Kaye, 2009). Irregularities in activity of the neurotransmitter serotonin, which plays a key role in regulating feelings of satiation after eating, may prompt binge episodes in people with bulimia (Hildebrandt et al., 2010). Antidepressant drugs that boost the availability of serotonin in the brain may help reduce binges.

Although we have seen promising results in treating eating disorders with psychological and drug therapies, recovery is typically a long-term process that is often punctuated by relapses and continuing symptoms (Agras et al., 2014; Fischer et al., 2014; Galsworthy-Francis , 2014; Pennesi & Wade, 2016).

Concept Chart 8.2 presents an overview of our discussion of hunger, obesity, and eating disorders.

Concept Chart 8.2   Hunger, Obesity, and Eating Disorders: Key Concepts

Hunger and Appetite	Obesity	Eating Disorders
The hypothalamus detects low blood sugar levels and depletion of fat in fat cells, leading to feelings of hunger that motivate eating. Hormones and neurotransmitters work on the hypothalamus to influence appetite and eating behavior.	Causes of obesity involve genetic, psychological, and environmental factors, including differences in metabolic rates, number of fat cells in the body, behavioral patterns (unhealthy diet and lack of exercise), and emotional and environmental cues that prompt overeating.	Cultural pressure imposed on young women to achieve an unrealistic standard of thinness is a major underlying factor in anorexia (self-starvation) and bulimia (binge eating followed by purging).

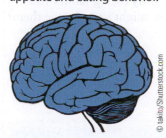
© takito/Shutterstock.com

© Shira Raz/Shutterstock.com

Psychological factors underlying eating disorders include issues of control and perfectionism, sexual or physical abuse during childhood, and family conflicts.

Biological factors implicated in eating disorders include genetics, abnormalities in brain mechanisms that control feelings of hunger and satiation, and irregularities in serotonin activity.

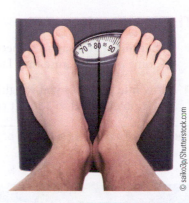
© saiko3p/Shutterstock.com

MODULE REVIEW   **8.2**   Hunger and Eating

Recite It

4. Explain how hunger and appetite are regulated.

(a) _____ processes in the brain regulate hunger and appetite. The (b) _____ plays a pivotal role. It senses changes in blood sugar levels and depletion of fat from fat cells, which leads to the feelings of hunger that motivate eating. Neurotransmitters and (c) _____ also play important roles in regulating hunger and appetite.

5. Identify causal factors in obesity.

Obesity is a complex problem that has multiple causes, including behavioral patterns, genetics, (d) _____ factors, and environmental and emotional factors. Genetics may affect basal metabolic rate and the number of (e) _____ cells in the body.

6. Identify and **describe** the types and causes of eating disorders.

(f) _____ _____ is an eating disorder in which people starve themselves because of exaggerated concerns about weight gain.

(g) _____ _____ is an eating disorder characterized by episodes of binge eating followed by purging. Purging is accomplished through self-induced vomiting or other means, such as excessive use of (h) _____.

Many factors are implicated in eating disorders. They include cultural pressure on young women to achieve unrealistic standards of (i) _____, issues of (j) _____ and perfectionism, childhood abuse, family conflicts, and possible disturbances in brain mechanisms that control hunger and satiety.

Recall It

1. Which of the following does *not* describe what happens physiologically after a person has not eaten for a while?

a. Blood sugar level drops.
b. Fat is released from fat cells.
c. The ventromedial hypothalamus signals that it is time to start eating.
d. The brain releases more neuropeptide Y.

2. If the lateral hypothalamus in a laboratory animal is stimulated, the animal

a. stops eating.
b. starves to death.
c. begins to eat even if it has just consumed a full meal.
d. becomes obese.

3. Match the terms on the left with the definitions on the right:

I. lateral hypothalamus

II. ventromedial hypothalamus

III. basal metabolic rate

a. the rate at which the body at rest burns calories

b. works like an on switch for eating

c. a genetically predetermined range for weight

IV. set point

d. works likes an off switch to signal when to stop eating

4. Irregularities in the regulation of the neurotransmitter _____ may be involved in prompting bulimic binges.

Think About It

- What might you say to someone who claims that people become obese because they lack willpower?

- How much should you weigh? Has your answer to this question changed as a result of our discussion of obesity?

Are you aware of your daily caloric intake? If not, should you be? Do you have any unhealthy eating habits you would like to change? If so, how might you change them?

Recite It *answers placed at the end of chapter.*

MODULE

8.3 Sexual Motivation

7 Identify and **describe** the four phases of the sexual response cycle.

8 Describe how researchers characterize the continuum of sexual orientation.

9 Describe the causes of sexual dysfunctions.

CONCEPT 8.14
Each society defines masculinity and femininity by imposing a set of gender-based expectations, called gender roles, that designate the behaviors and roles deemed appropriate for men and women.

© Agnieszka Guzowska/Shutterstock.com

gender identity The psychological sense of maleness or femaleness.

sexual orientation The directionality of one's erotic interests.

gender roles The cultural expectations imposed on men and women to behave in ways deemed appropriate for their gender.

Sexuality is another source of motivation, indeed an important source of motivation, and our experience of ourselves as sexual beings has a bearing on our sense of self. Our **gender identity** (sense of maleness or femaleness) and our **sexual orientation** (direction of erotic attraction) are essential parts of our self-identity. Society also imposes a set of expectations, called **gender roles**, that designate the behaviors and roles deemed appropriate for men and women. Gender roles stipulate how men and women should behave, how they should dress, what work they should do, and how they should interact with each other.

There exists great variety in human sexual expression, including a range of sexual practices such as oral sex, anal sex, and masturbation. Our bodies respond to many forms of sexual stimulation, but our sexual behavior is more strongly determined by cultural learning, personal values, and individual experiences than by biological drives or capacities for sexual response.

A recent large-scale, nationally representative survey of sexual behaviors among American adults shows more variety in sexual practices than existed a generation earlier (Healy, 2010; Herbenick et al., 2010; Reece et al., 2010). Although vaginal intercourse remains the most common sexual activity, other sexual behaviors such as genital stroking or masturbation, performed either by oneself or one's partner, as well as oral sex and experimentation with same-gender sex are more common today than was the case some 20 years earlier, the last time a major sex survey in the United States was conducted. Today, a majority of adults in the 18- to 49-year-old age range report engaging in oral sex. More than 20 percent of men age 25 to 49 and women age 20 to 39 reported engaging in anal sex during the past year. A majority of men (63 to 69 percent) in the 20- to 39-year-old age range report masturbating at least once during the past month, as do 39 to 44 percent of women

(National Survey of Sexual Health and Behavior [NSSHB], 2010). An intriguing finding that points to a possible communication gap occurring in America's bedrooms is that while 64 percent of women in a recent survey say they had achieved orgasm during their last sexual encounter, a much higher percentage of men (85 percent) report that their partners had achieved orgasm (Gardner, 2010).

The need for sexual gratification is an important source of motivation. In this module, we explore sexual motivation by examining how our bodies respond to sexual stimulation and the directionality, or orientation, of our erotic attractions and interests. Finally, we examine different types of sexual dysfunctions and how helping professionals treat these problems.

The Sexual Response Cycle: How Your Body Gets Turned On

Much of what we've learned about the physical response of the body to sexual stimulation comes from the pioneering research of William Masters and Virginia Johnson. They demonstrated that the body responds to sexual stimulation with a characteristic pattern of changes, which they called the **sexual response cycle.** They divided the sexual response cycle into four phases: *excitement, plateau, orgasm,* and *resolution* (Masters & Johnson, 1966). ■ Figures 8.5(a) and 8.5(b) show the levels of sexual arousal during the phases of the sexual response cycle in men and women, respectively. These changes are summarized in Table 8.2.

There are obvious gender differences in how our bodies respond to sexual stimulation. The penis in males becomes erect; the vagina in women becomes moist through a process called *vaginal lubrication.* Yet both of these markers of sexual excitement (arousal) reflect the same underlying biological process, **vasocongestion,** or pooling of blood in bodily tissues. Overall, the similarities in the sexual responses of men and women listed in Table 8.2 may surprise you. Yet there is one important difference. Unlike women, men enter a *refractory period* following orgasm. This is the period of time in which men are physiologically incapable of achieving another

CONCEPT 8.15
Landmark research by Masters and Johnson showed that the body's response to sexual stimulation can be characterized in terms of a sexual response cycle consisting of four phases: excitement, plateau, orgasm, and resolution.

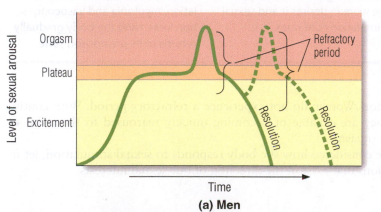

(a) Men

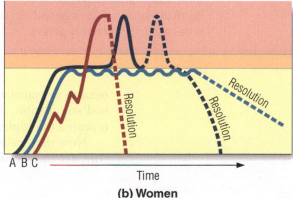

(b) Women

FIGURE 8.5 The Sexual Response Cycle
Here we see the level of sexual arousal across the four phases of the cycle. Men enter a refractory period after orgasm in which they become unresponsive to sexual stimulation. But as indicated by the broken line, men may become rearoused to the point of orgasm once the refractory period is past. Women do not enter a refractory period. Pattern A shows a woman's cycle with multiple orgasms, as indicated by the dotted line. Pattern B shows a response cycle in which the woman reaches the plateau stage but does not achieve orgasm. Pattern C shows a pattern leading to orgasm in which the woman quickly passes through the plateau phase.

sexual response cycle The term Masters and Johnson used to refer to the characteristic stages of physiological responses in the body to sexual stimulation.

vasocongestion Swelling of tissues with blood, a process that accounts for penile erection and vaginal lubrication during sexual arousal.

Table 8.2 Sexual Response Cycle: How Our Bodies Respond to Sexual Stimulation

Phase of Sexual Response	In Males	In Females	In Both Genders
Excitement phase	Vasocongestion results in erection.	Vasocongestion swells the vaginal tissue, the clitoris, and the area surrounding the opening of the vagina.	Vasocongestion of the genital tissue occurs.
	The testes begin to elevate.	Vaginal lubrication appears.	Heart rate, muscle tension (*myotonia*), and blood pressure increase.
	Skin on the scrotum tenses and thickens.	The inner two-thirds of the vagina expand, and the vaginal walls thicken and turn a deeper color.	Nipples may become erect.
Plateau phase	The tip of the penis turns a deep reddish-purple.	The inner two-thirds of the vagina expand fully.	Vasocongestion increases.
	The testes become completely elevated.	The outer third of the vagina thickens.	Myotonia, heart rate, and blood pressure continue to increase.
	Droplets of semen may be released from the penile opening before ejaculation.	The clitoris retracts behind its hood, and the uterus elevates and increases in size.	
Orgasm phase	Sensations of impending ejaculation lasting 2 to 3 seconds precede the ejaculatory reflex.	Contractions of the pelvic muscles surrounding the vagina occur.	Orgasmic release of sexual tension occurs, producing intense feelings of pleasure.
	Orgasmic contractions propel semen through the penis and out of the body.		Muscle spasms occur throughout the body; blood pressure, heart rate, and breathing rate reach a peak.
Resolution phase	Men become physiologically incapable of achieving another orgasm or ejaculation for a period of time called the refractory period.	Multiple orgasms may occur if the woman desires it and sexual stimulation continues.	Lacking continued sexual stimulation, myotonia and vasocongestion lessen and the body gradually returns to its prearoused state.

orgasm or ejaculation. Women do not experience a refractory period. With continued stimulation, they are capable of becoming quickly rearoused to the point of repeated (multiple) orgasms.

Now that we've considered how the body responds to sexual stimulation, let us consider the variations that exist in the direction of our sexual interests.

Sexual Orientation

Sexual orientation is not determined by sexual activity, but by the direction of a person's erotic attraction and romantic interests—whether one is sexually attracted toward members of one's sex, the opposite sex, or both sexes (Savin-Williams, Joyner, & Rieger, 2012). Heterosexuals are sexually attracted to members of the opposite sex. Gay males and lesbians are attracted to members of their own sex, and bisexuals are attracted to members of both sexes. Yet the boundaries between these different sexual orientations may not be as clearly drawn as you might think. We can conceptualize sexual orientation as a continuum with gradations of varying degres of bisexuality between exclusive homosexuality on one end and exclusive heterosexuality on the other. For example, people may identify themselves as primarily but not exclusively heterosexual or homosexual.

Several recent surveys shed light on the sexual orientations of Americans today. In a national health survey conducted by the Centers for Disease Control and Prevention, 96.6 percent of adult Americans aged 18 and over identified themselves as heterosexuals, 1.6 percent as gay or lesbian, and 0.7 percent as bisexual (Ward et al., 2014). (The remaining 1.1 percent of adults were divided between answering "something else" or said they didn't know or didn't provide an answer). Another survey showed that younger adults under the age of 30 are more likely than older adults to self-identify with varying degrees of bisexuality (YouGov, 2015). This suggests that sexual orientation is more fluid in young adulthood.

We should not confuse sexual orientation with sexual behavior. Occasional same-sex activity is reported by many people who identify themselves as heterosexuals. Twelve percent of adults in the YouGov survey who said they were completely heterosexual also reported having had a same-sex experience at some point in their lives. Another national survey found that among men, anal receptive sex (penile penetration) during the past year was reported by about 4 to 5 percent of respondents, which represents a much larger percentage than those who identify as gay (NSSHB, 2010). Similarly for women, the percentage, about 9 percent of women aged 20 to 24, who report giving oral sex to another woman in the past year is much higher than the percentage identifying as lesbians. Among men under the age of 60, between 5 and 8 percent of men reported giving oral sex to another man during the past year.

Theories of Sexual Orientation

Why do some people identify as homosexual while others say they are bisexual or heterosexual? Why are you the way you are? Though the causes of sexual orientation remain under study, one thing is clear: People don't choose to be gay or straight. We don't make a conscious decision to adopt a particular sexual orientation, as we might select a college major or a life partner.

Although early theories of sexual orientation focused on possible psychological roots, investigators today place a greater emphasis on biological factors, such as genetics and prenatal hormonal influences on the developing brain (Bailey et al., 2016). Identical (MZ) twins are more likely to have the same sexual orientation than fraternal (DZ) twins, a finding that squares with a genetic contribution to sexual orientation (Hyde, 2005; Zietsch et al., 2008). This pattern is found even among twins who were separated shortly after birth and raised in different families. But the fact that one identical twin may have a gay or straight sexual orientation doesn't necessarily mean the other twin will follow suit. Life experiences and environmental factors also influence development of sexual orientation (Bailey et al., 2016; Långström et al., 2008, 2010). Moreover, genetic factors appear to play a larger role in determining homosexuality in men than in women (LeVay, 2003).

What about the role of sex hormones? Researchers fail to find consistent differences in male or female sex hormones in adult gay males and lesbians in comparison with their heterosexual counterparts (Hines, 2011). However, the male sex hormone testosterone may play a role in shaping the developing brain during prenatal development in ways that affect the development of sexual orientation (Balthazart, 2012; LeVay, 2003; Savic, Garcia-Falgueras, & Swaab, 2010).

We also have evidence that the people who develop a gay or lesbian sexual orientation often showed gender-nonconforming behavior in early childhood, such as having preferred clothes, games, and toys typically associated with the opposite sex (Dawood, Bailey, & Martin, 2009; Lippa, 2008; Rieger & Savin-Williams, 2012). These early patterns of gender-nonconforming behavior may reflect genetic or

CONCEPT 8.16

Sexual orientation is generally conceptualized as a continuum ranging from exclusive homosexuality on one end to exclusive heterosexuality on the other end.

CONCEPT 8.17

Though the underlying causes of sexual orientation remain unclear, contemporary scholars believe that a combination of biological and environmental factors is involved.

Tetra Images/Getty Images

prenatal influences affecting the developing brain in utero. However, we should be careful not to overgeneralize. Many gay males and lesbians had interest patterns in childhood that were typical of their own gender. We should recognize, too, that gay males are found among the ranks of the most "macho" football and hockey players.

Let us also note that although biological factors may set the stage for the development of sexual orientation, psychological factors, such as developing self-perceptions early in life, may also play a contributing role. Many gay males have childhood recollections of feeling and acting "different" from their peers at a very young age—often as early as 3 or 4. They often recall being more sensitive than other boys and having fewer male buddies. Perhaps, as these boys mature, self-perceptions of differentness become transformed into erotic attractions. As psychologist Darryl Bem (1996) put it, what was exotic now becomes erotic. A similar process may occur in girls who develop a lesbian sexual orientation.

In sum, research on the origins of sexual orientation remains inconclusive. Most experts believe that sexual orientation is explained not by any single factor but, rather, by a combination of genes, hormones, and psychosocial factors interacting throughout the life span (Hines, 2011; Jannini et al., 2010; Långström et al., 2008). As it is possible to arrive at the same destination via different routes, we should allow for the possibility that multiple pathways are involved in explaining the development of sexual orientation (Garnets, 2002).

Sexual Dysfunctions

Occasional problems with sexual interest, arousal, or response are quite common and may affect virtually everyone at one time or another. Men may occasionally have difficulty achieving erections or may ejaculate sooner than they desire. Women may occasionally have problems becoming sexually aroused or reaching orgasm. When such problems become persistent and cause distress, they are classified as **sexual dysfunctions**.

Sexual dysfunctions involve problems relating to lack of sexual desire or interest, or difficulties becoming sexually aroused or achieving orgasm. Women are more likely than men to experience lack of sexual interest or desire and difficulty reaching orgasm (Goldstein et al., 2006; Leiblum et al., 2006). Men may also lack sexual desire or have problems with *erectile dysfunction* (difficulty or inability in achieving or maintaining erections) or *premature ejaculation* (rapid ejaculation with minimum stimulation and perceived lack of control over delaying ejaculation). The causes of sexual dysfunctions involve both biological and psychosocial factors.

Biological Causes

Neurological or circulatory conditions or diseases can interfere with sexual interest, arousal, or response. These include diabetes, multiple sclerosis, spinal cord injuries, epilepsy, complications from surgery (such as prostate surgery in men), side effects of certain medications, and hormonal problems. Psychoactive drugs, such as cocaine, alcohol, and narcotics, may dampen sexual interest or impair sexual responsiveness. Most cases of erectile disorder can be traced to biological factors, with circulatory problems topping the list (Chakraborty et al., 2013; Keller, Liang, & Lin, 2012).

Testosterone energizes sexual drives in both sexes, and deficiencies of the hormone can dampen sexual desire (Maggi, 2012; Davis et al., 2008). Although testosterone is a male sex hormone produced in the man's testes, it is also produced in smaller amounts in women's ovaries and in the adrenal glands of both men and

CONCEPT 8.18
Though occasional problems with sexual interest, arousal, or response are common, persistent problems that are the cause of personal distress are classified as sexual dysfunctions.

sexual dysfunctions Persistent or recurrent problems with sexual interest, arousal, or response.

women. That being said, most men and women with sexual dysfunctions have normal sex hormone levels. However, women whose adrenal glands and ovaries are surgically removed due to disease, and thus no longer produce testosterone, often report reduced sexual desire (Davis & Braunstein, 2012).

Psychosocial Causes

Psychosocial factors such as depression, relationship problems, and even stress can contribute to sexual dysfunctions (McCabe et al., 2010). Children raised in families in which negative attitudes toward sexuality prevail may encounter anxiety, guilt, or shame when they become sexually active, rather than sexual arousal and pleasure (Woo, Brotto, & Gorzalka, 2011). This is especially true of young women exposed to sexually repressive cultural attitudes. Such socialization pressures may discourage women from learning about their sexual responsiveness or inhibit them from asserting their sexual needs with their partners.

Some couples fall into a sexual routine, perhaps even a rut. Couples who fail to communicate their sexual preferences or to regularly invigorate their lovemaking routines may find themselves losing interest. Relationship problems can also impair a couple's sexual responsiveness, as conflicts and long-simmering resentments may be carried into bed.

Survivors of rape and other sexual traumas often develop deep feelings of disgust or revulsion toward sex. Not surprisingly, they often have difficulty in responding sexually, even with loving partners (Colangelo & Keefe-Cooperman, 2012; McCabe et al., 2010). Other emotional factors, especially anxiety, depression, and anger, can also lessen sexual interest or responsiveness.

Anxiety, especially **performance anxiety**, may make it impossible for a man to achieve or sustain an erection or for a woman to become adequately lubricated or achieve orgasm (Althof & Needle, 2011; Brotto et al., 2010; McCabe & Connaughton, 2014). Failure to perform then fuels further self-doubts and fears of repeated failure, which in turn heighten anxiety on subsequent occasions, leading to yet more failure experiences, and so on in a vicious cycle.

Premature ejaculation may arise from a failure to keep the level of stimulation below the man's ejaculatory threshold, or "point of no return." Though ejaculation is a reflex, men need to learn (usually through a trial-and-error procedure) to gauge their level of stimulation so that it does not exceed their ejaculatory threshold. They need to signal their partners to stop stimulation before this point so that their sensations can subside before resuming again.

Treatment of Sexual Dysfunctions

The good news is that most cases of sexual dysfunction can be treated successfully through either biological or psychological approaches, or with a combination approach. Sex therapy, a relatively brief form of psychological treatment, was pioneered by William Masters and Virginia Johnson (Masters & Johnson, 1970). In sex therapy, individuals, but usually couples, meet with a therapist or pair of male and female therapists who help them learn specific, behavioral techniques to overcome their sexual difficulties (Althof, 2010).

Biological therapies are also available to help people with sexual dysfunctions. Testosterone may be helpful in treating problems of low sexual interest or desire (Davis et al., 2008; Granata et al., 2012). Viagra and other similar drugs can help men with erectile dysfunction achieve more reliable erections (Qaseem et al., 2009). Viagra and similar drugs work by relaxing blood vessels in the penis, allowing them to expand and carry more blood to the penis, which is needed to induce and sustain an erection. Antidepressant drugs, such as Zoloft (generic name sertraline) and Paxil (generic name paroxetine), help delay ejaculation in men with premature ejaculation by increasing

CONCEPT 8.19
Underlying causes of sexual dysfunctions include biological factors, such as neurological or circulatory problems, and psychosocial factors, such as performance anxiety.

Sexually dysfunctional couples often have difficulty communicating their sexual needs and interests.

performance anxiety Anxiety experienced in performance situations stemming from a fear of negative evaluation of one's ability to perform.

Concept Chart 8.3 Sexual Response and Behavior

© macka/Shutterstock.com

Concept	Description	Additional Comments
Sexual response cycle	The characteristic pattern of bodily responses to sexual stimulation	According to Masters and Johnson, the sexual response cycle consists of four phases: excitement, plateau, orgasm, and resolution.
Sexual orientation	The direction of sexual attraction to one's own gender, to the opposite gender, or to both genders	The roots of sexual orientation remain obscure, but most investigators hold the view that genetic, hormonal, and environmental factors interact in the development of sexual orientation.
Sexual behavior	Includes masturbation, sexual intercourse, oral sex, and anal sex	Though the human body can respond to many forms of sexual stimulation, sexual behavior is strongly influenced by cultural learning, personal values, and individual experiences, not simply by biological drives or capacities for sexual response.
Sexual dysfunctions	Persistent problems with sexual interest, arousal, or response	The causes include biological factors (hormonal or medical problems) and psychosocial factors (guilt or anxiety, relationship issues, history of sexual trauma). Psychological and biological treatments are available to treat various types of sexual dysfunctions.

serotonin activity in the brain (Althof et al., 2014; Mohee & Eardley, 2011). Although research is ongoing, we still lack safe and effective pharmacological treatments for female sexual dysfunction. Before moving ahead, you may wish to review the major concepts relating to sexual motivation outlined in Concept Chart 8.3.

MODULE REVIEW 8.3 Sexual Motivation

Recite It

7. **Identify** and **describe** the four phases of the sexual response cycle.

The excitement phase is characterized by erection in the male and vaginal (a) _____ in the female. The plateau phase is an advanced state of arousal that precedes orgasm. The orgasm phase is characterized by involuntary (b) _____ of the pelvic musculature. During the (c) _____ phase, the body returns to its prearoused state.

8. **Describe** how researchers characterize the continuum of sexual orientation.

Most researchers conceptualize sexual orientation as a continuum with many gradations ranging from exclusive

(d) _____ on one end to exclusive (e) _____ on the other.

9. **Describe** the causes of sexual dysfunctions.

Sexual dysfunctions can have biological causes, such as declining hormone levels or health problems, and psychosocial causes, such as negative attitudes toward sex, communication problems, sexually traumatic experiences, and (f) _____ anxiety. They may be treated by a form of psychological treatment called (g) _____ therapy, by the use of therapeutic drugs, or by a combination of techniques.

Recall It

1. What aspect of our identity corresponds to our sense of maleness or femaleness?

2. Regarding the human sexual response cycle, match these terms with the following ones: (a) sexual release, intense pleasure; (b) body returns to prearoused state; (c) increased muscle tension and further increases in vasocongestion; (d) initial response to sexual stimulation.

   i. excitement phase   iii. plateau phase
   ii. orgasmic phase   iv. resolution phase

3. Which of the following statements best describes how the drug Viagra works?

   a. It increases sex drive.
   b. It relaxes blood vessels in the penis.
   c. It lowers blood pressure.
   d. It stimulates the muscles of the penis.

4. The failure to keep the level of stimulation below the man's ejaculatory threshold can lead to _____.

Think About It

■ Are you struggling with issues concerning your sexual orientation? Do you know someone who is? Are there resources on your campus or in your community that provide counseling services to people with these types of questions? How can you find out more about these services?

■ How do your sexual practices reflect your personal values? Which people have been the major influences on your sexual personal values?

Recite It *answers placed at the end of chapter.*

MODULE

8.4 Emotions

10 **Identify** the basic components of emotions and the six basic emotional expressions.

11 **Describe** the roles of gender and cultural factors in emotions.

12 **Identify** factors involved in human happiness.

13 **Explain** how the brain processes emotions.

14 **Describe** the major theories of emotion and **identify** the major theorists.

15 **Define** emotional intelligence and **evaluate** its importance.

16 **Describe** the polygraph technique and **evaluate** its reliability.

17 **Apply** techniques of anger management for controlling anger.

From the joy we feel at graduating college or landing a desirable job, to the sadness we feel at the loss of a loved one, to the ups and downs we experience in everyday life, our lives are filled with emotions. **Emotions** are complex feeling states that infuse our lives with color. We commonly say we are "red" with anger, "green" with envy, and "blue" with sadness. Imagine how colorless life would be without emotions. But what are emotions? Are particular emotional expressions recognized universally or only by members of the same culture? What is the physiological basis of emotions?

What Are Emotions?

Most people think of emotions simply as feelings, such as joy or anger. But psychologists view emotions as more complex feeling states that have three basic components: *bodily arousal* (nervous system activation), *cognitions* (the subjective or

emotions Feeling states that psychologists view as having physiological, cognitive, and behavioral components.

felt experience of the emotion, as well as the accompanying thoughts or judgments about people or situations that evoke the feeling), and *expressed behaviors* (outward expression of the emotion, such as approaching a love object or avoiding a feared one).

The physiological component of fear is bodily arousal. There is a degree of truth to the belief that we feel with our hearts. Strong emotions, such as fear and anger, are accompanied by activation of the sympathetic branch of the autonomic nervous system (ANS). As we noted in Chapter 2, activation of the sympathetic nervous system prompts the adrenal glands to release the hormones epinephrine and norepinephrine, which raise the body's level of arousal.

The cognitive component of fear includes what it feels like to be afraid, as well as the judgment that the situation is threatening. (If someone tosses a rubber snake at your feet, it may startle you, but it will not evoke fear when you appraise it as a fake.) The cognitive component of anger includes the judgment (cognitive appraisal) that events or the actions of others are unjust.

The behavioral expression of emotions generally takes two forms. We tend to approach objects or situations associated with pleasant emotions, such as joy or love, and avoid situations associated with fear, loathing, or disgust. When afraid, we approach the feared object in the hope of fighting it off, or we try to flee from it. Similarly, when angry, we tend to attack (approach) the object of our anger or to withdraw from it (that is, keep it at a distance). The behavioral component of emotions also encompasses ways in which we express emotions through facial features and other outward behaviors, such as gestures, tone of voice, and bodily posture.

Emotional Expression: Read Any Good Faces Lately?

Charles Darwin (1872) believed that emotions evolved because they have an adaptive purpose in helping species survive and flourish. Fear mobilizes animals to defend themselves in the face of a threatening predator; anger can be adaptive in provoking aggression that helps secure territory, resources, or mating partners. Darwin also recognized that the expression of emotions has communication value. For example, an animal displaying fear through its bodily posture or facial expression may signal others of its kind that danger lurks nearby. Darwin was the first to link specific facial expressions to particular emotions.

We can see the evolutionary roots of emotional expression in the similarity of the facial expressions of humans and nonhuman primates, such as gorillas. You don't need instructions to interpret the emotion expressed by the bared teeth of the ape and human shown in ■ Figure 8.6. This cross-species similarity in facial expression supports Darwin's view that human modes of emotional expression evolved from nonhuman primate ancestors (Chevalier-Skolnikoff, 1973).

FIGURE 8.6 Cross-Species Similarity in Facial Expression The bared teeth of both ape and man signal readiness to defend or to attack.

Facial Expressions of Emotion: Are They Universal?

Evidence suggests that six basic emotional expressions are universally recognized: anger, fear, disgust, sadness, happiness, and surprise (Ekman, 2003; Matsumoto, 2004) (see the Try This Out feature). In an early study, researchers had American students watch Japanese soap operas. Although the students didn't speak a word of Japanese, they recognized the emotions displayed by the characters simply by observing the facial expressions of the actors (Krauss, Curran, & Ferleger, 1983). Facial analysis tools developed by psychologist Paul Ekman, a leading authority on facial expressions of emotions, are now being used by airport screeners to detect telltale signs of emotions in people's faces in the effort to spot terrorists (Lipton, 2006).

A more recent study suggests that facial expressions of emotion are hardwired into the brain, rather than learned as the result of visual experience (Matsumoto

Try This Out   Reading Emotions in Facial Expressions

The same emotional expressions found in the streets of Chicago are found in the most distant corners of the world. The photographs accompanying this exercise show a man from a remote area of New Guinea. You probably have little difficulty recognizing the emotions he is portraying. Before reading further, match the following emotions to the numbers on the photos: (a) disgust, (b) sadness, (c) happiness, and (d) anger.

The man was asked to make faces as he was told stories involving the following: "Your friend has come and you are happy"; "Your child has died"; "You are angry and about to fight"; and "You see a dead pig that has been lying there a long time." So the correct answers are 1 (c), 2 (b), 3 (d), and 4 (a).

Paul Ekman, Ph.D/Paul Ekman Group, LLC

1._____   2._____   3._____   4._____

& Willingham, 2009). Investigators analyzed facial expressions of sighted and blind judo athletes based on photographs taken at the Olympic and Paralympic Games. Both sets of athletes used the same facial muscles in their emotional expressions, even though the blind athletes could not have acquired these responses through observation.

CONCEPT 8.22
Evidence supports the view that facial expressions of at least six basic emotions are recognized universally.

Cultural and Gender Differences in Emotions

Even though people the world over may recognize the same basic facial expressions of emotions, subtle differences exist across cultures in the appearance of these expressions. We can think of cultural differences in facial expressions as akin to nonverbal accents.

Psychologist Dacher Keltner of University of California at Berkeley calls attention to a particular type of nonverbal accent he describes as a national style of smiling. He notes that Americans tend to draw the corners of their lips up, showing their upper teeth, whereas people from Great Britain tend to draw their lips back as well as up, displaying their lower teeth (Max, 2005). The British smile may come across as a kind of suppressed grimace. See if you can tell the difference between the distinctive smiles of American actor Tom Cruise and British royal, Prince Charles, in the nearby photos.

Research has also uncovered cultural differences in how accurately emotions are recognized and how they are experienced and displayed. For example, people are generally more accurate when recognizing facial expressions of emotions in people of their own national, ethnic, and regional groups (Elfenbein & Ambady, 2002a, 2002b). In addition, certain emotions are more common in some cultures or even unique to a particular culture (Niiya, Ellsworth, & Yamaguchi, 2006). For example, Japanese people commonly report such emotions as *fureai* (feeling closely linked to others) and *oime* (an unpleasant feeling of indebtedness to others, similar to our

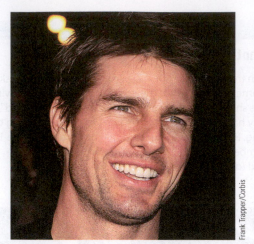 

Do people from different cultures or countries smile differently? Can you detect any differences in the smiles of American actor Tom Cruise and Prince Charles of England?

CONCEPT 8.23

Each culture has display rules that determine how emotions are expressed and how much emotion it is appropriate to express.

feeling of being "beholden"). These emotions are not unknown in the United States, but they are not as central to our lives as they are in Japan, where there is a greater cultural emphasis on communal values and mutual obligations.

Cultures also differ in how, or even whether, emotions are displayed. The term **display rules** refers to customs and social norms used to regulate the expression or display of emotion in a given culture (Fok et al., 2008; Matsumoto et al., 2005; Matsumoto et al., 2008). Display rules are learned as part of the socialization process and become so ingrained that they occur automatically among members of the same culture. Chinese and other East Asian cultures tend to frown on public displays of emotion, whereas emotions are expressed more openly in Mexican culture (Soto, Levenson, & Ebling, 2005). In East Asian cultures, people are expected to suppress their feelings in public; a failure to keep their feelings to themselves reflects poorly on their upbringing. The Japanese tend to hide negative emotions through smiling, which is one reason they tend to judge emotions in others based more on their tone of voice than their facial expressions (Tanaka et al., 2010). They tend to listen for emotional cues rather than read faces.

Cultures also have display rules governing the appropriate expression of emotions by men and women. In many cultures, women are given greater latitude than men in expressing certain emotions, such as joy, love, fear, and sadness, whereas men are permitted more direct displays of anger (Dittmann, 2003). Evidence shows that women tend to experience certain emotional states (joy, love, fear, sadness) more frequently than men (Brebner, 2003; Fischer et al., 2004). Yet the scientific jury is still out on whether there are gender differences in the experience of anger (Evers et al., 2005).

Women are generally better than men in expressing their feelings in both words and facial expressions and also in recognizing facial expressions of emotions in others (Lee et al., 2013; Spalek et al., 2015). Investigators suspect that women's brains may be wired differently, allowing them to be better able to perceive and recall emotional cues (Bianchin & Angrilli, 2011; Canli et al., 2002).

Men also tend to have more difficulty reading emotions in women's eyes than in men's eyes (Schiffer et al., 2013). However, we should consider some nuances when it comes to gender differences in emotions. For example, investigators report that women tend to be better at recognizing happy or sad faces, but men tend to hold an advantage when discerning angry faces (Bakalar, 2006b; Williams & Mattingley, 2006).

In Western cultures, men aren't supposed to cry or show their emotions or to smile very much. Not surprisingly, evidence shows that women tend to smile more than men (LaFrance, Hecht, & Paluck, 2003). However, the ideal of the stoic unemotional

display rules Cultural customs and norms that govern the display of emotional expressions.

male epitomized by Hollywood action heroes may be giving way to a new ideal: the "sensitive" male character.

Listening to music can also affect our emotional states. Did you ever notice how certain songs or melodies make you feel happier, whereas other music leaves you feeling sad or sorrowful? Exposure to romantic music may even make people more receptive to dating overtures. French researchers played songs with romantic lyrics in the background while young female participants waited to participate in a marketing study (Guéguen, Jacob, & Lamy, 2010). The female participants then interacted with a male confederate of the experimenter during the study, who—during a break—asked for their phone numbers to call them for a date. Guess what happened? Nearly double the number of women (52 percent) who had been exposed to romantic songs complied with the request for their phone numbers than those who had been exposed to neutral songs (28 percent) (SAGE Publications UK, 2010).

Happiness: What Makes You Happy?

Happiness may be a primary human emotion, but it has long been neglected by psychologists, who have focused mostly on understanding negative emotions such as fear, anger, and sadness. However, promoting human happiness is a key goal of *positive psychology,* a growing movement within psychology (see Chapter 1). The architects of the positive psychology movement believe that psychology should focus more on promoting human happiness and building human strengths and assets, such as the capacity to love and be loved, rather than just repairing negative emotions such as anxiety and depression.

What makes people happy? Is wealth the key? People may think they'd be a lot happier if they were wealthier, but evidence shows the link between money and happiness is largely an illusion (Kahneman et al., 2006). Wealth, and even good health, make only minor contributions to levels of happiness and life satisfaction (see, for example, Boyce, Brown, & Moore, 2010; Sussman & Shafir, 2012).

True, many people believe they would be much happier if they simply earned a lot more money, but evidence does not bear out this belief (Dunn & Norton, 2012; Proto & Rustichini, 2013). Although earning more money is linked to greater happiness at lower income levels, additional income beyond the level needed to meet a family's basic needs (about $75,000 in annual income) has little if any effect on personal happiness (see ■ Figure 8.7; Kahneman & Deaton, 2010; Munsey, 2010). Even members of the vaunted Forbes 400, a listing of the nation's wealthiest individuals, are only modestly happier than other people (Kesebir & Diener, 2008). One reason that greater wealth doesn't equate to greater happiness is that we tend to judge ourselves in relation to our peers; even people earning a high salary may not feel satisfied with their lives if others in their social network are earning much higher amounts (Frank, 2012). Consider too that although lottery winners often get an emotional boost from their winnings, their happiness tends to return to baseline levels within about a year (Corliss, 2003).

If not money, might marriage be the key to happiness? Generally speaking, married people are happier than single folks (Gallup Organization, 2005). But cause and effect may be muddled, as happier people might be more likely to get married or stay married. Turning again to the evidence, investigators find that whatever bounce in personal happiness newlyweds may experience tends to wear off within two years of marriage, with happiness levels then returning to the pre-wedding baseline (Lyubomirsky, 2012).

What, then, determines lasting happiness? Although research continues, evidence points to the importance of friends and religion (Deaton & Stone, 2013; Kesebir & Diener, 2008). Having close friendships is an important ingredient in happiness, so much so that social connections in childhood and adolescence more strongly predict whether

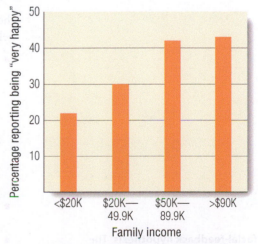

FIGURE 8.7 Happiness in Relation to Family Income
At around $50,000 a year, happiness begins to level off in relation to family income.

Source: Kahneman et al., 2006.

people will be happy in adulthood than does academic achievement (Olsson et al., 2012). We also find clusters of happy and unhappy people within social networks, lending support to the view that a person's happiness or unhappiness spreads through networks of friends, family members, and other social contacts like a social contagion (Fowler & Christakis, 2008; Roy-Byrne, 2009). In effect, whether or not you are happy may at least partly depend on having happy friends and family members.

Religion is also associated with happiness, and people who regularly participate in religious services are happier than less frequent attenders (Hout & Greeley, 2012). According to national surveys of Americans, the more frequently people participate in religious practices, the happier they tend to be. Researchers suspect that the happiness boost from religious practices comes from the emotional experiences of participating in religious services, not merely from socializing with others (Hout & Greeley, 2012).

Perhaps the greatest contribution overall to happiness is our inborn genetic potential. Genetic factors appear to play an important role in determining happiness (Chen et al., 2012). People may have a genetically determined "set point" for happiness, a level around which personal happiness tends to settle, despite the ups and downs of daily life (Wallis, 2005). Even so, happiness is not genetically fixed but can and does change through the course of a lifetime (Fujita & Diener, 2005; Inglehart et al., 2008). As we'll see next, we can nudge our genetic set point by enriching our lives in ways that boost happiness and well-being.

CONCEPT 8.24
People seem to have a particular "set point" for happiness, a level that remains fairly constant despite the ups and downs of life.

© Monkey Business Images/Shutterstock.com

Building Happiness

Positive psychology founder Martin Seligman (2003) argues that psychologists should become guides to help people lead the good life—the happy and meaningful life. He speaks of three kinds of human happiness: (1) *pleasure* of doing things, (2) *gratification* (being absorbed and engaged in life activities), and (3) *meaning* (finding personal fulfillment in life activities). Happiness is connected to doing things that are meaningful and personally fulfilling. Recent evidence echoes this view in showing that valuing time over the pursuit of money is associated with greater personal happiness (Whillans, Weidman, & Dunn, 2016).

Here are a few suggestions Seligman offers of things people can do in their daily lives to increase their personal happiness (adapted from Seligman, 2003; Seligman et al., 2005):

- *Gratitude visit.* Seligman believes that expressing gratitude is a key component of personal happiness. Close your eyes and visualize someone who has had a huge positive effect on your life—someone you never really thanked. Spend time during the next week writing a testimony of thanks to this person. Then schedule a visit to the person. When you arrive, read the testimonial and discuss with that person what he or she has meant to you. Gratitude visits can be infectious in a positive way. The recipients of the visit begin to think about the people *they* haven't thanked. They then make their own pilgrimage of thanks, which in turn can lead to a kind of daisy chain of gratitude and contentment (Pink, 2003).

- *Three blessings.* Every night, before going to bed, think of three things that went well during the day. Write them down and reflect on them.

- *One door closes, another opens.* Think about the times in your life that a door closed because of a death or a loss. Then think of a later experience in which a door opened. Come to appreciate the ebbs and flows of your experiences.

- *Savorings.* Plan a perfect day. But be sure to share it with another person.

All in all, happiness is not so much a function of what you've got as what you make of it. Happiness is most likely to be found in meaningful work, investment in family and community life, and development of strong spiritual or personal values.

facial-feedback hypothesis The belief that mimicking facial movements associated with a particular emotion will produce the corresponding emotional state.

Duchenne smile A genuine smile that involves contraction of a particular set of facial muscles.

The Facial-Feedback Hypothesis: Putting on a Happy Face

Can practicing smiling lift your mood? According to the **facial-feedback hypothesis**, mimicking the facial movements associated with an emotion will induce the corresponding emotional state. Just practicing smiling can induce more positive feelings, and either smiling or frowning can intensify the corresponding emotions even if the person is unaware of it (Davis, Senghas, & Ochsner, 2009; Soussignan, 2002). Practicing smiling several times a day may lift your spirits, at least temporarily, perhaps because it prompts you to recall pleasant experiences.

Yet the facial-feedback hypothesis has its limitations. A "put-on" smile is not the equivalent of a real one. Putting on a smile, the sort of smile you have when posing for family photos, may induce positive feelings, but is not accompanied by the feelings of enjoyment that lead to a genuine smile. In addition, these two types of smiles flex different facial muscles. We refer to a genuine smile as a **Duchenne smile**, after the French physician, Guillaume Duchenne de Boulogne (1806–1875), who discovered the facial muscles used to produce a genuine smile. You can see the difference between a genuine smile and a phony one in the photographs of emotions researcher Paul Ekman in ■ Figure 8.8.

Then there's the most enigmatic smile of all, that of the Mona Lisa. Recently, computer programmers created emotion-recognition software that could analyze facial features for telltale signs of emotions (Bohrn, Carbon, & Hutzler, 2010). By analyzing facial features such as the curvature of the lips and the crinkles around the eyes, researchers decoded the emotions expressed in the Mona Lisa portrait as composed of 83 percent happiness, 9 percent disgust, 6 percent fear, and 2 percent anger. No wonder Da Vinci's Mona Lisa has such an enigmatic smile.

CONCEPT 8.25
Evidence supports the view that practicing or mimicking facial movements associated with particular emotions can produce corresponding emotional states.

Paul Ekman, Ph.D./Paul Ekman Group, LLC

FIGURE 8.8 In Which Photo Is Paul Really Smiling?
As you probably guessed, the photo on the right shows a genuine smile; the smile in the photo on the left is simulated. One way to tell the difference is to look for crow's-feet around the eyes, a characteristic associated with genuine smiles.

How Your Brain Does Emotions

There is no one emotional center in the brain, nor any brain region that is solely responsible for any particular emotion such as fear or anger. Rather, emotional responses are regulated by complex brain networks located primarily in the limbic system and cerebral cortex (Barrett, 2015; Ray & Zald, 2011). You may recall from Chapter 2 that the limbic system includes the amygdala and hippocampus. The almond-shaped amygdala acts as a kind of emotional computer that evaluates threat potential and triggers fear responses to threatening objects or stimuli (Agren et al., 2012; Wood, Ver Hoef, & Knight, 2014). The amygdala controls—"gates"— the fear response, leading to behaviors associated with fear, such as freezing in place (Haubensak et al., 2010). For example, hearing people scream while riding a rollercoaster or attending a scary movie activates the amygdala, triggering a fear response (Arnal et al., 2015) ■ Figure 8.9 shows an example of activation of the amygdala in response to viewing a fearful face.

The hippocampus processes information relating to the context in which fear responses have been experienced. The hippocampus is involved in helping us remember place information or context and circumstances in which fear occurs, such as the bend in the road where we suddenly lost control of the car we were driving (Aamodt & Wang, 2008). The amygdala's role in emotions is not limited to fear; it is also involved in processing stimuli that elicit other emotional states, including grief and despair (Wang et al., 2005).

The cerebral cortex—the brain's "thinking center"—is connected to the limbic system and is a key player in processing fear and other emotions. It evaluates the meaning of emotionally arousing stimuli and plans and directs how to respond to them. It determines whether we should approach a stimulus (as in the case of a love

© Gianni Dagli Orti/CORBIS

Ah, her enigmatic smile. What is she really feeling? Researchers believe they may have an answer.

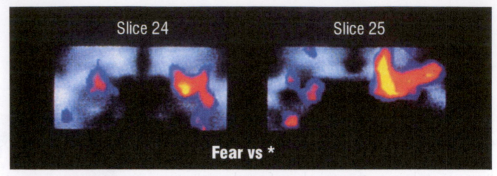

FIGURE 8.9 **Activation of Amygdala in Response to a Fearful Face**
Here we see functional MRI images of the amygdala in response to viewing a fearful face. More intense colors show greater activation in relation to a visual fixation point (control). Slice 24 shows the forward part of the amygdala, whereas Slice 25 shows the back part. The image is viewed as though the person were looking out from the page.

Source: National Institute of Mental Health (NIMH), 2001.

The fear you experience watching a scary movie is not just about what's happening on the screen; it's also about hearing people around you screaming, which triggers your amygdala to produce a fear response.

CONCEPT 8.26
The cerebral cortex and brain structures in the limbic system play key roles in regulating our emotional responses.

James–Lange theory The belief that emotions occur after people become aware of their physiological responses to the triggering stimuli.

interest or a pleasurable situation) or avoid one (as in the case of a threat). The cerebral cortex controls our subjective or felt experience of emotions, as well as our facial expressions of emotion.

There are differences in how the right and left cerebral hemispheres process emotions. Positive emotions, such as happiness, are associated with increased activity in the prefrontal cortex of the left cerebral hemisphere, whereas negative emotions, such as disgust, are associated with increased activity in the right prefrontal cortex (Davidson et al., 2002; Herrington et al., 2005). As noted in Chapter 2, the prefrontal cortex is the part of the frontal lobe that lies in front of the motor cortex. We're not sure why the hemispheres differ in this way, but studying these differences may yield important clues to the biological bases of emotional disorders like depression.

Theories of Emotion: Which Comes First—Feelings or Bodily Responses?

One night while I was driving home, my car hit an icy patch in the road and went out of control. The car spun completely around twice and wound up facing oncoming traffic. At that instant, I felt the way a deer must feel when it is caught in the headlights of a car bearing down on it—terrified and helpless. Fortunately, the cars coming toward me stopped in time, and I was able to regain control of my car. I arrived home safely but still shaking in fear. At the time, I didn't stop to consider the question many psychologists ponder: Did my awareness of my fear precede or follow my bodily response (shaking, sweating, heart pounding)? The *commonsense* view of emotion is that we first perceive a stimulus (the car spinning out of control), then feel an emotion (fear), and only then become physiologically aroused (heart pounding) and perform a behavioral response (tightly gripping the steering wheel). Yet one of the more enduring debates in psychology concerns which comes first—the feeling state (anger, fear, and so on) or our physiological or behavioral responses.

James–Lange Theory

William James (1890) argued that bodily reactions or sensations precede emotions. Because Carl Georg Lange, a Danish physiologist, proposed similar ideas independently, this view is called the **James–Lange theory**. James used the now classic example of confronting a bear in the woods. James asked the question, "Do we run from the bear because we are afraid, or do we become afraid because we run?" He answered this question by proposing that the response of running comes first. We see the bear. We run. Then we become afraid. We become afraid because we sense the particular pattern of bodily arousal associated with running, such as a pounding heart, rapid breathing, and muscular contractions (Friedman, 2010). Thus, emotions *follow* bodily reactions. In this view, we experience fear because we tremble; we experience the emotion of sadness because we cry. If this theory is correct, then my body would have reacted first when my car spun out of control. Only when I sensed my body's reaction would I have become consciously aware of fear.

James argued that distinct bodily changes are associated with each emotion. This is why fear feels different from other emotions, such as anger or love.

Cannon–Bard Theory

In the 1920s, physiologist Walter Cannon (1927) proposed a second major theory of emotions. He based his theory on research conducted by his laboratory assistant, Philip Bard. This theory, called the **Cannon-Bard theory**, challenged the James–Lange theory. It holds that the same bodily changes that result from the activation of the sympathetic nervous system accompany different emotions. Sympathetic activation makes our hearts race, our breathing quicken, and our muscles contract whether we are experiencing anger, fear, or sexual arousal. How could these common responses in the body evoke different emotions, as the James–Lange theory suggests? The Cannon–Bard theory proposes that the subjective experience of an emotion and the bodily reactions associated with it occur virtually simultaneously. In other words, our emotions accompany our bodily responses but are not caused by them. In simplest terms, the Cannon–Bard theory postulates that we see the bear, we experience fear and a pounding heart, and then we run.

Two-Factor Model

The **two-factor model**, which was developed in the 1960s, held that emotions depend on two factors: (1) a state of general arousal and (2) a cognitive interpretation, or *labeling* (Schachter, 1971; Schachter & Singer, 1962). According to this model, when we experience bodily arousal, we look for cues in the environment to explain why we feel aroused or excited. Your heart may race when you see a monster jump onto the movie screen in the latest horror movie; it may also race when your car spins out of control. Your arousal in the safe confines of the movie theater is likely to be labeled and experienced as "pleasurable excitement." But the same pattern of arousal experienced in the spinning car will probably be labeled and experienced as "sheer terror."

The two-factor model continues to generate interest, but it fails to account for the distinctive physiological features associated with different emotions. Anger may feel different from fear not merely because of how we label our arousal but also because it is associated with different bodily responses.

Experimental evidence also casts doubt on whether we must label the state of arousal to experience an emotion. Psychologist Robert Zajonc (1980, 1984) exposed subjects to brief presentations of Japanese ideographs (written symbols). Later, he found that subjects preferred particular characters they had seen, even if they had no recall of ever having seen these stimuli. Zajonc believes that some emotional responses, such as liking and disliking, may not involve any cognitive appraisal—that they may occur through mere exposure to a stimulus.

Dual-Pathway Model of Fear: "Feel First, Think Second"

According to the **dual-pathway model of fear** formulated by psychologist Joseph LeDoux (2000, 2003, 2008), the brain uses two pathways to process fear messages. An environmental stimulus (for example, seeing a car barreling down on you) is first

CONCEPT 8.27
The James–Lange theory proposes that emotions follow bodily reactions to triggering stimuli.

CONCEPT 8.28
The Cannon–Bard theory proposes that the subjective experience of an emotion and the bodily reactions associated with it occur virtually simultaneously.

CONCEPT 8.29
The two-factor model proposes that the combination of physiological arousal and cognitive appraisal (labeling) of the source of the arousal produces the specific emotional state.

Cannon–Bard theory The belief that emotional and physiological reactions to triggering stimuli occur almost simultaneously.

two-factor model The theory that emotions involve two factors: a state of general arousal and a cognitive interpretation (or labeling) of the causes of the arousal.

dual-pathway model of fear LeDoux's theory that the brain uses two pathways (a "high road" and a "low road") to process fear messages.

CONCEPT 8.30
The dual-pathway model suggests two
pathways for processing fear stimuli in the
brain: a "high road" leading to the cerebral
cortex and a "low road" leading to the
amygdala.

processed by the thalamus. From there, the information branches off, with one pathway (the "high road") leading to the cerebral cortex, the brain's thinking center where the threat can be evaluated more carefully. Another pathway (the "low road") leads directly to the amygdala in but a few thousandths of a second, allowing for a more immediate fear response to danger cues than if the signal had first passed through the cortex (see ■ Figure 8.10). The "low road" thus allows a faster response to danger cues. When it comes to fear, we tend to feel first and think second (Ropeik, 2012).

Suppose you are walking in the woods and see a curved object in the bush. This visual image is first processed by the thalamus, which makes a rough appraisal of the object as potentially dangerous (possibly a snake). The thalamus transmits this

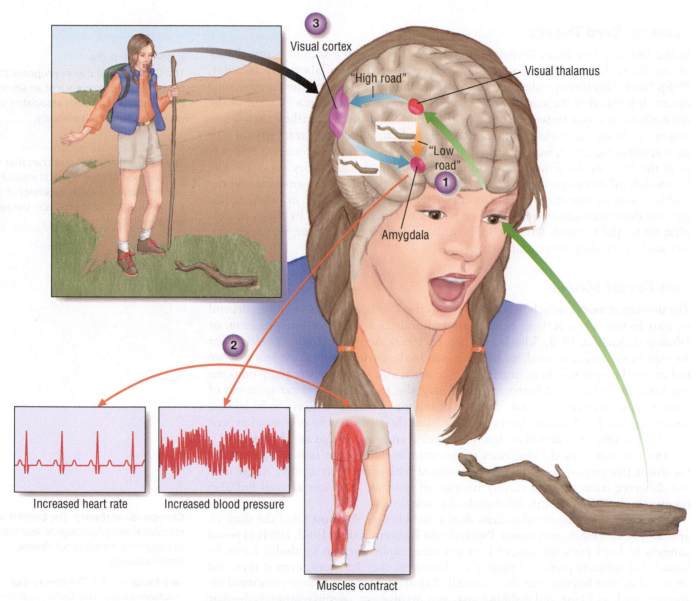

FIGURE 8.10 **LeDoux's Dual-Pathway Model of Fear**
LeDoux posits that fear messages are first processed in the thalamus and then branch off along two different pathways. One pathway, a "low road," goes directly to the amygdala, bypassing the higher thinking centers of the brain. The amygdala triggers a fear response that has multiple components. A "high road" leads to the cerebral cortex, where the message is interpreted more carefully. ("Relax. It's only a stick, not a snake.")

Source: Adapted from LeDoux, 1996.

information directly to the amygdala via the "low road," which prompts an immediate bodily response. Heart rate and blood pressure jump, and muscles throughout the body contract as the body prepares to respond quickly to a possible threat. The cortex, slower to respond, processes the information further. ("No, that's not a snake. It's just a stick.") From the standpoint of survival, it is better to act quickly on the assumption that the suspicious object is a snake and to ask questions later. Responding without thinking can be a lifesaver. As LeDoux puts it, "The time saved by the amygdala in acting on the thalamic information, rather than waiting for the cortical input, may be the difference between life and death. It is better to have treated a stick as a snake than not to have responded to a possible snake" (1994, p. 270). Whether the cortex interprets the object as a snake or a stick determines whether a fear response continues or is quickly quelled. The cortex is also responsible for producing the subjective or felt experience of fear.

What Does All This Mean?

Where do these various theories of emotions, as represented in ■ Figure 8.11, leave us? The James–Lange theory implies that distinctive bodily responses are associated with each emotion, whereas the Cannon–Bard theory postulates that a similar pattern of bodily responses accompanies different emotions. Both views may be at least partially correct. There certainly are common physiological responses associated with such emotions as fear, anger, and love, as the Cannon–Bard theory proposes. We feel our hearts beating faster when we are in the presence of a new love and when we are faced with an intruder in the night. Yet, as the James–Lange theory proposes, evidence shows there are also distinctive bodily reactions associated with different emotions (Friedman, 2010). For example, we may have the sensation of "cold feet" when we are afraid but not when we are angry because blood flow is reduced to our extremities in fear reactions but not in anger reactions. Anger is associated with a sharp rise in skin temperature, which may explain why we often describe people who are angry as "hot under the collar."

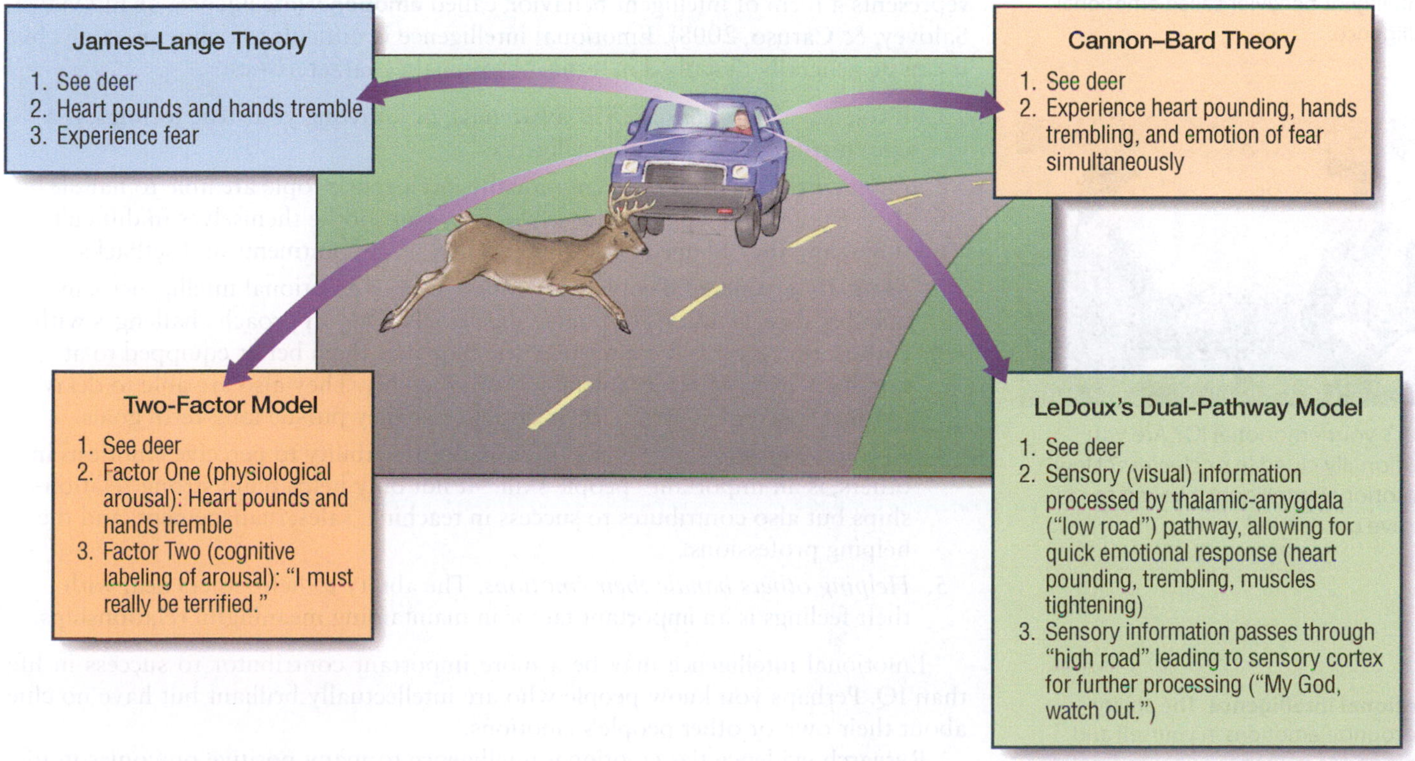

James–Lange Theory

1. See deer
2. Heart pounds and hands tremble
3. Experience fear

Cannon–Bard Theory

1. See deer
2. Experience heart pounding, hands trembling, and emotion of fear simultaneously

Two-Factor Model

1. See deer
2. Factor One (physiological arousal): Heart pounds and hands tremble
3. Factor Two (cognitive labeling of arousal): "I must really be terrified."

LeDoux's Dual-Pathway Model

1. See deer
2. Sensory (visual) information processed by thalamic-amygdala ("low road") pathway, allowing for quick emotional response (heart pounding, trembling, muscles tightening)
3. Sensory information passes through "high road" leading to sensory cortex for further processing ("My God, watch out.")

FIGURE 8.11 **Theoretical Models of Fear**

CONCEPT 8.31

The ability to recognize emotions in yourself and others and to regulate emotions effectively may represent a form of intelligent behavior called emotional intelligence.

What's your emotional IQ? Are you emotionally clued in or clueless? How is emotional intelligence linked to positive outcomes?

emotional intelligence The ability to recognize emotions in yourself and others and to manage your own emotions effectively.

Different emotions are also connected with different facial expressions. Blushing, for instance, is a primary characteristic of embarrassment. James considered facial expressions to be among the bodily responses that distinguish one emotion from another. Evidence favoring the facial-feedback hypothesis also provides some support for the James–Lange theory in showing that contractions of particular facial muscles (for example, smiling or frowning) can influence corresponding emotional states (Davis, Senghas, & Ochsner, 2009).

Emotions may precede cognitions under some conditions, as suggested by Zajonc's studies and by the dual-pathway model proposed by LeDoux. That emotions may occur before cognitions does not dismiss the important role that cognitions play in emotions. Whether you are angered when an instructor springs an unexpected assignment on you or frightened when a doctor points to a spot on your X-ray depends on the appraisal of the situation made in the cerebral cortex, not on automatic processing of stimuli by lower brain structures.

How we appraise events also depends on what the events mean to us personally (Lazarus, 2000). The same event, such as a pregnancy or a change of jobs, can lead to feelings of joy, fear, or even anger depending on the meaning the event has for the individual and its perceived importance. The nearby Try This Out feature offers an exercise in tracking your emotions.

The final chapter in the debate about how emotions are processed in the brain is still to be written. Yet the belief that distinctive bodily changes are associated with different emotions has had at least one practical implication. It is the basis of a method of lie detection, which is discussed later in this module.

Emotional Intelligence: How Well Do You Manage Your Emotions?

Some theorists believe that a person's ability to recognize and manage emotions represents a form of intelligent behavior, called **emotional intelligence**, or EI (Mayer, Salovey, & Caruso, 2008). Emotional intelligence is difficult to define precisely, but it can be generally described in terms of five main characteristics:

1. *Knowing your emotions.* Self-awareness, or knowing your true feelings, is a core feature of emotional intelligence.
2. *Managing your emotions.* Emotionally intelligent people are able to handle their emotions in appropriate ways. They can soothe themselves in difficult times, and they bounce back quickly from disappointments and setbacks.
3. *Motivating yourself.* People with a high level of emotional intelligence can marshal their emotions to pursue their goals. They approach challenges with enthusiasm, zeal, and confidence, which makes them better equipped to attain high levels of achievement and productivity. They also are able to delay gratification and constrain their impulses as they pursue long-term goals.
4. *Recognizing emotions in others.* Empathy, the ability to perceive emotions in others, is an important "people skill." It not only helps build strong relationships but also contributes to success in teaching, sales, management, and the helping professions.
5. *Helping others handle their emotions.* The ability to help others deal with their feelings is an important factor in maintaining meaningful relationships.

Emotional intelligence may be a more important contributor to success in life than IQ. Perhaps you know people who are intellectually brilliant but have no clue about their own or other people's emotions.

Research evidence ties emotional intelligence to many positive outcomes in life, including greater emotional well-being and life satisfaction, happier marriages, better job performance, greater success in medical school, and higher GPAs in college (see, for example, Choi & Kluemper, 2012; Davis & Humphrey, 2011; Joseph et al., 2015; Libbrecht et al., 2014; Schutte & Loi, 2014). People also tend to prefer working for an emotionally intelligent boss over one with a high IQ, so it's not surprising that many MBA programs now include measures of EI in their admissions process (Furnham, McClelland, & Mansi, 2012; Korn, 2013).

The Polygraph: Does It Work?

Let us end this module by commenting on the use of the polygraph, a device used to detect lying by comparing a person's responses to control (neutral) and test questions. It is based on the assumption that when people lie, they reveal telltale signs in breathing patterns, heart rates, and the electrical reactivity of the skin as the result of sweating. The polygraph measures patterns of bodily arousal, not lying per se. Many leading scientists, along with distinguished scientific groups such as the National Academy of Sciences, say the polygraph cannot accurately distinguish lying from the emotional reactions of honest people put in pressure situations (for example, Kluger & Masters, 2006). Another problem is that many seasoned liars can lie without any signs of nervousness or other telltale physiological reactions (Vrij, Granhag, & Porter, 2011). Unfortunately, false findings of polygraphs have damaged the lives of many innocent people. Though the polygraph may occasionally catch a person in a lie, it is not reliable enough to pass scientific muster. More sophisticated methods of detecting lying are in the experimental stage, such as measurement of minute facial movements associated with deception (Warren, Schertler, & Bull, 2009). That said, we still lack any reliable indicator of lying (Vrij, Granhag, & Porter, 2011), let alone anything akin to Pinocchio's nose, which grew each time the fictional character told a lie.

Concept Chart 8.4 provides an overview of the major concepts of emotion discussed in this module.

CONCEPT 8.32

Polygraphs are widely used, even though scientists remain skeptical of their ability to detect lying.

Is this person lying? The polygraph is widely used to detect lying, but critics claim it doesn't measure up to scientific standards of reliability.

Concept Chart 8.4	Major Concepts of Emotion	
	Concept	**Description**
	Facial expressions of emotion	Evidence from cross-cultural studies supports universal recognition of the facial expressions of six basic emotions: anger, fear, disgust, sadness, happiness, and surprise.
	Facial-feedback hypothesis	According to this hypothesis, mimicking facial movements associated with an emotion can produce the corresponding emotional state.
	Physiological bases of emotions	Emotions are accompanied by activation of the sympathetic branch of the autonomic nervous system. Emotions are processed by the structures of the limbic system (the amygdala and hippocampus) and by the cerebral cortex.

(Continued)

Concept Chart 8.4   (Continued)

	Concept	Description
	James–Lange theory of emotions	Emotions follow our bodily reactions to triggering stimuli—we become afraid because we run; we feel sad because we cry.
	Cannon–Bard theory of emotions	Emotions accompany bodily responses to triggering stimuli but are not caused by them.
	Two-factor model of emotions	The combination of physiological arousal and cognitive appraisal (labeling) of the source of the arousal produces the emotional state.
	LeDoux's dual-pathway model of fear	One pathway leads from the thalamus to the amygdala, which produces the initial fear response (bodily arousal), while a second pathway leads to the cortex, which further processes the fear stimulus and produces the conscious awareness of fear.
	Emotional intelligence	According to this concept, the ability to manage emotions effectively is a form of intelligent behavior.
	Polygraph	A device used to detect lying based on analysis of differences in physiological responses to control questions and test questions.

APPLYING PSYCHOLOGY in Daily Life

Managing Anger

CONCEPT 8.33
By identifying and correcting anger-inducing thoughts, people can gain better control over their anger and develop more effective ways of handling conflicts.

CONCEPT LINK
Chronic anger is not only a problem when it comes to controlling your temper; it can also increase your risk of developing coronary heart disease. See Module 10.2.

Do you know people who have problems controlling their temper? Do you yourself do things in anger that you later regret? Anger can be a catalyst for physical or verbal aggression. Even if you never express your anger through aggression, anger and hostility can take a toll on your health, putting you at increased risk of developing coronary heart disease (Chida & Steptoe, 2009) (see Chapter 10). Anger floods the body with stress hormones that may eventually damage your heart and arteries.

Cognitive theorists recognize that anger is prompted by a person's reactions to frustrating or provocative situations, not by the situations themselves. Though people often blame the "other guy" for making them angry, people make themselves angry by thinking angering thoughts or making anger-inducing statements to themselves. To gain better control over their anger, people need to identify and correct such thoughts and statements. By doing so, they can learn to avoid hostile confrontations and perhaps save wear and tear on their cardiovascular systems. Here are some suggestions psychologists offer for identifying and controlling anger:

- *Become aware of your emotional reactions in anger-provoking situations.* When you notice yourself getting "hot under the collar," take this as a cue to calm yourself down and think through the situation. Learn to replace anger-arousing thoughts with calming alternatives.
- *Review the evidence.* Might you be overreacting to the situation by taking it too personally? Might you be jumping to the conclusion that the other person means you ill? Are there other ways of viewing the person's behavior?

- *Practice more adaptive thinking.* For example, say to yourself, "I can handle this situation without getting upset. I'll just calm down and think through what I want to say."

- *Practice competing responses.* You can disrupt an angry response by conjuring up soothing mental images, by taking a walk, or by practicing self-relaxation. The time-honored practice of counting to 10 when you begin to feel angry may also help defuse an emotional response. If it doesn't, you can follow Mark Twain's advice and count to 100 instead. While counting, try to think calming thoughts.

- *Don't get steamed.* Others may do dumb or hurtful things, but you make yourself angry by dwelling on them. Take charge of your emotional responses by not allowing yourself to get steamed.

- *Oppose anger with empathy.* Try to understand what the other person is feeling. Rather than saying to yourself, "He's a miserable so-and-so who deserves to be punished," say, "He must really have difficulties at home to act like this. But that's his problem. I won't take it personally."

- *Congratulate yourself for responding assertively rather than aggressively.* Give yourself a mental pat on the back when you handle stressful situations with equanimity rather than with anger.

- *Scale back your expectations of others.* Perceptions of unfairness may result from the expectation that others "should" or "must" fulfill your needs or expectations. By scaling back your expectations, you're less likely to get angry with others when they disappoint you.

- *Modulate verbal responses.* Avoid raising your voice or cursing. Stay cool, even when others do not.

- *Learn to express positive feelings.* Expressing positive feelings can help diffuse negative emotions. Tell others you love them and care about them. They are likely to reciprocate in kind.

Think about situations in which you have felt angry or have acted in anger. How might you handle these situations differently in the future? What coping responses can you use to help you keep your cool? Table 8.3 offers some calming alternatives to thoughts that trigger anger.

Table 8.3 Anger Management: Replacing Anger-Inducing Thoughts with Calming Alternatives

Situation	Anger-Inducing Thoughts	Calming Alternatives
A provocateur says, "So what are you going to do about it?"	"That jerk. Who does he think he is? I'll teach him a lesson he won't forget!"	"He must really have a problem to act the way he does. But that's his problem. I don't have to respond at his level."
You get caught in a monster traffic jam.	"Why does this always happen to me? I can't stand this."	"This may be inconvenient, but it's not the end of the world. Don't blow it out of proportion. Everyone gets caught in traffic now and then. Just relax and listen to some music."
You're in a checkout line at the supermarket, and the woman in front of you is cashing a check. It seems as if it's taking hours.	"She has some nerve holding up the line. It's so unfair for someone to make other people wait. I'd like to tell her off!"	"It will take only a few minutes. People have a right to cash their checks in the market. Just relax and read a magazine while you wait."

(continued)

Table 8.3 *continued*

Situation	Anger-Inducing Thoughts	Calming Alternatives
You're looking for a parking spot when suddenly another car cuts you off and seizes a vacant space.	"No one should be allowed to treat me like this. I'd like to punch him out."	"Don't expect people always to be considerate of your interests. Stop personalizing things." Or "Relax, there's no sense going to war over this."
Your spouse or partner comes home several hours later than expected, without calling to let you know he or she would be late.	"It's so unfair. I can't let him (her) treat me like this."	Explain how you feel without putting your spouse or partner down.
You're watching a movie in a theater, and the people sitting next to you are talking and making a lot of noise.	"Don't they have any regard for others? I'm so angry with these people I could tear their heads off."	"Even if they're inconsiderate, it doesn't mean I have to get angry about it or ruin my enjoyment of the movie. If they don't quiet down when I ask them, I'll just change my seat or call the manager."

Source: From Jeffrey S. Nevid, Spencer A. Rathus, and Beverly Greene, *Abnormal Psychology in a Changing World*. Copyright © 2003 Prentice-Hall, Inc. Reproduced by permission of Pearson Education, Inc.

MODULE REVIEW   8.4   Emotions

Recite It

10. Identify the basic components of emotions and the six basic emotional expressions.

Psychologists conceptualize emotions as having a **(a)** _____ component (heightened bodily arousal), a **(b)** _____ component (a feeling state, as well as thoughts and judgments about experiences linked to the feeling state), and a **(c)** _____ component (approach or avoidance behaviors).

Evidence from cross-cultural studies supports the view that facial expressions of six basic emotions—anger, fear, disgust, sadness, happiness, and **(d)** _____—are universally recognized.

11. Describe the roles of gender and cultural factors in emotions.

Cultural differences, as well as some similarities, exist in how emotions are experienced. Each culture has rules, called **(e)** _____ rules, that determine how emotions are expressed and how much emotion is appropriate to express. Gender differences in emotional expression may reflect **(f)** _____ expectations.

12. Identify factors involved in human happiness.

Wealth is only modestly associated with personal happiness or life satisfaction above a subsistence level of income. Factors that predict happiness include social connectedness to others and **(g)** _____ commitment.

Happiness may also vary around a genetically influenced **(h)** _____ point. Still, there is much we can do to make our lives happier and more fulfilling.

13. Explain how the brain processes emotions.

Parts of the **(i)** _____ system, including the amygdala and the hippocampus, play key roles in emotional processing. The **(j)** _____ _____ interprets stimuli and plans strategies for either approaching or avoiding stimuli, depending on whether they are perceived as "friend" or "foe." The cortex also controls facial expression of emotions and is responsible for processing the felt experience of emotions.

14. Describe the major theories of emotion and **identify** the major theorists.

The major theories of emotions are the **(k)** _____-_____ theory (emotions occur after people become aware of their body's responses to triggering stimuli), the Cannon–Bard theory (emotional and physiological reactions to triggering stimuli occur almost **(l)** _____), the **(m)** _____-_____ model (emotions depend on an arousal state and labeling of the causes of the arousal), and LeDoux's dual-pathway model of fear (the **(n)** _____ responds to fear stimuli before the cerebral cortex gets involved).

15. Define emotional intelligence and **evaluate** its importance.

(o) _____ intelligence refers to the ability to recognize emotions in oneself and others and to manage emotions effectively. Emotional intelligence may have an important bearing on our success in life and ability to maintain intimate relationships.

16. Describe the polygraph technique and **evaluate** its reliability.

The polygraph is a device used to detect physiological responses believed to indicate when a person is (p) _____. However, we lack compelling scientific evidence that the polygraph can reliably detect lying.

17. Apply techniques of anger management for controlling anger.

Become aware of your emotional reactions in anger-provoking situations, review the evidence, practice more adaptive thinking, practice competing responses, don't get steamed, oppose anger with (q) _____, congratulate yourself for responding assertively rather than aggressively, scale back your expectations of others, and learn to express positive feelings.

Recall It

1. All of the following are basic components of emotion *except*
   a. bodily arousal.
   b. production of neuropeptide Y.
   c. cognition.
   d. expressed behavior.

2. Facial expressions of six basic emotions are recognized universally. What are these six emotions?

3. The belief that the subjective experience of an emotion and the bodily response that accompanies it occur at virtually the same time is the
   a. James–Lange theory.
   b. two-factor model.
   c. Cannon–Bard theory.
   d. dual-pathway model of fear.

4. Which of the following statements is *not* correct?
   a. Women are generally better able than men to express emotions in words.
   b. Women are generally better able than men to express emotions through facial expressions.
   c. In many cultures, men are given greater latitude in displaying anger.
   d. Evidence shows that men tend to smile more often than women.

Think About It

■ How is emotional intelligence different from general intelligence? In what ways might it become more important for success in life than general intelligence?

Recite It *answers placed at the end of chapter.*

THINKING CRITICALLY ABOUT PSYCHOLOGY

Based on your reading of this chapter, answer the following questions. Then, to evaluate your progress in developing critical thinking skills, compare your answers to the sample answers found in Appendix A.

People often think of thinking and feeling as opposite mental states. Is it correct to think of them as opposites? Why or why not?

Recite It Answers for Chapter 8

Module 8.1 1. (a) Motivation; (b) genetically; (c) complex; (d) Drive; (e) increase; (f) arousal; (g) optimal; (h) Incentive; (i) drive, 2. (j) Psychosocial; (k) achievement; (l) realistic, 3. (m) biological; (n) self-actualization **Module 8.2** 4. (a) Homeostatic; (b) hypothalamus; (c) hormones, 5. (d) metabolic; (e) fat, 6. (f) Anorexia nervosa; (g) Bulimia nervosa; (h) laxatives; (i) thinness; (j) control **Module 8.3** 7. (a) lubrication; (b) contractions; (c) resolution, 8. (d) homosexuality; (e) heterosexuality, 9. (f) performance; (g) sex **Module 8.4** 10. (a) physiological; (b) cognitive; (c) behavioral; (d) surprise, 11. (e) display; (f) cultural, 12. (g) religious; (h) set, 13. (i) limbic; (j) cerebral cortex, 14. (k) James–Lange; (l) simultaneously; (m) two-factor; (n) amygdala, 15. (o) Emotional, 16. (p) lying, 17. (q) empathy

Motivation: The "Whys" of Behavior

Biological Sources of Motivation

- **Instincts:** Inborn, species-specific responses as motives
- **Needs and Drives:** States of deficiency (needs) create drives that motivate behavior that result in drive reduction
- **Stimulus Motives:** Needs for exploration and optimal stimulation

Psychological Sources of Motivation

- **Incentives:** Rewards or goals that "pull" behavior
- **Psychosocial Needs:** Needs for friendship and achievement
- **Maslow's Need Hierarchy:** Biological and psychosocial needs ordered in a hierarchy

Self-Actualization
Fulfillment of individual potential

Esteem
Achievement, respect, prestige, status, approval

Love and Belongingness
Emotional intimacy, friendships, social connections

Safety
Safe and secure housing, protection from crime and harsh weather

Physiological
Hunger, thirst, avoidance of pain, sexual gratification, elimination

MODULE 8.2

Hunger and Eating

- **Control of Hunger:** Hypothalamus (brain's appetite regulator); brain chemicals act on hypothalamus to stimulate or curb appetite

Hypothalamus

Corpus callosum

1 Lateral hypothalamus

2 Ventromedial hypothalamus

Location of the Hypothalamus

Cross-section Showing Parts of the Hypothalamus

- **Obesity:** Many factors are involved including genetics, eating patterns, environmental influences, and emotions
- **Eating Disorders:** Anorexia nervosa (self-starvation and distorted body image) and bulimia (cycles of binge eating and purging); causes include social pressure to conform to ultrathin ideal, needs for perfectionism and control, genetic factors, irregularities in neurotransmitter functioning

MODULE 8.3

Sexual Motivation

- **Sexual Response Cycle:** Comprises four phases of (1) excitement, (2) plateau, (3) orgasm, and (4) resolution
- **Sexual Orientation:** Directionality of sexual attraction; causal factors most likely involve biological and psychosocial influences
- **Sexual Dysfunctions:** Problems in sexual interest, arousal, or response; causes include physical diseases and psychosocial factors such as relationship problems, performance anxiety, and negative attitudes toward sexuality

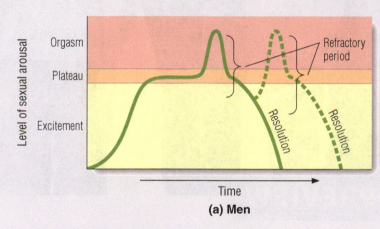
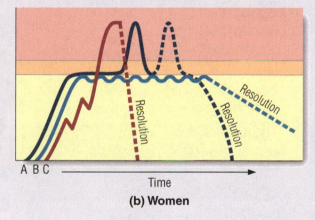

(a) Men   (b) Women

MODULE 8.4

Emotions

- **Components of Emotions:** Bodily arousal, cognitions, approach or avoidance behaviors
- **Universally Recognized Emotions:** Anger, fear, disgust, sadness, happiness, surprise
- **Key Brain Structures in Emotions:** Amygdala (fear-triggering center), hippocampus (remembering the context of the emotion), thalamus (initial processing center for fear-related messages), cerebral cortex (evaluating the threat)
- **Major Theories of Emotions:** James–Lange theory (see bear→run→feel afraid); Cannon–Bard theory (see bear→run and feel afraid); two-factor model (bodily arousal→labeling source of arousal→emotional state); dual-pathway model (the "low road" to the amygdala, the "high road" to the cerebral cortex)

LEARNING OBJECTIVES

After studying this chapter, you will be able to . . .

1 **Identify** and **describe** the stages of prenatal development and major threats to prenatal development.

2 **Identify** reflexes present at birth.

3 **Describe** the infant's sensory, perceptual, and learning abilities.

4 **Describe** the development of the infant's motor skills in the first year of life.

5 **Identify** and **describe** three types of infant temperament and three types of infant attachment styles.

6 **Identify** and **describe** the major parenting styles.

7 **Identify** and **describe** Erikson's stages of psychosocial development in childhood.

8 **Describe** Piaget's stages of cognitive development.

9 **Describe** Vygotsky's psychosocial theory of cognitive development.

10 **Describe** the physiological, cognitive, and psychosocial changes that occur during adolescence, and Erikson's beliefs about psychosocial development in adolescence.

11 **Describe** Kohlberg's stages of moral reasoning and **evaluate** his theory in light of Gilligan's criticism.

12 **Describe** the physical and cognitive changes that occur during adulthood and Erikson's stages of psychosocial development in early and middle adulthood.

13 **Describe** the physical and cognitive changes we can expect later in life, and Erikson's views on psychosocial development in late adulthood.

14 **Evaluate** the qualities associated with successful aging.

15 **Identify** the stages of dying proposed by Kübler-Ross.

16 **Apply** suggestions for living a longer and healthier life.

monkeybusinessimages/iStock/Getty Images

PREVIEW

Human Development

Keeping Peace at the Dinner Table

One of the things parents learn when they have a second child is the everyday meaning of the concept of equality. They learn that whatever they give to one child they must give to the other in equal measure. This lesson in parenting was driven home for me one day when we sat down at the dinner table to share a pizza. Everything was fine until we divided the last two slices between Daniella, then age 5, and Michael, who was then 11. I noticed Daniella's eyes beginning to well up with tears. I asked her what was wrong. She pointed to Michael's slice and said that his was bigger. Michael had already begun eating his slice, so it was clear that pulling a last-minute switch wouldn't ease her concern, let alone be fair to Michael. It was then that the heavy hammer of equality came down squarely on my head.

To resolve the situation, I drew upon a principle you'll read about in this chapter: the principle of *conservation*. This is the principle that the amount or size of a substance does not change merely as the result of a superficial change in its outward appearance. You don't increase the amount of clay by merely flattening or stretching it out. Neither do you increase the amount of a liquid by pouring it from a wider container into a narrower one, even though the liquid rises to a higher level in the narrower container. Although the principle of conservation may seem self-evident to an adult or older child, the typical 5-year-old has not mastered this concept. Knowing this, I quickly took a pizza slicer and divided Daniella's slice into two. "There," I said, "now you have twice as many slices as Michael." Michael gave me a quizzical look, as if he was wondering who on earth would fall for such an obvious trick. Daniella, on the other hand, looked at the two slices and quite happily started eating them, the tears receding. Peace at the Nevid dining table was restored, at least for the moment.

The pizza incident illustrates a theme that carries throughout our study of human development. It's not about applying principles of child psychology to keep peace at the dinner table. Rather, it's about understanding that the world of the child is very different from the world of the adolescent or adult. Children's cognitive abilities and ways of understanding the world change dramatically during childhood. As we continue our voyage of discovery through development, we'll find that many adolescents see themselves and the world quite differently than do their parents and other adults. Even in adulthood, people of 20-something or 30-something years see themselves and their place in the world quite differently than do those of more advanced years.

In this chapter, we trace the remarkable journey that is human development. Our story would be incomplete without first considering the important events that occur well before a child takes its first breath.

Did you know that...

- A fertilized egg cell is not yet attached to the mother's body during the first week or so after conception? (p. 325)
- There is no accepted safe limit for alcohol use during pregnancy? (p. 328)
- Baby geese followed a famous scientist around as if he were their mother? (p. 336)
- According to theorist Erik Erikson, the development of a sense of trust begins before the infant speaks its first word? (p. 341)
- It is normal for a 4-year-old to believe the moon has feelings? (p. 345)
- Despite what you may have heard, the percentage of teenagers who engage in sexual intercourse today is actually less than it was at the beginning of the new millennium? (p. 358)
- A midlife crisis may be more the exception than the rule during middle adulthood? (p. 363)
- The next best thing to a Fountain of Youth may be your neighborhood gym? (p. 370)

9.1 Prenatal Development: A Case of Nature and Nurture

1 **Identify** and **describe** the stages of prenatal development and major threats to prenatal development.

The branch of psychology that studies the systematic changes that occur during the life span is called **developmental psychology**. We can think of development progressing chronologically in terms of the stages shown in Table 9.1. We begin our story of human development by considering the important events that occur well before a child takes its first breath.

Prenatal development brings into focus the long-debated issue of how much of our development is due to nature (genes) and how much to nurture (the environment). Human development is best understood as a continuous interplay of heredity and experience (Leve et al., 2010; Meaney, 2010). Though some physical traits, such as hair color, are determined by only a single gene, complex behavioral traits such as intelligence and personality are influenced by multiple genes interacting with environmental factors (see, for example, Diamond, 2009; Gottesman & Hanson, 2005; Johnson et al., 2009).

Maturation, the biological unfolding of an organism according to its underlying genetic blueprint, largely determines how organisms, including ourselves, grow and develop physically. It explains why children of tall parents tend to be tall themselves and those with curly-haired parents tend to have curly hair. Yet development also depends on environmental factors, such as nutrition. The influences of nature and nurture begin to shape development even in the womb.

developmental psychology The branch of psychology that explores physical, emotional, cognitive, and social aspects of development.

maturation The biological unfolding of the organism according to the underlying genetic code.

Table 9.1 Stages of Development through the Life Span

Stage	Approximate Ages
Prenatal period	Conception to birth
Infancy period	Birth to 1 year
Toddler period	1 to 3 years
Preschool period	3 to 6 years
Middle childhood	6 to 12 years
Adolescence	12 to 18 years
Young adulthood	18 to 40 years
Middle adulthood	40 to 65 years
Late adulthood	65 years and older

Stages of Prenatal Development

Scientists believe that sexual reproduction began some 240 to 320 million years ago, long before humans ever strode upon the earth (Lahn & Page, 1999). They believe it began with a single chromosome that mutated to form the X and Y sex chromosomes that determine sex in mammals, including humans. The male of the species carries a combination of X and Y sex chromosomes, whereas the female carries two X chromosomes. Each reproductive cell or germ cell—the sperm in males and the ovum (egg cell) in females—contains only one copy of the two sex chromosomes. All other body cells have two sex chromosomes. Thus, a sperm cell carries either one X or one Y sex chromosome, whereas an ovum carries only one X. When an ovum is fertilized, the resulting combination (XX or XY) determines the baby's sex.

During **ovulation**, an ovum is released from one of the **ovaries** and then begins a slow journey through a **fallopian tube**. If fertilization occurs (the uniting of a sperm and an ovum), the resulting combination (XX or XY) of the sex chromosomes in the fertilized ovum determines the baby's sex. The single cell, called a **zygote**, that forms from the uniting of sperm and ovum soon undergoes cell division. First, it divides into two cells; then each of these two cells divides, forming four cells; each of these four cells divides, resulting in eight cells; and so on. In the months that follow, organ systems form as the developing organism increasingly takes on the form and structure of a human being.

A typical 9-month pregnancy is commonly divided into three trimesters, or 3-month periods. From the standpoint of prenatal development, we can also identify three major prenatal stages or periods: the germinal stage, which roughly corresponds to the first 2 weeks after conception; the embryonic stage, which spans the period of about 2 weeks to about 8 weeks after conception; and the fetal stage, which continues until birth (see ■ Figure 9.1).

The **germinal stage** spans the time from **fertilization** to implantation in the wall of the **uterus**. For the first three or four days following conception, the mass of dividing cells moves about the uterus before implantation. The process of implantation is not completed for perhaps another week or so.

The **embryonic stage** spans the period from implantation to about the eighth week of pregnancy. The major organ systems begin to take shape in the developing organism, which we now call the **embryo**. About three weeks into pregnancy, two ridges fold together to form the **neural tube**, from which the nervous system will develop. The head and blood vessels also begin to form at this time. By the fourth week, a primitive heart takes shape and begins beating. It will normally (and hopefully) continue beating without a break for at least the next 80, 90, or more years.

In this remarkable photograph of the dance of life, a single sperm is attempting to penetrate the egg covering. If it succeeds, the genetic material from both parents will combine into a single cell that marks the beginning of a new life.

ovulation The release of an egg cell (ovum) from the ovary.

ovaries The female gonads, which secrete the female sex hormones estrogen and progesterone and produce mature egg cells.

fallopian tube A straw-like tube between an ovary and the uterus through which an ovum passes after ovulation.

zygote A fertilized egg cell.

germinal stage The stage of prenatal development that spans the period from fertilization through implantation.

fertilization The union of sperm and ovum.

uterus The female reproductive organ in which the fertilized ovum becomes implanted and develops to term.

embryonic stage The stage of prenatal development from implantation through about the eighth week of pregnancy during which the major organ systems begin to form.

embryo The developing organism at an early stage of prenatal development.

neural tube The area in the embryo from which the nervous system develops.

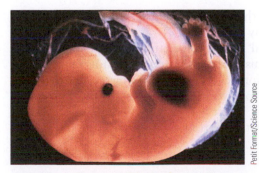

FIGURE 9.1 **Prenatal Development**
Dramatic changes in shape and form occur during prenatal development. Compare the embryo (a) at about 6 to 7 weeks of development with the fetus (b) at approximately 16 weeks. The fetus has already taken on a clearly recognizable human form.

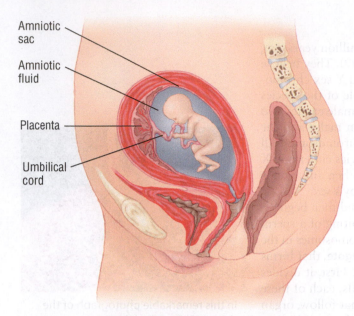

Amniotic sac

Amniotic fluid

Placenta

Umbilical cord

FIGURE 9.2 Structures in the Womb During prenatal development, the embryo lies in a protective enclosure within the uterus called the amniotic sac. Nutrients and waste materials are exchanged between mother and embryo/fetus through the placenta. The umbilical cord connects the embryo and fetus to the placenta.

CONCEPT 9.1

The fetus faces many risks, including maternal malnutrition and teratogens.

CONCEPT 9.2

Certain environmental influences or agents, called teratogens, may harm a developing embryo or fetus.

amniotic sac The uterine sac that contains the fetus.

placenta The organ that provides for the exchange of nutrients and waste materials between mother and fetus.

fetal stage The stage of prenatal development in which the fetus develops, beginning around the ninth week of pregnancy and lasting until the birth of the child.

fetus The developing organism in the later stages of prenatal development.

The embryo is suspended in a protective environment within the mother's uterus called the **amniotic sac** (see ■ Figure 9.2). Surrounding the embryo is amniotic fluid, which acts as a kind of shock absorber to cushion the embryo and fetus from damage that could result from the mother's movements. Nutrients and waste materials are exchanged between the mother and the embryo (and fetus) through the **placenta**. The embryo and later, the fetus, are connected to the placenta by the umbilical cord. The placenta allows nutrients and oxygen to pass from mother to fetus. Their blood streams do not mix.

The **fetal stage**, or stage of the **fetus**, begins around the 9th week of pregnancy and continues until the birth of the child. All of the major organ systems, as well as the fingers and toes, are formed by about the 12th week of prenatal development, which roughly corresponds to the end of the first trimester. They continue to develop through the course of the pregnancy. The fetus increases more than 30-fold in weight during the second trimester of pregnancy, from about 1 ounce to about 2 pounds. It grows from about 4 inches in length to about 14 inches. Typically the mother will feel the first fetal movements around the middle of the fourth month. By the end of the second trimester, the fetus approaches the *age of viability*, the point at which it becomes capable of sustaining life on its own. However, fewer than half of infants born at the end of the second trimester that weigh less than 2 pounds will survive on their own, even with the most intense medical treatment.

Threats to Prenatal Development

A pregnant woman requires adequate nutrition for the health of the fetus as well as for her own. Maternal malnutrition is associated with a greater risk of premature birth (birth prior to 37 weeks of gestation) and low birth weight (less than 5 pounds, or about 2,500 grams). Preterm and low-birth-weight babies face a higher risk of infant mortality and later developmental problems, including cognitive deficits and attention difficulties (for example, Lemons et al., 2001).

Women may receive prescriptions from their obstetricians for multivitamin pills to promote optimal fetal development. The federal government recommends that all women of childbearing age take 400 micrograms daily of the B vitamin folic acid and that pregnant women take 800 micrograms. Folic acid greatly reduces the risk of neural tube defects such as **spina bifida**, but only if it is taken early in pregnancy (Heseker, 2011).

The word **teratogen** is derived from the Greek root *teras,* meaning "monster." Teratogens include certain drugs taken by the mother, X-rays, environmental contaminants such as lead and mercury, and infectious organisms capable of passing through the placenta to the embryo or fetus. The risks posed by teratogens are greatest during certain critical periods of development. For example, teratogens that may damage the arms and legs are most likely to have an effect during the fourth through eighth weeks of development (see Concept Chart 9.1).

Let us now consider several of the most dangerous teratogens.

Infectious Diseases

Rubella (also called *German measles*) is a common childhood disease that can lead to serious birth defects, including heart disease, deafness, and intellectual disability (formerly called mental retardation), if contracted during pregnancy. Women exposed to

Concept Chart 9.1   Critical Periods in Prenatal Development

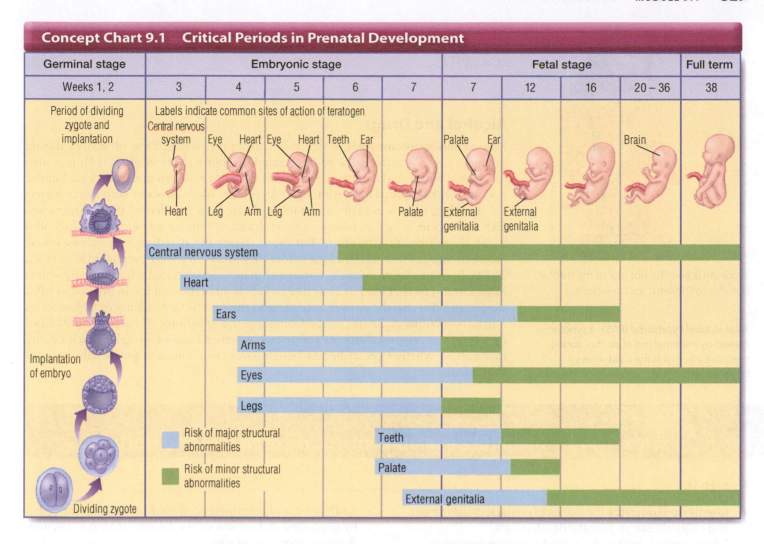

Germinal stage	Embryonic stage					Fetal stage				Full term
Weeks 1, 2	3	4	5	6	7	7	12	16	20 – 36	38

Period of dividing zygote and implantation

Implantation of embryo

Dividing zygote

Labels indicate common sites of action of teratogen

Central nervous system — Eye — Heart — Eye — Heart — Teeth — Ear — Palate — Ear — Brain

Heart — Leg — Arm — Leg — Arm — Palate — External genitalia — External genitalia

Central nervous system

Heart

Ears

Arms

Eyes

Legs

Teeth

Palate

External genitalia

Risk of major structural abnormalities

Risk of minor structural abnormalities

rubella in childhood acquire immunity to the disease. Those who lack immunity may be vaccinated before becoming pregnant to protect their future offspring.

Some sexually transmitted infections, such as HIV/AIDS and syphilis, may be transmitted from mother to child during pregnancy. Fortunately, aggressive treatment of HIV-infected mothers with the antiviral drug AZT greatly reduces the risk of maternal transmission of the virus to the fetus. Children born with congenital syphilis may suffer liver damage, impaired hearing and vision, and deformities in their teeth and bones. The risk of transmission can be reduced if the infected mother is treated effectively with antibiotics prior to the fourth month of pregnancy.

Smoking

Maternal smoking can have harmful consequences on the fetus and newborn, including miscarriage (spontaneous abortion), premature birth, low birth weight, and even infant mortality (Chertok, Luo, & Anderson, 2011; Heilbronner & Berlin, 2005). The more the mother smokes, the greater the risks. The risks extend to grade-school children, as those with mothers who smoked continuously during pregnancy show signs of abnormal brain development, including lower brain volumes and areas of thinning of neural tissue in the cerebral cortex (El Marroun et al., 2013).

Maternal smoking during pregnancy is also linked to increased risks of **sudden infant death syndrome (SIDS)** and lung problems, including childhood asthma, as

spina bifida A neural tube defect in which the child is born with a hole in the tube surrounding the spinal cord. Most cases are mild and do not involve any significant problems, but in severe cases, problems such as difficulty walking or performing daily activities without assistance may result.

teratogen An environmental influence or agent that may harm the developing embryo or fetus.

rubella A common childhood disease that can lead to serious birth defects if contracted by the mother during pregnancy (also called German measles).

sudden infant death syndrome (SIDS) The sudden and unexplained death of infants that usually occurs when they are asleep in their cribs.

Smoking is harmful not just to the mother, but also to the fetus and newborn.

fetal alcohol syndrome (FAS) A syndrome caused by maternal use of alcohol during pregnancy in which the child shows developmental delays and facial deformities.

well as to developmental problems such as reduced attention span, learning problems, and behavioral problems (for example, Goodwin et al., 2009; Trachtenberg et al., 2011).

Alcohol and Drugs

Fetal alcohol syndrome (FAS), which results from the mother's use of alcohol during pregnancy, is a leading cause of intellectual disability (May et al., 2014). It is also associated with facial deformities such as a flattened nose, an underdeveloped upper jaw, and widely spaced eyes. Although FAS is more likely to occur with heavy maternal drinking, there is actually no established safe limit for alcohol use in pregnancy. FAS may occur in babies whose mothers drank as little as a few ounces of alcohol a day during the first trimester. But more commonly it is found in babies whose mothers engaged in binge drinking before they knew they were pregnant (May et al., 2014). Even moderate drinking during pregnancy is associated with lower IQ scores in children (Lewis et al., 2012). Is there a safe level of alcohol use in pregnancy? Put simply and directly, the answer, according to the American Academy of Pediatrics, is a firm *no* (Williams, Smith, & the Committee on Substance Abuse, 2015). Alcohol or any other drug used during pregnancy, whether legal or illegal (illicit), or any medication, whether prescribed or bought over the counter, is potentially harmful to the fetus.

MODULE REVIEW   9.1   Prenatal Development: A Case of Nature and Nurture

Recite It

1. **Identify** and **describe** the stages of prenatal development and major threats to prenatal development.
   The germinal stage is the period from conception to (a) _____. The (b) _____ stage begins with implantation and extends to about the eighth week of development; it is characterized by differentiation of the major organ systems. The (c) _____ stage begins around the ninth week and continues until birth; it is characterized by continued maturation of the fetus's organ systems and dramatic increases in size.
   Threats include maternal diet, maternal diseases and disorders, and use of certain medications and drugs. Exposure to particular (d) _____ causes the greatest harm during critical periods of vulnerability.

Recall It

1. The first stage of prenatal development, which ends with implantation in the uterine wall, is called the _____ stage.

2. Name two major risks to the developing embryo or fetus.

3. Match the following terms to their descriptions: (a) the first stage of pregnancy; (b) a protective environment; (c) the organ in which nutrients and wastes are exchanged within the uterus; (d) a structure in the developing organism from which the nervous system develops.

   i. neural tube   iii. placenta
   ii. amniotic sac   iv. germinal stage

Think About It

■ Based on your reading of the text, what advice might you give someone about the risks posed by drinking alcohol or smoking during pregnancy?

■ Would you want to know if you or your partner were at risk for carrying a genetic abnormality? Why or why not? How would such knowledge affect your decisions about having children?

Recite It *answers placed at the end of chapter.*

MODULE

9.2 Infant Development

2 Identify reflexes present at birth.

3 Describe the infant's sensory, perceptual, and learning abilities.

4 Describe the development of the infant's motor skills in the first year of life.

It may seem that newborns do little more than sleep and eat, but, in fact, they come into the world with a wider range of responses than you might think. Even more remarkable are the changes that take place during development in the first two years of life. Let us enter the world of the infant and examine these remarkable changes.

Reflexes

A reflex is an unlearned, automatic response to a particular stimulus. Babies are born with a number of basic reflexes (see ■ Figure 9.3). For example, if you lightly touch a newborn's cheek, the baby will reflexively turn its head in the direction of the tactile (touch) stimulation. This is the **rooting reflex**, which, like many basic reflexes, has important survival value. It helps the baby obtain nourishment by orienting its head toward the breast or bottle. Another reflex that has survival value is the **eyeblink reflex**, the reflexive blinking of the eyes that protects the baby from bright light or foreign objects. Another is the **sucking reflex**, the rhythmic sucking action that enables an infant to obtain nourishment from breast or bottle. It is prompted whenever an object like a nipple or a finger is placed in the mouth.

Some reflexes appear to be remnants of our evolutionary heritage that may no longer serve any adaptive function. For example, if the infant is exposed to a loud noise, or if its head falls backward, the **Moro reflex** is elicited: The infant extends its arms, arches its back, and then brings its arms toward each other as if attempting to grab hold of someone. The **palmar grasp reflex**, or curling of the fingers around an object that touches the palm, is so strong that the infant can literally be lifted by its hands. In ancestral times, these reflexes may have had survival value by preventing

CONCEPT 9.3
Infants enter the world with some motor reflexes that may have had survival value among ancestral humans.

CONCEPT 9.4
Shortly after birth, infants are able to discern many different stimuli, including their mother's odor, face, and voice, as well as different tastes.

rooting reflex The reflexive turning of the newborn's head in the direction of a touch on its cheek.

eyeblink reflex The reflexive blinking of the eyes that protects the newborn from bright light and foreign objects.

sucking reflex Rhythmic sucking in response to stimulation of the tongue or mouth.

Moro reflex An inborn reflex, elicited by a sudden noise or loss of support, in which the infant extends its arms, arches its back, and brings its arms toward each other as though attempting to grab hold of someone.

palmar grasp reflex The reflexive curling of the infant's fingers around an object that touches its palm.

(a) Palmar grasp reflex (b) Rooting reflex

(c) Moro reflex

FIGURE 9.3 Infant Reflexes
The palmar grasp reflex (a) is so strong that the infant can literally be lifted by its hands. In the rooting reflex (b), the infant turns its head in the direction of a touch to its cheek. In the Moro reflex (c), when the infant is exposed to a noise or loss of support, it arches its back, extends its arms outward, and then brings the arms toward each other. What survival functions might these reflexes serve?

infants from falling as their mothers carried them around all day. The **Babinski reflex** involves a fanning out and curling of the toes and inward twisting of the foot when the sole of the foot is stroked.

Most newborn reflexes disappear within the first 6 months of life. The presence and later disappearance of particular reflexes at expected periods of time are taken as signs of normal neurological development.

During the first year of life, infants on average triple their birth weight from about 7 pounds to about 21 or 22 pounds. They also grow in height from about 20 inches to around 30 inches. The interconnections or synapses between neurons in the brain grow denser in the first two years of life, enabling the infant to organize its movements and engage the world by manipulating objects and acquiring knowledge about its environment. Between birth and adulthood, the brain will increase fourfold in volume. But perhaps most remarkable is the rapid development of the infant's abilities to sense, perceive, learn, and direct its movements.

Sensory, Perceptual, and Learning Abilities in Infancy

Infants are capable of sensing a wide range of sensory stimuli and of learning simple responses and retaining them in memory.

Sensory and Perceptual Ability

Ah, that beautiful face. Not only can newborns recognize their mother's face, but they also tend to show a preference for looking at her face over other faces.

Vision is the slowest of the senses to develop. Although the newborn's vision is blurry, its visual world is not a complete blur (see ■ Figure 9.4). For example, studies indicate that newborns show preferences for looking at facelike patterns and can also recognize

Babinski reflex The reflexive fanning out and curling of the infant's toes and inward twisting of its foot when the sole of the foot is stroked.

FIGURE 9.4 Newborn Vision and Face Recognition
To a newborn, a mother's face may appear as blurry as the photograph on the left. But a newborn can still recognize its mother's face and shows a preference for her face over other faces.

their mother's face (Colombo, Brez, & Curtindale, 2013). Not only can newborns recognize their mother's face, but they also tend to show a preference for looking at her face over other faces.

By 1 month of age, an infant can follow a moving object; by 2 months, the infant has developed basic color vision. Depth perception develops by around 6 months. Using a *visual cliff apparatus* consisting of a glass panel that covers an apparent sudden drop-off, Eleanor Gibson and Richard Walk (1960) showed that most infants about 6 months or older will hesitate and then refuse to crawl across to the deep side, indicating that they have developed depth perception (see ■ Figure 9.5).

Newborns can hear many different types of sounds. They are particularly sensitive to sounds falling within the frequency of the human voice and can discriminate their mother's voice from other voices. Even in the womb, fetuses respond more strongly, as shown by more forceful heart rate responses, to their mother's voice than to voices of female strangers (Kisilevsky et al., 2003). Remarkably, in just a few hours after birth, infants can differentiate sounds in their native language from those in a foreign tongue (Moon, Lagercrantz, & Kuhl, 2013). This suggests that exposure to sounds in the womb may predispose them to recognize similar sounds that later become incorporated in the language they develop. By several months of age, infants can differentiate among various speech sounds, such as between "ba" and "ma." The ability to discriminate among speech sounds helps prepare them for the development of language.

At 5 to 6 days of age, infants can detect their mother's odor. They react with a frown to the smell of rotten eggs but show a smile when they get a whiff of chocolate or bananas. Newborns can also discriminate among different tastes and show preferences for sweetness (no surprise!) (Raymond, 2000). They will suck faster and longer if given sweetened liquids than if given bitter, salty, or plain water solutions.

The perceptual world of the infant is not a blooming, buzzing confusion of meaningless stimuli, as people once believed. Rather, infants begin making meaningful discriminations among stimuli shortly after birth. For example, newborns are extremely sensitive to a soothing voice and to the way in which they are held. They can also recognize a scrambled picture of their mother's face just as well as a properly arranged picture of her face (Wingert & Brant, 2005).

By the age of 4 to 6 months, babies can discriminate among happy, angry, and neutral facial expressions and show a preference for faces reflecting their own racial characteristics (Bar-Haim et al., 2006; Saxe, Carey, & Kanwisher, 2004). What we don't know is what, if anything, different facial expressions mean to infants. We might think "Mom looks mad," but what infants make of different facial expressions remains unclear.

Learning Ability

Infants are capable of learning simple responses and retaining memories of these learned behaviors for days or even weeks. Infants as young as 6 or 7 months can also retain memories for faces (Pascalis et al., 1998) and for the sounds of particular words one day after hearing them (Houston & Jusczyk, 2003). Learning even occurs prenatally, as shown by newborns' preference for their mother's voice and for sounds reflecting their native language (Moon, Cooper, & Fifer, 1993).

Motor Development

Newborns' motor skills are not limited to simple reflexes. They can engage in some goal-directed behaviors, such as bringing their hands to their mouths to suck their thumbs, an ability that first appears prenatally during the third trimester. Minutes after birth, newborns can imitate their parents' facial expressions (Gopnik, 2000).

Mark Richards/PhotoEdit

FIGURE 9.5 **The Visual Cliff**
The visual cliff apparatus consists of a glass panel covering what appears to be a sudden drop-off. An infant who has developed depth perception will crawl toward a parent on the opposite end but will hesitate and refuse to venture into the "deep" end even if coaxed by the parent.

CONCEPT 9.5

Infants may seem to do little more than eat and sleep, but a closer look reveals they are both active learners and active perceivers of their environment.

CONCEPT 9.6

Motor development in infancy progresses rapidly through a series of steps from near immobility to coordinated running by around 18 months of age.

Imitative behavior may be the basis for shared communication between the infant and others. The infant and caregiver begin imitating each other's facial expressions in a kind of nonmusical duet (Trevarthen, 1995).

During the first 3 months, infants slowly begin replacing reflexive movements with voluntary, purposive movements. By the second or third month, they begin bringing objects to their mouths. By about 6 months, they can reliably grasp stationary objects and begin catching moving objects.

By 2 months of age, infants can lift their chins; by 5 months, they can roll over; and by 9 months, they can sit without support. By the end of the first year, infants will master the most difficult balancing problem they'll ever face in life: standing without support. Why is standing alone so difficult? Because of its smaller size, a 1-year-old will sway about 40 percent more while standing than will an adult and consequently will have less time to respond to balance disturbances to maintain itself in an upright position. To appreciate the challenge the 1-year-old faces when attempting to stand, imagine yourself trying to keep your balance while standing on a rope bridge that is constantly swaying. The development of motor skills, as outlined in Concept Chart 9.2, occurs in the same sequence among nearly all infants at about the same ages and in all cultures.

Concept Chart 9.2 Milestones in Infant Development

Approximate Ages	Sensory Skills and Learning Abilities	Motor Skills
Birth to 1 month	• Has blurry vision • Visually tracks a moving object • Sensitive to sounds within range of human voice • Shows preference for mother's voice and native language sounds (develops prenatally) • Detects mother's odor • Discerns certain pleasant or unpleasant basic odors • Shows taste preference for sweetness • Responds to a soothing voice • Discerns differences in how they are held • Shows preferences for facelike stimuli and responds to certain facial features	• Demonstrates basic reflexes • Sucks thumb • Mimics facial movements
2–3 months	• Discriminates direction of a moving object • Has developed basic color vision • Can discern differences in the tempo (beat) of a pattern of sounds • Discriminates among faces of different people • Learns simple responses and remembers them for several days (at 2 months) to several weeks (at 6 months)	• Lifts chin • Brings objects to mouth
4–6 months	• Develops depth perception • Discerns differences among certain facial expressions • Retains memory for certain faces	• Grasps stationary objects • Catches moving objects • Brings objects into field of view • Able to roll over

© saiko3p/Shutterstock.com

© iStockphoto.com/DaydreamsGirl

© iStockphoto.com/lostinbids

Concept Chart 9.2   (Continued)

Approximate Ages	Sensory Skills and Learning Abilities	Motor Skills
7–9 months	• Further development of depth perception and visual acuity	• Sits without support • Stands holding on
10–12 months	• Develops near 20/20 vision	• Walks holding on and without support

MODULE REVIEW   **9.2**   Infant Development

Recite It

2. Identify reflexes present at birth.

Reflexes include the rooting, eyeblink, sucking, Moro, (a) _____ grasp, and Babinski reflexes.

3. Describe the infant's sensory, perceptual, and learning abilities.

A newborn can detect objects visually (though not with perfect acuity) and can discriminate among different sounds, (b) _____, and tastes.

The ability to respond to depth cues and to discern facial expressions develops within the first (c) _____ months. Infants are also capable of learning simple responses and retaining (d) _____ of those responses.

4. Describe the development of the infant's motor skills in the first year of life.

During the first year, an infant acquires the ability to move its body, sit without support, turn over, crawl, and begin to stand and (e) _____ on its own.

Recall It

1. Match the following reflexes to the appropriate description: (a) rooting reflex; (b) eyeblink reflex; (c) sucking reflex; (d) Moro reflex.

  i. a rhythmic action that enables an infant to take in nourishment

  ii. a reflex action protecting one from bright lights and foreign objects

  iii. a grabbing movement, often in response to a loud noise

  iv. turning in response to a touch on the cheek; helps the baby find breast or bottle

2. What evidence (based on the sense of hearing) do we have to support the belief that a fetus is capable of learning?

3. Motor abilities develop extremely rapidly in infants. Which of the following is *not* a motor ability of a baby during the first year of life?

  a. imitation of parents' facial expressions
  b. development of voluntary, goal-directed movement
  c. balancing itself while sitting, without support
  d. speaking in complete sentences

Think About It

- What is the adaptive value of certain basic infant reflexes?

- Why is it incorrect to say that the world of the infant is merely a jumble of disconnected stimuli?

Recite It answers placed at the end of chapter.

MODULE

9.3 Years of Discovery: Emotional, Social, and Cognitive Development in Childhood

5 **Identify** and **describe** three types of infant temperament and three types of infant attachment styles.

6 **Identify** and **describe** the major parenting styles.

7 **Identify** and **describe** Erikson's stages of psychosocial development in childhood.

8 **Describe** Piaget's stages of cognitive development.

9 **Describe** Vygotsky's psychosocial theory of cognitive development.

Childhood is a period of wonderment, discovery, and, most of all, change. Here we examine the world of the growing child from the standpoint of emotional, social, and cognitive development, beginning with differences in temperament among infants. We then focus on two major stage theories of development, Erikson's stages of psychosocial development and Piaget's stages of cognitive development.

Stage theorists such as Erikson and Piaget believe that development remains relatively stable within each stage but then abruptly jumps to the next stage; that is, it occurs as sudden transformations or abrupt leaps rather than in smaller steps. (Kohlberg, another stage theorist, is discussed in the next module.) Though they recognize that many skills, such as vocabulary and arithmetical abilities, develop gradually through practice and experience, stage theorists argue that children must reach a stage of developmental readiness for such training and experience to matter.

Temperament: The "How" of Behavior

CONCEPT 9.7

Many psychologists believe that children differ in their basic temperaments and that these differences are at least partially determined by genetic factors.

Below, Janet, a mother of two, discusses the personalities of her two daughters, Tabitha (age 7) and Alicia (age 2½):

> *They're like day and night. Tabitha is the sensitive type. She's very tentative about taking chances or joining in with the other children. She can play by herself for hours. Just give her a book to read and she's in heaven. What can I say about Alicia? Where Tabitha will sit at the top of the slide and have to be coaxed to come down, Alicia goes down headfirst. Most kids her age stay in the part of the playground for the toddlers, but Alicia is off running to the big climbing equipment. She even thinks she's one of the older kids and tries to join them in their games. Can you picture that? Alicia is running after a baseball with the 6- and 7-year-olds.*

Ask parents who have two or more children and you're likely to hear a similar refrain: "They're just different. I don't know why they're different, but they just are."

We may attempt to explain these differences in terms of the construct of **temperament**. A temperament is a characteristic style of behavior, or disposition. Some theorists refer to temperament as the "how" of behavior—the characteristic way in which behavior is performed (Chess & Thomas, 1996). One child may display a cheerful temperament in approaching new situations, whereas another may exhibit a fearful or apprehensive temperament.

The most widely used classification of temperaments is based on a study of middle-class and upper-middle-class infants from the New York City area—the New York Longitudinal Study (NYLS) (Chess & Thomas, 1996). The investigators identified three general types of temperament that could be used to classify about two out of three of the children in the study group:

Can we predict how these infants are likely to behave in later childhood and even adulthood?

1. *Easy children.* These children are playful and respond positively to new stimuli. They adapt easily to changes; display a happy, engaging mood; and are quick to develop regular sleeping and feeding schedules. About 40 percent of the NYLS children were classified in this category.

2. *Difficult children.* These children react negatively to new situations or people, have irritable dispositions, and have difficulty establishing regular sleeping and feeding schedules. About 10 percent of the group fell into this category.

3. *Slow-to-warm-up children.* These children (called "inhibited children" by others) have low activity levels; avoid novel stimuli; require more time to adjust to new situations than most children; and typically react to unfamiliar situations by becoming withdrawn, subdued, or mildly distressed. This category described about 15 percent of the group.

The remaining 35 percent of the children studied represented a mixed group who could not be easily classified.

The distinct types of temperament observed in infancy predict later differences in adjustment (Rothbart, 2007; Volbrecht & Goldsmith, 2010). Easy infants are generally better adjusted as adults than infants with other temperaments. Fussier infants tend to have more conduct problems in childhood, especially among boys (Lahey et al., 2008). The slow-to-warm-up infants are more likely than other infants to be anxious or moody in childhood. But of the three temperament groups, the difficult, emotionally distressed infants are the ones most likely to develop mental health problems, especially depression, in later childhood and early adulthood (Bould et al., 2014; Kagan, 1997). However, they may also have positive qualities, such as being highly spirited and not becoming "pushovers."

Developmental psychologists believe temperament is shaped by both nature and nurture—that is, by genetics as well as environmental influences (Davies et al, 2013; Rothbart, 2012). Genes may shape basic temperament, but the degree to which genes become expressed in observable behavioral traits depends in part on the environment in which the child is raised (Thompson, 2012). But the question of whether it is possible to change basic temperament remains unanswered. Even if basic temperament cannot be changed, however, children are better able to adapt successfully to their environment when parents, teachers, and other caregivers take their underlying temperaments into account. For example, the difficult or slow-to-warm-up child may need more time and gentle encouragement when adjusting to new situations such as beginning school, making friends, or joining in play activities with other children. Complicating matters is that infants with more difficult temperaments tend to influence their parents to adopt harsher styles of parenting (Leve et al., 2010). We thus need to consider the mutual interactions between children and parents, as both influence each other.

Attachment behaviors are the ties that bind infants to their caregivers.

temperament A characteristic style of behavior or disposition.

Attachment: Binding Ties

In human development, **attachment** is the enduring emotional bond that infants and older children form with their caregivers. Do not confuse attachment with *bonding*, which is the parent's tie to the infant that may form in the hours following birth. Rather, attachment develops over time during infancy. Infants may crawl to be near their caregivers, pull or grab at them to maintain contact, and cry and show other signs of emotional distress when separated from them, even if only momentarily.

Attachment Behaviors in Other Animal Species

Many species exhibit attachment behaviors. Baby chimpanzees, tigers, and lions will cling for dear life to their mother's fur. The famed scientist Konrad Lorenz (1903–1989) studied imprinting in geese and other species. **Imprinting** is the formation of a strong bond of attachment to the first moving object seen after birth. A gosling (baby goose) will instinctively follow its mother wherever she goes. But goslings hatched in incubators will imprint on objects that happen to be present at their birth, including humans (Lorenz was one) and even mechanical toys. The goslings that imprinted on Lorenz followed him everywhere, even to the point of ignoring adult female geese.

In landmark research, psychologists Harry and Marguerite Harlow showed that baby monkeys developed attachment behaviors to inanimate objects placed in their cages (Harlow & Harlow, 1966). Newborn rhesus monkeys were separated from their mothers within hours of birth and raised in experimental cages in which various objects served as surrogate (substitute) mothers. In one early study, infant monkeys were raised in cages containing two types of surrogate mothers: a wire cylinder or a soft, terry cloth-covered cylinder (Harlow & Zimmermann, 1959). The infant monkeys showed clear preferences for the cloth mother, even when they were fed by an apparatus containing a bottle attached to the wire mother. Contact comfort apparently was a stronger determinant of attachment than food.

Goslings that imprinted on scientist Konrad Lorenz, dubbed Father Goose, followed him everywhere.

Attachment in Human Infants

Psychologist Mary Ainsworth developed a laboratory-based method, called the *strange situation,* to observe how infants react to separations and reunions with caregivers, typically their mothers (Ainsworth, 1979; Ainsworth et al., 1978). Based on these observations, Ainsworth noted three basic attachment styles in infants, one characterized by secure attachments and the other two by insecure attachments:

1. *Secure type (Type B).* These infants used their mothers as a secure base for exploring the environment, periodically looking around to check on her whereabouts and limiting exploration when she was absent. They sometimes cried when the mother left but warmly greeted her and were easily soothed by her when she returned. Soon they began exploring again. About 65 to 70 percent of middle-class samples of infants were classified as having secure attachments (Seifert & Hoffnung, 2000; Thompson, 1997). Cross-cultural studies indicate that most infants show a secure pattern of attachment (Main, 1996).

2. *Insecure-avoidant type (Type A).* These infants paid little attention to the mother when she was in the room and separated easily from her to explore the environment. They showed little distress when the mother departed and ignored her when she returned. About 20 percent of the infants in the typical sample fit this type (Thompson, 1997).

3. *Insecure-resistant type (Type C).* These infants clung to the mother and were reluctant to explore the environment despite the presence of desirable

attachment The enduring emotional bond that infants and older children form with their caregivers.

imprinting The formation of a strong bond of the newborn animal to the first moving object seen after birth.

toys. They showed a high level of distress when the mother departed and continued to experience some distress despite her attempts to comfort them when she returned. They also showed ambivalence or resistance toward the mother, first reaching out to her to be picked up and then pushing her away or twisting their bodies to get free of her. About 10 percent of the infants showed this attachment pattern.

In later studies, researchers identified a fourth type of attachment style, labeled *Type D* for *disorganized/disoriented* attachment (Cassidy, 2003; Padrón, Carlson, & Sroufe, 2014). These infants showed disorganized and unusual responses during separations and reunions, such as freezing in place or appearing dazed or confused when the mother left the room and was unable to approach her for support when she returned, even though they appeared fearful or distressed.

The Ainsworth method may not be appropriate for assessing attachment behaviors in children from cultures with different child-rearing practices. For example, Japanese cultural practices emphasize mother–infant closeness and interdependence, which may make it more difficult for these infants to manage brief separations from their mothers (Takahashi, 1990). More broadly, we need to recognize that substantial variations in attachment behaviors exist across cultures (Morelli, 2015). For example, Americans place a greater emphasis on exploration and independence in young children than do the Japanese.

Attachment styles forged in early infancy may have lasting consequences for later development (Holland & Roisman, 2010). The more securely attached infant is likely to be better adjusted in childhood and adolescence than the less securely attached infant, to have better peer relationships and self-esteem, and to exhibit fewer problem behaviors (for example, Cassidy & Shaver, 2008; Kerns & Richardson, 2005).

Psychologist Harry Harlow showed that baby monkeys preferred contact with a "cloth mother," even though a "wire mother" fed them.

Effects of Day Care on Attachment

Many working parents rely on organized day care centers to care for their young children during the day. Although concerns were raised in the past that full-time day care might interfere with the infant's attachment to its mother, recent evidence has failed to show any ill effects of day care placement on the security of infant–other attachments (NICHD, 1997; Sandlin-Sniffen, 2000). Higher-quality center-based day care and preschool care help foster independence and cooperative play and generally have positive effects on children's cognitive and language skills and emotional development (Auger et al., 2014; Loeb et al., 2004; Moyer, 2013).

Before we move on, refer to Concept Chart 9.3 to review the differences that researchers have observed in infant temperaments and attachment styles.

Child-Rearing Influences

Many factors influence a child's intellectual, emotional, and social development, including genetics, peer influences, and quality of parenting. Peer relationships provide the child with opportunities to develop socially competent behaviors in relating to others outside the family and as a member of a group. The acceptance and approval of peer group members help shape the child's developing self-esteem and sense of competence. Peer relationships can also have negative consequences (Monahan, Steinberg, & Cauffman, 2009). Children and adolescents have a strong need for peer acceptance and may be influenced by peers to engage in deviant activities they might never attempt on their own (Rubin, Bukowski, & Laursen, 2009).

Good parenting encompasses many qualities, including spending time with children (plenty of time!), modeling appropriate behaviors, helping children acquire skills to develop healthy peer relationships, stating rules clearly, setting limits, being consistent in correcting inappropriate behavior and praising good behavior, and

CONCEPT 9.10

Evidence shows that placing infants in day care does not prevent the development of secure attachments to their mothers.

CONCEPT 9.11

Peer relationships provide opportunities for children to develop social competencies and establish feelings of closeness and loyalty that can serve as the basis for later relationships.

CONCEPT 9.12

The quality of parenting is an important influence on children's intellectual, emotional, and social development.

Concept Chart 9.3 Differences in Temperaments and Attachment Styles

	Source	Major Types	General Characteristics
Temperaments	New York Longitudinal Study	Easy child	Playful; interested in new situations or novel stimuli; quickly develops regular sleeping and eating patterns
		Difficult child	Irritable; has difficulty adjusting to new situations or people and establishing regular sleeping and feeding schedules
		Slow-to-warm-up child	Shows low activity levels; becomes inhibited, withdrawn, or fretful when exposed to new situations
Attachment styles	Ainsworth's research using the *strange situation*	Secure type (Type B)	Uses mother as secure base to explore the environment; may be upset when she leaves but is easily comforted when she returns
		Insecure-avoidant type (Type A)	Pays little attention to mother when she is present and shows little distress when she leaves
		Insecure-resistant type (Type C)	Clings to mother; avoids venturing into unfamiliar situations; becomes very upset when mother leaves and fails to be comforted completely when she returns; shows some ambivalence or resistance toward mother
		Disorganized/ disoriented type (Type D)	Seems confused and disorganized in handling maternal separations and reunions; unable to seek support from mother when distressed

providing a warm, secure environment. Explaining to children how their behavior affects others can also help them develop more appropriate social behaviors (Kaplan, 2000). Children whose parents use discipline inconsistently, rely on harsh punishment, and are highly critical are more likely than others to develop problem behaviors at home and school and less likely to develop healthy peer relationships (Kilgore, Snyder, & Lentz, 2000).

Father's Influence

Although many studies of parent–child relationships focus on children and their mothers, we shouldn't lose sight of the importance of fathers in child development. Children whose fathers share meals with them, spend leisure time with them, and assist them with schoolwork tend to perform better academically than those with less engaged fathers (Cooksey & Fondell, 1996).

Children in two-parent, mother–father households tend to fare better academically and socially than those in households comprised either of mothers living with unmarried heterosexual partners or single-mother households, even after taking differences in income levels into account (Thomson, Hanson, & McLanahan, 1994). However, children raised by lesbian and gay parents tend to do as well in school and have relationships with peers that are as good as those of children of heterosexual parents (for example, Patterson, 2009; Wainright, Russell, & Patterson, 2004).

Mothers and fathers tend to differ in their parenting behavior. Compared to mothers, fathers typically provide less basic care (changing, feeding, bathing, and so on), but engage in more physically active play with their children (Parke, 2004). For example, a father might zoom the baby in the air ("play airplane"), whereas a mother might engage in more physically restrained games like peekaboo and patty-cake, and talk and sing soothingly to the infant (Berger, 2009a). However, greater physical play with fathers is not characteristic of all cultures. In Chinese, Malaysian, and Indian cultures, for example, fathers and mothers rarely engage in physical play with their children (Parke & Buriel, 1998).

Phase4Studios/Shutterstock.com

What does research evidence teach us about Dad's influence on a child's development? How do mothers and fathers tend to differ in parenting behaviors?

Cultural Differences in Parenting

Cultural learning has a strong bearing on child rearing, leading to variations across cultures in how children are raised (Gaskins, 2015). African American families, for example, tend to have strong kinship bonds and to involve grandmothers in more direct child care responsibilities than may be typical of other groups (Nevid, Rathus, & Greene, 2014). In traditional Hispanic families, the father is expected to be the provider and protector of the female, and the mother assumes full responsibility for child care (Javier, 2010). These traditional gender roles are changing, however, as more Hispanic women are entering the workforce and pursuing advanced educational opportunities.

Asian cultures tend to emphasize respect for parental authority, especially the father's, and warm maternal relationships (Berk, 2009; Nevid & Sta. Maria, 1999). All cultures help children move from a state of complete dependency in infancy toward assuming more responsibility for their own behavior. However, they vary in the degree to which they promote early independence in children and expect them to assume responsible roles within the family and community.

Parenting Styles

An important avenue of investigation into parenting influences on children's development focuses on differences in parenting styles. Diana Baumrind, a leading researcher in this area, identified three basic parenting styles: authoritative, authoritarian, and permissive (Baumrind, 1971, 1991):

1. *Authoritative style.* Authoritative parents set reasonable limits for their children but are not overcontrolling. The parent is the authority figure, firm but understanding, willing to give advice, but also willing to listen to children's concerns. Parents explain the reasons for their decisions rather than just "laying down the law." To Baumrind, authoritative parenting is the most successful parenting style. Evidence shows that children of authoritative parents tend to achieve the most positive outcomes in childhood and adolescence (Baumrind, 1971, 1991; Bornstein, Jager, & Steinberg, 2013). They tend to have high self-esteem and to be self-reliant, competent, and popular with peers. The flexible but firm child-rearing approach of authoritative parents encourages children to be independent and assertive but also respectful of the needs of others. Table 9.2 outlines some key steps in becoming an authoritative parent.

2. *Authoritarian style.* Authoritarian parents are rigid and overcontrolling. They expect and demand unquestioned obedience from their children. If children dare to ask why they are being told to do something, the answer

CONCEPT 9.13
Diana Baumrind identified three different parenting styles: authoritative, authoritarian, and permissive.

Table 9.2 Keys to Becoming an Authoritative Parent

Authoritative parents set firm limits but take the time to explain their decisions and to listen to their children's point of view. They also help children develop a sense of competence by setting reasonable demands for mature behavior. Here are suggestions for becoming an authoritative parent:

Rely on reason, not force.	Explain the rules, but keep explanations brief. When the child throws food against the wall, you can say, "We don't do that. That makes a mess, and I'll have to clean it up."
Show warmth.	Children's self-esteem is molded by how others, especially their parents, relate to them. Express your feelings verbally by using praise and physically by means of hugs, kisses, and holding hands when walking together. Praise the child for accomplishing tasks, even small ones.
Listen to your children's opinions.	Encourage children to express their opinions and feelings, but explain why it is important to follow the rules.
Set mature but reasonable expectations.	Encourage children to adopt more mature behaviors in line with their developmental level. If a child requires assistance, demonstrate how to perform the expected behavior, and give the child encouragement and feedback when he or she attempts it independently.

is likely to be "Because I say so." Authoritarian parents are unresponsive to their children's needs and rely on harsh forms of discipline while allowing their children little control over their lives. Children of authoritarian parents tend to be inhibited, moody, withdrawn, fearful, and distrustful of others. They are also at higher risk of becoming overweight (Rhee et al., 2006). The most negative outcomes in adolescence are found in boys with authoritarian parents. They typically perform more poorly in school; are more dependent and lacking in initiative and self-confidence; and tend to be conflicted, unhappy, and unfriendly toward peers (Baumrind, 1991; Bornstein, Jager, & Steinberg, 2013).

3. *Permissive style.* Permissive parents have an "anything goes" attitude toward raising their children. They may respond affectionately to children but be extremely lax in setting limits and imposing discipline. Children with permissive parents tend to be impulsive and lacking in self-control. Because they lack the experience of conforming to other people's demands, they may not develop effective interpersonal skills (Parke & Buriel, 1998).

Table 9.3 summarizes these three parenting styles. We need to take sociocultural realities into account when applying Baumrind's parenting styles. Some cultures emphasize authoritarian styles of parenting more than others do. It may be unfair or misleading to apply these categories when classifying parenting styles in other cultures that have different child-rearing traditions. Within our own society, authoritarian styles in families of lower socioeconomic status (SES) may represent a type of adaptation to stresses that families in poorer neighborhoods might face, such as heightened risks of violence and drug abuse. Parents in lower SES families may believe they need to enforce stricter limits on their children to protect them from these outside threats (Parke, 2004).

Table 9.3 Baumrind's Styles of Parenting

	Authoritative Style	Authoritarian Style	Permissive Style
Limit setting	High	High	Low
Style of discipline	Reasoning	Forceful	Lax
Maturity expectations	High	High	Low
Communications with children	High	Low	Moderate
Warmth and support	High	Low	High

Erikson's Stages of Psychosocial Development

Erik Erikson (1902–1994), a prominent psychodynamic theorist, emphasized the importance of social relationships in human development (Erikson, 1963). In his view, psychosocial development progresses through a series of stages that begin in early childhood and continue through adulthood. He believed our personalities are shaped by how we deal with a series of psychosocial crises or challenges during these stages. In this section, we focus on the four stages of psychosocial development that occur during childhood.

Trust Versus Mistrust

The first psychosocial challenge the infant faces is the development of a sense of trust toward its social environment. With a positive parent–child relationship in which parents treat the infant warmly and are responsive to its needs, a sense of trust and warmth toward others begins to develop (Easterbrooks et al., 2013). But if the parents are seldom there when the infant needs them, or if they are detached or respond coldly, the infant develops a basic mistrust of others. The world may seem a cold and threatening place.

Autonomy Versus Shame and Doubt

Erikson believed the central psychosocial challenge faced during the second and third years of life concerns autonomy. The child is now becoming mobile within the home and is "getting into everything." Parents may warmly encourage the child toward greater independence and nurture this newly developed sense of autonomy. However, if they demand too much too soon or make excessive demands that the child cannot meet (such as in the area of toilet training), the child may become riddled with feelings of self-doubt and shame that come to pervade later development, even into adulthood.

Initiative Versus Guilt

This stage, corresponding to the preschool years of 3 to 6, is a time of climbing gyms and play dates, a time at which the child is challenged to initiate actions and carry them out. Children who largely succeed in their efforts and are praised for their accomplishments will come to develop a sense of initiative and competence. In contrast, children who frequently fail to accomplish tasks and cannot seem to "get

CONCEPT 9.14
Erik Erikson described four stages of psychosocial development in childhood, each characterized by a particular life crisis or challenge: trust versus mistrust, autonomy versus shame and doubt, initiative versus guilt, and industry versus inferiority.

Table 9.4 Erik Erikson's Stages of Psychosocial Development in Childhood

Approximate Ages	Life Crisis	Major Challenge in Psychosocial Development
Infancy (birth to 1 year)	Trust versus mistrust	Developing a basic sense of trust in the caregiver and the environment
Toddlerhood (1 to 3 years)	Autonomy versus shame and doubt	Building a sense of independence and self-control
Preschool period (3 to 6 years)	Initiative versus guilt	Learning to initiate actions and carry them out
Elementary school period (6 to 12 years)	Industry versus inferiority	Becoming productive and involved

Source: Adapted from Erikson, 1963.

The Brain Loves a Puzzle

As you read ahead, use the information in the text to solve the following puzzle:

On a trip to the aquarium with his father, 5-year-old Kamau sees a whale for the first time and says, "Wow, what a big fish!" His father points out that the whale is not a fish, but Kamau seems puzzled and continues to call it a fish. Why would Kamau persist in calling a whale a fish?

Chad Ehlers/Getty Images

© cappi thompson/Shutterstock.com

things right" may develop feelings of guilt and powerlessness, especially if they are ridiculed or harshly criticized for their awkwardness or missteps.

Industry Versus Inferiority

At this stage, which corresponds to the elementary school period of 6 to 12 years, the child faces the central challenge of developing industriousness and self-confidence. If children believe they perform competently in the classroom and on the playing field in relation to their peers, they will likely become industrious by taking an active role in school and extracurricular activities. But if the pendulum swings too far in the other direction and failure outweighs success, feelings of inadequacy or inferiority may develop, causing the child to become withdrawn and unmotivated.

Table 9.4 provides an overview of Erikson's stages of psychosocial development in childhood. Though Erikson believed childhood experiences can have lasting effects on the individual's psychological development, he emphasized that later experiences in life may counter these earlier influences and lead eventually to more successful resolutions of these life challenges.

Cognitive Development

Seven-year-old Jason is upset with his younger brother Scott, age 3. Scott just cannot seem to get the basic idea of hide-and-seek. Every time Scott goes off to hide, he curls up in the corner of the room in plain sight of Jason. "You're supposed to hide where I can't see you," Jason complains. So Scott goes off and hides in the same spot, but now he covers his eyes. "Now you can't see me," he calls back to Jason. Though they live in the same home and share many family outings together, the world of a 3-year-old like Scott is very different from that of a 7-year-old like Jason. Let's consider how different they are by examining the changes in the way children think and reason as they progress through childhood. We begin with the work of the most influential theorist on cognitive development, Jean Piaget.

Piaget's Theory of Cognitive Development

Jean Piaget (1896–1980) is arguably the most important developmental theorist of all time—a "giant with a giant theory," to borrow a phrase from the social historian Morton Hunt (1993). Piaget, a Swiss developmentalist, believed the best way to understand how children think is to observe them closely as they interact with objects and solve problems. Much of his work was based on his observations of his own three children. He was less concerned with whether children answered questions correctly than with how they arrived at their answers.

To understand Piaget's theory of cognitive development, we must look at what he means by the term *schema*. To Piaget, a **schema** is an organized system of actions or a mental representation that people use to understand the world and interact with it (Piaget, 1952). The child is born with simple schemas comprising basic reflexes such as sucking. This schema obviously has adaptive value, because the infant needs to obtain nourishment from its mother's breast or the bottle by sucking.

Eventually the infant discovers that the schema works more effectively for some objects than for others. For my daughter Daniella, the sucking schema crashed the day we introduced her to an infant cup. Her dad demonstrated how to tip the cup at an angle to draw the liquid into the mouth. Daniella was unimpressed and continued to hold the cup upright and suck on its lip, which unhappily failed to produce the desired result.

Eventually schemas change as the child adapts to new challenges and demands. According to Piaget, **adaptation** is a process by which people adapt or change to function more effectively to meet challenges they face in the environment. Through adaptation, we adjust our schemas to meet the changing demands the environment imposes on us. Adaptation, in turn, consists of two complementary processes: *assimilation* and *accommodation*.

Assimilation is the process of incorporating new objects or situations into existing schemas. For example, newborns will reflexively suck any object placed in their mouths, such as a finger or even a piece of cloth. Daniella applied her sucking schema to an infant cup by attempting to suck on its lip. Older children develop classification schemas, which consist of mental representations of particular classes of objects. When Daniella was a toddler, she applied her "dog schema" to any nonhuman animal, including cats, horses, sheep, and even fish. To her, all were "bow-wows." And to 5-year-old Kamau (see earlier The Brain Loves a Puzzle), all marine life is assimilated to his schema of fish, even mammals like whales.

Assimilation is adaptive when new objects fit existing schemas, as when the infant sucks on the nipple of a baby bottle for the first time rather than the mother's breast. But horses and fish are not dogs, and infant cups cannot be sucked to draw liquid into the mouth. **Accommodation** is the process of altering existing schemas or creating new ones to deal with objects or experiences that don't fit readily into

CONCEPT 9.15
To Piaget, a schema is an action strategy or a mental representation that helps people understand and interact with the world.

CONCEPT LINK
People form mental images or representations called social schemas to make sense of their social environment, an example of which is the first impressions they form when meeting new people. See Module 14.1.

CONCEPT 9.16
In Piaget's view, adaptation to the environment consists of two complementary processes, assimilation and accommodation.

schema To Piaget, a mental framework for understanding or acting on the environment.

adaptation To Piaget, the process of adjustment that enables people to function more effectively in meeting the demands they face in the environment.

assimilation To Piaget, the process of incorporating new objects or situations into existing schemas.

accommodation To Piaget, the process of creating new schemas or modifying existing ones to account for new objects or experiences.

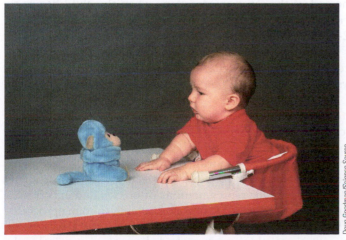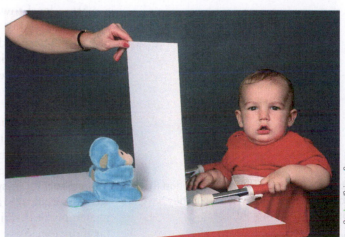

Infants who have not yet developed object permanence act as though objects that have disappeared from sight no longer exist.

existing schemas. Eventually Daniella developed a new "tipping schema" for using an infant cup: tipping it in her mouth so the contents would drip in.

Stages of Cognitive Development

In Piaget's view, the processes of assimilation and accommodation are ongoing throughout life. However, he held that the child's cognitive development progresses through a series of stages that occur in an ordered sequence at about the same ages in all children. Children at the different stages of cognitive development differ in how they view and interact with the world. Here we take a closer look at Piaget's four stages of cognitive development: the sensorimotor, preoperational, concrete operational, and formal operational stages.

Sensorimotor Stage: Birth to 2 Years. The sensorimotor stage spans a period of momentous growth in the infant's cognitive development. During this stage, which actually consists of six substages, the child becomes increasingly capable of performing more complex behaviors and skills. Piaget used the term *sensorimotor* because the infant explores its world by using its senses and applying its developing motor skills (body movement and hand control). The infant's intelligence is expressed through action and purposeful manipulation of objects.

At birth through 1 month, the infant's behaviors are limited to inborn reflexes, such as grasping and sucking. During months 1 through 8, the infant gains increasing voluntary control over some of its movements, such as by acquiring the ability to grasp objects placed above its crib. The infant is now beginning to act on the world and to repeat actions that have interesting effects, such as repeatedly squeezing a rubber duck to produce a squealing sound. By 8 to 12 months, the infant's actions are intended to reach a particular goal. The child will perform purposeful actions such as crawling to the other side of the room to open the bottom drawers of cabinets where toys are kept.

Early in the sensorimotor stage, infants are aware of an object's existence only if it is physically present. Out of sight is, quite literally, out of mind. If you block a 4-month-old's view of an object that he or she has been looking at, the child will immediately lose interest and begin looking at other objects. By about 8 months, the child will begin looking for a hidden object. Now, if you place a pillow over a teddy bear, she or he will push the pillow out of the way to get the toy. By this age, the child has begun to develop a concept of **object permanence**, the recognition that objects continue to exist even if they have disappeared from sight.

Piaget believed that object permanence is not yet complete at this point. It reaches a mature level toward the end of the sensorimotor stage when the child begins to acquire the ability to form a mental representation of an object that is not visibly present. One sign that 22-month-old Daniella had acquired object permanence was that she began asking for her brother Michael upon awakening. She apparently was able to retain a mental representation of Michael. Her parents tried not to take it personally that she always asked for Michael first!

Preoperational Stage: 2 to 7 Years. Piaget used the term *preoperational* to describe the cognitive abilities of children roughly ages 2 to 7 years because they lacked the ability to perform basic logical operations—to apply basic principles of logic to their experiences. During this period, however, extraordinary growth occurs in the ability to form mental or **symbolic representations** of the world, especially with the use of language. Specifically, a child forms symbolic representations of objects and experiences by naming or describing them in words. Language makes the child's thinking processes far more expansive and efficient than was possible in the sensorimotor stage.

Another form of representational thinking is make-believe or pretend play. In pretend play, children form mental representations that allow them to enact scenes

object permanence The recognition that objects continue to exist even if they have disappeared from sight.

symbolic representations A term referring to the use of words to represent (name) objects and describe experiences.

with characters that are not physically present. Pretend play becomes increasingly complex as children progress through the preoperational stage. By age 5 or 6, children are creating scenes with imagined characters or reenacting scenes they have seen on TV or in movies.

Though cognitive abilities expand dramatically during the preoperational stage, Piaget noted that the child's thinking processes are still quite limited. For example, the preoperational child demonstrates **egocentrism**, the tendency to view the world only from one's own point of view. Egocentric thinking doesn't mean the child is selfish or unconcerned about others; rather, the child at this stage lacks the cognitive ability to take another person's point of view or perspective. In the child's mind, he or she is the center of the universe. For example, 5-year-old Michelle wants to play with Mommy but doesn't understand that Mommy is tired and needs to rest. When Michelle feels like playing, she thinks Mommy should feel like playing too. In our earlier example, 3-year-old Scott is unable to take his brother's perspective when playing hide-and-seek. He doesn't realize that his hiding place is in plain view of his brother. He also assumes that because he cannot see his brother when he covers his own eyes, his brother cannot see him.

Egocentrism leads to another type of thinking typical of the preoperational child: **animistic thinking**. The child believes that inanimate objects like the moon, the sun, and the clouds have living qualities such as wishes, thoughts, and feelings just as she or he does. A 4-year-old, for instance, may think the moon is his friend and follows him as he walks home with his parents at night.

Two other limitations of the preoperational child's thinking are irreversibility and centration. **Irreversibility** is the inability to reverse the direction of a sequence of events to their starting point. **Centration** is the tendency to focus on only one aspect of a situation at a time to the exclusion of all other aspects.

Piaget illustrated these principles through his famous **conservation** tasks (see ■ Figure 9.6). (Conservation, the hallmark of the concrete operational stage, is discussed in the next section.) In a volume conservation task, the child is shown two identical glasses of water. Once the child agrees that the glasses contain the same amounts of water, the water in one glass is poured into a shorter, wider glass, which causes the water to come to rest at a lower level in the shorter glass than in the taller one. The preoperational child now insists that the taller, narrower glass contains more water. Because of centration, the child focuses on only one thing: the height of the column of water. Because of irreversibility, the child fails to recognize that the process can be reversed to its starting point—that pouring the water back into its original container would restore it to its original state (see Try This Out).

Concrete Operational Stage: 7 to 11 Years. The stage of concrete operations is marked by the development of conservation. To Piaget, conservation is the ability to recognize that the amount or quantity of a substance does not change if its outward appearance is changed, so long as nothing is either added to it or subtracted from it. The kinds of conservation tasks that stymied the 6-year-old become mere "child's play" to the average 7- or 8-year-old. The child at the concrete operational stage is able to mentally reverse the process in the conservation task and recognize that the amount of water doesn't change when poured into a container of a different shape. The child also becomes capable of decentered thinking, the ability to take into account more than one aspect of a situation at a time. The child now recognizes that a rise in the water level in the narrower container is offset by a change in the width of the column of water.

Which glass holds more juice? Preoperational children fail to recognize that the quantity of an object remains the same when placed in a different-sized container.

Try This Out
Learning Through Observation
You may be able to acquire more direct knowledge of children's cognitive development by serving as a volunteer in a nursery or preschool setting. To what extent does the cognitive development of preschoolers correspond to Piaget's concepts of egocentrism, animistic thought, centration, and irreversibility?

egocentrism To Piaget, the tendency to see the world only from one's own perspective.

animistic thinking To Piaget, the child's belief that inanimate objects have living qualities.

irreversibility To Piaget, the inability to reverse the direction of a sequence of events to their starting point.

centration To Piaget, the tendency to focus on only one aspect of a situation at a time.

conservation In Piaget's theory, the ability to recognize that the quantity or amount of an object remains constant despite superficial changes in its outward appearance.

Type of Conservation	① Initial Presentation	② Transformation	Question	③ Preoperational Child's Answer
Liquids	Two equal glasses of liquid	Pour one into a taller, narrower glass	Which glass contains more?	The taller one
Number	Two equal lines of checkers	Increase spacing of checkers in one line	Which line has more checkers?	The longer one
Mass	Two equal balls of clay	Squeeze one ball into a long, thin shape	Which piece has more clay?	The long one
Length	Two sticks of equal length	Move one stick	Which stick is longer?	The one that is farther to the right

FIGURE 9.6 **Examples of Piaget's Conservation Tasks**
Children are presented with a substance of a certain quantity. The substance is transformed in some superficial way. Children who have not yet developed the principle of conservation fail to recognize that the quantity of the substance remains the same.

Source: Adapted from Berger & Thompson, 1995.

The child's thinking at this stage also becomes much less egocentric. The child recognizes that other people's thoughts and feelings may differ from his or her own. The child can also perform simple logical operations, but only when they are tied to concrete examples. Seven-year-old Timmy can understand that if he has more baseball cards than Sally, and Sally has more than Sam, then he also has more than Sam. But Timmy would have great difficulty understanding the question if it were posed abstractly, such as "If A is greater than B and B is greater than C, is A greater than C?"

Formal Operational Stage The stage of **formal operations** is the final one in Piaget's theory—the stage of full cognitive maturity. In Western societies, formal operational thought tends to begin around puberty, at about age 11 or 12. However, not all children enter this stage at this time, and some never do, even as adults. Formal operations are characterized by the ability to think in abstract terms, to generate hypotheses, and to think deductively. With the development of formal operations, the person can think through hypothetical situations, including the "A is greater than B" example earlier. He or she can follow arguments from their premises to their conclusions and back again. We will return to this stage of cognitive development when we consider the thinking processes of the adolescent.

Piaget's Shadow: Evaluating His Legacy

In the annals of psychology, Piaget is a luminous figure who left a rich legacy that continues to guide an enormous amount of scholarly activity (Barrouillet, 2015).

formal operations The level of full cognitive maturity in Piaget's theory, characterized by the ability to think in abstract terms.

Piagetian concepts such as schemas, assimilation and accommodation, egocentricity, conservation, and irreversibility, among many others, provide researchers with a strong basis for understanding cognitive processes in children and how they change during development. Piaget was correct in recognizing the dramatic shifts in cognitive structures and abilities that occur during infancy and childhood. He encouraged us to view children not as passive responders to stimuli but as natural scientists who seek to understand the world and to operate on it.

At the same time, a number of criticisms of Piaget's theory have emerged (Hopkins, 2011). One frequent criticism is that his observations of children's cognitive abilities were limited to a small sample of children, including his own children. Another challenge is that cognitive development in childhood may be more variable from child to child than would be expected based on the fixed stages in Piaget's theory. Piaget may also have underestimated the abilities of young children. We noted earlier, for example, that even newborns can imitate facial expressions. Piaget believed this ability doesn't develop until late in the first year. Children may also develop object permanence and the ability to view events from other people's perspectives at earlier ages than Piaget's model would suppose (Aguiara & Baillargeon, 2002; Flavell, 1992).

Another frequent criticism of Piaget is that he failed to account for cultural differences in the timing by which these stages unfold. In some respects, Piaget was right: Evidence from cross-cultural studies shows that children do progress through the stages of cognitive development in the order Piaget described (Dasen, 1994). But cross-cultural evidence also shows that the ages at which children pass through these stages depend greatly on cultural factors.

Despite these challenges, Piaget's observations and teachings about how children develop have provided a guiding framework for generations of researchers to study and explore, and they will likely continue to do so for future generations.

Vygotsky's Sociocultural Theory of Cognitive Development

Whereas Piaget focused on children's understanding of their physical environment—the world of objects and things—the Russian psychologist Lev Vygotsky (1978, 1986) was concerned primarily with how children come to understand their social world. He believed that cultural learning is acquired through a gradual process of social interactions between children and parents, teachers, and other members of the culture. These interactions provide the basis for acquiring the knowledge that children need to solve everyday challenges and to meet the demands the culture imposes on them. In Vygotsky's view, the adult is the expert and the child is the novice, and the relationship between them is one of tutor and student.

To Vygotsky, children are born as cultural blank slates (Zukow-Goldring, 1997). They must learn the skills, values, and behaviors valued by the given culture. In American culture, this social knowledge includes such everyday behaviors as using the proper eating utensils, brushing teeth before bed, covering our mouths when we cough or sneeze, and waiting in line.

Vygotsky emphasized that social learning occurs within a **zone of proximal development (ZPD)**, also called the *zone of potential development*. The ZPD refers to the range between the skills children can currently perform and those they could perform if they received proper guidance and instruction. Working "in the zone" means providing less experienced individuals, or novices, with the support or instruction they need to advance beyond the level they would be able to accomplish on their own (Grusec et al., 2013; Holzman, 2009; Kleinspehn-Ammerlahn et al., 2011).

Concept Chart 9.4 provides an overview of the two theories of cognitive development reviewed in this module.

CONCEPT 9.18
Though Piaget continues to have an enormous impact on the field of developmental psychology, a number of challenges to his theory have surfaced.

CONCEPT 9.19
Vygotsky's theory of cognitive development emphasizes the role of social and cultural factors.

zone of proximal development (ZPD) In Vygotsky's theory, the range between children's present level of knowledge and their potential knowledge state if they receive proper guidance and instruction.

Concept Chart 9.4 Theories of Cognitive Development

	Theory	Overview
Piaget's theory of cognitive development		Emphasizes the role of adaptation in cognitive development as comprising two complementary processes, assimilation and accommodation.
Piaget's stages of cognitive development		The child progresses through a fixed sequence of stages involving qualitative leaps in ability and ways of understanding and interacting with the world.
	Sensorimotor stage (birth to 2 years)	The child uses its senses and developing motor skills to explore and act upon the world, and develops object permanence, which is the recognition that objects continue to exist even if they are not presently in sight.
	Preoperational stage (2 to 7 years)	The child uses language to symbolize objects and actions in words. Yet the child's thinking is limited by egocentrism, animistic thought, centration, and irreversibility.
	Concrete operational stage (7 to 11 years)	The child becomes able to perform simple logical operations tied to concrete problems. The child demonstrates conservation, or ability to recognize that the amount of a substance does not change if its shape or size is rearranged.
	Formal operational stage (begins around puberty, age 11 or 12)	The child or adolescent develops abstract reasoning abilities. Not all children, nor all adults, progress to this stage.
Evaluation of Piaget's theory		Though his theory remains a guiding framework for understanding cognitive development, it has been challenged in terms of the ages at which children acquire certain abilities and its lack of attention to cultural factors.
Vygotsky's sociocultural theory		Emphasizes the social interaction between children and adults as the basis for the child's acquisition of the skills, values, and behaviors needed to meet the demands imposed by the particular culture.

Photo credits (column): © Flashon Studio/Shutterstock.com; © pedalist/Shutterstock.com; © StockLite/Shutterstock.com; © Yuri Arcurs/Shutterstock.com

MODULE REVIEW 9.3 Years of Discovery: Emotional, Social, and Cognitive Development in Childhood

Recite It

5. **Identify** and **describe** three types of infant temperament and three types of infant attachment styles.

The three types are the (a) _____ child, the difficult child, and the (b) _____ child. Easy children have generally positive moods, react well to changes, and quickly develop regular feeding and sleep schedules. (c) _____ children have largely negative moods, react negatively to new situations and people, and have problems establishing regular feeding and sleep schedules. Slow-to-warm-up children tend to become (d) _____ when facing new situations, and experience mild levels of distress.

The three types of infant attachment styles are the secure type, the insecure-avoidant type, and the insecure-resistant type. The (e) _____ type of infant attaches to the mother and uses her as a secure base to explore the environment. The insecure-(f) _____ type freely explores the environment but tends to ignore the mother. The insecure-(g) _____ type clings excessively to the mother but shows ambivalence or resistance toward her.

6. **Identify** and **describe** the major parenting styles.

   (h) _____ parents expect mature behavior, use reasoning, and set firm limits. (i) _____ parents set firm limits but are overly controlling and rely on harsh styles of discipline. (j) _____ parents have an "anything goes" style characterized by a lax approach to limit setting.

7. **Identify** and **describe** Erikson's stages of psychosocial development in childhood.

   Erikson's stages are (1) trust versus (k) _____ (birth to 1 year), (2) (l) _____ versus shame and doubt (ages 1 to 3), (3) initiative versus (m) _____ (ages 3 to 6), and (4) (n) _____ versus inferiority (ages 6 to 12).

8. **Describe** Piaget's stages of cognitive development.

   In Piaget's theory, children in the sensorimotor stage, from birth to about 2 years, explore their world through their (o) _____, motor responses, and purposeful manipulation of objects. During the preoperational stage, from about 2 to 7 years of age, the child's thinking is more representational but is limited by centration, egocentricity, (p) _____ thinking, and irreversibility. The concrete operational stage, beginning around age 7 in Western cultures, is characterized by development of the principle of (q) _____ and the ability to draw logical relationships among concrete objects or events. The formal operational stage, the most advanced stage of cognitive development according to Piaget, is characterized by the ability to engage in (r) _____ thinking, generate hypotheses, and engage in abstract thought.

9. **Describe** Vygotsky's psychosocial theory of cognitive development.

   Vygotsky focused on how children acquire knowledge of their social world. He believed this knowledge is achieved through the interaction of the child (novice) with the parent (expert) within a zone of (s) _____ development that takes into account the child's present and potentially realizable knowledge structures.

Recall It

1. Unlike the developmental concept of bonding, attachment

   a. occurs in the hours of contact immediately after birth.
   b. takes time to develop, at least over the course of infancy.
   c. does not seem to be as crucial to a young child's well-being.
   d. refers to the parent's ties to the infant.

2. Match the following types of attachment identified by Ainsworth and other researchers to the following appropriate descriptions: (a) secure; (b) insecure-avoidant; (c) insecure-resistant; (d) disorganized/disoriented.

   i. child clings to mother, yet shows signs of ambivalence or negativity
   ii. mother is an important "base" for exploration; child is happy in mother's presence
   iii. child appears confused; seems unable to utilize mother for any support
   iv. child ignores mother when she is present and is unaffected by her departure or return

3. Parenting style is an important influence on children's development. Which of the following terms describes a parent who is warm, supportive, and consistent; who understands the child's point of view; and who communicates well?

   a. permissive   c. authoritative
   b. authoritarian   d. laissez-faire

4. In which of the following stages in Erikson's theory of psychosocial development do children compare their abilities to those of their friends and classmates?

   a. Stage 1: trust versus mistrust
   b. Stage 2: autonomy versus shame and doubt
   c. Stage 3: initiative versus guilt
   d. Stage 4: industry versus inferiority

5. In which stage does Piaget suggest a child learns by interacting with the environment through using his or her senses and developing motor skills?

   a. sensorimotor   c. concrete operational
   b. preoperational   a. formal operational

Think About It

■ Based on your reading of Baumrind's work on parent–child relationships, what do you think you need to do to become a better parent now or in the future?

■ Think of a child or young adult you know well. How do Erikson's stages of psychosocial development relate to this person's development in childhood? Which outcomes (trust versus mistrust, autonomy versus shame and doubt, initiative versus guilt, or industry versus inferiority) best describe the person's psychosocial development?

■ Think of examples of assimilation and accommodation in your own experience. In which situations were you able

to assimilate new information into existing schemas? In which situations did you need to alter your schemas or form new ones?

Recite It *answers placed at the end of chapter.*

MODULE

9.4 Adolescence

10 **Describe** the physiological, cognitive, and psychosocial changes that occur during adolescence and Erikson's beliefs about psychosocial development in adolescence.

11 **Describe** Kohlberg's stages of moral reasoning and **evaluate** his theory in light of Gilligan's criticism.

Adolescence is the link in the life chain between childhood and adulthood (Richter, 2006). The young person's body may seem to be sprouting in all directions at once. Adolescents may wonder what they will look like next year or even next month—who and what they will be. Intellectually, they may feel they are suddenly grown-ups, or expected to act as though they are, as they tackle more demanding subjects in middle school and high school and are expected to begin thinking seriously about what lies ahead for them when they leave high school. Yet their parents and teachers may continue to treat them as children—children masquerading in adult bodies who often must be restrained for their own good. Adolescents may find themselves in constant conflict with their parents over issues such as dating, using the family car, spending money, and _____ (you fill in the blank). At a time when young people are stretching their wings and preparing to fly on their own, they remain financially, and often emotionally, dependent on their parents. No wonder the early psychologist and founder of the American Psychological Association, G. Stanley Hall, characterized adolescence as a time of *sturm und drang*, or "storm and stress." Contemporary research bears out the belief that many young people, though certainly not all, experience adolescence as a turbulent, pressure-ridden period. Let us now consider the physical, cognitive, social, and emotional changes that occur during the years when many young people feel they are betwixt and between—no longer children but not quite adults.

Physical Development

CONCEPT 9.20

The major event in physical development in adolescence is puberty, the period of physical growth and sexual maturation during which we attain full sexual maturity.

adolescence The period of life beginning at puberty and ending with early adulthood.

puberty The stage of development at which individuals become physiologically capable of reproducing.

After the rapid growth that takes place during infancy, children typically gain 2 to 3 inches and 4 to 6 pounds a year until the growth spurt of adolescence. The spurt lasts for 2 to 3 years, during which time adolescents may shoot up 8 inches to 1 foot or more. Girls typically experience their growth spurt earlier than boys, so they may be taller than their male age mates for a while. But boys, on the average, eventually surpass girls in height and body weight. Boys also develop greater upper-body musculature.

The major landmark of physical development during adolescence is **puberty**, the period of life during which young people reach full sexual maturity (see ■ Figure 9.7). Puberty is not any single event, but a process that unfolds over time (Jay, 2006).

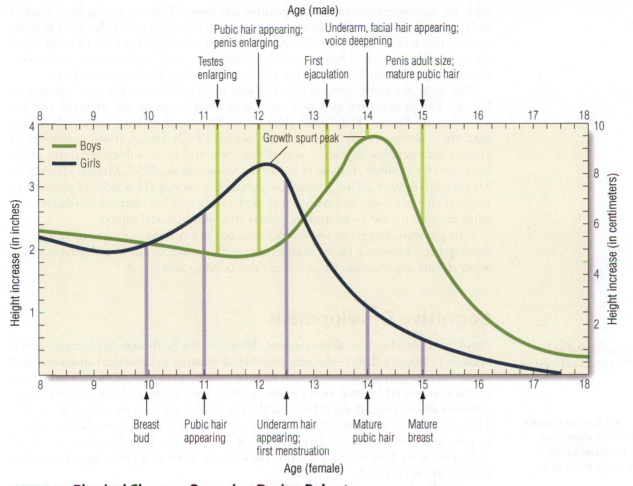

Age (male)

Pubic hair appearing;
penis enlarging

Underarm, facial hair appearing;
voice deepening

Testes
enlarging

First
ejaculation

Penis adult size;
mature pubic hair

Growth spurt peak

Boys
Girls

Breast
bud

Pubic hair
appearing

Underarm hair
appearing;
first menstruation

Mature
pubic hair

Mature
breast

Age (female)

FIGURE 9.7 Physical Changes Occurring During Puberty
This graph illustrates a number of changes occurring during puberty in boys and girls.
Note how the growth spurt begins sooner in girls than in boys. Note too that the graph
represents the average ages at which these changes occur and that growth patterns in
individuals often vary from these averages.

Source: Adapted from Seifert, Hoffnung, & Hoffnung, 2000.

It begins with the appearance of **secondary sex characteristics**, physical characteristics
that differentiate men and women but are not directly involved in reproduction, such
as pubic hair, breast development, and deepening of the voice. **Primary sex characteristics** also emerge; these are changes in sex organs directly involved in reproduction,
such as enlargement of the testes and penis in boys and of the uterus in girls. Puberty
lasts about 3 to 4 years, by the end of which time adolescents become physically
capable of reproduction.

Girls typically experience **menarche**, the beginning of menstruation, between ages
10 and 18, or at an average age of 12.5 years (CDC, 2015g). Girls today enter puberty and experience menarche at much earlier ages than girls in earlier generations.
The average European American girl today shows breast development and other
signs of puberty by age 10, as compared to age 15 at the beginning of the twentieth
century (Kantrowitz & Wingert, 1999). The average African American girl today
begins showing signs of puberty and experiences menarche at a somewhat earlier age
(Anderson, Dallal, & Must, 2003).

The timing of puberty may have different consequences for boys and girls. For
earlier-maturing boys, their greater size and strength give them an advantage in

secondary sex characteristics Physical
characteristics that differentiate males and
females but are not directly involved in
reproduction.

primary sex characteristics Physical
characteristics, such as the gonads, that
differentiate males and females and play a
direct role in reproduction.

menarche The first menstruation.

athletics and contribute to a more positive self-image. Later-maturing boys tend to be less popular than earlier-maturing boys and may be subject to ridicule or become socially ostracized (Berger, 2009b). Although early-maturing boys are more likely to engage in deviant social behavior such as drinking, smoking, or breaking the law, overall they generally have more positive outcomes than later-maturing boys.

For girls, the most obvious physical sign of maturation is the development of breasts. Earlier-maturing girls may encounter unwelcome sexual attention and believe they no longer "fit in" with their peers. They tend to have lower self-esteem than their later-maturing peers, a more negative body image, more symptoms of anxiety and depression, earlier sexual behavior, and more substance abuse problems (see, for example, Galvao et al., 2014; Mendle et al., 2016; Moore, Harden, & Mendle, 2014; Weir, 2016). Research suggests that the ways in which people react to physical changes associated with maturation, rather than the changes themselves, are what account for the social and emotional effects of pubertal timing.

The physical changes of adolescence may be the most obvious signs of adolescent development. However, major changes in cognitive abilities and social behavior also occur during adolescence. We consider these developments next.

Cognitive Development

People who develop formal operational thinking—the final stage of cognitive development in Piaget's theory—become capable of creating hypothetical situations and scenarios and playing them through in their minds. They can mount an argument in favor of something that runs counter to their own views and can imagine many different alternative futures (Flavell, Miller, & Miller, 2002; Schwartz et al., 2013). They are able to use deductive reasoning in which one derives conclusions about specific cases or individuals based on a set of premises. They become capable of deducing "who done it" on TV crime shows from clues to a crime long before the guilty party is revealed.

Not all adolescents, nor even all adults, reach the stage of formal operational thinking. Their thinking remains tied to concrete examples and relationships among objects rather than between ideas and abstract concepts. Whether or not formal operational thinking develops, many adolescents show certain forms of egocentric thinking. As Piaget noted, preschoolers show egocentrism with respect to their difficulty in seeing things from other people's points of view. Psychologist David Elkind (1985) believes that adolescent egocentrism typically reveals itself in two ways: through the imaginary audience and the personal fable.

The **imaginary audience** describes the adolescent's belief that other people are as keenly interested in his or her concerns and needs as the adolescent is. Adolescents may feel as though they are always on stage, as though all eyes are continually scrutinizing how they look, what they wear, and how they act (Frankenberger, 2000). They view themselves as the center of attention and feel extremely self-conscious and overly concerned about the slightest flaw in their appearance ("How could they not notice this blemish? Everybody will notice!").

The **personal fable** is an exaggerated sense of one's uniqueness and invulnerability. Adolescents may believe their life experiences or personal feelings are so unique that no one could possibly understand them, let alone have experienced them. When parents try to relate to what their adolescent is experiencing, they may be summarily rebuffed: "You can't possibly understand what I'm going through!"

Another aspect of the personal fable is the belief that "bad things can't happen to me." Adolescents often underestimate the risks of bad things happening to them (Reyna, 2013). They are more prone to taking risks than adults and their sense of personal invulnerability may contribute to risk-taking behaviors, such as reckless driving, unsafe sex, and drug use (Curry & Youngblade, 2006; Defoe et al., 2015).

CONCEPT 9.21
Adolescents who develop formal operational thinking become capable of solving abstract problems.

CONCEPT 9.22
Adolescents often show a form of egocentric thinking in which they believe their concerns and needs should be as important to others as they are to themselves.

imaginary audience The common belief among adolescents that they are the center of other people's attention.

personal fable The common belief among adolescents that their feelings and experiences cannot possibly be understood by others and that they are personally invulnerable to harm.

Even if adolescents know the risks they face, the risks may not deter them from engaging in risky behaviors associated with pleasurable or exciting experiences (Lewis, 2014; Roper, Vecera, & Vaidya, 2014). To be sure, not all adolescents are risk takers. Factors linked to increased risk taking in teens include poor school performance, family problems, having friends who engage in riskier behaviors, impulsivity, and availability of risk-taking opportunities (Albert, Chein, & Steinberg, 2013; Dir, Coskunpinar, & Cyders, 2014; Helfinstein, Mumford, & Poldrack, 2015; Stautz & Cooper, 2014). Adolescents are also more likely to engage in risky behaviors when they are with their friends than when they are alone (Knoll et al., 2015).

"How could they not notice?" Adolescents may constantly scrutinize their appearance and become overly concerned about the slightest flaw.

Bear in mind that the adolescent brain is still maturing, including that part of the brain, the prefrontal cortex, responsible for judgment, reasoning, and putting the brakes on risky or impulsive behavior (Casey, Kosofsky, & Bhide, 2014). Adolescents may be able to think logically and rationally, but, as psychiatrist David Fassler says, they "are more likely to act impulsively, on instinct, without fully understanding or analyzing the consequences of their actions" (cited in "Teens' Brains," 2007).

The developing cognitive abilities of adolescents change the way they see the world, including themselves, family and friends, and broad social and moral issues. These changes influence the ways people form judgments about questions of right and wrong, as we will see next.

Kohlberg's Stages of Moral Reasoning

Psychologist Lawrence Kohlberg (1927–1987) studied how individuals make moral judgments about conflict-laden issues. He was interested in the process by which people arrive at moral choices—what makes something right or wrong—rather than in the particular choices they make. He developed a methodology in which he presented subjects with hypothetical situations involving conflicting moral values, or moral dilemmas. Let's look at his most famous example (adapted from Kohlberg, 1969):

In Europe, a woman lies near death from a certain type of cancer. Only one drug that might save her is available, from a druggist in the same town who is charging ten times what it costs him to make it. Lacking this sum, the woman's husband, Heinz, attempts to borrow money from everyone he knows but can raise only about half the amount. Heinz tells the druggist his wife is dying and pleads with him to sell it for less so he can buy it now or allow him to pay for it later. The druggist refuses. Desperate, Heinz breaks into the druggist's store and steals the drug to give to his wife.

Now Kohlberg poses the questions: "Should Heinz have stolen the drug? Why or why not?" Here we have the making of a moral dilemma, a situation that pits two opposing moral values against each other—in this case, the moral injunction against stealing versus the human value of attempting to save the life of a loved one. Kohlberg believed that one's level of moral development is reflected in the way one reasons about the moral dilemma, not in whether one believes the behavior in question was right or wrong.

Based on his studies of responses to these types of hypothetical situations, Kohlberg determined that moral development progresses through a sequence of six stages organized into three levels of moral reasoning: the preconventional level, the conventional level, and the postconventional level.

Preconventional Level. Children at the *preconventional level* base their moral judgments on the perceived consequences of behavior. Kohlberg divided preconventional moral reasoning into two stages. Stage 1 is characterized by an *obedience and punishment orientation:* Good behavior is defined simply as behavior that avoids punishment by an external authority. In our example, we might reason that Heinz should take the drug because if he does not, he may be blamed for his wife's death; or he shouldn't take the drug because he could get caught and sent to jail. Stage 2 represents an *instrumental purpose orientation*: A behavior is judged good when it serves the person's needs or interests. Thus, we might reason that Heinz should have taken the drug because, by saving his wife, he would ensure that she'd be available to meet his needs for companionship, love, and support; or Heinz shouldn't have taken the drug because if he were caught and sent to jail, he would have done neither himself nor his wife any good.

Conventional Level. At the *conventional level*, moral reasoning is based on conformity with conventional rules of right and wrong. Individuals at this level recognize that the purpose of social rules is to preserve the social order and ensure harmonious relationships among people.

Stage 3 is characterized by a *"good boy–good girl" orientation*: Individuals believe that conformity with rules and regulations is important because of the need to be perceived by others as a "good boy" or a "good girl." They value the need to do the "right thing" in the eyes of others. Thus, Heinz should steal the drug because others would be displeased with him for failing to help save his wife's life; or Heinz should not steal the drug because if he is caught, he will bring dishonor on himself and his family.

Stage 4 has an *authority* or *law-and-order orientation*. Moral reasoning now goes beyond the need to gain approval from others: Rules must be obeyed and applied evenhandedly because they are needed for the orderly functioning of society. Each of us has a duty to uphold the law, simply because it is the law. Heinz should steal the drug because it is a husband's duty to protect his wife's life, but he must repay the druggist as soon as he is able and accept responsibility and punishment for breaking the law. Or Heinz should not steal the drug because although we may sympathize with his wish to save his wife's life, people cannot be permitted to break the law even when they face such dire circumstances.

Postconventional Level. Individuals generally reach the *postconventional level* of moral reasoning during adolescence, if they reach it at all. Postconventional reasoning involves applying one's own moral standards or abstract principles rather than relying on authority figures or blindly adhering to social rules or conventions (Haidt, 2008). The postconventional thinker believes that when laws are unjust, a moral person is bound to disobey them. In Kohlberg's (1969) studies, only about one in four people had reached the postconventional level by age 16. Even in adulthood, most people remain at the level of conventional moral reasoning.

Kohlberg identified two stages of postconventional moral reasoning. Stage 5, the *social contract orientation,* involves the belief that laws are based on mutual agreement among members of a society, but they are not infallible. They should be open to question rather than followed blindly out of respect for authority. Stage 5 reasoners weigh the rights of the individual against the rights of society. They might argue that although laws should be obeyed, protection of a life is a more important value than protection of property, and so an exception should be made in Heinz's case. Or they might reason that individuals must obey the law because the common good takes precedence over the individual good and that the ends, no matter how noble they may be, do not justify the means.

Stage 6 thinking involves adoption of *universal ethical principles,* an underlying set of self-chosen, abstract ethical principles that serve as a guiding framework for moral judgments. Beliefs in the sanctity of human life or in the "Golden Rule" exemplify such universal ethical principles. People at this stage are guided by their own internal moral compass, regardless of the dictates of society's laws or the opinions of others. They may believe that if laws devalue the sanctity of human life, it becomes

© schmettad/Shutterstock.com

CONCEPT 9.23

Psychologist Lawrence Kohlberg explored how individuals make moral judgments; his theory of moral development consists of a sequence of six stages organized in terms of three levels of moral reasoning.

immoral to obey them. Hence, it would be immoral for Heinz to obey laws that would ultimately devalue the sanctity of his wife's life. Kohlberg believed that very few people, even those within the postconventional level, reach Stage 6. Concept Chart 9.5 summarizes the six stages of moral reasoning in Kohlberg's model.

Kohlberg's model of moral development continues to foster understanding of how people develop a sense of morality. But does moral reasoning dictate moral behavior? Do people who achieve higher levels of moral reasoning in Kohlberg's system actually practice what they preach? The answer is complicated. There does appear to be some degree of overlap between a person's moral reasoning and a person's moral behavior. On the other hand, we need to account for environmental demands in particular situations to better understand whether we act in ways that are consistent with our moral beliefs (Hill & Roberts, 2010).

Evaluation of Kohlberg's Model

Kohlberg's classic studies set the stage for further research on moral reasoning that has continued to the present day (Hill & Roberts, 2010). Kohlberg's central belief that children and adolescents progress through stages of moral development has

Concept Chart 9.5   Kohlberg's Levels and Stages of Moral Development

	Stage of Moral Reasoning	Heinz Should Steal the Drug Because:	Heinz Should Not Steal the Drug Because:
LEVEL I Preconventional Level	Stage 1: Obedience and punishment orientation; behavior is judged good if it serves to avoid punishment	He would be blamed if his wife dies.	He would be punished for stealing if he were caught.
	Stage 2: Instrumental purpose orientation; behavior is judged good when it serves personal needs or interests	He needs his wife and she might die without it.	He would likely be sent to prison and his wife would probably die before he gets out.
LEVEL II Conventional Level	Stage 3: "Good boy–good girl" orientation; conforming with rules to impress others	He would lose people's respect if he didn't at least try to save his wife by stealing the drug.	Others will see him as a criminal, and that would bring shame and dishonor to his family.
	Stage 4: Authority or law-and-order orientation; obeying rules and laws because they are needed to maintain social order	He has a duty to protect his wife even if he might get punished for it.	People should not be permitted to break the law under any circumstances. The law must be respected.
LEVEL III Postconventional Level	Stage 5: Social contract orientation; viewing rules and laws as based on mutual agreement in the service of the common good	Though laws should be obeyed to maintain order in society, an exception should be made in Heinz's case because a law should not take precedence over protecting a human life.	He reasons that respect for the law outweighs individual needs no matter what the circumstances.
	Stage 6: Universal ethical principle orientation; adopting an internal moral code based on universal values that takes precedence over social rules and laws	Not stealing the drug would violate his belief in the absolute value of a human life.	Sometimes doing what we believe is right requires personal sacrifice. If he truly believes that stealing is worse than letting his wife die, he must not steal the drug.

Source: Adapted from Kohlberg, 1981.

been supported in later research (for example, Boom, Wouters, & Keller, 2007). However, critics question whether Kohlberg's developmental perspective captures the ways in which people form moral judgments and make morally laden decisions in their everyday lives (Krebs & Denton, 2005). Whether the developmental (stage-based) model should be replaced or refined remains an ongoing debate in the field (for example, Gibbs, 2006; Krebs & Denton, 2005). Critics also question whether Kohlberg's concept of postconventional thinking is more a reflection of his own personal ideals than a universal stage of moral development (Helwig, 2006).

Another debate is whether Kohlberg's model is biased on cultural or gender grounds. Kohlberg's model emphasizes ideals found primarily in Western cultures, such as individual rights and social justice. Cross-cultural evidence based on a study comparing moral reasoning in Americans and Indians did show cultural differences in the priorities placed on justice and interpersonal considerations (Miller & Bersoff, 1992). Americans placed greater value than did Indians on a justice orientation in determining morally correct choices—believing that what is just or fair governs what is right. Indians placed a greater weight on interpersonal responsibilities, such as upholding one's obligations to others and being responsive to other people's needs.

Harvard psychologist Carol Gilligan addressed the issue of gender bias in Kohlberg's work. She pointed out that Kohlberg's studies were based entirely on research with men. The voices of girls and women had not been heard.

Prior to her own work, researchers applying Kohlberg's model found that men often attained higher levels of moral reasoning than women did. Gilligan rejected the view that women are less capable of developing moral reasoning. Listening to women's voices, she argued that women tend to apply a different moral standard than men, one defined by a *care orientation* rather than a *justice orientation* adopted by men (Gilligan, 1982). Men would argue, based on abstract principles of justice and fairness, that Heinz should steal the drug because the value of life supersedes that of property. Young women, however, sought solutions that responded both to the druggist's need to protect his property and to Heinz's need to save his wife—solutions that expressed a caring attitude and the need to preserve the relationship between them. Gilligan argued that the moral standards of men and women represent two different ways of thinking about moral behavior, with neither one standing on higher moral ground than the other. However, because young women are less willing to apply abstract moral principles when facing ethical situations like that of Heinz, they may be classified at lower levels in Kohlberg's system.

Evidence shows that women do tend to place more emphasis on a care orientation, whereas men tend to place somewhat greater stress on a justice orientation (for example, Jaffee & Hyde, 2000; Jorgensen, 2006). Gilligan's work encourages investigators to listen to female voices and encourage young women to find and develop their own voices. However, as Gilligan herself recognizes, the human care ethic is not limited to women alone (Gilligan, 2011). Both men and women can apply a justice orientation and a care orientation when forming moral judgments.

Psychosocial Development

In this section, we examine the psychosocial development of adolescents as they negotiate the transition from childhood to young adulthood. Throughout, we focus on their relationships with parents and peers and the challenges they face in establishing a clear psychological identity of their own. We also consider an aspect of psychosocial development that often takes center stage during adolescence: sexuality.

Adolescent–Parent Relationships

Adolescent yearnings for independence often lead to some withdrawal from family members and to arguments with parents over issues of autonomy and decision

CONCEPT 9.24
Though evidence generally supports Kohlberg's stage model of moral reasoning, critics contend that his model may contain cultural and gender biases.

CONCEPT 9.25
Issues relating to independence come to the fore in the adolescent's social and personality development, but these issues often bring adolescents into conflict with their parents.

making. Some distancing from parents may be healthy during adolescence, as young people form meaningful relationships outside the family and develop a sense of independence and social competence. As it turns out, and despite the common belief, most adolescents and their parents say they love and respect one another and agree on many of the principal issues in life (Arnett, 2004; Collins & Laursen, 2006). Though disagreements with parents are common, serious conflict is neither normal nor helpful for adolescents (Smetana, Campione-Barr, & Metzger, 2006). Parents also influence their adolescents in more subtle ways, and not always for the better. For example, adolescents tend to mimic their parents' health-related behaviors, which may include negative behaviors such as smoking (Kodl & Mermelstein, 2004).

By psychologically separating from their parents, adolescents may begin to grapple with the major psychosocial challenge they face: developing a clear sense of themselves and of their future direction in life. As we will see next, the theorist Erik Erikson believed that the process of coming to terms with the question "Who am I?" represents the major life challenge of adolescence.

Who am I? Where am I headed in life? Theorist Erik Erikson emphasized the process of coming to terms with one's personal identity as the major psychosocial challenge facing adolescents.

Identity Versus Role Diffusion: Who Am I?

Earlier we saw that Erik Erikson believed children progress through a series of four stages of psychosocial development. Erikson's fifth stage of psychosocial development occurs during adolescence: the stage of *identity versus role diffusion*.

Issues of identity assume prominence during adolescence, as young people grapple with questions of "Who am I?" and "What am I good at?" and "Where am I headed?" The development of ethnic identity, of a connectedness with one's ethnic and cultural heritage, is an important part of the process of identity formation during adolescence, especially for adolescents of color (French et al., 2006; Fuligni, Witkow, & Garcia, 2005).

Ego identity is the attainment of a firm sense of self—who one is, where one is headed in life, and what one believes in. People who achieve ego identity clearly understand their personal needs, values, and life goals. Erikson coined the term **identity crisis** to describe the stressful period of soul-searching and serious self-examination that many adolescents experience when struggling to develop a set of personal values and direction in life. Although Erikson believed that an identity crisis is a normal part of the development of the healthy personality, some contemporary scholars use the term *exploration* rather than *crisis* to avoid implying that the process of examining one's different possibilities in life is inherently fraught with anguish and struggle (Arnett, 2004).

Adolescents who successfully weather an identity crisis emerge as their own people, as people who have achieved a state of ego identity. Ego identity, however, continues to develop throughout life. Investigators find that having a strong sense of personal identity in midlife is associated with higher levels of well-being (Sneed et al., 2012). Our occupational goals and our political, moral, and religious beliefs often change over time. Therefore, we may weather many identity crises in life.

Many adolescents or adults never grapple with an identity crisis. They may develop a firm sense of ego identity by modeling themselves after others, especially parents, without undergoing an identity crisis. Or they may fail to develop a clear sense of ego identity, remaining at sea, as it were, aimlessly taking each day as it comes. These individuals remain in a state of **role diffusion**, a confused and drifting state in which they lack a clear set of values and direction in life. They may be especially vulnerable to negative peer influences such as drug use.

Peer Relationships

As adolescents experiment with greater independence, peer relationships become increasingly important influences in their psychosocial development. "Fitting in" or

CONCEPT 9.26
To Erik Erikson, the major life challenge adolescents face is the development of a sense of ego identity, a coming to terms with the fundamental question, "Who am I?"

ego identity In Erickson's theory, the attainment of a psychological sense of knowing oneself and one's direction in life.

identity crisis In Erikson's theory, a stressful period of serious soul-searching and self-examination of issues relating to personal values and one's direction in life.

role diffusion In Erikson's model, a lack of direction or aimlessness with respect to one's role in life or public identity.

Though conflicts between adolescents and parents are common, most adolescents say they have good relationships with their parents.

Investigators find that use of online social networks like Facebook may actually help strengthen relationships in the real world.

CONCEPT 9.27

Peer pressure is an important influence in the social and emotional development of adolescents.

CONCEPT 9.28

Sexual maturation occurring during puberty leads to reproductive capability, whether or not youngsters are psychologically prepared for it.

belonging comes to play an even greater role in determining their self-esteem and emotional adjustment.

Young people today are likely to view social networking as a natural extension of their real-life circle of friends (wiseGEEK, 2012). Many adolescents today spend more time connecting with their friends through social media sites than through "face time." A recent study showed that online connections may actually strengthen real-life relationships (Reich, Subrahmanyam, & Espinoza, 2012). Many college students also use social networking to maintain contacts with friends from high school and to draw upon them for social support (Manago, Taylor, & Greenfield, 2012).

Parents are often concerned that their teenagers may "run with the wrong crowd." Peer pressure is a major factor in teenagers initiating sexual intercourse as well as their use of tobacco, alcohol, and marijuana (see, for example, Curran, Stice, & Chassin, 1997; Wills & Cleary, 1999). A strong parent–teen connection and close communication also has a protective effect against negative outcomes such as emotional and behavioral problems and use of alcohol and other drugs (Brody et al., 2010; Wagner et al., 2010).

Adolescent Sexuality

Adolescents may be more than just "hormones with feet," as one observer put it, but sexual thoughts and interests often do take center stage during this period. The average age of first intercourse decreased during the second half of the twentieth century and attitudes toward premarital sex became more permissive (Elias, Fullerton, & Simpson, 2015; Martinez & Abma, 2015). Yet the percentages of unmarried teenagers who engage in sexual intercourse is on the decline, dropping from more than 50 percent at the turn of the new millennium to about 42 percent today (CDC, 2015g). Teenage birth rates have also been declining steadily and now stand at their lowest levels in more than 70 years (CDC, 2015b; Hamilton & Chong, 2015). That said, the birth rate among U.S. teens still exceeds that of many other developed countries.

Although some teen mothers become pregnant to fill an emotional void or to rebel against their families, most teenage pregnancies result from failure to use contraceptives reliably. Many sexually active teenagers get caught up in their own personal fables that lead them to believe pregnancy is something that could not happen to them.

Unwed teenage mothers face serious obstacles to their educational and social development. They are more likely than other girls to live below the poverty level, to quit school, and to depend on public assistance (Arnett, 2004). Although the father (usually a teenager himself) is equally responsible for the pregnancy, he is usually absent or incapable of contributing to the child's support.

Why do some teens become sexually active whereas others abstain? For one thing, peer pressure, whether real or imagined, can promote or restrain sexual activity. Moral reasons, on the other hand, are often a basis for restraint. Teens who abstain may also be concerned about getting caught, becoming pregnant, or contracting a sexually transmitted disease. Other factors linked to sexual restraint among teens include the following (based on Aspy et al., 2008; Brown et al., 2006; Hardy & Raffaelli, 2003; McBride, Paikoff, & Holmbeck, 2003):

- Living in an intact family
- Having a family with low levels of conflict
- Having at least one parent who graduated from college

- Placing importance on religion and attending religious services frequently
- Having less exposure to sexual content in music, movies, television, and magazines

Many gay adolescents face the challenge of coming to terms with their sexuality against the backdrop of social condemnation and discrimination against gays in the broader culture (Meyer, 2003). Their struggle for self-acceptance often requires stripping away layers of denial about their sexuality. Some gay men and lesbians fail to achieve a "coming out" to themselves—that is, a personal acceptance of their sexual orientation—until young or middle adulthood. The process of achieving self-acceptance can be so difficult that many gay adolescents have suicidal thoughts or attempt suicide.

Before we leave our discussion of adolescence, it's important to note that most adolescents are generally happy and optimistic about their futures (Arnett, 2004). Though adolescents may have wider and more frequent changes in moods than adults, most of their mood swings fall within a mild range.

"We've been thinking a lot about what we want to do with your life."

© The New Yorker Collection 2002 David Sipress from cartoonbank.com.

MODULE REVIEW 9.4 Adolescence

Recite It

10. Describe the physiological, cognitive, and psychosocial changes that occur during adolescence and Erikson's beliefs about psychosocial development in adolescence.

Puberty spans the period of physical development that begins with the appearance of secondary sex characteristics and ends with the attainment of full (a) _____ maturity. Adolescents may progress to the stage of (b) _____ operations, which, according to Piaget, is denoted by the ability to engage in abstract thinking and reasoning. Egocentricity in adolescence involves concepts of the (c) _____ audience (believing everyone else is as concerned about us as we are ourselves) and the personal (d) _____ (an exaggerated sense of uniqueness and perceptions of personal invulnerability).
Erikson believed the achievement of a sense of who one is and what one stands for (ego (e) _____) is the major psychosocial challenge of adolescence.
Erikson coined the term *identity* (f) _____ to describe a period of serious soul-searching in which adolescents attempt to come to terms with their ego identity and future direction in life.

11. Describe Kohlberg's stages of moral reasoning and **evaluate** his theory in light of Gilligan's criticism.

At the preconventional level, moral judgments are based on the perceived (g) _____ of behavior. Behaviors that avoid punishment are good; those that incur punishment from an external authority are bad.
At the (h) _____ level, conformity with conventional rules of right and wrong are valued because of the need to do what others expect or because one has an obligation to obey the law.
At the (i) _____ level, moral judgments are based on value systems the individual develops through personal reflection, such as valuing the importance of human life and the concept of justice above that of the law. Postconventional thinking does not develop until adolescence, if ever.
Gilligan pointed out that (j) _____ model was based only on the responses of males and did not take female voices into account. Through her own research, Gilligan concluded that females tend to adopt a care orientation, whereas males tend to adopt a (k) _____ orientation. Other researchers have found that differences in moral reasoning between men and women are less clear-cut, although women have a greater tendency to adopt a care orientation.

Recall It

1. The physical growth period during which young people mature sexually and reach their full reproductive capacity is known as _____.

   a. adolescence
   c. formal operations
   b. menarche
   d. puberty

2. The beginning of menstruation is called _____.

3. What are two ways in which egocentric thinking becomes expressed during adolescence?

4. Lawrence Kohlberg posed moral dilemmas to children and then classified their responses. Children whose responses indicated that they based their moral judgments on the perceived consequences of actions were classified at the _____ level of moral reasoning.

   a. preconventional
   c. concrete operational
   b. conventional
   d. postconventional

5. Cite two types of biases for which Kohlberg's theory has been criticized.

6. According to Erikson, what is the major psychosocial challenge facing adolescents?

   a. trust versus mistrust
   b. initiative versus guilt
   c. identity versus role diffusion
   d. intimacy versus inferiority

Think About It

■ Was your adolescence a period of *sturm und drang* (storm and stress) or was it relatively peaceful? Why do you suppose some teenagers move through adolescence with relative ease, whereas others find it a difficult period? What made adolescence easy or difficult for you?

Recite It *answers placed at the end of chapter.*

MODULE

9.5 Early and Middle Adulthood

12 **Describe** the physical and cognitive changes that occur during adulthood and Erikson's stages of psychosocial development in early and middle adulthood.

Development doesn't stop with the end of puberty. Physical and psychological development is a continuing process that lasts a lifetime. Early adulthood encompasses the 20s and 30s. Middle adulthood spans the period from about age 40 to about age 60 or 65. In this module, we continue our journey through human development by examining the changes in our physical and psychological development that occur as we progress from early adulthood through middle age.

Physical and Cognitive Development

Physical and cognitive development tend to peak in early adulthood. During their 20s, most people are at their height in memory functioning, ability to learn new skills, sensory acuteness, muscle strength, reaction time, and cardiovascular condition.

By and large, people also perform best on standardized intelligence tests in early adulthood. Some decline in cognitive abilities occurs during middle and late adulthood, especially poorer memory functioning and longer reaction times (Blazer, Yaffe, & Karlawish, 2015). A type of intelligence needed to think quickly in solving problems, called **fluid intelligence**, or mental flexibility, begins to decline in middle and later adulthood. We use fluid intelligence to solve abstract reasoning problems, to identify patterns and relationships, to solve puzzles, and to remember names we have just heard or information we have just read (Salthouse, 2012; Sweatt, 2010). Fluid

fluid intelligence A form of intelligence associated with the ability to think abstractly and flexibly in solving problems.

intelligence relies on working memory, the type of memory that enables us to hold and manipulate information in mind, such as when we perform mental arithmetic or juggle two or more ideas in our head at the same time (see Chapter 6).

Another form of intelligence called **crystallized intelligence** tends to peak around middle age and remains relatively intact as we age (Blazer, Yaffe, & Karlawish, 2015; Hartshorne & Germine, 2015; Paul, 2013). This is the form of intelligence associated with wisdom and knowledge and includes mental abilities such as vocabulary and arithmetical skills. Some forms of crystallized intelligence, such as vocabulary, tend to increase as we age (Ben-David et al., 2015) (see ■ Figure 9.8).

Apart from the occasional social embarrassment of fumbling over people's names, expectable cognitive declines in midlife usually occur gradually and may not be noticeable or interfere with social or occupational functioning. These declines may also be offset by increased knowledge and experience.

Beginning in the late 20s, people start losing lean body tissue, especially muscle. With each passing decade, they tend to lose about 7 pounds of lean body mass as more and more lean tissue turns to fat (Evans & Rosenberg, 1991). From ages 20 to 70, people are likely to lose as much as 30 percent of their muscle cells.

With the loss of muscle tissue comes a gradual loss of muscle strength. A person can help offset this loss, however, by following a regular weight-bearing exercise program. Regular exercise, in combination with a proper diet, can also help prevent significant gains in weight. Major weight gains are neither a normal nor an inevitable consequence of aging.

The most dramatic physical change during middle age is the cessation of menstruation and reproductive capability in women. This biological event, called **menopause**,

CONCEPT 9.29
Though many cognitive abilities reach a peak in early adulthood, declines in memory functioning that normally occur with age may not interfere with occupational or social functioning.

CONCEPT 9.30
Menopause is a major life event for most women and may symbolize other issues they may face in middle adulthood, including changes in appearance, health, and sexuality.

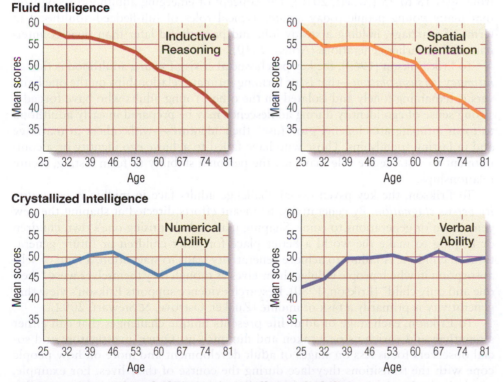

FIGURE 9.8 Age-Related Changes in Intellectual Ability
Crystallized intelligence, which includes abilities such as verbal ability (vocabulary comprehension) and numerical skills, remains relatively stable or may even improve as we age. The sharpest declines occur with fluid intelligence, the kind of intelligence needed for abstract reasoning skills, such as inductive reasoning and spatial orientation.

crystallized intelligence A form of intelligence associated with the use of knowledge or wisdom.

menopause The time of life when menstruation ends.

typically occurs in a woman's late 40s or early 50s. With menopause, the ovaries no longer ripen egg cells or produce the sex hormones estrogen and progesterone.

A persistent stereotype about menopause is that it signals the end of the woman's sexual appetite or drive. In fact, a woman's sex drive is fueled by the small amounts of male sex hormones (androgens) produced by her adrenal glands, not by estrogen. How a woman views menopause can have a strong bearing on her adjustment. Women who have been raised to believe menopause is connected with a loss of femininity may lose sexual interest or feel less sexually desirable. Others may actually feel liberated by the cutting of ties between sex and reproduction. A large-scale survey of post-menopausal women showed most were satisfied with their sexual activity, and most who expressed dissatisfaction actually wanted more, not less, sexual activity (Gass et al., 2011).

Unlike women, men can maintain fertility well into later adulthood. Men do experience a gradual decline in testosterone as they age, in contrast to the sharp decline in estrogen production that occurs in women during menopause. Although older adults may need to adjust to age-related changes in sexual response, such as allowing for more time to become sexually aroused, most report continued sexual interest and satisfying sexual relationships (Hillman, 2008; McCarthy & Pierpaoli, 2015; Ménard et al., 2015).

Psychosocial Development

The challenges of young adulthood have largely to do with sorting out adult roles and relationships. Psychologist Jeffrey Arnett coined the term **emerging adulthood** to describe the gradual transition from adolescence to adulthood that occurs roughly from ages 18 to 25 (Arnett, 2010). The concept of emerging adulthood recognizes that many young people today assume typical roles of full-fledged adulthood in terms of marriage, holding a steady job, and parenthood later than their counterparts did in earlier generations (Arnett, 2010).

To Erik Erikson (1963), the key psychosocial crisis of young adulthood is that of *intimacy versus isolation*—that is, of forming intimate relationships on the one hand versus remaining lonely and isolated on the other. Young adults who have forged a strong sense of ego identity during adolescence may be prepared in early adulthood to form intimate attachments—to "fuse" their identities—with others in marriage and in lasting friendships. Those who have failed to achieve ego identity or a commitment to a stable life role may lack the personal stability to form lasting, secure relationships.

To Erikson, the key psychosocial challenge adults face in midlife is *generativity versus stagnation*. By generativity, he meant efforts directed at shaping the new generation or generations to come. Shaping may include raising one's own children or helping to make the world a better place for other children or future generations of children. A failure to achieve generativity leads to stagnation, a kind of self-absorption in which people indulge themselves as though they themselves were "their one and only child" (Erikson, 1980). Research evidence supports Erikson's view that generativity is primarily a task of midlife (Zucker, Ostrove, & Stewart, 2002).

To Erikson, each stage of adult life presents unique challenges that can either strengthen and enrich us or weaken and diminish us. Other investigators and social observers focus less on stages of adult development and more on how people cope with the transitions they face during the course of their lives. For example, psychologist Daniel Levinson and his colleagues (1978) suggested that a *midlife transition* begins at about age 40. To Levinson, this age is a time of reckoning when we assess our lives in terms of whether we have reached the dreams we held in our youth. We may feel life is starting to slip away and realize we are now a full generation older than the youngest of the young adults. We may start to wonder

CONCEPT 9.31
Men experience a gradual decline in production of the male sex hormone testosterone as they age, but unlike women they may maintain reproductive capability well into late adulthood.

CONCEPT 9.32
Psychosocial development in early adulthood often centers on establishing intimate relationships and finding a place in the world.

CONCEPT 9.33
Erikson characterized the challenge faced by people in midlife as one of generativity versus stagnation.

CONCEPT 9.34
Although some people experience a midlife crisis, most appear to weather the changes in their middle years without a period of personal upheaval or state of crisis.

emerging adulthood The period of psychosocial development, roughly spanning the ages of 18 to 25, during which the person makes the transition from adolescence to adulthood.

whether we have more to look back on than forward to. Many middle-age adults compare their accomplishments to their earlier dreams and may despair if they find they have fallen short.

This midlife transition may trigger a **midlife crisis**: a sense of entrapment from the closing down of future options, of feeling that life is open-ended no more, of a loss of purpose or a sense of failure from not having fulfilled one's youthful ambitions or aspirations. Yet a midlife crisis is not inevitable and may in fact be more the exception than the rule (Lachman, 2004; Steger et al., 2006; Whitbourne, Lewis, & Schwartz, 2015). Many people in middle adulthood today are focusing on what they believe will be another three to four decades of promise rather than decline.

Concept Chart 9.6 at the end of the next module provides an overview of physical, cognitive, and psychosocial development during adulthood.

midlife crisis A state of psychological crisis, often occurring during middle adulthood, in which people grapple with the loss of their youth.

MODULE REVIEW 9.5 Early and Middle Adulthood

Recite It

12. Describe the physical and cognitive changes that occur during adulthood and Erikson's stages of psychosocial development in early and middle adulthood.

Beginning in their 20s, people start to experience a gradual decline in lean body mass and muscle tissue. (a) _____ intelligence—including rapid problem-solving ability and memory for lists of words, names, or text—tends to decline with increasing age during middle and late adulthood. (b) _____ intelligence remains relatively intact and may actually improve in some respects.

(c) _____, the cessation of menstruation, is the major physical marker of middle adulthood in women. Menopause is associated with a dramatic decline in estrogen production. Testosterone production in men also declines with age, but more gradually.

Erikson proposed the following stages of psychosocial development in adolescence and adulthood: ego (d) _____ versus role diffusion (adolescence), intimacy versus (e) _____ (early adulthood), (f) _____ versus stagnation (middle adulthood).

Recall It

1. In general, people perform best on standardized tests of intelligence

   a. in middle childhood.
   b. in adolescence.
   c. in early adulthood.
   d. at any time during their lives.

2. Which of the following statements about menopause is *not* true?

   a. Menopause is a normal physiological process.
   b. Menopause involves the cessation of menstruation.
   c. Loss of estrogen results in diminished sex drive.
   d. With menopause, the ovaries no longer produce ripened egg cells.

3. The major psychosocial challenge of early adulthood, according to Erikson, is that of

   a. role identity versus confusion.
   b. intimacy versus isolation.
   c. generativity versus stagnation.
   d. ego integrity versus despair.

4. Psychologist Daniel Levinson believes that at about the age of 40, people experience a time of reckoning or _____.

Think About It

■ What is your current "stage" of psychosocial development? Does your life reflect the issues and

challenges framed by Erikson and Levinson? If so, in what respects?

Recite It *answers placed at the end of chapter.*

MODULE

9.6 Late Adulthood

13 **Describe** the physical and cognitive changes we can expect later in life, and Erikson's views on psychosocial development in late adulthood.

14 **Identify** the qualities associated with successful aging.

15 **Identify** the stages of dying proposed by Kübler-Ross.

16 **Apply** suggestions for living a longer and healthier life.

CONCEPT 9.35
Americans are living longer than ever, on the average.

If you are fortunate enough, you may one day join the ranks of the fastest-growing segment of the population: people ages 65 and older. We are in the midst of a "graying of America," an aging of the population that has already begun to have profound effects on our society (see ■ Figure 9.9). About one in eight Americans (12.5 percent) is age 65 or older, a percentage that is expected to climb to 20 percent by the year 2030 (Vitiello, 2009).

Life expectancy in the United States and worldwide has been rising steadily (Murray et al., 2015). The average baby born today in the United States can expect to live 81 years (for females) or 76 years (for males) (Arias, 2016; CDC, 2015f). The average 65-year-old today can expect to live on the average to the age of 84.5 years for men and 86.6 for women (Olson, 2015).

A major determinant of psychological adjustment in later life is physical health status. For older adults in good health, reaching age 65 is experienced more as an extension of middle age than as entry into old age, particularly if they continue to work. The average 65-year-old today can expect to live to about age 83 for men or age 85 for women (Farrell, 2016).

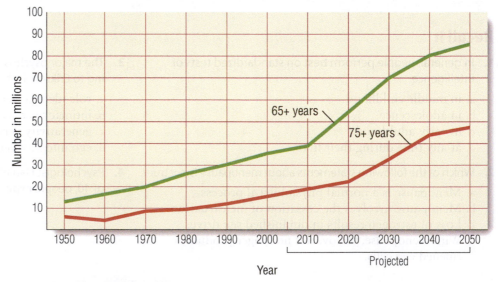

FIGURE 9.9 The Aging of America
The numbers of Americans over the age of 65 has been rising steadily and is projected to rise further through at least the first half of the twenty-first century.

Source: Centers for Disease Control and Prevention, National Center for Health Statistics, Health, United States, 2007, Figure 1. Data from the U.S. Census Bureau.

Physical and Cognitive Development

As we age, we experience a general decline in sensory and motor abilities. We continue to lose bone density as well as muscle mass, and our senses become less acute, especially our sense of smell (Rawson, 2006). The skin loses elasticity, and wrinkles and folds appear. Night vision fades and joints stiffen. Reaction times slow, so older drivers require more time to respond to traffic signals and changes in traffic conditions. Declines in the functioning of the immune system, the body's system of defense against disease-causing agents, makes older people more susceptible to illness, including life-threatening illnesses such as cancer.

"Good news, honey—seventy is the new fifty."

We noted in Module 9.5 that performance on tasks requiring fluid intelligence also tends to decline as people age. Older people typically require more time to solve problems and have greater difficulties with tasks involving pattern recognition, such as piecing together jigsaw puzzles. In addition, they may encounter more difficulties with memory for newly acquired information, such as remembering people's names or where they parked the car, and with *working memory*—keeping information briefly in mind while mulling it over or performing mental calculations (Sander, Lindenberger, & Werkle-Bergner, 2012; Yassa et al., 2011). Working memory seems to peak around age 30 (Hartshorne & Germine, 2015). Fortunately, age-related declines in memory are generally not significant enough to impair daily functioning. Some decline in mental processing speed needed to solve problems quickly is expected as people age (Park & McDonough, 2013; Robitaille et al., 2013). On the other hand, performance on tasks involving crystallized intelligence, such as tests of verbal ability and vocabulary skills, remains relatively intact as people age (Park & McDonough, 2013). Our fund of information and knowledge actually increases through much of the life span and only begins to decline around the well-advanced age of 90 (Park et al., 2002; Singer et al., 2003).

All told, most of us can expect to retain the bulk of our mental abilities throughout our lives. A long-term longitudinal study of cognitive ability shows that preserved intellectual ability in later life is associated with such factors as general physical health, engagement in stimulating activities, and openness to new experiences (Schaie, 1996, 2005).

But sadly, some people develop **dementia** in late adulthood. Dementia is characterized by a sharp decline in mental abilities, especially memory and reasoning ability. Importantly, note that dementia is *not* a normal consequence of aging (Gatz, 2007). It is a disease that damages or destroys brain tissue involved in higher mental functions, resulting in more severe memory loss than ordinary forgetfulness and difficulty performing routine activities. Let's put it this way: It is normal as we age to fumble when trying to remember someone's name or occasionally forgetting where we put our glasses (IOM, 2015; Jacob, 2015). But forgetting that you even wear glasses may well be a sign of dementia (Aamodt & Wang, 2008).

Dementia is caused by many physical conditions, including brain infections, tumors, Parkinson's disease, brain injuries, strokes, and chronic alcoholism. But the most common cause of dementia by far is **Alzheimer's disease**.

Alzheimer's disease, or AD, is an irreversible brain disease with a gradual onset that leads to a slow but progressive deterioration of mental functioning involving profound memory loss and impaired judgment and reasoning ability (Querfurth & LaFerla, 2010). About 5 million Americans suffer from AD, but as the general population continues to age, this number is expected to more than double to 13.8 million people by the year 2050 (Hebert et al., 2013; Wang, 2011). The disease is the sixth leading cause of death in the United States, claiming about 85,000 lives annually (CDC, 2015b,2015h). It affects about one in eight people age 65 or older and more

CONCEPT 9.36

In older adults, declines in problem-solving ability and memory functioning are typically not significant enough to impair daily functioning.

CONCEPT 9.37

A major longitudinal study on aging revealed that factors such as engagement in stimulating activities and openness to new experiences are associated with retention of intellectual functioning in later life.

dementia A condition involving a major deterioration or loss of mental abilities involved in memory, reasoning, judgment, and ability to carry out purposeful behavior.

Alzheimer's disease (AD) An irreversible brain disease with a progressive course of deterioration of mental functioning.

than one in three people over the age of 85 (Hebert et al., 2013; Querfurth & LaFerla, 2010). The disease can affect younger people, but is much less common than people over the age of 65.

AD is characterized by the formation of sticky masses of plaque (clumps of degenerative brain tissue) in the brain (Ossenkoppele et al., 2015; Underwood, 2015). These plaques are composed of a fibrous material called *beta-amyloid*. We don't yet know whether amyloid plaques play a causative role in AD or are merely a symptom of the disease. One line of inquiry suggests a possible causal role in which the formation of amyloid plaques leads to inflammation in the brain, which in turn causes damage to sensitive neural networks responsible for forming and maintaining memories (Bie et al., 2014). Though the cause or causes of AD remain unknown, we know that genetic factors play an important role in determining vulnerability to the disease (for example, Gillespie et al., 2016; Heck et al., 2015; Hooli et al., 2015; Tanzi, 2015).

As the disease progresses, people with AD require help selecting clothes, recalling names and addresses, and maintaining personal hygiene. They may start wandering and no longer be able to recognize family and friends or speak coherently. There is presently no cure for AD and the available drugs can only provide modest benefits in boosting memory and slowing the rate of decline (Dysken et al., 2014; Kuehn, 2012). Hopes lie in developing a better understanding of the formation of brain plaques in AD patients and possibly developing a vaccine against this terrible disease (Keaney et al., 2015; Winblad et al., 2012).

Remaining open to new experiences and challenges can help keep the mind sharp in later life.

Psychosocial Development

Erik Erikson characterized the central challenge of psychosocial development in late adulthood as one of *ego integrity versus despair.* He believed that the basic psychological challenge of later adulthood is the struggle to maintain a sense of meaning and satisfaction in life rather than drifting into a state of despair and bitterness. People who achieve a state of ego integrity are able to come to terms with their lives: to accept the joys and sorrows, and the successes and failures, that make up the totality of their life experiences. Erikson, who himself lived and worked productively into his 90s, was basically an optimist, believing we can remain fulfilled and maintain a sense of purpose at any stage of life and avoid falling into despair. Table 9.5 offers an overview of Erikson's stages of psychosocial development from adolescence through late adulthood.

A survey of former NFL players showed they were much more likely to report being diagnosed with Alzheimer's disease or other memory-related diseases than the national average. Suffering many blows to the head during their playing days may lead to the later development of dementia or other forms of cognitive impairment.

Other theorists, such as Daniel Levinson, also recognize that late adulthood is characterized by increasing awareness of the psychological and physical changes that accompany aging and the need to come to terms with death. He points out that one of the important life tasks older adults face is to rediscover the self—to understand who one is and find meaningful activities that continue to fill life with meaning and purpose—as well as to maintain connections with families and friends. Lacking connections to others and engagement in meaningful activities that imbue life with purpose can set the stage for a common problem in later life—depression. Many older adults, perhaps as many as one in five, experience periods of depressed mood, and 1 to 5 percent develop a full-fledged depressive disorder (Mackenzie et al., 2014; Mojtabai, 2014; Taylor, 2014). We should also note that suicide rates are much higher among middle age and older adults, especially older White males. Though effective psychological and drug treatments for depression in

Table 9.5 Erikson's Stages of Psychosocial Development During Adolescence and Adulthood

Life Period	Life Crisis	Major Challenge in Psychosocial Development
Adolescence	Identity versus role diffusion	To develop an occupational choice or public role and set of firmly held beliefs
Early adulthood	Intimacy versus isolation	To develop close intimate relationships and abiding friendships
Middle adulthood	Generativity versus stagnation	To contribute to the development and well-being of future generations
Late adulthood	Integrity versus despair	To maintain one's sense of dignity and psychological integrity

Source: Adapted from Erikson, 1963.

older adults are available, the disorder often goes untreated, partly because health care providers may focus more on the physical complaints of older adults than on their emotional concerns.

Despite the many challenges of late adulthood, including the aches and pains many older people face, many indices of emotional health, including happiness, life satisfaction, and a sense of well-being, are as high or even higher in older adults than in younger adults (Isaacowitz & Blanchard-Fields, 2012; Scheibe, 2012). Self-esteem, another important component of psychological adjustment, tends to rise during adolescence and through middle adulthood (ages 50 to 60) before declining toward the end of life (Orth & Robins, 2014; Orth, Maes, & Schmitt, 2015; Wagner et al., 2015).

There is much we can do to preserve our mental health as we age, such as maintaining social contacts and expanding social relationships by forming new friendships, which takes on added importance when coping with the loss of loved ones and old friends. As Cornell University psychologist Anthony Ong puts it, "We all age. It is how we age, however, that determines the quality of our lives" (Medical News Today, 2011). Developmental psychologists highlight the importance of several key characteristics associated with more successful aging:

1. *Selective optimization and compensation.* Successful aging is associated with the ability to optimize one's time and use available resources to compensate for shortcomings in physical energy, memory, or fluid intelligence (Freund, 2008). Rather than compete on the athletic field or in the business arena, where younger people may have the advantage, older adults may optimize their time by focusing on things that are more meaningful and important, such as visiting with family and friends more often—activities that allow them to pursue emotional goals that afford satisfaction. They may compensate for declining functioning by using written reminders, allowing themselves more time to learn new information, and using mechanical devices, such as hearing aids or canes, to compensate for loss of sensory or motor ability.

2. *Optimism.* Maintaining an optimistic frame of mind is linked to higher levels of life satisfaction and lower levels of depressive symptoms in later life (Chang & Sanna, 2001). Moreover, people who hold more positive views about aging tend to live longer—an average of 7.6 years longer—than those with more negative perceptions (Levy et al., 2002). Recent research also

Depression is a common emotional problem in late adulthood. What factors contribute to depression among older adults?

Concept Chart 9.6 Overview of Adult Development

	Early and Middle Adulthood	Late Adulthood
Physical development 	People tend to reach their physical and mental peaks in early adulthood. Declines in lean body tissue and muscle mass begin in the 20s. In middle age, women experience menopause, the cessation of menstruation, which is accompanied by a sharp drop in estrogen production. Men experience a more gradual reduction in testosterone as they age.	With aging, sensory acuity declines; muscles and bones lose mass; skin loses elasticity, causing wrinkles; reaction times increase; immune functioning declines.
Cognitive development 	Fluid intelligence tends to decline during middle and late adulthood, but crystallized intelligence tends to be relatively stable and may actually improve in some respects in middle and late adulthood. Memory ability may show the greatest age-related declines but typically does not have a significant impact on social or occupational functioning.	Alzheimer's disease and other forms of dementia are not normal aspects of aging but result from brain diseases or abnormalities.
Psychosocial development 	To Erikson, the psychosocial challenges of young and middle adulthood, respectively, involve *intimacy versus isolation* and *generativity versus stagnation*. Levinson focused on the important transitions that occur during stages of adulthood.	To Erikson, the psychosocial challenge of late adulthood involves *ego integrity versus despair*. Levinson focused on maintaining meaningful connections to others and engaging in activities that continue to imbue life with meaning. Depression is a major emotional concern for many older adults.

CONCEPT 9.40

Developmental psychologists have identified behavior patterns associated with successful aging, including selective optimization and compensation, optimism, and self-challenge.

shows that older adults who felt younger than their actual age had a lower death rate than those who felt their age or felt older than their actual age (Kelley, 2014; Rippon & Steptoe, 2015). There may be some truth to the familiar expression, "You're only as old as you feel."

3. *Self-challenge.* Seeking new challenges is a primary feature of successful adjustment at any age. The key for most older (and younger) adults is not to do less but to do more of the things that matter. Evidence shows that psychological factors such as maintaining a sense of purpose in life and having a sense of control over one's life is associated with greater longevity (Hill & Turiano, 2014; Steptoe, Deaton, & Stone, 2014; Turiano et al., 2014; Yager, 2014).

Concept Chart 9.6 provides an overview of adult development.

The Last Chapter: On Death and Dying

Now let us turn to a topic many of us would rather not think about: life's final transition, the one leading to death. When young, we may feel immortal. Our bodies may be strong and flexible, and our senses and minds sharp. We parcel thoughts about death and dying into a mental file cabinet to be opened much later in life, along with items like retirement, social security, and varicose veins. But death can occur at any age—by accident, violence, or illness. Death can also affect us deeply at any stage of life through the loss of loved ones. The issue of death raises questions well worth thinking about at any age, questions such as, Should I be an organ donor? How can I best leave my assets to those I care about? Shall I be buried or cremated? Shall I donate my body to science? Should I prepare a living will so that doctors will not need to use heroic measures to prolong my life when things are beyond hope?

Psychiatrist Elisabeth Kübler-Ross (1969) focused on how people cope with impending death. Based on her interviews with terminally ill people, she observed some common themes and identified five stages of dying through which many people pass.

1. *Denial.* At first, the person thinks, "It can't be me. I'm not really dying. The doctors made a mistake."

2. *Anger.* Once the reality of impending death is recognized, feelings of anger and resentment take center stage. Anger may be directed at younger or healthier people or toward the physicians who cannot save the person.

3. *Bargaining.* By the next stage, the person attempts to make a deal with God, such as promising to do good deeds in exchange for a few more months or years.

4. *Depression.* Depression reflects the growing sense of loss over leaving behind loved ones and losing life itself. A sense of utter hopelessness may ensue.

5. *Final acceptance.* As the person works through the earlier stages, he or she eventually achieves some degree of inner peace and acceptance. The person may still fear death, but comes to accept it with a kind of quiet dignity.

Kübler-Ross believed that family members and health professionals can help dying people by understanding the stages through which they are passing and helping them attain a state of final acceptance. Many dying people have experiences similar to those Kübler-Ross observed, but not everyone necessarily goes through each stage and not always in the order she proposed (Schneidman, 1983). Some dying people do not deny the inevitable but arrive at a rapid though painful acceptance of death. Some become hopelessly depressed; others experience mainly fear, and still others have rapidly shifting feelings.

CONCEPT 9.41
Elisabeth Kübler-Ross described the psychological experience of dying in terms of five identifiable stages.

MODULE REVIEW   9.6   Late Adulthood

Recite It

13. **Describe** the physical and cognitive changes we can expect later in life, and Erikson's views on psychosocial development in late adulthood.

We can expect a general decline in sensory and motor abilities, in immune system functioning, and in (a) _____ intelligence, memory for new information, and mental processing speed. However, cognitive changes are generally not severe enough to significantly impair daily functioning. (b) _____ disease and other forms of dementia are brain diseases, not normal consequences of aging. Erickson proposed that the major psychosocial challenge of late adulthood is one of finding a sense of (c) _____ (meaning and fulfillment in life) rather than falling into a state of despair.

14. **Identify** the qualities associated with successful aging.

Successful aging is associated with the ability to concentrate on what is important and meaningful, to maintain a (d) _____ outlook, and to continue to challenge oneself.

15. **Identify** the stages of dying that Kübler-Ross proposed.

The stages of dying are denial, (e) _____, bargaining, depression, and final acceptance.

16. **Apply** suggestions for living a longer and healthier life.

Suggestions include developing healthy exercise and nutrition habits, staying (f) _____ and helping others, managing stress, and exercising the mind.

Recall It

1. Which of the following cognitive skills is *not* likely to show a substantial decline as people age?

   a. rapid problem solving
   b. memory for new information
   c. speed at pattern recognition
   d. ability to apply acquired knowledge

2. List several factors that may help preserve intellectual functioning in later life.

3. What is closest in meaning to Erikson's term *ego integrity*?

   a. focusing attention on oneself
   b. achieving a sense of meaningfulness and satisfaction with one's life
   c. the development of generativity, or the ability to give of oneself to the next generation
   d. living an honest life

4. List three characteristics associated with successful aging.

Think About It

■ What key features of successful aging are highlighted in the text? How might you put this information to use in your own life?

■ Examine your own attitudes toward aging. How are your attitudes toward older adults affected by stereotypical perceptions?

Recite It *answers placed at the end of chapter.*

APPLYING PSYCHOLOGY in Daily Life

Living Longer, Healthier Lives

Longevity is partly determined by genes, a factor that for now lies beyond our control. But other factors enter the longevity equation. How people live—the behaviors and habits they acquire—may be even more important determinants of longevity. These lifestyle factors, such as exercise and dietary habits, contribute not just to longevity but also to the quality of life as people age. Young people who believe aging is a concern only for older people should take note that the earlier they establish healthier habits, the greater their chances will be of living a long, healthy life. Let's take a look at the healthier habits that may translate into living a longer and healthier life (Nevid & Rathus, 2010).

Developing Healthy Exercise and Nutrition Habits

Ponce de León, the Spanish explorer who searched for the mythical "Fountain of Youth," might have been more successful had he just stayed home and built a gym. Exercise at any age is healthful, but especially as we age, as it may slow down some effects of aging, such as loss of lean body mass, weight gain, and loss of bone and muscle strength. Regular exercise is also associated with a lower risk of certain cancers, such as cancer of the colon, and also helps lower the risk of other major killers such as heart disease, stroke, and diabetes, as well as the potentially disabling bone disorder **osteoporosis**. Weight-bearing exercise that requires working against gravity helps build bone density and keeps bones and muscles strong.

Evidence points to the value of regular exercise in helping people live longer and healthier lives (for example, Ekelund et al., 2015; Holme & Anderssen, 2015; Schnohr et al., 2015). Regular physical activity or vigorous exercise doesn't just keep the body strong, but also helps the mind stay sharp and helps combat depression, and may even reduce the risk of Alzheimer's disease (Berryman et al., 2014; Ferencz et al., 2014; Gill & Seitz, 2015; Merluzzi, 2015; Vidoni et al., 2015).

Exercise gets the blood flowing, including increased blood flow to the brain. It also helps us maintain a healthy weight. Because metabolism tends to slow down

CONCEPT 9.42

Longevity is partly determined by genetic inheritance and partly by factors people can directly control, such as a healthy diet, regular exercise, avoidance of harmful substances, and an active, involved lifestyle.

CONCEPT LINK

Taking care of your body, such as by taking frequent breaks, practicing relaxation skills, and exercising regularly, can help you cope more effectively with stress. See Module 10.1.

osteoporosis A bone disease characterized by a loss of bone density in which the bones become porous, brittle, and more prone to fracture.

with age, maintaining a healthy weight in middle and late adulthood requires compensating accordingly by curtailing calorie intake and exercising regularly to burn off excess calories.

Following a healthy, balanced diet is a key factor in promoting health and longevity (Anderson et al., 2011). Following a low-fat diet that is rich in fruits, vegetables, and whole grains can reduce the risks of potentially life-shortening diseases, such as coronary heart disease.

Developing healthy habits also extends to avoiding harmful substances. Tobacco use, illicit drug use, and excessive use of alcohol can lead to physical health problems that can cut life expectancy significantly (Rizzuto et al., 2012). Moreover, many lives, both young and old, have been lost to drug overdoses.

Staying Involved and Helping Others

Staying actively involved in meaningful activities and personal projects can contribute not only to preserving mental sharpness but also to emotional well-being (Lawton et al., 2002). Research evidence also gives credence to the familiar adage that it is better to give than to receive. A study of older adults showed that giving support to others was associated with a higher survival rate and was more strongly linked to extending longevity than was receiving support (Brown et al., 2003).

Managing Stress

In Chapter 10, you will learn how stress affects physical health and emotional well-being. Prolonged or intense stress can impair the immune system, the body's line of defense against disease-causing organisms and damaged cells. In turn, a weakened immune system makes people more likely to develop infectious diseases and less able to protect themselves from chronic diseases associated with aging such as hypertension, cancer, and heart disease. Stress management techniques can help take the distress out of stress and hopefully reduce the risk of developing stress-related disorders.

Exercising the Mind

Engaging the mind helps keep it healthy, especially as we age. Engaging in mentally stimulating activities and cognitive training programs helps strengthen mental functioning and memory in middle and late adulthood. Like strength training for toning muscles, cognitive training strengthens working memory and other mental skills and slows cognitive declines in older adults (Ngandu et al., 2015; Smith, 2014; Zinke et al., 2014).

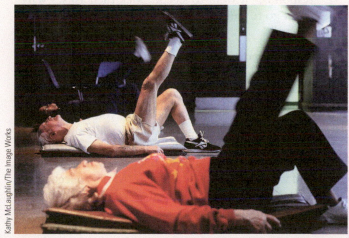

Exercise is not just for the young. Regular exercise in late adulthood can enhance longevity and physical health, as well as maintain mental sharpness.

Intellectual activities designed to preserve mental sharpness as we age include mentally challenging games (such as chess), crossword or jigsaw puzzles, reading, writing, painting, and sculpting, to name but a few. Learning new things, such as digital photography, yields positive effects on cognitive functioning in older adults (Park et al., 2014).

Do Healthy Habits Pay Off?

People who adopt healthier habits (avoiding smoking, remaining physically and socially active, following a healthy diet, controlling excess body weight, and avoiding excessive drinking) and who maintain favorable levels of blood cholesterol and blood pressure are more likely to live longer and healthier lives than those with unhealthier habits (Ekelund et al, 2015; Rizzuto et al., 2012; Schnohr et al., 2015; Willcox et al., 2006). The results of a large-scale study in the United Kingdom showed that people who adopted four healthy behaviors (nonsmoking, regular exercise, moderate alcohol consumption, and eating five servings of fruits and vegetables daily) lived an average of 14 years longer than others who adopted none of these four behaviors (Khaw et al., 2008).

Critical thinkers recognize that we cannot draw a cause-and-effect relationship between healthy habits and longevity based simply on a statistical relationship. Because longevity researchers may not be able to control whether people adopt healthier habits, they are generally limited to studying differences in outcomes between those who do and those who do not. Still, correlational relationships can point to possible causal relationships, and it stands to reason that adoption of healthier habits may help extend life.

All in all, it is wise to take stock of your health habits sooner rather than later. It is like salting away money for your later years: Developing healthy habits now and maintaining them throughout life are likely to boost your chances of living a longer and healthier life.

THINKING CRITICALLY ABOUT PSYCHOLOGY

Based on your reading of this chapter, answer the following questions. Then, to evaluate your progress in developing critical thinking skills, compare your answers to the sample answers found in Appendix A.

1. One evening after the sun sets, Nick asks his 3-year-old son Trevor, "Where did the sun go?" Trevor responds, "It went to sleep." Nick then asks, "Why did it go to sleep?" Trevor answers, "Because it was sleepy."

   Based on your understanding of Piaget's theory of cognitive development, explain why Trevor believes that the sun went to sleep because it was sleepy.

2. This critical thinking exercise asks you to apply Erikson's model of psychosocial development to yourself. To Erikson, *ego identity* is the achievement of a firm set of beliefs about who we are, what we believe, and where we are headed in life. Many college-age students are in the process of creating their ego identities. But creation takes time, and the process need not be completed by graduation. Psychologist James Marcia (Marcia, 1980, 2002; Marcia et al., 1993) identified four identity statuses that describe where people stand in their ego identities at any given time:

   Identity achievement describes people who have emerged from an identity crisis (a period of serious self-reflection) with a commitment to a relatively stable set of personal beliefs and to a course of action, such as following a major course of study in pursuing a particular career.

   Foreclosure describes people who have adopted a set of beliefs or a course of action without undergoing a period of serious self-exploration or self-examination. They have not gone through an identity crisis to arrive at their beliefs and occupational choices. Most base their commitments on what others, especially their parents, instilled in them.

   Moratorium is a state of identity crisis concerning one's beliefs or career choices. People in moratorium are currently working through their personal beliefs or struggling to determine which career course to pursue.

   Identity diffusion is the state describing people who are not yet committed to a set of personal beliefs or career choices and show no real interest in developing these commitments. Issues of ego identity have not yet taken center stage in their lives.

   Now think critically about yourself in relation to these categories:

   a. How would you determine your identity status in areas such as occupational choice and personal (political and moral) beliefs? What evidence would you need to make this determination? Bear in mind that you may have a different identity status in each area.

   b. Apply these criteria to yourself. Based on this self-appraisal, which identity status best describes your ego identity at this point in time in the areas of career choice and personal beliefs?

Recite It Answers for Chapter 9

Module 9.1 1. (a) implantation; (b) embryonic; (c) fetal; (d) teratogens   **Module 9.2** 2. (a) palmar, 3. (b) odors; (c) 6; (d) memories, 4. (e) walk
Module 9.3 5. (a) easy; (b) slow-to-warm-up; (c) Difficult; (d) withdrawn; (e) secure; (f) avoidant; (g) resistant, 6. (h) Authoritative; (i) Authoritarian;
(j) Permissive, 7. (k) mistrust; (l) autonomy; (m) guilt; (n) industry, 8. (o) senses; (p) animistic; (q) conservation; (r) deductive, 9. (s) proximal
Module 9.4 10. (a) sexual; (b) formal; (c) imaginary; (d) fable; (e) identity; (f) *crisis*, 11. (g) consequences; (h) conventional; (i) postconventional;
(j) Kohlberg's; (k) justice   **Module 9.5** 12. (a) Fluid; (b) Crystallized; (c) Menopause; (d) identity; (e) isolation; (f) generativity
Module 9.6 13. (a) fluid; (b) Alzheimer's; (c) integrity, 14. (d) positive, 15. (e) anger, 16. (f) involved

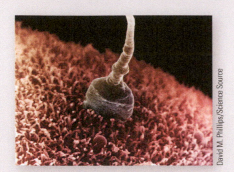

David M. Phillips/Science Source

MODULES 9.1, 9.2

Prenatal and Infant Development

Stages of Prenatal Development

- **Germinal Stage:** First 2 weeks after conception
- **Embryonic Stage:** From about 2 weeks to about 8 weeks after conception
- **Fetal Stage:** From about 8 weeks after conception until birth

Threats to Prenatal Development

- **Teratogens:** Dangerous influences to fetal health
- **Maternal Malnutrition:** Risk of premature birth and low birth weight

Infant Development

- **Reflexes:** Some have survival value
- **Sensory and Perceptual Abilities:** Not a buzzing confusion
- **Learning Ability:** Can learn and remember simple responses
- **Development of Motor Skills:** Occurs in same sequence and about same ages in all cultures

Mark Richards/PhotoEdit

Lew Merrim/Science Source

MODULE 9.3

Child Development

- **Individual Differences:** Temperaments (easy children, difficult children, slow-to-warm-up children); attachment styles (secure type [Type B], insecure-avoidant type [Type A], insecure-resistant type [Type C], disorganized/disoriented type [Type D])
- **Child-Rearing Influences:** Genetics, peer-group influences, parenting behaviors, and parenting styles
- **Erikson's Stages of Psychosocial Development:** Trust versus mistrust, autonomy versus shame and doubt, initiative versus guilt, industry versus inferiority
- **Theories of Cognitive Development:** Piaget's stages of cognitive development (sensorimotor stage, preoperational stage, concrete operational stage, formal operational stage); Vygotsky's sociocultural theory (zone of proximal development, or ZPD)

Adolescence

- **Physical Development:** Attainment of full sexual maturity during puberty
- **Psychosocial Development:** Marked by sometimes stormy but generally healthy adolescent–parent relationships, challenge of developing ego identity, and importance of peer relationships and emerging sexuality
- **Cognitive Development:** Characterized by Piaget's concept of formal operational thinking and Kohlberg's stages of moral reasoning; emergence of adolescent egocentricity (imaginary audience, personal fable)

Adult Development

Physical and Cognitive Development

- **Physical Maturity:** Reaches a peak in early 20s
- **Changes in Cognitive Functioning:** Fluid intelligence and memory functioning affected most by aging

Fluid Intelligence

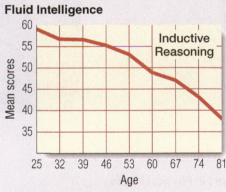

Crystallized Intelligence

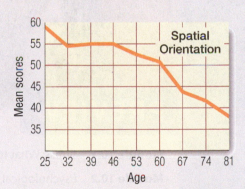

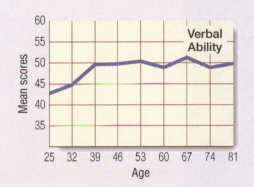

Psychosocial Development

- **Emerging Adulthood:** Adulthood is a gradual process that extends beyond adolescence
- **Erikson's Stages of Psychosocial Development:** Intimacy versus isolation (young adulthood), generativity versus stagnation (middle adulthood), ego integrity versus despair (late adulthood)
- **Coping with Age-Related Challenges:** Successful aging associated with selective optimization and compensation, optimism, and self-challenge; maintaining a sense of purpose and connection to others
- **Death and Dying:** Five stages in Kübler-Ross model (denial, anger, bargaining, depression, and final acceptance)

LEARNING OBJECTIVES

After studying this chapter, you will be able to . . .

1 **Define** stress in psychological terms.

2 **Identify** and **describe** the major sources of stress.

3 **Define** the general adaptation syndrome and **identify** its three stages.

4 **Evaluate** the effects of stress on the body's immune system.

5 **Identify** psychological factors that buffer the effects of stress.

6 **Apply** stress management techniques to daily life.

7 **Identify** psychological factors linked to coronary heart disease.

8 **Identify** psychological factors linked to cancer.

9 **Apply** knowledge of the transmission of sexually transmitted disease to steps we can take to protect ourselves from these diseases.

George Doyle/Stockbyte/Getty Images

PREVIEW

Psychology and Health

10

The Philosopher in the Morgue

The Paris morgue is a strange place for a famous philosopher to be rummaging about. But there among the corpses was the seventeenth-century French philosopher René Descartes (1596–1650) (Searle, 1996). You probably know Descartes for his famous statement "I think, therefore I am." Descartes believed that the mind and body are two fundamentally different entities. But if the mind and body are separate, there must be some connection between them. For example, if you decide to raise your arm and a fraction of a second later your arm moves up, the mind must have had an effect on the body. By examining corpses, Descartes hoped to find the part of the brain where the mind connected to the body. Despite his efforts to find the point of intersection of mind and body, modern science teaches that the mind and the body—the psychological and the physical—are much more closely intertwined than Descartes would ever have imagined. In this chapter, we examine the close links between our psychological health and our physical health. Sorry René, but the mind and body do not intersect at any one point; they are inextricably connected in many ways.

In previous chapters, we focused on how the workings of the body, especially the brain, affect mental experiences such as sensations, perceptions, emotions, and thinking. Here we look at the other side of the coin by considering how the mind affects the body—how psychological factors, especially stress, affect our health and well-being.

In this chapter, we examine the role of stress in our physical and mental health and look at the psychological factors that moderate the impact of stress. We then examine how psychological factors influence such major health problems as heart disease and cancer, the two leading killers of Americans. We will see that unhealthy behaviors and lifestyles, such as smoking and consumption of a high-fat diet, are linked to the risk of developing these life-threatening diseases. By better understanding the psychological links to physical illness, psychologists can develop health promotion programs to help people make healthful changes in their behaviors and lifestyles. Finally, we consider how each of us can apply psychological techniques and principles to better manage the stress we face in our daily lives.

Did you know that...

- Nearly half of Americans report that they experience health-related problems due to stress? (p. 378)
- Chronic anger may be harmful to your heart? (p. 400)
- The emotional stress of divorce or even college examinations may damage your health? (p. 390)
- Writing about traumatic experiences may boost the body's immune system? (p. 390)
- Socially isolated people have a higher risk of early death than socially engaged people? (p. 390)
- Optimistic people tend to live longer than pessimistic people? (p. 392)
- The major cause of cervical cancer is a sexually transmitted virus? (p. 402)
- Regular exercise can increase your resilience to stress? (p. 394)

MODULE

10.1 Stress: What It Is and What It Does to the Body

1 **Define** stress in psychological terms.

2 **Identify** and **describe** the major sources of stress.

3 **Define** the general adaptation syndrome and **identify** its three stages.

4 **Evaluate** the effects of stress on the body's immune system.

5 **Identify** psychological factors that buffer the effects of stress.

6 **Apply** stress management techniques to daily life.

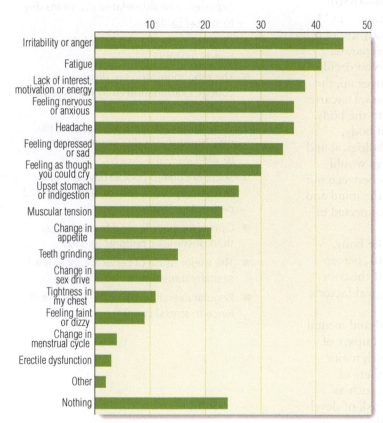

FIGURE 10.1 Physical and Psychological Symptoms Resulting from Stress

These figures show the percentages of Americans surveyed by the American Psychological Association who reported various psychological and physical symptoms resulting from stress during the past month.

Source: From *Physical Symptoms of Stress: American Psychological Association, Stress in American Findings.* Copyright © 2010 American Psychological Association. Reprinted by permission.

The study of interrelationships between psychology and physical health is called **health psychology**. Health psychologists work in universities, hospitals, and government agencies conducting research and using the knowledge they gain to develop health promotion and disease prevention programs.

Health psychologists are especially concerned with the effects of stress on physical health. But what is stress, and how does it affect our health?

Psychologists use the term **stress** to describe pressures or demands placed upon an organism to adjust or adapt to its environment. Stress is a fact of life. We may even need a certain amount of stress to remain active, alert, and energized. We can characterize these healthy forms of stress as good stress. But when stress increases to a point that it taxes our ability to cope, we may experience *distress*, which is an unpleasant state of physical or mental pain or suffering.

Distress may take the form of psychological problems, especially anxiety, depression, anger, and irritability, and physical health problems such as headache, fatigue, upset stomach, and such serious medical conditions as cardiovascular disorders (see ■ Figure 10.1).

Many Americans say that stress is on the rise. According to recent surveys by the American Psychological Association, one-third of Americans say they are facing extreme levels of stress in their lives, and more than 40 percent report adverse health effects from stress (American Psychological Association, 2007, 2010b). About 80 percent say their level of stress has increased or stayed the same in the past year, as compared to only 20 percent who say their stress has decreased (Bethune, 2013). And—wait, big surprise coming—younger adults in the Millennial generation (ages 18 to 33) reported higher levels of stress than did middle-aged and older adults (American Psychological Association, 2013; Martin, 2012).

Stress is taking a heavy toll on the emotional health of college students today. A recent national survey of first-year college students showed that student ratings of their emotional health had declined to record low levels (Higher Education Research Institute, 2011; Lewin, 2011). Increasing financial concerns are adding to academic and adjustment problems as sources of stress many students today face.

Sources of Stress

What stresses you out? School and work demands, relationship problems, traffic jams, or maybe the kinds of daily stress from needing to prepare meals, shop, or doing household chores? The American Psychological Association asked people to report on the major causes of stress in their lives. Concerns about money and work topped the list in 2015, with 67 percent and 65 percent of respondents, respectively, reporting these factors as significant sources of stress (APA, 2016a) (see ■ Figure 10.2).

Sources of stress are called **stressors**. We face many stressors in our lives. In this section, we examine a number of stressors, including daily hassles, life events or life changes, frustration, conflict, trauma, Type A behavior pattern, and pressure to adjust to a new culture, which is a stressor immigrant groups face.

Positive as well as negative experiences can be sources of stress. Happy or joyous events, such as having a baby, getting married, or graduating from college, are stressors because they impose demands on us to adjust or adapt. Positive changes in our lives, like negative ones, can tax our ability to cope, as any new parent will attest. How well we are able to cope with the stress we experience in our daily lives plays a key part in determining our mental and physical well-being.

How do Americans cope with stress? The top five ways of managing stress, according to the American Psychological Association survey, are listening to music (46 percent), exercising or walking (43 percent), going online or surfing the Internet (40 percent), watching TV or going to the movies (39 percent), and socializing with friends or family and reading (tied at 35 percent) (APA, 2016b). What do you do to cope with stress?

What are the stressors in your life?

CONCEPT 10.1
When the level of stress in our lives taxes our ability to cope, we may experience states of distress in the form of psychological or physical health problems.

CONCEPT 10.2
Stressors are sources of stress, such as hassles, life changes, frustration, and conflict.

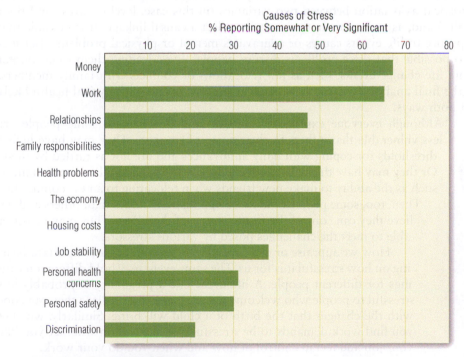

Causes of Stress
% Reporting Somewhat or Very Significant

FIGURE 10.2 Sources of Stress

Here are some things people say cause stress in their lives. How significant are these sources of stress in your life?

Source: Data derived from *Stress in America™ Survey*, American Psychological Association, 2016b.

health psychology The specialty in psychology that focuses on the interrelationships between psychological factors and physical health.

stress Pressure or demand placed on an organism to adjust or adapt.

stressors Sources of stress.

CONCEPT 10.3

Sources of chronic stress in our lives in-clude hassles, financial problems, job-re-lated problems, relationship problems, and persistent pain or other medical problems.

CONCEPT LINK

As we saw in Chapter 3, psychological factors may affect the severity of chronic pain and how people are able to cope with it. See Chapter 3's Applying Psychology in Daily Life feature.

Stress is taking a toll on the emotional well-being of college students today. Student ratings of their emotional health have recently hit record lows. What can you do to take the bite out of stress?

CONCEPT 10.4

People experiencing a greater number of life change events are at increased risk of physical health problems, but questions of cause and effect remain open to debate.

hassles Annoyances of daily life that impose a stressful burden.

chronic stress Continuing or lingering stress.

Hassles

Hassles are annoyances we commonly experience in our daily lives. Examples include traffic jams, household chores, coping with inclement weather, and balancing job demands and social relationships. Few, if any, of us are immune from daily hassles.

We may experience hassles on a daily basis, such as hunting for a parking spot in overcrowded parking lots. Others occur irregularly or unexpectedly, such as get-ting caught in a downpour without an umbrella. A single hassle may not amount to much in itself. But the accumulation of daily hassles contributes to the general level of **chronic stress** in our lives. Chronic stress is a state of persistent tension or pressure that can lead us to feel exhausted, irritable, and depressed. In addition to daily hassles, sources of chronic stress include ongoing financial problems, job-re-lated problems, marital or relationship conflicts, and persistent or recurrent pain or other chronic medical conditions.

Life Events

Stress can also result from major changes in life circumstances, which psychologists call *life events* or *life changes*. These may be negative events, such as the loss of a loved one or a job termination, or positive events, such as getting married, receiving a promotion, or having a baby. In other words, changes for better or for worse can impose stressful burdens that require adjustment. Unlike daily hassles, life events occur irregularly and sometimes unexpectedly. To determine how much stress is in your life, see the Try This Out feature.

People who experience greater numbers of life changes are more likely to suffer from psychological and physical health problems (Dohrenwend, 2006). We need to observe some caution when interpreting these data, however. Relationships be-tween life changes and psychological and physical problems are typically small, and the links are correlational. As you may recall from Chapter 1, a correlation is a statistical association between two variables (in this case, level of stress and poor health) and, as such, does not necessarily reflect a causal linkage. It is possible that exposure to life events causes or aggravates mental or physical problems. But it is also possible that these problems disrupt people's lives, leading them to encounter more life change events, such as job relocations or conflicts with family members. In the final analysis, relationships between life events and our physical health likely cut both ways.

Although everyone experiences hassles and life changes, some people are less vulnerable than others to these types of stressors. They may have higher thresholds for coping with daily annoyances and are not as rattled by them. Or they may have the skills needed to adjust to changes in life circumstances, such as the ability to make new friends when relocating to a new community.

Then, too, some people hold more optimistic attitudes than others and be-lieve they can control the future course of their lives. They may be better able to meet the challenges posed by various stressors.

How we appraise or evaluate a life event also has an important bear-ing on how stressful it is for us. The same event may hold different mean-ings for different people. A life event like a pregnancy is probably less stressful to people who welcome the pregnancy and believe they can cope with the changes that the birth of a child will bring. Similarly, whether you find work demands to be stressful may depend on whether you like your job and feel in control of how and when you do your work.

Frustration

Another major source of stress is **frustration**, the negative emotional state that occurs when our efforts to pursue our goals are blocked or thwarted. Adolescents

Try This Out   How Stressful Is Your Life?

The College Life Stress Inventory was designed to measure the amount of life stress experienced by college students. Circle the items in the inventory that you have experienced during the past year. Then compute your stress level by adding the stress ratings of the circled items. Use the scoring key to help you interpret your score.

Stress Rating	Event
100	Being raped
100	Finding out that you are HIV-positive
98	Being accused of rape
97	Death of a close friend
96	Death of a close family member
94	Contracting a sexually transmitted disease (other than AIDS)
91	Concerns about being pregnant
90	Finals week
90	Concerns about your partner being pregnant
89	Oversleeping for an exam
89	Flunking a class
85	Having a boyfriend or girlfriend cheat on you
85	Ending a steady dating relationship
85	Serious illness in a close friend or family member
84	Financial difficulties
83	Writing a major term paper
83	Being caught cheating on a test
82	Drunk driving
82	Sense of overload in school or work
80	Two exams in one day
77	Cheating on your boyfriend or girlfriend
76	Getting married
75	Negative consequences of drinking or drug use
73	Depression or crisis in your best friend
73	Difficulties with parents
72	Talking in front of a class
69	Lack of sleep
69	Change in housing situation (hassles, moves)
69	Competing or performing in public
66	Getting in a physical fight
66	Difficulties with a roommate
65	Job changes (applying, new job, work hassles)
65	Declaring a major or concerns about future plans
62	A class you hate
61	Drinking or use of drugs
60	Confrontations with professors
58	Starting a new semester
57	Going on a first date
55	Registration
55	Maintaining a steady dating relationship
54	Commuting to campus or work, or both
53	Peer pressures
53	Being away from home for the first time
52	Getting sick
52	Concerns about your appearance
51	Getting straight A's
48	A difficult class that you love
47	Making new friends; getting along with friends
47	Fraternity or sorority rush
40	Falling asleep in class
20	Attending an athletic event (for example, football game)

Scoring Key: You can gauge your overall level of stress by comparing your total score with the scores obtained by the developers of the scale based on a sample of 257 introductory psychology students. The average (mean) score was 1,247, and approximately two out of three students obtained scores ranging from 806 to 1,688. Though your total score may give you insight into how high your level of stress is, it does not reveal how much stress may be affecting you. Some people thrive on higher levels of stress than others. They may possess the coping skills and social support that they need to handle stress more effectively. But anyone can become overstressed as pressures and life changes continue to pile up. If you are facing a high level of stress in your life, perhaps you can reduce some of these sources of stress. You might also benefit by learning effective ways of handling stressors you cannot avoid. The Applying Psychology in Daily Life feature on page 393 offers some guidelines for managing stress that you may find helpful.

Source: From M. J. Renner and R. Scott Mackin, "College Life Stress Inventory," *Teaching of Psychology*, Vol. (1), p. 47. Copyright © 1998 Michael J. Renner and R. Scott Mackin, West Chester University of Pennsylvania. Reprinted by permission.

may feel frustrated when they want to drive, date, or drink alcoholic beverages but are told they are too young. People desiring higher education may be frustrated when they lack the financial resources to attend the college of their choice. We may frustrate ourselves when we set unrealistically high goals that we are unable to achieve.

frustration A negative emotional state experienced when one's efforts to pursue one's goals are thwarted.

🔗 **CONCEPT LINK**

As we saw in Chapter 8, incentive theory focuses on the "pull" or lure of goals and desired objects as an important source of motivation. See Module 8.1.

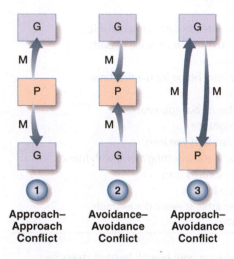

FIGURE 10.3 Types of Conflicts
① In an approach–approach conflict, the person (P) is motivated (M) to pursue two goals (G) but cannot pursue both of them at the same time. ② In an avoidance–avoidance conflict, the person is motivated to avoid each of two undesirable goals. ③ In an approach–avoidance conflict, the same goal has both positive and negative qualities. ④ In a multiple approach–avoidance conflict, the person faces two or more goals, each with positive and negative features.

CONCEPT 10.6
The four major types of psychological conflict are approach–approach, avoidance–avoidance, approach–avoidance, and multiple approach–avoidance conflict.

conflict A state of tension brought about by opposing response tendencies or motives operating simultaneously.

Conflict

Conflict is a state of tension resulting from the presence of two or more competing goals or response tendencies that demand resolution. People in conflict often vacillate, or shift back and forth, between competing goals. The longer they remain in conflict, the more stressed and frustrated they feel. Psychologists identify four major types of conflicts. Let us consider each in turn.

Approach–Approach Conflict. In an approach–approach conflict (see ■ Figure 10.3), you feel drawn toward two positive but mutually exclusive goals at the same time. You may need to decide between taking a vacation in the mountains or at the beach, or dating Taylor or Alex this weekend, or choosing between two attractive job offers. Though you may initially vacillate between the two goals, an approach–approach conflict is generally resolved by deciding on one course of action or another. The approach–approach conflict is generally considered the least stressful type of conflict.

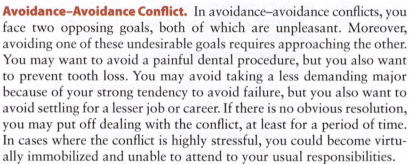

Avoidance–Avoidance Conflict. In avoidance–avoidance conflicts, you face two opposing goals, both of which are unpleasant. Moreover, avoiding one of these undesirable goals requires approaching the other. You may want to avoid a painful dental procedure, but you also want to prevent tooth loss. You may avoid taking a less demanding major because of your strong tendency to avoid failure, but you also want to avoid settling for a lesser job or career. If there is no obvious resolution, you may put off dealing with the conflict, at least for a period of time. In cases where the conflict is highly stressful, you could become virtually immobilized and unable to attend to your usual responsibilities.

Approach–Avoidance Conflict. In approach–avoidance conflicts, you face a goal that has both positive and negative qualities. You may want to ask someone for a date, but feel panic-stricken by fears of rejection. You may want to attend graduate school, but fear incurring heavy loans. Resolution of the conflict seems possible if you compare the relative pluses and minuses and then decide to commit yourself to either pursuing or abandoning the goal. But like a piece of metal within proximity of a magnet's two opposing poles, you may at first feel pulled toward the goal by its desirable qualities, only to be repelled by its unattractive qualities as you get closer to it.

Multiple Approach–Avoidance Conflict. The most complex type of conflict, multiple approach–avoidance conflict involves two or more goals, each with compelling positive and negative characteristics. You may, for example, want to pursue further training after graduation because it will expand your career options, but you are put off by the expense and additional time commitments involved. On the other hand, you may have a job opportunity that will get you started in a career now, but worry that you'll come to regret not having gone further with your education. Such conflicts can sometimes be resolved by combining both goals (getting started at the new job while taking night courses). At other times, the resolution comes from making a commitment to a course of action, even though it may entail nagging concerns about "the road not taken."

Conflicts are most easily resolved and least stressful when one goal is decidedly more attractive than another or when the positive qualities of a goal outweigh the negative. But when two goals pull you in opposite directions, or when the same goal both strongly attracts and repels you, you may experience high levels of stress and confusion about which course of action to pursue.

Traumatic Stressors

Traumatic stressors are potentially life-threatening events. Included in this category are natural or technological disasters (hurricanes, tornadoes, floods, nuclear accidents, and so on); combat experiences; serious accidents; physical or sexual assaults; a diagnosis of cancer, AIDS, or other life-threatening illness; and terrorist attacks, such as the horrific attacks on the United States on September 11, 2001, or the bombing at the Boston Marathon on April 15, 2013.

People who experience traumatic events may develop a psychological disorder called **post-traumatic stress disorder (PTSD)**, which is characterized by the occurrence of lingering psychological problems that may include the following:

CWB/Shutterstock.com

- *Avoidance of cues associated with the trauma.* People with PTSD may avoid situations or cues that may be reminders of the traumatic experience. A rape survivor may avoid traveling in the same part of town in which she was attacked. A combat veteran may avoid viewing war movies or socializing with service buddies.

- *Reexperiencing the traumatic event.* Such people may experience intrusive memories, images, or dreams of the traumatic experience. They may have flashbacks of the traumatic experience, as in combat veterans who have feelings of being back on the battlefield from time to time.

- *Impaired functioning.* They may experience depression or anxiety that interferes with their ability to meet ordinary responsibilities as workers, students, parents, or family members.

- *Heightened arousal.* They may be unusually tense or keyed up, find it difficult to relax or fall asleep, or have a heightened heart rate. They may also appear to be constantly on guard and show an exaggerated startle response to sudden noises.

- *Emotional numbing.* They may experience a numbing of emotional responses and find it difficult to feel love or other strong emotions.

Many trauma survivors suffer from PTSD, although their symptoms may not develop until months or years after the traumatic stressor. But it turns out that most people are resilient in the face of trauma and bounce back without the need for formal psychological treatment (Bonanno et al., 2010). Fewer than 10 percent of trauma survivors go on to develop PTSD (Delahanty, 2011).

PTSD is not limited to Western cultures. Researchers have found high rates of PTSD among earthquake survivors in Pakistan, hurricane survivors in Nicaragua, Khmer refugees who survived the "killing fields" of the Pol Pot War in Cambodia from 1975 to 1979, and survivors of the Balkan conflicts of the 1990s and the Iraq wars (Ali et al., 2012; Wagner, Schulz, & Knaevelsrud, 2011). Culture plays a role in determining not only the ways in which people manage and cope with traumatic experiences but also their vulnerability to PTSD and other psychological disorders arising from stress.

Type A Behavior Pattern

Do others describe you as hard-driving, competitive, impatient, and ambitious? Do you seem to take life at a faster pace than others? Does the idea of waiting in line or being stuck in traffic make you want to pull out your hair or pound your fists? If these characteristics ring true, your personality style probably fits the **Type A behavior pattern (TABP).**

CONCEPT 10.7
Traumatic events can be sources of intense stress that, in turn, can have profound, enduring effects on our psychological adjustment.

Adrees Latif/Reuters

Exposure to traumatic events, such as the mass killings in Newtown, Connecticut, can lead to the development of PTSD, a psychological disorder characterized by lingering problems in adjustment and psychological functioning.

post-traumatic stress disorder (PTSD) A psychological disorder involving a maladaptive reaction to traumatic stress.

Type A behavior pattern (TABP) A behavior pattern characterized by impatience, time urgency, competitiveness, and hostility.

CONCEPT 10.8
Chronic hostility is the component of the Type A behavior pattern most strongly linked to increased risk of heart disease.

On the road to a heart attack? A strong link exists between hostility and coronary heart disease.

People with the Type A behavior pattern (TABP) are impatient, competitive, and aggressive. They are constantly in a rush and have a strong sense of time urgency. They feel pressured to get the maximum amount done in the shortest possible amount of time. They tend to do everything fast; they talk fast, walk fast, even eat fast. They quickly lose patience with others, especially those who move or work more slowly than they would like. They may become hostile and prone to anger when others fail to meet their expectations. They are intense even at play. While others are content to bat the ball around on the tennis court, people with the Type A behavior pattern play to win at all costs. By contrast, those with the opposite personality style, sometimes called the Type B behavior pattern, take a slower, more relaxed pace in life. The nearby Try This Out feature can help you determine whether you fit the Type A profile.

It was once thought that people with the Type A profile stood a much greater risk than others of developing coronary heart disease (CHD), the nation's leading killer. However, research evidence linking the Type A profile to CHD has failed to show consistent results. But evidence did point to a stronger link between CHD and a component of the classic Type A profile, the personality trait of hostility (Eichstaedt et al., 2015; Everson-Rose et al., 2014). Hostile people tend to be angry much of the time, and strong negative emotions like anger increase the risk of developing coronary heart disease and other significant

---

Try This Out Are You Type A?

Check the appropriate column to indicate whether or not the item is generally true of you. Then consult the following scoring key to determine whether you fit the Type A profile.

YES	NO	Do you ...
☐	☐	Walk briskly from place to place or from meeting to meeting?
☐	☐	Strongly emphasize important words in your ordinary speech?
☐	☐	Think that life is by nature dog-eat-dog?
☐	☐	Get fidgety when you see someone complete a job slowly?
☐	☐	Urge others to complete what they're trying to express?
☐	☐	Find it exceptionally annoying to get stuck in line?
☐	☐	Envision all the things you have to do even when someone is talking to you?
☐	☐	Eat while you're getting dressed, or jot down notes while you're driving?
☐	☐	Catch up on work during vacations?
☐	☐	Direct the conversation to things that interest you?
☐	☐	Feel as if things are going to pot because you're relaxing for a few minutes?
☐	☐	Get so wrapped up in your work that you fail to notice beautiful scenery passing by?

☐	☐	Get so wrapped up in money, promotions, and awards that you neglect expressing your creativity?
☐	☐	Schedule appointments and meetings back to back?
☐	☐	Arrive early for appointments and meetings?
☐	☐	Make fists or clench your jaw to drive home your views?
☐	☐	Think that you've achieved what you have because of your ability to work fast?
☐	☐	Have the feeling that uncompleted work must be done *now* and fast?
☐	☐	Try to find more efficient ways to get things done?
☐	☐	Struggle always to win games instead of having fun?
☐	☐	Interrupt people who are talking?
☐	☐	Lose patience with people who are late for appointments and meetings?
☐	☐	Get back to work right after lunch?
☐	☐	Find that there's never enough time?
☐	☐	Believe that you're getting too little done, even when other people tell you that you're doing fine?

Scoring Key: "Yes" answers suggest a Type A behavior pattern—and the more items to which you answered "yes," the stronger your TABP. You should have little difficulty determining whether you are strongly or moderately inclined toward this behavior pattern—that is, if you are honest with yourself.

health problems (Kitayama et al., 2015). On the other hand, evidence links positive emotions to better health outcomes, such as lower blood pressure, as well as living a longer life (Ostir et al., 2006; Xu & Roberts, 2010). The lesson here is that emotional health is linked to living a longer and healthier life.

Before moving on, we should note that the question of whether the "hurry-up" features of the Type A behavior pattern contribute to health problems remains open to further study. Nonetheless, this behavior pattern is a modifiable source of stress. If you are seeking to reduce the level of stress in your life, a good place to start might be modifying Type A behavior. This chapter's Applying Psychology in Daily Life contains suggestions for reducing Type A behavior that you might find helpful.

Acculturative Stress

For immigrants, the demands of adjusting to a new culture can be a significant source of stress (Driscoll & Torres, 2013). Establishing a new life in one's adopted country can be a difficult adjustment, especially when there are differences in language and culture and few available job or training opportunities. One significant source of stress is pressure to become *acculturated*—to adapt to the values, linguistic preferences, and customs of the host or dominant culture. How does **acculturative stress**, which results from this burden, affect psychological health and adjustment?

Adjusting to a new society depends on a number of factors. For example, stress associated with economic hardship is a major contributor to adjustment problems in immigrant groups, as it is for members of the host culture. Less well acculturated immigrants often have difficulty gaining an economic foothold in the host country, which can lead to anxiety and depression. Exposure to racism and discrimination are other sources of stress that can take a toll on the physical and emotional health of immigrant and ethnic minority groups (Schmitt et al., 2014; Stevens-Watkins et al., 2014; Sutin, Stephan, & Terracciano, 2016; Torres & Vallejo, 2015).

Acculturation itself can be a double-edged sword. It can erode traditional family networks and values, leaving people more vulnerable to psychological problems in the face of stress and fostering undesirable behaviors such as substance abuse (Salas-Wright, Kagotho, & Vaughn, 2014; Zhang et al., 2013). Erosion of traditional cultural values may also help explain the greater likelihood of engaging in premarital intercourse among more acculturated Hispanic teens (Adam et al., 2005).

Withdrawal from the larger culture may prevent an individual from making the necessary adjustments to function effectively in a multicultural society. For many groups, making a successful transition to life in the United States is a process of balancing participation in the mainstream culture with maintaining their ethnic identity or cultural heritage. Investigators find that adjusting to the demands of the larger culture while maintaining one's own ethnic identity is associated with better psychological adjustment (LaFromboise, Albright, & Harris, 2010; Serrano-Villar & Calzada, 2016; Tran & Lee, 2010).

Before reading further, you may wish to review the sources of stress outlined in Concept Chart 10.1.

Ronnie Kaufman/Bridge/Corbis

Should immigrants adapt to the customs of the host culture or retain their identification with their traditional culture? Or should they do both?

CONCEPT 10.9

Acculturative stress is a source of stress faced by immigrants struggling to meet the demands of adjusting to a new culture.

CONCEPT LINK

As we saw in Chapter 4, acculturation plays an important role in explaining drug use and abuse. See Module 4.4.

a katz/Shutterstock.com

A strong sense of ethnic identity may help buffer stress, including acculturative stress.

acculturative stress Demands faced by immigrants in adjusting to a host culture.

Concept Chart 10.1 Sources of Stress

Source	Description	Key Points
Hassles	Common annoyances of everyday life	An accumulation may contribute to chronic stress, which can lead to impaired psychological and physical well-being.
Life events	Positive or negative changes in life circumstances that place demands on us to adapt	A high level of life change is associated with poorer psychological and physical health outcomes.
Frustration	A state of negative arousal resulting from the thwarting of efforts to attain personal goals	We feel frustrated when obstacles placed in our path prevent us from achieving our goals or when we set unattainable goals for ourselves.
Conflict	The state of tension that occurs when we feel torn between two opposing goals	Conflicts are most stressful when opposing goals are equally strong and no clear resolution is apparent.
Traumatic stressors	Sudden, life-threatening events	Traumatic events can tax our coping abilities to the limit. Trauma survivors may develop psychological disorders, such as PTSD.
Type A behavior pattern (TABP)	A behavior pattern characterized by impatience, competitiveness, aggressiveness, and time urgency	Hostility, a component of the TABP, is strongly linked to a higher risk of coronary heart disease.
Acculturative stress	Pressures imposed on immigrant people to adapt to the cultural and linguistic demands of the host country	Adjustment of immigrant groups depends on many factors, including economic opportunity, language proficiency, ethnic identification, and a supportive social network.

The Brain Loves a Puzzle

As you read ahead, use the information in the text to solve the following puzzle:

Why does stress make you sweat?

Inpix Creative/IndiaPicture/Alamy Stock Photo

general adaptation syndrome (GAS)
Selye's term for the general pattern of bodily responses to various forms of stress.

alarm stage The first stage of the general adaptation syndrome, involving mobilization of the body's resources to cope with an immediate stressor.

fight-or-flight response The body's built-in alarm system that allows it to quickly mobilize its resources to either fight or flee when faced with a threatening stressor.

The Body's Response to Stress

Much of what we know about the body's response to stress is the result of pioneering research by Hans Selye (1907–1982), the famed stress researcher known affectionately as "Dr. Stress."

The General Adaptation Syndrome

Selye recognized that specific stressors, such as an invading virus, do elicit specific reactions in the body. But layered over these specific responses is a more general response to stress, which he called the **general adaptation syndrome (GAS)** (also called the *stress response*). The body responds in a similar manner to various stressors—cold, noise, infectious agents, pressures on the job, or mental stress in the form of worry or anxiety. Investigating this syndrome led him to believe that the way the body responds to persistent stress is much like an alarm clock that does not shut off until its energy becomes depleted. The general adaptation syndrome consists of three stages, each of which we will consider.

Alarm Stage. The **alarm stage** is the body's first stage of response to a stressor, during which it prepares its defenses for action. Suppose a car ahead of you on the road suddenly veers out of control. This is an immediate stressful event. Your heart starts pounding faster, speeding the flow of blood to your extremities and providing your muscles with the oxygen and fuel they need to take swift action, such as performing an emergency maneuver to avoid a collision. The body's response during the alarm stage is called the **fight-or-flight response** because it is characterized by biological changes that prepare the body to deal with a threat either by fighting it off or fleeing from it.

The alarm stage is accompanied by strong physiological and psychological arousal. Our hearts pound, our breathing quickens, we are flooded with strong emotions such as terror, fright, anxiety, rage, or anger, and we sweat. Sweating in response to a threatening stressor is a feature of the body's fight-or-flight response. We also sweat when overheated, which helps the body cool down. Sweating in response to a threatening stressor is often dubbed "cold sweat."

Different stressful events may trigger the alarm stage of the GAS. The threat may be physical, as in an attack by an assailant, or psychological, as in an event that induces fear of failure (for example, a professor handing out an examination). In some people, the alarm is triggered whenever they meet a new person at a social gathering; they find themselves sweating heavily and feeling anxious, and they may become tongue-tied. In others, the body alarm system is activated whenever they visit the dentist. Whether the perceived threat is physical or psychological, the body's response is the same.

The alarm stage is like a "call to arms" that is prewired into the nervous system. The body's response to stress is a legacy inherited from our earliest ancestors, who faced many potential threats in their daily lives. A glimpse of a suspicious-looking object or a rustling sound in the bush might have cued them to the presence of a lurking predator, triggering the fight-or-flight response that helped prepare them to defend against a threat. But the fight-or-flight response didn't last long. If ancestral humans survived an immediate threat, their bodies returned to the normal state. If they failed, they simply perished. Even today, the fight-or-flight response can be a lifesaver in the face of a threatening situation.

Resistance Stage. Death may occur within the first few hours or days of exposure to a stressor that is so damaging (such as extreme cold) that its persistence is incompatible with life. But if survival is possible and the stressor continues, the body attempts to adapt to it as best it can. Selye called this part of the GAS the **resistance stage** (also called *adaptation stage*). During this stage, the body attempts to return to a normal biological state by restoring spent energy and repairing damage. Arousal remains high, though not as high as during the alarm reaction. This prolonged bodily arousal may be accompanied by such emotional reactions as anger, fatigue, and irritability.

Exhaustion Stage. If the stressor persists, the body may enter the final stage of the GAS—the **exhaustion stage**. Heart rate and respiration now *decrease* to conserve bodily resources. Yet with continued exposure to stress, the body's resources may become seriously depleted and the individual may develop what Selye called "diseases of adaptation"—stress-related disorders such as kidney disease, heart disease, allergic conditions, digestive disorders, and depression. Some people are hardier than others, but relentless, intense stress can eventually exhaust anyone. ■ Figure 10.4 shows the changes that occur in the body's level of resistance across the three stages of the GAS.

The body's stress response may have helped our ancient ancestors survive many of the physical threats they faced. Yet the alarm reaction in response to a threatening stressor was designed not to last very long. Our ancestors either escaped a predator or fought it off; within seconds, minutes perhaps, the threat was over and their bodies returned to their normal, prearoused state. The types of stress we face in contemporary life are more persistent. Our ancestors didn't need to juggle school and jobs, fight daily traffic jams, or face the daily grind of working a double shift to make ends meet. The reality is that for many of us the stressful demands of ordinary life repeatedly activate our alarm reactions day after day, year after year, eventually wearing down our bodies to a point we become more susceptible to stress-related disorders.

Psychologists have found behavioral differences in how men and women respond to stress. Women tend to engage in more nurturing behaviors during times of stress than do men, such as by comforting and soothing infants and children, and befriending others who might help protect them and their children from threats. We can describe women's stress-related behavior in terms of a "tend and befriend"

© Cengage Learning

Hans Selye

CONCEPT 10.10
The general adaptation syndrome (GAS) is a three-stage process by which the body responds to different types of stressors.

CONCEPT 10.11
The three stages in the general adaptation syndrome are the alarm stage, the resistance stage, and the exhaustion stage.

CONCEPT 10.12
During the alarm stage of the GAS, the body mobilizes its resources in the face of stress, preparing to fend off a threat by either fighting or fleeing.

CONCEPT 10.13
During the resistance stage of the GAS, the body conserves its resources to adapt to the effects of enduring stress.

CONCEPT 10.14
During the exhaustion stage of the GAS, continuing stress can lead to severe depletion of bodily resources and development of stress-related diseases.

resistance stage The second stage of the general adaptation syndrome, characterized by the body's attempt to adjust or adapt to persistent stress.

exhaustion stage The third stage of the general adaptation syndrome, characterized by depletion of bodily resources and a lowered resistance to stress-related disorders or conditions.

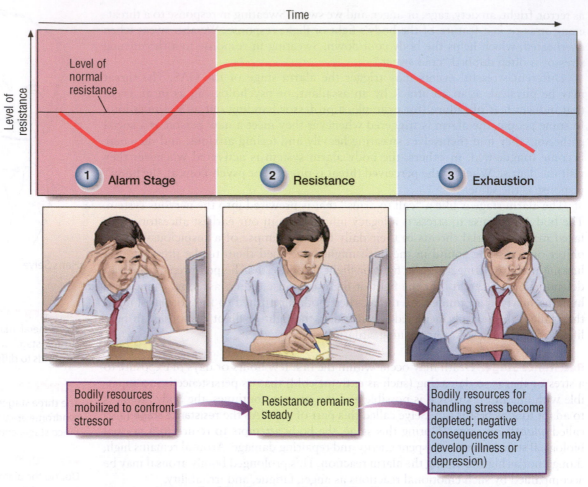

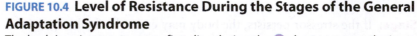

FIGURE 10.4 Level of Resistance During the Stages of the General Adaptation Syndrome

The body's resistance to stress first dips during the ① alarm stage, as the impact of the stressor takes a toll, but then increases as the body mobilizes its resources. Resistance remains steady through the ② resistance stage as the body attempts to cope with the stressor. But if the stressor persists, ③ exhaustion eventually sets in as bodily reserves needed to resist stress become dangerously depleted.

pattern (Taylor, 2007; Taylor et al., 2000). By contrast, men are more likely to react to stressful experiences by engaging in aggressive or hostile behavior in which the male hormone testosterone plays a pivotal role. Women's attachment and caregiving behaviors may be influenced by female reproductive and maternal hormones (Taylor et al., 2000).

Stress and the Endocrine System

The endocrine system is a system of ductless glands throughout the body that release secretions, called *hormones,* directly into the bloodstream (see Chapter 2). The hypothalamus, a small endocrine gland located in the midbrain, coordinates the endocrine system's response to stress. Like a series of falling dominoes, the chain reaction it sets off leads other glands to release their hormones.

Let's look closer at the falling dominoes. The body's stress regulatory process involves coordinated action within a group of endocrine organs that comprise the **hypothalamus pituitary adrenal (HPA) axis** (Hostinar et al., 2014). This gets a little complicated, but let's see how it works: When we are stressed, the hypothalamus

hypothalamus pituitary adrenal (HPA) axis The integrated system of endocrine glands involved in the body's response to stress.

FIGHT OR FLIGHT?
FIGHT OR FLIGHT?
FIGHT OR FLIGHT?
FIGHT OR FLIGHT?

KLANG!

5-25 www.gocomics.com

MoRE

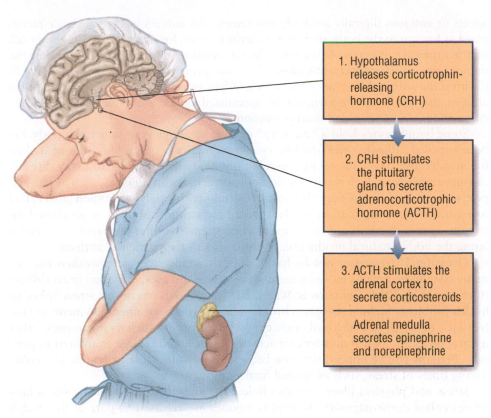

1. Hypothalamus releases corticotrophin-releasing hormone (CRH)

2. CRH stimulates the pituitary gland to secrete adrenocorticotrophic hormone (ACTH)

3. ACTH stimulates the adrenal cortex to secrete corticosteroids

Adrenal medulla secretes epinephrine and norepinephrine

Ghislain & Marie David De Lossy/The Image Bank/Getty Images

Fight or flight? Or friend or befriend? Women tend to adopt a "tend and be-friend" approach to dealing with stress, engaging in nurturing behaviors that may reflect the role of female reproductive hormones.

CONCEPT 10.15

The endocrine system plays a key role in the body's response to stress.

FIGURE 10.5 The Body's Response to Stress
Under stress, the body responds by releasing stress hormones (epinephrine and norepinephrine) from the adrenal medulla and corticosteroids from the adrenal cortex. These substances help the body prepare to cope with an immediate stressor. Stress hormones increase heart rate, respiration, and blood pressure, whereas secretion of corticosteroids leads to the release of stored reserves of energy.

secretes **corticotrophin-releasing hormone (CRH)**, which stimulates the pituitary gland to secrete a hormone of its own, **adrenocorticotrophic hormone (ACTH)**. ACTH travels through the bloodstream to the **adrenal glands**, the pair of small endocrine glands located just above the kidneys. ACTH stimulates the **adrenal cortex**, the outer layer of the adrenal glands, to release stress hormones called **corticosteroids** (or *cortical steroids*). These hormones help the body resist stress by making stored nutrients more available to meet the demands for energy that may be required to cope with stressful events.

The sympathetic nervous system gets involved too, by triggering the **adrenal medulla**, the inner layer of each adrenal gland, to secrete the stress hormones *epinephrine* and *norepinephrine*. These hormones make the heart pump faster, allowing more oxygen and nutrient-rich blood to reach the muscles where it is needed to allow the organism to either flee from a threatening stressor or fight it. The "racing heart" we experience during times of stress is the result of this surge of stress hormones. The body's response to stress is depicted in ■ Figure 10.5.

Stress and the Immune System

The *immune system* is the body's primary system of defense against infectious diseases and worn-out or diseased cells. The immune system fights disease in several ways. It dispatches billions of specialized white blood cells called **lymphocytes**. Lymphocytes constantly circulate throughout the body and remain on alert to the presence of foreign

corticotrophin-releasing hormone (CRH) A hormone released by the hypothalamus that induces the pituitary gland to release adrenocorticotrophic hormone.

adrenocorticotrophic hormone (ACTH) A pituitary hormone that activates the adrenal cortex to release corticosteroids (cortical steroids).

adrenal glands A pair of endocrine glands located just above the kidneys that produce various stress-related hormones.

adrenal cortex The outer layer of the adrenal glands that secretes corticosteroids (cortical steroids).

corticosteroids Adrenal hormones that increase the body's resistance to stress by increasing the availability of stored nutrients to meet the increased energy demands of coping with stressful events. Also called *cortical steroids*.

adrenal medulla The inner part of the adrenal glands that secretes the stress hormones epinephrine (adrenaline) and norepinephrine (noradrenaline).

lymphocytes White blood cells that protect the body against disease-causing organisms.

agents or **antigens** (literally *anti*body *gen*erators). An antigen is any substance recognized as foreign to the body, such as a bacterium, virus, foreign protein, or a body cell that has turned cancerous. As the term's literal meaning suggests, antigens activate the immune system to produce **antibodies**, which are specialized protein molecules that fit the invading antigen like a key fitting a lock. When antibodies lock into position on an antigen, they mark it for destruction by specialized "killer" lymphocytes that act like commandos on a search-and-destroy mission.

Some lymphocytes hold a "memory" of specific antigens to which the body has been exposed, allowing the immune system to render a quick blow the next time the invader appears. Thus we may develop immunity or resistance to many disease-causing antigens—which is why we do not contract certain illnesses, such as chicken pox, more than once. We may also acquire immunity through **vaccination** (also called *immunization*). A vaccination involves the administration of dead or weakened infectious agents that will not cause an infection themselves but are capable of stimulating the body's natural production of antibodies to the particular antigen.

Occasional stress may not be harmful, but chronic stress can weaken the immune system, making us more vulnerable to various diseases, including heart disease (Carlsson et al, 2014; Gianaros & Wager, 2015). Sources of chronic stress linked to health problems include divorce; chronic illness; prolonged unemployment; persistent lack of sleep; loss of loved ones; exposure to trauma such as hurricanes, other natural or technological disasters, or acts of violence; and college examination periods. Perhaps you've noticed that you become more vulnerable to "catching a cold" during times of stress, such as around final exams.

Stress and physical illness are also linked through the actions of the stress hormones called *corticosteroids*. Adrenal hormones are released as part of the body's reaction to stress. Although they help the body cope with stress, continued secretion of these hormones impairs the ability of the immune system to respond to invading pathogens. (Immune functioning also can be impaired by the use of synthetic steroids, such as those taken by some body builders and athletes.)

Stress hormones may even affect our relationship health. Evidence shows that newlyweds whose bodies pumped out more stress hormones during the first year of marriage were more likely to get divorced within ten years than were newlyweds with a lower stress response (Kiecolt-Glaser et al., 2003).

Psychological interventions can help combat stress and may even improve immunological functioning. For example, in people who encounter traumatic or stressful life experiences, the mere act of writing about these experiences helps reduce psychological and physical symptoms (Ironson et al., 2013; Travagin, Margola, & Revenson, 2015; Wisco, Sloan, & Marx, 2013).

Psychological Moderators of Stress

Here we examine psychological moderators that may lessen the impact of stress, including social support, self-efficacy, perceptions of control and predictability, psychological hardiness, and optimism (see ■ Figure 10.6).

Buffers Against Stress

Social support is a major factor in determining how well people cope with stress. It is even linked to how well the body's immune system works in fending off infections. Investigators find that more sociable people are more resistant to developing the common cold after voluntarily receiving injections of a cold virus than are less sociable volunteers (Cohen et al., 2003). Later research showed that people who are socially isolated or who live alone stand a higher risk of early death than more socially engaged people (Holt-Lunstad et al., 2015). The mechanism through which social connections may affect vulnerability to illness and premature death remains to be determined.

CONCEPT 10.16
Evidence suggests that stress can increase vulnerability to physical illness by impairing the functioning of the body's immune system.

CONCEPT 10.17
Social support, self-efficacy, perceptions of control and predictability, psychological hardiness, and optimism are psychological factors that moderate or buffer the effects of stress.

antigens Substances, such as bacteria and viruses, that are recognized by the immune system as foreign to the body and that induce it to produce antibodies to defend against them.

antibodies Protein molecules produced by the immune system that serve to mark antigens for destruction by specialized lymphocytes.

vaccination A method of acquiring immunity by means of injecting a weakened or partial form of an infectious agent that can induce production of antibodies but does not produce a full-blown infection.

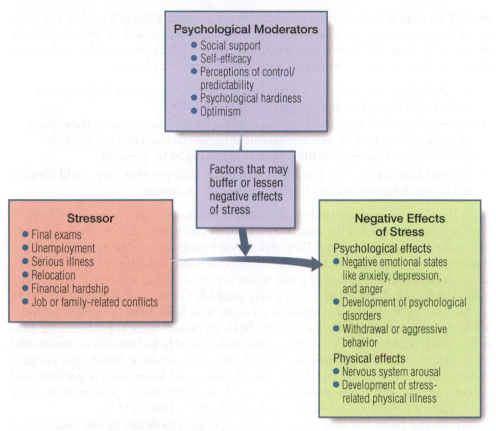

Psychological Moderators
- Social support
- Self-efficacy
- Perceptions of control/predictability
- Psychological hardiness
- Optimism

Factors that may buffer or lessen negative effects of stress

Stressor
- Final exams
- Unemployment
- Serious illness
- Relocation
- Financial hardship
- Job or family-related conflicts

Negative Effects of Stress
Psychological effects
- Negative emotional states like anxiety, depression, and anger
- Development of psychological disorders
- Withdrawal or aggressive behavior

Physical effects
- Nervous system arousal
- Development of stress-related physical illness

FIGURE 10.6 Psychological Moderators of Stress
Social support, self-efficacy, perceptions of control and predictability, psychological hardiness, and optimism are psychological moderators that help us better withstand the effects of stress.

Self-efficacy is the confidence we have in our ability to succeed in tasks we set out to accomplish. Self-efficacy acts as a buffer to stress, helping us withstand stressful demands we face in life (Schönfeld et al., 2016). People with high levels of self-efficacy tend to view stressful situations as challenges to be met than obstacles to overcome. Self-confidence in their abilities leads them to tackle stressors head-on and to persevere in the face or challenges or obstacles set in their path.

The impact of particular stressors varies with how predictable and controllable they seem to us (Koolhaas, de Boer, & Buwalda, 2006). Stressful events that seem more predictable and controllable, such as assignments or exams in school, tend to have less impact on us than other events, such as hurricanes or fluctuations in the stock market, which seem beyond our ability to either predict or control.

People also vary in whether they believe they can control what happens to them in life. Those with an *internal locus of control* believe that rewards or reinforcements in life are a direct consequence of their own actions (see Chapter 11). Those with an *external locus of control* believe their fate to be determined by external factors, such as fate or blind luck, rather than by their own efforts. "Internals" may be better able to marshal their efforts to cope with stressful events they experience because of their belief that they can control them. "Externals," on the other hand, may feel helpless and overwhelmed in the face of stressful events.

An internal locus of control is also a defining characteristic of **psychological hardiness**, a cluster of personality traits associated with an increased resilience to

psychological hardiness A cluster of traits (commitment, openness to challenge, internal locus of control) that may buffer the effects of stress.

Monkey Business Images/Shutterstock.com

stress. This term was introduced by psychologist Suzanne Kobasa based on her studies of business executives who maintained good physical health despite high levels of stress (Kobasa, 1979; Kobasa, Maddi, & Kahn, 1982). She and her colleagues identified three key traits associated with psychological hardiness:

- *Commitment.* The hardy executives had a strong commitment to their work and a belief that what they were doing was important.
- *Openness to challenge.* The hardy executives viewed the stressors they faced as challenges to be met, not as overwhelming obstacles. They believed that change is a normal part of life and not something to be dreaded.
- *Internal locus of control.* The hardy executives believed that they could control the future direction of their lives, for better or for worse.

In short, people with psychological hardiness accept stress as a normal challenge of life. They feel in control of the stress they encounter and believe that the challenges they face make life more interesting. They seek to solve problems, not to avoid them. They show "stick-to-itiveness." Psychological hardiness in linked to a number of positive outcomes, including ability to handle stress, higher grades in college, and better physical and mental health (Ouellette & DiPlacido, 2001; Sheard & Golby, 2007; Taylor et al., 2013).

Another buffer to stress is optimism. People who hold more optimistic attitudes are better able to handle stress and more likely to tackle stressful problems or difficulties directly rather than avoid them. Researchers find links between optimism and many positive health outcomes, including better cardiovascular health and immune system functioning, better psychological adjustment of heart disease patients and cancer patients, and lower death rates overall as compared to pessimists (Carver, 2014; Carver & Scheier, 2014; Hernandez et al., 2015; Jaffe, 2013).

We should point out that evidence tying optimism to better health outcomes is correlational, so we need to be careful about drawing causal inferences. Optimists may live longer because they tend to take better care of their health, not because of optimism per se (Brody, 2012). Still, doesn't it make sense to take an optimistic approach toward the stressors you face, seeing the glass as half full rather than half empty?

Let's turn the discussion around to you. What about your own outlook on life? Do you tend to be an optimist or a pessimist? The nearby Try This Out feature allows you to evaluate your outlook on life.

Try This Out   Are You an Optimist or a Pessimist?

Are you someone who looks on the bright side of things? Or do you expect bad things to happen? The following questionnaire may give you insight into whether you are an optimist or a pessimist.

Directions: Indicate whether or not each of the items represents your feelings by writing a number in the blank space according to the following code. Then turn to the scoring key at the end of the chapter.

    5 = strongly agree
    4 = agree
    3 = neutral
    2 = disagree
    1 = strongly disagree

1. _____ I believe you're either born lucky or, like me, born unlucky.

2. _____ My attitude is that if something can go wrong, it probably will.

3. _____ I think of myself more as an optimist than a pessimist.

4. _____ I generally expect things will work out in the end.

5. _____ I have these doubts about whether I will eventually succeed.

6. _____ I am hopeful about what the future holds for me.

7. _____ I tend to believe that "every cloud has a silver lining."

8. _____ I think of myself as a realist who thinks the proverbial class is half empty rather than half filled.

9. _____ I think the future will be rosy.

10. _____ Things don't generally work out the way I planned.

Source: From Jeffrey S. Nevid, Spencer A. Rathus, and Beverly Greene, *Abnormal Psychology in a Changing World*, 9th ed. Copyright © 2014 by Pearson Education. Reproduced by permission of Pearson Education, Inc.

APPLYING PSYCHOLOGY in Daily Life

Taking the Distress Out of Stress

We may not be able to eliminate all stress from our lives—indeed, a certain amount of stress might be good for us. But we can learn to cope more effectively so that stress doesn't lead to distress. Here, we summarize some of the basic skills needed to manage stress more effectively (adapted from Nevid & Rathus, 2013).

Maintain Stress at a Tolerable Level

Examine your daily life. Are you constantly running from place to place just to keep pace with all the demands on your time? Is it difficult to find time just to relax? Following are some suggestions for keeping stress within a manageable level:

- *Reduce daily hassles.* What can you do to reduce the stressful burdens of daily hassles? Might you rearrange your school or work schedule to avoid morning traffic jams? How about joining a car pool? You might still be stuck in traffic, but you can use that time to catch up on your reading rather than fighting traffic.

- *Know your limits.* Don't bite off more than you can chew. Avoid taking on more tasks than you can reasonably accomplish. Whenever possible, delegate responsibilities to others.

- *Follow a reasonable schedule.* Learn to schedule tasks so they don't pile up. In this way, you break down stressful tasks into more manageable doses. If stressful demands become too taxing, try to extend some deadlines to give yourself added time to finish your work.

- *Take frequent breaks.* When working on an assignment, take frequent breaks to refresh your mind and body.

- *Develop more effective time-management skills.* Use a monthly calendar to organize your activities and tasks. Schedule as many of your activities as you can in advance to ensure that you have enough time to accomplish your goals. But don't overschedule yourself. Allow yourself some free, unstructured time.

- *Learn to prioritize.* Use a monthly calendar to list the tasks you must accomplish each day. Prioritize your daily goals. Assign the number 1 to tasks you must accomplish, the number 2 to those you'd like to accomplish but are less essential, and the number 3 to tasks you'd like to accomplish if time permits. Then arrange your daily schedule to progress through your list.

Learn Relaxation Skills

Tone down your body's response to stress by learning to relax. Some people find that listening to music helps them unwind at the end of the day. Some like to curl up with a book (not a textbook—not even this one). Others use more formal relaxation techniques, such as biofeedback training (see Chapter 3), meditation (see Chapter 4), and deep breathing exercises. To practice deep breathing, breathe only through your nose. Take about the same amount of time breathing in as breathing out, and pace yourself by silently repeating a resonant-sounding word like "relax" on each out breath. Elongating the "x" sound can help you lengthen each breath to ensure that you breathe deeply and evenly. Many colleges offer seminars or workshops in stress management techniques where students can learn to develop relaxation skills. Why not check them out?

CONCEPT 10.18
Though stress may be an unavoidable part of life, how we cope with stress lies within our control.

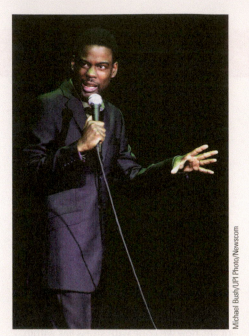

Humor can help relieve stresses of every-day life. Treating yourself to a comedy to-night may help relieve stressful burdens at least temporarily.

Work Out Daily Stress

Regular physical exercise increases resilience to stress and lessens the emotional consequences of stress, such as anxiety, depression, and burnout (Cecchini-Estrada et al., 2015; Kleijweg et al., 2013; Lindwall et al., 2014; Schoenfeld et al., 2013). Other evidence shows that sedentary adolescents tend to have higher levels of anxiety and depression than their more active counterparts (Monshouwer et al., 2013). Clinicians are now using exercise programs as a standard part of a treatment plan for depression (Kerling et al., 2015; Schuch et al., 2016). Exercise may also help prevent depression (Mammen & Faulkner, 2013). Clearly, the lesson here is that regular exercise or physical activity is good for body and mind.

Gather Information

People facing a serious illness may cope more effectively if they obtain information about their underlying condition rather than keeping themselves in the dark.

Expand Your Social Network

Social support helps people cope better during times of stress. You can expand your social network by forming relationships with others through participation in clubs and organizations sponsored at your college. The office of student life or counseling services at your college should be able to advise you about the availability of these resources.

Take in a Comedy Tonight

Humor can be an antidote to stress. A dose of humor not only makes us laugh, but it also provides at least temporary relief from stressful concerns of daily life.

Prevent Burnout

Burnout is a state of physical and emotional exhaustion and reduced personal effectiveness resulting from excessive work and life stress (Armon et al., 2014; Leiter et al., 2014). Job demands and caregiving responsibilities top the list of these stressors. Burnout is strongly associated with depression and is also linked to physical health problems such as cardiovascular disease (Bianchi, Schonfeld, & Laurent, 2015; Michel, 2016; Toker & Biron, 2012).

Taking steps to protect yourself from burnout can reap important benefits for your mental and physical health. To prevent burnout, experts recommend setting reasonable goals and limits, balancing work and personal life, and taking an active problem-focused approach to coping with stress (Rupert, Miller, & Dorociak, 2015; Shin et al., 2014). Set personal goals that are attainable and avoid pushing yourself beyond your limits. Learn to say "no" when people make excessive demands on you. Start delegating responsibilities, and learn to cut back on low-priority tasks when commitments begin piling up.

Replace Stress-Inducing Thoughts with Stress-Busting Thoughts

What you say to yourself under your breath about stressful events influences your adjustment to them. Do you react to disappointing events by blowing them out of proportion—treating them as utter disasters rather than as mere setbacks? Do you see events only in all-or-nothing, black-and-white terms—as either total successes or total failures? Do you place unrealistic expectations on yourself and then hold yourself accountable for failing to measure up? If you have thought patterns like these, you may benefit from replacing them with rational alternatives. Examples include: "This is a problem, not a catastrophe. I am a good problem solver. I can find a solution to this problem."

Taking a Problem-Solving Approach to Coping with Stress

Do you face stress head-on by seeking solutions to problems you face, or do you bury your head in a pillow and hope it all just goes away on its own? A study of high school students showed that adopting a problem-focused approach to coping with stress linked to better grades, life satisfaction, and more positive feelings about school (MacCann et al., 2012).

Don't Keep Upsetting Feelings Bottled Up

Keeping disturbing thoughts and feelings under wraps may place stressful demands on your autonomic nervous system, which in turn may weaken your immune system and make you more vulnerable to physical illness. Expressing your feelings about stressful or traumatic events may have positive effects on your emotional and physical health. In particular, consider writing down your feelings in a journal or sharing them with a trusted person or a helping professional.

Are you at risk of burnout? What steps can you take to relieve excessive stress due to work or other commitments?

Control Type A Behavior

People with the Type A behavior pattern place additional stressful demands on themselves by attempting to accomplish as much as possible in as little time as possible. Though it may not be feasible (or even desirable) to turn "hares" into "tortoises," we can all learn to modify Type A behavior, such as by reducing our sense of time urgency. Here are some behavioral changes that may be of help, even for people who are not bona fide Type A's:

- *Take things slower.* Slow down your walking pace. Enjoy looking at your surroundings rather than rushing past them.
- *Read books for enjoyment.* Spend time reading enjoyable books—perhaps that latest techno-thriller or a romance novel, but not a book designed to help you climb the corporate ladder.
- *Free yourself from digital overload.* When relaxing or vacationing, turn off your cell phone, tablet, or laptop and take a time-out from texting and surfing the Web.
- *Avoid rushing through your meals.* Don't wolf down your food. Take time to talk to your family members or dining companions.
- *Schedule breaks for yourself.* Go to the movies, visit art galleries and museums, or attend the theater or concerts. Give yourself a break from the stressful demands of daily life. Take up a hobby or pursue an interest that can help you unwind.
- *Set realistic daily goals.* Don't overschedule your activities or impose unrealistic demands on yourself. Lighten up.

What can you do to reduce Type A behavior?

Hostility, a component of the Type A behavior profile, is associated with quickness to anger. Suggestions for controlling anger are discussed in Chapter 8.

In sum, stress is an inescapable part of life. But handling stress more effectively can help you keep it at a manageable level and tone down your body's alarm reaction. Stress may be a fact of life, but it is a fact you can learn to live with.

MODULE REVIEW   10.1   Stress: What It Is and What It Does to the Body

Recite It

1. **Define** stress in psychological terms.

   The term (a) _____ refers to pressures and demands to adjust or adapt.

2. **Identify** and **describe** the major sources of stress.

   The major sources of stress include daily (b) _____ (minor annoyances of daily life), life (c) _____ (changes in life circumstances), frustration (negative emotional response when goal-seeking behavior is blocked), conflict (state of opposing motives), (d) _____ _____ behavior pattern (competitive demanding, hurry-up behavior pattern), traumatic events (natural or human-caused disasters), and pressures of acculturation faced by immigrant groups.

3. **Define** the general adaptation syndrome and **identify** its three stages.

   Stress activates a general pattern of physiological responses, described by Selye as the general adaptation syndrome, or GAS. GAS consists of the (e) _____ stage, the (f) _____ stage, and the (g) _____ stage.

4. **Evaluate** the effects of stress on the body's immune system.

   Persistent or severe stress can impair the functioning of the immune system, leaving us more susceptible to many illnesses, including the (h) _____ cold.

5. **Identify** psychological factors that buffer the effects of stress.

   Psychological buffers against stress include social support, self-(i) _____, perceptions of controllability and predictability, psychological (j) _____, and optimism.

6. **Apply** stress management techniques to daily life.

   Stress management techniques include maintaining stress at a tolerable level, learning (k) _____ skills, taking care of one's body, gathering information, expanding one's social network, using humor, preventing (l) _____, replacing stress-inducing thoughts with stress-busting thoughts, not keeping upsetting feelings bottled up, and controlling Type A behavior.

Recall It

1. (a) Provide a psychological definition of stress. (b) At what point does stress lead to distress?

2. Match the following types of stressors with the appropriate descriptions: (a) hassles; (b) life events; (c) conflict; (d) traumatic stressors.

   i. two or more competing goals where a choice must be made
   ii. common annoyances such as traffic jams and balancing work and social demands
   iii. major changes in life circumstances
   iv. potentially life-threatening events

3. The stage of the GAS characterized by the fight-or-flight response is the _____ stage.

4. List some psychological moderators of stress.

5. Which of the following are characteristics of the Type A behavior pattern?

   a. impatient, competitive, hard-driving behavior
   b. experiencing flashbacks, heightened arousal, and emotional numbness
   c. approach-avoidance conflicts or multiple approach-avoidance conflicts
   d. experiencing chronic stress or frustration

6. The body's general response to different kinds of stressors is called the _____ _____ syndrome.

Think About It

■ What is the role of the nervous system in the general adaptation syndrome? What is the role of the endocrine system?

■ Agree or disagree and support your answer: Stress can be healthy or unhealthy.

Recite It answers placed at the end of chapter.

MODULE **10.2** Psychological Factors in Physical Illness

7 **Identify** psychological factors linked to coronary heart disease.

8 **Identify** psychological factors linked to cancer.

9 **Apply** knowledge of the transmission of sexually transmitted disease to steps we can take to protect ourselves from these diseases.

Here's a shocker: Eventually we all die. But to what extent are our health and longevity a function of our behavioral patterns and lifestyles? What behaviors contribute to living healthier lives? What behaviors put our health at risk?

Our health and our longevity are affected by many lifestyle factors—what we eat, whether we exercise regularly, whether we use alcohol excessively or tobacco products, and whether we take steps to control obesity and high blood pressure (GBD 2013 Risk Factors Collaborators, 2015). The leading causes of death in the United States are not microbial agents like bacteria and viruses. They are unhealthy behaviors such as smoking (which contributes to cancer and heart disease), poor diet and inactivity (which contribute to obesity and heart disease), and excessive use of alcohol (which contributes to cancer and diseases of the liver). All told, unhealthy behaviors account for an estimated 40 percent of premature deaths in the United States (Schroeder, 2007).

Take a look at ■ Figure 10.7, which shows the numbers of deaths in the United States annually. More than one million lives are cut short each year due to unhealthy behaviors. Many of these deaths can be prevented if people adopted healthier behaviors, such as avoiding tobacco, seeking appropriate medical care to manage high blood pressure (hypertension) and cholesterol, exercising regularly, and reducing excess weight. Let's take a closer look at the types of unhealthy behaviors and lifestyles that contribute to the nation's two leading killer diseases: heart disease and cancer.

Coronary Heart Disease

The heart is composed of muscle tissue, which, like other body tissue, requires oxygen and nutrients carried through blood vessels called **arteries**. **Coronary heart disease (CHD)** is a cardiovascular (heart and artery) disorder in which the flow of blood to the heart becomes insufficient to meet its needs. In most cases, the underlying cause is **atherosclerosis**, the narrowing of arteries resulting from a buildup of fatty deposits called **plaque** along artery walls. Atherosclerosis impairs circulation of blood to the heart. It is the major form of **arteriosclerosis**, or "hardening of the arteries," a condition in which artery walls become thicker, harder, and less elastic.

Blood clots are more likely to become lodged in arteries narrowed by atherosclerosis. If a blood clot forms in a coronary artery (an artery that brings oxygen and nutrients to the heart), it may nearly or fully block the flow of blood

arteries Blood vessels that carry oxygen-rich blood from the heart through the circulatory system.

coronary heart disease (CHD) The most common form of heart disease, caused by blockages in coronary arteries, the vessels that supply the heart with blood.

atherosclerosis A form of arteriosclerosis involving the narrowing of artery walls resulting from the buildup of fatty deposits or plaque.

plaque In the circulatory system, fatty deposits that accumulate along artery walls.

arteriosclerosis A condition in which artery walls become thicker and lose elasticity. Commonly called *hardening of the arteries.*

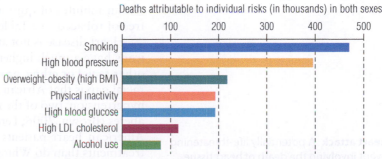

FIGURE 10.7 **Deaths Associated with Individual Risk Factors**

Source: Data drawn from Goodarz et al., 2009.

to a part of the heart, causing a **heart attack** or *myocardial infarction (MI)*. During a heart attack, heart tissue literally dies from lack of oxygenated blood. Whether or not one survives a heart attack depends on the extent of damage to heart tissue and to the electrical system of the body that controls the heart rhythm.

Heart disease is the nation's leading killer of both men and women, accounting for more 600,000 deaths annually in the United States, which translates into more than one out of every five deaths (CDC, 2015a, 2015b). Most of these deaths result from heart attacks. CHD is the leading form of heart disease and takes the lives of more women than all forms of cancer combined, including breast cancer. The good news, as we shall see, is that we can take steps to greatly reduce our risks of developing this killer disease.

Risk Factors for CHD

The risk of developing CHD varies with the number of risk factors a person possesses—factors such as age (CHD increases with age after about age 40), gender (men are at greater risk until about age 65), family history (heredity), hypertension (high blood pressure), smoking, obesity, diabetes, lack of physical activity, and high cholesterol levels (Bauchner, Fontanarosa, & Golub, 2013; Foody, 2013; James et al., 2014).

Some risk factors cannot be controlled: You cannot choose your parents or your gender or stop aging. Other factors, such as hypertension, smoking, obesity, diabetes, and cholesterol level, can be controlled through behavioral changes (diet and exercise) or appropriate medical treatment. Adopting healthier lifestyles (exercising regularly, avoiding smoking and excess alcohol use, maintaining a healthy weight, and following a healthy diet) is associated with lower risks of hypertension and heart disease (Bauchner, Fontanarosa, & Golub, 2014; Eckel et al., 2014; Mitka, 2013). Adoption of healthier lifestyles seems to be paying off, as deaths due to heart disease and stroke in the United States are on the decline (Ma et al., 2015; McGinnis, 2015).

A sedentary lifestyle is associated with double the risk of coronary heart disease (Manson et al., 2004). The good news is that by becoming more active, even seasoned couch potatoes can reduce their risk of cardiovascular disease (Borjesson & Dahlof, 2005; Meyers, 2007a). Smoking doubles the risk of heart attacks and is linked to more than one in five deaths from CHD. Fortunately, quitting smoking reduces the risks of premature death. (Some suggestions for quitting smoking are provided in the Try This Out feature on page 399) Many Americans have heeded the health message and quit smoking or never started in the first place. The percentage of Americans who smoke dropped from 43 percent in 1964 to about 19 percent today (CDC, 2015a; Frieden, 2014). Smokers who quit begin to reap health benefits within minutes of quitting, and the benefits increase the longer the person remains free of tobacco (see Table 10.1).

Heart disease is not an equal opportunity destroyer. Black (non-Hispanic) Americans have a much higher death rate due to coronary heart disease than Whites and other racial or ethnic groups in the United States (CDC, 2015b). One reason for this racial gap is that African Americans are much more likely to suffer from obesity and hypertension, two of the major risk factors for heart disease, as well as stroke and diabetes (Brown, 2006; Ferdinand & Ferdinand, 2009). Another reason is that African American heart patients and heart attack victims typically receive less aggressive treatments than do Whites (Chen et al., 2001; Stolberg, 2001). This dual standard of care may reflect unequal access to quality health care and discrimination by health care providers.

CONCEPT 10.19

Health-related behaviors, such as diet, exercise, and smoking, affect a person's risk of developing many physical disorders, including coronary heart disease.

CONCEPT LINK

As we saw in Chapter 4, smoking is the leading cause of premature death in the United States and worldwide. See Module 4.4.

CONCEPT 10.20

Risk factors for coronary heart disease include some factors you cannot control, such as heredity, and some you can, such as hypertension, physical activity, and tobacco use.

CONCEPT LINK

As we saw in Chapter 9, adopting healthy behaviors can help us lead longer and healthier lives. See Chapter 9's Applying Psychology in Daily Life feature.

heart attack A potentially life-threatening event involving the death of heart tissue due to a lack of blood flow to the heart. Also called *myocardial infarction*.

Try This Out   Steps to Quitting Smoking

The first step toward becoming a nonsmoker is making the decision to quit. Many smokers quit on their own. Others seek help from health professionals or organizations, like the American Lung Association, that offer smoking cessation programs either free of charge or at modest costs. If you decide to quit on your own, you may find the following suggestions helpful:

- *Set a quit date.* Set a date several weeks ahead when you intend to quit smoking completely. Tell your friends and family of your commitment to quit smoking by that date. Publicly announcing your intentions will increase the likelihood that you'll stick to your plan of action.

- *Taper off.* Begin reducing the number of cigarettes you smoke daily in anticipation of your quitting date. A typical schedule to follow is cutting back the number of cigarettes you smoke daily by 25 percent each week for three weeks before quitting completely during the fourth week. Lengthen the interval between cigarettes to keep your smoking rate down to your daily limit.

- *Limit exposure to smoking environments.* Restrict the locations in which you smoke. Limit smoking to one particular room in your house, or outside on your porch, terrace, or deck. Break the habit of smoking while watching TV or conversing on the phone.

- *Increase exposure to nonsmoking environments.* Spend more time in settings where smoking isn't permitted or customary, such as the library. Also, socialize more with nonsmokers and, to the extent possible, avoid socializing with friends who smoke. What other smoke-free settings can you think of?

- *Limit the availability of cigarettes.* Carry only as many cigarettes as you need to meet your daily limit. Never buy more than a pack at a time.

- *Practice competing responses when tempted to smoke.* Preceding and following your quit date, substitute responses that are incompatible with smoking whenever you feel the urge to smoke. Delay reaching for a cigarette. Practice relaxation exercises. Exercise instead of smoking until the urge passes. Take a bath or a walk around the block (without your cigarettes). Use sugar-free mints or gum as substitutes whenever you feel the urge to smoke.

- *Mentally rehearse the benefits of not smoking.* Imagine yourself living a longer, healthier, non-coughing life.

- *Learn to cope, not smoke.* Learn healthier ways of coping with negative feelings, such as anxiety, sadness, and anger, rather than reaching for a cigarette.

Once you have quit smoking completely, remove all smoking-related paraphernalia from your house, including ashtrays and lighters. Remove as many cues as possible that were associated with your smoking habit. Establish a nonsmoking rule in your house, and request that friends and family members respect it. Ask others to be especially patient with you in the days and weeks following your quit date. Ask others not to smoke in your presence (explain that you have recently quit and would appreciate their cooperation). If you should lapse, don't despair. Make a commitment then and there not to have another cigarette. Many people succeed completely after a few near misses.

Table 10.1   Health Benefits of Quitting Smoking

After You Quit Smoking . . .

20 minutes	Heart rate drops
12 hours	Carbon monoxide level in the blood drops to normal
2 days	Ability to smell and taste improves
2 to 3 weeks	Heart attack risk begins to drop and lung function improves; walking becomes easier
1 month	Coughing and shortness of breath decrease
1 year	Risk of heart disease is cut in half
5 years	Risk of stroke is reduced to that of a nonsmoker
10 years	Risk of dying from lung cancer is about half that of a continuing smoker
15 years	Risk of coronary heart disease returns to the level of people who have never smoked

Source: NYC Department of Health and Mental Hygiene, 2010.

© Sagasan/Shutterstock.com

CONCEPT 10.21

Negative emotions, such as anger, anxiety, and depression, may have damaging effects on the cardiovascular system.

Emotions and Your Heart

As noted earlier, hostility is the component of the Type A behavior profile most strongly linked to an increased risk of coronary heart disease. Hostile people are angry much of the time, and chronic anger increases the risk of hypertension and CHD (Chida & Steptoe, 2009; Denollet & Pedersen, 2009).

Persistent emotional arousal may damage the cardiovascular system due to the effects of the stress hormones epinephrine (adrenaline) and norepinephrine (noradrenaline). These hormones are released during emotional states of anger and anxiety. They accelerate heart rate, raise blood pressure, and increase the strength of heart contractions, resulting in a greater burden on the heart and circulatory system.

The added burden of persistent stress on the cardiovascular system may eventually lead to heart-related problems, especially in vulnerable people. Stress hormones (primarily epinephrine) also increase the stickiness of blood-clotting factors, which in turn may heighten the risk of potentially dangerous blood clots that can lead to heart attacks or strokes. Stress hormones, especially adrenaline, also trigger the body's sweat response, which explains why people often sweat when they face a stressful social or job situation (Reddy, 2013).

Persistent emotional distress in the form of depression, anxiety, and chronic anger or hostility also take a toll on the cardiovascular system, raising the risk of heart disease and stroke (Everson-Rose et al., 2014; Lambiase et al., 2014; Lichtman et al., 2014). Psychologists are developing ways of helping chronically angry or anxious people learn to control their emotional responses to reduce their risks of CHD and other serious health problems.

Cancer

CONCEPT 10.22

If everyone practiced cancer-preventative behaviors, hundreds of thousands of lives would be saved each year.

The word *cancer* may strike more fear in people's hearts than any other word in the English language. The fear is understandable. More than one out of every five deaths in the United States is caused by cancer. About 1.5 million Americans receive the dreaded diagnosis of cancer each year, and more than a half million die from the disease (Centers for Disease Control, 2015b, 2015f; National Cancer Institute, 2010). The good news is that the cancer death rate has been declining steadily, in large part because of improved screening and treatment (Hampton, 2015).

Cancer is a disease in which body cells exhibit uncontrolled growth. The body normally manufactures new cells only when they are needed. The genes in our cells direct them to replicate in orderly ways. But in cancer, cells lose the ability to regulate their growth. They multiply even when they are not needed, leading to the formation of masses of excess body tissue called **malignant tumors**. Malignant or cancerous tumors may spread to other parts of the body, where they invade healthy tissue. Cancerous tumors damage vital body organs and systems, leading to death in many cases. Cancers can form in any body tissue or organ. There are many causes of cancer, including genetics, exposure to cancer-causing chemicals, even exposure to some viruses, and use of harmful substances, especially tobacco.

Risk Factors for Cancer

malignant tumors Uncontrolled growths of body cells that invade surrounding tissue and spread to other parts of the body.

Some risk factors for cancer, like family history and age (older people are at greater risk), are unavoidable. The good news is that other factors can be controlled through lifestyle changes. We could prevent more than half of all cancers if people adopted healthier behaviors, such as by avoiding smoking, following a healthy, low-fat diet, controlling excess body weight, limiting alcohol use, exercising regularly, and limiting sun exposure (that is, ultraviolet light causes skin cancer) (for example, see Colditz, Wolin, & Gehlert, 2012; Snowden, 2009). If everyone practiced such cancer-preventive behaviors, hundreds of thousands of lives would be saved each year (see Table 10.2).

Smoking. You probably know that smoking causes lung cancer, which is the leading cancer killer of men and women. Nearly 90 percent of lung cancer deaths are directly attributable to smoking. But smoking is also linked to many other cancers, including colorectal (colon or rectal) cancer. Overall, cigarette smoking accounts for about one-third of all cancer deaths in the United States. Other means of using tobacco, such as pipe and cigar smoking and smokeless tobacco, like dip or chew, also can cause cancer.

Psychological support groups can help cancer patients cope with the disease.

Diet and Alcohol Consumption. High levels of consumption of saturated fat, the type of fat found in meat and dairy products, is linked to two leading cancer killers: prostate cancer in men and colorectal cancer. Obesity, which itself is linked to following a high-fat diet, is also associated with increased risk of some cancers (Gorman, 2012; Taubes, 2012). Smoking and diet are not the only behavioral factors associated with higher risks of cancer. Heavy alcohol consumption raises the risk of several cancers, including those of the mouth, pharynx, larynx, and esophagus (Jayasekara et al., 2015).

Sun Exposure. Prolonged sun exposure can lead to **basal cell carcinoma**, the most common type of skin cancer but also the least dangerous. This form of cancer, which accounts for 75 percent of skin cancers, typically appears on the head, neck, and hands—areas of the body frequently exposed to the sun. It is readily curable so long as it is detected at an early stage and removed surgically. Severe sunburns early in life increase the risk of developing the least common but most deadly form of skin cancer, **melanoma**, which accounts for about 5 percent of skin cancers and claims about 8,000 lives in the United States annually (Kalb, 2001). To protect ourselves from skin cancer, we need to limit our exposure to the sun and use a sunscreen whenever exposure exceeds a few minutes.

Table 10.2 Behaviors That Can Help Prevent Cancer

- Avoid tobacco use.

- If you use alcohol, limit consumption to one drink per day for women or two drinks per day for men.

- Maintain a physically active lifestyle.

- Follow a healthy diet and limit intake of saturated fat.

- Maintain a healthy weight.

- Avoid unprotected exposure to the sun.

- Get regular medical examinations and follow recommended cancer screening procedures (ask your health care provider).

basal cell carcinoma A form of skin cancer that is easily curable if detected and removed early.

melanoma The most deadly form of skin cancer.

Stress. Is the risk of developing cancer related to stress? Unfortunately, we don't yet have a clear answer, as research evidence is mixed. We also lack clear evidence that psychological treatment can help cancer patients live longer or that adopting particular coping styles, such as a "fighting spirit," boosts the odds of surviving cancer (Antoni, 2012; Coyne et al., 2009). That said, many cancer patients benefit psychologically from counseling to help them cope with potentially devastating emotional effects of cancer, especially feelings of depression, anxiety, and hopelessness (e.g., Cleary & Stanton, 2015; Hopko et al., 2015; Stagl et al., 2015; Stanton et al., 2013).

Sexual Behavior and STDs: Are You Putting Yourself at Risk?

AIDS (*acquired immune deficiency syndrome*) has become one of history's worst epidemics. More than 30 million people worldwide are living with HIV, the virus that causes AIDS (Kaiser Family Foundation, 2012). AIDS has claimed more than 650,000 lives in the United States, and many millions more around the world since the start of the epidemic (CDC, 2015c). Approximately 50,000 people in the United States contract HIV annually (Satcher, Hook III, & Coleman, 2015).

HIV is transmitted by contact with infected bodily fluids, generally through intimate sexual contact or needle sharing. HIV attacks and disables the body's immune system, making the person vulnerable to other infections the body is normally able to fend off.

HIV/AIDS is the most threatening **sexually transmitted disease (STD)** (also called a *sexually transmitted infection* or STI), but it is far from the most common. Approximately one million people in the United States are living with HIV or AIDS, but genital herpes is believed to affect more than 50 million Americans (Herpes Statistics, 2014). More than a million new cases of *chlamydia*, the most common bacterial STD, are reported annually in the United States (CDC, 2013b). Some 20 million Americans are infected with *human papilloma viruses* (HPVs), the group of viruses that causes genital warts. Most sexually active people can expect to contract HPV at some point in their lives (CDC, 2010d).

Many STDs, not just HIV/AIDS, pose serious threats to our health. HPV, for example, is responsible for almost all cases of cervical cancer (CDC, 2013c). Fortunately, an effective vaccine is now available that protects women from strains of HPV that cause most forms of cervical cancer. However, the vaccine does not protect women who have already been infected with the virus or against some less common types of HPV not covered by the vaccine.

Treatment

Though antibiotics can cure bacterial forms of STDs, they are of no use against viral STDs. Antiviral drugs may help control viral STDs, such as HIV/AIDS and genital herpes, but they cannot eliminate the infectious organisms from the body.

The lack of a cure for viral STDs, including HIV/AIDS, and awareness of the risks posed by untreated bacterial STDs underscore the importance of prevention and early treatment. The use of antiviral drugs can control the infection for decades, raising hopes that HIV/AIDS may become a chronic but manageable disease. The lack of a cure for viral STDs, as well as awareness of the risks posed by untreated bacterial STDs, underscores the importance of prevention and early treatment.

Arming yourself with information about the modes of transmission of these diseases, early signs of infection, and available treatments is an important step in

CONCEPT 10.23

Many STDs, not just HIV/AIDS, pose serious threats to our health.

CONCEPT 10.24

Modifiable behaviors such as unprotected sex and needle sharing are major risk factors for transmission of sexually transmitted diseases, including HIV/AIDS.

sexually transmitted disease (STD) A disease caused by an infectious agent that is spread by sexual contact. Also called a *sexually transmitted infection* or STI.

protecting yourself from STDs (see Table 10.3). But information alone does not reduce the risks of transmitting STDs: It must be put into practice through changes in behavior. The next section, "Prevention," lists suggestions for safer sexual practices and medical screening.

Prevention

The only sure way to prevent the sexual transmission of STDs is to practice life-long abstinence or to maintain a monogamous relationship with an uninfected partner who is also monogamous. Short of that, we can speak of reducing risk from sexual contact rather than eliminating it entirely, of practicing *safer* sex rather than *safe* sex. To lower our risk, we can avoid unsafe sexual and injection practices and take steps to ensure that we detect and treat any STDs we may have. Here are some guidelines that can lower the risk of contracting an STD or suffering the consequences of an untreated STD (adapted from Nevid, Rathus, & Greene, 2014):

1. *Be careful in your choice of sex partners.* Get to know the person's sexual background before engaging in sexual activity. (Even so, getting to know someone is no guarantee that the person is not carrying HIV or some other infectious agent.)

2. *Avoid multiple partners,* especially partners who themselves may have multiple partners.

3. *Communicate your concerns.* Be assertive with your partner. Openly state your concerns about the risks of AIDS and other STDs and the need to practice safer sex.

4. *Avoid engaging in sexual contact with anyone with a sore or blister around the genitals.* Inspect your partner's sex organs before having any sexual contact. Rashes, blisters, chancres, discharges, warts, disagreeable odors, and so on should be treated as warning signs of a possible infection. But be aware that some STDs, including HIV infection, do not have any obvious signs.

5. *Avoid unprotected sexual contact.* Latex condoms (not "natural" condoms, which are more porous) offer the most reliable protection against the spread of HIV during sexual contact.

6. *Obtain a medical evaluation* if you suspect that you may have been exposed to a sexually transmitted disease.

7. *Get regular medical checkups* to detect and treat disorders you may not be aware you have.

8. *When in doubt, don't.* Abstain from intimate sexual contact if you have any doubts about whether it is potentially harmful. Your safety and that of your partner should be your top priority.

You may want to review Concept Chart 10.2, which highlights some key points about psychological risk factors in physical disorders.

Table 10.3 Major Types of STDs

	Mode of Transmission	Symptoms	Treatment
Bacterial STDs			
Gonorrhea	Sexual contact (vaginal, oral, or anal intercourse); from mother to newborn during childbirth	Men may have a yellowish, thick penile discharge and burning urination; though most women do not show early symptoms, some have increased vaginal discharge, burning urination, and irregular menstrual bleeding.	Antibiotics
Syphilis	Sexual contact; by touching an infectious chancre (sore)	A round, painless, but hard chancre develops at the site of infection within 2 to 4 weeks; symptoms progress through additional stages if left untreated.	Antibiotics
Chlamydia in women, or nongonococcal urethritis (NGU) in men	Sexual contact; touching an eye after contact with genitals of an infected partner; from infected mother to newborn during childbirth	Most women are symptom-free, but some have frequent and painful urination, lower abdominal pain and inflammation, and vaginal discharge. Men, too, are generally symptom-free but may have gonorrhea-like symptoms.	Antibiotics
Viral STDs			
HIV/AIDS	Sexual contact; needle sharing; receiving contaminated blood; from mother to fetus during pregnancy or from mother to child during childbirth or breastfeeding	Infected people may be initially symptom-free or have mild flu-like symptoms, but may progress to develop full-blown AIDS.	Antiviral drugs may help control the virus but do not cure the disease.
Genital herpes	Sexual contact	Painful, reddish bumps appear around the genitals, thighs, buttocks, or in the vagina or on the cervix in women. The bumps may develop into blisters or sores that fill with pus and break open before healing over.	Antiviral drugs can help control outbreaks but do not rid the body of the virus.
Viral hepatitis	Sexual contact, especially anal contact in the case of hepatitis A; contact with infected fecal matter; transfusion of contaminated blood (especially for hepatitis B and C)	Symptoms range from absence of symptoms to mild flu-like symptoms to more severe symptoms, such as fever, abdominal pain, vomiting, and "jaundiced" (yellowish) skin and eyes.	Bed rest and possible use of the drug alpha interferon in cases of hepatitis C
Genital warts	Sexual contact; contact with infected towels or clothing	Painless warts resembling cauliflowers may develop on the genitals, the internal reproductive organs, around the anus, or in the rectum.	Warts may be removed, but the virus (HPV) remains in the body.

Concept Chart 10.2 Psychological Risk Factors in Physical Disorders

	Health Problem	Psychological or Behavioral Risk Factors	Healthier Habits
	Coronary heart disease	Smoking, unhealthy diet, lack of physical activity, chronic anger or anxiety	Avoid tobacco use, get regular exercise, control anger and anxiety, limit dietary fat, reduce excess weight, and practice stress management techniques.
	Cancer	Smoking, high-fat diet, heavy alcohol consumption, unsafe sun exposure, inactivity, possible role of stress	Avoid tobacco use and excessive alcohol consumption, adopt a regular exercise routine, use sunscreen, and reduce excess weight.
	Sexually transmitted diseases	Unsafe sexual and injection practices	Practice abstinence, maintain a monogamous relationship with an uninfected partner, practice safer sex techniques, avoid needle sharing, and have regular medical checkups.

MODULE REVIEW 10.2 Psychological Factors in Physical Illness

Recite It

6. Apply stress management techniques to daily life.

Stress management techniques include maintaining stress at a tolerable level, learning (a) _____ skills, taking care of one's body, gathering information, expanding one's social network, using humor, (b) _____ burnout, replacing stress-inducing thoughts with stress-busting thoughts, not keeping upsetting feelings bottled up, and controlling Type A behavior.

7. Identify psychological factors linked to coronary heart disease.

Behaviors such as smoking, inactivity, and adopting an unhealthy diet as well as psychological traits such as

(c) _____ are associated with an increased risk of heart disease.

8. Identify psychological factors linked to cancer.

Unhealthy behaviors, such as smoking and consumption of a (d) _____-fat diet, are linked to an increased risk of various forms of cancer.

9. Apply knowledge of the transmission of sexually transmitted disease to steps we can take to protect ourselves from these diseases.

We can reduce our chances of contracting an STD by avoiding unsafe sexual and (e) _____ practices.

Recall It

1. Match the following terms with the appropriate descriptions: (a) arteriosclerosis; (b) myocardial infarction (MI); (c) plaque; (d) atherosclerosis.
   i. narrowing of vessels carrying blood to the heart
   ii. fatty deposits on artery walls
   iii. a heart attack (blood clot blocks blood flow in a coronary artery)
   iv. thicker, harder, and less elastic artery walls

2. (a) List some of the major risk factors for coronary heart disease. (b) Which of these are we able to control?

3. Smoking _____ the risk of suffering a heart attack.
   a. doubles
   b. triples
   c. quadruples
   d. has no effect on

4. Bacterial forms of STDs include
   a. HIV/AIDS.
   b. HPV.
   c. genital herpes.
   d. chlamydia.

Think About It

- What risk factors do you have for cardiovascular disease that you can control? What steps do you need to take to control these factors?

- What steps are you taking to protect yourself from the risk of cancer? What steps are you taking to ensure early detection of cancer?

Recite It *answers placed at the end of chapter.*

THINKING CRITICALLY ABOUT PSYCHOLOGY

Based on your reading of this chapter, answer the following questions. Then, to evaluate your progress in developing critical thinking skills, compare your answers to the sample answers found in Appendix A.

Every now and then, we hear claims touting some miracle drug, vitamin, hormone, or alternative therapy that promises to enhance health and vitality, cure or prevent disease, or even reverse the effects of aging. Some of these claims are outright hoaxes. Others take promising scientific leads and exaggerate or distort the evidence. Still others tout psychological therapies as cures for medical conditions on the basis of unsupported testimonials. Although the federal watchdog agency, the Food and Drug Administration (FDA), regulates health claims for drugs and medications, many of the substances found in your health food store or neighborhood supermarket purporting to have disease-preventive or antiaging effects are classified as foods and are not regulated as drugs. It's basically a case of "buyer beware."

Critical thinkers do not take health claims at face value. They recognize that alternative therapies and health care products may not work as promised and could even be harmful. Another concern is that people advocating particular therapies may have a vested interest in getting consumers to try their services or use their products, and may play fast and loose with the truth.

Use your critical thinking skills to read between the lines in evaluating health claims. What do you think the following claims for products found in your neighborhood health store actually mean?

- Designed to enhance vitality and well-being
- Promotes muscle growth
- Recommended by leading physicians
- Backed by advanced research
- Supercharge your metabolism!

Recite It Answers for Chapter 10

Module 10.1   1. (a) stress, 2. (b) hassles; (c) changes; (d) Type A, 3. (e) alarm; (f) resistance; (g) exhaustion, 4. (h) common, 5. (i) efficacy; (j) hardiness, 6. (k) relaxation; (l) burnout   **Module 10.2**   6. (a) relaxation; (b) preventing, 7. (c) hostility; (d) high, 9. (e) injection

Scoring Key for Optimism Scale

To compute your overall score, you first need to reverse your scores on Items 1, 2, 5, 8, and 10. This means that a 1 becomes 5, a 2 becomes a 4, a 3 remains the same, a 4 becomes a 2, and a 5 becomes a 1. Then sum your scores. Total scores can range from 10 (lowest optimism) to 50 (highest optimism). Scores around 30 indicate that you are neither strongly optimistic nor pessimistic. Although we do not have norms for this scale, you may consider scores in the 31 to 39 range as indicating a moderate level of optimism, whereas those in the 21 to 29 range indicate a moderate level of pessimism. Scores of 40 or above suggest higher levels of optimism, whereas those of 20 or below suggest higher levels of pessimism.

MODULE 10.1

Stress: What It Is and What It Does to the Body

What Is Stress?

- Pressure to adjust or cope with environmental demands or challenges

Sources of Stress

- Hassles
- Life Events
- Frustration
- Conflict
- Traumatic Stressors
- Type A Behavior Pattern
- Acculturation

Types of Conflicts

- Approach–Approach
- Avoidance–Avoidance
- Approach–Avoidance
- Multiple Approach–Avoidance

 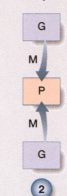 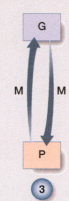 

①	②	③	④
Approach–Approach Conflict	Avoidance–Avoidance Conflict	Approach–Avoidance Conflict	Multiple Approach–Avoidance Conflict

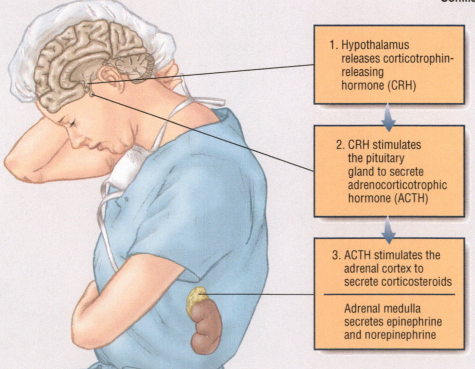

1. Hypothalamus releases corticotrophin-releasing hormone (CRH)

2. CRH stimulates the pituitary gland to secrete adrenocorticotrophic hormone (ACTH)

3. ACTH stimulates the adrenal cortex to secrete corticosteroids

Adrenal medulla secretes epinephrine and norepinephrine

The Body's Response to Stress

- **General Adaptation Syndrome:** Comprises three stages: alarm stage, resistance stage, exhaustion stage
- **Stress and the Endocrine System:** Coordinated response within HPA axis
- **Stress and the Immune System:** Chronic stress can weaken immune system responses

Ghislain & Marie David De Lossy/The Image Bank/Getty Images

Psychological Moderators of Stress

- **Social Support:** A helping hand in times of stress
- **Self-Efficacy:** Confidence in handling stressful challenges
- **Predictability and Controllability:** Stress is more manageable when it is predictable and controllable
- **Psychological Hardiness:** Commitment, challenge, and control
- **Optimism:** Believing the proverbial glass is half full

Managing Stress

- Maintain stress at a tolerable level
- Develop relaxation skills
- Take care of your body
- Gather information
- Expand your social network
- Prevent burnout
- Replace stress-inducing thoughts with stress-busting thoughts
- Control Type A behavior

MODULE 10.2

Psychological Factors in Physical Illness

Behavioral Risk Factors

- **Coronary Heart Disease:** Smoking, unhealthy diet, inactivity, hostility, and chronic negative emotions
- **Cancer:** Smoking, high-fat diet, excessive sun exposure

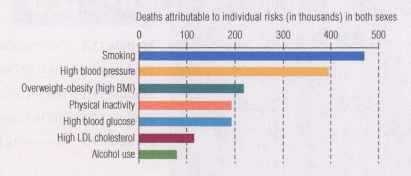

Deaths attributable to individual risks (in thousands) in both sexes

LEARNING OBJECTIVES

After studying this chapter, you will be able to . . .

1 **Define** the concept of personality.

2 **Identify** and **describe** the three levels of consciousness and three structures of personality in Freud's psychoanalytic theory.

3 **Identify** and **describe** the stages in Freud's theory of psychosexual development.

4 **Describe** the personality theories of Jung, Adler, and Horney.

5 **Describe** the trait theories of Allport, Cattell, Eysenck, and the Big Five model.

6 **Evaluate** the genetic basis of personality traits.

7 **Describe** the social-cognitive theories of Rotter, Bandura, and Mischel.

8 **Describe** the self-theory of humanistic theorist Carl Rogers.

9 **Explain** the difference between the concepts of self in collectivistic and individualistic cultures.

10 **Apply** suggestions for enhancing self-esteem.

11 **Identify** the two major types of personality tests, **describe** their features, and **evaluate** self-report and projective personality tests.

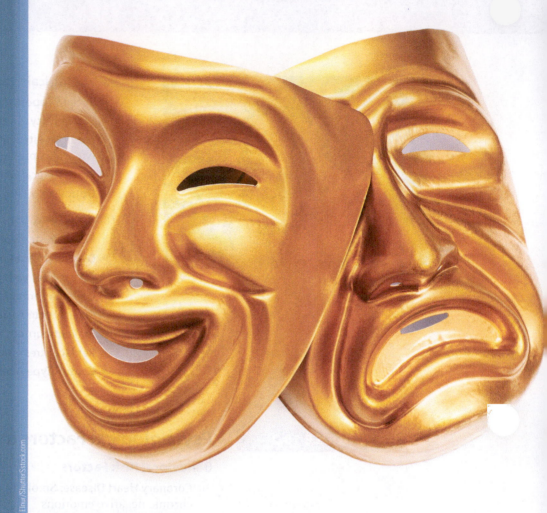

©Elnur/ShutterStock.com

PREVIEW

Personality

11

The Person in the Bathroom Mirror

Who is that person that stares back at you in the bathroom mirror? Do you know the person well, or is she or he still something of a mystery? How would you describe the person you see? What is special or unique about the person? How is the person similar to other people you know? How is the person different? Do you like the person you see? What would you like to change about the person you see?

This chapter is about the person in the mirror—you. It is also about every other human. Specifically, we are interested in *personality,* the relatively stable set of psychological characteristics and behavior patterns that make individuals unique and that account for the consistency of their behavior over time. Personality is a composite of the ways in which individuals relate to others and adapt to the demands placed on them by the environment.

The study of personality involves the attempt to describe and explain the characteristics that make each of us unique as individuals. Psychologists seek to understand these characteristics by drawing upon knowledge from the many other areas of psychology discussed elsewhere in the text. They consider how learning experiences, biological factors, social and cultural influences, and cognitive and developmental processes shape the people we become.

In this chapter, we consider the views of several leading personality theorists. Each brings a different perspective to bear on the study of personality. Some theorists, including Sigmund Freud, the originator of psychodynamic theory, emphasize unconscious influences on personality. They believe our personalities are shaped by a struggle between opposing forces within the mind that occurs outside the range of ordinary consciousness.

Other theorists, called trait theorists, view personality as composed of underlying traits that account for the consistency in our behavior from one situation to another. Social-cognitive theorists view personality in terms of our individual learning history and ways of thinking. To humanistic psychologists, such as Carl Rogers and Abraham Maslow, our personality is the expression of our unique potential as human beings. We explore these different perspectives and examine what each has to say about personality, beginning with the psychodynamic model of personality espoused by Freud and his followers.

Did you know that...

- According to Sigmund Freud, slips of the tongue may reveal hidden motives and wishes of which we are unaware? (p. 417)

- The Big Five is not the name of a new NCAA basketball conference but the label used to describe the leading trait theory of personality today? (p. 423)

- Your personality traits help predict how well you are likely to do in college? (p. 424)

- Conscientiousness typically increases during young adulthood when people need to adjust to increasing work and family responsibilities? (p. 424)

- More conscientious people tend to live longer? (p. 424)

- Extraverted students tend to have more Facebook friends as well as more friends in the real world? (p. 425)

- A leading humanistic theorist, Carl Rogers, believed that children should receive love and approval unconditionally from their parents regardless of their behavior at any particular point in time? (p. 434)

- According to a widely held view in the nineteenth century, you can learn about a person's character by examining the bumps on the person's head? (p. 439)

11.1 The Psychodynamic Perspective

1 **Define** the concept of personality (from chapter introduction).

2 **Identify** and **describe** the three levels of consciousness and three structures of personality in Freud's psychoanalytic theory.

3 **Identify** and **describe** the stages in Freud's theory of psychosexual development.

4 **Describe** the personality theories of Jung, Adler, and Horney.

CONCEPT 11.1

The study of personality involves efforts to understand our uniqueness as individuals and the characteristics that account for consistencies in our behavior over time.

CONCEPT 11.2

Freud developed the first psychodynamic theory of personality, the belief that personality is shaped by underlying conflicts between opposing forces within the mind.

Sigmund Freud

Mansell/Time Life Pictures/Getty Images

personality The relatively stable constellation of psychological characteristics and behavioral patterns that account for our individuality and consistency over time.

psychoanalytic theory Freud's theory of personality that holds that personality and behavior are shaped by unconscious forces and conflicts.

conscious To Freud, the part of the mind corresponding to the state of present awareness.

Sigmund Freud was the architect of the first major theory of **personality**, called **psychoanalytic theory**. The central idea underlying his theory of personality is the belief that a dynamic struggle takes place within the human psyche (mind) between unconscious forces. For this reason, Freud's views and those of his followers are often called *psychodynamic theory*. In this module, we first discuss Freud's ideas and then describe the contributions of other theorists in the psychodynamic tradition who followed in Freud's footsteps.

Sigmund Freud: Psychoanalytic Theory

In the tradition of Darwin, Freud recognized that we share with nonhuman animals certain common processes that have *survival* as their aim. We need to breathe, feed, and eliminate bodily wastes. And to survive as a species, we need to reproduce. Freud believed we are endowed with a sexual instinct that has as its purpose the preservation of the species. He later would add an aggressive instinct to explain human aggression. Yet Freud believed that giving free rein to these instincts might tear apart the very fabric of society and of the family unit itself. To live in an ordered society, he maintained, humans need to control their primitive sexual and aggressive impulses. In other words, humans need to channel their sexual and aggressive instincts in socially appropriate ways so as to live harmoniously with one another. They need to learn that aggression or sexual touching is unacceptable except in socially acceptable contexts, such as the football field (aggressive impulses) and the marital bed (sexual impulses).

Freud developed psychoanalytic theory to account for how the mind accomplishes the task of balancing these conflicting demands of instinct and social acceptability. His theory of personality is complex, but it can be represented in terms of four major concepts: levels of consciousness, structure of personality, defense mechanisms, and stages of psychosexual development.

Levels of Consciousness: The Conscious, the Preconscious, and the Unconscious

We can liken Freud's model of the human mind to a giant iceberg. Like an iceberg, which has much of its mass hidden below the surface of the water, most of the mind lies below the surface of conscious awareness (see ■ Figure 11.1). Freud represented the mind as consisting of three levels of consciousness: the **conscious**, the **preconscious**, and the **unconscious**. The conscious is the tip of the iceberg. It is the level of consciousness that corresponds to our present awareness—what we are thinking or feeling at any given moment in time. The preconscious holds information we've stored from previous life experience or prior learning. This information can be retrieved from memory and brought into awareness at any time. Your telephone number, for example, is information stored in the preconscious that you can bring into awareness when needed.

The unconscious mind is like the large mass of the iceberg lying under the surface of the water. It contains primitive sexual and aggressive impulses as well as memories of troubling emotional experiences (for example, traumatizing events) and unacceptable sexual or aggressive wishes or ideas. Freud believed the contents of the unconscious mind can only be brought into consciousness with great difficulty, if at all. You cannot summon them to consciousness simply by mental focusing, as you might bring to mind your telephone phone number or the name of your high school. With so much of the contents of the mind mired in the unconscious, we remain unaware of our deepest wishes, ideas, and urges.

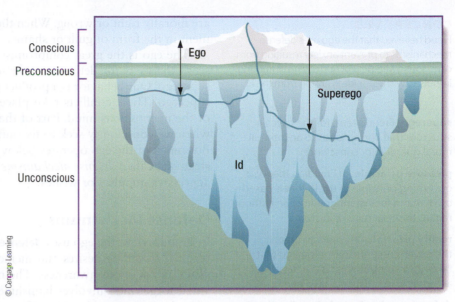

© Cengage Learning

FIGURE 11.1 Levels of Consciousness in Freud's Theory
The human mind in Freudian theory can be likened to an iceberg in which only the tip rises above the level of conscious awareness. Though information held in the preconscious can be brought into the conscious mind at any time, much of the contents of the mind—including many of our deepest wishes, ideas, and urges—remain mired in the dark recesses of the unconscious.

The Structure of Personality: Id, Ego, and Superego

Freud proposed that personality consists of three mental entities called **id**, **ego**, and **superego**. The balance and interactions of these three parts of the personality largely determine our behavior and our ability to function effectively in meeting the life challenges we face. Freud did not consider these mental entities to be actual structures we could locate in the brain. Rather, he conceived of them as hypothetical concepts that represent the opposing forces within the personality.

As Figure 11.1 shows, the id (literally, "it") operates only in the unconscious. The id contains our baser animal drives and instinctual impulses, including hunger, thirst, elimination, sex, and aggression. The id stirs us to action to ensure that our basic biological needs are met. It is the only psychic structure present at birth and follows what Freud called the **pleasure principle**, the demand for instant gratification without regard to social rules or customs. In essence, the id wants what it wants when it wants it. Think of the infant. When a need arises, such as hunger or elimination, the infant demands immediate satisfaction of that need. It doesn't wait patiently until an appropriate time comes to feed or to move its bowels. The infant soon finds that not every demand is instantly gratified. It finds it must cope with frustration and learn to delay gratification. So a second part of the mind forms during the first year of life that is responsible for organizing ways to handle delays of gratification. Freud called this entity ego. The ego represents "reason and good sense" (Freud, 1933/1964, p. 76).

The ego operates according to the **reality principle**, the basis for operating in the world by taking into account what is practical and acceptable. The ego seeks ways to satisfy the demands of the id without incurring social disapproval. The id may motivate you to rise from your chair and seek nourishment when you are hungry. But the ego enables you to make a sandwich and keeps you from grabbing food from someone else's plate.

The superego is our internal moral guardian or conscience. By 3 to 5 years of age, during middle childhood, it splits off from the ego, forming through a process of internalizing the moral teachings of parents or other significant figures. Part of the superego may be available to consciousness, the part that corresponds to our moral convictions—our personal beliefs about right and wrong. But much of the superego operates in the unconscious, standing in judgment of whether the actions of the ego

CONCEPT 11.3
Freud believed that the mind consists of three levels of consciousness: the conscious, the preconscious, and the unconscious.

CONCEPT 11.4
Freud believed that personality consists of three mental entities: the id, the ego, and the superego.

preconscious To Freud, the part of the mind whose contents can be brought into awareness through focused attention.

unconscious To Freud, the part of the mind that lies outside the range of ordinary awareness and that holds troubling or unacceptable urges, impulses, memories, and ideas.

id Freud's term for the psychic structure existing in the unconscious that contains our baser animal drives and instinctual impulses.

ego Freud's term for the psychic structure that attempts to balance the instinctual demands of the id with social realities and expectations.

Freud believed that the ego uses defense mechanisms to prevent anxiety resulting from conscious awareness of underlying disturbing impulses, wishes, or ideas arising from the id.

superego Freud's term for the psychic structure that corresponds to an internal moral guardian or conscience.

pleasure principle In Freudian theory, a governing principle of the id that is based on demand for instant gratification without regard to social rules or customs.

reality principle In Freudian theory, the governing principle of the ego that takes into account what is practical and acceptable in satisfying basic needs.

defense mechanisms In Freudian theory, the reality-distorting strategies of the ego to prevent awareness of anxiety-evoking or troubling ideas or impulses.

repression In Freudian theory, a type of defense mechanism involving motivated forgetting of anxiety-evoking material.

denial In Freudian theory, a defense mechanism involving the failure to recognize a threatening impulse or urge.

are morally right or wrong. When they are not, the superego can impose self-punishment in the form of guilt or shame.

The ego is the great compromiser. It stands between the superego and the id. It seeks to satisfy the demands of the id without offending the moral standards of the superego. Our behavior is a product of the dynamic struggles among the id, ego, and superego. These conflicts take place outside of conscious awareness, on the stage of the unconscious mind. Part of the ego rises to the level of consciousness, such as when we consciously seek to fix ourselves a sandwich in response to hunger pangs. But much of the ego operates below the surface of consciousness, where it employs strategies called *defense mechanisms* to prevent awareness of unacceptable sexual or aggressive impulses or wishes.

Defense Mechanisms

In Freud's view, the ego uses **defense mechanisms** to prevent the anxiety that would result if troubling desires and memories residing in the unconscious were fully realized in conscious awareness. The major defense mechanism—**repression**, or motivated forgetting—involves banishment to the unconscious of unacceptable wishes, fantasies, urges, and impulses (Boag, 2006).

Repression permits people to remain outwardly calm and controlled even though they harbor hateful or lustful urges under the surface of awareness. Yet repressed desires or memories may become revealed in disguised forms, such as in dream symbols and in slips of the tongue (so-called *Freudian slips*) (Freud, 1938). To Freud, slips of the tongue may reveal underlying motives and wishes kept hidden by repression. If a friend intends to say "I know what you're saying" but it comes out as "I hate what you're saying," perhaps the friend is expressing repressed hateful impulses (Nevid, Rathus, & Greene, 2014). Other defense mechanisms Freud identified include **denial, reaction formation, rationalization, projection, sublimation, regression,** and **displacement** (see Table 11.1).

Table 11.1 **Major Defense Mechanisms in Psychodynamic Theory**		
Type of Defense Mechanism	**Description**	**Example**
Repression	Expulsion from awareness of unacceptable ideas or motives	A person remains unaware of harboring hateful or destructive impulses toward others.
Regression	The return of behavior that is typical of earlier stages of development	Under stress, a college student starts biting his nails or becomes totally dependent on others.
Displacement	The transfer of unacceptable impulses away from their original objects onto safer or less threatening objects	A worker slams a door after his boss chews him out.
Denial	Refusal to recognize a threatening impulse or desire	A person who nearly chokes someone to death acts afterward like it was "no big deal."
Reaction formation	Behaving in a way that is the opposite of one's true wishes or desires in order to keep these repressed	A sexually frustrated person goes on a personal crusade to stamp out pornography.
Rationalization	The use of self-justifications to explain away unacceptable behavior	When asked why she continues to smoke, a woman says, "Cancer doesn't run in my family."
Projection	Imposing one's own impulses or wishes onto another person	A sexually inhibited person misinterprets other people's friendly approaches as sexual advances.
Sublimation	The channeling of unacceptable impulses into socially constructive pursuits	A person channels aggressive impulses into competitive sports.

Though defense mechanisms may be a normal process of adjusting to the unreasonable demands of the id, they can give rise to abnormal behavior. For example, a man who sexually assaults a woman may rationalize to himself that "she had it coming" rather than directly confront his aggressive urges. A person who regresses to a dependent infantile-like state during times of extreme stress may be shielded from the anxiety of facing the stressful situation but be unable to function effectively.

Stages of Psychosexual Development

In Freud's view, personality develops through five psychosexual stages of development. He considered these stages to be psychosexual in nature because they involve changes in how the child seeks physical pleasure from sexually sensitive parts of the body, called **erogenous zones**. He further believed that physical activities connected to basic life functions, such as feeding, elimination, and reproduction, are basically "sexual" because they are inherently pleasurable. So an infant sucking at the mother's breast or eliminating bodily wastes is performing acts that are sexual in Freud's view. And why are these activities pleasurable? The answer, Freud believed, is clear: They are essential to survival. The infant needs to suck to obtain nourishment. If sucking weren't pleasurable, the infant wouldn't do it and would likely die. As the child progresses through the stages of psychosexual development, the primary erogenous zone shifts from one part of the body to another.

Psychological conflicts may emerge during each psychosexual stage of development. These conflicts, which often arise from receiving too much or too little gratification, can lead to the development of **fixations**—personality traits or behavior patterns characteristic of the particular stage. It's as though one's personality gets "stuck" at an early level of development. Let us briefly consider these five stages and the conflicts that may emerge during each one.

Oral Stage. The **oral stage** spans the period of birth through about 12 to 18 months of age. During this stage, the primary erogenous zone is the mouth. The infant seeks sexual pleasure through sucking at its mother's breast and mouthing (taking into the mouth) or, later, biting objects that happen to be nearby, including the parents' fingers. Whatever fits into the mouth goes into the mouth. Too much gratification in the oral stage may lead to oral fixations in adulthood such as smoking, nail biting, alcohol abuse, and overeating. Too little gratification, perhaps from early weaning, may lead to the development of traits that suggest a failure to have needs met for nurturance and care during infancy, such as passivity, clinging dependence, and a pessimistic outlook.

Anal Stage. By about the age of 18 months, the child has entered the **anal stage**. The anal cavity becomes the primary erogenous zone as the child develops the ability to control elimination by contracting and releasing the sphincter muscles at will. Yet this stage, which lasts until about age 3, is set for conflict between the parents and the child around the issue of toilet training. To earn the parents' approval and avoid their disapproval, the child must learn to "go potty" at the appropriate time and to delay immediate gratification of the need to eliminate whenever the urge is felt.

In Freud's view, anal fixations reflect either too harsh or too lenient toilet training. Training that is too harsh may lead to traits associated with the so-called **anal-retentive personality**, such as perfectionism and extreme needs for self-control, orderliness, cleanliness, and neatness. Extremely lax training may lead to an opposite array of traits associated with the **anal-expulsive personality**, such as messiness, lack of self-discipline, and carelessness.

Phallic Stage. During the phallic stage, which roughly spans the ages of 3 to 6, the erogenous zone shifts to the phallic region—the penis in males and the clitoris in

reaction formation In Freudian theory, a defense mechanism involving behavior that stands in opposition to one's true motives and desires so as to prevent conscious awareness of them.

rationalization In Freudian theory, a defense mechanism involving the use of self-justification to explain away unacceptable behavior, impulses, or ideas.

projection In Freudian theory, a defense mechanism involving the projection of one's own unacceptable impulses, wishes, or urges onto another person.

sublimation In Freudian theory, a defense mechanism involving the channeling of unacceptable impulses into socially sanctioned behaviors or interests.

regression In Freudian theory, a defense mechanism in which an individual, usually under high levels of stress, reverts to a behavior characteristic of an earlier stage of development.

displacement In Freudian theory, a defense mechanism in which an unacceptable sexual or aggressive impulse is transferred to an object or person that is safer or less threatening than the original object of the impulse.

erogenous zones Parts of the body that are especially sensitive to sexual or pleasurable stimulation.

fixations Constellations of personality traits characteristic of a particular stage of psychosexual development, resulting from either excessive or inadequate gratification at that stage.

oral stage In Freudian theory, the first stage of psychosexual development, during which the infant seeks sexual gratification through oral stimulation (sucking, mouthing, and biting).

anal stage In Freudian theory, the second stage of psychosexual development, during which sexual gratification is centered on processes of elimination (retention and release of bowel contents).

anal-retentive personality In Freudian theory, a personality type characterized by perfectionism and excessive needs for self-control as expressed through extreme neatness and punctuality.

anal-expulsive personality In Freudian theory, a personality type characterized by messiness, lack of self-discipline, and carelessness.

© Dmitry Naumov/Shutterstock.com

CONCEPT 11.6

Freud believed that personality develops through five stages of psychosexual development: the oral, anal, phallic, latency, and genital stages.

CONCEPT LINK

In contrast to Freud, the psychodynamic theorist Erik Erikson posited stages of psychosocial development that begin in early childhood and continue through adulthood. See Modules 9.3 to 9.6.

CONCEPT 11.7

As a group, neo-Freudians placed a lesser emphasis on sexuality than did Freud and a greater emphasis on the roles of conscious choice, self-direction, creativity, and ways of relating to others.

phallic stage In Freudian theory, the third stage of psychosexual development, marked by erotic attention on the phallic region (penis in boys, clitoris in girls) and the development of the Oedipus complex.

Oedipus complex In Freudian theory, the psychological complex in which the young boy or girl develops incestuous feelings toward the parent of the opposite gender and perceives the parent of the same gender as a rival.

Electra complex The term given by some psychodynamic theorists to the form of the Oedipus complex in young girls.

castration anxiety In Freudian theory, unconscious fear of removal of the penis as punishment for having unacceptable sexual impulses.

females. Conflicts with parents over masturbation (self-stimulation of the phallic area) may emerge at this time. But the core conflict of the **phallic stage** is the **Oedipus complex**, which involves the development of incestuous desires for the parent of the opposite sex, leading to rivalry with the parent of the same sex. Freud named the Oedipus complex after the ancient Greek myth of Oedipus the King—the tragic story of Oedipus who unwittingly slew his father and married his mother. He believed that this ancient tale revealed a fundamental human truth about psychosexual development. Some of Freud's followers dubbed the female version of the Oedipus complex the **Electra complex**, after another figure in ancient Greek tragedy, Electra, who avenged her father's death by killing his murderers—her own mother and her mother's lover.

In Freud's view, boys normally resolve the conflict by forsaking their incestuous wishes for their mother and identifying with their rival—their father. Girls normally surrender their incestuous desires for their father and identify with their mother. Identification with the parent of the same sex leads to the development of gender-based behaviors. Boys develop aggressive and independent traits associated with masculinity, and girls develop nurturant and demure traits associated with femininity. Another by-product of the Oedipus complex is development of the superego—the internalization of parental values in the form of a moral conscience.

Freud believed that the failure to successfully resolve Oedipal conflicts may cause boys to become resentful of strong masculine figures, especially authority figures. For either boys or girls, failure to identify with the parent of the same gender may lead to the development of traits associated with the opposite gender and perhaps, according to Freud, to the development of homosexuality.

Freud also believed that young boys develop **castration anxiety**, the fear that their father will punish them for their sexual desires for their mother by castrating them. An unconscious fear of castration motivates boys to forsake their incestuous desires for their mother and to identify with their father. In Freud's view, girls experience **penis envy**, or jealousy of boys for having a penis. Penis envy leads girls to feel inferior or inadequate in relation to boys and to unconsciously blame their mother for bringing them into the world so "ill-equipped." But fears of losing their mother's love and protection over their incestuous desires for their fathers prompts girls to forsake these incestuous desires and to identify with their mother. As girls become sexually mature, they forsake their wish to have a penis of their own (to "be a man") for a desire to have a baby—that is, as a kind of penis substitute for their missing penis. Bear in mind that Freud believed the Oedipus complex, with its incestuous desires, rivalries, and castration anxiety and penis envy, largely occurs at an unconscious level. On the surface, all may seem quiet, masking the turmoil occurring within.

Latency Stage The turbulent psychic crisis of the phallic period gives way to a period of relative tranquility—the **latency stage**, spanning the years between about 6 and 12. The latency stage is so named because of the belief that sexual impulses remain latent (dormant) during this time.

Genital Stage Children enter the **genital stage** at about the time of puberty. The forsaken incestuous desires for the parent of the opposite sex give rise to yearnings for more appropriate sexual partners of the opposite gender. Girls may be attracted to boys who resemble "dear old Dad" while boys may seek "the kind of girl who married dear old Dad." Sexual energies seek expression through mature (genital) sexuality in the form of sexual intercourse in marriage and the bearing of children.

See Table 11.2 for a summary of Freud's psychosexual stages of development.

Table 11.2 Freud's Psychosexual Stages of Development

Psychosexual Age	Approximate Zone	Erogenous Zone	Source of Sexual Pleasure	Source of Conflict	Adult Characteristics Associated with Conflicts at This Stage
Oral	Birth to 12 to 18 months	Oral cavity	Sucking, biting, and mouthing	Weaning	Oral behaviors such as smoking, alcohol use, nail biting; dependency; passivity; pessimism
Anal	18 months to 3 years	Anal region	Retention and release of bodily waste	Toilet training	Anal-retentive versus anal-expulsive traits
Phallic	3 to 6 years	Penis in boys; clitoris in girls	Masturbation	Masturbation; Oedipus complex	Homosexuality; resentment of authority figures in men; unresolved penis envy in women
Latency	6 years to puberty	None	None (focus on play and school activities)	None	None
Genital	Puberty to adulthood	Genitals (penis in men; vagina in women)	Return of sexual interests expressed in mature sexual relationships	None	None

Other Psychodynamic Approaches

Freud attracted a host of followers, many of whom are recognized as important personality theorists in their own right. These followers held views that differed from Freud's in some key respects, but they retained certain central tenets of psychodynamic theory, especially the belief that behavior is influenced by unconscious conflicts within the personality. Yet, as a group, the theorists who followed in Freud's footsteps (often called *neo-Freudians*) placed a lesser emphasis on sexual and aggressive motivations and a greater emphasis on social relationships and the workings of the ego, especially the development of a concept of the self. Here we discuss the major ideas of several of the leading neo-Freudians: Carl Jung, Alfred Adler, and Karen Horney. The contributions of another neo-Freudian, Erik Erikson, were discussed in Chapter 9.

Carl Jung: Analytical Psychology

Carl Gustav Jung (1875–1961) was once part of Freud's inner circle, but he broke with Freud as he developed his own distinctive views of personality. Jung shared with Freud the beliefs that unconscious conflicts influence human behavior and that defense mechanisms distort or disguise people's underlying motives. However, he placed greater emphasis on the present than on infantile or childhood experience as well as greater emphasis on conscious processes, such as self-awareness and pursuit of self-directed goals (Boynton, 2004; Kirsch, 1996).

Jung believed that people possess both a **personal unconscious**, which consists of repressed memories and impulses, and a **collective unconscious**, or repository of accumulated ideas and images in the unconscious mind that is shared among all humans and passed down genetically through the generations. The collective unconscious contains primitive images called **archetypes** that reflect ancestral or universal human experiences, including images such as an omniscient and all-powerful God, the young hero, and the fertile and nurturing mother figure. Jung believed that while these images remain unconscious, they influence our dreams and waking thoughts and emotions. It is the collective unconscious, Jung maintained, that explains similarities among cultures in dream images, religious symbols, and artistic expressions (such as movie heroes and heroines).

penis envy In Freudian theory, jealousy of boys for having a penis.

latency stage In Freudian theory, the fourth stage of psychosexual development, during which sexual impulses remain latent or dormant.

genital stage In Freudian theory, the fifth and final stage of psychosexual development, which begins around puberty and corresponds to the development of mature sexuality and emphasis on procreation.

personal unconscious Jung's term for an unconscious region of mind comprising a reservoir of the individual's repressed memories and impulses.

collective unconscious In Jung's theory, a part of the mind containing ideas and archetypal images shared among humankind that have been transmitted genetically from ancestral humans.

archetypes Jung's term for the primitive images contained in the collective unconscious that reflect ancestral or universal experiences of human beings.

The young hero is a Jungian archetype, as is the wise old man and the mother figure. Jung believed that these symbols of universal human experiences are embedded in a part of the mind he called the collective unconscious.

Karen Horney

Alfred Adler: Individual Psychology

Alfred Adler (1870–1937) was another member of Freud's inner circle who broke away to develop his own theory of personality. Adler called his theory **individual psychology** because of its emphasis on the unique potential of each individual. He believed that conscious experience plays a greater role in our personalities than Freud had believed. The **creative self** is what he called the part of the personality that is aware of itself and organizes goal-seeking behavior. As such, our creative self strives toward overcoming obstacles that lie in the path of pursuing our potentials, of becoming all that we seek to become.

Adler is perhaps best known for his concept of the **inferiority complex**. He believed that because of their small size and limited abilities, all children harbor feelings of inferiority to some degree. How they compensate for these feelings influences their emerging personalities. Feelings of inferiority lead to a desire to compensate, which Adler called the **drive for superiority** or *will-to-power*. The drive for superiority may motivate us to try harder and achieve worthwhile goals, such as professional accomplishments and positions of prominence. Or it may lead us to be domineering or callous toward others, to perhaps step on or over people as we make our way up the professional or social ladder.

Karen Horney: An Early Voice in Feminine Psychology

One of the staunchest critics of Freud's views on female development was one of his own followers, Karen Horney (1885–1952) (pronounced *HORN-eye*), a German physician and early psychoanalyst who became a prominent theorist in her own right. Horney accepted Freud's belief that unconscious conflicts shape personality, but she focused less on sexual and aggressive drives and more on the roles of social and cultural forces. She also emphasized the importance of parent–child relationships. When parents are harsh or uncaring, children may develop a deep-seated form of anxiety she called **basic anxiety**, which is associated with the feeling of "being isolated and helpless in a potentially hostile world" (cited in Quinn, 1987, p. 41). Children may also develop a deep form of resentment toward their parents, which she labeled **basic hostility**. Horney believed, as did Freud, that children repress their hostility toward their parents out of fear of losing them or suffering their reprisals. Yet repressed hostility generates more anxiety and insecurity.

Horney rejected Freud's belief that a female's sense of inferiority derives from penis envy. She argued that if women feel inferior, it is because they envy men their social power and authority, not their penises (Stewart & McDermott, 2004). Horney even raised the possibility that men may experience "womb envy" over the obvious "physiological superiority" of women with respect to their biological capacity for creating and bringing life into the world.

Evaluating the Psychodynamic Perspective

Psychodynamic theory remains the most detailed and comprehensive theory of personality yet developed. Many of the terms Freud introduced—such as ego, superego, repression, fixation, and defense mechanisms—are used today in everyday language, although perhaps not precisely in the ways that Freud defined them.

Perhaps the major contribution of Freud and later psychodynamic thinkers was to put the study of the unconscious mind on the map (Lothane, 2006). To know oneself, Freud believed, means to plumb the depths of our unconscious mind, to ferret out the unconscious motives that underlie our behavior. As we shall see in Chapter 13, Freud developed a method of psychotherapy, called *psychoanalysis,* that focuses on helping people gain insight into the unconscious motives and conflicts that he believed were at the root of their problems.

Psychodynamic theory has had its critics, however. Many, including some of Freud's own followers, believe Freud placed too much importance on sexual and

CONCEPT 11.8

Although the psychodynamic perspective has had a major impact on psychology and beyond, critics contend that it lacks support from rigorous scientific studies for many of its key concepts.

individual psychology Adler's theory of personality, which emphasizes the unique potential of each individual.

creative self In Adler's theory, the self-aware part of personality that organizes goal-seeking efforts.

aggressive drives and too little emphasis on the role of social relationships in the development of personality. Other psychodynamic thinkers, including Horney, did place greater emphasis on social influences in personality development. Another challenge to Freud is the lack of evidence to support many of the principles on which his theory is based, including his beliefs in castration anxiety, penis envy, and the universality of the Oedipus complex. Some critics question whether the Oedipus complex even exists at all (see Kupfersmid, 1995).

Other critics challenged the progression and timing of Freud's psychosexual stages of development. Still others challenged psychodynamic theory itself as resting almost entirely on evidence gathered from a relatively few case studies. Case studies may be open to varied interpretations. Moreover, the few individuals who are subjects of case studies may not be representative of people in general.

Perhaps the greatest limitation of the psychodynamic approach is the difficulty in scientifically testing many of its key concepts, especially those involving the unconscious mind. The scientific method requires that theories lend themselves to testable hypotheses. By their nature, unconscious processes are not open to direct observation or scientific measurement, which makes them difficult—some would say impossible—to study scientifically. Still, a number of investigators today are seeking to objectively test certain aspects of psychodynamic theory, including the role of defense mechanisms (e.g., Cramer, 2000; Westen & Gabbard, 2002).

Concept Chart 11.1 provides an overview of the psychodynamic perspective on personality. In subsequent modules, we will consider other leading perspectives on personality—namely, the trait, social-cognitive, and humanistic approaches.

inferiority complex In Adler's theory, a concept involving the influence that feelings of inadequacy or inferiority in young children have on their developing personalities and desires to compensate.

drive for superiority Adler's term for the motivation to compensate for feelings of inferiority. Also called the *will-to-power*.

basic anxiety In Horney's theory, a deep-seated form of anxiety in children that is associated with feelings of being isolated and helpless in a world perceived as potentially threatening and hostile.

basic hostility In Horney's theory, deep feelings of resentment that children may harbor toward their parents.

Concept Chart 11.1   Major Concepts in Psychodynamic Theory

	Concept	Description	Summary
Freud's Psychoanalytic Theory	Levels of consciousness	The mind consists of three levels of consciousness: the conscious, the preconscious, and the unconscious.	Only a small part of the mind is fully conscious. The unconscious mind, the largest part of the mind, contains our baser drives and impulses.
	Structure of personality	Id, ego, and superego	Existing only in the unconscious, the id is a repository of instinctual impulses. The ego seeks to satisfy the demands of the id through socially acceptable ways without offending the superego, the moral guardian of the self.
	Governing principles	Pleasure principle and reality principle	The id follows the pleasure principle, the demand for instant gratification regardless of social necessities. The ego follows the reality principle, by which gratification of impulses must be weighed in terms of social acceptability and practicality.
	Defense mechanisms	The ego uses defense mechanisms to conceal or distort unacceptable impulses, thus preventing them from rising into consciousness.	The major defense mechanisms include repression, regression, projection, rationalization, denial, reaction formation, sublimation, and displacement.
	Stages of psychosexual development	Sexual motivation is expressed through stimulation of different body parts or erogenous zones as children mature.	The five stages of psychosexual development are oral, anal, phallic, latency, and genital. Overgratification or undergratification can lead to personality features or fixations characteristic of that stage.
Other Theories	Key points	Greater emphasis on the ego and social relationships than was the case with Freud, and lesser emphasis on sexual and aggressive motivation	Carl Jung's analytical psychology introduced concepts of the personal unconscious, archetypes, and the collective unconscious. Alfred Adler's individual psychology emphasized self-awareness, goal striving, and ways in which people compensate for underlying feelings of inadequacy or inferiority. Karen Horney focused on ways in which people relate to each other and the importance of parent–child relationships.

MODULE REVIEW   11.1   The Psychodynamic Perspective

Recite It

1. **Define** the concept of personality (from chapter introduction).

   We can define (a) _____ as the composite set of psychological characteristics and behavior patterns that distinguish one person from another and that account for (b) _____ of the person's behavior over time and from situation to situation.

2. **Identify** and **describe** the three levels of consciousness and three structures of personality in Freud's psychoanalytic theory.

   According to Freud, the three levels of consciousness are the conscious, the (c) _____, and the unconscious. The conscious represents your present awareness; the preconscious represents the region of the mind that contains information you can readily retrieve from memory; and the (d) _____ represents a darkened region of the mind that contains primitive urges, wishes, and troubling memories that cannot be directly summoned to consciousness. Freud represented personality as composed of three mental structures: the id, the ego, and the (e) _____. The ego attempts to satisfy the sexual and aggressive urges of the (f) _____ in ways that avoid social disapproval or condemnation from the superego, the internal moral guardian or conscience.

3. **Identify** and **describe** the stages in Freud's theory of psychosexual development.

   The stages of psychosexual development are ordered as follows: (g) _____ (focus on oral activities of sucking and biting), (h) _____ (focus on purposeful control of excretion), (i) _____ (focus on the phallic region, the penis in boys and clitoris in girls), (j) _____ (dormant sexual desires), and (k) _____ (full expression of mature sexuality focused on genital sexuality and procreation).

4. **Describe** the personality theories of Jung, Adler, and Horney.

   Jung believed in both a (l) _____ unconscious and a shared unconscious he called the (m) _____ unconscious.
   Adler developed the concept of the (n) "_____ complex," the tendency to compensate for feelings of inferiority by developing a drive to (o) _____ ("drive for superiority").
   Horney challenged Freud's ideas about female psychology and focused on the emotional effects in children of impaired relationships with their (p) _____.

Recall It

1. Psychoanalytic theory attempts to explain how humans balance
   a. sexual instincts and social standards.
   b. demands for productivity with demands for leisure.
   c. desire for wealth with desires for sexual reproduction.
   d. basic biological needs with self-actualization needs.

2. To Freud, the part of the mind that organizes efforts to satisfy basic impulses in ways that avoid social condemnation is the
   a. id.   c. ego.
   b. superego.   d. preconscious.

3. To Freud, the psychosexual developmental stage during which a young boy experiences the Oedipus complex is the
   a. oral stage.   c. phallic stage.
   b. anal stage.   d. genital stage.

4. Match the following terms with their descriptions: (a) defense mechanisms; (b) repression; (c) Freudian slip; (d) projection.
   i. motivated forgetting
   ii. accidentally revealing underlying thoughts
   iii. aimed at shielding the self from anxiety
   iv. imposing one's own impulses or desires on others

5. Which of the following psychodynamic theorists supported the view that humans share a collective unconscious?
   a. Carl Jung   c. Erik Erikson
   b. Karen Horney   d. Alfred Adler

Think About It

■ Underlying the psychodynamic perspective is the belief that we are not aware of the deeper motives and impulses that drive our behavior. Do you agree? Why or why not?

■ Can you identify any of your behaviors that might be examples of defense mechanisms? How would you even know?

Recite It answers placed at the end of chapter.

11.2 The Trait Perspective

5 **Describe** the trait theories of Allport, Cattell, Eysenck, and the Big Five model.

6 **Evaluate** the genetic basis of personality traits.

Like psychodynamic theorists, trait theorists look within the personality to explain behavior. But the structures of personality they bring into focus are not opposing mental states or entities. Rather, they believe that personality consists of a distinctive set of relatively stable or enduring characteristics or dispositions called **traits**. They use personality traits to predict how people are likely to behave in different situations. For example, they may describe Rosa as having personality traits such as cheerfulness and outgoingness. Based on these traits, they might predict that she is likely to be involved in many social activities and to be the kind of person people describe as always having a smile on her face. We might describe Derek, however, as having traits such as suspiciousness and introversion. Based on these traits, they might expect Derek to shun social interactions and to feel that people are always taking advantage of him.

Trait theorists are interested in learning how people differ in their underlying traits. They are also interested in measuring traits and understanding how traits are organized or structured within the personality. Some trait theorists believe that traits are largely innate or inborn; others argue that traits are largely acquired through experience. In this module, we focus on the contributions of several prominent trait theorists, beginning with an early contributor to the trait perspective, Gordon Allport.

Gordon Allport: A Hierarchy of Traits

To Gordon Allport (1897–1967), personality traits are inherited but are influenced by experience. He claimed that traits could be ranked within a hierarchy in relation to the degree to which they influence behavior (Allport, 1961). **Cardinal traits** are at the highest level. They are pervasive characteristics that influence a person's behavior in most situations. For example, we might describe the cardinal trait in Martin Luther King's personality as the commitment to social justice. Yet Allport believed that relatively few people possess such dominant traits. More common but less wide-reaching traits are **central traits**, the basic building blocks of personality that influence behavior in many situations. Examples of central traits are characteristics such as competitiveness, generosity, independence, arrogance, and fearfulness—the kinds of traits you would generally use when describing the general characteristics of other people's behavior. At a more superficial level are **secondary traits**, such as preferences for particular styles of clothing or types of music, which affect behavior in fewer situations.

Raymond Cattell: Mapping the Personality

Trait theorist Raymond Cattell (1905–1998) believed that there are two basic levels of traits (Cattell, 1950, 1965). **Surface traits** lie on the "surface" of personality. They are characteristics of personality that can be inferred from observations of behavior. Surface traits are associated with adjectives commonly used to describe personality, such as friendliness, stubbornness, emotionality, and carelessness. Cattell observed that surface traits often occur together. A person others see as stubborn also tends to be perceived as rigid and foul tempered. These linkages suggested that there is a deeper level of personality consisting of more general, underlying traits that give rise

The Brain Loves a Puzzle

As you read ahead, use the information in the text to solve the following puzzle:

How might your personality traits contribute to living a longer and healthier life?

Jose Luis Pelaez Inc/Blend Images/Getty Images

CONCEPT 11.9
Allport believed that personality traits are ordered in a hierarchy of importance from cardinal traits at the highest level through central traits and secondary traits at the lower levels.

CONCEPT 11.10
Raymond Cattell believed the structure of personality consists of two levels of traits: surface traits that correspond to ordinary descriptions of personality, and a deeper level comprising more general traits, called source traits, that give rise to surface traits.

traits Relatively enduring personal characteristics.

cardinal traits Allport's term for the more pervasive dimensions that define an individual's general personality.

central traits Allport's term for personality characteristics that have a widespread influence on the individual's behavior across situations.

secondary traits Allport's term for specific traits that influence behavior in relatively few situations.

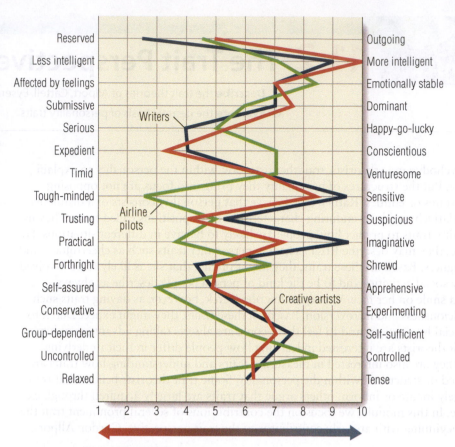

FIGURE 11.2 **Cattell's 16PF**
The 16PF is a personality test that compares individuals on 16 source traits or key dimensions of personality, each of which is represented on a continuum ranging from one polar extreme to the other. Here we see the average scores of samples composed of three occupational groups: creative artists, airline pilots, and writers. Notice the differences in the personalities in these groups. For example, compared to the other groups, airline pilots tend to be more controlled, self-assured, and relaxed—traits that should help put airline passengers at ease.

Source: Adapted from Cattell, Eber, & Tatsuoka, 1970.

surface traits Cattell's term for personality traits at the surface level that can be gleaned from observations of behavior.

source traits Cattell's term for traits at a deep level of personality that are not apparent in observed behavior but must be inferred based on underlying relationships among surface traits.

introversion–extraversion Tendencies toward being solitary and reserved on the one end or outgoing and sociable on the other end.

to surface traits. To explore this deeper level, Cattell used statistical techniques to map the structure of personality by analyzing the relationships among surface traits (Horn, 2001). Through this work, he derived a set of more general factors of personality, which he called **source traits**. Cattell went on to construct a paper-and-pencil personality scale to measure 16 source traits, which he called the Sixteen Personality Factor Questionnaire, or 16PF. Each trait on the 16PF is represented on a continuum, such as "reserved versus outgoing." ■ Figure 11.2 compares the scores of groups of writers, airline pilots, and creative artists on the 16PF. To compare your personality with those in Figure 11.2, see the Try This Out feature.

Hans Eysenck: A Simpler Trait Model

In contrast to Cattell's model, which organized personality traits into a complex hierarchy, Hans Eysenck (1916–1997) constructed a simpler model of personality. This model describes personality using three major traits (Eysenck, 1981):

1. **Introversion-extraversion**—People who are introverted are solitary, reserved, and unsocial, whereas those who are extraverted are outgoing, talkative, cheerful, friendly, and people oriented.

Table 11.3 Eysenck's Personality Types

	Extraverted		
Emotionally Unstable (High Neuroticism)	**Unstable/Extraverted** Restless Excitable Changeable Active Impulsive Aggressive	Outgoing Talkative Sociable Lively Carefree Easygoing **Stable/Extraverted**	**Emotionally Stable (Low Neuroticism)**
	Unstable/Introverted Anxious Moody Pessimistic Quiet Unsociable Reserved	Controlled Passive Thoughtful **Stable/Introverted** Calm Reliable Careful	
	Introverted		

2. **Neuroticism**—People who are high on neuroticism, or emotional instability, tend to be tense, anxious, worrisome, restless, and moody. Those who are low on neuroticism tend to be relaxed, calm, stable, and even-tempered.

3. **Psychoticism**—People who are high on psychoticism are perceived as cold, antisocial, hostile, and insensitive. Those who are low on psychoticism are described as warm, sensitive, and concerned about others.

Eysenck classified people according to four basic personality types based on combinations of introversion–extraversion and neuroticism: (1) extraverted-neurotic, (2) extraverted-stable, (3) introverted-stable, and (4) introverted-neurotic (Eysenck, 1982). Table 11.3 shows these four types, represented by the four quadrants of the table, along with commonly observed characteristics identified with each type.

Eysenck believed that biological differences are responsible for variations in personality traits from person to person. He argued that introverts inherit a nervous system that operates at a higher level of arousal than does that of extraverts. Consequently, introverts require less stimulation to maintain an optimal level of arousal. An introvert would be most comfortable enjoying quiet activities. Extraverts may require more stimulation to raise their arousal to optimal levels, which could explain why they are drawn to more exciting activities. It would come as no surprise to Eysenck that a group of mountain climbers who were attempting to scale Mt. Everest, the world's tallest peak, scored high on extraversion (Egan & Stelmack, 2003). They were also low on neuroticism (emotional instability), which is a good thing if you happen to be climbing the face of a mountain.

The Five-Factor Model of Personality: The "Big Five"

The most widely used trait model of personality today is the **five-factor model (FFM)**, or Big Five model (McCrae et al., 2004). This model captures the five broad factors most consistently found in research on personality traits across a number

neuroticism Tendencies toward emotional instability, anxiety, and worry.

psychoticism Tendencies to be perceived as cold and antisocial.

five-factor model (FFM) The dominant contemporary trait model of personality, consisting of five broad personality factors: neuroticism, extraversion, openness, agreeableness, and conscientiousness.

Conscientiousness tends to increase from late adolescence through early adulthood as people assume more career and family responsibilities.

CONCEPT 11.11

Eysenck believed that the combinations of three general traits of introversion–extraversion, neuroticism, and psychoticism could be used to classify basic personality types.

CONCEPT 11.12

The five-factor model of personality—the Big Five—identifies the five most common personality factors derived from research on personality.

of cultures (Hofstee, 2003; McCrae & Terracciano, 2005; Widiger, 2005). The Big Five isn't so much a new set of personality traits as a consolidation and integration of traits previously identified by Cattell, Eysenck, and other trait theorists. In fact, the first two traits, *neuroticism* and *extraversion,* parallel those in Eysenck's model. The three other factors making up the Big Five are *openness to new experiences, agreeableness,* and *conscientiousness* (see Table 11.4). Researchers believe that Big Five factors have a substantial genetic component (Lewis & Bates, 2014; Smillie, 2013).

The Big Five is useful in predicting many behaviors, including how well students do in college. Neuroticism (emotional instability) is linked to lower grades, whereas conscientiousness is associated with higher grades and with stronger performance motivation (setting goals and pursuing them) (e.g., Cheng & Ickes, 2009; Conrad & Patry, 2012; Poropat, 2009; Vedel, 2014). Lower levels of neuroticism and higher levels of extraversion and agreeableness are associated with better mental health (Lamers et al., 2012). Similarly, higher neuroticism (lower emotional stability) tracks to poorer adjustment among adolescents and greater likelihood of depression among college students (Hutchinson & Williams, 2007; Vazsonyi et al., 2015). Moreover, more agreeable people tend to be more giving and cooperative, report greater satisfaction in their relationships, and tend to drive more safely (less aggressively) than less agreeable people (Cellar, Nelson, & Yorke, 2000; Graziano & Tobin, 2009; White, Hendrick, & Hendrick, 2004). But these personality factors are not fixed. For example, conscientiousness tends to increase in early adulthood from about age 18 to about age 40, which represents the time of life when people tend to take on more career and family responsibilities (Bleidorn, 2015). Put more plainly, it is typically during young adulthood that reality bites and that people face the need to develop more conscientious habits to meet their developing adult responsibilities.

One of the Big Five factors, conscientiousness, also ties into longevity (Friedman et al., 2014; Jokela et al., 2013). Higher conscientiousness is associated with living a longer and healthier life, in part because conscientious people tend to take better care of their health (controlling their weight, not smoking, exercising regularly) and avoid reckless behaviors, such as unsafe driving (Bogg & Roberts, 2013; Friedman et al., 2014; Israel et al., 2014; Shanahan et al., 2014).

Success in school may have more to do with personality traits than intelligence (Poropat, 2014). To achieve academic success, students need to be able to organize

Table 11.4 **The Big Five Trait Model**

Personality Factor	Description
Neuroticism	Prone to anxiety, worry, guilt, emotional instability versus relaxed, calm, secure, emotionally stable
Extraversion	Outgoing, friendly, enthusiastic, fun loving versus solitary, shy, serious, reserved
Openness to new experiences	Imaginative, curious, intellectual, open to nontraditional values versus conforming, practical, conventional
Agreeableness	Sensitive, warm, tolerant, easy to get along with, concerned with other's feelings and needs versus cold, suspicious, hostile, callous
Conscientiousness	Reliable, responsible, self-disciplined, ethical, hard working, ambitious versus disorganized, unreliable, lax, impulsive, careless

Sources: Adapted from Costa & McCrae, 1992a, 1992b; Goldberg, 1993; McCrae & Costa, 1986, 1996.

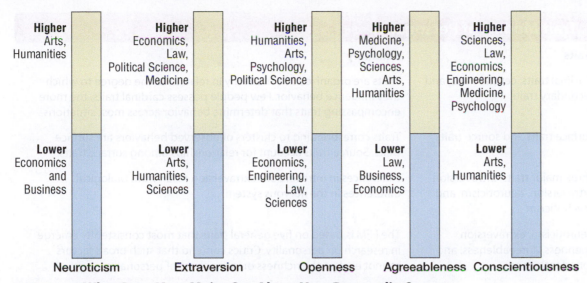

Higher Arts, Humanities	**Higher** Economics, Law, Political Science, Medicine	**Higher** Humanities, Arts, Psychology, Political Science	**Higher** Medicine, Psychology, Sciences, Arts, Humanities	**Higher** Sciences, Law, Economics, Engineering, Medicine, Psychology
Lower Economics and Business	**Lower** Arts, Humanities, Sciences	**Lower** Economics, Engineering, Law, Sciences	**Lower** Law, Business, Economics	**Lower** Arts, Humanities
Neuroticism	Extraversion	Openness	Agreeableness	Conscientiousness

FIGURE 11.3 What Does Your Major Say About Your Personality?
Comparisons between college students in different major areas of study show some interesting personality differences. How well does your major suit your personality?

Source: Vedel, 2016.

and apply themselves and be open to new learning and experiences—traits which map to Big Five traits of conscientiousness and openness. The good news is that personality can change over time, especially traits of conscientiousness and openness to new experiences (Letzring, Edmonds, & Hampson, 2014).

Personality differences also emerge when we compare students in different major areas of study. A recent review of students in North American and European universities showed some intriguing differences (Vedel, 2016) (see ■ Figure 11.3). Did you know, for example, that students in the humanities, the arts, and psychology and political science, tend to be more open to new experiences than those in economics, engineering, or the law?

Big Five traits also relate to how people use social networking sites. More extraverted students tend to use Facebook more often and to update their social activities more frequently than do less extraverted students (Eftekhar, Fullwood, & Morris, 2014; Marshall, Lefringhausen, & Ferenczi, 2015; Lee, Ahn, & Kim, 2014). More extraverted students also tend to have more Facebook friends, as well as more friends in the real world. This suggests that extraversion in the real world carries over to the online world of social media.

What else might your online behavior tell us about your personality? To find out, investigators analyzed digital footprints, in this case the "likes" people post on Facebook (Youyou, Kosinski, & Stillwell, 2015). They also had participants take a personality test measuring the Big Five traits. They then matched their personality scores to judgments that other people who knew them well made of their personality traits and to predictions made by a computer based on the person's "likes." The computer analysis of "likes" did rather well, better in fact than using other people as judges. The computer needed only 10 likes to outperform a work colleague, 70 likes to beat the judgments made by friends, and 300 likes to outperform a person's spouse. A takeaway message from this research is that our likes, whether they are Mexican food, romantic walks on the beach, or bungee jumping, provide digital footprints a computer can analyze to reveal aspects of our personalities. We might even get to the point when computers "know" us better than we know ourselves.

Extraverted people tend to have more friends in both the real and virtual worlds than do less extraverted people.

Concept Chart 11.2 Trait Models of Personality

Trait Theorist/Model	Traits	Summary
Gordon Allport	Cardinal traits, central traits, and secondary traits	Traits are organized in a hierarchy in relation to the degree to which they influence behavior. Few people possess cardinal traits, the more encompassing traits that determine behavior across most situations.
Raymond Cattell	Surface traits and source traits	Traits corresponding to clusters of observed behaviors are surface traits. Source traits account for relationships among surface traits.
Hans Eysenck	Three major traits: introversion–extraversion, neuroticism, and psychoticism	Differences in introversion–extraversion result from biological differences in the nervous system.
Five-Factor Model (FFM): The Big Five	Neuroticism, extraversion, openness, agreeableness, and conscientiousness	The FFM is based on five general traits that most consistently emerge in research on personality. Critics contend that such broad factors cannot explain the richness or uniqueness of personality.

Investigators also learned from studying social media sites that young adults who are higher on neuroticism (more poorly adjusted) tend to present more of a fake or idealized image of themselves on their Facebook profiles (Michikyan, Subrahmanyam, & Dennis, 2014). They may not feel that others would want to interact with them if their profiles were a more accurate depiction of their true selves.

Is the Big Five the final word on describing the structure of personality? Perhaps not. For one thing, the Big Five factors may not be as independent of each other as many investigators believe. Or perhaps more factors (a *Big Seven?*), or a different set of factors, may provide a better approximation of the individual variations among people in their psychological traits that we conceptualize as personality (Loehlin, 2012; Simms, 2007). Then again, perhaps any model that reduces personality to only a few broadly defined categories fails to capture the richness and uniqueness of personality or account for an individual's behavior in specific contexts.

In Concept Chart 11.2, you'll find a review of the major trait models of personality.

The Genetic Basis of Traits: Moving Beyond the Nature–Nurture Debate

CONCEPT 11.13

Psychologists are moving beyond the nature–nurture debate to examine how heredity and environment interact in the development of personality.

CONCEPT LINK

The interaction of genetic and environmental factors is implicated in the development of many psychological disorders, such as schizophrenia. See Module 13.5.

Evidence supports the role of genetics in many personality traits, including the Big Five traits, as well as shyness, aggressiveness, sociability, and novelty seeking (for example, Archontaki, Lewis, & Bates, 2012; Laceulle et al., 2013; Lewis & Bates, 2014). Overall, about 40 percent of the variability in personality traits among people may be explained by genetics, whereas environmental factors account for about 60 percent (Vukasović & Bratko, 2015).

Researchers today are moving beyond the old nature–nurture debate. They understand that the relationship between biology and environment is a two-way street. Genetic factors influence the development of personality traits, and environmental influences, such as life experiences, affect the developing brain in ways that influence personality development.

Evaluating the Trait Perspective

Let us note on the positive side of the ledger that the trait perspective has intuitive appeal. People commonly use trait terms when describing their own and other people's personalities. We might describe Samantha as cold or callous, but think of Li Ming as kind and compassionate. Thus, trait theories are useful to the extent that they provide convenient categories or groupings of traits that people commonly use. Trait theories have also proved to be useful in the development of many personality tests, including Cattell's 16PF and the Eysenck Personality Inventory. Psychologists use these tests to compare how people score on different traits.

Personality traits tend to be relatively stable over time (Costa & McCrae, 2006; Roberts, Walton, & Viechtbauer, 2006a, 2006b). That said, we should not think of personality as fixed early in life or "set like plaster" by the time we enter adulthood. Rather, personality traits often do change over time, although at a somewhat slower pace as the person ages (Boyce, Wood, & Powdthavee, 2012; Mroczek, 2014). For example, people tend to become more agreeable (friendlier) as they age, and as mentioned earlier, more conscientious (Lucas & Donnellan, 2009). These types of changes indicate that people tend to become better adapted to their environments as they get older.

Trait theories do have their drawbacks, however. Perhaps the major criticism is that trait theories merely attach a label to behavior rather than explaining it. Consider the following example:

1. You can always count on Mary. She's very reliable.
2. Why is Mary reliable? Because she is a conscientious person.
3. How do you know she is a conscientious person? Because she's reliable.

This is an example of *circular reasoning*—that is, explaining Mary's behavior on the basis of a trait ("conscientiousness"), which you infer based on observing the very same behaviors you are trying to explain. Traits may offer nothing more than shorthand descriptions of the behaviors we observe in others, with little to offer in explaining the underlying causes of the behaviors. Even as descriptions, trait theories are based on broadly defined traits, such as the Big Five, that may not fully capture the unique characteristics of individuals.

Another argument against trait theories is that behavior may not be as stable across time and situations as trait theorists suppose. How you act with your boss, for example, may be different from how you act around the house. How you relate to people today may be very different from how you related to people in the past. Learning theorists argue that we need to take into account environmental or situational factors, such as stimulus cues and reinforcements, in order to more accurately predict behavior (Sherman, Nave, & Funder, 2010).

A developing consensus in the field is emerging around the concept of *interactionism*—the belief that both personality traits and situational factors, and the interactions between them, influence behavior (Fleeson & Noftle, 2009; Sherman et al., 2015; Webster, 2009). Situational factors clearly affect behavior in that people tend to act differently in different situations depending upon the particular demands they face. But we also need to account for the fact that people tend to have typical ways of acting that cut across various situations.

Measurement of personality traits in humans is well established, but what about assessing personality traits in other species, such as dogs, cats, or apes? Investigators find that people who rate orangutans higher on Big Five personality traits of extraversion, neuroticism, and agreeableness also tend to rate the animals higher on general well-being—findings that dovetail with research with both chimpanzees and humans (Stambor, 2006b; Weiss, King, & Perkins, 2006). Personality traits in apes are also related to greater longevity, as research with

CONCEPT 11.14
Though trait theories provide convenient ways of describing personality features, they have been criticized on grounds of circular reasoning and failure to account for differences in behavior across situations.

DULLO/Renee Lynn/Corbis

Many dog and cat owners believe their pets have distinct personalities. Recent evidence indicates that judgments of personality traits in dogs achieve as much agreement among raters as judgments of traits in humans. Do other animals have personalities? What do you think?

gorillas shows links between greater extraversion and longer lifespans (Gartner, 2015; Weiss et al., 2013). We also have evidence that people tend to agree in their ratings of personality traits of apes (Weiss et al., 2015). But we still face the fundamental question of whether it's the case that animals themselves have distinct personalities or that people merely impose human categories onto other species? What do you think?

MODULE REVIEW   11.2   The Trait Perspective

Recite It

5. **Describe** the trait theories of Allport, Cattell, Eysenck, and the Big Five model.

Allport distinguished between (a) _____ traits (pervasive characteristics that govern behavior), (b) _____ traits (more commonly found general characteristics around which behavior is organized), and (c) _____ traits (interests or dispositions that influence behavior in specific situations).
Cattell believed that traits are organized in terms of (d) _____ traits (consistencies in a person's observed behavior) and (e) _____ traits (general, underlying traits that account for relationships among surface traits).

Eysenck believed that variations in personality could generally be explained in terms of three major traits: introversion–extraversion, (f) _____, and psychoticism.
The Big Five (neuroticism, extraversion, (g) _____, agreeableness, conscientiousness) are five broad dimensions or traits that have consistently emerged in personality research.

6. **Evaluate** the genetic basis of personality traits.

Genetic influences are implicated in many personality traits, including neuroticism, shyness, aggressiveness, and (h) _____ seeking. Scientists today are exploring how genes interact with (i) _____ influences in the development of personality.

Recall It

1. In the field of personality, relatively stable or enduring characteristics or dispositions are called _____.

2. In Gordon Allport's view, the most common characteristics that form the basic building blocks of personality are

   a. cardinal traits.   c. secondary traits.
   b. central traits.   d. universal traits.

3. The 16PF Questionnaire, developed by Raymond Cattell, is designed to measure

   a. source traits.   c. introversion–extraversion.
   b. surface traits.   d. psychoticism traits.

4. Among the personality psychologists discussed in this module, who described personality on the basis of three major traits?

5. The personality dimensions of neuroticism, extraversion, openness, agreeableness, and conscientiousness together constitute

   a. the Eysenck Personality Inventory.
   b. the 16PF.
   c. the Big Five model of personality.
   d. the MMPI.

6. Name some of the personality characteristics for which a genetic link has been supported.

Think About It

■ What psychological traits would you use to describe your personality? What traits do you believe others might use to describe you? How do you account for any differences?

■ Do you believe that your personality traits are fixed or unchangeable? Or might your personality be open to adjustment here and there? What would you like to change about yourself and how you relate to others?

Recite It *answers placed at the end of chapter.*

11.3 The Social-Cognitive Perspective

7 Describe the social-cognitive theories of Rotter, Bandura, and Mischel.

Some psychologists proposed models of personality that were quite different from those of Freud and the trait theorists. Behaviorists such as John Watson and B. F. Skinner believed that personality is shaped by environmental influences (rewards and punishments), not by unconscious influences, as in Freud's theory, or by underlying traits, as the trait theorists believed. The behaviorists believed that personality consists of the sum total of an individual's learned behavior. Consider your own personality as a behaviorist might view it. Others may see you as friendly and outgoing; but to a behaviorist, terms like *friendly* and *outgoing* are merely labels describing a set of behaviors, such as showing an interest in others and participating in a wide range of social activities.

Behaviorists believe that behavior is learned on the basis of classical and operant conditioning. Rather than probe the depths of your unconscious to understand the roots of your behavior, behaviorists might explore how you were reinforced in the past for displaying friendly and outgoing behaviors. People with different histories of rewards and punishments develop different patterns of behavior. If Maisha is respectful and conscientious in her work habits, it is because she has been rewarded for this kind of behavior in the past. If Tyler spends more time socializing than studying, it is likely he has been reinforced more for social interactions than for academic performance.

Many learning theorists today adopt a broader view of learning than did the traditional behaviorists, such as Watson and Skinner. This contemporary model, called **social-cognitive theory**, maintains that to explain behavior we need to take into account cognitive and social aspects of behavior, not just the rewards and punishments to which we are exposed in the environment. These social and cognitive variables include expectancies we hold about the outcomes of our behavior, the values we place on rewards, and the learning that occurs through imitating the behavior of others we observe interacting in social situations. To social-cognitive theorists, personality comprises not only learned behavior but also the ways individuals think about themselves and the world around them. They believe that people act upon the environment in pursuing their goals, not just react to it (Bandura, 2006). The three primary contributors to social-cognitive theory are the psychologists Julian Rotter, Albert Bandura, and Walter Mischel.

Julian Rotter: The Locus of Control

To Julian Rotter (1990), explaining and predicting behavior involves knowing an individual's reinforcement history as well as the person's expectancies and subjective values. **Expectancies** are your personal predictions of the outcomes of your behavior. For example, students who hold a positive expectancy about schoolwork believe that studying will improve their chances of getting good grades. **Subjective value** is the worth you place on desired outcomes. A dedicated student will place a high subjective value on getting good grades. In this instance, a student with high positive expectancy and high subjective value would be more likely to study for a forthcoming exam than someone who does not link studying with grades or who does not care about grades.

CONCEPT 11.15
To behaviorists, the concept of personality refers to the sum total of an individual's learned behavior.

CONCEPT 11.16
Social-cognitive theorists expanded traditional learning theory by focusing on the cognitive and social-learning aspects of behavior.

CONCEPT 11.17
Social-cognitive theorists believe that personality consists of individuals' repertoires of behavior and ways of thinking about themselves and the world.

social-cognitive theory A contemporary learning-based model that emphasizes the roles of cognitive and environmental factors in determining behavior.

expectancies In social-cognitive theory, personal predictions about the outcomes of behavior.

subjective value In social-cognitive theory, the importance individuals place on desired outcomes.

CONCEPT 11.18
Rotter believed that our ability to explain and predict behavior depends on knowing an individual's reinforcement history as well as the person's expectancies, subjective values, and perceptions of control.

CONCEPT LINK

Perceptions of control and predictability are important factors in determining a person's ability to cope with stressful life events. See Module 10.1.

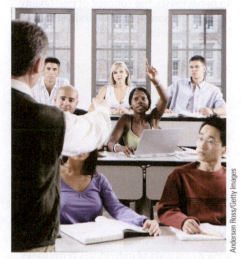

Belief in one's ability to succeed in college, or high academic self-efficacy, is actually a stronger predictor of college grades than either high school grades or standardized test scores.

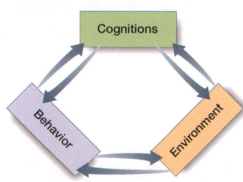

FIGURE 11.4 Bandura's Model of Reciprocal Determinism
Bandura believes that cognitions, behaviors, and environmental factors are reciprocally determined, which means that they mutually influence each other.

Source: Adapted from Bandura, 1986.

CONCEPT 11.19
Bandura's model of reciprocal determinism holds that cognitions, behaviors, and environmental factors mutually influence each other.

Rotter also believed that people acquire general expectancies about their ability to obtain reinforcements in their lives. Some, for example, have an internal **locus of control** (*locus* is the Latin word for "place"). They believe they can obtain reinforcements through their work and effort. People with an external locus of control (LOC) believe that outcomes in life, and the rewards or reinforcements they receive, are controlled by external forces beyond their control, such as luck or fate. Locus of control is linked to various outcomes. For example, an external locus is linked to symptoms of depression and anxiety (Cheng et al., 2013). People with an internal LOC are more likely than "externals" to succeed in school (Gifford, Briceño-Perriott, & Mianzo, 2006), to cope with pain (Coughlin et al., 2000), and, in overweight people, make changes in diet and exercise patterns (Holt, Clark, & Kreuter, 2001).

Albert Bandura: Reciprocal Determinism and the Role of Expectancies

Albert Bandura sees people as active agents in directing their lives (Bandura, 2006, 2008b, 2010). As Bandura notes, "They [people] are not simply onlookers of their behavior. They are contributors to their life circumstances, not just products of them" (Bandura, 2006, p. 164). His model of **reciprocal determinism** holds that cognitions, behaviors, and environmental factors influence each other (see ■ Figure 11.4). Bandura focuses on the interaction between what we do (our behavior) and what we think (our cognitions). For example, suppose a motorist is cut off by another motorist on the road. The first motorist may think angering thoughts, such as "I'm going to teach that guy a lesson." These thoughts or cognitions increase the likelihood of aggressive behavior (for example, cutting in front of the other motorist). The aggressive behavior, in turn, affects the social environment (the other motorist responds aggressively). The other motorist's actions then led the first to have even more angering thoughts ("I can't let him get away with that!"), which, in turn, led to more aggressive behavior. This vicious cycle of escalating aggressive behavior and angering thoughts may result in an incident of *road rage,* which can have tragic consequences.

Bandura (1989, 1997) emphasized the role of observational learning, or learning by observing and imitating the behavior of others in social contexts. He also emphasized the importance of two cognitive variables: outcome expectations and efficacy expectations.

Outcome expectations are predictions of the outcomes of behavior. You are more likely to drink alcohol in a social situation if you believe it will be a pleasant experience and perhaps increase your self-confidence than if you think it will make you sick or act silly.

Efficacy expectations are predictions you hold about your ability to perform tasks or behaviors you set out to accomplish. People with high self-efficacy stay the course when confronting difficult challenges. They are likely to undertake challenges and persevere in the face of adversity because they believe they can surmount obstacles placed in their path. People with low self-efficacy tend to give up easily in the face of difficulties (Bandura, 2006). Success also boosts efficacy expectations. This is one reason that success experiences are important to children and adults alike.

Self-efficacy is linked to success in a number of ways. High levels of academic performance self-efficacy in students (believing they will succeed in class if they apply themselves) is a stronger predictor of college GPA than even high school GPA or SAT or ACT scores (Richardson, Abraham, & Bond, 2012). Ex-smokers with greater self-efficacy are less likely to relapse after quitting smoking and more likely to maintain regular physical activity (Gwaltney et al., 2009). People high in self-efficacy also tend to do better than others in mending their lives following calamitous events, such as natural disasters and terrorist attacks (Benight & Bandura, 2004).

Walter Mischel: Situation Versus Person Variables

Walter Mischel's (1973) theoretical model overlaps to a large extent with Rotter's and Bandura's. Mischel argued that behavior is influenced by both **situation variables**, which are environmental factors such as rewards and punishments, and **person variables**, or internal personal factors. Two of these person variables, *expectancies* and *subjective values,* have the same meaning as in Rotter's model. But Mischel adds other person variables, including

- *Competencies,* or the knowledge and skills we possess, such as the ability to play an instrument or to speak a foreign language;
- *Encoding strategies,* or personal perceptions of events, such as whether we see a sudden gift of a basket of flowers as a gesture of love or as a way of making amends; and
- *Self-regulatory systems and plans,* or ability to plan a course of action to achieve our goals and to reward ourselves for accomplishing them.

In Mischel's view, as in Bandura's, environmental and personal factors interact to produce behavior. In predicting a specific person's behavior, we need to take into account what we know about the person as well as the situation at hand.

In his more recent work, Mischel has focused on the interactions of emotions (affects) and cognitions (for example, Mischel, 2009). One example is how negative feeling states such as depression cast a dim outlook on the ways that people encode experiences and form expectancies about future outcomes. But Mischel also recognizes that emotional reactions, in turn, depend on how we interpret and label experiences, a point to which we shall return when we consider cognitive theories of depression in Chapter 13.

Evaluating the Social-Cognitive Perspective

Learning theorists have increased our understanding of how behavior is influenced by environmental factors, such as a history of rewards and punishments. Reinforcement principles are now applied in a wide range of programs, including those designed to help parents learn better parenting skills and to help children learn more effectively in the classroom. Learning theory has also given rise to a major contemporary model of psychotherapy, *behavior therapy,* in which learning principles are applied to help people deal with emotional and behavioral problems (see Chapter 14).

Social-cognitive theorists broadened the scope of learning theory to include cognitive influences on learning and the recognition that much of what we learn occurs by observing others in social contexts. Today, many behavior therapists subscribe to a broader treatment model, called *cognitive-behavioral therapy,* or *CBT* (see Chapter 14), which incorporates cognitive as well as behavioral approaches to therapy and mirrors the teachings of the social-cognitive theorists. But perhaps the most important influence of the social-cognitive theorists is that they have presented us with a view of people as active seekers and interpreters of information, not just responders to environmental influences. Indeed, many psychologists have come to believe that behavior is best explained by the reciprocal interactions between the person and the environment.

To some of its critics, social-cognitive theory presents a limited view of personality because it fails to account for the roles of unconscious influences and heredity. To others, specifically trait theorists, social-cognitive theorists fail to take personality traits into account when attempting to explain underlying consistencies in behavior across situations. Social-cognitive theorists would counter that traits don't explain behavior

Uli Wiesmeier/Cusp/Corbis

"I can do this." Bandura's social-cognitive model of personality emphasizes the importance of cognitive factors such as self-efficacy—the belief in our ability to accomplish tasks we set out to do.

CONCEPT 11.20
Mischel proposed that behavior is influenced both by environmental factors, called situation variables, and by internal personal factors, called person variables.

CONCEPT 11.21
Though social-cognitive theory broadened traditional learning theory, critics claim that it doesn't account for unconscious processes and genetic factors in personality.

locus of control In Rotter's theory, one's general expectancies about whether one's efforts can bring about desired outcomes or reinforcements.

reciprocal determinism Bandura's model in which cognitions, behaviors, and environmental factors influence and are influenced by each other.

outcome expectations Bandura's term for our personal predictions about the outcomes of our behavior.

efficacy expectations Bandura's term for the expectancies we have regarding our ability to perform behaviors we set out to accomplish.

situation variables Mischel's term for environmental influences on behavior, such as rewards and punishments.

Concept Chart 11.3   Behavioral and Social-Cognitive Perspectives on Personality

	Traditional Behaviorism	Social-Cognitive Theory
	Personality is the sum total of an individual's learned behavior; distinctive patterns of behavior are determined by differences in learning experiences.	Personality consists of both learned behaviors and ways of thinking. We need to attend to the role of cognitions and observational learning to explain and predict behavior, not just to the role of environmental influences such as rewards and punishments.

© Elnur/ShutterSstock.com

but merely attach labels to behavior—and, moreover, that behavior is not as consistent across situations as trait theorists may suppose. Finally, social-cognitive theory is criticized by those who believe that it focuses too little on subjective experience, such as self-awareness and the flow of consciousness. Social-cognitive theorists may believe that the emphasis they place on cognitive factors, such as expectancies and subjective values, addresses these concerns. As you'll see next, subjective experience takes center stage in another perspective on personality, the humanistic approach. But first you may want to review Concept Chart 11.3, which summarizes the major concepts associated with the behavioral and social-cognitive perspectives on personality.

person variables Mischel's term for internal personal factors that influence behavior, including competencies, expectancies, and subjective values.

MODULE REVIEW   11.3   The Social-Cognitive Perspective

Recite It

7. Describe the social-cognitive theories of Rotter, Bandura, and Mischel.

Rotter believed that to explain and predict behavior we need to take into account a person's (a) _____ (personal predictions about the outcomes of events) and (b) _____ values (worth placed on particular goals).

Bandura proposed the principle of (c) _____ determinism—the belief that cognitions, behaviors,

and environmental factors mutually influence each other.

Mischel proposed that both (d) _____ variables (environmental influences such as rewards and punishments) and (e) _____ variables (factors relating to the person such as competencies, expectancies, (f) _____ strategies, subjective values, and self-regulatory systems and plans) are needed to explain and predict behavior.

Recall It

1. Unlike Freudian and trait theorists, behaviorists believe that personality is due to

  a. deep, underlying unconscious conflicts.
  b. the sum total of a person's history of reinforcements and punishments.
  c. the ways we think about ourselves and the world.
  d. the ways we think about others in the world.

2. According to Julian Rotter, the individual who expects a good outcome due to hard work and effort has a(n) _____ locus of control.

  a. internal   **c.** external
  b. positive   **d.** negative

3. Describe Albert Bandura's concept of *reciprocal determinism.*

4. Match the following terms with the appropriate descriptions: (a) self-efficacy; (b) situation variables; (c) competencies; (d) encoding strategies.

  i. personal perceptions of events
  ii. belief in personal effectiveness
  iii. personal knowledge and skills
  iv. environmental influences

MODULE 11.4 The Humanistic Perspective

8 Describe the self-theory of humanistic theorist Carl Rogers.

9 Explain the difference between the concepts of self in collectivistic and individualistic cultures.

10 Apply suggestions for enhancing self-esteem.

Humanistic psychology departed from the psychodynamic and behaviorist schools in proposing that conscious choice and personal freedom are central features of what it means to be a human being (Grogan, 2013). To humanistic psychologists, we are not puppets whose movements are controlled by strings pulled by the unconscious mind or the environment; rather, we are endowed with the ability to make free choices that give meaning and personal direction to our lives. Two of the major contributors to humanistic thought were the American psychologists Carl Rogers (1902–1987) and Abraham Maslow (1908–1970).

Carl Rogers: The Importance of Self

Rogers (1961, 1980) believed that each of us possesses an inner drive that leads us to strive toward *self-actualization*—toward realizing our own unique potentials. The roadway toward self-actualization is an unfolding process of self-discovery and self-awareness, of tapping into our true feelings and needs, accepting them as our own, and acting in ways that genuinely reflect them. To Rogers and other humanists, personality is expressed through the conscious experience of directing ourselves toward fulfilling our unique potentials as human beings.

Rogers believed that the self is the center of the human experience. Thus it is no surprise that he referred to his theory of personality as **self-theory**. To Rogers, the self is the executive part of your personality that organizes how you relate to the world. It is the sense of being "I" or "me"—the person who looks back at you in the mirror, the sense of being a distinct individual with your own likes, dislikes, needs, and values. The self also includes the impressions you have of yourself, impressions that constitute your *self-concept*. The theory of personality Rogers developed reflects the importance of coming to know yourself and being true to yourself, regardless of what others might think or say.

One of the primary functions of the self, as Rogers viewed it, is to develop self-esteem, or a degree of liking for ourselves. Rogers noted that self-esteem at first mirrors how other people value us, or fail to value us. For this reason, he believed it is crucial for parents to bestow on their children **unconditional positive regard**, or

CONCEPT 11.22
Rogers's theory of personality emphasizes the importance of the self, the sense of the "I" or "me" that organizes how you relate to the world.

CONCEPT LINK
The importance of the self is emphasized in the model of therapy Rogers developed, called client-centered therapy. See Module 14.1.

self-theory Rogers's model of personality, which focuses on the importance of the self.

unconditional positive regard Valuing another person as having intrinsic worth, regardless of the person's behavior at the particular time.

The makings of unconditional positive regard?

Psychologist Kenneth Clark observing as an African American child selects a White doll over a Black doll to play with.

conditional positive regard Valuing a person only when the person's behavior meets certain expectations or standards.

self-ideals Rogers's term for the idealized sense of how or what we should be.

acceptance of a person's basic worth regardless of whether their behavior pleases or suits us. In other words, Rogers believed that parents should prize their children regardless of their behavior at any particular moment in time. In this way, children learn to value themselves as having intrinsic worth, rather than judging themselves as either good or bad depending on whether they measure up to other people's expectations or demands. Rogers didn't mean that parents should turn a blind eye toward undesirable behavior. Parents do not need to accept all of their children's behavior; they can correct their children's poor behavior without damaging their self-esteem. However, parents need to clarify that it is the *behavior* that is undesirable, not the child.

Unfortunately, many parents show **conditional positive regard** toward their children. They bestow approval only when the children behave "properly." Children given conditional positive regard may learn to think of themselves as being worthwhile only when they are behaving in socially approved ways. Their self-esteem may become shaky, as it comes to depend on what other people think of them at a particular moment in time. To maintain self-esteem, they may need to deny their genuine feelings, interests, and desires. They learn to wear masks or to don social facades to please others. Their sense of themselves, or self-concept, may become so distorted that they feel like strangers to themselves. They may come to question who they really are.

Our self-esteem is ultimately a function of how close we come to meeting our **self-ideals**—our idealized sense of who or what we should be. When these ideals are shaped by what others expect of us, we may have a hard time measuring up to them. Our self-esteem may plummet. The model of therapy Rogers developed, called *client-centered therapy* (also called *person-centered therapy;* see Chapter 14), helps people get in touch with their true feelings and come to value and prize themselves.

Rogers was an optimist who believed in the essential worth and goodness of human nature. He believed that people become hurtful toward each other only when their own pathways toward self-actualization are blocked or stymied by obstacles. Parents can help their children in this personal voyage of discovery by bestowing on them unconditional approval, even if the children's developing interests and values differ from their own.

As you reflect on the importance of self-esteem, consider the results of a classic 1939 study by Kenneth and Mamie Clark on the self-esteem of African American preschool children. They discovered that the children preferred playing with a white doll over a black one and attributed more positive characteristics to the white doll—a result they believed reflected the negative effects of segregation on self-esteem. In the intervening years, many other researchers have examined self-esteem in African Americans using a number of different methods. The findings? Overall, African American children, adolescents, and adults actually show higher levels of self-esteem, on average, than Whites (Hafdahl & Gray-Little, 2002; Zeigler-Hill & Wallace, 2011). One explanation of the self-esteem advantage among young African Americans is that they tend to have a stronger sense of ethnic identity than young Whites.

A study of Facebook use among African American college students showed that displaying their photographs and personal interests on social networking sites provided a means of signaling their racial identity (Lee, 2011). Ethnic identity in people of color is a strong predictor of self-esteem and helps buffer the emotional effects of racism and discrimination (Pierre & Mahalik, 2005; Tynes et al., 2012; Umaña-Taylor, 2004). One reason for the link between ethnic identity and self-esteem is that ethnic identity among people of color contributes to a stronger sense of community and greater social connections to others of similar backgrounds (Rivas-Drake, 2012).

Abraham Maslow: Scaling the Heights of Self-Actualization

Like Rogers, Maslow, who we discussed in Chapter 8, believed in an innate human drive toward self-actualization—toward becoming all that we are capable of being (Maslow, 1970, 1971). To Maslow, this drive toward self-actualization shapes our personality by motivating us to develop our unique potentials as human beings. He believed that if people were given the opportunity, they would strive toward self-actualization. Yet he recognized that few of us become fully self-actualized. In the humanistic view, personality is perhaps best thought of as a continuing process of personal growth and realization—more a road to be followed than a final destination.

Humanistic psychologists, following the principles established by Maslow and Rogers, noted that each of us has unique feelings, desires, and needs. Therefore, we cannot completely abide by the wishes of others and still be true to ourselves. The path to psychological health is paved with awareness and acceptance of *all* parts of ourselves, warts and all.

Let's not leave our discussion of humanistic concepts of the self without discussing the important role that culture plays in the development of our self-concept.

Culture and Self-Identity

How you define yourself may depend on the culture in which you were raised. If you were raised in a **collectivistic culture**, you might define yourself in terms of the social roles you assume or the groups to which you belong (Markus & Kitayama, 1991; Triandis & Suh, 2002). You might say, "I am a Korean American" or "I am Jonathan's father." By contrast, if you were raised in an **individualistic culture**, you are likely to define yourself in terms of your unique individuality (the characteristics that distinguish you from others) and your personal accomplishments. You might say, "I am a systems analyst" or "I am a caring person." Differences also exist among individuals within cultures in how they define their self-identity.

Many cultures in Asia, Africa, and Central and South America are considered collectivistic, whereas those of the United States, Canada, and many Western European countries are characterized as individualistic. Collectivistic cultures value the group's goals over the individual's. They emphasize communal values such as harmony, respect for authority and for one's elders, conformity, cooperation, interdependence, and conflict avoidance. For example, traditional Filipino culture emphasizes deference to elders at any cost (Nevid & Sta. Maria, 1999). Filipino children are taught to never disrespect their older siblings, no matter how small the age difference and, in many cases, regardless of who is "right."

RyFlip/Shutterstock.com

Individualistic cultures, by contrast, emphasize values relating to independence and self-sufficiency. They idealize rugged individualism as personified in tales of the nineteenth-century American West. Despite differences between individualistic and collectivistic cultures, the mind possesses the ability to think both individualistically and collectivistically depending on the circumstances (Oyserman, Coon, & Kemmelmeier, 2002).

Extremes of either individualism or collectivism can have undesirable outcomes. Excessive collectivism may stifle creativity, innovation, and personal initiative, whereas excessive individualism may lead to unmitigated greed and exploitation.

CONCEPT 11.23
Whereas Freud was primarily concerned with our baser instincts, Maslow focused on the highest reaches of human endeavor, the process of realizing our unique potentials.

CONCEPT 11.24
Whether we define ourselves in terms of our individuality or the social roles that we perform is influenced by the values of the culture in which we are raised.

collectivistic culture A culture that emphasizes people's social roles and obligations.

individualistic culture A culture that emphasizes individual identity and personal accomplishments.

CONCEPT 11.25
The humanistic perspective focuses on the need to understand conscious experience and one's sense of self, but difficulties exist in studying private, subjective experiences and in measuring such core concepts as self-actualization.

Monkey Business Images/Shutterstock.com

Evaluating the Humanistic Perspective

The humanistic perspective provided much of the impetus for the broad social movement of the 1960s and 1970s, in which many people searched inward to find direction and meaning in their lives. It renewed the age-old debate about free will and determinism and focused attention on the need to understand the subjective or conscious experiences of individuals. Rogers's method of therapy, *client-centered therapy*, remains highly influential. And perhaps most important of all, humanistic theorists helped restore to psychology the concept of self—that center of our conscious experience of being in the world.

Yet the very strength of the humanistic viewpoint, its focus on conscious experience, is also its greatest weakness when approached as a scientific endeavor. Ultimately your conscious experience is known or knowable only to an audience of one—you. As scientists, how can humanistic psychologists ever be certain that they are measuring with any precision the private, subjective experience of another person? Humanistic psychologists might answer that we should do our best to study conscious experience scientifically, for to do less is to ignore the very subject matter—human experience—we endeavor to know. Indeed, they have been joined by cognitive psychologists in developing methods to study conscious experience, including rating scales and thought diaries that allow people to make public their private experiences—to report their thoughts, feelings, and attitudes in systematic ways that can be measured reliably.

Critics also contend that the humanistic approach's emphasis on self-fulfillment may lead some people to become self-indulgent and so absorbed with themselves that they develop a lack of concern for others. Even the concept of self-actualization poses challenges. For one thing, humanistic psychologists consider self-actualization to be a drive that motivates behavior toward higher purposes. Yet how do we know that this drive exists? If self-actualization means different things to different people—one person may become self-actualized by pursuing an interest in botany, another by becoming a skilled artisan—how can we ever measure self-actualization in a standardized way? To this, humanistic psychologists might respond that because people are unique, we should not expect to apply the same standard to different people.

Concept Chart 11.4 provides a summary of the major concepts in the humanistic perspective on personality.

Concept Chart 11.4 The Humanistic Perspective: Key Points

	Concept	Summary	Key Principle
© iofoto/Shutterstock.com	Rogers's self-theory	The self is the executive or organizing center of the personality—the "I" that determines how we relate to the world and pursue our goals.	People who are not encouraged in their upbringing to develop their individuality and uniqueness—but instead are valued only when they meet other people's expectations—tend to develop distorted self-concepts.
© Carlos Neto/Shutterstock.com	Maslow's concept of self-actualization	Self-actualization is a key element of personality and human motivation.	If given the chance, people will strive toward achieving self-actualization, a goal that is better thought of as a continuing journey than as a final destination.
© Christopher Futcher/Shutterstock.com	Culture and self-identity	Self-identity may be influenced by collectivistic or individualistic cultural values.	Collectivistic cultures foster the development of communal or interdependent concepts of the self, whereas individualistic cultures encourage definitions of the self that embody individuality and uniqueness.

APPLYING PSYCHOLOGY *in Daily Life*

Building Self-Esteem

The humanistic psychologists Carl Rogers and Abraham Maslow recognized the importance of self-esteem in developing a healthy personality. When our self-esteem is low, it is usually because we see ourselves as falling short of some ideal. Yet our self-esteem is not a fixed quality; it goes through ups and downs throughout the course of life (Robins et al., 2002). Enhancing self-esteem is important, as evidence links higher self-esteem in adolescence to better emotional and physical health, lower levels of criminal behavior, and greater financial success in adulthood (Trzesniewski et al., 2006). We can boost self-esteem by developing our competencies—skills and abilities that enable us to achieve our goals and that enhance our sense of self-worth. But to build self-esteem, we must also challenge perfectionistic expectations and learn to accept ourselves when we inevitably fall short of our ideals.

CONCEPT 11.26
Self-esteem, rather than being a fixed quality, can be enhanced by developing competencies and adopting more realistic goals and expectations.

Acquire Competencies: Become Good at Something

Social-cognitive theorists recognize that our self-esteem is related to the skills or competencies we can marshal to meet the challenges we face. Competencies include academic skills such as reading, writing, and math; artistic skills such as drawing and playing the piano; athletic skills such as walking a balance beam and throwing a football; social skills such as knowing how to start conversations; and job or occupational skills. The more competencies we possess, especially in areas that matter most to us, the better we feel about ourselves.

Competencies can be acquired through training and practice. You may not be able to throw a baseball at 90 miles per hour unless you have certain genetic advantages in arm strength and coordination. However, most skills can be developed within a normal range of genetic variation. Most people can learn to play the piano well, although only a few can become concert pianists. Indeed, most people can achieve a majority of the skills valued in our society.

Set Realistic, Achievable Goals

Part of boosting self-esteem is setting realistic goals. This does not mean that you should not strive to be the best that you can be. It does mean that you may find it helpful to evaluate your goals in light of your true needs and capabilities.

Enhance Self-Efficacy Expectations

Success breeds success. You can enhance your self-efficacy expectations by choosing tasks that are consistent with your interests and abilities and working at them. Start with smaller, clearly achievable goals. Meeting these challenges will boost your self-confidence and encourage you to move toward more challenging goals. Regard the disappointments that life inevitably has in store as opportunities to learn from your mistakes, not as signs of ultimate failure.

© ViLevi/Shutterstock.com

Create a Sense of Meaningfulness in Your Life

To psychologically healthy individuals, life is not just a matter of muddling through each day. Rather, each day provides opportunities to pursue higher purposes. There are many different kinds of meaning in life, many different purposes. Some people find meaning in connecting themselves spiritually to something larger—whether it be a specific religion or the cosmos. Other people find meaning in community, among those who share a common ethnic identity and cultural heritage. Still others find meaning in love and family. Their spouses and their children provide them with a sense of fulfillment. People may also find meaning in their work.

Challenge Perfectionistic Expectations

Many of us withdraw from life challenges because of unreasonable demands we impose on ourselves to be perfect in everything we attempt. If you place perfectionistic demands on yourself, consider an attitude shift. Try lightening up on yourself and adopting more realistic expectations based on a fair-minded appraisal of your strengths and weaknesses. You may not measure up to an idealized image of perfection, but chances are you already have some abilities and talents you can cultivate, thus bolstering your self-esteem.

Challenge the Need for Constant Approval

Psychologist Albert Ellis believed that an excessive need for social approval is a surefire recipe for low self-esteem (Ellis, 1977; Ellis & Ellis, 2011). He recognized that incurring disapproval from others, even significant others, is an inevitable part of life. Ellis challenges us to consider whether experiencing disapproval is truly as awful or intolerable as we might have thought. He encourages us to replace irrational needs for approval with more rational expectations that can help bolster our self-esteem, especially when we run into people who fail to appreciate our finer points.

Comparing yourself to others on social media sites can lead you to feel that other people have better lives.

Robin Beckham/BEEPstock/Alamy Stock Photo

Avoid Comparing Facebook Profiles

Do you spend time comparing your Facebook profile with those of your 50, 100, 300, 500, or more "friends"? If so, findings from a recent study of state university students in Utah suggest your self-esteem may take a hit. Students who spent more time on Facebook perceived others to be happier themselves and to have better lives (Chou & Edge, 2012). Moreover, those with more "friends" they did not know personally were also more likely to think other people had better lives.

MODULE REVIEW **11.4** The Humanistic Perspective

Recite It

8. **Describe** the self-theory of humanistic theorist Carl Rogers.

In Rogers's view, the (a) _____ is the organized center of our experience. The self naturally moves toward self-(b) _____, or development of its unique potential.

Movement toward self-actualization is assisted when the person receives unconditional (c) _____ regard

(noncontingent approval) from others. By contrast, when approval is contingent on "proper" behavior, the person may develop a distorted self-concept and become detached from his or her genuine feelings and needs.

9. **Explain** the difference between the concepts of self in collectivistic and individualistic cultures.

(d) _____ cultures view the self in terms of the role or place of the individual within the social group or society.

(e) _____ cultures emphasize the uniqueness or individuality of the self.

10. **Apply** suggestions for enhancing self-esteem.

Some suggestions for boosting self-esteem include acquiring (f) _____, setting realistic, achievable goals, enhancing self-efficacy expectations, creating a sense of meaningfulness in life, challenging (g) _____ expectations, challenging the need for constant approval, and avoiding comparing Facebook profiles.

Recall It

1. Which statement best describes the humanistic belief about our freedom to make personal choices in our lives?

   a. The ability to make conscious choices is true only of people who were raised in cultures that encouraged them to think freely.
   b. Free will is but an illusion.
   c. The choices we make are largely determined by the social influences we encounter.
   d. Our free will is a basic feature of our humanity.

2. Self-actualization involves
   a. self-awareness and self-discovery.
   b. tapping into one's true feelings and needs.
   c. acknowledging and acting upon one's individual characteristics.
   d. all of the above.

3. What did Rogers believe was the center of our experience of being human?

4. Defining oneself in terms of the roles one plays within the group or society is most likely to occur in
   a. a collectivist culture.
   b. an individualistic culture.
   c. Western European cultures.
   d. traditional U.S. culture.

Think About It

■ How does your cultural background affect your goals and ambitions? Your values? Your self-identity? Your relationships with others? Do you think you would have developed a different personality had you been raised in another culture? Why or why not?

■ Do you consider yourself more of an individualist or a collectivist? How are your views of yourself connected with your cultural background?

Recite It answers placed at the end of chapter.

MODULE **11.5 Personality Tests**

11 **Identify** the two major types of personality tests, **describe** their features, and **evaluate** self-report and projective personality tests.

Let us now move from attempts to describe or explain personality to ways of measuring it. Attempts to measure personality actually have a long history. In the eighteenth and nineteenth centuries, many well-respected scientists believed one could make reasonable judgments about a person's character and mental abilities by examining the bumps on a person's head, or even the shape of the person's nose. According to **phrenology**, a popular view at the time, you could judge people's character and mental abilities based on the pattern of bumps on their heads. Such

phrenology The now-discredited view that one can judge a person's character and mental abilities by measuring the bumps on his or her head.

CONCEPT 11.27
Self-report personality inventories are widely used measures of personality in which a person's response options are limited so as to make scoring them objective.

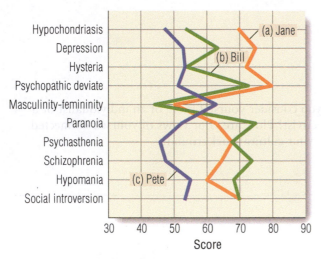

FIGURE 11.5 Sample MMPI-2 Profiles

(a) Jane is a 21-year-old woman who was admitted to a psychiatric facility following a suicide attempt; (b) Bill is a 34-year-old schizophrenia patient; and (c) Pete is a well-adjusted, 25-year-old editor.

Note: Scores of 50 are average. Scores on masculinity–femininity are keyed here in the masculine direction for females and in the feminine direction for males.

personality tests Structured psychological tests that use formal methods of assessing personality.

views have long been debunked. We no longer believe you can assess people's personality traits by their superficial biological characteristics.

The methods psychologists use today to assess personality include case studies, interviews, observational techniques, and experimental studies (see Chapter 1). But the most widely used method for learning about personality is based on the use of formal **personality tests**. The two major types of personality tests are self-report personality inventories and projective tests.

Self-Report Personality Inventories

Self-report personality inventories are structured psychological tests in which individuals are given a set of questions to answer about themselves in the form of "yes–no," "true–false," or "agree–disagree" types of response formats. Self-report personality inventories are also called **objective tests**. They are not objective in the same sense that your bathroom scale is an objective measure of your weight. Unlike scales of weight, they rely on people's opinions or judgments as to whether they agree or disagree with particular statements. The tests are objective in the sense that they can be scored objectively because the responses they require are limited to a few choices, such as true or false. They are also considered objective because they were constructed from evidence gathered from research studies. Some self-report personality tests measure single dimensions of personality, such as assertiveness or hostility. Others attempt to capture multiple dimensions of personality. A leading example of a multidimensional personality test is the Minnesota Multiphasic Personality Inventory (MMPI), the most widely used self-report personality inventory in the world (Camara, Nathan, & Puente, 2000).

Minnesota Multiphasic Personality Inventory (MMPI)

Do you like fashion magazines? Are you frequently troubled by feelings of anxiety or nervousness? Do you feel that others "have it in for you"? What might your answers to questions such as these tell us about your underlying personality or mental health?

These questions model the items found in the MMPI, now in a revised edition called the MMPI-2 (Butcher, 2000). The MMPI-2 consists of 567 true–false items that yield scores on ten clinical scales (see Table 11.5) and additional scales measuring other personality dimensions and response tendencies.

The MMPI was constructed to help clinicians diagnose mental disorders. Items are grouped on particular scales if they tend to be answered differently by particular diagnostic groups than by normal reference groups. For example, an item such as "I feel moody at times" would be placed on the depression scale if it tended to be endorsed more often by people in a depressed group than by normal controls. The more items a person endorses in the same direction as the diagnostic group, the higher the score the person receives on the scale.

When scoring the MMPI, one converts raw scores (number of items scored in the same direction as the diagnostic group) into **standard scores**, which are then plotted on a graph similar to the one shown in ■ Figure 11.5. Scores of 65 or higher on the clinical scales are considered clinically elevated or abnormally high. Examiners take into account the elevations on individual scales and the pattern of relationships among the scale scores to form impressions of individuals' personality characteristics and their possible psychological problems. For another use of personality tests, see the nearby Try This Out above.

Evaluation of Self-Report Personality Tests

A large body of evidence supports the validity of self-report personality inventories such as the MMPI (for example, Graham, 2006; Sellbom, Graham, & Schenk, 2006;

Table 11.5 Clinical Scales of the MMPI-2

Scale Number and Label	Items Similar to Those Found on MMPI Scale	Sample Traits of High Scorers
1. Hypochondriasis	I am frequently bothered by an upset stomach. At times, my body seems to ache all over.	Many physical complaints, cynical defeatist attitudes, often perceived as whiny, demanding
2. Depression	Nothing seems to interest me anymore. My sleep is often disturbed by worrisome thoughts.	Depressed mood; pessimistic, worrisome, despondent, lethargic
3. Hysteria	I sometimes become flushed for no apparent reason. I tend to take people at their word when they're trying to be nice to me.	Naive, egocentric, little insight into problems, immature; develops physical complaints in response to stress
4. Psychopathic deviate	My parents often disliked my friends. My behavior sometimes got me into trouble at school.	Difficulties incorporating values of society; rebellious, impulsive, antisocial tendencies; strained family relationships; poor work and school history
5. Masculinity–femininity*	I like reading about electronics. (M) I would like the work of an interior decorator. (F)	Males endorsing feminine attributes: cultural and artistic interests, effeminate, sensitive, passive. Females endorsing male interests: aggressive, masculine, self-confident, active, assertive, vigorous
6. Paranoia	I would have been more successful in life but people didn't give me a fair break. It's not safe to trust anyone these days.	Suspicious, guarded, blames others, resentful, aloof, may have paranoid delusions
7. Psychasthenia	I'm one of those people who have to have something to worry about. I seem to have more fears than most people I know.	Anxious, fearful, tense, worried, insecure, difficulties concentrating, obsessional, self-doubting
8. Schizophrenia	Things seem unreal to me at times. I sometimes hear things that other people cannot hear.	Confused and illogical thinking, feels alienated and misunderstood, socially isolated or withdrawn, may have blatant psychotic symptoms such as hallucinations or delusional beliefs, or may lead a detached lifestyle
9. Hypomania	I sometimes take on more tasks than I can possibly get done. People have noticed that my speech is sometimes pressured or rushed.	Energetic, possibly manic, impulsive, optimistic, sociable, active, flighty, irritable, may have overly inflated or grandiose self-image or unrealistic plans
10. Social introversion*	I don't like loud parties. I was not very active in school activities.	Shy, inhibited, withdrawn, introverted, lacks self-confidence, reserved, anxious in social situations

*The construction of these scales was based on nonclinical comparison groups.

Source: From Jeffrey S. Nevid, Spence A. Rathus, and Beverly Greene, *Abnormal Psychology in a Changing World*. Copyright © 2003 by Prentice Hall, Inc. Reproduced by permission of Pearson Education, Inc.

Veltri et al., 2009). The MMPI provides a wealth of information about a person's interests, areas of concern, needs, and ways of relating to others, and assists therapists in making diagnoses of psychological or mental disorders. However, it should not be used by itself to make a diagnosis. A high score on the depression scale does not necessarily mean that a person has a depressive disorder, for example. Yet the person may share certain personality traits or complaints in common with people who do, which may be important for treatment providers to know.

Self-report personality inventories have several strengths. They are relatively inexpensive to administer and score—in fact, many can be machine-scored and interpreted by computer. People may also be more willing to disclose personal information on paper-and-pencil tests than when facing an interviewer. Most important, the results

self-report personality inventories Structured psychological tests in which individuals are given a limited range of response options to answer a set of questions about themselves.

objective tests Tests of personality that can be scored objectively and that are based on a research foundation.

standard scores Scores that represent an individual's relative deviation from the mean of the standardization sample.

of these tests may be used to predict a wide range of behaviors, including the ability to relate effectively to others and to achieve positions of leadership or dominance.

Reliance on self-report data in personality tests such as the MMPI can introduce potential biases, however. Some responses may be outright lies. Others may be prone to more subtle distortions, such as tendencies to respond in a socially desirable direction—in other words, to put one's best foot forward. The more sophisticated self-report scales, including the MMPI, have validity scales that help identify response biases. Yet even these scales may not be able to eliminate all sources of bias (McGovern & Nevid, 1986; Nicholson et al., 1997).

Projective Tests

CONCEPT 11.28

Projective tests are based on the belief that the ways in which people respond to ambiguous stimuli are determined by their underlying needs and personalities.

In **projective tests**, people are presented with a set of unstructured or ambiguous stimuli, such as inkblots, that can be interpreted in various ways. Projective tests are based on the belief in psychodynamic theory that people transfer, or "project," their unconscious needs, drives, and motives onto their responses to unstructured or vague stimuli. Unlike objective tests, projective tests have a response format that is not restricted to "yes–no" or multiple-choice answers or other limited response options. Accordingly, an examiner must interpret the subject's responses, thus bringing more subjectivity to the procedure. Here we focus on the two most widely used projective tests, the Rorschach test and the Thematic Apperception Test (TAT) (Camara, Nathan, & Puente, 2000).

Rorschach Test

FIGURE 11.6 What Does This Look Like to You?
The Rorschach test is based on the assumption that people project aspects of their own personalities onto their responses to ambiguous figures, such as inkblots.

As a child growing up in Switzerland, Hermann Rorschach (1884–1922) amused himself by playing a game of dripping ink and folding the paper to make symmetrical inkblot figures. He noticed that people would perceive the same blots in different ways and came to believe that their responses revealed something about their personalities. His fascination with inkblots earned him the nickname *Klex,* which means "inkblot" in German. Rorschach, who went on to become a psychiatrist, turned his childhood pastime into the psychological test that bears his name. Unfortunately, Rorschach did not live to see how popular and influential his inkblot test would become. He died at the age of 37 from complications following a ruptured appendix, only months after the publication of his test (Exner, 2002).

The Rorschach test consists of ten cards similar to the one in ■ Figure 11.6. Five have splashes of color, and the others are in black and white and shades of gray. Subjects are asked what each blot looks like. After the responses to each card are obtained, the examiner conducts a follow-up inquiry to probe more deeply into the person's responses.

Scoring Rorschach responses is a complex task. The scoring is based on such features as content (what the blot looked like—a "bat," for example) and form level (consistency of the response with the actual shape of the blot). Poor form level may indicate problems with perceiving reality clearly or perhaps an overly fertile imagination. Those who see formless figures dominated by color—who see reddened areas as "blood," for instance—may have difficulties controlling their emotions. The content of the response may indicate underlying conflicts with others. For example, someone who sees only animal figures and no human forms may have difficulties relating to other people.

Thematic Apperception Test

projective tests Personality tests in which ambiguous or vague test materials are used to elicit responses that are believed to reveal a person's unconscious needs, drives, and motives.

Harvard psychologist Henry Murray developed the Thematic Apperception Test (TAT) in the 1930s (Murray, 1938). The test consists of a set of pictures depicting ambiguous scenes that may be interpreted differently. The subject is asked to tell a story about the scene, what led up to these events, and what the eventual outcome will be. Murray believed that the stories people tell reveal aspects of their own personalities, or projections of their own psychological needs and conflicts into the events they describe. For example, people whose stories consistently touch upon themes of parental rejection may be saying something about their own underlying psychological issues.

Evaluation of Projective Tests

One drawback of projective tests is that the scoring of test responses is largely based on the examiner's subjective impressions. Two examiners may disagree on the scoring of the form level of a particular Rorschach response, for example. Although more structured scoring systems have been developed (for example, Exner, 1993), questions remains about whether interpretations of Rorschach responses are valid or useful.

Another problem with projective tests is *stimulus pull*. Despite efforts to make stimuli ambiguous, they often contain cues, such as sad-looking faces in the TAT, that may elicit (pull for) certain types of responses. In such cases, responses may involve reactions to the stimulus properties of the test materials themselves rather than projections of one's underlying personality (Murstein & Mathes, 1996).

Although the value of the Rorschach continues to be debated, recent evidence supports the validity of some Rorschach interpretations, especially responses indicative of impaired thinking and perceptual processing (Mihura et al., 2013, 2015; Wood et al., 2015). However, critics of the Rorschach claim it lacks the overall validity and usefulness needed for clinical assessment of personality or emotional disorders (for example, Garb, Klein, & Grove, 2002; Wood et al., 2010, 2015). Without any clear resolution in sight, the debate over the clinical value of the Rorschach is likely to continue. Concept Chart 11.5 compares the methods of assessment and forms of therapy associated with each of the major perspectives on personality covered in this chapter.

Concept Chart 11.5 Overview of Theoretical Perspectives on Personality

Theoretical Model	Key Theorists	Major Concepts	Assessment Techniques	Associated Therapy
Psychoanalytic	Freud	Personality is influenced by an unconscious dynamic struggle among the id, the ego, and the superego.	Interviews, projective techniques	Psychoanalysis (discussed in Chapter 14)
Psychodynamic (neo-Freudians)	Adler, Jung, Horney, Erikson	Social factors and development of self are more important influences on personality than sexual motivation.	Interviews, projective techniques	Psychodynamic therapy (discussed in Chapter 14)
Trait	Allport, Cattell, Eysenck	Personality consists of a set of underlying traits that account for the characteristic ways people act in different situations.	Self-report personality inventories, such as Cattell's 16PF	None
Behaviorism	Watson, Skinner	Personality consists of learned behavior acquired through classical and operant conditioning.	Behavioral observation	Behavior therapy (discussed in Chapter 14)
Social-cognitive	Rotter, Bandura, Mischel	Personality consists of the individual's repertoire of behaviors and ways of thinking about the world.	Behavioral observation, interviewing, self-report measures, thought checklists	Cognitive-behavioral therapy (discussed in Chapter 14)
Humanistic	Rogers, Maslow	Personality consists of the subjective experience of being in the world, organized around a concept of the self.	Interviews, self-concept measures	Rogers's client-centered therapy (discussed in Chapter 14)

MODULE REVIEW **11.5** Personality Tests

Recite It

11. **Identify** the two major types of personality tests, **describe** their features, and **evaluate** self-report and projective personality tests.

(a) _____ personality tests are psychological tests that consist of sets of questions that people answer about themselves by using limited response options. They are classified as objective tests because they use objective methods of (b) _____ and are based on a research foundation.

(c) _____ tests are based on the use of ambiguous test materials that are answered in ways believed to reflect

(d) _____ of the person's unconscious needs, drives, and motives.

Self-report or (e) _____ personality tests predict a wide range of behaviors and are efficient and inexpensive to administer and score. However, they should not be used alone to make a diagnosis of a psychological disorder. Controversy persists among psychologists about the validity of (f) _____ tests. Though evidence backs up the use of some Rorschach responses, the general usefulness of the test as a method of assessment continues to be debated.

Recall It

1. What are two major types of personality tests?

2. Which of the following is *not* correct with regard to the Minnesota Multiphasic Personality Inventory?

   a. It was originally designed to detect mental disorders.
   b. Scales are composed of items that differentiate responses of people from particular diagnostic groups from those of people in a normal reference group.
   c. It is the most widely used self-report personality inventory in the world.
   d. Test responses to self-report personality inventories are free of response biases.

3. A test score that represents the relative deviation of a person's score from the mean of the standardization sample is called a _____ score.

4. Which of the following statements about projective tests is *true*?

   a. Projective tests rely upon limited response options, such as "yes–no" type questions.
   b. Projective tests are based on the Freudian defense mechanism of regression.
   c. Projective tests are most closely associated with the behaviorist perspective.
   d. Projective tests were developed to help reveal unconscious desires and motives.

Think About It

- Have you ever taken a personality test? What, if anything, do you believe you learned about your personality?

- Consider the debate over the validity of projective tests. Do you believe that people reveal underlying aspects of

their personality in their responses to unstructured stimuli, such as inkblots? Why or why not?

Recite It answers placed at the end of chapter.

THINKING CRITICALLY ABOUT PSYCHOLOGY

Based on your reading of this chapter, answer the following questions. Then, to evaluate your progress in developing critical thinking skills, compare your answers to the sample answers found in Appendix A.

Personality and astrology: Is your personality all in the stars? What's in store for you? Let's

see what the stars say about "Geminis" and "Scorpios":

Gemini (May 21–June 20): It is now time to focus on meeting your personal needs. Your energy level is high, and you can make the best use of your personal resources. There are many creative opportunities available to you, but you will need to apply yourself to take full advantage of them. You are the type of person who can go beyond what others expect of you. You are facing an important financial decision that can have a great impact on your future. But allow others to counsel you in reaching the best decision. All in all, now is the time to fully enjoy the many blessings in your life.

Scorpio (October 23–November 21): Your best-laid plans may need to be altered because of an unforeseen development. This can cause stress with others, but you will be able to use your sense of humor to ease the situation. You are a caring person whose concern for others shines through. Even though the next month or two may be unsettled, it is best to stay calm. Pursue what is important to you and take advantage of the romantic opportunities you may find or discover. Above all, maintain that sense of humor through trying times and don't accept more responsibilities than you can handle.

Believers in astrology hold that our personalities and destinies are fixed at the time of our birth by the positions of the sun, the moon, and the planets in the zodiac. Do you believe your personality was determined by the alignment of the heavens at the time of your birth? Do you read the astrology charts in your local newspaper? Do you believe them?

Astrology can be traced back thousands of years and still attracts many adherents, even among people with advanced education. More than 30 percent of college students polled in a survey expressed beliefs in astrology (Duncan, Donnelly, & Nicholson, 1992).

Another study examined scores on the Eysenck Personality Inventory (EPI) in relation to the birth positions of the sun and moon. The results failed to confirm beliefs that such personality factors as extraversion and neuroticism conform to astrological predictions (Clarke, Gabriels, & Barnes, 1996). Other research points to the same conclusion—namely, that there is no scientific basis for astrology (Crowe, 1990; Dean, Mather, & Kelly, 1996). Given the absence of

scientific evidence supporting astrology, why does it remain so popular?

One reason may be the *Barnum effect*—the tendency to believe overgeneralized descriptions of personality as accurate descriptions of oneself. The "Barnum" after whom the effect is named was the famous nineteenth-century circus showman P. T. Barnum, who once said, "There's a sucker born every minute." The next time you glance at an astrology forecast in your local paper, notice how often the statements are phrased in general terms that can apply to just about anyone (for example, "Now is the time to focus on your personal needs . . .," "Even though the next month or two may be unsettled . . ."). Look again at the astrological readings for "Geminis" and "Scorpios" given. Chances are that you will identify with characteristics found in both descriptions, regardless of your particular date of birth.

The Barnum effect may also explain the continued popularity of other pseudosciences, such as psychic reading and fortune-telling. The special "insights" into our futures that psychics and fortune-tellers claim they have are based on general characteristics that fit just about everyone ("You are likely to encounter some financial difficulty . . ."). In addition, they tend to be good observers who notice subtle cues in their clients' attire, gestures, or responses to leading questions that they can use to personalize their predictions.

Another contributor to beliefs in astrology and other pseudosciences is the tendency for people to filter information about themselves in terms of how it reflects upon them. For instance, we tend to give greater credence to information that confirms a positive image of ourselves than to information that casts us in a negative light. Notice that the astrology readings shown previously contain many positive attributes (for example, "caring person," "sense of humor"). The tendency to place greater emphasis on information that bolsters a positive self-image is called the *self-serving bias*—a bias that also accounts for the tendency of people to take credit for their successes and to explain away their failures or disappointments (see Chapter 12).

Now it's your turn to try a little critical thinking. Explain how another type of cognitive bias, the *confirmation bias* (see Chapter 7), contributes to beliefs in astrology.

Recite It Answers for Chapter 11

Module 11.1 1. (a) personality; (b) consistency, 2. (c) preconscious; (d) unconscious; (e) superego; (f) id, 3. (g) oral; (h) anal; (i) phallic; (j) latency; (k) genital, 4. (l) personal; (m) collective; (n) "inferiority; (o) excel; (p) parents **Module 11.2** 5. (a) cardinal; (b) central; (c) secondary; (d) surface; (e) source; (f) neuroticism; (g) openness to new experiences, 6. (h) novelty; (i) environmental **Module 11.3** 7. (a) expectancies; (b) subjective; (c) reciprocal; (d) situation; (e) person; (f) encoding **Module 11.4** 8. (a) self; (b)actualization; (c) positive, 9. (d) Collectivistic; (e) Individualistic, 10. (f) competencies; (g) perfectionistic **Module 11.5** 11. (a) Self-report; (b) scoring; (c) Projective; (e) objective; (f) projective

MODULE 11.1

The Psychodynamic Perspective

Freud's Psychoanalytic Theory

- **Three Levels of Consciousness**: Conscious, preconscious, unconscious
- **Three Structures of Personality**: Id (primitive drives), ego ("reason and good sense"), superego (moral conscience)
- **Defense Mechanisms**: Shielding the self from awareness of troubling impulses and memories; examples include repression, displacement, and projection
- **Stages of Psychosexual Development**: Oral stage (birth to 2 years), anal stage (18 months to 3 years), phallic stage (3 to 6 years), latency stage (6 to puberty), genital stage (puberty to adulthood)

Other Psychodynamic Theorists

- **Carl Jung's Analytical Psychology**: Personal unconscious, collective unconscious, archetypes
- **Alfred Adler's Individual Psychology**: Creative self, inferiority complex, drive for superiority
- **Karen Horney**: Basic anxiety and basic hostility; criticized Freud over theory of female development

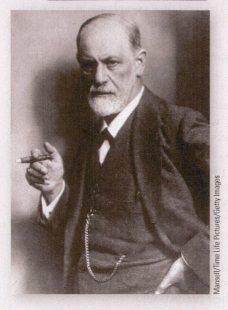

Mansell/Time Life Pictures/Getty Images

MODULE 11.2

The Trait Perspective

Major Trait Theorists

- **Gordon Allport**: Three levels of traits (cardinal, central, specific)
- **Raymond Cattell**: Two levels of traits (surface traits apparent in behavior versus deeper source traits reflecting underlying structure of personality)
- **Hans Eysenck**: three trait model (extraversion, neuroticism, psychoticism)

Contemporary Trait Theories

- **Big Five Model**: Consolidation of earlier trait models, comprising five broad traits (extraversion, neuroticism, openness, agreeableness, conscientiousness)
- **Trait-Situational Interactionism**: Behavior involves interaction of traits and situational factors
- **Genetic Bases of Traits**: Personality traits derive from combination of genetic factors and life experiences

MODULE 11.3

The Social-Cognitive Perspective

Social Cognitive Theorists

- **Julian Rotter**: Expectancies, locus of control
- **Albert Bandura**: Reciprocal determinism, outcome and efficacy expectations
- **Walter Mischel**: Person variables and situation variables

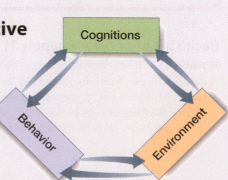

Extraverted

Unstable/Extraverted	**Stable/Extraverted**
Restless	Outgoing
Excitable	Talkative
Changeable	Sociable
Active	Lively
Impulsive	Carefree
Aggressive	Easygoing

Emotionally Unstable (High Neuroticism) — **Emotionally Stable (Low Neuroticism)**

Unstable/Introverted	**Stable/Introverted**
Anxious	Controlled
Moody	Passive
Pessimistic	Thoughtful
Quiet	Calm
Unsociable	Reliable
Reserved	Careful

Introverted

MODULE 11.4

The Humanistic Perspective

- **Carl Rogers:** Emphasis on the self; importance of self-understanding and self-acceptance
- **Abraham Maslow:** Emphasis on self-actualization
- **Culture and Self-Identity:** Collectivistic versus individualistic cultures

© iofoto/Shutterstock.com

MODULE 11.5

Personality Tests

- **Self-Report Personality Inventories:** Inventories of likes and dislikes, emotional problems, and attitudes. The person's responses are compared to those of normal and clinical samples (for example, MMPI-2)
- **Projective Tests:** Projecting underlying needs and conflicts in responses to ambiguous stimuli (for example, Rorschach Inkblot Test and TAT)

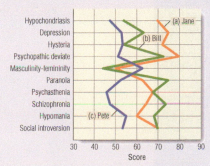

LEARNING OBJECTIVES

After studying this chapter, you will be able to . . .

1. **Identify** the major influences on first impressions and **explain** why first impressions often become lasting impressions.

2. **Identify** and **describe** cognitive biases that influence causal attributions.

3. **Identify** three components of attitudes and **describe** the sources of attitudes and the pathways involved in changing attitudes through persuasive appeals.

4. **Describe** cognitive dissonance theory and **explain** how cognitive dissonance can be reduced.

5. **Identify** factors that influence attraction.

6. **Identify** the components of love identified in the triangular model of love.

7. **Describe** the decision-making model of helping and **identify** factors that influence helping behavior.

8. **Define** prejudice, **explain** how it develops, and **apply** your knowledge to ways of reducing it.

9. **Identify** factors that contribute to human aggression.

10. **Define** social identity and **evaluate** cultural factors involved in social identity.

11. **Describe** the basic finding of Asch's classic study on conformity and **identify** factors that influence conformity.

12. **Explain** the psychological bases of manipulative sales tactics.

13. **Describe** the findings of Milgram's classic study and **evaluate** why his methods were controversial.

14. **Evaluate** the effects of the presence of others on performance.

15. **Define** groupthink and **explain** how it can lead to wrong decisions.

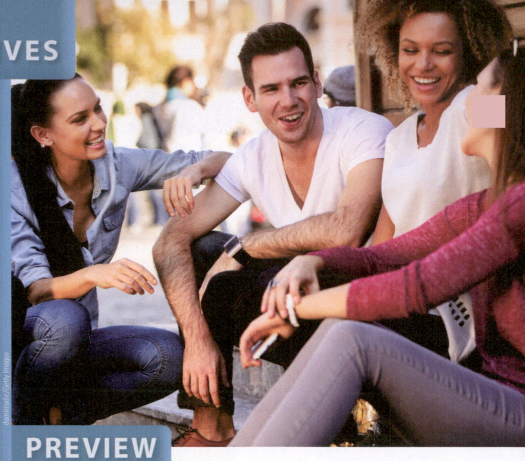

damircudic/Getty Images

PREVIEW

Social Psychology

12

In the Company of Others

A stranger faints on a crowded street as you pass by. Several people gather about the fallen person. Do you offer assistance or continue on your way?

You participate in a psychology experiment in which you and other members of a group are asked to determine which of two lines is longer. One person after another chooses the line that looks shorter to you. Now comes your turn. Do you go along with the crowd or stand your ground and select the line you think is longer?

A man and a woman are standing on a street corner speaking privately in Italian. The man hands the woman an envelope, which she puts in her handbag. What do you make of this interaction? Do you suppose it was a lover's note that was passed between them? Or do you think it was an exchange related to Mafia business?

You volunteer for a psychology experiment on the effects of electric shock on learning. You are instructed to administer to another participant what you are told are painful shocks each time the other participant gives a wrong answer. At first you refuse. But the experimenter insists you continue and tells you the shocks will cause no serious harm to the other participant. You would still refuse such an unreasonable demand, wouldn't you?

These questions fall within the domain of *social psychology*, the study of people interacting with people. Social psychology is the subfield of psychology that deals with how our thoughts, feelings, and behaviors are influenced by our social interactions with others and the culture in which we live.

In this chapter, we touch upon these questions and others as we explore how we perceive others in our social environment, how we relate to them, and how we are influenced by them. We consider what social psychologists have learned about these social processes, beginning with how we perceive others and how our perceptions of others influence our behavior.

Did You Know That . . .

- We literally begin forming an impression of other people in a fraction of a second of catching a glimpse of them? (p. 450)
- Adolescents tend to disclose more about themselves and use fewer privacy settings on Facebook than do adults? (p. 451)
- Japanese are more likely than Americans to attribute their success to luck or fate than to themselves? (p. 453)
- Your attitudes may be shaped in part by your genes? (p. 454)
- In our society, it pays to be tall—literally? (p. 460)
- The common stereotype that "girls can't do math" may discourage young women from pursuing promising career opportunities in engineering and the sciences? (p. 460)
- Most people who participated in a famous but controversial study administered what they believed to be painful and dangerous electric shocks to other people when instructed to do so by the experimenter? (p. 478)
- Studying in the presence of others who are also hitting the books is likely to increase how hard you study? (p. 480)

12.1 Perceiving Others

1 **Identify** the major influences on first impressions and **explain** why first impressions often become lasting impressions.

2 **Identify** and **describe** cognitive biases that influence causal attributions.

3 **Identify** three components of attitudes and **describe** the sources of attitudes and the pathways involved in changing attitudes through persuasive appeals.

4 **Describe** cognitive dissonance theory and **explain** how cognitive dissonance can be reduced.

People from East Asian cultures are typically more reserved about disclosing personal information when meeting new people.

© AP Images/Chiaki Tsukumo

In Chapter 3, we explored the ways in which we perceive the physical world of objects and shapes. As we turn to the study of **social psychology**, we focus on the ways in which we perceive the social world, composed of the people whom we see and with whom we interact in our daily lives. **Social perception** is the process by which we come to form an understanding of our social environment based on observations of others, personal experiences, and information we receive. In this section, we examine three major aspects of social perception: forming impressions of others, making sense of the causes of our own and other people's behaviors, and developing attitudes that incline us to respond to people, issues, and objects in positive or negative ways.

Impression Formation: Why First Impressions Count So Much

Impression formation is the process involved by which we form an opinion or impression of another person. We form first impressions quickly. Just how quickly? Evidence from the research lab shows that people begin forming impressions upon catching a glimpse of a person, literally in the blink of an eye or a mere fraction of a second (Gregoire, 2015; Todorov & Porter, 2014).

What does this mean for us? Why is it important? Think about the fact that when you are meeting a blind date or interviewing for a job, the person greeting you may well have sized you up before you even get to say a word. Although impressions may well change as people get to know you better, you never get a second chance to make a first impression. It's best to make that first impression count in your favor.

First impressions count so much because they tend to be long-lasting and difficult to change, even in the face of discrepant information (Gawronski et al., 2010; Gregoire, 2015). First impressions also influence how we relate to people. Suppose you meet a number of people at a party or social gathering. Within the first few minutes of talking to them—perhaps even the first few seconds—you begin forming impressions that will be hard to change. Even before you begin talking to someone, you have already started to size up their surface characteristics, such as how they look and how they dress. Let us examine some of the factors that influence impression formation, including personal disclosure, social schemas, stereotyping, and self-fulfilling prophecies.

Personal Disclosure: Going Beyond Name, Rank, and Serial Number

We generally form more favorable impressions of people who are willing to disclose personal information about themselves. But revealing too much too soon can lead

social psychology The subfield in psychology that deals with how our thoughts, feelings, and behaviors are influenced by our social interactions with others.

social perception The processes by which we form impressions, make judgments, and develop attitudes about the people and events that constitute our social world.

impression formation The process of developing an opinion or impression of another person.

people to form a negative impression (Anderson et al., 2011; Park, Jin, & Jin, 2011). People who disclose too much about themselves in the first stages of a social relationship tend to be perceived by others as less secure, less mature, and more poorly adjusted than those who are more restrained regarding what they say about themselves. Cultural differences also come into play in determining how much disclosure is deemed acceptable. People in East Asian societies, such as China and Japan, tend to disclose less about themselves than do people in the West (Kim & Sherman, 2007; Nevid & Sta. Maria, 1999).

In this age of social media, people often disclose more information about themselves on social media sites like Facebook than they do in face-to-face interactions. "*Hey mom, what's on your Facebook?*" was the title of a recent psychology study of self-disclosure by adolescents and adults (Muise & Desmarais, 2012). It turned out that adolescents reported disclosing more about themselves and used fewer privacy settings than did adults. Bear in mind that whatever you disclose about yourself may be discoverable by potential employers who scour the Internet to find information about prospective job candidates.

Impressions as Social Schemas: Why Early Impressions Are Hard to Budge

An impression is a type of **social schema** or mental representation we form about people in our social environment. One reason that first impressions tend to be long-lasting is that we filter new information about people through the earlier impressions or social schemas we have formed about them. Let's say we have a favorable impression (a social schema) of someone we recently met. If that person then does something annoying or upsetting to us, we're more likely to look for extenuating factors to explain away the person's undesirable behavior ("He must be having a bad day") than we are to alter our existing impression. On the other hand, when we form a negative impression of someone, we're more likely to ignore or explain away positive information we later receive about that person.

Stereotyping: Judging Groups, Not Individuals

We all have preconceived ideas about groups of people, called **stereotypes**, that influence our first impressions (Aronson, Wilson, & Akert, 2004). Stereotypes are sets of beliefs about the characteristics, attributes, and behaviors of members of a particular group or category. For example, we might stereotype fraternity members as big drinkers or people who wear glasses as intelligent.

Stereotypes influence first impressions. Recall the couple speaking in Italian on the street corner. Did you think they were engaged in a romantic exchange or in illegal, Mafia-related activities? Both interpretations are based on stereotypes of Italians as romantic or crooks (Lepore & Brown, 1997). As the example suggests, stereotypes may include positive attributes (romantic in this case) or negative attributes (criminal). However, stereotypes about members of other social or ethnic groups are usually more negative than those about members of one's own group.

Social psychologists believe that stereotyping is a normal cognitive tendency, a kind of cognitive shorthand that simplifies the process of making social judgments (Nelson, 2002). Upon meeting someone for the first time, we automatically classify the person as belonging to a particular group or category. Stereotypes allow us to more efficiently use stored information about other groups instead of expending cognitive resources to evaluate each individual member of the groups we encounter. Efficient, perhaps—but not necessarily accurate.

Stereotyping on the basis of race, ethnicity, gender, age, disability, body weight, or sexual orientation can lead us to make inferences about people that prove to be unfounded as we get to know them as individuals. Once stereotypes are formed, they tend to stick and become resistant to change even in the face of contrary information.

CONCEPT 12.1
Our preconceived ideas influence the impressions we form of people even before we meet them.

CONCEPT 12.2
The amount of personal information we disclose affects the impressions that other people form of us.

CONCEPT 12.3
By filtering information through existing social schemas, first impressions become lasting impressions.

Think twice about what you post online! Future employers may check you out on social networking websites. Your photos may also be tagged by friends and posted on their pages long after you thought you had deleted them.

social schema A mental image or representation that we use to understand our social environment.

stereotypes The tendency to characterize all members of a particular group as having certain characteristics in common.

Stereotyping can damage group relations and be used to justify social inequities. For example, many Europeans during the time of colonial expansion held a stereotyped belief that Blacks lacked the ability to govern themselves, which they used as a justification for colonial rule in Africa. Stereotypes of obese people as lazy and undisciplined may lead employers to unfairly pass them over for jobs or promotions.

Self-Fulfilling Prophecies: What Goes Around Comes Around

When you form an initial impression of someone, you may act toward the person in a way that mirrors your impression. Let's say you form an impression of someone as unfriendly. This belief can become a type of **self-fulfilling prophecy** if it leads you to be somewhat standoffish when interacting with the person and he or she responds in kind. Self-fulfilling prophecies may also lead to underperformance in school. Teachers who expect students to do poorly may convey their lower expectations to their students. Students may then begin thinking less of themselves, which can sap their motivation, leading them to underperform.

© buruhtan/Shutterstock.com

Attributions: Why the Pizza Guy Is Late

The pizza guy delivers your pizza 30 minutes late. Do you believe the guy was loafing on the job or that some external influence (for example, traffic, orders backing up) caused the delay? What about the times *you* arrive late? Are you likely to reach the same judgments about your own behavior as you do when explaining the behavior of others?

An **attribution** is a personal explanation of the causes of behavior or events we observe. When interpreting our social world, we act like personal scientists who seek to understand underlying causes. We tend to explain events by attributing them to either dispositional causes or situational causes. **Dispositional causes** are internal factors, such as the internal traits, needs, or personal choices of the person involved (the "actor"). **Situational causes** are external or environmental factors, such as the pressures or demands imposed upon the actor. Saying that the pizza guy is late because he is a loafer invokes a dispositional cause. Saying he is late because several other pies were in the oven at the time invokes a situational cause. Social psychologists have found that attributions can be affected by certain cognitive biases, such as the *fundamental attribution error*, the *actor–observer effect*, and the *self-serving bias*.

Fundamental Attribution Error

Social psychologist Fritz Heider (1958) proposed that people tend to focus more on the behavior of others than on the circumstances in which the behavior occurs. Consequently, they tend to overlook situational influences when explaining other people's behavior. The **fundamental attribution error** is a term that social psychologists use to describe the tendency to attribute behavior to internal causes, such as traits like intelligence or laziness, without regard to the situational influences that come to bear on people.

Note a cross-cultural difference. People in individualistic cultures such as the United States and Canada are more likely to commit fundamental attribution errors than those in collectivist cultures such as China, Japan, and Taiwan (Chen, Jing, & Lee, 2012; Kitayama et al., 2003). Collectivist cultures tend to emphasize external causes of behavior that stem from the social environment, such as obligations imposed on people. Individualistic cultures, by contrast, emphasize individuality and autonomy of the self. People from these cultures are quicker to assume that behavior results from internal factors, such as traits, attitudes, or motives.

CONCEPT 12.4

We tend to explain events by attributing them to either dispositional or situational causes—that is, to factors within either the individual or the environment.

CONCEPT 12.5

People tend to overemphasize internal causes and to overlook situational influences when explaining other people's behavior.

CONCEPT 12.6

The actor–observer effect leads us to attribute the behavior of others to dispositional internal causes but to explain our own behavior in terms of the situational demands we face in the environment.

self-fulfilling prophecy An expectation that helps bring about the outcome that is expected.

attribution An assumption about the causes of behavior or events.

dispositional causes Causes relating to the internal characteristics or traits of individuals.

situational causes Causes relating to external or environmental events.

fundamental attribution error The tendency to attribute behavior to internal causes without regard to situational influences.

The Actor–Observer Effect

When people commit the fundamental attribution error, they ignore the external circumstances that influence the behavior of others. But do we commit the same error when explaining our own behavior? Apparently not. Social psychologists have identified another type of cognitive bias that comes into play, called the **actor–observer effect**—the tendency to attribute the causes of one's own behavior to external factors, such as situational demands, while attributing other people's behavior to internal causes or dispositions. If you do poorly on an exam, you're likely to attribute your poor performance to external causes—the exam wasn't fair, you didn't have time to study, the material you studied wasn't on the exam, and so on. But when someone else does poorly, you're likely to think the person lacked the ability to do well or was too lazy to study.

Heider (1958) attributed the actor–observer effect to differences in perspective. As an actor, you look outward to the environment, so the situation engulfs your view. But your perspective as an observer is engulfed by your view of the actor within the situation. Recent research indicates that the actor–observer effect may be weaker than many people suspect and limited to certain situations, such as when the actor and observer know each other very well (Malle, 2006).

Self-Serving Bias

A specific type of attributional bias in performance situations is the **self-serving bias**—the tendency to attribute personal successes to internal or dispositional causes and personal failures to external or situational causes. In other words, people tend to take credit for their successes but disclaim responsibility for their failures. If you get a good grade on an exam, you are likely to attribute it to your ability or talent—an internal attribution ("I got an A"). Yet you are likely to attribute a poor grade to an external cause beyond your control—an external attribution ("I didn't have enough time to study" or "The questions were unfair").

The self-serving bias—letting failures flow off our backs while taking success to heart—helps bolster self-esteem. Members of sports teams show a similar bias. They make more internal attributions about the success of their teams after victories ("We played well as a team") than defeats ("They were just lucky") (Sherman, Kim, & Heejung, 2005).

The self-serving bias is widespread in Western cultures, such as the United States and Canada, but it is found much less frequently in East Asian cultures, such as Japan, China, and Taiwan (DeAngelis, 2003; Heine et al., 2001). Unlike Americans, the Japanese tend to attribute their successes to luck and their failures to lack of ability or talent. The self-serving bias may be embedded within a cultural ethic in the United States and other individualistic Western cultures that value the protection of self-esteem (Markus & Kitayama, 1991). The opposite tendency (valuing self-criticism and humility) is found more often in collectivist cultures, such as in China or Japan (Oyserman, Coon, & Kemmelmeier, 2002). In these cultures, people are more attuned to their responsibilities to the group than to their individuality or the need to enhance their individual self-esteem. Blaming oneself for personal failure affirms one's responsibility to the social group and the need to work harder to improve one's performance in the future.

Attitudes: How Do You Feel About . . . ?

What are your attitudes toward gun control laws, sport utility vehicles (SUVs), and vegetarian diets? An **attitude** is an evaluation or judgment of either liking or disliking a person, object, or social issue (Bohner & Dickel, 2011). We can conceptualize attitudes as comprising three components: (1) *cognitions* (sets of beliefs), (2) *emotions* (feelings of

CONCEPT 12.7
Another type of cognitive bias, the self-serving bias, comes into play in accounting for the tendency of people to take credit for their successes but explain away their failures.

CONCEPT LINK
As discussed in Chapter 7, cognitive biases can impair our ability to make rational or sound decisions. See Module 7.1.

CONCEPT 12.8
The self-serving bias is widespread in Western cultures but virtually absent in some Eastern cultures.

CONCEPT 12.9
To social psychologists, attitudes are judgments of liking or disliking that can be conceptualized in terms of three components: cognitions, emotions, and behaviors.

CONCEPT LINK
You'll recall from Chapter 8 that emotions also include three basic components: bodily arousal, cognitions, and expressed behaviors. See Module 8.4.

actor–observer effect The tendency to attribute the causes of one's own behavior to situational factors while attributing the causes of other people's behavior to internal factors or dispositions.

self-serving bias The tendency to take credit for our accomplishments and to explain away our failures or disappointments.

attitude A positive or negative evaluation of people, objects, or issues.

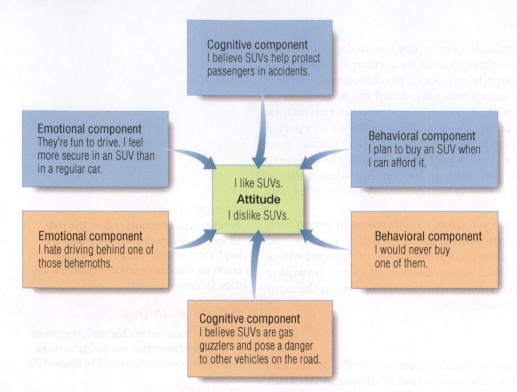

FIGURE 12.1 Attitudes
The attitudes we hold consist of cognitive, emotional, and behavioral components.

CONCEPT 12.10

Our social environments shape the attitudes we develop, but research points to possible genetic influences as well.

CONCEPT 12.11

Though attitudes predispose us to act in certain ways, they are not very strong predictors of behavior.

cognitive dissonance theory The belief that people are motivated to resolve discrepancies between their behavior and their attitudes, beliefs, or perceptions.

elaboration likelihood model (ELM) A theoretical model that posits two channels by which persuasive appeals lead to attitude change: a central route and a peripheral route.

liking or disliking), and (3) *behaviors* (inclinations to act positively or negatively). For example, you may hold favorable or unfavorable views about SUVs, feel positively or negatively toward them, and be either inclined or disinclined to purchase one if you were shopping for a vehicle (see ■ Figure 12.1).

The importance we ascribe to attitudes is a function of their personal relevance. Our attitudes toward sport utility vehicles (love them, hate them) will be more important to us if we happen to be considering buying one. Yet it's also the case that the more often we express a particular attitude, the more important it is likely to become to us (Roese & Olson, 1994). Think of an example in which your behavior was inconsistent with your attitudes or beliefs. Were you motivated to reconcile these discrepancies? Or did you simply ignore them?

Source of Attitudes

Our attitudes are acquired from many sources in our social environment—our parents, teachers, peers, personal experiences, and media sources such as newspapers, television, and movies. Not surprisingly, people from similar backgrounds tend to hold similar attitudes. Yet evidence also points to a possible genetic contribution (Abrahamson, Baker, & Caspi, 2002; Smith et al., 2011). Twins reared apart show a surprising degree of shared attitudes on a range of issues that cannot be explained by a common environmental influence. We shouldn't think that people inherit any gene or genes for a particular attitude, such as favoring stricter gun control laws or not. Rather, we can think about genetics influencing factors, such as intelligence or personality traits, that increase the likelihood of developing a particular set of attitudes. That said, genetic factors appear to be less important determinants of attitudes than environmental influences (DeAngelis, 2004).

Attitudes and Behavior: Not as Strong a Link as You Might Expect

Attitudes may not carry over into behavior. You may hold favorable attitudes toward environmental issues but still purchase a high-performance car that guzzles gas. Or you may have a favorable attitude toward a particular product but purchase a competing product. Overall, attitudes are only modestly related to behavior (Wallace et al., 2005). The lack of consistency reflects many factors, especially situational constraints. We may have an inclination to act in a certain way but be unable to carry out the action because of the particular demands we face in that particular situation. For example, you may hold a positive attitude toward a specific charity but be unable to make a contribution to the latest fund drive because you are running short of cash or need the money for another important purpose. Under other conditions, however, attitudes are more strongly linked to behavior—such as when the attitudes are more stable, are held with greater confidence or certainty, when they relate specifically to the behavior at hand, when the person is free to perform or not perform the behavior, and when the attitude can be more readily recalled from memory (for example, Glasman & Albarracín, 2006; Olson & Maio, 2003).

Cognitive Dissonance: Maintaining Consistency Between Your Attitudes and Behavior

What happens when your actions deviate from your attitudes? Say you believe in protecting the environment but buy a gas-guzzling car. Are you likely to change your behavior (buy a different car)? Or would you change your beliefs, perceptions, or attitudes about the importance of protecting the environment or the risks posed by gas guzzlers? In other words, how would you iron out the kinks between your cognitions and your behavior? Or would you even bother?

According to **cognitive dissonance theory**, inconsistencies between attitudes and behavior lead to a state of dissonance, or emotional discomfort (Festinger, 1957). This uncomfortable state motivates people to change their attitudes or behaviors to make them more compatible (Aronson, Wilson, & Akert, 2004). There are several ways in which people can reduce cognitive dissonance (Cooper, 2011; Matz & Wood, 2005). They can change their behavior to fit their attitudes or beliefs, change their attitudes or beliefs to fit their behavior, attempt to explain away any inconsistencies between their behavior and their attitudes or beliefs, or simply ignore any discrepancies. For example, smokers who believe that smoking causes cancer but continue to smoke may reduce cognitive dissonance by altering their behavior (quitting smoking), altering their beliefs (adopting the belief that smoking isn't really all that harmful), or using a form of rationalization to explain away the inconsistency ("Cancer doesn't run in my family"). Yet perhaps the most common way of reducing dissonance is not to change either beliefs or behavior but simply to ignore inconsistencies until they fade away ("I'll worry about my smoking when I get older") (Newby-Clark, McGregor, & Zanna, 2002). ■ Figure 12.2 illustrates some ways of reducing cognitive dissonance. As we'll see in the Applying Psychology in Daily Life feature, salespeople, advertisers, fund-raisers, and others who try to influence us often use strategies that seek to take advantage of our need for consistency in our behavior and attitudes.

Spencer Grant/PhotoEdit

Think of an example in which your behavior was inconsistent with your attitudes or beliefs. Were you motivated to reconcile these discrepancies? Or did you simply ignore them?

CONCEPT 12.12

Cognitive dissonance theory holds that people are motivated to reconcile discrepancies between their behavior and their cognitions.

CONCEPT 12.13

According to the elaboration likelihood model, attitude change occurs through either a central processing route or a peripheral processing route.

Persuasion: The Fine Art of Changing People's Minds

We are constantly bombarded with messages attempting to persuade us to change our beliefs and attitudes. Commercials on radio and TV, and advertisements in newspapers and magazines and on the Internet, attempt to persuade us to adopt more favorable attitudes toward advertised products and to purchase them. Political candidates and political action groups seek to sway us to support their candidacies and causes. Doctors, religious leaders, teachers, friends, and family members regularly urge us to change our behaviors, beliefs, and attitudes in ways they believe would be beneficial to us.

Short of secluding ourselves in an isolated cabin in the woods, we can hardly avoid persuasive appeals. But how do such appeals lead to attitude change? And what factors are likely to increase their effectiveness?

The Elaboration Likelihood Model: Two Pathways to Persuasion

A leading model of attitude change is the **elaboration likelihood model (ELM)** (Petty & Briñol, 2008). According to this model, people are more likely

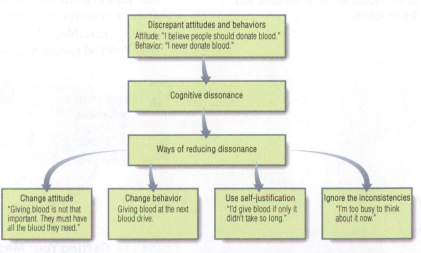

FIGURE 12.2 Ways of Reducing Cognitive Dissonance

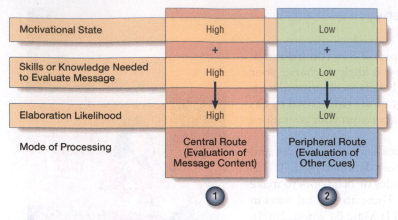

FIGURE 12.3 Elaboration Likelihood Model

According to the elaboration likelihood model, attitude change occurs through one of two routes of cognitive processing—❶ a central route or ❷ a peripheral route. When elaboration likelihood is high, we attend more carefully to the content of the message itself. When it is low, as when we are distracted or disinterested, we attend to peripheral cues unrelated to the content of the message.

CONCEPT 12.14

The effectiveness of persuasive appeals is influenced by variables relating to the source, the message itself, and the recipient.

to carefully evaluate ("elaborate") a persuasive message when their motivational state is high (that is, when they are willing to exert the mental effort needed to evaluate the message) and when they possess the skills or knowledge needed to evaluate the information (see ■ Figure 12.3).

When evaluation likelihood is high, attitude change occurs via a *central route* of processing information, whereby people carefully evaluate the content of the message. When elaboration likelihood is low, attitude change occurs through a *peripheral route* of cognitive processing, whereby people focus on cues not centrally related to the content of the message. Let us use the example of a televised political debate. Assume that viewers are alert, well informed about the issues, and interested in the views the candidates hold. Under these conditions, elaboration likelihood is high and attitude change is likely to occur through a central processing route by which the viewers carefully evaluate the arguments the respective candidates make. Conversely, if the viewers are distracted, fatigued, or uninterested in the issues, they are not likely to carefully evaluate each candidate's message. Attitude change occurring under these conditions is likely to be based on peripheral cues that are not directly related to the content of the candidate's message, such as the physical attractiveness of the candidate. In other words, the viewers may be persuaded to endorse candidates on the basis of how they look in the debate rather than how they stand on the issues.

Advertisers often take advantage of the peripheral route of attitude change by using leading sports stars as commercial spokespeople. Celebrity endorsers needn't even mention the distinctive qualities of the product. Just using the product or wearing it may be sufficient to convey the message that the advertiser wants to get across.

Variables Influencing Persuasion. Some persuasive appeals are more effective than others. Persuasion is influenced by many variables, as shown in ■ Figure 12.4, including those relating to the source, the message, and the recipient (Littlejohn, 2002; Visser & Cooper, 2003; Whiting et al., 2012):

- *Source variables.* Source variables are features of the communicator who presents the message. Communicators are generally more persuasive when they are perceived as *credible* (knowledgeable and trustworthy), *likable* (attractive and personable), and *similar* to the receiver in key respects (for example, a former substance abuser may be more successful in persuading current substance abusers to accept treatment than a person who has never abused drugs).

- *Message variables.* Messages that contain emotional appeals are often persuasive. Political candidates, for example, frequently appeal to voters' fears when

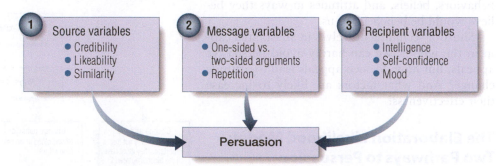

FIGURE 12.4 Getting Your Message Across: Factors in Persuasive Appeals
The effectiveness of persuasive appeals depends upon ❶ characteristics of the source of the message, ❷ the message itself, and ❸ the recipient of the message.

they characterize their opponents as "soft" on national security issues. Presenting both sides of an argument is generally more effective than presenting only one side, so long as the communicator refutes the other side. Messages that run counter to the perceived interests of the communicator tend to be perceived as more credible. Not surprisingly, people paid great attention a few years ago when a member of the R. J. Reynolds family of tobacco growers spoke out on the dangers of smoking. Third, the more often we are exposed to a message, the more favorably we are likely to evaluate it, but only up to a point. When the message is repeated often enough, people may come to believe it, whether or not it is true. But with further repetition, irritation and tedium begin to set in, and acceptance of the message begins to decline.

Direct eye contact may backfire in making a persuasive pitch if it makes the receiver uncomfortable.

- *Recipient variables.* No one is immune to persuasive appeals, but some people are easier to persuade than others. Those of low intelligence or low self-confidence are generally more susceptible to persuasive appeals. People also tend to be more receptive to persuasive messages when they are in a positive mood rather than a negative one. A good mood may motivate people to see things in a more positive light. And despite the common belief that eye contact boosts persuasive appeals, psychologists in a recent study found just the opposite, that direct eye contact actually decreased the ability to change a person's attitudes about a political issue (Chen et al., 2013). Though direct eye contact may convey interest in the other person, it may also make the receiver feel uncomfortable or even threatened, especially when it is lasts beyond a few seconds (Moyer, 2016).

The major influences on social perception are reviewed in Concept Chart 12.1.

Concept Chart 12.1 Perceiving Others

Topic	What It Is	Influences on Social Perception
Initial impressions	Initial evaluation (liking or disliking) of others	Initial impressions are influenced by physical appearance, attire, stereotypes, and degree of personal disclosure. They are difficult to dislodge because we tend to filter new information through them and because they may become self-fulfilling prophecies.
Attributions	Personal explanations of the causes of behavior	Attributional biases affecting social perception include the fundamental attribution error, the actor–observer effect, and the self-serving bias.
Attitudes	Judgments of liking or disliking people, objects, and issues	Attitudes are influenced by the social environment and possibly by genetic factors. They do not necessarily predict behavior. According to the elaboration likelihood model, attitude change occurs through either a central or peripheral route of processing, depending on the degree to which the message is elaborated. The effectiveness of persuasive appeals depends on source variables, recipient variables, and message variables.

MODULE REVIEW 12.1 Perceiving Others

Recite It

1. **Identify** the major influences on first impressions and **explain** why first impressions often become lasting impressions.

   First impressions are influenced by surface characteristics, such as physical appearance and attire, and by stereotypes and personal (a) _____.

   First impressions may become lasting impressions when people reconcile discrepant information with their existing impressions, or social (b) _____. Impressions may also become self-(c)_____ prophecies.

2. **Identify** and **describe** cognitive biases that influence causal attributions.

The (d) _____ _____ error is an overemphasis on internal or dispositional causes of behavior to the exclusion of situational factors.

The actor–(e)_____ effect is the tendency to explain our own behavior in terms of the demands of the situation while explaining the behavior of others in terms of internal or dispositional causes.

The self-(f) _____ bias bolsters self-esteem in that it involves attributing personal success to one's talents or abilities while explaining personal failure in terms of external causes.

3. **Identify** three components of attitudes and **describe** the sources of attitudes and the pathways involved in changing attitudes through persuasive appeals.

Psychologists conceptualize attitudes as having three components: (g) _____, emotions, and behaviors.

The social environment, which encompasses our relationships and experiences with others as well as our exposure to mass (h) _____, is the learning ground for the acquisition of attitudes. Genetic factors may also play a role.

The (i) _____ _____ model explains attitude change in response to persuasive appeals through two pathways, a central pathway based on careful evaluation of the (j) _____ of a message and a (k) _____ pathway, based on incidental or peripheral cues not directly associated with the content of the message.

4. **Describe** cognitive dissonance theory and **explain** how cognitive dissonance can be reduced.

Cognitive (l) _____ theory holds that inconsistencies between our behavior and our attitudes, beliefs, or perceptions produce a state of psychological tension or (m) _____ that motivates efforts to reconcile these inconsistencies.

Cognitive dissonance may be reduced by changing one's behavior to be (n) _____ with one's attitudes or beliefs, changing one's attitudes or beliefs to fit one's (o) _____, attempting to rationalize any inconsistency between behavior and attitudes or beliefs, or simply (p) _____ any discrepancies.

Recall It

1. A mental image or representation we use to understand our social environment is called a social _____.

2. When we interpret a behavior or an event, we usually see it as due to either _____ or _____ causes.

3. The fundamental attribution error refers to an underestimation or overestimation of internal factors?

4. Give a social-psychological definition of the term *attitude*.

5. Discrepancies between behavior and attitudes may produce an unpleasant state of tension called _____.

6. Match the following terms with the appropriate descriptions: (a) peripheral processing route; (b) source variable(s); (c) message variable(s); (d) recipient variable(s).

   i. the tendency of repetition to lead to more favorable evaluations
   ii. when people are not likely to carefully evaluate message contents
   iii. the relationship between low self-confidence and greater susceptibility to persuasion
   iv. credibility, likability, and similarity

Think About It

■ Why do first impressions tend to become lasting impressions?

■ Do you have a tendency to take credit for your successes and explain away your failures? How might the self-serving bias prevent you from learning from your mistakes and taking appropriate steps to prevent them in the future?

Recite It *answers placed at the end of chapter.*

12.2 Relating to Others

5 **Identify** factors that influence attraction.

6 **Identify** the components of love identified in the triangular model of love.

7 **Describe** the decision-making model of helping and **identify** factors that influence helping behavior.

8 **Define** prejudice, **explain** how it develops, and **apply** your knowledge to ways of reducing it.

9 **Identify** factors that contribute to human aggression.

Social psychologists are interested in how individuals relate to each other in their social environments. We may categorize ways of relating to others in terms of positive and negative interactions. Attraction, love, and helping are positive interactions. Negative ways of relating include prejudiced behavior and aggression. In this module, we examine what psychologists have learned about these positive and negative ways of relating to others.

Attraction: Getting to Like (or Love) You

In nature, attraction is the tendency for two objects or bodies to be drawn toward each other, like the opposite poles of a magnet. In psychology, **attraction** describes feelings of liking others as well as having positive thoughts about them and inclinations to act positively toward them. Attraction is not limited to romantic or sexual attraction. Social psychologists use the term more broadly to include other kinds of attraction as well, such as feelings of liking toward friends. Here we consider key determinants of attraction as well as that special type of attraction we associate with romantic love. Psychologists have identified several key determinants of attraction, including similarity, physical attractiveness, proximity, and reciprocity.

Similarity

Like birds of a feather, we are generally attracted to people with whom we share similar values and attitudes (Rushton & Bons, 2005; Ullrich & Krueger, 2010). We also tend to like people who are similar to us in characteristics such as physical appearance, social class, race, height, musical tastes, and intelligence. People also tend to select mates who are similar to themselves on attitudes, religious views, and values (Luo & Klohnen, 2005). People are even more likely to marry others whose first or last names resemble their own (Jones et al., 2004).

Why are people attracted to similar others? The most widely held view is that similarity is gratifying because each person in the relationship serves to validate, reinforce, and enhance the other's self-concept. If you echo my sentiments about movies, politics, and the like, I might feel better about myself.

Does this mean that relationships are doomed to fail if two people (roommates, friends, or lovers) differ in their attitudes, interests, or tastes? Not necessarily. For one thing, no two people are identical in all respects (fortunately so!). At least some common ground is necessary to anchor a relationship, but every successful relationship still requires compromise and accommodation to keep it afloat. Not surprisingly, the attitudes of dating partners tend to become more closely aligned over time (Davis & Rusbult, 2001).

Recent research suggests that when people consider the personality traits of an ideal romantic partner, they tend to be interested in partners who have similar

CONCEPT 12.15
Attraction is influenced by similarity, physical attractiveness, proximity, and reciprocity.

attraction Feelings of liking for others, together with having positive thoughts about them and inclinations to act toward them in positive ways.

traits but have them to a greater degree (Figueredo, Sefcek, & Jones, 2006). That is, they seek partners with similar Big Five personality traits as their own but who are somewhat more conscientious, extraverted, and agreeable, while also less neurotic than themselves.

Physical Attractiveness

We might like to think we are attracted to romantic partners because of their inner qualities. However, we tend to be attracted to others because of their outer packaging, not their inner soul. Physical attractiveness is a major factor in determining both interpersonal and sexual or romantic attraction (Eastwick et al., 2013; Lippa, 2012). Note some gender differences, however. Men typically place greater emphasis than women on physical attractiveness of dating partners and mates, whereas women tend to put more emphasis on social status (Ha et al., 2012; Meltzer et al., 2014). But when it comes to casual sexual relationships, both men and women tend to place a premium on physical attractiveness of partners (Li & Kenrick, 2006; Nevid, 1984; Stambor, 2006a).

Our physical appearance affects how others perceive us. People tend to adopt a "what is beautiful is also good stereotype" in judging attractive people not simply as more attractive, but also as psychologically better adjusted, more intelligent, competent, extraverted, and socially skillful than less attractive people (for example, Little, Burt, & Perret, 2006; Lorenzo, Biesanz, & Human, 2010; Segal-Caspi, Roccas, & Sagiv, 2012). Yet there are exceptions to the "beautiful is good" stereotype: Attractive people are typically judged as more vain and less modest than their less attractive peers (Feingold, 1992).

No surprise perhaps, but attractive people tend to attract each other in dating and marital relationships. Evidence shows strong relationships between the attractiveness of dating partners and marital couples (Lee et al., 2008). A recent study examining dating patterns among members of a website (HotorNot.com), in which people rate the physical attractiveness of other members, showed that more attractive people tend to prefer dating more attractive others (Lee et al., 2008). When we do find a mismatch, we shouldn't be surprised to find that the less attractive partner compensates by having greater wealth or social position than the more attractive partner.

In our society, it also pays to be tall—literally. Evidence shows that height is associated with higher incomes (Dittmann, 2004; Tyrrell et al., 2016). The reason, investigators suspect, is that taller workers tend to be favored for sales and executive positions (Judge & Cable, 2004). Even standing tall by adopting a type of power pose induces feelings of powerfulness, increases tendencies to take more risks, and even boosts levels of testosterone in both men and women (Carney, Cuddy, & Yap, 2010; Huang et al., 2011).

Beauty may be in the eye of the beholder, but beholders tend to view beauty in highly similar ways. People tend to agree on whom they find attractive or not attractive. Two cues linked to perceived attraction are symmetrical facial features and a clear complexion (Fink & Penton-Voak, 2002; Fink et al., 2006).

Perceptions of the ideal female face vary little across cultures (Langlois et al., 2000). In one study, investigators asked groups of White, Euro-American students, and recently arrived Asian and Hispanic students to judge the attractiveness of photographs of Asian, Hispanic, Black, and White women (Cunningham et al., 1995). Judgments of physical beauty were generally consistent for photographs of members of the different groups. Faces rated as more attractive typically had such features as high cheekbones and eyebrows, widely spaced eyes, a small nose, thin cheeks, a large smile, a full lower lip, a small chin, and a fuller hairstyle. Both male and female raters tended to judge the same faces as attractive; they also tended to agree that faces of women with more feminine features were more attractive than those

Evidence suggests that it pays to be tall—literally. Researchers find that taller people typically earn more than shorter workers. How might you explain this finding?

Bikeriderlondon/Shutterstock.com

with more masculine features (Angier, 1998). Yet perhaps surprisingly, both male and female raters generally found male faces with more feminine features to be more attractive. The more refined and delicate features of a youthful Leonardo DiCaprio, for example, are preferred over the more squared-jawed, masculinized features of a young Arnold Schwarzenegger (Angier, 1998).

Although some features of physical beauty appear to be universal, cultural differences certainly do exist. In certain African cultures, for example, feminine beauty is associated with such physical features as long necks and round, disk-like lips. Female plumpness is valued in some societies, whereas in others, including our own, the female ideal is associated with an unrealistic standard of thinness (see Chapter 8). In our society, both men and women tend to value slenderness in potential partners (Fales et al., 2016), but social pressures to be thin are placed disproportionately on women.

One explanation for why people who fall short of a physical ideal are likely to be saved from a lifetime of dinners for one is the **matching hypothesis,** the prediction that people will seek partners who are similar to themselves in physical attractiveness and other characteristics (Sprecher & Fehr, 2011; Taylor et al., 2011). Evidence generally supports the matching hypothesis, but as noted previously, when mismatches in physical attractiveness occur, it's often the case that the less attractive partner compensates by having greater wealth or social position than the more attractive partner.

When rating male faces, both men and women tend to rate those having more feminine features, such as the refined and delicate features of a Johnny Depp or Robert Pattinson, as more attractive than those with more masculinized features, such as those of Dwayne "The Rock" Johnson.

Proximity

Friendship patterns are strongly influenced by physical **proximity**. If you live in a college dormitory, your friends are more likely to live down the hall than across campus. Your earliest friends were probably children who lived next door or down the block from you.

Proximity increases the chances of interacting with others and getting to know them better, thus providing a basis for developing feelings of attraction toward them. Another explanation for the positive effects of proximity on attraction is the tendency for people to have more in common with people who live nearby or attend the same classes. Similarity in attitudes and background can increase feelings of liking. Proximity can also increase negative attraction, or dislike. Repeated contact with someone you dislike may intensify negative feelings.

Reciprocity. **Reciprocity** is the tendency to like others who like us back. We typically respond in kind to people who compliment us, do us favors, or tell us how much they like us. Reciprocal interactions build upon themselves, leading to feelings of liking. Yet we may be wary of people who compliment us too quickly or seem to like us too much before they get to know us. We may suspect that they want something from us or are not very discriminating.

When it comes to romantic attraction, playing hard to get by holding back whether you are attracted to someone may make you hard to forget. Recently, investigators told female college students that a group of college men had rated their desirability, along with the desirability of other women, based on their Facebook profiles (Whitchurch, Wilson, & Gilbert, 2011). Some women were told the men liked them the best, whereas other women were told men gave them only average ratings. Other women were left to wonder, being told only that the men's ratings wouldn't be revealed to them and that the men might have liked them best or might

matching hypothesis The belief that people tend to pair off with others who are similar to themselves in physical attractiveness and other characteristics.

proximity Nearness or propinquity.

reciprocity The principle that people tend to like others who like them back.

have rated them as average. Now it was the women's turn to rate the guys based on their Facebook profiles. In reality, but unbeknownst to the women, the "male students" were actually a fiction, a concoction the experimenter used to manipulate liking. Which group of women do you think gave the men the highest ratings? It turned out the reciprocity principle was supported, as women who were told the men had rated them highest returned the favor, rating the men higher than did women in the condition in which they were told they were average-looking . But women in the uncertainty condition (Did he like me best or not?) gave the men the highest ratings of all, supporting the view that keeping people guessing about how much you like them might just pique their interest in wanting to get to know you better. In other words, if a man wants to attract a woman's attention, perhaps he should think again about first poking her on Facebook (Cloud, 2011b).

Love: The Deepest Emotion

The subject of love has long intrigued and puzzled poets and philosophers. Only recently, however, have psychologists applied the scientific method to the study of love. Psychologists consider love to be both a motive (a need or want that drives us) and an emotion (or feeling state). According to a leading contemporary view of love, Robert Sternberg's (1988, 1997) triangular model, we can conceptualize love in terms of three basic components (see ■ Figure 12.5):

1. *Intimacy,* the close bond and feeling of attachment between two people, including their desire to share their innermost thoughts and feelings
2. *Passion,* an intense sexual desire for the other person
3. *Decision/commitment,* the recognition that one loves the other person (decisional component) and is committed to maintaining the relationship through good times and bad (commitment component)

Decision and commitment need not go hand in hand. A person may acknowledge being in love but not be ready or willing to make a lasting commitment.

Sternberg believes that different combinations of these three basic components characterize different types of loving relationships (see Table 12.1). In his view,

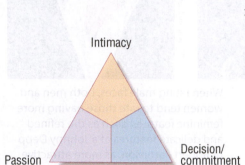

FIGURE 12.5 **Sternberg's Triangular Model of Love**

CONCEPT 12.16
Sternberg's triangular model of love proposes that different types of loving relationships can be characterized by different combinations of three basic components of love: intimacy, passion, and decision/commitment.

Table 12.1 Types of Love According to Sternberg's Triangular Model

Nonlove	A relationship in which all three components of love are absent. Most of our personal relationships are of this type—casual acquaintanceships that do not involve any elements of love.
Liking	A friendship in which intimacy is present but passion and decision/commitment are not.
Infatuation	A kind of "love at first sight," in which one experiences passionate desire for another person but in which there is neither intimacy nor decision/commitment.
Fatuous (foolish) love	The type of love associated with whirlwind romances and "quickie marriages," in which both passion and decision/commitment are present but intimacy is not.
Empty love	A kind of love characterized by the commitment to maintain a relationship that lacks passion and intimacy.
Romantic love	Love characterized by the combination of passion and intimacy but that lacks decision/commitment.
Consummate love	The complete measure of love, which combines passion, intimacy, and decision/commitment. Maintaining consummate love is often harder than achieving it.
Companionate love	A kind of love that combines intimacy with decision/commitment. We may see this kind of love in marriages in which passion is lacking, but has been replaced by a kind of committed and close friendship or partnership.

Source: Adapted from Sternberg, 1988.

romantic love combines intimacy and passion but is lacking in decision/commitment. Romantic love may burn brightly but soon flicker out. On the other hand, it may develop into a more abiding form of love called consummate love, which combines all three components: intimacy, passion, and decision/commitment. Consummate love may be more of an ideal for many couples than an enduring reality. In companionate love, the type of love found in many long-term marriages, intimacy and commitment remain strong even though passion has ebbed.

Sternberg proposes that relationships are balanced when the love triangles of both partners are well matched or closely overlapping; that is, when partners are similar in their levels of passion, intimacy, and commitment. But relationships may fizzle, rather than sizzle, when partners differ in these love components. For example, one partner may want to make a lasting commitment to the relationship, whereas the other's idea of making a commitment is deciding to stay the night.

Next we turn to another positive way of relating to others—helping others in time of need. We begin with a tragic story of nonhelping in which a young woman was brutally attacked and people who heard her agonizing screams did nothing to help her.

Helping Behavior: Lending a Hand to Others in Need

Even now, more than 50 years after the 1964 murder of 28-year-old Kitty Genovese on a quiet street in Queens, New York, the shock remains. Kitty screamed for help as an assailant viciously attacked her, stabbing her again and again until she lay dying from her wounds. From their nearby apartment windows, a number of witnesses (the exact number is unclear) heard Kitty's screams or saw the attack. But none rushed to her aid, although at least one person reportedly called the police, but not until after the first attack (Manning, Levine, & Collins, 2007). This tragic case prompted serious scientific inquiry into factors that determine helping behavior. Why do some bystanders help a stranger in need while others just pass by?

Is there something so callous in human nature that we would turn our backs on someone in need of assistance, even people in dire emergencies? If so, how are we to explain the countless acts of simple kindness of people who selflessly help people in need, let alone the heroic acts of people who risk their lives in emergency situations to save others? Consider the heroic efforts of the firefighters and police officers who responded to the terrorist attack on the World Trade Center on September 11, 2001, many of whom lost their lives in a valiant attempt to save others. Let us also recognize the heroic efforts of first responders in the Boston Marathon bombing, including many civilians who rushed to the site of the explosion to help the injured despite the obvious dangers to themselves. Clearly, the question is not whether people will help others in need but under what conditions they will help.

Helping is a form of **prosocial behavior**, or behavior that is beneficial to others. Psychologist C. Daniel Batson, a leading authority on helping, distinguishes between two types of motives that underlie helping behavior (Batson et al., 2002; Batson & Powell, 2003). One type of helping arises from *altruistic* motives—the pure, unselfish desire to help others without expecting anything in return. But another type is based on self-centered motives, such as the desire to help someone make oneself look good in the eyes of others or to avoid feeling guilty from failing to help. Batson believes that altruistic helping results from the helper's identification with the plight of the victim. By putting ourselves in the victim's shoes, so to speak, we are able to empathize with the person's suffering, which prompts us to take action. Batson's belief in pure altruism is not universally accepted, as some social psychologists believe that all forms of helping benefit the helper to a certain extent.

Bruce Ayres/Stone/Getty Images

In Sternberg's model, consummate love combines intimacy, passion, and decision/commitment. Consummate love may not be as enduring as companionate love, which combines intimacy and decision/commitment but lacks passion. But even couples for whom the flames of passion have ebbed may occasionally stir the embers.

The Brain Loves a Puzzle

As you read ahead, use the information in the text to solve the following puzzle:

If you were to collapse on the street and needed immediate help, why would you be less likely to receive help if the street was crowded than if there were but a few people nearby?

Andy Ryan/Stone/Getty Images

CONCEPT 12.17

Helping may be motivated by both altruistic and self-centered motives.

prosocial behavior Behavior that benefits others.

Altruistic acts take many forms, including selfless acts of heroism, as in the case of hundreds of firefighters who lost their lives in the effort to save others on September 11, 2001.

CONCEPT 12.18

According to the decision-making model, bystander intervention depends on a series of decisions leading to intervention.

CONCEPT 12.19

Helping behavior is influenced by situational and individual factors and by social norms.

bystander intervention Helping a stranger in distress.

social norms Standards that define what is socially acceptable in a given situation.

Bystander Intervention: Deciding to Get Involved—Or Not

The decision-making model of helping behavior proposed by Bibb Latané and John Darley (1970) explains **bystander intervention** in terms of a decision-making process that can be broken down into a series of five decisions (see ■ Figure 12.6). First, people must decide that a need for help exists. Second, they must decide that the situation is a clear emergency. Third, they must decide to assume personal responsibility for providing assistance. Fourth, they must decide what kind of help to give. Fifth, they must decide to implement this course of action.

Consider again the people who witnessed Kitty Genovese's murder but did nothing. Why didn't they help? The critical thinking exercise at the end of the chapter poses this question for you to answer. For now, however, let us examine what social psychologists have learned about the factors that affect helping behavior. Some of these factors may shed light on the inaction of those witnesses.

Influences on Helping

Many factors influence a person's willingness to help, including the following:

- *Situational ambiguity*. In an ambiguous situation in which it is not clear what is happening, people are much less likely to offer assistance than in situations involving a clear-cut emergency (Baron, Branscombe, & Byrne, 2009). People are also less likely to help in unfamiliar environments than in familiar ones (for example, when they are in strange cities rather than in their hometowns).

- *Perceived cost*. The likelihood of helping increases as the perceived cost to ourselves declines. We are more likely to lend our class notes to someone we believe will return them than to a person who doesn't appear trustworthy.

- *Diffusion of responsibility*. The presence of others may diffuse the sense of individual responsibility (Fischer et al., 2011). If you suddenly felt faint and were about to pass out on the street, you would be more likely to receive help if there were only a few bystanders than if the street were crowded with pedestrians. With fewer people present, it becomes more difficult to point to the "other guy" as the one responsible for taking action. If everyone believes the other guy will act, then no one acts.

- *Similarity*. People are more willing to help others whom they perceive to be similar to themselves—people who share a common background and beliefs. They are even more likely to help others who dress the way they do than those wearing different attire (Cialdini, 2007). People also tend to be more willing to help relatives than unrelated people (Gaulin & McBurney, 2001).

- *Empathy*. Having empathy, or understanding of a person's feelings or pain, is associated with a greater likelihood of helping a person in need (Batson, 2009; Penner et al., 2005).

- *Facial features*. People with baby-faced features are more likely to elicit help than people with more mature facial features (Keating et al., 2003).

- *Mood and gender*. People are generally more willing to help others when they are in a good mood (Baron, Branscombe, & Byrne, 2009). Despite changes in traditional gender roles, it remains the case that women in need are more likely to get help from strangers than are men in need.

- *Attributions of the cause of need*. People are much more likely to help others they judge to be innocent victims than those they believe have brought their problems on themselves (Batson, 1998). Thus, they may fail to lend assistance to homeless people and drug addicts whom they feel "deserve what they get."

- *Social norms*. **Social norms** prescribe behaviors that are expected of people in social situations. The social norm of "doing your part" in helping a worthy cause places a demand on people to help, especially in situations where their

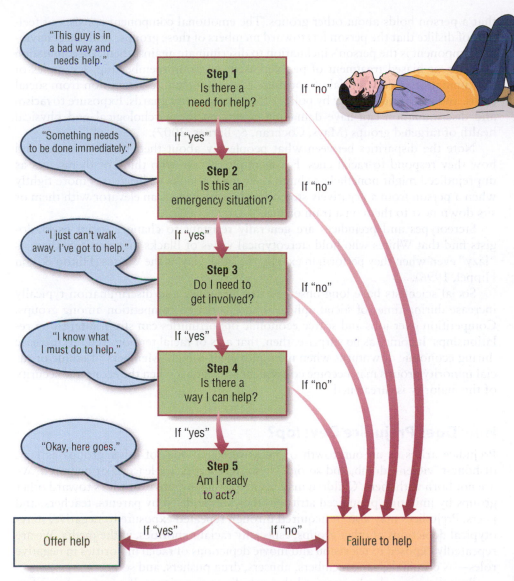

FIGURE 12.6 A Decision-Making Model of Helping

"This guy is in a bad way and needs help."

Step 1
Is there a need for help?

If "no"

If "yes"

"Something needs to be done immediately."

Step 2
Is this an emergency situation?

If "no"

If "yes"

"I just can't walk away. I've got to help."

Step 3
Do I need to get involved?

If "no"

If "yes"

"I know what I must do to help."

Step 4
Is there a way I can help?

If "no"

If "yes"

"Okay, here goes."

Step 5
Am I ready to act?

If "no"

If "yes"

Offer help

Failure to help

behavior is observed by others (Gaulin & McBurney, 2001). For example, people are more likely to make a charitable donation when they are asked to do so by a coworker in full view of others than when they receive an appeal in the mail in the privacy of their own homes.

Let us now explore negative ways of relating to others, including prejudice and discrimination as well as human aggression.

Prejudice: Attitudes That Harm

Prejudice is a preconceived attitude, usually unfavorable, that is formed without critical thought or evaluation of the facts. Some prejudices reflect positive biases, such as when we prejudge members of our own ethnic or religious group more favorably than members of other groups. But most prejudices reflect negative biases against other groups or categories on the basis of race, ethnicity, social class, gender, age, and occupational, disability, or social status.

Prejudice, like other attitudes, consists of cognitive, emotional, and behavioral components. The cognitive component is the set of biased beliefs and stereotypes

Would you help this man? What influences the decision to help a person in need?

prejudice A preconceived opinion or attitude about an issue, person, or group.

CONCEPT 12.20
Social psychologists conceptualize prejudice, as they do other types of attitudes, as consisting of cognitive, emotional, and behavioral components.

that a person holds about other groups. The emotional component consists of feelings of dislike that the person has toward members of these groups. And the behavioral component is the person's inclination to discriminate against them. **Discrimination** is unfair or biased treatment of people based on group membership. Examples of discrimination include denial of housing or job opportunities, exclusion from social clubs, and increased scrutiny by police officers or security guards. Exposure to **racism** and discrimination can have damaging effects on the psychological and physical health of targeted groups (Mays, Cochran, & Barnes, 2007).

Note the disparities between what people say about their racial attitudes and how they respond to racial cues. For example, people who think of themselves as unprejudiced might nonetheless clutch their pocketbooks or briefcases more tightly when a person from a negatively stereotyped group boards an elevator with them or sits down next to them on a train or bus.

Stereotypes and prejudices are generally resistant to change. Social psychologists find that Whites who hold stereotypical views of Blacks may perceive them as "lazy" even when they perform in exactly the same way as the Whites (Hilton & von Hippel, 1996).

Social scientists have long observed that prejudice and discrimination typically increase during times of social upheaval and increased competition among groups. Competition over jobs and scarce economic opportunities can strain intergroup relationships. It comes as no surprise, then, that acts of racial tensions tend to increase during economic downturns when unemployment is high. Members of ethnic or racial minority groups may become convenient scapegoats when the economic security of the majority is threatened.

How Does Prejudice Develop?

CONCEPT 12.21
Prejudice develops as an outgrowth of negative stereotypes and is acquired in the same way that other attitudes are learned.

Prejudice arises as an outgrowth of negative stereotypes of other groups as lazy, dishonest, violent, dumb, and so on. These stereotypes are learned or acquired. We are not born with them. Children may begin forming negative attitudes toward other groups by imitating prejudiced attitudes they see modeled by parents, teachers, and peers. Prejudices may also be acquired through repeated exposure to negative, stereotypical depictions of other groups, especially racial minorities, in the media. We are repeatedly exposed to television and movie depictions of racial minorities in negative roles—as criminals, gang members, abusers, drug pushers, and so on.

Prejudice may also be acquired through direct experience. If a person has a few experiences with members of a particular group who are cold or nasty, he or she may overgeneralize and develop a stereotyped belief that all members of the particular group share these characteristics.

Though we may differ in the prejudices we acquire, we all harbor some prejudices. The universality of prejudice points to a basic cognitive tendency we have to parse our social environment into two general categories: people who belong to the same groups as we do and those who do not belong. Social psychologists describe these social categories as **in-groups** (one's own social, religious, ethnic, racial, and national groups) and **out-groups** (all other groups) (Culotta, 2012).

Prejudice develops when our thinking becomes biased in such a way that we attribute more negative characteristics to members of out-groups and more positive characteristics to members of in-groups. These two biased ways of thinking are called **out-group negativism** (also called *out-group prejudice*) and **in-group favoritism** (or *in-group bias*), respectively (Balliet, Wu, & Dreu, 2014; Effron & Knowles, 2015). Negative stereotypes of out-groups—beliefs that "we" are better than "they"—bolster the self-esteem of in-group members. Labeling other groups as dumb, lazy, dishonest, and so on makes us feel good in comparison.

Another type of biased thinking associated with prejudice is **out-group homogeneity**, which is the tendency to perceive members of other racial or ethnic

discrimination Unfair or biased treatment of people based on their membership in a particular group or category.

racism Negative bias held toward members of other racial groups.

in-groups Social, religious, ethnic, racial, or national groups with which one identifies.

out-groups Groups other than those with which one identifies.

out-group negativism A cognitive bias involving the predisposition to attribute more negative characteristics to members of out-groups than to those of in-groups.

in-group favoritism A cognitive bias involving the predisposition to attribute more positive characteristics to members of in-groups than to those of out-groups.

out-group homogeneity A cognitive bias describing the tendency to perceive members of out-groups as more alike than members of in-groups.

groups as being alike or *homogeneous* while perceiving members of one's own group as being "different as snowflakes" (Nelson, 2002). This bias can lead people to think that members of other groups all "look alike" and may explain why people are generally better able to remember faces of members of their own race or ethnicity than those of other groups (Anzures et al., 2013). One prominent explanation of out-group homogeneity, the *exemplar model,* holds that people are likely to know more in-group members than out-group members and so can more easily recall differences among people within their own groups.

The cognitive bases of prejudice may have evolved over thousands of generations. As social psychologist Martin Fishbein (1996) argues, ancestral humans organized themselves into tribal groups that shared a common language and culture, and they needed to keep their guard up against threats posed by outsiders—people from other groups who might harm them or kill them. Stereotyping other groups as "dangerous" or "evil" may have served an adaptive function to these early humans, who had good reason to fear outsiders. In the multicultural society of today, however, the adaptive demands we face are very different. We need to learn to get along with people of diverse backgrounds and to avoid branding people who are different from ourselves with unwarranted stereotypes.

Why Are Some People More Prejudiced Than Others?

Learning experiences play a key role in explaining individual differences in prejudice. Children exposed to the teachings of less prejudiced parents are likely to develop less prejudiced attitudes than are children of more intolerant parents. Low-prejudiced individuals also tend to differ in their cognitive style. They tend to look more at similarities among people than at differences, a cognitive framework that psychologists call a *universalist orientation* (Phillips & Ziller, 1997). By contrast, people with more prejudiced attitudes emphasize differences among people and use ethnicity as a basis for judging people.

An underlying personality type called the **authoritarian personality** is associated with prejudiced attitudes (Ludeke, Johnson, & Bouchard, 2013; Roets, Au, & Van Hiel, 2016). Theodore Adorno and his colleagues (1950) coined this term to describe a cluster of personality traits that include rigidity and excessive concern with obedience and respect for authority. Individuals with authoritarian personalities are prone to hate people who are different from themselves and those they perceive as weak or downtrodden.

How Does Stereotyping Affect Stereotyped Groups?

Members of stereotyped and stigmatized groups may be "on guard" for cues or signals associated with stereotypes like "girls can't do math" or "Blacks don't do well on IQ tests." This "on-guard" phenomenon, labeled **stereotype threat**, hangs like a "threat in the air." It can trigger negative expectations in people from stereotyped groups, leading to underperformance in testing situations in which these stereotypes are evoked. Drawing attention to the stereotype that males typically have an edge in math abilities may undermine math performance in women by diverting their attention to worrying about how they are doing rather than focusing on the test questions (Boucher, Rydell, & Murphy, 2015; Passolunghi et al., 2014).

Negative stereotypes can become internalized by members of stereotyped groups, sapping their motivation to succeed, lowering self-esteem, and leading them to perceive themselves as inadequate or inferior. Thus, the stereotypical belief that "girls can't do math" may discourage young women from pursuing promising career opportunities in engineering and the sciences. The negative stereotype can become a type of self-fulfilling prophecy, as underperformance serves to confirm the negative stereotype.

CONCEPT 12.22

The cognitive bases of prejudice reflect tendencies to separate people into two basic categories, in-groups and out-groups, and to attribute more negative characteristics to out-group members and more positive characteristics to in-group members.

CONCEPT LINK

As we saw in Chapter 7, we use mental categories or concepts to group objects, events, and ideas according to their common features. See Module 7.1.

CONCEPT 12.23

Individual differences in prejudice may be explained by learning experiences, personality traits, and the tendency to emphasize either similarities or differences between people.

CONCEPT 12.24

Stereotyping and prejudice negatively affect stereotyped groups in a number of ways, producing lowered expectations and internalization of negative stereotypes.

authoritarian personality A personality type characterized by rigidity, prejudice, and excessive concerns with obedience and respect for authority.

stereotype threat A sense of threat evoked in people from stereotyped groups when they believe they may be judged or treated stereotypically.

Try This Out
Examining Prejudice

Interview two or three friends or acquaintances from different ethnic or religious backgrounds. Ask them to describe any experiences they may have had in which they encountered prejudice or discrimination. How did these experiences affect them? How did they affect their perceptions of their social environment? Of themselves? How did they cope with these experiences? Based on your reading of the text, how might you counter your own tendencies to think in stereotyped or prejudiced ways?

What can be done to counter stereotypes and prejudices? Social psychologists suggest some possible remedies (also see the nearby Try This Out).

What Can We Do to Reduce Prejudice?

Albert Einstein said that "It is harder to crack a prejudice than an atom." Despite the challenge, psychologists have developed models for reducing prejudice. Perhaps the best known model is the **contact hypothesis** that psychologist Gordon Allport formulated in 1954. He proposed that the best way to reduce prejudice and intergroup tension was to bring groups into closer contact with each other. But he recognized that intergroup contact alone was not sufficient. Under some conditions, intergroup contact may increase negative attitudes by making differences between groups more apparent. Allport outlined the following four conditions he believed must be present for intergroup contact to have a desirable effect on reducing prejudice and intergroup tension. Note that an important question remains as to whether these conditions represent more of an ideal than an achievable reality in today's world (Dixon, Durrheim, & Tredoux, 2005; Dixon et al., 2010).

- *Social and institutional support.* People in positions of authority must be clearly behind the effort to bring groups closer together.
- *Acquaintance potential.* Opportunities must exist for members of different groups to become better acquainted with each other. With opportunities for more face-to-face contact, members of different groups have a better chance of finding common ground and increasing empathy and trust (Beelmann & Heinemann, 2014; Hodson, 2011). Having closer contact may also disconfirm negative stereotypes that different groups hold about each other.
- *Equal status.* Increased opportunities for contact with members of other groups who occupy subordinate roles may actually reinforce existing stereotypes and prejudices. When opportunities exist for members of different groups to meet on an equal footing, it becomes more difficult to maintain prejudiced beliefs.
  - *Intergroup cooperation.* Working cooperatively to achieve a common goal can help reduce intergroup bias by bringing members of different groups closer together (Hodson, 2011; Pettigrew & Tropp, 2006). Whether it involves a baseball team, a work team in the office, or citizens banding together to fight a common cause, cooperation can foster feelings of friendliness and mutual understanding.

Combating prejudice and discrimination begins with the lessons we teach our children in the home and at school. Teaching empathy may be one way to reduce prejudice. *Empathy* is the ability to take the perspective of other people and understand their feelings. Popular movies that allow us to share emotional experiences of members of stigmatized groups—films such as *The Help*, *Schindler's List*, and *The Color Purple*—may be useful in promoting more accepting and tolerant attitudes. Enforcing laws against discrimination and encouraging tolerance are societal measures that help combat prejudice and discrimination.

We as individuals can also take steps to counter prejudiced thinking. Simply telling ourselves not to think in stereotypical terms may actually strengthen these beliefs by bringing them more readily to mind (Sherman et al., 1997). Though stereotypical and biased attitudes may occur automatically or unconsciously, evidence suggests it is possible to change these attitudes (Ashburn-Nardo, Voils, & Monteith, 2001; Dasgupta & Greenwald, 2001). Social psychologists offer a number of suggestions that may help reduce prejudiced and stereotypical thinking, including repeated practice rejecting these thoughts when they occur, rehearsing more positive mental images of out-group members, taking part in cooperative works or projects in which we

CONCEPT 12.25

According to Allport, intergroup contact can help reduce prejudice, but only under conditions of social and institutional support, acquaintance potential, equal status, and intergroup cooperation.

contact hypothesis Allport's belief that under certain conditions, increased intergroup contact helps reduce prejudice and intergroup tension.

get to interact with people of different backgrounds, and participating in diversity education, such as workshops or seminars on prejudice and intergroup conflict (for example, Nelson, 2002; Pettigrew et al., 2011; Rudman, Ashmore, & Gary, 2001).

Human Aggression: Behavior That Harms

Far too often in human history, these negative attitudes toward members of other groups have set the stage for violent behavior in the form of killing and warfare. Are human beings inherently aggressive? Or is aggression a form of learned behavior that can be modified by experience? Psychologists and other scientists have many opinions about the nature of human aggression. Let us consider what the major perspectives in psychology might teach us about our capacity to harm one another.

Is Human Aggression Instinctual?

Some theorists believe that aggression in humans and other species is based on instinct. For example, the famed ethologist Konrad Lorenz (1966) believed that the fighting instinct is a basic survival mechanism in many animal species. Predators need to survive by instinctively attacking their prey. The more fortunate animals on which they prey survive by either instinctively fleeing from these attacks or fighting them off. In Lorenz's view, aggression can be an adaptive response that increases the chances of survival of predator and prey. But what of human aggression? Might it also be explained by instinct?

Contemporary theorists believe that human aggression is far too complex to be based on instinct. Human aggression takes many forms, from organized warfare and acts of terrorism to interpersonal forms of violent behavior such as muggings, spousal abuse, and sexual assaults. These different forms of aggression reflect a variety of political, cultural, and psychological motives. Moreover, instinct theories neither fail to account for the important roles that learning and culture play in shaping behavior, nor do they explain the diversity that exists in human aggression. Violence is unusual in some cultures but all too common in others, unfortunately including our own.

Theorists today believe that human aggression cannot be explained by any one cause. Accordingly, we next consider the multiple factors that contemporary theorists believe contribute to human aggression, including biological influences, learning influences, sociocultural influences, use of alcohol, emotional states, and environmental influences (Anderson & Bushman, 2003; DeWall, Anderson, & Bushman, 2011; Hamburg, 2012).

Biological Influences

We are making progress toward understanding the biological underpinnings of aggression. For example, investigators recently identified genes linked to violent or impulsive behavior (Meyer-Lindenberg et al., 2006). Researchers have also implicated abnormalities in neural circuitry in the brain that regulate anger, which is often an emotional trigger for aggressive behavior (Davidson, Putnam, & Larson, 2000). Another focus of study is the neurotransmitter serotonin, which is involved in brain circuits responsible for curbing impulsive behavior (Carver, Johnson, & Joormann, 2008). Serotonin serves as a kind of "behavioral seat belt" or "emergency brake" for restraining aggressive impulses (Raine, 2008). That said, we need further evidence that directly ties deficiencies in serotonin, or perhaps irregularities in how serotonin is used in the brain, to aggressive behavior.

CONCEPT 12.26

Like other forms of human behavior, aggression is too complex to be reduced to the level of instinct.

These empty shoes of gunshot victims in the United States provide a poignant reminder of the consequences of violent behavior.

CONCEPT 12.27

The biological underpinnings of aggression reflect genetic, hormonal, and neurotransmitter influences.

"You've been charged with driving under the influence of testosterone."

William Haefeli/The New Yorker Collection/www.cartoonbank.com

CONCEPT 12.28

Social-cognitive theorists view aggression as learned behavior that is acquired through observational learning and reinforcement.

CONCEPT 12.29

Sociocultural theorists explore the social stressors that contribute to aggressive behavior, including poverty, child abuse and neglect, family breakdown, and exposure to violence.

CONCEPT 12.30

Alcohol is linked to aggressive behavior through its effects on loosening inhibitions, impairing the ability to weigh the consequences of behavior and interpret social cues, and reducing sensitivity to punishment-related cues.

CONCEPT LINK

As discussed in Chapter 4, alcohol use is linked to many crimes of violence. See Module 4.4.

The male sex hormone testosterone clearly plays an important role in aggressive behavior in other animal species, but its role in human aggression is complex and depends on other factors (Mehta & Beer, 2010; Trainor & Nelson, 2012). Not all aggressive or violent men have high testosterone levels, nor do all—or even most—men with high testosterone levels engage in violent behavior. Clearly the factors involved in aggression are more complex than levels of hormones circulating in the bloodstream.

Evolutionary psychology points to possible ancestral roots of violence (Gorelik, Shackelford, & Weekes-Shackelford, 2012). Among ancestral humans, aggression may have benefited men in their primary role as hunters. Ancestral women, so far as we know, primarily engaged in food gathering and child care roles in which aggressiveness may have been counterproductive. Perhaps the greater aggressiveness we find in males today is explained in part by inherited tendencies passed down through generations from ancestral times.

Learning Influences

The social-cognitive theorist Albert Bandura (2008a) highlights the role of observational learning in the development of aggressive behavior. He notes that children learn to imitate aggressive behavior that they observe in the home, the schools, and the media, especially television (see Module 5.3 in Chapter 5). Young boys, for example, may learn by observing their peers or by watching male characters on television that conflicts are to be settled with fists or weapons, not with words.

Aggressive or violent children often come from homes in which parents and other family members modeled aggression. Reinforcement also contributes to the learning of aggressive behavior. If children are rewarded for aggressive behavior, such as by receiving approval or respect from peers, or by getting their way, they are more likely to repeat the same behavior. Indeed, people in general are more likely to resort to aggressive behavior if they have failed to learn alternative ways of resolving conflicts. Violent behavior may be perpetuated from generation to generation as children who are exposed to violence in the home learn that violent behavior is an acceptable way to settle disagreements.

Sociocultural Influences

Sociocultural theorists encourage us to consider the broader social contexts in which aggression takes place. Interpersonal violence often occurs against a backdrop of social stressors such as poverty, prolonged unemployment, lack of opportunity, child abuse and neglect, family breakdown, and exposure to violence in the family and community. Children who are abused by their parents may fail to develop the secure loving attachments to their parents that would otherwise provide the basis for acquiring empathy and concern for others. Not surprisingly, abused children often display violent behavior in childhood and adulthood (Urquiza & Blacker, 2011).

Violence may also be used as a social influence tactic—a means of coercion by which individuals seek to compel others to comply with their wishes. We need only consider such examples as the "mob enforcer" who uses strong-arm tactics to obtain compliance or the abusive husband who uses physical force or threat of force to get his wife to accede to his demands.

Alcohol Use

Investigators find strong links between alcohol use and violent behaviors such as domestic violence, homicide, and rape (Boles & Miottoa, 2003; Fals-Stewart, 2003). Alcohol loosens inhibitions or restraints on impulsive behavior, including acts of impulsive violence. It also impairs our ability to weigh the consequences of our actions, reduces our sensitivity to cues that signal the threat of punishment, and leads us to misperceive other people's motives as malevolent. Not everyone who drinks becomes aggressive, of course. Relationships between alcohol use and aggression may be influenced by the user's biological sensitivity to alcohol as well as by the social demands of the situation in which provocation occurs, such as a bar versus the family home.

Emotional States

Psychologists have long recognized that certain negative emotions, especially frustration and anger, may trigger aggression. As we learned in Chapter 10, frustration is a negative emotional state that is induced when our efforts to reach a goal are thwarted or blocked. Though frustration often leads to aggression, other outcomes are possible. You may feel frustrated when someone behind you in a movie theater talks throughout the picture, prompting a *state of readiness* to respond aggressively either verbally or physically (Geen, 1998). But whether you actually respond aggressively may depend on your expectation that an aggressive response will yield a positive outcome and your history of aggressive behavior, among other factors. Questions remain about whether aggression is necessarily preceded by frustration. The cool, premeditated aggression of a mob "hit man" does not fit the pattern of frustration-induced aggression.

Anger is another negative emotion that can induce aggressive responses in some individuals. We might think of the husband who strikes out violently at his wife when she says something that angers him or the child abuser who lashes out angrily when a child is slow to comply with a demand. People who think angering thoughts ("I can't let him/her get away with this . . .") or who blow minor provocations out of proportion are more likely to respond aggressively in conflict situations than those who think calmer thoughts.

CONCEPT 12.31
Frustration and anger are negative emotions that may serve as triggers for aggression.

Environmental Influences

People may get hot under the collar as the outdoor temperature rises, but are they more likely to become aggressive? Indeed they are. Environmental psychologists find that aggressive behavior increases with rising temperatures, although it may begin to decline at very high temperatures (Anderson et al., 2000; Sorg & Taylor, 2011).

Hot temperatures incite aggression by increasing states of bodily arousal (heart rates and blood pressure increase) and inducing angry, hostile thoughts and feelings, leading to a readiness to respond aggressively to even minor social provocations (Anderson et al., 2000; Dahl, 2013). As a leading researcher in the field, Brad Bushman of Ohio State University, puts it, "If someone cuts you off in traffic, you're much more likely to honk at them or flip them off if it's a hot day rather than a cool day" (quoted in Dahl, 2013). Links between rising temperature and aggression raise some interesting questions that might be pursued through more formal study: Might the use of air conditioning in prisons reduce the problems of inmate violence? Might air conditioning have a similar effect in reducing aggression in the workplace or in schools?

Might baseball pitchers be more likely to throw at hitters when temperatures rise? Based on an analysis of more than 50,000 major league baseball games, investigators found that pitchers were indeed much more likely to hit batters at high temperatures in games in which their own players had been hit by an opposing pitcher earlier in the game (Larrick et al., 2011). The investigators reasoned that hot temperatures incite retaliation by leading players to attribute more hostile intentions to opposing players when their teammates are hit by a pitch, and by reducing their inhibitions.

Before reading further, you may want to review the positive (helping) and negative ways of relating to others outlined in Concept Chart 12.2.

CONCEPT 12.32
High temperatures are linked to aggressive behavior, perhaps because they induce angry, hostile thoughts and feelings that become expressed in aggressive behavior.

Concept Chart 12.2 Relating to Others

	Concept	Description	More About It
Determinants of Helping	Decision-making processes	The Latané and Darley decision-making model comprises five steps: (1) recognizing that a need for help exists, (2) interpreting the situation as an emergency, (3) assuming personal responsibility for helping, (4) determining the type or kind of help needed, and (5) deciding to implement a course of action	Helping is based on a decision-making process involving the appraisal of the situation at hand as well as one's personal responsibility and resources to address it.
	Influences on helping	Includes factors such as situational ambiguity, perceived cost, diffusion of responsibility, similarity, empathy, facial features, mood and gender effects, attributions of the cause of need, and social norms	Helping depends on a combination of personal and situational factors.
Negative Ways of Relating	Prejudice	A cluster of (mostly) negative beliefs, feelings, and behavioral tendencies toward members of other groups	Efforts to reduce prejudice can be directed at increasing intergroup contacts under conditions of social and institutional support, acquaintanceship potential, equal status, and cooperativeness, by practicing nonstereotyped ways of thinking and seeking opportunities for contact with people of other social groups, and by instilling nonprejudiced attitudes in children by setting an example of tolerance.
	Aggression	Takes many forms, from organized warfare to interpersonal violence, such as assaults, rapes, and partner abuse	Many factors are implicated in human aggression, including biological, learning, sociocultural, emotional, and environmental influences, and alcohol use.

MODULE REVIEW **12.2** Relating to Others

Recite It

5. **Identify** factors that influence attraction.

   The major determinants of attraction include similarity, physical (a) _____, proximity, and reciprocity.

6. **Identify** the components of love identified in the triangular model of love.

   According to Sternberg's triangular model, the components of love are intimacy, (b) _____, and decision/commitment.

7. **Describe** the decision-making model of helping and **identify** factors that influence helping behavior.

   The decision-making model holds that bystander intervention is based on a series of (c) _____ that must be made before helping occurs.

   Factors that influence helping behavior include the ambiguity of the situation, perceived (d) _____, diffusion of (e) _____, similarity, empathy, facial features, mood and gender, attributions of the cause of need, and social (f) _____.

8. **Define** prejudice, **explain** how it develops, and **apply** your knowledge to ways of reducing it.

   (g) _____ is a preconceived attitude or bias, usually unfavorable, that is formed without critical thought or evaluation.

   Prejudice derives from negative group (h) _____ to which people are exposed in their social environment. The development of prejudice may also reflect basic (i) _____ processes that evolved over thousands of generations.

   Individual differences in prejudice may be explained by differences in learning experiences, (j) _____ personality traits, and the adoption of a (k) _____ orientation.

   Prejudice may be reduced by creating opportunities for (l) _____ contact that have strong social and institutional support, are based on equal status relationships, allow acquaintanceships to develop, and emphasize (m) _____ rather than competition.

9. Identify factors that contribute to human aggression.

Contemporary theorists attempt to explain human (n) _____ on the basis of biological influences, learning influences, sociocultural influences, alcohol use, emotional states, and environmental influences.

Recall It

1. Name several key factors that determine attraction.

2. Regarding physical attractiveness, which of the following statements is *incorrect*?

   a. Men tend to place greater emphasis on the physical attractiveness of their partners than do women.
   b. Standards for physical attractiveness cross cultural boundaries.
   c. Attractive people tend to be more favorably judged on many personality traits.
   d. People tend to rate male and female faces as more attractive when they have more masculine characteristics.

3. What is the proper order of the steps involved in determining whether bystanders will become involved in helping someone in need?

   a. Assume personal responsibility for helping.
   b. Determine that the situation is a true emergency.
   c. Implement the chosen course of action.
   d. Determine that a true need for help exists.
   e. Choose what kind of help to provide.

4. Prejudice, like other attitudes, consists of (a) cognitive, (b) emotional, and (c) behavioral components. Describe the major features of each component as they relate to prejudice.

5. What are the four conditions that Allport said must be met for intergroup contact to reduce prejudice?

Think About It

■ To what extent was your attraction to your friends and romantic partners a function of similarity of attitudes, backgrounds, physical attractiveness, proximity, and reciprocity?

■ Do you believe that people can be completely altruistic or selfless? Or might there be underlying self-serving motives even in acts of kindness and self-sacrifice? Explain.

■ Suppose you were asked to develop a proposal to improve intergroup relations among students of different ethnic groups on campus by bringing them together. What factors do you think would determine whether your efforts are successful?

Recite It answers placed at the end of chapter.

MODULE **12.3** **Group Influences on Individual Behavior**

10 **Define** social identity and **evaluate** cultural factors involved in social identity.

11 **Describe** the basic finding of Asch's classic study on conformity and **identify** factors that influence conformity.

12 **Explain** the psychological bases of manipulative sales tactics.

13 **Describe** the findings of Milgram's classic study and **evaluate** why his methods were controversial.

14 **Evaluate** the effects of the presence of others on performance.

15 **Define** groupthink and **explain** how it can lead to wrong decisions.

The view that humans are social creatures was expressed perhaps most clearly by the sixteenth-century English poet John Donne, who wrote "no man is an island, sufficient unto himself." We influence others and are influenced by them in turn. In this module, we consider ways in which others influence our behavior and even our self-concepts. We examine the tendency to conform our behavior to social pressure, even when we consider such demands unreasonable or immoral. We examine situations where the presence of others may enhance our performance and those where it may not. Finally, we explore the phenomenon of *groupthink* and see how group influences can sometimes lead to bad decisions. The Applying Psychology in Daily Life feature examines the social influences underlying persuasive sales tactics and the steps people can take to avoid manipulative sales approaches.

CONCEPT 12.33

Our social or group identity is an important part of our psychological identity or self-concept.

© IInteractimages/Shutterstock.com

personal identity The part of our psychological identity that involves our sense of ourselves as unique individuals.

social identity The part of our psychological identity that involves our sense of ourselves as members of particular groups. Also called *group identity*.

Our Social Selves: "Who Are We?"

Many social psychologists separate psychological identity or self-concept into two parts: **personal identity** (individual identity) and **social identity** (group identity) (Ellemers, Spears, & Doosje, 2002; Verkuyten & De Wolf, 2007). Your personal identity ("Who am I?") is the part of your psychological makeup that distinguishes you as a unique individual. You might think of yourself as a caring, creative person who likes pepperoni pizza, jazz, and sci-fi movies. Your social identity ("Who are we?") is your sense of yourself as a member of the various family, kinship, religious, national, and social groups to which you belong. You might refer to this part of your identity by saying, "I am a Catholic. . . . I am a software developer. . . . I am a Mexican American. . . . I am Jonathan's dad." Our social identity converts the "I" to the "we." Social or ethnic identity is for many people the core aspect of who they are.

Social psychologists believe we have a fundamental need to be members of groups—in other words, to belong. Our social identity tends to rub off on our self-esteem (see the nearby Try This Out feature). We are likely to feel better about ourselves when someone of the same ethnicity, religion, or even locality accomplishes something special.

Social identity is generally a more prominent part of one's psychological identity in collectivist cultures, such as those in the Far East, than it is in individualistic societies in the West (Fiske et al., 1998). In collectivist cultures, individuals have a stronger desire to fulfill their social obligations to the group, whereas Western societies emphasize a more individualistic or autonomous sense of self. People in Western cultures tend to define themselves less by what they share in common with others and more in terms of their unique abilities, interests, and attributes (Chen, Jing, & Lee, 2012). They expect to stand out from the crowd—being themselves means becoming unique individuals. Yet there are variations within Western cultures. Women tend to place a greater emphasis on an interdependent sense of self—defining themselves more in terms of their roles as mothers, wives, daughters, and so on, whereas men tend to have a more independent sense of self (Cross & Madson, 1997).

Try This Out Sign on the Dotted Line

Sign your name on the line below:

_____

Sign your name again, but now imagine that you are signing as the president of the United States:

_____

Were your signatures the same size? Psychologist Richard Zweigenhaft (1970) found that students penned larger signatures when they were signing as president. Zweigenhaft also found that signatures of college professors were larger than those of blue-collar university employees. The social roles we play, as student, employee, husband or wife, or even president, are part of our social identity. Holding a high-status position bolsters our self-image, which may be reflected in the size of our signatures.

Conformity: Bending the "I" to Fit the "We"

You would not get arrested if you arrived at work in your pajamas, but you probably would hear some snickering comments or be asked to go home and change. Then again, perhaps pajama wearing might become something of a new fashion statement. You might actually be thought of as a trendsetter. Well, perhaps not. In any event, we are expected to conform our behavior to prevailing social standards or norms. Though social norms don't carry the force of law, violation of these standards can incur social disapproval. If we deviate too far from social standards, we might even lose our friends or jobs or alienate our family members.

Conformity affects many aspects of our daily behavior, from the clothes we wear for specific occasions, to the custom of covering our mouths and saying "excuse me" when we sneeze, to choosing a college to attend ("You're going to State, like your brother, right?"). Conformity pressures may also lead us to date or even marry the kinds of people whom others deem acceptable.

We conform not only to general social norms but also to group or peer norms. Young people who color their hair purple may not be conforming to the standards of mainstream society, but they are conforming to those of their peer group—just as their parents are to their own.

We might consider ourselves to be free thinkers who can resist pressures to conform when we don't see eye to eye with others. But the results of a classic study by psychologist Solomon Asch (1956) lead us to recognize that we may conform more than we think. Asch set out to study independence, not conformity. He believed that if participants in the study were faced with a unanimous group judgment that was obviously false, they would stick to their guns, resist pressures to conform, and report the correct information. He was wrong.

Asch placed individuals in a group consisting of people who were actually in league with the experimenter. The group was presented with the task of choosing the one line among a group of three that was the same length as a test line (see ■ Figure 12.7). But the twist was that the other group members—all confederates of the experimenter—unanimously made the wrong choice. Now it was the individual's turn. Would the person go along with the group and make an obviously incorrect choice? Asch was surprised by the results. Bowing under the pressure to conform, three out of four of the college students who participated in the study gave at least one incorrect answer in a series of trials.

Why were people so willing to conform in the Asch experiment, even to the extent of claiming that something was true when it was obviously false? Subsequent research established at least three reasons: (1) People assume the majority must be correct; (2) they are so concerned about being accepted by the group that they don't care whether their judgments were correct; (3) they feel it is easier to go along with the group—to "fit in with the crowd"—than to disagree (Cialdini & Trost, 1998; Jetten & Hornsey, 2015). Even so, some groups are more susceptible to pressures to conform than others (Horry et al., 2012; Toelch & Dolan, 2015). Women, by a small margin, are more likely to conform than men. People from collectivist cultures such as China tend to conform more than people from individualistic cultures such as the United States, Canada, and Great Britain. And conformity tends to be greater among people with low self-esteem, low self-confidence, social shyness, and a strong desire to be liked by the group. More generally, conformity tends to decline with age from childhood through older adulthood (Pasupathi, 1999).

Conformity is also influenced by situational factors. In the Asch paradigm, people were more likely to conform when they were required to disclose their responses publicly rather than privately, when the size of the group increased to about four or five people (beyond that number, conformity leveled off with increasing group size), and when more ambiguous stimuli were used (Cialdini & Trost, 1998; Toelch & Dolan, 2015). Yet just one dissenting voice in the group—one fellow traveler down the road of defection—can override group influence, regardless of the size of the group (Morris, Miller, & Spangenberg, 1977).

CONCEPT 12.34
When we conform, we behave in ways that adhere to social norms.

CONCEPT 12.35
People are more likely to conform than they might think, even to the extent of claiming that something is true when they know it to be false.

conformity The tendency to adjust one's behavior to actual or perceived social pressures.

FIGURE 12.7 **Stimuli Similar to Those Used in the Asch Conformity Studies**

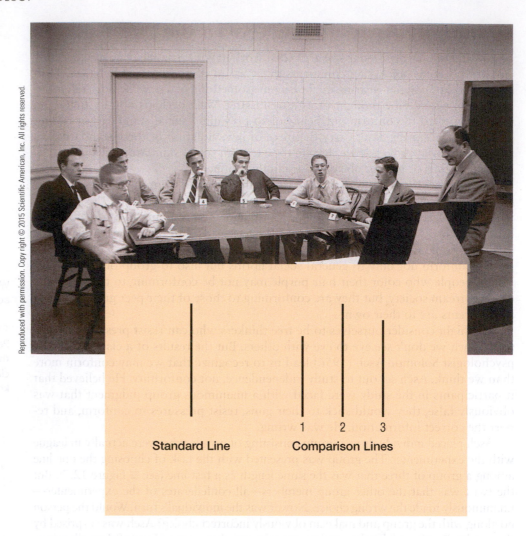

Standard Line   Comparison Lines
                         1   2   3

CONCEPT 12.36

Many factors influence conformity, including personal and situational characteristics.

Asch believed that conformity can stifle individuality and independence. Yet some degree of conformity may help groups to function more smoothly. After all, sneezing on someone might be taken as a social affront; covering our noses and mouths and saying "excuse me" afterward shows respect for other people's rights.

APPLYING PSYCHOLOGY *in Daily Life*

Compliance: Doing What Others Want You to Do

compliance The process of acceding to the requests or demands of others.

Compliance is the process of acceding to the requests or demands of others. One factor influencing compliance is authority. Appeals from a recognized authority figure are often extremely influential. You may be more willing to follow your doctor's advice about making changes in your diet than advice from your next-door neighbor. Another factor is *social validation*. We tend to use the actions of others as a standard or social norm for judging the appropriateness of our own behavior (Cialdini & Goldstein, 2004). Thus, we are more likely to donate to a charity appeal if we find out that other people in the office are giving than if they are not.

Marketers often get us to comply with sales pitches by first softening us up with snowball questions (*How are you today?*) before landing the sales punch (Fennis, Janssen, & Vohs, 2009).

The desire for consistency is yet another important determinant of compliance (Woolston, 2012). Salespeople, advertisers, fund-raisers, and others try to get us to comply with their requests by using consistency to their advantage. Several market-honed techniques succeed because they first obtain a person's commitment to a particular course of action that is consistent with a later requested action. Here are three examples:

1. *Lowball technique.* Say a car salesperson offers you an attractive price, only to pull the offer minutes later, claiming the sales manager couldn't approve it or the allowance offered for your trade-in came in lower than expected. You are then offered a higher price, which the salesperson swears is the best possible price. This is the **lowball technique** at work. Committing yourself to the prior action of accepting a lower price may make you more likely to follow through on the subsequent, more costly action.

2. *Bait-and-switch technique.* In the **bait-and-switch technique,** a marketer advertises merchandise at an unusually low price. When people come to buy the merchandise, they learn that it is actually of inferior quality or is sold out or back-ordered. Then comes the switch, as they are shown more expensive merchandise for sale. Here again the person making the pitch capitalizes on the desire for consistency. Prospective buyers who expressed an initial interest in the merchandise are often more receptive to buying more expensive merchandise than they would be otherwise.

3. *Foot-in-the-door technique.* In the **foot-in-the-door technique,** the person making an appeal first asks for a small favor that will almost certainly be granted. After obtaining initial compliance, the person raises the ante by asking for a larger, related favor. Evidence shows that people who agree to smaller requests are more likely to comply with larger ones, apparently due to the desire for consistency (Guadagno & Cialdini, 2010). In an early example, Patricia Pliner and her colleagues (1974) showed that people who agreed to wear a lapel pin promoting a local charity were subsequently more willing to make a monetary donation to the charity. Yet investigators find that only those people with a strong need for consistency show evidence of the foot-in-the-door effect (Cialdini, Trost, & Newsom, 1995).

Another sales strategy is the **door-in-the-face technique,** in which saying no to a first request increases the likelihood of compliance with a later request (Pansu, Lima, & Fointiat, 2014). Though it doesn't always work (Henderson & Burgoon, 2013), this strategy takes advantage of the psychological principle of *reciprocity*. First comes a large unreasonable request, which is rejected out of hand. Then the person making the request offers a lesser alternative in the form of a smaller request, which is actually what the person wanted in the first place. This smaller request is more likely to be accepted following rejection of the larger, unreasonable request than it would be had it been presented first. Why? Recall the concept of reciprocity. When requesters appear willing to compromise by withdrawing the original request in favor of a smaller one, people receiving the request may feel obliged to reciprocate by becoming more accommodating themselves.

Let's turn the discussion around to you. The Try This Out feature on page 478 offers the opportunity to practice your skills at resisting persuasive sales tactics.

CONCEPT 12.37
Need for consistency, social validation, reciprocity, and perceptions of authority are important determinants of compliance.

Bob Daemmrich/The Image Works

Are you being lowballed? What are some common types of manipulative sales tactics? What psychological principles underlie these tactics? What would you do if you were lowballed?

lowball technique A compliance technique based on obtaining a person's initial agreement to purchase an item at a lower price before revealing hidden costs that raise the ultimate price.

bait-and-switch technique A compliance technique based on "baiting" a person by making an unrealistically attractive offer and then replacing it with a less attractive offer.

foot-in-the-door technique A compliance technique based on securing compliance with a smaller request as a prelude to making a larger request.

door-in-the-face technique A compliance technique in which refusal of a large, unreasonable request is followed by a smaller, more reasonable request.

Try This Out What Do You Say Now?

You are in the market for a new car. The salesperson shows you a model you like, and after haggling for a while, you settle on a price that seems fair to you. The salesperson then says, "Let me get this approved by my manager and I'll be right back." What would you say to protect yourself against the types of influence tactics described in the text? For each of the following examples, write your response in the following provided column. Then compare your answers with sample responses at the end of the chapter.

Type of Tactic	What the Salesperson Says	What Do You Say Now?
Lowball technique	"I'm sorry. He says we can't let it go for this amount. It has nothing to do with you, but he's getting more pressure from the boss. Maybe if we went back to him with another two or three hundred dollars, he'd accept it."	_____ _____ _____ _____
Bait-and-switch technique	"My manager tells me that we're having difficulty placing orders for that model. Something to do with a strike in Osaka. We can definitely get the LX version, however. It's got some great features."	_____ _____ _____ _____
Foot-in-the-door technique	"Okay, we can get you the car." After completing some of the paperwork, the salesman slips in the following comment: "You know, you really should think about this factory-installed security system. You can never be too safe these days."	_____ _____ _____ _____

Obedience to Authority: When Does It Go Too Far?

The study of **obedience** to authority has implications that go far beyond psychology. The atrocities of the Nazi regime in Germany preceding and during World War II raised disturbing questions about the tendency of soldiers and even ordinary citizens to obey authority figures in the commission of horrific acts. Many individuals, including civilians, participated in the Holocaust—the systematic genocide of the Jewish population of Europe. When later called to account for their deeds, many Nazis claimed they were "only following orders." Years afterward, American soldiers who participated in a massacre of civilians in the village of My Lai during the Vietnam War would offer a similar defense.

Yale University psychologist Stanley Milgram developed a unique and controversial research program to find out whether ordinary Americans would perform clearly immoral actions if they were instructed to do so. Milgram's decision to study obedience to immoral authority was rooted in his Jewish heritage and his determination to better understand the atrocities ordinary German citizens committed during the Holocaust (Blass, 2009). Participants in his studies were residents of New Haven, Connecticut, and surrounding areas who answered newspaper ads requesting participants for studies on learning and memory. They ranged in age from 20 to 50 and included teachers, engineers, salespeople, and laborers. Some were college graduates; others had not even completed elementary school. When they arrived at the lab, they were told that they would be participating in a study designed to test the effects of punishment on learning. They would play the role of a "teacher." Another person to whom they were introduced would be the "learner."

The learner was seated in one room, the teacher in an adjoining room. The teacher was placed in front of a console that was described as a device for administering electric

obedience Compliance with commands or orders issued by others, usually people in a position of authority.

shocks to the learner. The console consisted of a series of levers with labels ranging from "Slight Shock" to "Danger: Severe Shock." The learner was presented with a list of word pairs to memorize. Then one word in each pair was presented and the learner's task was to respond with the correct word with which it had been paired in the list. The teacher was instructed that following each incorrect response from the learner, he was to deliver an electric shock. With each additional error, the voltage of the shock was to increase by 15 volts.

Unbeknown to the teachers, the learners were confederates of the experimenter. It was all part of an elaborate ruse. The experiment was not actually intended to study learning. What it tested was the teacher's willingness to inflict pain on another person when instructed to do so. No actual shocks were given. The learner's incorrect responses were all predetermined. But to the "teachers," it was all too real.

Each teacher was informed that although the shocks might be extremely painful, they would cause "no permanent tissue damage" to the learner. To provide teachers with a sense of what a mild shock felt like, they were administered an electric shock corresponding to 45 volts. As the number of errors mounted, the teacher was instructed to increase the voltage until it reached the "danger" level. Most teachers were visibly upset when given the order to raise the shock level to apparently hazardous levels. When they hesitated, the experimenter simply instructed them: "The experiment requires that you continue." If they still hesitated, the experimenter pressured them further, telling them: "It is absolutely essential that you continue. . . . You have no other choice. . . . You must go on." Now, would they comply and throw the switch? Would you?

The results were disturbing (Milgram, 1963, 1974). Some participants disobeyed experimenter commands to inflict what they perceived to be painful and potentially dangerous shocks on learners (Packer, 2008). Most initially protested but eventually relented to continuing pressure from the experimenter. Of the 40 original participants, 26 (65 percent) obeyed every order, including the one to deliver the highest voltage shock (Abma, 2013). In another experimental condition, the teachers could hear the learner screaming to be let go and pounding on the wall. Even so, 25 of the 40 participants administered the full series of shocks (Elms, 1995). In a variation in which participants themselves did not throw the switch activating the shock but instructed others (actually confederates) to do so, the rate of obedience rose to 92.5 percent (Meeus & Raaijmakers, 1995). Placing the learner in the same room as the participant reduced obedience, but 40 percent still obeyed. Milgram later obtained similar results with female participants and groups of college undergraduates (Milgram, 1974).

The disturbing findings of the Milgram studies may help us better understand the behavior of ordinary people who participated in seemingly inexplicable and horrific events such as the behavior of German citizens in the Holocaust and mass suicides at the behest of cult leaders. Milgram's studies may teach us how good people can commit bad deeds in situations where they are led to blindly follow authority.

Yet many critics have contended that laboratory-based experimental claims should not be generalized to the destructive obedience found in Nazi Germany or other real-life atrocities. One related argument is that participants may not have believed that anything terrible was happening to the "learner"—after all, this was a respected university and someone would have stopped them if it were truly dangerous. *Wouldn't they?* In fact, a majority of Milgram's participants believed that the "learner" was receiving significant levels of pain (Meeus & Raaijmakers, 1995). Even when Milgram moved his laboratory away from the hallowed halls of the university to a dingy storefront in a commercial district, nearly half of the participants (48 percent) complied (Milgram, 1974).

Milgram's studies sparked much controversy, much of it concerning the ethics of deceiving participants in research studies and the emotional aftereffects of raising people's awareness that they were capable of such behavior. The ethical issues raised by the Milgram experiments informed the development of the set of ethical

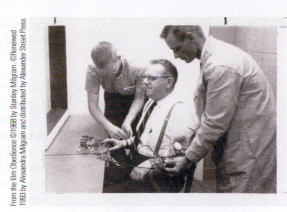

From the film Obedience ©1968 by Stanley Milgram. ©Renewed 1993 by Alexandra Milgram and distributed by Alexander Street Press

The participant in the Milgram studies was led to believe that the "learner," as shown here, would receive electric shocks following each wrong answer. If you were a participant, would you have obeyed the experimenter even as the learner cried out for help?

CONCEPT 12.38

In the classic Milgram studies of obedience, ordinary people were willing to obey the dictates of an external authority even to the extent of inflicting what they believed were serious and even dangerous shocks to other supposed participants.

guidelines later adopted by the American Psychological Association to protect the welfare of participants in psychological research (Benjamin & Simpson, 2009). (See Chapter 1 for a discussion of ethical principles in psychology.)

Are people today as likely as those in Milgram's time to comply with unreasonable and immoral demands? We don't have a definitive answer because ethical restrictions imposed since Milgram's time make a full replication of his experiment out of bounds for contemporary investigators (Burger, 2009; Elms, 2009). However, a partial replication that administered the Milgram procedure but stopped well short of the highest level of shock (so as to avoid imposing undue stress on participants) showed similar rates of compliance to those in Milgram's original work (Burger, 2009). We should caution, however, that some psychologists have raised reservations about the procedures used in the partial replication study (see Elms, 2009; Miller, 2009; Twenge, 2009).

Why Do People Obey Immoral Commands?

The **legitimization of authority** is one explanation of the behavior of participants in Milgram's studies. We are taught from an early age to obey authority figures such as parents and teachers and not to question or second-guess them. This early socialization prepares us to comply when directed to do so by a legitimate authority figure, be it a police officer, a government or military official, or a scientist. Another likely reason for obedience is **social validation** (also called social comparison). Participants in Milgram's studies may have lacked any basis for knowing what other people would do in a similar situation. The only basis for social comparison was the example the experimenter set. For people in Nazi Germany, seeing respected others perform atrocities may have served to legitimize their activities not only as socially acceptable but, more disturbingly, as admirable. People are generally more willing to comply with more extreme requests once they have shown a willingness to comply with lesser requests. Once participants began to deliver shocks to "learners," they may have found it increasingly difficult to stop—just as soldiers who have been trained to respond unstintingly to commands may not hesitate to follow orders, even immoral ones.

Evaluating Milgram's Legacy

Scholars continue to debate the methods Milgram used and the ultimate significance of his findings (Brannigan, Nicholson, & Cherry, 2015). Perhaps the ultimate significance of Milgram's studies is to remind us to look inward to our capacity for blind and destructive obedience. As some have observed, the Milgram studies may indicate that we do too good a job at socializing young people to be obedient to authority (Vecchio, 1997). Perhaps more emphasis should be placed on personal responsibility for one's actions, a teaching that might go a long way toward preventing destructive obedience.

Now we consider ways in which the presence of groups may influence individual performance—for better or worse.

Social Facilitation and Social Loafing: When Are You Likely to Perform at Your Best?

Do you perform better when you work in front of others? **Social facilitation** is the term social psychologists use to refer to the tendency for people to work better or harder when they work in the presence of others than when they work alone (Mendes, 2007). Social facilitation helps explain why you may study better when studying in a group or in the library than when studying alone. Having others around may present something of a challenge or even a threat, which energizes your performance and brings out the best in you. When you are studying alone, you have no handy

legitimization of authority The tendency to grant legitimacy to the orders or commands of people in authority.

social validation The tendency to use other people's behavior as a standard for judging the appropriateness of one's own behavior.

social facilitation The tendency to work better or harder in the presence of others than when alone.

social comparison, as there's no one around to compare your behavior against. In the library, you may take your cues from others who have their heads buried in their books and measure your performance against theirs. A historical footnote: The first research example of social facilitation may be from 1898, when researchers reported that cyclists who "rode with others performed better" (Joyce & Baker, 2008).

On the other hand, the presence of others does not always *improve* performance. According to noted social psychologist Robert Zajonc (1965), the presence of others increases the performance of dominant responses. In the case of simple or well-learned tasks, the dominant response will usually be the correct response. However, for complex tasks in which the dominant response may be incorrect, the presence of others tends to impair performance. So, if you are a good typist, you may type faster when others are present than when you are alone. But if you need to solve complex math problems, having an audience would likely slow your performance.

Social loafing is the tendency for people to apply less effort when they work as members of a group than when they work on their own. Perhaps you have observed social loafing in work that you did as part of a team effort. Did one or more members of the team fail to apply themselves as much as they could?

Underlying social loafing is the tendency for people to conserve individual effort when they expect that other team members will pick up the slack (Plaks & Higgins, 2000). But social loafing is not inevitable. It is more likely to occur when individual performance is not evaluated. It can be reduced by making tasks more appealing, increasing the visibility of each individual's performance in the group, holding each member accountable for his or her own contributions, and giving public feedback of individual performance (Hoeksema van Orden, Gaillard, & Buunk, 1998; Levine & Moreland, 1998).

Groupthink: How Can Smart People Make Dumb Decisions?

This was the question President John F. Kennedy asked his advisers in the aftermath of the disastrous invasion of Cuba at the Bay of Pigs in 1961, when Cuban forces easily defeated a brigade of U.S.-backed Cuban exiles. Yale psychologist Irving Janis (1997) believed that stupidity wasn't the explanation. To Janis, the fault lay in a flawed approach to group decision making that he termed **groupthink**.

Groupthink is the tendency for members of a group to become so concerned with reaching a consensus that they lose the ability to critically evaluate the problem before them. Groupthink can be likened to a kind of "tunnel vision" in which the group's perspective is limited to a single point of view (Nowak, Vallacher, & Miller, 2003).

In groupthink, the pressure to conform to majority opinion squelches any serious debate, which can lead groups to make less effective decisions than if dissenting opinions were aired (Jetten & Hornsey, 2015). Janis believed that groupthink is more likely to occur under conditions in which (1) members are strongly attached to the group, (2) an external threat is present, and (3) there is a strong-minded leader directing the group. Group members may not want to "rock the boat" by expressing a dissenting opinion or they may have a misplaced confidence that the leader and other group members must be right.

In late 2008, a month before taking office as president, Barack Obama reflected on the risks posed by groupthink:

> One of the dangers in a White House, based on my reading of history, is that you get wrapped up in groupthink, and everybody agrees with everything, and there's no discussion and there are no dissenting views. (Quoted in Cohen, 2008)

Critics point out that research evidence supporting the groupthink model is mixed (Kerr & Tindale, 2004). But Janis's recommendations for avoiding negative effects of groupthink are well worth considering at any level of decision making:

- Group members should be encouraged to consider all alternatives and carefully weigh the evidence on all sides of an issue.
- The group leader should avoid stating any preferences as the group begins its work.

CONCEPT 12.40
The presence of others may enhance individual performance on simple tasks but impair performance on more complex tasks.

CONCEPT 12.41
In social loafing, people fail to pull their own weight because they believe others will pick up the slack.

Hill Street Studios/Blend/Glow Images

Does the presence of others help or hinder your ability to perform at your best? Evidence teaches that the presence of others may impair performance of complex tasks but strengthen performance of simple or well-learned tasks.

CONCEPT 12.42
When groups tackle a problem, they may become so focused on reaching a consensus that they fail to critically examine the issues before them.

social loafing The tendency to expend less effort when working as a member of a group than when working alone.

groupthink Janis's term for the tendency of members of a decision-making group to be more focused on reaching a consensus than on critically examining the issues at hand.

Concept Chart 12.3 Group Influences on Identity and Behavior	
Sources of Group Influence	**Description**
Conformity	Adherence to social standards or norms
Obedience	Adherence to the commands of external authority
Social facilitation	Improvement in performance occurring when we perform in front of others
Social loafing	Impaired performance occurring when our individual effort is obscured by a group effort
Groupthink	The tendency for groups to emphasize consensus building rather than thoughtful consideration of the issues

- Outsiders should be called upon to offer their opinions and analyses.
- Group members or outsiders should be encouraged to play the role of "devil's advocate."
- The group should be subdivided into smaller groups to independently review the issues that are before the larger group.
- Several group meetings should be held to reassess the situation and evaluate any new information before final decisions are reached.

Concept Chart 12.3 summarizes the group influences on identity and behavior discussed in this module.

MODULE REVIEW 12.3 Group Influences on Individual Behavior

Recite It

10. Define social identity and **evaluate** cultural factors involved in social identity.

Social identity (also called group identity) is our (a) _____ self—that part of our self-concept that relates to our family and social roles and the collective identities we share with members of our own religious, ethnic, fraternal, or national groups. Social identities play a stronger role in (b) _____ cultures than (c) _____ cultures.

11. Describe the basic finding of Asch's classic study on conformity and **identify** factors that influence conformity.

Asch showed that people often (d) _____ to group judgments, even when those judgments are obviously false.

Factors that influence conformity include gender, cultural background, self-(e) _____, social shyness, desire to be liked by a group, age, and situational features such as public disclosure, group size, and stimulus (f) _____.

12. Explain the psychological bases of manipulative sales tactics.

Manipulative sales techniques such as the *lowball technique*, the *bait-and-switch technique*, and the *foot-in-the-door technique* rely on the desire for (g) _____, whereas the *door-in-the-face technique* relies on the psychological principle of (h) _____.

13. Describe the findings of Milgram's classic study and **evaluate** why his methods were controversial.

Milgram found that people from various walks of life could be induced to obey unreasonable or even immoral commands given by an (i) _____ figure.

The use of (j) _____, as well as the potential emotional aftereffects of raising awareness of participants' capabilities for such behavior, led to controversy over Milgram's methods.

14. Evaluate the effects of the presence of others on performance.

The presence of others may (k) _____ performance in simple, well-learned tasks but impair performance in complex tasks.

People may exert less than their best effort in a group task when they know others will pick up the slack and their performance will not be individually (l) _____.

15. **Define** groupthink and **explain** how it can lead to wrong decisions.

Groupthink is group decision making on the basis of reaching a (m) _____ within the group rather than a critical evaluation of the issues, which sometimes can lead to wrong decisions when groups fail to objectively weigh the facts at hand.

Recall It

1. Our _____ identity reflects the fundamental need to be part of a group.

2. Which of the following statements is *not* correct with regard to characteristics associated with greater levels of conformity?
   a. Individuals who conform assume that the majority must be correct.
   b. Individuals who conform exhibit greater independence and self-esteem.
   c. Individuals who conform find it difficult to disagree with group opinion.
   d. Public disclosure leads to more conformity than disclosing responses in private.

3. In Milgram's classic study, what percentage of original participants administered the full series of electric shocks (that is, to the highest level)?

4. Social facilitation is likely to lead to _____ performance on simpler, well-known tasks and _____ performance on less familiar or more difficult tasks.
   a. enhanced, impaired
   b. impaired, enhanced
   c. enhanced, enhanced
   d. impaired, impaired

5. The phenomenon of groupthink explains how
   a. groups often make better-informed decisions than individuals.
   b. groups often make bad decisions because of the desire to maintain harmony within the group.
   c. group members tend to think in similar ways because of their similar backgrounds.
   d. groups often make good decisions because of the desire to reach a consensus.

Think About It

■ Agree or disagree with this statement, and support your answer: "Had I been a participant in the Milgram study, I would have refused to comply with the experimenter's demands."

Recite It answers placed below.

THINKING CRITICALLY ABOUT PSYCHOLOGY

Based on your reading of this chapter, answer the following questions. Then, to evaluate your progress in developing critical thinking skills, compare your answers to the sample answers found in Appendix A.

Why didn't they help? A number of people reportedly witnessed Kitty Genovese being stabbed to death or heard screams but did nothing. Based on your reading of the factors influencing helping behavior, speculate on the reasons why these bystanders failed to help.

Recite It Answers for Chapter 12

Module 12.1 1. (a) disclosures; (b) schemas; (c) fulfilling, **2.** (d) fundamental attribution; (e) observer; (f) serving, **3.** (g) cognitions; (h) media; (i) elaboration likelihood; (j) content; (k) peripheral, **4.** (l) dissonance; (m) dissonance; (n) consistent; (o) behavior; (p) ignoring **Module 12.2 5.** (a) attractiveness, **6.** (b) passion, **7.** (c) decisions; (d) cost; (e) responsibility; (f) norms, **8.** (g) Prejudice; (h) stereotypes; (i) cognitive; (j) authoritarian; (k) universalist (l) intergroup; (m) cooperation, **9.** (n) aggression **Module 12.3 10.** (a) social; (b) collectivist; (c) individualistic, **11.** (d) conform; (e) esteem; (f) ambiguity, **12.** (g) consistency; (h) reciprocity, **13.** (i) authority; (j) deception, **14.** (k) improve; (l) evaluated, **15.** (m) consensus

Sample Responses to Try This Out, "What Do You Say Now?"

■ Lowball technique: You might say, "Sorry, that's my best offer. We agreed on a price and I expect you to stick to it."

■ Bait-and-switch technique: You might say, "If I wanted the LX version I would have asked for it. If you're having difficulty getting the car I want, then it's your problem. Now, what are you going to do for me?"

■ Foot-in-the-door technique: You might say, "If you want to lower the price of the car, we can talk about it. But the price I gave you is all I can afford to spend."

MODULE 12.1

Perceiving Others

Factors in Impression Formation

- Personal disclosure
- Social schemas
- Stereotyping
- Self-fulfilling prophecies
- Attributions
- Fundamental attribution error
- Actor–observer effect
- Self-serving bias

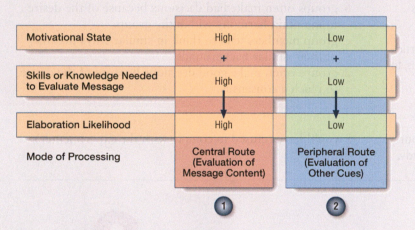

Motivational State	High	Low
	+	+
Skills or Knowledge Needed to Evaluate Message	High	Low
	↓	↓
Elaboration Likelihood	High	Low
Mode of Processing	Central Route (Evaluation of Message Content)	Peripheral Route (Evaluation of Other Cues)
	①	②

Attitudes

- **Components:** Cognitions, emotions, and behavior
- **Sources:** Parents, teachers, peers, personal experiences, media, and possible genetic influences
- **Cognitive Dissonance:** Discomfort arising from discrepancies between beliefs or attitudes and behavior
- **Elaboration Likelihood Model:** Persuasion works through either a central route (evaluation of the content of the message) or a peripheral route (focus on incidental cues)

MODULE 12.2

Relating to Others

Positive Ways of Relating

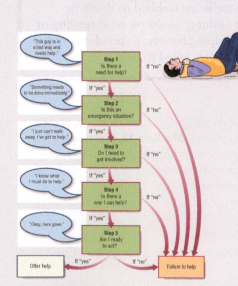

- **Factors Influencing Attraction:** Similarity, physical attractiveness, proximity, reciprocity
- **Triangular Model of Love:** Intimacy, passion, and decision/commitment components
- **Decision-Making Model of Bystander Intervention:** Predicts likelihood of bystanders helping a person in need
- **Factors Influencing Helping:** Situational ambiguity, perceived cost, diffusion of responsibility, similarity, empathy, facial features, gender and mood effects, attributions of the cause of need, social norms

Negative Ways of Relating

- **Factors Relating to Prejudice and Discrimination:** Negative stereotyping, in-group favoritism and out-group negativism, out-group homogeneity, authoritarian personality, and stereotype threat
- **Influences on Aggression:** Biological, learning, sociocultural, and environmental factors; use of alcohol; emotional states

Group Influences on Individual Behavior

Social Versus Personal Identity

- **Social Identity:** Ethnic, group, and role identity
- **Personal Identity:** Individual identity

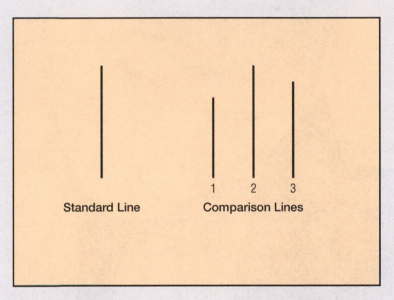

Standard Line   Comparison Lines

1   2   3

Conformity

- **Asch Experiments:** Conforming to group judgments
- **Factors Influencing Conformity:** Individual differences and situational factors

Obedience to Authority

- **Milgram's Studies:** Obedience to unreasonable or immoral commands
- **Controversies:** Ethical issues, relevance of findings to real-life atrocities
- **Factors Influencing Obedience to Authority:** Legitimization of authority, social validation

Hill Street Studios/Blend/Glow Images

Other Social Influences

- **Social Facilitation:** Performing better when others are present
- **Social Loafing:** Sloughing off in group work
- **Groupthink:** Putting consensus building above careful decision making

485

LEARNING OBJECTIVES

After studying this chapter, you will be able to . . .

1 **Identify** criteria used to distinguish normal behavior from abnormal behavior, and **apply** these criteria to the case examples of Claire and Phil.

2 **Identify** the major contemporary models of abnormal behavior.

3 **Describe** the features of psychological disorders and **explain** how they are classified in the *DSM* system.

4 **Identify** and **describe** types of anxiety-related disorders and underlying causal factors in these disorders.

5 **Identify** and **describe** types of dissociative and somatic symptom and related disorders and underlying causal factors in these disorders.

6 **Identify** and **describe** two major types of mood disorders and underlying causal factors in these disorders.

7 **Identify** factors linked to risk of suicide.

8 **Describe** the features of schizophrenia and underlying causal factors.

9 **Explain** the development of schizophrenia based on the diathesis-stress model.

10 **Define** the concept of personality disorders.

11 **Describe** the features of antisocial personality disorder and borderline personality disorder and underlying causal factors in these disorders.

PREVIEW

Psychological Disorders

The "Garlic Lady"

It was about 2:00 A.M. when the police brought Claire to the emergency room. She seemed to be about 45; her hair was matted, her clothing was disheveled, and her face was fixed in a blank stare. She clutched a clove of garlic in her right hand. She did not respond to the interviewer's questions: "Do you know where you are? Can you tell me your name? Can you tell me if anything is bothering you?"

The police officers filled in the details. Claire had been found meandering through town along the painted line that divided the main street, apparently oblivious to the cars swerving around her. She was waving the clove of garlic in front of her. She said nothing to the officers when they arrived on the scene, but she offered no resistance.

Claire was admitted to the hospital and taken to the psychiatric ward. The next morning, she was brought before the day staff, still clutching the clove of garlic, and was interviewed by the chief psychiatrist. She said little, but her intentions could be pieced together from mumbled fragments. Claire said something about "devils" who were trying to "rob" her mind. The garlic was meant to protect her. She had decided that the only way to rid the town of the "devils" that hounded her was to walk down the main street, waving the garlic in front of her. Claire would become well known to the hospital. This was but one of a series of such episodes.

"Pretty Grisly Stuff"

Phil was 42, a police photographer. It was his job to take pictures at crime scenes. "Pretty grisly stuff," he admitted, "corpses and all." Phil was married and had two teenage sons. He sought a psychological consultation because he was bothered by fears of being confined in enclosed spaces. Many situations evoked his fears. He was terrified of becoming trapped in an elevator and took the stairs whenever possible. He felt uncomfortable sitting in the backseat of a car. He had lately become fearful of flying, although in the past he had worked as a news cameraperson and would often fly to scenes of news events at a moment's notice—usually by helicopter.

"I guess I was younger then and more daring," he related. "Sometimes I would hang out of the helicopter to shoot pictures with no fear at all. But now, just thinking about flying makes my heart race. It's not that I'm afraid the plane will crash. I just start trembling when I think of them closing that door, trapping us inside. I can't tell you why."

In this chapter, we examine the behavior of people like Claire and Phil—behavior that psychologists would consider abnormal. Let us begin by examining the criteria that psychologists use to determine when

Did you know that...

- Psychological disorders affect just about everyone in one way or another? (p. 493)
- Some people are so afraid of leaving the house that they literally are unable to go out to buy a quart of milk? (p. 496)
- If there is a spider in a room full of people, the person with a spider phobia is likely to be the first one to notice it and point it out? (p. 496)
- Some people have lost all feeling in an arm or leg but remain strangely unconcerned about their ailments? (p. 502)
- Women are nearly twice as likely as men to develop major depression? (p. 506)
- Older adults are more likely to commit suicide than teens? (p. 511)
- Adolescents who have a friend who attempted suicide are more likely than others to attempt suicide themselves? (p. 512)
- People labeled as psychopaths are not psychotic? (p. 519)

behavior crosses the line between normal and abnormal. Later we will explore different kinds of abnormal behavior patterns that psychologists and other professionals classify as psychological or mental disorders.

The descriptions in this chapter may raise your awareness about psychological problems of people you know, or perhaps even problems you've faced yourself. But it is not intended to make you a diagnostician. If the problems discussed in the chapter hit close to home, it makes sense to discuss your concerns with a qualified professional.

13.1 What Is Abnormal Behavior?

1 **Identify** criteria used to distinguish normal behavior from abnormal behavior, and **apply** these criteria to the case examples of Claire and Phil.

2 **Identify** the major contemporary models of abnormal behavior.

3 **Describe** the features of psychological disorders and **explain** how they are classified in the *DSM* system.

CONCEPT 13.1

Psychologists use several criteria in determining whether behavior is abnormal, including unusualness, social deviance, emotional distress, maladaptive behavior, dangerousness, and faulty perceptions or interpretations of reality.

Determining whether behavior is abnormal is a more complex problem than it may seem at first blush. Most of us get anxious or depressed from time to time, but our behavior is not abnormal. The same behavior may be deemed normal under some circumstances but abnormal in others. For example, anxiety during a job interview is normal, but anxiety experienced whenever you board an elevator is not. Deep feelings of sadness are appropriate when you lose a loved one, but not when things are going well or following a mildly upsetting event that others take in stride.

Charting the Boundaries Between Normal and Abnormal Behavior

Where, then, might we draw the line between normal and abnormal behavior? Psychologists typically identify abnormal behavior based on a combination of the following criteria (Nevid, Rathus, & Greene, 2014):

1. *Unusualness.* Behavior that is unusual, or experienced by only a few, may be abnormal—but not in all cases or situations. Surely it is unusual for people to report "hearing voices" or, like Claire, to walk through town warding off demons. Yet uncommonness, by itself, is not sufficient to be deemed abnormal. Exceptional behavior, such as the ability to hit a three-point jump shot with some regularity or to become a valedictorian, is also unusual, but it is not abnormal.

2. *Social deviance.* All societies establish standards or social norms that define socially acceptable behaviors. Deviation from these norms is often used as a criterion for labeling behavior as abnormal. The same behavior might be considered abnormal in some contexts but perfectly acceptable in others. For example, we might consider it abnormal to shout vulgarities at strangers in the street. Yet shouting vulgarities at an umpire or referee who misses an important call in a ball game may fall within the range of acceptable social norms, however offensive it might be.

© IMAGENFX/Shutterstock.com

3. *Emotional distress.* States of emotional distress, such as anxiety or depression, are considered abnormal when inappropriate, excessive, or prolonged relative to the person's situation.

4. *Maladaptive behavior.* Behavior is maladaptive when it causes personal distress, is self-defeating, or is associated with significant health, social, or occupational problems. For example, abuse of alcohol or other drugs may threaten an individual's health and ability to function in meeting life's responsibilities.

5. *Dangerousness.* Violent or dangerous behavior is another criterion for which we need to examine the social context. For example, engaging in behavior that is dangerous to oneself or others may be an act of bravery in times of war, but not in peacetime. Hockey players and football players regularly engage in physically aggressive behavior that may be dangerous to themselves or their opponents, but their behavior in athletic competitions is often rewarded with lucrative contracts and endorsement deals. Apart from the sanctioned contexts of warfare and sports, however, violent behavior is likely to be considered abnormal.

6. *Faulty perceptions or interpretations of reality.* **Hallucinations** ("hearing voices" or seeing things that are not there) involve distorted perceptions of reality. Similarly, fixed but unfounded beliefs, called **delusions**, such as believing that FBI agents are listening in on your phone conversations, represent faulty interpretations of reality (unless of course the FBI really is tapping your phone).

As we shall see next, the cultural context in which behavior occurs must also be evaluated when making judgments about whether behavior is abnormal.

Cultural Bases of Abnormal Behavior

Psychologists take the cultural context into account when making judgments about abnormal behavior. They realize that the same behavior can be normal in one culture but abnormal in another. For example, in the majority American culture, "hearing voices" is deemed abnormal. Yet among some Native American peoples, it is considered normal for individuals to hear the voices of their recently deceased relatives. They believe that the voices of the departed call out as their spirit ascends to the afterworld (Kleinman, 1987). Such behavior, because it falls within the normal spectrum of the culture in which it occurs, is not deemed abnormal—even if it may seem so to people from other cultures.

In addition, abnormal behavior patterns may be expressed differently in different cultures. For example, people in Western cultures may experience anxiety in the form of excessive worries about finances, health, or jobs. Among some native African peoples and Australian aboriginal peoples, anxiety may be expressed in the form of fears of witchcraft or sorcery (Kleinman, 1987). Evidence shows that Chinese people tend to put greater emphasis on physical symptoms of depression, such as headaches, fatigue, and weakness, and less emphasis on feelings of sadness, than do people from Western cultures (Kalibatseva & Leong, 2011; Zhou et al., 2011).

Alternatively, the same behavior may be judged to be abnormal at some points in time but not at others. The American Psychiatric Association once classified homosexuality as a type of mental disorder, but no longer does so. Many professionals today consider homosexuality a variation of sexual behavior rather than an abnormal behavior pattern.

Applying the Criteria

Reconsider the examples of Claire and Phil, described at the start of this chapter. Was their behavior abnormal? Claire's behavior certainly met several of the criteria

CONCEPT 13.2
Behavior that is deemed to be normal in some cultures may be considered abnormal in others.

Igor Akimov/Corbis News/Corbis

Is this man abnormal? Abnormality must be judged in relation to cultural standards. Are heavy body tattooing and piercings a sign of abnormality or a fashion statement?

hallucinations Perceptions ("hearing voices" or seeing things) experienced in the absence of corresponding external stimuli.

delusions Fixed but patently false beliefs, such as believing that one is being hounded by demons.

of abnormal behavior. It was clearly unusual as well as socially deviant, and it represented what most people would take to be a delusion—believing you are protecting the community from demons. It was also clearly maladaptive and dangerous, as it put at risk not only Claire herself but also the drivers who were forced to swerve out of the way to avoid hitting her.

Phil, on the other hand, had good contact with reality. He understood that his fears exceeded the dangers he faced. Yet his phobia was a source of considerable emotional distress and was maladaptive because it impaired his ability to carry out his occupational and family responsibilities. We might also employ a criterion of unusualness here. Relatively few people have such fears of confinement that they avoid flying or taking elevators. Yet, as we have noted, unusualness alone is not a sufficient criterion for abnormality.

Although the behaviors of these individuals invoke different criteria, they could all be considered abnormal. Overall, professionals apply multiple criteria when making judgments about abnormality.

Models of Abnormal Behavior

Abnormal behavior has existed in all societies, even though the view of what is or is not abnormal varies from culture to culture and has changed over time. In some cases, these explanations have led to humane treatment of people with abnormal behavior, but more frequently, people deemed to be "mad" or mentally ill have been treated cruelly or harshly.

Early Beliefs

> **CONCEPT 13.3**
> Throughout much of Western history, the prevailing view of abnormal behavior was based on a concept of demonic possession.

Throughout much of Western history, from ancient times through the Middle Ages, people thought that those displaying abnormal behavior were controlled by supernatural forces or possessed by demonic spirits. Beliefs in supernatural causes of abnormal behavior, especially the doctrine of demonic possession, held sway until the rise of scientific thinking in the seventeenth and eighteenth centuries. The treatment of choice for demonic possession—*exorcism*—was used to ferret out satanic forces or the Devil himself from the afflicted person's body. If that didn't work, there were even more forceful "remedies," such as the torture rack. Not surprisingly, many recipients of these "cures" attempted to the best of their ability to modify their behavior to meet social expectations.

The Medical Model

> **CONCEPT 13.4**
> With the rise of scientific thought, attention began to shift from religious dogma to scientific or naturalistic explanations of human behavior.

The eighteenth and nineteenth centuries were times of rapid advances in medical science. Among the more notable advances were the development of a vaccine against the ancient scourge of smallpox, the discovery of the bacterial causes of diseases such as anthrax and leprosy, and the introduction of antiseptics in surgery to prevent infections. It was against this backdrop of medical discovery and shifts from religious dogma to scientific or naturalistic explanations of human behavior that the first modern model of abnormal behavior was developed, the **medical model**. The medical model is based on the belief that abnormal behavior patterns are *mental illnesses or* brain diseases that have a biological basis and can be classified on the basis of their particular characteristics or symptoms (Deacon, 2013).

medical model A framework for understanding abnormal behavior patterns as symptoms of underlying brain disorders or diseases.

Psychological Models

Even as the medical model was taking shape, theorists were actively developing psychological models of abnormal behavior. The first major psychological model of abnormal behavior was the psychodynamic model that Sigmund Freud developed. Freud believed that abnormal behavior arises from unconscious conflicts that remain unresolved from childhood. These conflicts result from the need to control instinctual sexual and aggressive impulses from the unconscious mind or to channel them into socially acceptable outlets. Psychological symptoms (for example, a phobia) are merely outward expressions of this inner turmoil. The person may be aware of the symptom (the phobia) but not of the unconscious conflicts that gave rise to it. Contemporary psychodynamic theorists differ from Freud in some respects, but they retain the central belief that unconscious conflicts are at the root of abnormal behavior patterns.

At about the time that Freud was plumbing the depths of the unconscious, behaviorists were exploring the role of learning in the development of abnormal behavior. Pavlov's discovery of the conditioned response gave the early behaviorist movement a model for studying how maladaptive behaviors, such as phobias, could be learned or acquired through experience. The behavioral model is based on the belief that most forms of abnormal behavior are learned in the same ways that normal behavior is learned. Among the early demonstrations of the role of learning in the development of abnormal behavior was the experiment with "Little Albert" (discussed in Chapter 5). In this experiment, John B. Watson and his colleague Rosalie Rayner (1920) induced a fear of white rats in a young boy by presenting a noxious stimulus (loud banging sound) whenever a rat was brought close to the child. The repeated pairing of the conditioned stimulus (rat) and unconditioned stimulus (loud banging) instilled a conditioned response (fear evoked by the rat itself).

The humanistic model offers another psychological perspective on abnormal behavior. Humanistic theorists such as Carl Rogers and Abraham Maslow rejected the belief that human behavior is the product of either unconscious processes or simple conditioning. Human beings, they argued, possess an intrinsic ability to make conscious choices and to strive toward self-actualization. Abnormal behavior develops when people encounter roadblocks on the path toward personal growth or self-actualization. To satisfy the demands of others to think, feel, and act in certain ways, people may become detached from their true selves and develop a distorted self-image that can lead to emotional problems such as anxiety and depression. Humanistic theorists believe that people with psychological problems need to become more aware of their true feelings and come to accept themselves for who they truly are.

Cognitive theorists, such as Albert Ellis and Aaron Beck, believe that irrational or distorted thinking leads to emotional problems and maladaptive behavior. Examples of faulty styles of thinking include magnifying or exaggerating the consequences of negative events ("making mountains out of molehills") and interpreting events in an overly negative way, as though one were seeing things through blue-colored glasses.

The Sociocultural Model

The sociocultural model views the causes of abnormal behavior within the broader social and cultural contexts in which the behavior develops. Theorists in this tradition believe that abnormal behavior may have more to do with social ills or failures of society than with problems within the individual. They examine a range of social and cultural influences on behavior, including social class, poverty, ethnic and cultural background, and racial and gender discrimination. Sociocultural theorists believe that stress of coping with poverty and social disadvantage can eventually take its toll on mental health. Consistent with this view, evidence shows a number of psychological disorders including mood disorders, substance-related disorders, and schizophrenia occur proportionately more often among poor and socially

CONCEPT 13.5

Psychodynamic, behavioral, humanistic, and cognitive models focus on the psychological roots of abnormal behavior.

CONCEPT LINK

These major psychological models also give rise to different forms of psychotherapy. See Module 14.1.

© Irin-k/Shutterstock.com

CONCEPT 13.6

The sociocultural model views abnormal behavior in terms of the social and cultural contexts in which it occurs.

disadvantaged groups (Kirkbride et al., 2012; Sareen et al., 2011). Minority youth often face stressors such as acculturation, poverty, and discrimination, which may help explain findings that they have higher rates of anxiety and depression (Anderson & Mayes, 2010).

Sociocultural theorists also focus on the effects of labeling people as mentally ill. They recognize that because of social prejudices, people who are labeled mentally ill are often denied job or housing opportunities and become stigmatized or marginalized in society. These theorists join with other professionals in arguing for greater understanding and support for people with mental health problems.

The Biopsychosocial Model. We have many different models to explain abnormal behavior. We shouldn't conclude that one particular model is necessarily right and all the others wrong. Each of these models—medical, psychological, and sociocultural—has something unique to offer our understanding of abnormal behavior. None offers a complete view.

Abnormal behavior presents us with many puzzles as we attempt to unravel its causes. How are our mental functions affected by biology—by genes, brain structures, and neurotransmitter systems? What psychological factors, such as underlying motives or conflicts, personality traits, cognitions, and learned behaviors, are involved? And how is our behavior affected by society and culture?

Many psychologists today subscribe to the **biopsychosocial model**—the view that abnormal behavior is best explained by complex interactions of biological, psychological, environmental, and sociocultural factors (Nigg, 2013; Smith, 2012; Weir, 2012b). We are only beginning to put together the pieces of what has turned out to be a very complicated puzzle—the subtle and often complex patterns of underlying factors that give rise to abnormal behavior patterns.

A prominent example of the biopsychosocial model is the **diathesis-stress model**. According to this model, certain people have a vulnerability or predisposition, called a **diathesis,** which increases their risk of developing a particular disorder. A diathesis is usually genetic in nature, but can involve psychological factors such as maladaptive personality traits or dysfunctional thinking patterns. If a diathesis for a particular disorder is present, then the likelihood of the disorder emerging depends on the level of stress the person encounters (Pruessner et al., 2011). If the person faces a low level of life stress or has effective skills for handling stress, the disorder may never emerge even in the presence of a diathesis. However, the stronger the diathesis, the less stress is likely to be needed for the disorder to develop (see ■ Figure 13.1). In some cases, the diathesis may be so strong that the disorder develops even under the most benign life circumstances.

CONCEPT 13.7
Today there is increasing convergence toward a biopsychosocial model of abnormal behavior, which focuses on the contributions and interactions of biological and psychosocial influences.

biopsychosocial model An integrative model for explaining abnormal behavior patterns in terms of the interactions of biological, psychological, and sociocultural factors.

diathesis-stress model A type of biopsychosocial model that relates the development of disorders to the combination of a diathesis, or predisposition, usually genetic in origin, and exposure to stressful events or life circumstances.

diathesis A vulnerability or predisposition to developing a disorder.

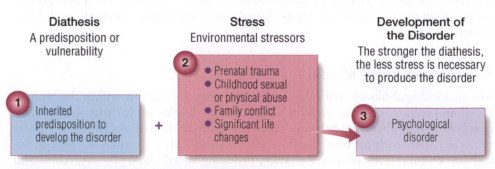

FIGURE 13.1 **The Diathesis-Stress Model**
The diathesis-stress model posits that the development of particular disorders involves an interaction of a ❶ predisposition (diathesis), usually genetic in nature, and ❷ exposure to life stress, which leads to ❸ the development of psychological disorders.

Source: Adapted from Nevid, Rathus, & Greene, 2008.

What Are Psychological Disorders?

Distinctive patterns of abnormal behavior are classified as **psychological disorders**—also known as *mental disorders* or *mental illnesses* within the medical model. Psychological disorders involve disturbances of mood, behavior, thought processes, or perception that result in significant personal distress or impaired functioning. Examples of psychological disorders include schizophrenia, anxiety-related disorders such as phobias and panic disorder, and mood disorders such as major depression.

How Many Are Affected?

Chances are that you or someone you know will be affected by a psychological disorder at one time or another. Nearly half (46 percent) of adult Americans develop diagnosable psychological disorders at some point in their lifetimes (Kessler, Berglund, et al., 2005; see ■ Figure 13.2). About one-fourth of adults (26 percent) experience a psychological disorder in any given year (Kessler, Chiu, et al., 2005; The WHO World Mental Health Survey Consortium, 2004). If we also take into account the economic costs of diagnosing and treating these disorders, and the lost productivity and wages that result from them, it is fair to say that virtually everyone is affected by psychological disorders.

How Are Psychological Disorders Classified?   One reference book found on the shelves of virtually all mental health professionals and probably dog-eared from repeated use is the *Diagnostic and Statistical Manual of Mental Disorders*, or *DSM*—now in a 5th edition called the *DSM-5* (APA, 2013). The manual contains descriptions and diagnostic criteria for every recognized psychological disorder, which are called *mental disorders* in the manual. The *DSM* classifies mental disorders on the basis of their distinctive features or symptoms and organizes them into groupings of disorders that have similar features or symptom profiles.

Though the *DSM* is the most widely used diagnostic system, questions remain about the reliability and validity of some disorders and the criteria used to arrive at those diagnoses (First, 2012; Frances & Widiger, 2012; Zimmerman et al., 2006). A frequent criticism, especially among psychologists, is that the *DSM* relies too heavily on a medical model conceptualization that abnormal behaviors represent symptoms of underlying mental disorders or illnesses. Yet many clinicians find the listing of specific criteria for particular disorders very helpful in making diagnostic judgments. Perhaps it is best to consider the *DSM* as a work in progress rather than as a finished product.

The following modules describe the prominent symptoms of major forms of psychological or mental disorders, the rates of occurrence of these disorders, and theories about their underlying causes. See Concept Chart 13.1 for a listing of the major contemporary models of abnormal behavior.

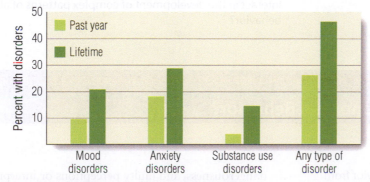

FIGURE 13.2 Prevalence of Psychological Disorders
Nearly half of adult Americans suffer from a diagnosable psychological disorder at some point in their lives. About one in four suffers from a current disorder.

Sources: Kessler, Berglund et al., 2005; Kessler, Chiu, et al., 2005; based on data from National Comorbidity Survey Replication (NCS-R).

CONCEPT 13.8
Psychological disorders are patterns of disturbed behavior, mood, thinking, or perception that cause personal distress or impaired functioning.

CONCEPT 13.9
The *DSM*, the diagnostic system used most widely for classifying psychological or mental disorders, provides criteria clinicians use to diagnose these disorders.

psychological disorders Abnormal behavior patterns characterized by disturbances in behavior, thinking, perceptions, or emotions that are associated with significant personal distress or impaired functioning. Also called *mental disorders* or *mental illnesses*.

Concept Chart 13.1   Contemporary Models of Abnormal Behavior

	Model	Focus	Key Questions
	Medical model	Biological underpinnings of abnormal behavior	What roles do neurotransmitters, genetics, and brain abnormalities play in abnormal behavior?
Psychological Models	Psychodynamic model	Unconscious conflicts and motives underlying abnormal behavior	How do particular symptoms represent or symbolize unconscious conflicts? What are the childhood roots of a person's problem?
	Behavioral model	Learning experiences that shape the development of abnormal behavior	How are abnormal patterns of behavior learned? What role does the environment play in explaining abnormal behavior?
	Humanistic model	Roadblocks to self-awareness and self-acceptance	How do a person's emotional problems reflect a distorted self-image? What roadblocks did the person encounter in the path toward self-realization?
	Cognitive model	Faulty thinking underlying abnormal behavior	What styles of thinking characterize people with particular types of psychological disorders? What roles do personal beliefs, thoughts, and ways of interpreting events play in the development of abnormal behavior patterns?
	Sociocultural model	Social ills contributing to the development of abnormal behavior, such as poverty, racism, and prolonged unemployment; relationships between abnormal behavior and ethnicity, gender, culture, and socioeconomic level	What relationships exist between social class status and risks of psychological disorders? Are there gender or ethnic group differences in various disorders? How are these explained? What are the effects of stigmatization on people who are labeled mentally ill?
	Biopsychosocial model	Interactions of biological, psychological, and sociocultural factors in the development of abnormal behavior	How might genetic or other factors predispose individuals to psychological disorders in the face of life stress? How do biological, psychological, and sociocultural factors interact in the development of complex patterns of abnormal behavior?

MODULE REVIEW   **13.1**   **What Is Abnormal Behavior?**

Recite It

1. **Identify** criteria used to distinguish normal behavior from abnormal behavior and **apply** these criteria to the case examples of Claire and Phil.

    There are several criteria, including unusualness, social (a) _____, emotional distress, maladaptive behavior,

dangerousness, and faulty perceptions or interpretations of (b) _____. Claire demonstrated unusual behavior, social deviant behavior, dangerous and maladaptive behavior, and faulty (c) _____ of reality. Phil demonstrated unusual and maladaptive behavior and (d) _____ distress.

2. **Identify** the major contemporary models of abnormal behavior.

The major contemporary models are the medical model, the psychological model, the sociocultural model, and the (e) _____ model.

3. **Describe** the features of psychological disorders and **explain** how they are classified in the *DSM* system.

Varying in symptoms and severity, (f) _____ disorders (also called *mental disorders*) are disturbances in

behavior, thought processes, or emotions associated with significant personal distress or impaired functioning. The (g) _____ classifies mental or psychological disorders based on distinctive features or symptoms of disorders and organizes them in grouping of disorders having similar features or symptoms.

Recall It

1. List the six criteria for defining abnormal behavior discussed in the text.

2. _____ are distorted perceptions of reality; _____ are fixed but unfounded beliefs.

    a. Delusions; hallucinations
    b. Dreams; fantasies
    c. Fantasies; dreams
    d. Hallucinations; delusions

3. The explanation for abnormal behavior during much of the history of Western civilization was

    a. brain malfunction or chemical disorder.
    b. harsh and cruel treatment by close family members.
    c. possession by demons or supernatural forces.
    d. falsehoods or other retaliation spread by a sufferer's enemies.

4. Match the following psychological models for abnormal behavior with the appropriate descriptions: (a) psychodynamic; (b) behavioral; (c) humanistic; (d) cognitive.

    i. distorted self-image, loss of sense of true self
    ii. faulty styles of thinking, exaggeration of negative aspects of events
    iii. learned patterns of behavior
    iv. unresolved unconscious conflicts dating from childhood

Think About It

■ Why is it important to consider the cultural context when determining abnormal behavior? Can you think of any

examples of behaviors that are deemed acceptable in some cultures but not in others?

Recite It answers placed at the end of chapter.

MODULE # 13.2 Anxiety-Related Disorders

4 **Identify** and **describe** types of anxiety-related disorders and underlying causal factors in these disorders.

Anxiety is an emotional state of uneasiness or distress associated with worry or apprehension about the future. There is a lot to be anxious about—our health, our jobs, our families, climate change, the state of the nation and the world. Indeed, anxiety can be an adaptive response in some situations. It can motivate us to study before an exam and to seek regular medical checkups, for example. But when anxiety is excessive in a given situation or interferes with the ability to function, it can become abnormal. *Fear* is the term we use to describe anxiety experienced in specific situations, as when boarding an airplane or taking a final exam.

CONCEPT 13.10
Anxiety-related disorders are psychological disorders characterized by excessive or inappropriate anxiety reactions.

The National League starting pitcher in the 2015 All-Star game, Zack Greinke, has struggled with social anxiety disorder for years. He says that taking medication and working with a sports psychologist helped him control his anxiety. Though he recognizes it may return in the future, he no longer thinks about it or feels stressed about it.

CONCEPT 13.11
The major types of anxiety-related disorders are phobias, panic disorder, generalized anxiety disorder, obsessive-compulsive disorder, and post-traumatic stress disorder.

"It was as big as my head, I swear!" Investigators find that the more afraid people are of spiders, the larger they perceive them to be.

phobias Excessive or irrational fears of particular objects or situations.

social anxiety disorder A type of anxiety disorder involving excessive fear of social situations. Also called *social phobia*.

Types of Disorders

Anxiety-related disorders are among the most common psychological disorders, affecting about one in five U.S. adults—more than 40 million people in total (Torpy, Burke, & Golub, 2011). These disorders are characterized by excessive or inappropriate anxiety reactions. Here we focus on several major types of anxiety-related disorders that are grouped in a diagnostic category of anxiety disorders in the *DSM-5*: phobias, panic disorder, and generalized anxiety disorder. We also discuss another anxiety-related disorder, obsessive-compulsive disorder (OCD), which was formerly classified as an anxiety disorder, but was moved in the *DSM-5* to a new diagnostic category comprising disorders characterized by compulsive behavior problems. Posttraumatic stress disorder (PTSD), another type of anxiety-related disorder, was discussed in Chapter 10.

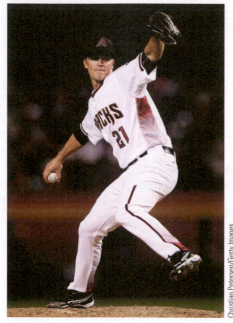

Christian Petersen/Getty Images

Phobias

Phobias are irrational or excessive fears of particular objects or situations. The *DSM-5* classifies three types of phobic disorders: *social anxiety disorder (social phobia)*, *specific phobia*, and *agoraphobia*. People with **social anxiety disorder** have intense fears of social interactions, such as meeting others, dating, or giving a speech or presentation in class. People with **specific phobia** have excessive fears of specific situations or objects, such as animals, insects, heights (**acrophobia**), or enclosed spaces (**claustrophobia**). People with **agoraphobia** have more general fears of venturing into open places or going out in public.

People with phobias are constantly alert to threatening stimuli. If there is a spider in a room full of people, a person with a spider phobia is usually the first one to notice it and point it out (Purkis, Lester, & Field, 2011). Fear also affects perception. The more strongly a person fears spiders, the bigger that person perceives them to be (Vasey et al., 2012).

People with claustrophobia may refuse to use elevators despite the inconvenience of climbing many flights of stairs several times a day. Those with agoraphobia may become literally housebound, unable even to go to the local store to buy a quart of milk. Those with social phobia may have difficulty maintaining a normal social life. People with phobias usually recognize that their fears are irrational or excessive, but they still avoid the objects or situations they fear.

Panic Disorder

People with **panic disorder** experience sudden episodes of sheer terror called *panic attacks*. Panic attacks are characterized by intense physical symptoms: profuse sweating, nausea, numbness or tingling, flushes or chills, trembling, chest pain, shortness of breath, and pounding of the heart. These symptoms may lead people to think they are having a heart attack, or "going crazy," or losing control. A specific attack can last anywhere from a few minutes to more than an hour. A young man who suffered a series of panic attacks recounted what it felt like: "All of a sudden, I felt a tremendous wave of fear for no reason at all. My heart was pounding, my chest hurt, and it was getting harder to breathe. I thought I was going to die."

Panic attacks initially seem to come "out of the blue." Yet they can later be connected with the situations in which they occur, such as shopping in a crowded department store or riding on a train. Agoraphobia, too, sometimes develops in people with panic disorder when they begin avoiding public places out of fear of having panic attacks while away from the security of their homes.

Pro golfer Charlie Beljan suffered a panic attack while playing in a professional tournament. Although he played through the attack and went on to win the tournament, he feared that something was terribly wrong with his heart. The shortness of breath and pounding heart that often occur during a panic attack may be mistaken for signs of an impending heart attack. Charlie was taken by ambulance from the golf course to a local hospital for medical tests, which showed, fortunately, that his heart was fine.

Generalized Anxiety Disorder

People with **generalized anxiety disorder (GAD)** experience persistent anxiety that is not tied to any particular object or situation. In such cases, the anxiety has a "free-floating" quality, as it seems to travel with the person from place to place. The hallmark feature of GAD is excessive worry (Stefanopoulou et al., 2014; Stein & Sareen, 2015). People with GAD are chronic worriers who tend to worry over just about everything. They seldom if ever are free of worry. Other characteristics of GAD include shakiness, inability to relax, fidgeting, and feelings of dread and foreboding (Donegan & Dugas, 2012).

Obsessive-Compulsive Disorder

Have you ever had a thought you couldn't shake off? Have you ever felt compelled to repeat the same behavior again and again? People with **obsessive-compulsive disorder (OCD)** experience persistent obsessions and/or compulsions. Obsessions are nagging, intrusive thoughts the person feels unable to control and that engender anxiety. Compulsions are repetitive behaviors or rituals the person feels compelled to perform again and again. Some people with this disorder become obsessed with the thought that germs contaminate their skin and spend hours each day compulsively washing their hands or showering. Others repeatedly perform checking rituals upon leaving the house to ensure that the doors and windows are securely locked and the gas jets on the stove are turned off.

What do you fear? Where do we draw the line between ordinary fear and phobias?

Causes of Anxiety-Related Disorders

Nearly everyone experiences anxiety from time to time, but only some people develop anxiety-related disorders. Although we don't know precisely why these disorders develop, we can identify biological and psychological factors that contribute to them and surmise that an interaction of these factors affects their development.

Biological Factors

Investigators are beginning to make headway in understanding the biological underpinnings of anxiety. Studies of twins and adoptees point to an important role for genetic factors in many anxiety-related disorders (Mattheisen et al., 2014; Taylor & Jang, 2011).

Genetic factors may affect brain circuitry involved in the body's response to threatening stimuli. Recent evidence suggests that the amygdala, the fear-generating part of the limbic system in the brain, may be overreactive in people with anxiety-related disorders, making them especially anxious or jumpy in response to threatening cues (Denny et al., 2015; Grant, 2014). In panic disorder, disturbances in neurotransmitter functioning in the brain may trigger an internal alarm system that induces feelings of panic in susceptible people. In people with OCD, the brain may be continually sending messages that something is

specific phobia Phobic reactions involving specific situations or objects.

acrophobia Excessive fear of heights.

claustrophobia Excessive fear of enclosed spaces.

agoraphobia Excessive, irrational fear of being in public places.

panic disorder A type of anxiety disorder involving repeated episodes of sheer terror called panic attacks.

generalized anxiety disorder (GAD) A type of anxiety disorder involving persistent and generalized anxiety and worry.

obsessive-compulsive disorder (OCD) A psychological disorder involving the repeated occurrence of obsessions and/or compulsions.

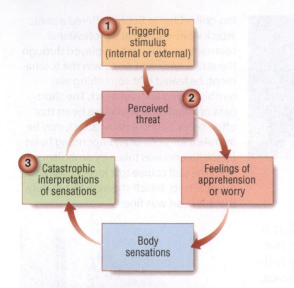

FIGURE 13.3 Cognitive Model of Panic

Cognitive theorists conceptualize panic disorder in terms of an interaction of physiological and cognitive factors: ❶ A triggering stimulus or cue, such as sudden lightheadedness, sets the cycle in motion. ❷ The stimulus is perceived as threatening, leading to apprehension (feelings of anxiety and worry), which leads to bodily sensations, such as a tightening feeling in the chest. ❸ These sensations are misconstrued as signs of an impending catastrophe, such as a heart attack, which reinforces perceptions of threat, leading to yet more anxiety and more catastrophic thoughts, resulting in a vicious cycle that can quickly spiral into a panic attack.

Source: Adapted from Clark, 1986.

CONCEPT 13.12

Both biological factors, such as disturbed neurotransmitter functioning, and psychological factors, such as learning experiences, are implicated as causal influences in anxiety-related disorders.

terribly wrong and requires immediate attention—a situation that may lead to obsessional, worrisome thoughts. The compulsions associated with OCD may be linked to abnormalities in brain circuits that ordinarily put the brakes on repetitive, ritualistic behaviors (Hsieh et al., 2014; Szeszko et al., 2008).

Psychological Factors

Some phobias may be learned via classical conditioning in which a previously neutral or benign stimulus becomes paired with an aversive stimulus (Field, 2006; Kim & Jung, 2006). A person bitten by a dog during childhood may come to develop a fear of dogs or other animals; a person trapped in an elevator for hours may acquire a fear of elevators or of confinement in other enclosed spaces. The previously neutral stimulus is the conditioned stimulus (CS), the aversive stimulus is the unconditioned stimulus (US), and the acquired fear response is the conditioned response (CR).

Operant conditioning may help account for avoidance behavior. Avoidance of the phobic object or situation (as when a person with an elevator phobia takes the stairs instead of the elevator) is negatively reinforced by relief from anxiety. However, though avoiding a fearful situation may offer short-term relief from anxiety, it doesn't help people overcome their fears. (The principle of negative reinforcement is discussed in Chapter 5.)

Negative reinforcement (relief from anxiety) may also contribute to obsessive-compulsive disorder. People with OCD often become trapped in a repetitive cycle of obsessive thinking and compulsive behavior. Obsessive thoughts ("my hands are covered with germs") trigger anxiety, which, in turn, is partially relieved through performance of a compulsive ritual (repetitive hand-washing). In effect, the solution to obsessive thinking (performing the compulsive ritual) becomes the problem (Salkovskis et al., 2003). However, because relief from the obsessive thoughts is at best incomplete or fleeting, the thoughts soon return, prompting yet more compulsive behavior—and so on in a continuing cycle.

A cognitive model of panic disorder focuses on the interrelationship between biological and psychological factors. From this perspective, panic disorder arises from misinterpretation of relatively minor changes in bodily sensations (for example, sudden light-headedness or dizziness) as signs of imminent catastrophe, such as an impending heart attack or loss of control. As a result of these catastrophic misinterpretations, the person experiences symptoms of anxiety (sweating, racing heart), which, like falling dominoes, lead to yet more catastrophic thinking, which in turn induces more anxiety symptoms, and so on in a cycle that quickly spirals into a full-blown panic attack (see ■ Figure 13.3). Internal cues (dizziness, heart palpitations) and external cues (boarding a crowded elevator) that have been associated with panic attacks in the past may also become conditioned stimuli (CS's) that elicit anxiety or panicky symptoms when the person encounters them.

Cognitive factors also come into play in other anxiety-related disorders. Social phobias, for example, arise from excessive concerns about social embarrassment or being judged negatively by others. In sum, anxiety disorders involve a complex interplay of biological and psychological factors. Before going further, you may wish to review the summary of anxiety-related disorders presented in Concept Chart 13.2.

Concept Chart 13.2   Anxiety-Related Disorders

Type of Disorder	Lifetime Prevalence in Population (approx.)	Symptoms	Associated Features
Agoraphobia	1.4% to 2%	Fear and avoidance of public places	This generally develops secondarily to panic disorder, as the person attempts to avoid situations in which attacks have occurred or in which help might be unavailable in the event of an attack.
Panic disorder	5.1%	Repeated panic attacks accompanied by persistent concern about future attacks	Panic attacks have strong physiological symptoms; beginning attacks occur without warning; this disorder may be accompanied by agoraphobia.
Generalized anxiety disorder	5.7%	Persistent, excessive levels of anxiety and worry	Anxiety has a free-floating quality in that it is not tied to particular objects or situations.
Specific phobia	12.5%	Fear and avoidance of a specific object or situation	Avoidance of the phobic object or situation is negatively reinforced by relief from anxiety.
Social anxiety disorder	12.1%	Fear and avoidance of social situations or performance situations	This involves underlying fear of rejection, humiliation, or embarrassment in social situations.
Obsessive-compulsive disorder	2% to 3%	Recurrent obsessions and/or compulsions	A repetitive cycle may ensue in which obsessive thoughts engender anxiety that, in turn, is partially relieved (negatively reinforced) by performing the compulsive ritual.

Sources: Prevalence data based on American Psychiatric Association, 2013; Conway et al., 2006; Grant, Hasin, Blanco et al., 2006; Grant, Hasin, Stinson et al., 2006; Kessler, Berglund, et al., 2005; Kessler, Chiu, et al., 2005; Snyder et al., 2015; Stein & Sareen, 2015.

MODULE REVIEW 13.2 Anxiety-Related Disorders

Recite It

4. Identify and **describe** types of anxiety-related disorders and underlying causal factors in these disorders.

(a) _____-related disorders involve excessive or inappropriate anxiety reactions. These include anxiety-related disorders such as agoraphobia, panic disorder, social anxiety disorder, (b) _____ anxiety disorder, specific phobia, and obsessive-compulsive disorder. Causal factors include psychological factors such as prior (c) _____ experiences and thinking patterns, and biological factors, such as genetic influences, imbalances of (d) _____ in the brain, and underlying brain abnormalities.

Recall It

1. The relief from anxiety associated with performing a compulsive ritual in people with OCD is a

   a. type of conditioned stimulus.
   b. type of unconditioned stimulus.
   c. form of negative reinforcement.
   d. form of positive reinforcement.

2. Acrophobia and claustrophobia are two examples of _____ phobia.

3. Match the following anxiety-related disorders with the appropriate descriptions: (a) phobic disorder; (b) panic disorder; (c) generalized anxiety disorder; (d) obsessive-compulsive disorder.

   i. sudden onset; intense fear and dread
   ii. excessive, persistent worry
   iii. irrational, extreme fear of a particular object or situation
   iv. repeated, uncontrollable thoughts or behaviors

Think About It

- Apply learning principles to explain the development of certain types of anxiety-related disorders, including specific fears and obsessive-compulsive disorder.

- Is anxiety normal? What might evolutionary psychologists say about the survival value of

anxiety? When does a normal response become abnormal?

- Have you ever "panicked"? Do you think you suffered a true panic attack? Why or why not?

Recite It *answers placed at the end of chapter.*

MODULE ## 13.3 Dissociative and Somatic Symptom and Related Disorders

5 **Identify** and **describe** types of dissociative and somatic symptom and related disorders and underlying causal factors in these disorders.

Among the most puzzling psychological disorders are *dissociative disorders* and *somatic symptom and related disorders.* People with dissociative disorders may show multiple personalities, have amnesia that cannot be explained by physical causes, or even assume a completely new self-identity. The dissociative disorders are fodder for countless television melodramas and soap operas. In real life, they are relatively uncommon, even rare. Indeed, there is controversy among professionals as to whether multiple personality (now called *dissociative identity disorder*) even exists.

Although they have different symptoms or characteristics, dissociative disorders and somatic symptom and related disorders are often grouped together because of the classic view that they involve psychological defenses against anxiety. Here we examine several of these mystifying disorders, beginning with dissociative disorders.

Dissociative Disorders

Dissociative disorders involve problems with memory or changes in consciousness or self-identity that fracture the continuity or wholeness of the individual's personality. Normally we know who we are and where we've been. We may forget how we spent last weekend, but we don't suddenly lose the capacity to remember whole chunks of our lives or abruptly shift back and forth between very different personalities. Dissociative disorders, however, affect the ability to maintain a cohesive sense of self or unity of consciousness, resulting in unusual, even bizarre behavior. Here we consider two major types of dissociative disorders: dissociative identity disorder and dissociative amnesia.

Dissociative Identity Disorder

Consider the following case history:

dissociative disorders A class of psychological disorders involving changes in consciousness, memory, or self-identity.

[Margaret explained that] she often "heard a voice telling her to say things and do things." *It was, she said, "a terrible voice" that sometimes threatened to "take over completely."* *When it was finally suggested to [Margaret] that she let the voice "take over," she closed*

her eyes, clenched her fists, and grimaced for a few moments during which she was out of contact with those around her. Suddenly she opened her eyes and one was in the presence of another person. Her name, she said, was "Harriet." Whereas Margaret had been paralyzed, and complained of fatigue, headache, and backache, Harriet felt well, and she at once proceeded to walk unaided around the interviewing room. She spoke scornfully of Margaret's religiousness, her invalidism, and her puritanical life, professing that she herself liked to drink and "go partying" but that Margaret was always going to church and reading the Bible. "But," she said impishly and proudly, "I make her miserable—I make her say and do things she doesn't want to." At length, at the interviewer's suggestion, Harriet reluctantly agreed to "bring Margaret back," and after more grimacing and fist clenching, Margaret reappeared, paralyzed, complaining of her headache and backache, and completely amnesiac for the brief period of Harriet's release from prison. (Adapted from Nemiah, 1988, p. 248)

In **dissociative identity disorder (DID)**, commonly called *multiple personality* or *split personality,* two or more distinct personalities exist within the same individual. Each of these alternate personalities (also called *alter personalities*) has its own distinctive traits, manner of speech, and memories. In some cases, there is a core personality that is generally known to the outside world and hidden alternate personalities that reveal themselves at certain times or in certain situations. Sometimes the alternate personalities compete for control. The alter personalities may lack any memory of events experienced by other alter personalities or even any knowledge of the existence of alters (Huntjens et al., 2005). The alter personalities may represent different genders, ages, sexual orientations, or—as in the case of Margaret—conflicting sexual urges. One personality may be morally upright, another licentious; one heterosexual, another homosexual. The dominant personality may be unaware of the existence of these alternates, though the person may vaguely recognize that something is wrong. People with dissociative identity disorder often present with more than two alternate personalities, sometimes even with 20 or more alters.

Dissociative Amnesia

People with *dissociative amnesia* (first discussed in Chapter 6) experience a loss of memory for information about themselves or their life experiences. The absence of any physical cause for their amnesia (a blow to the head, a neurological condition, or drug or alcohol abuse) suggests that the disorder is psychological in nature. The information lost to memory is usually a traumatic or stressful experience that the person may be motivated to forget. A soldier returning from the battlefield or a survivor of a serious accident may have no memory of the battle or the accident. These memories sometimes return, perhaps gradually in bits and pieces, or suddenly all at once. Much less common, except in the imaginations of soap opera writers, is *generalized amnesia* in which people forget their entire lives. They forget who they are, what they do for a living, and whom they are married or related to. More commonly, however, amnesia involves loss of memory for specific events or periods of time linked to traumatic experiences.

Causes of Dissociative Disorders

Dissociative amnesia may represent an attempt to disconnect or dissociate one's conscious state from awareness of traumatic experiences or other sources of psychological pain or conflict. Dissociative symptoms may protect the self from anxiety that might occur if these memories and experiences became fully conscious. Similarly, individuals with dissociative identity disorder may split off parts of themselves from consciousness. Severe, repetitive physical or sexual abuse in childhood, usually beginning before the age of 5, figures prominently in case histories of people with DID (Dale et al., 2009; Spiegel, 2006).

CONCEPT 13.13
In dissociative identity disorder, the personality is split into two or more distinct alternate personalities residing within the same individual.

CONCEPT 13.14
In dissociative amnesia, people experience a loss of memory for personal information that cannot be explained by a blow to the head or some other physical cause.

CONCEPT 13.15
The formation of alternate personalities in dissociative identity disorder may represent a psychological defense against trauma or unbearable abuse.

dissociative identity disorder (DID) A type of dissociative disorder characterized by the appearance of multiple personalities in the same individual.

Karl Gehring/Contributor/Getty Images

"Does anybody know me?" Diagnosed with a type of amnesia linked to severe stress, 40-year-old Jeffrey Ingram searched for his identity for more than a month, eventually winding up in Denver asking people there for help. Family members in Washington State recognized him when he appeared on a TV news program asking if anybody knew him. When he returned home, he still had no memory, but reported that it felt like home to him. His mother reported he had had a similar incident in the past and had never fully regained his memory.

Many people with DID were highly imaginative as children, often creating games of make-believe. Perhaps in these early years, they used their fertile imaginations to split off parts of themselves in order to distance themselves psychologically from the abusive situations they faced. Over time, these parts may have become consolidated as distinct personalities. In adulthood, they may continue to use their alternate personalities to block out memories of childhood trauma and of the conflicting emotions that these experiences evoked. The alternate personalities themselves may represent a psychological means of expressing the deep-seated hatred and anger they are unable to integrate within their primary personalities.

Some psychologists believe DID is a rare but genuine disorder that involves a way of coping with terrible physical and sexual abuse dating back to childhood. But there are dissenting voices. Among these are scholars who doubt the existence of DID, ascribing the behavior to a form of attention-seeking role-playing (Boysen & VanBergen, 2014). Perhaps troubled individuals with a history of abuse might inadvertently be cued by their therapists to enact alternate personalities that help them make sense of the confusing and conflicting emotions they experience, eventually identifying so closely with the role they are performing that it becomes a reality to them. This description is not meant to suggest that people with DID are faking their alternate selves, any more than we would suggest that you are faking your behavior whenever you adopt the role of a student, spouse, or worker. Whatever the underlying process in DID may be, authorities agree that people with the disorder need help dealing with the underlying traumas they have experienced and working through the often conflicting emotions and impulses these brutal experiences evoked.

Somatic Symptom and Related Disorders

The diagnostic category of **somatic symptom and related disorders** (formerly called *somatoform* disorders) applies to abnormal behavior patterns associated with physical symptoms (Dimsdale & Levenson, 2013). The word *somatic* derives from the Greek "soma," meaning "body." People with somatic symptom disorders and related disorders may have physical (somatic) symptoms or complaints that cannot be explained medically. Or they may hold a belief that their symptoms are signs of a grave or life-threatening illness, despite reassurances from their doctors to the contrary.

Conversion Disorder

In **conversion disorder**, a person suffers a loss of, or significant change in, a physical function, such as inability to lift an arm (hysterical paralysis), a loss of vision (hysterical blindness), or a loss of feeling in a hand or arm (anesthesia). Yet there is no physical cause that can account for these neurological symptoms (Rickards & Silver, 2014).

Conversion disorder (called *functional neurological symptom disorder* in *DSM-5*) figured prominently in the history of psychology. It was conversion disorder—called *hysteria* or *hysterical neurosis* at the time—that attracted a young physician named Sigmund Freud to study the psychological bases of abnormal behavior. Conversion disorder or hysteria is uncommon or even rare today, but appears to have been more frequent in Freud's day. In Freud's time, hysteria was considered a female problem; however, experience with male soldiers in combat who suffer a loss of function (blindness or paralysis) that cannot be explained medically has taught us that the disorder can affect both men and women.

If you suddenly lost feeling in your hand, you would probably be quite upset. But curiously, some people with conversion symptoms appear indifferent to their situations—a phenomenon called *la belle indifférence* ("beautiful indifference"). This lack of concern suggests that the symptoms may be of psychological value to

somatic symptom and related disorders A class of psychological disorders involving physical ailments or complaints that cannot be explained by organic causes or that involve exaggerated concerns about the seriousness of these symptoms.

conversion disorder A psychological disorder characterized by a change in or loss of a physical function that cannot be explained by medical causes.

the individual, perhaps representing a way of avoiding anxiety associated with painful or stressful conflicts or situations. We should note, however, that hysteria and conversion symptoms are sometimes incorrectly diagnosed in people who turn out to have bona fide medical conditions (Stone et al., 2006).

Somatic Symptom Disorder

Some people become preoccupied with the belief that something is terribly wrong with their health, despite medical reassurances to the contrary. The traditional term for this psychological condition, **hypochondriasis**, is no longer used in the *DSM* system because of its pejorative or negative connotation. Although the term *hypochondriasis* continues to be used widely by professionals and lay people, the *DSM-5* applies a more benign diagnostic term, *somatic symptom disorder*, to most cases of people who formerly would have been diagnosed with hypochondriasis.

People with somatic symptom disorder have real physical complaints or symptoms. However, their excessive concerns about their symptoms significantly affect their thoughts, feelings, and behaviors in daily life. They may believe their symptoms are signs of a serious or life-threatening illness such as cancer or heart disease (Abramowitz & Braddock, 2011; Skritskaya et al., 2012). They do not feel reassured when their doctors tell them they are not gravely ill, believing their doctors missed something or are incompetent. They also don't realize how their anxiety contributes to their physical complaints—for example, leading to sweating, dizziness, rapid heartbeat, and other signs of sympathetic nervous system arousal.

Causes of Somatic Symptom and Related Disorders

To Freud, the hysterical or conversion symptom (for example, loss of movement in a limb) is a sign of a struggle between opposing motives in the unconscious mind. On one side are sexual or aggressive impulses of the id seeking expression; on the other side are forces of restraint, marshaled by the ego. The ego seeks to protect the self from the flood of anxiety that would occur if these unacceptable impulses were to become fully conscious. It employs defense mechanisms, especially repression, to keep these impulses buried in the unconscious. The leftover energy from these impulses becomes "strangulated," or cut off from its source, and is then converted into physical symptoms like paralysis or blindness (Aybek et al., 2014). One problem with Freud's view, however, is that it doesn't explain how conversion occurs—that is, how leftover sexual or aggressive energy becomes channeled into particular physical symptoms.

Freud also believed that the symptom itself both symbolizes the underlying struggle and serves an underlying purpose. For instance, hysterical paralysis of the arm serves the purpose of preventing the person from using the arm to act out an unacceptable sexual (for example, masturbatory) or aggressive (for example, murderous) impulse. The symptom has yet another function, called **secondary gain**. It can prevent the individual from having to confront stressful or conflict-laden situations. If Freud was correct in his belief that conversion symptoms serve hidden purposes, it may explain why many people with conversion appear strangely unconcerned or untroubled about their symptoms.

Learning theorists, too, recognize that conversion symptoms may serve a secondary role of helping individuals avoid painful or anxiety-evoking situations. (The bomber pilot who develops hysterical night blindness, or failure to be able to see at night, may avoid the danger of night missions, for example.)

People with conversion disorders may also be reinforced by others for adopting a "sick role," drawing sympathy and support from them and being relieved of

CONCEPT 13.16
People with conversion disorder experience a loss of a physical function that defies any medical explanation.

CONCEPT 13.17
People with hypochondriasis mistakenly believe that their minor physical complaints are signs of serious underlying illness.

hypochondriasis A psychological disorder in which there is excessive concern that one's physical complaints are signs of underlying serious illness.

secondary gain Reward value of having a psychological or physical symptom, such as release from ordinary responsibilities.

CONCEPT 13.18
Though Freudian and learning theory explanations of somatic symptom disorders differ, they both focus on the anxiety-reducing role of somatic symptoms.

ordinary work or household responsibilities. This is not meant to suggest that these individuals are consciously faking their symptoms. They may be deceiving themselves, but they do not appear to be deliberately attempting to deceive others.

Cognitive theorists focus on cognitive biases associated with somatic symptom and related disorders (for example, Fulton, Marcus, & Merkey, 2011; Weck et al., 2015). People with hypochondriasis, for example, may "make mountains out of molehills" by misinterpreting bodily sensations as signs of underlying catastrophic causes (cancer, heart disease, and so on). In this respect, they resemble people with panic disorder, who tend to misinterpret bodily sensations as signs of an impending catastrophe (that is, having a heart attack or going crazy).

Dissociative and somatic symptom disorders are summarized in Concept Chart 13.3.

Concept Chart 13.3   Dissociative and Somatic Symptom and Related Disorders

Type of Disorder	Lifetime Prevalence	Features	Comments
Dissociative identity disorder	Rare	Multiple personalities emerge within the same individual	May represent a type of psychological defense against trauma or unbearable abuse from childhood
Dissociative amnesia	Rare	Memory loss that cannot be explained as the result of head trauma or other physical cause	Typically involves loss of memories associated with specific traumatic events
Conversion disorder	Rare, but is reported in 5% of patients referred to neurology clinics	A loss or change of physical function that cannot be explained by a medical condition	May have been much more common in Freud's day than in our own
Somatic symptom disorder	Unknown, but may affect between 5% and 7% of the general population	Excessive concerns about one's physical symptoms to the point that it significantly interferes with one's thoughts, feelings, or behaviors in daily life	May have features similar to those of anxiety-related disorders

Source: Prevalence rates based on American Psychiatric Association, 2013.

MODULE REVIEW 13.3 Dissociative and Somatic Symptom and Related Disorders

Recite It

5. **Identify** and **describe** types of dissociative and somatic symptom and related disorders and underlying causal factors in these disorders.

Dissociative disorders involve disturbances in memory, consciousness, or identity that affect the ability to maintain an integrated sense of (a) _____. These disorders include dissociative (b) _____ disorder and dissociative (c) _____. Exposure to childhood abuse figures prominently in the backgrounds of people with dissociative identity disorder, leading theorists to believe that the disorder may represent a psychological (d) _____

that protects the self from troubling memories or feelings. Avoidance of painful or troubling memories is also implicated in dissociative amnesia.

People with (e) _____ symptom and related disorders place undue concern on the meaning of physical complaints or have physical complaints that cannot be accounted for by organic causes. Freud believed that conversion disorder represents the transformation of inner psychological conflicts into physical symptoms. Learning theorists focus on the (f) _____-reducing roles of somatic symptom and related disorders, whereas cognitive theorists focus on underlying cognitive biases.

Recall It

1. In _____ identity disorder, a person exhibits multiple personalities.

2. Dissociative amnesia
   a. involves a clear physical underlying cause.
   b. does not seem to be related to a particular traumatic event.
   c. involves extensive and permanent memory loss.
   d. has no apparent neurological cause.

3. What are some common characteristics of individuals with dissociative identity disorder?
   a. Their early childhood experiences include severe and prolonged abuse.
   b. They tend to be highly imaginative as youngsters.
   c. Their alternate personalities have very different and distinctive traits.
   d. All of the above are correct.

4. Conversion disorder (is or is not?) caused by underlying physical problems.

Think About It

■ Do you believe that dissociative identity disorder is a true disorder? Or do you think it is an exaggerated form of role-playing? Explain your answer.

Recite It answers placed at the end of chapter.

MODULE 13.4 Mood Disorders

6 **Identify** and **describe** types of mood disorders and underlying causal factors in these disorders.

7 **Identify** factors linked to risk of suicide.

Most people have occasional ups and downs, but those with **mood disorders** have more severe or persistent disturbances of mood. These mood disturbances limit their ability to function and may even sap their will to live. It is normal to feel sad when unfortunate events occur and to be uplifted when fortune shines on us. But people with mood disorders often feel down when things are going right. Or they remain down following a disappointing experience long after others would have snapped back. Some people with mood disorders have exaggerated mood swings. Their moods may alternate between dizzying heights and abysmal depths.

Types of Mood Disorders

Here we focus on two major forms of mood disorder: major depression and bipolar disorder.

Major Depression

In **major depression** (also called *major depressive disorder*), people typically feel sad or "down in the dumps" and may experience feelings of worthlessness, changes in sleep or appetite, lethargy, and loss of interest in pleasurable activities. Major depression occurs in episodes that can last months or even a year or longer, especially

CONCEPT 13.19
Two of the major types of mood disorders are major depression and bipolar disorder.

CONCEPT 13.20
In major depression, people have a dampening of mood to the point that they may become unmotivated, lose interest in pleasurable activities, develop feelings of worthlessness, or attempt suicide.

mood disorders A class of psychological disorders involving disturbances in mood states, such as major depression and bipolar disorder.

major depression The most common type of depressive disorder, characterized by periods of downcast mood, feelings of worthlessness, and loss of interest in pleasurable activities.

Many psychologists believe that the stressors many women face today contribute to their increased risk of depression.

when untreated, and has a high rate of recurrence (Hölzel et al., 2011; Smith, 2015). Unfortunately, despite the availability of safe and effective treatments, about half of Americans who suffer from major depression do not receive professional care (González et al., 2010). Latinos and African Americans are less likely than other ethnic groups to receive care.

People with major depression may feel they cannot get out of bed to face the day. They may be unable to make decisions, even about small things, such as what to have for dinner. They may be unable to concentrate. They may feel helpless or say that they don't "care" anymore. They may have recurrent thoughts of suicide or even attempt suicide.

Nearly one in five U.S. adults (17 percent) suffer from major depression at some point in their lives (Conway et al., 2006; Forgeard et al., 2012). About one in twelve adults (nearly 8 percent) are currently experiencing major depression (National Center for Health Statistics, 2012b). Worldwide, depression accounts for more years lost to disability than any other condition, including heart disease and cancer (Smith, 2015).

Women are nearly twice as likely as men to develop major depression (about 12 percent for men versus 21 percent for women) (Hyde, Mezulis, & Abramson, 2008). Although underlying hormonal or other biological differences between men and women may play a role in explaining this gender gap, we need to also consider the greater stress burdens that many women carry in today's society (Eagly et al., 2012). Women are more likely to encounter significant stressors such as physical and sexual abuse, poverty, single parenthood, and sexism. Even when both spouses work, women typically shoulder the bulk of household and child care chores. Women also are more likely than men to provide support for aging family members or those coping with disabling medical conditions.

Differences in how men and women cope with emotional distress also come into play. The late psychologist Susan Nolen-Hoeksema suggested that men are more likely to distract themselves from their emotional concerns, such as by going to a favorite hangout to get their mind off their problems (Nolen-Hoeksema, 2008, 2012). By contrast, women tend to ruminate or brood about their problems. Distraction may temporarily blunt emotional responses, but ruminating or dwelling on problems can amplify a person's emotional distress, setting the stage for depression (Koster et al., 2011). Then again, turning to alcohol to blunt negative feelings can lead to other problems, such as substance abuse. To raise your awareness of the signs of depression, see the Try This Out feature on page 507.

CONCEPT 13.21

People with bipolar disorder experience dramatic mood swings.

bipolar disorder A type of mood disorder characterized by mood swings from extreme elation (mania) to severe depression.

manic episodes Periods of mania, or unusually elevated mood and extreme restlessness.

Bipolar Disorder

People with **bipolar disorder** (formerly called *manic depression*) experience mood swings that shift between periods of euphoric or elevated mood, or **manic episodes** (mania), and periods of depression. They may have intervening periods of normal moods. During a manic episode, people may feel unusually euphoric or become extremely restless, excited, talkative, and argumentative. They may spend lavishly, drive recklessly, destroy property, or become involved in sexual escapades that appear out of character with their usual personalities. Even those who care about such individuals may find them abrasive. Other symptoms are pressured speech (talking too rapidly), flight of ideas (jumping from topic to topic), and an inflated sense of self-worth (grandiosity). During manic episodes, people may become delusional (hold false beliefs) or undertake tasks well beyond their abilities, such as writing a symphony or solving world hunger. Or they may show poor judgment, such as by giving away their life savings. They may have boundless energy and little need for sleep. Then, when their moods sink into depression, they may feel hopelessness and despair. Some people with bipolar disorder commit suicide on the

Try This Out Are You Depressed?

Many people suffer depression in silence out of ignorance or shame. They believe that depression is not a real problem because it doesn't show up on an X-ray or CT scan. They think it's just all in their heads. Or they may feel that asking for help is an admission of weakness and that they should bear it on their own.

Although a diagnosis of a depressive disorder can only be made by a qualified professional, the National Institutes of Health provides a listing of common signs of symptoms of depression. Take a moment to determine whether any of the following items apply to you:

	YES	NO
1. Persistent sad, anxious, or "empty" feelings	____	____
2. Feelings of hopelessness or pessimism	____	____
3. Feelings of guilt, worthlessness, or helplessness	____	____
4. Irritability, restlessness	____	____
5. Loss of interest in activities or hobbies once pleasurable, including sex	____	____
6. Fatigue and decreased energy	____	____

7. Difficulty concentrating, remembering details, and making decisions	____	____
8. Insomnia, early-morning wakefulness, or excessive sleeping	____	____
9. Overeating, or appetite loss	____	____
10. Thoughts of suicide, suicide attempts	____	____
11. Aches or pains, headaches, cramps, or digestive problems that do not ease even with treatment.	____	____

Evaluating your responses: Not everyone with a depressive disorder reports the same symptoms. Symptoms also vary with respect to their severity, frequency, and duration. If you have experienced two or more of these signs and symptoms for two or more weeks, you may wish to consult with a mental health professional for a more complete evaluation. However, if you indicated that you have been thinking about death or suicide (#10), you should seek an immediate consultation. If you don't know where to go, contact your college counseling center, a mental health center in your neighborhood, or your health care provider.

Source: Adapted from National Institute of Mental Health, National Institutes of Health. *Depression*. Retrieved from http://www.nimh.nih.gov/health/topics/depression/index.shtml#part3

way down, apparently wanting to avoid the depths of depression they have learned to expect. About 1 percent of the U.S. population develops bipolar disorder at some point in their lives (Frye, 2011; Merikangas & Pato, 2009).

Causes of Mood Disorders

Like anxiety-related disorders, mood disorders are believed to have both psychological and biological causes.

Psychological Factors

Several psychological models of depression have been proposed. The classic psychodynamic view espoused by Freud (1917/1957) and his followers held that depression involves anger turned inward against the self. By contrast, the behavioral model focuses on the role of reinforcement. To maintain motivation, one needs a balance between output and input, between the efforts one expends and the reinforcement or rewards one receives back. In the behavioral view, depression results from a loss or shortfall in reinforcement, especially reinforcement one receives from others in the way of attention, approval, and emotional support. Loss of reinforcement may occur for many reasons. The death of a spouse or close friend removes the person as a potential source of reinforcement. A young person attending college away from home may feel cut off from high school friends and have difficulty forming new social

CONCEPT 13.22
Psychological causes implicated in mood disorders include changes in reinforcement levels, distorted ways of thinking, depressive attributional style, and stress.

CONCEPT LINK
Cognitive therapy is a form of psychotherapy that focuses on helping distressed individuals recognize and correct distorted or self-defeating ways of thinking. See Module 14.1.

networks that might provide opportunities for reinforcement. The more depressed people become, the less motivated they may be to make the effort to find new sources of reinforcement. In some cases, reinforcement opportunities may abound, but the person lacks effective social skills to establish and maintain relationships that lead to reinforcing interactions.

Cognitive theorists believe that the ways in which people interpret events in their lives contribute to the development of emotional disorders such as depression and anxiety. One of the most influential cognitive theorists is the psychiatrist Aaron Beck, the developer of cognitive therapy (discussed in Chapter 14). Beck and his colleagues (Beck, Freeman, et al., 2006; Beck, Rush et al., 1979) believe having a negatively biased or distorted way of thinking makes a person more vulnerable to depression when he or she encounters disappointing or unfortunate life events. Just as wearing a pair of dark sunglasses puts a darkened tint on your perception of the world, distorted and negative thinking serves as a kind of mental filter that puts a negative slant on how people interpret their life experiences, especially disappointing experiences such as getting a bad grade or losing a job. A minor disappointment is blown out of proportion—experienced more as a crushing blow than as a mild setback.

Beck and his colleagues identify a number of these faulty thinking patterns, called *cognitive distortions,* that they believe increase a person's vulnerability to depression following negative life events. The more these distorted thinking patterns come to dominate a person's thinking, the greater the vulnerability to depression is likely to be. Table 13.1 lists cognitive distortions most closely associated with depression.

Another psychological model of depression, the **learned helplessness model**, suggests that people become depressed when they come to believe that they are helpless to control the reinforcements in their lives. This concept, developed by psychologist Martin Seligman (1973, 1975), is based on experiments showing that laboratory animals who were exposed to inescapable shocks failed to learn to avoid the shocks when the conditions changed in such a way as to make escape possible. The animals seemed to give up trying, becoming lethargic and unmotivated—behaviors that resembled depression in people. Seligman proposed that exposure to uncontrollable situations may induce a learned helplessness effect in humans, leading to depression. In essence, when repeated efforts prove futile, the person may eventually give up trying and sink into a state of depression.

Seligman and his colleagues later revised the helplessness model to include cognitive factors (Abramson, Seligman, & Teasdale, 1978). In particular, they borrowed from social psychology (discussed in Chapter 12) the concept of **attributional style**, which refers to the characteristic ways in which individuals explain the causes of events that happen to them. The reformulated helplessness model proposes that attributions vary along three dimensions: *internal versus external, global versus specific,* and *stable versus unstable.*

Consider a negative event, such as receiving a poor grade on a math test. An internal attribution fixes blame on oneself ("I screwed up"), whereas an external attribution places responsibility on external factors ("The exam was too hard"). A global attribution treats the cause as reflecting generally on one's underlying personality or abilities ("I'm really not very good at math"), whereas a specific attribution knocks it down to size ("I tripped up on the equations"). A stable attribution treats the cause as more or less permanent ("I'll never be able to learn this stuff"), whereas an unstable attribution views it as changeable ("Next time I'll be better prepared"). People who tend to explain disappointments and failures by attributing them to *internal, global,* and *stable* causes have a **depressive attributional style** that predisposes them to depression when they face such negative events, according to Seligman and his colleagues.

learned helplessness model The view that depression results from the perception of a lack of control over the reinforcements in one's life that may result from exposure to uncontrollable negative events.

attributional style A person's characteristic way of explaining outcomes of events in his or her life.

depressive attributional style A characteristic way of explaining negative events in terms of internal, stable, and global causes.

Table 13.1 Cognitive Distortions Linked to Depression

Type of Cognitive Distortion	Description	Example
All-or-nothing thinking	Viewing events in black or white terms, as either all good or all bad	Do you view a relationship that ended as a total failure, or are you able to see some benefits in the relationship? Do you consider any less-than-perfect performance as a total failure?
Misplaced blame	Tendency to blame or criticize yourself for disappointments or setbacks while ignoring external circumstances	Do you automatically assume that it's your fault when things don't go as planned?
Misfortune telling	Tendency to think that one disappointment will inevitably lead to another	If you get a rejection letter from a job you applied for, do you assume that all the other applications you sent will meet the same fate?
Negative focusing	Focusing your attention only on the negative aspects of your experiences	When you get a job evaluation, do you overlook the praise and focus only on the criticism?
Dismissing the positives	Snatching defeat from the jaws of victory by trivializing or denying your accomplishments; minimizing your strengths or assets	When someone compliments you, do you find some way of dismissing it by saying something like "It's no big deal" or "Anyone could have done it"?
Jumping to conclusions	Drawing a conclusion that is not supported by the facts at hand	Do you usually or always expect the worst to happen?
Catastrophizing	Exaggerating the importance of negative events or personal flaws (making mountains out of molehills)	Do you react to a disappointing grade on a particular examination as though your whole life is ruined?
Emotion-based reasoning	Reasoning based on your emotions rather than on a clear-headed evaluation of the available evidence	Do you think that things are really hopeless because it feels that way?
Shouldisms	Placing unrealistic demands on yourself that you *should* or *must* accomplish certain tasks or reach certain goals	Do you feel that you *should* be further along in your life than you are now? Do you feel you *must* ace this course or else? (Not that it wouldn't be desirable to ace the course, but is it really the case that you *must*?)
Name-calling	Attaching negative labels to yourself or others as a way of explaining your own or others' behavior	Do you label yourself *lazy* or *stupid* when you fall short of reaching your goals?
Mistaken responsibility	Assuming that you are the cause of other people's problems	Do you automatically assume that your partner is depressed or upset because of something you said or did (or didn't say or do)?

Source: Adapted from Burns, 1980; Nevid & Rathus, 2010; Nevid, Rathus, & Greene, 2014.

People with depression show evidence of negative, distorted thinking, just as cognitive theorists propose (for example, Baer et al., 2012; Koster et al., 2011). Similarly, people who attribute their failures and disappointments to internal, stable, and global factors are at greater risk of depression, just as the reformulated helplessness theory would predict (Hamilton et al., 2015). Yet questions remain about whether distorted thinking or attributional styles are causal factors in depression or effects of depression (Baer et al., 2012; LaGrange et al., 2011). Perhaps depression leads people to

"Why do I always screw up?" Cognitive theorists believe that the way in which we interpret negative events has an important bearing on our proneness to depression in the face of disappointing life experiences.

CONCEPT 13.23

Biological causes implicated in mood disorders include disturbances in neurotransmitter functioning in the brain and genetic influences.

CONCEPT LINK

Psychiatric drugs are chemicals used to normalize neurotransmitter functioning in the brain. See Module 14.2.

develop negative, distorted thoughts and to adopt a depressive attributional style, rather than the other way around. In all likelihood, causal linkages work both ways, such that thinking styles affect moods and moods affect thinking styles.

Life stress also contributes to the development and recurrence of mood disorders (Conway, Rutter, & Brown, 2016; Hammen, 2015; Koenders et al., 2014; Liu & Alloy, 2010). Examples of stressful life events linked to mood disorders include the loss of a loved one, prolonged unemployment, serious physical illness, marital problems or separation, divorce, pressures at work, and financial hardship. The availability of social support helps people withstand stressful life events, so it's not surprising that people who live alone face a greater risk of depression (Pulkki-Raback et al., 2012).

Biological Factors

Depression is linked to irregularities in the workings of certain neurotransmitters in the brain, especially the neurotransmitter serotonin (Cumming et al., 2016; Tessier et al., 2015). Drugs that help relieve depression, called *antidepressants,* increase levels of neurotransmitters in the brain, especially *serotonin* as well as *norepinephrine.* The widely used antidepressants, Prozac and Zoloft, for instance, increase serotonin levels in the synapse by interfering with the reuptake (absorption) of this mood-regulating chemical by the transmitting neuron. As a result, more of the chemical remains active in the synapse.

But we shouldn't think that depression is caused by a mere deficiency of certain neurotransmitters in the brain. After all, antidepressants usually take weeks and sometimes months to work, even though they boost brain levels of the neurotransmitters they target within a few days or even a few hours of use (Shive, 2015). More complex processes are at work, perhaps involving an oversensitivity of receptors on receiving neurons where neurotransmitters dock or an imbalance in the numbers of these receptors (either too many or too few) (Cipriani et al., 2009; Oquendo et al., 2007). We also have growing evidence from brain imaging studies of patients with mood disorders that points to abnormalities in parts of the brain involved in regulating thinking processes, memory, and emotions, especially the prefrontal cortex and the hippocampus (for example, Kaiser et al., 2015; Klauser et al., 2014; Nenadic et al., 2015; Phillips & Swartz, 2014; Schmaal et al., 2015).

Genetic factors also play an important role in explaining vulnerability to major depression and an even stronger role in bipolar disorder (Duffy et al., 2014; Okbay et al., 2016; Whisman, Johnson, & Rhee, 2014). Researchers are now zeroing in on genes linked to mood disorders, many of which are involved—not surprisingly—in regulating neurotransmitter functioning (Zhang et al., 2014; Zhao et al, 2014). We should caution, however, that biological causes of mood disorders are not the only contributing factors. Psychological factors, such as stress and negative thinking patterns, also play important roles. All things considered, mood disorders are complex phenomena involving a number of factors interacting in complex ways we are still trying to unravel (Dunn et al., 2015) (see Concept Chart 13.4).

Suicide

What would you say is the second leading cause of death, after motor vehicle accidents, among young people 15 to 24 years of age? AIDS? Drugs? The answer is suicide (CDC, 2015b; Joffe, 2015). About one million adult Americans (about one in 200) make a suicide attempt each year, and more than 40,000 "succeed" in taking their own lives (CDC, 2015f; Olfson et al., 2014). On college campuses, we lose more than 1,000 students each year to suicide. Sadly, suicide rates in the United

Concept Chart 13.4   Mood Disorders

	Type of Disorder	Lifetime Prevalence (approx.)	Symptoms	Associated Features
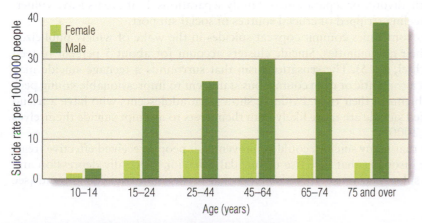	Major depression	12% in men, 21% in women, 16.5% overall	Downcast mood, feelings of hopelessness and worthlessness, changes in sleep patterns or appetite, loss of motivation, loss of pleasure in pleasant activities	Following a depressive episode, the person may return to his or her usual state of functioning, but recurrences are common.
	Bipolar disorder	1%	Periods of shifting moods between mania and depression, perhaps with intervening periods of normal mood	Manic episodes are characterized by pressured speech, flight of ideas, poor judgment, hyperactivity, and inflated mood and sense of self.

Sources: Prevalence data based on American Psychiatric Association, 2013; Conway et al., 2006.

States are increasing at an alarming rate, jumping 24 percent from 1999 through 2014 (Young, 2016).

Who Is Most at Risk?

Suicide cuts across every stratum of our society. Yet certain factors are related to an increased risk:

- *Age.* Though much attention is focused on adolescent suicides, suicide rates are generally higher among middle age and older adults, especially males age 75 and above (Curtin, Warner, & Hedegaard, 2016; Mills et al., 2013) (see ■ Figure 13.4). However, suicide rates are rising most rapidly among middle age women and young girls age 10 to 14.

- *Gender.* More women attempt suicide, but about three times as many men complete the act (Curtin, Warner, & Hedegaard, 2016). Why do more women

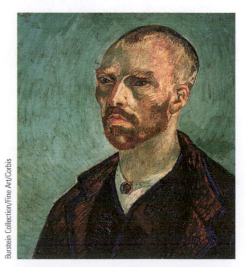

"Starry, Starry Night." The artist Vincent van Gogh suffered from terrible bouts of depression that eventually led to his suicide at the age of 37 from a self-inflicted gunshot wound. In this melancholy self-portrait, his eyes and facial countenance reveal the despair with which he struggled through much of his life.

FIGURE 13.4 **Suicide Rates in Relation to Age**
As you can see, suicide rates increase in middle and late adulthood.
Sources: Centers for Disease Control and Prevention, 2009c. Data from Curtin, Warner, & Hedegaard, 2016.

attempt suicide but more men succeed? The primary reason is that men typically use more lethal means, especially firearms. Women are more apt to use pills, poison, or other methods that may be less lethal.

- *Race/ethnicity.* White (European) Americans and Native Americans are more likely to take their own lives than are African Americans and Hispanic Americans (CDC, 2015b; Gone & Trimble, 2012). The highest suicide rates in the United States are reported among Native American youth and young adults (Meyers, 2007b; O'Keefe et al, 2014). The widespread sense of hopelessness among Native Americans arising from lack of opportunities and segregation from the dominant culture helps set the stage for alcohol and drug abuse, which are often preludes to depression and suicide.

CONCEPT 13.24

Most suicides are linked to depression and, especially, to feelings of utter hopelessness.

Causal Factors in Suicide

Suicide is closely linked to major depression, and even more strongly to bipolar disorder, and to deep feelings of hopelessness and worthlessness that often accompany mood disorders (Chen et al., 2014; Jeon et al., 2014). Feelings of hopelessness about the future combined with a sense of worthlessness or helplessness can lead to the overwhelming feelings of distress that many suicidal individuals experience. Stressful life events can also serve as triggers for suicidal thoughts and behaviors (Liu & Miller, 2014).

Like depression, suicide is linked to biochemical factors, including dysfunctions in serotonin functioning in the brain, and to genetic factors, possibly involving genes that play a role in regulating serotonin functioning (Petersen et al., 2014; Shinozaki et al., 2013; Sullivan et al., 2015). Serotonin helps curb excess nervous system activity. Irregularities in the use of serotonin in the brain may cause a **disinhibition effect**—the removal of inhibitions that might otherwise constrain impulsive behavior, including impulses to commit suicide.

Drug and/or alcohol dependence are important risk factors in suicide. Use of alcohol may lead people to act impulsively, with the result that suicidal thoughts are carried over into action. Other psychological disorders, such as schizophrenia and PTSD, as well as prolonged unemployment and serious medical illness, also figure into many suicides (for example, Ceskova, Prikryl, & Kasparek, 2011; Conner et al., 2014; DeVylder et al., 2015).

Suicide expert Edwin Shneidman (1987) also points to a lack of coping responses among people who attempt or commit suicide. Suicidal people may see no other way of resolving their problems or ending their unendurable psychological or physical pain. In addition, suicide is linked to *exit events,* or losses of supportive people through death, divorce or separation, or family separations. Exit events leave vulnerable people feeling stripped of crucial sources of social support.

Teenagers sometimes commit copycat suicides in the wake of widely publicized suicides in their communities. Suicide clusters account for about 5 percent of teen suicides (Richtel, 2015). The sensationalism that surrounds a teenage suicide may make it seem a romantic or even courageous statement to impressionable young people with problems of their own. Evidence shows that adolescents who have a friend who attempted suicide are more likely than their peers to attempt suicide themselves (Blum et al., 2000).

It is clear that many suicides could be prevented if people received effective treatment for the disorders that give rise to suicidal behavior, especially depression and alcohol and substance abuse. It is also clear that myths about suicide abound (see Table 13.2).

disinhibition effect The removal of normal restraints or inhibitions that serve to keep impulsive behavior in check.

Table 13.2 Myths About Suicide

Myth	Fact
People who threaten suicide are only seeking attention.	Not so. People who go on to commit suicide often give clear clues concerning their intentions, such as disposing of their possessions or suddenly making arrangements for a burial plot.
A person must be insane to attempt suicide.	Most people who attempt suicide may feel hopeless, but they are not insane (that is, out of touch with reality).
Talking about suicide with a person with depression may prompt the person to attempt it.	An open discussion of suicide with a person with depression does not prompt the person to attempt it. In fact, extracting a promise that the person will not attempt suicide before calling or visiting a mental health worker may well *prevent* a suicide.
People who attempt suicide and fail aren't serious about killing themselves.	Most people who commit suicide have made previous unsuccessful attempts.
If someone threatens suicide, it is best to ignore it so as not to encourage repeated threats.	Though some people do manipulate others by making idle threats, it is prudent to treat every suicidal threat as genuine and to take appropriate action.

APPLYING PSYCHOLOGY in Daily Life

Suicide Prevention

"I don't believe it. I saw him just last week and he looked fine."
"She sat here just the other day, laughing with the rest of us. How were we to know what was going on inside her?"
"I knew he was depressed, but I never thought he'd do something like this. I didn't have a clue."
"Why didn't she just call me?" (Nevid, Rathus, & Greene, 2014)

We may respond to the news of a suicide of a friend or family member with shock or with guilt that we failed to pick up any warning signs. Yet even professionals have difficulty predicting whether someone is likely to commit suicide. But when signs are present, the time to take action is now. Encourage the person, calmly but firmly, to seek professional assistance. Offer to accompany the person to a helping professional—or make the first contact yourself.

Facing the Threat

Suppose a friend confides in you that he or she is contemplating suicide. You know your friend has been going through a difficult time and has been depressed. You didn't think it would come to this, however. You want to help but are unsure about what to do. It's normal to feel frightened, even flustered. Here are some suggestions to consider if you ever face this situation. Because the situation at hand may call for specific responses, they are offered as general guidelines, not as direct instructions.

1. *Recognize the seriousness of the situation.* Don't fall for the myth of thinking that people who talk about suicide are not truly serious. Treat any talk of suicide as a clear warning sign.
2. *Take implied threats seriously.* Some suicidal people don't come right out and say they are planning to kill themselves. They might say something like "I just don't feel I can go on anymore."

CONCEPT 13.25
A suicide threat should be taken seriously, and the immediacy of the threat should be assessed, but above all, professional help should be sought at the first opportunity.

3. *Express understanding.* Engage the person in conversation to allow his or her feelings to be expressed. Show that you understand how troubled the person is. Don't dismiss his or her concerns by saying something like "Everyone feels like this from time to time. It'll pass."

4. *Focus on alternatives.* Tell the person that he or she may find other ways of dealing with the problems, even if they are not apparent at the moment.

5. *Assess the immediate danger.* Ask the person whether he or she has made a specific plan to commit suicide. If the person plans to use guns or drugs kept at home, prevent the person from returning home alone.

6. *Enlist the person's agreement to seek help.* Insist that the person accompany you to a health professional or nearby hospital emergency room. If that's not immediately possible, call a health professional or suicide prevention hotline. Help is available by calling 1-800-SUICIDE or a local crisis center or health center.

7. *Accompany the person to seek help.* Above all, don't leave the person alone. If you do get separated for any reason, or if the person refuses help and leaves, call a mental health professional, suicide hotline service, or the police for assistance.

MODULE REVIEW 13.4 Mood Disorders

Recite It

6. Identify and **describe** two major types of mood disorders and underlying causal factors in these disorders.

Mood disorders are disturbances in (a) _____ that are unusually severe or prolonged. Two of the major types of mood disorders are major depression and bipolar disorder. Suspected causal factors in mood disorders include genetic factors, biochemical imbalances in (b) _____ activity in the brain, changes in (c) _____ patterns, and dysfunctional thinking patterns.

7. Identify factors linked to risk of suicide.

Groups at highest risk for suicide include older (d) _____ men and Native Americans. Men are more likely than women to "succeed" at suicide attempts because they tend to use more lethal means. Most suicides result from deep feelings of (e) _____ and despair. Teenagers have been known to commit (f) _____ suicides.

Recall It

1. The type of mood disorder characterized by severe mood swings is called _____.

2. Which factors may help explain the greater prevalence of depression in women than men? (Identify at least one factor.)

3. The widely used antidepressant Prozac boosts levels of the neurotransmitter _____ by interfering with the _____ of this chemical by the transmitting neuron.

4. In Seligman's early research on learned _____, animals who were earlier exposed to inescapable shock failed to try to escape shock when it became possible to do so.

Think About It

- Which, if any, of the errors in thinking and negative attributions mentioned in the text describe how you typically explain disappointing events in your life? How do your thinking patterns affect your moods? Your motivation? Your feelings about yourself? How might you change your ways of thinking about negative experiences in the future?

- How do bipolar disorders differ from the ordinary "ups and downs" of everyday life?

Recite It answers placed at the end of chapter.

MODULE

13.5 Schizophrenia

8 Describe the features of schizophrenia and underlying causal factors.

9 Explain the development of schizophrenia based on the diathesis-stress model.

Schizophrenia is the disorder that most closely corresponds to popular concepts of insanity, madness, or lunacy. The word *schizophrenia* comes from Greek roots meaning "split brain." In schizophrenia, the mind is stripped of the intimate connections among thoughts, perceptions, and feelings. Individuals with this disorder may giggle in the face of disaster, hear or see things that aren't physically present, or maintain beliefs that are firmly held but patently false.

Schizophrenia affects about 1 percent of the adult population worldwide (Balter, 2014; Dhindsa & Goldstein, 2016). Nearly 1 million people are treated for schizophrenia each year in the United States, with about one-third receiving hospitalized care.

Schizophrenia is characterized by bizarre, irrational behavior, such as in the case of Claire, who was convinced she was protecting the populace from demons. The disorder is somewhat more common in men than in women. Men also tend to develop the disorder a bit earlier than women and to experience a more severe form of the disorder. Schizophrenia follows a lifelong course and typically develops in late adolescence or early adulthood, at about the time that people are beginning to make their way in the world (Walker et al., 2010). It occurs about as frequently in other cultures as in our own, although the particular symptoms may vary from culture to culture.

Symptoms of Schizophrenia

Schizophrenia is a **psychotic disorder**—that is, a disorder in which an individual confuses reality with fantasy, seeing or hearing things that aren't there (hallucinations) or holding fixed but patently false beliefs (delusions) (Balter, 2014; McCarthy-Jones et al., 2014). *Hallucinations* are perceptions that occur in the absence of external stimuli. They may affect different senses. Auditory hallucinations ("hearing voices") are most common. Visual hallucinations (seeing things that are not there) and other sensory hallucinations (sensing odors or having taste sensations without any physical stimulus) are much less common. *Delusions* may represent many different themes, but the most common are themes of persecution, such as the belief that demons or "the Devil" are trying to harm the person.

People with schizophrenia may exhibit bizarre behavior, incoherent speech, and illogical thinking. They may not know the time of day, or what day or year it is. Or where they are. Or *who* they are. Note that not all of these symptoms must be present for a diagnosis of schizophrenia to be given.

Many people with schizophrenia exhibit a **thought disorder**, a breakdown in the logical structure of thinking and speech characterized by *loose associations* between expressed ideas. Normally, our thoughts are tightly connected or associated; one thought follows another in a logical sequence. But in people with schizophrenia, there may be an absence of logical connections between thoughts. The ideas expressed are strung loosely together or jumbled in such a way that a listener is unable to follow the person's train of thought. In severe cases, speech becomes completely incoherent or incomprehensible. The person may begin to form meaningless words or mindless rhymes.

CONCEPT 13.26

Schizophrenia is a puzzling and disabling disorder that fills the mind with distorted perceptions, false ideas, and loosely connected thoughts.

The Brain Loves a Puzzle

As you read ahead, use the information in the text to solve the following puzzle:

Genetics plays an important role in schizophrenia, but why is it the case that scientists have been unable to find the gene that causes schizophrenia and probably never will?

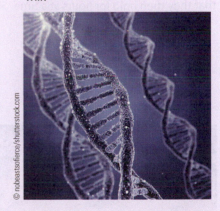

© nobeastsofierce/shutterstock.com

schizophrenia A severe and chronic psychological disorder characterized by disturbances in thinking, perception, emotions, and behavior.

psychotic disorder A psychological disorder, such as schizophrenia, characterized by a "break" with reality.

thought disorder A breakdown in the logical structure of thought and speech, revealed in the form of a loosening of associations.

The body position of people showing catatonic behavior can sometimes be molded by others into unusual postures that they then hold for hours at a time.

Even among identical twins who share 100 percent genetic overlap, there is less than a 50 percent chance that if one twin develops schizophrenia, the other will as well. Clearly, genetic and nongenetic influences are involved.

The more flagrant signs of schizophrenia, such as hallucinations, delusions, bizarre behavior, and thought disorder, are behavioral excesses classified as **positive symptoms**. Yet people with schizophrenia may also have behavioral deficits or **negative symptoms**, such as extreme withdrawal or social isolation, apathy, and lack of facial expressions or emotions (Fusar-Poli et al., 2014; Hartmann et al., 2015; Kring et al., 2013). Positive symptoms may fade after acute episodes, but negative symptoms are typically more enduring, making it difficult for the person with schizophrenia to meet demands of daily life.

In rare cases, patients with schizophrenia show **catatonic** behavior, remaining in a motionless state or stupor in which they appear unresponsive to the environment. They may maintain a fixed or rigid posture for hours and then abruptly shift into a highly agitated state. Although they may be mute or uncommunicative during these episodes, they later may report that they heard what others were saying at the time. Less commonly, they may show **waxy flexibility**, a behavior pattern in which their body position can be molded by others (like wax) into unusual, even uncomfortable positions that they then hold for hours at a time.

Causes of Schizophrenia

Schizophrenia remains a puzzling—indeed, mystifying—disorder. Though we have not solved the puzzle, researchers have made substantial progress in putting many of the pieces into place. Many investigators today consider schizophrenia to be a brain disorder involving abnormal brain development that leads to confused or irrational thinking, incoherent or jumbled speech, faulty perceptions, and difficulty functioning in social and occupational roles (Walker et al., 2010; Zalesky et al., 2015). Let's take a closer look at some of the contributing factors.

Genetic Factors

A large and ever-growing body of evidence indicates that schizophrenia is strongly affected by genetic factors (e.g., Agerbo et al., 2015; Cannon, 2016; Dhindsa & Goldstein, 2016; Jones et al., 2016; Ruzzo & Geschwind, 2016). The closer the genetic relationship a person shares with someone who has schizophrenia, the greater the likelihood the person will also have or develop schizophrenia. Consistent with a genetic contribution, monozygotic or identical twins are more likely to share the disorder in common (a concordance rate of about 45 to 50 percent) than are dizygotic or fraternal twins (about a 17 percent concordance rate).

We also know that adopted children whose biological parents had schizophrenia are more likely to develop schizophrenia themselves than are adopted children whose parents did not have the disorder (Tienari et al., 2003). All in all, investigators believe that multiple genes are involved in creating a genetic predisposition or susceptibility to schizophrenia (Schizophrenia Working Group, 2014). Any one gene may have only a small effect on its own, but a combination of certain genes may greatly increase the risk of developing the disorder. Scientists are trying to pinpoint these genes and the effects they have on brain development and functioning (for example, Dickinson et al., 2014; Greenhill et al., 2015; Greenwood et al., 2016; Siegert et al., 2015, among many others).

Although genetics clearly plays an important role in the development of schizophrenia, genes do not tell the whole story. Consider that only about 13 percent of people who have a parent with schizophrenia develop the disorder themselves. Consider also that if one identical twin has schizophrenia, the other twin, though genetically identical, has a 45 to 50 percent chance of having the disorder as well. If only genetics were involved, we would expect 100 percent concordance among monozygotic twins. In short, genetic vulnerability is not genetic inevitability. People at high genetic risk for schizophrenia may only go on to develop the disorder if they experience significant life stressors (Tienari et al., 2004). Some types of stressors have a biological basis, such as early brain trauma. But others may be environmental or psychological in origin, such as child abuse or neglect or persistent and intense family conflict.

Biochemical Imbalances

Researchers suspect that biochemical or neurotransmitter imbalances in nerve pathways in the brain, especially those involving the neurotransmitter dopamine, are involved in the development of schizophrenia (Keshavan, Nasrallah, & Tandon, 2011; Steeds, Carhart-Harris, & Stone, 2014). Dopamine is suspected because *antipsychotic drugs* that help control hallucinations and delusions reduce dopamine activity by blocking dopamine receptors in the brain, preventing molecules of dopamine from docking at receptor sites (Abbott, 2010). Yet the brains of patients with schizophrenia do not appear to produce too much dopamine. Rather, dopamine receptors may be overly sensitive to the chemical (Grace, 2010; Valenti et al., 2011). It is hoped that future research will clarify the underlying biomolecular processes.

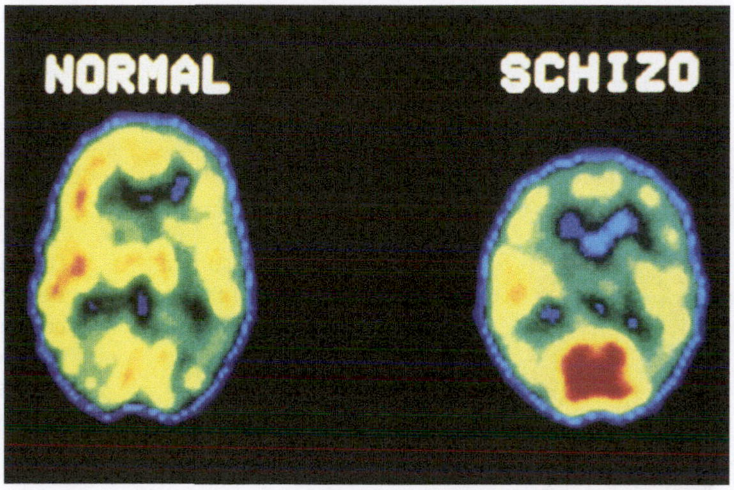

Brain Abnormalities

Scanning the brains of schizophrenia patients consistently shows evidence of brain abnormalities (Bohlken et al., 2016; Guo et al., 2015; Sun et al., 2015; Zhang et al., 2015) (see ■ Figure 13.5). For example, patients with schizophrenia often show structural changes in the brain, especially enlarged ventricles, which are hollow spaces associated with the loss of brain tissue. We don't yet know what causes this loss or shrinkage of brain tissue, but abnormal brain development may begin prenatally when brain structures are first forming or in early childhood when they are developing further (King, St-Hilaire, & Heidkamp, 2010; Walker et al., 2010).

Areas of the brain that appear most affected in people with schizophrenia are the prefrontal cortex (PFC) and parts of the limbic system, as well as the connections between these regions (see, for example, Anticevic, Murray, & Barch, 2015; Baker et al., 2014; Bohlken et al., 2016; Slifstein et al., 2015). The PFC is the "thinking part" of the brain—the part responsible for keeping information in mind (that is, working memory), organizing thoughts and behavior, and formulating and carrying out goals and plans. These are the very functions that are often disrupted in schizophrenia (Kaller et al., 2014).

The limbic system plays key roles in forming new memories and processing emotions—functions too that are often disturbed in patients with schizophrenia. In a landmark study reported in 2016, investigators linked genetic variations associated with schizophrenia to a process of thinning of connections (synapses) between neurons in the prefrontal cortex of the brain (Carey, 2016; Dhindsa & Goldstein, 2016; Sekar et al., 2016). This thinning of neuronal connections, a process likened to pruning a tree, may help explain defects in brain circuitry that give rise to the types of problems with disturbed thinking and perception we see in schizophrenia patients.

Psychosocial Influences

Psychosocial influences, such as significant life stress, may interact with a genetic vulnerability in the development of schizophrenia. The belief that schizophrenia results from an interaction of a *diathesis* (a vulnerability factor such as a genetic predisposition) and stressful life experiences is represented in the form of the *diathesis-stress model* (Zubin & Spring, 1977) (review Figure 13.1). Sources of stress may include biological factors, such as prenatal or early brain trauma; psychosocial factors, such

CONCEPT 13.28
The diathesis-stress model holds that schizophrenia results from the interaction of a genetic predisposition and stressful life events or trauma.

Science Source

FIGURE 13.5 Brain Images of Schizophrenia Patients Versus Normal Controls
Here we see PET scan images of metabolic activity in the brains of patients with schizophrenia versus normal controls. Note the lower level of activity in the frontal lobes of the brains of patients with schizophrenia (denoted by less yellow and red in the upper part of the brain images in the lower row). This evidence supports the belief that schizophrenia involves abnormalities in the frontal lobes of the brain, and more specifically, in the prefrontal cortex.

positive symptoms Symptoms of schizophrenia involving behavioral excesses, such as hallucinations and delusions.

negative symptoms Behavioral deficits associated with schizophrenia, such as withdrawal and apathy.

catatonic Relating to catatonia, a condition involving states of stupor and unresponsiveness to the environment.

waxy flexibility A feature of catatonia characterized by maintaining a body position or posture in which the person was placed by others.

as being raised in an abusive family environment or experiencing disturbed patterns of communication in the family; and negative life events, such as the loss of a loved one or failure in school. Though we lack a precise understanding of how these factors fit together, one possibility is that genetic and stressful influences combine to produce abnormalities in the brain that interfere with thinking, memory, and perceptual processes, leading eventually to the welter of confusing thoughts and perceptions that we see in people with schizophrenia.

The symptoms and suspected causes of schizophrenia are summarized in Concept Chart 13.5.

Concept Chart 13.5 Schizophrenia

	Description	Symptoms	Probable Causes
© Tramper/Shutterstock.com	A chronic psychotic disorder affecting about 1% of the population	Delusions, hallucinations, bizarre behavior, incoherent or loosely connected speech, inappropriate emotions or lack of emotional expression, social withdrawal, and apathy	An interaction of a genetic predisposition and life stress; underlying brain abnormalities

MODULE REVIEW 13.5 Schizophrenia

Recite It

8. **Describe** the features of schizophrenia and underlying causal factors.

   Schizophrenia is a psychotic disorder, meaning that it is characterized by a break with (a) _____. Gross confusion, delusions, and hallucinations are common symptoms in patients with schizophrenia. Precise causes are unknown, but suspected causes include biological factors such as a (b) _____ predisposition, disturbed neurotransmitter activity in the brain (irregularities in (c) _____

   transmission), brain abnormalities (loss of brain tissue and abnormalities in brain circuitry), and stress.

9. **Explain** the development of schizophrenia based on the diathesis-stress model.

   The diathesis-stress model postulates that schizophrenia results from an interaction of a genetic predisposition ((d) _____) and (e) _____ life experiences.

Recall It

1. More (males or females?) are affected by schizophrenia.

2. A person showing _____ behavior may remain motionless for hours and then abruptly become highly agitated.

3. About how many people will develop schizophrenia if they have an identical (MZ) twin with this disorder?
   a. 10 to 15 percent   c. 45 to 50 percent
   b. 20 to 25 percent   d. more than 50 percent

4. Scientists believe that abnormalities involving the neurotransmitter _____ are closely linked to the development of schizophrenia.
   a. serotonin
   b. dopamine
   c. epinephrine
   d. acetylcholine

Think About It

- In what sense does schizophrenia correspond to the Greek roots from which it derives its name?

- Have you known anyone who was diagnosed with schizophrenia? How did the disorder affect the person's behavior and ability to function? How is the person functioning today?

Recite It *answers placed at the end of chapter.*

13.6 Personality Disorders

10 **Define** the concept of personality disorders.

11 **Describe** the features of antisocial personality disorder and borderline personality disorder and underlying causal factors in these disorders.

People with **personality disorders** show excessively rigid and maladaptive patterns of behavior that make it difficult for them to adjust to the demands they face in their daily lives and to form long-term, satisfying relationships. These maladaptive behaviors reflect extreme variations on underlying personality traits, such as excessive emotionality, undue suspiciousness, and excessive dependency. Personality disorders become so deeply ingrained that they are highly resistant to change in many cases.

There are many different types of personality disorders. Our focus is on two of the most widely studied types, **antisocial personality disorder (APD or ASPD)** and **borderline personality disorder** (see Concept Chart 13.6).

Antisocial Personality Disorder

People with antisocial personalities (sometimes called *psychopaths* or *sociopaths*) show a flagrant disregard for the rules of society and a lack of concern for the welfare of others. They are not psychotic; they maintain contact with reality. But they often act on impulse—doing what they want when they want. They typically are irresponsible, treat others callously, and take advantage of others for their own needs or personal gain (Marcus, Fulton, & Edens, 2012). They may engage in criminal or other antisocial behaviors. They may also lack remorse for their misdeeds or mistreatment of others and appear to be untroubled by anxiety or undeterred by the threat of punishment or by punishment itself.

Some people with antisocial personalities engage in criminal behavior, but most are law abiding. They may display a high level of intelligence and a superficial charm that attracts others. APD is found more often among men than women, with estimates of lifetime rates of 3 to 6 percent in men and 1 percent in women (American Psychiatric Association, 2013; Cale & Lilienfeld, 2002; Kessler et al., 1994).

Causal Factors in Antisocial Personality Disorder

Evidence points to a role for biological factors in the development of antisocial personality disorder, including genetic factors and brain abnormalities (Meier et al., 2011; Raine, 2008). Brain-imaging studies link antisocial personality disorder to abnormalities in the prefrontal cortex, the part of the brain responsible for regulating

CONCEPT 13.29

People with personality disorders exhibit excessively rigid patterns of behavior that ultimately make it difficult for them to relate to others or meet the demands that are placed upon them.

CONCEPT 13.30

Features of antisocial personality disorder include showing a blatant disregard for social rules and regulations, antisocial behavior, impulsivity, irresponsibility, lack of remorse for wrongdoing, and a tendency to take advantage of others.

personality disorders A class of psychological disorders characterized by rigid personality traits that impair people's ability to adjust to the demands they face in the environment and that interfere with their relationships with others.

antisocial personality disorder (APD or ASPD) A type of personality disorder characterized by callous attitudes toward others and by antisocial and irresponsible behavior.

borderline personality disorder A type of personality disorder characterized by unstable emotions and self-image.

Concept Chart 13.6 Overview of Two Major Types of Personality Disorders

Disorder	Lifetime Prevalence in Population (approx.)	Symptoms	Associated Features
Antisocial personality disorder	Upwards of 6% in men, 1% in women	A pattern of antisocial and irresponsible behavior; callous treatment of others; lack of remorse for wrongdoing	Lacks empathy for others and may take advantage of people or fail to meet their commitments
Borderline personality disorder	1.6%–5.9%	Unstable moods and stormy relationships with others; unstable self-image; lack of impulse control	May engage in self-destructive behaviors, such as cutting themselves

Sources: American Psychiatric Association, 2013; Cale & Lilienfeld, 2002; Kernberg & Michels, 2009; Kessler et al., 1994; Paris, 2010.

AP Images/David J. Philip

Serial killer Henry Lee Lucas was a career drifter who fits the stereotype of people with antisocial personality. Although many people with antisocial personalities do not run afoul of the law, they show other antisocial behaviors such as irresponsibility, callousness in the treatment of others, and lack of remorse for misdeeds.

emotions, controlling impulsive aggressive behavior, and weighing the consequences of one's actions (Motzkin et al., 2011; Schiffer et al., 2014). Still, we don't yet know how many people with antisocial personality disorder actually have underlying brain abnormalities.

People with antisocial personalities may have a genetic predisposition to crave higher levels of stimulation to maintain an optimum level of arousal. They may become quickly bored with routine activities and turn to more dangerous activities that provide immediate thrills, such as alcohol and drug use, racing cars or motorcycles, high-stakes gambling, or risky sexual encounters.

What role does the environment play? Research shows that many people with APD were raised in families characterized by lack of parental warmth and nurturing, as well as parental neglect, abuse, rejection, and use of harsh punishment (Johnson et al., 2006; Lobbestael & Arntz, 2009). A history of emotional or physical abuse in childhood may lead to a failure to develop a sense of empathy or concern for the welfare of others. It may also lead to a failure to develop a moral compass or sense of conscience. This lack of empathy and moral values may explain why people with APD act in a callous way toward others. In all likelihood, then, both genetic and environmental factors contribute to the development of APD, as is the case with many forms of abnormal behavior (Meier et al., 2011).

Borderline Personality Disorder

CONCEPT 13.31

People with borderline personality disorder have abrupt shifts in mood, lack a coherent sense of self, act impulsively, and often have stormy relationships with others.

People with borderline personality disorder (BPD) tend to have stormy relationships with others, dramatic mood swings, difficulty controlling their emotions, and an unstable self-image (Krause-Utz et al., 2013; Lazarus et al., 2014; Santangelo et al., 2014). They have turbulent moods that can range from anger and irritability to depression and anxiety. They may feel a deep emptiness inside that reflects their unstable self-image and lack of a clear identity or direction in life. Fear of abandonment and difficulty being alone lead them to become excessively clinging or dependent on others, which may push away the very people on whom they depend. They tend to act on impulse without considering the consequences and have difficulty regulating their emotions, especially anger, acting out by hurting or mutilating themselves, such as by cutting themselves (Millon, 2011). Impulsive behaviors may take the form of spending sprees, gambling and drug binges, unsafe sexual activity, reckless driving, binge eating, and shoplifting.

Here a man with BPD speaks about his impulsive anger:

When I feel I cannot control my surroundings, I become nervous and angry. It gets much worse when I am under stress. Everything negative comes in full blast and overwhelms me.

*When triggered, I can go from perfectly calm to full-blown, white-hot rage within a frac-
tion of a second. . . . I think that my temper comes from the abuse I suffered when I was
a child. At some point, I decided that I didn't have to take my parents' abuse anymore.
Raging back became a matter of survival. . . . So now, it's hard for me to feel concerned
about the other person's feelings—in fact, I want them to hurt because they've hurt me.*
(Mason & Kreger, 1998, pp. 39–41)

People with BPD often have alternating feelings toward others, which shift
abruptly from complete adulation when they feel others are meeting their needs to
utter loathing when they feel rejected or frustrated. Psychoanalysts refer to this process as "splitting," which is the tendency to perceive people in either all good or all
bad terms and to abruptly shift from one extreme to the other in one's perceptions of
others. Not surprisingly, people with BPD tend to have a history of stormy, turbulent
relationships. Partners whom they adored and depended upon become treated with
utter contempt when they feel their needs are not being met.

Borderline personality disorder affects from 1.6% to 5.9% of the general adult
population (Kernberg & Michels, 2009; Paris, 2010). Women are more frequently
diagnosed with the disorder, but it is unclear whether women truly are more likely to
be affected or simply more likely to be diagnosed with the disorder. Many historical
figures have been thought to have features of borderline personality disorder, including Marilyn Monroe, Lawrence of Arabia, Adolf Hitler, and the philosopher Søren
Kierkegaard.

Causal Factors in Borderline Personality Disorder

Causal factors in BPD continue to be studied, but histories of physical or sexual
abuse or neglect in childhood often figure prominently in many cases (Golier et al.,
2003; McLean & Gallop, 2003). Psychoanalytic theorists, like Otto Kernberg
(1975), believe that people with BPD are unable to develop a cohesive concept of
themselves and others in early childhood, resulting in the difficulties they encounter
in synthesizing the contradictory (good and bad) elements of themselves and others
into complete, stable wholes. Rather than recognizing that people are sometimes
loving and sometimes rejecting, they shift back and forth in their appraisal of others
between pure idealization and utter hatred.

Brain-imaging studies show abnormalities in parts of the brain involved in regulating emotions and restraining impulsive behaviors, especially aggressive behaviors
(Bøen et al., 2013; Siegle, 2008; Yager, 2014). An intriguing possibility requiring
further study is that the prefrontal cortex fails to restrain impulsive behaviors at
times of strong negative emotions (Silbersweig et al., 2008). Genetic factors also play
a role, perhaps by influencing underlying brain structures and functions (Reichborn-
Kjennerud et al., 2013). BPD, like many other forms of abnormal behavior, appears
to involve an interaction of genetics and life experiences (Gunderson, 2011).

CONCEPT 13.32
Evidence points to an interaction of environmental and biological factors in the
development of personality disorders.

MODULE REVIEW **13.6** Personality Disorders

Recite It

10. Define the concept of personality disorders.

(a) _____ disorders are deeply ingrained patterns of behavior that become maladaptive because they either cause personal distress or impair the person's ability to relate to others.

11. Describe the features of antisocial personality disorder and
borderline personality disorder and underlying causal factors
in these disorders.

Characteristics associated with (b) _____ personality disorder include impulsivity, irresponsibility, a
callous disregard for the rights and feelings of others,
and antisocial behavior. A number of causal factors are
implicated, including environmental factors, such as a
family environment characterized by a lack of parental
warmth, neglect, rejection, and use of harsh (c) _____,

and biological factors, such as a genetic predisposition, abnormalities in higher brain centers that control (d) _____ behavior, and a greater need for arousing stimulation.

(e) _____ personality disorder is characterized by problems in forming a stable self-image, maintaining stable

moods and relationships, and difficulty controlling (f) _____. Evidence points to such factors as a history of childhood abuse or (g) _____, genetic influences, and brain abnormalities involving mechanisms that regulate control of impulsive behaviors.

Recall It

1. What are personality disorders?

2. Investigators link antisocial personality disorder to abnormalities in what area of the brain?

3. Match the following characteristics to either (a) antisocial personality disorder or (b) borderline personality disorder:

   i. turbulent relationships with others
  ii. lack of empathy
 iii. need for higher levels of stimulation
 iv. unstable self-image

Think About It

■ What are the differences between criminality and antisocial personality? Or are they one and the same? Explain.

■ Have you known anyone with a personality disorder? What factors might have led to the development of

these problem personality traits? How did these traits affect the person's relationships with others? With you?

Recite It answers placed at the end of chapter.

THINKING CRITICALLY ABOUT PSYCHOLOGY

Based on your reading of this chapter, answer the following questions. Then, to evaluate your progress in developing critical thinking skills, compare your answers to the sample answers found in Appendix A.

1. Ron, a 22-year-old stock clerk in an auto parts store, sought a consultation with a psychologist because he was feeling "down in the dumps." He explained that he was involved in a three-year-long relationship with Katie. The relationship followed a seesawing pattern of numerous breakups and brief reconciliations. Most of the breakups occurred after incidents in which Ron became angry when he felt Katie was becoming distant from him. On one occasion, he accused her of sitting too far away from him in the car. If she was in a bad mood, he assumed it was because she didn't really want to be with him. The relationship meant everything to him, he told the psychologist, saying further that "I don't know what I'd do if she left me, you know, for good. I've got to figure out how to make this relationship work" (adapted from Nevid, Rathus, & Greene, 2014).

   Review the characteristic errors in thinking associated with depression listed in Table 13.2. Give some examples of these cognitive errors in Ron's thinking.

2. Lonnie, a 38-year-old chemical engineer for a large pharmaceutical company, sought a consultation at the urging of his wife, Maria. He told the psychologist that Maria had grown exasperated over his "little behavioral quirks." It seems that Lonnie was a compulsive checker. Whenever the two of them would leave their apartment, he would insist on returning to check and recheck that the gas jets were turned off, the windows were shut, the door was securely locked, and the refrigerator door was tightly shut. Sometimes he'd get as far as the garage before the compulsion to return to the apartment would strike. He would apologize to Maria and leave her fuming. When retiring to bed at night, he performed an elaborate ritual of checking and rechecking to see that everything was secure. But even then, he would often bolt out of bed to check everything again, which would disturb Maria's sleep. Leaving for vacation was especially troublesome, as it required checking rituals that consumed the better part of the morning. Yet he would still be bothered by nagging doubts that would plague him throughout his trip. Lonnie recognized that his compulsive behavior was wrecking his marriage and causing him

emotional distress. However, he feared that giving it up would leave him defenseless against the anxieties it helped to ease (adapted from Nevid, Rathus, & Greene, 2014).

Review the six criteria used to define abnormal behavior. Which of these criteria do you think would apply to Lonnie's case? Which wouldn't apply?

Recite It Answers for Chapter 13

Module 13.1 1. (a) deviance; (b) reality; (c) interpretations; (d) emotional, 2. (e) biopsychosocial, 3. (f) psychological; (g) *DSM*

Module 13.2 4. (a) Anxiety; (b) generalized; (c) learning; (d) neurotransmitters   **Module 13.3** 5. (a) self; (b) identity; (c) amnesia; (d) defense; (e) somatic; (f) anxiety   **Module 13.4** 6. (a) mood; (b) neurotransmitter; (c) reinforcement, 7. (d) White; (e) hopelessness; (f) copycat

Module 13.5 8. (a) reality; (b) genetic; (c) dopamine, 9. (d) diathesis; (e) stressful   **Module 13.6** 10. (a) Personality, 11. (b) antisocial; (c) punishment; (d) impulsive; (e) Borderline; (f) impulses; (g) neglect

Psychological Disorders

What Is Abnormal Behavior?

Diathesis
A predisposition or vulnerability

Stress
Environmental stressors

Development of the Disorder
The stronger the diathesis, the less stress is necessary to produce the disorder

1 Inherited predisposition to develop the disorder

+

2
- Prenatal trauma
- Childhood sexual or physical abuse
- Family conflict
- Significant life changes

3 Psychological disorder

Criteria for Determining Abnormal Behavior

- Unusualness
- Social Deviance
- Emotional Distress
- Maladaptive Behavior
- Dangerousness
- Faulty Perceptions or Interpretations of Reality

Models of Abnormal Behavior

- **Early Beliefs:** Dominated by supernatural or demonic forces
- **Medical Model:** Abnormal behavior as medical illness
- **Psychological Models:** Psychodynamic, behavioral, humanistic, and cognitive models
- **Sociocultural Model:** Abnormal behavior rooted in social ills
- **Biopsychosocial Model:** Interaction of multiple factors, as represented by the diathesis-stress model

Psychological Disorders

- **Prevalence of Psychological Disorders:** Nearly one in two adults affected at some point in their lives
- **Classification of Psychological Disorders:** *DSM* diagnostic system provides specific criteria clinicians use to diagnose mental or psychological disorders.

Anxiety-Related Disorders

- **Phobias:** Excessive or inappropriate fear reactions, such as a specific phobia, social anxiety disorder, and agoraphobia
- **Panic Disorder:** Intense anxiety reactions called panic attacks
- **Generalized Anxiety Disorder:** Anxiety not limited to specific objects or situations
- **Obsessive-Compulsive Disorder:** Bothersome obsessive thoughts and compulsive rituals
- **PTSD:** Maladaptive reactions to traumatic stress (discussed in Chapter 10)

Phovoir/Shutterstock.com

Dissociative and Somatic Symptom and Related Disorders

Dissociative Disorders

- **Dissociative Identity Disorder:** Formerly called multiple personality; involves a splitting of the self into alternate personalities
- **Dissociative Amnesia:** Memory loss resulting from psychological causes

Somatic Symptom and Related Disorders

- **Conversion Disorder:** A loss or major change in bodily function that cannot be explained medically
- **Hypochondriasis (now labeled somatic symptom disorder in most cases):** Mistakenly believing that physical symptoms are signs of underlying serious illness

MODULE 13.4

Mood Disorders

- **Major Depression:** Periods of significant downcast mood and loss of interest and pleasure
- **Bipolar Disorder:** Mood swings from extremely elevated moods to periods of deep depression

Burstein Collection/Fine Art/Corbis

MODULE 13.5

Schizophrenia

- **Key Features:** Break with reality and severely impaired cognitive and social functioning

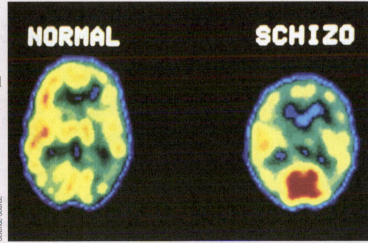

Science Source

MODULE 13.6

Personality Disorders

- **Key Features:** Rigid, maladaptive behavior patterns that interfere with interpersonal relationships and ability to meet life demands

Two Major Types

- **Antisocial Personality Disorder:** Callous treatment of others, disregard for rules of society, lack of remorse for misdeeds, irresponsible behavior, and antisocial behavior
- **Borderline Personality Disorder:** Unstable self-image, turbulent relationships, unstable moods, and lack of impulse control

LEARNING OBJECTIVES

iStockphoto.com/Aina555

PREVIEW

Methods of Therapy

14

"The Beast is Back"

My body aches intermittently, in waves, as if I had malaria. I eat with no appetite, simply because the taste of food is one of my dwindling number of pleasures. I am tired, so tired. Last night I lay like a pile of old clothes, and when David came to bed I did not stir. Sex is a foreign notion. At work today I am forgetful; I have trouble forming sentences, I lose track of them halfway through, and my words keep getting tangled. I look at my list of things to do today, and keep on looking at it; nothing seems to be happening. Things are sad to me. This morning I thought of the woman who used to live in my old house, who told me she went to Sears to buy fake lace curtains. It seemed a forlorn act—having to save your pennies, not being able to afford genuine lace. (Why? A voice in my head asks. The curtains she bought looked perfectly nice.) I feel as if my brain were a lump of protoplasm with tiny circuits embedded in it, and some of the wires keep shorting out. There are tiny little electrical fires up there, leaving crispy sections of neurons smoking and ruined.

I don't even know when this current siege began—a week ago? A month ago? The onset is so gradual, and these things are hard to tell. All I know is, the Beast is back.

It is called depression, and my experiences with it have shaped my life—altered my personality, affected my most intimate relationships, changed the course of my career—in ways I will probably never be fully aware of.

Source: Thompson, 1995.

In this chapter, we discuss ways of helping people like the woman in this case example who suffer from psychological disorders. As we shall see in Modules 14.1 and 14.2, help takes many forms, including psychotherapy and biomedical therapies such as drug therapy and electroconvulsive therapy (ECT). We will then review the information that informed consumers need to know—and the questions they need to ask—when seeking the assistance of mental health professionals.

Did you know that...

- Psychologists in three states can now prescribe psychiatric medications upon completing a specialized training program? (p. 529)
- Sigmund Freud believed that clients bring into the therapeutic relationship the underlying conflicts they have had with important people in their lives? (p. 530)
- Gestalt therapists have their clients talk to an empty chair? (p. 533)
- People with a fear of heights can encounter what it feels like to peer over a 33rd-floor balcony while remaining at ground level? (p. 535)
- Some therapists are using Internet-delivered therapy and computerized programs as add-ons to traditional therapy and even as stand-alone treatments? (p. 535)
- Cognitive therapists believe that emotional disorders arise from the ways in which we interpret our life experiences, not from the experiences themselves? (p. 536)
- Antidepressant drugs are used to treat many types of psychological disorders, not just depression? (p. 550)
- Stimulant drugs are used to help hyperactive children? (p. 551)

14.1 Types of Psychotherapy

1 **Identify** the major types of mental health professionals.

2 **Define** psychotherapy.

3 **Identify** the major types of psychotherapy and the developers of these therapies and **describe** techniques used in these different types of psychotherapy.

4 **Identify** and **describe** forms of therapy that involve more than the individual client.

5 **Evaluate** evidence regarding the effectiveness of psychotherapy.

6 **Identify** and **describe** cultural factors that affect the practice of psychotherapy.

7 **Apply** steps you can take to obtain help for a psychological problem.

CONCEPT 14.1

Psychotherapy consists of one or more verbal interactions between a therapist and a client and is used to help people understand and resolve their psychological problems.

CONCEPT 14.2

Mental health services are offered by different types of professionals who vary in their training backgrounds and areas of competence.

CONCEPT 14.3

Psychodynamic therapy is based on the belief that insight into unresolved psychological conflicts originating in childhood can help people overcome psychological problems.

psychotherapy A verbal form of therapy derived from a psychological framework that consists of one or more treatment sessions with a therapist.

psychoanalysis Freud's method of psychotherapy; it focuses on uncovering and working through the unconscious conflicts that he believed were at the root of psychological problems.

psychoanalysts Practitioners of psychoanalysis who are schooled in the Freudian tradition.

Psychotherapy is a psychologically based form of treatment used to help people better understand their emotional or behavioral problems and resolve them. It consists of a series of verbal interactions between a therapist and a client, which is why it is often referred to as "talk therapy." In some forms of psychotherapy, there is an ongoing back-and-forth dialogue between the therapist and client, whereas in others, especially in classical psychoanalysis, the client does most or virtually all of the talking. There are many different types of psychotherapy, literally hundreds of types, but the most widely used derive from the major psychological models of abnormal behavior discussed in Chapter 13: the psychodynamic, behavioral, humanistic, and cognitive models. Although most forms of psychotherapy focus on the individual, some therapists extend their model of treatment to couples, families, and groups of unrelated individuals.

Before we consider the major forms of psychotherapy, have a look at Table 14.1, which lists the major types of helping professionals who provide mental health services. Note the differences in their training backgrounds and areas of expertise.

Psychodynamic Therapy

What comes to mind when you think of psychotherapy? If you picture a person lying on a couch and talking about the past, especially early childhood, you are probably thinking of **psychoanalysis**, the original form of *psychodynamic therapy*. Psychodynamic therapies share in common the belief that psychological problems are rooted in unconscious psychological conflicts dating from childhood. They also assume that gaining insight into these conflicts and working through them in the light of the individual's adult personality are the key steps toward restoring psychological health (Johansson et al., 2010).

Traditional Psychoanalysis: Where Id Was, Ego Shall Be

Psychoanalysis, the form of psychotherapy Sigmund Freud developed, is based on the belief that unconscious conflicts originating in childhood give rise to psychological problems. Practitioners of psychoanalysis are called **psychoanalysts**, or *analysts* for short. Recall from Chapter 11 that Freud believed that conflicts over primitive sexual or aggressive impulses cause the ego to employ *defense mechanisms,* especially *repression,* to keep these impulses out of conscious awareness. In some instances, these unconscious impulses threaten to leak into consciousness, resulting in feelings of anxiety. The person may report feeling anxious or experience a sense of dread or foreboding but have no idea about its cause. In other instances, the energy attached to the impulse is channeled or converted into a physical symptom, as in cases of hysterical blindness or paralysis. The symptom itself, such as the inability to move an arm, serves a hidden purpose: It prevents the person from acting upon the underlying impulse.

Thus, for example, a person with hysterical paralysis becomes unable to use an arm to engage in unacceptable sexual acts such as masturbation. Similarly, a person with a fear of heights may harbor unconscious self-destructive impulses that are kept in check by avoiding height situations in which the person might lose control over the impulse to jump. The task of therapy, Freud believed, is to help people

Table 14.1 Major Types of Mental Health Professionals

Clinical Psychologists

Clinical psychologists have earned a doctoral degree in psychology (either a PhD, Doctor of Philosophy; PsyD, Doctor of Psychology; or an EdD, Doctor of Education) from an accredited college or university and have passed a licensing examination. Clinical psychologists specialize in administering psychological tests, diagnosing mental disorders, and practicing psychotherapy. Until a few years ago, they were not permitted to prescribe psychiatric drugs. However, as of this writing, three states (New Mexico, Louisiana, and Illinois) had enacted laws granting prescription privileges to psychologists who complete specialized training programs (American Psychological Association, 2014; Robiner, Tumlin, & Tompkins, 2013). Whether other states will follow suit remains to be seen. However, the granting of prescription privileges to psychologists remains a hotly contested issue between psychologists and psychiatrists and within the field of psychology itself.

Counseling Psychologists

Counseling psychologists hold doctoral degrees in psychology and have passed a licensing examination. They typically provide counseling to people with psychological problems falling within a milder range of severity than those treated by clinical psychologists, such as difficulties adjusting to college or uncertainties regarding career choices. Many counseling psychologists in college settings are also involved in providing appropriate services to students covered by the Americans with Disabilities Act (ADA).

Psychiatrists

Psychiatrists have earned a medical degree (MD) and have completed residency training programs in psychiatry, which usually are three years in length. They are physicians who specialize in the diagnosis and treatment of psychological disorders. As licensed physicians, they can prescribe psychiatric drugs and may employ other medical techniques, such as electroconvulsive therapy (ECT). Many also practice psychotherapy based on training they receive during their residency programs or in specialized training institutes.

Clinical or Psychiatric Social Workers

Clinical or psychiatric social workers have earned a master's degree in social work (MSW) and use their knowledge of community agencies and organizations to help people with severe mental disorders receive the services they need. Many clinical social workers practice psychotherapy or specific forms of therapy, such as marital or family therapy.

Psychoanalysts

Psychoanalysts are typically either psychiatrists or psychologists who have completed extensive additional training in psychoanalysis. They are required to undergo psychoanalysis themselves as part of their training.

Counselors

Counselors have typically earned a master's degree and work in private practice settings, as well as in public schools, college testing and counseling centers, and hospitals and health clinics. Many states certify mental health counselors at the master's level of training to provide counseling services to people in the community. Many counselors specialize in vocational evaluation, marital or family counseling, or substance abuse counseling. Counselors may also focus on providing psychological assistance to people with milder forms of disturbed behavior or those struggling with a chronic or debilitating illness or recovering from a traumatic experience.

Psychiatric Nurses

Psychiatric nurses are typically RNs who have completed a master's program in psychiatric nursing. They may work in a psychiatric facility or in a group medical practice where they treat people suffering from severe psychological disorders.

CONCEPT 14.4

Freud devised a number of techniques, including free association, dream analysis, and interpretation, to help clients gain awareness of their unconscious conflicts.

CONCEPT LINK

As we saw in Chapter 4, Freud believed that dreams have both manifest (transparent) and latent (symbolic) content. See Module 4.2.

CONCEPT 14.5

Freud believed that the ability to understand the transference relationship is essential to the client's success in psychoanalysis.

free association A technique in psychoanalysis in which the client is encouraged to say anything that comes to mind.

dream analysis A technique in psychoanalysis in which the therapist analyzes the underlying or symbolic meaning of the client's dreams.

interpretation In psychoanalysis, the therapist's attempt to explain connections between what the client discloses during therapy and his or her unconscious conflicts.

insight In Freudian theory, the realization or awareness of underlying unconscious wishes and conflicts.

resistance In psychoanalysis, the blocking that occurs when therapy touches upon anxiety-evoking thoughts or feelings.

transference relationship The tendency of clients to reenact earlier conflicted relationships in their lives in the relationships they develop with their therapists.

countertransference The tendency for therapists to relate to clients in ways that mirror the relationships they've had with important figures in their own lives.

gain insight into their unconscious conflicts and work them through—to shine the conscious light of the ego on the darkest reaches of the id. With self-insight, the ego would no longer need to maintain defensive behaviors or psychological symptoms that shield the self from the inner turmoil. The ego would then be free to focus its efforts on pursuing more constructive interests, such as work and love relationships.

Freud used psychoanalysis to probe the unconscious mind for these inner conflicts, a lengthy process that typically would take years. He believed that unconscious conflicts are not easily brought into consciousness, so he devised several techniques to help clients gain awareness of them, including free association, dream analysis, and interpretation.

Free Association. In **free association**, clients are instructed to say anything that crosses their mind, no matter how trivial or irrelevant it may seem. Freud believed these free associations would eventually work their way toward uncovering deep-seated wishes and desires that reflect underlying conflicts. In classical psychoanalysis, a client lies on a couch with the analyst sitting off to the side, out of the client's direct view, saying little. By remaining detached, the analyst hopes to create an atmosphere that encourages the client to focus inwardly on his or her own thoughts.

Dream Analysis. In **dream analysis**, the analyst helps the client gain insight into the symbolic or *latent* content of dreams, as opposed to the overt or *manifest* content (see Chapter 4). Freud called dreams the "royal road to the unconscious." He encouraged clients to freely associate to the manifest content of their dreams, hoping that doing so would lead to a better understanding of the dreams' hidden meanings.

Interpretation. **Interpretation** is an explanation of the connections between the client's behavior and verbal expressions—how the client acts and what the client says—and the client's unconscious motives and conflicts. By offering interpretations, the analyst helps the client gain **insight** into the unconscious origins of the problem.

Interpretation of the client's **resistance** plays an important role in psychoanalysis. Resistance is the blocking that occurs when therapy evokes anxiety-related thoughts and feelings that touch upon underlying conflicts or issues. The client may suddenly draw a blank when free associations touch upon sensitive areas, or "forget" to show up for an appointment when deeper issues are being discussed. Psychoanalysts interpret signs of resistance as clues to important underlying issues or concerns that need to be addressed in therapy.

The most important use of interpretation, in Freud's view, is analysis of the **transference relationship**. Freud believed that clients reenact troubled, conflicted relationships with others in the context of the relationship they develop with the analyst. A female client may respond to the analyst as a "father figure," perhaps transferring her ambivalent feelings of love and hate toward her own father onto the therapist. A young man may view the analyst as a competitor or rival, reenacting an unresolved Oedipal conflict from his childhood. By interpreting the transference relationship, the analyst raises the client's awareness about how earlier conflicted relationships intrude upon the client's present relationships. Freud believed that the client's ability to come to an understanding of the transference relationship is an essential ingredient in a successful analysis.

Transference is a two-way street. Freud himself recognized that he sometimes responded to clients in ways that carried over from his relationships with others. He called this process **countertransference** and believed that it damaged the therapeutic relationship. A male therapist, for example, may react to a male client as a competitor or rival or to a female client as a rejecting love interest.

Modern Psychodynamic Approaches: More Ego, Less Id

Traditional psychoanalysis is a lengthy, intensive process. It may require three to five sessions a week for many years. Some contemporary psychoanalysts continue to practice in much the same way as Freud did. However, many psychodynamic therapists today focus less on sexual issues and the remote past and more on the client's present relationships (Knoblauch, 2009). Moreover, because many modern analysts adopt a briefer therapy format, they tend to take a more direct approach to exploring how clients' underlying defenses and transference issues cause problems in how they relate to others—a process likened to "peeling an onion" (Gothold, 2009; Rosso, Martini, & Maina, 2012). One obvious difference is that many analysts today prefer to have their clients sit facing them, rather than lying on a couch. There is also more dialogue between analyst and client, and clients typically come to only one or two sessions a week (Grossman, 2003).

In the following exchange, we see an example of the give-and-take between a contemporary psychoanalyst and a young adult patient. The analyst focuses on the client's competitiveness with him. In an analytic framework, this competitiveness represents the transference of the client's unresolved Oedipal rivalry with his own father:

Many modern psychoanalysts have replaced the traditional couch with more direct, face-to-face verbal interactions with clients.

Client:	I continue to have success, but I have been feeling weak and tired. I saw my doctor yesterday and he said there's nothing organically wrong.
Analyst:	Does anything come to mind in relation to weak and tired feelings?
Client:	I'm thinking of the way you looked last year after you came out of the hospital. (The patient was referring to a hospitalization that, in fact, I had the previous year during which time our treatment sessions were suspended.)
Analyst:	Do you recall how you felt when you saw me looking that way?
Client:	It made me upset, even guilty.
Analyst:	But why guilty?
Client:	I'm not sure why I said that. There was nothing to feel guilty about.
Analyst:	Perhaps you had some other feelings.
Client:	Well, it's true that at one point I felt faintly pleased that I was young and vigorous and you seemed to be going downhill. . . .
Analyst:	. . . Clearly you're not very comfortable when you contrast your state with mine—to your advantage.
Client:	Well, you know, I've never felt comfortable when thinking of myself outdoing you in any way. . . .
Analyst:	. . . Perhaps your weak and tired feelings represent an identification with me brought on by your feeling guilty about your successes, since that implies that you are outdoing me. . . . Your discomfort with feeling that in certain respects you're surpassing me is posing a problem for you.

Source: Silverman, 1984, pp. 226–227.

Humanistic Therapy

Humanistic therapists believe that human beings possess free will and can make conscious choices that enrich their lives. The methods of therapy developed within the humanistic tradition emphasize the client's subjective, conscious experiences. Humanistic therapists focus on what the individual is experiencing at the particular moment in time, rather than on the distant past. It's not that they view the past as unimportant; they believe that past experiences do affect present behavior and feelings. But they emphasize that change must occur in the present, in the *here and now*. The two major forms of humanistic therapy are *client-centered therapy,* developed by Carl Rogers, and *gestalt therapy,* developed by Fritz Perls.

CONCEPT 14.6
Compared to traditional psychoanalysis, modern forms of psychodynamic therapy are briefer, allow for more interaction between therapist and client, and focus more on the ego.

CONCEPT 14.7
Humanistic therapies emphasize subjective, conscious experience and development of one's unique potential.

CONCEPT LINK
As we saw in Chapter 8, Maslow believed the highest level of human motivation involves self-actualization, the drive to realize one's unique potential. See Module 8.1.

Client-Centered Therapy

Rogers (Rogers, 1951; Raskin, Rogers, & Witty, 2011) believed that when children are valued only when they behave in ways that please others, they may become psychologically detached from parts of themselves that meet with disapproval or criticism. They may become so good at playing the "good boy" or "good girl" role that they develop a distorted self-concept—a view of themselves that does not reflect who they really are and what they truly feel. Well-adjusted people make choices that are consistent with their own unique selves, needs, and values. But people with a distorted self-concept remain largely strangers to themselves.

The form of therapy that Rogers developed, *client-centered therapy* (also called, *person-centered therapy*), focuses on the exploration of the self. Client-centered therapists seek to create a warm and accepting therapeutic environment in which clients feel safe to explore their innermost feelings and become more accepting of their true selves. The therapist takes a *nondirective* approach by allowing the client to take the lead and set the tone. The therapist's role is to reflect back the client's feelings in a supportive manner so as to encourage self-exploration and self-acceptance. Here, Rogers illustrates how a client-centered counselor uses reflection to help a client clarify and further explore her feelings:

Client: Now—one of the things that . . . had worried me was . . . living at the dorm, it's hard—not to just sort of fall in with a group of people . . . that aren't interesting, but just around. . . . So, now I find that I'm . . . getting away from that group a little bit . . . and being with a group of people . . . I really find I have more interests in common with.

Counselor: That is, you've really chosen to draw away from the group you're just thrown in with by chance, and you pick people whom you want more to associate with. Is that it?

Client: That's the idea. . . . They [my roommates] . . . had sort of pulled me in with a group of their friends that I wouldn't have picked myself, especially. And . . . so that I found that all my time was being taken up with these people, and now I'm beginning to seek out people that I prefer myself . . . rather than being drawn in with the bunch.

Counselor: You find it a little more possible, I gather, to express your real attitudes in a social situation . . . [to] make your own choice of friends. . . .

Client: . . . I tried to see if I was just withdrawing from this bunch of kids I'd been spending my time with. . . . It's not a withdrawal, but it's more of an assertion of my real interest.

Counselor: M-hm. In other words, you've tried to be self-critical in order to see if you're just running away from the situation, but you feel really, it's an expression of your positive attitudes.

Client: I—I think it is.

Source: Rogers, 1951, pp. 154–155.

Rogers believed that effective therapists display three qualities that are necessary to create an atmosphere of the emotional support needed for clients to benefit from therapy:

1. *Unconditional positive regard.* The therapist is unconditionally accepting of the client as a person, even though he or she may not approve of all the client's choices or behaviors.
2. *Empathy.* The therapist demonstrates *empathy,* the ability to accurately mirror or reflect back the client's experiences and feelings—to see the world through the client's eyes or frames of reference. By entering the client's

CONCEPT 14.8
Carl Rogers believed that for therapists to be effective, they must demonstrate empathy and unconditional positive regard for their clients as well as genuineness in their expression of feelings.

"Strip down to your ego and the doctor will be in shortly."

subjective world, the therapist encourages the client to do likewise—to get in touch with deeper feelings of which he or she may be only dimly aware.

3. *Genuineness.* The therapist is able to express genuine feelings and demonstrates that one's feelings and actions can be congruent or consistent. Even when the therapist is feeling bored or down, it is best to express these feelings, so as to encourage the client to do the same, rather than distorting true feelings or concealing them.

Gestalt Therapy

Fritz Perls (1893–1970), the originator of gestalt therapy, was trained as a psychoanalyst but became dissatisfied with the lack of emphasis on the client's subjective experiences in the present. Perls was influenced by Gestalt psychology and believed that it was important to help clients blend the conflicting parts of their personalities into an integrated whole or "gestalt" (Philippson, 2012). Unlike client-centered therapists, who attempt to create a warm and accepting atmosphere, gestalt therapists take a direct and even confrontational approach in helping clients get in touch with their underlying feelings. They repeatedly challenge clients to express how they are feeling at each moment in time—in the here and now (Francesetti et al., 2014). They don't let them off the hook by allowing them to slide into discussing events from their past or to ramble in general, abstract terms about their feelings or experiences.

Nuwatphoto/Shutterstock.com

Gestalt therapists use role-playing exercises to help clients integrate their inner feelings into their conscious experience (Nevis, 2014). In the *empty chair* technique, therapists place an empty chair in front of the clients. Clients are told to imagine that someone with whom they have had a troubled relationship (mother, father, spouse, boss) is sitting in the chair and to express their feelings toward that person. In this way, clients feel they can safely express their innermost feelings and unmet needs without fear of criticism from the other person.

Perls also had clients role-play different parts of their own personalities. One part might bark a command, like "Take chances. Get involved." A more restrained part might bark back, "Play it safe. Don't risk it." By helping the individual become more aware of these opposing parts, gestalt therapists hope to bring about an integration of the client's personality that may take the form of a compromise between opposing parts.

Behavior Therapy

In **behavior therapy** (also called *behavior modification*), therapists systematically apply principles of learning to help individuals make adaptive changes in their behavior. Behavior therapists believe that psychological problems are largely learned and thus can be unlearned. Like humanistic and cognitive therapies, behavior therapy addresses the client's present situation, not the distant past. But behavior therapy focuses directly on changing problem behaviors, rather than on exploring the client's feelings. Behavior therapy is relatively brief, usually lasting weeks or months rather than years.

Methods of Fear Reduction

Behavior therapists use several techniques to treat phobias, including systematic desensitization, gradual exposure, and modeling. In **systematic desensitization**, the client is first trained in skills needed to deeply relax muscle groups in the body. The therapist and client then work together to construct a **fear hierarchy**, which is an

CONCEPT 14.9
Fritz Perls, who developed gestalt therapy, believed that therapists should help clients blend the conflicting parts of their personalities into an integrated whole or "gestalt."

CONCEPT 14.10
Behavior therapy involves the systematic application of learning principles to weaken undesirable behaviors and strengthen adaptive behaviors.

behavior therapy A form of therapy that involves the systematic application of the principles of learning.

systematic desensitization A behavior therapy technique for treating phobias through the pairing of exposure in imagination to fear-inducing stimuli and states of deep relaxation.

fear hierarchy An ordered series of increasingly fearful objects or situations.

Through gradual exposure, people with phobias learn to handle fearful situations more effectively, sometimes assisted by a therapist or supportive others.

CONCEPT 14.11

To help people overcome phobic responses, behavior therapists use learning-based techniques such as systematic desensitization, gradual exposure, and modeling.

gradual exposure A behavior therapy technique for treating phobias based on direct exposure to a series of increasingly fearful stimuli. Also called *in-vivo* (*"real-life"*) *exposure.*

modeling A behavior therapy technique for overcoming phobias and acquiring more adaptive behaviors, based on observing and imitating models.

ordered series of fearful stimuli scaled from the least to the most fearful. For example, a person with a spider phobia might create a hierarchy that might range from looking at a picture of a spider in a book on the low end to having a harmless spider placed on the hand on the high end. The therapist then guides the client to induce deep relaxation. Once a state of deep relaxation is achieved, the client imagines confronting the least threatening stimulus in the fear hierarchy. If anxiety occurs, the client stops imagining the fearful stimulus and restores deep relaxation before trying the exercise again. When the client remains relaxed during imagined exposures to the least threatening stimulus on several trials, he or she progresses to the next stimulus in the hierarchy. This procedure is repeated for each step in the hierarchy. The objective is to use relaxation as an incompatible response to fear, so as to weaken the bonds between the stimuli and the fear they evoke.

Behavior therapists also use **gradual exposure** (also called *in vivo exposure,* meaning exposure in "real life") to help people overcome phobias. Clients progress gradually at their own pace through a series of real-life encounters with phobic stimuli in a safe environment. The exposure exercises are ordered in a hierarchy ranging from the least fearful to the most fearful situation. In this way, they learn to confront fearful situations they had previously avoided. Exposure therapy is based on a learning model that proposes that fear should extinguish (lessen or disappear) as the result of repeated exposure to fearful stimuli in the absence of disturbing consequences ("nothing bad happening").

Clients may first be taught self-relaxation skills they can use during exposure trials. They may be trained to use calming self-statements to help them cope with these encounters—statements they can repeat to themselves under their breath (for example, "I can do this. Just take a few deep breaths and the fear will pass.").

A sample hierarchy for a person with an elevator phobia might include the following steps:

1. Standing outside the elevator
2. Standing in the elevator with the door open
3. Standing in the elevator with the door closed
4. Taking the elevator down one floor
5. Taking the elevator up one floor
6. Taking the elevator down two floors
7. Taking the elevator up two floors
8. Taking the elevator down two floors and then up two floors
9. Taking the elevator down to the basement
10. Taking the elevator up to the highest floor
11. Taking the elevator all the way down and then all the way up

Gradual exposure can help people overcome specific fears, such as fear of riding on trains or elevators, as well as social phobias, such as fear of meeting new people or speaking in public (Choy, Fyer, & Lipsitz, 2007; Hofmann, 2008; McEvoy, 2008). A person with a social phobia might be instructed to create a hierarchy of fearful social situations. The person would then learn relaxation skills and begin a series of exposure trials, beginning with the least stressful social situation and working upward in the hierarchy to the most stressful situation. Gradual exposure is also used to help people with post-traumatic stress disorder (PTSD) overcome anxiety by directly confronting situations and related cues that are linked to the traumas they experienced (Cusack et al., 2015; Henslee & Coffey, 2010). (See Chapter 10 for further discussion of PTSD.)

A form of observational learning called **modeling** may be used to help people overcome fears and acquire more adaptive behaviors. Modeling involves observing and imitating desirable behaviors in others. People who lack social skills, for example, may be asked to observe more socially skillful people interacting with others. Psychologist Albert Bandura pioneered the use of modeling in helping people overcome phobias, such as fears of snakes, dogs, and other small animals (Bandura, Blanchard, & Ritter, 1969).

Behavior therapists today have adapted the technology of virtual reality to create simulated environments in which phobic people can confront virtual representations of fearful stimuli (Turner & Casey, 2014). For example, using a specialized helmet and gloves connected to a computer, a phobic person with a fear of heights can simulate a ride in a glass-enclosed virtual elevator or peer out over a virtual balcony on the 33rd floor. With this form of exposure therapy, called **virtual reality therapy**, therapists can simulate real-life environments, including some that would be difficult to arrange in reality (for example, simulated airplane takeoffs). Virtual therapy has been shown to be effective in treating a wide range of anxiety-related problems, including fear of heights, social phobia, fear of flying, and fear of spiders (for example, Anderson et al., 2013; Coelho et al., 2009; DeAngelis, 2012).

Therapists are also beginning to incorporate Internet-delivered treatments and computerized programs used in addition to traditional therapy or as stand-alone or self-guided treatments (see, for example, El Alaoui et al., 2015; Kuester, Niemeyer, & Knaevelsrud, 2016; Pennant et al., 2015; Richards et al., 2015; Silfvernagel et al., 2015; Smith et al., 2015; Spence et al., 2014; Wootton et al., 2015). In one example, researchers equipped patients with electronic devices that prompted them (like "tweets") several times a day to report about their symptoms, whether they had taken their medication, and whether they had used any drugs (Swendsen, Ben-Zeev, & Granholm, 2010). Next up are therapeutic programs embedded in smartphone apps and software programs that can be used as adjuncts (additions) to standard treatment, or even as stand-alone treatments, for psychological problems such as anxiety, depression, and even alcohol abuse (Clough & Casey, 2015; Gonzalez & Dulin, 2015). For example, apps like Beating the Blues, MoodGYM, and the Stress and Anxiety Companion are intended to help people struggling with stress and emotional problems (Berger, Boettcher, & Caspar, 2014; Eells et al., 2014). However, we need further research in order to determine whether these therapeutic apps are truly effective (Anthes, 2016; Leigh & Flatt, 2015).

Aversive Conditioning

In **aversive conditioning**, a form of classical conditioning, stimuli associated with an undesirable response are paired with aversive stimuli, such as an electric shock or a nausea-inducing drug. The idea is to make these stimuli elicit a negative response (fear or nausea) that would discourage the person from performing the undesirable behavior. For example, adults who are sexually attracted to children might receive a mild but painful electric shock when they view sexually provocative pictures of children. Or in alcoholism treatment, a nausea-inducing drug could be paired with sniffing or sipping an alcoholic beverage. A recent example showed that exposing smokers to smells of cigarettes paired with those of rotten eggs or fish reduced the amount of smoking the following day (Arzi et al., 2014). Clearly, this is not a stand-alone treatment, but these results indicate that aversive conditioning, even when implemented during sleep, may be a useful addition to a formal treatment program.

In treating alcoholism, the nausea-inducing drug is the unconditioned stimulus (US) and nausea is the unconditioned response (UR). The alcoholic beverage becomes a conditioned stimulus (CS) that elicits nausea (CR) when it is paired repeatedly with the US. Unfortunately, the effects of aversive conditioning are often temporary; outside the treatment setting, the aversive stimulus no longer accompanies the undesirable behavior. Partly for this reason, aversive conditioning is not in widespread use, although it may be useful as a component of a broader treatment program.

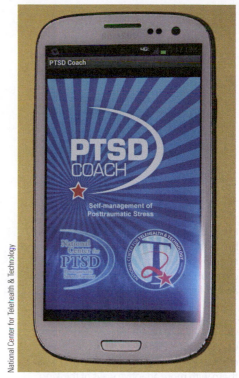

National Center for Telehealth & Technology

Therapists are now using electronic aids and apps, such as the PTSD Coach developed by the U.S. government, to help patients monitor their symptoms and access services they need.

CONCEPT 14.12
Aversive conditioning applies principles of classical conditioning to create an unpleasant response to stimuli associated with undesirable behaviors.

CONCEPT LINK
As we saw in Chapter 5, the principles of classical conditioning can be used to explain a wide range of behaviors, from fear responses to drug cravings. See Module 5.1.

CONCEPT 14.13
Behavior therapists apply operant conditioning principles to strengthen desirable behavior and weaken or eliminate undesirable behavior.

virtual reality therapy A form of exposure therapy in which virtual reality is used to simulate real-world environments.

aversive conditioning A form of behavior therapy in which stimuli associated with undesirable behavior are paired with aversive stimuli to create a negative response to these stimuli.

Operant Conditioning Methods

Behavior therapists apply operant principles of reinforcement and punishment to help strengthen desirable behavior and weaken undesirable behavior. For example, therapists may train parents to reward children for appropriate behavior and to withdraw attention (a social reinforcer) following problem behavior to weaken or eliminate it. Or they may train parents to use mild forms of punishment, such as a *time-out* procedure, in which children are removed from a rewarding environment when they misbehave and "sit out" for a prescribed period of time before resuming other activity.

In Chapter 5, you were introduced to another operant conditioning technique, the *token economy,* a behavior modification program used in mental health facilities and other settings such as schools. For example, residents of mental health facilities may receive tokens, or plastic chips, as positive reinforcers for performing certain desirable behaviors such as self-grooming, tidying their rooms, and socializing appropriately with others. Tokens can then be exchanged for tangible reinforcers such as extra privileges or candy. Token economy programs have been used successfully in mental health facilities and residential treatment facilities.

Cognitive-Behavioral Therapy

Cognitive-behavioral therapy (CBT) combines behavioral techniques, such as gradual exposure, with cognitive techniques that focus on helping clients recognize and correct faulty beliefs and ways of thinking (Rachman, 2015). Cognitive-behavioral therapists draw upon the principles and techniques of cognitive models of therapy, such as those pioneered by psychologist Albert Ellis and psychiatrist Aaron Beck, whose work we consider in the next section.

Cognitive Therapy

Cognitive therapists focus on helping people change how they think. Their techniques are based on the view that distorted or faulty ways of thinking underlie emotional problems (for example, anxiety disorders and depression) as well as self-defeating or maladaptive behavior. In short, they argue that emotional problems are not caused by negative events or life experiences but, rather, by ways in which people interpret their experiences. As William Shakespeare penned in *Hamlet,* "there is nothing either good or bad, but thinking makes it so."

Shakespeare certainly didn't mean that misfortunes are painless or easy to cope with. Rather, he seemed to imply that the ways in which we think about upsetting events can either heighten or diminish our discomfort and affect how we cope with life's misfortunes. Several hundred years later, cognitive therapists would adopt Shakespeare's simple but elegant expression as a kind of motto for their approach to therapy.

Cognitive therapies are relatively brief forms of treatment (involving months rather than years). Like practitioners of the humanistic approach, they focus more on what is happening in the present than on what happened in the distant past. Clients are given homework assignments to help them identify, evaluate, and challenge distorted thoughts as they occur and develop adaptive behaviors and rational ways of thinking. The two major cognitive therapies today are *rational emotive behavior therapy,* which was developed by Ellis, and *cognitive therapy,* which was developed by Beck.

Rational Emotive Behavior Therapy: The Importance of Thinking Rationally

Albert Ellis (1913–2007) developed **rational emotive behavior therapy (REBT)** based on his view that irrational or illogical thinking is at the root of emotional problems

---

CONCEPT 14.14

Many behavior therapists subscribe to a broader concept of behavior therapy called cognitive behavioral therapy, which focuses on changing maladaptive thoughts and beliefs as well as problem behaviors.

CONCEPT 14.15

Cognitive therapists help clients challenge maladaptive thoughts and beliefs and replace them with more adaptive ways of thinking.

Albert Ellis

cognitive-behavioral therapy (CBT) A form of therapy that combines behavioral and cognitive treatment techniques.

rational emotive behavior therapy (REBT) Developed by Albert Ellis, a form of therapy based on identifying and correcting irrational beliefs that are thought to underlie emotional and behavioral difficulties.

Table 14.2 Examples of Irrational Beliefs According to Ellis

- You absolutely must have love and approval from virtually all the people who are important to you.

- You must be completely competent in all your activities to feel worthwhile.

- It is awful and catastrophic when life does not go the way you want it to go. Things are awful when you don't get your first choices.

- People must treat each other fairly, and it is horrible when they don't.

- It's awful and terrible when there is no clear or quick solution to life's problems.

- Your past must continue to affect you and determine your behavior.

Source: Adapted from Ellis, 1991.

(Ellis, 2011; Ellis & Ellis, 2011). To overcome these problems, the therapist must teach the client to recognize these irrational beliefs and replace them with logical, self-enhancing beliefs. Ellis viewed this process as a kind of "pounding away" at the client's irrational beliefs until the client is persuaded to change these beliefs and replace them with more logical ways of thinking.

Ellis contends that irrational beliefs often take the form of *shoulds* and *musts*, such as the belief that we must have the approval of all of the important people in our lives all of the time. Ellis notes that although the desire for approval is understandable, it is irrational to believe we will always garner approval or that we couldn't possibly survive without it. REBT encourages clients to replace irrational beliefs (such as those listed in Table 14.2) with rational ones and learn more adaptive ways of dealing with their life situations.

To Ellis, negative emotional reactions, such as anxiety and depression, are not the direct result of life experiences. Rather, they stem from the irrational beliefs we hold about these experiences. Irrational beliefs are illogical because they are based on a distorted, exaggerated appraisal of the situation, not on the facts at hand. Ellis uses an "ABC" approach to explain the causes of emotional distress. This model can be diagrammed as follows:

Activating event ➜ *Beliefs* ➜ *Consequences*

Consider a person who feels worthless and depressed after getting a poor grade on a college exam (see ■ Figure 14.1). The poor grade is the *activating event* (A). The *consequences* (C), or outcomes, are feelings of depression. But the activating event (A) does not lead directly to the emotional consequences (C). Rather, the event is filtered through the person's *beliefs* (B) ("I'm just a complete jerk. I'll never succeed."). People often have difficulty identifying their underlying beliefs (B)—in part, because they are generally more aware of their feelings than what they are thinking when responding to an event (A) and, in part, because the event (A) and emotional consequences (C) occur so closely together that the event seems to be the direct cause of the emotion. People may also have difficulty focusing inwardly on their thoughts to reflect on what they are telling themselves about their experiences. Ellis recognizes

CONCEPT 14.16

Rational emotive behavior therapy is based on the view that irrational beliefs cause people to suffer emotional distress in the face of disappointing life experiences.

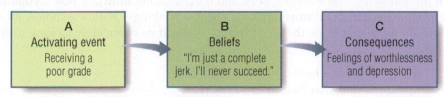

FIGURE 14.1 **The Ellis "ABC" Model**

Maria Managing Anxiety With ABC's

A Activating Event

B Beliefs & Self-Talk

"Tomorrow morning, it's my turn to give a five minute speech in class." (Activating events can be anticipated events.)

"I must do well or I'll be humiliated and feel worthless. I-can't-stand everyone watching me so closely. Why does school have to be so hard? I'll never be any good at speaking in front of people."

Causes

C Consequences:
Emotional & Behavioral Consequences

D Dispute

"My heart is speeding up; my hands are starting to tremble; and I'm starting to feel sick to my stomach just thinking about giving this impossible speech."

"My demanding that I must do well is causing me to feel really anxious. Although I don't like it, I can stand others evaluating me. If my speech isn't great, I can live with it. Besides, my teacher says I'm improving."

© Lynn Clark, SOS Help for Emotions, www.sosprograms.com

CONCEPT 14.17
Cognitive therapy focuses on helping clients identify and correct distorted thoughts and beliefs that have no basis in reality.

cognitive therapy Developed by Aaron Beck, a form of therapy that helps clients recognize and correct distorted patterns of thinking associated with negative emotional states.

that disappointment is an understandable reaction in the face of upsetting or frustrating events. But when people exaggerate the consequences of negative events, they convert disappointment into depression and despair.

Ellis later added a "D" (dispute) to the ABC model by helping clients challenge or dispute their irrational beliefs. The accompanying cartoon, "Maria Managing Anxiety with ABC's," illustrates the ABCD model in relation to a common source of anxiety, public speaking. REBT also helps people develop more effective interpersonal behaviors to replace self-defeating or maladaptive behavior. Therapists give clients specific tasks or homework assignments, such as disagreeing with an overbearing relative or asking someone for a date. They also help clients practice or rehearse more adaptive behaviors.

Cognitive Therapy: Correcting Errors in Thinking

Cognitive therapy helps people identify and correct errors in thinking and replace them with rational alternatives (Beck, 2006; Beck & Dozois, 2011; Beck & Weishaar, 2011). The developer of cognitive therapy, psychiatrist Aaron Beck (b. 1921), believes that faulty thinking about life experiences is at the root of negative emotional states such as depression. Distorted or faulty thoughts act like tinted glasses that darken a person's perceptions of life experiences (Smith, 2009).

Beck used cognitive techniques on himself long before he developed cognitive therapy. He suffered from childhood phobias that continued to plague him as an adult, including a fear of tunnels (Hunt, 1993). He traced the origin of the phobia to a fear of suffocation he had developed as a child following a severe case of whooping cough. He succeeded in overcoming the phobia by repeatedly pointing out to himself how his expectations of the dangers of traveling through tunnels had no basis in reality.

Beck refers to errors in thinking as "cognitive distortions." For example, he believes that people with depression tend to magnify or exaggerate the consequences of negative events and to blame themselves for disappointments in life while ignoring the role of external circumstances. Cognitive therapists give clients homework assignments in which they are to record the distorted thoughts that accompany their negative emotional responses and practice substituting rational alternative thoughts (see the Try This Out feature on page 539).

Another type of homework assignment is *reality testing,* in which clients are encouraged to test out their negative beliefs to determine whether they are valid. For example, a client with depression who feels unwanted by everyone might be asked to call two or three friends on the phone to gather data about how the friends react to the calls. The therapist might then ask the client to report on the assignment: "Did they immediately hang up the phone? Or did they seem pleased that you called? Did they express any interest at all in talking to you again or getting together sometime? Does the evidence support the conclusion that *no one* has any interest in you?"

In the following case example, Beck and his colleagues illustrate how a cognitive therapist challenges the distortions in a client's thinking—in this instance, all-or-nothing thinking that leads the client to judge herself as completely lacking in self-control:

Client:	I don't have any self-control at all.
Therapist:	On what basis do you say that?
Client:	Somebody offered me candy and I couldn't refuse it.

Try This Out   Replacing Distorted Thoughts with Rational Alternatives

For each of the following automatic thoughts, fill in a rational alternative response. If necessary, refer again to Table 13.1 (p. 509) for a listing of the common types of cognitive distortions. Sample rational alternatives can be found at the end of the chapter.

Automatic Thought	Type of Cognitive Distortion	Rational Alternative
1. This relationship is a disaster, a complete disaster.	All-or-nothing thinking	_____
2. I'm falling apart. I can't handle this.	Catastrophizing	_____
3. Things must really be awful for me to feel this way.	Emotion-based reasoning	_____
4. I know I'm going to flunk this course.	Jumping to conclusions	_____
5. _____'s problems are really my fault.	Mistaken responsibility	_____
6. I'm just a loser.	Name-calling	_____
7. Someone my age should be further along than I am.	Shouldism	_____
8. It would be awful if I don't get this job.	Catastrophizing	_____
9. I know that if _____ got to know me, he/she would not like me.	Jumping to conclusions	_____
10. All I can think about are the negatives.	Negative focusing	_____

Therapist: Were you eating candy every day?

Client: No, I just ate it this once.

Therapist: Did you do anything constructive during the past week to adhere to your diet?

Client: Well, I didn't give in to the temptation to buy candy every time I saw it at the store. . . . Also, I did not eat any candy except that one time when it was offered to me and I felt I couldn't refuse it.

Therapist: If you counted up the number of times you controlled yourself versus the number of times you gave in, what ratio would you get?

Client: About 100 to 1.

Therapist: So if you controlled yourself 100 times and did not control yourself just once, would that be a sign that you are weak through and through?

Client: I guess not—not through and through [smiles].

Source: Adapted from Beck et al., 1979, p. 68.

Aaron Beck

REBT and cognitive therapy are similar in many respects. Both focus primarily on helping people replace dysfunctional thoughts and beliefs with more adaptive, rational ones. The major difference may be one of therapeutic style: The REBT therapist typically adopts a more direct and sometimes confrontational approach in disputing the client's irrational beliefs, whereas the cognitive therapist usually takes a gentler, more collaborative approach to help clients identify and correct distortions in their thinking.

The differences between specific psychotherapies are not as clear-cut as they may seem. On the one hand, there is a blurring of lines between cognitive and behavioral therapies in the sense that we can classify the cognitive therapies of Ellis and Beck as forms of cognitive-behavioral therapy. Both rely on behavioral and cognitive techniques to help people develop more adaptive behaviors and to change dysfunctional thinking patterns. On the other hand, many therapists identify themselves with an even broader eclectic approach, as we will see next.

Eclectic Therapy

Therapists who practice **eclectic therapy** look beyond the theoretical barriers that divide one school of psychotherapy from another. They integrate principles and techniques representing different approaches in designing treatments they believe would provide the maximum benefits for a particular client (Prochaska & Norcross, 2010). In a particular case, an eclectic therapist might use behavior therapy to help a client change problem behaviors and psychodynamic approaches to help the client develop insight into underlying conflicts.

Eclecticism is the second most popular therapeutic orientation among clinical psychologists, according to results of a recent survey of clinical psychologists (see ■ Figure 14.2). Eclectic therapists may have learned through experience the value of drawing upon different points of view.

Not all therapists subscribe to an eclectic approach. Many believe that the differences between schools of therapy are so compelling that therapeutic integration is neither desirable nor achievable. Trying to combine them, they argue, leads to a veritable hodgepodge of techniques that lacks a cohesive conceptual framework. Nevertheless, the movement toward eclecticism continues to grow within the therapeutic community.

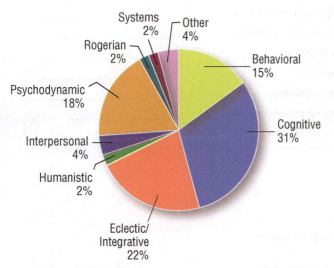

FIGURE 14.2 Therapeutic Orientations of Clinical Psychologists

According to a recent survey of clinical psychologists, the integrative/eclectic orientation is the second most widely endorsed therapeutic orientation (at 22 percent), after cognitive (31 percent).

Source: Adapted from Norcross & Karpiak (2012).

eclectic therapy A therapeutic approach that draws upon principles and techniques representing different schools of therapy.

group therapy A form of therapy in which clients are treated within a group format.

family therapy Therapy for troubled families that focuses on changing disruptive patterns of communication and improving the ways in which family members relate to each other.

Group, Family, and Couple Therapy

Group therapy brings people together in small groups to help them explore and resolve their problems. Compared to individual therapy, it offers several advantages. For one thing, because the therapist treats several people at a time, group therapy is generally less costly than individual therapy. For another, it may be particularly helpful for people experiencing interpersonal problems such as loneliness, shyness, and low self-esteem. These individuals often benefit from interacting with supportive others in a group treatment program. The give-and-take within the group may help improve a member's social skills. And clients in group therapy can learn how others in the group have coped with similar problems in their lives.

Group therapy may not be for everyone. Some clients prefer the individual attention of a therapist. They may feel that one-on-one therapy provides an opportunity for a deeper exploration of their emotions and experiences. They may also be reluctant to disclose their personal problems to other members of a group. Or they may feel too inhibited to relate comfortably to others in a group, even if they themselves are perhaps the ones for whom group interaction is most beneficial.

Group therapists can offset some of these drawbacks by creating an atmosphere that promotes trust and self-exploration. In particular, they require that information disclosed by group members is kept in strict confidence, ensure that group members relate to each other in a supportive and nondestructive fashion, and prevent any single member from monopolizing their attention or dominating the group. In short, effective group therapists attempt to provide each member with the attention he or she needs.

Family therapy helps troubled families learn to communicate better and resolve their differences. The family, not the individual, is the unit of treatment. Family therapists view the family unit as a complex social system in which individuals play certain roles (Gehar, 2009). In many cases, there is one family member whom the family brands as the source of the family's problems. Effective family therapists demonstrate how the problems of this individual are symptomatic of larger problems in the family involving a breakdown in the family system, not in the individual per se. They help dysfunctional families change how family members interact and relate to one another so that members can become more accepting and supportive of each other's needs and differences.

In **couple therapy** (often called *marital therapy* when applied to married couples), the couple is the unit of the treatment. Couple therapy builds healthier relationships by helping couples learn to communicate better and work out solutions to their problems (Baucom et al., 2015; Doss et al., 2015). Couple therapists identify power struggles and lack of communication as among the typical problems faced by troubled couples seeking help. Their aim is to help open channels of communication between partners and encourage them to share personal feelings and needs in ways that do not put each other down.

Group therapy brings together small groups of people to help them explore and work through their psychological problems.

Is Psychotherapy Effective?

Yes, psychotherapy works. A wealth of scientific findings supports the effectiveness of psychotherapy. Yet questions remain about whether some forms of therapy are more effective than others.

Measuring Effectiveness

The strongest body of evidence supporting the effectiveness of psychotherapy comes from controlled studies in which people who received psychotherapy are compared with those who were placed in waiting-list control groups. Investigators commonly use a statistical technique called **meta-analysis** to average the results across a large number of such studies.

An early but influential meta-analysis was conducted by Mary Lee Smith, Gene Glass, and Thomas Miller (1980). Based on an analysis of more than 400 controlled studies comparing particular types of therapy (psychodynamic, behavioral, humanistic, and so on) against control groups, they reported that the average person receiving psychotherapy achieved better outcomes than did 80 percent of people in waiting-list control groups (see ■ Figure 14.3). More recent meta-analyses also point to better outcomes for people treated with psychotherapy than for those in control groups (see, for example, Cuijpers et al., 2010; Driessen et al., 2010; Shedler, 2010; Town et al., 2012).

The greatest gains in therapy are typically achieved during the first few months of treatment. Fifty percent of people who participate in psychotherapy show significant improvement within the first 21 sessions (Anderson & Lambert, 2001; Lambert, Hansen, & Finch, 2001). Many other patients respond with additional treatment. But not everyone benefits from therapy, and some people even deteriorate. Then too, we should recognize that some people who receive other forms of treatment, such as drug therapy, have negative outcomes.

Which Therapy Is Best?

To say that therapy overall is effective does not mean that all therapies are equally effective, or that one form of therapy is as good as any other for a particular problem. Using the statistical tool of meta-analysis, investigators find that different forms of psychotherapy produce about the same magnitude or size of effects (benefits) when

CONCEPT 14.20

A wealth of scientific findings supports the effectiveness of psychotherapy, but questions remain about whether some forms of therapy are more effective than others.

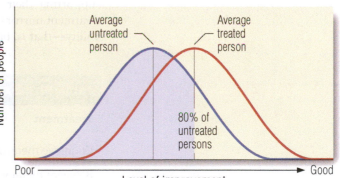

FIGURE 14.3 Effectiveness of Psychotherapy
A meta-analysis of more than 400 outcome studies showed that the average therapy client achieved greater improvement than 80 percent of untreated controls.

Source: Adapted from Smith, Glass, & Miller, 1980.

couple therapy Therapy that focuses on helping distressed couples resolve their conflicts and develop more effective communication skills.

meta-analysis A statistical technique for averaging results across a large number of studies.

they are compared with control groups or with one another (Kivlighan et al., 2015; Wampold et al., 2011).

Does this mean that different therapies are about equally effective? Not necessarily. For one thing, cognitive-behavioral therapy (CBT) seems to have a slight edge overall in comparison to other treatment approaches (Marcus et al., 2014). But we also need to ask which therapy works best for which particular problems. For example, evidence shows that CBT works well in treating a wide range of disorders, including panic disorder, social anxiety, phobias, posttraumatic stress disorder, obsessive-compulsive disorder, depression, and bulimia (see, for example, Barth et al., 2016; Crino, 2015; Glasofer & Devlin, 2013; Hofmann et al., 2012; McKay et al., 2014; Mørkved et al., 2014; Öst et al., 2015; Rapee et al., 2013; Thimm & Antonsen, 2014; Weitz et al., 2015).

Evidence also supports the effectiveness of contemporary forms of psychodynamic therapy in treating psychological disorders such as depression, borderline personality disorder, social anxiety disorder, and bulimia (see, for example, Bögels et al., 2014; Driessen et al., 2015; Keefe et al., 2014; Leichsenring et al., 2013, 2014; Leichsenring & Schauenburg, 2014; Poulsen et al., 2014; Shedler, 2010). Humanistic therapies may have their greatest benefits in helping individuals develop a more cohesive sense of self, connect with their innermost feelings, and mobilize their efforts toward self-actualization.

The Movement Toward Evidence-Based Treatments

A major development in recent years is the growing emphasis on evidence-based treatments or EBTs—that is, treatments shown to be effective in carefully designed empirical studies (Church et al., 2014; McHugh & Barlow, 2010). A partial listing of these evidence-based therapies, which are also called *empirically supported treatments*, or ESTs, is shown in Table 14.3. Other treatments may be added to the list as evidence supporting their effectiveness becomes available. The emphasis on evidence-based treatment mirrors the larger concern in the health community on the need for accountability—that is, basing practice on treatments that have been shown to work.

Table 14.3 Examples of Empirically Supported Treatments (ESTs)

Treatment	Effective in Treating
Cognitive therapy	Depression
Behavior therapy	Depression
	People with developmental disabilities
	Enuresis ("bed-wetting")
	Headache
	Agoraphobia and specific phobia
	Obsessive-compulsive disorder
Cognitive-behavioral therapy (CBT)	Panic disorder
	Generalized anxiety disorder
	Bulimia
	Smoking cessation
Interpersonal psychotherapy (a structured brief form of psychodynamic therapy)	Depression

What Accounts for the Benefits of Therapy?

Might the benefits of therapy have to do with the common characteristics shared by different therapies? These common characteristics are called **nonspecific factors** because they are not limited to any one therapy. They include a positive expectation of treatment success, as well as aspects of the interpersonal relationship between client and therapist, such as the *therapeutic alliance*—that is, the attachment the client feels toward the therapist and the therapy (Goldfried, 2012; Norcross & Lambert, 2014). The quality of the therapeutic alliance is strongly associated with better outcomes in therapy (see, for example, Arnow et al., 2013; Laska, Gurman, & Wampold, 2014; Zilcha-Mano et al., 2014). Having a positive expectancy or sense of hopefulness that problems can be overcome can become a self-fulfilling prophecy by motivating clients to mobilize their efforts to resolve their problems. Responses to positive expectancies are called **placebo effects** or *expectancy effects*. In all likelihood, the benefits of psychotherapy involve a combination of specific factors, such as the particular techniques used, and nonspecific factors (for example, Raykos et al., 2014).

Multicultural Issues in Treatment

In our multicultural society, therapists treat people from diverse ethnic and racial groups. Members of ethnic and racial minorities may have different customs, beliefs, and philosophies than members of the dominant majority culture, and therapists must be aware of these differences to provide successful treatment (Alarcón, Oquendo, & Wainberg, 2014; Hwang, 2011). For example, with African American clients, therapists need to understand the long history of extreme racial discrimination and oppression to which African Americans have been exposed in our society. This history of negative treatment and cultural oppression may lead African Americans to develop a heightened sense of suspiciousness or reserve toward Whites, including White therapists, as a type of coping skill—a defense against exploitation. They may thus be hesitant to disclose personal information in therapy, especially during the early stages. Therapists should not press for disclosure or confuse culturally laden suspiciousness with paranoid thinking.

The traditional value in Asian cultures of keeping one's feelings to oneself, especially negative emotions, may conflict with the emphasis in psychotherapy on open expression of emotions. Culturally competent therapists recognize that Asian clients who appear passive or emotionally restrained when judged by Western standards may be responding in ways that are culturally appropriate and should not be judged as shy, uncooperative, or avoidant (Hwang, 2006). Moreover, the emphasis on collective or group values in Asian cultures over those of the individual may conflict with the emphasis in Western psychotherapy on the importance of individuality and self-determination.

Value conflicts may also come into play in therapeutic situations involving Latinos from traditional Hispanic backgrounds. Traditional Hispanic cultures place a strong value on interdependency among family members—a value that may clash with the emphasis on independence and self-reliance in mainstream U.S. culture. Treatment providers need to be respectful of this difference and avoid imposing their own values on Latino clients. In working with Latinos as well as other ethnic groups, therapists must also be sensitive to the linguistic preferences of the people they serve.

Culturally sensitive therapists also need to respect and understand the customs, cultures, and values of the people they treat (Chu et al., 2016; Kaufman et al., 2013). In working with Native Americans, for example, they may find it helpful to bring elements of tribal culture into the therapy setting, such as healing ceremonies that are part of the client's cultural or religious traditions. Native American clients may

CONCEPT 14.21
Evidence points to both specific and nonspecific factors in accounting for the benefits of psychotherapy.

CONCEPT 14.22
Therapists are trained to be sensitive to cultural differences among the different groups of people they treat.

nonspecific factors General features of psychotherapy, such as attention from a therapist and mobilization of positive expectancies or hope.

placebo effects Positive outcomes of an experiment resulting from a participant's positive expectations about the treatment rather than from the treatment itself.

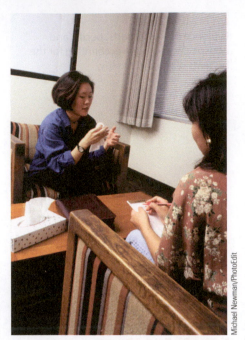

Michael Newman/PhotoEdit

Culturally sensitive therapy is structured to create a more receptive therapeutic environment for people from varied cultural backgrounds.

expect therapists to do most of the talking, consistent with the traditional healer role within their culture.

Therapists also need to demonstrate that treatment methods they use work effectively with members of particular ethnic groups they treat (see, for example, Chavira et al., 2014; Collado, Lim, & MacPherson, 2016; Windsor, Jemal, & Alessi, 2015). In short, therapists need to adapt their treatment approaches to clients from diverse backgrounds. Therapists also need to be aware of their own cultural biases to avoid stereotyping clients from other cultural groups. When a therapist's own cultural biases are left unexamined, they can quickly become destructive of the therapeutic relationship.

The mental health system also needs to do a better job of providing quality care to all groups. An influential report by the U.S. Surgeon General concluded that minority group members typically receive lower quality care and have less access to care than other Americans (U.S. Department of Health and Human Services, 2001; see Table 14.4). Consequently, minority group members typically shoulder a greater mental health burden because their mental disorders go undiagnosed and untreated.

Table 14.4 Disparities in Mental Health Care: Culture, Race, and Ethnicity

Disparities

- As compared to other groups, racial or ethnic minorities have less access to mental health care and receive lower quality care.

Causes

- Minority group members are more likely to lack health insurance.

- Minority group members lack access to treatment providers who are similar in ethnicity or who possess appropriate language skills.

- The lingering stigma about mental illness discourages minority group members from seeking help.

- Few treatment providers are in rural or isolated locations where minority group members, especially Native Americans, may reside.

Vision for the Future

- Expand the scientific base to better understand relationships between mental health and sociocultural factors such as acculturation, stigma, and racism.

- Improve access to treatment—for example, by improving language access and geographic availability of mental health services.

- Reduce barriers to mental health care, such as costs of services and the societal stigma toward mental illness.

- Improve quality of care—for example, by individualizing treatment to the person's age, gender, race, ethnicity, and culture.

- Increase minority representation among mental health treatment providers.

- Promote mental health by strengthening supportive families and working to eradicate contributors to mental health problems, such as poverty, community violence, racism, and discrimination.

Source: U.S. Department of Health and Human Services, 2001.

Concept Chart 14.1 summarizes the differences among the types of psychotherapy discussed in this module.

Concept Chart 14.1	Major Types of Psychotherapy: How They Differ			

David Buffington/Getty images

Type of Therapy	Focus	Length	Therapist's Role	Techniques
Classical psychoanalysis	Insight into unconscious causes of behavior	Long, at least several years	Passive, interpretive	Free association, dream analysis, interpretation
Modern psychodynamic approaches	Insight-oriented, but focus is more on ego functioning and current relationships than is the case in Freudian psychoanalysis	Briefer than traditional analysis	Probing; engaging client in back-and-forth discussion	More direct analysis of client's defenses and transference relationships; less use of free association
Humanistic, client-centered therapy	Promotes self-growth by helping clients become more aware of, and accepting of, their inner feelings, needs, and interests	Varies	Nondirective; allows client to lead, with therapist serving as an empathic listener	Demonstrating empathy, unconditional positive regard, and genuineness to create a warm and accepting therapeutic atmosphere
Humanistic, gestalt therapy	Helps clients develop a unified sense of self by bringing into present awareness their true feelings and conflicts with others	Brief, sometimes only a few sessions	Directive, engaging, even confrontational	Empty chair technique and other role-playing exercises
Behavior therapy	Changes problem behavior through use of learning-based techniques tailored to the specific problem	Brief, lasting perhaps 10 to 20 sessions	Direct, active problem solving	Systematic desensitization, exposure therapy, aversion therapy, operant conditioning techniques
Cognitive-behavioral therapy	Focuses on changing both maladaptive cognitions and overt behaviors	Brief, usually lasting 10 to 20 sessions	Direct, active problem solving	Combines cognitive and behavioral techniques
Rational emotive behavior therapy	Helps clients replace irrational beliefs with more adaptive, logical alternatives	Brief, typically 10 to 20 sessions	Directive, challenging, sometimes confrontational	Identifying and disputing irrational beliefs, with behavioral homework assignments
Cognitive therapy	Helps clients identify and correct faulty styles of thinking	Brief, typically 10 to 20 sessions	Collaborative process of engaging client in an effort to logically examine beliefs and find evidence to support or refute them	Identifying and correcting distorted thoughts; specific homework assignments including thought recording and reality testing

Getting Help

CONCEPT 14.23
Though consumers face a bewildering array of mental health services providers, they can do a number of things to ensure that they receive quality care.

© Marcin Balcerzak/Shutterstock.com

In most areas in the United States and Canada, telephone and Internet directories have pages upon pages of clinics and health professionals. Many people have no idea whom to call for help. If you don't know where to go or whom to see, you can take a number of steps to ensure that you receive appropriate care.

1. *Seek recommendations from respected sources,* such as your family physician, course instructor, clergyperson, or college health service.

2. *Seek a referral from a local medical center or local community mental health center.* When making inquiries, ask about the services that are available or about opportunities for referral to qualified treatment providers in the area.

3. *Seek a consultation with your college counseling center or health services center.* Most colleges and universities offer psychological assistance to students, generally without charge.

4. *Contact professional organizations for recommendations.* Many local or national organizations maintain a referral list of qualified treatment providers in your area. If you would like to consult a psychologist, contact the American Psychological Association in Washington, DC (by telephone at 202-336-5650 or on the Internet at www.apa.org), and ask for local referrals in your area. Alternatively, you can call your local or state psychology association in the United States or your provincial or territorial psychological association in Canada.

5. *Let your fingers or computer mouse do the walking—but be careful!* Look under "psychologists," "physicians," "social workers," or "marriage, family, child, and individual counselors," in the Yellow Pages or online listings. However, be wary of professionals who take out large ads and claim to be experts in treating many different kinds of problems.

6. *Make sure the treatment provider is a licensed member of a recognized mental health profession, such as psychology, medicine, counseling, or social work.* In many states, anyone can set up practice as a "therapist," even as a "psychotherapist." These titles may not be limited by law to licensed practitioners. Licensed professionals clearly display their licenses and other credentials in their offices, usually in plain view. If you have any questions about the licensure status of a treatment provider, contact the licensing board in your state, province, or territory.

7. *Inquire about the type of therapy being provided (for example, psychoanalysis, family therapy, behavior therapy).* Ask the treatment provider to explain how his or her particular type of therapy is appropriate to treating the problems you are having.

8. *Inquire about the treatment provider's professional background.* Ask about the person's educational background, supervised experience, and credentials. An ethical practitioner will not hesitate to provide this information.

9. *Inquire whether the treatment provider has had experience treating other people with similar problems.* Ask about their results and how they were measured.

10. *Once the treatment provider has had the opportunity to conduct a formal evaluation of your problem, discuss the diagnosis and treatment plan before making any commitments to undertake treatment.*

11. *Ask about costs and insurance coverage.* Ask what types of insurance the provider accepts and whether co-payments are required on your part. Ask whether the provider will adjust his or her fees on a sliding scale that takes your income and family situation into account. If you are eligible for Medicaid or Medicare, inquire whether the treatment provider accepts these types of coverage. College students may also be covered by their parents' health insurance plans or by student plans offered by their colleges. Find out if the treatment provider participates in any health maintenance organization to which you may belong.

12. *Find out about the treatment provider's policies regarding charges for missed or canceled sessions.*

13. *If medication is to be prescribed, find out how long a delay is expected before it starts working.* Also inquire about possible side effects, and about which side effects should prompt you to call with questions. Don't be afraid to seek a second opinion before undergoing any course of medication.

14. *If the treatment recommendations don't sound quite right to you, discuss your concerns openly.* An ethical professional will be willing to address your concerns rather than feeling insulted.

15. *If you still have any doubts, request a second opinion.* An ethical professional will support your efforts to seek a second opinion. Ask the treatment provider to recommend other professionals—or select your own.

16. *Be wary of online therapy services.* The use of online counseling and therapy services, as well as self-guided smartphone apps and Internet-based therapy modules, is growing rapidly, even as psychologists and other mental health professionals raise the yellow flag of caution. Counselors and therapists are offering help to people with emotional problems via Skype, email, video calls, and other electronic means. Concerns arise because unqualified practitioners may be taking advantage of unwary consumers, as we lack a system for ensuring that online therapists have the appropriate credentials and licensure to practice. Moreover, conducting treatment sessions by typing on a computer or using a cell phone may prevent therapists from evaluating the many nonverbal cues and gestures they can observe in face-to-face sessions that might signal deeper levels of emotional distress (Drum & Littleton, 2014). Many of the self-help therapy apps on the market today also lack solid evidence supporting their effectiveness. Despite these concerns, many psychologists believe that electronic means of providing therapy and counseling services can have therapeutic value when proper safeguards and evidence of effectiveness are established.

Blend Images/Alamy Stock Photo

Would you be willing to Skype a therapist? Why or why not?

MODULE REVIEW   14.1   Types of Psychotherapy

Recite It

1. **Identify** the major types of mental health professionals.

   The major types of professionals who provide mental health services are clinical and (a) _____ psychologists, psychiatrists, clinical or psychiatric social workers, psychoanalysts, counselors, and (b) _____. They vary in their training backgrounds as well as in the services they provide.

2. **Define** psychotherapy.

   Psychotherapy is a (c) _____ form of therapy intended to help people overcome psychological or personal problems.

3. **Identify** the major types of psychotherapy and the developers of these therapies and **describe** techniques used in these different types of psychotherapy.

   Psychodynamic therapy is an insight-oriented approach to therapy based on Freud's model, which he called (d) _____. The psychodynamic therapist helps clients uncover and work through the (e) _____ conflicts dating from childhood that are believed to be at the root of their problems.
   Carl Rogers was the major developer of (f) _____ therapy, which focuses primarily on the client's subjective, (g) _____ experience in the here and now.
   Behavior therapy involves the systematic application of (h) _____ principles to help people unlearn maladaptive behaviors and acquire more adaptive behaviors. The techniques of behavior therapy include (i) _____ desensitization, gradual exposure, modeling, aversive conditioning, and methods based on operant conditioning. Cognitive-behavioral therapy is a broader form of behavior therapy that incorporates both behavioral and (j) _____ techniques in treatment. Cognitive therapies, such as rational emotive behavior therapy (REBT) developed by Albert (k) _____ and cognitive therapy developed by Aaron (l) _____, focus on modifying the individual's maladaptive thoughts and beliefs that are believed to underlie emotional problems, such as anxiety and depression, and self-defeating or maladaptive forms of behavior.
   In (m) _____ therapy, therapists adopt principles or techniques from different schools of therapy.

4. **Identify** and **describe** forms of therapy that involve more than the individual client.

   (n) _____ therapy is a form of psychotherapy in which several individuals receive treatment at the same time in a group format.

   (o) _____ therapy helps conflicted families learn to resolve their differences, clarify communications, resolve role conflicts, and avoid tendencies toward _____ individual family members.

   (p) _____ therapy is used to help distressed couples improve their communication skills and resolve their differences.

5. **Evaluate** evidence regarding the effectiveness of psychotherapy.

   (q) _____-analyses show that people who participate in psychotherapy are more likely to achieve a good outcome than those who remain untreated. There is a continuing debate about whether some forms of therapy are better than others. Evidence supports the effectiveness of particular forms of therapy, called (r) _____ supported treatments, for specific disorders.

6. **Identify** and **describe** cultural factors that affect the practice of psychotherapy.

   Cultural factors to be considered include differences in (s) _____ beliefs, customs, values, and linguistic preferences between therapists and clients, as well as the therapists' own cultural biases and (t) _____ tendencies.

7. **Apply** steps you can take to obtain help for a psychological problem.

   Seek recommendations from respected sources or a (u) _____ from a local medical center or local community mental health center, seek a consultation with your college (v) _____ center or health services center, contact professional organizations for recommendations or (carefully) use the Yellow Pages or other directories, check out the provider's licensure status, find out about the type of therapy provided and about the provider's professional background and experience in treating similar types of problems, ask about costs and insurance coverage and cancellation fees, and if medication is prescribed, inquire about possible side effects and length of time before it starts working, directly discuss any concerns you may have with the mental health provider, and if you have doubts, seek a (w) _____ opinion.

Recall It

1. Match the following concepts from psychodynamic therapy with the appropriate descriptions: (a) free association; (b) insight; (c) resistance; (d) transference relationship.

   i. understanding the unconscious origins of a problem
   ii. responding to the analyst as a "father figure"
   iii. blocking that occurs when emotionally sensitive topics arise
   iv. saying whatever comes to mind

2. Name three important qualities shown by an effective client-centered therapist.

3. Jonathan's therapist trains him to use deep muscle relaxation and helps him construct a fear hierarchy. Which behavior therapy technique is the therapist likely to be using?

4. The form of therapy that holds that irrational beliefs underlie the development of psychological problems is _____.

5. List two advantages and two disadvantages of group therapy.

Think About It

■ Which approach to therapy would you prefer if you were seeking help for a psychological problem? Why would you prefer this approach?

■ What cultural factors should therapists take into account when providing services to members of diverse cultural or racial groups?

Recite It answers placed at the end of chapter.

MODULE ## 14.2 Biomedical Therapies

8 **Identify** the major classes of psychiatric drugs and specific drugs in each class.

9 **Evaluate** the advantages and disadvantages of these drugs.

10 **Describe** other forms of biomedical therapy and **explain** why they are controversial.

11 **Describe** the functions of the modern community mental health center.

12 **Evaluate** whether the policy of deinstitutionalization has been successful.

Remarkable gains have been made in treating a wide range of psychological disorders with biomedical forms of treatment, which most often involve the use of **psychotropic drugs** (also called *psychiatric* or *psychotherapeutic drugs*). Today, about one in five adults in the United States are taking psychotropic drugs (Smith, 2012). Despite their success, psychiatric drugs have limitations, including unwelcome side effects and potential for abuse. Other forms of biomedical treatment, such as electroconvulsive therapy (ECT) and psychosurgery, are more controversial.

Drug Therapy

Neurotransmitters ferry nerve impulses from one neuron to another. But irregularities in the workings of neurotransmitters in the brain are implicated in a wide range of psychological disorders, including anxiety disorders, mood disorders, eating disorders, and schizophrenia. Scientists have developed drugs that work on neurotransmitters in the brain to help regulate moods and thinking processes. These drugs, called *psychotropic drugs* or *psychiatric drugs,* help relieve symptoms of psychological disorders ranging from panic disorder to depression to schizophrenia. However, they are not cures. There are three major groupings of psychotropic drugs: *antianxiety drugs*, *antidepressants*, and *antipsychotics*.

psychotropic drugs Psychiatric drugs used in the treatment of psychological or mental disorders.

Zigy Kaluzny/Stone/Getty Images

CONCEPT 14.24
Psychotropic drugs work on neurotransmitter systems in the brain to help regulate moods and thinking processes.

CONCEPT LINK
As we saw in Chapter 2, neurotransmitters are chemicals that carry nerve messages from neuron to neuron. See Module 2.1.

CONCEPT 14.25
Three major classes of psychotropic drugs are antianxiety drugs, antidepressants, and antipsychotics.

CONCEPT LINK
As we saw in Chapter 2, these psychotropic drugs work as either agonists or antagonists depending on their actions on particular neurotransmitter systems. See Module 2.1.

Antianxiety Drugs

Antianxiety drugs (sometimes called *minor tranquilizers*) help quell anxiety, induce calmness, and reduce muscle tension. The most widely used antianxiety drugs are minor tranquilizers such as *diazepam* (Valium), *chlordiazepoxide* (Librium), and *alprazolam* (Xanax). They act on the neurotransmitter *gamma-aminobutyric acid*—or GABA for short (first discussed in Chapter 2). GABA is an inhibitory neurotransmitter, which means that it inhibits the flow of nerve impulses and thus prevents neurons in the brain from overly exciting their neighbors. The most widely used antianxiety drugs, including Valium, Librium, and Xanax, make GABA receptors more sensitive, which enhances the chemical's calming (inhibitory) effects.

Antidepressants

Antidepressants increase levels of the neurotransmitters norepinephrine and serotonin in the brain. There are three major types of antidepressants: **tricyclics, monoamine oxidase (MAO) inhibitors**, and **selective serotonin reuptake inhibitors (SSRIs)**.

The tricyclics, which include *imipramine* (Tofranil) and *amitriptyline* (Elavil), raise brain levels of norepinephrine and serotonin by interfering with the reuptake process by which these chemical messengers are reabsorbed by the transmitting cells. MAO inhibitors, which include *phenelzine* (Nardil) and *tranylcypromine* (Parnate), inhibit the action of the enzyme *monoamine oxidase,* which normally breaks down (degrades) these neurotransmitters in the synapse. The SSRIs, which include *fluoxetine* (Prozac) and *sertraline* (Zoloft), have more specific effects on raising levels of serotonin in the brain by interfering with its reuptake. These drugs increase the availability of serotonin in the synaptic gap between neurons, which increases the activity of serotonin neurons in the brain. Although tricyclics and SSRIs are about equally effective, the SSRIs are generally preferred because they typically produce less severe side effects and are less dangerous in overdose situations (Gartlehner et al., 2008; Mori, Lockwood, & McCall, 2015).

Did you know that antidepressants are used in treating other psychological disorders besides depression? These drugs have therapeutic effects in treating a wide range of disorders, including bulimia nervosa, panic disorder, social phobia, post-traumatic stress disorder, generalized anxiety disorder, and obsessive-compulsive disorder (see, for example, Grant, 2014; Maia & Cano-Colino, 2015; Pampaloni et al., 2009; Stein & Sareen, 2015). Why do antidepressants have such broad-ranging effects? One reason is that neurotransmitters, especially serotonin, are involved in regulating emotional states such as anxiety and depression. Another reason, as noted in Chapter 8, is that serotonin plays a key role in regulating appetite. Antidepressants such as Zoloft that specifically target this neurotransmitter may help reduce episodes of binge eating associated with bulimia (Mitchell, Roerig, & Steffen, 2013).

Antipsychotics

Antipsychotics (sometimes called *major tranquilizers*) are powerful drugs used to treat schizophrenia and other psychotic disorders. The first class of antipsychotic drugs were *phenothiazines,* which included the drugs Thorazine and Mellaril. The introduction of these drugs in the 1950s revolutionized the treatment of schizophrenia, making it possible to control the more flagrant symptoms of the disorder, such as hallucinations and delusions. With their symptoms largely controlled on maintenance doses of these drugs, many patients with schizophrenia were able to leave the confines of state hospitals and return to their families and communities.

Phenothiazines and a newer generation of antipsychotic drugs (called "atypical" antipsychotics) block the action of the neurotransmitter dopamine at receptor sites in the brain. Though the underlying causes of schizophrenia remain unknown, researchers suspect that the disorder arises from disturbances in neural pathways that utilize dopamine (see Chapter 13).

The newer generation of atypical antipsychotics (for example, *clozapine*, *risperidone*, and *olanzapine*) are about as effective as phenothiazines but have largely replaced the earlier drugs because they carry fewer neurological side effects (McEvoy et al., 2014; Rosenheck & Lin, 2014).

Other Psychiatric Drugs

Mood-stabilizing drugs, such as the powdered form of the metallic element *lithium*, help stabilize mood swings in people with bipolar disorder and reduce the risks of recurrent manic episodes (Lichta, 2010; Ogawa et al., 2014). Other mood stabilizers include anticonvulsant drugs that are also used in the treatment of epilepsy (Reid et al., 2013).

Stimulant drugs, such as Ritalin and Concerta, are used to improve attention spans and reduce disruptive behavior in hyperactive children. Nearly 7 percent of young people in the 6- to 17-year age range are now receiving stimulant medications (Olfson, Druss, & Marcus, 2015). These drugs appear to work by increasing activity of the neurotransmitter dopamine in the frontal lobes of the cerebral cortex, the parts of the brain that regulate attention and control impulsive or acting-out behavior (Devilbiss & Berridge, 2008).

Evaluating Psychotropic Drugs

Therapeutic drugs can provide some relief from troubling psychological symptoms, but they are not panaceas. None produces a cure, nor do all patients respond well to them. Although antidepressants can help relieve depression, their effects are not nearly as dramatic as we see represented in many drug commercials on TV (Kennedy, Young, & Blier, 2011; McClintock et al., 2011). Complete relief from depression occurs in fewer than 40 percent of patients treated with antidepressant medication alone (Anthes, 2014).

Another limitation of psychiatric drugs is that relapses are quite common when patients stop taking them (Donovan et al., 2010). Relapses occur even among patients who continue to take psychiatric drugs (Mulder et al., 2009). One reason why relapses are so common is that psychiatric drugs do not teach patients new skills they can use to solve their problems, handle stress, and cope with disappointments they may face in the future. Relapses may be lessened if psychological treatment is combined with use of psychiatric drugs (Guidi, Tomba, & Fava, 2016). The bottom line is that we cannot expect to solve the problems we face in life with a pill (Sroufe, 2012).

Psychiatric drugs also carry risks of some troubling side effects, including drowsiness (from antianxiety drugs), dry mouth and problems with sexual response (from antidepressants), and muscular tremors, rigidity, and even severe movement disorders (from antipsychotic drugs). Drugs can also have adverse, sometimes even dangerous, effects. For example, use of antidepressants may increase the risk of suicidal thinking or behavior in children and adolescents (Brent & Gibbons, 2014; Friedman, 2014; Miller et al., 2014). Lithium needs to be closely monitored because of potential toxic effects. It can also produce mild impairments in memory.

Clozapine (Clozaril), one of a newer generation of antipsychotics, appears to be at least as effective as earlier antipsychotics in controlling symptoms of schizophrenia—but with fewer neurological side effects than the earlier antipsychotics (Correll & Shenk, 2009). However, other complications with these newer antipsychotics have emerged, including significant weight gain and metabolic disorders associated with increased risk of sudden death from heart disease and stroke (Foley & Morley, 2011; Stroup et al., 2011).

CONCEPT 14.26
Psychotropic drugs help control symptoms of psychological disorders, but they do not cure the disorders.

antianxiety drugs Drugs that combat anxiety.

antidepressants Drugs that combat depression by affecting the levels or activity of neurotransmitters.

tricyclics A class of antidepressant drugs that increase the availability of neurotransmitters in the brain by interfering with the reuptake of these chemicals by transmitting neurons.

monoamine oxidase (MAO) inhibitors A class of antidepressant drugs that increase the availability of neurotransmitters in the brain by inhibiting an enzyme, monoamine oxidase, that breaks down or degrades them in the synapse.

selective serotonin reuptake inhibitors (SSRIs) A class of antidepressant drugs that work specifically on increasing availability of the neurotransmitter serotonin by interfering with its reuptake.

antipsychotics Drugs used in the treatment of psychotic disorders that help alleviate hallucinations and delusional thinking.

Psychiatric drugs may help control symptoms, but they are not a cure. We cannot expect to solve the problems we face in life with a pill.

Some psychiatric drugs, such as the antianxiety drug Valium, can lead to psychological and physical dependence (addiction) if used regularly over time. Valium can also be very dangerous, even deadly, in overdoses or if mixed with alcohol or other drugs. Some people come to depend on antianxiety drugs to cope with life's travails rather than confronting the sources of their anxiety or relationship problems.

Critics also claim that the large numbers of children on psychiatric drugs such as Ritalin and antidepressants suggests that many mental health professionals are too eager to find a "quick fix" for complex problems (Sroufe, 2012). We also know little about the long-term effects of Ritalin and other stimulant drugs on the developing brain (Geller, 2006). On the other hand, advocates of drug therapy point to benefits of using psychiatric drugs to control symptoms in children with serious psychological problems and to the risks of leaving these children untreated or undertreated (Kluger, 2003).

Are psychiatric drugs more effective than psychotherapy in treating depression? Investigators report that cognitive therapy practiced by experienced therapists is at least as effective as antidepressants in treating depression and leads to more lasting gains, even in cases of moderate to severe depression (Beck & Dozois, 2011; Holmes, Craske, & Graybiel, 2014; Mondin et al., 2015). Investigators also find that behavioral approaches to treatment that focus on increasing rewarding activities and goal-directed behaviors compare favorably with cognitive therapy and antidepressant medication (Dimidjian et al., 2011; Houghton, Curran, & Ekers, 2011). All things considered, some people with depressive or anxiety-related disorders respond better to psychological treatment alone, some to drug therapy alone, and some to a combination of both treatments (see, for example, Craighead & Dunlop, 2014; Cuijpers, 2014; Hollon et al., 2014; Huhn et al., 2014; Simpson, 2014; Thase, 2014).

Electroconvulsive Therapy

CONCEPT 14.27

Many mental health professionals view electroconvulsive therapy as a treatment of last resort for severe depression in cases where less invasive treatments have failed.

Electroconvulsive therapy (ECT) sounds barbaric. A jolt of electricity is passed through the patient's head. It is strong enough to cause convulsions similar to those of a grand mal epileptic seizure. Yet it often produces dramatic relief from severe depression and can be a lifesaver for people who are suicidally depressed. When receiving ECT, the patient is first anesthetized to prevent any pain or discomfort. Muscle relaxants are used to prevent injuries that may result from the convulsive jerking that ensues. The person awakens shortly afterward, with no memory of the procedure. ECT typically involves a series of 6 to 12 treatments over several weeks.

ECT is used almost exclusively in the treatment of severe depression, especially in cases that are unresponsive to other forms of treatment (Faedda et al., 2010; Kennedy et al., 2009). More than 100,000 people receive ECT annually in the United States (Wilson, 2011). We're not certain how ECT works in relieving depression. Most probably it alters levels of neurotransmitters in brain circuits that control moods. However, it is associated with a high rate of relapse in the weeks and months following a course of treatment (Prudic et al., 2004). ECT may also produce memory loss, especially for events occurring around the time of treatment. In light of these concerns, it is not surprising that many health professionals view ECT as a treatment of last resort.

electroconvulsive therapy (ECT) A form of therapy for severe depression that involves the administration of an electrical shock to the head.

psychosurgery Brain surgery used to control violent or deviant behavior.

prefrontal lobotomy A surgical procedure in which neural pathways in the brain are severed in order to control violent or aggressive behavior.

Psychosurgery

Psychosurgery is a procedure in which the brain is surgically altered to control deviant or violent behavior. The most widely practiced form of psychosurgery in the past was the **prefrontal lobotomy**, developed in the 1930s by Portuguese neurologist António Egas Moniz. In a prefrontal lobotomy, nerve pathways between the frontal lobe and lower brain centers are severed to control a patient's violent or aggressive behavior. More than 1,000 patients underwent the procedure before it was eliminated because of serious complications, including death in some cases. Meanwhile, the introduction of psychiatric drugs offered a less radical alternative to controlling aberrant behavior. A sad footnote to this story was that one of Moniz's own patients (for whom the treatment failed) later shot him, leaving his legs paralyzed.

More sophisticated psychosurgery techniques have been introduced in recent years, involving surgical alterations limited to smaller areas of the brain. These procedures are presently experimental and used rarely—and, again, only as a treatment of last resort—in some cases of severe obsessive-compulsive disorder, bipolar disorder, and major depression (Carey, 2009; D'Astous et al., 2013). Concerns remain—understandably so—about the safety and effectiveness of these experimental procedures (Carey, 2011; Silver, 2013).

A less invasive but still experimental surgical technique involves deep brain stimulation (Islam et al., 2015). In one example, surgeons implanted electrodes in specific areas of the brain in patients with severe obsessive-compulsive disorder (OCD). A pacemaker-like device was used to stimulate the electrodes to transmit electrical signals into surrounding brain tissue, which blocks brain circuitry believed to be overactive in severe forms of OCD (Denys et al., 2010). Deep brain stimulation is also being tested as a treatment for severe depression that fails to respond to less invasive treatments (see, for example, Blomsted et al., 2011). Other brain stimulation techniques for treating depression are also being studied, including magnetic stimulation of deep areas in the brain (Holtzheimer & McDonald, 2014; Liu et al., 2014; Nauczyciel et al., 2014; Plewnia et al., 2014).

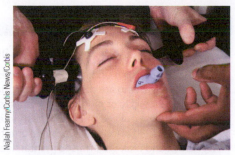

In electroconvulsive therapy (ECT), an electric current is passed through the head while the patient is anesthetized. It often produces dramatic relief from severe depression, but relapses are common.

The Movement Toward Community-Based Care

By the 1950s, the public outcry over deplorable conditions in mental hospitals had led to a call for reform. The result was the community mental health system, which began to take shape in the 1960s. The hope was that community-based facilities would provide people suffering from schizophrenia or other severe and persistent psychological disorders with alternatives to long-term hospitalization. The advent of antipsychotic drugs, which helped control the flagrant symptoms of schizophrenia, was an additional impetus for the massive exodus of chronic mental patients from state institutions that began in earnest during the 1960s.

The social policy that redirected care of people with severe mental disorders from state mental hospitals toward community-based treatment settings is called **deinstitutionalization.** As a result of this policy, the back wards of many mental hospitals were largely vacated. Many state mental hospitals were closed entirely and were replaced by community-based mental health centers and residential treatment facilities. The state hospital census in the United States dropped from about 550,000 in 1955 to fewer than 40,000 today.

Today, community-based mental health centers offer a variety of services, including outpatient care, day treatment programs, and crisis intervention (see the Try This Out feature on page 554). Supervised residential facilities, such as halfway houses, help formerly hospitalized patients make the transition to community life. The contemporary mental hospital now exists as a resource to provide patients with more structured treatment alternatives that may be needed during times of crisis and a protective living environment for long-term patients who are unable to manage the challenges of adjusting to life in the community.

The objectives of deinstitutionalization are certainly laudable. But the question remains: Has it succeeded in its goal of reintegrating mental patients into their

CONCEPT 14.28
The community mental health movement offers the hope that mental patients can be reintegrated into society, but in far too many cases, it remains a hope as yet unfulfilled.

deinstitutionalization A policy of reducing the population of mental hospitals by shifting care from inpatient facilities to community-based outpatient facilities.

communities? Unfortunately, deinstitutionalization receives at best a mixed grade. Critics claim that mental hospitals today are like revolving doors, repeatedly admitting patients and then rapidly discharging them once they become stabilized. Far too many patients fail to receive the comprehensive range of psychological and support services they need to adapt successfully to community living (Lieberman, 2010). Most people suffering from severe psychiatric disorders, such as schizophrenia, live in their own communities, but only about half of them currently receive treatment (Torrey, 2011). Some simply fall through the cracks of the mental health system and are left to fend for themselves. Many of the homeless people seen wandering about or sleeping in bus terminals have unrecognized mental health and substance abuse problems but are not receiving the help they need (Price, 2009c). Understaffed and underfunded, community-based mental health facilities continue to struggle to meet the demands of a generation of people with severe mental health problems who have come of age during the era of deinstitutionalization.

Not surprisingly, more intensive community-based programs that match services to the needs of people with severe and persistent mental health problems generally achieve better results (see, for example, Coldwell & Bender, 2007). More intensive outreach efforts are especially important if we are to reach the large numbers of psychiatric homeless people who fail to seek out mental health services on their own (Price, 2009c). All in all, perhaps it is best to think of deinstitutionalization as a work in progress rather than a failed policy.

Concept Chart 14.2 summarizes the major types and uses of the psychotropic drugs discussed in this module.

Concept Chart 14.2	Major Types and Uses of Psychotropic Drugs			
	Generic Name	**Brand Name**	**Clinical Uses**	**Possible Side Effects or Complications**
Antianxiety Drugs	Diazepam	Valium	Treatment of anxiety and insomnia	Drowsiness, fatigue, impaired coordination, nausea
	Chlordiazepoxide	Librium		
	Lorazepam	Ativan		
	Alprazolam	Xanax		

Concept Chart 14.2   (Continued)

	Generic Name	Brand Name	Clinical Uses	Possible Side Effects or Complications
Antidepressant Drugs	**Tricyclics**			
	Imipramine	Tofranil	Depression, bulimia, panic disorder	Changes in blood pressure, heart irregularities, dry mouth, confusion, skin rash
	Amitriptyline	Elavil		
	Doxepin	Sinequan		
	MAO Inhibitors			
	Phenelzine	Nardil	Depression	Dizziness, headache, sleep disturbance, agitation, anxiety, fatigue
	Selective Serotonin Reuptake Inhibitors			
	Fluoxetine	Prozac	Depression, bulimia, panic disorder, obsessive-compulsive disorder, posttraumatic stress disorder (Zoloft)	Nausea, constipation, diarrhea, vomiting, anxiety, insomnia, sweating, dry mouth, sexual side effects, dizziness, drowsiness
	Sertraline	Zoloft		
	Paroxetine	Paxil		
	Citalopram	Celexa		
	Other Antidepressant Drugs			
	Bupropion	Wellbutrin, Zyban	Depression, nicotine dependence	Dry mouth, insomnia, headaches, nausea, constipation, tremors
	Venlafaxine	Effexor	Depression	Nausea, constipation, dry mouth, drowsiness, insomnia, dizziness, anxiety
Antipsychotic Drugs	**Phenothiazines**			
	Chlorpromazine	Thorazine	Schizophrenia and other psychotic disorders	Movement disorders, drowsiness, restlessness, dry mouth, blurred vision, muscle rigidity
	Thioridazine	Mellaril		
	Fluphenazine	Prolixin		
	Atypical Antipsychotics			
	Risperidone	Risperdal	Schizophrenia and other psychotic disorders	Difficulty sitting still, constipation, dizziness, drowsiness, weight gain
	Clozapine	Clozaril	Schizophrenia and other psychotic disorders	Potentially lethal blood disorder, seizures, fast heart rate, drowsiness, dizziness, nausea
	Olanzapine	Zyprexa	Schizophrenia and other psychotic disorders	Drowsiness, low blood pressure, dizziness, heart palpitations, fatigue, constipation, weight gain
Antimanic Drugs	Lithium carbonate	Eskalith	Manic episodes and stabilization of mood swings associated with bipolar disorder	Tremors, thirst, diarrhea, drowsiness, weakness, lack of coordination
	Divalproex sodium	Depakote		Nausea, vomiting, dizziness, abdominal cramps, sleeplessness
Stimulant Drugs	Methylphenidate	Ritalin	Attention deficit/hyperactivity disorder (ADHD)	Nervousness, insomnia, nausea, dizziness, heart palpitations, headache; may temporarily retard growth

MODULE REVIEW 14.2 Biomedical Therapies

Recite It

8. Identify the major classes of psychiatric drugs and specific drugs in each class.

The major classes of psychiatric drugs are (a) _____ agents (for example, Valium, Xanax), (b) _____ (for example, Elavil, Prozac), and (c) _____ (for example, Thorazine, Clozaril). Other drugs, such as lithium and Ritalin, are used to treat specific disorders.

9. Evaluate the advantages and disadvantages of these drugs.

Psychiatric drugs can help relieve or control symptoms of many psychological disorders, including anxiety disorders, mood disorders, and schizophrenia, but they are not (d) _____.
The major disadvantages of these drugs are the occurrence of troubling side effects, high (e) _____ rates following discontinuance, and, in some cases, possible chemical dependence.

10. Describe other forms of biomedical therapy and **explain** why they are controversial.

(f) _____ involves the administration of brief pulses of electricity to the brain. It is used to treat severe depression, especially in cases that do not respond to other treatments. However, ECT is controversial because of the invasive nature of the treatment and because it can cause (g) _____ loss for events occurring around the time of treatment.

(h) _____ is the use of surgical procedures on the brain to control deviant or violent behavior. It is rarely used today because of concerns about the safety and effectiveness of these procedures.

11. Describe the functions of the modern community mental health center.

Community-based mental health centers are treatment facilities that provide a comprehensive range of mental health services and other supportive services to psychiatric patients in the (i) _____ in which they reside.

12. Evaluate whether the policy of deinstitutionalization has been successful.

The policy of deinstitutionalization remains a promise not yet fulfilled, as many patients fail to receive the services they need to adjust successfully to the (j) _____.

Recall It

1. Psychiatric drugs are used to regulate _____ in the brain.

2. The drugs Valium and Xanax are examples of which class of psychiatric drugs?

3. A widely used treatment for childhood hyperactivity involves the use of
   a. extensive psychotherapy.
   b. a stimulant drug.
   c. lithium.
   d. gamma-aminobutyric acid.

4. Psychiatric drugs are widely used because they
   a. teach people how to solve their problems.
   b. correct nutritional deficiencies that give rise to psychological disorders.
   c. help reduce and control symptoms of psychological disorders.
   d. cure most types of psychological disorders.

5. Electroconvulsive therapy (ECT) is used
   a. only after successful treatment with antidepressant drugs.
   b. in treating severe cases of schizophrenia as well as depression.
   c. in treating mild to moderate cases of depression.
   d. in treating cases of severe depression, especially when other approaches have proved unsuccessful.

Think About It

- Do you know children who have been treated with stimulant medication for hyperactivity and attention problems? What were the outcomes? Do you believe that stimulant medication is used too often or not often enough?

- What are the advantages and disadvantages of psychotropic drugs? Would you consider using psychotropic drugs if you developed an anxiety disorder or a mood disorder? Why or why not?

- If you or someone you know needed mental health services, where would you turn? How might you find out what types of mental health services are available in your college and your community?

Recite It *answers placed at the end of chapter.*

THINKING CRITICALLY ABOUT PSYCHOLOGY

Based on your reading of this chapter, answer the following questions. Then, to evaluate your progress in developing critical thinking skills, compare your answers to the sample answers found in Appendix A.

Lauren has been depressed since the breakup of her relationship with her boyfriend two months ago. She is crying frequently, has difficulty getting out of bed in the morning, and has been losing weight. She claims she doesn't feel like eating. She tells the psychologist that she hasn't ever felt like hurting herself, but wavers when asked if she feels she might reach a point where she would consider ending her life. She says she feels like a failure and that no one will ever want her. Looking down at the floor, she tells the psychologist, "Everyone's always rejected me. Why should this be any different?"

Review the major approaches to therapy (psychodynamic, humanistic, behavioral, cognitive) and biomedical treatments discussed in this chapter. Then briefly describe how each might be used to help someone like Lauren.

Key to Sample Rational Alternatives in Try This Out (p. 539)

1. We've got problems, but it's not a complete disaster. It's better to think of ways of making it better than to think the worst.

2. I sometimes feel overwhelmed, but I've handled things like this before. I need to take things a step at a time to get through this.

3. Just because it feels that way doesn't make it so.

4. Focus on getting through this course, not on jumping to conclusions.

5. Stop taking the blame for other people's problems. There are many reasons why _____ has these problems that have nothing to do with me.

6. Stop dumping on yourself. Focus on what you need to do.

7. It doesn't help compare myself to others. All I can expect of myself is to do the best I can.

8. It would be upsetting, but it wouldn't be the end of the world. It's awful only if I make it so.

9. What evidence do I have for believing that? People who get to know me like me more often than not.

10. Putting everything in context, it's really not so bad.

Recite It Answers for Chapter 14

Module 14.1 1. (a) counseling; (b) nurses, 2. (c) verbal, 3. (d) psychoanalysis; (e) unconscious; (f) client-centered; (g) conscious; (h) learning; (i) systematic; (j) cognitive; (k) Ellis; (l) Beck; (m) eclectic, 4. (n) Group; (o) Family, blaming; (p) Couple, 5. (q) Meta; (r) empirically, 6. (s) cultural; (t) stereotyping, 7. (u) referral; (v) counseling; (w) second   **Module 14.2** 8. (a) antianxiety; (b) antidepressants; (c) antipsychotics, 9. (d) cures; (e) relapse, 10. (f) ECT; (g) memory; (h) Psychosurgery, 11. (i) communities, 12. (j) community.

VISUAL OVERVIEW
Methods of Therapy

Types of Psychotherapy

Psychodynamic Therapy

- **Traditional Psychoanalysis:** "Where id is, ego shall be"
- **Major Techniques:** Free association, dream analysis, interpretation, analysis of transference relationship
- **Modern Psychodynamic Approaches:** More direct "give-and-take" between therapist and client, greater focus on ego functioning

Behavior Therapy

- **Methods of Fear Reduction:** Gradual exposure, systematic desensitization, modeling
- **Aversive Conditioning:** Eliciting a negative response to undesirable stimuli
- **Operant Conditioning Techniques:** Applying principles of reinforcement to strengthen more adaptive behaviors
- **Cognitive-Behavioral Therapy:** Combining cognitive and behavioral techniques

Humanistic Therapy

- **Carl Rogers, Client-Centered Therapy:** Focuses on enhancing self-understanding and self-acceptance; nondirective approach, emphasizes unconditional positive regard, empathy, and genuineness in therapeutic relationship
- **Fritz Perls, Gestalt Therapy:** Integrating parts of the personality into a cohesive whole or "gestalt"; uses role-playing exercises such as the "empty chair" technique

Cognitive Therapy

- **Beck's Cognitive Therapy:** Replacing distorted thoughts and beliefs with rational alternatives
- **Ellis's Rational Emotive Behavior Therapy:** Uses the ABC model to help clients correct irrational beliefs

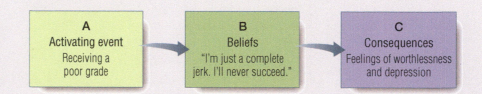

A	B	C
Activating event	Beliefs	Consequences
Receiving a poor grade	"I'm just a complete jerk. I'll never succeed."	Feelings of worthlessness and depression

Other Therapies

- **Eclectic Therapy:** Using different approaches tailored to particular cases
- **Group, Family, and Couple Therapy:** Expanding treatment beyond the individual client

Effectiveness of Psychotherapy

- **Meta-Analysis:** Average person receiving psychotherapy achieves a better outcome than 80 percent of untreated controls
- **Evidence-Based Therapies:** Specific types of therapy that demonstrate effectiveness in carefully controlled studies

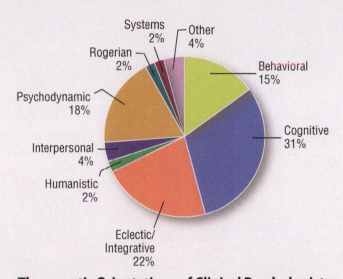

Therapeutic Orientations of Clinical Psychologists

MODULE 14.2 — Biomedical Therapies

Drug Therapy

- **Antianxiety Drugs:** Valium, Librium, Xanax
- **Antidepressants:** Tricyclics, monoamine oxidase (MAO) inhibitors, and selective serotonin reuptake inhibitors (SSRIs)
- **Antipsychotics:** Used to treat schizophrenia and other psychotic disorders
- **Other Psychiatric Drugs:** Mood stabilizers (anticonvulsant drugs) to treat bipolar disorder; Ritalin for childhood hyperactivity

Other Biomedical Therapies

- **Electroconvulsive Therapy (ECT):** Used to treat severe depression, but can cause memory loss for recent past events
- **Psychosurgery:** Rarely used because of serious complications

Appendix A

Sample Answers to **Thinking Critically About Psychology** Questions

CHAPTER 1 THE SCIENCE OF PSYCHOLOGY

1. Unfortunately, a basic flaw in the research design casts serious doubt on the experimenter's conclusions. The experimenter did not use random assignment as the basis for assigning participants to the experimental (sleep learning) or control (nonparticipating) groups. Rather, students who responded to the invitation to participate constituted the experimental group, and the control group was selected from nonparticipating students from the same class. Lacking random assignment, we have no way of knowing whether differences between the two groups were due to the independent variable (sleep learning) or to the characteristics of participants comprising these groups.

2. In the absence of random assignment, it is conceivable that the more motivated and committed students opted to participate and that these students would have achieved higher test grades than the nonparticipating students, whether or not they had participated in the sleep learning study.

3. To provide a fairer test of the sleep learning method, the experimenter should have randomly assigned students to experimental and control groups. Experimenters use random assignment to equate groups on differences that may exist among individuals in level of ability or other participant characteristics.

CHAPTER 2 BIOLOGICAL FOUNDATIONS OF BEHAVIOR

1. Fortunately for Gage, the rod that penetrated his skull did not damage structures in the brain stem that control basic bodily processes, such as breathing and heart rate. However, the rod did damage the prefrontal cortex, the part of the brain responsible for personality and other higher mental functions.

2. The prefrontal cortex, which was damaged in the accident, helps us weigh the consequences of our actions and inhibit impulsive behaviors, including aggressive behaviors.

CHAPTER 3 SENSATION AND PERCEPTION

1. The woman located an area on the map where the missing man might be found. But her success at locating the missing man could be explained in a number of ways other than ESP. It could have been a lucky guess. Or perhaps the woman used the process of elimination to systematically narrow the possible search areas by ruling out those

in which the police had already focused their efforts. Or perhaps she arrived at a possible location by identifying areas where a person would be likely to have wandered off. What other explanations can you generate that do not rely on positing the existence of ESP?

2. To evaluate whether the woman's predictions were likely to have been mere chance events, we would need to know how often her predictions turn out to be right. In other words, we'd need to know whether her success rate significantly exceeds chance expectations. But even if she turned out to be right more often than you would expect by chance alone, we still couldn't conclude that her success was attributable to ESP rather than to more conventional explanations.

CHAPTER 4 CONSCIOUSNESS

1. No, the evidence does not directly demonstrate that ethnicity or race is the differentiating factor in rates of drug use. Statistics comparing rates of drug use in ethnic or racial groups may be misleading if they fail to take into account possible confounding factors, such as differences between groups in education and income levels or characteristics of the neighborhoods in which people of different ethnic or racial groups may live.

2. African Americans have disproportionately high rates of unemployment, and people who are unemployed tend to abuse drugs more often. Blacks and other ethnic minorities are also more likely than Whites to be poor and to live in socially distressed neighborhoods. People living under such conditions are more likely to use drugs than are more affluent people who live in more secure neighborhoods. Investigators who controlled for differences in types of neighborhoods found that African Americans were no more likely than (non-Hispanic) Whites to use crack cocaine (USDHHS, 1999). Other investigators who controlled for education and income level found that Black Americans were actually less likely than White Americans to develop alcohol or drug dependence problems (Anthony, Warner, & Kessler, 1994).

CHAPTER 5 LEARNING

1. the poison; 2. the sheep meat; 3. nausea; 4. taste aversion to sheep meat

CHAPTER 6 MEMORY

1. It is likely that the second man rehearsed the information by repeating the license plate number to himself a number of times. Acoustic rehearsal is generally a more efficient method of holding information in short-term memory and transferring it to long-term memory than trying to keep a visual image of a stimulus in mind.

2. The woman apparently had memorized the song phonologically (by sound) rather than semantically (by meaning).

CHAPTER 7 THINKING, LANGUAGE, AND INTELLIGENCE

1a. The shepherd led the sheep to reverse direction and move back behind the ambulance, thus freeing the ambulance to move ahead without obstruction.

1b. The medical technician relied on a mental set for making one's way past a crowd.

2a. The availability heuristic and the representativeness heuristic may help explain John's poor investment decisions. The availability heuristic applies when we base our decisions on whatever happens to come most readily to mind—in John's case, the news reports of the day or comments he hears from others. When using the representativeness heuristic, we treat small samples of occurrences as though they were representative of occurrences in general. An individual news report about a company may be a poor indication of the company's overall financial health or future prospects. Comments from others may be even less trustworthy as a basis for making sound investment decisions.

2b. As John's investment adviser, you should probably recommend that he adopt a sound investment strategy and stick to it rather than base his investment decisions on daily news reports or comments from others.

CHAPTER 8 MOTIVATION AND EMOTION

People commonly think of thoughts and feelings as opposites. You may have heard people say how they feel with their hearts, but think with their heads. Though poets take license with the view that the human heart can "feel," critical thinkers question underlying assumptions, including the assumption that thoughts and feelings are independent of each other (let alone the assumption that the heart has feelings). Psychologists conceptualize emotions as complex feeling states that have important cognitive (thinking) components. They believe that our emotions reflect our cognitions (beliefs, judgments, appraisals, and so on) about our experiences. For example, anger reflects a judgment we make that we have been treated unfairly, whereas fear reflects an appraisal of a situation or object as threatening. In this view, thoughts are bridges to our emotions. To better understand emotions, we need to better understand the interconnections between thoughts and feelings.

CHAPTER 9 HUMAN DEVELOPMENT

1. Three-year-old children like Trevor show a type of thinking pattern that Piaget called animistic thinking— the tendency to attribute human qualities to inanimate objects, such as the sun and the clouds. To Trevor, the sun has feelings ("gets sleepy") and engages in behaviors ("goes to sleep"), just as people do.

2a. To determine your identity status, you first need to decide whether you have achieved a commitment in each area (that is, occupational choice, political and moral beliefs). A commitment represents either the adoption of a relatively firm set of beliefs or the pursuit of a course of action consistently over time. Critical thinkers weigh the validity of claims in terms of the evidence at hand— in this case, claims of achieving a commitment. What evidence would you seek to support these claims? Here are some examples of the types of criteria you may wish to apply:

- Showing evidence in your actions and pronouncement to others of a relatively permanent or unswerving commitment to an occupational choice, political philosophy, or set of moral values
- Being able to describe your beliefs or actions in an organized and meaningful way
- Pursuing a course of action consistent with your career choice and your political and moral beliefs or values

2b. Now you need to carefully evaluate whether you experienced an identity crisis to arrive at any of the commitments you have achieved. Bearing in mind, again, that critical thinkers weigh the evidence at hand, consider that evidence of an identity crisis might be based on meeting the following criteria:

- Having undergone a serious examination of alternatives before arriving at a commitment (or are now undergoing this serious examination)
- Having devoted serious effort toward developing a commitment (or are now devoting a serious effort)
- Having gathered information (or are now gathering information) to seriously evaluate different points of view or courses of action

Classify yourself in the *identity achievement* status in a given area (career choice, political and moral beliefs) if you have developed a commitment to a set of beliefs or a course of action and underwent an identity crisis to arrive at this commitment. Place yourself in the *moratorium* status if you are presently in a state of identity crisis and are making active efforts to arrive at a commitment. Place yourself in the *foreclosure* category if you developed a commitment without having first experienced an identity crisis. Classify yourself in the *identity diffusion* category if you have neither achieved a commitment (that is, currently lack a clear career course or a firmly held set of beliefs or values) nor are currently struggling to arrive at one.

CHAPTER 10 PSYCHOLOGY AND HEALTH

1. The claims may mean the following: We may have designed our product to enhance vitality and well-being, but we cannot claim that it actually accomplishes this purpose.

2. Our product contains amino acids that the body uses to build muscle, but so do many other sources of protein, including meat and dairy products.

3. We hired a few physicians with respectable credentials who said they would recommend our product, and we paid them for their endorsements.

4. By *backed*, we mean that we conducted research on our product. We're not saying what our research actually found or whether the studies were well designed or carried out by impartial investigators. And when we say *advanced*, we're simply referring to any research method that went beyond just asking people if they liked our product.

5. We're not really sure what we mean by "supercharge," but it sounded good in the advertising copy.

CHAPTER 11 PERSONALITY

The confirmation bias leads us to give credence to information that confirms our preexisting beliefs and to ignore contrary evidence. Thus, for example, we are more likely to believe astrological readings when they conform to beliefs we already hold about ourselves than when they provide contrary information. Because astrological readings contain general personality descriptions that apply to a wide range of people, it's not surprising that many individuals believe these descriptions are true of themselves.

CHAPTER 12 SOCIAL PSYCHOLOGY

Why didn't they help? Though we will never know for certain, several hypotheses can be offered based on factors that have been shown to influence bystander behavior:

- *Situational ambiguity.* It was dark, and witnesses may not have had a direct view of the situation. Perhaps they were confused or uncertain about what was happening and whether it was a true emergency.
- *Diffusion of responsibility.* Even if the witnesses recognized the situation as an emergency, perhaps they weren't willing to assume personal responsibility for getting involved. Or perhaps they thought others would act, so they didn't need to. Or perhaps they thought it was "none of their business."
- *Perceived cost.* Perhaps the witnesses believed the cost of helping would be too great—including

possible injury or loss of their own lives. But what about the minimal cost involved in calling the police? Perhaps they didn't want to accept a personal role in the incident and become involved in a lengthy court case.

- *Attributions of the cause of need.* Perhaps the witnesses reasoned that the victim deserved what she got. Perhaps they figured the assailant was her boyfriend or husband and that she shouldn't have chosen such a partner.

What do you think is the likely explanation? What do you think you would do in a similar situation?

CHAPTER 13 PSYCHOLOGICAL DISORDERS

1. Ron's thought patterns illustrate several cognitive distortions or errors in thinking, including mistaken responsibility (assuming his girlfriend's bad moods were a response to him), catastrophizing (exaggerating the consequences of breaking off the relationship), and jumping to conclusions (assuming that when his girlfriend sat farther away from him in the car it meant she was trying to distance herself emotionally).

2. Lonnie's behavior appears to meet four of the six listed criteria: (a) unusualness (relatively few people are troubled by such obsessive concerns or compulsive rituals), (b) social deviance (repeated checking may be considered socially unacceptable behavior), (c) emotional distress (his compulsive behavior was a source of emotional distress), and (d) maladaptive behavior (his checking rituals were damaging his marital relationship). His behavior does not meet the criterion of dangerousness, because it does not appear to have posed any danger to him or others. Nor does he exhibit faulty perceptions or interpretations of reality, such as experiencing hallucinations or holding delusional beliefs.

CHAPTER 14 METHODS OF THERAPY

A psychodynamic therapist might help Lauren explore how her present relationships and feelings of rejection are connected with disappointments she may have experienced in other relationships, including her early relationships with her parents. A humanistic therapist might help Lauren learn to accept and value herself for who she is, regardless of how others respond to her, and not to judge herself by other people's expectations. A cognitive-behavioral therapist might help Lauren increase reinforcing or pleasurable activities in her life and identify and correct distorted thinking patterns ("Everyone's always rejected me. Why should this be any different?"). Biomedical treatment might involve antidepressant medication, or perhaps even electroconvulsive therapy if her depression deepens and fails to respond to other treatment approaches.

Appendix B

Answers to Recall It Questions

CHAPTER 1
Module 1.1: 1. Wilhelm Wundt; 2. c; 3. behaviorism; 4. b; 5. a; 6. psychodynamic perspective. **Module 1.2:** 1. Basic, applied; 2. (a) iv, (b) i, (c) ii, (d) iii; 3. c; 4. b. **Module 1.3:** 1. c; 2. d; 3. experimental method; 4. d; 5. b.

CHAPTER 2
Module 2.1: 1. b; 2. soma; 3. sensory neurons, motor neurons, and interneurons; 4. a; 5. b. **Module 2.2:** 1. central, peripheral; 2. central; 3. the sympathetic branch of the autonomic nervous system; 4. a. **Module 2.3:** 1. d; 2. (a) iv, (b) i, (c) iii, (d) ii; 3. d; 4. temporal lobes. **Module 2.4:** 1. c; 2. b; 3. a; 4. a. **Module 2.5:** 1. c; 2. left, right; 3. c; 4. d; 5. b. **Module 2.6:** 1. endocrine; 2. b; 3. homeostasis; 4. pituitary. **Module 2.7:** 1. c; 2. c; 3. a; 4. familial association studies, twin studies, and adoptee studies; 5. b.

CHAPTER 3
Module 3.1: 1. c; 2. b; 3. sensory adaptation. **Module 3.2:** 1. d; 2. rods, cones; 3. occipital; 4. (a) iv; (b) vi; (c) i; (d) ii; (e) v; (f) iii. **Module 3.3:** 1. amplitude and frequency; 2. basilar membrane; 3. (a) i; (b) v; (c) vi; (d) iv; (e) iii; (f) ii. **Module 3.4:** 1. b; 2. some 5,000 or more; 3. pheromones; 4. touch, pressure, warmth, cold, and pain; 5. d; 6. kinesthetic. **Module 3.5:** 1. perception; 2. b; 3. perceptual set; 4. connectedness; 5. interposition; 6. a; 7. b.

CHAPTER 4
Module 4.1: 1. a; 2. selectivity; 3. d. **Module 4.2:** 1. circadian; 2. c; 3. restorative; 4. (i) c, (ii) b, (iii) d, (iv) a. **Module 4.3:** 1. transcendental meditation; 2. hypnotic analgesia; 3. neodissociation theory. **Module 4.4:** 1. psychoactive; 2. d; 3. depressants; 4. b; 5. tranquilizers; 6. dopamine.

CHAPTER 5
Module 5.1: 1. stimulus generalization; 2. d; 3. c; 4. b; 5. b. **Module 5.2:** 1. a; 2. radical behaviorism; 3. response, reinforcement; 4. d; 5. c. **Module 5.3:** 1. cognitive learning; 2. a; 3. latent learning; 4. b.

CHAPTER 6
Module 6.1: 1. procedural; 2. d; 3. (i) d, (ii) b, (iii) a, (iv) c. **Module 6.2:** 1. proactive; 2. a; 3. spaced, massed; 4. b. **Module 6.3:** 1. neuronal networks; 2. b; 3. long-term potentiation (LTP); 4. a.

CHAPTER 7
Module 7.1: 1. concepts; 2. logical, natural; 3. b; 4. d. **Module 7.2:** 1. b; 2. a; 3. relativity; 4. c. **Module 7.3:** 1. (i) d, (ii) a, (iii) b, (iv) c; 2. cultural; 3. triarchic theory; 4. d.

CHAPTER 8
Module 8.1: 1. motivation; 2. (i) d, (ii) a, (iii) c, (iv) b; 3. stimulus motives; 4. incentive value; 5. d. **Module 8.2:** 1. c; 2. c; 3. (i) b, (ii) d, (iii) a, (iv) c; 4. serotonin. **Module 8.3:** 1. gender identity; 2. (a) ii, (b) iv, (c) iii, (d)i; 3. b; 4. premature ejaculation. **Module 8.4:** 1. b; 2. anger, fear, disgust, sadness, happiness, and surprise; 3. c; 4. d.

CHAPTER 9
Module 9.1: 1. germinal; 2. maternal malnutrition, teratogens; 3. (a) iv, (b) ii, (c) iii, (d) i. **Module 9.2:** 1. (a) iv, (b) ii, (c) i, (d) iii; 2. Fetuses show a preference for their mothers' voices; 3. d. **Module 9.3:** 1. b; 2. (a) ii, (b) iv, (c) i, (d) iii; 3. c; 4. d; 5. a. **Module 9.4:** 1. d; 2. menarche; 3. imaginary audience and personal fable; 4. a; 5. gender and cultural biases; 6. c. **Module 9.5:** 1. c; 2. c; 3. b; 4. midlife transition. **Module 9.6:** 1. d; 2. general physical health, involvement in stimulating activities, openness to new experiences; 3. b; 4. selective optimization and compensation, optimism, and self-challenge.

CHAPTER 10
Module 10.1: 1. (a) pressures or demands placed upon an organism to adjust or adapt to its environment, (b) when stress reaches a level that taxes our ability to cope effectively; 2. (a) ii, (b) iii, (c) i, (d) iv; 3. alarm; 4. social support, self-efficacy, perceptions of control and predictability, psychological hardiness,

and optimism; 5. a; 6. general adaptation. **Module 10.2:** 1. (a) iv, (b) iii, (c) ii, (d) i; 2. (a) age, gender, heredity, lack of physical activity, obesity, high cholesterol, diabetes, high blood pressure, (b) all but the first three can potentially be controlled; 3. a; 4. d.

CHAPTER 11

Module 11.1: 1. a; 2. c; 3. c; 4. (a) iii, (b) i, (c) ii, (d) iv; 5. a. **Module 11.2:** 1. traits; 2. b; 3. a; 4. Hans Eysenck; 5. c; 6. shyness, neuroticism, aggressiveness, novelty seeking. **Module 11.3:** 1. b; 2. a; 3. Thoughts, behaviors, and environmental factors mutually influence each other; 4. (a) ii, (b) iv, (c) iii, (d) i.**Module 11.4:** 1. d; 2. d; 3. the self; 4. a. **Module 11.5:** 1. self-report personality tests and projective tests; 2. d; 3. standard; 4. d.

CHAPTER 12

Module 12.1: 1. schema; 2. dispositional, situational; 3. overestimation; 4. an evaluation or judgment of liking or disliking a person, object, or social issue; 5. cognitive dissonance; 6. (a) ii, (b) iv, (c) i, (d) iii. **Module 12.2:** 1. similarity, physical attractiveness, proximity, reciprocity; 2. d; 3. The correct order is (d), (b), (a), (e), (c); 4. (a) biased beliefs and stereotypes, (b) feelings of dislike toward target, (c) discrimination; 5. social and institutional support, acquaintance potential, equal status, intergroup cooperation. **Module 12.3:** 1. social; 2. b; 3. 65 percent; 4. a; 5. b.

CHAPTER 13

Module 13.1: 1. unusualness, social deviance, emotional distress, maladaptive behavior, dangerousness, faulty perceptions or interpretations of reality; 2. d; 3. c; 4. (a) iv, (b) iii, (c) i, (d) ii. **Module 13.2:** 1. c; 2. specific; 3. (a) iii, (b) i, (c) ii, (d) iv. **Module 13.3:** 1. dissociative; 2. d; 3. d; 4. (is not). **Module 13.4:** 1. bipolar disorder; 2. Women appear to be exposed to greater stress and are more likely to ruminate or dwell on their problems; 3. serotonin, reabsorption or reuptake; 4. helplessness. **Module 13.5:** 1. males; 2. catatonic; 3. c; 4. b. **Module 13.6:** 1. excessively rigid patterns of behavior, difficulty adjusting to external demands and relating to other people; 2. frontal lobes; 3. (i) b, (ii) a, (iii) a, (iv) b.

CHAPTER 14

Module 14.1: 1. (a) iv, (b) i, (c) iii, (d) ii; 2. unconditional positive regard, empathy, genuineness; 3. systematic desensitization; 4. rational-emotive behavior therapy; 5. The advantages of group therapy include its lower cost and the fact that clients can gain experience relating to others and learn from others how to cope with problem situations; its disadvantages include a lower level of individual attention and clients' potential fear of revealing very personal matters to other members of the group. **Module 14.2:** 1. neurotransmitters; 2. antianxiety drugs; 3. b; 4. c; 5. d.

Appendix C

Statistics in Psychology

Dennis Hinkle   Towson University
Leping Liu   Towson University

The word *statistics* means different things to different people. Weatherpeople report daily weather statistics, such as high and low temperatures, amount of rainfall, and the average temperatures recorded for this day in history. Sportscasters flood us with statistics that include players' batting averages, fielding percentages, and ratios of home runs to times at bat. And in televised football games, commentators give half-time statistics that include total yards rushing and total yards passing.

Psychologists, too, use statistics. But to them, statistics are procedures for analyzing and understanding the results of research studies. For example, research evidence shows that night-shift workers in sensitive positions tend to be sleepier and less alert than day-shift workers. Investigators in these studies used statistical techniques to determine whether the two groups of workers—night-shift and day-shift workers—differed from each other, *on the average*, on measures of sleepiness and alertness, among other variables. Psychologists also use statistics for describing the characteristics of particular groups of people, including themselves. In Chapter 1, for example, you learned about the characteristics of psychologists with respect to their ethnicities and places of employment.

Fundamental theories in modern psychology would not exist without the application of statistics in psychological research. Psychologists rely on statistics to explain the results of their research studies, as well as to provide empirical evidence to support or refute particular theories or beliefs. For example, investigators used statistical techniques to refute the original version of the *linguistic relativity hypothesis*, which was based on the theory that language determines how we think (see Chapter 7). In this case, statistical analysis of the research findings supported an alternative theory—that cultural factors influence how we think. We all need to understand statistics to become more knowledgeable consumers of psychological research. For example, we need to understand how the IQ scores of people in the general population are distributed in order to determine the relative standing of a particular score (again, see Chapter 7). And when seeking psychological assistance, we need to know which forms of therapy have been shown through methods of statistical analysis to be effective for which types of psychological problems (see the discussion in Chapter 14 about *empirically supported treatments*). Whatever the reason for using statistics, researchers and consumers alike should understand the information that statistics provide and the conclusions that can be drawn from them.

Populations and Samples

The terms *population* and *sample* are used frequently in psychological research involving statistical analysis. By definition, a *population* includes all members of a specified group, such as "all residents living in Washington, D.C.," "all patients in a psychiatric hospital at a specified time who are being treated for various psychological disorders," or "all students enrolled in an introductory psychology class in a particular university during the fall semester." In many research situations, however, it is not feasible to include all members of a given population. In such instances, a

Table 1 Final Examination Scores for Freshman Psychology Students

68	52	69	51	43	36	44	35	54	57	55	56
55	54	54	53	33	48	32	47	47	57	48	56
65	57	64	49	51	56	50	48	53	56	52	55
42	49	41	48	50	24	49	25	53	55	52	56
64	63	63	64	54	45	53	46	50	40	49	41
45	54	44	55	63	55	62	56	50	46	49	47
56	38	55	37	68	46	67	45	65	48	64	49
59	46	58	47	57	58	56	59	60	62	59	63
56	49	55	50	43	45	42	46	53	40	52	41
42	33	41	34	56	32	55	33	40	45	39	46
38	43	37	44	54	56	53	57	57	46	56	45
50	40	49	39	47	55	46	54	39	56	38	55
37	29	36	30	37	49	36	50	36	44	35	45
42	43	41	42	52	47	51	46	63	48	62	49
53	60	52	61	49	55	48	56	38	48	37	47

subset or segment of the population, called a *sample*, is selected to participate, and only the members of that sample are included in the research study.

Descriptive Statistics and Inferential Statistics

The study of statistics can be divided into two broad categories: descriptive statistics and inferential statistics. Investigators use **descriptive statistics** to describe data (that is, to classify and summarize information expressed in numerical form), and they use **inferential statistics** to make generalizations about a population by studying results based on a sample drawn from the population.

Descriptive and inferential statistics have three main purposes in scientific inquiry:

1. *To describe*
2. *To relate*
3. *To compare*

These approaches form a general framework for applying statistical procedures that allow researchers to interpret the results of a study, draw conclusions, make generalizations and inferences from samples to populations, and provide a focus for future studies. In the remainder of this appendix, we provide an overview of these three approaches to statistical analysis.

Using Statistics to Describe

The simplest application of statistics involves describing a distribution of scores collected from a group of individuals. Suppose, for example, that we have the final examination scores for 180 freshman psychology students, as shown in Table 1. To describe this distribution of scores, we must (1) identify the shape of the distribution, (2) compute the "average" score, and (3) determine the variability of the scores.

descriptive statistics Procedures used for classifying and summarizing information in numerical form—in short, for describing data.

inferential statistics Procedures for making generalizations about a population by studying the characteristics of samples drawn from the population.

Table 2 Frequency Distribution of Final Examination Scores Using Class Intervals

Class Interval	f
65–69	6
60–64	15
55–59	37
50–54	30
45–49	42
40–44	22
35–39	18
30–34	7
25–29	2
20–24	1

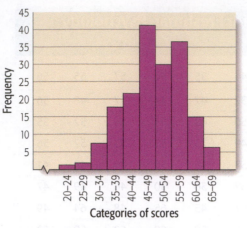

FIGURE 1 Histogram of Final Examination Scores

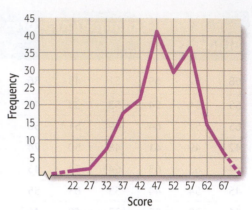

FIGURE 2 Frequency Polygon of Final Examination Scores

Frequency Distribution

The first step in describing a distribution of scores is to develop a **frequency distribution** for individual scores or categories of scores.

Table 2 shows a frequency distribution constructed by combining our 180 scores into categories, called *class intervals*, beginning with the category of scores 20 to 24 and ending with the category of scores 65 to 69. Note that the categories with the most scores are 45 to 49, which contains 42 scores, and 55 to 59, which contains 37 scores. We can depict this frequency distribution using a type of bar graph, called a histogram. As shown in Figure 1, a **histogram** depicts the frequencies of class intervals of scores using bars of different lengths. Thus, for example, the class interval of 45 to 49 is represented by a bar with a value of 42.

Another way of graphing a frequency distribution is to use a **frequency polygon**, as shown in Figure 2. Here, the frequencies of class intervals are plotted at the intervals' midpoints, which are then connected with straight lines.

Measures of Central Tendency

The second step in describing a distribution of scores is to compute the **central tendency** of the scores. Central tendency is an indicator of the average score in a distribution of scores. Three different statistical measures of central tendency are available. Researchers can determine the **mode** (most frequent score), the **median** (middle score), or the **mean** (arithmetic average).

As an example, consider the following distribution: 2, 5, 9, 10, 12, 13, 13. The mode is 13, which is the score that occurs most often. The median is the score that slices the distribution of scores in half (half of the scores fall above the median and half fall below). The median is 10, because three scores fall above this value and three fall below.

The mean is the most often used measure of central tendency. To find the mean ($\overline{X}$), sum all the scores (X) and then divide the sum by the number of scores. Symbolically,

$$\overline{X} = \Sigma X/n$$

where ΣX is the sum of all the scores and n is the total number of scores. For the previous distribution of scores, the mean would be computed as follows:

$$\overline{X} = 64/7 = 9.14$$

frequency distribution A tabulation that indicates the number of times a given score or group of scores occurs.

histogram A graph that depicts the frequencies of individual scores or categories of scores, using bars of different lengths.

frequency polygon A graph on which the frequencies of class intervals are at their midpoints, which are then connected with straight lines.

central tendency A central point on a scale of measurement around which scores are distributed.

mode The most frequent score in a distribution of scores.

median The middle score in a distribution, above and below which half of the scores fall.

mean The arithmetic average of the scores in a distribution.

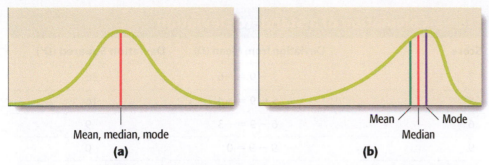

FIGURE 3 **Comparisons of the Mode, Median, and Mean in Two Distributions**

As you can see, the mode, median, and mean sometimes represent different values.

Similarly, for the final examination scores for the 180 freshman psychology students, the mean would be computed as follows:

$$\overline{X} = 8860/180 = 49.22$$

In other cases, such as the distribution shown in Figure 3(a), the mean, median, and mode are represented by the same value. But when the distribution is skewed ("tilted" to the right or left), as in Figure 3(b), the mean, median, and mode do not coincide.

What is the best measure of central tendency? The answer depends on what we want to know. If we're interested in finding out what score has been received most often on an examination, we would use the mode. But the most frequently occurring score may not be the best representation of how the class performed on the average. For that determination, we could use the median, which indicates the middle score in the distribution—that is, the score below which half of the scores fall and above which half of the scores fall. By knowing the median, we could specify which score separates the top half of the class from the bottom half.

We could also use the mean, which provides us with the arithmetic average of the whole class. But one limitation of the mean is that it is greatly influenced by extreme scores. Consider the following example of the distribution of salaries for employees in a small manufacturing company:

Position	Number of Employees	Salary	Measure of Central Tendency
President/CEO	1	$350,000	
Executive vice president	1	120,000	
Vice presidents	2	95,000	
Controller	1	60,000	
Senior salespeople	3	58,000	Mean
Junior salespeople	4	40,000	
Foreman	1	36,000	Median
Machinists	12	30,000	Mode

In this example, the mean is greatly influenced by one very high score—the salary of the president/CEO. If you were the chairperson of the local machinists' union, which measure of central tendency would you use to negotiate a new wage agreement? Alternatively, which would you use if you represented management's position in the negotiations?

Table 3 Calculation of a Standard Deviation

Score	Deviation from Mean (D)	Deviation Squared (D^2)
3	$3 - 9 = -6$	36
5	$5 - 9 = -4$	16
6	$6 - 9 = -3$	9
9	$9 - 9 = 0$	0
12	$12 - 9 = 3$	9
13	$13 - 9 = 4$	16
15	$15 - 9 = 6$	36
$X = 63/7 = 9$		$\Sigma D^2 = 122$

Standard Deviation $= \sqrt{\Sigma D^2 / n} = \sqrt{122/7} = \sqrt{17.43} = 4.17$

Another consideration in choosing the best measure concerns how it is to be used. If we wish to generalize from samples to populations, the mean has a distinct advantage. It can be manipulated mathematically in ways that are inappropriate for the median or the mode. But if the purpose is primarily descriptive, then the measure that best characterizes the data should be used. In general, reporting all three measures of central tendency provides the most accurate description of a given distribution.

Measures of Variability

The final step in describing a distribution of scores is to compute the **variability** of the scores. Variability is the spread of scores throughout the distribution of scores. One measure of variability is the **range** of scores, or the difference between the highest and lowest scores in the distribution. The final examination scores for the 180 freshman psychology students range from a low of 24 to a high of 69, so the range would be $69 - 24 = 45$.

Another, more commonly used measure of variability is the **standard deviation (SD)**, conceptually defined as the average difference between each individual score and the mean of all scores in the data set. A large standard deviation suggests considerable variability (spread) of scores around the mean, whereas a small standard deviation indicates little variability. Table 3 illustrates the computations involved in calculating the standard deviation based on a hypothetical data set. (The standard deviation of the 180 final examination scores is 8.98.)

The Normal Distribution

The histogram for the 180 final examination scores in Figure 1 illustrates a commonly observed phenomenon in psychological data—namely, that the majority of scores tend to fall in the middle of the distribution, with fewer scores in the extreme categories. For many measures used in psychological research, score distributions have this general shape and are said to resemble a "bell-shaped curve," which is otherwise known as a "normal curve" or "normal distribution." In statistics, the true normal distribution is a mathematical model. However, when the shape of a particular score distribution closely aligns with a normal distribution, we can use the general properties of the normal distribution to describe the distribution of actual scores under study. The normal distribution provides a good description of

variability In statistics, the spread or dispersion of scores throughout the distribution.

range A measure of variability that is given by the difference in value between the highest and lowest scores in a distribution of scores.

standard deviation (SD) A measure of variability defined as the average difference between each individual score and the mean of all scores in the data set. More precisely, the square root of the average of the squared deviations of individual scores from the mean.

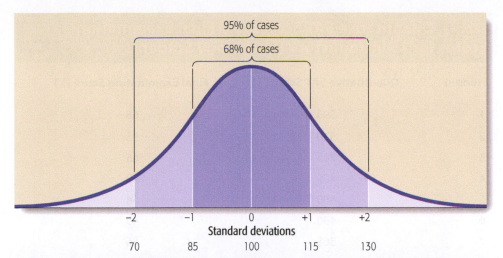

FIGURE 4 A Normal Distribution Showing the Approximate Percentages of Cases Falling Within One and Two Standard Deviations from the Mean

the distribution of many sets of data, such as measures of intelligence and achievement. Moreover, in a normal distribution, the mean, median, and mode all have the same value, so we can use the standard deviation to describe a particular score in the distribution relative to all scores in the distribution.

In a normal distribution, such as the one shown in Figure 4, half of all cases fall above the mean and half fall below. Based on the properties of the normal distribution, we can determine the percentages of cases that fall within each segment of the distribution. For example, approximately 68 percent of cases fall within one standard deviation above and below the mean (between −1.0 and +1.0), and approximately 95 percent of cases fall within two standard deviations above and below the mean (between −2.0 and +2.0).

The properties of the normal distribution can also be used to describe the distance between a score and the mean. Scores on most IQ tests, for example, are distributed with a mean of 100 and a standard deviation of 15. Thus, an IQ score of 115 would be about one standard deviation above the mean. We use the term **standard score** (also called a *z-score*) to refer to a transformed score that indicates how many standard deviations the actual (raw) score is above or below the mean. For example, the standard score corresponding to a raw score of 115, based on a mean of 100 and a standard deviation of 15, would be +1.0. Similarly, we could say that a score of 70 is two standard deviations below the mean; in this case, the standard score would be −2.0. These standard score properties of the normal distribution are critical in applying inferential statistical procedures in psychological research.

Using Statistics to Relate

A second application of statistics involves determining the relationship between two variables. As an example, let's say we want to determine the relationship between quantitative SAT scores and final examination scores, using the data for 15 introductory psychology students shown in Table 4.

The Scatterplot: Plotting the Data

Our first step would be to enter these data in a **scatterplot**, a type of graph that represents the "scatter" of scores obtained by plotting each individual's scores on two variables. The two variables can be symbolized by the terms *X* and *Y*.

standard score A transformed score that indicates the number of standard deviations a corresponding raw score is above or below the mean. Also called a *z-score*.

scatterplot A graph in which pairs of scores are plotted for each research participant on two variables.

Table 4 Quantitative SAT Scores and Final Examination Scores for 15 Introductory Psychology Students

Student	Quantitative SAT Score (X)	Final Examination Score (Y)
1	595	68
2	520	55
3	715	65
4	405	42
5	680	64
6	490	45
7	565	56
8	580	59
9	615	56
10	435	42
11	440	38
12	515	50
13	380	37
14	510	42
15	565	53
Σ	8,010	772
	$\overline{X} = 534.00$	$\overline{Y} = 51.47$
	$S_X = 96.53$	$S_Y = 10.11$

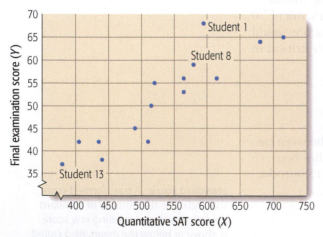

FIGURE 5 Scatterplot Illustrating the Relationship Between Final Examination (Y) and Quantitative SAT Scores (X)

In Figure 5, each point represents the paired measurements for each of the fifteen students, three of whom—Students 1, 8, and 13—are labeled specifically. (For example, the point for Student 1 represents the paired scores "SAT = 595" and "Final Score = 68.") Notice that these points form a pattern that starts in the lower left corner and ends in the upper right corner of the scatterplot. This pattern occurs when there is a positive relationship, or *positive correlation*, between the two variables. A positive correlation between two variables means that higher scores on one variable are associated with higher scores on the other variable. The pattern shown in Figure 5 thus illustrates that students with higher SAT scores tend to have higher final examination scores, and vice versa.

Different scatterplot patterns emerge as a result of different types of relationships between two variables. Three of these patterns are illustrated in Figure 6. Pattern A depicts a positive correlation between two variables. Pattern B depicts a negative correlation—a relationship in which higher scores on one variable are associated with lower scores on the other variable. And Pattern C is a scatterplot in which the points have neither an upward nor a downward trend. This last pattern occurs in situations where there is a zero correlation (no relationship) between the two variables.

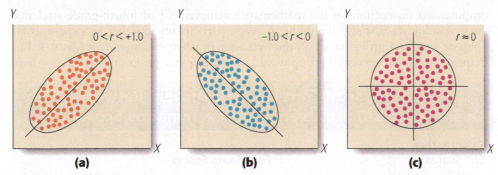

FIGURE 6 **Scatterplots Illustrating Varying Degrees of Relationship Between X and Y**

The Correlation Coefficient: Calculating the Relationship Between Two Variables

The scatterplot gives us a visual representation of the relationship between two variables. But researchers also use a statistical measure that provides a more precise indication of both the magnitude (strength) and direction of the relationship (positive or negative). The statistical measure of the relationship between two variables is called the correlation coefficient (expressed by the letter r). The range of values for positive *correlation coefficients* is from 0 (minimum) to +1.0 (maximum); the range of values for negative correlation coefficients is from 0 (minimum) to −1.0 (maximum).

Table 5 shows a worked-out example of the computations involved in calculating a correlation coefficient based on the data presented in Table 4. The correlation coefficient is found to be +0.90, which represents a very high, positive relationship between SAT scores and final examination scores. In other words, as we saw earlier, freshmen with higher SAT scores tend to achieve higher scores in their psychology exams.

Table 6 provides some rules of thumb for interpreting the magnitude of a correlation coefficient.

Using One Variable to Predict Another

An important use of correlational statistics is prediction. If two variables are correlated, we can predict scores on one variable based upon scores on the other variable. For example, after determining the relationship between SAT scores and final examination scores for our 15 introductory psychology students, let's suppose that we want to predict the final examination scores of similar students based upon our knowledge of their SAT scores. The process of prediction involves developing a mathematical equation that incorporates the paired sets of scores on the two variables obtained in the study. This equation can then be used to predict final examination scores based on SAT scores for comparable groups of students. The accuracy of the prediction reflects the magnitude of the correlation between the variables: The higher the correlation, the better the prediction. If a strong relationship exists between the two variables, knowing how students score on the SAT would allow us to make fairly accurate predictions about how they will perform in their psychology courses.

Using Statistics to Compare

A third application of statistics involves comparing two or more groups. Let's say, for example, that an educational psychologist is interested in examining the effects of computerized instruction on the mathematics achievement of fourth-grade students. The psychologist's first step would be to assign participants to either an experimental group or a control group based on the technique of *random assignment* (discussed in Chapter 1). The experimental group would use a computer program that allows them

Table 5 Calculation of Correlation Coefficient Between Quantitative SAT Scores and Final Examination Scores

Quantitative SAT Scores		Final Exam Scores		
X	X^2	Y	Y^2	XY
595	354,025	68	4,624	40,460
520	270,400	55	3,025	28,600
715	511,225	65	4,225	46,475
405	164,025	42	1,764	17,010
680	462,400	64	4,096	43,520
490	240,100	45	2,025	22,050
565	319,225	56	3,136	31,640
580	336,400	59	3,481	34,220
615	378,225	56	3,136	34,440
435	189,225	42	1,764	18,270
440	193,600	38	1,444	16,720
515	265,225	50	2,500	25,750
380	144,400	37	1,369	14,060
510	260,100	42	1,764	21,420
565	319,225	53	2,809	29,945
8,010	4,407,800	772	41,162	424,580

$$\text{Raw Score Formula} = \frac{n\Sigma X \Sigma Y}{\sqrt{n\Sigma X^2 - (\Sigma X)^2}\sqrt{n\Sigma Y^2 - (\Sigma Y)^2}}$$

$$= \frac{15(424,580) - (8,010)(772)}{\sqrt{12(4,407,800) - (8,010)^2}\sqrt{15(41,162) - (772)^2}}$$

$$= 0.90$$

Table 6 Rules of Thumb for Interpreting the Size of a Correlation Coefficient

Size of Correlation	Interpretation
.90 to 1.00 (−.90 to −1.00)	Very high positive (negative) correlation
.70 to .90 (−.70 to −.90)	High positive (negative) correlation
.50 to .70 (−.50 to −.70)	Moderate positive (negative) correlation
.30 to .50 (−.30 to −.50)	Low positive (negative) correlation
.00 to .30 (.00 to −.30)	Little if any correlation

to acquire mathematical concepts through interactive on-screen exercises, whereas the control group would receive standard classroom instruction. Then, at the conclusion of the study, both groups would be tested on a mathematics achievement test.

Let's further suppose that the results of the initial descriptive data analysis are as follows:

	Control Group	Experimental Group
Mean (X)	62.4	77.6
Standard Deviation (SD)	15.8	16.3

Using these data, the educational psychologist would be able to describe the performance of the two groups by examining their means and standard deviations. Note, however, that for drawing conclusions and making generalizations from these data, inferential statistical procedures would also be needed.

Beyond Description: Using Inferential Statistics

Descriptive statistics allow us to summarize data, but the meaning of these statistical measures cannot be fully understood through descriptive statistics alone. In psychological research, it is important to determine whether the size of a correlation coefficient, or the difference between the means of two groups, is statistically significant. *Statistical significance* indicates that the results obtained from a study are unlikely to have been due to chance or to the random fluctuations that would be expected to occur among scores in the general population.

Statistical significance can be determined only through the use of statistical techniques, called inferential statistics, that enable us to draw conclusions from our data and to make inferences and generalizations from samples to the populations from which they are drawn.

Stating the Null Hypothesis

The first step in using inferential statistics is to state a **null hypothesis** for the study in question. Defined literally, the word *null* refers to something of no value or significance. By the same token, a null hypothesis is a prediction that a given finding has no value or significance. For the study of the relationship between SAT scores and final examination scores, we can state the following null hypothesis: "There is *no relationship* between the two variables." And for the study of the difference between experimental and control groups on the question of computerized versus standard instruction, we can offer this null hypothesis: "There is *no difference* between the two groups."

Testing the Null Hypothesis

The main purpose of inferential statistics is to test the null hypothesis. Using these techniques, scientific investigators can apply principles of probability to determine whether relationships between variables or differences between groups are large enough to be unlikely to be due to chance. In the process, they typically apply a criterion by which an outcome is judged to be significant when its likelihood of arising from chance is less than 5 percent. In other words, if the probability that an outcome would occur by chance alone is less than 5 percent, they would say that the finding is

null hypothesis A prediction of no difference between groups or no relationship between variables.

statistically significant. Depending on the nature of the research, researchers may set either more stringent or more liberal criteria for determining the threshold at which they would represent a given finding as statistically significant.

Let's return to our example of the 15 introductory psychology students. First, if the correlation coefficient between their SAT scores and final examination scores is high enough to reach a level of statistical significance, we would reject the null hypothesis of "no relationship." In other words, we would conclude that the correlation is significantly different from zero (which in itself means "no relationship"). Second, in applying inferential statistics to the prediction of scores on one variable from scores on another, we would say that the null hypothesis is that SAT scores do not predict final examination scores. But because there *is* a statistically significant relationship between these two variables, our conclusion (based on probability theory) would be that SAT scores are a significant predictor of final examination scores.

Inferential statistics are used in a similar way when investigating differences between two or more groups. These statistical techniques involve mathematical constructs based on probability theory for determining whether differences between sample means are large enough to reject the null hypothesis of "no difference." If the difference between the means of the computer instruction group and the classroom instruction group is large enough to meet the threshold of statistical significance, we would reject the null hypothesis and conclude that the difference between the groups is statistically significant. The underlying rationale is that when group differences between samples of research participants on measures of interest meet the threshold for statistical significance, they are unlikely to reflect chanceful variations that would be expected to occur on these measures in the population in general.

Summing Up

In this brief introduction to statistics, we have provided some basic terminology, identified several approaches to using statistics in psychological research, and discussed descriptive and inferential statistics as well as their general application in research studies. We have also offered a convenient way of categorizing the main purposes of statistics: (1) to describe, (2) to relate, and (3) to compare. An understanding of all these aspects of statistics is necessary not only for researchers in psychology but also for consumers of research results.

Glossary

absolute threshold The smallest amount of a given stimulus a person can sense.

accommodation In perception, the process by which the lens changes its shape to focus images more clearly on the retina. To Piaget, the process of creating new schemas or modifying existing ones to account for new objects or experiences.

acculturative stress Demands faced by immigrants in adjusting to a host culture.

achievement motivation The motive or desire to achieve success.

acronym A word composed of the first letters of a series of words.

acrophobia Excessive fear of heights.

acrostic A verse or saying in which the first or last letter of each word stands for something else.

action potential An abrupt change from a negative to a positive charge of a nerve cell, also called a *neural impulse*.

activation–synthesis hypothesis The proposition that dreams represent the brain's attempt to make sense of the random discharges of electrical activity that occur during REM sleep.

actor–observer effect The tendency to attribute the causes of one's own behavior to situational factors while attributing the causes of other people's behavior to internal factors or dispositions.

acupuncture An ancient Chinese practice of inserting and rotating thin needles in various parts of the body in order to release natural healing energy.

adaptation To Piaget, the process of adjustment that enables people to function more effectively in meeting the demands they face in the environment.

adolescence The period of life beginning at puberty and ending with early adulthood.

adoptee studies Studies that examine whether adoptees are more similar to their biological or adoptive parents with respect to their psychological traits or to the disorders they develop.

adrenal cortex The outer layer of the adrenal glands that secretes corticosteroids (cortical steroids).

adrenal glands A pair of endocrine glands located just above the kidneys that produce various stress-related hormones.

adrenal medulla The inner part of the adrenal glands that secretes the stress hormones epinephrine (adrenaline) and norepinephrine (noradrenaline).

adrenocorticotrophic hormone (ACTH) A pituitary hormone that activates the adrenal cortex to release corticosteroids (cortical steroids).

afterimage The visual image of a stimulus that remains after the stimulus is removed.

agonists Drugs that either increase the availability or effectiveness of neurotransmitters or mimic their actions.

agoraphobia Excessive, irrational fear of being in public places.

alarm stage The first stage of the general adaptation syndrome, involving mobilization of the body's resources to cope with an immediate stressor.

alcoholism A chemical addiction characterized by impaired control over the use of alcohol and physiological dependence on it.

algorithm A step-by-step set of rules that will always lead to a correct solution to a problem.

all-or-none principle The principle by which neurons will fire only when a change in the level of excitation occurs that is sufficient to produce an action potential.

altered states of consciousness States of awareness during wakefulness that are different than the person's usual waking state.

Alzheimer's disease (AD) An irreversible brain disease with a progressive course of deterioration of mental functioning.

amnesia Loss of memory.

amniotic sac The uterine sac that contains the fetus.

amphetamines A class of synthetically derived stimulant drugs, such as methamphetamine or "speed."

amygdala A set of almond-shaped structures in the limbic system believed to play an important role in aggression, rage, and fear.

anal stage In Freudian theory, the second stage of psychosexual development, during which sexual gratification is centered on processes of elimination (retention and release of bowel contents).

anal-expulsive personality In Freudian theory, a personality type characterized by messiness, lack of self-discipline, and carelessness.

anal-retentive personality In Freudian theory, a personality type characterized by perfectionism and excessive needs for self-control as expressed through extreme neatness and punctuality.

animistic thinking To Piaget, the child's belief that inanimate objects have living qualities.

antagonists Drugs that block the actions of neurotransmitters by occupying the receptor sites in which the neurotransmitters dock.

anterograde amnesia Loss or impairment of the ability to form or store new memories.

antianxiety drugs Drugs that combat anxiety.

antibodies Protein molecules produced by the immune system that serve to mark antigens for destruction by specialized lymphocytes.

antidepressants Drugs that combat depression by affecting the levels or activity of neurotransmitters.

antigens Substances, such as bacteria and viruses, that are recognized by the immune system as foreign to the body and that induce it to produce antibodies to defend against them.

antipsychotics Drugs used in the treatment of psychotic disorders that help alleviate hallucinations and delusional thinking.

antisocial personality disorder (APD or ASPD) A type of personality disorder characterized by callous attitudes toward others and by antisocial and irresponsible behavior.

aphasia Loss or impairment of the ability to understand or express language.

applied research Research that attempts to find solutions to specific problems.

archetypes Jung's term for the primitive images contained in the collective unconscious that reflect ancestral or universal experiences of human beings.

arousal theory The belief that whenever the level of stimulation dips below an organism's optimal level, the organism seeks ways of increasing it.

arteries Blood vessels that carry oxygen-rich blood from the heart through the circulatory system.

arteriosclerosis A condition in which artery walls become thicker and lose elasticity. Commonly called *hardening of the arteries*.

assimilation To Piaget, the process of incorporating new objects or situations into existing schemas.

association areas Areas of the cerebral cortex that piece together sensory information to form meaningful perceptions of the world and perform higher mental functions.

atherosclerosis A form of arteriosclerosis involving the narrowing of artery walls resulting from the buildup of fatty deposits or plaque.

attachment The enduring emotional bond that infants and older children form with their caregivers.

attitude A positive or negative evaluation of people, objects, or issues.

attraction Feelings of liking for others, together with having positive thoughts about them and inclinations to act toward them in positive ways.

attribution An assumption about the causes of behavior or events.

attributional style A person's characteristic way of explaining outcomes of events in his or her life.

audition The sense of hearing.

auditory nerve The nerve that carries neural impulses from the ear to the brain, which gives rise to the experience of hearing.

authoritarian personality A personality type characterized by rigidity, prejudice, and excessive concerns with obedience and respect for authority.

autonomic nervous system (ANS) The part of the peripheral nervous system that automatically regulates involuntary bodily processes, such as breathing, heart rate, and digestion.

availability heuristic The tendency to judge events as more likely to occur when information pertaining to them comes readily to mind.

aversive conditioning A form of behavior therapy in which stimuli associated with undesirable behavior are paired with aversive stimuli to create a negative response to these stimuli.

avoidance learning The learning of behaviors that allow an organism to avoid an aversive stimulus.

avoidance motivation The motive or desire to avoid failure.

axon The tubelike part of a neuron that carries messages away from the cell body toward other neurons.

Babinski reflex The reflexive fanning out and curling of the infant's toes and inward twisting of its foot when the sole of the foot is stroked.

bait-and-switch technique A compliance technique based on "baiting" a person by making an unrealistically attractive offer and then replacing it with a less attractive offer.

basal cell carcinoma A form of skin cancer that is easily curable if detected and removed early.

basal ganglia An assemblage of neurons lying in the forebrain that is important in controlling movement and coordination.

basic anxiety In Horney's theory, a deep-seated form of anxiety in children that is associated with feelings of being isolated and helpless in a world perceived as potentially threatening and hostile.

basic hostility In Horney's theory, deep feelings of resentment that children may harbor toward their parents.

basic research Research focused on acquiring knowledge even if such knowledge has no direct practical application.

basilar membrane The membrane in the cochlea that is attached to the organ of Corti.

behavior modification (B-mod) The systematic application of learning principles to strengthen adaptive behavior and weaken maladaptive behavior.

behavior therapy A form of therapy that involves the systematic application of the principles of learning.

behavioral perspective An approach to the study of psychology that focuses on the role of learning and importance of environmental influences in explaining behavior.

behaviorism The school of psychology that holds that psychology should limit itself to the study of overt, observable behavior.

binocular cues Cues for depth that involve both eyes, such as retinal disparity and convergence.

biofeedback training (BFT) A method of learning to control certain bodily responses by using information from the body transmitted by physiological monitoring equipment.

biopsychosocial model An integrative model for explaining abnormal behavior patterns in terms of the interactions of biological, psychological, and sociocultural factors.

bipolar cells A layer of interconnecting cells in the eye that connect photoreceptors to ganglion cells.

bipolar disorder A type of mood disorder characterized by mood swings from extreme elation (mania) to severe depression.

blind spot The area in the retina where the optic nerve leaves the eye and that contains no photoreceptor cells.

borderline personality disorder A type of personality disorder characterized by unstable emotions and self-image.

bottom-up processing A mode of perceptual processing by which the brain recognizes meaningful patterns by piecing together bits and pieces of sensory information.

brain The mass of nerve tissue encased in the skull that controls virtually everything we are and everything we do.

brainstem The "stalk" in the lower part of the brain that connects the spinal cord to higher regions of the brain.

brainstorming A method of promoting divergent thinking by encouraging people to propose as many solutions to a problem as possible without fear of being judged negatively by others, no matter how far-fetched their proposals may be.

brightness constancy The tendency to perceive objects as retaining their brightness even when they are viewed in dim light.

Broca's area An area of the left frontal lobe involved in speech.

bystander intervention Helping a stranger in distress.

Cannon–Bard theory The belief that emotional and physiological reactions to triggering stimuli occur almost simultaneously.

cardinal traits Allport's term for the more pervasive dimensions that define an individual's general personality.

carpentered-world hypothesis An attempt to explain the Müller-Lyer illusion in terms of the cultural experience of living in a carpentered, right-angled world like our own.

case study method An in-depth study of one or more individuals.

castration anxiety In Freudian theory, unconscious fear of removal of the penis as punishment for having unacceptable sexual impulses.

catatonic Relating to catatonia, a condition involving states of stupor and unresponsiveness to the environment.

central nervous system The part of the nervous system that consists of the brain and spinal cord.

central tendency A central point on a scale of measurement around which scores are distributed.

central traits Allport's term for personality characteristics that have a widespread influence on the individual's behavior across situations.

centration To Piaget, the tendency to focus on only one aspect of a situation at a time.

cerebellum A structure in the hindbrain involved in controlling coordination and balance.

cerebral cortex The wrinkled, outer layer of gray matter that covers the cerebral hemispheres; controls higher mental functions, such as thought and language.

cerebral hemispheres The right and left masses of the cerebrum, which are joined by the corpus callosum.

cerebrum The largest mass of the forebrain, consisting of two cerebral hemispheres.

chromosomes Rodlike structures in the cell nucleus that house an individual's genes.

chronic stress Continuing or lingering stress.

chunking The process of enhancing retention of a large amount of information by breaking it down into smaller, more easily recalled chunks.

circadian rhythm The pattern of fluctuations in bodily processes that occur regularly each day.

clairvoyance The ability to perceive objects and events without using the known senses.

classical conditioning The process of learning by which a previously neutral stimulus comes to elicit a response identical or similar to one that was originally elicited by another stimulus as the result of the pairing or association of the two stimuli.

claustrophobia Excessive fear of enclosed spaces.

clinical psychologists Psychologists who use psychological techniques to evaluate and treat individuals with mental or psychological disorders.

closure The perceptual principle that people tend to piece together disconnected bits of information to perceive whole forms.

cochlea The snail-shaped organ in the inner ear that contains sensory receptors for hearing.

cognitive-behavioral therapy (CBT) A form of therapy that combines behavioral and cognitive treatment techniques.

cognitive dissonance theory The belief that people are motivated to resolve discrepancies between their behavior and their attitudes, beliefs, or perceptions.

cognitive learning Learning that occurs without the opportunity of first performing the learned response or being reinforced for it.

cognitive map A mental representation of an area that helps an organism navigate its way from one point to another.

cognitive perspective An approach to the study of psychology that focuses on the processes by which we acquire knowledge.

cognitive psychology The branch of psychology that focuses on such mental processes as thinking, problem solving, decision making, and use of language.

cognitive therapy Developed by Aaron Beck, a form of therapy that helps clients recognize and correct distorted patterns of thinking associated with negative emotional states.

collective unconscious In Jung's theory, a part of the mind containing ideas and archetypal images shared among humankind that have been transmitted genetically from ancestral humans.

collectivistic culture A culture that emphasizes people's social roles and obligations.

color constancy The tendency to perceive an object as having the same color despite changes in lighting conditions.

comparative psychologists Psychologists who study behavioral similarities and differences among animal species.

compliance The process of acceding to the requests or demands of others.

computer-assisted instruction A form of programmed instruction in which a computer is used to guide a student through a series of increasingly difficult questions.

concepts Mental categories for classifying events, objects, and ideas on the basis of their common features or properties.

conceptual combinations Combinations of two or more concepts into one concept, resulting in the creation of a novel idea or application.

conceptual expansion Expanding familiar concepts by applying them to new uses.

concordance rates In twin studies, the percentages of cases in which both members of twin pairs share the same trait or disorder.

conditional positive regard Valuing a person only when the person's behavior meets certain expectations or standards.

conditioned emotional reaction (CER) An emotional response to a particular stimulus acquired through classical conditioning.

conditioned response (CR) An acquired or learned response to a conditioned stimulus.

conditioned stimulus (CS) A previously neutral stimulus that comes to elicit a conditioned response after it has been paired with an unconditioned stimulus.

conditioned taste aversion An aversion to a particular food or beverage acquired through classical conditioning.

conduction deafness A form of deafness, usually involving damage to the middle ear, in which there is a loss of conduction of sound vibrations through the ear.

cones Photoreceptors that are sensitive to color.

confirmation bias The tendency to maintain allegiance to an initial hypothesis despite strong evidence to the contrary.

conflict A state of tension brought about by opposing response tendencies or motives operating simultaneously.

conformity The tendency to adjust one's behavior to actual or perceived social pressures.

connectedness The principle that objects positioned together or moving together will be perceived as belonging to the same group.

conscious To Freud, the part of the mind corresponding to the state of present awareness.

consciousness A state of awareness of ourselves and of the world around us.

conservation In Piaget's theory, the ability to recognize that the quantity or amount of an object remains constant despite superficial changes in its outward appearance.

consolidation The process of converting short-term memories into long-term memories.

constructionist theory A theory that holds that memory is not a replica of the past but a representation, or *reconstruction*, of the past.

consumer psychologists Psychologists who study why people purchase particular products and brands.

contact hypothesis Allport's belief that under certain conditions, increased intergroup contact helps reduce prejudice and intergroup tension.

continuity The principle that a series of stimuli will be perceived as representing a unified form.

control groups Groups of participants in a research experiment who do not receive the experimental treatment or intervention.

convergence A binocular cue for distance based on the degree of tension required to focus two eyes on the same object.

convergent thinking The attempt to narrow down a range of alternatives to converge on the one correct answer to a problem.

conversion disorder A psychological disorder characterized by a change in or loss of a physical function that cannot be explained by medical causes.

cornea A transparent covering on the eye's surface through which light enters.

coronary heart disease (CHD) The most common form of heart disease, caused by blockages in coronary arteries, the vessels that supply the heart with blood.

corpus callosum The thick bundle of nerve fibers that connects the two cerebral hemispheres.

correlation coefficient A statistical measure of association between variables that can vary from −1.00 to +1.00.

correlational method A research method used to examine relationships between variables, which are expressed in the form of a statistical measure called a correlation coefficient.

corticosteroids Adrenal hormones that increase the body's resistance to stress by increasing the availability of stored nutrients to meet the increased energy demands of coping with stressful events. Also called *cortical steroids*.

corticotrophin-releasing hormone (CRH) A hormone released by the hypothalamus that induces the pituitary gland to release adrenocorticotrophic hormone.

counseling psychologists Psychologists who help people clarify their goals and make life decisions or find ways of overcoming problems in various areas of their lives.

countertransference The tendency for therapists to relate to clients in ways that mirror the relationships they've had with important figures in their own lives.

couple therapy Therapy that focuses on helping distressed couples resolve their conflicts and develop more effective communication skills.

creative self In Adler's theory, the self-aware part of personality that organizes goal-seeking efforts.

creativity Originality of thought associated with the development of new, workable products or solutions to problems.

critical thinking The adoption of a skeptical, questioning attitude and careful scrutiny of claims or arguments.

crystallized intelligence A form of intelligence associated with the use of knowledge or wisdom.

CT (computed tomography) scan A computer-enhanced imaging technique in which an X-ray beam is passed through the body at different angles to generate a three-dimensional image of bodily structures (also called a CAT scan, short for computed axial tomography).

culture-fair tests Tests designed to eliminate cultural biases.

daydreaming A form of consciousness during a waking state in which one's mind wanders to dreamy thoughts or fantasies.

decay theory A theory of forgetting that posits that memories consist of traces laid down in the brain that gradually deteriorate and fade away over time (also called *trace theory*).

decision making A form of problem solving in which we must select a course of action from among the available alternatives.

declarative memory Memory of facts and personal information that requires a conscious effort to bring to mind (also called *explicit memory*).

defense mechanisms In Freudian theory, the reality-distorting strategies of the ego to prevent awareness of anxiety-evoking or troubling ideas or impulses.

deinstitutionalization A policy of reducing the population of mental hospitals by shifting care from inpatient facilities to community-based outpatient facilities.

delirium A mental state characterized by confusion, disorientation, difficulty in focusing attention, and excitable behavior.

delusions Fixed but patently false beliefs, such as believing that one is being hounded by demons.

dementia A condition involving a major deterioration or loss of mental abilities involved in memory, reasoning, judgment, and ability to carry out purposeful behavior.

dendrites Rootlike structures at the end of axons that receive neural impulses from neighboring neurons.

denial In Freudian theory, a defense mechanism involving the failure to recognize a threatening impulse or urge.

deoxyribonucleic acid (DNA) The basic chemical material in chromosomes that carries an individual's genetic code.

dependent variables The effects or outcomes of an experiment that are believed to be dependent on the values of the independent variables.

depolarization A positive shift in the electrical charge in the neuron's resting potential, making it less negatively charged.

depressants Drugs, such as alcohol and barbiturates, that dampen central nervous system activity.

depressive attributional style A characteristic way of explaining negative events in terms of internal, stable, and global causes.

descriptive statistics Procedures used for classifying and summarizing information in numerical form—in short, for describing data.

detoxification A process of clearing drugs or toxins from the body.

developmental psychologists Psychologists who focus on processes involving physical, cognitive, social, and personality development.

developmental psychology The branch of psychology that explores physical, emotional, cognitive, and social aspects of development.

diathesis A vulnerability or predisposition to developing a disorder.

diathesis-stress model A type of biopsychosocial model that relates the development of disorders to the combination of a diathesis, or predisposition, usually genetic in origin, and exposure to stressful events or life circumstances.

dichromats People who can see some colors but not others.

difference threshold The minimal difference in the magnitude of energy needed for people to detect a difference between two stimuli.

discrimination Unfair or biased treatment of people based on their membership in a particular group or category.

discriminative stimulus A cue that signals that reinforcement is available if the subject makes a particular response.

disinhibition effect The removal of normal restraints or inhibitions that serve to keep impulsive behavior in check.

displacement In Freudian theory, a defense mechanism in which an unacceptable sexual or aggressive impulse is transferred to an object or person that is safer or less threatening than the original object of the impulse.

display rules Cultural customs and norms that govern the display of emotional expressions.

dispositional causes Causes relating to the internal characteristics or traits of individuals.

dissociative amnesia A psychologically based form of amnesia involving the "splitting off" from memory of traumatic or troubling experiences.

dissociative disorders A class of psychological disorders involving changes in consciousness, memory, or self-identity.

dissociative identity disorder (DID) A type of dissociative disorder characterized by the appearance of multiple personalities in the same individual.

divergent thinking The ability to conceive of new ways of viewing situations and new uses for familiar objects.

divided consciousness A state of awareness characterized by divided attention to two or more tasks or activities performed at the same time.

door-in-the-face technique A compliance technique in which refusal of a large, unreasonable request is followed by a smaller, more reasonable request.

double-blind studies In drug research, studies in which both participants and experimenters are kept uninformed about which participants are receiving the active drug and which are receiving the placebo.

dream analysis A technique in psychoanalysis in which the therapist analyzes the underlying or symbolic meaning of the client's dreams.

drifting consciousness A state of awareness characterized by drifting thoughts or mental imagery.

drive A state of bodily tension, such as hunger or thirst, that arises from an unmet need.

drive for superiority Adler's term for the motivation to compensate for feelings of inferiority. Also called the *will-to-power*.

drive reduction Satisfaction of a drive.

drive theory The belief that behavior is motivated by drives that arise from biological needs that demand satisfaction.

drug abuse Maladaptive or dangerous use of a chemical substance.

drug addiction Drug dependence accompanied by signs of physiological dependence, such as the development of a withdrawal syndrome.

drug dependence A severe drug-related problem characterized by impaired control over the use of the drug.

dual-pathway model of fear LeDoux's theory that the brain uses two pathways (a "high road" and a "low road") to process fear messages.

Duchenne smile A genuine smile that involves contraction of a particular set of facial muscles.

dyslexia A learning disorder characterized by impaired ability to read.

eardrum A sheet of connective tissue separating the outer ear from the middle ear that vibrates in response to auditory stimuli and transmits sound waves to the middle ear.

echoic memory A sensory store for holding a mental representation of a sound for a few seconds after it registers in the ears.

eclectic therapy A therapeutic approach that draws upon principles and techniques representing different schools of therapy.

educational psychologists Psychologists who study issues relating to the measurement of intelligence and the processes involved in educational or academic achievement.

EEG (electroencephalograph) A device that records electrical activity in the brain.

efficacy expectations Bandura's term for the expectancies we have regarding our ability to perform behaviors we set out to accomplish.

ego Freud's term for the psychic structure that attempts to balance the instinctual demands of the id with social realities and expectations.

egocentrism To Piaget, the tendency to see the world only from one's own perspective.

ego identity In Erickson's theory, the attainment of a psychological sense of knowing oneself and one's direction in life.

eidetic imagery A lingering mental representation of a visual image (commonly called *photographic memory*).

elaboration likelihood model (ELM) A theoretical model that posits two channels by which persuasive appeals lead to attitude change: a central route and a peripheral route.

elaborative rehearsal The process of strengthening new memories by forming meaningful associations between the information and existing memories or knowledge.

Electra complex The term given by some psychodynamic theorists to the form of the Oedipus complex in young girls.

electrical recording As a method of investigating brain functioning, a process of recording the electrical changes that occur in a specific neuron or groups of neurons in the brain in relation to particular activities or behaviors.

electrical stimulation As a method of investigating brain functioning, a process of electrically stimulating particular parts of the brain to observe the effects on behavior.

electroconvulsive therapy (ECT) A form of therapy for severe depression that involves the administration of an electrical shock to the head.

electromyographic (EMG) biofeedback A form of BFT that involves feedback about changes in the level of muscle tension in the forehead or elsewhere in the body.

embryo The developing organism at an early stage of prenatal development.

embryonic stage The stage of prenatal development from implantation through about the eighth week of pregnancy during which the major organ systems begin to form.

emerging adulthood The period of psychosocial development, roughly spanning the ages of 18 to 25, during which the person makes the transition from adolescence to adulthood.

emotional intelligence The ability to recognize emotions in yourself and others and to manage your own emotions effectively.

emotions Feeling states that psychologists view as having physiological, cognitive, and behavioral components.

empirical approach A method of developing knowledge based on evaluating evidence gathered from experiments and careful observation.

endocrine system The body's system of glands that release their secretions, called hormones, directly into the bloodstream.

endorphins Natural chemicals released in the brain that have pain-killing and pleasure-inducing effects.

engram Lashley's term for the physical trace or etching of a memory in the brain.

environmental psychologists Psychologists who study relationships between the physical environment and behavior.

enzymes Organic substances that produce certain chemical changes in other organic substances through a catalytic action.

epilepsy A neurological disorder characterized by seizures that involve sudden, violent discharges of electrical activity in the brain.

episodic memory Memory of personal experiences.

erogenous zones Parts of the body that are especially sensitive to sexual or pleasurable stimulation.

escape learning The learning of behaviors that allow an organism to escape from an aversive stimulus.

ethics review committees Committees that evaluate whether proposed studies meet ethical guidelines.

evolutionary psychology A branch of psychology that focuses on the role of evolutionary processes in shaping behavior.

exhaustion stage The third stage of the general adaptation syndrome, characterized by depletion of bodily resources and a lowered resistance to stress-related disorders or conditions.

expectancies In social-cognitive theory, personal predictions about the outcomes of behavior.

experimental method A method of scientific investigation involving the manipulation of independent variables and observation or measurement of their effects on dependent variables under controlled conditions.

experimental psychologists Psychologists who apply experimental methods to the study of behavior and mental processes.

explicit memory Memory accessed through conscious effort.

extinction The gradual weakening and eventual disappearance of a conditioned response.

extrasensory perception (ESP) Perception that occurs without benefit of the known senses.

extrinsic motivation Motivation reflecting a desire for external rewards, such as wealth or the respect of others.

eyeblink reflex The reflexive blinking of the eyes that protects the newborn from bright light and foreign objects.

facial-feedback hypothesis The belief that mimicking facial movements associated with a particular emotion will produce the corresponding emotional state.

fallopian tube A straw-like tube between an ovary and the uterus through which an ovum passes after ovulation.

familial association studies Studies that examine the degree to which disorders or characteristics are shared among family members.

family therapy Therapy for troubled families that focuses on changing disruptive patterns of communication and improving the ways in which family members relate to each other.

fear hierarchy An ordered series of increasingly fearful objects or situations.

feature detectors Specialized neurons in the visual cortex that respond only to particular features of visual stimuli, such as horizontal or vertical lines.

fertilization The union of sperm and ovum.

fetal alcohol syndrome (FAS) A syndrome caused by maternal use of alcohol during pregnancy in which the child shows developmental delays and facial deformities.

fetal stage The stage of prenatal development in which the fetus develops, beginning around the ninth week of pregnancy and lasting until the birth of the child.

fetus The developing organism in the later stages of prenatal development.

fight-or-flight response The body's built-in alarm system that allows it to quickly mobilize its resources to either fight or flee when faced with a threatening stressor.

five-factor model (FFM) The dominant contemporary trait model of personality, consisting of five broad personality factors: neuroticism, extraversion, openness, agreeableness, and conscientiousness.

fixations Constellations of personality traits characteristic of a particular stage of psychosexual development, resulting from either excessive or inadequate gratification at that stage.

flashbulb memories Enduring memories of emotionally charged events that seem permanently seared into the brain.

fluid intelligence A form of intelligence associated with the ability to think abstractly and flexibly in solving problems.

focused awareness A state of heightened alertness in which one is fully absorbed in the task at hand.

foot-in-the-door technique A compliance technique based on securing compliance with a smaller request as a prelude to making a larger request.

forebrain The largest and uppermost part of the brain; contains the thalamus, hypothalamus, limbic system, basal ganglia, and cerebral cortex.

forensic psychologists Psychologists involved in the application of psychology to the legal system.

formal operations The level of full cognitive maturity in Piaget's theory, characterized by the ability to think in abstract terms.

fovea The area near the center of the retina that contains only cones and that is the center of focus for clearest vision.

fraternal twins Twins who developed from separate zygotes and so have 50 percent of their genes in common (also called dizygotic, or DZ, twins).

free association A technique in psychoanalysis in which the client is encouraged to say anything that comes to mind.

free recall A type of recall task in which individuals are asked to recall as much information as they can about a particular topic in any order.

frequency distribution A tabulation that indicates the number of times a given score or group of scores occurs.

frequency polygon A graph on which the frequencies of class intervals are at their midpoints, which are then connected with straight lines.

frequency theory The belief that pitch depends on the frequency of vibration of the basilar membrane and the volley of neural impulses transmitted to the brain via the auditory nerve.

frontal lobes The parts of the cerebral cortex, located at the front of the cerebral hemispheres, that are considered the "executive center" of the brain because of their role in higher mental functions.

frustration A negative emotional state experienced when one's efforts to pursue one's goals are thwarted.

functional fixedness The tendency to perceive objects as limited to the customary functions they serve.

functionalism The school of psychology that focuses on the adaptive functions of behavior.

fundamental attribution error The tendency to attribute behavior to internal causes without regard to situational influences.

ganglion cells Nerve cells in the back of the eye that transmit neural impulses in response to light stimulation, the axons of which make up the optic nerve.

gate-control theory of pain The belief that a neural gate in the spinal cord opens to allow pain messages to reach the brain and closes to shut them out.

gender identity The psychological sense of maleness or femaleness.

gender roles The cultural expectations imposed on men and women to behave in ways deemed appropriate for their gender.

general adaptation syndrome (GAS) Selye's term for the general pattern of bodily responses to various forms of stress.

generalized anxiety disorder (GAD) A type of anxiety disorder involving persistent and generalized anxiety and worry.

genes Basic units of heredity that contain an individual's genetic code.

genital stage In Freudian theory, the fifth and final stage of psychosexual development, which begins around puberty and corresponds to the development of mature sexuality and emphasis on procreation.

genotype An organism's genetic code.

germ cells Sperm and egg cells from which new life develops.

germinal stage The stage of prenatal development that spans the period from fertilization through implantation.

geropsychologists Psychologists who focus on psychological processes involved in aging.

gestalt A German word meaning "unitary form" or "pattern."

gestalt psychology The school of psychology that holds that the brain structures our perceptions of the world in terms of meaningful patterns or wholes.

glands Body organs or structures that produce secretions called hormones.

glial cells Small but numerous cells in the nervous system that support neurons and that form the myelin sheath found on many axons.

gonads Sex glands (testes in men and ovaries in women) that produce sex hormones and germ cells (sperm in the male and egg cells in the female).

gradual exposure A behavior therapy technique for treating phobias based on direct exposure to a series of increasingly fearful stimuli. Also called *in-vivo ("real-life") exposure.*

grammar The set of rules governing how symbols in a given language are used to form meaningful expressions.

group therapy A form of therapy in which clients are treated within a group format.

groupthink Janis's term for the tendency of members of a decision-making group to be more focused on reaching a consensus than on critically examining the issues at hand.

hair cells The auditory receptors that transform vibrations caused by sound waves into neural impulses that are then transmitted to the brain via the auditory nerve.

hallucinations Perceptions ("hearing voices" or seeing things) experienced in the absence of corresponding external stimuli.

hallucinogens Drugs that alter sensory experiences and produce hallucinations.

hassles Annoyances of daily life that impose a stressful burden.

health psychologists Psychologists who focus on the relationship between psychological factors and physical health.

health psychology The specialty in psychology that focuses on the interrelationships between psychological factors and physical health.

heart attack A potentially life-threatening event involving the death of heart tissue due to a lack of blood flow to the heart. Also called *myocardial infarction.*

heritability The degree to which heredity accounts for variations on a given trait within a population.

heuristic A rule of thumb for solving problems or making judgments or decisions.

hidden observer Hilgard's term for a part of consciousness that remains detached from the hypnotic experience but aware of everything that happens during it.

hierarchy of needs Maslow's concept that there is an order to human needs, which starts with basic biological needs and progresses to self-actualization.

hindbrain The lowest and, in evolutionary terms, oldest part of the brain; includes the medulla, pons, and cerebellum.

hippocampus A structure in the limbic system involved in memory formation.

histogram A graph that depicts the frequencies of individual scores or categories of scores, using bars of different lengths.

homeostasis The tendency of systems to maintain a steady, internally balanced state.

hormones Secretions from endocrine glands that help regulate bodily processes.

humanistic perspective An approach to the study of psychology that applies the principles of humanistic psychology.

humanistic psychology The school of psychology that believes that free will and conscious choice are essential aspects of the human experience.

hypnosis An altered state of consciousness characterized by focused attention, deep relaxation, and heightened susceptibility to suggestion.

hypnotic age regression A hypnotically induced experience that involves reexperiencing past events in one's life.

hypnotic analgesia A loss of feeling or responsiveness to pain in certain parts of the body occurring during hypnosis.

hypochondriasis A psychological disorder in which there is excessive concern that one's physical complaints are signs of underlying serious illness.

hypothalamus A small, pea-sized structure in the forebrain that helps regulate many vital bodily functions, including body temperature and reproduction, as well as emotional states, aggression, and responses to stress.

hypothalamus pituitary adrenal (HPA) axis The integrated system of endocrine glands involved in the body's response to stress.

hypothesis A precise prediction about the outcomes of an experiment.

iconic memory A sensory store for holding a mental representation of a visual image for a fraction of a second.

id Freud's term for the psychic structure existing in the unconscious that contains our baser animal drives and instinctual impulses.

identical twins Twins who developed from the same zygote and so have identical genes (also called monozygotic, or MZ, twins).

identity crisis In Erikson's theory, a stressful period of serious soul-searching and self-examination of issues relating to personal values and one's direction in life.

imaginary audience The common belief among adolescents that they are the center of other people's attention.

immune system The body's system of defense against disease.

implicit memory Memory accessed without conscious effort.

impression formation The process of developing an opinion or impression of another person.

imprinting The formation of a strong bond of the newborn animal to the first moving object seen after birth.

inattentional blindness The failure to notice something right in front of your eyes because your attention is directed elsewhere.

incentive theory The belief that our attraction to particular goals or objects motivates much of our behavior.

incentive value The strength of the "pull" of a goal or reward.

incentives Rewards or other stimuli that motivate us to act.

independent variables Factors that are manipulated in an experiment.

individual psychology Adler's theory of personality, which emphasizes the unique potential of each individual.

individualistic culture A culture that emphasizes individual identity and personal accomplishments.

industrial/organizational (I/O) psychologists Psychologists who study people's behavior at work.

inferential statistics Procedures for making generalizations about a population by studying the characteristics of samples drawn from the population.

inferiority complex In Adler's theory, a concept involving the influence that feelings of inadequacy or inferiority in young children have on their developing personalities and desires to compensate.

informed consent Agreement to participate in a study following disclosure of information about the purposes and nature of the study and its potential risks and benefits.

in-group favoritism A cognitive bias involving the predisposition to attribute more positive characteristics to members of in-groups than to those of out-groups.

in-groups Social, religious, ethnic, racial, or national groups with which one identifies.

insight In Freudian theory, the realization or awareness of underlying unconscious wishes and conflicts.

insight learning The process of mentally working through a problem until the sudden realization of a solution occurs.

insomnia Difficulty falling asleep, remaining asleep, or returning to sleep after nighttime awakenings.

instinct theory The belief that behavior is motivated by instinct.

instinctive behaviors Genetically programmed, innate patterns of response

that are specific to members of a particular species.

intellectual disability A generalized deficit or impairment in intellectual and social skills.

intelligence The capacity to think and reason clearly and to act purposefully and effectively in adapting to the environment and pursuing one's goals.

intelligence quotient (IQ) A measure of intelligence based on performance on tests of mental abilities, expressed as a ratio between one's mental age and chronological age or derived from the deviation of one's scores from the norms for those of one's age group.

interference theory The belief that forgetting is the result of the interference of memories with each other.

interneurons Nerve cells within the central nervous system that process information.

interpretation In psychoanalysis, the therapist's attempt to explain connections between what the client discloses during therapy and his or her unconscious conflicts.

intoxicant A chemical substance that induces a state of drunkenness.

intrinsic motivation Motivation reflecting a desire for internal gratification, such as the self-satisfaction derived from accomplishing a particular goal.

introspection Inward focusing on mental experiences, such as sensations or feelings.

introversion–extraversion Tendencies toward being solitary and reserved on the one end or outgoing and sociable on the other end.

ions Electrically charged chemical particles.

iris The pigmented, circular muscle in the eye that regulates the size of the pupil to adjust to changes in the level of illumination.

irreversibility To Piaget, the inability to reverse the direction of a sequence of events to their starting point.

James-Lange theory The belief that emotions occur after people become aware of their physiological responses to the triggering stimuli.

jet lag A disruption of sleep–wake cycles caused by the shifts in time zones that accompany long-distance air travel.

kinesthesia The sense that keeps us informed about movement of the parts of the body and their position in relation to each other.

language A system of communication composed of symbols (words, hand signs, and so on) that are arranged according to a set of rules (grammar) to form meaningful expressions.

language acquisition device Chomsky's concept of an innate, prewired mechanism in the brain that allows children to acquire language naturally.

latency stage In Freudian theory, the fourth stage of psychosexual development, during which sexual impulses remain latent or dormant.

latent learning Learning that occurs without apparent reinforcement and that is not displayed until reinforcement is provided.

lateral hypothalamus A part of the hypothalamus involved in initiating, or "turning on," eating.

lateralization The specialization of the right and left cerebral hemispheres for particular functions.

law of effect Thorndike's principle that responses that have satisfying effects are more likely to recur, whereas those that have unpleasant effects are less likely to recur.

laws of perceptual organization The principles identified by Gestalt psychologists that describe the ways in which the brain groups bits of sensory stimulation into meaningful wholes or patterns.

learned helplessness model The view that depression results from the perception of a lack of control over the reinforcements in one's life that may result from exposure to uncontrollable negative events.

learning A relatively permanent change in behavior acquired through experience.

legitimization of authority The tendency to grant legitimacy to the orders or commands of people in authority.

lens The structure in the eye that focuses light rays on the retina.

lesioning In studies of brain functioning, the intentional destruction of brain tissue in order to observe the effects on behavior.

levels-of-processing theory The belief that how well or how long information is remembered depends on the depth of encoding or processing.

limbic system A formation of structures in the forebrain that includes the hippocampus, amygdala, and parts of the thalamus and hypothalamus.

linguistic relativity hypothesis The proposition that the language we use determines how we think and how we perceive the world (also called the *Whorfian hypothesis*).

locus of control In Rotter's theory, one's general expectancies about whether one's efforts can bring about desired outcomes or reinforcements.

logical concepts Concepts with clearly defined rules for membership.

long-term memory (**LTM**) The memory subsystem responsible for long-term storage of information.

long-term potentiation (**LTP**) The long-term strengthening of neural connections as the result of repeated stimulation.

lowball technique A compliance technique based on obtaining a person's initial agreement to purchase an item at a lower price before revealing hidden costs that raise the ultimate price.

lucid dreams Dreams in which the dreamer is aware that he or she is dreaming.

lymphocytes White blood cells that protect the body against disease-causing organisms.

mainstreaming The practice of placing children with special needs in a regular classroom environment.

maintenance rehearsal The process of extending retention of information held in short-term memory by consciously repeating the information.

major depression The most common type of depressive disorder, characterized by periods of downcast mood, feelings of worthlessness, and loss of interest in pleasurable activities.

malignant tumors Uncontrolled growths of body cells that invade surrounding tissue and spread to other parts of the body.

manic episodes Periods of mania, or unusually elevated mood and extreme restlessness.

mantra A sound or phrase chanted repeatedly during transcendental meditation.

massed versus spaced practice effect The tendency for retention of learned material to be greater with spaced practice than with massed practice.

matching hypothesis The belief that people tend to pair off with others who are similar to themselves in physical attractiveness and other characteristics.

maturation The biological unfolding of the organism according to the underlying genetic code.

mean The arithmetic average of the scores in a distribution.

median The middle score in a distribution, above and below which half of the scores fall.

medical model A framework for understanding abnormal behavior patterns as symptoms of underlying physical disorders or diseases.

meditation A process of focused attention that induces a relaxed, contemplative state.

medulla A structure in the hindbrain involved in regulating basic life functions, such as heartbeat and respiration.

melanoma The most deadly form of skin cancer.

memory The system that allows us to retain information and bring it to mind.

memory encoding The process of converting information into a form that can be stored in memory.

memory retrieval The process of accessing and bringing into consciousness information stored in memory.

memory storage The process of retaining information in memory.

menarche The first menstruation.

menopause The time of life when menstruation ends.

mental age A representation of a person's intelligence based on the age of people who are capable of performing at the same level of ability.

mental image A mental picture or representation of an object or event.

mental set The tendency to rely on strategies that worked in similar situations in the past but that may not be appropriate to the present situation.

meta-analysis A statistical technique for averaging results across a large number of studies.

midbrain The part of the brain that lies on top of the hindbrain and below the forebrain.

midlife crisis A state of psychological crisis, often occurring during middle adulthood, in which people grapple with the loss of their youth.

migraine headaches Prolonged, intense headaches brought on by changes in blood flow in blood vessels in the brain.

mindfulness meditation A form of meditation in which one adopts a state of nonjudgmental attention to the unfolding of experience on a moment-to-moment basis.

mirror neurons Neurons that fire both when an action is performed and when the same action is merely observed.

misinformation effect A form of memory distortion that affects eyewitness testimony and that is caused by misinformation provided during the retention interval.

mnemonic A device for improving memory.

mode The most frequent score in a distribution of scores.

modeling A behavior therapy technique for overcoming phobias and acquiring more adaptive behaviors, based on observing and imitating models.

monoamine oxidase (MAO) inhibitors A class of antidepressant drugs that increase the availability of neurotransmitters in the brain by inhibiting an enzyme, monoamine oxidase, that breaks down or degrades them in the synapse.

monochromats People who have no color vision and can see only in black and white.

monocular cues Cues for depth that can be perceived by each eye alone, such as relative size and interposition.

mood disorders A class of psychological disorders involving disturbances in mood states, such as major depression and bipolar disorder.

Moro reflex An inborn reflex, elicited by a sudden noise or loss of support, in which the infant extends its arms, arches its back, and brings its arms toward each other as though attempting to grab hold of someone.

morphemes The smallest units of meaning in a language.

motivation Factors that activate, direct, and sustain goal-directed behavior.

motives Needs or wants that drive goal-directed behavior.

motor cortex A region of the frontal lobes involved in regulating body movement.

motor neurons Neurons that convey nerve impulses from the central nervous system to muscles and glands.

MRI (magnetic resonance imaging) A technique that uses a magnetic field to create a computerized image of internal bodily structures.

multiple intelligences Gardner's term for the distinct types of intelligence that characterize different forms of intelligent behavior.

multiple sclerosis (MS) A disease of the central nervous system in which the myelin sheath that insulates axons is damaged or destroyed.

myelin sheath A layer of protective insulation that covers the axons of certain neurons and helps speed transmission of nerve impulses.

narcolepsy A sleep–wake disorder characterized by sudden unexplained "sleep attacks" during the day.

narcotics Addictive drugs that have pain-relieving and sleep-inducing properties.

natural concepts Concepts with poorly defined or fuzzy rules for membership.

naturalistic observation method A method of research based on careful observation of behavior in natural settings.

nature–nurture debate The debate in psychology about the relative influences of genetics (nature) and environment (nurture) in determining behavior.

need A state of deprivation or deficiency.

need for achievement The need to excel in one's endeavors.

negative reinforcement The strengthening of a response through the removal of a stimulus after the response occurs.

negative symptoms Behavioral deficits associated with schizophrenia, such as withdrawal and apathy.

neodissociation theory A theory of hypnosis based on the belief that hypnosis represents a state of dissociated (divided) consciousness.

nerve A bundle of axons from different neurons that transmit nerve impulses.

nerve deafness Deafness associated with nerve damage, usually involving damage to the hair cells or to the auditory nerve itself.

nervous system The network of nerve cells and support cells for communicating and processing information from within and outside the body.

neural tube The area in the embryo from which the nervous system develops.

neurogenesis The process by which new neurons are formed.

neuromarketing An emerging field of marketing that examines brain responses to advertisements and brand-related messages.

neuromodulators Chemicals released in the nervous system that influence the sensitivity of the receiving neuron to neurotransmitters.

neuronal networks Memory circuits in the brain that consist of complicated networks of nerve cells.

neurons Nerve cells.

neuropsychologists Psychologists who study relationships between the brain and behavior.

neuroticism Tendencies toward emotional instability, anxiety, and worry.

neurotransmitters Chemical messengers that transport nerve impulses from one nerve cell to another.

neutral stimulus (NS) A stimulus that before conditioning does not produce a particular response.

nightmare disorder A type of sleep–wake disorder involving a pattern of frequent, disturbing nightmares.

nodes of Ranvier Gaps in the myelin sheath that create noninsulated areas along the axon.

nonspecific factors General features of psychotherapy, such as attention from a therapist and mobilization of positive expectancies or hope.

norms The standards used to compare an individual's performance on a test with the performance of others.

null hypothesis A prediction of no difference between groups or no relationship between variables.

obedience Compliance with commands or orders issued by others, usually people in a position of authority.

object permanence The recognition that objects continue to exist even if they have disappeared from sight.

objective tests Tests of personality that can be scored objectively and that are based on a research foundation.

observational learning Learning by observing and imitating the behavior of others (also called *vicarious learning* or *modeling*).

obsessive-compulsive disorder (OCD) A psychological disorder involving the repeated occurrence of obsessions and/or compulsions.

occipital lobes The parts of the cerebral cortex, located at the back of both cerebral hemispheres, that process visual stimuli.

Oedipus complex In Freudian theory, the psychological complex in which the young boy or girl develops incestuous feelings toward the parent of the opposite gender and perceives the parent of the same gender as a rival.

olfaction The sense of smell.

olfactory bulb The area in the front of the brain above the nostrils that receives sensory input from olfactory receptors in the nose.

olfactory nerve The nerve that carries impulses from olfactory receptors in the nose to the brain.

operant conditioning The process of learning in which the consequences of a response determine the probability that the response will be repeated.

operant response A response that operates on the environment to produce certain consequences.

operational definition A definition of a variable based on the procedures or operations used to measure it.

opponent-process theory A theory of color vision that holds that the experience of color results from opposing processes involving two sets of color receptors, red-green receptors and blue-yellow receptors, and that another set of opposing receptors, black-white, is responsible for detecting differences in brightness.

optic nerve The nerve that carries neural impulses generated by light stimulation from the eye to the brain.

oral stage In Freudian theory, the first stage of psychosexual development, during which the infant seeks sexual gratification through oral stimulation (sucking, mouthing, and biting).

organ of Corti A gelatinous structure in the cochlea containing the hair cells that serve as auditory receptors.

ossicles Three tiny bones in the middle ear (the hammer, anvil, and stirrup) that vibrate in response to vibrations of the eardrum.

osteoporosis A bone disease characterized by a loss of bone density in which the bones become porous, brittle, and more prone to fracture.

outcome expectations Bandura's term for our personal predictions about the outcomes of our behavior.

out-group homogeneity A cognitive bias describing the tendency to perceive members of out-groups as more alike than members of in-groups.

out-group negativism A cognitive bias involving the predisposition to attribute more negative characteristics to members of out-groups than to those of in-groups.

out-groups Groups other than those with which one identifies.

oval window The membrane-covered opening that separates the middle ear from the inner ear.

ovaries The female gonads, which secrete the female sex hormones estrogen and progesterone and produce mature egg cells.

overlearning Practice repeated beyond the point necessary to reproduce material without error.

ovulation The release of an egg cell (ovum) from the ovary.

palmar grasp reflex The reflexive curling of the infant's fingers around an object that touches its palm.

pancreas An endocrine gland located near the stomach that produces the hormone insulin.

panic disorder A type of anxiety disorder involving repeated episodes of sheer terror called panic attacks.

parapsychology The study of paranormal phenomena.

parasympathetic nervous system The branch of the autonomic nervous system that regulates bodily processes, such as digestion, that replenish stores of energy.

parietal lobes The parts of the cerebral cortex, located on the side of each cerebral hemisphere, that process bodily sensations.

Parkinson's disease A progressive brain disease involving destruction of dopamine-producing brain cells and characterized by muscle tremors, shakiness, rigidity, and difficulty in walking and controlling fine body movements.

penis envy In Freudian theory, jealousy of boys for having a penis.

perception The process by which the brain integrates, organizes, and interprets sensory impressions to create representations of the world.

perceptual constancy The tendency to perceive the size, shape, color, and brightness of an object as remaining the same even

when the image it casts on the retina changes.

perceptual set The tendency for perceptions to be influenced by one's expectations or preconceptions.

performance anxiety Anxiety experienced in performance situations stemming from a fear of negative evaluation of one's ability to perform.

peripheral nervous system (PNS) The part of the nervous system that connects the spinal cord and brain with the sensory organs, muscles, and glands.

person variables Mischel's term for internal personal factors that influence behavior, including competencies, expectancies, and subjective values.

personal fable The common belief among adolescents that their feelings and experiences cannot possibly be understood by others and that they are personally invulnerable to harm.

personal identity The part of our psychological identity that involves our sense of ourselves as unique individuals.

personal unconscious Jung's term for an unconscious region of mind comprising a reservoir of the individual's repressed memories and impulses.

personality The relatively stable constellation of psychological characteristics and behavioral patterns that account for our individuality and consistency over time.

personality disorders A class of psychological disorders characterized by rigid personality traits that impair people's ability to adjust to the demands they face in the environment and that interfere with their relationships with others.

personality psychologists Psychologists who study the psychological characteristics and behaviors that distinguish us as individuals and lead us to act consistently over time.

personality tests Structured psychological tests that use formal methods of assessing personality.

PET (positron emission tomography) scan An imaging technique in which a radioactive sugar tracer is injected into the bloodstream and used to measure levels of activity of various parts of the brain.

phallic stage In Freudian theory, the third stage of psychosexual development, marked by erotic attention on the phallic

region (penis in boys, clitoris in girls) and the development of the Oedipus complex.

phenotype The observable physical and behavioral characteristics of an organism, representing the influences of the genotype and environment.

pheromones Chemical substances that are emitted by many species and that have various functions, including sexual attraction.

phobias Excessive or irrational fears of particular objects or situations.

phonemes The basic units of sound in a language.

photoreceptors Light-sensitive cells (rods and cones) in the eye upon which light registers.

phrenology The now-discredited view that one can judge a person's character and mental abilities by measuring the bumps on his or her head.

physiological dependence A state of physical dependence on a drug caused by repeated usage that changes body chemistry.

physiological perspective An approach to the study of psychology that focuses on the relationships between biological processes and behavior.

physiological psychologists Psychologists who focus on the biological underpinnings of behavior.

pineal gland A small endocrine gland in the brain that produces the hormone melatonin, which is involved in regulating sleep–wake cycles.

pitch The highness or lowness of a sound that corresponds to the frequency of the sound wave.

pituitary gland An endocrine gland in the brain that produces various hormones involved in growth, regulation of the menstrual cycle, and childbirth.

place theory The belief that pitch depends on the place along the basilar membrane that vibrates the most in response to a particular auditory stimulus.

placebo An inert substance or experimental condition that resembles the active treatment.

placebo effects Positive outcomes of an experiment resulting from a participant's positive expectations about the treatment rather than from the treatment itself.

placenta The organ that provides for the exchange of nutrients and waste materials between mother and fetus.

plaque In the circulatory system, fatty deposits that accumulate along artery walls.

plasticity The ability of the brain to adapt itself after trauma or surgical alteration.

pleasure principle In Freudian theory, a governing principle of the id that is based on demand for instant gratification without regard to social rules or customs.

polyabusers People who abuse more than one drug at a time.

polygenic traits Traits that are influenced by multiple genes interacting in complex ways.

pons A structure in the hindbrain involved in regulating states of wakefulness and sleep.

population All the individuals or organisms that constitute particular groups.

positive psychology A contemporary movement within psychology that emphasizes the study of human virtues and assets, rather than weaknesses and deficits.

positive reinforcement The strengthening of a response through the introduction of a stimulus after the response occurs.

positive symptoms Symptoms of schizophrenia involving behavioral excesses, such as hallucinations and delusions.

posthypnotic amnesia An inability to recall what happened during hypnosis.

posthypnotic suggestion A hypnotist's suggestion that the subject will respond in a particular way following hypnosis.

posttraumatic stress disorder (PTSD) A psychological disorder involving a maladaptive reaction to traumatic stress.

precognition The ability to foretell the future.

preconscious To Freud, the part of the mind whose contents can be brought into awareness through focused attention.

prefrontal cortex (PFC) The area of the frontal lobe that lies in front of the motor cortex and that is involved in higher mental functions, including thinking, planning, impulse control, and weighing the consequences of behavior.

prefrontal lobotomy A surgical procedure in which neural pathways in the brain are severed in order to control violent or aggressive behavior.

prejudice A preconceived opinion or attitude about an issue, person, or group.

premenstrual syndrome (PMS) A cluster of physical and psychological symptoms occurring in the few days preceding the menstrual flow.

primacy effect The tendency to recall items better when they are learned first.

primary drives Innate drives, such as hunger, thirst, and sexual desire, that arise from basic biological needs.

primary mental abilities Seven basic mental abilities that Thurstone believed constitute intelligence.

primary reinforcers Reinforcers, such as food or sexual stimulation, that are naturally rewarding because they satisfy basic biological needs or drives.

primary sex characteristics Physical characteristics, such as the gonads, that differentiate males and females and play a direct role in reproduction.

prime A stimulus or cue that affects a person's subsequent behavior without the person being aware of its impact.

proactive interference A form of interference in which material learned earlier interferes with retention of newly acquired information.

problem solving A form of thinking focused on finding a solution to a particular problem.

procedural memory Memory of how to do things that require motor or performance skills.

programmed instruction A learning method in which complex material is broken down into a series of small steps that learners master at their own pace.

projection In Freudian theory, a defense mechanism involving the projection of one's own unacceptable impulses, wishes, or urges onto another person.

projective tests Personality tests in which ambiguous or vague test materials are used to elicit responses that are believed to reveal a person's unconscious needs, drives, and motives.

prosocial behavior Behavior that benefits others.

prospective memory Memory of things one plans to do in the future.

proximity The principle that objects that are near each other will be perceived as belonging to a common set.

psychiatrists Medical doctors who specialize in the diagnosis and treatment of mental or psychological disorders.

psychoactive drugs Chemical substances that affect a person's mental or emotional state.

psychoanalysis Freud's method of psychotherapy; it focuses on uncovering and working through unconscious conflicts he believed were at the root of psychological problems.

psychoanalysts Practitioners of psychoanalysis who are schooled in the Freudian tradition.

psychoanalytic theory Freud's theory of personality that holds that personality and behavior are shaped by unconscious forces and conflicts.

psychodynamic perspective The view that behavior is influenced by the struggle between unconscious sexual or aggressive impulses and opposing forces that try to keep this threatening material out of consciousness.

psychokinesis The ability to move objects by mental effort alone.

psychological dependence A pattern of compulsive or habitual use of a drug to satisfy a psychological need.

psychological disorders Abnormal behavior patterns characterized by disturbances in behavior, thinking, perceptions, or emotions that are associated with significant personal distress or impaired functioning. Also called *mental disorders* or *mental illnesses*.

psychological hardiness A cluster of traits (commitment, openness to challenge, internal locus of control) that may buffer the effects of stress.

psychology The science of behavior and mental processes.

psychophysics The study of the relationship between features of physical stimuli, such as the intensity of light and sound, and the sensation we experience in response to these stimuli.

psychosocial needs Needs that reflect interpersonal aspects of motivation, such as the need for friendship or achievement.

psychosurgery Brain surgery used to control violent or deviant behavior.

psychotherapy A verbal form of therapy derived from a psychological framework that consists of one or more treatment sessions with a therapist.

psychotic disorder A psychological disorder, such as schizophrenia, characterized by a "break" with reality.

psychoticism Tendencies to be perceived as cold and antisocial.

psychotropic drugs Psychiatric drugs used in the treatment of psychological or mental disorders.

puberty The stage of development at which individuals become physiologically capable of reproducing.

punishment The introduction of an aversive stimulus or the removal of a reinforcing stimulus after a response occurs, which leads to the weakening or suppression of the response.

pupil The black opening inside the iris that allows light to enter the eye.

questionnaire A written set of questions or statements to which people reply by marking their responses on an answer form.

racism Negative bias held toward members of other racial groups.

radical behaviorism The philosophical position that free will is an illusion or myth and that human and animal behavior is completely determined by environmental and genetic influences.

random assignment A method of randomly assigning subjects to experimental or control groups.

random sampling A method of sampling in which each individual in the population has an equal chance of being selected.

range A measure of variability that is given by the difference in value between the highest and lowest scores in a distribution of scores.

rapid-eye-movement (REM) sleep The stage of sleep that involves rapid eye movements and that is most closely associated with periods of dreaming.

rational emotive behavior therapy (REBT) Developed by Albert Ellis, a form of therapy based on identifying and correcting irrational beliefs that are thought to underlie emotional and behavioral difficulties.

rationalization In Freudian theory, a defense mechanism involving the use of self-justification to explain away unacceptable behavior, impulses, or ideas.

reaction formation In Freudian theory, a defense mechanism involving behavior that stands in opposition to one's true motives and desires so as to prevent conscious awareness of them.

reality principle In Freudian theory, the governing principle of the ego that takes into account what is practical and acceptable in satisfying basic needs.

recency effect The tendency to recall items better when they are learned last.

receptor site A site on the receiving neuron in which neurotransmitters dock.

reciprocal determinism Bandura's model in which cognitions, behaviors, and environmental factors influence and are influenced by each other.

reciprocity The principle that people tend to like others who like them back.

recognition task A method of measuring memory retention that assesses the ability to select the correct answer from among a range of alternative answers.

reconditioning The process of relearning a conditioned response following extinction.

reflex An automatic, unlearned response to particular stimuli.

refractory period A temporary state in which a neuron is unable to fire in response to continued stimulation.

regression In Freudian theory, a defense mechanism in which an individual, usually under high levels of stress, reverts to a behavior characteristic of an earlier stage of development.

reinforcer A stimulus or event that increases the probability that the response it follows will be repeated.

reliability The stability of test scores over time.

replication The attempt to duplicate findings.

representativeness heuristic A rule of thumb for making a judgment that assumes a given sample is representative of the larger population from which it is drawn.

repression In Freudian theory, a type of defense mechanism involving motivated forgetting of anxiety-evoking material.

resistance In psychoanalysis, the blocking that occurs when therapy touches upon anxiety-evoking thoughts or feelings.

resistance stage The second stage of the general adaptation syndrome, characterized by the body's attempt to adjust or adapt to persistent stress.

resting potential The electrical potential across the cell membrane of a neuron in its resting state.

reticular formation A weblike formation of neurons involved in regulating states of attention, alertness, and arousal.

retina The light-sensitive layer of the inner surface of the eye that contains photoreceptor cells.

retinal disparity A binocular cue for distance based on the slight differences in the visual impressions formed in both eyes.

retrieval cues Cues associated with the original learning that facilitate the retrieval of memories.

retrieval theory The belief that forgetting is the result of a failure to access stored memories.

retroactive interference A form of interference in which newly acquired information interferes with retention of material learned earlier.

retrograde amnesia Loss of memory of past events.

retrospective memory Memory of past experiences or events and previously acquired information.

reuptake The process by which neurotransmitters are reabsorbed by the transmitting neuron.

rods Photoreceptors that are sensitive only to the intensity of light (light and dark).

role diffusion In Erikson's model, a lack of direction or aimlessness with respect to one's role in life or public identity.

rooting reflex The reflexive turning of the newborn's head in the direction of a touch on its cheek.

rubella A common childhood disease that can lead to serious birth defects if contracted by the mother during pregnancy (also called German measles).

samples Subsets of a population.

savings method A method of testing memory retention by comparing the numbers of trials needed to learn material with the number of trials needed to relearn the material at a later time.

scatterplot A graph in which pairs of scores are plotted for each research participant on two variables.

schedule of continuous reinforcement A system of dispensing a reinforcement each time a response is produced.

schedule of partial reinforcement A system of reinforcement in which only a portion of responses is reinforced.

schedules of reinforcement Predetermined plans for timing the delivery of reinforcement.

schema To Piaget, a mental framework for understanding or acting on the environment.

schizophrenia A severe and chronic psychological disorder characterized by disturbances in thinking, perception, emotions, and behavior.

school psychologists Psychologists who evaluate and assist children with learning problems or other special needs.

scientific method A method of inquiry involving careful observation and use of experimental methods.

secondary drives Drives that are learned or acquired through experience, such as the drive to achieve monetary wealth.

secondary gain Reward value of having a psychological or physical symptom, such as release from ordinary responsibilities.

secondary reinforcers Learned reinforcers, such as money, that develop their reinforcing properties because of their association with primary reinforcers.

secondary sex characteristics Physical characteristics that differentiate males and females but are not directly involved in reproduction.

secondary traits Allport's term for specific traits that influence behavior in relatively few situations.

selective attention The process by which we attend to meaningful stimuli and filter out irrelevant or extraneous stimuli.

selective serotonin-reuptake inhibitors (SSRIs) A class of antidepressant drugs that work specifically on increasing availability of the neurotransmitter serotonin by interfering with its reuptake.

self-actualization The motive that drives individuals to express their unique capabilities and fulfill their potentials.

self-fulfilling prophecy An expectation that helps bring about the outcome that is expected.

self-ideals Rogers's term for the idealized sense of how or what we should be.

self-report personality inventories Structured psychological tests in which individuals are given a limited range of response options to answer a set of questions about themselves.

self-serving bias The tendency to take credit for our accomplishments and to explain away our failures or disappointments.

self-theory Rogers's model of personality, which focuses on the importance of the self.

semantic memory Memory of facts and general information about the world.

semantic network model A representation of the organizational structure of long-term memory in terms of a network of associated concepts.

semantics The set of rules governing the meaning of words.

semicircular canals Three curved, tubelike canals in the inner ear that are involved in sensing changes in the direction and movement of the head.

sensation The process by which we receive, transform, and process stimuli from the outside world to create sensory experiences of vision, touch, hearing, taste, smell, and so on.

sensory adaptation The process by which sensory receptors adapt to constant stimuli by becoming less sensitive to them.

sensory memory The storage system that holds memory of sensory impressions for a very short time.

sensory neurons Neurons that transmit information from sensory organs, muscles, and inner organs to the spinal cord and brain.

sensory receptors Specialized cells that detect sensory stimuli and convert them into neural impulses.

sensory register A temporary storage device for holding sensory memories.

serial position effect The tendency to recall items at the start or end of a list better than items in the middle of a list.

set point theory The belief that brain mechanisms regulate body weight around a genetically predetermined "set point."

sexual dysfunctions Persistent or recurrent problems with sexual interest, arousal, or response.

sexual orientation The directionality of one's erotic interests.

sexual response cycle The term Masters and Johnson used to refer to the characteristic stages of physiological responses in the body to sexual stimulation.

sexually transmitted disease (STD) A disease caused by an infectious agent that is spread by sexual contact. Also called a *sexually transmitted infection* or STI.

shape constancy The tendency to perceive an object as having the same shape despite differences in the images it casts on the retina as the viewer's perspective changes.

shaping A process of learning that involves the reinforcement of increasingly closer approximations of the desired response.

short-term memory (STM) The memory subsystem that allows for retention and processing of newly acquired information for a maximum of about 30 seconds (also called *working memory*).

signal-detection theory The belief that the detection of a stimulus depends on factors involving the intensity of the stimulus, the level of background stimulation, and the biological and psychological characteristics of the perceiver.

similarity The principle that objects that are similar will be perceived as belonging to the same group.

single-blind studies In drug research, studies in which subjects are kept uninformed about whether they are receiving the experimental drug or a placebo.

situation variables Mischel's term for environmental influences on behavior, such as rewards and punishments.

situational causes Causes relating to external or environmental events.

size constancy The tendency to perceive an object as having the same size despite changes in the images it casts on the retina as the viewing distance changes.

skin senses The senses of touch, pressure, warmth, cold, and pain that involve stimulation of sensory receptors in the skin.

Skinner box An experimental apparatus developed by B. F. Skinner for studying relationships between reinforcement and behavior.

sleep apnea Temporary cessation of breathing during sleep.

sleep terror disorder A type of sleep–wake disorder involving repeated episodes of intense fear during sleep, causing the person to awake abruptly in a terrified state.

sleep–wake disorders A diagnostic category of psychological or mental disorders involving disturbed sleep patterns.

sleepwalking disorder A sleep–wake disorder characterized by repeated episodes of sleepwalking.

social anxiety disorder A type of anxiety disorder involving excessive fear of social situations. Also called *social phobia*.

social-cognitive theory A contemporary learning-based model that emphasizes the roles of cognitive and environmental factors in determining behavior.

social desirability bias The tendency to respond to questions in a socially desirable manner.

social facilitation The tendency to work better or harder in the presence of others than when alone.

social identity The part of our psychological identity that involves our sense of ourselves as members of particular groups. Also called *group identity*.

social loafing The tendency to expend less effort when working as a member of a group than when working alone.

social norms Standards that define what is socially acceptable in a given situation.

social perception The processes by which we form impressions, make judgments, and develop attitudes about the people and events that constitute our social world.

social psychologists Psychologists who study group or social influences on behavior and attitudes.

social psychology The subfield in psychology that deals with how our thoughts, feelings, and behaviors are influenced by our social interactions with others.

social schema A mental image or representation that we use to understand our social environment.

social validation The tendency to use other people's behavior as a standard for judging the appropriateness of one's own behavior.

sociocultural perspective An approach to the study of psychology that emphasizes the role of social and cultural influences on behavior.

soma The cell body of a neuron that contains the nucleus of the cell and carries out the cell's metabolic functions.

somatic nervous system The part of the peripheral nervous system that transmits information between the central nervous system and the sensory organs and muscles; also controls voluntary movements.

somatic symptom and related disorders A class of psychological disorders involving physical ailments or complaints that cannot be explained by organic causes or that involve exaggerated concerns about the seriousness of these symptoms.

somatosensory cortex The part of the parietal lobe that processes information about touch and pressure on the skin, as well as the position of the parts of our bodies as we move about.

source traits Cattell's term for traits at a deep level of personality that are not apparent in observed behavior but must be inferred based on underlying relationships among surface traits.

specific phobia Phobic reactions involving specific situations or objects.

spina bifida A neural tube defect in which the child is born with a hole in the tube surrounding the spinal cord. Most cases are mild and do not involve any significant problems, but in severe cases, problems such as difficulty walking or performing daily activities without assistance may result.

spinal cord The column of nerves that transmits information between the brain and the peripheral nervous system.

spinal reflex A reflex controlled at the level of the spinal cord that may involve as few as two neurons.

spine The protective bony column that houses the spinal cord.

split-brain patients People with a corpus callosum that has been surgically severed.

spontaneous recovery The spontaneous return of a conditioned response following extinction.

sport psychologists Psychologists who apply psychology to understanding and improving athletic performance.

standard deviation (SD) A measure of variability defined as the average difference between each individual score and the mean of all scores in the data set. More precisely, the square root of the average of the squared deviations of individual scores from the mean.

standardization The process of establishing norms for a test by administering the test to large numbers of people who constitute a standardization sample.

standard score A transformed score that indicates the number of standard deviations a corresponding raw score is above or below the mean. Also called a *z-score*.

standard scores Scores that represent an individual's relative deviation from the mean of the standardization sample.

states of consciousness Levels of consciousness ranging from alert wakefulness to deep sleep.

statistics The branch of mathematics involving the tabulation, analysis, and interpretation of numerical data.

stereotype threat A sense of threat evoked in people from stereotyped groups when they believe they may be judged or treated stereotypically.

stereotypes The tendency to characterize all members of a particular group as having certain characteristics in common.

stimulant A drug that activates the central nervous system, such as amphetamines and cocaine.

stimulus discrimination The tendency to differentiate among stimuli so that stimuli that are related to the original conditioned stimulus, but not identical to it, fail to elicit a conditioned response.

stimulus generalization The tendency for stimuli that are similar to the conditioned stimulus to elicit a conditioned response.

stimulus motives Internal states that prompt inquisitive, stimulation-seeking, and exploratory behavior.

stress Pressure or demand placed on an organism to adjust or adapt.

stressors Sources of stress.

stroboscopic movement A type of apparent movement based on the rapid succession of still images, as in motion pictures.

structuralism The school of psychology that attempts to understand the structure of the mind by breaking it down into its component parts.

structured interview An interview in which a set of specific questions is asked in a particular order.

subjective value In social-cognitive theory, the importance individuals place on desired outcomes.

sublimation In Freudian theory, a defense mechanism involving the channeling of unacceptable impulses into socially sanctioned behaviors or interests.

subliminal perception Perception of stimuli that are presented below the threshold of conscious awareness.

sucking reflex Rhythmic sucking in response to stimulation of the tongue or mouth.

sudden infant death syndrome (SIDS) The sudden and unexplained death of infants that usually occurs when they are asleep in their cribs.

superego Freud's term for the psychic structure that corresponds to an internal moral guardian or conscience.

superstitious behavior In Skinner's view, behavior acquired through coincidental association of a response and a reinforcement.

surface traits Cattell's term for personality traits at the surface level that can be gleaned from observations of behavior.

survey method A research method in which structured interviews or

questionnaires are used to gather information about groups of people.

symbolic representations A term referring to the use of words to represent (name) objects and describe experiences.

sympathetic nervous system The branch of the autonomic nervous system that accelerates bodily processes and releases stores of energy needed to meet increased physical demands.

synapse The small fluid-filled gap between neurons through which neurotransmitters carry neural impulses.

syntax The rules of grammar that determine how words are ordered within sentences or phrases to form meaningful expressions.

systematic desensitization A behavior therapy technique for treating phobias through the pairing of exposure in imagination to fear-inducing stimuli and states of deep relaxation.

taste buds Pores or openings on the tongue containing taste cells.

taste cells Nerve cells that are sensitive to tastes.

telepathy Communication of thoughts from one mind to another that occurs without using the known senses.

temperament A characteristic style of behavior or disposition.

temporal lobes The parts of the cerebral cortex lying beneath and somewhat behind the frontal lobes that are involved in processing auditory stimuli.

teratogen An environmental influence or agent that may harm the developing embryo or fetus.

terminal buttons Swellings at the tips of axons from which neurotransmitters are dispatched into the synapse.

testes The male gonads, which produce sperm and secrete the male sex hormone testosterone.

thalamus A structure in the forebrain that serves as a relay station for sensory information and that plays a key role in regulating states of wakefulness and sleep.

theory A formulation that accounts for relationships among observed events or experimental findings in ways that make them more understandable and predictable.

thermal biofeedback A form of BFT that involves feedback about changes in

temperature and blood flow in selected parts of the body; used in the treatment of migraine headaches.

thinking The process of mentally representing and manipulating information.

thought disorder A breakdown in the logical structure of thought and speech, revealed in the form of a loosening of associations.

three-stage model A model of memory that posits three distinct stages of memory: sensory memory, short-term memory, and long-term memory.

thyroid gland An endocrine gland in the neck that secretes the hormone thyroxin, which is involved in regulating metabolic functions and physical growth.

tip-of-the-tongue (TOT) phenomenon An experience in which people are sure they know something but cannot seem to bring it to mind.

token economy program A form of behavior modification in which tokens earned for performing desired behaviors can be exchanged for positive reinforcers.

tolerance A form of physical habituation to a drug in which increased amounts are needed to achieve the same effect.

top-down processing A mode of perceptual processing by which the brain identifies patterns as meaningful wholes rather than as piecemeal constructions.

traits Relatively enduring personal characteristics.

transcendental meditation (TM) A form of meditation in which practitioners focus their attention by repeating a particular mantra.

transference relationship The tendency of clients to reenact earlier conflicted relationships in their lives in the relationships they develop with their therapists.

triarchic theory of intelligence Sternberg's theory of intelligence that posits three aspects of intelligence: analytic, creative, and practical.

trichromatic theory A theory of color vision that posits that the ability to see different colors depends on the relative activity of three types of color receptors in the eye (red, green, and blue-violet).

trichromats People with normal color vision who can discern all the colors of the visual spectrum.

tricyclics A class of antidepressant drugs that increase the availability of neurotransmitters in the brain by interfering with the reuptake of these chemicals by transmitting neurons.

twin studies Studies that examine the degree to which concordance rates between twin pairs for particular disorders or characteristics vary in relation to whether the twins are identical or fraternal.

two-factor model The theory that emotions involve two factors: a state of general arousal and a cognitive interpretation (or labeling) of the causes of the arousal.

Type A behavior pattern (TABP) A behavior pattern characterized by impatience, time urgency, competitiveness, and hostility.

unconditional positive regard Valuing another person as having intrinsic worth, regardless of the person's behavior at the particular time.

unconditioned response (UR) An unlearned response to a stimulus.

unconditioned stimulus (US) A stimulus that elicits an unlearned response.

unconscious In Freudian theory, the part of the mind that lies outside the range of ordinary awareness and that contains primitive drives and instincts.

uterus The female reproductive organ in which the fertilized ovum becomes implanted and develops to term.

vaccination A method of acquiring immunity by means of injecting a weakened or partial form of an infectious agent that can induce production of antibodies but does not produce a full-blown infection.

validity The degree to which a test measures what it purports to measure.

variability In statistics, the spread or dispersion of scores throughout the distribution.

variable A factor or measure that varies within an experiment or among individuals.

vasocongestion Swelling of tissues with blood, a process that accounts for penile erection and vaginal lubrication during sexual arousal.

ventromedial hypothalamus A part of the hypothalamus involved in regulating feelings of satiety.

vestibular sacs Organs in the inner ear that connect the semicircular canals.

vestibular sense The sense that keeps us informed about balance and the position of our body in space.

virtual reality therapy A form of exposure therapy in which virtual reality is used to simulate real-world environments.

visual illusions Misperceptions of visual stimuli.

volley principle The principle that relates the experience of pitch to the alternating firing of groups of neurons along the basilar membrane.

volunteer bias The type of bias that arises when people who volunteer to participate in a survey or research study have characteristics that make them unrepresentative of the population from which they were drawn.

waxy flexibility A feature of catatonia characterized by maintaining a body position or posture in which the person was placed by others.

Weber's law The principle that the amount of change in a stimulus needed to detect a difference is given by a constant ratio or fraction, called a constant, of the original stimulus.

Wernicke's area An area of the left temporal lobe involved in processing written and spoken language.

withdrawal syndrome A cluster of symptoms associated with abrupt withdrawal from a drug.

zone of proximal development (ZPD) In Vygotsky's theory, the range between children's present level of knowledge and their potential knowledge state if they receive proper guidance and instruction.

zygote A fertilized egg cell.

References

Aamodt, S., & Wang, S. (2008). *Welcome to your brain: Why you lose your car keys but never forget how to drive and other puzzles of everyday life.* London: Bloomsbury.

Abbott, A. (2010). Levodopa: The story so far. *Nature, 466,* S6–S7. doi: 10.1038/466S6a

ABC News. Democrats smell a rat in GOP ad. (2000, September 13). Retrieved from http://abcnews .go.com/Politics /story?id=122936&page=1# .UcNBSLvLhr8

Abma, R. (2013). Rewriting Milgram. *Science, 341,* 1454. doi: 10.1126/science.1244504

Abrahamson, A. C., Baker, L. A., & Caspi, A. (2002). Rebellious teens? Genetic and environmental influences on the social attitudes of adolescents. *Journal of Personality and Social Psychology, 83,* 1392–1408. doi: 10.1234/12345678

Abramowitz, J. S., & Braddock, A. E. (2011). *Hypochondriasis and health anxiety: Advances in psychotherapy—evidence-based practice.* Cambridge, MA: Hogrefe Publishing.

Abramson, L. T., Seligman, M. E. P., & Teasdale, J. D. (1978). Learned helplessness in humans: Critique and reformulation. *Journal of Abnormal Psychology, 87,* 49–74.

Adam, M. B., McGuire, J. K., Walsh, M., Basta, J., & LeCroy, C. (2005). Acculturation as a predictor of the onset of sexual intercourse among Hispanic and white teens. *Archives of Pediatrics & Adolescent Medicine, 159,* 261–265.

Adelson, R. (2005, February). Hues and views. *Monitor on Psychology, 36*(2), 26–29.

Ader, R., & Cohen, N. (1982). Behaviorally conditioned immunosuppression and murine systemic lupus erythematosus. *Science, 215,* 1534–1536.

Adorno, T. W., Frenkel-Brunswik, E., Levinson, D., & Sanford, R. N. (1950). *The authoritarian personality.* New York: Harper.

Afifi, T. O., Mota, N. P., Dasiewicz, P., MacMillan, H. L., & Sareen, J. (2012). Physical punishment and mental disorders: Results from a nationally representative U.S. sample. *Pediatrics,* published online ahead of print July 2, 2012. doi: 10.1542/peds.2011-2947

Afraz, A., Pashkam, M. V., & Cavanagh, P. (2010). Spatial heterogeneity in the perception of face and form attributes. *Current Biology, 20,* 2112–2116. doi: 10.1016/j.cub.2010.11.017

Agerbo, E., Sullivan, P. F., Vilhjálmsson, B. J., Pedersen, C. B., Mors, O., Børglum, A. D., . . . Mortensen, P. B. (2015). Polygenic risk score, parental socioeconomic status, family history of psychiatric disorders, and the risk for schizophrenia: A Danish population-based study and meta-analysis. *JAMA Psychiatry, 72,* 635–641. doi: 10.1001/jamapsychiatry.2015.0346

Agras, W. S., Lock, J., Brandt, H., Bryson, S. W., Dodge, E., Halmi, K. A., . . . Woodside, B. (2014). Comparison of 2 family therapies for adolescent anorexia nervosa: A randomized parallel trial. *JAMA Psychiatry, 71,* 1279–1286. doi: 10.1001/jamapsychiatry.2014.1025

Agren, T., Engman, J., Frick, A., Björkstrand, J., Larsson, E. M., Furmark, T., . . . Fredrikson, M. (2012). Disruption of reconsolidation erases a fear memory trace in the human amygdala. *Science, 337,* 1550. doi: http://dx.doi .org/10.1126/science.1223006

Aguiara, A., & Baillargeon, R. (2002). Developments in young infants' reasoning about occluded objects. *Cognitive Psychology, 45,* 267–336.

Ainsworth, M. D. S. (1979). Infant-mother attachment. *American Psychologist, 34,* 932–937. doi: 10.1016/ S0010-0285(02)00005-1

Ainsworth, M. D. S., Blehar, M. C., Waters, E., & Wall, S. (1978). *Patterns of attachment: A psychological study of the Strange Situation.* Hillsdale, NJ: Erlbaum.

Alarcón, R. D., Oquendo, M. A., & Wainberg, M. L. (2014). Depression in a Latino man in New York. *American Journal of Psychiatry, 171,* 506–508. doi: 10.1176/appi.ajp.2013.13101292

Albert, D., Chein, J., & Steinberg, L. (2013). The teenage brain: Peer influences on adolescent decision making. *Current Directions in Psychological Science, 22,* 114–120. doi: 10.1177/0963721412471347

Ali, M., Farooq, N., Bhatti, M. A., & Kuroiwa, C. (2012). Assessment of prevalence and determinants of posttraumatic stress disorder in survivors of earthquake in Pakistan using Davidson Trauma Scale. *Journal of Affective Disorders, 136,* 238–243.

Allport, G. W. (1961). *Pattern and growth in personality.* New York: Holt, Rinehart & Winston.

Allsop, D. J., Copeland, J., Norberg, M. M., Fu, S., Molnar, A., Lewis, J., & Budney, A. J. (2012). Quantifying the clinical significance of cannabis withdrawal. *PLOS ONE, 7*(9), e44864. doi: 10.1371/journal. pone.0044864

Althof, S. E. (2010). What's new in sex therapy? *Journal of Sexual Medicine, 7,* 5–13.

Althof, S. E., McMahon, C. G., Waldinger, M. D., Serefoglu, E. C., Shindel, A. W., Adaikan, P. G., . . . Torres, L. O. (2014). An update of the International Society of Sexual Medicine's Guidelines for the Diagnosis and Treatment of Premature Ejaculation (PE). *Journal of Sexual Medicine, 11,* 1392-1422. doi: 10.1111/ jsm.1250

Althof, S. E., & Needle, R. B. (2011). Sex therapy in male sexual dysfunction. *Current Clinical Urology, Part 5,* 731–738.

doi: Ameli, R. (2014). 25 lessons in mindfulness: Now time for healthy living. *LifeTools: Books for the general public series.* Washington, D.C.: American Psychological Association.

American College Health Association. (2011). *National College Health Assessment—Reference Group Data Report, Fall 2011.* Hanover, MD: Author.

American Psychiatric Association (APA). (2013). *DSM-5: Diagnostic and statistical manual of mental disorders* (5th ed.). Washington, D.C.: Author.

American Psychological Association (2002). Ethical principles of psychologists and code of conduct. *American Psychologist, 57,* 1060–1073.

American Psychological Association (2003, July). *Employment settings for PhD: 2001.* Washington, D.C.: APA Research Office.

American Psychological Association (2004, April). *Current major fields of APA membership by membership status, 2002.* Washington, D.C.: APA Research Office.

American Psychological Association (2007, October 25). *Stress a major health problem in the U.S., warns APA.* Washington, D.C.: Author. Retrieved from www .apa.org /news/press /releases/2007/10/stress.aspx

American Psychological Association (2010, January). *2010: Race/ethnicity of doctorate recipients in psychology in the past 10 years.* APA Center for Workforce Studies. Retrieved from https:// www.apa.org/workforce/publications/10-race/index .aspx

American Psychological Association (2010a, January 6). Few gender differences in math abilities, worldwide study finds. *ScienceDaily.* Retrieved July 6, 2013, from http://www.apa.org/news/press /releases/2010/01/gender-math.aspx

American Psychological Association (2010b). *Stress in America 2011: Executive summary.* Retrieved from www.apa.org/news/press/releases/stress-exec -summary.pdf, p. 8

American Psychological Association (2013). *Stress by generation.* Retrieved from www.apa.org/news/press /releases /stress/2012/generations.aspx

American Psychological Association (2014, June 25). *APA applauds landmark Illinois Law allowing psychologists to prescribe medications.* Retrieved from http://www.apa.org/news/press/releases/2014/06 /prescribe-medications.aspx

American Psychological Association (2015, July). *2005–13: Demographics of the U.S. Psychology Workforce.* Center for Workforce Studies, APA Center for Workforce Studies. Retrieved from https:// www.apa.org/workforce/publications/13-dem-acs /index.aspx?tab=4

American Psychological Association (2016a, March 10). *Discrimination linked to increased stress, poorer health, American Psychological Association survey finds.* Retrieved from http://www.apa .org/news/press/releases/2016/03/impact-of -discrimination.aspx

American Psychological Association (2016b). Stress in America: The impact of discrimination. *Stress in America™ Survey.* Washington, D.C.: American Psychological Association.

Anderson, A. L., Harris, T. B., Tylavsky, F. A., Perry, S. E., Houston, D. K., Hue, T. F., . . . Health ABC Study. (2011). Dietary patterns and survival of older adults. *Journal of the American Dietetic Association, 111,* 84–91. doi: 10.1016/j.jada.2010.10.012

Anderson, C. A., Anderson, K. B., Dorr, N., DeNeve, K. M., & Flanagan, M. (2000). Temperature and aggression. *Advances in Experimental Social Psychology, 32,* 63–133.

Anderson, C. A., & Bushman, B. J. (2003). Human aggression. *Annual Review of Psychology, 53,* 27–51. doi: 10.1146/ annurev.psych.53.100901.135231

Anderson, E. M., & Lambert, M. J. (2001). A survival analysis of clinically significant change in outpatient psychotherapy. *Professional Psychology: Research and Practice, 57,* 875–888.

Anderson, E. R., & Mayes, L. C. (2010). Race/ethnicity and internalizing disorders in youth: A review. *Clinical Psychology Review, 30,* 338–48. doi: 10.1016/j. cpr.2009.12.008

Anderson, P. L., Price, M., Edwards, S. M., Obasaju, M. A., Schmertz, S. K., Zimand, E., . . . Calamaras, M. R. (2013). Virtual reality exposure therapy for social anxiety disorder: A randomized controlled trial. *Journal of Consulting and Clinical Psychology, 81,* 751–760. doi: 10.1037/a0033559

Anderson, S. E., Dallal, G. E., & Must, A. (2003). Relative weight and race influence average age at menarche: Results from two nationally representative surveys of U.S. girls studied 25 years apart. *Pediatrics, 111,* 844–850.

Angier, N. (1998, September 1). Nothing becomes a man more than a woman's face. *The New York Times,* p. F3.

Angier, N. (2009, October 27). A molecule of motivation, dopamine excels at its tasks. *The New York Times,* pp. D1, D3

Anstee, Q. M., Knapp, S., Maguire, E. P., Hosie, A. M., Thomas, P., Mortensen, M., . . . Thomas, H. C. (2013) . Mutations in the Gabrb1 gene promote alcohol consumption through increased tonic inhibition. *Nature Communications, 4,* doi: 10.1038/ncomms3816

Anthes, E. (2014). Depression: A change of mind. *Nature, 515,* 185–187. doi: 10.1038/515185a

Anthes, E. (2016, April 6). Mental health: There's an app for that. *Nature.* Retrieved from http://www .nature.com/news/mental-health-there-s-an-app-for-that-1.19694

Anticevic, A., Murray, J. D., & Barch, D. M. (2015). Bridging levels of understanding in schizophrenia through computational modeling. *Clinical Psychological Science, 3,* 433–459. doi: 10.1177/2167702614562041

Antoni, M. H. (2012). Psychosocial intervention effects on adaptation, disease course and biobehavioral processes in cancer. *Brain, Behavior, and Immunity,* May 22. Epub ahead of print.

Anzures, G., Quinn, P. C., Pascalis, O., Slater, A. M., Tanaka, J. W., & Lee, L. (2013). Developmental origins of the other-race effect. *Current Directions in Psychological Science, 22,* 173–178. doi: 10.1177/0963721412474459

Aoyagi, M. W., Portenga, S. T., Poczwardowski, A., Cohen, A. B., & Statler, T. (2012). Reflections and directions: The profession of sport psychology past, present, and future. *Professional Psychology: Research and Practice, 43,* 32–38. doi: 10.1037/a0025676

Apovian, C. M. (2016). The obesity epidemic: Understanding the disease and the treatment. *New England Journal of Medicine, 374,* 177–179. doi: 10.1056/NEJMe1514957

Arcelus, J., Mitchell, A. J., Wales, J., & Nielsen, S. (2011). Mortality rates in patients with anorexia nervosa and other eating disorders: A meta-analysis of 36 studies. *Archives of General Psychiatry, 68,* 724.

Archer, J. (2006). Testosterone and human aggression: An evaluation of the challenge hypothesis. *Neuroscience & Biobehavioral Reviews, 30,* 319–345.

Archontaki, D., Lewis, G., J., & Bates, T. C. (2012). Genetic influences on psychological well-being: A nationally representative twin study. *Journal of Personality, 81,* 221–230. doi: 10.1111/j.1467-6494. 2012.00787.x

Arias, E. (2016, April). Changes in life expectancy by race and Hispanic Origin in the United States, 2013–2014. National Center for Health Statistics (NCHS). *NCHS Data Brief No. 244.* Retrieved from http://www.cdc .gov/nchs/products/databriefs/db244.htm

Armon, G., Melamed, S., Toker, S., Berliner, S., & Shapira, I. (2014). Joint effect of chronic medical illness and burnout on depressive symptoms among employed adults. *Health Psychology, 33,* 264–272. doi: 10.1037/a0033712

Armstrong, L., & Rimes, K. A. (2016). Mindfulness-based cognitive therapy for neuroticism (stress vulnerability): A pilot randomized study. *Behavior Therapy, 47,* 287–298. doi: 10.1016/j.beth.2015.12.005

Arnal, L. H., Flinker, A., Kleinschmidt, A., Giraud, A.-L., & Poeppel, D. (2015). Human screams occupy a privileged niche in the communication soundscape. *Current Biology, 25,* 2051–2056. doi: http://dx.doi. org/10.1016/j.cub.2015.06.043

Arnett, J. J. (2004). *Adolescence and emerging adulthood: A cultural approach* (2nd ed.). Upper Saddle River, NJ: Pearson/Prentice Hall.

Arnett, J. J. (2010). Oh, grow up! Generational grumbling and the new life stage of emerging adulthood—Commentary on Trzesniewski & Donnellan (2010). *Perspectives on Psychological Science, 5,* 89–92. doi: 10.1177/1745691609357016

Arnold, C. (2011). Why sleep is good for you. *Scientific American, 304*(1), 26.

Arnow, B. A., Steidtmann, D., Blasey, C., Manber, R., Constantino, M. J., Klein, D. N., . . . Kocsis, J. H. (2013).Therapeutic alliance and treatment outcome in two psychotherapies for chronic depression. *Journal of Consulting and Clinical Psychology, 81,* 627–638. doi: 10.1037/a0031530

Aronson, E., Wilson, T. D., & Akert, R. M. (2004). *Social psychology: Media and research update* (5th ed.). Upper Saddle River, NJ: Prentice Hall.

Arzi, A.,. Holtzman, Y., Samnon, P., Eshel, N., Harel, E., & Sobel, N. (2014). Olfactory aversive conditioning during sleep reduces cigarette-smoking behavior. *Journal of Neuroscience, 3,* 15382. doi: 10.1523/ JNEUROSCI.2291-14.2014

Asch, S. E. (1956). Studies of independence and conformity: I. A minority of one against a unanimous majority. *Psychological Monographs, 70,* 70.

Ashburn-Nardo, L., Voils, C. I., & Monteith, M. J. (2001). Implicit associations as the seeds of intergroup bias: How easily do they take root? *Journal of Personality and Social Psychology, 81,* 789–799.

Ashby, F. G., & Maddox, W. T. (2005). Human category learning. *Annual Review of Psychology, 56,* 149–178.

Ashmore, J. (2004). Hearing: Channel at the hair's end. *Nature, 432,* 685–686.

Ashton, M. C., & Leeb, E. (2014). Orthogonal factors of mental ability? A response to Hampshire et al.

Personality and Individual Differences, 60, 13–15. doi: 10.1016/j.paid.2013.09.032

Aspy, C. B., Vesely, S. K., Oman, R. F., Rodine, S., Marshall, L., & McLeroy, K. (2008). Parental communication and youth sexual behavior. *Journal of Adolescence, 30,* 449–466. doi: 10.1016/j.adolescence.2006.04.007

Association for Psychological Science (2010, April 30). Out of mind, out of sight: Blinking eyes indicate mind wandering. *ScienceDaily.* Retrieved from https://www.sciencedaily.com/releases/2010/04 /100429153959.htm

Atkinson, R. C., & Shiffrin, R. M. (1971). The control of short-term memory. *Scientific American, 225,* 82–90.

Atlas, L. Y., & Wager, T. D. (2014). A meta-analysis of brain mechanisms of placebo analgesia: Consistent findings and unanswered questions. *Handbook of Experimental Pharmacology, 225,* 37–69.

Auger, A., Farkas, G., Burchinal, M. R., Duncan, G. J., &Vandell, D. L. (2014). Preschool center care quality effects on academic achievement: An instrumental variables analysis. *Developmental Psychology, 50,* 2559–2571. doi: http://dx.doi.org/10.1037/a0037995

Averhart, C. J., & Bigler, R. S. (1997). Shades of meaning: Skin tone, racial attitudes, and constructive memory in African American children. *Journal of Experimental Child Psychology, 67,* 363–388.

Avins, A. L. (2012). Needling the status quo. *Archives of Internal Medicine, 172,* 1454. doi: http://dx.doi .org/10.1001/archinternmed.2012.4198

Aybek, S., Nicholson, T. R., Zelaya, F., O'Daly, O. G., Craig, T. J., David, A. S., . . . Kanaan, R. A. (2014). Neural correlates of recall of life events in conversion disorder. *JAMA Psychiatry, 71,* 52–60. doi: 10.1001 /jamapsychiatry.2013.2842

Azañón, E., Longo, M. R., Soto-Faraco, S., & Haggard, P. (2010). The posterior parietal cortex remaps touch into external space. *Current Biology, 20,* 1304–1309. doi: 10.1016/j.cub.2010.05.063

Azar, B. (1996, April). Musical studies provide clues to brain functions. *APA Monitor, 27*(4), 1, 4.

Azar, B. (2006, January). Wild findings on animal sleep. *Monitor on Psychology, 37*(1), 54–55.

Azzi, A., Dallmann, R., Casserly, A., Rehrauer, H., Patrignani, A., Maier, B., . . . Brown, S. A. (2014). Circadian behavior is light-reprogrammed by plastic DNA methylation. *Nature Neuroscience, 17,* 377–382. doi: http://dx.doi.org/10.1038/nn.3651

Bäckström, T., Andreen, L., Birzniece, V., Björn, L., Johansson, I. M., Nordenstam-Haghjo, . . . Zhu, D. (2003). The role of hormones and hormonal treatments in premenstrual syndrome. *CNS Drugs, 17*(5), 325–342.

Baddeley, A. (2012). Working memory: Theories, models, and controversies. *Annual Review of Psychology, 63,* 1–29. doi: 10.1146/annurev-psych-120710-100422

Baer, R. A., Peters, J. R., Eisenlohr-Moula, T. A., Geiger, P. J., & Sauer, S. E. (2012). Emotion-related cognitive processes in borderline personality disorder: A review of the empirical literature. *Clinical Psychology Review, 32,* 359–369. doi: 10.1016/j.cpr.2012.03.00

Bailey, J. M., Vasey, P. L., Diamond, L. M., Breedlove, S. M., Vilain, E., & Epprecht, M. (2016). Sexual orientation, controversy, and science. *Psychological Science in the Public Interest, 17,* 45.doi: 10.1177/1529100616637616

Bakalar, N. (2006a, April 18). Research ties lack of sleep to risk for hypertension. *The New York Times,* p. F7.

Bakalar, N. (2006b, June 13). Men are better than women at ferreting out that angry face in a crowd. *The New York Times,* p. F5.

Bakalar, N. (2012). Sensory science: Partners in flavour. *Nature, 486,* S4–S5. doi: 10.1038/486S4a

Baker, J. T., Holmes, A. J., Masters, G. A., Yeo, B. T. T., Krienen, F., Buckner, R. L., . . . Öngür, D. (2014). Disruption of cortical association networks in schizophrenia and psychotic bipolar disorder. *JAMA Psychiatry, 71,* 109–118. doi: 10.1001/jamapsychiatry.2013.3469

Bakes, K. (2013, December). Sedative and opioid abuse in adolescents. Retrieved from http://www.jwatch.org/na32837/2013/12/12/sedative-and-opioid-abuse-adolescents?query=etoc_jwpsych

Balliet, D., Wu, J., & Dreu, C. K. W. (2014). Ingroup favoritism in cooperation: A meta-analysis. *Psychological Bulletin, 140,* 1556–1581. doi: http://dx.doi.org/10.1037/a0037737

Balter, M. (2014). Talking back to madness. *Science, 343,* 1190–1193. doi 10.1126/science.343.6176.1190

Balthazart, J. (2012). *The biology of homosexuality.* New York : Oxford University Press.

Bandler, R., Jr. (2006). Predatory aggression: Midbrain-pontine junction rather than hypothalamus as the critical structure? *Aggressive Behavior, 1,* 261–266.

Bandura, A. (1986). *Social foundations of thought and action: A social-cognitive theory.* Englewood Cliffs, NJ: Prentice Hall.

Bandura, A. (1989). Social cognitive theory. In R. Vasta (Ed.), *Annals of child development: Theories of child development: Revised formulations and current issues.* Greenwich, CT: JAI Press.

Bandura, A. (1997). *Self-efficacy: The exercise of control.* New York: Freeman.

Bandura, A. (2006). Toward a psychology of human agency. *Perspectives on Psychological Science, 1,* 164–180.

Bandura, A. (2008a). Observational learning. In W. Donsbach (Ed.), *International encyclopedia of communication* (Vol. 7, pp. 3359–3361). Oxford, U.K.: Blackwell.

Bandura, A. (2008b). An agentic perspective on positive psychology. In S. J. Lopez (Ed.), *Positive psychology: Exploring the best in people* (Vol. 1, pp. 167–196). Westport, CT: Greenwood Publishing Company.

Bandura, A. (2009). Vicarious learning. In D. Matsumoto (Ed.), *Cambridge dictionary of psychology.* Cambridge, U.K.: Cambridge University Press.

Bandura, A. (2010). Agency. In D. Carr (Ed.), *Encyclopedia of life course and human development.* New York: Macmillan.

Bandura, A., Blanchard, E. B., & Ritter, B. (1969). The relative efficacy of desensitization and modeling approaches for inducing behavioral, affective, and cognitive changes. *Journal of Personality and Social Psychology, 13,* 173–199.

Bandura, A., Ross, S. A., & Ross, D. (1963). Imitation of film-mediated aggressive models. *Journal of Abnormal Psychology, 66,* 3–11.

Banyard, P., & Flanagan, C. (2006). *Ethical issues and guidelines in psychology.* New York: Routledge.

Barabási, A.-L. (2007). Network medicine—From obesity to the "diseasome." *New England Journal of Medicine, 357,* 404–407.

Baranzini, S. E., Mudge, J., van Velkinburgh, J. C., Khankhanian, P., Khrebtukova, I., Miller, N. A., . . . Kingsmore, S. F. (2010). Genome, epigenome and RNA sequences of monozygotic twins discordant for multiple sclerosis. *Nature, 464,* 1351. doi: 10.1038/nature08990

Barber, T. X. (1999). A comprehensive three-dimensional theory of hypnosis. In I. Kirsch, A. Capafons, E. Cardeña-Buelna, & S. Amigó (Eds.), *Clinical hypnosis and self-regulation: Cognitive-behavioral perspectives* (pp. 21–48). Washington, D.C.: American Psychological Association.

Bar-Haim, Y., Ziv, T., Lamy, D., & Hodes, R. M. (2006). Nature and nurture in own-race face processing. *Psychological Science, 17,* 159–163.

Barnett, W. S., & Hustedt, J. T. (2005). Head Start's lasting benefits. *Infants & Young Children, 18,* 16–24.

Baron, R. A., Branscombe, N. R., & Byrne, D. (2009). *Social psychology* (12th ed.). Boston: Pearson/Allyn and Bacon.

Barrett, L. S. (2015, August 2). What emotions are (and aren't). *The New York Times Review,* p. 10.

Barrouillet, P. (2015). Theories of cognitive development: From Piaget to today. *Developmental Review, 38,* 1–12. doi: 10.1016/j.dr.2015.07.004

Barth, J., Munder, T., Gerger, H., Nüesch, E., Trelle, S., Znoj, H, & Cuijpers, P. (2016). Comparative efficacy of seven psychotherapeutic interventions for patients with depression: A network meta-analysis. *Focus, 14,* 229–243.

Bartho, P., Hirase, H., Monconduit, L., Zugaro, M., Harris, K. D., & Buzsaki, G. (2004). Characterization of neocortical principal cells and interneurons by network interactions and extracellular features. *Journal of Neurophysiology, 92,* 600–608.

Bartholow, B. D., & Heinz, A. (2006). Alcohol and aggression without consumption: Alcohol cues, aggressive thoughts, and hostile perception bias. *Psychological Science, 17,* 30–37.

Bartoshuk, L. (2007, January). *Do you taste what I taste? Using genetic variation in taste to teach about taste, diet and health.* Paper presented at the National Institute for the Teaching of Psychology, St. Petersburg, FL.

Bartz, J. A. (2016). Oxytocin and the pharmacological dissection of affiliation. *Current Directions in Psychological Science, 25,* 104–110. doi: 10.1177/0963721415626678

Batalla, A., Bhattacharyya, A., Yücel, M., Fusar-Poli, P., Crippa, J. A., Nogué, S., . . . Martin-Santos, R. (2013). Structural and functional imaging studies in chronic cannabis users: A systematic review of adolescent and adult findings. *PLoS ONE.* Retrieved from http://journals.plos.org/plosone/article?id=10.1371/journal.pone.0055821

Batson, C. D. (1998). Altruism and prosocial behavior. In D. T. Gilbert, S. T. Fiske, & G. Lindzey (Eds.), *The handbook of social psychology* (Vol. 2, 4th ed., pp. 282–316). Boston: McGraw-Hill.

Batson, C. D. (2009). These things called empathy: Eight related but distinct phenomena. In J. Decety & W. Ickes (Eds.), *The social neuroscience of empathy* (pp. 3–15). Cambridge, MA: MIT Press.

Batson, C. D., Ahmad, N., Lishner, D. A., & Tsang, J. (2002). Empathy and altruism. In C. R. Snyder &

S. J. Lopez (Eds.), *Handbook of positive psychology* (pp. 485–498). New York: Oxford University Press.

Batson, C. D., & Powell, A. A. (2003). Altruism and prosocial behavior. In T. Millon & M. J. Lerner (Eds.), *Handbook of psychology: Personality and social psychology* (Vol. 5, pp. 463–484). New York: Wiley.

Bauchner, H., Fontanarosa, P. B., & Golub, R. M. (2013). Updated guidelines for management of high blood pressure: Recommendations, review, and responsibility [Editorial]. *Journal of the American Medical Association, 311,* 477–478. doi: 10.1001/jama.2013.284432

Baucom, B. R., Atkins, D. C., Rowe, L. S., Doss, B. D., & Christensen, A. (2015). Prediction of treatment response at 5-year follow-up in a randomized clinical trial of behaviorally based couple therapies. *Journal of Consulting and Clinical Psychology, 83,* 103–114. doi: http://dx.doi.org/10.1037/a0038005

Baumeister, R. F., Campbell, J. D., Krueger, J. I., & Vohs, K. D. (2003). Does high self-esteem cause better performance, interpersonal success, happiness, or healthier lifestyle? *Psychological Science in the Public Interest, 4,* 1–44.

Baumrind, D. (1971). Current patterns of parental authority. *Developmental Psychology, 4*(1, Part 2), 1–103.

Baumrind, D. (1991). Parenting styles and adolescent development. In J. Brooks-Gunn, R. Lerner, & A. C. Petersen (Eds.), *Encyclopedia of adolescence* (pp. 746–758). New York: Garland.

Beck, A. T. (2006). How an anomalous finding led to a new system of psychotherapy. *Nature Medicine, 12,* 1139–1141.

Beck, A. T., & Dozois, D. J. A. (2011). Cognitive therapy: Current status and future directions. *Annual Review of Medicine, 62,* 397–409. doi: 10.1146/annurev-med-052209-100032

Beck, A. T., Freeman, A., Davis, D. D., & Associates. (2006). *Cognitive therapy of personality disorders* (2nd ed.). New York: Guilford Press.

Beck, A. T., Rush, A. J., Shaw, B. F., & Emery, G. (1979). *Cognitive therapy of depression.* New York: Guilford Press.

Beck, A. T., & Weishaar, M. E. (2011). Cognitive therapy. In R. J. Corsini & D. Wedding (Eds.), *Current psychotherapies* (9th ed). Belmont, CA: Brooks/Cole.

Beck, H. P., Levinson, S., & Irons, G. (2009). Finding Little Albert: A journey to John B. Watson's infant laboratory. *American Psychologist, 64,* 605–614. doi: 10.1037/a0071234

Beck, M. (2011, November 15). Scan reveal where hurtful signals lie; teaching patient to short-circuit them. *The Wall Street Journal,* p. D1.

Beck, M., & Schatz, A. (2014, January 17). American eating habits take a healthier turn. *The Wall Street Journal,* pp. A1, A2.

Beelmann, A., & Heinemann, K. S. (2014). Preventing prejudice and improving intergroup attitudes: A meta-analysis of child and adolescent training program. *Journal of Applied Developmental Psychology, 35,* 10–24. doi: http://dx.doi.org/10.1016/j.appdev.2013.11.002

Begley, S. (2011a, January 10/17). Can you build a better brain? *Newsweek,* pp. 40–45.

Begley, S. (2011b, November 7/14). Stop! You can't afford it. *Newsweek,* pp. 50–53. Bell, B. T., & Dittmar,

H. (2011). Does media type matter? The role of identification in adolescent girls' media consumption and the impact of different thin-ideal media on body image. *Sex Roles, 65,* 478–490. doi: 10.1007/s11199-011-9964-x

Belleville, G., Foldes-Busque, G., Dixon, M., Marquis-Pelletier, E., Barbeau, S., Poitras, J., . . . Marchand, A. (2012). Impact of seasonal and lunar cycles on psychological symptoms in the ED: An empirical investigation of widely spread beliefs. *General Hospital Psychiatry, S0163-8343,* 320–329. doi: 10.1016/j.genhosppsych.2012.10.002

Bellis, M. (2001, April 14). *Your about.com guide to inventors.* Retrieved from http://inventors.about.com/science/ inventors/library/bl/bl12_ 2a_u.htm

Belluck, P. (2000, October 18). New advice for parents: Saying "That's great!" may not be. *The New York Times,* p. A18.

Bem, D. J. (1996). Exotic becomes erotic: A developmental theory of sexual orientation. *Psychological Review, 103,* 320–335.

Bempechat, J., & Shernoff, D. J. (2012). Parental influences on achievement motivation and student engagement. In S. L. Christenson, A. L. Reschly, & C. Wylie (Eds.), *Handbook of research on student engagement* (pp. 315–342). New York: Springer.

Ben-David, B. M., Erel, H., Goy, H., & Schneider, B. A. (2015). "Older is always better": Age-related differences in vocabulary scores across 16 years. *Psychology and Aging, 30,* 856–862. doi: http://dx.doi.org/10.1037/pag0000051

Benight, C. C., & Bandura, A. (2004). Social cognitive theory of posttraumatic recovery: The role of perceived self-efficacy. *Behaviour Research and Theory, 42,* 1129–1148.

Benjamin, L. T. (1988). *A history of psychology: Original source and contemporary research.* New York: McGraw-Hill.

Benjamin, L. T. (1997). The origin of psychological species: History of the beginnings of American Psychological Association Divisions. *American Psychologist, 51,* 725–732.

Benjamin, L. T. (2000). The psychology laboratory at the turn of the 20th century. *American Psychologist, 55,* 318–321.

Benjamin, L. T., Jr. (2009, January). The birth of American intelligence testing. *Monitor on Psychology, 40*(1), 20–21.

Benjamin, L. T., Jr., & Simpson, J. A. (2009). The power of the situation: The impact of Milgram's obedience studies on personality and social psychology. *American Psychologist, 64,* 12–19. doi: 10.1037/a0014077

Bennett, J. (2009). Gene therapy for color blindness. *New England Journal of Medicine, 361,* 2483–2484.

Benowitz, N. L. (2010). Nicotine addiction. *New England Journal of Medicine, 362,* 2295–2303.

Benson, E. (2003, February). Intelligence across cultures. *Monitor on Psychology, 34*(2), 56–58.

Berger, K. S. (2009a). *The developing person through childhood* (5th ed.). New York: Worth Publishers.

Berger, K. S. (2009b). *The developing person through childhood and adolescence* (8th ed.). New York: Worth Publishers.

Berger, K. S., & Thompson, R. A. (1995). *The developing person through childhood and adolescence* (4th ed.). New York: Worth Publishers.

Berger, T., Boettcher, J., & Caspar, F. (2014). Internet-based guided self-help for several anxiety

disorders: A randomized controlled trial comparing a tailored with a standardized disorder-specific approach. *Psychotherapy, 51,* 207–219. doi: 10.1037/a0032527

Bergeron, J., Langlois, J., & Cheang, H. S. (2014). An examination of the relationships between cannabis use, driving under the influence of cannabis and risk-taking on the road. *Revue Européenne de Psychologie Appliquée/European Review of Applied Psychology, 64,* 101–109. doi: 10.1016/j.erap.2014.04.001

Bergman, B. G., Greene, M. C., Hoeppner, B. B., Slaymaker, V., & Kelly, J. F. (2013). Psychiatric co-morbidity and 12-step participation: A longitudinal investigation of treated young adults. *Alcoholism: Clinical and Experimental Research, 38,* 501–510. doi: 10.1111/acer.12249

Berk, L. E. (2009). *Child development* (8th ed.). Needham Heights, MA: Pearson Education.

Berko Gleason, J., & Ratner, N. (Eds.). (2009). *The development of language* (7th ed.). Boston: Allyn & Bacon.

Bernard, L. L. (1924). *Instinct.* New York: Holt, Rinehart & Winston.

Berners-Lee, R. (with Fischetti, M.). (1999). *Weaving the Web: The original design and ultimate destiny of the World Wide Web by its inventor.* London: Orion Business.

Bernstein, D. M., & Loftus, E. F. (2009). The consequences of false memories for food preferences and choices. *Perspectives on Psychological Science, 4,* 135–139. doi: 10.1111/j.1745-6924.2009.01113.x

Berrington de Gonzalez, B., Hartge, P., Cerhan, J. R., Flint, A. J., Hannan, L., MacInnis, R. J., . . . Thun, M. J. (2010). Body-mass index and mortality—prospective analysis of 1.46 million white adults. *New England Journal of Medicine, 363,* 2211–2219. doi: 10.1056/NEJMoa1000367

Berry, J. A., Cervantes-Sandoval, I., Nicholas, E. P., & Davis, R. L. (2012). Dopamine is required for learning and forgetting in drosophila. *Neuron, 74,* 530. doi: 10.1016/j.neuron.2012.04.007

Berryman, N., Bherer, L., Nadeau, S., Lauzière, S., Lehr, L., Bobeuf, L., . . . Bosquet, L. (2014). Multiple roads lead to Rome: Combined high-intensity aerobic and strength training vs. gross motor activities leads to equivalent improvement in executive functions in a cohort of healthy older adults. *Age, 36,* 9710. doi: 10.1007/s11357-014-9710-8

Bersamin, M. M., Paschall, M. J., Saltz, R. F., & Zamboanga, B. L. (2012). Young adults and casual sex: The relevance of college drinking settings. *Journal of Sex Research, 49,* 274–281. doi: 10.1080/00224499.2010.548012

Bethune, S. (2013, February 7). Health care system falls short on stress management. Press Release, American Psychological Association. Author: Washington, D.C.

Bezdjian, S., Baker, L. A., & Tuvblad, C. (2011). Genetic and environmental influences on impulsivity: A meta-analysis of twin, family and adoption studies. *Clinical Psychology Review, 31,* 1209–1223. doi: 10.1016/j.cpr.2011.07.005

Bianchi, R., Schonfeld, I. S., & Laurent, E. (2015). Burnout–depression overlap: A review. *Clinical Psychology Review, 36,* 28–41.

Bianchin, M., & Angrilli, A. (2011). Gender differences in emotional responses: A psychophysiological study. *Physiology & Behavior, 105,* 925–932.

Bie, B., Wu, J., Yang, H., Xu, J. J., Brown, D. L., & Naguib, M. (2014). Epigenetic suppression of neuroligin 1 underlies amyloid-induced memory deficiency. *Nature Neuroscience, 17,* 223–231. doi: 10.1038/nn.3618 [9]

Bishop, E. G., Cherny, S. S., Corleya, R., Plomin, R., DeFriesa, J. C., & Hewitt, J. K. (2003). Developmental genetic analysis of general cognitive ability from 1 to 12 years in a sample of adoptees, biological siblings, and twins. *Intelligence, 31,* 31–49.

Blake, A. B., Nazarian, M., & Castel, A. D. (2015). The Apple of the mind's eye: Everyday attention, metamemory, and reconstructive memory for the Apple logo. *The Quarterly Journal of Experimental Psychology, 68,* 858–685. doi: 10.1080/17470218.2014.1002798

Blakeslee, S. (2005, November 22). This is your brain under hypnosis. *The New York Times,* pp. F1, F4.

Blashill, A., J., & Wilhelm, S. (2013). Body image distortions, weight, and depression in adolescent boys: Longitudinal trajectories into adulthood. *Psychology of Men & Masculinity, 15,* 445-445. doi: 10.1037/a0034618

Blass, T. (2009). From New Haven to Santa Clara: A historical perspective on the Milgram obedience experiments. *American Psychologist, 64,* 37–45.

Blazer, D. G., Yaffe, K., & Karlawish, J. (2015, April 15). Cognitive aging: A report from the Institute of Medicine. *Journal of the American Medical Association.* Retrieved from http://jama.jamanetwork.com/article.aspx?articleid=2276710

Bleidorn, W. (2015). What accounts for personality maturation in early adulthood? *Current Directions in Psychological Science, 24,* 245–252. doi: 10.1177/0963721414568662

Blom, K., Tillgren, H. T., Wiklund, T., Danlycke, E., Forssén, M., Söderström, A., . . . Kaldo. V. (2015). Internet- vs. group-delivered cognitive behavior therapy for insomnia: A randomized controlled non-inferiority trial. *Behaviour Research and Therapy, 70,* 47–55. doi: 10.1016/j.brat.2015.05.002

Blomsted, P., Sjöberg, R. L., Hansson, M., Bodlund, O., & Hariz, M. I. (2011). Deep brain stimulation in the treatment of depression. *Acta Psychiatrica Scandinavica, 123,* 4–11. doi: 10.1111/j.1600-0447.2010.01625.x

Blum, R. W., Beuhring, T., Shew, M. L., Bearinger, L. H., Sieving, R. E., & Resnick, M. D. (2000). The effects of race/ethnicity, income, and family structure on adolescent risk behaviors. *American Journal of Public Health, 90,* 1879–1884.

Boag, S. (2006). Freudian repression, the common view, and pathological science. *Review of General Psychology, 10,* 74–86.

Bøen, E., et al. (2013). Regional cortical thinning may be a biological marker for borderline personality disorder. *Acta Psychiatrica Scandinavica, 130,* 193–204. doi: 10.1111/acps.12234

Bögels, S. M., Wijts, P., Oort, F. J., & Sallaerts, S. J. M. (2014). Psychodynamic psychotherapy versus cognitive behavior therapy for social anxiety disorder: An efficacy and partial effectiveness trial. *Depression and Anxiety, 31,* 5, 363–373. doi: 10.1002/da.22246

Bogg, T., & Roberts, B. W. (2013). The case for conscientiousness: Evidence and implications for a personality trait marker of health and longevity. *Annals of Behavioral Medicine, 45,* 278–288. doi: 10.1007/s12160- 012-9454-6

Bohlken, M. M., Brouwer, R. M., Mandl, R. W., Van den Heuvel, M. P., Hedman, A. M., De Hert, M., . . . Hulshoff Pol, H. E. (2016). Structural brain connectivity as a genetic marker for schizophrenia. *JAMA Psychiatry, 73*, 11–19. doi: 10.1001/jamapsychiatry.2015.1925

Bohner, G., & Dickel, N. (2011). Attitudes and attitude change. *Annual Review of Psychology, 62*, 391–417. doi: 10.1146/annurev.psych.121208.131609

Bohrn, I., Carbon, C.-C., & Hutzler, F. (2010). Mona Lisa's smile—Perception or deception? *Psychological Science, 21*, 378–380. doi: 10.1177/0956797610362192

Boles, S. M., & Miottoa, K. (2003). Substance abuse and violence: A review of the literature. *Aggression and Violent Behavior, 8*, 155–174.

Bolhuis, J. J., & Wynne, C. D. L. (2009). Can evolution explain how minds work? *Nature, 458*, 832–833.

Bollmann, F., Art, J., Henke, J., Schrick, K., Besche, V., Bros, M., . . . Pautz, A. (2014). Resveratrol post-transcriptionally regulates pro-inflammatory gene expression via regulation of KSRP RNA binding activity. *Nucleic Acids Research, 42*, 12555–12569. doi: 10.1093/nar/gku1033

Bonanno, G. A., Brewin, C. R., Kaniasty, K., & La Greca, A. M. (2010). Weighing the costs of disaster: Consequences, risks, and resilience in individuals, families, and communities. *Psychological Science in the Public Interest, 11*, 1–49. doi: 10.1177/1529100610387086

Bongaarts, J., Pelletier, F., & Gerland, P. (2010a). How many more AIDS deaths? *The Lancet, 375*, 103–104. doi: 10.1016/S0140-6736(09)61756-6

Bongaarts, J., Pelletier, F., & Gerland, P. (2010b). Global trends in AIDS mortality. In R. G. Rogers & E. M. Crimmins (Eds.), *International handbook of adult mortality.* New York: Springer.

Boom, J., Wouters, H., & Keller, M. A. (2007). A cross-cultural validation of stage development: A Rasch re-analysis of longitudinal socio-moral reasoning. *Cognitive Development, 22*, 213–229.

Boone, L., Soenens, B., & Luyten, P. (2014). When or why does perfectionism translate into eating disorder pathology? A longitudinal examination of the moderating and mediating role of body dissatisfaction. *Journal of Abnormal Psychology, 123*, 412–418. doi: 10.1037/a0036254

Bootzin, R. R., & Epstein, D. R. (2011). Understanding and treating insomnia. *Annual Review of Clinical Psychology, 7*, 435–458. doi: 10.1146/annurev.clinpsy.3.022806.091516

Borjesson, M., & Dahlof, B. (2005). Physical activity has a key role in hypertension therapy. *Lakartidningen, 102*, 123–124, 126, 128–129.

Bornstein, M. H., Jager, J., & Steinberg, L. D. (2013). Adolescents, parents, friends/peers: A relationships model. R. M. Lerner, M. A. Easterbrooks, & J. Mistry (Eds.), *Handbook of psychology, developmental psychology* (Vol. 6, 2nd ed., pp. 393–434). Hoboken, NJ: Wiley.

Boskind-White, M., & White, W. C. (1983). *Bulimarexia: The binge-purge cycle.* New York: Norton.

Boucher, K. L., Rydell, R. J., & Murphy, M. C. (2015). Forecasting the experience of stereotype threat for others. *Journal of Experimental Social Psychology, 58*, 56–62.

Bould, H., Araya, R., Pearson, R. M., Stapinski, L., Carnegie, R., & Joinson, C. (2014). Association between early temperament and depression at 18 years. *Depression and Anxiety, 31*, 729–736. doi: 10.1002/da.22294

Bourke, P., & Shaw, H. (2014). Spontaneous lucid dreaming frequency and waking insight. *Dreaming, 24*, 152–159. doi: 10.1037/a0036908

Boyce, C. J., Brown, G. D. A., & Moore, S. C. (2010). Money and happiness: Rank of income, not income, affects life satisfaction. *Psychological Science, 21*, 471–475. doi: 10.1177/0956797610362671

Boyce, C. J., Wood, A. M., & Powdthavee, N. (2012). Is personality fixed? Personality changes as much as "variable" economic factors and more strongly predicts changes to life satisfaction. *Social Indicators Research, 111*, 1–19. doi: 10.1007/s11205-012-0006-z

Boynton, R. S. (2004, January 11). In the Jung archives. *The New York Times Book Review*, p. 8.

Boysen, G. A., & VanBergen, A. (2014). Simulation of multiple personalities: a review of research comparing diagnosed and simulated dissociative identity disorder. *Clinical Psychology Review, 34*, 14–28. doi: 10.1016/j.cpr.2013.10.008

Bradshaw, J. (2008, July/August). Consulting authority expanding for RxP psychologist. *The National Psychologist*, p. 7.

Brady, K. R., McCauley, J. L., & Back, S. E. (2016). Prescription opioid misuse, abuse, and treatment in the United States: An update. *American Journal of Psychiatry, 173*, 18–26.

Brandler, W. M., Morris, A. P., Evans, D. M., Scerri, D. S., Kemp, J. P., Timpson, N. J., . . . Paracchini, S. (2013). Common variants in left/right asymmetry genes and pathways are associated with relative hand skill. *PLoS Genetics, 9*, e1003751. doi: 10.1371/journal.pgen.1003751

Brannan, M. E., & Petrie, T. A. (2011). Psychological well-being and the body dissatisfaction-bulimic symptomatology relationship: An examination of moderators. *Eating Behaviors, 12*, 233–241. doi: 10.1016/j.eatbeh.2011.06.002

Brannigan, A., Nicholson, I., & Cherry, F. (2015). Introduction to the special issue: Unplugging the Milgram machine. *Theory & Psychology, 25*, 551–563.

Brant, A. M., Munakata, Y., Boomsma, D. I., DeFries, J. C., Haworth, C. M. A., Keller, M. C., . . . Martin, N. G. (2013). The nature and nurture of high IQ: An extended sensitive period for intellectual development. *Psychological Science, 24*, 1487–1495. doi: 10.1177/0956797612473119

Brawn, T. P., Nusbaum, H. C., & Margoliash, D. (2010). Sleep-dependent consolidation of auditory discrimination learning in adult starlings. *Journal of Neuroscience, 30*, 609–613. doi: 10.1523/JNEUROSCI.4237-09.2010

Brebner, J. (2003). Gender and emotions. *Personality and Individual Differences, 34*, 387–394.

Brent, D. Q., & Gibbons, R. (2014). Initial dose of antidepressant and suicidal behavior in youth: Start low, go slow. *JAMA Internal Medicine, 174*, 909–911. doi: 10.1001/jamainternmed.2013.14016.

Brewer, N., & Wells, G. L. (2011). Eyewitness identification. *Current Directions in Psychological Science, 20*, 24–27. doi: 10.1177/0963721410389169

Brewer, W. F., & Treyens, J. C. (1981). Role of schemata in memory for places. *Cognitive Psychology, 13*, 207–230.

Brewin C. R., & Andrews B. (2014). Why it is scientifically respectable to believe in repression: A response to Patihis, Ho, Tingen, Lilienfeld, and Loftus (2014). *Psychological Science, 25*, 1964–1966.

Bridge, D. J., & Paller, K. A. (2012). Neural correlates of reactivation and retrieval-induced distortion. *Journal of Neuroscience, 32*, 12144. doi: 10.1523/JNEUROSCI.1378-12.2012

Bridge, D. J., & Voss, J. L. (2014). Hippocampal binding of novel information with dominant memory traces can support both memory stability and change. *Journal of Neuroscience, 34*, 2203. doi: 10.1523/JNEUROSCI.3819-13.2014

Briley, D. A., & Tucker-Drob, E. M. (2013). Explaining the increasing heritability of cognitive ability across development: A meta-analysis of longitudinal twin and adoption studies. *Psychological Science, 24*, 1704–1713. doi: 10.1177/0956797613478618

Brister, H. A., Sher, K. J., & Fromme, K. (2011). 21st birthday drinking and associated physical consequences and behavioral risks. *Psychology of Addictive Behaviors, 25*, 573–582. doi: 10.1037/a0025209

Brody, G. H., Beach, S. R. H., Philibert, R. A., Chen, Y.-F., Lei, M.-K., McBride, M. V., & Brown, A. C. (2009). Parenting moderates a genetic vulnerability factor in longitudinal increases in youths' substance use. *Journal of Consulting and Clinical Psychology, 77*, 1–11. doi: 10.1037/a0012996

Brody, G. H., Chen, Y.-F., Kogan, S. M., Murry, V. M., & Brown, A. C. (2010). Long-term effects of the strong African American families program on youths' alcohol use. *Journal of Consulting and Clinical Psychology, 78*, 281–285. doi: 10.1037/a0018552

Brody, J. (2012, May 22). A richer life by seeing the glass half full. *The New York Times*, p. D7.

Brody, J. E. (2006, April 18). A slight change in habits could lull you to sleep. *The New York Times*, p. F7.

Brody, J. E. (2015, December 8). It's not just drivers driven to distraction. *The New York Times*, p. D5.

Brooks, J. X., Carriot, J., & Cullen, K. E. (2015). Learning to expect the unexpected: rapid updating in primate cerebellum during voluntary self-motion. *Nature Neuroscience, 18*, 1310–1317. doi: 10.1038/nn.4077

Brotto, L. A., Bitzer, J., Laan, E., Leiblum, S., & Luria, M. (2010). Women's sexual desire and arousal disorders. *Journal of Sexual Medicine, 7*, 586–614.

Brown, J. D., L'Engle, K. L., Pardun, C. J., Guo, G., Kenneavy, K., & Jackson, C. (2006). Sexy media matter: Exposure to sexual content in music, movies, television, and magazines predicts Black and White adolescents' sexual behavior. *Pediatrics, 117*, 1018–1027.

Brown, M. J. (2006). Hypertension and ethnic group. *British Medical Journal, 332*, 833–836.

Brown, P. L., & Jenkins, H. M. (2009). On the law of effect. In D. Shanks (Ed.), *Psychology of learning.* Thousand Oaks, CA: Sage.

Brown, S. L., Nesse, R. M., Vinokur, A. D., & Smith, D. M. (2003). Providing social support may be more beneficial than receiving it: Results from a prospective study of mortality. *Psychological Science, 14*, 320–327.

Bruner, J. S., & Minturn, A. L. (1955). Perceptual identification and perceptual organization. *Journal of General Psychology, 53*, 21–28.

Bryant, R. A., & Mallard, D. (2002). Hypnotically induced emotional numbing: A real simulating analysis. *Journal of Abnormal Psychology, 111*, 203–207.

Buddie, A. M., & Testa, M. (2005). Rates and predictors of sexual aggression among students and nonstudents. *Journal of Interpersonal Violence, 20,* 713–724.

Bulik, C. M., Marcus, M. D., Zerwas, S., Levine, M. D., & La Via, M. (2012). The changing "weights-cape" of bulimia nervosa. *American Journal of Psychiatry, 169,* 1031–1036. doi: 10.1176/appi.ajp.2012.12010147

Burger, J. M. (2009). Replicating Milgram: Would people still obey today? *American Psychologist, 64,* 1–11.

Burke, T. M., Markwald, R. R., McHill, A. W., Chinoy, E. D., Snider, J. A., Bessman, S. C., . . . Wright, K. P. (2015). Effects of caffeine on the human circadian clock in vivo and in vitro. *Science Translational Medicine, 7,* 305. doi: 10.1126/scitranslmed.aac5125

Burns, D. D. (1980). *Feeling good: The new mood therapy.* New York: Morris.

Burns, J. W., Nielson, W. R., Jensen, M. P., Heapy, A., Czlapinski, R., & Kerns, R. D. (2015). Specific and general therapeutic mechanisms in cognitive behavioral treatment of chronic pain. *Journal of Consulting and Clinical Psychology, 83,* 1–11. doi: http://dx.doi.org/10.1037/a0037208

Bushdid, C., Magnasco, M. O., Vosshall, L. B., & Keller, A. (2014). Humans can discriminate more than 1 trillion olfactory stimuli. *Science, 343,* 1370–1372. doi: 10.1126/science.1249168

Buss, D. M. (2008). *Evolutionary psychology* (3rd ed.). Boston: Allyn & Bacon.

Busuttil, R., W., & Klintmalm, G. B (2015). *Transplantation of the liver.* Philadelphia: Elsevier.

Butcher, J. N. (2000). Revising psychological tests: Lessons learned from the revision of the MMPI. *Psychological Assessment, 12,* 263–271.

Buzsáki, G. (2013). Cognitive neuroscience: Time, space and memory. *Nature, 497,* 568–569. doi: 10.1038/497568a

By the numbers. (2014, January). *Monitor on Psychology, p. 13*

Cabeza, R., & Moscovitch, M. (2013). Memory systems, processing modes, and components: Functional neuroimaging evidence. *Perspectives on Psychological Science, 8,* 49–55. doi: 10.1177/1745691612469033

Caetano, R. (1987). Acculturation and drinking patterns among U.S. Hispanics. *British Journal of Addiction, 82,* 789–799.

Calderon de Anda, F., Pollarolo, G., Santos Da Silva, J., Camoletto, P. G., Feiguin, F., & Dotti, C. G. (2005). Centrosome localization determines neuronal polarity. *Nature, 436,* 704–708.

Cale, E. M., & Lilienfeld, S. O. (2002). Sex differences in psychopathy and antisocial personality disorder. A review and integration. *Clinical Psychology Review, 22,* 1179–1207.

Camara, W. J., Nathan, J. S., & Puente, A. E. (2000). Psychological test usage: Implications in professional psychology. *Professional Psychology: Research and Practice, 31,* 141–154.

Campos, A. (2014). Gender differences in imagery. *Personality and Individual Differences, 59,* 107–111. doi: 10.1016/j.paid.2013.12.010

Canli, T., Desmond, J. E., Zhao, Z., & Gabrieli, J. D. E. (2002). Sex differences in the neural basis of emotional memories. *Proceedings of the National Academy of Sciences, 99*(16), 10789–10794.

Cannon, T. D. (2016). Deciphering the genetic complexity of schizophrenia. *JAMA Psychiatry, 73,* 5–6. doi: 10.1001/jamapsychiatry.2015.2111.

Cannon, W. (1927). The James-Lange theory of emotions: A critical examination as an alternative theory. *American Journal of Psychology, 39,* 106–112.

Carey, B. (2009, November 26). Surgery for mental ills offers both hope and risk. *The New York Times Online.* Retrieved from www.nytimes.com

Carey, B. (2011). Wariness on surgery of the mind. *The New York Times, Science Times,* pp. D5, D6.

Carey, B. (2014, May 14). Remembering, as an extreme sport. *The New York Times.* Retrieved from www.nytimes.com

Carey, B. (2016, January 28). Scientists home in on cause of schizophrenia. *The New York Times,* pp. A1, A17.

Carhart-Harris, R. L., Muthukumaraswamy, S., Roseman, L., Kaelen, M., Droog, W., Murphy, K., . . . Nutt, D. J. (2016). Neural correlates of the LSD experience revealed by multimodal neuroimaging. *Proceedings of the National Academy of Sciences (PNAS), 113,* 4853–4858. doi: 10.1073/pnas.1518377113

Carlsson, E., Frostell, A., Ludvigsson, J., & Faresjo, M. (2014). Psychological stress in children may alter the immune response. *The Journal of Immunology, 192,* 2071. doi: 10.4049/jimmunol.1301713

Carmody, T. P., Duncan, C., Simon, J. A., Solkowitz, S., Huggins, J., Lee, S., & Delucchi, K. (2008). Hypnosis for smoking cessation: A randomized trial. *Nicotine & Tobacco Research, 10,* 811–818.

Carney, D. R., Cuddy, A. J. C., & Yap, A. J. (2010). Power posing: Brief nonverbal displays affect neuroendocrine levels and risk tolerance. *Psychological Science, 21,* 1363–1368. doi: 10.1177/0956797610383437

Carpenter, S. (2000, October). A taste expert sniffs out a long-standing measurement oversight. *Monitor on Psychology, 31*(9), 20–21.

Carpenter, S. (2013, January). Awakening to sleep. *Monitor on Psychology, 44,* 40–45.

Carroll., L. (2004, February 10). Parkinson's research focuses on links to genes and toxins. *The New York Times,* p. F5.

Carroll, S. B. (2009, October 19). For fish in coral reefs, it's useful to be smart. *The New York Times.* Retrieved from www .nytimes.com

Carter, C. S. (2014). Oxytocin pathways and the evolution of human behavior. *Annual Review of Psychology, 65,* 17–39. doi: 10.1146/annurev-psych-010213-115110

Carver, C. S. (2014). Dispositional optimism. *Trends in Cognitive Sciences, 18,* 293–299. doi: http://dx.doi.org/10.1016/j.tics.2014.02.003

Carver, C. S., Johnson, S. L., & Joormann, J. (2008). Serotonergic function, two-mode models of self-regulation, and vulnerability to depression: What depression has in common with impulsive aggression. *Psychological Bulletin, 134,* 912–943. doi: 10.1111/j.1467-8721.2009.01635

Carver, C. S., Johnson, S. L., & Joormann, J. (2009). Two-mode models of self-regulation as a tool for conceptualizing effects of the serotonin system in normal behavior and diverse disorders. *Current Directions in Psychological Science, 18,* 195–199.

Carver, C. S., & Scheier, M. F. (2014). Dispositional optimism. *Trends in Cognitive Sciences, 18,*

293–2994. doi: http://dx.doi.org/10.1016/j.tics.2014.02.003

Casey, B. J., Kosofsky, B.E., & Bhide, P. G. (2014). *Teenage brains: Think different?* Basel, Switzerland: Karger.

Cassidy, J. (2003). Continuity and change in the measurement of infant attachment: Comment on Fraley and Spieker. *Developmental Psychology, 39,* 409–412.

Cassidy, J., & Shaver, P. R. (Eds.). (2008). *Handbook of attachment* (2nd ed.). New York: Guilford.

Cattell, R. B. (1950). *Personality: A systematic, theoretical, and factual study.* New York: McGraw-Hill.

Cattell, R. B. (1965). *The scientific analysis of personality.* Baltimore, MD: Penguin.

Cattell, R. B., Eber, H. W., & Tatsuoka, M. M. (1970). *Handbook for the Sixteen Personality Factor Questionnaire (16PF).* Champaign, IL: Institute for Personality and Ability Testing.

Cecchini-Estrada, J.-A., Méndez-Giménez, A., Cecchini, C., Moulton, M., & Rodríguez, C. (2015). Exercise and Epstein's TARGET for treatment of depressive symptoms: A randomized study. *International Journal of Clinical and Health Psychology, 15,* 191–199. doi: 10.1016/j.ijchp.2015.05.001

Cellar, D. F., Nelson, Z. C., & Yorke, C. M. (2000). The five-factor model and driving behavior: Personality and involvement in vehicular accidents. *Psychological Reports, 86,* 454–456.

Centers for Disease Control and Prevention. (2009a). Cigarette smoking among adults and trends in smoking cessation: United States, 2008. *Morbidity and Mortality Weekly Report, 58*(44), 1227–1232.

Centers for Disease Control and Prevention. (2009b). Obesity and overweight. *FastStats.* Washington, D.C.: Author. Retrieved from www.cdc.gov/nchs/fastats/overwt.htm

Centers for Disease Control and Prevention. (2009c). *Suicide rates among persons ages 10 years and older, by race/ethnicity and sex, United States, 2002–2006.* Washington, D.C.: Author. Retrieved from www.cdc.gov/violenceprevention /suicide/statistics/rates02.html

Centers for Disease Control and Prevention (CDC). (2010a). *Fast stats: Illegal drug use.* Retrieved from www.cdc.gov /nchs/fastats

Centers for Disease Control and Prevention (CDC). (2010b, June). *Obesity and overweight.* Retrieved from www.cdc.gov/nchs /fastats/overwt.htm.

Centers for Disease Control and Prevention (CDC). (2010c). FDA licensure of bivalent human papillomavirus vaccine (HPV2, Cervarix) for use in females and updated HPV vaccination recommendations from the Advisory Committee on Immunization Practices (ACIP). *Morbidity and Mortality Weekly Report, 59,* 626.

Centers for Disease Control and Prevention (CDC). (2010d, December 17). Sexually transmitted diseases treatment guidelines, 2010. *Morbidity and Mortality Weekly Report, 5,* No. RR-12.

Centers for Disease Control and Prevention (CDC), (2011a, May 17). *Insufficient sleep is a public health epidemic.* Retrieved from www.cdc.gov/Features /dsSleep/index.html

Centers for Disease Control and Prevention (CDC). (2011b). Vital signs: Current cigarette smoking among adults aged ≥18 years—United States, 2005–2010. *Morbidity and Mortality Weekly Report, 60,* 1207–1212.

Centers for Disease Control and Prevention (CDC). (2012a). Health, United States: 2012. Retrieved from www.cdc.gov /nchs/data/hus/hus12.pdf#018

Centers for Disease Control and Prevention (CDC). (2012b). Sexual experience and contraceptive use among female teens—United States, 1995, 2002, and 2006–2010. *Morbidity and Mortality Weekly Report, 61*, 297.

Centers for Disease Control and Prevention (CDC). (2012c). Vital signs: Binge drinking prevalence, frequency, and intensity among adults—United States, 2010. *Morbidity and Mortality Weekly Report. Journal of the American Medical Association, 307*, 908–910.

Centers for Disease Control and Prevention. (2013a). *Suicide and self-inflicted injury*. Retrieved from http://www.cdc.gov /nchs/fastats/suicide.htm. Updated May 30, 2013.

Centers for Disease Control and Prevention (CDC). (2013b). *Reported STDs in the United States. 2013 national data for chlamydia, gonorrhea, and syphilis. CDC fact sheet*. Retrieved from http://www.cdc.gov /nchhstp/newsroom/docs/STD-Trends-508.pdf

Centers for Disease Control and Prevention (CDC). (2013c, February). *HPV vaccines*. Retrieved from http://www.cdc.gov/hpv/vaccine.html

Centers for Disease Control and Prevention (CDC). (2014, June). *A new report finds that excessive alcohol use accounts for one in 10 deaths among working-age adults ages 20–64 years in the United States*. Retrieved from http://www.cdc.gov/media /releases/2014/p0626-excessive-drinking.html

Centers for Disease Control and Prevention (CDC). (2015a), August 25). *Current cigarette smoking among adults in the United States*. Retrieved from http://www.cdc.gov/tobacco/data_statistics/fact _sheets/adult_data/cig_smoking/

Centers for Disease Control and Prevention (CDC). (2015b). *Health, United States, 2014.* Retrieved from http://www.cdc.gov/nchs/hus.htm

Centers for Disease Control and Prevention (CDC). (2015c). *HIV in the United States: At a glance*. Retrieved from http://www.cdc.gov/hiv/statistics/basics /ataglance.html

Centers for Disease Control and Prevention (CDC). (2015d). *Assault or homicide*. Retrieved from http:// www.cdc.gov/nchs/fastats/homicide.htm

Centers for Disease Control and Prevention (CDC). (2015e). *HIV/AIDS: Basic statistics.* Retrieved from http://www.cdc.gov/hiv/statistics/basics.html

Centers for Disease Control and Prevention (CDC). (2015f, February 2). *Fast stats: Deaths and mortality*. Retrieved from ww.cdc.gov/nchs/fastats/deaths.htm

Centers for Disease Control and Prevention (CDC). (2015g, January 20). *Fast stats: Reproductive health*. Retrieved from http://www.cdc.gov/nchs/fastats /reproductive-health.htm

Centers for Disease Control and Prevention (CDC). (2015h, April 8). *Fast stats: Alzheimer's disease*. Retrieved from http://www.cdc.gov/nchs/fastats /alzheimers.htm

Centers for Disease Control and Prevention (CDC). (2015i, April 29). *Fast stats: Depression*. Retrieved from http://www.cdc.gov/nchs/fastats/alzheimers.htm

Cepeda, N. J., Pashler, H., Vul, E., Wixted, J. T., & Rohrer, D. (2006). Distributed practice in verbal recall tasks: A review and quantitative synthesis. *Psychological Bulletin, 132*, 354–380.

Cesario, J. (2014). Priming, replication, and the hardest science. *Perspectives on Psychological Science, 9*, 40–48, doi: 10.1177/1745691613513470

Ceskova, E., Prikryl, R., & Kasparek, T. (2011). Suicides in males after the first episode of schizophrenia. *Journal of Nervous & Mental Disease, 199*, 62–64. doi: 10.1097/NMD.0b013e31820448e4

Chan, J. C. K., Thomas, A. K., & Bulevich, J. B. (2009). Recalling a witnessed event increases eyewitness suggestibility: The reversed testing effect. *Psychological Science, 20*, 66–73. doi: 10.1111/j.1467-9280.2008.02245.x

Chance, P. (2009). *Learning and behavior* (6th ed.). Belmont, CA: Cengage.

Chang, A.-M., Aeschbach, D., Duffy, J. F., & Czeisler, C. A. (2014). Evening use of light-emitting eReaders negatively affects sleep, circadian timing, and next-morning alertness. *PNAS, 112*, 1232–1237. doi: 10.1073/pnas.1418490112

Chang, E. C., & Sanna, L. J. (2001). Optimism, pessimism, and positive and negative affectivity in middle-aged adults: A test of a cognitive-affective model of psychological adjustment. *Psychology and Aging, 16*, 524–531.

Chang, S. W. C., Barter, J. W., Ebitz, R. B., Watson, K. K., & Platt, M. L. (2012). Inhaled oxytocin amplifies both vicarious reinforcement and self reinforcement in rhesus macaques *(Macaca mulatta)*. *Proceedings of the National Academy of Sciences, 109*, 959–964. doi: 10.1073/pnas.1114621109

Chapman, C. D., Nilsson, E. K., Nilsson, V. C., Cedernaes, J., Rångtell, F. H., Vogel, H., . . . Benedict, C. (2013). Acute sleep deprivation increases food purchasing in men. *Obesity, 21*, E555–560. doi: 10.1002/oby.20579

Chavira, D. A., Golinelli, D., Sherbourne, C., Stein, M. B., Sullivan, G., Bystritsky, A., . . . Craske, M. (2014). Treatment engagement and response to CBT among Latinos with anxiety disorders in primary care. *Journal of Consulting and Clinical Psychology, 82*, 392–403. doi: 10.1037/a0036365

Chen, F. F., Jing, Y., & Lee, J. M. (2012). "I" value competence but "we" value social competence: The moderating role of voters' individualistic and collectivistic orientation in political elections. *Journal of Experimental Social Psychology, 48*, 1350–1355. doi: http://dx.doi.org/10.1016/j.jesp.2012.07.006

Chen, F. S., Minson, J. A., Schöne, M., & Heinrichs, M. (2013). In the eye of the beholder: Eye contact increases resistance to persuasion. *Psychological Science, 24*, 2254–2261. doi: 10.1177/0956797613491968

Chen, J., Rathore, S. S., Radford, M. J., Wang, Y., & Krumholz, H. M. (2001). Racial differences in the use of cardiac catheterization after acute myocardial infarction. *New England Journal of Medicine, 344*, 1443–1449.

Chen, L., Liu, Y. H., Zheng, Q. W., Xiang, Y. T., Duan, Y. P., Yang, F. D., . . . Si, T. M. (2014). Suicide risk in major affective disorder: Results from a national survey in China. *Journal of Affective Disorders, 155*, 174–179. doi: 10.1016/j.jad.2013.10.046

Chen, X., Wang, R., Zee, P., Lutsey, P. L., Javaheri, S., Alcántara, C., . . . Redline, S. (2015). Racial/ethnic differences in sleep disturbances: The multi-ethnic study of atherosclerosis (MESA). *Sleep, 38*, 877–888. doi: 10.5665/sleep.4732

Chen, Z., & Cowan, N. (2005). Chunk limits and length limits in immediate recall: A reconciliation.

Journal of Experimental Psychology: Learning, Memory, and Cognition, 31, 1235–1249.

Cheng, C., Cheung, S.-F., Chio, J. H.-M., & Chan, M.-P. S. (2013). Cultural meaning of perceived control: A meta-analysis of locus of control and psychological symptoms across 18 cultural regions. *Psychological Bulletin, 139*, 152–188. doi: 10.1037/a0028596

Cheng, W., & Ickes, W. (2009). Conscientiousness and self-motivation as mutually compensatory predictors of university-level GPA. *Personality and Individual Differences, 47*, 817–822. doi: 10.1016/j. paid.2009.06.029

Cherkin, D. C., Sherman, K. J., Balderson, B. H., Cook, A. J., Anderson, M. L., Hawkes, R. J., . . . Turner, J. A. (2016). Effect of mindfulness-based stress reduction vs cognitive behavioral therapy or usual care on back pain and functional limitations in adults with chronic low back pain. *Journal of the American Medical Association, 315*, 240–1249. doi: 10.1001/ jama.2016.2323

Chernyak, Y., & Lowe, M. R. (2010). Motivations for dieting: Drive for thinness is different from drive for objective thinness. *Journal of Abnormal Psychology, 119*, 276–281. doi: 10.1037/a0018398

Chertok, I. R. A., Luo, J., & Anderson, R. H. (2011). Association between changes in smoking habits in subsequent pregnancy and infant birth weight in West Virginia. *Maternal and Child Health Journal, 15*, 249–254. doi: 10.1007/s10995-010-0582-y

Chess, S., & Thomas, A. (1996). *Temperament: Theory and practice*. New York: Brunner/Mazel.

Chetrit, J., Ballion, B., Laquitaine, S., Belujon, P., Morin, S., Taupignon, A., . . . Benazzouz, A. (2009). Involvement of basal ganglia network in motor disabilities induced by typical antipsychotics. *PLOS ONE, 4*(7), e6208. doi: 10.1371/journal. pone.0006208

Chevalier-Skolnikoff, S. (1973). Facial expression of emotion in nonhuman primates. In P. Ekman (Ed.), *Darwin and facial expression: A century of research in review* (pp. 11–82). New York: Academic Press.

Chida, Y., & Steptoe, A. (2009). The association of anger and hostility with future coronary heart disease: A meta-analytic review of prospective evidence. *Journal of the American College of Cardiology, 53*, 936–946. doi: 10.1016/j.jacc.2008.11.044

Chih, B., Engelman, H., & Scheiffele, P. (2005). Control of excitory and inhibitory synapse formation by neuroligins. *Science, 307*, 1324–1328.

Choi, S., & Kluemper, D. H. (2012). The relative utility of differing measures of emotional intelligence. *European Review of Applied Psychology, 62*, 121–127. doi: http://dx.doi .org/10.1016/j.erap.2012.01.002

Chomsky, N. (1965). *Aspects of the theory of syntax*. Cambridge, MA: MIT Press.

Chou, H. T.-G., & Edge, N. (2012). "They are happier and having better lives than I am": The impact of using Facebook on perceptions of others' lives. *Cyberpsychology, Behavior, and Social Networking, 15*, 117–121. doi: 10.1089 /cyber.2011.0324

Choy, Y., Fyer, A. J., & Lipsitz, J. D. (2007). Treatment of specific phobia in adults. *Clinical Psychology Review, 27*, 266–286.

Christakis, N. A., & Fowler, J. H. (2007). The spread of obesity in a large social network over 32 years. *New England Journal of Medicine, 357*, 370–379.

Chu, J., Leino, A., Pflum, S., & Sue, S. (2016). A model for the theoretical basis of cultural competency to guide psychotherapy. *Professional Psychology: Research and Practice, 47,* 18–29. doi: http://dx.doi.org/10.1037/

Chua, H. F., Boland, J. E., & Nisbett, R. E. (2005). Cultural variation in eye movements during scene perception. *Proceedings of the National Academy of Sciences, 102,* 12629–12633.

Church, D., Feinstein, D., Palmer-Hoffman, J., Stein, P. K., & Tranguch, A. (2014). Empirically supported psychological treatments: The challenge of evaluating clinical innovations. *Journal of Nervous & Mental Disease, 202,* 699–709. doi: 10.1097/NMD.0000000000000188

Cialdini, R. B. (2007). *Influence: The psychology of persuasion.* New York: HarperCollins.

Cialdini, R. B., & Goldstein, N. J. (2004). Social influence: Compliance and conformity. *Annual Review of Psychology, 55,* 591–621.

Cialdini, R. B., & Trost, M. R. (1998). Social influence: Social norms, conformity, and compliance. In D. T. Gilbert, S. T. Fiske, & G. Lindzey (Eds.), *The handbook of social psychology* (Vol. 2, 4th ed., pp. 151–192). Boston: McGraw-Hill.

Cialdini, R. B., Trost, M. R., & Newsom, J. T. (1995). Preference for consistency: The development of a valid measure and the discovery of surprising behavioral implications. *Journal of Personality and Social Psychology, 69,* 318–328.

Cicero, T. J, Ellis, M. S., Surratt, H. L., & Kurtz, S. P. (2014). The changing face of heroin use in the United States: A retrospective analysis of the past 50 years. *JAMA Psychiatry, 71,* 821–826. doi: 10.1001/jamapsychiatry.2014.366

Cicognani, E., & Zani, B. (2011). Alcohol use among Italian University students: The role of sensation seeking, peer group norms and self-efficacy. *Journal of Alcohol and Drug Education, 55,* 17–36.

Cipriani, A., La Ferla, T., Furukawa, T. A., Signoretti, A., Nakagawa, A., Churchill, R., . . . Barbuil, C. (2009). Sertraline versus other antidepressive agents for depression. *Cochrane Database of Systematic Reviews, 2.* doi: 10.1002/14651858.CD006117.pub2

Clark, D. M. (1986). A cognitive approach to panic. *Behaviour Research and Therapy, 24,* 461–470.

Clarke, D., Gabriels, T., & Barnes, J. (1996). Astrological signs as determinants of extroversion and emotionality: An empirical study. *Journal of Psychology, 130,* 131–140.

Clayton, R. B., Leshner, G., & Almond, A. (2015). The extended iSelf: The impact of iPhone separation on cognition, emotion, and physiology. *Journal of Computer-Mediated Communication, 20,* 119–135. doi: 10.1111/jcc4.12109

Cleary, E. H., & Stanton, A. L. (2015). Mediators of an Internet-based psychosocial intervention for women with breast cancer. *Health Psychology, 34,* 477–485. doi: http://dx.doi.org/10.1037/hea0000170

Cloud, J. (2011a, March 7). Beyond drugs: How alternative treatments can ease pain. *Time,* pp. 80–88.

Cloud, J. (2011b, February 10). *Facebook and love: Why women are attracted to guys who play hard to get.* Retrieved from http://healthland.time.com

Clough, B. A., & Casey, L. M. (2015). The smart therapist: A look to the future of smartphones and mHealth technologies in psychotherapy. *Professional Psychology: Research and Practice, 46,* 147–153. doi: http://dx.doi.org/10.1037/pro0000011

Cludius, B., Stevens, S., Bantin, T., Gerlach, A. L., & Hermann, C. (2013). The motive to drink due to social anxiety and its relation to hazardous alcohol use. *Psychology of Addictive Behaviors, 27,* 806–813. doi: 10.1037/a0032295

Coelho, C. M., Waters, A. M., Hine, T. J., & Wallis, G. (2009). The use of virtual reality in acrophobia research and treatment. *Journal of Anxiety Disorders, 23,* 563–574. doi: 10.1016/j.janxdis.2009.01.014

Cohen, R. (2008, December 16). Piercing the bubble of presidential isolation. *The Washington Post.* Retrieved from http://www.washingtonpost.com/wp-dyn/content/article/2008/12/15/AR2008121502394.html

Cohen, S., Doyle, W. J., Alper, C. M., Janicki-Deverts, D., & Turner, R. B. (2009). Sleep habits and susceptibility to the common cold. *Archives of Internal Medicine, 169,* 62–66.

Cohen, S., Doyle, W. J., Turner, R., Alper, C. M., & Skoner, D. P. (2003). Sociability and susceptibility to the common cold. *Psychological Science, 14,* 389–395.

Cohen, S., Frank, E., Doyle, W. J., Skoner, D. P., Rabin, B. S., & Gwaltney, J. M., Jr. (1998). Types of stressors that increase susceptibility to the common cold in healthy adults. *Health Psychology, 17,* 214–223.

Cohen, S., Kozlovsky, N., Matar, M. A., Kaplan, Z., Zohar, J., & Cohen, H. (2012). Post-exposure sleep deprivation facilitates correctly timed interactions between glucocorticoid and adrenergic systems, which attenuate traumatic stress responses. *Neuropsychopharmacology, 37,* 2388–2404. doi: 10.1038/npp.2012.94

Colangelo, J. J., & Keefe-Cooperman, K. (2012). Understanding the impact of childhood sexual abuse on women's sexuality. *Journal of Mental Health Counseling, 34*(1), 14–37.

Colditz, G. A., Wolin, K. Y., & Gehlert, S. (2012). Applying what we know to accelerate cancer prevention. *Science Translational Medicine, 4,* 127. doi: 10.1126/scitranslmed.3003218

Coldwell, C. M., & Bender, W. S. (2007). The effectiveness of assertive community treatment for homeless populations with severe mental illness: A meta-analysis. *American Journal of Psychiatry, 164,* 393–399.

Collado, A., Lim, A. C., & MacPherson, L. (2016). A systematic review of depression psychotherapies among Latinos. *Clinical Psychology Review, 45,* 193–209. doi: 10.1016/j.cpr.2016.04.001

Collins, A. M., & Loftus, E. F. (1975). A spreading-activation theory of semantic processing. *Psychological Review, 82,* 407–428.

Collins, W. A., & Laursen, B. (2006). Parent-adolescent relationships. In P. Noller & J. A. Feeney (Eds.), *Close relationships: Functions, forms and processes* (pp. 111–125). Hove, U.K.: Psychology Press/Taylor & Francis.

Colombo, J., Brez, C. C., & Curtindale, L. M. (2013). Infant perception and cognition. R. M. Lerner, M. A. Easterbrooks, & J. Mistry (Eds.), *Handbook of psychology, developmental psychology* (Vol. 6, 2nd ed., pp. 61–90). Hoboken, NJ: Wiley.

Comas-Diaz, L. (2011a). Multicultural psychotherapies. In R. J. Corsini & D. Wedding (Eds.), *Current psychotherapies* (9th ed.). Belmont, CA: Brooks/Cole.

Comas-Diaz, L. (2011b). *Multicultural care: A clinician's guide to cultural competence.* Washington, DC: American Psychological Association.

Combe, E., & Wexler, M. (2010). Observer movement and size constancy. *Psychological Science, 21,* 667–675. doi: 10.1177/0956797610367753

Compton, W., Conway, K. P., Stinson, F. S., Colliver, J. D., & Grant, B. F. (2005). Prevalence and comorbidity of DSM-IV antisocial syndromes and specific drug use disorders in the United States: Results from the National Epidemiologic Survey on Alcohol and Related Conditions. *Journal of Clinical Psychiatry, 66,* 676–685.

Confer, J. C., Easton, J. A., Fleischman, D. S., Goetz, C. D., Lewis, D. M. G., Perilloux, C., & Buss, D. M. (2010). Evolutionary psychology: Controversies, questions, prospects, and limitations. *American Psychologist, 65,* 110–126 . doi: 10.1037/a0018413

Connelly, M. (2013). Cognitive behavioral therapy for treatment of pediatric chronic migraine. *Journal of the American Medical Association, 310,* 2617–2618. doi: 10.1001/jama.2013.282534

Conner, K. R., Bossarte, R. M., Hea, H., Arora, J., Lu, N., Tua, X. M., . . . Katz, I. R. (2014). Posttraumatic stress disorder and suicide in 5.9 million individuals receiving care in the veterans health administration health system. *Journal of Affective Disorders, 166,* 1–5.

Connor, C. E. (2010). A new viewpoint on faces. *Science, 330,* 764–765. doi: 10.1126/science.1198348

Conrad, N., & Patry, M. W. (2012). Conscientiousness and academic performance: A mediational analysis. *International Journal for SoTL, 6.* Retrieved from http://academics.georgiasouthern.edu/ijsotl/v6n1.html

Conway, C. C., Rutter, L. A., & Brown, T. A. (2016). Chronic environmental stress and the temporal course of depression and panic disorder: A trait-state-occasion modeling approach. *Journal of Abnormal Psychology, 125,* 53–63. doi: http://dx.doi.org/10.1037/abn0000122

Conway, K. P., Compton, W., Stinson, F. S., & Grant, B. F. (2006). Lifetime comorbidity of DSM-IV mood and anxiety disorders and specific drug use disorders: Results from the National Epidemiologic Survey on Alcohol and Related Conditions. *Journal of Clinical Psychiatry, 67,* 247–257.

Cook, M. B., & Smallman, H. S. (2008). Human factors of the confirmation bias in intelligence analysis: Decision support from graphical evidence landscapes. *Human Factors: The Journal of the Human Factors and Ergonomics Society, 50,* 745–754. doi: 10.1518/001872008X354183

Cook, R., Bird, G., Catmur, C., Press, C., & Heyes, C. (2014). Mirror neurons: From origin to function. *Behavioral and Brain Sciences, 37,* 177–192. doi: http://dx.doi.org/10.1017/S0140525X13000903

Cooksey, E. C., & Fondell, M. M. (1996). Spending time with his kids: Effects of family structure on fathers' and children's lives. *Journal of Marriage and Family, 58,* 693–707.

Cooney, G. M., Dwan, K., Greig, C. A., Lawlor, D. A., Rimer, J., Waugh, F. R., . . . Mead, G. E. (2013). Exercise for depression. *The Cochrane Library.* doi: 10.1002/14651858.CD004366.pub6

Cooper, J. (2011). Cognitive dissonance theory. In A. W. Kruglanski, P. A. M. Van Lange, & E. T. Higgins (Eds.), *Handbook of theories of social psychology* (Vol. 1, pp. 378–399). Thousand Oakes, CA: Sage.

Copeland, W., Shanahan, L., Miller, S., Costello, E. J., Angold, A., & Maughan, B. (2010). Outcomes of early pubertal timing in young women: A prospective population-based Study. *American Journal of Psychiatry, 167,* 1218–1225.

Corbett, J., Saccone, N. L., Foroud, T., Goate, A., Edenberg, H., Nurnberger, J., . . . Rice, J. P. (2005). A sex-adjusted and age-adjusted genome screen for nested alcohol dependence diagnoses. *Psychiatric Genetics, 15,* 25–30.

Corliss, R. (2003, January 20). Is there a formula for joy? *Time Magazine,* pp. 44–46.

Cornelis, M. C., El-Sohemy, A., Kabagambe, E. K., & Campos, H. (2006). Coffee, CYP1A2 genotype, and risk of myocardial infarction. *Journal of the American Medical Association, 295,* 1135–1141.

Correll, C., & Shenk, E. (2009). Tardive dyskinesia and new antipsychotics. *Current Opinion in Psychiatry, 21,* 151–156. doi: 10.1097/YCO.0b013e3282f53132

Costa, P. T., & McCrae, R. R. (1992a). Four ways five factors are basic. *Personality and Individual Differences, 13,* 653–665.

Costa, P. T., & McCrae, R. R. (1992b). Normal personality assessment in clinical practice: The NEO Personality Inventory. *Psychological Assessment, 4,* 5–13.

Costa, P. T., & McCrae, R. R. (2006). Changes in personality and their origins: Comment on Roberts, Walton, and Viechtbauer (2006). *Psychological Bulletin, 132,* 26–28.

Costello, F. J., & Keane, M. T. (2001). Testing two theories of conceptual combination: Alignment versus diagnosticity in the comprehension and production of combined concepts. *Journal of Experimental Psychology: Learning, Memory, and Cognition, 27,* 255–271.

Cottrell, J. M., Newman, D., A., & Roisman, G. I. (2015). Explaining the black–white gap in cognitive test scores: Toward a theory of adverse impact. *Journal of Applied Psychology, 100,* 1713–1736. doi: http://dx.doi.org/10.1037/apl0000020

Coughlin, A. M., Bandura, A. S., Fleischer, T. D., & Guck, T. P. (2000). Multidisciplinary treatment of chronic pain patients: Its efficacy in changing patient locus of control. *Archives of Physical Medicine and Rehabilitation, 81,* 739–740.

Coviello, L., Sohn, Y., Kramer, A. D. I., Marlow, C., Franceschetti, M., Christakis, N. A., . . . Fowler, J. H., (2014) . Detecting emotional contagion in massive social networks. *PLoS ONE, 9,* e90315. doi: 10.1371/journal.pone.0090315n

Coyne, J. C., Thombs, B. D., Stefanek, M., & Palmer, S. C. (2009). Time to let go of the illusion that psychotherapy extends the survival of cancer patients: Reply to Kraemer, Kuchler, and Spiegel (2009). *Psychological Bulletin, 135,* 179–182.

Craddock, T. J. A., Tuszynski, J. A., & Hameroff, S. (2012). Cytoskeletal Signaling: Is memory encoded in microtubule lattices by CaMKII phosphorylation? *PLOS Computational Biology, 8,* e1002421. doi: 10.1371/journal.pcbi.1002421

Craig, A. W., Loureiro, Y., K., Wood, S., & Vendemia, J. M. C. (2011). Suspicious minds: exploring neural processes during exposure to deceptive advertising. *Journal of Marketing Research, 49,* 361–372. doi: 10.1509/jmr.09.0007

Craighead, W. E., & Dunlop, B. W. (2014). Combination psychotherapy and antidepressant medication treatment for depression: For whom, when, and how. *Annual Review of Psychology, 65,* 267–300. doi: 10.1146/annurev.psych.121208.131653

Craik, F. I. M., & Lockhart, R. S. (1972). Levels of processing: A framework for memory research. *Journal of Verbal Learning and Verbal Behavior, 11,* 671–684.

Cramer, P. (2000). Defense mechanisms in psychology today: Further processes for adaptation. *American Psychologist, 55,* 637–646.

Crespo-Facorro, B. , Pérez-Iglesias, R-O., Mata, I., Ramirez-Bonilla, M., Martínez-Garcia, O., Pardo-Garcia, G., . . . Vázquez-Barquero, J. L. (2011). Effectiveness of haloperidol, risperidone and olanzapine in the treatment of first-episode non-affective psychosis: Results of a randomized, flexible-dose, open-label 1-year follow-up comparison. *Journal of Psychopharmacology, 219,* 225–233. doi: 10.1177/0269881110388332

Creswell, J. D., Taren, A. A., Lindsay, E. K., Greco, C. M., Gianaros, P. J., Fairgrieve, A., . . . Ferris, J. L. (2016). Alterations in resting state functional connectivity link mindfulness meditation with reduced interleukin-6: A randomized controlled trial. *Biological Psychiatry, 80,* 53–61. doi: http://dx.doi.org/10.1016/j.biopsych.2016.01.008

Crino, R. D. (2015). Psychological treatment of obsessive compulsive disorder: An update. *Australas Psychiatry, 23,* 347–349. doi: 10.1177/1039856215590030

Crockett, M. J. (2009). The neurochemistry of fairness: Clarifying the link between serotonin and prosocial behavior. *Annals of the New York Academy of Sciences, 1167,* 76–86.

Cross, S. E., & Madson, L. (1997). Models of the self: Self-construals and gender. *Psychological Bulletin, 122,* 89–103.

Crowe, R. A. (1990). Astrology and the scientific method. *Psychological Reports, 67,* 163–191.

Croy, I., Olgun, S., & Joraschky, P. (2011). Basic emotions elicited by odors and pictures. *Emotion, 6,* 1331–1335. doi: 10.1037/a0024437

Csicsvari, J., Henze, D. A., Jamieson, B., Harris, K. D., Sirota, A., Bartho, P., Wise, K. D., & Buzsaki, G. (2003). Massively parallel recording of unit and local field potentials with silicon-based electrodes. *Journal of Neurophysiology, 90,* 1314–1323.

Cuijpers, P. (2014). Combined pharmacotherapy and psychotherapy in the treatment of mild to moderate major depression? *JAMA Psychiatry, 71,* 747–748. doi: 10.1001/jamapsychiatry.2014.277.

Cuijpers, P., van Straten, A., Schuurmans, J., van Oppen, P., Hollon, S. D., & Andersson, G. (2010). Psychotherapy for chronic major depression and dysthymia: A meta-analysis. *Clinical Psychology Review, 30,* 51–62. doi: 10.1016/j.cpr.2009.09.003

Culotta, E. (2012). Roots of racism. *Science, 336,* 825–827. doi: 10.1126/science.336.6083.825

Cumming, P., Gryglewski,, G., Kranz, G. S., Lanzenberger, R. (2016). Commentary: the serotonin transporter in depression: Meta-analysis of in vivo and post mortem findings and implications for understanding and treating depression. *Journal of Affective Disorders, 199,* 21–22.

Cunningham, M. R., Roberts, A. R., Barbee, A. P., Druen, P. B., & Wu, C.-H. (1995). "Their ideas of beauty are, on the whole, the same as ours." *Journal of Personality and Social Psychology, 68,* 261–279.

Curran, P. J., Stice, E., & Chassin, L. (1997). The relation between adolescent alcohol use and peer alcohol use: A longitudinal random coefficients model.

Journal of Consulting and Clinical Psychology, 65, 130–140.

Curry, L. A., & Youngblade, L. M. (2006). Negative affect, risk perception, and adolescent risk behavior. *Journal of Applied Developmental Psychology, 27,* 468–485.

Curtin, S. C., Warner, M., & Hedegaard, H. (2016, April). Increase in suicide in the United States, 1999–2014. *NCHS Data Brief,* No. 241. Hyattsville, MD: National Center for Health Statistics.

Cusack, K., Jonas, D. E., Forneris, C. A., Wines, C., Sonis, J., Middleton, J. C. , . . . Gaynes, B. N. (2015). Psychological treatments for adults with posttraumatic stress disorder: A systematic review and meta-analysis. *Clinical Psychology Review, 43,* 128–141. doi: 10.1016/j.cpr.2015.10.003.

Cynkar, A. (2007, June). The changing gender composition of psychology. *Monitor on Psychology, 38*(6), 46–47.

Cyranoski, D. (2011). Neuroscience: Thought experiment. *Nature, 469,* 148–149. doi: 10.1038/469148a

Dahl, M. (2013, July 4). Heat waves lead to hot tempers—and here's why. *NBCNEWS.com.* Retrieved from http://www.today.com/health/heat-waves-lead-hot-tempers-heres-why-6C10436073

Dale, K. Y., Berg, R., Elden, A., Ødegård, A., & Holte, A. (2009). Testing the diagnosis of dissociative identity disorder through measures of dissociation, absorption, hypnotizability and PTSD: A Norwegian pilot study. *Journal of Trauma & Dissociation, 10,* 102–112. doi: 10.1080/15299730802488478

Dalen, K., Ellertsen, B., Espelid, I., & Grønningsaeter, A. G. (2009). EMG feedback in the treatment of myofascial pain dysfunction syndrome. *Acta Odontologica Scandinavica, 44,* 279–284.

Darwin, C. A. (1872). *The expression of the emotions in man and animals.* London: J. Murray.

Dasen, P. R. (1994). Culture and cognitive development from a Piagetian perspective. In W. J. Lonner & R. Malpass (Eds.), *Psychology and culture.* Boston: Allyn & Bacon.

Dasgupta, N., & Greenwald, A. G. (2001). On the malleability of automatic attitudes: Combating automatic prejudice with images of admired and disliked individuals. *Journal of Personality and Social Psychology, 81,* 800–814.

D'Astous, M., Cottin, S., Roy, M., Picard, C., & Cantin, L. (2013). Bilateral stereotactic anterior capsulotomy for obsessive-compulsive disorder: Long-term follow-up. *Journal of Neurology, Neurosurgery & Psychiatry, 84,* 1208–1213. doi: 10.1136/jnnp-2012-303826

Datta, S. (2011). Pontine-wave generator: A key player in REM sleep-dependent memory consolidation. In B. N. Mallick, S. R. Pandi-Perumal, R. W. McCarley, & A. R. Morrison (Eds.), *Rapid eye movement sleep: Regulation and function* (pp. 140–150). New York: Cambridge University Press.

Davelaar, E. J., Goshen-Gottstein, Y., Ashkenazi, A., Haarmann, H. J., & Usher, M. (2005). The demise of short-term memory revisited: Empirical and computational investigations of recency effects. *Psychological Review, 112*(1), 3–42.

Davidson, R. J., Pizzagalli, D., Nitschke, J. B., & Putnam, K. (2002). Depression: Perspectives from affective neuroscience. *Annual Review of Psychology, 53,* 545–574.

Davidson, R. J., Putnam, K. M., & Larson, C. L. (2000). Dysfunction in the neural circuitry of emotion regulation—A possible prelude to violence. *Science, 289,* 591–594.

Davies, P. T., Cicchetti, D., Hentges, R., & Sturge-Apple, M. L. (2013). The genetic precursors and the advantageous and disadvantageous sequelae of inhibited temperament: An evolutionary perspective. *Developmental Psychology, 49,* 2285–2300. doi: 10.1037/a0032312

Davis, J. I., Senghas, A., & Ochsner, K. N. (2009). How does facial feedback modulate emotional experience? *Journal of Research in Personality, 43,* 822–829. doi: 10.1016/j.jrp.2009.06.005

Davis, J. L., & Rusbult, C. E. (2001). Attitude alignment in close relationships. *Journal of Personality and Social Psychology, 81,* 65–84.

Davis, K., Christodoulou, J., Seider, S., & Gardner, H. (2011). The theory of multiple intelligences. In R. J. Sternberg & S. B. Kaufman (Eds.), *Cambridge handbook of intelligence* (pp. 485–503). Cambridge, UK: Cambridge University Press.

Davis, M. C., Zautra, A. J., Wolf, L. D., Tennen, H., & Yeung, E. W. (2015). Mindfulness and cognitive-behavioral interventions for chronic pain: Differential effects on daily pain reactivity and stress reactivity. *Journal of Consulting and Clinical Psychology, 83,* 24–35. doi: http://dx.doi.org/10.1037/a0038200

Davis, S. K., & Humphrey, N. (2011). Emotional intelligence predicts adolescent mental health beyond personality and cognitive ability. *Personality and Individual Differences, 52,* 144–149. doi: 10.1016/j.paid.2011.09.016

Davis, S. R., & Braunstein, G. D. (2012). Efficacy and safety of testosterone in the management of hypoactive sexual desire disorder in menopausal women. *The Journal of Sexual Medicine, 9,* 1134–1148.

Davis, S. R., Moreau, M., Kroll, R., Bouchard, C., Panay, N., Gass, M., . . . APHRODITE Study Team. (2008). Testosterone for low libido in postmenopausal women not taking estrogen. *New England Journal of Medicine, 359,* 2005–2017.

Dawood, K., Bailey, J. M., & Martin, N. G. (2009). Genetic and environmental influences on sexual orientation. In Y.-K. Kim (Ed.), *Handbook of behavior genetics* (pp. 269–279). New York: Springer.

Day, B. L., & Fitzpatrick, R. C. (2005). The vestibular system. *Current Biology, 15,* R583–R586.

Deacon, B. J. (2013). The biomedical model of mental disorder: A critical analysis of its validity, utility, and effects on psychotherapy research. *Clinical Psychology Review,* in press. doi: http://dx.doi.org/10.1016/j.cpr.2012.09.007

Dean, G., Mather, A., & Kelly, I. W. (1996). Astrology. In G. Stein (Ed.), *The encyclopedia of the paranormal.* Buffalo, NY: Prometheus.

DeAngelis, T. (2003, February). Why we overestimate our competence. *Monitor on Psychology, 34,* 60–62.

DeAngelis, T. (2004, April). Are beliefs inherited? *Monitor on Psychology, 35,* 50–51.

DeAngelis, T. (2012). A second life for practice? *Monitor on Psychology, 43*(3), 48.

Deary, I. J. (2012). Intelligence. *Annual Review of Psychology, 63,* 453–482. doi: 10.1146/annurev-psych-120710-100353

Deaton, A., & Stone, A. A. (2013). Two happiness puzzles. *American Economics Review, 103,* 591–597. doi: 10.1257/aer.103.3.591 [8]

de Bono, E. (1970). *Lateral thinking: Creativity step by step.* New York: Harper & Row.

DeCasper, A. J., & Fifer, W. P. (2008). Of human bonding: Newborns prefer their mother's voices. In M. Gauvian & M. Cole, *Readings on the development of children* (pp. 53–57). New York: Macmillan.

Defoe, I. N., Dubas, J. S., Figner, B., & van Aken, M. A. G. (2015). A meta-analysis on age differences in risky decision making: Adolescents versus children and adults. *Psychological Bulletin, 141,* 48–84. doi: http://dx.doi.org/10.1037/a0038088

de Groot, J. H. B., Smeets, M. A. M., Rowson, M. R., Bulsing, P. J., Blonk, C. G., Wilkinson, J. E., . . . Semin, G. R. (2015). A sniff of happiness. *Psychological Science, 26,* 684–700. doi: 10.1177/0956797614566318

Delahanty, D. L. (2011). Toward the predeployment detection of risk for PTSD. *American Journal of Psychiatry, 168,* 9–11. doi: 10.1176/appi.ajp.2010.10101519 [10]

De la Herran-Arita, A. K., Kornum, B. R., Mahlios, J., Jiang, W., Lin, L., . . . Mignot, E. (2013). CD4 T cell autoimmunity to hypocretin/orexin and cross-reactivity to a 2009 H1N1 Influenza A Epitope in narcolepsy. *Science Translational Medicine, 5,* 216ra176. doi: 10.1126/scitranslmed.3007762

Delaney, P. F., Sahakyan, L., Kelley, C. M., & Zimmerman, C. A. (2010). Remembering to forget: The amnesic effect of daydreaming. *Psychological Science, 21,* 1036–1042. doi: 10.1177/0956797610374739

Denny, B. T., Fan, J., Liu, X., Ochsner, K. N., Guerreri, S., Mayson, S. J., . . . Koenigsberg, H. W. (2015). Elevated amygdala activity during reappraisal anticipation predicts anxiety in avoidant personality disorder. *Journal of Affective Disorders, 172,* 1–7. doi: 10.1016/j.jad.2014.09.017

Denollet, J., & Pedersen, S. S. (2009). Anger, depression, and anxiety in cardiac patients: The complexity of individual differences in psychological risk. *Journal of the American College of Cardiology, 53,* 947–949. doi: 10.1016/j.jacc.2008.12.006

Denys, D., Mantione, M., Figee, M., van den Munckhof, P., Koerselman, F., Westenberg, H., . . . Schuurman, R. (2010). Deep brain stimulation of the nucleus accumbens for treatment-refractory obsessive-compulsive disorder. *Archives of General Psychiatry, 67,* 1061–1068. doi: 10.1001/archgenpsychiatry.2010.122

Derringer, J., Krueger, R. F., Dick, D. M., Saccone, S., Grucza, R. A., Agrawal, A., . . . Gene Environment Association Studies (GENEVA) Consortium. (2010). Predicting sensation seeking from dopamine genes: A candidate-system approach. *Psychological Science, 9,* 1282–1290. doi: 10.1177/0956797610380699

Derrington, A. M. (2004). Visual mechanisms of motion analysis and motion perception. *Annual Review of Psychology, 55,* 181–205.

Desbordes, G., Negi, L. T., Pace, T. W. W., Wallace, B. A., Raison, C. L., . . . Schwartz, E. L. (2012). Effects of mindful-attention and compassion meditation training on amygdala response to emotional stimuli in an ordinary, non-meditative state. *Frontiers in Human Neuroscience, 6,* 292. doi: 10.3389/fnhum.2012.00292.E

Devilbiss, D. M., & Berridge, C. W. (2008). Cognition-enhancing doses of methylphenidate preferentially increase prefrontal cortical neuronal responsiveness. *Biological Psychiatry, 64,* 626–635. doi: 10.1016/j.biopsych.2008.04.037

DeVylder, J. E., Lukens, E. P., Link, B. G., & Lieberman, J. A. (2015). Suicidal ideation and suicide attempts among adults with psychotic experiences data from the Collaborative Psychiatric Epidemiology Surveys. *JAMA Psychiatry, 72,* 219–225. doi: 10.1001/jamapsychiatry.2014.2663

DeWall, C. N., Anderson, C. A., & Bushman, B. J. (2011). The general aggression model: Theoretical extensions to violence. *Psychology of Violence, 1,* 245–258. doi: 10.1037/a0023842

Dewsbury, D. A. (2000). Issues in comparative psychology at the dawn of the 20th century. *American Psychologist, 55,* 750–753.

Dhindsa, R. S., &. Goldstein, D. B. (2016). Schizophrenia: From genetics to physiology at last. *Nature, 530,* 162–163. doi: 10.1038/nature16874

Diamond, A. (2009). The interplay of biology and the environment broadly defined. *Developmental Psychology, 45,* 1–8. doi: 10.1037/a0014601

Dickinson, D., Straub, R. E., Trampush, J. W., Gao, Y., Feng, N., Xie, B., . . . Weinberger, D. R. (2014). Differential effects of common variants in SCN2A on general cognitive ability, brain physiology, and messenger RNA expression in schizophrenia cases and control individuals. *JAMA Psychiatry, 71,* 647-656. doi: 10.1001/jamapsychiatry.2014.157

Diehm, R., & Armatas, C. (2004). Surfing: An avenue for socially acceptable risk-taking, satisfying needs for sensation seeking and experience seeking. *Personality and Individual Differences, 36,* 663–677.

Dietrich, T., Walter, C., Oluwagbemigun, K., Bergmann, M., Pischon, T., Pischon, N.,. . . . Boeing, H. (2015). Smoking, smoking cessation, and risk of tooth loss: The EPIC-Potsdam Study. *Journal of Dental Research, 94,* 1369–1375. doi: 10.1177/0022034515559896

Di Iorio, C. R., Watkins, T. J., Dietrich, M. S., Cao, A., Blackford, J. U., Rogers, B., . . . Cowan, R. L. (2011). Evidence for chronically altered serotonin function in the cerebral cortex of female 3,4-methylenedioxymethamphetamine polydrug users. *Archives of General Psychiatry, 69,* 399–409. doi: 10.1001/archgenpsychiatry.2011.156

Dimidjian, S., Barrera, M. Jr., Martell, C., Muñoz, R. F., & Lewinsohn, P. M. (2011). The Origins and current status of behavioral activation treatments for depression. *Annual Review of Clinical Psychology, 7,* 1–38. doi: 10.1146/annurev-clinpsy-032210-104535

Dimidjian, S., & Segal, Z. V. (2015). Prospects for a clinical science of mindfulness-based intervention. *American Psychologist, 70,* 593-620. doi: http://dx.doi.org/10.1037/a0039589

Dimsdale, J. E., & Levenson, J. (2013). What's next for somatic symptom disorder? *American Journal of Psychiatry, 170,* 1393–1395. doi: 10.1176/appi.ajp.2013.13050589

Dir, A. L., Coskunpinar, A., & Cyders, M. A. (2014). A meta-analytic review of the relationship between adolescent risky sexual behavior and impulsivity across gender, age, and race. *Clinical Psychology Review, 34,* 551–562.doi: 10.1016/j.cpr.2014.08.004

Dismukes, R. K. (2012) Prospective memory in workplace and everyday situations. *Current Directions in Psychological Science, 21,* 215–220. doi: 10.1177/0963721412447621

Distracted driving: Habits of San Diego drivers revealed. (2013, April 10). Retrieved from http://www.sciencedaily.com/releases/2013/04/130410154625.htm

Dittmann, M. (2003, March). Anger across the gender divide. *Monitor on Psychology, 34*(3), 52–53.

Dittmann, M. (2004, July/August). Standing tall pays off, study finds. *Monitor on Psychology, 35*(7), 14.

Dixon, J., Durrheim, K., & Tredoux, C. (2005). Beyond the optimal contact strategy: A reality check for the contact hypothesis. *American Psychologist, 60,* 697–711. [12]

Dixon, J., Tropp, L. R., Durrheim, K., & Tredoux, C. (2010). "Let them eat harmony": Prejudice-reduction strategies and attitudes of historically disadvantaged groups. *Current Directions in Psychological Science, 19,* 76–80. doi: 10.1177/0963721410363366

Dmochowski, J. P., Bezdek, M. A., Abelson, B. P., Johnson, J. S., Schumacher, E. H., & Parra, L. C. (2014). Audience preferences are predicted by temporal reliability of neural processing. *Nature Communications, 5,* 4567. doi: 10.1038/ncomms5567

Dobson, K. S., Hollon, S. D., Dimidjian, S., Schmaling, K. B., Kohlenberg, R. J., Gallop, R. J., . . . Jacobson, N. S. (2008). Randomized trial of behavioral activation, cognitive therapy, and antidepressant medication in the prevention of relapse and recurrence in major depression. *Journal of Consulting and Clinical Psychology, 76,* 468–477. doi: 10.1037/0022-006X.76.3.468

Dohrenwend, B. P. (2006). Inventorying stressful life events as risk factors for psychopathology: Toward resolution of the problem of intracategory variability. *Psychological Bulletin, 132,* 477–495.

Domjan, M. (2005). Pavlovian conditioning: A functional perspective. *Annual Review of Psychology, 56,* 179–206.

Donaldson, S. I., Csikszentmihalyi, M., & Nakamura, J. (Eds.) (2011). *Applied positive psychology: Improving everyday life, health, schools, work, and society. Series in applied psychology.* New York: Routledge/Taylor & Francis Group.

Donegan, E., & Dugas, M. J. (2012). Generalized anxiety disorder: A comparison of symptom change in adults receiving cognitive-behavioral therapy or applied relaxation. *Journal of Consulting and Clinical Psychology, 80,* 490–496. doi: 10.1037/a0028132

Donovan, M. R., Glue, P., Kolluri, S., & Emir, B. (2010). Comparative efficacy of antidepressants in preventing relapse in anxiety disorders—A meta-analysis. *Journal of Affective Disorders, 123,* 9–16. doi: 10.1016/j.jad.2009.06.021

Doss, B. D., Mitchell, A., Georgia, E. J., Biesen, J. N., & Rowe, L. S. (2015). Improvements in closeness, communication, and psychological distress mediate effects of couple therapy for veterans. *Journal of Consulting and Clinical Psychology, 83,* 405–415. doi: http://dx.doi.org/10.1037/a0038541

Dougherty, D. M., Mathias, C. W., Marsh, D. M., Moeller, F. G., & Swann, A. C. (2004). Suicidal behaviors and drug abuse: Impulsivity and its assessment. *Drug and Alcohol Dependence, 76,* S93–S105.

Draheim, C., Hicks, K. L., & Engle, R. W. (2016). Combining reaction time and accuracy: The relationship between working memory capacity and task switching as a case example. *Perspectives on Psychological Science, 11,* 133–155. doi: 10.1177/1745691615596990

Drew, T., Võ, M., L.-H., & Wolfe, J. M. (2013). The invisible gorilla strikes again: Sustained inattentional blindness in expert observers. *Psychological Science, 24,* 1848–1853. doi: 10.1177/0956797613479386

Drews, F. A., Pasupathi, M., & Strayer, D. L. (2008). Passenger and cell phone conversations in simulated driving. *Journal of Experimental Psychology: Applied, 14,* 392–400. doi: 10.1037/a0013119

Driessen, E., Cuijpers, P., de Maat, S. C. M., Abbass, A. A., de Jonghe, F., & Dekker, J. J. M. (2010). The efficacy of short-term psychodynamic psychotherapy for depression: A meta-analysis. *Clinical Psychology Review, 30,* 25–36. doi: 10.1016/j.cpr.2009.08.010

Driessen, E., Hegelmaier, L. M., Abbass, A. A., Barber, J. P., Dekker, J. J. M., Vane, H. L., . . . Cuijpers, P. (2015). The efficacy of short-term psychodynamic psychotherapy for depression: A meta-analysis update. *Clinical Psychology Review, 30,* 25–36. doi: 10.1016/j.cpr.2009.08.010

Driscoll, M. W., & Torres, L. (2013). Acculturative stress and Latino depression: The mediating role of behavioral and cognitive resources. *Cultural Diversity and Ethnic Minority Psychology, 19,* 373–382. doi: 10.1037/a0032821

Drowsy driving an increasing hazard. (2013, October 28). *ScienceDaily.* Retrieved from http://www .sciencedaily.com/releases/2013/10/131028162054.htm

Drum, K. B., & Littleton, H. L. (2014). Therapeutic boundaries in telepsychology: Unique issues and best practice recommendations. *ProfessionalPsychology: Research and Practice, 45,* 309–315. doi: http://dx .doi.org/10.1037/a0036127

Dubovsky, S. (2014, March 14). How light alters circadian rhythms: An animal study. *NEJM Journal Watch.* Retrieved from http://www.jwatch.org /na33910/2014/03/14/how-light-alters-circadian -rhythms-animal-study?query=etoc_jwpsych

Duffy, A., Horrocks, J., Doucette, S., Keown-Stoneman, C., McCloskey, S., & Grof, P. (2014). The developmental trajectory of bipolar disorder. *The British Journal of Psychiatry, 204,* 122–128. doi: 10.1192/ bjp.bp.113.126706

Dumay, N. (2015). Sleep not just protects memories against forgetting, it also makes them more accessible. *Cortex, S0010-9452*(15), 00209-9. doi: 10.1016/j.cortex.2015.06.007

Duncan, D. F., Donnelly, J. W., & Nicholson, T. (1992). Belief in the paranormal and religious belief among American college students. *Psychological Reports, 70,* 15–18.

Duncker, K. (1945). On problem-solving. *Psychological Monographs, 58*(Whole No. 270).

Dunn, E., & Norton, M. (2012, July 8). Don't indulge. Be happy. *The New York Times Sunday Review,* pp. SR1, 7.

Dunn, E. C., Brown, R. C., Dai, Y., Rosand, J., Nugent, N. R., Amstadter, A. B., . . . Smoller, J. W. (2015). Genetic determinants of depression. *Harvard Review of Psychiatry, 23,* 1. doi: 10.1097/ HRP.0000000000000054

Dweck, C. (1997, June). Cited in B. Murray, "Verbal praise may be the best motivator of all." *APA Monitor, 28*(6), 26.

Dysken, M. W., Sano, M., Asthana, S., Vertrees, J. E., Pallaki, M., Llorente, M., . . . Guarino, P. G. (2014). Effect of Vitamin E and memantine on functional decline in Alzheimer Disease: The TEAM-AD VA Cooperative Randomized Trial. *Journal of the American Medical Association, 311,* 33–44. doi: 10.1001/ jama.2013.282834.

Eagly, A. H., Eaton, A., Rose, S. M., Riger, S., & McHugh, M. C. (2012). Feminism and psychology: Analysis of a half-century of research on women and gender. *American Psychologist, 67,* 211–230. doi: 10.1037/a0027260

Easterbrooks, M. A., Bartlett, J. D., Beeghly, M., & Thompson, R. A. (2013). Social and emotional development in infancy. In M. Lerner, M. A. Easterbrooks, & J. Mistry (Eds.), *Handbook of psychology, developmental psychology* (Vol. 6, 2nd ed., pp. 91–120). Hoboken, NJ: Wiley.

Eastwick, P. W., Luchies, L. B., Finkel, E. J., & Hunt, L. L. (2013). The predictive validity of ideal partner preferences: A review and meta-analysis. *Psychological Bulletin, 140,* 623–665. doi: 10.1037/a0032432

Ebbinghaus, H. (1885). *Über das Gedachtnis.* Leipzig: Duncker & Humblot.

Eberlein, T. (1997). *Child magazine's guide to whining.* New York: Pocket Books.

Eckel, R. H., Jakicic, J. M., Ard, J. D., de Jesus, J., Miller, N. H., Hubbard, MD, V. S., . . . Yanovski, S. Z. (2014). AHA/ACC prevention guideline 2013 AHA/ACC guideline on lifestyle management to reduce cardiovascular risk: A Report of the American College of Cardiology/American Heart Association Task Force on Practice Guidelines. *Circulation, 129,* S76–S99. doi: 10.1161/01.cir.0000437740.48606.d1

Edenberg, H. J., Strother, W. N., McClintick, J. N., Tian, H., Stephens, M., Jerome, R. E., . . . McBride, W. J. (2005). Gene expression in the hippocampus of inbred alcohol-preferring and nonpreferring rats. *Genes, Brain and Behavior, 4,* 20–30.

Edwards, R. R., Campbell, C., Jamison, R. N., & Wiech, K. (2009). The neurobiological underpinnings of coping with pain. *Current Directions in Psychological Science, 18,* 237–241. doi: 10.1111/j.1467-8721.2009.01643.x

Eells, T. D., Barrett, M. S., Wright, J. H., & Thase, M. (2014). Computer-assisted cognitive–behavior therapy for depression. *Psychotherapy, 51,* 191–197. doi: 10.1037/a0032406

Effron, D. A., & Knowles, E. D. (2015). Entitativity and intergroup bias: How belonging to a cohesive group allows people to express their prejudices. *Journal of Personality and Social Psychology, 108,* 234–253. doi: http://dx.doi.org/10.1037/pspa0000020

Eftekhar, A., Fullwood, C., & Morris, N. (2014). Capturing personality from Facebook photos and photo-related activities: How much exposure do you need? *Computers in Human Behavior, 37,* 162–170. doi: http://dx.doi.org/10.1016/j.chb.2014.04.048

Eftekhari, A., Ruzek, J. I., Crowley, J. J., Rosen, C. S., Greenbaum, M. A., & Karlin, B. E. (2013). Effectiveness of national implementation of prolonged exposure therapy in Veterans Affairs care. *JAMA Psychiatry, 70,* 949–955. doi: 10.1001/jamapsychiatry.2013.36

Egan, S., & Stelmack, R. M. (2003). A personality profile of Mount Everest climbers. *Personality and Individual Differences, 34,* 1491–1494.

Eichstaedt, J. C., Schwartz, H. A., Kern, M. L., Park, G., Labarthe, D. R., Merchant, R. M., . . . Seligman, M. E. P. (2015). Psychological language on Twitter predicts county-level heart disease mortality. *Psychological Science, 26,* 159–169. doi: 10.1177/0956797614557867

Eisner, R. (2005, January). Study suggests cognitive deficits in MDMA-only drug abusers. *NIDA Notes, 19*(5). Retrieved from www.nida.nih.gov

Ekelund, U., Ward, H. A., Norat, T., Luan, J., May, A. M., Weiderpass, E., . . . Riboli, E. (2015). Physical activity and all-cause mortality across levels of overall and abdominal adiposity in European men and women: The European Prospective Investigation into Cancer and Nutrition Study (EPIC). *American Journal of Clinical Nutrition, 30,* 25–36. doi: 10.1016/j. cpr.2009.08.010

Ekman, P. (2003). *Emotions revealed: Recognizing faces and feeling to improve communication and emotional life.* New York: Times Books.

El Alaoui, S., Hedman, E., Kaldo, V., Hesser, H., Kraepelien, M., Andersson, . . . Lindefors, N. (2015). Effectiveness of Internet-based cognitive–behavior therapy for social anxiety disorder in clinical psychiatry. *Journal of Consulting and Clinical Psychology, 83,* 902–914. doi: http://dx.doi.org/10.1037/a0039198

Elfenbein, H. A., & Ambady, N. (2002a). Is there an in-group advantage in emotion recognition? *Psychological Bulletin, 128,* 243–249.

Elfenbein, H. A., & Ambady, N. (2002b). On the universality and cultural specificity of emotion recognition: A meta-analysis. *Psychological Bulletin, 128,* 203–235.

Elias, V. L., Fullerton, A. S., & Simpson, J. M. (2015). Long-term changes in attitudes toward premarital sex in the United States: Reexamining the role of cohort replacement. *Journal of Sex Research, 52,* 129–139.

Elkind, D. (1985). Egocentrism redux. *Developmental Review, 5,* 218–226.

Ellemers, N., Spears, R., & Doosje, B. (2002). Self and social identity. *Annual Review of Psychology, 53,* 161–186.

Ellenbogen, J. M., Hulbert, J. C., Stickgold, R., Dinges, D. F., & Thompson-Schill, S. L. (2006). Interfering with theories of sleep and memory: Sleep, declarative memory, and associative interference. *Current Biology, 16,* 1290–1294. doi: 10.1016/j.cub.2006.05.024

Elliot, A. J., & Maier, M. A. (2014). Color psychology: Effects of perceiving color on psychological functioning in humans. *Annual Review of Psychology, 65,* 95–120. doi: 10.1146/annurev-psych-010213-115035

Elliot, A. J., Niesta Kayser, D., Greitemeyer, T., Lichtenfeld, S., Gramzow, R. H., Maier, M. A., . . . Liu, H. (2010). Red, rank, and romance in women viewing men. *Journal of Experimental Psychology: General, 139,* 399–417. doi: 10.1037/a0019689

Ellis, A. (1977). The basic clinical theory of rational-emotive therapy. In A. Ellis & R. Grieger (Eds.), *Handbook of rational-emotive therapy.* New York: Springer.

Ellis, A. (1991). *Reason and emotion in psychotherapy.* New York: Carol Publishing.

Ellis, A. (2011). Rational emotive behavior therapy. In R. J. Corsini & D. Wedding (Eds.), *Current psychotherapies* (9th ed.). Belmont, CA: Brooks/Cole.

Ellis, A., & Ellis, D. J. (2011). *Rational emotive behavior therapy: Theories of psychotherapy.* Washington, DC: American Psychological Association.

El Marroun, H., Schmidt, M. N., Franken, I. H. A., Jaddoe, V. W. V., Hofman, A., van der Lug, A.,. . . White, T. (2013). Prenatal tobacco exposure and brain morphology: A prospective study in young children. *Neuropsychopharmacology, 39,* 792–800. doi: 10.1038/npp.2013.273

Elms, A. C. (1995). Obedience in retrospect. *Journal of Social Issues, 51,* 21–31.

Elms, A. C. (2009). Obedience lite. *American Psychologist, 64,* 32–36.

Else-Quest, N. M., Hyde, J. S., & Linn, M. C. (2010). Cross-national patterns of gender differences in

mathematics: A meta-analysis. *Psychological Bulletin, 136,* 103–127. doi: 10.1037/a0018053

Eny, K. M., Wolever, T. M. S., Fontaine-Bisson, B., & El- Sohemy, A. (2008). Genetic variant in the glucose transporter type 2 (GLUT 2) is associated with higher intakes of sugars in two distinct populations. *Physiolgenomics, 33,* 355–360. doi: 10.1152/physiolgenomics.00148.2007

Erasmus, V., Daha, T. J., Brug, H., Richardus, J. H., Behrendt, M. D., Vos, M. C., . . . van Beeck, E. F. (2010). Systematic review of studies on compliance with hand hygiene guidelines in hospital care. *Infection Control and Hospital Epidemiology, 31,* 283–294. doi: http://dx.doi.org/ 10.1086/650451

Erdleyi, M. H. (2010). The ups and downs of memory. *American Psychologist, 65,* 623–633. doi: 10.1037/a0020440

Erikson, E. H. (1963). *Childhood and society* (2nd ed.). New York: Norton.

Erikson, E. H. (1980). *Identity and the life cycle.* New York: Norton.

Espay, A. J., Norris, M. M., Eliassen, J. C., Dwivedi, A., Smith, M. S., Banks, C., . . . Szaflarski, J. P. (2015). Placebo effect of medication cost in Parkinson disease: A randomized double-blind study. *Neurology, 84,* 794–802. doi: 10.1212/WNL.0000000000001282

Evans, W., & Rosenberg, I. H. (1991). *Biomarkers: The 10 determinants of aging you can control.* New York: Simon & Schuster.

Evers, C., Fischer, A. H., Mosquera, P. M. R., & Manstead, A. S. R. (2005). Anger and social appraisal: A "spicy" sex difference? *Emotion, 5,* 258–266.

Everson-Rose, S. A., Roetker, N. S., Lutsey, P. L., Kershaw, K. N., Longstreth, W. T., Sacco, R. L., . . .Alonso, A. (2014). Chronic stress, depressive symptoms, anger, hostility, and risk of stroke and transient ischemic attack in the multi-ethnic study of atherosclerosis. *Stroke, 45,* 2318–2323. doi: 10.1161/STROKEAHA.114.004815

Exner, J. E. (1993). *The Rorschach: A comprehensive system: Vol. 1. Basic foundations* (3rd ed.). New York: Wiley.

Exner, J. E., Jr. (2002). Early development of the Rorschach test. *Academy of Clinical Psychology Bulletin, 8,* 9–24.

Eysenck, H. J. (Ed.). (1981). *A model for personality.* New York: Springer.

Eysenck, H. J. (1982). *Personality, genetics, and behavior.* New York: Praeger.

Faedda, G. L., Becker, I., Baroni, A., Tondo, L., Aspland, E., & Koukopoulos, A. (2010). The origins of electroconvulsive therapy: Prof. Bini's first report on ECT. *Journal of Affective Disorders, 120,* 12–15. doi: 10.1016/j.jad.2009.01.023

Fagan, J. F., & Holland, C. R. (2002). Equal opportunity and racial differences in IQ. *Intelligence, 30,* 361–387.

Fales, M. R., Frederiack, D. A., Garcia, J. R., Gildersleeve, K. A., Haselton, M. G., & Fisher, H. E. (2016). Mating markets and bargaining hands: Mate preferences for attractiveness and resources in two national U.S. studies. *Personality and Individual Differences, 88,* 78–87.

Falkner, A. L., Grosenick, L., Davidson, T. J., Deisseroth, K., & Lin, D. (2016). Hypothalamic control of male aggression-seeking behavior. *Nature Neuroscience, 19,* 596–604. doi: 10.1038/nn.4264

Fals-Stewart, W. (2003). The occurrence of partner physical aggression on days of alcohol consumption: A longitudinal diary study. *Journal of Consulting and Clinical Psychology, 71,* 41–52.

Farell, B. (2006). Orientation-specific computation in stereoscopic vision. *Journal of Neuroscience, 26,* 9098–9106.

Farrell, C. (2016, January 30). Annuities as an alternative to shaky markets? Be wary. *The New York Times,* p. B5.

Farrell, M. T., & Abrams, L. (2011). Tip-of-the-tongue states reveal age differences in the syllable frequency effect. *Journal of Experimental Psychology: Learning, Memory, and Cognition, 37,* 277–285. doi: 10.1037/a0021328

Farstad, S. M., McGeown, L., & von Ranson, K. M. (2016). Eating disorders and personality, 2004–2016: A systematic review and meta-analysis. *Clinical Psychology Review, 46,* 91–108.

Fassihi, A., Akrami, A., Esmaeili,V., & Diamond, M. E. (2014). Tactile perception and working memory in rats and humans. *Proceedings of the National Academy of Sciences, 111,* 2331–2336. doi: 10.1073/pnas.1315171111

Feingold, A. (1992). Good-looking people are not what we think. *Psychological Bulletin, 111,* 304–341.

Feinstein, J. S., Adolphs, R., Damasio, A., & Trane, D. (2010). The human amygdala and the induction and experience of fear. *Current Biology, 21,* 34–38. doi: 10.1016/j.cub.2010.11.04

Fennis, B. M., Janssen, L., & Vohs, K. D. (2009). Acts of benevolence: A limited-resource account of compliance with charitable requests. *Journal of Consumer Research, 35,* 906–924. doi: 10.1086/593291

Ferdinand, K. C., & Ferdinand, D. P. (2009). Cardiovascular disease disparities: Racial/ethnic factors and potential solutions. *Current Cardiovascular Risk Reports, 3,* 187–193. doi: 10.1007/s12170-009-0030-y

Ferencz, B., Laukka, E. J., Welmer, A.-K., Kalpouzos, G., Angleman, S., Keller, L., . . . Bäckman, L. (2014). The benefits of staying active in old age: Physical activity counteracts the negative influence of PICALM, BIN1, and CLU risk alleles on episodic memory functioning. *Psychology and Aging, 29,* 440–449. doi: 10.1037/a0035465

Ferrari, P. F., & Rizzolatti, G. (Eds). (2015). *New frontiers in mirror neurons research.* Oxford, UK: Oxford Press.

Ferrè, E. R., Lopez, C., & Haggard, P. (2014). Anchoring the self to the body: Vestibular contribution to the sense of self. *Psychological Science, 25,* 2106–2108. doi: 10.1177/0956797614547917

Ferri, M., Amato, L., & Davoli, M. (2006). Alcoholics Anonymous and other 12-step programmes for alcohol dependence. *The Cochrane Database of Systematic Reviews,* No. 3. Retrieved from http://dx.doi.org/10.1002/14651858 .CD005032.pub2

Festinger, L. (1957). *A theory of cognitive dissonance.* Palo Alto, CA: Stanford University Press.

Fiedler, K. (2008). Language: A toolbox for sharing and influencing social reality. *Perspectives on Psychological Science, 3,* 38–47. doi: 10.1111/j.1745-6916.2008.00060.x

Field, A. (2006). I don't like it because it eats sprouts: Conditioning preferences in children. *Behaviour Research and Therapy, 44,* 439–455.

Fields, H. (2012, April). Fragrant flashbacks smells rouse early memories. *APS Observer, 5.* Retrieved from www.psychologicalscience.org/index.php/publications/observer/2012/april-12/fragrant-flashbacks.html

Fields, R. D. (2013). Neuroscience: Map the other brain. *Nature*. Retrieved from http://www.nature.com/news/neuroscience-map-the-other-brain-1.13654

Figueredo, A. J., Sefcek, J. A., & Jones, D. N. (2006). The ideal romantic partner: Absolute or relative preferences in personality? *Personality and Individual Differences, 41,* 431–441.

Filbey, F. M., Aslan, S., Calhoun, V., D., Spence, J. S., Damaraju, E., Caprihan, A., . . . Segall, J. (2014). Long-term effects of marijuana use on the brain. *PNAS, 111,* 16913–16918. doi: 10.1073/pnas.1415297111

Filevich, E., Dresler, M., Brick, T.R., &Kühn, S. (2015). Metacognitive mechanisms underlying lucid dreaming. *The Journal of Neuroscience, 35,* 1082–1088. doi: 10.1523/JNEUROSCI.3342-14.2015

Fink, B., Neave, N., Manning, J. T., & Grammer, K. (2006). Facial symmetry and judgements of attractiveness, health and personality. *Personality and Individual Differences, 41,* 491–499.

Fink, B., & Penton-Voak, I. (2002). Evolutionary psychology of facial attractiveness. *Current Directions in Psychological Science, 11,* 154–158.

Finley, J. R., Benjamin, A. S., & McCarley, J. S. (2014). Metacognition of multitasking: How well do we predict the costs of divided attention? *Journal of Experimental Psychology: Applied, 20,* 158–165. doi: 10.1037/xap0000010

First, M. B. (2012). A practical prototypic system for psychiatric diagnosis: The ICD-11 Clinical descriptions and diagnostic guidelines. *World Psychiatry, 11,* 24–25.

Fischer, A. H., Mosquera, P. M. R., van Vianen, A. E. M., & Manstead, A. S. R. (2004). Gender and culture differences in emotion. *Emotion, 4,* 87–94.

Fischer, P., Krueger, J. I., Greitemeyer, T., Vogrincic, C., Kastenmüller, A., Frey, D., . . . Kainbacher, M. (2011). The bystander-effect: A meta-analytic review on bystander intervention in dangerous and non-dangerous emergencies. *Psychological Bulletin, 137,* 517–537. doi: 10.1037/a0023304

Fischer, S., Meyer, A. H., Dremmel, D., Schlup, B., & Munsch, S. (2014). Short-term cognitive-behavioral therapy for binge eating disorder: Long-term efficacy and predictors of long-term treatment success. *Behaviour Research and Therapy, 58,* 36–42. doi: 10.1016/j.brat.2014.04.007

Fishbein, M. D. (1996). *Peer prejudice and discrimination: Evolutionary, cultural, and developmental dynamics.* Boulder, CO: Westview Press.

Fiske, A. P., Kitayama, S., Markus, H. R., & Nisbett, R. E. (1998). The cultural matrix of social psychology. In D. T. Gilbert, S. T. Fiske, & G. Lindzey (Eds.), *The handbook of social psychology* (Vol. 2, 4th ed., pp. 915–981). Boston: McGraw-Hill.

Fitzsimons, G. M., Chartrand, T. L., & Fitzsimons, G. J. (2008). Automatic effects of brand exposure on motivated behavior: How Apple makes you "think different." *Journal of Consumer Research, 35,* 21–35. Retrieved from www.journals.uchicago.edu/doi/pdf/10.1086/527269

Flagel, S. B., Clark, J. J., Robinson, T. E., Mayo, L., Czuj, A., Willuhn, I., . . . Akil, H. (2011). A selective role for dopamine in stimulus–reward learning. *Nature, 469,* 53–57. doi: 10.1038/nature09588

Flavell, J. H. (1992). Cognitive development: Past, present, and future. *Developmental Psychology, 28,* 998–1005.

Flavell, J. H., Miller, P. H., & Miller, S. A. (2002). *Cognitive development* (4th ed.). Upper Saddle River, NJ: Prentice Hall.

Fleeson, W., & Noftle, E. E. (2009). In favor of the synthetic resolution to the person–situation debate. *Journal of Research in Personality, 43,* 150–154. doi: 10.1016/j.jrp.2009.02.008

Flegal, K. M., Graubard, B. L., Williamson, D. F., & Gail, M. H. (2005). Excess deaths associated with underweight, overweight, and obesity. *Journal of the American Medical Association, 293,* 1861–1867.

Flegal, K. M., Kit, B., Orpana, H., & Graubard, B. I. (2013). Association of all-cause mortality with overweight and obesity using standard body mass index categories: A systematic review and meta-analysis. *Journal of the American Medical Association, 309,* 71–82. doi: 10.1001/jama.2012.113905.

Florian, C., Vecsey, C. G., Halassa, M. M., Haydon, P. G., & Abel, T. (2011). Astrocyte-derived adenosine and a1 receptor activity contribute to sleep loss-induced deficits in hippocampal synaptic plasticity and memory in mice. *Journal of Neuroscience, 31, 6956.*

Flynn, J. R. (2013). *Are we getting smarter? Rising IQ in the twenty-first century.* Cambridge, UK: Cambridge University Press.

Fok, H. K., Hui, C. M., Bond, M. H., Matsumoto, D., & Yoo, S. H. (2008). Integrating personality, context, relationship, and emotion type into a model of display. *Journal of Research in Personality, 42,* 133–150. doi: 10.1016/j.jrp.2007.04.005

Foley, D. L., & Morley, K. J. (2011). Systematic review of early cardiometabolic outcomes of the first treated episode of psychosis. *Archives of General Psychiatry, 68,* 609–616. doi: 10.1001/archgenpsychiatry.2011.2

Foody, J. (2013, November 12). Guidelines for a heart-healthy lifestyle. *NEJM Journal Watch.* Retrieved from http://www.jwatch.org/na32827/2013/11/12/guidelines-heart-healthy-lifestyle?query=etoc_jwgenmed

Ford, E. S., Maynard, L. M., & Li, C. (2014). Trends in mean waist circumference and abdominal obesity among US adults, 1999–2012. *Journal of the American Medical Association, 312,* 1151. doi: 10.1001/jama.2014.8362

Forgeard, M. J. C., Haigh, E. A. P., Beck, A. T., Davidson, R. J., Henn, F. A., Maier, S. F., . . . Seligman, M. (2012). Beyond depression: Toward a process-based approach to research, diagnosis, and treatment. *Clinical Psychology: Science and Practice, 18,* 275–299. doi: 10.1111/j.1468-2850.2011.01259.x

Forney, J. J., Buchman-Schmitt, J. M., Keel, P. K., & Frank G, K. (2016). The medical complications associated with purging. *International Journal of Eating Disorders, 49,* 249–259. doi: 10.1002/eat.22504

Forster, S., & Lavie, N. (2014). Distracted by your mind? Individual differences in distractibility predict mind wandering. *Journal of Experimental Psychology: Learning, Memory, and Cognition, 40,* 251–260. doi: 10.1037/a0034108

Fountain, H. (2007, June 19). Cockroaches conditioned to salivate at a scent, not Pavlov's dinner bell. *The New York Times.* Retrieved from www.nytimes.com

Fowler, J. H., & Christakis, N. A. (2008). Dynamic spread of happiness in a large social network: Longitudinal analysis over 20 years in the Framingham

Heart Study. *British Medical Journal, 337,* 2338. doi: 10.1136/bmj.a2338

Fox, M. (2014, January 9). What's in a sugar pill? Maybe more than you think. *NBC News.* Retrieved from http://www.nbcnews.com/health/whats-sugar-pill-maybe-more-you-think-2D11880962

Fox, M. (2015, November 12). 'Real progress': Percentage of U.S. smokers plummets, CDC finds. *MSNBC.com.* Retrieved from www.msnbc.com

Frances, A. J., & Widiger, T. (2012). Psychiatric diagnosis: Lessons from the DSM-IV past and cautions for the DSM-5 future. *Annual Review of Clinical Psychology, 8,* 109–130. doi: 10.1146/annurev-clinpsy-032511-143102

Francesetti, G., Gecele, M., Roubal, J., Greenberg, L. (2014). Gestalt therapy in clinical practice: From psychopathology to the aesthetics of contact. In G. Francesetti, M. Gecele, & J. Roubal (Eds.), *Gestalt therapy book series,* Kindle Edition.

Frank, R. H. (2012). The Easterlin Paradox revisited. *Emotion, 12,* 1188–1191. doi: 10.1037/a0029969

Frankenberger, K. D. (2000). Adolescent egocentrism: A comparison among adolescents and adults. *Journal of Adolescence, 23,* 343–354.

Franklin, T. B., Russig, H., Weiss, I. C., Gräff, J., Linder, N., Michalon, A., . . . Mansuy, I. M. (2011). Epigenetic transmission of the impact of early stress across generations. *Biological Psychiatry, 68,* 408–415.

Franko, D. L., Keshaviah, A., Eddy, K. T., Krishna, M., Davis, M. C., Keel, P. K., . . . Herzog, D. B. (2013). A longitudinal investigation of mortality in anorexia nervosa and bulimia nervosa. *American Journal of Psychiatry, 170,* 917–925. 10.1176/appi.ajp.2013.12070868

Freemon, F. R. (1981). *Organic mental disease.* Jamaica, NY: Spectrum.

French, S. E., Seidman, E., Allen, L., & Aber, J. L. (2006). The development of ethnic identity during adolescence. *Developmental Psychology, 42,* 1–10.

Frenda, S. J., Nichols, R. M., & Loftus, E. F. (2011). Current issues and advances in misinformation research. *Current Directions in Psychological Science, 20,* 20–23. doi: 10.1177/0963721410396620

Freud, S. (1900). The interpretation of dreams. In J. Strachey (Ed.), *The standard edition of the complete psychological works of Sigmund Freud: Vol. 8.* London: Hogarth Press.

Freud, S. (1917/1957). Mourning and melancholia. In J. Rickman (Ed.), *A general selection from the works of Sigmund Freud.* Garden City, NY: Doubleday.

Freud, S. (1933/1964). New introductory lectures. In A.J. Strachey (Ed.), *Standard edition of the complete psychological works of Sigmund Freud* (Vol. 22). London: Hogarth.

Freud, S. (1938). *The psychopathology of everyday life.* Harmondsworth, UK: Pelican Books.

Freund, A. M. (2008). Successful aging as management of resources: The role of selection, optimization, and compensation. *Research on Human Development, 5,* 94–106.

Frieden, T. R. (2014). Tobacco control progress and potential. *Journal of the American Medical Association, 311,* 133–134. doi: 10.1001/jama.2013.284534.

Friederici, A. D., & Singer, W. (2015). Grounding language processing on basic neurophysiological principles. *Trends in Cognitive Sciences, 19,* 329–338. doi: http://dx.doi.org/10.1016/j.tics.2015.03.012

Friedman, B. H. (2010). Feelings and the body: The Jamesian perspective on autonomic specificity of emotion. *Biological Psychology, 84,* 383–393. doi: 10.1016/j.biopsycho.2009.10.006

Friedman, H. S., Kern, M. L., Hampson, S. E., & Duckworth, A. L. (2014). A new life-span approach to conscientiousness and health: Combining the pieces of the causal puzzle. *Developmental Psychology, 50,* 1377–1389. doi: 10.1037/a0030373

Friedman, R. A. (2014). Antidepressants' black-box warning—10 years later. *New England Journal of Medicine, 371,* 1666–1668. doi: 10.1056/NE-JMp1408480

Friedmann, P. D. (2013). Alcohol use in adults. *New England Journal of Medicine, 368,* 365–373. doi: 10.1056/NEJMcp1204714

Friedrich, M., Wilhelm, I., Born, J., & Friederici, A. D. (2015). Generalization of word meanings during infant sleep. *Nature Communications, 6,* 6004. doi: 10.1038/ncomms7

Fruzzetti, A. E., Toland, K., Teller, S. A., & Loftus, E. F. (1992). Memory and eyewitness testimony. In M. M. Gruneberg & P. E. Morris (Eds.), *Aspects of memory: The practical aspects* (Vol. 1, 2nd ed., pp. 18–50). Florence, KY: Taylor & Francis/Routledge.

Frye, M. A. (2011). Bipolar disorder—a focus on depression. *New England Journal of Medicine, 364,* 51–59.

Fujita, F., & Diener, E. (2005). Life satisfaction set point: Stability and change. *Journal of Personality and Social Psychology, 88,* 158–164.

Fuligni, A. J., Witkow, M., & Garcia, C. (2005). Ethnic identity and the academic adjustment of adolescents from Mexican, Chinese, and European backgrounds. *Developmental Psychology, 41,* 799–811.

Fulton, J. J., Marcus, D. K. & Merkey, T. (2011). Irrational health beliefs and health anxiety. *Journal of Clinical Psychology, 67,* 527–538. doi: 10.1002/jclp.20769

Furnham, A., McClelland, A., & Mansi, A. (2012). Selecting your boss: Sex, age, IQ and EQ factors. *Personality and Individual Differences, 53,* 552–556.

Fusar-Poli, P., Papanastasiou, E., Stahl, D., Rocchetti, M., Carpenter, W., Shergill, S., . . . McGuire, P. (2014). Treatments of negative symptoms in schizophrenia: Meta-analysis of 168 randomized placebo-controlled trials. *Schizophrenia Bulletin, 41,* 892–899. doi: 10.1093/schbul/sbu170

Galak, J., LeBoeuf, R. A., Nelson, L. D., & Simmons, J. P. (2012). Correcting the past: Failures to replicate psi. *Journal of Personality and Social Psychology, 103,* 933–948. doi: 10.1037/a0029709

Galanter, E. (1962). Contemporary psychophysics. In R. Brown, E. Galanter, H. Hess, & G. Mandler (Eds.), *New directions in psychology.* New York: Holt, Rinehart & Winston.

Gallese, V., Gernsbacher, M. A., Heyes, C. Hickok, G., & Iacoboni, M. (2011). Mirror neuron forum. *Perspectives on Psychological Science, 6,* 369–407. doi: 10.1177/1745691611413392

Gallistel, C. R. (2006). Dopamine and reward: Comment on Hernandez et al. (2006). *Behavioral Neuroscience, 120,* 992–994.

Gallup Organization. (2005). *Americans' Personal Satisfaction, 2005.* Retrieved from www.gallup.com

Gallup, G. G., Jr., & Frederick, D. A. (2010). The science of sex appeal: An evolutionary perspective. *Review of General Psychology, 14,* 240–250. doi: 10.1037/a0020451

Galsworthy-Francis, L. (2014). Cognitive behavioral therapy for anorexia nervosa: A systematic review. *Clinical Psychology Review, 34,* 54–72. doi: 10.1016/j.cpr.2013.11.001

Galvao, T. F., Silva, M. T., Zimmermann, I. R., Souza, K. M., Martins, S. S., & Pereira, M. G. (2014). Pubertal timing in girls and depression: A systematic review. *Journal of Affective Disorders, 155,* 13–19.

Garb, H. N., Klein, D. F., & Grove, W. M. (2002). Comparison of medical and psychological tests. *The American Psychologist, 57,* 137–138.

Garcia, J., & Koelling, R. A. (1966). Relation of cue to consequence in avoidance learning. *Psychonomic Science, 4,* 123–124.

Garcia, J., & Koelling, R. A. (1971). The use of ionizing rays as a mammalian olfactory stimulus. In H. Autrum et al. (Eds.), *Handbook of sensory physiology: Vol. 4. Chemical senses* (Part 1). New York: Springer-Verlag.

Garcia, J., & Koelling, R. A. (2009). Specific hungers and poison avoidance as adaptive specialization of learning. In D. Shanks (Ed.), *Psychology of learning.* Thousand Oaks, CA: Sage.

Gardner, A. (2010, October 4). *Variety spices up Americans' sex lives, survey says.* Retrieved from www.businessweek.com /lifestyle/content/health-day/643856.html

Gardner, H. (1998). Are there additional intelligences? The case for naturalist, spiritual, and existential intelligences. In J. Kane (Ed.), *Education information, and transformation* (pp. 111–131). Upper Saddle River, NJ: Prentice Hall.

Gardner, H. (2006). *Multiple intelligences: New horizons in theory and practice.* New York: Basic Books.

Gardner, H. (2011 edition). *Frames of mind: The theory of multiple intelligences.* New York: Basic Books.

Gardner, R. A., & Gardner, B. T. (1969). Teaching sign language to a chimpanzee. *Science, 165,* 664–672.

Gardner, R. A., & Gardner, B. T. (1978). Comparative psychology and language acquisition. *Annals of the New York Academy of Science, 309,* 37–76.

Garnets, L. D. (2002). Sexual orientations in perspective. *Cultural Diversity and Ethnic Minority Psychology, 8,* 115–129.

Gartlehner, G., Gaynes, B. N., Hansen, R. A., Thieda, P., DeVeaugh-Geiss, A., Krebs, E. E., . . . Lohr, K. N. (2008). Comparative benefits and harms of second-generation antidepressants: Background paper for the American College of Physicians. *Annals of Internal Medicine, 149,* 734–750. Retrieved from www.ncbi.nlm.nih.gov/pubmed/19017592

Gartner, M. C. (2015). Pet personality: A review. *Personality and Individual Differences, 75,* 102–113. doi: 10.1016/j.paid.2014.10.042

Garwood, S. G., Cox, L., Kaplan, V., Wasserman, N., & Sulzer, J. (1980). Beauty is only "name deep": The effect of first name in ratings of physical attraction. *Journal of Applied Social Psychology, 10,* 431–435.

Gaskins, S. (2015). Childhood practices across cultures: Play and household work. In L. A. Jensen (Ed.), *Oxford handbook of human development and culture.* New York: Oxford University Press.

Gass, M. L. S., Cochrane, B. B., Larson, J. C., Manson, J. E., Barnabei, V. M., Brzyski, R. G., . . . Barad, D. H. (2011). Patterns and predictors of sexual activity among women in the Hormone Therapy trials of the Women's Health Initiative. *Menopause, 18,* 1160. doi: 10.1097/gme.0b013e3182227ebd.

Gatz, M. (2007). Commentary on evidence-based psychological treatments for older adults. *Psychology and Aging, 22,* 52–55.

Gaulin, S. J. C., & McBurney, D. (2001). *Psychology: An evolutionary approach.* Upper Saddle River, NJ: Prentice Hall.

Gawronski, B., Rydell, R. J., Vervliet, B., & De Houwer, J. (2010). Generalization versus contextualization in automatic evaluation. *Journal of Experimental Psychology: General, 139,* 683–701. doi: 10.1037/a0020315

Gazzaniga, M. (1999). The interpreter within: The glue of conscious experience. *Cerebrum, 1*(1), 68–78.

Gazzaniga, M. S. (1992). *Nature's mind.* New York: Basic Books.

Gazzaniga, M. S. (1995). Consciousness and the cerebral hemispheres. In M. S.

GBD 2013 Risk Factors Collaborators. (2015). Global, regional, and national comparative risk assessment of 79 behavioural, environmental and occupational, and metabolic risks or clusters of risks in 188 countries, 1990–2013: A systematic analysis for the Global Burden of Disease Study 2013. *The Lancet, 386,* 2287–2323. doi: 10.1016/S0140-6736(15)00128-2

Geen, R. G. (1998). Aggression and antisocial behavior. In D. T. Gilbert, S. T. Fiske, & G. Lindzey (Eds.), *The handbook of social psychology* (Vol. 2, 4th ed., pp. 317–356). Boston: McGraw-Hill.

Gehar, D. R. (2009). *Mastering competencies in family therapy.* Belmont, CA: Brooks/Cole, Cengage Learning.

Geier, A., Wansink, B., & Rozin, P. (2012). Red potato chips: Segmentation cues can substantially decrease food intake. *Health Psychology, 31,* 398–401. doi: 10.1037/a0027221

Geier, A. B., Rozin, P., & Doros, G. (2006). Unit bias: A new heuristic that helps explain the effect of portion size on food intake. *Psychological Science, 17,* 521–525.

Gel, S., Gohl, E. L. K., Sailor, K. A., Kitabatake, Y., Ming, G., & Song, H. (2006). GABA regulates synaptic integration of newly generated neurons in the adult brain. *Nature, 439,* 589–593.

Gelfand, A. (2014, September 15). Finally, migraine-specific preventive therapy is on the horizon. *NEJM Journal Watch Neurology.* Retrieved from https://mail.google.com/mail/u/0/#inbox /14881317cf1e3506

Geller, B. (2006, October 16). Early use of methylphenidate: The jury on neuronal effects is still out. *Journal Watch Psychiatry.* Retrieved from http://psychiatry.jwatch.org /cgi/content/full/2006/1016/2

Geller, B. (2015, May 22). It's all in the family: Children's parasomnias are often familial, decrease over time. *NEJM Journal Watch.* Retrieved from http://www.jwatch.org/na37906/2015/05/22/its-all -family-childrens-parasomnias-are-often-familial?query =etoc_jwpeds

Gelstein, S., Yeshurun, Y., Rozenkrantz, L., Shushan,S., Frumin, I., Roth, Y., . . . Sobel, N. (2011). Human tears contain a chemosignal. *Science, 331,* 226–230. doi: 10.1126/science.1198331

Gémes, K., Janszky, I., Laugsand, L. E., László, K. D., Ahnve, S., Vatten, L. J., & Mukamal, K. J. (2015).

Alcohol consumption is associated with a lower incidence of acute myocardial infarction: Results from a large prospective population-based study in Norway. *Journal of Internal Medicine*, in press. doi: 10.1111/joim.12428

Gene linked to Alzheimer's. (2013). *Nature, 493*, 454–455. doi: 10.1038/493454d

Gene mutation for excessive alcohol drinking found. (2013, November 26). *ScienceDaily*. Retrieved from http://www.sciencedaily.com/releases/2013/11/131126123931.htm

Geraerts, E., Lindsay, D. S., Merckelbach, H., Jelicic, M., Raymaekers, L., Arnold, M. M., . . . Schooler, J. W. (2009). Cognitive mechanisms underlying recovered-memory experiences of childhood sexual abuse. *Psychological Science, 20*, 92–98. doi: 10.1111/j.1467-9280.2008.02247.x

Gerkin, R. C., & Castro, J. B. (2015). The number of olfactory stimuli that humans can discriminate is still unknown. *eLife,4*. doi: 10.7554/eLife.08127

German, T. P., & Barrett, H. C. (2005). Functional fixedness in a technologically sparse culture. *Psychological Science, 16*, 1–5.

Gertner, Y., Fisher, C., & Eisengart, J. (2006). Learning words and rules: Abstract knowledge of word order in early sentence comprehension. *Psychological Science, 17*, 684–691.

Gianaros, P. J., & Wager, T. D. (2015). Brain-body pathways linking psychological stress and physical health. *Current Directions in Psychological Science, 24*, 313–321.

Gibbs, J. C. (2006). Should Kohlberg's cognitive developmental approach to morality be replaced with a more pragmatic approach? Comment on Krebs and Denton (2005). *Psychological Review, 113*, 666–671.

Gibson, E. J., & Walk, R. D. (1960, April). The visual cliff. *Scientific American*, pp. 64–71.

Gifford, D. D., Briceño-Perriott, J., & Mianzo, F. (2006). Locus of control: Academic achievement and retention in a sample of university first-year students. *Journal of College Admission, 191*, 18–25.

Gifford, R. (2014) Environmental psychology matters. *Annual Review of Psychology, 65*, 541–579. doi: 10.1146/annurev-psych-010213-115048

Gill, S. S., & Seitz, D. P. (2015). Lifestyles and cognitive health: What older individuals can do to optimize cognitive outcomes. *Journal of the American Medical Association, 314*, 774–775. doi: 10.1001/jama.2015.9526

Gillespie, A. K., Jones, E., A., Lin, Y.-H., Karlsson, M. P., Kay, K., Yoon, S. Y., . . . Huang, Y. (2016). Apolipoprotein E4 causes age-dependent disruption of slow gamma oscillations during hippocampal sharp-wave ripples. *Neuron, 90*, 740–751. doi: 10.1016/j.neuron.2016.04.009

Gilligan, C. (1982). *In a different voice: Psychological theory and women's development*. Cambridge, MA: Harvard University Press.

Gilligan, C. (2011). *Joining the resistance*. Oxford, UK: Polity Press.

Girgenti, M. J., LoTurco, J. J., & Maher, B. J. (2012). 1ZNF804a regulates expression of the schizophrenia-associated genes PRSS16, COMT, PDE4B, and DRD2. *PLoS ONE*, e32404. doi: 10.1371/journal.pone.0032404

Glasman, L. R., & Albarracín, D. (2006). Forming attitudes that predict future behavior: A meta-analysis of the attitude-behavior relation. *Psychological Bulletin, 132*, 778–822.

Glasofer, D. R., & Devlin, M. J. (2013). Cognitive behavioral therapy for bulimia nervosa. *Psychotherapy, 50*, 537–542. doi: 10.1037/a0031939

Goebel, M. U., Trebst, A. E., Steiner, J., Xie, Y. F., Exton, M. S., Frede, S., . . . Schedlowski, M. (2002). Behavioral conditioning of immunosuppression is possible in humans. *FASEB Journal, 16*, 1869–1873.

Goetzmann, W. N., Kim, D., Kumar, A., & Wang, Q. (2014). Weather-induced mood, institutional investors, and stock returns. *Review of Financial Studies, 28*, 73. doi: 10.1093/rfs/hhu063

Goldberg, L. R. (1993). The structure of phenotypic personality traits. *American Psychologist, 48*, 26–34.

Golder, S. A., & Macy, M. W. (2011). Diurnal and seasonal mood vary with work, sleep, and daylength across diverse cultures. *Science, 333*, 1878–1881.

Goldfried, M. R. (2012). On entering and remaining in psychotherapy. *Clinical Psychology: Science and Practice, 19*, 125–128. doi: 10.1111/j.1468-2850.2012.01278.x

Goldstein, I., Meston, C., Davis, S., & Traish, A. (Eds.). (2006). *Female sexual dysfunction*. New York: Parthenon.

Golier, J. A., Yehuda, R., Bierer, L. M., Mitropoulou, V., New, A. S., Schmeidler, J., . . . Siever, L. J. (2003). The relationship of borderline personality disorder to posttraumatic stress disorder and traumatic events. *American Journal of Psychiatry, 160*, 2018–2024.

Golinkoff, R. M., & Hirsh-Pasek, K. (2006). Baby wordsmith: From associationist to social sophisticate. *Current Directions in Psychological Science, 15*, 30–33.

Goncalves, A., Claggett, B., Jhund, P. S., Rosamond, W., Deswal, A., Aguilar, D., . . . Solomon, S. D. (2015). Alcohol consumption and risk of heart failure: The Atherosclerosis Risk in Communities Study. *European Heart Journal, 36*, 946–935. doi: 10.1093/eurheartj/ehu514

Gone, J. P., & Trimble, J. E. (2012). American Indian and Alaska Native mental health: Diverse perspectives on enduring disparities. *Annual Review of Clinical Psychology, 8*, 131–160.

Gonsalves, B. D., & Cohen, N. J. (2010). Brain imaging, cognitive processes, and brain networks. *Perspectives on Psychological Science, 5*, 744–752. doi: 10.1177/1745691610388776

González, H. J., Vega, W. A., Williams, D. R., Tarraf, W., West, B. T., & Neighbors, H. W. (2010). Depression care in the United States: Too little for too few. *Archives of General Psychiatry, 67*, 37–46.

Gonzalez, V. M., & Dulin, P. L. (2015). Comparison of a smartphone app for alcohol use disorders with an Internet-based intervention plus bibliotherapy: A pilot study. *Journal of Consulting and Clinical Psychology, 83*, 335–345. doi: http://dx.doi.org/10.1037/a0038620

Goodarz, D., Ding, E. L., Mozaffarian, D., Taylor, B., Rehm, J., Murray, C. J. L., & Ezzati, M. (2009). The preventable causes of death in the United States: Comparative *risk assessment of dietary, lifestyle, and metabolic risk factors. PLOS Medicine, 6*(4), e1000058.

Goodwin, R. D., Canino, G., Ortega, A. N., & Bird, H. R. (2009). Maternal mental health and childhood asthma among Puerto Rican youth: The role of prenatal smoking. *Journal of Asthma, 46*, 726–730. doi: 10.1080/02770900903072051

Gopnik, A. (2000, December 24). Children need childhood, not vocational training. *The New York Times Week in Review*, p. 6.

Gordon-Larsen, P. (2008). Obesity epidemiology. *New England Journal of Medicine, 359*, 1299–1300.

Gorelik, G., Shackelford, T. K., & Weekes-Shackelford, V. A. (2012). Human violence and evolutionary consciousness. *Review of General Psychology, 16*, 343–356. doi: 10.1037/a0027991

Gorman, C. (2012, January). Five hidden dangers of obesity: Excess weight can harm health in ways that may come as a surprise. *Scientific American*. Retrieved from www.scientificamerican.com/article.cfm?id=five-hidden-dangers-of-obesity

Goschke, T., & Bolte, A. (2012). On the modularity of implicit sequence learning: Independent acquisition of spatial, symbolic, and manual sequences. *Cognitive Psychology, 65*, 284–320.

Gosling, S., D., & Mason, W. (2015). Internet research in psychology. *Annual Review of Psychology, 66*, 877–902. doi: 10.1146/annurev-psych-010814-015321

Gothold, J. J. (2009). Peeling the onion: Understanding layers of treatment. *Annals of the New York Academy of Sciences, 1159*, 301–312.

Gottesman, I. I., & Hanson, D. R. (2005). Human development: Biological and genetic processes. *Annual Review of Psychology, 56*, 263–286.

Gottfredson, L. S., & Deary, I. J. (2004). Intelligence predicts health and longevity, but why? *Current Directions in Psychological Science, 13*, 1–4.

Grace, A. A. (2010). Ventral hippocampus, interneurons, and schizophrenia: A new understanding of the pathophysiology of schizophrenia and its implications for treatment and prevention. *Current Directions in Psychological Science, 19*, 232–237. doi: 10.1177/0963721410378032s

Graham, J. R. (2006). *MMPI-2: Assessing personality and psychopathology* (4th ed.). New York: Oxford University Press.

Granata, A. R., Pugni, V., Rochira, V., Zirilli, L., & Carani, C. (2012). Hormonal regulation of male sexual desire: The role of testosterone, estrogen, prolactin, oxytocin, and others. In M. Maggi (Ed.), *Hormonal therapy for male sexual dysfunction* (pp. 72–82). Hoboken, NJ: Wiley.

Grant, B. F., Hasin, D. S., Blanco, C., Stinson, F. S., Chou, S. P., Goldstein, R. B., . . . Huang, B. (2006). The epidemiology of social anxiety disorder in the United States: Results from the National Epidemiologic Survey on Alcohol and Related Conditions. *Journal of Clinical Psychiatry, 66*, 1351–1361.

Grant, B. F., Hasin, D. S., Stinson, F. S., Dawson, D. A., Goldstein, R. B., Smith, S., . . . Saha, T. D. (2006). The epidemiology of DSM-IV panic disorder and agoraphobia in the United States: Results from the National Epidemiologic Survey on Alcohol and Related Conditions. *Journal of Clinical Psychiatry, 67*, 363–374.

Grant, J. E. (2014). Obsessive–compulsive disorder. *New England Journal of Medicine, 371*, 646–653. doi: 10.1056/NEJMcp1402176

Grant, S., LaBrie, J. W., Hummer, J. F., & Lac, A. (2012). How drunk am I? Misperceiving one's level of intoxication in the college drinking environment. *Psychology of Addictive Behaviors, 26*, 51–58. doi: 10.1037/a0023942

Gray, R. (2011). Links between attention, performance pressure, and movement in skilled motor action.

Current Directions in Psychological Science, 20, 301. doi: 10.1177/0963721411416572

Graziano, W. G., & Tobin, R. M. (2009). Agreeableness. In M. R. Leary & R. H. Hoyle (Eds.), *Handbook of individual differences in social behavior* (pp. 46–61). New York: Guilford.

Greenhill, S. D., Juczewski, K., de Haan, A. M., Seaton, G., Fox, K., & Hardingham, N. R. (2015). Adult cortical plasticity depends on an early postnatal critical period. *Science, 349,* 424. doi: 10.1126/science.aaa8481

Greenwood, T. A., Lazzeroni, L. C., Calkins, M. E., Freedman, R., Green, M. R., Gur, R. E., . . . Braff, D. L. (2016). Genetic assessment of additional endophenotypes from the Consortium on the Genetics of Schizophrenia Family Study. *Schizophrenia Research, 170,* 30–40. doi: http://dx.doi.org/10.1016/j.schres.2015.11.008

Greer, M. (2004, April). General cognition also makes the difference on the job, study finds. *Monitor on Psychology, 35*(4), 12.

Gregoire, C. (2015, May). How to make the perfect first impression (according to science). *The Huffington Post.* Retrieved from http://www.huffingtonpost.com/2014/05/30/the-science-and-art-of-fi_n_5399004.html?ncid=txtlnkusaolp00000592

Grogan, J. (2013). *Encountering America: Humanistic psychology, sixties culture and the shaping of the modern self.* New York: HarperPerennial.

Grossman, L. (2003, January 20). Can Freud get his job back? *Time,* pp. 48–51.

Grover, S., Chakrabarti, S., Ghormode, D., Agarwal, M., Sharma, A., & Avasthi, A. (2015). Catatonia in inpatients with psychiatric disorders: A comparison of schizophrenia and mood disorders. *Psychiatry Research, 229,* 919–925. doi: 10.1016/j.psychres.2015.07.020

Groves, R. M., Fowler, F. J., Jr., Couper, M. P., Lepkowski, J. M., Singer, E., & Tourangea, R. (2009). *Survey methodology.* Hoboken, NJ: Wiley.

Grusec, J. E., Chaparro, M. P., Johnston, M., & Sherman, A. (2013). Social development and social relationships in middle childhood. In R. M. Lerner, M. A. Easterbrooks, & J. Mistry (Eds.), *Handbook of psychology, developmental psychology* (Vol. 6, 2nd ed., pp. 243–264). Hoboken, NJ: Wiley.

Guadagno, R. E., & Cialdini, R. B. (2010). Preference for consistency and social influence: A review of current research findings. *Social Influence, 5,* 152–163.

Gubbels, S. P., Woessner, D. W., Mitchell, J. C., Ricci, A. J., & Brigande, A. J. (2008). Functional auditory hair cells produced in the mammalian cochlea by in utero gene transfer. *Nature Online.* Retrieved from www.nature.com/nature/journal/vaop/ncurrent/abs/nature07265.html

Guéguen, N., Jacob, C., & Lamy, L. (2010). "Love is in the air": Effects of songs with romantic lyrics on compliance with a courtship request. *Psychology of Music, 38,* 303–307. doi: 10.1177/0305735609360428

Guidi, J., Tomba, E., & Fava, G. A. (2016). The sequential integration of pharmacotherapy and psychotherapy in the treatment of major depressive disorder: A meta-analysis of the sequential model and a critical review of the literature. *American Journal of Psychiatry, 173,* 128–137. doi: http://dx.doi.org/10.1176/appi.ajp.2015.15040476

Guilford, J. P., Christensen, P. R., Merrifield, P. R., & Wilson, R. C. (1978). *Alternate uses: Form B, Form C.* Orange, CA: Sheridan Psychological Services.

Gunderson, J. G. (2011). Borderline personality disorder. *New England Journal of Medicine, 364,* 2037–2042.

Guo, J. Y., Huhtaniska, S. Miettunen, J., Jääskeläinen, E., Kiviniemi, V., Nikkinen, J., . . . Murray, G. K. (2015). Longitudinal regional brain volume loss in schizophrenia: Relationship to antipsychotic medication and change in social function. *Schizophrenia Research, 168,* 297–304. doi: 10.1016/j.schres.2015.06.016

Gustavson, C. R., & Garcia, J. (1974). Aversive conditioning: Pulling a gag on the wily coyote. *Psychology Today, 8,* 68–72.

Gustavson, C. R., Garcia, J., Hawkins, W. G., & Rusiniak, K. W. (1974). Coyote predation control by aversive conditioning. *Science, 184,* 581–583.

Gwaltney, C. J., Metrik, J., Kahler, C. W., & Shiffman, S. (2009). Self-efficacy and smoking cessation: A meta-analysis. *Psychology of Addictive Behaviors, 23,* 56–66. doi: 10.1037/a0013529

Gyatso, T. (2003, April 26). The monk in the lab. *The New York Times,* p. A29.

Ha, T., van den Berg, J. E. M., Engels, R. C. M. E., & Lichtwarck-Aschoff, A. (2012). Effects of attractiveness and status in dating desire in homosexual and heterosexual men and women. *Archives of Sexual Behavior, 41,* 673–682. doi: 10.1007/s10508-011-9855-9

Hafdahl, A. R., & Gray-Little, B. (2002). Explicating methods in reviews of race and self-esteem: Reply to Twenge and Crocker (2002). *Psychological Bulletin, 128,* 409–416.

Haider, B., Duque, A., Hasenstaub, A. R., & McCormick, D. A. (2006). Neocortical network activity in vivo is generated through a dynamic balance of excitation and inhibition. *The Journal of Neuroscience, 26,* 4535–4545.

Haidt, J. (2008). Morality. *Perspectives on Psychological Science, 3,* 65–72. doi: 10.1111/j.1745-6916.2008.00063.x

Hakim, D. (2003, October 25). New luxury-car specifications: Styling. Performance. Aroma. *The New York Times,* pp. A. 1, C2.

Halbreich, U., O'Brien, S., Eriksson, E., Bäckström, T., Yonkers, K. A., & Freeman, E.W. (2006). Are there differential symptom profiles that improve in response to different pharmacological treatments of premenstrual syndrome/premenstrual dysphoric disorder? *CNS Drugs, 20,* 523–547.

Halpern, D. F. (2004). A cognitive-process taxonomy for sex differences in cognitive abilities. *Current Directions in Psychological Science, 13,* 135–139.

Ham, L. S., & Hope, D. A. (2003). College students and problematic drinking: A review of the literature. *Clinical Psychology Review, 23,* 719–759.

Hamburg, D. (2012). Preventing mass violence. *Science, 336,* 775. doi: 10.1126/science.1223918

Hamilton, B. E., & Chong, L. L. (2015). *U.S. and state trends on teen births, 1990–2013.* National Center for Health Statistics. Retrieved from http://blogs.cdc.gov/nchs-data-visualization/2015/08/14/us-and-state-trends-on-teen-births-1990-2013/

Hamilton, J. L., Stange, J. P., Abramson, L. Y., & Alloy, L. B. (2015). Stress and the Development of cognitive vulnerabilities to depression explain sex differences in depressive symptoms during adolescence. *Clinical Psychological Science, 3,* 702–714.doi: 10.1177/2167702614545479

Hamilton, S. P. (2008). Schizophrenia candidate genes: Are we really coming up blank? *American Journal of Psychiatry, 165,* 420–423. doi: 10.1176/appi.ajp.2008.08020218

Hammen, C. (2015). Stress sensitivity in psychopathology: Mechanisms and consequences. *Journal of Abnormal Psychology, 124,* 152–154. doi: http://dx.doi.org/10.1037/abn0000040

Hammond, D. C. (2007). Review of the efficacy of clinical hypnosis with headaches and migraines. *International Journal of Clinical & Experimental Hypnosis, 55,* 207–219.

Hampshire, A., Highfield, R. R., Parkin, B. L., & Owen, A. M. (2012). Fractionating human intelligence. *Neuron, 76,* 1225–1237. doi: http://dx.doi.org/10.1016/j.neuron.2012.06.022

Hampshire, A., Parkin, B., Highfield, R., & Owen, A. M. (2014). Brief response to Ashton and colleagues regarding fractionating human intelligence. *Personality and Individual Differences, 60,* 16–17.

Hampton, T. (2015). Report describes trends in US cancer incidence and mortality rates. *Journal of the American Medical Association, 313,* 2014. doi: 10.1001/jama.2015.4359

Hamre, K. (2013). Obesity: Multiple factors contribute. *Nature, 493,* 480. doi: 10.1038/493480c

Hardy, S. A., & Raffaelli, M. (2003). Adolescent religiosity and sexuality: An investigation of reciprocal influences. *Journal of Adolescence, 26,* 731–739.

Hargreaves, D. A., & Tiggemann, M. (2009). Muscular ideal media images and men's body image: Social comparison processing and individual vulnerability. *Psychology of Men & Masculinity, 10,* 109–119. doi: 10.1016/j.bodyim.2004.10.002

Harlow, H. F., & Harlow, M. K. (1966). Learning to love. *American Scientist, 54,* 244–272.

Harlow, H. F., Harlow, M. K., & Meyer, D. R. (1950). Learning motivated by a manipulation drive. *Journal of Experimental Psychology, 40,* 228–234.

Harlow, H. F., & Zimmermann, R. R. (1959). Affectional responses in the infant monkey. *Science, 130,* 421–432.

Harriger, J. A., Calogero, R. M., Witherington, D. C., & Smith, J. E. (2010). Body size stereotyping and internalization of the thin ideal in preschool girls. *Sex Roles, 63,* 609–620. doi: 10.1007/s11199-010-9868-1

Harris, J. L., Bargh, J. A., & Brownell, K. D. (2009). Priming effects of television food advertising on eating behavior. *Health Psychology, 28,* 404–413. doi: 10.1037/a0014399

Harshman, R. A., & Paivio, A. (1987). Paradoxical sex differences in self-reported imagery. *Canadian Journal of Psychology, 41,* 287–302.

Hartmann, E. (2011). *The nature and functions of dreaming.* New York: Oxford University Press.

Hartmann, E. (2012). The dream is not a series of perceptions to which we respond logically (or not). The dream is an imaginative creation: A comment on Hobson et al. Dream logic—The inferential reasoning paradigm. *Dreaming, 22,* 74–77. doi: 10.1037/a0026141

Hartmann, M. N., Kluge, A., Kalis, A., Mojzisch, A., Tobler, P. N., & Kaiser, S. (2015). Apathy in schizophrenia as a deficit in the generation of options for action. *Journal of Abnormal Psychology, 124,* 309–318. doi: http://dx.doi.org/10.1037/abn0000048

Hartshorne, J. K., & Germine, L. T. (2015). When does cognitive functioning peak? The asynchronous rise and fall of different cognitive abilities across the life span. *Psychological Science, 26,* 433–443. doi: 10.1177/0956797614567339

Harvey, A. G., & Tang, N. K. Y (2012). (Mis)perception of sleep in insomnia: A puzzle and a resolution. *Psychological Bulletin, 138,* 77–101. doi: 10.1037/a0025730

Harvey, A. G., Bélanger, L., Talbot, L., Eidelman, P., Beaulieu-Bonneau, S., Fortier-Brochu, E., . . . Morin, C. M. (2014). Comparative efficacy of behavior therapy, cognitive therapy, and cognitive behavior therapy for chronic insomnia: A randomized controlled trial. *Journal of Consulting and Clinical Psychology, 82,* 670–683. doi: 10.1037/a0036606

Hassert, D. L., Miyashita, T., & Williams, C. L. (2004). The effects of peripheral vagal nerve stimulation at a memory-modulating intensity on norepinephrine output in the basolateral amygdala. *Behavioral Neuroscience, 118,* 79–88.

Hatzigeorgiadis, A., Zourbanos, N., Galanis, E., & Theodorakis, Y. (2011). Self-talk and sports performance: A meta-analysis. *Perspectives on Psychological Science, 6,* 348–356. doi: 10.1177/1745691611413136

Haubensak, W., Kunwar, P.S ., Cai, H., Ciocchi, S., Wall, N.R., Ponnusamy, R., . . . Anderson, D. J. (2010). Genetic dissection of an amygdala microcircuit that gates conditioned fear. *Nature, 468,* 270. doi: 10.1038/nature09553

Haynes, J.-D., & Rees, G. (2006). Decoding mental states from brain activity in humans. *Nature Neuroscience Review, 7,* 524–534.

Haynos, A. F., & Fruzzetti, A. E. (2011). Anorexia nervosa as a disorder of emotion dysregulation: Evidence and treatment implications. *Clinical Psychology: Science and Practice, 18,* 183–202. doi: 10.1111/j.1468-2850.2011.01250.x

Healy, M. (2010, October 5). *Americans are branching out sexually, survey finds.* Retrieved from www.latimes.com/health /la-sci-sex-survey-20101005,0,587370.story

Heavy toll from alcohol. (2014). *Journal of the American Medical Association, 312,* 688. doi: 10.1001/jama.2014.9637.

Hebb, D. O. (1955). Drive and the CNS (central nervous system). *Psychological Review, 62,* 243–254.

Hebert, L. E., Weuve, J., Scherr, P. A., & Evans, D. A. (2013). Alzheimer disease in the United States (2010–2050) estimated using the 2010 census. *Neurology.* Retrieved from www.neurology.org/content /early/2013/02/06 /WNL.0b013e31828726f5.short

Heck, A., Fastenrath, M., Coynel, D., Auschra, B., Bickel, H., Freytag, V., . . . Papassotiropoulos, A. (2015). Genetic analysis of association between calcium signaling and hippocampal activation, memory performance in the young and old, and risk for sporadic Alzheimer Disease. *JAMA Psychiatry, 72,* 1029–1036. doi: 10.1001/jamapsychiatr

Heffernan, V. (2011, January 9). Against headphones. *The New York Times Magazine,* pp. 16–17.

Hehman, E., Mania, E. W., & Gaertner, S. L. (2010). Where the division lies: Common in-group identity moderates the cross-race facial-recognition effect. *Journal of Experimental Social Psychology, 46,* 445–448. doi: 10.1016/j.jesp.2009.11.008

Heider, E. (1958). *The psychology of interpersonal relations.* New York: Wiley.

Heilbronner, C., & Berlin, I. (2005). Maternal smoking during pregnancy induces obstetrical and fetal complications but also has an impact on newborns, infants, children and adults. *European Journal of Obstetrics and Gynecology and Reproductive Biology, 34*(7, Pt. 1), 679–686.

Heine, S. J., Kitayama, S., Lehman, D. R., Takata, T., Ide, E., Leung, C., & Matsumoto, H. (2001). Divergent consequences of success and failure in Japan and North America: An investigation of self-improving motivations and malleable selves. *Journal of Personality and Social Psychology, 81,* 599–615.

Heinemann, L. A. J., Minh, T. D., Filonenko, A., & Uhl-Hochgräber, K. (2010). Explorative evaluation of the impact of severe premenstrual disorders on work absenteeism and productivity. *Women's Health Issues, 20,* 58–65. doi: 10.1016/j.whi.2009.09.005

Helfinstein, S. M., Mumford, J. A., & Poldrack, R. A. (2015). If all your friends jumped off a bridge: The effect of others' actions on engagement in and recommendation of risky behaviors. *Journal of Experimental Psychology: General, 144,* 12–17. doi: http://dx.doi.org/10.1037/xge0000043

Helms, J. E. (1992). Why is there no study of culture equivalence in standardized cognitive ability testing? *American Psychologist, 47,* 1083–1101.

Helwig, C. C. (2006). Rights, civil liberties, and democracy across cultures. In M. Killen & J. G. Smetana (Eds.), *Handbook of moral development* (pp. 185–210). Mahwah, NJ: Erlbaum.

Henderlong, J., & Lepper, M. R. (2002). The effects of praise on children's intrinsic motivation: A review and synthesis. *Psychological Bulletin, 128,* 774–795.

Henderson, M. D., & Burgoon, E. M. (2013). Why the door-in-the-face technique can sometimes backfire: A construal-level account. *Social Psychological and Personality Science.* Retrieved from http://spp.sagepub.com/content/early/2013/10/03 /1948550613506719

Henrickson, H. C., Crowther, J. H., & Harrington, E. F. (2010). Ethnic identity and maladaptive eating: Expectancies about eating and thinness in African American women. *Cultural Diversity and Ethnic Minority Psychology, 16,* 87–93.

Henslee, A. M., & Coffey, S. F. (2010). Exposure therapy for posttraumatic stress disorder in a residential substance use treatment facility. *Professional Psychology, Research and Practice, 41,* 34–40. doi: 10.1016/j.brat.2010.02.002

Hepper, P. G., Shahidullah, S., & White, R. (1990). Origins of fetal handedness. *Nature, 347,* 431.

Herbenick, D., Reece, M., Schick, V., Sanders, S., Dodge, B., & Fortenberry, J. D. (2010). Sexual behavior in the United States: Results from a national probability sample of males and females ages 14–94. *Journal of Sexual Medicine, 7* (Supp. 5), 255–265. doi: 10.1111/j.1743-6109.2010.02012.x

Hergenhahn, B. R. (2009). *An introduction to the history of psychology* (6th ed.). Belmont, CA: Cengage Learning.

Hernandez, I., & Preston, J. L. (2012). Disfluency disrupts the confirmation bias. *Journal of Experimental Social Psychology, 49,* 178–182.

Hernandez, R., Kershaw, K. N., Siddique, J., Boehm, J. K., Kubzansky, L. D., Diez-Roux, A., . . . Lloyd-Jones, D. M. (2015). Optimism and cardiovascular health: Multi-ethnic study of atherosclerosis (MESA). *Health Behavior and Policy Review, 2,* 62–73. doi: 10.14485/HBPR.2.1.6

Heron, M. (2010, March 31). *Deaths: Leading causes for 2006 National Vital Statistics Reports, 58*(14).

Herpes statistics: How common is genital herpes (HSV-2)? (2014). Retrieved from http://justherpes.com/facts/genital-herpes-statistics-us-hsv2/

Herrington, J. D., Mohanty, A., Koven, N. S., Fisher, J. E., Stewart, J. L., Banich, M., . . . Heller, W. (2005). Emotion-modulated performance and activity in left dorsolateral prefrontal cortex. *Emotion, 5,* 200–207.

Herrmann, D. J., & Palmisano, M. (1992). The facilitation of memory performance. In M. Gruneberg & P. Morris (Eds.), *Aspects of memory: The practical aspects* (Vol. 1, 2nd ed., pp. 147–167). London: Routledge.

Heseker, H. (2011). Folic acid and other potential measures in the prevention of neural tube defects. *Annals of Nutrition and Metabolism, 59,* 41–45. doi: 10.1159/000332126

Higher Education Research Institute, UCLA Graduate School of Education & Information Studies (2011, January 26). *Incoming college students rate emotional health at record low, annual survey finds.* Retrieved from www.heri.ucla.edu /pr-display.php?prQry=55

Hildebrandt, T., Alfano, L., Tricamo, M., & Pfaff, D. W. (2010). Conceptualizing the role of estrogens and serotonin in the development and maintenance of bulimia nervosa. *Clinical Psychology Review, 30,* 655–668. doi: 0.1016/j.cpr.2010.04.011

Hilgard, E. R. (1977). *Divided consciousness: Multiple controls in human thought and action.* New York: Wiley.

Hilgard, E. R. (1994). A neodissociation theory. In S. Lynn & J. W. Rhue (Eds.), *Dissociation: Clinical and theoretical perspectives* (pp. 83–104). New York: Guilford Press.

Hill, P. L., & Roberts, B. W. (2010). Propositions for the study of moral personality development. *Current Directions in Psychological Science, 19,* 380–383. doi: 10.1177/0963721410389168

Hill, P. L., & Turiano, N. A. (2014). Purpose in life as a predictor of mortality across adulthood. *Psychological Science, 25,* 1482–1486. doi: 10.1177/0956797614531799.

Hillman, J. (2008). Sexual issues and aging within the context of work with older adult patients. *Professional Psychology: Research and Practice, 39,* 290–297. doi: 10.1037/0735-7028.39.3.290

Hilmert, C. J., Kulik, J. A., & Christenfeld, N. J. S. (2006). Positive and negative opinion modeling: The influence of another's similarity and dissimilarity. *Journal of Personality and Social Psychology, 90,* 440–452.

Hilton, J. L., & von Hippel, W. (1996). Stereotypes. In J. T. Spence, J. M. Darley, & D. J. Foss (Eds.), *Annual Review of Psychology* (Vol. 47, pp. 237–271). Palo Alto, CA: Annual Reviews.

Hines, M. (2011). Prenatal endocrine influences on sexual orientation and on sexually differentiated childhood behavior. *Frontiers in Neuroendocrinology, 32,* 170–182.

Hingson, R. W., Zha, W., & Weitzmanet, E. R. (2009). Magnitude of and trends in alcohol-related mortality and morbidity among U.S. college students ages 18 to 24, 1998–2005. *Journal of Studies on Alcohol and Drugs, 16,* 12–20. doi: 10.1146/annurev.publhealth.26.021304.144652

Hinman, R. S., McCrory, P., Pirotta, M., Relf, I., Forbes, A., Crossley, K. M., . . . Bennell, K. L.

(2014). Acupuncture for chronic knee pain: A randomized clinical trial. *Journal of the American Medical Association, 312,* 1313–1322. doi: 10.1001/jama.2014.12660

Hirshkowitz, M., Whiton, K., Albert, S. M., Alessi, C., Bruni, O., DonCarlos, L., . . . Ware, J. C. (2015). National Sleep Foundation's sleep time duration recommendations: Methodology and results summary. *Sleep Health, 1,* 40–43. Hirst, W., & Phelps, E. A. (2016). Flashbulb memories. *Current Directions in Psychological Science, 25,* 36–41. doi: 10.1177/0963721415622487

Hirst, W., Phelps, E. A., Meksin, R., Vaidya, C. J., Johnson, M. K., Mitchell, K. J., . . . Olsson, A. (2015). Ten-year follow-up of a study of memory for the attack of September 11, 2001: Flashbulb memories and memories for flashbulb events. *Journal of Experimental Psychology: General, 144,* 604–623. doi: http://dx.doi.org/10.1037/xge0000055

Hispanics to total 30 percent of US population by 2050. (2014, September 1). *NBCNEWS.com.* Retrieved from http://www.nbcnews.com/news/latino/hispanics-total-30-percent-us-population-2050-n193206

Hobson, J. A. (1999). *Consciousness.* New York: Scientific American Library.

Hobza, D. L., & Rochlen, A. B. (2009). Gender role conflict, drive for muscularity, and the impact of ideal media portrayals on men. *Psychology of Men & Masculinity, 10,* 120–130. doi: 10.1037/a0015040

Hodson, G. (2011). Do ideologically intolerant people benefit from intergroup contact? *Current Directions in Psychological Science, 20,* 154–159.

Hoeksema van Orden, C. Y. D., Gaillard, A. W. K., & Buunk, B. P. (1998). Social loafing under fatigue. *Journal of Personality and Social Psychology, 75,* 1179–1190.

Hofmann, S. G. (2008). Cognitive processes during fear acquisition and extinction in animals and humans: Implications for exposure therapy of anxiety disorders. *Clinical Psychology Review, 28,* 200–211.

Hofmann, S. G., Asnaani, A., Vonk, I. J. J., Sawyer, A. T., & Fang, A. (2012). The efficacy of cognitive behavioral therapy: A review of meta-analyses. *Cognitive Therapy and Research, 36,* 427–440. doi: 10.1007/s10608-012-9476-1

Hofstee, W. K. B. (2003). Structures of personality traits. In T. Millon & M. J. Lerner (Eds.), *Handbook of psychology: Personality and social psychology* (Vol. 5, pp. 231–256). New York: Wiley.

Hojjat, M., & Cramer, D. (Eds.) (2013). *Positive psychology of love. Series in positive psychology.* New York: Oxford University Press.

Holden, C. (2009, July). A face for Phineas Gage. *Science, 325,* 521.

Holford, T. R., Meza, R., Warner, K. E., Meernik, C., Jeon, J., Moolgavkar, S. H., . . . Levy, D. T. (2014). *Journal of the American Medical Association, 311,* 164–171. doi: 10.1001/jama.2013.285112.

Holland, A. S., & Roisman, G. (2010). Adult attachment security and young adults' dating relationships over time: Self-reported, observational, and physiological evidence. *Developmental Psychology, 46,* 552–557. doi: 10.1037/a0018542

Hollon, S. D., DeRubeis, R. J., Fawcett, J., Amsterdam, J. D., Shelton, R. C., Zajecka, J., . . . Gallop, R. (2014). *JAMA Psychiatry, 7,* 1157–1164. doi: 10.1001/jamapsychiatry.2014.1054.

Holme, I., & Anderssen, S. A. (2015). Increases in physical activity is as important as smoking cessation for reduction in total mortality in elderly men: 12 years of follow-up of the Oslo II study. *British Journal of Sports Medicine, 49,* 743–748. doi: 10.1136/bjsports-2014-094522

Holmes, E. A., Craske, M. G., & Graybiel, A. M. (2014). Psychological treatments: A call for mental-health science. *Nature, 511.* Retrieved from http://www.nature.com/news/psychological-treatments-a-call-for-mental-health-science-1.15541

Holohan, M. (2014, September 24). *Fat suit diet: How our friends influence the way we eat.* Retrieved from http://www.today.com/health/fat-suit-diet-how-our-friends-influence-way-we-eat-2D80172483

Holt, C. L., Clark, E. M., & Kreuter, M. W. (2001). Weight locus of control and weight-related attitudes and behaviors in an overweight population. *Addictive Behaviors, 26,* 329–340.

Holt-Lunstad, J., Smith, T. B., Baker, M., Harris, T., & Stephenson, D. (2015). Loneliness and social isolation as risk factors for mortality: A meta-analytic review. *Perspectives on Psychological Science, 10,* 227–237. doi: 10.1177/1745691614568352

Holtom-Viesel, A., & Allan, S. (2014). A systematic review of the literature on family functioning across all eating disorder diagnoses in comparison to control families. *Clinical Psychology Review, 34,* 29–43. doi: 10.1016/j.cpr.2013.10.005.

Holtzheimer, P. E., & McDonald, W. E. (Eds.). (2014). *A clinical guide to transcranial magnetic stimulation.* New York: Oxford University Press.

Hölzel, B., K., Lazar, S. W., Gard, T., Schuman-Olivier, Z., Vago, D. R., & Ott, U. (2011). How does mindfulness meditation work? Proposing mechanisms of action from a conceptual and neural perspective. *Perspectives on Psychological Science, 6,* 537–559. doi: 10.1177/1745691611419671

Holzman, L. (2009). *Vygotsky at work and play.* New York: Routledge/Taylor & Francis Group.

Hooli, B. V., Lill,C. M., Mullin,K., Qiao, D., Lange,C., Bertram, L., & Tanzi, R. E. (2015). PLD3 gene variants and Alzheimer's disease. *Nature, 520,* E7–E8. doi: 10.1038/nature14040

Hopkin, M. (2008, May 5). Fat cell numbers stay constant through adult life. *Nature News.* Retrieved from www. nature.com/news/2008/080505/full/news.2008.800.html. doi: 10.1038/news.2008.800

Hopkins, J. R. (2011, December). The enduring influence of Jean Piaget. *APS Observer, 24*(10), 35–36.

Hopkins, W. D., & Cantalupo, C. (2008). Theoretical speculations on the evolutionary origins of hemispheric specialization. *Current Directions in Psychological Science, 17,* 2133–237. doi: 10.1111/j.1467-8721.2008.00581.x

Hopko, D. R., Cannity, K., McIndoo, C. C., File, A. A., Ryba, M. M., Clark, C. G., . . . Bell, J. L. (2015). Behavior therapy for depressed breast cancer patients: Predictors of treatment outcome. *Journal of Consulting and Clinical Psychology, 83,* 225–231. doi: http://dx.doi.org/10.1037/a0037704

Hor, H., Bartesaghi, L, Kutalik, Z., Vicário, J. L., de Andrés, C., Pfister, C., . . . & Peraita-Adrados, R. (2011). A missense mutation in myelin oligodendrocyte glycoprotein as a cause of familial narcolepsy with cataplexy. *American Journal of Human Genetics, 89,* 474–479. doi: 10.1016/j.ajhg.2011.08.007

Horn, J. (2001). Raymond Bernard Cattell (1905–1998). *American Psychologist, 56,* 71–72.

Horowitz, S. (2012). *The universal sense: How hearing shapes the mind.* Bloomsbury Publishing Plc.: Kindle Edition.

Horry, R., Palmer, M. A., Sexton, M. L., & Brewer, N. (2012). Memory conformity for confidently recognized items: The power of social influence on memory reports. *Journal of Experimental Social Psychology, 48,* 783–786. doi: 10.1016/j.jesp.2011.12.010

Hostinar, C. E., Sullivan, R. M., & Gunnar, M. R. (2014). Psychobiological mechanisms underlying the social buffering of the hypothalamic–pituitary–adrenocortical axis: A review of animal models and human studies across development. *Psychological Bulletin, 140,* 256–282. doi: 10.1037/a0032671

Hothersall, D. (1995). *History of psychology* (3rd ed.). New York: McGraw-Hill.

Houghton, S., Curran, J., & Ekers, D. (2011). Behavioural activation in the treatment of depression. *Mental Health Practice, 14,* 18–23.

Houston, D. M., & Jusczyk, P. W. (2003). Infants' long-term memory for the sound patterns of words and voices. *Journal of Experimental Psychology: Human Perception and Performance, 29,* 1143–1154.

Hout, M., & Greeley, A. (2012). Religion and happiness. In P. V. Marsden (Ed.), *Social trends in American life: Findings from the General Social Survey since 1972* (pp. 288–314). Princeton, NJ: Princeton University Press.

Hsieh, H. J., Lue, K. H., Tsai, H. C., Lee, C. C., Chen, S. Y., & Kao, P. F. (2014). L-3,4-dihydroxy-6-[F-18] fluorophenylalanine positron emission tomography demonstrating dopaminergic system abnormality in the brains of obsessive-compulsive disorder patients . *Psychiatry and Clinical Neurosciences, 68,* 292–298. doi: 10.1111/pcn.12139

Hu, M.-C., Davies, M., & Kandel, D. B. (2006). Epidemiology and correlates of daily smoking and nicotine dependence among young adults in the United States. *American Journal of Public Health, 96,* 299–308.

Huang, L., Galinsky, A. D., Gruenfeld, D. H., & Guillory, L. E (2011). Powerful postures versus powerful roles: Which is the proximate correlate of thought and behavior? *Psychological Science, 22,* 95–102. doi: 10.1177/0956797610391912

Hubel, D. H. (1988). *Eye, brain, and vision.* New York: Scientific American Library.

Hubel, D. H., & Wiesel, T. N. (1979). Brain mechanisms of vision. *Scientific American, 241,* 130–144.

Hudson, J. I., Hiripi, E., Pope, H. G., Jr., & Kessler, R. C. (2006). Prevalence and correlates of eating disorders in the National Comorbidity Survey Replication. *Biological Psychiatry, 61,* 348–358.

Huesmann, L. R., Moise-Titus, J., Podolski, C.-L., & Eron, L. D. (2003). Longitudinal relations between children's exposure to TV violence and their aggressive and violent behavior in young adulthood: 1977–1992. *Developmental Psychology, 39,* 201–221.

Huey, E. D., Krueger, F., & Grafman, J. (2006). Representations in the human prefrontal cortex. *Current Directions in Psychological Science, 15,* 167–171.

Huhn, M., Tardy, M., Spineli, L. M., Kissling, W., Förstl, H., Pitschel-Walz, G., . . . Leucht, S. (2014). Efficacy of pharmacotherapy and psychotherapy for adult psychiatric disorders: A systematic overview of meta-analyses. *JAMA Psychiatry, 71,* 706–715. doi: 10.1001/jamapsychiatry.2014.112

Hull, C. L. (1943). *Principles of behavior*. New York: Appleton-Century-Crofts.

Hull, C. L. (1952). *A behavior system*. New Haven, CT: Yale University Press.

Hummingbirds: Small brains, long memories. (2006, March 6). Retrieved from www.msnbc.msn.com /id/11697039/

Hunt, M. (1993). *The story of psychology*. New York: Anchor Books.

Hunt, R. R., & Worthen, J. B. (Eds.). (2006). *Distinctiveness and memory*. New York: Oxford University Press.

Huntjens, R. J. C., Peters, M. L., Postma, A., Woertman, L., Effting, M., & van der Hart, O. (2005). Transfer of newly acquired stimulus valence between identities in dissociative identity disorder (DID). *Behaviour Research and Therapy, 43*, 243–255.

Hutchinson, J. G., & Williams, P. G. (2007). Neuroticism, daily hassles, and depressive symptoms: An examination of moderating and mediating effects. *Personality and Individual Differences, 42*, 1367–1378.

Hutchison, R. M., Chidiac, P., & Leung, L. S. (2009). Hippocampal long-term potentiation is enhanced in urethane-anesthetized RGS2 knockout mice. *Hippocampus, 19*, 687–691.

Hwang, W.-C. (2006). The psychotherapy adaptation and modification framework: Application to Asian Americans. *American Psychologist, 61*, 702–715.

Hwang, W.-C. (2011). Cultural adaptations: A complex interplay between clinical and cultural issues. *Clinical Psychology: Science and Practice, 18*, 238–241. doi: 10.1111/j.1468-2850.2011.01255

Hyde, J. S. (2005). The genetics of sexual orientation. In J. S. Hyde (Ed.), *Biological substrates of human sexuality* (pp. 9–20). Washington, D.C.: American Psychological Association.

Hyde, J. S. (2014). Gender similarities and differences. *Annual Review of Psychology, 65*, 373–398. doi: 10.1146/annurev-psych-010213-115057

Hyde, J. S., Mezulis, A. H., & Abramson, L. Y. (2008). The ABCs of depression: Integrating affective, biological, and cognitive models to explain the emergence of the gender difference in depression. *Psychological Review, 115*, 291–313.

Hyman, R. (2010). Meta-analysis that conceals more than it reveals: Comment on Storm et al. (2010). *Psychological Bulletin, 136*, 486–490. doi: 10.1037/a001967

Inglehart, R., Foa, F., Peterson, C., & Welzel, C. (2008). Development, freedom, and rising happiness: A global perspective (1981–2007). *Perspectives on Psychological Science, 3*, 264–285. doi: 10.1111/j.1745-6924.2008.00078.x

Instant recall. (2000, February 14). *Newsweek*, p. 8.

Institute of Medicine (2015). *Cognitive aging: Progress in understanding and opportunities for action. Report Brief, April 2015*. Retrieved from http://www. iom.edu/~/media/Files/Report%20Files/2015 /Cognitive_aging/Cognitive%20Aging%20report %20brief.pdf

Ip, G. W., Chiu, C.-Y., & Wan, C. (2006). Birds of a feather and birds flocking together: Physical versus behavioral cues may lead to trait- versus goal-based group perception. *Journal of Personality and Social Psychology, 90*, 368–381.

Ironson, G., O'Cleirigh, C., Leserman, J., Stuetzle, R., Fordiani, J., Fletcher, M.A., . . . Schneiderman, N. (2013). Gender-specific effects of an augmented written emotional disclosure intervention on posttraumatic, depressive, and HIV-disease-related outcomes: A randomized, controlled trial. *Journal of Consulting and Clinical Psychology, 81*, 284–298. doi: 10.1037/a0030814

Irwin, M. R. (2015). Why sleep is important for health: A psychoneuroimmunology perspective. *Annual Review of Psychology, 66*, 143–172. doi: 10.1146/annurev-psych-010213-115205

Isaacowitz, D. M., & Blanchard-Fields, F. (2012). Linking process and outcome in the study of emotion and aging. *Perspectives on Psychological Science, 7*, 3–17. doi: 10.1177/1745691611424750

Isaacson, W. (2007). *Einstein: His life and universe*. New York: Simon & Schuster.

Islam, L., Franzinia, A., Messina, G., Scaroneb, S., & Gambinib, O. (2015). Deep brain stimulation of the nucleus accumbens and bed nucleus of stria terminalis for obsessive-compulsive disorder: A case series. *World Neurosurgery, 83*, 657–663. doi: 10.1016/j.wneu.2014.12.024

Israel, S., Moffitt, T. E., Belsky, D. W., Hancox, R. J., Poulton, R., Roberts, B., . . . Caspi, A. (2014). Translating personality psychology to help personalize preventive medicine for young adult patients. *Journal of Personality and Social Psychology, 106*, 484–498. doi: 10.1037/a0035687

Jacob, J. (2015). IOM Report on Cognitive Aging. *Journal of the American Medical Association, 313*, 2415. doi: 10.1001/jama.2015.6577

Jacobs, G. H., & Nathans, J. (2009, March). Color vision: How our eyes reflect primate evolution. *Scientific American*. Retrieved from www.sciam.com /article.cfm?id=evolution -of-primate-color-vision

Jaffe, E. (2013, September). The link between personality and immunity. *APS Observer, 26*, 27–30.

Jaffee, S., & Hyde, J. S. (2000). Gender differences in moral orientation: A meta-analysis. *Psychological Bulletin, 126*, 703–726.

Jahnke, C. J., & Nowaczyk, R. H. (1998). *Cognition*. Upper Saddle River, NJ: Prentice Hall.

James, L. E., & MacKay, D. G. (2001). H.M., word knowledge and aging: Support for a new theory of long-term retrograde amnesia. *Psychological Science, 12*, 485–492.

James, P. A., Oparil, S., Carter, B. L., Cushman, W. C., Dennison-Himmelfarb, C., Handler, J., . . . Ortiz, E. (2014). 2014 evidence-based guideline for the management of high blood pressure in adults: Report from the panel members appointed to the Eighth Joint National Committee. *Journal of the American Medical Association, 31*, 507–520. doi: 10.1001/jama.2013.284427.

James, S. D. (2015, May 17). Generation deaf: Doctors warn of dangers of ear buds. *NBCnews.com*. Retrieved from http://www.nbcnews.com/health/health-news/generation-deaf-doctors-warn-dangers-ear-buds-n360041

James, W. (1890/1970). *The principles of psychology* (Vol. 1). New York: Holt.

Jan, J. E., Reiter, R. J., Wasdell, M. B., & Bax, M. (2009). The role of the thalamus in sleep, pineal melatonin production, and circadian rhythm sleep disorders. *Journal of Pineal Research, 46*, 1–7. doi: 10.1111/j.1600-079X.2008.00628

Janis, I. L. (1997). Groupthink. In R. P. Vecchio (Ed.), *Leadership: Understanding the dynamics of power and influence in organizations* (pp. 163–176). Notre Dame, IN: University of Notre Dame Press.

Jannini, E. A., Blanchard, R., Camperio-Ciani, A., & Bancroft, J. (2010). Male homosexuality: Nature or culture. *Journal of Sexual Medicine, 7*, 3245–3253.

Järnefelt, H. Sallinen, M., Luukkonen, R., Kajastec, S., Savolainen, A., & Hublina, C. (2014). Cognitive behavioral therapy for chronic insomnia in occupational health services: Analyses of outcomes up to 24 months post-treatment. *Behaviour Research and Therapy, 56*, 16–21. doi: org/10.1016/j.brat.2014.02.007

Javier, R. (2010). Acculturation and changing roles. In J. S. Nevid & S. A. Rathus (Eds.), *Psychology and the challenges of life: Adjustment and growth* (p. 336). Hoboken, NJ: Wiley.

Jay, M. S. (2006). The tempo of puberty. *The Journal of Pediatrics, 148*, 732–733.

Jayasekara, H., MacInnis, R. J., Room, R., & English, D. R. (2015). Long-term alcohol consumption and breast, upper aero-digestive tract and colorectal cancer risk: A systematic review and meta-analysis. *Alcohol and Alcoholism, 51*, 315–330. doi: 10.1093/alcalc/agv110

Jefferson, D. J. (2005, August 8). America's most dangerous drug. *Newsweek*, pp. 41–48.

Jensen, M. P. (2008). The neurophysiology of pain perception and hypnotic analgesia: Implications for clinical practice. *The American Journal of Clinical Hypnosis, 25*, 123–148.

Jeon, H. J., Park, J.-I., Fava, M., Mischoulon, D., Sohn, J. H., Seong, S., . . . Choe, M. J. (2014). Feelings of worthlessness, traumatic experience, and their comorbidity in relation to lifetime suicide attempt in community adults with major depressive disorder. *Journal of Affective Disorders, 166*, 206–212.

Jetten, J., & Hornsey, M. J. (2015). Deviance and dissent in groups. *Annual Review of Psychology, 65*, 461–485. doi: 10.1146/annurev-psych-010213-115151

Jha, P., & Peto, R. (2014). Global effects of smoking, of quitting, and of taxing tobacco. *New England Journal of Medicine, 370*, 60–68. doi: 10.1056/NEJMra1308383

Jha, P., Ramasundarahettige, C., Landsman, V., Rostron, B., Thun, M., Anderson, R. N., McAfee, T., & Peto, R. (2013). 21st-century hazards of smoking and benefits of cessation in the United States. *New England Journal of Medicine, 368*, 341–350. doi: 10.1056/NEJMsa1211128

Ji, D., & Wilson, M. A. (2007). Coordinated memory replay in the visual cortex and hippocampus during sleep. *Nature Neuroscience, 10*, 100–107.

Joe, S., Baser, E., Breeden, G., Neighbors, H. W., & Jackson, J. S. (2006). Prevalence of and risk factors for lifetime suicide attempts among Blacks in the United States. *Journal of the American Medical Association, 296*, 2112–2123.

Joffe, A. (2015, May 27). Preventing youth suicide. *NEJM Journal Watch*. Retrieved from http://www .jwatch.org/na37964/2015/05/27/preventing-youth -suicide?query=etoc_jwpeds

Johansson, A., Sundbom, E., Höjerback, T., & Bodlund, O. (2010). A five-year follow-up study of Swedish adults with gender identity disorder. *Archives of Sexual Behavior, 39*, 1429–1437. doi: 10.1007/s10508-009-9551-1

Johnson, C. K. (2010). 1 in 5 U.S. teens has hearing loss, new study says. Retrieved from www.msnbc.msn.com /id/38742752/ns/health-kids_and_parenting/

Johnson, D. A., & Rubin, S. (2011). Effectiveness of interactive computer-based instruction: A review of studies published between 1995 and 2007. *Journal of Organizational Behavior Management, 31,* 55–94, doi: 10.1080/01608061.2010.541821

Johnson, D. C., Thom, N. J., Stanley, E. A., Haase, L., Simmons, A. N., Shih, P. B., . . . Paulus, M. P. (2014). Modifying resilience mechanisms in at-risk individuals: A controlled study of mindfulness training in Marines preparing for deployment. *American Journal of Psychiatry, 171,* 844–853. doi: 10.1176/appi. ajp.2014.13040502

Johnson, D. F. (2000). Cultivating the field of psychology: Psychological journals at the turn of the century and beyond. *American Psychologist, 55,* 1144–1147.

Johnson, J. G., Cohen, P., Chen, H., Kasen, S., & Brook, J. S. (2006). Parenting behaviors associated with risk for offspring personality disorder during adulthood. *Archives of General Psychiatry, 63,* 579–587.

Johnson, W., Turkheimer, E., Gottesman, I. I., & Bouchard, T. J., Jr. (2009). Beyond heritability: Twin studies in behavioral research. *Current Directions in Psychological Science, 18,* 217–220.

Johnston, L. D., O'Malley, P. M., Bachman, J. G., & Schulenberg, J. E. (2010a). *Marijuana use is rising; ecstasy use is beginning to rise; and alcohol use is declining among U.S. Teens.* University of Michigan News Service: Ann Arbor, MI. Retrieved from www .monitoringthefuture.org

Johnston, L D., O'Malley, P. M., Bachman, J. G., & Schulenberg, J. E. (2010b). *Monitoring the Future, National Survey Results on Drug Use: Overview of Key Findings, 2009* (NIH Publication No. 10-7583). Bethesda, MD: National Institute on Drug Abuse, May 2010.

Johnston, L. D., O'Malley, P. M., Bachman, J. G., & Schulenberg, J. E. (2012a). *Monitoring the Future national survey results on drug use, 1975–2011. Volume I: Secondary school students.* Ann Arbor: Institute for Social Research, The University of Michigan.

Johnston, L. D., O'Malley, P. M., Bachman, J. G., & Schulenberg, J. E. (2012b, December 19). *The rise in teen marijuana use stalls, synthetic marijuana use levels, and use of 'bath salts' is very low.* University of Michigan News Service: Ann Arbor, MI. Retrieved from www.monitoringthefuture.org

Jokela, M., Batty, G. D., Nyberg, S. T., Virtanen, M., Nabi, H., Singh-Manoux, A., . . . Kivimäki M. (2013). Personality and all-cause mortality: Individual-participant meta-analysis of 3,947 deaths in 76,150 adults. *American Journal of Epidemiology, 178,* 667–675. doi: 10.1093/aje/kwt170.

Jonas, D. E., Amick, H. R., Feltner, C., Bobashev, G., Thomas, K., Wines, R., . . . Garbutt, J. C. (2014). Pharmacotherapy for adults with alcohol use disorders in outpatient settings: A systematic review and meta-analysis. *Journal of the American Medical Association, 311,* 1889–1900. doi: 10.1001/jama.2014.3628.

Jones, H. J., Stergiakouli, E., Tansey, K. E., Hubbard, L., Heron, J., Cannon, M., . . . Zammit, S. (2016). Phenotypic manifestation of genetic risk for schizophrenia during adolescence in the general population. *JAMA Psychiatry, 73,* 221–228. doi: 10.1001/jamapsychiatry.2015.3058

Jones, J. R., Tackenberg, M. C., & McMahon, D. G. (2015). Manipulating circadian clock neuron firing rate resets molecular circadian rhythms and behavior. *Nature Neuroscience, 18,* 373–375. doi: 10.1038/nn.3937

Jones, J. T., Pelham, B. W., Carvallo, M., & Mirenberg, M. C. (2004). How do I love thee? Let me count the Js: Implicit egotism and interpersonal attraction. *Journal of Personality and Social Psychology, 87,* 665–683.

Jorgensen, G. (2006). Kohlberg and Gilligan: Duet or duel? *Journal of Moral Education, 35,* 179–196.

Joseph, D. L., Jin, J., Newman, D. A., & O'Boyle, E. H. (2015). Why does self-reported emotional intelligence predict job performance? A meta-analytic investigation of mixed EI. *Journal of Applied Psychology, 100,* 298–342. doi: http://dx.doi.org/10.1037/a0037681

Joyce, N., & Baker, D. B. (2008, July/August). The early days of sport psychology. *Monitor on Psychology, 39*(7), 28–29.

Judge, T. A., & Cable, D. M. (2004). Income: Preliminary test of a theoretical model. *Journal of Applied Psychology, 89,* 428–441.

Junco, R. (2015). Student class standing, Facebook use, and academic performance. *Journal of Applied Developmental Psychology, 36,* 18–29.

Kagan, J. (1997). Biology and the child. In W. Damon (Editor-in-Chief) & N. Eisenberg (Vol. Ed.), *Handbook of child psychology: Social, emotional, and personality development* (Vol. 3, 5th ed., pp. 177–236). New York: Wiley.

Kahneman, D., & Deaton, A. (2010). High income improves evaluation of life but not emotional well-being. *Proceedings of the National Academy of Sciences, 107,* 16489–16493.

Kahneman, D., & Frederick, S. (2005). A model of heuristic judgment. In K. J. Holyoak & R. G. Morrison (Eds.), *The Cambridge handbook of thinking and reasoning* (pp. 267–293). Cambridge, U.K.: Cambridge University Press.

Kahneman, D., & Klein, G. (2009). Conditions for intuitive expertise: A failure to disagree. *The American Psychologist, 64*(6), 515–526.

Kahneman, D., Krueger, A. B., Schkade, D., Schwarz, N., & Stone, A. A. (2006). Would you be happier if you were richer? A focusing illusion. *Science, 312,* 1908–1910.

Kaiser Family Foundation (2012). HIV/AIDS: The state of the epidemic after 3 decades. *Journal of the American Medical Association, 308,* 330. doi: 10.1001/jama.2012.8700

Kaiser, R. H., Andrews-Hanna, J. R., Wager, T. D., & Pizzagalli, D. A. (2015). Large-scale network dysfunction in major depressive disorder: A meta-analysis of resting-state functional connectivity. *JAMA Psychiatry, 72,* 603–611. doi: 10.1001/jamapsychiatry.2015.0071

Kalb, C. (2001, August 20). Overexposed. *Newsweek,* pp. 34–38.

Kaldo, V., Jernelöv, S., Blom, K., Ljótsson, B., Brodin, M., Jörgensen, M., Kraepelien, M., . . . Lindefors, N. (2015). Guided internet cognitive behavioral therapy for insomnia compared to a control treatment: A randomized trial. *Behaviour Research and Therapy, 71,* 90–100. doi: 10.1016/j.brat.2015.06.001.

Kalibatseva, Z., & Leong, F. T. L. (2011). Depression among Asian Americans: Review and recommendations. *Depression Research and Treatment.* Retrieved from www.hindawi .com/journals/drt/2011/320902/

Kaller, C, P., Loosli, S. V., Rahm, B., Gössel, A., Schieting, S., Hornig, T.,... Katzev, M. (2014). Working memory in schizophrenia: Behavioral and neural evidence for reduced susceptibility to item-specific proactive interference. *Biological Psychiatry, 76,*

486–494. doi: 10.1016/j.biopsych.2014.03.012. Epub 2014, March 19.

Kalueff, A. V., & Nutt, D. J. (2006). Role of GABA in anxiety and depression. *Depression and Anxiety, 24,* 495–517.

Kam-Hansen, S., Jakubowski, M., Kelley, J. M., Kirsch, I., Hoaglin, D. C., Kaptchuk, T. J., . . . Burstein, R. (2014). Altered placebo and drug labeling changes the outcome of episodic migraine attacks. *Science Translational Medicine, 8,* 218ra5.

Kandel, E. R. (1995). Cellular mechanisms of learning and memory: Synaptic integration. In E. R. Kandel, J. H. Schwartz, & T. M. Jessel (Eds.), *Essentials of neural science and behavior.* Norwalk, CT: Appleton & Lange.

Kandel, E. R., & Hawkins, R. D. (1993). The biological basis of learning and individuality. In *Mind and brain: Readings from Scientific American Magazine* (pp. 40–53). New York: W. H. Freeman & Co.

Kantowitz, B. H., Roediger, H. L. III, & Elmes, D. G. (2009). *Experimental psychology* (9th ed.). Belmont, CA: Cengage Learning.

Kantrowitz, B., & Wingert, P. (1999, October 18). The truth about teens. *Newsweek,* pp. 62–72.

Kaplan, P. S. (2000). *A child's odyssey: Child and adolescent development* (3rd ed.). Belmont, CA: Wadsworth.

Kaufman, A. S., & Lichtenberger, E. O. (2006). *Assessing adolescent and adult intelligence* (3rd ed.). Hoboken, NJ: Wiley.

Kaufman, C. E., Beals, J., Croy, C., Jiang, L., Novins, D. K., & the AI-SUPERPFP Team Aurora CO US. (2013). Multilevel context of depression in two American Indian tribes. *Journal of Consulting and Clinical Psychology, 81,* 1040–1051. doi: 10.1037/a0034342

Kaye, W. (2009). Eating disorders: Hope despite mortal risk. *American Journal of Psychiatry, 166,* 139–1311. doi: 10.1176/appi.ajp.2009.09101424

Kazlauskaite, A., Kondapalli, C., Gourlay, R., Campbell, D., Ritorto, M. S., Hofmann, K.,...Muqit, M. (2014). Parkin is activated by PINK1-dependent phosphorylation of ubiquitin at Serine65. *Biochemical Journal, 460,* 127–139. doi: 10.1042/BJ20140334

Kean, S. (2014, May 3). Beyond the damaged brain. *The New York Times Sunday Review.* Retrieved from www.nytimes.com

Keaney, J., Walsh, D. M., O'Malley, T., Hudson, N., Crosbie, D. E., Loftus, T.,... Campbell, M. (2015). Autoregulated paracellular clearance of amyloid-β across the blood-brain barrier. *Science Advances, 8,* e1500472. doi: 10.1126/sciadv.1500472

Keating, C. F., Randall, D., Kendrick, T., & Gutshall, K. (2003). Do babyfaced adults receive more help? The (cross-cultural) case of the lost resume. *Journal of Nonverbal Behavior, 27,* 89–109.

Keefe, J. R., McCarthy, K. S., Dinger, U., Zilcha-Mano, S., & Barber, J. P. (2014). A meta-analytic review of psychodynamic therapies for anxiety disorders. *Clinical Psychology Review, 34,* 309–323. doi: 10.1016/j.cpr.2014.03.004.

Keller, J. J., Liang, Y., & Lin, H. (2012). Association between multiple sclerosis and erectile dysfunction: A nationwide case-control study. *Journal of Sexual Medicine.* doi: 10.1111/j.1743-6109.2012.02746.x.

Keller, M. C., Fredrickson, B. L., Ybarra, O., Côté, S., Johnson, K., Mikels, J.,... Wager, T. (2005). A warm heart and a clear head: The contingent effects of weather on mood and cognition. *Psychological Science, 16*, 724–731.

Keller, S. N., & Brown, J. D. (2002). Media interventions to promote responsible sexual behavior. *Journal of Sex Research, 39*, 1–6.

Kelley, K. J. (2014, December 16). Young at heart: Feeling younger than your actual age linked to lower mortality. *NEJM Journal Watch*. Retrieved from http://www.jwatch.org/fw109641/2014/12/16/young-heart-feeling-younger-your-actual-age-linked-lower?query=pfw

Kelsoe, J. R. (2010). A gene for impulsivity. *Nature, 468*, 1049–1050 . doi: 10.1038/4681049a

Kendler, K. S. (2005a). Psychiatric genetics: A methodologic critique. *American Journal of Psychiatry, 162*, 3–11.

Kendler, K. S. (2005b). "A gene for . . .": The nature of gene action in psychiatric disorders. *American Journal of Psychiatry, 162*, 1243–1252.

Kendler, K. S., & Gardner, C. O. (2010). Dependent stressful life events and prior depressive episodes in the prediction of major depression: The problem of causal inference in psychiatric epidemiology. *Archives of General Psychiatry, 67*, 1120–1127. doi: 10.1001/archgenpsychiatry.2010.136

Kendler, K. S., Schmitt, E., Aggen, S. H., & Prescott, C. A. (2008). Genetic and environmental influences on alcohol, caffeine, cannabis, and nicotine use from early adolescence to middle adulthood. *Archives of General Psychiatry, 65*, 674–682. Retrieved from http://archpsyc.ama-assn.org /cgi/content /abstract/65/6/674

Kendler, K. S., Sundquist, K., Ohlsson, H., Palmér, K., Maes, H., Winkleby, M. A., & Sundquist, J. (2012). Genetic and familial environmental influences on the risk for drug abuse: A National Swedish Adoption Study. *Archives of General Psychiatry, 69*, 690–697. doi: 10.1001/archgenpsychiatry.2011.2112

Kendler, K. S., Thornton, L. M., Gilman, S. E., & Kessler, R. C. (2000). Sexual orientation in a U.S. national sample of twin and nontwin sibling pairs. *American Journal of Psychiatry, 157*, 1843–1846.

Kendzerska, T., Gershon, A. S., Hawker, G., Tomlinson, G., & Leung. R. S. (2014). Obstructive sleep apnea and incident diabetes: A historical cohort study. *American Journal of Respiratory and Critical Care Medicine, 190*, 218–225. doi: 10.1164 /rccm.201312-2209OC

Kennedy, P. (2011, September 14). The cyborg in us all. *The New York Times Magazine*, pp. 24–26.

Kennedy, S. H., Milev, R., Giacobbe, P., Ramasubbu, R., Lam, R. W., Parikh, S. V., . . . Canadian Network for Mood and Anxiety Treatments (CANMAT). (2009). Canadian Network for Mood and Anxiety Treatments (CANMAT) clinical guidelines for the management of major depressive disorder in adults: IV. Neurostimulation therapies. *Journal of Affective Disorders, 117*, S44–S53. doi: 10.1111/j.1399-5618.2006.00432.x

Kennedy, S. H., Young, A. H., & Blier, P. (2011). Strategies to achieve clinical effectiveness: Refining existing therapies and pursuing emerging targets. *Journal of Affective Disorders, 132*, S21–S28. doi: 10.1016/j.jad.2011.03.048

Kenrick, D. T., Griskevicius, V., Neuberg, S. L., & Schaller, M. (2010). Renovating the pyramid of needs: Contemporary extensions built upon ancient foundations. *Perspectives on Psychological Science, 5*, 292–314. doi: 10.1177/1745691610369469

Kerling, A., Tegtbur,U., Gützlaff, E., Kück, M., Borchert, L., Ates, Z., . . . Kahl, K. G. (2015). Effects of adjunctive exercise on physiological and psychological parameters in depression: A randomized pilot trial. *Journal of Affective Disorders, 177*, 1–6.

Kern, A., Albarran-Zeckler, R., Walsh, H. E., & Smith, R. G. (2012). Apo-ghrelin receptor forms heteromers with DRD2 in hypothalamic neurons and is essential for anorexigenic effects of DRD2 agonism. *Neuron, 73*, 317–332. doi: 10.1016/j.neuron.2011.10.038

Kernberg, O. F. (1975). *Borderline conditions and pathological narcissism*. New York: Jason Aronson.

Kernberg, O. F., & Michels, R. (2009). Borderline personality disorder. *American Journal of Psychiatry, 166*, 505–508.

Kerns, K. A., & Richardson, R. A. (2005). *Attachment in middle childhood*. New York: Guilford.

Kerr, N. L., & Tindale, R. S. (2004). Group performance and decision making. *Annual Review of Psychology, 55*, 623–655.

Kesebir, P., & Diener, E. (2008). In pursuit of happiness: Empirical answers to philosophical questions. *Perspectives on Psychological Science, 3*, 117–125. doi: 10.1111/j.1745-6916.2008.00069.x

Keshavan, M. S., Nasrallah, H. A., & Tandon, R. (2011). Schizophrenia, "Just the Facts" 6. Moving ahead with the schizophrenia concept: From the elephant to the mouse. *Schizophrenia Research, 127*, 3–13.

Kessler, R. C., Berglund, P. A., Demler, O., Jin, R., & Walters, E. E. (2005). Lifetime prevalence and age-of-onset distributions of DSM-IV disorders in the National Comorbidity Survey Replication (NCS-R). *Archives of General Psychiatry, 62*, 593–602.

Kessler, R. C., Chiu, W. T., Demler, O., & Walters, E. E. (2005). Prevalence, severity, and comorbidity of 12-month DSM-IV disorders in the National Comorbidity Survey Replication. *Archives of General Psychiatry, 62*, 617–627.

Kessler, R. C., McGonagle, K. A., Zhao, S., & Nelson, C. B. (1994). Lifetime and 12-month prevalence of DSM-III-R psychiatric disorders in the United States: Results from the National Comorbidity Survey. *Archives of General Psychiatry, 51*, 8–19.

Keyes, K. M., Maslowsky, J., Hamilton, A., & Schulenberg, J. (2015). The great sleep recession: Changes in sleep duration among US adolescents, 1991–2012. *Pediatrics, 135*, 460–468. doi: 10.1542/peds.2014-2707

Khaw, K. T., Wareham, N., Bingham, S., Welch, A., Luben, R., & Day, N. (2008). Combined impact of health behaviours and mortality in men and women: The EPIC-Norfolk Prospective Population study. *PLOS Med, 5*(1), e12. Retrieved from http://medicine.plosjournals.org/perlserv/?request=get-document&doi=10.1371/journal.pmed.0050012

Khoury, B., Sharma, M., Rush, S. E., & Fournier, C. (2015). Mindfulness-based stress reduction for healthy individuals: A meta-analysis. *Journal of Psychosomatic Research, 78*, 519–528. doi: 10.1016/j.jpsychores.2015.03.009

Kiecolt-Glaser, J. K., Bane, C., Glaser, R., & Malarkey, W. B. (2003). Love, marriage, and divorce: Newlyweds' stress hormones foreshadow relationship changes. *Journal of Consulting and Clinical Psychology, 71*, 176–188.

Kiecolt-Glaser, J. K., Marucha, P. T., Atkinson, C., & Glaser, R. (2001). Hypnosis as a modulator of cellular immune dysregulation during acute stress. *Journal of Consulting and Clinical Psychology, 69*, 674–682.

Kiesner, J. (2009). Physical characteristics of the menstrual cycle and premenstrual depressive symptoms. *Psychological Science, 20*, 763–770.

Kihlstrom, J. F. (2005). Is hypnosis an altered state of consciousness or what? *Contemporary Hypnosis, 22*, 34–38.

Kihlstrom, J. F. (2015). Dynamic versus cognitive unconscious. In *The encyclopedia of clinical psychology*. Published online by John Wiley & Sons. doi: 10.1002/9781118625392.wbecp275En

Kilgore, K., Snyder, J., & Lentz, C. (2000). The contribution of parental discipline, parental monitoring, and school risk to early-onset conduct problems in African American boys and girls. *Developmental Psychology, 36*, 835–845.

Killingsworth, M., A, & Gilbert, D. T. (2010). A wandering mind is an unhappy mind. *Science, 330*, 932. doi: 10.1126 /science.1192439

Kim, H. S., & Sherman, D. K. (2007). "Express yourself": Culture and the effect of self expression on choice. *Journal of Personality and Social Psychology, 92*, 1–11.

Kim, J. J., & Jung, M. W. (2006). Neural circuits and mechanisms involved in Pavlovian fear conditioning: A critical review. *Neuroscience and Biobehavioral Reviews, 30*, 188–202.

Kim, K. H. (2005). Can only intelligent people be creative? A meta-analysis. *Journal of Secondary Gifted Education, 16*, 57–66.

King, B. H., Toth, K. E., Hodapp, R. M., & Dykens, E. M. (2009). Intellectual disability. In B. J. Sadock, V. A. Sadock, & P. Ruiz (Eds.), *Comprehensive textbook of psychiatry* (9th ed.) (pp. 3444–3474). Philadelphia: Lippincott Williams & Wilkins.

King, S., St-Hilaire, A., & Heidkamp, D. (2010). Prenatal factors in schizophrenia. *Current Directions in Psychological Science, 19*, 209–213. doi: 10.1177/0963721410378360

Kirkbride, J. B., Jones, P. B., Ullrich, S., & Coid, J. W. (2012). Social deprivation, inequality, and the neighborhood-level incidence of psychotic syndromes in East London. *Schizophrenia Bulletin*, in press. doi: 10.1093/schbul /sbs151

Kirp, D. L. (2006, July 23). After the bell curve. *The New York Times Magazine*, pp. 5–16.

Kirsch, I. (1996). Hypnotic enhancement of cognitive-behavioral weight loss treatments: Another meta-reanalysis. *Journal of Consulting and Clinical Psychology, 64*, 517–519.

Kirsch, I., & Lynn, S. J. (1995). Altered state of hypnosis: Changes in the theoretical landscape. *American Psychologist, 50*(10), 846–858.

Kish, A. M., & Newcombe, P. A. (2015). "Smacking never hurt me!": Identifying myths surrounding the use of corporal punishment. *Personality and Individual Differences, 87*, 121–129. doi: 10.1016/j.paid.2015.07.035

Kisilevsky, B. S., Hains, S. M. J., Lee, K., Xie, X., Huang, H., Ye, H.-H., . . . Wang, Z. (2003). Effects of experience on fetal voice recognition. *Psychological Science, 14*, 220–224.

Kistemaker, D. A., Faber, H., & Beek, P. J. (2009). Catching fly balls: A simulation study of the

Chapman strategy. *Human Movement Science, 28,* 236–249. doi: 10.1016 /j.humov.2008.11.001

Kitayama, S., Duffy, S., Kawamura, T., & Larsen, J. T. (2003). Perceiving an object and its context in different cultures: A cultural look at new look. *Psychological Science, 14,* 201–206.

Kitayama, S., Park, J., Boylan, J. M., Miyamoto, Y., Levine, C. S., Markus, H. R., . . . Ryff, C. D. (2015). Expression of anger and ill health in two cultures: An examination of inflammation and cardiovascular risk. *Psychological Science, 26,* 211–220. doi: 10.1177/0956797614561268

Kivlighan III, D. M., Goldberg, S. B., Abbas, M., Pace, B. T., Yulish, N. E., Thomas, J. G., . . . Wampold, B. E. (2015). The enduring effects of psychodynamic treatments vis-à-vis alternative treatments: A multilevel longitudinal meta-analysis. *Clinical Psychology Review, 40,* 1–14. doi: 10.1016/j.cpr.2015.05.003

Klass, P. (2011, March 8). On the left hand, answers aren't easy. *The New York Times,* pp. D1, D6.

Klauer, S. G., Guo, F., Simons-Morton, B. G., Ouimet, M. C., Lee, S. E., & Dingus, T. A. (2014). Distracted driving and risk of road crashes among novice and experienced drivers. *New England Journal of Medicine, 370,* 54–59. doi: 10.1056/NEJMsa1204142

Klauser, P., Fornito, A., Lorenzetti, V., Davey, C. G., Dwyer, D. B., Allen, N. B., . . . Yücel, M. (2014). Cortico-limbic network abnormalities in individuals with current and past major depressive disorder. *Journal of Affective Disorders, 173,* 45–52. doi: 10.1016/j.jad.2014.10.041

Kleiman, M. A. R., Caulkins, J. P., & Hawken, A. (2012, April 21–22). Rethinking the war on drugs. *The Wall Street Journal,* p. C1.

Kleinman, A. (1987). Anthropology and psychiatry: The role of culture in cross-cultural research on illness. *British Journal of Psychiatry, 151,* 447–454.

Kleinspehn-Ammerlahn, A., Riediger, M., Schmiedek, F., von Oertzen, Timo, T., Li, S.-C., . . . Lindenberger, U. (2011). Dyadic drumming across the lifespan reveals a zone of proximal development in children. *Developmental Psychology, 47,* 632–644. doi: 10.1037/a0021818

Klimstra, T. A., Frijns, T., Keijsers, L., Denissen, J. A., Raaijmakers, Q. A. W., van Aken, M. A. G., . . . Meeus, W. H. J. (2011). Come rain or come shine: Individual differences in how weather affects mood. *Emotion, 11,* 1495–1499. doi: 10.1037/a0024649

Kluger, J. (2003, October 26). Medicating young minds. *Time Magazine.* Retrieved from www.time.com

Kluger, J., & Masters, C. (2006, August 28). How to spot a liar. *Time Magazine,* pp. 46–48.

Knoblauch, S. (2009). From self psychology to selves in relationship: A radical process of micro and macro expansion in conceptual experience. In W. Coburn & N. Vanderhide (Eds.), *Self and systems, Annals of the New York Academy of Sciences, 1159,* 262–278.

Knoedler, A. J., Hellwig, K. A., & Neath, I. (1999). The shift from recency to primacy with increasing delay. *Journal of Experimental Psychology: Learning, Memory, and Cognition, 25,* 474–487.

Knoll, L. J., Magis-Weinberg, L., Speekenbrink, M., & Blakemore, S.-J. (2015). Social influence on risk perception during adolescence. *Psychological Science, 26,* 583–592. doi: 10.1177/0956797615569578

Knutson, B., Rick, S., Wimmer, G. E., Prelec, D., & Loewenstein, G. (2007). Neural predictors of purchases. *Neuron, 53,* 147–156.

Kobasa, S. C. (1979). Stressful life events, personality, and health: An inquiry into hardiness. *Journal of Personality and Social Psychology, 37,* 1–11.

Kobasa, S. C., Maddi, S. R., & Kahn, S. (1982). Hardiness and health: A prospective study. *Journal of Personality and Social Psychology, 42,* 168–177.

Kodl, M. M., & Mermelstein, R. (2004). Beyond modeling: Parenting practices, parental smoking history, and adolescent cigarette smoking. *Addictive Behaviors, 29,* 17–32.

Koegelenberg, C. F. N., Noor, F., Bateman, E. D., van Zyl-Smit, R. N., Bruning, A., O'Brien, J. A., . . . Irusen, E. M. (2014). Efficacy of varenicline combined with nicotine replacement therapy vs varenicline alone for smoking cessation: A randomized clinical trial. *Journal of the American Medical Association, 312,* 155. doi: http://dx.doi.org/10.1001 /jama.2014.7195

Koenders, M. A., Giltay, E. J., Spijker, A. T., Hoencamp, E., Spinhoven, P., & Elzinga, B. M. (2014). Stressful life events in bipolar I and II disorder: Cause or consequence of mood symptoms? *Journal of Affective Disorders, 161,* 55–64. doi: 10.1016/j.jad.2014.02.036

Koh, H. K., & Sebelius, K. G. (2012). Ending the tobacco epidemic. *Journal of the American Medical Association, 308,* 767–768. doi: 10.1001/jama.2012.9741

Kohlberg, L. (1969). *Stages in the development of moral thought and action.* New York: Holt, Rinehart and Winston.

Kohlberg, L. (1981). *The philosophy of moral development.* San Francisco: Harper & Row.

Köhler, W. (1927). *The mentality of apes.* New York: Harcourt Brace.

Koko the gorilla calls for the dentist. (2004, August 8). *Cable News Network.* Retrieved from www.cnn.com

Koltko-Rivera, M. E. (2006). Rediscovering the later version of Maslow's hierarchy of needs: Self-transcendence and opportunities for theory, research, and unification. *Review of General Psychology, 10,* 302–317.

Komaroff, A. L. (2004, March 25). Sleep improves insight. *Journal Watch Psychiatry.* Retrieved from http://psychiatry .jwatch.org/cgi/content /full/2004/325/10?qetoc

Koolhaas, J. M., de Boer, S. F., & Buwalda, B. (2006). Stress and adaptation: Toward ecologically relevant animal models. *Current Directions in Psychological Science, 15,* 109–112.

Korn, M. (2013, May 2). B-schools know how you think, but how do you feel? *The Wall Street Journal,* p. B1.

Kosinski, M., Matz, S. C, Gosling, S. D., Popov, V., & Stillwell, D. (2016, March). Facebook as a research tool. *Monitor on Psychology, 47,* 70–75.

Kosslyn, S. M., Thompson, W. L., Costantini-Ferrando, M. F., Alpert, N. M., & Spiegel, D. (2000). Hypnotic visual illusion alters color processing in the brain. *American Journal of Psychiatry, 157,* 1279–1284.

Koster, E. H. W., De Lissnyder, E., Derakshan, N., & De Raedt, R. (2011). Understanding depressive rumination from a cognitive science perspective: The impaired disengagement hypothesis. *Clinical Psychology Review, 31,* 138–145. doi: 10.1016/j.cpr.2010.08.005

Kounios, J., & Beeman, M. (2009). The Aha! moment: The cognitive neuroscience of insight. *Current Directions in Psychological Science, 18,* 210–216. doi: 10.1111/j.1467-8721.2009.01638.x

Kramer, A. (2015). When the circadian clock becomes blind. *Science, 347,* 476–477. doi: 10.1126/science.aaa5085

Krantz, M. J., & Mehler, P. S. (2004). Treating opioid dependence: Growing implications for primary care. *Archives of Internal Medicine, 164,* 277–288.

Krause-Utz, A., Sobanski, E., Alm, B., Valerius, G., Kleindienst, N., Bohus, M., . . .Schmahl, D. (2013). Impulsivity in relation to stress in patients with borderline personality disorder with and without co-occurring attention-deficit /hyperactivity disorder: An exploratory study. *Journal of Nervous & Mental Disease, 201,* 116–123. doi: 10.1097/NMD.0b013e31827f6462

Krauss, R. M., Curran, N. M., & Ferleger, N. (1983). Expressive conventions and the cross-cultural perception of emotion. *Basic and Applied Social Psychology, 4,* 295–305. Krebs, D. L., & Denton, K. (2005). Toward a more pragmatic approach to morality: A critical evaluation of Kohlberg's model. *Psychological Review, 112,* 629–649.

Kreuger, K. A., & Dayan, P. (2009). Flexible shaping: How learning in small steps helps. *Cognition, 10,* 380–394.

Kring, A., M., Gur, R. E., Blanchard, J. J., Horan, W. P., & Reise, S. P. (2013). The Clinical Assessment Interview for Negative Symptoms (CAINS): Final development and validation. *American Journal of Psychiatry, 170,* 165–172. doi: 10.1176/appi.ajp.2012.12010109

Kros, C. (2005). Hearing: Aid from hair force. *Nature, 433,* 810–811.

Kross, E., Verduyn, P., Demiralp, E., Park, J., Lee, D. S., Lin, N., Shablack, H.., . . . Ybarra, O. (2013). Facebook use predicts declines in subjective well-being in young adults. *PLoS ONE, 8,* e69841. doi: 10.1371/journal.pone.0069841

Ksir, C. J., Hart, C. L., & Ray, O. S. (2008). *Drugs, society, and human behavior* (12th ed.). New York: McGraw-Hill.

Kübler-Ross, E. (1969). *On death and dying.* New York: Macmillan.

Kuehn, B. M. (2012). Challenge to Alzheimer drug. *Journal of the American Medical Association, 308,* 2557. doi: 10.1001 /jama.2012.156122

Kuehn, B. M. (2013). Sleep may help remove harmful molecules from the brain. *The Journal of the American Medical Association, 310,* 2140. doi: 10.1001/jama.2013.283499

Kuehn, B. M. (2013). Teen perceptions of marijuana risks shift: Use of alcohol, illicit drugs, and tobacco declines. *Journal of the American Medical Association, 309,* 429–430. doi: 10.1001/jama.2012.211240

Kuester, A., Niemeyer, H., & Knaevelsrud, C. (2016). Internet-based interventions for posttraumatic stress: A meta-analysis of randomized controlled trials. *Clinical Psychology Review, 43,* 1–16. doi: 10.1016/j.cpr.2015.11.004

Kuncel, N. R., Hezlett, A. A., & Ones, D. S. (2004). Academic performance, career potential, creativity, and job performance: Can one construct predict them all? *Journal of Personality and Social Psychology, 86,* 148–161.

Kupfersmid, J. (1995). Does the Oedipus complex exist? *Psychotherapy, 32,* 535–547.

Kusnecov, A. W. (2001). Behavioral conditioning of the immune system. In A. Baum, T. A. Revenson, &

J. E. Singer (Eds.), *Handbook of health psychology* (pp. 105–116). Mahwah, NJ: Erlbaum.

Kwon, D. (2016). First drug to treat progressive multiple sclerosis. *Scientific American Mind, 27*(1), 14.

La Mela, C., Maglietta, M., Caini, S., Case, G. P., Lucarelli, S., . . . Ruggiero, G. M. (2015). Perfectionism, weight and shape concerns, and low self-esteem: Testing a model to predict bulimic symptoms. *Eating Behaviors, 19*, 155–158. doi: 10.1016/j.eatbeh.2015.09.002

Labonté, B., Suderman, M., Maussion, G., Navaro, L., Yerko, V., Mahar, I., . . . Turecki, G. (2012). Genome-wide epigenetic regulation by early-life trauma. *Archives of General Psychiatry, 69*, 722–731. doi: 10.1001/archgenpsychiatry.2011.2287

Laceulle, O. M., Ormel, J., Aggen, S. H., Neale, M. C., & Kendler, K. S. (2013). Genetic and environmental influences on the longitudinal structure of neuroticism: A trait-state approach. *Psychological Science, 24*, 1780–1790. doi: 10.1177/0956797613481356

Lachman, M. E. (2004). Development in midlife. *Annual Review of Psychology, 55*, 305–331.

Ladabaum, U., Mannalithara, A., Parvathi, A., Myer, A., & Singh, G. (2014). Obesity, abdominal obesity, physical activity, and caloric intake in US adults: 1988 to 2010. *The American Journal of Medicine, 127*, 717–727.

Laeng, B., Sirois, S., & Gredeback. G. (2012). Pupillometry: A window to the preconscious? *Perspectives on Psychological Science, 7*, 18. doi: 10.1177/1745691611427305

LaFrance, M., Hecht, M. A., & Paluck, E. L. (2003). The contingent smile: A meta-analysis of sex differences in smiling. *Psychological Bulletin, 129*, 325–334.

LaFromboise, T. D., Albright, K., & Harris, A. (2010). Patterns of hopelessness among American Indian adolescents: Relationships by levels of acculturation and residence. *Cultural Diversity and Ethnic Minority Psychology, 16*, 68–76. doi: 10.1037/a0016181

LaGrange, B., Cole, D. A., Jacquez, F., Ciesla, J., Dallaire, D., Pineda, A., Truss, A., . . . Felton, J. (2011). Disentangling the prospective relations between maladaptive cognitions and depressive symptoms. *Journal of Abnormal Psychology, 120*, 511–527. doi: 10.1037/a0024685

Laguna, A., Schintu, N., Nobre, A., Alvarsson, A., Volakakis, N., Jacobsen, J. K., . . . Perlmann, T. (2015). Dopaminergic control of autophagic-lysosomal function implicates Lmx1b in Parkinson's disease. *Nature Neuroscience, 18*, 826–835. doi: 10.1038/nn.4004

Lahey, B. B., Van Hulle, C. A., Keenan, K., Rathouz, P. J., D'Onofrio, B. M., Rodgers, J. L., & Waldman, I. D. (2008). Temperament and parenting during the first year of life predict future child conduct problems. *Journal of Abnormal Child Psychology, 36*, 1139–1158. doi: 10.1007/s10802-008 -9247-3

Lahn, B. T., & Page, D. C. (1999). Four evolutionary strata on the human X chromosome. *Science, 286*, 964–967.

Lamberg, L. (2006). Rx for obesity: Eat less, exercise more, and—maybe—get more sleep. *Journal of the American Medical Association, 295*, 2341–2344.

Lambert, M. J., Hansen, N. B., & Finch, A. E. (2001). Patient-focused research: Using patient outcome data to enhance treatment effects. *Journal of Consulting and Clinical Psychology, 69*, 159–172.

Lambiase, M. J., Kubzansky, L. D., & Thurston, R. C. (2014). Prospective study of anxiety and incident stroke. *Stroke, 45*, 438–443.

Lamers, S. M. A., Westerhof, G. J., Kovács, V., & , Bohlmeijer, E. T. (2012). Differential relationships in the association of the Big Five personality traits with positive mental health and psychopathology. *Journal of Research in Personality, 46*, 517–524. doi: http://dx.doi.org/10.1016 /j.jrp.2012.05.012

Lamiell, J. T. (2013). On psychology's struggle for existence: Some reflections on Wundt's 1913 essay a century on. *Journal of Theoretical and Philosophical Psychology, 33*, 205–215.

Lanaj, K., Johnson, R. E., & Barnes, C. M. (2014). Beginning the workday yet already depleted? Consequences of late-night smartphone use and sleep. *Organizational Behavior and Human Decision Processes, 124*, 11–23.

Lane, A., Luminet, O., Rimé, B., Gross, J. J., de Timary, P., & Mikolajczak, M. (2012). Oxytocin increases willingness to socially share one's emotions. *International Journal of Psychology, 48*, 676–681. doi: 10.1080/00207594.2012.677540 Langlois, J. H., Kalakanis, L., Rubenstein, A. J., Larson, A., Hallam, M., & Smoot, M. (2000). Maxims or myths of beauty? A meta-analytic and theoretical review. *Psychological Bulletin, 126*, 390–423.

Långström, N., Rahman, Q., Carlström, E., & Lichtenstein, P. (2008, June 7). Genetic and environmental effects on same-sex sexual behavior: A population study of twins in Sweden. *Archives of Sexual Behavior.* doi: 10.1007/s10508-008-9386-1

Långström, N., Rahman, Q., Carlström, E., & Lichtenstein, P. (2010). Genetic and environmental effects on same-sex sexual behavior: A population study of twins in Sweden. *Archives of Sexual Behavior, 39*, 75–80. doi: 10.1007/s10508 -008-9386-1

Lanza, S. T., Vasilenko, S. A., Dziak, J. J., & Butera, N. M. (2015). Trends among U.S. high school seniors in recent marijuana use and associations with other substances: 1976–2013. *Journal of Adolescent Health, 57*, 198. doi: 10.1016/j.jadohealth.2015.04.006

Larrick, R. P., Timmerman, T. A., Carton, A. M., & Abrevay, J. (2011). Temper, temperature, and temptation: Heat-related retaliation in baseball. *Psychological Science, 22*, 423–428.

Laska, K. M., Gurman, A. S., & Wampold, B. E. (2014). Expanding the lens of evidence-based practice in psychotherapy: A common factors perspective. *Psychotherapy, 51*, 467–481. doi: http://dx.doi .org/10.1037/a0034332

Latané, B., & Darley, J. M. (1970). *The unresponsive bystander: Why doesn't he help?* New York: Appleton-Century-Crofts.

Laumann, E. O., Gagnon, J. H., Michael, R. T., & Michaels, S. (1994). *The social organization of sexuality: Sexual practices in the United States.* Chicago: University of Chicago Press.

Laumann, E. O., Paik, A., Glasser, D. B., Kang, J.-H., Wang, T., Levinson, B., . . . Gingell, C. (2006). *A cross-national study of subjective sexual well-being among older women and men: Findings from the Global Study of Sexual Attitudes and Behaviors.* Retrieved from www.npr.org

Lawton, M. P., Moss, M. S., Winter, L., & Hoffman, C. (2002). Motivation in later life: Personal projects and well-being. *Psychology and Aging, 17*, 539–547.

Lazaros, K. G., Barttfeld, P., Havlin, S., Sigman, M., & Makse, H. E. (2012). Collective behavior in the spatial spreading of obesity. *Scientific Reports, 2*, 454. doi: 10.1038/srep00454

Lazarus, R. S. (2000). Toward better research on stress and coping. *American Psychologist, 55*, 665–673.

Lazarus, S. A., Cheavens, J. S., Festa, F., & Rosenthal, M. Z. (2014). Interpersonal functioning in borderline personality disorder: A systematic review of behavioral and laboratory-based assessments. *Clinical Psychology Review, 34*, 193–205. doi: 10.1016/j.cpr.2014.01.007

Leahey, T. (2014). The decline and fall of introspection. *PsycCRITIQUES, 59*(3). Retrieved from http://psqtest.typepad.com/blogPostPDFs /TheDeclineandFallofIntrospection-2014-59-3.pdf

LeBel, E. P., & Peters, K. R. (2011). Fearing the future of empirical psychology: Bem's evidence of PSI as a case study of deficiencies in modal research practice. *Review of General Psychology, 15*, 371–379.

Leding, J. K. (2012). False memories and persuasion strategies. *Review of General Psychology, 16*, 256–268. doi: 10.1037 /a0027700

LeDoux, J. (2003). The emotional brain, fear, and the amygdala. *Cellular and Molecular Neurobiology, 23*, 727–738.

LeDoux, J. E. (1994, June). Emotion, memory, and the brain. *Scientific American, 270*, 32–39.

LeDoux, J. E. (1996). *The emotional brain.* New York: Touchstone.

LeDoux, J. E. (2000). Emotion circuits in the brain. *Annual Review of Neuroscience, 23*, 155–184.

LeDoux, J. E. (2008). Amygdala. *Scholarpedia, 3*(4), 2698. Retrieved from www.scholarpedia.org/article/Amygdala

Lee, E. B. (2011). Young, Black, and connected: Facebook usage among African American college students. *Journal of Black Studies, 43*, 336–354.

Lee, E., Ahn, J., Kim, Y. J. (2014). Personality traits and self-presentation at Facebook. *Personality and Individual Differences, 69*, 162–167. doi: 10.1016/j.paid.2014.05.020

Lee, L., Loewenstein, G., Ariely, D., Hong, J., & Young, J. (2008). If I'm not hot, are you hot or not? Physical-attractiveness evaluations and dating preferences as a function of one's own attractiveness. *Psychological Science, 19*, 669–677. doi: 10.1111/j.1467-9280.2008.02141

Lee, N. C., Krabbendam, L., White, T. P., Meeter, M., Banaschewski, T., Barker, G. J., . . . IMAGEN Consortium (2013). Do you see what I see? Sex differences in the discrimination of facial emotions during adolescence. *Emotion, 13*, 1030–1040. doi: 10.1037/a0033560

Lehrer, J. (2012). *Imagine how creativity works.* Boston: Houghton Mifflin.

Leiblum, S. R., Koochaki, P. E., Rodenberg, C. A., Barton, I. P., & Rosen, R. C. (2006). Hypoactive sexual desire disorder in postmenopausal women: U.S. results from the Women's International Study of Health and Sexuality (WISHeS). *Menopause, 13*, 46–56.

Leibowitz, H. W. (1971). Sensory, learned, and cognitive mechansims of size perception. *Annals of the New York Academy of Sciences, 1988*, 47–62.

Leichsenring, F., Salzer, S., Beutel, M. E., Herpertz, S., Hiller, W., Hoyer, J., . . . Leibing, E. (2013). Psychodynamic therapy and cognitive-behavioral therapy in social anxiety disorder: A multicenter randomized controlled trial. *American Journal of Psychiatry, 170*, 759–767. doi: 10.1176/appi.ajp.2013.12081125

Leichsenring, F., Salzer, S., Beutel, M. E., Herpertz, S., Hiller, W., Hoyer, J., . . . Leibing, E. (2014). Long-term outcome of psychodynamic therapy and cognitive-behavioral therapy in social anxiety disorder. *American Journal of Psychiatry, 171*, 1074–1082. doi: 10.1176/appi.ajp.2014.13111514

Leichsenring, F., & Schauenburg, H. (2014). Empirically supported methods of short-term psychodynamic therapy in depression: Towards an evidence-based unified protocol. *Journal of Affective Disorders, 169*, 128–143. doi: 10.1016/j.jad.2014.08.007

Leigh, S., & Flatt, S. (2015). App-based psychological interventions: Friend or foe? *Evidence Based Mental Health, 18*, 97–99. doi: 10.1136/eb-2015-102203

Leiter, M. P. (Ed.), Bakker, A. B.(Ed.), & Maslach, C. (Ed.). (2014). *Burnout at work: A psychological perspective. Current issues in work and organizational psychology.* New York: Psychology Press.

Lemons, J. A., Baur, C. R., Oh, W., Korones, S. B., Papile, L. A., Stoll, B. J., . . . Stevenson, D. K. (2001). Very low birth weight outcomes of the National Institute of Child Health and Human Development neonatal research network, January 1995 through December 1996. *Pediatrics, 107*, 1.

Lepore, L., & Brown, R. (1997). Category and stereotype activation: Is prejudice inevitable? *Journal of Personality and Social Psychology, 72*, 275–287.

Lerner, B. H. (2011). Drunk driving, distracted driving, moralism, and public health. *New England Journal of Medicine.* Retrieved from http://healthpolicyandreform.nejm.org/ ?p=15251&query=home

Letzring, T. D., Edmonds, G. W., & Hampson, S. E. (2014). Personality change at mid-life is associated with changes in self-rated health: Evidence from the Hawaii Personality and Health Cohort. *Personality and Individual Differences, 58*, 60–64. doi: 10.1016/j.paid.2013.10.002

Leutgeb, S. (2008, March 21). Detailed differences. *Science, 319*, 1623–1624. doi: 10.1126/science.1156724

LeVay, S. (2003). *The biology of sexual orientation.* Retrieved from https://webcache.googleusercontent.com/search?q=cache:bwZm3hRe9XAJ:faculty.txwes.edu/jbrown06 /course3/documents /TheBiologyofSexualOrientation .doc+&cd =4&hl=en&ct=clnk&gl=us

Leve, L. D., Harold, G. T., Ge, X., Neiderhiser, J. M., & Patterson, G. (2010). Refining intervention targets in family-based research: Lessons from quantitative behavioral genetics. *Perspectives on Psychological Science, 5*, 516–526. doi: 10.1177/1745691610383506

Levine, J. M., & Moreland, R. L. (1998). Small groups. In D. T. Gilbert, S. T. Fiske, & G. Lindzey (Eds.), *The handbook of social psychology* (Vol. 2, 4th ed., pp. 415–469). Boston: McGraw-Hill.

Levine, M. (1994). *Effective problem solving* (2nd ed.). Englewood Cliffs, NJ: Prentice Hall.

Levinson, D. J., with Darrow, C. N., Klein, E. R., Levinson, M. H., & McKee, B. (1978). *The seasons of a man's life.* New York: Knopf.

Levy, B. R., Pilver, C., Chung P. H., & Slade, M. D. (2014). Subliminal strengthening: Improving older individuals' physical function over time with an implicit-age-stereotype intervention. *Psychological Science, 25*, 2127–2135. doi: 10.1177/0956797614551970

Levy, B. R., Slade, M. D., Kunkel, S. R., & Kasl, S. V. (2002). Longevity increased by positive self-perceptions of aging. *Journal of Personality and Social Psychology, 83*, 261–270.

Lewin, T. (2011, January 26). Record level of stress found in college freshman. *The New York Times*, pp. A1, A18.

Lewis, G. J., & Bates, T. C. (2014). How genes influence personality: Evidence from multi-facet twin analyses of the HEXACO dimensions. *Journal of Research in Personality, 51*, 9–17. doi: http://dx.doi.org/10.1016/j.jrp.2014.04.004

Lewis, S. J., Zuccolo, L., Smith, G. D., Macleod, J., Rodriguez, S., Draper, E. S., . . . Gray, R. (2012). Fetal alcohol exposure and IQ at age 8: Evidence from a population-based birth-cohort study. *PLOS ONE, 7*(11), e49407. doi: 10.1371/journal.pone.0049407

Lewis, T. (2014, January 14). Teen brains really are wired to seek rewards. *LiveScience.* Retrieved from livescience.com

Li, N. P., & Kenrick, D. T. (2006). Sex similarities and differences in preferences for short-term mates: What, whether, and why. *Journal of Personality and Social Psychology, 90*, 468–489.

Libbrecht, N., Lievens, F., Carette, B., & Côté, S. (2014). Emotional intelligence predicts success in medical school. *Emotion, 14*, 64–73. doi: 10.1037/a0034392

Lichta, R. W. (2010). A new BALANCE in bipolar I disorder. *The Lancet, 375*, 350–352. doi: 10.1016 / S0140-6736(09)61970-X

Lichtman, J. H., Froelicher, E. S., Blumenthal, J. A., Carney, R. M., Doering, L V., Frasure-Smith, N., . . . on behalf of the American Heart Association Statistics Committee of the Council on Epidemiology and Prevention and the Council on Cardiovascular and Stroke Nursing (2014). Depression as a risk factor for poor prognosis among patients with acute coronary syndrome: Systematic review and recommendations: A scientific statement from the American Heart Association. *Circulation.* Retrieved from http://circ.ahajournals.org/content/early/2014/02/24 /CIR.0000000000000019

Lieberman, J. S. A. (2010). Psychiatric care shortage: What the future holds. *Medscape Psychiatry and Mental Health.* Retrieved from www.medscape.com

Lien, M.-C., Ruthruff, E., & Johnston, J. C. (2006). Attentional limitations in doing two tasks at once: The search for exceptions. *Current Directions in Psychological Science, 15*, 89–93.

Lilienfeld, S. O., & Arkowitz, H. (2009). "Lunacy and the full moon." *Scientific American.* Retrieved from www.scientificamerican.com/article.cfm?id=lunacy-and-the-full-moon

Lim, J., & Dinges, D. F. (2010). A meta-analysis of the impact of short-term sleep deprivation on cognitive variables. *Psychological Bulletin, 136*, 375–389. doi: 10.1037/a0018883

Limebeer, C. L., & Parker, L. A. (2006). Effect of conditioning method and testing method on strength of lithium-induced taste aversion learning. *Behavioral Neuroscience, 120*, 963–969.

Lin, L., Stamm, K., & Christidis, P. (2015, July/August). Is psychology becoming more diverse? *Monitor on Psychology*, p. 17.

Lin, L. Y., Sidani, J. E., Shensa, A., Radovic, A., Miller, E., Colditz, J. B., . . . Primack, B. A. (2016). Association between social media use and depression among U.S. young adults. *Depression and Anxiety, 33*, 323–331. doi: 10.1002/da.22466

Lin, Z., & Murray, S.O. (2014). Unconscious processing of an abstract concept. *Psychological Science, 25*, 296–298. doi: 10.1177/0956797613504964

Linde, K., Allais, G., Brinkhaus, B., Manheimer, E., Vickers, A., & White, A. R. (2009a). Acupuncture for tension-type headache. *Cochrane Database of Systematic Reviews*, Issue 1. doi: 10.1002/14651858.CD007587

Linde, K., Allais, G., Brinkhaus, B., Manheimer, E., Vickers, A., & White, A. R. (2009b). Acupuncture for migraine prophylaxis. *Cochrane Database of Systematic Reviews*, Issue 1. doi: 10.1002/14651858.CD001218.pub2

Linde, K., Streng, A., Jürgens, S., Hoppe, A., Brinkhaus, B., Witt, C., . . . Melchart, D. (2005). Acupuncture for patients with migraine: A randomized controlled trial. *Journal of the American Medical Association, 293*, 2118–2125.

Lindwall, M., Gerber, M., Jonsdottir, I. H., Börjesson, M., & Ahlborg Jr., G. (2014). The relationships of change in physical activity with change in depression, anxiety, and burnout: A longitudinal study of Swedish healthcare workers. *Health Psychology, 33*, 1309–1318. doi: http://dx.doi.org/10.1037/a0034402

Lippa, R. A. (2008). The relation between childhood gender nonconformity and adult masculinity-femininity and anxiety in heterosexual and homosexual men and women. *Sex Roles, 59*, 684–693. doi: 10.1007/s11199-008-9476-5

Lippa, R. A. (2012). Effects of sex and sexual orientation on self-reported attraction and viewing times to images of men and women: Testing for category specificity. *Archives of Sexual Behavior, 41*, 149–160.

Lipton, E. (2006, August 16). Faces, too, are searched as U.S. airports try to spot terrorists. *The New York Times*, pp. A1, A10.

Little, A. C., Burt, D. M., & Perrett, D. I. (2006). What is good is beautiful: Face preference reflects desired personality. *Personality and Individual Differences, 41*, 1107–1118.

Littlejohn, S. W. (2002). *Theories of human communication* (7th ed.). Belmont, CA: Wadsworth.

Liu B., Zhang, Y., Zhang, L., & Lingjiang, L. (2014). Repetitive transcranial magnetic stimulation as an augmentative strategy for treatment-resistant depression: A meta-analysis of randomized, double-blind and sham-controlled study. *BMC Psychiatry, 14*, 342. doi: 10.1186/s12888-014-0342-4

Liu, R. T., & Alloy, L. B. (2010). Stress generation in depression: A systematic review of the empirical literature and recommendations for future study. *Clinical Psychology Review, 30*, 582–593. doi: 10.1016/j.cpr.2010.04.010

Liu, R. T., & Miller, I. (2014). Life events and suicidal ideation and behavior: A systematic review. *Clinical Psychology Review, 34*, 181–192. doi: http://dx.doi.org/10.1016/j.cpr.2014.01.006

Liu, Y., Wheaton, A. G., Chapman, D. P., Cunningham, T. J., Lu, H., & Croft, J. B. (2016). Prevalence of healthy sleep duration among adults—United States, 2014. *Morbidity and Mortality Weekly Report (MMWR), 65*, 137–141. doi: http://dx.doi.org/10.15585/mmwr.mm6506a1

Lobbestael, J., & Arntz, A. (2009). Emotional, cognitive and physiological correlates of abuse-related stress in borderline and antisocial personality disorder. *Behaviour Research and Therapy, 34*, 571–586. doi: 10.1016/j.brat.2009.09.015

Locke, A. E., Kahali, B., Berndt, S. I., Justice, A. E., Pers, T. H., Day, F. R., . . . Speliotes, E. K. (2015). Genetic studies of body mass index yield new insights for obesity biology. *Nature, 518* (7538), 197. doi: 10.1038/nature14177

Lockley, S. W., Cronin, J. W., Evans, E. E., Cade, B. E., Lee, C. J., Landrigan, C. P., . . . Harvard Work Hours, Health and Safety Group. (2004). Effect of reducing interns' weekly work hours on sleep and attentional failures. *New England Journal of Medicine, 351,* 1829–1837.

Loeb, S., Fuller, B., Kagan, S. L., & Carrol, B. (2004). Child care in poor communities: Early learning effects of type, quality, and stability. *Child Development, 75,* 4765.

Loehlin, J. C. (2012). The general factor of personality: What lies beyond? *Personality and Individual Differences, 54,* 52–56. doi: http://dx.doi.org/10.1016/j .paid.2012.08.006

Loft, S. (2014). Applying psychological science to examine prospective memory in simulated air traffic control . *Current Directions in Psychological Science, 23,* 326–331. doi: 10.1177/0963721414545214

Loftus, E. F. (1993). The reality of repressed memories. *American Psychologist, 48,* 518–537.

Loftus, E. F. (1997, September). Creating false memories. *Scientific American, 277,* 70–75.

Loftus, E. F. (2004). Memories of things unseen. *Current Directions in Psychological Science, 13,* 145–147.

Loftus, E. F., Miller, D. G., & Burns, H. J. (1978). Semantic integration of verbal information into a visual memory. *Journal of Experimental Psychology: Human Learning and Memory, 4,* 19–31.

Lorayne, H. (2002). *The complete guide to memory mastery.* Hollywood, FL: Fell Publishers.

Lorenz, K. (1966). *On aggression.* New York: Harcourt Brace Jovanovich.

Lorenzo, G. L., Biesanz, J. C., & Human, L. J. (2010). What is beautiful is good and more accurately understood: Physical attractiveness and accuracy in first impressions of personality. *Psychological Science, 21,* 1777–1782. doi: 10.1177/095679761038804

Lothane, Z. (2006). Freud's legacy—Is it still with us? *Psychoanalytic Psychology, 23,* 285–301.

Lovén, J., Herlitz, A., & Rehnman, J. (2011). Women's own-gender bias in face recognition memory: The role of attention at encoding. *Experimental Psychology, 58,* 333–340.

Lu, J., & Zuo, Y. (2015). Neuroscience: Forgetfulness illuminated. *Nature, 525,* 324–325. doi: 10.1038/ nature15211

Lu, S. (2015, April). Great expectations. *Monitor on Psychology, 46*(4), 50.

Lucas, R. E., & Donnellan, M. B. (2009). Age differences in personality: Evidence from a nationally representative Australian sample. *Developmental Psychology, 45,* 1353–1363.

Ludeke, S., Johnson, W., & Bouchard, T. J., Jr., (2013). "Obedience to traditional authority:" A heritable factor underlying authoritarianism, conservatism and religiousness. *Personality and Individual Differences, 55,* 375–380. doi: 10.1016/j.paid.2013.03.018

Luo, S., & Klohnen, E. C. (2005). Assortative mating and marital quality in newlyweds: A couple-centered approach. *Journal of Personality and Social Psychology, 88,* 304–326.

Lupski, J. R. (2007). Structural variation in the human genome. *New England Journal of Medicine, 356,* 1169–1171.

Luria, A. R. (1968). *The mind of a mnemonist.* New York: Basic Books.

Lynn, S. J., Boycheva, E., Barnes, S., Barretta, N., Barretta, P., Geary, B. B., et al. (2008). To assess or not assess hypnotic suggestibility? That is the question. *American Journal of Clinical Hypnosis, 51,* 161–165.

Lyubomirsky, S. (2012, December 2). New love: A short shelf life. *The New York Times Sunday Review,* pp. 1, 6.

Ma, J., Ward, E. M., Siegel, R. L., & Jemal, A. (2015). Temporal trends in mortality in the United States, 1969–2013. *Journal of the American Medical Association, 314,* 1731–1739. doi: 10.1001/jama.2015.12319.sciencedaily.com/re- leases/2015/10/151029111924.htm

Mabe, A. G., Forney, K. J., & Keel, P. K. (2014). Do you "like" my photo? Facebook use maintains eating disorder risk. *International Journal of Eating Disorders, 47,* 516–523. doi: 10.1002/eat.22254

MacCann, C., Lipnevich, A. A., Burrus, J., & Roberts, R. D. (2012).The best years of our lives? Coping with stress predicts school grades, life satisfaction, and feelings about high school. *Learning and Individual Differences, 22,* 235–241. doi: 10.1016/j. lindif.2011.08.004

Macey, P. M., Kumar, R., Woo, M. A., Yan-Go, F. L., & Harper, R. M. (2013). Heart rate responses to autonomic challenges in obstructive sleep apnea. *PLoS ONE, 8,* e76631. doi: 10.1371/journal. pone.0076631

MacGregor, J. N., Ormerod, T. C., & Chronicle, E. P. (2001). Information processing and insight: A process model of performance on the nine-dot and related problems. *Journal of Experimental Psychology: Learning, Memory, and Cognition, 27,* 176–201.

Mackenzie, C. S., El-Gabalawy, R., Chou, K. L., & Sareen, J. (2014). Prevalence and predictors of persistent versus remitting mood, anxiety, and substance disorders in a national sample of older adults. *American Journal of Geriatric Psychiatry, 22,* 854–865. doi: 10.1016/j.jagp.2013.02.007.

MacKillop, J., McGeary, J. E., & Ray, L. A. (2010). Genetic influences on addiction: Alcoholism as an exemplar. In D. Ross, P. Collins, & D. Spurrett (Eds.), *What is addiction?* (pp. 53–98). Cambridge, MA: MIT Press.

Maggi, M. (2012). *Hormonal therapy for male sexual dysfunction.* Hoboken, NJ: Wiley.

Maggiolini, A., Cagnin, C., Crippa, F., Persico, A., & Rizzi, P. (2010). Content analysis of dreams and waking narratives. *Dreaming, 20,* 60–76. doi: 10.1037/ a0018824

Maia, T. V., & Cano-Colino, M. (2015). The role of serotonin in orbitofrontal function and obsessive-compulsive disorder. *Clinical Psychological Science, 3,* 460–482. doi: 10.1177/2167702614566809

Maier, N. R. F. (1931). Reasoning in humans: II. The solution of a problem and its appearance in consciousness. *Journal of Comparative Psychology, 12,* 181–194.

Main, M. (1996). Introduction to the special section on attachment and psychopathology: 2. Overview of the field of attachment. *Journal of Consulting and Clinical Psychology, 64,* 237–243.

Major, G. C., Doucet, E., Trayhurn, P., Astrup, A., & Tremblay, A. (2007). Clinical significance of adaptive thermogenesis. *International Journal of Obesity, 31,* 204–212.

Malinowski, J. E., & Horton, C. L. (2014). The effect of time of night on wake–dream continuity. *Dreaming, 24,* 253–269.

Malle, B. A. (2006). The actor–observer asymmetry in attribution: A (surprising) meta-analysis. *Psychological Bulletin, 132,* 895–891.

Malouff, J., Rooke, S., & Schutte, N. (2008). The heritability of human behavior: Results of aggregating meta-analyses. *Current Psychology, 27,* 153–161. doi: 10.1007/s12144-008-9032-z

Mammen, G., & Faulkner, G. (2013). Physical activity and the prevention of depression: A systematic review of prospective studies. *American Journal of Preventive Medicine, 45,* 649–657.

Manago, A. M., Taylor, T., & Greenfield, P. (2012). Me and my 400 friends: The anatomy of college students' Facebook networks, their communication patterns, and well-being. *Developmental Psychology, 48,* 369–380. doi: 10.1037/a0026338

Mandelman, S. D., & Grigorenko, E. L. (2011). Intelligence: Genes, environments, and their interactions. In R. J. Sternberg & S. B. Kaufman (Eds.), *Cambridge handbook of intelligence* (pp. 85–106). Cambridge, UK: Cambridge University Press.

Mann, K., Vollstädt-Klein, S., Leménager, T., Fauth-Bühler, M. H. D., Hoffmann, S., Zimmermann, U. S., . . . Smolka, M. N. (2014). Predicting naltrexone response in alcohol-dependent patients: The contribution of functional magnetic resonance imaging. *Alcoholism: Clinical and Experimental Research, 38,* 2754–2762. doi: 10.1111/acer.12546.

Manning, R., Levine, M., & Collins, A. (2007). The Kitty Genovese murder and the social psychology of helping: The parable of the 38 witnesses. *American Psychologist, 62,* 555–562.

Manson, J. E., Skerrett, P. J., Greenland, P., & VanItallie, T. B. (2004). The escalating pandemics of obesity and sedentary lifestyle a call to action for clinicians. *Archives of Internal Medicine, 164,* 249–258.

Manuck, S. B., & McCaffery, J. M. (2014). Gene-environment interaction. *Annual Review of Psychology, 65,* 41–70. doi: 10.1146/annurev-psych-010213-115100

Marcia, J. E. (1980). Identity in adolescence. In J. Adelson (Ed.), *Handbook of adolescent psychology* (pp. 159–187). New York: Wiley.

Marcia, J. E. (2002). Identity and psychosocial development in adulthood. *Identity, 2,* 7–28.

Marcia, J. E., Waterman, A. S., Matteson, D. R., Archer, S. L., & Orlofsky, J. L. (Eds.). (1993). *Ego identity: A handbook for psychosocial research.* New York: Springer-Verlag.

Marcus, D. K., Fulton, J. J., & Edens, J. F. (2012). The two-factor model of psychopathic personality: Evidence from the Psychopathic Personality Inventory. *Personality Disorders: Theory, Research, and Treatment, 3,* 140–154.

Marcus, D. K., O'Connell, D., Norris, A. L., & Sawaqdeh, A. (2014). Is the Dodo bird endangered in the 21st century? A meta-analysis of treatment comparison studies. *Clinical Psychology Review, 34,* 519–530. doi: 10.1016/j.cpr.2014.08.001

Markel, H. (2003, September 3). Lack of sleep takes it toll on student psyches. *The New York Times, Science Times,* p. F6.

Markus, H. R., & Kitayama, S. (1991). Culture and the self: Implications for cognition, emotion, and motivation. *Psychological Review, 98,* 224–253.

Marsh, R. L., Hicks, J. L., & Cook, G. I. (2005). On the relationship between effort toward an ongoing task and cue detection in event-based prospective memory.

Journal of Experimental Psychology: Learning, Memory, and Cognition, 31, 68–75.

Marshall, T. C., Lefringhausen, K., & Ferenczi, N. (2015). The Big Five, self-esteem, and narcissism as predictors of the topics people write about in Facebook status updates. *Personality and Individual Differences, 85*, 35–40. doi: 10.1016/j.paid.2015.04.039

Martin, C. (2015, August 16). Finding a niche for the accidental spectacles. *The New York Times*, p. BU3.

Martin, S. (2012, March). "Our health at risk": APA's latest survey finds that many Americans don't understand how stress can undermine their health. *Monitor on Psychology, 43*(3), 18.

Martindale, C. (2001). Oscillations and analogies: Thomas Young, MD, RFS, genius. *American Psychologist, 56*, 342–345.

Martinez, G. M., & Abma, J. C. (2015). *Sexual activity, contraceptive use, and childbearing of teenagers aged 15–19 in the United States*. U.S. Department of Health and Human Services, National Center for Health Statistics. NCHS Data Brief, No. 209.

Martinez, M. A., & Craighead, L. W. (2015). Toward person(ality)-centered treatment: How consideration of personality and individual differences in anorexia nervosa may improve treatment outcome. *Clinical Psychology: Science and Practice, 22*, 296–314. doi: 10.1111/cpsp.12111

Maruyama, K., Sato, S., Ohira, T., Maeda, K., Noda, H., Kubota, Y., ... Iso, H. (2008). The joint impact on being overweight of self reported behaviours of eating quickly and eating until full: Cross sectional survey. *British Medical Journal, 337*, 2002. doi: 10.1136/bmj.a2002

Maslow, A. H. (1943). A theory of human motivation. *Psychological Review, 50*, 370–396.

Maslow, A. H. (1969). The farther reaches of human nature. *Journal of Transpersonal Psychology, 1*, 1–9.

Maslow, A. H. (1970). *Motivation and personality* (2nd ed.). New York: Harper & Row.

Maslow, A. H. (1971). *Farther reaches of human nature*. New York: Viking Penguin.

Maslow, A. H. (1987). *Motivation and personality* (3rd ed.), edited by R. Frager, J. Fadiman, C. McReynolds, & R. Cox. Boston: Addison Wesley.

Mason, B. J., Crean, R., Goodell, V., Light, J. M., Quello, S., Shadan, F., ... Rao, S. (2012). A proof-of-concept randomized controlled study of gabapentin: Effects on cannabis use, withdrawal and executive function deficits in cannabis-dependent adults. *Neuropsychopharmacology, 37*, 1689–1698. doi: 10.1038/npp.2012.37:1689

Mason, P. T., & Kreger, R. (1998). *Stop walking on eggshells*. Oakland, CA: New Harbinger Publications.

Masters, W. H., & Johnson, V. E. (1966). *Human sexual response*. Boston: Little, Brown.

Masters, W. H., & Johnson, V. E. (1970). *Human sexual inadequacy*. Boston: Little, Brown.

Masuda, T., & Nisbett, R. E. (2001). Attending holistically versus analytically: Comparing the context sensitivity of Japanese and Americans. *Journal of Personality and Social Psychology, 81*, 992–934.

Matsumoto, D. (2004). Paul Ekman and the legacy of universals. *Journal of Research in Personality, 38*, 45–51.

Matsumoto, D., & Willingham, B. (2009). Spontaneous facial expressions of emotion in congenitally and non-congenitally blind individuals. *Journal of Person-*

ality and Social Psychology, 96, 1–10. doi: 10.1037/a0014037

Matsumoto, D., Yoo, S. H., Hirayama, S., & Petrova, G. (2005). Development and validation of a measure of display rule knowledge: The Display Rule Assessment Inventory. *Emotion, 5*, 23–40.

Matsumoto, D., Yoo, S. H., Nakagawa, S., & Multinational Study of Cultural Display Rules. (2008). Culture, emotion regulation, and adjustment. *Journal of Personality and Social Psychology, 94*, 925–937. doi: 10.1037/0022-3514.94.6.925

Mattheisen, M., Samuels, J. F., Wang, Y., Greenberg, B. D., Fyer, A. J., McCracken, J. T., ... Nestadt, G. (2014). Genome-wide association study in obsessive-compulsive disorder: Results from the OCGAS. *Molecular Psychiatry, 20*, 337–344. doi: 10.1038/mp.2014.43

Matthews, S. E. (2012, June 12). Why we go for doughnuts when we're sleep-deprived. *MyHealthNewsDaily*. Retrieved from http://todayhealth.today.msnbc.msn.com/_news/2012/06/12/12188651-why-we-go-for-doughnuts -when-were-sleep-deprived?lite

Matz, D. C., & Wood, W. (2005). Cognitive dissonance in groups: The consequences of disagreement. *Journal of Personality and Social Psychology, 88*, 22–37.

Max, D. T. (2005, December 11). National smiles. *The New York Times Magazine*, p. 82.

Max-Planck-Gesellschaft (2011, May 14). Sense of smell: Single giant interneuron in locusts controls activity in 50,000 neurons, enabling sparse codes for odours. *ScienceDaily*. Retrieved from https://www.sciencedaily.com/releases/2011/05/110513112248.htm

May, C. (2016, February). The value of careful thought. *APS Observer, 29*(2), 37–39.

May, P. A., Baete, A., Russo, J., Elliott, A. J., Blankenship, J., Kalberg, W. O., ... Hoyme, H. E. (2014). Prevalence and characteristics of fetal alcohol spectrum disorders. *Pediatrics, 13*, 855. doi: 10.1542/peds.2013-3319

Mayer, J. D., Salovey, P., & Caruso, D. R. (2008). Emotional intelligence: New ability or eclectic traits. *American Psychologist, 63*, 503–517. doi: 10.1037/0003-066X.63.6.503

Mays, V. M., Cochran, S. D., & Barnes, N. W. (2007). Race, race-based discrimination, and health outcomes among African Americans. *Annual Review of Psychology, 58*, 201–225.

McBride, C. K., Paikoff, R. L., & Holmbeck, G. N. (2003). Individual and familial influences on the onset of sexual intercourse among urban African American adolescents. *Journal of Consulting and Clinical Psychology, 71*, 159–167.

McCabe M., Leiblum, S. R, Chevret-Measson, M., Hartmann, U., Levine, S. B., McCabe, M., Plaut, M., ... Wylie, K. (2010). Psychological and interpersonal dimensions of sexual function and dysfunctions. *Journal of Sexual Medicine, 7*, 327–336.

McCabe, M. P., & Connaughton, C. (2014). Psychosocial factors associated with male sexual difficulties. *Journal of Sex Research, 51*, 31–42.

McCann, S., Moeri, O., Jimenez, S. I., Scott, C., & Gries, G. (2015). Developing a paired-target apparatus for quantitative testing of nest defense behavior by vespine wasps in response to con- or heterospecific nest defense pheromones. *Journal of Hymenoptera Research, 246*, 151. doi: 10.3897/JHR.46.6585

McCarthy, B., & Pierpaoli, C. (2015). Sexual challenges with aging: Integrating the GES approach in an

elderly couple. *Journal of Sex & Marital Therapy, 41*, 72–82. doi: 14681994.2014.931689

McCarthy-Jones, S., Trauer, T., Mackinnon, A., Sims, E., Thomas, N., & Copolov, D. L. (2014). A new phenomenological survey of auditory hallucinations: Evidence for subtypes and implications for theory and practice. *Schizophrenia Bulletin, 40*, S275–S284.

McClelland, D. C. (1958). Risk-taking in children with high and low need for achievement. In J. W. Atkinson (Ed.), *Motives in fantasy, action, and society*. Princeton, NJ: Van Nostrand.

McClelland, D. C. (1985). *Human motivation*. Glenview, IL: Scott, Foresman.

McClintock, S. M., Husain, M. M., Wisniewski, S. R., Nierenberg, A. A., Stewart, J. W., Trivedi, M. H., ... Rush, J. (2011). Residual symptoms in depressed outpatients who respond by 50% but do not remit to antidepressant medication. *Journal of Clinical Psychopharmacology, 31*, 180. doi: 10.1097/JCP.0b013e31820ebd2c

McCrae, C. S., Bramoweth, A. D., Williams, J., Roth, A., & Mosti, C. (2014). Impact of brief cognitive behavioral treatment for insomnia on health care utilization and costs. *Journal of Clinical Sleep Medicine, 15*, 127–135. doi: 10.5664/jcsm.3436

McCrae, R. R., & Costa, P. T., Jr. (1986). Clinical assessment can benefit from recent advances in personality psychology. *American Psychologist, 41*, 1001–1003.

McCrae, R. R., & Costa, P. T., Jr. (1996). Toward a new generation of personality theories: Theoretical contexts for the five-factor model. In J. S. Wiggins (Ed.), *The five-factor model of personality: Theoretical perspectives*. New York: Guilford Press.

McCrae, R. R., Costa, P. T., Jr., Martin, T. A., Oryol, V. E., Rukavishnikov, A. A., Senin, I. G., ... Urbánek, T. (2004). Consensual validation of personality traits across cultures. *Journal of Research in Personality, 38*, 17–20.

McCrae, R. R., & Terracciano, A. (2005). Personality profiles of cultures: Aggregate personality traits. *Journal of Personality and Social Psychology, 89*, 407–425.

McDaniel, M. A., LaMontagne, P., Beck, S. M., Scullin, M. K., & Braver, T. S. (2013). Dissociable neural routes to successful prospective memory. *Psychological Science, 24*, 1791–1800. doi: 10.1177/0956797613481233

McDougall, W. (1908). *An introduction to social psychology*. New York: Methuen.

McEvoy, J. P., Byerly, M., Hamer, R. M., Dominik, R., Swartz, M. S., Rosenheck, R. A., ... Stroup, T. S. (2014). Effectiveness of paliperidone palmitate vs haloperidol decanoate for maintenance treatment of schizophrenia: A randomized clinical trial. *Journal of the American Medical Association, 311*, 1978–1987. doi: 10.1001/jama.2014.4310

McEvoy, P. M. (2008). Effectiveness of cognitive behavioural group therapy for social phobia in a community clinic: A benchmarking study. *Behaviour Research and Therapy, 45*, 3030–3040.

McGinnis, J. M. (2015). Mortality trends and signs of health progress in the United States. Improving understanding and action. *Journal of the American Medical Association, 314*, 1699–1700. doi: 10.1001/jama.2015.12391

McGovern, F. J., & Nevid, J. S. (1986). Evaluation apprehension on psychological inventories in a prison-based setting. *Journal of Consulting and Clinical Psychology, 54,* 576–578.

McHugh, R. K., & Barlow, D. H. (2010). The dissemination and implementation of evidence-based psychological treatments: A review of current efforts. *American Psychologist, 65,* 73–84. doi: 10.1037/a0018121

McKay, D., Sookman, D., Neziroglu, F., Wilhelm, S., Stein, D. J., Kyrios, M., . . . Veale, D. (2014). *Psychiatry Research, 225,* 236–246. doi: http://dx.doi.org/10.1016/j.psychres.2014.11.058

McLean, L. M., & Gallop, R. (2003). Implications of childhood sexual abuse for adult borderline personality disorder and complex posttraumatic stress disorder. *American Journal of Psychiatry, 160,* 369–371.

McNally, R. J., & Geraerts, E. (2009). A new solution to the recovered memory debate. *Perspectives on Psychological Science, 4,* 126–134. doi: 10.1111/j.1745-6924.2009.01112.x

McNulty, J. K., & Fincham, F. D. (2012). Beyond positive psychology? Toward a contextual view of psychological processes and well-being. *American Psychologist, 67,* 101–110.

Meadows, G. N., Shawyer, F., Enticott, J. C., Graham, A. L., Judd, F., Martin, P. R., . . . Segal, Z. (2014). Mindfulness-based cognitive therapy for recurrent depression: A translational research study with 2-year follow-up. *Australian and New Zealand Journal of Psychiatry, 48,* 743–755.

Meaney, M. J. (2010). Epigenetics and the biological definition of gene × environment interactions. *Child Development, 81,* 41–79. doi: 10.1111/j.1467-8624.2009.01381.x

Medical News Today. (2011). *Are positive emotions good for your health in old age?* Retrieved from www.medicalnewstoday .com/articles/214442.php

Mednick, S., Makovski, T., Cai, D., & Jiang, Y. (2009). Sleep and rest facilitate implicit memory in a visual search task. *Vision Research, 49,* 2557–2565. doi: 10.1016/j.visres.2009.04.011

Meeus, W. H. J., & Raaijmakers, Q. A. W. (1995). Obedience in modern society: The Utrecht studies. *Journal of Social Issues, 51,* 155–175.

Mehta, P. H., & Beer, J. (2010). Neural mechanisms of the testosterone–aggression relation: The role of orbitofrontal cortex. *Journal of Cognitive Neuroscience, 22,* 2357–2368.

Meier, M. H., Slutske, W. S., Heath, A. C., & Martin, N. G. (2011). Sex differences in the genetic and environmental influences on childhood conduct disorder and adult antisocial behavior. *Journal of Abnormal Psychology, 120,* 377–388. doi: 10.1037/a0022303

Melamed, S., Shirom, A., Toker, S., Berliner, S., & Shapira, I. (2006). Burnout and risk of cardiovascular disease: Evidence, possible causal paths, and promising research directions. *Psychological Bulletin, 132,* 327–353.

Meltzer, A. L., McNulty, J. K., Jackson, G. L., & Karney, B. R. (2014). Men still value attractiveness in a long-term mate more than women. *Journal of Personality and Social Psychology, 106,* 435–440.

Melzack, R., & Wall, P. D. (1965). Pain mechanisms: A new theory. *Science, 150,* 971–979.

Melzack, R., & Wall, P. D. (1983). *The challenge of pain.* New York: Basic Books.

Ménard, A. D., Kleinplatz, P. J., Rosen, L., Lawless, S., Paradis, N., Campbell, M., . . . Huber, J. D. (2015).

Individual and relationship contributors to optimal sexual experiences in older men and women. *Sexual and Relationship Therapy, 30,* 78–93.

Mendes, W. B. (2007). Social facilitation. In R. Baumeister & K. Vohs (Eds.), *Encylopedia of social psychology.* Thousand Oaks, CA: Sage.

Mendle, J., Moore, S. R., Briley, D. A., & Harden, K. P. (2016). Puberty, socioeconomic status, and depression in girls: Evidence for gene × environment interactions. *Clinical Psychological Science, 4,* 3–16. In press. doi: 10.1177/2167702614563598

Merchant, J. (2016, January 26). *How meditation, placebos and virtual reality help power 'mind over body.'* Retrieved from http://www.npr.org

Merikangas, K. R., & Pato, M. (2009). Recent developments in the epidemiology of bipolar disorder in adults and children: Magnitude, correlates, and future directions. *Clinical Psychology: Science and Practice, 16,* 121–133. doi: 10.1111 /j.1468-2850.2009.01152.x

Merkow, M. B., Burke, J. F., & Kahana, M. J. (2015). The human hippocampus contributes to both the recollection and familiarity components of recognition memory. *Proceedings of the National Academy of Sciences, 112,* 14378–14383. doi: 10.1073/pnas.1513145112

Merluzzi, A. (2015, February). Cognitive shields. *APS Observer, 28*(2), 21–24.

Merwin, R. M. (2011). Anorexia nervosa as a disorder of emotion regulation: Theory, evidence, and treatment implications. *Clinical Psychology: Science and Practice, 18,* 208–214. doi: 10.1111/j.1468-2850.2011.01252

Metcalfe, J. (1986). Feelings of knowing in memory and problem solving. *Journal of Experimental Psychology: Learning, Memory, and Cognition, 12,* 288–294.

Meyer, B., Yuen, K. S., Ertl, M., Polomac, N., Mulert, C., Büchel, C., . . . Kalisch, R. (2015). Neural mechanisms of placebo anxiolysis. *Journal of Neuroscience, 35,* 7365–7373. doi: 10.1523/JNEUROSCI.4793-14.2015

Meyer, I. H. (2003). Prejudice, social stress, and mental health in lesbian, gay, and bisexual populations: Conceptual issues and research evidence. *Psychological Bulletin, 129,* 674–697.

Meyer-Lindenberg, A., Buckholtz, J. W., Kolachana, B., Hariri, A. R., Pezawas, L., Blasi, G., . . . Weinberger, D. R. (2006). Neural mechanisms of genetic risk for impulsivity and violence in humans. *Proceedings of the National Academy of Sciences, 103,* 6269–6274.

Meyers, L. (2005, November). Psychologists back increased parity, prescriptive authority and professional access. *Monitor on Psychology, 36*(10), 42–43.

Meyers, L. (2007a, January). Building a strong heart. *Monitor on Psychology, 38,* 52–54.

Meyers, L. (2007b, February). A struggle for hope. *Monitor on Psychology, 38,* 30–31.

Michel, A. (2016, February). Burnout and the brain. *APS Observer, 29*(2), 27–31.

Michikyan, M., Subrahmanyam, K., & Dennis, J. (2014). Can you tell who I am? Neuroticism, extraversion, and online self-presentation among young adults. *Computers in Human Behavior, 33,* 179–183. doi: http://dx.doi.org/10.1016/j.chb.2014.01.010

Mihura, J. L., Meyer, G. J., Bombel, G., & Dumitrascu, N. (2015). Standards, accuracy, and questions of bias

in Rorschach meta-analyses: Reply to Wood, Garb, Nezworski, Lilienfeld, and Duke (2015). *Psychological Bulletin, 141,* 250–260.

Mihura, J. L., Meyer, G. J., Dumitrascu, N., & Bombel, G. (2013). The validity of individual Rorschach variables: Systematic reviews and meta-analyses of the comprehensive system. *Psychological Bulletin, 139,* 548–605. doi: 10.1037/a0029406

Milgram, S. (1963). Behavioral study of obedience. *Journal of Abnormal and Social Psychology, 67,* 371–378.

Milgram, S. (1974). *Obedience to authority.* New York: Harper & Row.

Miller, A. G. (2009). Reflections on "'Replicating Milgram'" (Burger, 2009). *American Psychologist, 64,* 20–27.

Miller, G. (2007). Hunting for meaning after midnight. *Science, 315,* 1360.

Miller, G. (2011). Sweet here, salty there: Evidence for a taste map in the mammalian brain. *Science, 333,* 213. doi: 10.1126/science.333.6047.1213

Miller, J. G., & Bersoff, D. M. (1992). Culture and moral judgment: How are conflicts between justice and interpersonal responsibilities resolved? *Journal of Personality and Social Psychology, 62,* 541–554.

Miller, K. D. (2015, October 11). Will you ever be able to upload your brain? *The New York Times Sunday Review,* p. 6.

Miller, M., Swanson, S. A., Azrael, D., Pate, V., & Stürmer, T. (2014). Antidepressant dose, age, and the risk of deliberate self-harm. *JAMA Internal Medicine, 174,* 899–909. doi: 10.1001/jamainternmed.2014.1053

Miller, P. A., Wallis, G., Bex, P. J., & Arnold, D. H. (2015). Reducing the size of the human physiological blind spot through training. *Current Biology, 25,* R747. doi: 10.1016/j.cub.2015.07.026

Miller, S. L., & Maner, J. K. (2010). Scent of a woman: Men's testosterone responses to olfactory ovulation cues. *Psychological Science, 21,* 276–283. doi: 10.1177/0956797609357733

Millon, T. (2011). *Disorders of personality: Introducing a DSM/ICD spectrum from normal to abnormal* (3rd ed.). Hoboken, NJ: Wiley.

Mills, P. D., Watts, B. V., Huh, T. J. W., Boar, S., & Kemp, J. (2013). Helping elderly patients to avoid suicide: A review of case reports from a national veterans affairs database. *Journal of Nervous & Mental Disease, 201,* 12–16. doi: 10.1097 /NMD.0b013e-31827ab29c

Mischel, W. (1973). Toward a cognitive social learning reconceptualization of personality. *Psychological Review, 80,* 252–283.

Mischel, W. (2009). From personality and assessment (1968) to personality science, 2009. *Journal of Research in Personality, 43,* 282–290. doi: 10.1016/j.jrp.2008.12.037

Mischel, W., & Brooks, D. (2011). The news from psychological science: A conversation between David Brooks and Walter Mischel. *Perspectives on Psychological Science, 6,* 515–520. doi: 10.1177/1745691611425013

Mitchell, J. E., Roerig, J., & Steffen, K. (2013). Biological therapies for eating disorders. *International Journal of Eating Disorders, 46,* 470–477. doi: 10.1002

Mitchell, J. M., O'Neil, J. P., Janabi, M., Marks, S. M., Jagust, W. J., & Fields, H. L. (2012). Alcohol consumption induces endogenous opioid release in the human orbitofrontal cortex and nucleus accumbens. *Science Translational Medicine, 4*, 116ra6. doi: 10.1126/scitranslmed.3002902

Mitka, M. (2013). Groups release new, updated guidelines to reduce heart disease risk factors. *Journal of the American Medical Association, 310*, 2602–2604. doi: 10.1001/jama.2013.284084.

Miyamichi, K., Amat, F., Moussavi, G., Wang, C., Wickersham, I., Wall, N. R., . . . Luo, L. (2010). Cortical representations of olfactory input by trans-synaptic tracing. *Nature.* Published online. Retrieved from www.hfsp.org/frontier-science/awardees-articles/cortical-representations-olfactory-input

Mohee, A., & Eardley, I. (2011). Medical therapy for premature ejaculation. *Therapeutic Advances in Urology, 3*, 211–222.

Mojtabai, R., (2014). Diagnosing depression in older adults in primary care. *New England Journal of Medicine, 370*, 1180–1182. doi: 10.1056/NEJMp1311047

Monaco, J. D., Rao, G., Roth, E. D., & Knierim, J. J. (2014). Attentive scanning behavior drives one-trial potentiation of hippocampal place fields. *Nature Neuroscience, 17*, 725–731. doi: 10.1038/nn.3687

Monahan, K. C., Steinberg, L., & Cauffman, E. (2009). Affiliation with antisocial peers, susceptibility to peer influence, and antisocial behavior during the transition to adulthood. *Developmental Psychology, 45*, 1520–1530. doi: 10.1037 /a0017417

Mondin, T. C., Cardoso, T. de A., , Jansen, K., Silva G., Souza, L. D., & Silva, R. A. (2015). Long-term effects of cognitive therapy on biological rhythms and depressive symptoms: A randomized clinical trial. *Journal of Affective Disorders, 15*, 1–9. doi: 10.1016/j.jad.2015.08.014.

Monshouwer, K., Ten Have, M., van Poppel, M., Kemper, H., & Vollebergh, W. (2013). Possible mechanisms explaining the association between physical activity and mental health: Findings from the 2001 Dutch Health Behaviour in School-Aged Children Survey. *Clinical Psychological Science, 1*, 67–74. doi: 10.1177/2167702612450485

Moon, C., Cooper, R. P., & Fifer, W. P. (1993). Two-day-olds prefer their native language. *Infant Behavior and Development, 16*, 495–500.

Moon, C., Lagercrantz, H., & Kuhl, P. K. (2013). Language experienced in utero affects vowel perception after birth: A two-country study. *Acta Paediatrica, 102*, 156–160. doi: 10.1111/apa.12098

Moore, A. S. (2014, November 2). This is your brain on drugs. *New York Times Education Life*, p. 17.

Moore, S. R., Harden, K. P., & Mendle, J. (2014). Pubertal timing and adolescent sexual behavior in girls. *Developmental Psychology, 50*, 1734–1745. doi: http://dx.doi.org/10.1037/a0036027

Morbidity and Mortality Weekly Report (MMWR). (2015, October 22). *Cigarette, cigar, and marijuana use among high school students: United States, 1997–2013.* Retrieved from http://www.mdlinx.com/psychiatry/top-medical-news/article/2015/10/22/4

Morelli, G. (2015). The evolution of attachment theory and cultures of human attachment in infancy and early childhood. In L. A. Jensen (Ed.), *Oxford handbook of human development and culture.* New York: Oxford University Press.

Mori, N., Lockwood, L., & McCall, W. V. (2015). Current antidepressant therapy: A critical

examination. *Psychiatric Annals, 45*, 456–462. doi: 10.3928/00485713-20150901-04

Mørkved, N., Hartmann, K., Aarsheim, L. M., Holen, D., Milde. A. M., Bomyea, J., . . . Thorp, S. R. (2014). A comparison of narrative exposure therapy and prolonged exposure therapy for PTSD. *Clinical Psychology Review, 34*, 453–467. doi: 10.1016/j.cpr.2014.06.005

Morris, W. N., Miller, R. S., & Spangenberg, S. (1977). The effects of dissenter position and task difficulty on conformity and response conflict. *Journal of Personality, 45*, 251–256.

Moser, M., Franklin, S. F., & Handler, J. (2007). The nonpharmacologic treatment of hypertension: How effective is it? An update. *The Journal of Clinical Hypertension, 9*, 209–216.

Mostafa, T., El Khouly, G., & Hassan, A. (2012). Pheromones in sex and reproduction: Do they have a role in humans? *Journal of Advanced Research, 3*, 1–9.

Motivala, S. J., & Irwin, M. R. (2007). Sleep and immunity: Cytokine pathways linking sleep and health outcomes. *Current Directions in Psychological Science, 16*, 21–25.

Motzkin, J. C., Newman, J. P., Kiehl, K. A., & Koenigs, M. (2011). Reduced prefrontal connectivity in psychopathy. *Journal of Neuroscience, 31*, 17348–17357. doi: 10.1523 /JNEUROSCI.4215-11.2011

Moyer, M. W. (2013, August 23). *The day care dilemma.* Retrieved from http://www.psychologicalscience.org /index.php/news/the-day-care-dilemma.html

Moyer, M. W. (2016, January). Eye contact: How long is too long? *Scientific American Mind, 27*(1), 8.

Mroczek, D. (2014). Personality plasticity, healthy aging, and interventions. *Developmental Psychology, 50*, 1470–1474. doi: 10.1037/a0036028

Muise, A., & Desmarais, S. (2012). Hey Mom, what's on your Facebook? Comparing Facebook disclosure and privacy in adolescents and adults. *Social Psychological and Personality Science, 3*, 48–54. doi: 10.1177/1948550611408619

Mulder, R. T., Frampton, C. M. A., Luty, S. E., & Joyce, P. R. (2009). Eighteen months of drug treatment for depression: Predicting relapse and recovery. *Journal of Affective Disorders, 114*, 263–270. doi: 10.1016/j.jad.2008.08.002

Müller, C. A., Geisel, O., Banas, R., & Heinz, A. (2014). Current pharmacological treatment approaches for alcohol dependence. *Expert Opinion on Pharmacotherapy, 15*, 471–481. doi: 10.1517/14656566.2014.876008. Epub 2014Jan 23.

Mumford, M. D., Medeiros, K. E., & Partlow, P. J. (2012). Creative thinking: Processes, strategies, and knowledge. *The Journal of Creative Behavior, 46*, 30–47.

Munsey, C. (2010, October). Does marriage make us happy? *Monitor on Psychology*, pp. 20–21.

Murray, C J. L., GBD 2013 DALYs, & HALE Collaborators (2015). Global, regional, and national disability-adjusted life years (DALYs) for 306 diseases and injuries and healthy life expectancy (HALE) for 188 countries, 1990–2013: A systematic analysis for the Global Burden of Disease Study 2013. *The Lancet, 386*, 2145–2191. doi: 10.1016/S0140-6736(15)61340-X

Murray, H. A. (1938). *Explorations in personality.* New York: Oxford University Press.

Murstein, B. I., & Mathes, S. (1996). Projection on projective techniques pathology: The problem that is not

being addressed. *Journal of Personality Assessment, 66*, 337–349.

Naci, L., Cusack, R., Jia, V. Z., & Owen, A. M. (2013). The brain's silent messenger: Using selective attention to decode human thought for brain-based communication. *Journal of Neuroscience, 33*, 9385. doi: http://dx.doi.org/10.1523/JNEUROSCI.5577 -12.2013

Nash, R. A., Nash, A., Morris, A., & Smith, S. L. (2015). Does rapport-building boost the eyewitness eyeclosure effect in closed questioning? *Legal and Criminological Psychology*, in press. doi: 10.1111/lcrp.12073

Nassauer, S. (2013). The psychology of small packages. *The Wall Street Journal*, pp. D1, D4.

National Cancer Institute, National Institutes of Health, U.S. Department of Health and Human Services. (2010). *2008–2009 annual report: President's Cancer Panel: Reducing environmental cancer risk: What we can do now.* Bethesda, MD: Author.

National Center for Health Statistics. (2012a). *Health, United States, 2012: In brief.* Hyattsville, MD.

National Center for Health Statistics. (2012b). *Health, United States, 2011: With special feature on socioeconomic status and health.* Hyattsville, MD.

National Council on Patient Information and Education (NCPIE). (2013a). *Taking action to prevent and address prescription drug abuse.* Retrieved from www.talkaboutrx.org/college_resource_kit.jsp

National Council on Patient Information and Education (NCPIE) (2013b). *Get the facts: prescription drug abuse on college campuses.* Retrieved from www.talkaboutrx.org /documents/GetTheFacts.pdf

National Highway Transportation and Safety Administration (NHSTA). (2013). *What is distracted driving?* Retrieved from www.distraction.gov/content/get-the -facts/facts-and -statistics.html

National Institute of Environment Health Sciences. (2001). Brainteaser quizzes. *NIEHS kids' pages.* Washington, D.C.: National Institutes of Health. Retrieved from www.niehs .nih.gov/kids/questionstx.htm

National Institute of Mental Health. (2001). *Seeing our feelings: Imaging emotion in the brain* (NIH Publication No. 01-460). Bethesda, MD: Author.

National Institute on Drug Abuse (NIDA). (2013, September). *MDMA (Ecstasy/Molly).* Retrieved from https://www.drugabuse.gov/drugs-abuse/mdma-ecstasymolly

National Institutes of Health (NIH), National Institute on Alcohol Abuse and Alcoholism (2015, December). *College drinking.* Retrieved from http://pubs.niaaa.nih .gov/publications/CollegeFactSheet/CollegeFactSheet.pdf

National Survey of Sexual Health and Behavior (NSSHB). (2010). Findings from the National Survey of Sexual Health and Behavior. *Journal of Sexual Medicine, 7* (Supp. 5).

National Women's Health Information Center, U.S. Department of Health and Human Services, Office on Women's Health. (2009, August 10). *Genital herpes.* Retrieved from http://www.womenshealth.gov/faq /genital-herpes .cfm#b

Nauczyciel, C., Le Jeune, F., Naudet, F., Douabin, S., Esquevin, A., Vérin, M., . . . Millet, B. (2014). Repetitive transcranial magnetic stimulation over the orbitofrontal cortex for obsessive-compulsive disorder: A double-blind, crossover study. *Translational Psychiatry, 9*, e436. doi: 10.1038/tp.2014.62

Nawrot, M., Nordenstrom, B., & Olson, A. (2004). Disruption of eye movements by ethanol intoxication affects perception of depth from motion parallax. *Psychological Science, 15,* 858–865.

Neighbors, C., Lee, C. M., Atkins, D. C., Lewis, M. A., Kaysen, D., Mittmann, A., . . . Larimer, M. A. (2012). A randomized controlled trial of event-specific prevention strategies for reducing problematic drinking associated with 21st birthday celebrations. *Journal of Consulting and Clinical Psychology, 80,* 850–862. doi: 10.1037/a0029480

Nelson, T. D. (2002). *The psychology of prejudice.* Boston: Allyn and Bacon.

Nemiah, J. C. (1988). Psychoneurotic disorders. In A. M. Nicholi, Jr. (Ed.), *The new Harvard guide to psychiatry* (pp. 234–258). Cambridge, MA: Belknap Press.

Nenadic, I., Maitra ,R., Dietzek, M., Langbein, K., Smesny, S., Sauer, H., . . . Gaser, C. (2015). Prefrontal gyrification in psychotic bipolar I disorder vs. schizophrenia. *Journal of Affective Disorders, 185,* 104–107. doi: 10.1016/j.jad.2015.06.014

Nestoriuc, Y., & Martin, A. (2007). Efficacy of biofeedback for migraine: A meta-analysis. *Radiology Source, 128,* 111–127.

Nestoriuc, Y., Rief, W., & Martin, A. (2008). Meta-analysis of biofeedback for tension-type headache: Efficacy, specificity, and treatment moderators. *Journal of Consulting and Clinical Psychology, 76,* 379–396. doi: 10.1037/0022-006X.76.3.379

Nettelbeck, T., & Wilson, C. (2005). Intelligence and IQ: What teachers should know. *Educational Psychology, 25,* 609–630.

Neuroscience News. (2010, December 17). The fearless SM: Woman missing amygdala. Retrieved from http://neurosciencenews.com/sm-fearless-woman -missing-amygdala/

Nevid, J. S. (1984). Sex differences in factors of romantic attraction. *Sex Roles, 11,* 401–411.

Nevid, J. S. (2010). Implicit measures of consumer response: The search for the Holy Grail of marketing research. Introduction to special issue. *Psychology and Marketing, 27,* 913–910. doi: 10.1002/mar.2036

Nevid, J. S. (2011, May/June). Teaching the millennials. *APS Observer, 24*(5), 153–156.

Nevid, J. S., & Carmony, T. M. (2002). Traditional versus modular format in presenting textual material in introductory psychology. *Teaching of Psychology, 29,* 237–238.

Nevid, J. S., & Lampmann, J. L. (2003). Effects on content acquisition of signaling key concepts in text material. *Teaching of Psychology, 30,* 227–229.

Nevid, J. S., & Rathus, S. A. (2010). *Psychology and the challenges of life* (11th ed.). New York: Wiley.

Nevid, J. S., & Rathus, S. A. (2013). *Psychology and the challenges of life* (12th ed.). New York: Wiley.

Nevid, J. S., Rathus, S. A., & Greene, B. (2006). *Abnormal psychology in a changing world* (6th ed.). Upper Saddle River, NJ: Prentice Hall.

Nevid, J. S., Rathus, S. A., & Greene, B. (2008). *Abnormal psychology in a changing world* (7th ed.). Upper Saddle River, NJ: Prentice Hall.

Nevid, J. S., Rathus, S. A., & Greene, B. (2014). *Abnormal psychology in a changing world* (9th ed.). Upper Saddle River, NJ: Pearson Education.

Nevid, J. S., & Sta. Maria, N. (1999). Multicultural issues in qualitative research. *Psychology and Marketing, 16,* 305–325.

Nevis, E. C. (2014) (Ed.). *Gestalt therapy: Perspectives and applications* (Rev. edition). Cleveland, IN: Gestalt Press.

New Parkinson's disease chemical messenger discovered. (2014, May 27). *ScienceDaily.* Retrieved from http://www.sciencedaily.com/releases/2014/03 /140327222452.htm

Newby-Clark, I. R., McGregor, I., & Zanna, M. P. (2002). Thinking and caring about cognitive inconsistency: When and for whom does attitudinal ambivalence feel uncomfortable? *Journal of Personality and Social Psychology, 82,* 157–166.

Ng, M., Fleming, T., Robinson, M., Thomson, B., Graetz, N., Margono, C., . . . Gakidou, E. (2014). Global, regional, and national prevalence of overweight and obesity in children and adults during 1980–2013: A systematic analysis for the Global Burden of Disease Study 2013. *The Lancet, 384,*766–781. doi: 10.1016/S0140-6736(14)60460-8

Ngandu, T., Lehtisalo, J., Solomon, A., Levälahti, E., Ahtiluoto, S., Antikainen, R., & Kivipelto, M. (2015). A 2 year multidomain intervention of diet, exercise, cognitive training, and vascular risk monitoring versus control to prevent cognitive decline in at-risk elderly people (FINGER): A randomised controlled trial. *Lancet.* Retrieved from http://dx .doi.org/10.1016/S0140-6736(15)60461-5

NICHD Early Child Care Research Network. (1997). The effects of infant child care on infant-mother attachment security: Results of the NICHD study of early child care. *Child Development, 68,* 860–879.

Nicholson, R. A., Mouton, G. J., Bagby, R. M., Buis, T., Peterson, S. A., & Buigas, R. A. (1997). Utility of MMPI-2 indicators of response distortion: Receiver operating characteristic analysis. *Psychological Assessment, 9,* 471–479.

Nickerson, R. A., & Adams, M. J. (1979). Long-term memory for a common object. *Cognitive Psychology, 11,* 287–307.

NIDA Notes (2004, December). 2003 survey reveals increase in prescription drug abuse, sharp drop in abuse of hallucinogens. *NIDA Notes, 19*(4), 14.

Nielsen, J. A., Zielinski, B. A., Ferguson, M. A., Lainhart, J. E., & Anderson, J. S. (2013). An evaluation of the left-brain vs. right-brain hypothesis with resting state functional connectivity magnetic resonance imaging. *PLoS ONE, 8,* e71275. doi: 10.1371/journal.pone.0071275

Nigg, J. T. (2013). Commentary: Gene by environment interplay and psychopathology—in search of a paradigm. *Journal of Child Psychology and Psychiatry, 54,* 1150–1152. doi: 10.1111/jcpp.12134

Niiya, Y., Ellsworth, P. C., & Yamaguchi, S. (2006). Amae in Japan and the United States: An exploration of a "culturally unique" emotion. *Emotion, 6,* 279–295.

Nisbett, R. E., Aronson, J., Blair, C., Dickens, W., Flynn, J., Halpern, D., & Turkheimer, E. (2012a). Group differences in IQ are best understood as environmental in origin. *American Psychologist, 67,* 503–504. doi: 10.1037 /a0029772

Nisbett, R. E., Aronson, J., Blair, C., Dickens, W., Flynn, J., Halpern, D. E., & Turkheimer, E. (2012b). Intelligence: New findings and theoretical developments. *American Psychologist, 6,* 130–159. doi: 10.1037/ a0026699

Nolen-Hoeksema, S. (2008). It is not what you have; it is what you do with it: Support for Addis's gendered

responding framework. *Clinical Psychology: Science and Practice, 15,* 178–181.

Nolen-Hoeksema, S. (2012). Emotion regulation and psychopathology: The role of gender. *Annual Review of Clinical Psychology, 8,* 161–187. doi: 10.1146 /annurev -clinpsy-032511-143109

Noonan, D. (2006, June 6). A little bit louder, please. *Newsweek,* pp. 42–45.

Norcross, J. C., & Karpiak, C. P. (2012). Clinical psychologists in the 2010s: 50 years of the APA Division of Clinical Psychology. *Clinical Psychology: Science and Practice, 19,* 1–12. doi: 10.1111/j.1468 -2850.2012.01269

Norcross, J. C., & Lambert, M. J. (2014). Relationship science and practice in psychotherapy: Closing commentary. *Psychotherapy, 51,* 398–403. doi: http:// dx.doi.org/10.1037/a0037418

Nosek, B. A., Banaji, M. R., & Greenwald, A. G. (2003). Math male, me female, therefore math—me. *Journal of Personality and Social Psychology, 83,* 44–59.

Novotney, A. (2013, November). No such thing as 'right-brained' or 'left-brained,' new research finds. *Monitor on Psychology, 44,* 10

Nowak, A., Vallacher, R. R., & Miller, M. E. (2003). Social influence and group dynamics. In T. Millon & M. J. Lerner (Eds.), *Handbook of psychology: Personality and social psychology* (Vol. 5, pp. 383–418). New York: Wiley.

Nowak, D. A., Bösl, K., Podubeckà, J., & Carey, J. R. (2010). Noninvasive brain stimulation and motor recovery after stroke. *Restorative Neurology and Neuroscience, 28,* 531–544. doi: 10.3233/RNN-2010-0552

Nyberg, L., Lövdén, M., Riklund, K., Lindenberger, U., & Bäckman, L. (2012). Memory aging and brain maintenance. *Trends in Cognitive Sciences, 16,* 292. doi: 10.1016 /j.tics.2012.04.005

NYC Department of Health and Mental Hygiene. (2010). *Tobacco control.* Retrieved from www.nyc .gov

O'Connor, A. (2012). Sleep apnea is linked to a higher risk of cancer. *The New York Times,* p. D5.

O'Keefe, V. M., Wingate, L. R., Tucker, R. P., Rhoades-Kerswill, S., Slish, M. L., & Davidson, C. L. (2014). Interpersonal suicide risk for American Indians: Investigating thwarted belongingness and perceived burdensomeness. *Cultural Diversity and Ethnic Minority Psychology, 20,* 61–67. doi: 10.1037/ a0033540

Oberauer, K., & Kliegl, R. (2004). Simultaneous cognitive operations in working memory after dual-task practice. *Journal of Experimental Psychology: Human Perception and Performance, 30,* 689–707.

O'Connor, A. (2015). A fresh look at sleep needs. *The New York Times,* p. D2.

Ogawa, Y., Tajika, A., Takeshima, N., Hayasaka, Y., & Furukawa, T. A. (2014). Mood stabilizers and antipsychotics for acute mania: A systematic review and meta-analysis of combination/augmentation therapy versus monotherapy. *CNS Drugs, 28,* 989–1003. doi: 10.1007/s40263-014-0197-8

Ogden, C. L., Carroll, M. D., Kit, B. K., & Flegal, K. M. (2014). Prevalence of childhood and adult obesity in the United States, 2011–2012. *Journal of the American Medical Association, 311,* 806–814. doi: 10.1001/jama.2014.732

Ohayon, M. M., Mahowald, M. W., Dauvilliers, Y., Krystal, A. D., & Leger, D. (2012). Prevalence and comorbidity of nocturnal wandering in the US adult general population. *Neurology, 78,* 1583. doi: 10.1212/WNL.0b013e3182563

Okbay, A., Baselmans, B. M., De Neve, J. E., Turley, P., Nivard, M. G., Fontana, M. A., . . . Cesarini, D. Genetic variants associated with subjective well-being, depressive symptoms, and neuroticism identified through genome-wide analyses. *Nature Genetics, 48,* 624–633. doi: 10.1038/ng.3552

Okun, M. S. (2014). Deep-brain stimulation: Entering the era of human neural-network modulation. *New England Journal of Medicine, 371,* 1369–1373. doi: 10.1056/NEJMp1408779

Olfson, M., Druss, B. G., & Marcus, S. C. (2015). Trends in mental health care among children and adolescents. *New England Journal of Medicine, 372,* 2029–2038. doi: 10.1056/NEJMsa1413512

Olfson, M., Marcus, S. C., & Bridge, J. A. (2014). Focusing suicide prevention on periods of high risk. *Journal of the American Medical Association, 311,* 1107–1108. doi: 10.1001/jama.2014.501.

Olson, E. (2015, January 10). When outside factors dictate retirement age. *The New York Times,* p. B4.

Olson, J. M., & Maio, G. R. (2003). Attitudes in social behavior. In T. Millon & M. J. Lerner (Eds.), *Handbook of psychology: Personality and social psychology* (Vol. 5, pp. 299–326). New York: Wiley.

Olsson, C. A., McGee, R., Nada-Raja, S, & Williams, S. M. (2012). A 32-year longitudinal study of child and adolescent pathways to well-being in adulthood. *Journal of Happiness Studies, 13,* 1–15. doi: 10.1007/s10902-012-9369-8

Onion, A. (2000, September 12). Subliminal signals: All in the mind. Retrieved from http://abcnews.go.com /Technology /story?id=119954&page=1# .UcNC8bvLhr8

Oquendo, M. A., Hastings, R. S., Huang, Y., Simpson, N., Ogden, R. T., Hu, X. Z., . . . Parsey, R. V. (2007). Brain serotonin transporter binding in depressed patients with bipolar disorder using positron emission tomography. *Archives of General Psychiatry, 64,* 201–208.

Orchowski, L. M., Mastroleo, N. R., & Borsari, B. (2012). Correlates of alcohol-related sex among college students. *Psychology of Addictive Behaviors, 26,* 782–790. doi: 10.1037/a0027840

Ormerod, T. C., MacGregor, J. N., & Chronicle, E. P. (2002). Dynamics and constraints in insight problem solving. *Journal of Experimental Psychology: Learning, Memory, and Cognition, 28,* 791–799.

Orth, U., Maes, J., & Schmitt, M. (2015).Self-esteem development across the life span: A longitudinal study with a large sample from Germany. *Developmental Psychology, 51,* 248–259.

Orth, U. & Robins, R. W. (2014). The development of self-esteem. *Current Directions in Psychological Science, 23,* 381–387. doi: 10.1177/0963721414547414

Ortigue, S., Bianchi-Demicheli, F., Patel, N., Frum, C., & Lewis, J. W. (2010). Neuroimaging of love: fMRI meta-analysis evidence toward new perspectives in sexual medicine. *The Journal of Sexual Medicine, 7,* 3451–3552. doi: 10.1111/j.1743-6109.2010.01999.x

Osborne, A. F. (1963). *Applied imagination: Principles and procedures of creative problem solving.* New York: Scribners.

Ossenkoppele, R., Jansen, W. J., Rabinovici, G. D., Knol, D. L., van der Flier, W. M., van Berckel, B. N. M., . . . Amyloid PET Study Group (2015). Prevalence of amyloid pet positivity in dementia syndromes: A meta-analysis. *Journal of the American Medical Association, 313,* 1939–1949. doi: 10.1001/jama.2015.4669

Öst, L.-G., Havnen, A., Hansen, B., & Kvale, G. (2015). Cognitive behavioral treatments of obsessive–compulsive disorder. A systematic review and meta-analysis of studies published 1993–2014. *Clinical Psychology Review, 40,* 156–169. doi: 10.1016/j.cpr.2015.06.003

Ostir, G. V., Berges, I. M., Markides, K. S., & Ottenbacher, K. J. (2006). Hypertension in older adults and the role of positive emotions. *Psychosomatic Medicine, 68,* 727–733.

Ouellette, S. C., & DiPlacido, J. (2001). Personality's role in the protection and enhancements of health: Where the research has been, where it is stuck, how it might move. In A. Baum, T. A. Revenson, & J. E. Singer (Eds.), *Handbook of health psychology* (pp. 175–194). Mahwah, NJ: Erlbaum.

Overstreet, N. M., Quinn, D. M., & Agocha, V. B. (2010). Beyond thinness: The influence of a curvaceous body ideal on body dissatisfaction in Black and White women. *Sex Roles, 63,* 91–103. doi: 10.1007/s11199-010-9792-4

Oyserman, D., Coon, H. M., & Kemmelmeier, M. (2002). Rethinking individualism and collectivism: Evaluation of theoretical assumptions and meta-analyses. *Psychological Bulletin, 128,* 3–72.

Özgen, E. (2004). Language, learning, and color perception. *Current Directions in Psychological Science, 13,* 95–102.

Pabst, A., Kraus, L., Piontek, D., Mueller, S., & Demmel, R. (2014). Direct and indirect effects of alcohol expectancies on alcohol-related problems. *Psychology of Addictive Behaviors, 28,* 20–30. doi: 10.1037/a0031984

Pacheco-Lopez, G., Niemi, M. B., Kou, W., Harting, M., Fandrey, J., & Schedlowski, M. (2005). Neural substrates for behaviorally conditioned immunosuppression in the rat. *Journal of Neuroscience, 25,* 2330–2337.

Packer, D. J. (2008). Identifying systematic disobedience in Milgram's Obedience experiments: A meta-analytic review. *Perspectives on Psychological Science, 3,* 301–304. doi: 10.1111/j.1745-6924.2008.00080.x

Padrón, E., Carlson, E. A., & Sroufe, L. A. (2014). Frightened versus not frightened disorganized infant attachment: Newborn characteristics and maternal caregiving. *American Journal of Orthopsychiatry, 84,* 201–208.

Palfai, T. P., & Weafer, J. (2006). College student drinking and meaning in the pursuit of life goals. *Psychology of Addictive Behaviors, 20,* 131–134.

Pampaloni, I., Sivakumaran, T., Hawley, C. J., Al Allaq, A., Farrow, J., Nelson, S., & Fineberg, N. A. (2009). High-dose selective serotonin reuptake inhibitors in OCD: A systematic retrospective case notes survey. *Journal of Psychopharmacology, 24,* 1439–1445. doi: 10.1177/0269881109104850

Pancsofar, N., & Vernon-Feagans, L. (2006). Mother and father language input to young children: Contributions to later language development. *Journal of Applied Developmental Psychology, 27,* 571–587.

Pansu, P., Lima, L, & Fointiat, V. (2014). When saying no leads to compliance: The door-in-the-face

technique for changing attitudes and behaviors towards smoking at work. *RevueEuropéenne de Psychologie Appliquée/European Review of Applied Psychology, 64,* 19–27.

Papadatou-Pastou, M., Martin, M., Munafò, M. R., & Jones, G. V. (2008). Sex differences in left-handedness: A meta-analysis of 144 studies. *Psychological Bulletin, 134,* 677–699. doi: 10.1037/a0012814

Paris, J. (2010). Estimating the prevalence of personality disorders in the community. *Journal of Personality Disorders, 24,* 405–411.

Park, A., Sher, K. J., Wood, P. K., & Krull, J. L. (2009). Dual mechanisms underlying accentuation of risky drinking via fraternity/sorority affiliation: The role of personality, peer norms, and alcohol availability. *Journal of Abnormal Psychology, 118,* 241–255. doi: 10.1037/a0015126

Park, D. C., Lautenschlager, G., Hedden, T., Davidson, N. S., Smith, A. D., & Smith, P. K. (2002). Models of visuospatial and verbal memory across the adult life span. *Psychology and Aging, 17,* 299–320.

Park, D. C., Lodi-Smith, J., Drew, L., Haber, S., Hebrank, A., Bischof, G. N., . . . Aamodt, W. (2014). The impact of sustained engagement on cognitive function in older adults: The Synapse Project. *Psychological Science, 25,* 103–112. doi: 10.1177/0956797613499592

Park, D. C., & McDonough, I. M. (2013). The dynamic aging mind: Revelations from functional neuroimaging research. *Perspectives on Psychological Science, 8,* 62–67, doi: 10.1177/1745691612469034

Park, N., Jin, B., & Jin, S. A. (2011). Effects of self-disclosure on relational intimacy in Facebook. *Computers in Human Behavior, 27,* 1974–1983.

Parke, R. D. (2004). Development in the family. *Annual Review of Psychology, 55,* 365–399.

Parke, R. D., & Buriel, R. (1998). Socialization in the family: Ethnic and ecological perspectives. In W. Damon (Editor-in-Chief) & N. Eisenberg (Vol. Ed.), *Handbook of child psychology: Social, emotional, and personality development* (Vol. 3, 5th ed., pp. 463–552). New York: Wiley.

Parker-Pope, T. (2009, January 13). A problem of the brain, not the hands: Group urges phone ban for drivers. *The New York Times,* p. D5.

Parloff, R. (2003, February 3). Is fat the next tobacco? *Fortune,* pp. 51–54.

Pascalis, O., deHaan, M., Nelson, C. A., & de Schonen, S. (1998). Long-term recognition memory for faces assessed by visual paired comparison in 3- and 6-month-old infants. *Journal of Experimental Psychology: Learning, Memory, and Cognition, 24,* 249–260.

Passolunghi, M. C., Ferreira, T. I. R., & Tomasetto, C. (2014). Math-gender stereotypes and math-related beliefs in childhood and early adolescence. *Learning and Individual Differences, 34,* 70–76.

Pasupathi, M. (1999). Age differences in response to conformity pressure for emotional and nonemotional material. *Psychology and Aging, 14,* 170–174.

Patihis, L., Lilienfeld, S. O., Ho, L. Y., & Loftus, E. F. (2014). Unconscious repressed memory is scientifically questionable. *Psychological Science, 25,* 1967–1968. doi: 10.1177/0956797614547365

Patrick, M. E., & Schulenberg, J. E. (2011). How trajectories of reasons for alcohol use relate to trajectories of binge drinking: National panel data spanning late adolescence to early adulthood. *Developmental Psychology, 47,* 311–317.

Patterson, C. J. (2009). *Lesbian & gay parents & their children: Summary of research findings*. Retrieved from www.apa.org /pi/lgbc/publications/lgpsummary .html

Patterson, D. R., & Jensen, M. P. (2003). Hypnosis and clinical pain. *Psychological Bulletin, 129,* 495–521.

Paul, A. M. (2013, August 15). 10 ways we get smarter as we age. *Time.* Retrieved from http://ideas.time .com/2013/08/15/10-ways-we-get-smarter-as-we -age/#ixzz2cv2jXJ8W

Paulos, J. A. (2009, December 12). Mammogram math. *The New York Times Magazine,* pp. 19–20.

Payne, J. D., & Kensinger, E. A. (2010). Sleep's role in the consolidation of emotional episodic memories. *Current Directions in Psychological Science, 19,* 290–295. doi: 10.1177/096372141038397

Paz-Alonso, P. M., Gallego, P., & Ghetti. S. (2013). Age differences in hippocampus-cortex connectivity during true and false memory retrieval. *Journal of the International Neuropsychological Society, 19,* 1031. doi: 10.1017/S1355617713001069

Pazda, A. D., & Elliot, A. J. (2012). The color of attraction: How red influences physical appeal. In M. Paludi (Ed.), *The psychology of love.* Santa Barbara, CA: Praeger.

Pazda, A. D., Elliot, A. J., & Greitemeyer, T. (2012). Sexy red: Perceived sexual receptivity mediates the red-attraction relation in men viewing women. *Journal of Experimental Social Psychology, 48,* 787–790. doi: 10.1016/j.jesp.2011.12.009

Pazzaglia, M. (2015). Body and odors: Not just molecules, after all. *Current Directions in Psychological Science, 24,* 329–333. doi: 10.1177 /0963721415575329

Pearson, H. (2006, September 18). Distaste for sprouts in the genes. *News@Nature.com.* Retrieved from www .nature .com/news/2006/060918/full/060918-1.html

Pearson, J. (2014). New directions in mental-imagery research: The binocular-rivalry technique and decoding fMRI patterns. *Current Directions in Psychological Science, 23,* 178–183. doi: 10.1177/0963721414532287

Peciña, M., Bohnert, A. S., Sikora, M., Avery, E. T., Langenecker, S. A., Mickey, B. I., . . . Zubieta, J. K. (2015). Association between placebo-activated neural systems and antidepressant responses: Neurochemistry of placebo effects in major depression. *JAMA Psychiatry, 30,* 1–8. doi: 10.1001/jamapsychia-try.2015.1335

Pedersen, D. M., & Wheeler, J. (1983). The Müller-Lyer illusion among Navajos. *Journal of Social Psychology, 121,* 3–6.

doi: Pennant, M. E., Loucas, C. E., Whittington, C., Creswell, C., Fonagy, P., Fugglee, P., . . . Kendall, T. (2015). Computerised therapies for anxiety and depression in children and young people: A systematic review and meta-analysis. *Behaviour Research and Therapy, 67,* 1–18.

Penner, L. A., Dovidio, J. F., Piliavin, J. A., & Schroeder, D. A. (2005). Prosocial behavior: Multilevel perspectives. *Annual Review of Psychology, 56,* 365–392.

Pennesi, J. L., & Wade. T. D. (2016). A systematic review of the existing models of disordered eating: Do they inform the development of effective interventions? *Clinical Psychology Review, 43,* 175–192. doi: 10.1016/j.cpr.2015.12.004

Pepper, T. (2005, February 21). Inside the head of an applicant. *Newsweek,* pp. E24–E26.

Perlis, R. H., Ostacher, M., Fava, M., Nierenberg, A. A., Sachs, G. S., & Rosenbaum, J. F. (2010). Assuring that double-blind is blind. *American Journal of Psychiatry, 167,* 2502–2552. doi: 10.1176/appi. ajp.2009.09060820

Perrinet, L. U., & Bednar, J. A. (2015). Edge co-occurrences can account for rapid categorization of natural versus animal images. *Scientific Reports, 5,* 11400. doi: 10.1038/srep11400

Personality outsmarts intelligence at school: Conscientiousness and openness key to learning. (2014, December 17). *ScienceDaily.* Retrieved from http:// www.sciencedaily.com/releases/2014/12 /141217090812.htm

Pesant, N., & Zadra, A. (2004). Working with dreams in therapy: What do we know and what should we do? *Clinical Psychology Review, 24,* 489–512.

Petersen, L., Sørensen, T. I. A., Andersen, P. K., Mortensen, P. B., & Hawton, K. (2014). Genetic and familial environmental effects on suicide attempts: A study of Danish adoptees and their biological and adoptive siblings. *Journal of Affective Disorders, 155,* 273–277.

Peterson, M. A., & Skow, E. (2008). Inhibitory competition between shape properties in figure–ground perception. *Journal of Experimental Psychology: Human Perception and Performance, 34,* 251–267. doi: 10.1037/0096 -1523.34.2.251

Petit, D., Pennestri, M. H., Paquet, J., Desautels, A., Zadra, A., Vitaro, F., . . . Montplaisir, J. (2015). Childhood sleepwalking and sleep terrors: A longitudinal study of prevalence and familial aggregation. *JAMA Pediatrics.* Retrieved from http://dx.doi.org /10.1001/jamapediatrics.2015.127

Pettigrew, T. F., & Tropp, L. R. A. (2006). A meta-analytic test of intergroup contact theory. *Journal of Personality and Social Psychology, 90,* 751–783.

Pettigrew, T. F., Tropp, L. R., Wagner, U., & Christ, O. (2011). Recent advances in intergroup contact. International *Journal of Intercultural Relations, 35,* 271–280.

Petty, R. E., & Briñol, P. (2008). Persuasion: From single to multiple to metacognitive processes. *Perspectives on Psychological Science, 3,* 137–147. doi: 10.1111/j.1745-6916.2008.00071

Philippson, P. (2012). *Gestalt therapy: Roots and branches—Collected papers.* London, England: Karnac Books.

Phillips, M. L., & Swartz, H. A. (2014). A critical appraisal of neuroimaging studies of bipolar disorder: toward a new conceptualization of underlying neural circuitry and a road map for future research. *American Journal of Psychiatry, 171,* 829–843. doi: 10.1176/appi.ajp.2014.13081008

Phillips, S. T., & Ziller, R. C. (1997). Toward a theory and measure of the nature of nonprejudice. *Journal of Personality and Social Psychology, 72,* 420–434.

Piaget, J. (1952). *The origins of intelligence in children.* New York: International Universities Press.

Pierre, M. R., & Mahalik, J. R. (2005). Examining African self-consciousness and Black racial identity as predictors of Black men's psychological well-being. *Cultural Diversity and Ethnic Minority Psychology, 11,* 28–40.

Pietschnig, J., & Voracek, M. (2015). One century of global IQ Gains: A formal meta-analysis of the Flynn Effect (1909–2013). *Perspectives on Psychological Science, 10,* 282–306. doi: 10.1177/1745691615577701

Pink, D. (2003, December 14). Gratitude visits. *The New York Times Magazine,* p. 73.

Pinker, S. (1994). *The language instinct.* New York: William Morrow.

Pinker, S. (2003). Language as an adaptation to the cognitive niche. In M. H. Christiansen & S. Kirby (Eds.), *Language evolution* (pp. 16–37). New York: Oxford University Press.

Pinto, P. R., McIntyre, T., Almeida, A., & Araújo-Soares, V. (2011). The mediating role of pain catastrophizing in the relationship between pre-surgical anxiety and acute postsurgical pain after hysterectomy. *Pain, 153,* 218–226. doi: 10.1016/j. pain.2011.10.020

Pittler, M. H., & Ernst, E. (2005, May 31). Complementary therapies for reducing body weight: A systematic review. *International Journal of Obesity, 29,* 1030–1038. doi: 10.1038/sj.ijo.0803008

Plaks, J. E., & Higgins, E. T. (2000). Pragmatic use of stereotyping in teamwork: Social loafing and compensation as a function of inferred partner-situation fit. *Journal of Personality and Social Psychology, 79,* 962–974.

Plaza, M., Gatignol, P., Leroy, M. , & Duffau, H. (2009). Speaking without Broca's area after tumor resection. *Neurocase, 9,* 1–17.

Plewnia, C., Pasqualetti, P., Große, S., Schlipf, S., Wasserka, B., Zwissler, B., & Fallgatter, A. (2014). Treatment of major depression with bilateral theta burst stimulation: A randomized controlled pilot trial. *Journal of Affective Disorders, 156,* 219–223. doi: 10.1016/j.jad.2013.12.025

Pliner, P. H., Hart, H., Kohl, J., & Saari, D. (1974). Compliance without pressure: Some further data on the foot-in-the door technique. *Journal of Experimental Social Psychology, 10,* 17–22.

Plomin, R., & Haworth, C. M. A. (2009). Genetics of high cognitive abilities. *Journal of Behavior Genetics, 39,* 347–349. doi: 10.1007/s10519-009-9277-9

Plomin, R., & Petrill, S. A. (1997). Genetics and intelligence: What's new. *Intelligence, 24,* 53–57.

Pokhrel, P., Herzog, T. A., Sun, P., Rohrbach, L. A., & Sussman, S. (2013). Acculturation, social self-control, and substance use among Hispanic adolescents. *Psychology of Addictive Behaviors, 27,* 674–686. doi: 10.1037/a0032836

Polderman, T. J. C., Benyamin, B., de Leeuw, C. A., Sullivan, P. F., van Bochoven, A., Visscher, P. M., & Posthuma, D. (2015). Meta-analysis of the heritability of human traits based on fifty years of twin studies. *Nature Genetics, 47,* 702–709. doi: 10.1038/ng.3285

Poldrack, R. A. (2010). Mapping mental function to brain structure: How can cognitive neuroimaging succeed? *Perspectives on Psychological Science, 5,* 753–761. doi: 10.1177/1745691610388777

Pollick, A. S., & de Waal, F. B. M. (2007). Ape gestures and language evolution. *Proceedings of the National Academy of Sciences, Online Edition.* doi: 10.1073/ pnas.0702624104

Polusny, M. A., Erbes, C. R., Thuras, P., Moran, A., Lamberty, G. J., Collins, R. C., . . . Lim, K. O. (2015). Mindfulness-based stress reduction for posttraumatic stress disorder among veterans. *Journal of the American Medical Association, 314,* 456. doi: 10.1001/ jama.2015.8361

Pomerantz, J. R., & Portillo, M. C. (2011). Grouping and emergent features in vision: Toward a theory of basic Gestalts. *Journal of Experimental Psychology: Human Perception and Performance, 37,* 1331–1349. doi: 10.1037/a0024330

Pomplun, M., Silva, E. J., Ronda, J. M., Cain, S. W., Münch, M. Y., Czeisler, C. A., . . . Duffy, J. F. (2012). The effects of circadian phase, time awake, and imposed sleep restriction on performing complex visual tasks: Evidence from comparative visual search. *The Journal of Vision, 26,* 14. doi: 10.1167/12.7.14. doi 10.1167/12.7.14

Poropat, A. E. (2009). A meta-analysis of the five-factor model of personality and academic performance. *Psychological Bulletin, 135,* 322–338. doi: 10.1037/a0014996

Poulin, M. (2012, December). Our genes want us to be altruists. *APS Observer, 25,* pp. 11–15.

Poulsen , S., Lunn, S., Daniel, S. I. F., Folke, S., Mathiesen, B. B., Katznelson, H., . . . Fairburn C. G. (2014). A randomized controlled trial of psychoanalytic psychotherapy or cognitive-behavioral therapy for bulimia nervosa. *American Journal of Psychiatry, 171,* 109–113.

Powers, S. W., Kashikar-Zuck, S. M., Allen, J. R., LeCates, S. L., Slater, S. K. , Zafar, M., . . . Hershey, A. D. (2013). Cognitive behavioral therapy plus amitriptyline for chronic migraine in children and adolescents: A randomized clinical trial. *Journal of the American Medical Association, 310,* 2622–2630. doi: 10.1001/jama.2013.282533

Premack, D. (1971). Language in chimpanzees. *Science, 172,* 808–822.

Price, M. (2009a, January). The left brain knows what the right hand is doing. *Monitor on Psychology, 40*(1), 60–63.

Price, M. (2009b, January). Lateral of the sexes. *Monitor on Psychology, 40*(1), 62.

Price, M. (2009c, December). More than shelter. *Monitor on Psychology, 40*(11), 59–62.

Price, T. S., & Jaffee, S. R. (2008). Effects of the family environment: Gene–environment interaction and passive gene–environment correlation. *Developmental Psychology, 44,* 305–315. doi: 10.1037/0012-1649.44.2.305

Priebe, N. J., & Ferster, D. (2010). Neuroscience: Each synapse to its own. *Nature, 464,* 1290–1291. doi: 10.1038/4641290b

Prochaska, J. O., & Norcross, J. C. (2010). *Systems of psychotherapy* (7th ed.). Pacific Grove, CA: Brooks/Cole, Cengage Learning.

Proffitt, D. R. (2006). Distance perception. *Current Directions in Psychological Science, 15,* 131–135.

Proto, E., & Rustichini. A. (2013). A reassessment of the relationship between GDP and life satisfaction. *PLoS ONE, 8,* e79358. doi: 10.1371/journal.pone.0079358

Protzko, J., Aronson, J., & Blair, C. (2013). How to make a young child smarter: Evidence from the database of raising intelligence. *Perspectives on Psychological Science, 8,* 25–40. doi: 10.1177/1745691612462585

Provine, R. R. (2004). Laughing, tickling and the evolution of speech and self. *Current Directions in Psychological Science, 13,* 215–218.

Prudic, J., Olfson, M., Marcus, S. C., Fuller, R. B., & Sackheim, H. A. (2004). Effectiveness of electroconvulsive therapy in community settings. *Biological Psychiatry, 55,* 301–312.

Pruessner, M., Iyer, S. N., Faridi, K., Joober, R., & Malla, A. K. (2011). Stress and protective factors in individuals at ultra-high risk for psychosis, first episode psychosis and healthy controls. *Schizophrenia Research, 129,* 29–35.

Pulkki-Raback, L., Kivimaki, M., Ahola, K., Joutsenniemi, K., Elovainio, M., Rossi, H., . . Virtanen, M. (2012). Living alone and antidepressant medication use: A prospective study in a working-age population. *BMC Public Health, 12,* 236. doi: 10.1186/1471-2458-12-236

Purdie, M. P., Norris, J., Davis, K. C., Zawacki, T., Morrison, D. M, George, W. H., . . . Kiekel, P.A. (2011). The effects of acute alcohol intoxication, partner risk level, and general intention to have unprotected sex on women's sexual decision making with a new partner. *Experimental and Clinical Psychopharmacology, 19,* 378–388.

Purkis, H. M., Lester, K. J., & Field, A. P. (2011). But what about the Empress of Racnoss? The allocation of attention to spiders and doctor who in a visual search task is predicted by fear and expertise. *Emotion, 11,* 1484–1488.

Qaseem, A., Snow, V., Denberg, T. D., Casey, D. E., Jr., Forciea, M. A., Owens, D. K., & Shekelle, P. (2009). Testing and pharmacologic treatment of erectile dysfunction: A clinical practice guideline from the American College of Physicians. *Annals of Internal Medicine.* Retrieved from www.annals.org/content/early/2009/10/19/0000605-200911030-00151.abstract?sid=4f936910 ee83-44d8-8f48-1f7f7124d93c

Querfurth, H. W., & LaFerla, F. M. (2010). Alzheimer's Disease. *New England Journal of Medicine, 362,* 329–344.

Quinn, P. C., & Liben, L. S. (2008). A sex difference in mental rotation in young infants. *Psychological Science, 19,* 1067–1070. doi: 10.1111/ j.1467-9280.2008.02201

Quinn, S. (1987). *A mind of her own: The life of Karen Horney.* New York: Summit Books.

Quiroga, R. Q., Fried, I., & Koch, C. (2013, February). Brain cells for grandmother. *Scientific American, 308,* 31–35.

Rabasca, L. (2000, March). Listening instead of preaching. *Monitor on Psychology, 31*(3), 50–51.

Rachman, S. (2015). The evolution of behaviour therapy and cognitive behaviour therapy. *Behaviour Research and Therapy, 64,* 1–8.

Radel, M., Vallejo, R. L., Iwata, N., Aragon, R., Long, J. C., Virkkunen, M., & Goldman, D. (2005). Haplotype based localization of an alcohol dependence gene to the 5q34? Aminobutyric acid Type A gene cluster. *Archives of General Psychiatry, 62,* 47–55.

Raine, A. (2008). From genes to brain to antisocial behavior. *Current Directions in Psychological Science, 17,* 323–328. doi: 10.1111/j.1467-8721.2008.00599

Ramamoorthi, K., Fropf, R., Belfort, G. M., Fitzmaurice, H. L., McKinney, R. M., Neve, R. L., Otto, T., . . . Lin, Y. (2011). Npas4 regulates a transcriptional program in CA3 required for contextual memory formation. *Science, 334,* 1669–1675. doi: 10.1126/science.1208049

Ramirez, S., Liu, X., Lin, P.-A., Suh, J., Pignatelli, M., Redondo, R. L., . . . Tonegawa, S. (2013). Creating a false memory in the hippocampus. *Science, 341* (6144), 387. doi: 10.1126/science.1239073

Randall, K. (2015, November 3). Neuropolitics, where campaigns try to read your mind. *The New York Times.* Retrieved from http://www.nytimes.com/2015/11/04/world/americas/neuropolitics-where-campaigns-try-to-read-your-mind.html

Rapee, R. M., MacLeod, C., Carpenter, L.,. Gaston, J. E., Frei, J., Peters, L., & Baillie, A. J. (2013). Integrating cognitive bias modification into a standard cognitive behavioural treatment package for social phobia: A randomized controlled trial. *Behaviour Research and Therapy, 51,* 207–215.

Raskin, N. J., Rogers, C. R., & Witty, M. C. (2011). Person-centered therapy. In R. J. Corsini & D. Wedding (Eds.), *Current psychotherapies (9th ed.).* Belmont, CA: Brooks/Cole.

Rawson, N. E. (2006). Olfactory loss in aging. *Science of Aging Knowledge Environment, 5,* e6.

Ray, R. A. (2012). Clinical neuroscience of addiction: Applications to psychological science and practice. *Clinical Psychology: Science and Practice, 19,* 154–166. doi: 10.1111/j.1468-2850.2012.01280

Ray, R., & Zald, D. H. (2011). Anatomical insights into the interaction of emotion and cognition in the prefrontal cortex. *Neuroscience & Biobehavioral Reviews, 36,* 479–501. doi: 10.1016/j.neubiorev.2011.08.005

Raykos, B. C., McEvoy, P. M., Erceg-Hurn, D., Byrne, S. M., Fursland, A. & Nathan, P. (2014). Therapeutic alliance in enhanced cognitive behavioural therapy for bulimia nervosa: Probably necessary but definitely insufficient. *Behavior Research and Therapy, 57,* 65–71.

Raymond, J. (2000, Fall/Winter). The world of the senses. *Newsweek Special Issue,* pp. 16–18.

Raymond, J. (2013, September 13). You will look better with sleep, but you have to wear your mask. Retrieved from http://www.today.com/health/you-will-look-better-sleep-you-have-wear-your-mask-8C11150914

Rayner, K., Schotter, E. R. Masson, M. E., J., Potter, M. C. & Treiman, R. (2016). So much to read, so little time: How do we read, and can speed reading help? *Psychological Science in the Public Interest, 17*(1), 4–34. doi: 10.1177/1529100615623267

Read, J. P., Wood, M. D., Kahlera, C. W., Maddock, J. E., & Palfaid, T. P. (2003). Examining the role of drinking motives in college student alcohol use and problems. *Psychology of Addictive Behaviors, 17,* 13–23.

Reddy, S. (2013, February 5). Why stress makes you sweat. *The Wall Street Journal,* pp. D1, D2.

Reece, M., Herbenick, D., Schick, V., Sanders, S. A., Dodge, B., & Fortenberry, D. (2010). Sexual behaviors, relationships, and perceived health among adult men in the United States: Results from a national probability sample. *Journal of Sexual Medicine, 7* (Supp. 5), 291–304. doi: 10.1111/j.1743-6109.2010.02009.x

Reese-Weber, M. (2000). Middle and late adolescents' conflict resolution skills with siblings: Associations with interparental and parent-adolescent conflict resolution. *Journal of Youth and Adolescence, 29,* 697–711.

Reese-Weber, M., & Marchand, J. E. (2002). Family and individual predictors of late adolescents' romantic relationships. *Journal of Youth and Adolescence, 31,* 197–206.

Reeve, C. L., & Bonaccio, S. (2011). The nature and structure of "intelligence." In T. Chamorro-Premuzic, S. von Stumm, & A. Furnham (Eds.), *The*

Wiley-Blackwell handbook of individual differences (pp. 187–216). Hoboken, NJ: Wiley.

Reich, S. M., Subrahmanyam, K., & Espinoza, G. (2012). Friending, IMing, and hanging out face-to-face: Overlap in adolescents' online and offline social networks. *Developmental Psychology, 48,* 356–368. doi: 10.1037/a0026980

Reichborn-Kjennerud, T., Ystrom, E., Neale, M. C., Aggen, S. H., Mazzeo, S. E., Knudsen, G. P., . . . Kendler, K S. (2013). Structure of genetic and environmental risk factors for symptoms of DSM-IV borderline personality disorder. *JAMA Psychiatry, 70,* 206–1214. doi: 10.1001/jamapsychiatry.2013.1944.

Reid, J. G., et al. (2013). Lamotrigine in psychiatric disorders. *The Journal of Clinical Psychiatry, 74,* 675–684. doi: 10.4088/JCP.12r08046

Reiss, D., Neiderhiser, J. M., Hetherington, E. M., & Plomin, R. (2000). *The relationship code: Deciphering genetic and social influences on adolescent development.* Cambridge, MA: Harvard University Press.

Reitz, C., Honig, L., Vonsattel, J. P., Tang, M.-X., & Mayeux, R. (2009). Memory performance is related to amyloid and tau pathology in the hippocampus. *Journal of Neurology, Neurosurgery, and Psychiatry, 80,* 715–721. doi: 10.1136 /jnnp.2008.154146

Rescorla, R. A. (1988). Pavlovian conditioning: It's not what you think it is. *American Psychologist, 43,* 151–160.

Rescorla, R. A. (2009). A theory of Pavlovian conditioning: Variations in the effectiveness of reinforcement and nonreinforcement. In D. Shanks (Ed.), *Psychology of learning.* Thousand Oaks, CA: Sage.

Reuter, M., Frenzel, C., Walter, N. T., Markett, S., & Montag, C. (2010). Investigating the genetic basis of altruism: The role of the COMT Val158Met polymorphism. *Social Cognitive and Affective Neuroscience.* Retrieved from http://scan.oxfordjournals.org /content/early/2010/10/28/scan.nsq083.full.pdf. doi: 10.1093/scan/nsq083

Reyna, V. F. (2013). Psychology: Good and bad news on the adolescent brain. *Nature, 503,* 48–49. doi: 10.1038/nature12704

Reynolds, C. F. III, & O'Hara, R. (2013). DSM-5 sleep-wake disorders classification: Overview for use in clinical practice. *American Journal of Psychiatry, 170,* 1099–1101. doi: 10.1176/appi. ajp.2013.13010058

Rhee, K. E., Lumeng, J. C., Appugliese, D. P., Kaciroti, N., & Bradley, R. H. (2006). Parenting styles and overweight status in first grade. *Pediatrics, 117,* 2047–2054.

Richards, D., Richardson, T., Timulak, L., & McElvaney, J. (2015). The efficacy of internet-delivered treatment for generalized anxiety disorder: A systematic review and meta-analysis. *Internet Interventions, 2,* 272–282. doi: http://dx.doi.org/10.1016/j .invent.2015.07.003

Richardson, M., Abraham, C., & Bond, R. (2012). Psychological correlates of university students' academic performance: A systematic review and meta-analysis. *Psychological Bulletin, 138,* 353–387. doi: 10.1037/ a0026838

Richmond, L. L., Redick, T. S., & Braver, T. S. (2015). Remembering to prepare: The benefits (and costs) of high working memory capacity. *Journal of Experimental Psychology: Learning, Memory, and Cognition, 41,* 1764–1777. doi: http://dx.doi.org/10.1037 /xlm0000122

Richtel, M. (2015, April 26). Push, don't crush, the students. *The New York Times Sunday Review,* pp. 1, 7.

Richter, L. M. (2006). Studying adolescence. *Science, 312,* 1902–1905.

Rickards, H., & Silver, J. (2014). Don't know what they are, but treatable? Therapies for conversion disorder. *Journal of Neurology, Neurosurgery, and Psychiatry, 85,* 830–831.

Rieger, G., & Savin-Williams, R. C. (2012). Gender nonconformity, sexual orientation, and psychological well-being. *Archives of Sexual Behavior, 41,* 611–621. doi: 10.1007/s10508-011-9738-0

Rippon, I., & Steptoe, A. (2015). Feeling old vs being old: Associations between self-perceived age and mortality. *JAMA Internal Medicine, 175,* 307–309. doi: 10.1001/jamainternmed.2014.6580.

Ritchie, S. J., Wiseman, R., & French, C. C. (2012). Failing the future: Three unsuccessful attempts to replicate Bem's 'Retroactive facilitation of recall' effect. *PLOS ONE, 7,* e33423. doi: 10.1371/journal. pone.0033423

Rivas-Drake, D. (2012). Ethnic identity and adjustment: The mediating role of sense of community. *Cultural Diversity and Ethnic Minority Psychology, 18,* 210–215. doi: 10.1037/a0027011

Rizzuto, D., Orsini,, N., Qiu, C., Wang, H.-X., & Fratiglioni, L. (2012). Lifestyle, social factors, and survival after age 75: Population based study. *British Medical Journal, 345,* e5568. Retrieved from http:// dx.doi.org/10.1136/bmj.e5568

Roberts, A. I., Vick, S.-J., Roberts, S. G. B., & Menzel, C. R. (2014). Chimpanzees modify intentional gestures to coordinate a search for hidden food. *Nature Communications, 5,* 3088. doi: 10.1038/ ncomms4088.

Roberts, B. W., Walton, K. E., & Viechtbauer, W. (2006a). Patterns of mean-level change in personality traits across the life course: A meta-analysis of longitudinal studies. *Psychological Bulletin, 132,* 1–25.

Roberts, B. W., Walton, K. E., & Viechtbauer, W. (2006b). Personality traits change in adulthood: Reply to Costa and McCrae (2006). *Psychological Bulletin, 132,* 29–32.

Roberts, T. A., & Ryan, S. A. (2002). Tattooing and high-risk behavior in adolescents. *Pediatrics, 110,* 1058–1063.

Robiner, W. N., Tumlin, T. R., & Tompkins, T. L. (2013). Psychologists and medications in the era of interprofessional care: Collaboration is less problematic and costly than prescribing. *Clinical Psychology: Science and Practice, 20,* 489–507. doi: 10.1111/ cpsp.12054

Robins, R. W., Trzesniewski, K. H., Tracy, J. L., Gosling, S. D., & Potter, J. (2002). Global self-esteem across the life span. *Psychology and Aging, 17,* 423–434.

Robitaille, A., Piccinin, A. M., Muniz-Terrera, G., Hoffman, L, Johansson, B, Deeg, D., . . . Hofer, S. M. (2013). Longitudinal mediation of processing speed on age-related change in memory and fluid intelligence. *Psychology and Aging, 28,* 887–901. doi: 10.1037/a0033316

Rodriguez, J., Umaña-Taylor, A., Smith, E. P., & Johnson, D. J. (2009). Cultural processes in parenting and youth outcomes: Examining a model of racial-ethnic socialization and identity in diverse populations. *Cultural Diversity and Ethnic Minority Psychology, 15,* 106–111. doi: 10.1037/a0015510

Roediger, III, H.L., & DeSoto, K.A. (2014). Forgetting the presidents. *Science, 346*(6213), 1106–1109. doi: 10.1126/science.1259627

Roese, N. J., & Olson, J. M. (1994). Attitude importance as a function of repeated attitude expression. *Journal of Experimental Social Psychology, 30,* 39–51.

Roets, A., Au, E. W. M., & Van Hiel, A. (2016). Can authoritarianism lead to greater liking of out-groups? The intriguing case of Singapore. *Psychological Science,* in press.

Rogers, C. R. (1951). *Client-centered therapy: Its current practice, implications, and theory.* Boston: Houghton Mifflin.

Rogers, C. R. (1961). *On becoming a person.* Boston: Houghton Mifflin.

Rogers, C. R. (1980). *A way of being.* Boston: Houghton Mifflin.

Ropeik, D. (2012, September 30). Inside the mind of worry. *The New York Times Sunday Review,* p. 11.

Roper, Z. J. J., Vecera, S. P., & Vaidya, J. G. (2014). Value-driven attentional capture in adolescence. *Psychological Science, 108,* 10367–10371. doi: 10.1073/ pnas.1104047108

Rosch, E. (1975). Cognitive representation of semantic categories. *Journal of Experimental Psychology: General, 105,* 192–223.

Rosch-Heider, E., & Olivier, D. C. (1972). The structure of the color space in naming and memory for two languages. *Cognitive Psychology, 3,* 337–354.

Rosenheck, R., & Lin, H. (2014). Noninferiority of perphenazine vs. three second-generation antipsychotics in chronic schizophrenia. *Journal of Nervous & Mental Disease, 202,* 18–24. doi: 10.1097/ NMD.0000000000000065

Roskes, M., Elliot, A. J., & De Dreu, C. K. W. (2014). Why is avoidance motivation problematic, and what can be done about it? *Current Directions in Psychological Science, 23,* 133–138. doi: 10.1177/0963721414524224

Rosso, G., Martini, B., & Maina, G. (2012). Brief dynamic therapy and depression severity: A single-blind, randomized study. *Journal of Affective Disorders, 19,* S0165–0327. doi: 10.1016/j.jad.2012.10.017.

Rothbart, M. K., (2007). Temperament, development, and personality. *Current Directions in Psychological Science, 16,* 207–212.

Rothbart, M. K. (2012). *Becoming who we are: Temperament and personality in development.* New York: Guilford Press.

Rothen, N., Meier, B., & Ward, J. (2012). Enhanced memory ability: Insights from synaesthesia. *Neuroscience & Biobehavioral Reviews, 36,* 1952–1963.

Rotter, J. B. (1990). Internal versus external control of reinforcement: A case history of a variable. *American Psychologist, 45,* 489–493.

Roy-Byrne, P. (2009, January 12). With a little help from my friends: The happiness effect. *Journal Watch Psychiatry.* Retrieved from http://psychiatry.jwatch. org/cgi/content/full/2009/112/1

Rozin, P., Bauer, R., & Catanese, D. (2003). Food and life, pleasure and worry, among American college students: Gender differences and regional similarities. *Journal of Personality and Social Psychology, 85,* 132–141.

Rubin, K. H., Bukowski, W. M., & Laursen, B. (Eds.). (2009). *Handbook of peer interactions, relationships, and groups.* New York: Guilford.

Rudman, L. A., Ashmore, R. D., & Gary, M. L. (2001). "Unlearning" automatic biases: The malleability of implicit prejudice and stereotypes. *Journal of Personality and Social Psychology, 81,* 856–868.

Rupert, P. A., Miller, A. O., & Dorociak, K. E. (2015). Preventing burnout: What does the research tell us? *Professional Psychology: Research and Practice, 46,* 168–174. doi: http://dx.doi.org/10.1037/a0039297

Rupp, R. (1998). *Committed to memory: How we remember and why we forget.* New York: Crown.

Rushton, J. P., & Bons, T. A. (2005). Mate choice and friendship in twins: Evidence for genetic similarity. *Psychological Science, 16,* 555–559.

Rutherford, B. R., Pott, E., Tandler, J. M., Wall, M. M., Roose, S. P., & Lieberman, J. A. (2014). Placebo response in antipsychotic clinical trials: A meta-analysis. *JAMA Psychiatry, 71,* 1409–1421. doi: 10.1001/jamapsychiatry.2014.1319

Ruzzo, E. K., & Geschwind, D. H. (2016). Schizophrenia genetics complements its mechanistic understanding. *Nature Neuroscience.* Published online, March 21, 2016. doi: 10.1038/nn.4277

Ryan, R. M., & Deci, E. L. (2000). Self-determination theory and the facilitation of intrinsic motivation, social development, and well-being. *American Psychologist, 55,* 68–78.

Sacchet, M. D., LaPlante, R. A., Wan, Q., Pritchett, D. L., Lee, A .K. C., Hamalainen, C. I., . . . Jones, S. R. (2015). Attention drives synchronization of alpha and beta rhythms between right inferior frontal and primary sensory neocortex. *Journal of Neuroscience, 35,* 2074. doi: 10.1523/JNEUROSCI.1292-14.2015

SAGE Publications UK. (2010, June 18). Love ballad leaves women more open to a date. *ScienceDaily.* Retrieved July 8, 2013, from https://www.sciencedaily.com/releases/2010/06/100618112139.htm

Saggino, A., Pezzuti, L., Tommasi, M., Cianci, L., Colom, R., & Orsini. A. (2014). Null sex differences in general intelligence among elderly. *Personality and Individual Differences, 63,* 53–57. doi: http://dx.doi.org/10.1016/j.paid.2014.01.047

Sagioglou, C., & Greitemeyer, T. (2014). Facebook's emotional consequences: Why Facebook causes a decrease in mood and why people still use it. *Computers in Human Behavior, 35,* 359–363. doi: http://dx.doi.org/10.1016/j.chb.2014.03.003

Sahin, N.T., Pinker, S., Cash, S.S., Schomer, D., & Halgren, E. (2009). Sequential processing of lexical, grammatical, and phonological information within Broca's area. *Science, 326,* 445–449.

Sakai, K. L. (2005). Language acquisition and brain development. *Science, 310,* 815–819.

Salas-Wright, C.P., Kagotho, N., & Vaughn M.. G. (2014). Mood, anxiety, and personality disorders among first and second-generation immigrants to the United States. *Psychiatry Research,* S0165-1781(14)00742-2. doi: 10.1016/j.psychres.2014.08.045

Salkovskis, P. M., Thorpe, S. J., Wahl, K., Wroe, A. L., & Forrester, E. (2003). Neutralizing increases discomfort associated with obsessional thoughts: An experimental study with obsessional patients. *Journal of Abnormal Psychology, 112,* 709–715.

Salthouse, T. (2012). Consequences of age-related cognitive declines. *Annual Review of Psychology, 63,* 201–226.

Samalin, N., & Whitney, C. (1997, December). When to praise. *Parents Magazine,* pp. 51–55.

Sánchez-Ortuño, M. M., & Edinger, J. D. (2010). A penny for your thoughts: Patterns of sleep-related beliefs, insomnia symptoms and treatment outcome. *Behavior Research and Therapy, 48,* 125–133. doi: 10.1016/j.brat.2009.10.003

Sanchez-Romera, J. F., Lopez, J., Bandin, C., Colodro-Conde, L., Madrid, J. A., Garaulet, M., . . . Ordoñana, J. R. (2014). Individual differences in chronobiology. Genetic and environmental factors. *Personality and Individual Differences, 60 Supplement,* S31–S32.

Sandell, M. A., & Breslin, P. A. S. (2006). Variability in a taste-receptor gene determines whether we taste toxins in food. *Current Biology, 16,* R792–R794.

Sander, M. C., Lindenberger, U., & Werkle-Bergner, M. (2012). Lifespan age differences in working memory: A two-component framework. *Neuroscience & Biobehavioral Reviews, 36,* 2007–2033. doi: 10.1016/j.neubiorev.2012.06.004.

Sandlin-Sniffen, C. (2000, November 2). How are we raising our children? *St. Petersburg Times.* Retrieved from www .psycport.com/news/2000/11/02 /eng-sptimes_floridian /eng-sptimes_floridian_071015 _110_905256867409.html

Santangelo, P., Reinhard, I., Mussgay, L, Steil, R., Sawitzki, G., Klein, C., . . . Ebner-Priemer, U. W. (2014). Specificity of affective instability in patients with borderline personality disorder compared to posttraumatic stress disorder, bulimia nervosa, and healthy controls. *Journal of Abnormal Psychology, 123,* 258–272. doi: 10.1037/a0035619

Saphire-Bernstein, S., Way, B. M., Kim, H. S., Sherman, D. K., & Taylor, S. E. (2011). Oxytocin receptor gene (OXTR) is related to psychological resources. *Proceedings of the National Academy of Sciences, 108,* 15118. doi: 10.1073/pnas.1113137108

Sareen, J., Afifi, T. O., McMillan, K. A., & Asmundson, G. J. G. (2011). Relationship between household income and mental disorders: Findings from a population-based longitudinal study. *Archives of General Psychiatry, 68,* 419. doi: 10.1001/archgenpsychiatry.2011.15

Sasaki, S., Sata, F., Katoh, S., Saijo, Y., Nakajima, S., Washino, N., . . . Kishi, R. (2008). Adverse birth outcomes associated with maternal smoking and polymorphisms in the N-nitrosamine-metabolizing enzyme genes NQO1 and CYP2E1. *American Journal of Epidemiology, 167,* 6. doi: 10.1093/aje/kwm360

Satcher, D., Hook III, E. W., & Coleman, E. (2015). Sexual health in America: Improving patient care and public health. *Journal of the American Medical Association, 314,* 765–766. doi: 10.1001/jama.2015.6831.

Sauerland, M., & Sporer, S. L. (2009). Fast and confident: Postdicting eyewitness identification accuracy in a field study. *Journal of Experimental Psychology: Applied, 15,* 46–62. Retrieved from www .allacademic.com/meta/p228794_index.html

Saulny, S. (2011, March 24). Census data presents rise in multiracial population of youths. *The New York Times.* Retrieved from nytimes.com

Savage-Rumbaugh, S., Shanker, S. G., & Taylor, T. J. (1998). *Apes, language, and the human mind.* New York: Oxford University Press.

Savic, I., Garcia-Falgueras, A., & Swaab, D. F. (2010). Sexual differentiation of the human brain in relation to gender identity and sexual orientation. In I. Savic (Ed.), *Sex differences in the human brain, their underpinnings and implications: Progress in brain research, 186,* 41–64. New York: Elsevier.

Savin-Williams, R. C., Joyner, K., & Rieger, G. (2012). Prevalence and stability of self-reported sexual orientation identity during young adulthood. *Archives of Sexual Behavior, 41,* 103–110.

Saxe, R., Carey, S., & Kanwisher, N. (2004). Understanding other minds: Linking developmental psychology and functional neuroimaging. *Annual Review of Psychology, 55,* 87–124.

Sayim, B., Westheimer, G., & Herzog, M. H. (2010). Gestalt factors modulate basic spatial vision. *Psychological Science, 21,* 641–644. doi: 10.1177/0956797610368811

Scammell, T. E. (2015). Narcolepsy. *NEJM, 373,* 2654–2662. doi: 10.1056/NEJMra1500587

Schachter, S. (1971). *Emotion, obesity, and crime.* New York: Academic Press.

Schachter, S., & Singer, J. E. (1962). Cognitive, social, and physiological determinants of emotional state. *Psychological Review, 69,* 377–399.

Schafer, S. M., Colloca, L., & Wager, T. D. (2015). Conditioned placebo analgesia persists when subjects know they are receiving a placebo. *Pain, 16,* 412–420. doi: 10.1016/j.jpain.2014.12.008

Schaie, K. W. (1996). *Intellectual development in adulthood: The Seattle Longitudinal Study.* Cambridge, U.K.: Cambridge University Press.

Schaie, K. W. (2005). *Developmental influences on intelligence: The Seattle Longitudinal Study.* New York: Oxford University Press. doi: 10.1093/acprof:oso/9780195156737.001.0001

Scheibe, S. (2012). The golden years of emotion: Lifespan research. *APS Observer.* Retrieved from www .psychologicalscience.org/index.php/publications /observer/2012/november-12/the-golden-years-of -emotion.html

Schenkman, L. (2010, November 11). Daydreaming is a downer. *Science.* Retrieved from http://news. sciencemag.org/2010/11/daydreaming-downer

Schiffer, B., Pawliczek, C., Müller, B., Forsting, M., Gizewski, E., Leygraf, N., . . . Hodgins. S. (2014). Neural mechanisms underlying cognitive control of men with lifelong antisocial behavior. *Psychiatry Research: Neuroimaging, 222,* 43–51. doi: 10.1016/j .pscychresns.2014.01.008

Schiffer, B., Pawliczek, C., Müller, B. W., Gizewski, E. R., & Walter, H. (2013). Why don't men understand women? Altered neural networks for reading the language of male and female eyes. *PLoS ONE, 8,* e60278. doi: 10.1371/journal.pone.0060278

Schizophrenia Working Group of the Psychiatric Genomics Consortium (2014). Biological insights from 108 schizophrenia-associated genetic loci. *Nature, 511,* 421–427. doi: 10.1038/nature13595

Schmaal, L., Veltman, D. J., van Erp, T. G. M., Sämann, P. G., Frodl, T., Jahanshad, N., . . . ENIGMA-Major Depressive Disorder Working Group. (2015). Subcortical brain alterations in major depressive disorder: Findings from the ENIGMA Major Depressive Disorder working group. *Molecular Psychiatry, 21,* 806–812. doi: 10.1038/mp.2015.69

Schmitt, M. T., Branscombe, N. R., Postmes, T., & Garcia, A. (2014). The consequences of perceived discrimination for psychological well-being: A meta-analytic review. *Psychological Bulletin, 140,* 921–948. doi: 10.1037/a0035754

Schneidman, E. S. (1983). On abolishing "death": An etymological note. *Suicide and Life Threatening Behavior, 13,* 176–178.

Schnohr, P., O'Keefe, J. H., Marott, J. L., Lange, P., & Jensen, G. B. (2015). Dose of jogging and long-term mortality: The Copenhagen City Heart Study. *Journal of American College of Cardiology, 65*, 411–419. doi: 10.1016/j.jacc.2014.11.023

Schoenfeld, T. J., Rada, P., Pieruzzini, P. R., Hsueh, B., & Gould, E. (2013). Physical exercise prevents stress-induced activation of granule neurons and enhances local inhibitory mechanisms in the dentate gyrus. *Journal of Neuroscience, 33*, 7770. doi: 10.1523/JNEUROSCI.5352-12.2013

Schönfeld, P., Brailovskaia, B., Bieda, A., Zhang,X. C., & Margraf, J. (2016). The effects of daily stress on positive and negative mental health: Mediation through self-efficacy. *International Journal of Clinical and Health Psychology, 16*, 1–10. doi: 10.1016/j.ijchp.2015.08.005

Schroeder, S. A. (2007). We can do better—Improving the health of the American people. *New England Journal of Medicine, 357*, 1221–1228.

Schuch, F. B., Vancampfort, D., Richards, J., Rosenbaum, S., Ward, P. B., & Stubbs, B. (2016). Exercise as a treatment for depression: A meta-analysis adjusting for publication bias. *Journal of Psychiatric Research, 77*, 42–51. doi: 10.1016/j.jpsychires.2016.02.023

Schunk, D. H., Pintrich, P. R., & Meece, J. (2008). *Motivation in education: Theory, research, and applications* (3rd ed.). Upper Saddle River, NJ: Pearson Education.

Schutte, N. S., & Loi, N. M. (2014). Connections between emotional intelligence and workplace flourishing. *Personality and Individual Differences, 66*, 134–139. doi: http://dx.doi.org/10.1016/j.paid.2014.03.031

Schwab, A. P. (2009). Putting cognitive psychology to work: Improving decision-making in the medical encounter. *Social Science & Medicine, 67*, 1861–1869.

Schwartz, S. J., Donnellan, M. B., Ravert, R. D., Luyckx, K., & Zamboanga, B. L. (2013). Identity development, personality, and well-being in adolescence and emerging adulthood: Theory, research, and recent advances. In R. M. Lerner, M. A. Easterbrooks, & J. Mistry (Eds.), *Handbook of psychology, developmental psychology* (Vol. 6, 2nd ed., pp. 339–364). Hoboken, NJ: John Wiley.

Schwartz, S. J., Unger, J. B., Zamboanga, B. L., & Szapocznik, J. (2010). Rethinking the concept of acculturation: Implications for theory and research. *American Psychologist, 65*, 237–251.

ScienceDaily (2014, January 19). *Mechanism identified in Alzheimer's-related memory loss.* Retrieved from http://www.sciencedaily.com/releases/2014/01/140119142456.htm

Science News (2016, April 11). *Brain on LSD revealed: First scans show how the drug affects the brain.* Retrieved from https://www.sciencedaily.com/releases/2016/04/160411153006.htm
Scriba, M. F., Ducrest, A.-L., Henry, I., Vyssotski, A. L., Rattenborg, N. C., & Roulin, A. (2013). Linking melanism to brain development: Expression of a melanism-related gene in barn owl feather follicles covaries with sleep ontogeny. *Frontiers in Zoology, 10*, 42. doi: 10.1186/1742-9994-10-42

Searle, J. R. (1996). Dualism: Descartes' legacy. *The philosophy of mind: The Superstar Teachers Series* [Audiotape]. Springfield, VA: The Teaching Company.

Segal-Caspi, L., Roccas, S., & Sagiv, L. (2012). Don't judge a book by its cover, revisited: Perceived and reported traits and values of attractive women. *Psychological Science, 23*, 1112–1116. doi: 10.1177/0956797612446349

Segall, M. H. (1994). A cross-cultural research contribution to unraveling the nativist/empiricist controversy. In J. Lonner & R. Malpass (Eds.), *Psychology and culture* (pp. 135–138). Boston: Allyn & Bacon.

Segall, M. H., Campbell, D. T., & Herskovits, M. J. (1963). Culture differences in the perception of geometric illusions. *Science, 139*, 769–771.

Segall, M. H., Campbell, D. T., & Herskovits, M. J. (1966). *The influence of culture on visual perception.* Indianapolis, IN: Bobbs-Merrill.

Seifert, K. L., & Hoffnung, R. J. (2000). *Child and adolescent development.* Boston: Houghton Mifflin.

Seifert, K. L., Hoffnung, R. J., & Hoffnung, M. (2000). *Lifespan development* (2nd ed.). Boston: Houghton Mifflin.

Sejnowski, T. & Delbruck, T. (2012, October). The language of the brain. *Scientific American, 307*(4), 54–59.

Sekar, A., Bialas, A. R., de Rivera, H., Davis, A., Hammond, T. R., Kamitaki, N., . . . McCarroll, S. A. (2016). Schizophrenia risk from complex variation of complement component. *Nature, 530*, 177–183. doi: 10.1038/nature16549 doi

Sekuler, A. B., & Bennett, P. J. (2001). Generalized common fate: Grouping by common luminance changes. *Psychological Science, 12*, 437–444.

Seligman, M. E. P. (1973). Fall into helplessness. *Psychology Today, 7*, 43–48.

Seligman, M. E. P. (1975). *Helplessness: On depression, development, and death.* San Francisco, CA: Freeman.

Seligman, M. E. P. (2003, August). *Positive psychology: Applications to work, love, and sports.* Paper presented at the meeting of the American Psychological Association, Toronto, Canada.

Seligman, M. E. P., Steen, T. A., Park, N., & Peterson, C. (2005). Positive psychology progress: Empirical validation of interventions. *American Psychologist, 60*, 410–421.

Sellbom, M., Graham, J. R., & Schenk, P. W. (2006). Incremental validity of the MMPI-2 Restructured Clinical (RC) Scales in a private practice sample. *Journal of Personality Assessment, 86*(2), 196–205.

Seo, D., Patrick, C. J., & Kennealy, P. J. (2008). Role of serotonin and dopamine system interactions in the neurobiology of impulsive aggression and its comorbidity with other clinical disorders. *Aggression and Violent Behavior, 13*, 383–395. doi: 10.1016/j.avb.2008.06.003

Serrano-Villar, M., & Calzada, E. J. (2016). Ethnic identity: Evidence of protective effects for young, Latino children. *Journal of Applied Developmental Psychology, 42*, 21–30.

Shackelford, T. K., & Goetz, A. T. (2012). *The Oxford handbook of sexual conflict in humans.* New York: Oxford University Press.

Shanahan, M. J., Hill, P. L, Roberts, B. W., Eccles, J., & Friedman, H. S. (2014). Conscientiousness, health, and aging: The life course of personality model. *Developmental Psychology, 50*, 1407–1425. doi: 10.1037/a0031130

Shanker, S. G., & Savage-Rumbaugh, E. S. (1999). Kanzi: A new beginning. *Animal Learning & Behavior, 27*, 24–25.

Sheard, M., & Golby, J. (2007). Hardiness and undergraduate academic study: The moderating role of commitment. *Personality and Individual Differences, 43*, 579–588.

Shedler, J. (2010). The efficacy of psychodynamic psychotherapy. *American Psychologist, 65*, 98–109. doi: 10.1037/a0018378

Sher, L. (2005). Suicide and alcoholism. *Nordic Journal of Psychiatry, 59*, 152.

Sherman, D. K., Kim, H. S., & Heejung, S. (2005). Is there an "I" in "team"? The role of the self in group-serving judgments. *Journal of Personality and Social Psychology, 88*, 108–120.

Sherman, J. W., Stroessner, S. J., Loftus, S. T., & Deguzman, G. (1997). Stereotype suppression and recognition memory for stereotypical and nonstereotypical information. *Social Cognition, 15*, 205–215.

Sherman, R. A., Nave, C. S., & Funder, D. C. (2010). Situational similarity and personality predict behavioral consistency. *Journal of Personality and Social Psychology, 99*, 330–343. doi: 10.1037/a0019796

Sherman, R. A., Rauthmann, J. F., Brown, N. A., Serfass, D. G., & Jones, A. B. (2015). The independent effects of personality and situations on real-time expressions of behavior and emotion. *Journal of Personality and Social Psychology, 109*, 872-888. doi: http://dx.doi.org/10.1037/pspp0000036

Shin, H., Park, Y. M., Ying, J. Y., Kim, B., Noh, H., & Lee, S. M. (2014). Relationships between coping strategies and burnout symptoms: A meta-analytic approach. *Professional Psychology: Research and Practice, 45*, 44–56. doi: 10.1037/a0035220

Shinozaki, G., Romanowicz, M., Passov, V., Rundell, J., Mrazek, D., & Kung, S. (2013). State dependent gene–environment interaction: Serotonin transporter gene–child abuse interaction associated with suicide attempt history among depressed psychiatric inpatients. *Journal of Affective Disorders, 147*, 373–378.

Shive, H. (2015, July 23). When it comes to depression, serotonin deficiency may not be to blame. *Texas A&M Health Sciences Center Press Release.* Retrieved from http://news.tamhsc.edu/?post=when-it-comes-to-depression-serotonin-deficiency-may-not-be-to-blame

Shneidman, E. (2005). Prediction of suicide revisited: A brief methodological note. *Suicide and Life-Threatening Behavior, 35*, 1–2.

Shneidman, E. S. (1987). Ten commonalities of suicide and their implications for response. *Crisis, 7*, 88–93.

Shors, T. J. (2014). The adult brain makes new neurons, and effortful learning keeps them alive. *Current Directions in Psychological Science, 23*, 311-318. doi: 10.1177/0963721414540167

Shungin, D., Winkler, T. W., Croteau-Chonka, D. C., Ferreira, T., Locke, A. E., Mägi, G., . . . Scherag, A. (2015). New genetic loci link adipose and insulin biology to body fat distribution. *Nature, 518*, 187–196. doi: 10.1038/nature14132

Sibille, E., & Lewis, D. A. (2006). SERT-ainly involved in depression, but when? *American Journal of Psychiatry, 163*, 8–11.

Siegal, M., Varley, R., & Want, S. C. (2001). Mind over grammar: Reasoning in aphasia and development. *Trends in Cognitive Sciences, 5*, 296–301.

Siegert, S., Seo, J., Kwon, E. J., Rudenko, A., Cho, S., Wang, W., . . . Tsai, L.-H. (2015).The schizophrenia risk gene product miR-137 alters presynaptic plasticity. *Nature Neuroscience.* Retrieved from http://www.nature.com/neuro/journal/vaop/ncurrent/full/nn.4023.html (2015) doi: 10.1038/nn.4023

Siegle, G. J. (2008). Brain mechanisms of borderline personality disorder at the intersection of cognition, emotion, and the clinic. *American Journal of Psychiatry, 164,* 1776–1779.

Silbersweig, D., Clarkin, J. F., Goldstein, M., Kernberg, O. F., Tuescher, O., Levy, K. N., . . . Stern, E. (2008). Failure of frontolimbic inhibitory function in the context of negative emotion in borderline personality disorder. *American Journal of Psychiatry, 164,* 1832.

Silfvernagel, K., Gren-Landell, M., Emanuelsson, M., Carlbring, P., & Andersson, G. (2015). Individually tailored internet-based cognitive behavior therapy for adolescents with anxiety disorders: A pilot effectiveness study. *Internet Interventions, 2,* 297–302. doi: http://dx.doi.org/10.1016/j.invent.2015.07.002

Silver, J. (2013, June 27). Psychosurgery for OCD: Some respond in the long run. *NEJM Journal Watch.* Retrieved from http://www.jwatch.org/na31340/2013/06/27/psychosurgery-ocd-some-respond-long-run?query=etoc_jwpsych#sthash.2EyJZeRs.dpuf

Silverman, L. H. (1984). Beyond insight: An additional necessary step in redressing intrapsychic conflict. *Psychoanalytic Psychology, 1,* 215–234.

Simms, L. J. (2007). The Big Seven model of personality and its relevance to personality pathology. *Journal of Personality, 75,* 65–94.

Simons, D. J. (2014). The value of direct replication. *Perspectives on Psychological Science, 9,* 76–80. doi: 10.1177/1745691613514755

Simons, D. J., & Chabris, C. F. (2011). What people believe about how memory works: A representative survey of the U.S. population. *PLoS ONE, 6,* e22757. doi: 10.1371/journal.pone.0022757

Simpson, H. B. (2014). Cognitive-behavioral therapy vs risperidone for augmenting serotonin reuptake inhibitors in obsessive-compulsive disorder: A randomized clinical trial serotonin reuptake inhibitor augmentation. *JAMA Psychiatry, 70,* 1190–1199. doi: 10.1001/jamapsychiatry.2013.1932

Singer, N. (2010, November 14). Making ads that whisper to the brain. *The New York Times,* p. BU4.

Singer, T., Verhaeghen, P., Ghisletta, P., Lindenberger, U., & Baltes, P. B. (2003). The fate of cognition in very old age: Six-year longitudinal findings in the Berlin Aging Study (BASE). *Psychology and Aging, 18,* 318–331.

Singleton, R. A., Jr., & Wolfson, A. R. (2009). Alcohol consumption, sleep, and academic performance among college students. *Journal of Studies on Alcohol and Drugs, 70,* 355.

Skinner, B. F. (1961). *Cumulative record* (3rd ed.) Englewood Cliffs, NJ: Prentice Hall.

Skritskaya, N. A., Carson-Woing, A. R., Moeller, J. R., Shen, S., Barsky, A. J., & Fallo, B. A. (2012). A clinician-administered severity rating scale for illness anxiety: Development, reliability and validity of the H-YBOCS-M. *Depression and Anxiety, 29,* 652–664.

Slifstein, M., van de Giessen, E., Van Snellenberg, J., Thompson, J. L, Narendran, R., Gil, R., . . . Abi-Dargham, A. (2015). Deficits in prefrontal cortical and extrastriatal dopamine release in schizophrenia: A positron emission tomographic functional magnetic resonance imaging study. *JAMA Psychiatry, 72,* 316–324. doi: 10.1001/jamapsychiatry.2014.2414

Slutske, W. S. (2005). Alcohol use disorders among U.S. college students and their non-college-attending peers. *Archives of General Psychiatry, 62,* 321–327.

Smallwood, J., & Schooler, J. W. (2015). The science of mind wandering: Empirically navigating the stream of consciousness. *Annual Review of Psychology, 66,* 487–518. doi: 10.1146/annurev-psych-010814-015331

Smetana, J. G., Campione-Barr, N., & Metzger, A. (2006). Adolescent development in interpersonal and societal contexts. *Annual Review of Psychology, 57,* 255–284.

Smilek, D., Carriere, J. S., & Cheyne, J. A. (2010). Out of mind, out of sight: Eye blinking as indicator and embodiment of mind wandering. *Psychological Science, 21,* 786–789. doi: 10.1177/0956797610368063

Smillie, L. D. (2013). Extraversion and reward processing. *Current Directions in Psychological Science, 22,* 167–172. doi: 10.1177/0963721412470133

Smith, A. R., Hames, J. L., & Joiner, T. E. Jr. (2013). Status update: Maladaptive Facebook usage predicts increases in body dissatisfaction and bulimic symptoms. *Journal of Affective Disorders, 149,* 235–240. doi: 10.1016/j.jad.2013.01.032.

Smith, B. J. (2012, June). Inappropriate prescribing. *Monitor on Psychology, 43,* 36–40.

Smith, D. B. (2009, Autumn). The doctor is in. *The American Scholar.* Retrieved from www.theamericanscholar.org/the-doctor-is-in/

Smith, K. (2010). Settling the great glia debate. *Nature, 468,* 160–162. doi: 10.1038/468160a

Smith, K. (2014, March). Cognitive training slows cognitive decline, major study finds. *Monitor on Psychology, 45*(3), 10.

Smith, K. (2015). Mental health: A world of depression. *Nature, 515,* 180–181. doi: 10.1038/515180a

Smith, K. B., Oxley, D. R., Hibbing, M. V., Alford, J. R., & Hibbing, J. R. (2011). Linking genetics and political attitudes: Reconceptualizing political ideology. *Political Psychology, 32,* 369–397. doi: 10.1111/j.1467-9221.2010.00821.x

Smith, M. L., Glass, G. V., & Miller, T. I. (1980). *The benefits of psychotherapy.* Baltimore, MD: Johns Hopkins University Press.

Smith, M. T., & Perlis, M. L. (2006). Who is a candidate for cognitive-behavioral therapy for insomnia? *Health Psychology, 25,* 15–19.

Smith, P., Scott, R., Eshkevari, E., Jatta, F., Leigh, E., Harris, V., . . . Yule, W. (2015). Computerised CBT for depressed adolescents: Randomised controlled trial. *Behaviour Research and Therapy, 73,* 104–110.

Sneed, J. R., Whitbourne, S. K., Schwartz, S. J., & Huang, S. (2012). The relationship between identity, intimacy, and midlife well-being: Findings from the Rochester Adult Longitudinal Study. *Psychology and Aging, 27,* 318–323. doi: 10.1037/a0026378

Sneider, J. T., , Hamilton, D. A., Cohen-Gilbert, J. E., Crowley, D. J., Rosso, I. M., & Silveri, M. (2015). Sex differences in spatial navigation and perception in human adolescents and emerging adults. *Behavioural Processes, 111,* 42–50.

Snowden, R. V. (2009, February 25). Even moderate alcohol use increases risk of certain cancers in women. *ACS News,* Press Release.

Snyder, H. R., Kaiser, R. H., Warren, S. L., & Heller, W. (2015). Obsessive-compulsive disorder is associated with broad impairments in executive function: A meta-analysis. *Clinical Psychological Science, 3,* 301–330. doi: 10.1177/2167702614534210

Sorg, E.T., & Taylor, R. B. (2011). Community-level impacts of temperature on urban street robbery. *Journal of Criminal Justice, 39,* 463–470.

Soto, J. A., Levenson, R. W., & Ebling, R. (2005). Cultures of moderation and expression: Emotional experience, behavior, and physiology in Chinese Americans and Mexican Americans. *Emotion, 5,* 154–165.

Soussignan, R. (2002). Duchenne smile, emotional experience, and autonomic reactivity: A test of the facial feedback hypothesis. *Emotion, 2,* 52–74.

Spalek, K., Fastenrath, M., Ackermann, S., Auschra, B., Coynel, X., Frey, J.,. . . Milnik, A. (2015). Sex-dependent dissociation between emotional appraisal and memory: A large-scale behavioral and fMRI Study. *Journal of Neuroscience, 35,* 920–935. doi: 10.1523/JNEUROSCI.2384-14.2015

Spearman, C. (1927). *The abilities of man.* New York: Macmillan.

Spence, J. Titov, N., Jones, M. P., Dear, B. F., & Solley, K. (2014). Internet-based trauma-focused cognitive behavioural therapy for PTSD with and without exposure components: A randomised controlled trial. *Journal of Affective Disorders, 162,* 73–80.

Sperry, R. W. (1982). Some effects of disconnecting the cerebral hemispheres. *Science, 217,* 1223–1226.

Spiegel, D. (2006). Recognizing traumatic dissociation. *American Journal of Psychiatry, 163,* 566–568.

Sprecher, S., & Fehr, B. (2011). Dispositional attachment and relationship-specific attachment as predictors of compassionate love for a partner. *Journal of Social and Personal Relationships, 28,* 558–574.

Sprenger, C., Eippert, F., Finsterbusch, J., Bingel, U., Rose, M., & Büchel, C. (2012). Attention modulates spinal cord responses to pain. *Current Biology, 22,* 1019–1022. doi: 10.1016/j.cub.2012.04.006

Springen, K., & Kantrowitz, B. (2004, May 10). Alcohol's deadly triple threat. *Newsweek,* pp. 90–92.

Springer, S. P., & Deutsch, G. (1993). *Left brain, right brain* (4th ed.). New York: Freeman.

Squeglia, L. M., Sorg, S. F., Schweinsburg, A. D., Wetherill, R. R., Pulido, C., & Tapert, S. F. (2012). Binge drinking differentially affects adolescent male and female brain morphometry. *Psychopharmacology, 220,* 529–539.

Sroufe, L. A. (2012, January 28). Ritalin gone wrong. *The New York Times Review.* Retrieved from www.nytimes.com

Staddon, J. E. R., & Cerutti, D. T. (2003). Operant conditioning. *Annual Review of Psychology, 54,* 115–144.

Stagl, J. M., Antoni, M. H., Lechner, S. C., Bouchard, L. C., Blomberg, B. B., Glück, S., . . . Carver, C. S. (2015). Randomized controlled trial of cognitive behavioral stress management in breast cancer: A brief report of effects on 5-year depressive symptoms. *Health Psychology, 34,* 176–180. doi: http://dx.doi.org/10.1037/hea0000125

Stahre, M., Roeber, J., Kanny, D., Brewer, R. D., & Zhang, X. (2014). Contribution of excessive alcohol consumption to deaths and years of potential life lost in the United States. *Preventing Chronic Disease, 11,* 130293. doi: 10.5888/pcd11.130293

Stallen, M., De Dreu, C. K. W., Shalvi, S., Smidts, A., & Sanfey, A. G. (2012). The herding hormone: Oxytocin stimulates in-group conformity. *Psychological Science, 23,* 1288–1292. doi: 10.1177/0956797612446026

Stambor, Z. (2006a, April). Both sexes seek attractiveness in one-night stand partners. *Monitor on Psychology, 37*(4), 12.

Stambor, Z. (2006b, April). Extraversion, agreeableness linked to happiness in orangutans. *Monitor on Psychology, 37*(4), 10.

Stamm, K., Christidis, P., Hamp, A., & Nigrinis, A. (2014, July/August). *How many psychology doctorates are awarded by U.S. institutions?* American Psychological Association Center for Workforce Studies. Retrieved from http://www.apa.org /monitor/2014/07-08/datapoint.aspx

Stanley, D. J., & Spence, J. R. (2014). Expectations for replications: Are yours realistic? *Perspectives on Psychological Science, 9,* 305–318. doi: 10.1177/1745691614528518

Stanton, A. L., Luecken, L. J., MacKinnon, D. P., & Thompson, E. H. (2013). Mechanisms in psychosocial interventions for adults living with cancer: Opportunity for integration of theory, research, and practice. *Journal of Consulting and Clinical Psychology, 81,* 318–335. doi: 10.1037/a0028833

Stautz, K., & Cooper, A. (2014). Deconstructing impulsivity to better understand adolescent risk-taking. *Personality and Individual Differences, 60,* S4. doi: http://dx.doi.org/10.1016/j.paid.2013.07.152

Steeds, H., Carhart-Harris, R. L., & Stone, J. M. (2014). Drug models of schizophrenia. *Therapeutic Advances in Psychopharmacology, 5,* 43–58. doi: 10.1177/2045125314557797

Stefanopoulou, E., Hirsch, C. R., Hayes, S., Adlam, A., & Coker, S. (2014). Are attentional control resources reduced by worry in generalized anxiety disorder? *Journal of Abnormal Psychology, 123,* 330–335. doi: 10.1037/a0036343

Steger, M. F., Frazier, P., Oishi, S., & Kaler, M. (2006). The meaning in life questionnaire: Assessing the presence of and search for meaning in life. *Journal of Counseling Psychology, 53,* 80–93. doi: 10.1037/0022-0167.53.1.80

Stein, M. B., & Sareen, J. (2015). Generalized anxiety disorder. *New England Journal of Medicine, 373,* 2059–2068. doi: 10.1056/NEJMcp1502514

Steinberg, D., Levine, E., Askew, S., Foley, P., & Bennett, G. (2013). Daily text messaging for weight control among racial and ethnic minority women: Randomized controlled pilot study. *Journal of Medical Internet Research, 15,* e244. doi: 10.2196/jmir.2844

Steptoe, A., Deaton, A., & Stone, A. A. (2014). Subjective wellbeing, health, and ageing. *The Lancet, 385,* 640–648. doi: 10.1016/S0140-6736(13)61489-0

Stern, P. (2013). Connection, connection, connection... *Science, 342,* 577. doi: : 10.1126/science.342.6158.577

Sternberg, R. J. (1988). Triangulating love. In R. J. Sternberg & M. J. Barnes (Eds.), *The psychology of love.* New Haven: Yale University Press.

Sternberg, R. J. (1997). Construct validation of a triangular love scale. *European Journal of Social Psychology, 27,* 313–335.

Sternberg, R. J. (2001a). *Beyond IQ: A triarchic theory of human intelligence.* New York: Cambridge University Press.

Sternberg, R. J. (2001b). What is the common thread of creativity? Its dialectical relation to intelligence and wisdom. *American Psychologist, 56,* 360–362.

Sternberg, R. J. (2003). Giftedness according to the theory of successful intelligence. In N. Colangelo & G. Davis (Eds.), *Handbook of gifted education* (pp. 88–99). Boston MA: Allyn and Bacon.

Sternberg, R. J., & Grigorenko, E. L. (2008). Ability testing across cultures. In L. A. Suzuki & J. G. Ponterotto (Eds.), *Handbook of multicultural assessment* (3rd ed., pp. 449–470). San Francisco, CA: Jossey-Bass.

Sternberg, R. J., Grigorenko, E. L., & Kidd, K. K. (2005). Intelligence, race, and genetics. *American Psychologist, 60,* 46–59.

Stevens-Watkins, D., Perry, B., Pullen, E., Jewell, J., & Oser, C. B. (2014). Examining the associations of racism, sexism, and stressful life events on psychological distress among African-American women. *Cultural Diversity and Ethnic Minority Psychology, 20,* 561–569. doi: http://dx.doi.org/10.1037/a0036700

Stewart, A. J., & McDermott, C. (2004). Gender in psychology. *Annual Review of Psychology, 55,* 519–544.

Stickgold, R. (2011). The role of REM sleep in memory consolidation, enhancement, and intergration. In B. N. Mallick, S. R. Pandi-Perumal, R. W. McCarley, & A. R. Morrison (Eds.), *Rapid eye movement sleep: Regulation and function* (pp. 328–337). New York: Cambridge University Press.

Stickgold, R., & Wehrwein, P. (2009, April 27). Sleep now, remember later. *Newsweek,* p. 56.

Stolberg, S. G. (2001, May 10). Blacks found on short end of heart attack procedure. *The New York Times,* p. A20.

Stone, J., Smyth, R., Carson, A., Lewis, S., Prescott, R., Warlow, C., & Sharpe, M. (2006). La belle indifférence in conversion symptoms and hysteria: Systematic review. *British Journal of Psychiatry, 188,* 204–209.

Story, P. A., Hart, J. W., Stasson, M. F., & Mahoney, J. M. (2009). Using a two-factor theory of achievement motivation to examine performance-based outcomes and self-regulatory processes. *Personality and Individual Differences, 46,* 391–395. doi: 10.1016/j.paid.2008.10.023

Stothart, C., Mitchum, A., & Yehnert, C. (2015). The attentional cost of receiving a cell phone notification. *Journal of Experimental Psychology: Human Perception and Performance, 41,* 893–897. doi: http://dx.doi.org/10.1037/xhp0000100

Strayer, D. L., & Drews, F. A. (2007). Cell-phone-induced driver distraction. *Current Directions in Psychological Science, 16,* 128–131.

Strollo, P. J., Jr., Soose, R. J., Maurer, J. T., de Vries, N., Cornelius, J., Froymovich, O., . . . the STAR Trial Group. (2014). Upper-airway stimulation for obstructive sleep apnea. *New England Journal of Medicine, 370,* 139–149. doi: 10.1056/NEJMoa1308659

Stroup, T. S., McEvoy, J. P., Ring, K. D., Hamer, R. H., LaVange, L. M., Swartz, M. S., . . . Schizophrenia Trials Network. (2011). A randomized trial examining the effectiveness of switching from olanzapine, quetiapine, or risperidone to aripiprazole to reduce metabolic risk: Comparison of antipsychotics for metabolic problems (CAMP). *American Journal of Psychiatry, 168,* 947–956. doi: 10.1176 /Appi. Ajp.2011.10111609

Suarez-Almazor, M. E., Looney, C., Liu, Y. F., Cox, V., Pietz, K., Marcus, D. M., . . . Street, R. L. (2010). A randomized controlled trial of acupuncture for osteoarthritis of the knee: Effects of patient-provider communication. *Arthritis Care & Research, 62,* 1229–1236. doi: 10.1002 /acr.20225

Substance Abuse and Mental Health Services Administration (SAMSHA). (2005). *Overview of findings from the 2002 National Survey on Drug Use and Health* (Office of Applied Studies, NHSDA Series H-21 DHHS Publication No. SMA 03-3774). Rockville, MD: Author. Retrieved from www.samhsa.gov/ data /nhsda/overview/2k2Overview.htm

Substance Abuse and Mental Health Services Administration (SAMSHA). (2010a). *Results from the 2008 National Survey on Drug Use and Health: National Findings,* Updated 2010. Retrieved from http://oas .samhsa.gov /NSDUH/2K8NSDUH/tabs/toc.htm

Substance Abuse and Mental Health Services Administration (SAMHSA). (2010b). *Results from the 2009 National Survey on Drug Use and Health: National Findings.* Office of Applied Studies, NSDUH Series H-38A, HHS Publication No. SMA 10-4586. Rockville, MD: Author.

Substance Abuse and Mental Health Services Administration (SAMSHA). (2013, January). *State estimates of nonmedical use of prescription pain relievers.* Retrieved from www.samhsa.gov/data/2k12 /NSDUH115/sr115-nonmedical-use-pain-relievers.htm

Substance Abuse and Mental Health Services Administration (SAMHSA). (2014). *Results from the 2013 National Survey on Drug Use and Health: Summary of National Findings.* NSDUH Series H-48, HHS Publication No. (SMA) 14-4863. Rockville, MD: Author.

Substance Abuse and Mental Health Services Administration (SAMHSA). (2015). *Behavioral Health Trends in the United States: Results from the 2014 National Survey on Drug Use and Health.* Retrieved from http://www.samhsa.gov/data/sites/default/files /NSDUH-FRR1-2014/NSDUH-FRR1-2014.pdf

Sugita, M., & Shiba, Y. (2005). Genetic tracing shows segregation of taste neuronal circuitries for bitter and sweet. *Science, 309,* 781–785.

Sullivan, G. M., Oquendo, M. A., Milak, M., Miller, J. M., Burke, A., Ogden, R. T.,... Mann, J. J. (2015). Positron emission tomography quantification of serotonin1a receptor binding in suicide attempters with major depressive disorder. *JAMA Psychiatry, 72,* 169–178. doi: 10.1001/jamapsychiatry.2014.240

Sun, H., Lui, S., Yao, L., Deng, W., Xiao, Y., Zhang, W., . . . Gong, Q. (2015). Two patterns of white matter abnormalities in medication-naive patients with first-episode schizophrenia revealed by diffusion tensor imaging and cluster analysis. *JAMA Psychiatry, 72,* 678–686. doi: 10.1001/jamapsychiatry.2015.0505.

Sussman, A. B., & Shafir, E. (2012). On assets and debt in the psychology of perceived wealth. *Psychological Science, 23,* 101–108. doi: 10.1177/0956797611421484

Sutin, A. R., Stephan, Y., & Terracciano, A. (2016). Perceived discrimination and personality development in adulthood. *Developmental Psychology, 52,* 155–163. doi: http://dx.doi.org/10.1037/dev0000069

Sweatt, J. D. (2010). Epigenetics and cognitive aging. *Science, 328,* 701–702. doi: 10.1126/science.1189968

Sweeney, C. (2009, July 29). Banking on a chemical reaction. *The New York Times,* p. E3.

Swendsen, J., Ben-Zeev, D., & Granholm, E. (2010). Real-time electronic ambulatory monitoring of substance use and symptom expression in schizophrenia. *American Journal of Psychiatry, 168,* 202–209. doi: 10.1176/appi.ajp.2010.10030463

Szalma, J. L., & Hancock, P. A. (2011). Noise effects on human performance: A meta-analytic synthesis. *Psychological Bulletin, 137,* 682–707. doi: 10.1037/a0023987

Szeszko, P. R., Christian, C., MacMaster, F., Lencz, T., Mirza, Y., Taormina, P., Easter, P., . . . Rosenberg, D. R. (2008). Gray matter structural alterations in psychotropic drug-naive pediatric obsessive-compulsive disorder: An optimized voxel-based morphometry study. *American Journal of Psychiatry, 16,* 1299–1307.

Szymenowicza, A., & Furnham, A. (2011). Gender differences in self-estimates of general, mathematical, spatial and verbal intelligence: Four meta-analyses. *Learning and Individual Differences, 21,* 493–504. doi: 10.1016 /j.lindif.2011.07.001

Takahashi, M., Shimizu, H., Saito, S., & Tomoyori, H. (2006). One percent ability and ninety-nine percent perspiration: A study of a Japanese memorist. *Journal of Experimental Psychology: Learning, Memory, and Cognition, 32,* 1195–1200.

Takahashi, Y. (1990). Separation distress of Japanese infants in the strange situation. *Research and Clinical Center for Child Development, 12,* 141–150.

Talarico, J. M., & Rubin, D. C. (2003). Confidence, not consistency, characterizes flashbulb memories. *Psychological Science, 14,* 455–461.

Tanaka, A., Koizumi, A., Imai, H., Hiramatsu, S., Hiramoto, E., & de Gelder, G. (2010). I feel your voice: Cultural differences in the multisensory perception of emotion. *Psychological Science, 19,* 1259–1262. doi: 10.1177/0956797610380698

Tanzi, R. E. (2015). TREM2 and risk of Alzheimer's Disease—Friend or foe? *New England Journal of Medicine, 372,* 2564–2565. doi: 10.1056/NEJMcibr1503954

Taubes, G. (2012). Unraveling the obesity-cancer connection. *Science, 335,* 28–32. doi: 10.1126/science.335.6064.28

Tavernise, S. (2012). Obesity in young is seen as falling in several cities. *The New York Times,* December 11. Retrieved from nytimes.com

Tavernisejan, S. (2014). List of smoking-related illnesses grows significantly in U.S. report. *The New York Times,* p. A15.

Tayler, K. K., Tanaka, K. Z., Reijmers, L. G., & Wiltgen, B. J. (2012). Reactivation of neural ensembles during the retrieval of recent and remote memory. *Current Biology, 21,* 99–106. doi: 10.1016/j.cub.2012.11.019

Taylor, L. S., Fiore, A. T., Mendelsohn, G. A., & Cheshire, C. (2011). "Out of my league": A real-world test of the matching hypothesis. *Personality and Social Psychology Bulletin, 37,* 942–954. doi: 10.1177/0146167211409947

Taylor, M. K., Pietrobon, R., Taverniers, J., Leon, M. R., & Fern, B. F. (2013). Relationships of hardiness to physical and mental health status in military men: A test of mediated effects. *Journal of Behavioral Medicine, 36,* 1–9.

Taylor, S., & Jang, K. L. (2011). Biopsychosocial etiology of obsessions and compulsions: An integrated behavioral–genetic and cognitive–behavioral analysis. *Journal of Abnormal Psychology, 120,* 174–186. doi: 10.1037/a0021403

Taylor, S. E. (2007). Social support. In H. S. Friedman & R. C. Silver (Eds.), *Foundations of health psychology* (pp. 145–171). New York: Oxford University Press.

Taylor, S. E., Klein, L. C., Lewis, B. P., Gruenewald, T. L., Gurung, R. A., & Updegraff, J. A. (2000). Biobehavioral responses to stress in females: Tend-and-befriend, not fight-or-flight. *Psychological Review, 7,* 411–429.

Taylor, W. D. (2014). Depression in the elderly. *New England Journal of Medicine, 371,* 1228–1236. doi: 10.1056/NEJMcp1402180

te Nijenhuis, J. (2013). The Flynn effect, group differences, and g loadings. *Personality and Individual Differences, 55,* 224–228.

Teens' brains hold key to their impulsiveness. (2007, December 3). Retrieved from www.msnbc.msn.com /id/21997683/

Tellegen, A., Lykken, D. T., Bouchard, T. J., & Wilcox, K. J. (1988). Personality similarity in twins reared apart and together. *Journal of Personality and Social Psychology, 54,* 1031–1039.

Terrace, H. S. (2005). Metacognition and the evolution of language. In H. S. Terrace & J. Metcalfe (Eds.), *The missing link in cognition: Origins of self-reflective consciousness* (pp. 84–115). New York: Oxford University Press.

Tervaniemi, M., Kruck, S., De Baene, W., Schröger, E., Alter, K., & Friederici, A. D. (2009). Top-down modulation of auditory processing: Effects of sound context, musical expertise and attentional focus. *European Journal of Neuroscience, 30,* 1636–1642. doi: 10.1111/j.1460-9568.2009.06955.x

Tessier, A., Chemiakine, A., Inbar, B., Bagchi, S., Ray, R. S., Palmiter, R. D., . . . Ansorge, M. S. (2015). Activity of raphe serotonergic neurons controls emotional behaviors. *Cell Reports, 13,* 1965–1976. doi: http://dx.doi.org/10.1016/j.celrep.2015.10.061

Thase, M. E. (2014). Large-scale study suggests specific indicators for combined cognitive therapy and pharmacotherapy in major depressive disorder. *JAMA Psychiatry, 71,* 1101–1102. doi: 10.1001/jamapsychiatry.2014.1524.

The Lancet. (2011). No mental health without physical health. *The Lancet, 377,* 611. doi: 10.1016/S0140-6736(11)60211-0

The psychological toll of the smartphone. (2014, May/June). *APS Observer, 27* (5). Retrieved from http://www.psychologicalscience.org/index.php/publications /observer/2014/may-june-14/the-psychological-toll-of -the-smartphone.html

The way a room is lit can affect the way you make decisions. (2014, February 20). *ScienceDaily.* Retrieved from http://www.sciencedaily.com/releases/2014/02/140220132004.htm

Theocharopoulou, F., Cocks, N., Pring, T., & Dipper, L. T. (2015). TOT phenomena: Gesture production in younger and older adults. *Psychology and Aging, 30,* 245–252. doi: http://dx.doi.org/10.1037/a0038913

Thiede, B. R., Mann, Z. F., Chang, W., Ku, Y.-C., Son, Y. K., Lovett, M., . . . Corwin, J. T. (2014). Retinoic acid signalling regulates the development of tonotopically patterned hair cells in the chicken cochlea. *Nature Communications, 20,* 3840. doi: 10.1038/ncomms4840

Thimm, J. C., & Antonsen, L. E. (2014). Effectiveness of cognitive behavioral group therapy for depression in routine practice. *BMC Psychiatry, 14,* 292. doi: 10.1186/s12888-014-0292-x

Thompson, P. M., Hayashi, K. M., Simon, S. L., Geaga, J. A., Hong, M. S., Sui, Y., . . . London, E. D. (2004). Structural abnormalities in the brains of human subjects who use methamphetamine. *Journal of Neuroscience, 30,* 6028–6036.

Thompson, R. A. (1997). Early sociopersonality development. In W. Damon (Editor-in-Chief) & N. Eisenberg (Vol. Ed.), *Handbook of child psychology: Social, emotional, and personality development* (Vol. 3, 5th ed., pp. 25–104). New York: Wiley.

Thompson, R. A. (2012). Twenty-first century temperament. *Journal of Applied Developmental Psychology, 33,* 269–271.

Thompson, R. R. (2005). In search of memory traces. *Annual Review of Psychology, 56,* 1–23.

Thompson, T. (1995). *The beast: A journey through depression.* New York: Putnam.

Thomson, E., Hanson, T. L., & McLanahan, S. S. (1994). Family structure and child well-being:

Economic resources vs. parental behaviors. *Social Forces, 73,* 221–242.

Thorndike, E. L. (1905). *The elements of psychology.* New York: Seiler.

Thun, M. J., Carter, B. D., Feskanich, D., Freedman, N. D., Prentice, R., Lopez, A. D., . . . Gapstur, S. M. (2013). 50-year trends in smoking-related mortality in the United States. *New England Journal of Medicine, 368,* 351–364. doi: 10.1056/NEJMsa1211127

Thurstone, L. L., & Thurstone, T. G. (1941). Factorial studies of intelligence. *Psychometric Monographs, 94*(2).

Tienari, P., Wynne, L. C., Läksy, K., Moring, J., Nieminen, P., Sorri, A., . . . Wahlberg, K. E. (2003). Genetic boundaries of the schizophrenia spectrum: Evidence from the Finnish adoptive family study of schizophrenia. *American Journal of Psychiatry, 160,* 1587–1594.

Tienari, P., Wynne, L. C., Sorri, A., Lahti, I., Laksy, K., Moring, J., . . . Wahlberg, K. (2004). Genotype-environment interaction in schizophrenia spectrum disorder. *British Journal of Psychiatry, 184,* 216–222.

Tierney, J. (2007, August 28). A world of eloquence in an upturned palm. *The New York Times,* pp. 1, 4.

Tiggemann, M., & Miller, J. (2010). The Internet and adolescent girls' weight satisfaction and drive for thinness. *Sex Roles, 63,* 79–90. doi: 10.1007/s11199-010-9789-z

Todorov, A., & Porter, J. M. (2014). Misleading first impressions: Different for different facial images of the same person. *Psychological Science, 25,* 1404–1417. doi: 10.1177/0956797614532474

Toelch, U., & Dolan R. J. (2015). Informational and normative influences in conformity from a neurocomputational perspective. *Trends in Cognitive Science, 19,* 579–589. doi: 10.1016/j.tics.2015.07.007

Toker, S., & Biron, M. (2012). Job burnout and depression: Unraveling their temporal relationship and considering the role of physical activity. *Journal of Applied Psychology, 97,* 699–710. doi: 10.1037/a0026914

Tolman, E. C., & Honzik, C. H. (1930). Introduction and removal of reward, and maze performance in rats. *University of California Publications in Psychology, 4,* 257–275.

Tomlinson, K. L., Tate, S. R., Anderson, K. G., McCarthy, D. M., & Brown, S. A. (2006). An examination of self-medication and rebound effects: Psychiatric symptomatology before and after alcohol or drug relapse. *Addictive Behaviors, 31,* 461–474.

Tononi, G., & Cirelli, C. (2014). Sleep and the price of plasticity: From synaptic and cellular homeostasis to memory consolidation and integration. *Neuron, 81,* 12. doi: 10.1016/j.neuron.2013.12.025

Toomey, R., Lyons, M. J., Eisen, S. A., Xian, H., Chantarujikapong, S., Seidman, L. J., . . . Tsuang, M. T. (2003). A twin study of the neuropsychological consequences of stimulant abuse. *Archives of General Psychiatry, 60,* 303–310.

Topolinski, S., & Reber, R. (2010). Gaining insight into the "Aha" experience. *Current Directions in Psychological Science, 19,* 402–405. doi: 10.1177/0963721410388803

Torpy, J. M., Burke, A., E., & Golub, R. M. (2011). Generalized anxiety disorder. *Journal of the American Medical Association, 305,* 522.doi: 10.1001/jama.305.5.522

Torres, L., & Vallejo, L. G. (2015). Ethnic discrimination and Latino depression: The mediating role of traumatic stress symptoms and alcohol use. *Cultural Diversity and Ethnic Minority Psychology, 21,* 517–526. doi: http://dx.doi.org/10.1037/cdp0000020

Torrey, E. F. (2011). The association of stigma with violence. *American Journal of Psychiatry, 168,* 325. doi: 10.1176/appi.ajp.2011.10121710

Town, J. M., Diener, M. J., Abbass, A., Leichsenring, F., Driessen, E., & Rabung, S. (2012). A meta-analysis of psychodynamic psychotherapy outcomes: Evaluating the effects of research-specific procedures. *Psychotherapy, 49,* 276–290. doi: 10.1037/a0029564

Trachtenberg, F. L., Haas, E. A., Kinney, H. C., Stanley, C., & Krous, H. F. (2011). Risk factor changes for sudden infant death syndrome after initiation of back-to-sleep campaign. *Pediatrics, 129,* 630–638. doi: 10.1542 /peds.2011-1419

Trahan, L. H., Stuebing, K. K., Fletcher, J. M., & Hiscock, M. (2014). The Flynn effect: A meta-analysis. *Psychological Bulletin, 140,* 1332–1360. doi: http://dx.doi.org/10.1037/a0037173

Trainor, B. C., & Nelson, R. J. (2012). Neuroendocrinology of aggression. In G. Fink, D. W. Pfaff, & J. E. Levine (Eds.), *Handbook of neuroendocrinology* (pp. 509–520). London, UK: Elsevier.

Tran, A. G. T. T., & Lee, R. M. (2010). Perceived ethnic–racial socialization, ethnic identity, and social competence among Asian American late adolescents. *Cultural Diversity and Ethnic Minority Psychology, 16,* 169–178. doi: 10.1037/a0016400

Trauer, J. M., Qian, M. Y., Doyle, J. S., Rajaratnam, S. M. W., & Cunningham, D. (2015). Cognitive behavioral therapy for chronic insomnia: A systematic review and meta-analysis. *Annals of Internal Medicine, 163,* 191–204. doi: 10.7326/M14-2841

Travagin, G., Margola, D., & Revenson, T. A. (2015). How effective are expressive writing interventions for adolescents? A meta-analytic review. *Clinical Psychology Review, 36,* 42–55. doi: 10.1016/j.cpr.2015.01.003

Trevarthen, C. (1995). Mother and baby—Seeing artfully eye to eye. In R. L. Gregory et al. (Eds.), *The artful eye* (pp. 157–200). New York: Oxford University Press.

Triandis, H. C., & Suh, E. M. (2002). Cultural influences on personality. *Annual Review of Psychology, 53,* 133–160.

Trivedi, B. P. (2012). Neuroscience: Hardwired for taste. *Nature, 486,* S7–S9 (2012, June 21). doi: 10.1038/486S7a

Trzesniewski, K. H., Donnellan, M. B., Moffitt, T. E., Robins, R. W., Poulton, R., & Caspi, A. (2006). Low self-esteem during adolescence predicts poor health, criminal behavior, and limited economic prospects during adulthood. *Developmental Psychology, 42,* 381–390.

Turiano, N. A., Chapman, B. P., Agrigoroaei, S., Infurna, F. J., & Lachman, M. (2014). Perceived control reduces mortality risk at low, not high, education levels. *Health Psychology, 33,* 883–890. doi: 10.1037/hea0000022

Turk-Browne, N. B. (2013). Functional interactions as big data in the human brain science. *Science, 342,* 580–584. doi: 10.1126/science.1238409

Turkington, C. (1996). *12 steps to a better memory.* New York: MacMillan.

Turnbull, C. (1961). *The forest people.* New York: Simon & Schuster.

Turner, J. A., Mancl, L., & Aaron, L. A. (2006). Short- and long-term efficacy of brief cognitive-behavioral therapy for patients with chronic temporomandibular

disorder pain: A randomized, controlled trial. *Pain, 121,* 181–194.

Turner, W. A., & Casey, L. M. (2014). Outcomes associated with virtual reality in psychological interventions: Where are we now? *Clinical Psychology Review, 34,* 634–644.

Tweney, R. D., & Budzynski, C. A. (2000). The scientific status of American psychology in 1900. *American Psychologist, 55,* 1014–1017.

Twenge, J. M. (2009). Change over time in obedience: The jury's still out, but it might be decreasing. *American Psychologist, 64,* 28–31.

Tynes, B. M., Umaña-Taylor, A. J., Rose, C. A., Lin, J., & Anderson, C. J. (2012). Online racial discrimination and the protective function of ethnic identity and self-esteem for African American adolescents. *Developmental Psychology, 48,* 343–355. doi: 10.1037/a0027032

Tyrrell, J., Jones, S. E., Beaumont, R., Astley, C. M, Lovell, R., Yaghootkar, H., . . . Frayling, T. M. (2016). Height, body mass index, and socioeconomic status: Mendelian randomisation study in UK Biobank. *British Medical Journal, 8,* 352. doi: 10.1136/bmj.i582

Tzourio-Mazoyer, N., Petit, L., Razafim, A., Crivello, F., Zago, L., Jobard,G., . . . Mazoyer, B. (2010). Left hemisphere lateralization for language in right-handers. *The Journal of Neuroscience, 30,* 13314 –13318.

U.S. Department of Health and Human Services (2001). *National Household Survey on Drug Abuse: Highlights 2000.* Retrieved from www.samhsa.gov [14]

U.S. Preventive Services Task Force. (2009). Folic acid for the prevention of neural tube defects: U.S. Preventive Services Task Force recommendation statement. *Annals of Internal Medicine, 150,* 626–631. Retrieved from www.ahrq.gov /clinic/uspstf09/folicacid /folicart.htm

Uhlmann, E., & Swanson, J. (2004). Exposure to violent video games increases automatic aggressiveness. *Journal of Adolescence, 27,* 41–52.

Ullrich, J., & Krueger, J. I. (2010). Interpersonal liking from bivariate attitude similarity. *Social Psychological and Personality Science, 1,* 214–221. doi: 10.1177/1948550610368315

Umaña-Taylor, A. J. (2004). Ethnic identity and self-esteem: Examining the role of social context. *Journal of Adolescence, 27,* 139–146.

Underwood, E. (2015). Alzheimer's amyloid theory gets modest boost. *Science, 349,* 464. doi: 10.1126/science.349.6247.464

Unhavaithaya, Y., & Orr-Weaver, T. L. (2012). Polyploidization of glia in neural development links tissue growth to blood-brain barrier integrity. *Genes Dev., 26(1),* 31–36.

University College London (2010, July 19). Part of the brain that tracks limbs in space discovered. *ScienceDaily.* Retrieved from https://www.sciencedaily.com /releases/2010/07/100715123406.htm

University of Michigan (2011, December 21). Do you hear what I hear? Noise exposure surrounds us. *ScienceDaily.* Retrieved from www.sciencedaily.com /releases/2011/12/111221211233.htm

Unsworth, N. Fukuda, K., Awh, E., & Vogel, E. K. (2014). Working memory and fluid intelligence: Capacity, attention control, and secondary memory retrieval. *Cognitive Psychology, 71,* 1–26. doi: http://dx.doi.org/10.1016/j.cogpsych.2014.01.003

Unsworth, N., Heitz, R. P., & Parks, N. A. (2008). The importance of temporal distinctiveness for forgetting

over the short term. *Psychological Science, 19,* 1078–1081. doi: 10.1111/j.1467-9280.2008.02203.x

Urquiza, A. J., & Blacker, D. (2011). Parent-child interaction therapy for sexually abused children. In P. Goodyear-Brown (Ed.), *Handbook of child sexual abuse: Identification, assessment, and treatment.* New York: Wiley.

Vaitl, D., Birbaumer, N., Gruzelier, J., Jamieson, G. A., Kotchoubey, B., Kübler, A., . . . Weiss, T. (2005). Psychobiology of altered states of consciousness. *Psychological Bulletin, 131,* 98–127.

Valenti, O., Cifelli, P., Gill, K. M, & Grace, A. A. (2011). Antipsychotic drugs rapidly induce dopamine neuron depolarization block in a developmental rat model of schizophrenia. *Journal of Neuroscience, 31,* 12330–12338. doi: 10.1523 /JNEUROSCI.2808-11.2011

Van Bavel, J. J., & Cunningham, W. A. (2012). A social identity approach to person memory: Group membership, collective identification, and social role shape attention and memory. *Personality and Social Psychology Bulletin, 38,* 1566–1578. doi: 10.1177/0146167212455829

van der Velden, A. M., Kuyken, W., Wattar, U., Crane, C., Pallesen, K. J., Dahlgaard, J., Fjorback, L. O., . . . Piet, J. (2015). A systematic review of mechanisms of change in mindfulness-based cognitive therapy in the treatment of recurrent major depressive disorder. *Clinical Psychology Review, 37,* 26–39. doi: 10.1016/j.cpr.2015.02.001

Van Horn, J. D., Irimia, A., Torgerson, C. M., Chambers, M. C., & Kikinis, R. (2012). Mapping connectivity damage in the case of Phineas Gage. *PLOS ONE, 7,* e37454. doi: 10.1371/journal.pone.0037454

Van Horn, L. (2014). A diet by any other name is still about energy. *Journal of the American Medical Association, 312,* 900–901. doi: 10.1001/jama.2014.10837

Van Oystaeyen, A., Oliveira, R., Holman, L., Van Zweden, J. S., Romero, C., Oi, C. A., . . . Wenseleers, T. (2014). Conserved class of queen pheromones stops social insect workers from reproducing. *Science, 343,* 287–290.

Vasey, M. W., Vilensky, M. R., Heath, J. H., Harbaugh, C. N., Buffington, A. G., & Fazio, R. H. (2012). It was as big as my head, I swear! *Journal of Anxiety Disorders, 26,* 20. doi: 10.1016/j.janxdis.2011.08.009

Vazsonyi, A. T., Ksinan, A., Mikuška, J., & Jiskrova, G. (2015). The Big Five and adolescent adjustment: An empirical test across six cultures. *Personality and Individual Differences, 83,* 234–244. doi: 10.1016/j.paid.2015.03.049

Vecchio, R. P. (1997). *Leadership: Understanding the dynamics of power and influence in organizations.* Notre Dame, IN: University of Notre Dame Press.

Vedel, A. (2014). The Big Five and tertiary academic performance: A systematic review and meta-analysis. *Personality and Individual Differences, 71,* 66–76. doi: 10.1016/j.paid.2014.07.011

Vedel, A. (2016). Big Five personality group differences across academic majors: A systematic review. *Personality and Individual Differences, 92,* 1–10. doi: 10.1016/j.paid.2015.12.011

Veilleux, J. C., Colvin, P. J., Anderson, J., York, C., & Heinz, A. J. (2010). A review of opioid dependence treatment: Pharmacological and psychosocial interventions to treat opioid addiction. *Clinical Psychology Review, 30,* 155–166. doi: 10.1016/j.cpr.2009.10.006

Veltri, C. O., Graham, J. R., Sellbom, M., Ben-Porath, Y. S., Forbey, J. D., O'Connell, C., . . . White, R. S.

(2009). Correlates of MMPI-A scales in acute psychiatric and forensic samples. *Journal of Personality Assessment, 91,* 288–300. [11]

Verkuyten, M., & De Wolf, A. (2007). The development of in-group favoritism: Between social reality and group identity. *Developmental Psychology, 43,* 901–911. [12]

Verwijmeren, T., Karremans, J. C., Bernritter, S. F., Stroebe, W., & Wigbold, D. H. J. (2013). Warning: You are being primed! The effect of a warning on the impact of subliminal ads. *Journal of Experimental Social Psychology, 4,* 1124–1129. doi: 10.1016/j.jesp.2013.06.010

Verwijmeren, T., Karremans, J. C., Stroebe, W., & Wigboldus, D. H. J. (2011). The workings and limits of subliminal advertising: The role of habits. *Journal of Consumer Psychology, 21,* 206–213.

Vetter, I., Kapitzke, D., Hermanussen, S., Monteith, G. R., & Cabot, P. J. (2006). The effects of pH on beta-endorphin and morphine inhibition of calcium transients in dorsal root ganglion neurons. *The Journal of Pain, 7,* 488–499.

Vickers, A. J., Cronin, A. M., Maschino, A. C., Lewith, G., MacPherson, H., Foster, N. E., . . . Acupuncture Trialists' Collaboration. (2012). Acupuncture for chronic pain: Individual patient data meta-analysis. *Archives of Internal Medicine, 172,* 1444. doi: http://dx.doi.org/10.1001 /archinternmed.2012.3654

Vidoni , E. D., Johnson , D. K., Morris, J. K., Van Sciver, A., Greer, C. S., Billinger, S. A., . . . Burns, J. M. (2015). Dose-response of aerobic exercise on cognition: A community-based, pilot randomized controlled trial. *PLoS ONE, 10,* e0131647. doi: 10.1371/journal.pone.0131647

Visser, B. A., Ashton, M. C., & Vernon, P. A. (2006). Beyond g: Putting multiple intelligences theory to the test. *Intelligence, 34,* 487–502.

Visser, P. S., & Cooper, J. (2003). Attitude change. In M. Hogg & J. Cooper (Eds.), *Sage handbook of social psychology.* London: Sage Publications.

Vitevitch, M. S., & Goldstein, R. (2014). Keywords in the mental lexicon. *Journal of Memory and Language, 73,* 131. doi: 10.1016/j.jml.2014.03.005

Vitiello, M. V. (2009). Recent advances in understanding sleep and sleep disturbances in older adults: Growing older does not mean sleeping poorly. *Current Directions in Psychological Science, 18,* 316–320. doi: 10.1111/j.1467-8721.2009.01659.x

Vock, M., Preckel, G., & Holling, H. (2011). Mental abilities and school achievement: A test of a mediation hypothesis. *Intelligence, 39,* 357–369.

Vogel, G. (2015). Identifying the gene switch that turns fat cells bad. *Science.* Retrieved from http://news .sciencemag.org/biology/2015/08/identifying-gene -switch-turns-fat-cells-bad

Voisin, J., Bidet-Caulet, A., Bertrand, O., & Fonlupt, P. (2006). Listening in silence activates auditory areas: A functional magnetic resonance imaging study. *Journal of Neuroscience, 26,* 273–278.

Volbrecht, M. M., & Goldsmith, H. H. (2010). Early temperamental and family predictors of shyness and anxiety. *Developmental Psychology, 46,* 1192–1205. doi: 10.1037 /a0020616

Volkow, N. D. (2006). Map of human genome opens new opportunities for drug abuse research. *NIDA Notes, 20*(4), 3.

Voss, U. (2011, November/December). Unlocking the lucid dream. *Scientific American Mind.* Retrieved from www.sciamdigital.com/index.cfm?fa=Products.

ViewIssuePreview&ARTICLEID_CHAR=220732B9 -237D-9F22-E8DDD91116658076

Voyer, D., & Voyer, S. D. (2014). Gender differences in scholastic achievement: A meta-analysis. *Psychological Bulletin, 140,* 1174–1204. doi: 10.1037/a0036620

Vrij, A., Granhag, P. A., & Porter, S. (2011). Pitfalls and opportunities in nonverbal and verbal lie detection. *Psychological Science in the Public Interest, 11,* 89–121. doi: 10.1177/1529100610390861

Vukasović, T., & Bratko, D. (2015). Heritability of personality: A meta-analysis of behavior genetic studies. *Psychological Bulletin, 141,* 769–785. doi: http://dx.doi.org/10.1037/bul0000017

Vygotsky, L. S. (1978). *Mind in society: The development of higher psychological processes.* Cambridge, MA: Harvard University Press.

Vygotsky, L. S. (1986). *Thought and language.* Cambridge, MA: MIT Press. (Original work published 1934.)

Wadden, T. A., Butryn, M. L., Hong, P. S., & Tsai, A. G. (2014). Behavioral treatment of obesity in patients encountered in primary care settings: A systematic review. *Journal of the American Medical Association, 312,* 1779–1791. doi: 10.1001/jama.2014.14173

Wade, N. (2007, May 1). Among chimps and bonobos, the hand often does the talking. *The New York Times,* p. F3.

Wade, T. D., Wilksch, S. M., Paxton, S. J., Byrne, S. M., & Austin, S. B. (2015). How perfectionism and ineffectiveness influence growth of eating disorder risk in young adolescent girls. *Behaviour Research and Therapy, 66,* 56–63. doi: 10.1016/j.brat.2015.01.007

Wagemans, J., Elder, J. H., Kubovy, M., Palmer, S. E., Peterson, M. A., Singh, M., . . . von der Heydt, R. (2012a). A century of Gestalt psychology in visual perception: I. Perceptual grouping and figure–ground organization. *Psychological Bulletin, 138,* 1172–1217. doi: 10.1037/a0029333

Wagemans, J., Feldman, J., Gepshtein, S., Kimchi, R., Pomerantz, J., van der Helm, P. A., . . . van Leeuwen, C. (2012b). A century of Gestalt psychology in visual perception: II. Conceptual and theoretical foundations. *Psychological Bulletin, 138,* 1218–1252. doi: 10.1037/a0029334

Wagenmakers, E. J., Wetzels, R., Borsboom, D., & van der Maas, H. (2011). Why psychologists must change the way they analyze their data: The case of psi. *Journal of Personality and Social Psychology, 100,* 426–432. doi: 10.1037/a0022790

Wagner, B., Schulz, W., & Knaevelsrud, C. (2011). Efficacy of an Internet-based intervention for posttraumatic stress disorder in Iraq: A pilot study. *Psychiatry Research, 30,* 85–88. doi: 10.1016/j.psychres.2011.07.026

Wagner, J., Hoppmann, C., Ram, N., & Gerstorf, D. (2015). Self-esteem is relatively stable late in life: The role of resources in the health, self-regulation, and social domains. *Developmental Psychology, 51,* 136–149. doi: http://dx.doi.org/10.1037/a0038338

Wagner, K. D., Ritt-Olson, A., Chou, C.-P., Pokhrel, P., Duan, L., Baezconde-Garbanati, L., . . . Unger, J. B. (2010). Associations between family structure, family functioning, and substance use among Hispanic /Latino adolescents. *Psychology of Addictive Behaviors, 24,* 98–108. doi: 10.1037/a0018497

Wagner, U., Gais, S., Haider, H., Verleger, R., & Born, J. (2004). Sleep inspires insight. *Nature, 427,* 352–355.

Wagstaff, G. F., & Frost, R. (1996). Reversing and breaching posthypnotic amnesia and hypnotically

created pseudomemories. *Contemporary Hypnosis, 13*(3), 191–197.

Wagstaff, J. (2006, September 29). Facial non-recognition: At least there's one thing humans are better at than computers. *The Wall Street Journal.* Retrieved from www.wsj.com

Wainright, J. L., Russell, S. T., & Patterson, C. J. (2004). Psychosocial adjustment, school outcomes, and romantic relationships of adolescents with same-sex parents. *Child Development, 75,* 1886–1898.

Waldman, I. D., Weinberg, R. A., & Scarr, S. (1994). Racial-group differences in IQ in the Minnesota Transracial Adoption Study: A reply to Levin and Lynn. *Intelligence, 19,* 29–44.

Walker, E., Shapiro, D., Esterberg, M. & Trotman, H. (2010). Neurodevelopment and schizophrenia: Broadening the focus. *Psychological Science, 19,* 204–208. doi: 10.1177/0963721410377744

Walker, R. (2008, October 5). Team Speedo USA parka. *The New York Times Magazine,* p. 22.

Wallace, D. S., Paulson, R. M., Lord, C. G., & Bond, C. F. (2005). Which behaviors do attitudes predict? Meta-analyzing the effects of social pressure and perceived difficulty. *Review of General Psychology, 9,* 214–227.

Wallis, C. (2005). The new science of happiness. *Time Magazine,* pp. A3–A9.

Wampold, B. E., Stephanie, L. B., Laska, K. M., Del Re, A. C., Baardseth, T. P., Flückiger, C., Minamic, T., . . . Gunn, W. (2011). Evidence-based treatments for depression and anxiety versus treatment-as-usual: A meta-analysis of direct comparisons. *Clinical Psychology Review, 31,* 1304–1312. doi: 10.1016/j.cpr.2011.07.012

Wang, L., McCarthy, G., Song, A. W., & LaBar, K. S. (2005). Amygdala activation to sad pictures during high-field (4 tesla) functional magnetic resonance imaging. *Emotion, 5,* 12–22.

Wang, S. S. (2011, April 19). New guidelines for spotting Alzheimer's. *The Wall Street Journal,* p. D4.

Wansink, B. (2013, April). Fooled by food. *Nutrition-Action Health Letter, 40*(3), pp. 3–7.

Wansink, B., & van Ittersum, K. (2013). Portion size me: Plate-size induced consumption norms and win-win solutions for reducing food intake and waste. *Journal of Experimental Psychology: Applied, 19,* 320–332. doi: 10.1037/a0035053

Ward, B. W., Dahlhamer, J. M., Galinsky, A. M., & Joestl, S. S. (2014). Sexual orientation and health among U.S. adults: National Health Interview Survey, 2013. *National Health Statistics Reports, 77,* 1–10.

Ward, D., & Lasen, M. (2009). An overview of needs theories behind consumerism. *Journal of Applied Economic Sciences, 4.* Retrieved from http://mpra .ub.uni-muenchen.de/13090/

Ward, T. B. (2004). Cognition, creativity, and entrepreneurship. *Journal of Business Venturing, 19,* 173–188.

Ward, T. B. (2007). Creative cognition as a window on creativity. *Methods, 42,* 28–37.

Wargo, E. (2008, May). Talk to the hand: New insights into the evolution of language and gesture. *APS Observer, 21*(5), 16–22.

Warren, G., Schertler, E., & Bull, P. (2009). Detecting deception from emotional and unemotional cues. *Journal of Nonverbal Behavior, 33,* 59–69. doi: 10.1007/s10919-008-0057-7

Watanabe, H., & Mizunami, M. (2007). Pavlov's cockroach: Classical conditioning of salivation in an insect. *PLOS ONE, 2*(6), e529.

Watson, J. B. (1924). *Behaviorism*. New York: Norton.

Watson, J. B., & Rayner, R. (1920). Conditioned emotional reactions. *Journal of Experimental Psychology, 3*, 1–14.

Weaver, J. (2012, March 1). Twitter reveals people are happiest in the morning. Retrieved from http://www.scientificamerican.com/article/happy-in-the-morning/

Webster, G. D. (2009). The person-situation interaction is increasingly outpacing the person-situation debate in the scientific literature: A 30-year analysis of publication trends, 1978–2007. *Journal of Research in Personality, 43*, 278–279. doi: 10.1016/j.jrp.2008.12.030

Weck, F., Neng, J. M. B., Richtberg, S., Jakob, M., & Stangier, U. (2015). Cognitive therapy versus exposure therapy for hypochondriasis (health anxiety): A randomized controlled trial. *Journal of Consulting and Clinical Psychology, 83*, 665–676. doi: http://dx.doi.org/10.1037/ccp0000013

Wei, Y., Krishnan, G. P., & Bazhenov, M. (2016). Synaptic mechanisms of memory consolidation during sleep slow oscillations. *Journal of Neuroscience, 36*, 4231. doi: 10.1523/JNEUROSCI.3648-15.2016

Weidemann, G., Satkunarajah, M., & Lovibond, P. F. (2016). I think, therefore eyeblink: The importance of contingency awareness in conditioning. *Psychological Science, 27*, 467–475. doi: 10.1177/0956797615625973

Weiland, B. J., Welsh, R. C., Yau, W.-Y. W, Zucker, R. A., Zubieta, J.-K., & Heitzeg, M. M. (2012). Accumbens functional connectivity during reward mediates sensation-seeking and alcohol use in high-risk youth. *Drug and Alcohol Dependence, 128*, 130–139. doi: 10.1016/j.drugalcdep.2012.08.019

Weinberger, J., & Westen, D. (2008). RATS, we should have used Clinton: Subliminal priming in political campaigns. *Political Psychology, 29*, 631–651.

Weir, K. (2012a, December). Big kids. *Monitor on Psychology, 43*, 58–63.

Weir, K. (2012b, June). The roots of mental illness. *Monitor on Psychology, 43*, 30–33.

Weir, K. (2015, November). Marijuana and the developing brain. *Monitor on Psychology*, 48–52.

Weir, K. (2016a, March). The risks of earlier puberty. *Monitor on Psychology, 47*(3), 41–44.

Weir, K. (2016b, March). Positive feedback. *Monitor on Psychology, 47*(3), 50–55.

Weiss, A., Gartner, M. C., Gold, K. C., & Stoinski, T. S. (2013). Extraversion predicts longer survival in gorillas: An 18-year longitudinal study. *Proceedings of the Royal Society B: Biological Sciences, 280*, 1471. doi: 10.1098 /rspb.2012.2231

Weiss, A., King, J. E., & Perkins, L. (2006). Personality and subjective well-being in orangutans (*Pongo pygmaeus* and *Pongo abelii*). *Journal of Personality and Social Psychology, 90*, 501–511.

Weiss, A., Staes, N., Pereboom, J. J. M., Inoue-Murayama, M., Stevens, J. M. G., & Eens, M. (2015). Personality in bonobos. *Psychological Science, 26*, 1430–1439. doi: 10.1177/0956797615589933

Weisz, C., Glowatzki, E., & Fuchs, P. (2009). The postsynaptic function of type II cochlear afferents. *Nature, 461*, 1126. doi: 10.1038/nature08487

Weitz, E. S., Hollon, S. D., Twisk, J., van Straten, A., Huibers, M. J. H., David, D., . . . Cuijpers, P. (2015). Baseline depression severity as moderator of depression outcomes between cognitive behavioral therapy vs pharmacotherapy: An individual patient data meta-analysis. *JAMA Psychiatry, 72*, 1102–1109. doi: 10.1001/jamapsychiatry.2015.1516.

Wells, G. L., & Olson, E. A. (2003). Eyewitness testimony. *Annual Review of Psychology, 54*, 277–295.

Westen, D., & Gabbard, G. O. (2002). Developments in cognitive neuroscience: I. Conflict, compromise, and connectionism. *Journal of the American Psychoanalytic Association, 50*, 53–98.

Westera, W. (2012). The eventful genesis of educational media. *Education and Information Technologies, 17*, 345–360. doi: 10.1007/s10639-011-9162-z

Whillans, A., Weidman, A., and Dunn, E. (2016). Valuing time over money is associated with greater happiness. *Social Psychological and Personality Science*. Retrieved from http://spp.sagepub.com/content/early/2016/01/04/1948550615623842

Whisman, M. A., Johnson, D. P., & Rhee, S. H. (2014). A behavior genetic analysis of pleasant events, depressive symptoms, and their covariation. *Clinical Psychological Science, 2*, 535–544. doi: 10.1177/2167702613512793

Whitbourne, S. K., Lewis, T. R., & Schwartz, S. J., (2015, August). *Meaning in life and subjective well-being across adult age groups*. Paper presented at the meeting of the American Psychological Association, Toronto, Canada.

Whitchurch, E. R., Wilson, T. D., & Gilbert, D. T. (2011). "He loves me, he loves me not . . ." Uncertainty can increase romantic attraction. *Psychological Science, 22*, 172–175. doi: 10.1177/0956797610393745

White, H., R., Fleming, C. B., Kim, M. J., Catalano, R. F., & McMorris, B. J. (2008). Identifying two potential mechanisms for changes in alcohol use among college-attending and non-college-attending emerging adults. *Developmental Psychology, 44*, 1625–1639. doi: 10.1037/a0013855

White, J. K., Hendrick, S. S., & Hendrick, C. (2004). Big five personality variables and relationship constructs. *Personality and Individual Differences, 37*, 1519–1530.

Whiting, S. W., Maynes, T. D., Podsakoff, N. P., & Podsakoff, P. M. (2012). Effects of message, source, and context on evaluations of employee voice behavior. *Journal of Applied Psychology, 97*, 159–182. doi: 10.1037/a0024871.

WHO World Mental Health Survey Consortium, The. (2004). Prevalence, severity, and unmet need for treatment of mental disorders in the World Health Organization World mental health surveys. *Journal of the American Medical Association, 29*, 2581–2590.

Whorf, B. L. (1956). Science and linguistics. In J. B. Carroll (Ed.), *Language, thought, and reality: Selected writings of Benjamin Lee Whorf*. Cambridge, MA: MIT Press.

Widiger, T. A. (2005). Five factor model of personality disorder: Integrating science and practice. *Journal of Research in Personality, 39*, 67–83.

Wilcox, L. M., & Duke, P. A. (2003). Stereoscopic surface interpolation supports lightness constancy. *Psychological Science, 14*, 525–530.

Wilhelm, I., Diekelmann, S., Molzow, I., Ayoub, A., Mölle, M., & Born, J. (2011). Sleep selectively enhances memory expected to be of future relevance. *Journal of Neuroscience, 31*, 1563–1569. doi: 10.1523/JNEUROSCI.3575-10.201

Willcox, B. J., He, Q., Chen, R., Yano, K., Masaki, K. H., Grove, J. S., . . . Curb, J. D. (2006). Midlife risk factors and healthy survival in men. *Journal of the American Medical Association, 296*, 2343–2350.

Williams, J. F., Smith, V. C., & the Committee on Substance Abuse. (2015). Fetal alcohol spectrum disorders. *Pediatrics, 136*. Retrieved from http://pediatrics.aappublications.org/content/136/5/e1395

Williams, M. A., & Mattingley, J. B. (2006). Do angry men get noticed? *Current Biology, 16*, R402–R404.

Williams, W. M., & Ceci, S. J. (2014, November 2). Academic science isn't sexist. *The New York Times Sunday Review*, p 12.

Willingham, D. B. (2007). *Cognition: The thinking animal* (3rd ed.). Upper Saddle River, NJ: Pearson/Prentice Hall.

Willis, J. O., Dumont, R., & Kaufman, A. S. (2011). Factor-analytic models of intelligence. In R. J. Sternberg, & S. B. Kaufman (Eds.), *Cambridge handbook of intelligence* (pp. 39–56). Cambridge, UK: Cambridge University Press.

Wills, T. A., & Cleary, S. D. (1999). Peer and adolescent substance use among 6th–9th graders: Latent growth analyses of influence versus selection mechanisms. *Health Psychology, 18*, 453–463.

Willyard, C. (2011, January). Men: A growing minority? *American Psychological Association gradPsych Magazine*, p. 40.

Wilson, D. (2011, January 24). The risk level of electroshock devices is under an F.D.A. review. *The New York Times*, D1, D4.

Wilson, S. M., Galantucci, S., Carmela, M., Tartaglia, K. R., Patterson, D. K., Henry, M. L., . . . Gorno-Tempini, M. L. (2011) . Syntactic processing depends on dorsal language tracts. *Neuron, 72*, 397. doi: 10.1016/j.neuron.2011.09.014

Winblad, B., Andreasen, N., Minthon, L., Floesser, A., Imbert, G., Dumortier, T., Maguire, R. P., . . .Graf, A. (2012). Safety, tolerability, and antibody response of active Aβ immunotherapy with CAD106 in patients with Alzheimer's disease: Randomised, double-blind, placebo-controlled, first-in-human study. *The Lancet Neurology, 11*, 597–604. doi: 10.1016/S1474-4422(12)70140-0

Windsor, L. C., Jemal, A., & Alessi, E. J. (2015). Cognitive behavioral therapy: A meta-analysis of race and substance use outcomes. *Cultural Diversity and Ethnic Minority Psychology, 21*, 300-313. doi: http://dx.doi.org/10.1037/a0037929

Wingert, P., & Brant, M. (2005, August 15). Reading your baby's mind. *Newsweek*, pp. 33–39.

Wisco, B. E., Sloan, D. M., & Marx, B. P. (2013). Cognitive emotion regulation and written exposure therapy for posttraumatic stress disorder. *Clinical Psychological Science, 1*, 435–442. doi: 10.1177/2167702613486630

wiseGEEK. (2012). What is the Facebook Generation? Retrieved from www.wisegeek.com/what-is-the-facebook -generation.htm

Wixted, J. T. (2004). The psychology and neuroscience of forgetting. *Annual Review of Psychology, 55*, 235–269.

Wixted, J. T. (2005). A theory about why we forget what we once knew. *Current Directions in Psychological Science, 14*, 6–9.

Wixted, J. T., Mickes, L., Clark, S. E., Gronlund, S. D., & Roediger III, H. L. (2015). Initial eyewitness confidence reliably predicts eyewitness identification accuracy. *American Psychologist, 70*, 515–526.

Wollan, M. (2015, May 17). How to fall asleep. *The New York Times Magazine*, p. 25.

Woo, J. S. T., Brotto, L. A., & Gorzalka, B. B. (2011). The role of sex guilt in the relationship between culture and women's sexual desire. *Archives of Sexual Behavior, 40*(2), 385–394.

Wood, J. M., Garb, H. N., Nezworski, M. T., Lilienfeld, S. O., Duke, M. C. A. (2015). A second look at the validity of widely used Rorschach indices: Comment on Mihura, Meyer, Dumitrascu, and Bombel (2013). *Psychological Bulletin, 141,* 236–249. doi: http://dx.doi.org/10.1037/a0036005

Wood, J., M., Lilienfeld, S. O, Nezworski, M. T, Garb, H. N., Allen, K. H., & Wildermuth, J. L. (2010). Validity of Rorschach Inkblot scores for discriminating psychopaths from nonpsychopaths in forensic populations: A meta-analysis. *Psychological Assessment, 22,* 336–349. doi: 10.1037/a0018998

Wood, K. H., Ver Hoef, L. W., & Knight, D. C. (2014). The amygdala mediates the emotional modulation of threat-elicited skin conductance response. *Emotion, 14,* 693–700. doi: 10.1037/a0036636

Woolston, C. (2012, April 28). 'Weapons of persuasion' from Robert Cialdini. *The Los Angeles Times.* Retrieved from health@latimes.com

Wootton, B. M., Dear, B. F., Johnston, L., Terides, M. D., & Titov, N. (2015). Self-guided internet-delivered cognitive behavior therapy (iCBT) for obsessive–compulsive disorder: 12 month follow-up. *Internet Applications, 2,* 243–247. doi: http://dx.doi.org/10.1016/j.invent.2015.05.003

World Health Organization (WHO). (2015). *1.1 billion people at risk of hearing loss; WHO highlights serious threat posed by exposure to recreational noise.* Retrieved from http://www.who.int/mediacentre/news/releases/2015/ear-care/en/

Wu, J. Q., Appleman, E. R., Salazar, R. D., & Ong J. C. (2015). Cognitive behavioral therapy for insomnia comorbid with psychiatric and medical conditions: A meta-analysis. *JAMA Internal Medicine, 175,* 1461–1472. doi: 10.1001/jamainternmed.2015.3006

Xie, L., Kang, H., Xu, Q., Chen, M. J., Liao, Y., Thiyagarajan, M., . . . Nedergaard, M. (2013). Sleep drives metabolite clearance from the adult brain. *Science, 342,* 373–377.

Xu, A. J., & Labroo, A. A. (2013). Incandescent affect: Turning on the hot emotional system with bright light. *Journal of Consumer Psychology, 24,* 207–216. doi: 10.1016/j.jcps.2013.12.007

Xu, J., & Roberts, R. E. (2010). The power of positive emotions: It's a matter of life or death—Subjective well-being and longevity over 28 years in a general population. *Health Psychology, 29,* 9–19. doi: 10.1037/a0016767

Yager, J. (2014, January 10). Borderline brains. *NEJM Journal Watch.* Retrieved from www.jwatch.org

Yang, L., & Colditz. G. A. (2015). Prevalence of overweight and obesity in the United States, 2007–2012. *JAMA Internal Medicine, 175,* 1412–1413. doi: 10.1001/jamainternmed.2015.2405

Yassa, M. A., Mattfeld, A. T., Stark, S. M., Stark, C. E. L. (2011). Age-related memory deficits linked to circuit-specific disruptions in the hippocampus. *Proceedings of the National Academy of Sciences.* Retrieved from www.pnas.org/cgi/doi/10.1073/pnas.1101567108.

Yates, D. (2011). Sleep: Visualizing dreams. *Nature Reviews Neuroscience, 12,* 706. doi: 10.1038/nrn3149

Yonkers, K. A., O'Brien, P. M. S., & Eriksson, E. (2008). Premenstrual syndrome. *The Lancet, 371,* 1200–1210. doi: 10.1016/S0140-6736(08)60527-9

YouGov (2015, August 15). A third of young Americans say they aren't 100% heterosexual. *YouGov.* Retrieved from https://today.yougov.com

/news/2015/08/20/third-young-americans-exclusively-heterosexual/

Young, K. (2016, April). Suicide rates in U.S. have risen steadily since 1999. *NEJM Journal Watch.* Retrieved from https://mail.google.com/mail/u/0/#inbox/1543da6bc93e657b

Your memory is no video camera: It edits the past with present experiences. (2014, February 4). *ScienceDaily.* Retrieved from http://www.sciencedaily.com/releases/2014/02/140204185651.htm

Youyou, W., Kosinski, M., & Stillwell, D. (2015). Computer-based personality judgments are more accurate than those made by humans. *PNAS, 112,* 1036–1040. doi: 10.1073/pnas.1418680112

Yule, G. (2014). *The study of language* (5th ed). Cambridge, UK: Cambridge University Press.

Zajonc, R. (1965). Social facilitation. *Science, 149,* 269–274.

Zajonc, R. B. (1980). Feeling and thinking: Preferences need no inferences. *American Psychologist, 35,* 151–175.

Zajonc, R. B. (1984). On the primacy of affect. *American Psychologist, 39,* 117–123.

Zak, P. J. (2012, April 27). The trust molecule. *The Wall Street Journal,* pp. C1, C2.

Zalesky, A., Pantelis, C., Cropley, V., Fornito, A., Cocchi, L., McAdams, H.,… Gogtay, N. (2015). Delayed development of brain connectivity in adolescents with schizophrenia and their unaffected siblings. *JAMA Psychiatry, 72 ,* 900–908. doi: 10.1001/jamapsychiatry.2015.0226.

Zamboanga, F. L., Olthuis, J. V., Kenney, S. R., Correia, C. J., Van Tyne, K., Ham, L. S.,… Borsari, B. (2014). Not just fun and games: A review of college drinking games research from 2004 to 2013. *Psychology of Addictive Behaviors, 28,* 682–695. doi: http://dx.doi.org/10.1037/a0036639

Zeigler-Hill, V., & Wallace, M. T. (2011). Racial differences in narcissistic tendencies. *Journal of Research in Personality, 45,* 456–467. doi: 10.1016/j.jrp.2011.06.001

Zell, E., Krizan, Z., & Teeter, S. R. (2015). Evaluating gender similarities and differences using metasynthesis. *American Psychologist, 70,* 10–20. doi: http://dx.doi.org/10.1037/a0038208

Zhang, J., Fang, L., Wu, Y. W., & Wieczorek, W. F. (2013). Depression, anxiety, and suicidal ideation among Chinese Americans: A study of immigration-related factors. *Journal of Nervous and Mental Disease, 201,*17–22. doi: 10.1097/NMD.0b013e-31827ab2e2

Zhang, L.S., Hu, L., Li, X., & Zhang, J. (2014). The DRD2 rs1800497 polymorphism increase the risk of mood disorder: Evidence from an update meta-analysis. *Journal of Affective Disorders, 158,* 71–77. doi: 10.1016/j.jad.2014.01.015

Zhang, W., Deng, W., Yao, L., Xiao, Y., Li, F., Liu, J., . . . Gong, MQ. (2015). Brain structural abnormalities in a group of never-medicated patients with long-term schizophrenia. *AJP, 172,* 995–1003. doi: http://dx.doi.org/10.1176/appi.ajp.2015.14091108

Zhao, X., Sun, L., Sun, Y. H., Ren, C., Chen, J., Wu, Z., . . . Lv, X. L. (2014). Association of HTR2A T102C and A-1438G polymorphisms with susceptibility to major depressive disorder: A meta-analysis. *Neurological Science, 35,* 1857–1866. doi: 10.1007/s10072-014-1970-7

Zhong, C. B. (2010). You are how you eat: Fast food and impatience. *Psychological Science, 21,* 619–622. doi: 10.1177/0956797610366090

Zhou, W., Yang, X., Chen, K., Cai, P., He, S., & Jiang, Y. (2014). Chemosensory communication of gender through two human steroids in a sexually dimorphic manner. *Current Biology, 24,* 1091–1095. doi: 10.1016/j.cub.2014.03.035

Zhou, X., Dere, J., Zhu, X., Yao, S., Chentsova-Dutton, Y. E., & Ryder, A. J. (2011). Anxiety symptom presentations in Han Chinese and Euro-Canadian outpatients: Is distress always somatized in China? *Journal of Affective Disorders, 135,* 111–114.

Zhu, P. J., Huang, W., Kalikulov, D., Yoo, J. W., Placzek, A. N., Stoica, L., . . . Costa-Mattioli , M. (2011). Suppression of PKR promotes network excitability and enhanced cognition by interferon-γ-mediated disinhibition. *Cell, 147,* 1384–1396. doi: 10.1016/j.cell.2011.11

Zietsch, B. P., Morley, K. I., Shekar, S. N., Verweij, K. J. H., Keller, M. C., Macgregor, S., . . . Martin, N. G. (2008). Genetic factors predisposing to homosexuality may increase mating success in heterosexuals. *Evolution and Human Behavior, 29,* 424–433.

Zilcha-Mano, S., Dinger, U., McCarthy, K. S., & Barber, J. P. (2014). Does alliance predict symptoms throughout treatment, or is it the other way around? *Journal of Consulting and Clinical Psychology, 82,* 931–935. doi: http://dx.doi.org/10.1037/a0035141

Zimmerman, M., McGlinchey, J. B., Young, D., & Chelminski, I. (2006). Diagnosing major depressive disorder: III. Can some symptoms be eliminated from the diagnostic criteria? *Journal of Nervous & Mental Disease, 194,* 313–317.

Zinke, K., Zeintl, M., Rose, N. S., Putzmann, J., Pydde, A., & Kliegel, M. (2014). Working memory training and transfer in older adults: Effects of age, baseline performance, and training gains. *Developmental Psychology, 50,* 304–315. doi: 10.1037/a0032982

Zubin, J., & Spring, B. (1977). Vulnerability—A new view of schizophrenia. *Journal of Abnormal Psychology, 86,* 103–126.

Zucker, A. N., Ostrove, J. M., & Stewart, A. J. (2002). College-educated women's personality development in adulthood: Perceptions and age differences. *Psychology and Aging, 2,* 236–244.

Zuckerman, M. (1980). Sensation seeking. In H. London & J. Exner (Eds.), *Dimensions of personality* (pp. 487–549). New York: Wiley.

Zuckerman, M. (2004). The shaping of personality: Genes, environments, and chance encounters. *Journal of Personality Assessment, 82,* 11–22.

Zuger, A. (1997, August 19). Removing half of brain improves young epileptics' lives. *The New York Times,* p. C4.

Zukow-Goldring, P. (1997). A social ecological realist approach to the emergence of the lexicon: Educating attention to amodal invariants in gesture and speech. In C. Dent-Read & P. Zukow-Goldring (Eds.), *Evolving explanations of development: Ecological approaches to organism-environment systems* (pp. 199–250). Washington, D.C.: American Psychological Association.

Zweigenhaft, R. L. (1970). Signature size: A key to status awareness. *Journal of Social Psychology, 81,* 49–54.

Name Index

Subject Index

Page numbers in italics refer to information in tables, figures, illustrations, and captions.